Mastering Psychology

Fourth Edition

Lester A. Lefton
University of South Carolina

Laura Valvatne
New Mexico State University at Carlsbad

ALLYN AND BACON
Boston London Toronto Sydney Tokyo Singapore

Executive Editor: Susan Badger
Senior Editorial Assistant: Dana Lamothe
Editorial-Production Administrator: Rowena Dores
Editorial-Production Service: York Production Services
Cover Administrator: Linda Dickinson
Composition Buyer: Linda Cox
Manufacturing Buyer: Louise Richardson
Text Designer: Helane M. Prottas
Cover Designer: Design Ad Cetera

A Division of Simon & Schuster, Inc.
160 Gould Street
Needham Heights, Massachusetts 02194

Library of Congress Cataloging-in-Publication Data

Lefton, Lester A.
Mastering psychology / Lester A. Lefton, Laura Valvatne. — 4th ed.
p. cm.
Includes bibliographical references and index.
ISBN 0-205-13189-1
1. Psychology. I. Valvatne, Laura. II. Title.
BF121.L423 1992
150—dc20 91-31656
CIP

Printed in the United States of America
10 9 8 7 6 5 4 3 2 1 96 95 94 93 92 91

CREDITS
Page 9: T. Van Dyke/Sygma. 16T: The Bettmann Archive; 16B: Psychology Archives. 17L: Library of Congress; 17R: The Bettmann Archive. 18T: The Bettmann Archive; 18B: Historical Picture Service. 28: Superstock. 40: CNRI-Science Library/Photo Researchers Inc. 41L: S. Murphy/TSW-
(Credits continued on p. I-21)

Contents

CHAPTER 6 MEMORY 200

Preface

Writing this fourth edition of *Mastering Psychology* was an exciting opportunity to organize, explain, and generate new ideas for more effective learning and teaching. It was a creative challenge that we undertook with enthusiasm and a commitment to helping students master psychology's principles and concepts.

Thanks to the helpful feedback we have received from adoptors and students, this edition of *Mastering Psychology* continues the text-plus-study guide combination it pioneered in its first edition. It also continues to focus on teaching the science of psychology, and on showing how psychology applies to everyday issues and concerns in the lives of students.

Keeping abreast of new teaching trends and concerns, we have refined *Mastering Psychology*'s proven pedagogy to address today's classroom needs. These changes include a new modular organization for teaching flexibility and student mastery, and new pedagogy based on what we call "SQ3R *plus*," involving writing and critical thinking.

Features of the New Edition: Organization, Themes, and Content

Today, teaching introductory psychology can be a major challenge. Our discipline has grown so large that it is difficult to cover the field comprehensively and coherently. To meet this challenge, we have chosen to use a new modular structure, breaking chapters into smaller units that build and connect into a coherent, meaningful picture of psychology's past and present. The result is a textbook organized into 15 chapters that comprise 33 short modules. Instructors might choose to assign either all 15 chapters and all 33 modules, in the order in which they are currently presented, or some subset of chapters and modules in the order they would prefer. This organization allows for greater flexibility for instructors who wish to individualize their course, and the brief modules facilitates student comprehension of the material.

Themes. Interrelationships among concepts, disciplines, and perspectives form the thematic foundations of this textbook. For example, while encouraging students to think critically about research, we show them that application follows directly from research and that applied situations often prompt further research. We further suggest ways in which students may consider the implications of research for their own lives. To connect the subdisciplines of psychology, we show students how biology relates to therapy, and learning relates to personality, as well as how motivation, learning, and personality all interplay to create adjustment or maladjustment. Past and present psychological perspectives are linked by frequently highlighting traditional psychology while featuring topics of contemporary interest to students, in order to present a refreshing, intellectually accurate view of psychology, which integrates high-interest topics of the 1990s with classic issues and research concerns.

Content. This edition offers a full and clear presentation of core content areas, such as learning, memory, and perception, while also featuring many important contemporary topics, such as childrearing, gender differences, performance appraisal, and testing issues. Current concerns such as brief therapy, codependence, and substance abuse are also covered, along with brain plasticity, sexual dysfunctions, and Alzheimer's disease. These high-interest topics are presented in a way that integrates contemporary science and application and shows how they flow directly from traditional psychology. To ensure that the fourth edition of *Mastering Psychology* is up-to-date, most of the research cited has taken place in the past few years, including hundreds of research citations in the early 1990s.

Writing. Every line of this new edition was written with an emphasis on clear exposition and an inviting, upbeat style. While avoiding oversimplification of difficult issues, the key concepts are explained directly and concretely. Personal anecdotes have been included, to bring the ideas to life for students.

Pedagogical Features

To build a strong text, each basic element must be strong and able to stand alone. We have tried to build on those essential elements by sharpening existing pedagogical features and developing new ones. The key elements of *Mastering Psychology* fall into nine major pedagogical features:

- ▲ Overviews and summaries
- ▲ Learning objectives
- ▲ SQ3R *plus*
- ▲ Critical thinking: application and research
- ▲ Key terms
- ▲ Building tables
- ▲ Progress checks

- Self-tests
- Connections

Overviews and Summaries. Each chapter begins with an overview outlining the modules within the chapter and what is to be covered within each module. Each module opens with learning objectives and a review of SQ3R *plus;* it ends with a structured summary of key concepts in that module, organized by major headings and page-referenced to appropriate places for review in the text. A self-test keyed to learning objectives is also included at the end of each module.

Learning Objectives. Learning objectives are used to organize and structure each module. They spell out to students the key ideas and concepts that must be mastered in that module. These learning objectives are repeated in the margins at appropriate places in the text, in interim progress checks, and also in the final self-test, which concludes each module.

SQ3R *plus.* Both research and practical experience show that when students *survey* the text to set goals for studying, *question* as they *read,* and stop occasionally to *recite* and *review,* they learn better. Further reinforcement and learning is accomplished when they *write* a summary of key points and *reflect* on hypotheses, evidence, and implications. We suggest to students that they use the technique of *SQ3R plus:* survey, question, read, recite, and review—plus write and reflect, to improve their mastery of basic material and to practice their thinking skills as well.

Critical Thinking: Application and Research. One of the major goals of this new edition is to foster critical thinking. In every chapter, highlighted boxes focus on either applications of psychology or an understanding of the research process. At the end of each of these boxes, a series of critical thinking questions asks the students to consider and reconsider the evidence and implications of the findings presented.

Key Terms. Important concepts and terms are highlighted in bold type, within the text. These terms are also repeated in the margins, where a full definition is provided. At the end of each module, key terms are listed in alphabetical order with a page reference as to where the key term may be found, for review and reinforcement.

Building Tables. A major structural and pedagogical element in this text is the presentation of major theories and concepts in a way that shows the development of ideas. The "building tables" pioneered in previous editions have been expanded in this fourth edition. In these tables, each new set of concepts is summarized and added to the existing summaries of previously mastered concepts, which helps students to make comparisons and contrasts, and to integrate new concepts they are learning. In addition, the "building tables" are an excellent aid for study and review.

Progress Checks. Every few pages, the text includes a progress check for students. Keyed to learning objectives, the progress checks allow them to evaluate their progress and to go back and review the material until they have mastered it. Answers to the progress checks for students are found at the end of the text.

Self-tests. At the end of every module is a multiple-choice self-test, also keyed to learning objectives. This self-test allows students to evaluate how well they have mastered the whole module. Answers to all of the self-tests for students are found at the end of the text.

Connections. At the end of each chapter is a connections table that provides cross-references for major, high-interest topics, covered in modules throughout the book. Students can use connections tables to learn more about various areas of interest and to see the interrelated nature of psychology.

Building an integrated modular text is a difficult balancing act. In addition, our goal has been to carefully select and present the essentials of psychology, along with interesting examples, a wealth of pedagogy, and a high level of scholarship. This task has been made somewhat easier, however, because both of us have been teaching introductory psychology for many years. We have taught thousands of students at our respective institutions and have interacted with hundreds of psychology instructors. We have been given guidance by our publisher, advice from our colleagues, and feedback from hundreds of previous users of our textbook; this input has changed and improved the textbook with each edition. We hope we have struck an appropriate balance of pedagogy, research, and application, which allows students to master psychology in an effective, intellectually honest, and stimulating manner. Nonetheless, once again, we invite both students and instructors to participate in the process by contributing comments and suggestions. Please write us:

Professor Lester A. Lefton
Department of Psychology
University of South Carolina
Columbia, South Carolina
29208

Professor Laura Valvatne
Department of Psychology
New Mexico State University
at Carlsbad
Carlsbad, New Mexico 88220

Annotated Instructor's Edition and Supplements for Instructors

Another convenient new feature offered with *Mastering Psychology* (4th edition) is the *Annotated Instructor's Edition,* to assist professors in planning their course and in fostering student involvement and understanding. It includes a comprehensive and detailed instructor's section bound into the front of the book and detailed annotations in the margin of each chapter, with teaching suggestions, examples, demonstrations, visual aids, test answers, and learning objectives. In addition to the *Annotated Instructor's Edition,* a wide array of supplementary materials are available, including a superb set of transparencies; a set of 70 ready-to-duplicate handouts and activities; a lengthy computer-ready test-item file; *Psych Science,* an interactive, computer simulation of real-life experiments; and an extensive videotape library. All of these supplements, and more, are keyed to the *Annotated Instructor's Edition.*

Acknowledgments

Over the 3 years during which this text has been developed, we have been encouraged and given help by a number of students and instructors. They have helped us immeasurably by sharpening our point of view, focusing our vision, and needling us when we have become too sharp or critical. The development of this edition was facilitated in great measure by the comments and criticisms of the following individuals who provided editorial input; we are especially thankful to them: George Armstrong, *Bucks County Community College*; Andre Cedras, *Macomb Community College*; David Cuevas, *El Paso Community College*; Diane Davis, *Oakton Community College*; Ernest Furchtgott, *University of South Carolina*; Mary Hanna, *Wayne County Community College*; Elton Quinton, *University of Louisville*; Jenelle L. Schuler, *Delgado Community College*; H. Stuart Smith, Jr., *Tidewater Community College*; and Paul Susen, *Mt. Wachusett Community College*.

We would also like to thank instructors who were helpful in the development of previous editions of this book and of *Psychology,* fourth edition. Their numbers run into the hundreds and we are thankful to all of them. We thank especially the following instructors: Lewis Aiken, *Pepperdine University*; Brian Bate, *Cuyahoga Community College—Western Campus;* George Bishop, *University of Texas—San Antonio;* Jay Braun, *Arizona State University;* John Caruso, *Southeastern Massachusetts University;* Winifred Curtis, *Community College of Rhode Island;* Donald Devers, *Northern Virginia Community College;* Leslie Fisher, *Cleveland State University;* Linda Flickinger, *St. Clair Community College;* Mark Garrison, *Kentucky State University;* Richard Harris, *Kansas State University;* Morton Hoffman, *Metropolitan State College;* Kermit Hoyenga, *Western Illinois University;* William Kalberer, *California State University—Chico;* Dennis Karpowitz, *University of Kansas;* Harold Kiess, *Framingham State College;* Jack Kirshenbaum, *Fullerton Community College;* James Knight, *Humboldt State University;* Wayne Lesko, *Marymount University;* Sheldon Malev, *Westchester Community College;* Richard Maslow, *Delta College;* James Matiya, *Moraine Valley Community College;* Robert Meyer, *University of Louisville;* Jerry Mikosz, *Moraine Valley Community College;* Dirk Steiner, *Louisiana State University;* David Townsend, *Montclair State College;* Benjamin Wallace, *Cleveland State University;* William Wallace, *Marshall University;* John Williams, *Westchester Community College;* and Patrick Williams, *Wharton County Junior College.*

We would like to acknowledge the reviewers of the previous edition: Mike Aamodt, *Radford University;* Elizabeth A. Andrews, *Westbrook College;* Cheryl B. Bradley, *Central Virginia Community College;* Allen R. Branum, *South Dakota State University;* Judith Bridges, *University of Connecticut at Hartford;* Garvin Chastain, *Boise State University;* John S. Childers, *East Carolina University;* Steven G. Cole, *Texas Christian University;* Ray V. Coleman, *Mt. Washusett Community College;* James R. Counsil, *North Dakota State University;* Gene Cunningham, *Henry Ford Community College;* Paul F. Cunningham, *Rivier College;* Faye Dumbrot, *University of Akron;* Dick Eglsae, *Sam Houston State;* Peter Flynn, *Northern Essex Community College;* Roger G. Gaddis, *Gardner-Webb College;* Kurt F. Geisinger, *Fordham University;* Judith L. Gibbons, *St. Louis University;* Charles A. Graessle, *Olivet College;* Thomas D. Graves, *Mesa College;* David Griese, *SUNY—Farmingdale;* Janice L. Hartgrove-Freile, *North Harris County College;* Edgar E. Hawkes, *Virginia Commonwealth University;* Irwin Kahn, *Ferris State College;* George Kaluger, *Shippensburg University;* Jack A. Kapchan, *University of Miami;* Carole A. Kendig, *Seton Hall University;* Hal Kiess, *Framingham State College;* James M. Knight, *Humboldt State University;* Richard A. Kribs III, *Motlow State Community College;* Velton Lacefield, *Prairie State College;* Linda L. Lamwers, *St. Cloud State University;* Phil Lau, *DeAnza Community College;* Wayne A. Lesko, *Marymount University;* Richard J. McCarbery, *Lorain County Community College;* Lynn McCutcheon, *Northern Virginia Community College;* Ann McNeer, *Polk Community College;* Dale H. Melton, *Manatee Community College;* Henry L. Moreland, *Florida Community College at Jacksonville;* Ronald Murdoff, *San Joaquin Delta College;* Linden Nelson, *Cal Poly, San Luis Obispo;* Bobby J. Poe, *Belleville Area College;* Paula M. Popovich, *Ohio University;* Randy P. Quevillon, *University of South Dakota;* Harve E. Rawson, *Hanover College;* Rosemary Reed, *Seattle Community College;* George C. Rogers, *Massachusetts Bay Community College;* Lawrence I. Rosenkoetter, *Bethany College;* Michael J. Ross, *St. Louis University;* Tirzah Schutzengel, *Bergen Community College;* Donald M. Stanley, *North Harris County College;* K. W. Steere, *Manchester Community College;* Dirk D. Steiner, *Louisiana State University;* Roger L. Terry, *Hanover College;* Louis Tharp, *Long Beach City College;* Benjamin Wallace, *Cleveland State University;* Robert T. Wiater, *Bergen Community College;* Jerry J. Wisner, *Florida Community College at Jacksonville;* and Bonnie M. Wright, *Gardner-Webb College.*

In addition to the reviewers, a number of people helped us handle the day-to-day details of developing this text. We thank Marcia Gardner, who helped us coordinate references, and Jodi Helton, who helped coordinate permissions. We are especially appreciative to Gregory Cutler from North Dakota State University, who prepared the basic manuscript for the instructor's manual and the annotations that occur in the *Annotated Instructor's Edition.* As we expanded upon and modified Greg's work, we came to appreciate even more the quality of his endeavor. We thank David Kramer Haller for helping to coordinate the restructuring of the *Annotated Instructor's Edition.* David kept track of myriad details and facilitated meeting deadlines.

Working as authors with Allyn and Bacon is a special treat because they have such a strong commitment to the discipline of psychology. Individuals in many areas of the company have provided us information and feedback from instructors. We thank the managers and sales representatives who wrote and called us regularly with feedback from instructors. We especially thank Mark Berrafato, Judy Shaw, Bob Dillman, Jerry Higgins, Bill Tomlinson, and Leslie Wardrop, who coordinated much of this feedback. We thank Lou Kennedy, who is a key member of the marketing team. We thank Joyce Nilsen and Nancy Forsyth, who worked out in the field, helped arrange for class tests of the manuscript, and are long-time friends and mentors of this project. We also thank Sandi Kirshner for her involvement in this project on many levels; Sandi has been a friend and mentor for over a decade, and her insight and energy are unparalleled. We thank Judy Fiske, John Gilman, Bill Barke, and John Isley; each in their own quiet and sometimes mysterious ways helped us launch this project, maintain a level of excellence and a commitment to pedagogy, and produce a fine teaching and learning tool.

We are also appreciative to the production and editorial staff at our publisher, Allyn and Bacon. Producing a text such as this with its highly technical design and many elements turns out to be a monumental task. Rowena Dores and Mary Jo Gregory handled the day-to-day elements of production with skill and a dedication to fine book making. Their accomplishments are evident on every page of this text. We also thank Elaine Ober for her watchful eye on our project and Dana Lamothe who kept track of details, coordinated a host of editorial tasks, and facilitated our work on a range of fronts.

Gathering data from instructors, helping us find our focus, and reviewing our manuscript as it developed has been the principal job of the editorial team. The developmental editing of Beth Brooks is stamped on every page; we are thankful for her creative efforts. The overall responsibility for the editorial development this book has been in the skilled hands of Executive Editor Susan Badger. Susan's years of experience, insight into the field of psychology, and understanding of sound pedagogy has been crucial in helping us develop a book that appeals to both students and instructors. A seemingly endless dialogue took place between Susan and us, and we are most appreciative for her insights. Susan also goes the extra distance to ensure that every detail has been handled, that quality is maintained, and that the best book possible is produced. We consider ourselves privileged to work with her.

We dedicate this book to our students; on a daily basis they inspire, challenge, and stimulate us. We wrote this book for them, that they might better understand the discipline that we find so exciting.

To the Student: Learning to Learn

When Ben, a graduate student in psychology, first learned about the learning and memory strategies of SQ3R *plus*, he exclaimed, "Thank God! All these years I thought it was me—that there was something wrong with *me* that made learning such a struggle. Now I see, I just never was taught how to go about it."

Ben's feelings are not at all unique to him. Many students who have completed high school or their GED and have entered college realize that although they always were expected to learn in school, none of their teachers had ever really taught them how to do it. Now, wanting more than ever to make their educational experience worthwhile and meaningful, both young and older adult learners are usually delighted to finally discover *new tactics for learning*. In this section, we describe some study, learning, and memory strategies that are known to make scholastic efforts more effective and fulfilling. Whether you are a student who has already developed an effective approach to study or a student who, after all these years of being in school, still hopes to find ways that make learning less of a struggle, we think this chapter will give you some sound ideas for mastering the content of psychology—and the content of all your other courses as well.

What Does It Take to Learn and Remember?

Educational (or "instructional") psychologists focus their attention on instruction and academic learning and know a lot about what it takes for a person to learn in school, and the information in this chapter comes primarily from their research findings about teaching, thinking, and learning.

The three most important characteristics of effective study are:

- Being actively involved in the learning process.
- Making new information meaningful by linking your existing life experiences and knowledge (what you already know) to new information (what you are learning for the first time).
- Taking responsibility for your own learning.

These characteristics are important to learning for several reasons. The first characteristic, *active learning* or *active participation,* means that you interact with new information so that it becomes alive and challenging. Instead of passively yawning over lifeless facts that refuse to stay in mind long enough even to pass a test, an active learner makes the facts alive and important by wrestling and dancing with them and really getting to know them. By simply using your own thoughts, asking and answering your own questions, and organizing information in ways that make sense to you, you become an active learner. When you are an active learner, the facts become more than facts—they become meaningful and stay with you. This suggests the second characteristic of effective learning.

To *generate personal meaning* out of new material (so that it becomes relevant to your life and needs), you must find ways to connect yourself, your knowledge, and your life experiences to the material you are studying. People have a natural tendency to do this, but by knowing that learning and memory are enhanced when you create personal meaning, you will be more likely in the future to do it intentionally. When you can relate new information to your own life by connecting it to your past or present, to problems you need to solve, or to events in the world, you make it important, and you are much more likely to understand it, remember it, and use it.

The third characteristic of effective study, *taking responsibility* for your own learning, is essential, because no one can do your learning for you. We do not learn much just by being present in class and skimming over printed words on a page. To learn means to change, and to change, we must experience things for ourselves. Teachers (and textbooks) can present ideas and try to make them interesting; but only you can learn those ideas for yourself, and only you can make them meaningful to your life. For this reason, it is important to take responsibility not only for how you go about learning, but also for how you will shape and mold the ideas that are presented to you.

SQ3R *plus*: A Reading and Study Method for Active Participation

In the 1930s and 1940s, Francis P. Robinson, a psychologist teaching at Ohio State University began counseling students who were having trouble passing their courses in college. As a result of his interactions with students who found learning to be a struggle, Robinson developed a five-step, easily remembered, organized, and effective study system to help students become successful learners. His system, abbreviated by the acronym SQ3R, reminds learners to *survey, question, read, recite,* and *review* when they are reading from textbooks (Robinson, 1970). SQ3R has been used effectively and successfully by college students since 1941—it is a tried-and-true active reading and study method, which is why it is the reading strategy most recommended by psychology teachers. Over 50 years have passed since Professor Robinson first described SQ3R. In this time, many variations of the strategy have been used, although most variations have only changed the words used to describe the steps. In *Mastering Psychology,* we show you how to use the original SQ3R strategy. In addition, because Professor Robinson encouraged students to *write* down ideas and *reflect* on ideas as a part of the SQ3R strategy, we have added these two activities in our description of SQ3R to remind you to use them. For this reason, from here on, we refer to the strategy as SQ3R *plus*. The following describes how and why SQ3R *plus* works and how *Mastering Psychology* is organized to help you make use of it.

Step 1: Survey

If you were about to drive across the country for the first time in your life, what would you do to plan your trip? You probably would take some time to look at a road map to get an idea of what roads to use, places where you can stop for gas, food, and rest, how long it might take to get from one place to the next, and what places of special interest might be worth taking time to explore. Just as a road map helps plan a trip, the survey step of SQ3R *plus* allows you to plan your study sessions.

Before you begin to read an assignment, take a little time—5 minutes or so—to survey your assignment. *Surveying* simply means to skim over the pages of the assignment and to pay attention to special features that you observe while doing so. In *Mastering Psychology,* when you survey:

- ▲ Quickly read the **page-referenced list of topics** at the beginning of the chapter, the chapter's opening paragraphs, which provide a brief **overview** of the chapter, and the **learning objectives** listed at the beginning of the module you have been assigned to read.
- ▲ Scan **topic headings** printed throughout the module because you may want to turn some of these into questions as a part of the "Q" in SQ3R *plus*.
- ▲ Look at the **photographs, art work, tables,** and **graphs**—these will help you get a more concrete picture of ideas you will be studying.
- ▲ Take time to scan the **building tables**—these will give you a preview of concepts that you will want to compare and contrast as you read, so that you can learn the similarities and differences among theories presented in a module.
- ▲ Pay attention to other special features, such as print styles, the use of color in the text, and where **progress checks** are located. You may want to plan a break or the end of your study session at progress check locations.

Your purpose in surveying the chapter is to (1) *see how the chapter or module is organized,* (2) *form an idea of what is to be learned,* and (3) *set goals for the amount of material you realistically can cover in the time you have allotted for your study session.* Just as a road map helps you to know where you are headed so that you can wisely plan a trip, surveying an assignment lets you know what ideas and concepts are coming up so that you can organize your thoughts and notes around the information as you read.

> Before reading on, take some time to survey one chapter in this text so that you can (a) practice the survey step of SQ3R *plus* and (b) get an idea of how this book is organized. Stop now and survey any chapter in the text.

As you surveyed a chapter, you probably noticed that *Mastering Psychology* provides you with directions, in the form of numbered learning objectives at the beginning of each study module. These objectives are formal statements of what you must do to show mastery of key concepts in psychology. Consider them carefully, and refer to them frequently as you study. To help you spot where the text begins discussing the information needed to fulfill each learning objective, they are also printed in the margins on appropriate text pages. You can use the margin learning objective statements to review what you are supposed to learn. Later, after you have checked your progress check and self-test answers, you also can use the margin learning objective numbers to locate the appropriate text pages for restudying and reviewing the material.

Step 2: Question

Have you ever considered having a conversation with the author of the book you are reading? In a way, that is what you will do as you participate in Step 2 of SQ3R *plus,* by asking questions as you study. While surveying your assignment and later when you are reading, ask questions about the information being presented, and then try to find answers to them. Here are two ways to begin asking questions:

- ▲ Turn the topic headings and subheadings printed in the text into questions. For example, the heading "Psychology As a Career" on page 5 of this book could be converted into the question, "If I major in psychology, what type of job could I get?" For a heading such as "Dreams" on page 135 you could ask, "Why do I dream?"
- ▲ Pretend that you are having a conversation with the authors of your text, and ask who, when, where, what, why, and how questions. For example, you could ask questions such as, "What is so important about that? How can you be sure this is true? Why are you giving me two versions of the same story? How will this information be useful to me?"

When you ask and answer questions such as these, you are using the *reflect* activity of SQ3R *plus.* Professor Robinson knew that reflection is important to true learning, and it is one of the reasons why he encouraged students to ask questions.

Asking your own questions before and while you read will increase your interest, involvement, and concentration because, with each question you ask, you will have the goal of finding an answer. The question stage of SQ3R *plus* will be even more effective if you take the time to *write* down both your questions before you read and your answers while you are reading. If you cannot find the answer to a question you have asked, try rewording your question, or seek help from other students, your professor, or library resources.

> Before you read on, take a few minutes to make questions out of the remaining topic headings in this chapter. Then, as you continue on with your reading see whether you can answer your questions. Remember, it is a good idea to *write* questions and answers on paper. Also, if you already have a question for the authors, you are doing a great job—you are beginning to *reflect* already.

Step 3: Read

Do you recall a time when you eagerly began to read an assignment for one of your courses and when you got to the bottom of the page, you realized that although your eyes had been scanning the words, your mind had been wandering in a daydream? This happens to most of us on occasion, but when it happens often, studying becomes frustrating.

When you read without seeking to discover answers or just to be able to say, "I did my homework," your passive approach to study usually leads to drifting thoughts instead of learning. If you really want to use your study time effectively you need to do things that keep your mind on the task at hand—you need to actively participate in your own learning by digging out facts and making sense out of the material you are trying to learn.

Active reading takes place when you interact with the information on the page. After you have surveyed the assignment and have converted topic headings into some initial questions about the text material, begin reading. As you read:

- ▲ Find answers for your initial questions.
- ▲ Read the margin learning objective statements each time you come across one, so that you can focus on what to learn in the section you are reading.
- ▲ Continue asking and answering your own questions as if you were having a dialogue with the authors concerning the information you are covering.
- ▲ Whenever you can, try to find ways to make the information personally relevant to your own life. One way you can do this is by thinking of examples from your past and present life experiences or the lives of people you know. Another way to make things relevant is to think about how you could use the information to make a difference in your work, your relationships, or in understanding yourself.

Focusing on what you want to learn, continually asking and answering your own questions as you read, and finding ways to make the material relevant to your own life will help you be an active participant and a successful learner.

> If you have been following the instructions in the blue boxes and have been asking and answering your own questions as you read, as well as *writing* summaries and *reflecting* on what is being said, you are well on your way to perfecting the art of active reading. Keep up the good work, and continue on.

Step 4: Recite

To *recite* means to repeat something from memory. It is a form of rehearsal, something like rehearsing lines for a play, but when reciting to become an educated person, you usually do not want to rehearse the lines exactly as they were stated in the original source or in the same way each time—instead, you will want to put things into your own words.

In this book, we recommend that you recite at the end of each main topic discussed (when you have completed a section of text and have come upon a new topic heading). Also, an effective place for reciting material is when you come to a progress check. Before completing the progress check, practice recalling ideas about the material you have just read.

You can approach the recitation step in at least three ways. All three involve using the *plus* activity of *writing;* and, using all three of the following approaches will prove to be most effective:

- Refer to the questions you asked, and answer them again, in your own words, from memory, and in writing.
- Return to the **learning objectives** (listed at the opening of the assigned module) and the list of **key terms** (listed at the end of each module), and, in your own words, *write* summaries of everything you can remember about them.
- In your own words, write a summary of each topic and subtopic discussed in the module before you move on to read the next topic or subtopic.

All of these approaches to recitation are effective because you become an active participant in learning when you put ideas into your own words. If you can do this without feeling tongue-tied or confused, then you can feel fairly certain that you have gone a step beyond rote learning (memorized, parroted ideas) and that you are beginning to really understand the material.

When you recite, it is important that you *write* your ideas down or speak them out loud (you might just move your lips or whisper) because otherwise, thoughts can flutter in and out of your mind as a butterfly flutters from one flower to the next. Putting your ideas into written, spoken, or even artistic forms (such as drawing a sketch) allows you to catch your weak areas: These concrete activities force you to notice gaps in your understanding of ideas.

After reciting ideas from memory, complete the **progress check** and then refer to the **answer section at the back of the book,** to check your answers. The progress checks will let you see how successful you have been in digging out and remembering some of the facts and ideas presented in the text. If you give an incorrect answer to any of the progress check questions, take time to go back into the text discussion to understand the correct answer. The learning objective reference numbers will help you locate the information you need.

> Take a few minutes now to recite what you have learned. See what you can recall about this step, and in your own words, *write* answers to questions you have asked and summaries for other key points described. Next, look back to see how well you learned and remembered.

Step 5: Review

The review step of SQ3R *plus* encourages you to double-check your understanding and your accuracy when recalling the material you have studied. With this step, try to pull together key terms, concepts, and subtopics within a module or chapter, so that you have a complete, organized understanding about the main topic. During this stage of learning, find ways to store the information in long-term memory by making it meaningful. Here are some ways that you can review the material:

- Read the **module summary,** and look back in the text if something presented there seems unfamiliar or unclear to you.
- Restudy your own questions and answers, and compare them with the text material.
- Check the **learning objectives** and list of **key terms,** to see whether you can remember important information about them.
- Restudy the **progress checks,** to be sure you understand the correct answers.
- Review the **building tables.**
- *Reflect* on ideas so that they become more than just facts and words to put in your head.
- Check back through the text and your notes, to be sure you are remembering things accurately.

After thoroughly reviewing, take the **self-test** as if it were a graded test given in class. The results of the self-test will give you *immediate feedback* about how well you have learned some of the material in the module. If you miss any questions on the self-test, use the learning objective reference number given in the **answer section at the back of the text,** to return to the appropriate discussion in the text; restudy and review these concepts.

> Before practicing the review strategy of SQ3R *plus,* take some time to recite all that you can remember about what you have studied. Then review, checking to see which points you remembered and which ones you may have forgotten. When checking back, be sure to see whether you remembered things accurately, and *reflect* again about what you have studied.

plus . . .

The *write* and *reflect* learning activities described below are not additional steps in SQ3R *plus* because as we have said, you do them as a part of SQ3R. The following ideas about the *plus* system will help you understand why writing and reflecting are important to SQ3R and how to do these activities well.

Write

When you *write* a summary of key points, in your own words, you increase the quality and quantity of your learning and memory. To put text ideas into your own words means that you restate the ideas in words that are meaningful to you. When you do this, it is important that you think about what has been said in the text and that you restate what has been said in words that work for you and that accurately reflect the concepts and information presented.

Scientific knowledge advances when investigators challenge what has been said or view existing knowledge in different ways. However, before you can effectively challenge or question the information presented here, you must understand what was actually said in the text. Keep yourself from getting off track when you put ideas into your own words: Take the time to really think about what the words in the text mean. This can help you to avoid making errors at test time or passing along mistaken information. On the other hand, if you don't put ideas into your own words, you may not understand what is being said when ideas are restated in different words. If you have only learned the ideas through straight memorization of the text's words, you will probably have trouble when the ideas are reworded, such as on a test or in a class discussion. If you really want to learn well, take time to understand what has been said, then say it again, combining words that come from your own vocabulary with key terms that you have learned in the text. Putting ideas into your own words makes them a part of you.

When you use your own words, you are beginning to *reflect* on ideas, and when you *write*, you make a permanent record of your thoughts that you can use later as a reference when you study for a test or want to rediscover something you have already learned. Both of these activities—using your own words and writing them down—show that you are involved in the three most important characteristics of effective study (described in the outset of this introduction): You are *actively involved, making new information meaningful,* and *taking responsibility for your own learning.*

Reflect

Take the time to *reflect* on the hypotheses, evidence, and implications of the material and on its relevance to *your* life. *When you reflect on what you are studying, you become not only an active learner, but also a critical thinker—a person who will be able to make good use of the information learned.* You can reflect by thinking about the following:

- ▲ Hypotheses (What main ideas were presented and investigated?)
- ▲ Evidence (What research studies and examples were given to support these ideas?)
- ▲ Implications (How could this information help to improve life? How could this situation or practice cause problems in a person's life? What is still unknown or not discussed in regard to this topic?)
- ▲ Relevance (How can you put this information to work for you in your own life?)

Also, when you *reflect,* feel free to challenge the material you have studied. Do you agree or disagree with what was said? Why? What evidence do you have from your own knowledge or experience to support or to disprove the ideas?

If you still feel somewhat uncertain about how to reflect on information, you can start practicing in *Mastering Psychology* by using the featured sections, titled **Understanding the Research Process** and **Applying Psychology,** found in each chapter. At the end of these discussions, you will find questions that will prompt you to reflect.

Another important characteristic of reflecting is to make connections among concepts presented on a page, within a topic discussion, within a module, within a chapter, from chapter to chapter, from the textbook to class discussions, and from your psychology class to things you learn in other classes, from the news media, and from discussions with friends. At the end of each chapter in this text, you will find a **connections table.** You can use these connections tables to get a glimpse of how ideas in psychology are related, and from there, you can reflect, using your own thoughts, to see why these relationships might be important. *By reflecting and connecting ideas, we become more knowledgeable, better educated, and wiser people.*

Individual Differences: How They Affect the Way We Learn

The word *individual* implies that each one of us is unique. These differences among individuals influence the way in which each person perceives and acts upon the world; they influence the way in which each person interprets instruction and learns most effectively. The degree to which you benefit from *Mastering Psychology* and from your psychology class will have a lot to do with your expectations and your awareness of your own learning styles, preferences, and personal attributes.

To modify an old saying, "Meaning is in the eye of the beholder." The way in which you perceive and interpret things, such as the meaning and importance of course content, your teachers' motives, and the difficulty or ease of a particular course, has a lot to do with the way you behold the event. With this in mind, if you find yourself feeling out of sync, frustrated with assignments, angry with your teachers, or just plain lost with what is going on in class, you might find it helpful to talk with others. A new perspective offered by one of your peers, a teacher, a tutor, or a friend could make all the difference in the world to your success in college.

Our individual differences are the result of inherited characteristics and learned behavior. Because of these two forces, we differ in our styles of learning and our preferences for learning. For instance, some people are *visual learners*—they learn more easily if they can watch a demonstration, look at a chart, or view a video about the information they are learning; other people are *auditory learners*—they learn more effectively if they can listen to a lecture or discussion of the subject; and still others are *kinesthetic learners*—they learn best if they can have a hands-on experience, with the subject at hand. Most individuals use all three of these learning styles in a distinctly individual way, with a particular strength in using one of the styles. Some people, however, seem to learn equally as well through all three of these sensory modalities, although this type of style is fairly rare (Reinert, 1976). The sensory modality through which you learn best—your learning modality—is a part of your learning style. By being aware of your personal and unique learning style, you will learn better because you will know what you need in order to learn best.

Learning preferences are also important to your learning style and include things such as preferring either total silence or background noise while studying, preferring an informal classroom arrangement or a formal one, and preferring to study alone or with others. Other individual characteristics that influence the way we learn include our expectations of ourselves and others, our attention span, our motives for taking a class, our family and cultural background, and our personality, self-esteem, and ability to cope with stressful events.

Just knowing that you have a unique learning style, including your individual modality, preferences, and personal attributes, can be helpful to your success as a student because by knowing this, you can begin to observe yourself to discover what works for you and what does not, what feels comfortable to you and what does not. From these self-observations, you can begin to make choices that will enhance your efforts at studying and learning.

On-Campus Learning Assistance Centers: A Place to Get Help and to Discover More About Your Style

If you are interested in finding out more about your particular learning style, check with your psychology teacher or the learning development or learning assistance center on your campus. They will probably have assessment tools designed to evaluate your individual learning style, tutors to help you understand material from your classes, suggestions for how you can make the most out of your personal strengths, and learning materials to help you improve your proficiency in specific study skills and strategies. For example, most college learning assistance centers have materials that can help you learn effective time-scheduling strategies, listening techniques, note-taking skills, and test-taking skills, and even information on how to write a term paper or how to overcome test anxiety.

Some Final Comments

Students who succeed in college take responsibility for their own learning; they make and follow a study schedule; they observe themselves as learners, to determine what study methods and learning arrangements work well and feel comfortable, and they make adjustments when the learning process is not working effectively. They get involved and participate actively in all aspects of their study, learning, and classroom activities; they exchange ideas with their peers; they are inquisitive, asking and answering questions and continually reflecting on what they have learned. They make good use of learning and memory systems such as SQ3R *plus,* and they feel confident and at ease with the learning process.

Being a competent student does not come naturally or easily for most people. It takes self-discipline, realistic scheduling, and a true desire to learn. Becoming a confident and competent learner takes time and practice, so go easy on yourself if you make mistakes or don't quite live up to your expectations of yourself. The important thing to remember is that almost anyone who wants to be a successful student can be one. In the end, the day-by-day progress you make will lead you to your goals. We sincerely hope you enjoy your experience with *Mastering Psychology.*

Module 1 ► DEFINING PSYCHOLOGY AND CAREERS IN PSYCHOLOGY 2

Module 2 ► PSYCHOLOGY PAST AND PRESENT: HOW PSYCHOLOGISTS EXPLORE AND UNDERSTAND HUMAN BEHAVIOR 14

Chapter 1

What Is Psychology?

Each chapter of this book begins with a one-page overview of the chapter contents. This chapter presents an overview of the science of psychology. As a science, psychology has a rich and diverse set of methods that help both researchers and practitioners study behavior and mental processes. The overall goal of this chapter is to present the scope and the principal techniques of psychological inquiry.

The chapter's first module begins with the definition of psychology—the study of behavior and mental process. The wide array of careers that a psychologist can choose is explored, including both research careers and careers that involve the delivery of mental health services. Both researchers and deliverers of direct mental health services work together to enrich the discipline.

The methods and techniques have matured over the years, as the discipline has grown from a fledgling outgrowth of philosophy, to a full-blown, multisubspeciality science. This development is the focus of the chapter's second module. All psychologists have as a cornerstone of their training the understanding of research in its various forms. Principal among those forms is the scientific method, including the experiment. Only through the scientific method and experimental techniques can psychology be fully understood. Indeed, it was a lack of thorough sophistication on the part of early researchers that limited the usefulness of their early research findings. Early researchers did not make full use of scientific methods as we know them today. Only after the Second World War was the broad range of human behavior considered and scrutinized scientifically.

Today, psychologists are employed to teach, conduct research, deliver mental health services, evaluate programs, and help businesses achieve the most that they can. In some ways, psychology's arm stretches out widely into other disciplines, which is why a study of it becomes so important to our understanding of the human endeavor.

Module 1

Defining Psychology and Careers in Psychology

LEARNING OBJECTIVES

When you have mastered the material in this module, you will be able to

Defining Psychology (pp. 4–5)

1.1 Describe the field of psychology and identify its four major goals (p. 4).

Careers in Psychology (pp. 5–7)

1.2 Identify the similarities and differences in the training and specialization of psychologists, psychiatrists, and psychoanalysts (p. 5).

1.3 Give examples of the types of careers that are available to people with doctoral, master's, and bachelor's degrees in psychology (p. 6).

What Psychologists Do (pp. 8–10)

1.4 Describe human services, applied psychology, and experimental psychology and characterize subfields of each (p. 8).

SQ3R
- ▲ **Survey** to set goals for studying.
- ▲ Ask **questions** as you **read.**
- ▲ Stop occasionally to **recite** and **review**.

plus
- ▲ **Write** a summary of key points.
- ▲ **Reflect** on the hypotheses, evidence, and implications of this material and on the relevance it has to *your* life.

Note: *Study, learning, and memory strategies are discussed in the "To the Student" section on pages xiv–xix. If you have not yet done so, you may want to read that section now.*

It is 8:00 P.M. on a Monday night. In the Eastside co-ed dormitory, the lights are blazing, and the muffled sounds of music, voices, and a ringing telephone can be heard. Let's take a closer look at the students living on the second floor. . . .

At the pay phone in the hallway, Keri is grinning as she tells her mother about her A on the physiology exam and her acceptance into the premed program. Her hard work is paying off, and her parents are very proud of her achievements. As Keri hangs up, she can't help wondering for the millionth time how her older brother, Jack, could be so different from her. At 23, he has dropped out of college and is barely supporting himself with a minimum wage job at a fast-food restaurant. "I know he's smart," she thinks to herself, "but he just doesn't have my energy or motivation. Did my parents do something wrong in raising him? Or was he just born the way he is—like our Uncle Bob?"

Across the hall in the Eastside dorm, Miguel is lying on his bed staring at the ceiling. The letter dangling in his hand is from his girlfriend, Pam, who attends college in another state. She writes that she has met someone new and wants to break off their relationship. Miguel closes his eyes and feels himself falling into a deep black pit of depression. "Why *shouldn't* I be depressed?" he thinks. "We've been together for more than a year, and I thought things were going really well. . . . I thought we were in love." Miguel stays in his room for more than an hour, thinking of Pam, then he gets up and walks down the hall with a look of contentment on his face. "I guess I'm not really depressed after all," he thinks. "When you stop to think about it, maybe we weren't so right for each other. Besides, that girl who sits next to me in psychology class is kind of cute."

Two doors down from Miguel, Chris is worried about her grandmother, who has just been diagnosed with Alzheimer's disease. She thinks back to last summer when her grandmother kept calling her by her sister's name and repeated things that she had just said. Chris shivers as she wonders what her grandmother will be like next summer. "There must be *something* the doctors can do. What if it's hereditary? Will my Dad get it? Will I get it?"

In the lounge at the end of the hallway, Sandra, Harry, and Rick are involved in a heated discussion about the value of SAT scores. "Look, colleges have been using SATs for a long time, to decide who to admit. They're fair, and they're accurate," asserts Sandra, who received high scores when she took the tests. "You're crazy," retorts Harry. "SATs only measure your ability to take a test—not what you know, or how well you'll do in college. My SAT scores were terrible, and look at how well I'm doing this semester." "Harry's right," Rick says. "And besides, I think they're unfair to people from minorities or the inner city who don't have the same opportunities and experiences that we had."

Mark smiles as he closes his trigonometry book and turns off the desk lamp. His freshman year was going really well—better than he or his parents had even hoped. In kindergarten, Mark had been held back a year when his teacher described him as hyperactive and lacking social skills. Mark remembered hating school, being frustrated by his lessons and teased by his classmates—until a school psychologist tested him for dyslexia and enrolled him in special classes. With individual attention and extra help, Mark began to do better in school. He worked hard to make it to college. Today, he wonders whether he will be able to achieve his goal of becoming an architect, whether he will continue to need extra help, and whether some of his classes will prove too difficult. How far can he go? How far can any of us go to achieve our goals?

Unlike her classmates who live in a dormitory, Samantha faces different challenges. Samantha had to leave her studying to pick up her 11-month-old son from a child care center. She wonders whether Billy is okay and whether he missed her. Samantha faces problems of finding good child care, working part-time to pay tuition and rent, family hassles about her single parenthood, and the pressures of a 12-unit class load. Trying to rush from college to the child care center to home, and to study, shop, and see her son—all at age 19—puts Samantha at a real disadvantage. Migraine headaches, feeling that it is all too much, and trying to do it alone are making Samantha's experience of college one of a pressure cooker. Unlike Mark, she knows she can do the work; unlike Keri, she doesn't have enough time to study to get A's; but Samantha keeps going, one day at a time, always attempting to reach her goal of self-sufficiency. She knows that education is one of the keys to her independence, and she attempts to cope with her stressors. However, she wonders, is she coping as well as she could? She asks whether child care is helping or hurting her son—or does it matter? Is trying to do it all worthwhile?

These students are faced with questions, problems, and experiences that highlight the diversity of life experiences. Their concerns are our concerns, and their questions are our questions. What do you think? Why can brothers and sisters turn out so differently? Is motivation something we are born with, or is it learned through life? How can we best cope with feelings of depression or anxiety? How can physical problems affect our behavior? Are SATs and intelligence tests the best ways to measure intelligence? Can we overcome weaknesses, disabilities, and family problems to achieve our goals? Are there limits to what we can do?

Psychologists try to answer all of these questions and hundreds more. They focus on why people behave the way they do. They study the brain, behavior, and mental processes to determine how a person's biological, physical, and social world affect day-to-day behaviors and interactions. Our goal in writing this book is to convey the diversity of the field of psychology and to provide a basis for understanding behavior, mental processes, and experiences in ways that can benefit anyone in everyday life. Before we describe what psychologists do and how they do it, let us first define psychology.

Defining Psychology

Learning Objective 1.1
Describe the field of psychology, and identify its four major goals.

What exactly is psychology? We begin with a simple broad definition: **Psychology** is the science of behavior and mental processes. We then expand on this simple definition: Because psychology is a *science,* psychologists use scientific principles, methods, and procedures. They use precise procedures and carefully defined methods to present an organized body of knowledge and to make inferences (discussed later in the chapter). As a science, psychology is committed to

- *Objectivity*—Evaluating research and theory on their own merits without bias or preconceived ideas
- *Accuracy*—gathering data from the laboratory and the real world in precise ways
- *Healthy skepticism*—viewing data and theory cautiously until results are repeated and verified

psychology: The science of behavior and mental processes.

Aspects of Psychology

Because psychologists study mental processes and behavior, they observe most all aspects of human functioning—overt actions, mental processes, emotional responses, and physiological reactions:

- *Overt actions* are any directly observable and measurable movements or the products of such movements. Walking, talking, playing, kissing, gestures, and expressions are examples of overt behavior. Products of overt behavior might be term papers that you write, the mess in your bedroom, or your finely tuned body if you exercise regularly.
- *Mental processes* include your thoughts about being angry or happy or sad about something, your ideas, or your reasoning processes.
- *Emotional responses* include anger, regret, lust, happiness, or depression.
- *Physiological reactions* are closely associated with emotional responses and include an increased heart rate when you are excited, biochemical changes when light stimulates your eye, or reactions to stress, such as high blood pressure and ulcers.

theory: A synthesis of interrelated ideas and facts put forward to summarize, explain, and predict behavior and mental processes.

psychologist: A person who studies behavior and uses behavioral principles in scientific research or in applied settings for the treatment of emotional or other mental problems.

The first psychologists only studied the mind and mental processes. Later psychologists focused only on overt behavior. Today, psychologists study both mental processes and behavior, to see how organisms affect and are affected by the social, physical, and biological world.

Aims and Scope of Psychology

The goals of psychology are to *describe* the basic components of behavior, to *explain* the causes of behavior, to *predict* behavior, and, potentially, to *manage* behavior. Psychology describes and explains behavior in order to predict behavior and to help people manage it. Therefore, some psychologists do basic research to uncover, explore, and understand the principles of behavior. They measure and describe behavior in a scientific way, using verifiable observations and carefully controlled research methods. Because behavior and mental processes are not always directly observable, psychologists must sometimes infer the thought processes, emotions, and motivations behind the actions they observe in both human beings and animals. From their research, psychologists develop theories to explain, predict, and help manage behavior. **Theory** refers to a collection of interrelated ideas and facts put forward to explain and predict behavior and mental processes. In sum, psychology is a problem-solving science rooted in research and scientific principles. For most psychologists, their work is a search for the causes of behavior. It is an exploration, an adventure, into understanding behavior and mental processes.

Careers in Psychology

Psychologists study nearly every aspect of life, not only to understand how people behave but also to help them lead happier, healthier, more productive lives. Some people mistakenly assume that psychologists primarily assist those suffering from debilitating mental disorders such as schizophrenia or severe depression, but only a portion of all psychologists do this kind of work.

Learning Objective 1.2
Identify the similarities and differences in the training and specialization of psychologists, psychiatrists, and psychoanalysts.

Psychologists are professionals who have learned to study behavior and to apply research findings in a variety of settings; most have advanced degrees, usually Ph.D.s (doctorates of philosophy). Many psychologists also train for an additional year or two in a specialized area, such as mental health and therapy, perception, physiology, child development, learning, teaching, or conducting scientific research or meeting clients in a laboratory setting, or hospital.

clinical psychologist: A person who views behavior and mental processes from a psychological perspective and who uses that knowledge to treat persons with serious emotional or behavioral problems or to do research into the causes of behavior.

psychiatrist: a doctor who has completed a medical residency specializing in the study of behavior and the treatment of patients with emotional and physiological disorders.

psychoanalyst: A person (usually a psychiatrist) who has studied the technique of psychoanalysis and who uses it in treating people with emotional problems.

The oldest and largest professional organization for psychologists is the American Psychological Association (APA). Founded in 1892, its purpose is to advance psychology as a science, a profession, and a means of promoting human welfare. Today, the APA has more than 68,000 members, with the majority holding doctoral degrees from accredited universities. In addition, there are more than 25,000 student affiliates.

The APA is not the sole voice of psychology. Many specialty groups have emerged over the years; for example, organizations consisting mainly of developmental, behavioral, cognitive, or neuroscience psychologists have formed. Recently, the American Psychological Society (APS) has formed; it has a large membership of psychologists with academic interests and focuses on scientific research (rather than practice or applied) interests. As a new organization, the future of the APS is still unclear; but it has great potential for assuming a leadership role as a voice for researchers in psychology.

Differences Among Practitioners

People often confuse clinical psychologists, psychiatrists, and psychoanalysts. All are mental health practitioners who help people with serious emotional and behavioral problems, but each looks at behavior differently. **Clinical psychologists** usually have Ph.D.s in psychology and view behavior and emotions from a psychological perspective. In contrast, **psychiatrists** are physicians (medical doctors) who specialize in the treatment of disturbed behavior. Patients who see psychiatrists often have physical and emotional problems. Because of their medical training, psychiatrists can prescribe drugs and can admit patients for hospitalization. Clinical psychologists and psychiatrists often see a similar mix of clients and sometimes work together as part of a mental health team. Most psychologists and psychiatrists support collaborative efforts. However, a friendly rivalry exists between the two disciplines because of their sometimes very different points of view.

Clinical psychologists generally have more extensive training in assessment, research, and psychological treatment of emotional problems than psychiatrists do. Their nonmedical perspective alters their roles in hospital settings and allows them to view patients differently than psychiatrists do (Kingsbury, 1987). Instead, psychiatrists use a medical approach, which often involves making assumptions about behavior—for example, that abnormal behavior is diseaselike in nature—that psychologists do not make.

Psychoanalysts are usually psychiatrists who have training in a specific method of treating people with emotional problems. Their treatment method, *psychoanalysis,* was originated by Freud and includes the study of unconscious motivation and dream analysis. (Freud, unconscious motivation, and dream analysis are described in Module 2 of this chapter.) Psychoanalysis often requires a course of daily therapy sessions; each patient's treatment may last several years.

Psychology as a Career

Learning Objective 1.3
Give examples of the types of careers that are available to people with doctor's, master's and bachelor's degrees in psychology.

Psychology is a diverse and exciting field that attracts many college students who like the idea of helping others. Every year, almost all the approximately 3,000 new holders of doctorate degrees in psychology accept jobs directly related to their training (Pion, Bramblett, & Wicherski, 1987). There are more than 100,000 psychologists in the United States. If you are considering becoming a psychologist or entering a related field, there is good news: unemployment among psychologists is low, and new psychologists continue to find employment in areas related

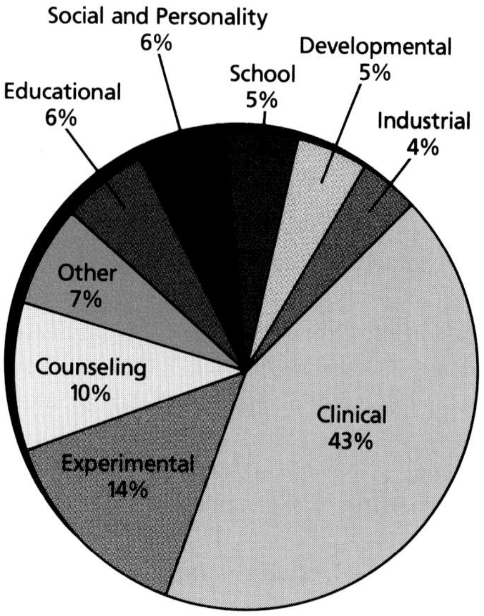

Figure 1.1

The percentage of psychologists who work in different branches of psychology is shown here. Although the numbers vary from year to year, over the last decade, the human service fields of clinical counseling, and school psychology have accounted for more than half of the membership of the APA.

to their graduate training (see Figure 1.1). Most experts agree that employment opportunities will continue to improve.

Training is the key to employment. For example, a psychologist who (1) obtains a Ph.D. from an accredited program in clinical psychology, (2) does an internship in a state hospital, and (3) becomes licensed will have a wide variety of job opportunities available in both the private and the public sectors. Sixty-two percent of the doctoral membership of the APA deliver human services. Doctoral-level psychologists provide more than 50 million hours of treatment annually to 4–10 million people (Howard, Kopta, Krause, & Orlinsky, 1986; Stapp, Tucker, & VandenBos, 1985). Individuals with master's degrees can function in a variety of settings, and even those with bachelor's degrees can play an important role in the delivery of psychological services. Salary, responsibilities, and working conditions tend to be commensurate with an individual's level of training.

Becoming a psychologist is difficult but rewarding. State hospitals employ both bachelor's and master's level psychologists to work with groups of impaired individuals. School systems often hire master's level school psychologists to administer and interpret tests and to work with school children. Business and industry employ bachelor's and master's level psychologists in personnel departments and in other positions, to evaluate the success of ongoing programs. Many psychology teachers at community colleges, junior colleges, and vocational schools are master's level psychologists. University psychologists spend most of their time researching and teaching.

As a helping profession with deep scientific roots, psychology continues to attract an increasing number of women. The number of women in graduate training programs has doubled in the past 20 years. Data suggest that this trend is likely to continue (Russo & Denmark, 1987). Today, women are presidents of national, regional, and local psychological organizations, and their thoughts and work often dominate the psychological journals (Russo & Denmark, 1987). Although proportionately more women than men are entering psychology, women are also more likely than men to be employed on a part-time basis (Stapp, Fulcher, & Wicherski, 1984).

Progress Check 1.1

Complete each of the following sentences with one of the options provided.

(L.O. 1.1) a. As a science, psychology is committed to objectivity, accuracy, and ________. (promoting a "leading edge" philosophy / healthy skepticism)

(L.O. 1.1) b. When psychologists observe thoughts, ideas, and reasoning, they are studying ________. (overt actions / mental processes / emotions)

(L.O. 1.1) c. The behaviors and mental processes that psychologists study ________ always observable. (are / are not)

(L.O. 1.1) d. A synthesis of interrelated ideas and facts put forth to explain and predict behavior and mental processes is the definition of ________. (psychology / science / a theory)

(L.O. 1.2) e. Psychiatrists are ________ who specialize in the treatment of disturbed behavior. (medical doctors / Ph.D. psychologists)

(L.O. 1.2) f. ________ generally have more extensive training in assessment, research, and psychological treatment of emotional problems. (Psychiatrists / Psychoanalysts / Clinical psychologists)

(L.O. 1.2) g. ________ is a specific treatment method that includes the study of unconscious motivation and dream analysis. (Psychiatry / Psychoanalysis)

(L.O. 1.3) h. Psychology graduates with ________ degrees provide more than 50 million hours of psychological treatment each year. (bachelor's / master's / doctoral)

What Psychologists Do

Learning Objective 1.4
Describe applied psychology, human services, and experimental psychology, and characterize subfields of each.

The three main fields of psychology—applied psychology, human services, and experimental psychology—have much in common. Actually, human services is a subfield of applied psychology, but it comprises such a large proportion of psychologists that it is generally considered a separate field of psychology. All consider research and theory to be the cornerstone of their approach. In addition, a human service provider may also do research, and a researcher who works in a university may also provide human services to the university or the community at large. For example, learning principles discovered in an experimental laboratory may be applied by a human services psychologist to help an alcoholic patient. Similarly, problems discovered by therapists challenge researchers to investigate causes in the laboratory. Let's look at each of these areas within psychology.

Applied Psychology

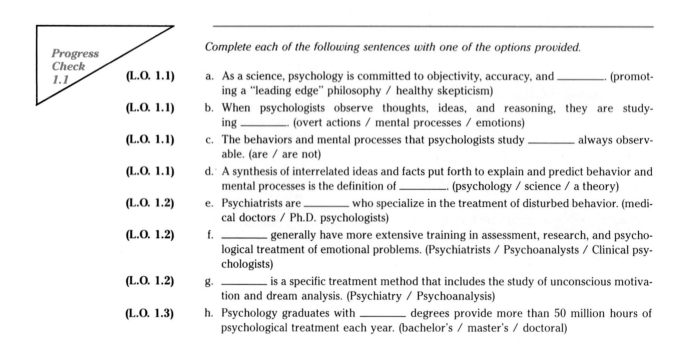

Applied psychologists do research and then use that research to solve everyday practical problems. Actually, psychologists working in the human service field who treat people with emotional problems function as applied psychologists, but so do many other psychologists who use psychological principles in business, government, or institutions such as hospitals. (Applied psychologists who work in the human services field are considered separately.) For example, *engineering psychologists* (sometimes called human factors psychologists) focus on using psychological principles to help people use machines efficiently (for example, determining how to design the most easy-to-use automated bank-teller or the most pleasing computer screen). *Educational psychologists* focus on how learning proceeds in the classroom, how intelligence affects performance, and the relationship between personality and learning. *Forensic psychologists* focus on legal issues, the court, and correctional systems. They often work with the courts in evaluating whether an inmate is ready for parole, or whether a specific rehabilitation program is achieving its goals. *Health psychologists* focus on the way that life-style changes can facilitate health improvement. They devise techniques for helping people with medical and psychological problems. *Sports psychology* is an emerging field that focuses on brain—behavior interactions, the role of sports in healthful life-styles, and the motivation and preparation of athletes in sports-related activities. *Industrial/organizational* psychologists are concerned with the way that employers evaluate employees; they focus on personnel selection, employee motivation, work behavior, and work appraisals. They apply psychological research and theory to organizational problems (such as productivity, turnover, absenteeism, and management—labor relations) and work in personnel offices, universities, and businesses to help evaluate organizational programs. Human-service psychology considered next is a special area of applied psychology and is usually considered a discrete key area of psychology.

Human Service Fields

Many applied psychologists work in settings in which they teach people to cope more effectively by applying behavioral principles. Their aim is to help people solve problems and to promote well-being. Within the human service area are the subfields of clinical, counseling, community, and school psychology.

Clinical Psychology. Clinical psychologists specialize in helping clients with behavior problems such as anger, shyness, depression, or marital discord. Their aim is to promote well-being. Clinical psychologists work either in private practice or at a hospital, mental institution, or social service agency. They administer psychological tests, interview potential clients, and use psychological methods to treat emotional problems. Many universities employ psychologists to help students and staff adjust to the pressures of academic life. In universities, clinical psychologists may also be research psychologists and often have laboratories where they research the causes of abnormal behavior.

Counseling Psychology. Counseling psychologists, like clinical psychologists, work with people who have emotional problems. Counseling psychologists often help people with career planning, marriage and family problems, and effective parenting. Traditionally, the problems presented by clients of counseling psychologists are less serious than those presented by clients of clinical psychologists. However, since the 1980s, counseling psychologists have increasingly become engaged in psychotherapy and other activities that were previously performed exclusively by clinical psychologists. Counseling psychologists may work for public agencies such as mental health centers, hospitals, and universities. Many work in college or university counseling bureaus where they help students adjust to the university atmosphere and provide vocational and educational guidance.

Community psychologists take an action-oriented approach to helping people help themselves, as in the aftermath of the San Francisco earthquake.

Community Psychology. Community psychologists work for mental health agencies, state governments, and private organizations. They strengthen existing social support networks and stimulate the formation of new networks to meet a variety of challenges. Their goals are to help individuals and their neighborhoods or communities to grow, develop, and plan for the future. Community psychology emerged in response to the widespread desire for an action-oriented approach to individual and social adjustment, and one key element of community psychology is community involvement to effect social change.

School Psychology. School psychology aims to implement comprehensive psychological services (Fagan, 1986). Many school psychologists see their primary job as helping students, teachers, parents, and others to understand each other.

Today, there are more than 30,000 school psychologists, most of whom work in educational systems.

School psychologists' jobs vary with their level of training. Those with bachelor's degrees usually only administer tests. Those with master's degrees administer and interpret tests and help teachers with classroom-related problems. Psychologists with Ph.D.s perform all those tasks and also influence school policies and procedures (Bardon, 1983). They establish communication among parents, teachers, administrators, and other psychologists at the school. They also provide information to teachers and parents about students' progress and advise them how to help students to achieve more.

Experimental Psychology

Experimental psychology, the other major field of psychology, focuses on identifying and understanding the basic processes involved in behavior and mental processes. Experimental psychology is an approach. When a psychologist says that he or she is an experimental psychologist, it means that the researcher uses a set of *techniques;* experimental psychology does *not* define the *topics* that a psychologist examines. (We examine some of these techniques in Module 2 in this chapter.) Thus, applied psychologists are involved in experimental research, and many experimental psychologists teach in university settings and do research as well.

Experimental psychology covers many areas of interest, some of which overlap with fields outside of psychology. An experimental psychologist may be interested in visual perception, in how people learn language or solve problems, in how hormones influence behavior, in the neurochemistry of the brain, in eye movements, or in the components of emotions. Four key fields of experimental psychology are developmental psychology, social psychology, cognitive psychology, and physiological psychology. *Developmental psychology* focuses on the emotional, physical, and intellectual changes that take place over the life span of organisms. Increasingly, psychologists are looking at behavior from a developmental perspective, asking how a particular behavior changes as people mature physically, emotionally, and intellectually. *Social psychology* studies the ways in which people affect an individual's behavior and thoughts, particularly the ways in which people interact with one another. Social psychologists examine how the presence of others affects attitude formation, how aggressive behavior emerges, when people are willing to help others, and how and when people form intimate relationships. Social psychology, with its wide scope of interests, has emerged as a dominant field in psychology. *Cognitive psychology* focuses on thought processes, especially the relationships among learning, memory, and perception. Cognitive psychologists often examine how organisms process and interpret information based on some internal representations in memory. *Physiological psychology* (sometimes called neuropsychology) tries to understand the relationship of the brain and its mechanisms to behavior. Drugs, hormones, and even brain transplants are examined. This research often involves specialized techniques for studying behavior.

Goal of This Book

The goal of this book is to introduce you to the basic theories and principles of psychology. Some of what you learn may point you in directions that help you resolve everyday problems. For example, how does your life history affect your future development? How much do your thoughts about yourself and others determine what you will do tomorrow? How can an understanding of personality and motivation help you interact with other people? How can the principles of memory be applied to improving your skills and grades?

Some of the specific information may help you or other readers to cope with difficult situations. For example, an understanding of personality and motivation may help some individuals deal with their underachieving children. Knowledge about depression and its causes may help still others cope with rejection in dating. Understanding the origins, symptoms, and treatment of illness may help families deal with feelings about a beloved grandmother's Alzheimer's disease.

Psychologists address all of these issues and many more. In the following chapters, you will explore psychological topics such as the effects of drugs on behavior, various mental disorders and forms of therapy, the processes of perception and memory, and the physical, mental, and social development of human beings from birth through death. We hope this book will provide you with a fundamental understanding of the principles of human behavior and some effective problem-solving tools you can use for the rest of your life.

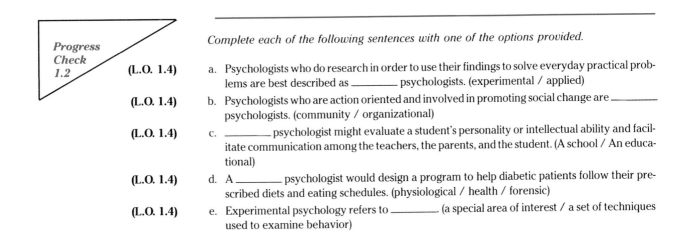

Progress Check 1.2

Complete each of the following sentences with one of the options provided.

(L.O. 1.4) a. Psychologists who do research in order to use their findings to solve everyday practical problems are best described as ________ psychologists. (experimental / applied)

(L.O. 1.4) b. Psychologists who are action oriented and involved in promoting social change are ________ psychologists. (community / organizational)

(L.O. 1.4) c. ________ psychologist might evaluate a student's personality or intellectual ability and facilitate communication among the teachers, the parents, and the student. (A school / An educational)

(L.O. 1.4) d. A ________ psychologist would design a program to help diabetic patients follow their prescribed diets and eating schedules. (physiological / health / forensic)

(L.O. 1.4) e. Experimental psychology refers to ________. (a special area of interest / a set of techniques used to examine behavior)

Module Summary

Defining Psychology

- *Psychology* is the science of behavior and mental processes, which studies every aspect of an organism's functioning—overt actions, mental processes, emotional responses, and physiological reactions (pp. 4–5).
- *Overt actions* refer to any directly observable and measurable movements in the organism, or the results of such movements. *Mental processes* include ideas, reasoning processes, and any thoughts about being angry or happy or sad. *Emotional responses* refer to anger, regret, lust, happiness, depression, and so on. Psychologists also study *physiological reactions,* which include things such as an increased heart rate when the subject is excited or biochemical changes when light stimulates the subject's eye (p. 5).
- Psychologists attempt to *describe* the basic components of behavior, to understand and *explain* them, to *predict* them, and possibly even to *manage* them (p. 5).

Careers in Psychology

- A *psychologist* is someone who has obtained a graduate degree in psychology (typically a Ph.D.) and who studies behavioral principles (p. 5).
- A *psychiatrist* is a medical doctor who has specialized in the treatment of disordered behavior (p. 6).

What Psychologists Do

- A master's degree or a doctorate in psychology requires years of study but opens doors to many fields of endeavor. Opportunities for individuals with bachelor's degrees are more limited but still varied (p. 7).
- The three main fields of psychology—applied psychology, human services, and experimental psychology—all consider research and theory to be the cornerstone of the psychological approach (pp. 8–9).
- A large group of psychologists are *experimental psychologists,* whose focus is usually teaching and research (p. 10).

KEY TERMS

clinical psychologist, p. 6
psychiatrist, p. 6
psychoanalyst, p. 6
psychologist, p. 5
psychology, p. 4
theory, p. 5

SELF-TEST

Module 1

- Before taking the Self-Test, **recite** and **review.**
- Use the key at the back of the text to *correct* your answers.
- *Restudy* pages that correspond to any questions you answered incorrectly.

1. Modern psychologists define psychology as the science of
   a. the mind and emotional disturbance.
   b. psychoanalysis and mental illness.
   c. self-esteem and life-style.
   d. behavior and mental processes.
2. As a science, psychology is committed to *objectivity.* This means that psychologists
   a. develop theories based on common sense.
   b. use personal judgment when drawing conclusions about research findings.
   c. attempt to keep their own expectations and opinions from biasing their evaluation of research and theory.
   d. reject studies that provide socially unapproved explanations for the causes of some human behaviors.
3. Which of the following are the major goals of psychology?
   a. describe, explain, predict, and manage behavior
   b. strengthen desirable behavior and suppress undesirable behavior
   c. explore, discover, invent, and understand behavioral responses
   d. identify, diagnose, treat, and cure behavior problems
4. A similarity among clinical psychologists, psychiatrists, and psychoanalysts is that people in all three professions
   a. are medical doctors who have graduated with M.D. degrees.
   b. can prescribe medications such as tranquilizers and antidepressants.
   c. consider themselves mental health practitioners.
   d. consider research one of their most important activities.
5. Cross out the statement about psychoanalysts that is *false.*
   a. Psychoanalysts are frequently psychiatrists.
   b. Psychoanalysts use a specialized treatment method called "behavior modification."
   c. Psychoanalysts often meet with their clients on a daily basis for several years.
   d. Psychoanalysts look for unconscious motivations and use dream analysis to treat emotional problems.
6. A person with a bachelor's degree in psychology could reasonably expect to be employed by a
   a. corporation to evaluate personnel training programs.
   b. school system to interpret IQ or personality tests.
   c. mental health hospital as a licensed clinical psychologist.
   d. university as a psychology professor.
7. The main difference between clinical and counseling psychologists is
   a. their ability to conduct research within the job setting.
   b. the type of agency, private or public, that employs them.
   c. that counseling psychologists have traditionally worked with less serious behavior problems, but this may be changing.
   d. that clinical psychologists only see people with emotional problems, whereas counseling psychologists only see people with family adjustment problems.
8. ____________ psychology focuses on the emotional, physical, and intellectual changes that take place over the life span.
   a. Health
   b. Educational
   c. Physiological
   d. Developmental

Module 2

Psychology Past and Present: How Psychologists Explore and Understand Human Behavior

LEARNING OBJECTIVES

When you have mastered the material in this module, you will be able to

A History of Psychology. Past and Present Schools of Thought (pp. 15–20)

2.1 Characterize the eight major schools of psychology, including the similarities and differences among them, and describe the eclectic perspective (p. 15).

Techniques Used to Study Behavior (pp. 20–28)

2.2 Explain why animals are sometimes used in psychological research (p. 20).

2.3 Make a distinction between correlations and cause-and-effect relationships (p. 21).

2.4 Describe the specific components of a typical psychology experiment; explain what is meant by a *significant difference* (p. 22).

2.5 Explain how researchers can avoid problems created by the self-fulfilling prophecy and the Hawthorne effect (p. 25).

2.6 Describe four nonexperimental research methods and identify the strengths and weaknesses of each (p. 25).

Applying Research Findings (pp. 28–29)

2.7 Explain why the evaluation of research findings and subsequent application of those findings requires time and caution (p. 28).

SQ3R
- ▲ **Survey** to set goals for studying.
- ▲ Ask **questions** as you **read.**
- ▲ Stop occasionally to **recite** and **review**.

plus
- ▲ **Write** a summary of key points.
- ▲ **Reflect** on the hypotheses, evidence, and implications of this material and on the relevance it has to *your* life.

A former psychology student, Madelyn Jordan, sat in her therapist's office, in a comfortable wing-backed chair. This was her fourth session with her therapist, and she was beginning to feel at ease with the surroundings. She knew that in a minute or two the therapist would emerge from her outer office, where she was probably making some phone calls. In her psychology class, Madelyn had learned about the many different types of psychotherapy and the various ways that psychologists approach therapy. Therefore, she was able to select a therapist who used techniques with which she felt comfortable. Madelyn's therapist uses an approach that lets her see how some of her thoughts cause her to feel inadequate. Together, she and her therapist find more positive ways for Madelyn to think about events in her life so that she can free herself from worry.

Madelyn's therapy helped her see that psychology has a great deal to offer. She has realized that her ideas about the study of the mind were limited in scope before she studied psychology and started her therapy. In many ways, Madelyn's realizations paralleled the changes that have taken place in the field of psychology. Early psychologists adopted narrow, stern, and unbending views of the mind and behavior. As the discipline matured, new topics were introduced, and only in the past 20 years has the full realization of the role of thought and behavior come under scientific scrutiny.

As you study the history of psychology, it is likely that your views of the discipline, like Madelyn's will widen in their scope. We begin this module with a look back at the history of psychology.

A History of Psychology: Past and Present Schools of Psychological Thought

Learning Objective 2.1 Characterize the eight major schools of psychology, including the similarities and differences among them, and describe the eclectic perspective.

Psychologists use many different perspectives to analyze human behavior. These perspectives have been developed over time—across the history of psychology. They serve to orient researchers and provide them with a frame of reference, a way of looking at things. A specific approach to the study of behavior is a *school of psychological thought.* This section discusses the development of schools of psychological thought (summarized in Table 2.1 on the next page).

You will see that the study of behavior and mental processes has had a roller-coaster history, the emphasis shifting from one topic to another. Initially, psychologists studied only the mind. Later they focused only on overt behavior. Most

structuralism: A school of psychology founded on ideas that were initiated by Wundt; proponents believed that psychology should study the contents of consciousness; structuralists developed and used the technique called "introspection."

introspection: The technique of examining the contents of the mind through both self-report and the careful examination of thoughts and feelings.

TABLE 2.1 Summary of schools of psychology

School	Focus	Early leader
Structuralism	Structures of the mind	Wundt
Functionalism	Functions of the mind	James
Gestalt	Properties of perceptual experience	Wertheimer
Psychoanalysis	Unconscious mental processes	Freud
Behaviorism	Overt, observable behavior	Watson
Humanistic	Individual growth, personal responsibility, and free will	Maslow
Cognitive	Thought processes	Various
Biological	Basic biological mechanisms and structures	Various

Wilhelm Wundt

Edward B. Titchener

recently, mental processes are again being carefully considered along with observable behavior.

Structuralism: The Contents of Consciousness

The first widely accepted school of thought was developed by Wilhelm Wundt (1832–1920). In 1879, Wundt founded the first psychological laboratory in Leipzig, Germany, and he is considered to be the founder of the discipline. Before Wundt, the field of psychology did not exist; psychological questions were within the domain of philosophy, medicine, or theology.

Edward B. Titchener (1867–1927) was an Englishman who popularized Wundt's ideas, along with his own, in the United States and the English-speaking world. Titchener and other adherents of **structuralism** considered conscious experience the proper subject matter of psychology. Instead of looking at the broad range of behavior and mental processes that psychologists consider today, they tried to look inside a person by studying the contents of the mind. They attempted to observe the inner working of the mind to find the simple elements of conscious experience.

Titchener used the technique of **introspection** or self-examination—the description and analysis by a person of what he or she is thinking and feeling. Wundt and Titchener also conducted some of the first experiments in psychology. They studied the speed of thought by observing reaction times to simple tasks; for example, they changed elements of the environment, such as the intensity of a sound to which a person was listening, and recorded reaction time.

By today's standards, the structuralists focused too narrowly on conscious experience. They confused many aspects of psychological functioning by changing many things all at once, and they measured several things all at once. Thus, their results allowed for few if any generalizations, and they made little headway in describing the nature of the mind.

Functionalism: How Does the Mind Work?

Before long, a new school of thought—**functionalism**—developed and brought with it a new way of thinking about behavior. As an outgrowth of structuralism, functionalism tried to discover how and why the mind *functions* (hence the name) and its relation to consciousness. Functionalists sought to understand how people adapted to their environment.

William James

Sigmund Freud

With William James (1842–1910) at its head, functionalism was the first truly American psychology. James, a physician and professor of anatomy at Harvard University, argued that knowing the contents of consciousness (structuralism) was too limited; a psychologist had to know how those contents worked together, how they functioned. Through such knowledge, a psychologist could understand how the mind (consciousness) guided behavior.

The early schools of psychological thought were soon replaced by different conceptualizations of psychology: Gestalt, psychoanalysis, behaviorism, and cognitive and humanistic approaches.

functionalism: A school of psychology that developed out of structuralism. Concerned with how and why the conscious mind works, its main aim was to know how the contents of consciousness worked together; principal proponents were James and Hall.

Gestalt psychology: [gesh-TALT] A school of psychology that argues that behavior cannot be studied in parts but must be viewed as a whole; Gestalt psychologists focused on the unity of perception and thinking.

Gestalt Psychology: Examining Wholes

At the same time that some psychologists were grappling with structuralism and functionalism, others were developing very different approaches. One such approach was **Gestalt psychology.** Gestalt psychologists, such as Max Wertheimer and Kurt Koffka, found Wundt's and Titchener's structuralism too limiting. They argued that it is necessary to study a person's total experience—not just parts of the mind or behavior (*Gestalt* means "configuration").

Gestalt psychologists suggested that conscious experience is more than simply the sum of its parts. Arguing that the mind takes the elements of experience and organizes them to form something unique, Gestalt psychologists analyzed the world in terms of perceptual frameworks. By analyzing the whole experience, the patterns of a person's perceptions and thoughts, one can understand the mind and its workings. Eventually, Gestalt psychology became a major influence in many areas of psychology, for example, in therapy. However, as broad as its influence would become, Gestalt approaches never achieved as wide a following as did psychoanalysis.

Psychoanalysis: Probing the Unconscious

One of the first to develop a theory about emotional disturbance was Sigmund Freud (1856–1939). Freud was a physician interested in helping people overcome anxiety. He focused on the causes and treatment of emotional disturbances. Freud worked from the premise that unconscious processes direct daily behavior; he ultimately developed techniques, such as free association and dream interpretation, to explore those unconscious processes. He emphasized the idea that child-

psychoanalytic approach: [SIE-ko-an-uh-LIT-ick] The theory developed by Freud, who was interested in how personality develops and in the treatment of maladjustment. His approach focused on the unconscious and on how it directs day-to-day behavior.

hood experiences influence future adult behaviors and that sexual energy fuels day-to-day behavior.

Freud's approach is the **psychoanalytic approach,** or *psychoanalysis.* Psychoanalytic theories assume that maladjustment is a consequence of anxiety resulting from unresolved conflicts and forces of which a person may not be aware. The psychoanalytic perspective has undergone many changes since it was first devised by Freud; at times, it seems only loosely connected to Freud's basic ideas. Chapter 10 discusses Freud's theory of personality, and Chapter 14 discusses psychoanalysis as the therapeutic technique derived from his theory.

Behaviorism: Observable Behavior

In the early years of the 20th century, American psychology moved from studying the contents of the mind to studying overt behavior. At the forefront of that movement was John B. Watson (1878–1958), the founder of **behaviorism.** Watson argued that there is no reasonable, objective way to observe the human mind. He contended that observable behavior, not the private contents of consciousness, is the proper subject matter of psychology. According to Watson, psychologists should study only activities that can be objectively observed and measured.

After Watson, other American researchers have extended and developed behaviorism. Behaviorists such as Harvard psychologist B. F. Skinner (1904–1990) attempted to explain the causes of behavior by cataloging and describing the relations among events in the environment (*stimuli*) and a person's or animals' reactions (*responses*). Skinner's behaviorism led the way to thousands of research studies on conditioning and human behavior, a special focus on stimuli and responses, and efforts to control behavior through learning principles (Skinner, 1990). The terms *learning theory, behavior modification,* and *behavioral psychology* refer to this school of psychology.

John B. Watson

The behaviorists' perspective focuses on how observable responses are learned, modified, and forgotten. It usually focuses on current behavior and how it is acquired or modified rather than on inherited characteristics or early childhood experiences. A fundamental assumption of behavioral theorists is that disordered behavior can be reshaped and that appropriate, worthwhile behavior can be substituted through the traditional learning techniques described in Chapter 5.

Early behaviorists took a stern, unbending view of the scope of psychology by refusing to study mental phenomena. Behaviorists today take a broader view; most behavioral psychologists study a wider range of human behavior, including mental phenomena and especially thought processes.

B. F. Skinner

Humanistic Psychology: Free Will

Another school of thought that figures into the landscape of modern psychology is **humanistic psychology,** which arose in response to psychoanalytic and behavioral views. The humanists see people as good and striving to fulfill themselves, whereas psychoanalytically oriented theorists saw people as fraught with inner conflict, and behaviorists were too narrowly focused on stimulus–response relations. Humanistic psychologists see people as having *free will,* the ability to choose the paths they take in life. In other words, humanists believe that human beings have control of their lives.

This approach emphasizes the uniqueness of the human experience and the idea that human beings have the ability to determine or at least powerfully affect their own destiny. Humanistic psychologists assert that human beings are conscious, creative, and born with an innate desire to fulfill themselves. They say that psychologists must examine human behavior individually. Proponents of the humanistic view, such as Abraham Maslow and Carl Rogers (whom we study in Chapter 10), believe that human beings have both a desire for **self-actualization**—that is, fulfillment of their human potential—and the ability to create their own perceptions and choose their own experiences of reality (Andrews, 1989). Although this approach is appealing, it is difficult or impossible to test experimentally (Sappington, 1990).

Cognitive Psychology: Thinking Again

Many psychologists realized that strict behaviorism had limitations; they especially reacted to its narrow focus on observable behavior. As an outgrowth of behaviorism (and a reaction to it), **cognitive psychology** focuses on thought processes and mental activities involved in perception, memory, learning, and thinking. Cognitive psychology focuses on the mental processes involved in behavior, such as how people solve problems and appraise situations as threatening. Cognitive psychology is sometimes seen as antibehaviorist, but it is not. Cognitive psychology views the strict behavioral approach as incomplete, as missing a key component—mental processes. Cognitive psychology is not restricted to a single area; it is an approach that spans many psychological fields. For example, cognitive psychologists are sometimes clinicians working with maladjusted clients, helping them to identify more realistic ideas about the world so that they might change their own behavior, to adjust more effectively.

Biological Perspective: Predispositions

Increasingly, researchers are turning to biology to explain some human behavior. The **biological perspective** (sometimes called a neuroscience perspective) focuses on how physical mechanisms affect emotions, thoughts, desires, and sensory experiences. Those with a biological perspective tend to examine psychological issues from the viewpoint of how inherited and biological structures affect mental processes and behavior. Genetic abnormalities, problems in the central nervous system, and hormonal changes are often the focus of those who adopt a biological perspective. Researchers such as Kety, Gottesman, and Rosenthal (discussed in Chapter 15) are often cited as leaders of a biological perspective.

Eclecticism: The Best of Everything

Psychologists realize that a complex relationship exists among the factors that affect both overt behavior and mental processes. Therefore, most American psychologists who are involved in applied psychology, especially clinical psychology, are **eclectic** in their approach and their perspective. Instead of studying only one aspect of behavior or taking only one approach to treatment, they use a variety of approaches to evaluate data, theory, or therapy.

An eclectic orientation allows a researcher or practitioner to view a problem from several orientations. For example, consider *depression,* the disabling mood disorder in which people become exceedingly sad, which affects 10–20% of men and women in America at some time in their life (Chapter 13 discusses depression at length). From a biological perspective alone, people become depressed because of changes in brain chemistry. From a behavioral point of view alone, people learn to be depressed and sad because of faulty reward systems in their environment. The psychoanalytic perspective suggests that people become depressed because their early childhood experiences caused them to form a negative outlook on life. Humanists argue that depression is often caused by people choosing inaction because of poor role models. The cognitive perspective suggests that depres-

behaviorism: A school of psychology that rejects the study of the contents of consciousness; instead, it focuses on describing and measuring only what is observable, either directly or through assessment instruments.

humanistic psychology: The school of psychology that emphasizes the uniqueness of the human experience and the idea that human beings have free will to determine their destiny.

self-actualization: The process by which individuals strive to fulfill themselves; proposed by humanistic psychologists.

cognitive psychology: A school of psychology that focuses on the thought processes and mental activities involved in perception, memory, learning, and thinking.

biological perspective: Examines psychological issues based on how heredity and biological structures affect behavior; it focuses on how physical mechanisms create emotions, feelings, thoughts, and desires.

eclectic: [ek-LECK-tick] A combination of theories, facts, or techniques; in clinical psychology, this term usually describes the practice of using whatever therapy techniques are appropriate for an individual client rather than relying exclusively on the techniques of one school of psychology.

sion is made worse by the interpretations (thoughts) an individual might adopt about a situation. An eclectic position recognizes the complex nature of depression and acknowledges each of the possible contributions; an eclectic practitioner evaluates the person, the depression, and the context in which the person is depressed.

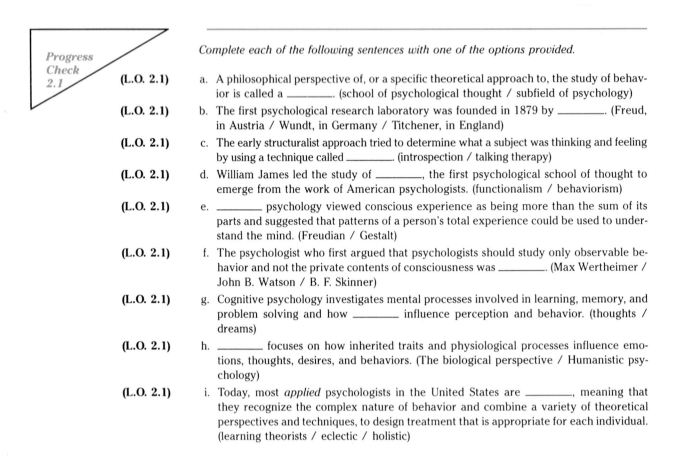

Progress Check 2.1

Complete each of the following sentences with one of the options provided.

(L.O. 2.1) a. A philosophical perspective of, or a specific theoretical approach to, the study of behavior is called a ________. (school of psychological thought / subfield of psychology)

(L.O. 2.1) b. The first psychological research laboratory was founded in 1879 by ________. (Freud, in Austria / Wundt, in Germany / Titchener, in England)

(L.O. 2.1) c. The early structuralist approach tried to determine what a subject was thinking and feeling by using a technique called ________. (introspection / talking therapy)

(L.O. 2.1) d. William James led the study of ________, the first psychological school of thought to emerge from the work of American psychologists. (functionalism / behaviorism)

(L.O. 2.1) e. ________ psychology viewed conscious experience as being more than the sum of its parts and suggested that patterns of a person's total experience could be used to understand the mind. (Freudian / Gestalt)

(L.O. 2.1) f. The psychologist who first argued that psychologists should study only observable behavior and not the private contents of consciousness was ________. (Max Wertheimer / John B. Watson / B. F. Skinner)

(L.O. 2.1) g. Cognitive psychology investigates mental processes involved in learning, memory, and problem solving and how ________ influence perception and behavior. (thoughts / dreams)

(L.O. 2.1) h. ________ focuses on how inherited traits and physiological processes influence emotions, thoughts, desires, and behaviors. (The biological perspective / Humanistic psychology)

(L.O. 2.1) i. Today, most *applied* psychologists in the United States are ________, meaning that they recognize the complex nature of behavior and combine a variety of theoretical perspectives and techniques, to design treatment that is appropriate for each individual. (learning theorists / eclectic / holistic)

Techniques Used to Study Behavior

If you ever have the opportunity to tour a psychologist's laboratory, take the tour. Even better, if you have an opportunity to assist a psychologist in research, take advantage of it. Your appreciation of psychology will grow immensely because of the experience. Although psychologists use some of the same techniques as other scientists, they must refine these techniques to deal with the uncertainties of human behavior. Psychologists have developed an arsenal of techniques and methods for investigating patterns of behavior, some of which are unique to psychology.

Animals and Human Beings

Learning Objective 2.2
Explain why animals are sometimes used in psychological research.

Psychologists study behavior in both animals and human beings. By studying how animals and human beings react under different circumstances, psychologists learn about the basic principles of behavior and the possibilities for applying these principles.

Some experimental psychologists study behavior by observing it first in animals and then generalizing the principles they discover to human behavior. For example, years ago, Pavlov discovered the fundamentals of classical conditioning (discussed in Chapter 5) by conducting experiments on salivating dogs. These fundamentals of classical conditioning have been used to explain how some children develop a generalized fear or phobic reaction to harmless situations, animals, or objects.

Using animals in research studies allows experimenters to isolate simple aspects of behavior and to eliminate the complex distractions and variables that arise in studies involving human beings. Also because most animals have shorter life spans than human beings, studying animals enables experimenters to control the life history of the organism being studied, to perform autopsies to obtain information, and to study several generations in a short time.

Many people object to the use of animals in research, but there are no known realistic alternatives at present (Gallup & Suarez, 1985). For example, experiments on laboratory rats reveal much about the addictive properties of cocaine and its adverse effects on behavior; of course, doing similar experiments on human beings would be unethical. In addition, many people with incurable diseases and disorders can only hope for a cure through animal research and experimentation (Feeney, 1987). Nonetheless, most researchers are sensitive to the needs of animals (Novak & Suomi, 1988), and the APA has strict ethical guidelines for animal research. Though research on animals is only a small part (about 7%) of the research published in psychological journals (Miller, 1985), the conflict between animal psychologists and animal rights activists has been around for many years and is likely to continue for many more to come (Dewsbury, 1990).

Psychologists more often work with human participants, traditionally called **subjects.** In such research, psychologists investigate many of the same processes they do with animals, and they design experiments specifically for human subjects. Psychologists conduct research both in laboratory settings and in naturalistic environments. (The differences between laboratory and naturalistic settings are explored later in this module.) They generally try to place their research findings and interpretations in a framework of real-world problems and perspectives. Their ultimate aims are to understand and to make reliable predictions about the complexities of human behavior and thus to help people manage their lives.

Systematic Explorations: Correlation Versus Causation

Learning Objective 2.3
Make a distinction between correlations and cause-and-effect relationships.

The typical research process is usually systematic and begins with a specific question. However, sometimes a researcher searching for the cause of a particular behavior or the answer to a particular question may unexpectedly find an answer to another problem. Although researchers may discover some things accidentally, they always follow up their research *systematically;* that is, they try to consider all the aspects of a situation that might cause an organism to behave as it does.

Ordinarily, observation may show that two types of behavior often occur together, but this does not necessarily mean that one behavior causes the other. For example, beer consumption increased sharply from 1900 to 1990; at the same time, life expectancy has increased sharply. These two events have paralleled one another but are unrelated (i.e., beer consumption was not the cause of life expectancy increases, nor were life expectancy increases the cause of increased beer consumption). Only controlled experiments permit researchers to make *cause-and-effect statements*—to make inferences about the causes of behavior.

subject: An individual who participates in an experiment and whose behavior is observed for research data collection; subjects are sometimes called "participants."

An important point to remember is that *correlated events are not necessarily causally related.* Two events are *correlated* when the increased presence (or ab-

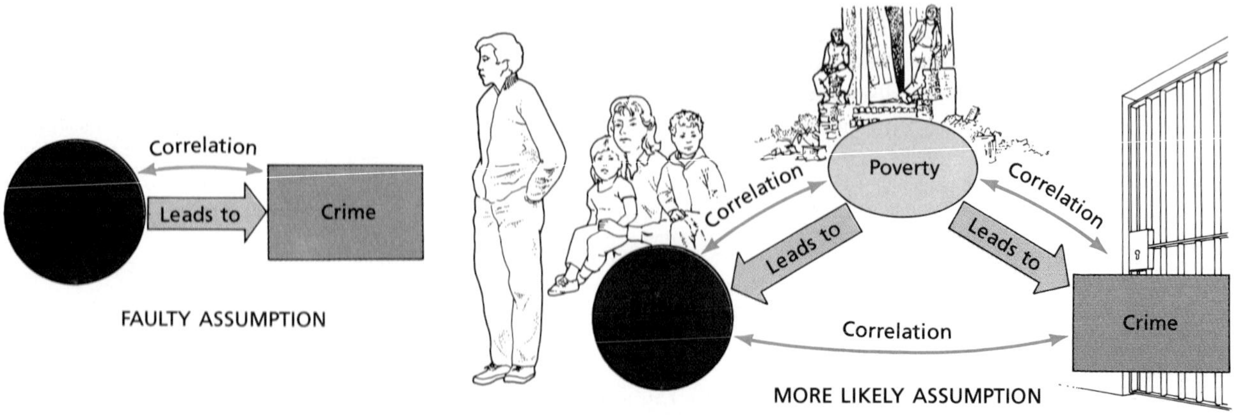

Figure 2.1

Correlations do not show causation. When research shows that broken homes and crime are correlated, it does not show causation. Poverty, a third variable, may be the cause of both crime and broken homes.

sence) of a particular situation (or a particular feature of a situation) is regularly associated with a high (or low) presence of another situation, event, or situational feature. For example, if a researcher finds that children from broken homes have more emotional problems than other children, he or she can state that there is a correlation. However, these data do not permit causal statements; that is, we cannot conclude that broken homes cause emotional problems. Even though broken homes provide an atmosphere conducive to emotional stress in children, too many other variables can also contribute to emotional problems, so we cannot state with certainty that broken homes *cause* later emotional disturbances. By contrast, events are causally related when one event makes another event occur—when one event or situation is contingent on the other.

Thus, although a correlation shows that a relationship exists between two characteristics of a situation, a person, or an event, that relationship may result from a common cause (i.e., both factors or characteristics are affected by a third one, not by each other; see Figure 2.1) or from the method used to gather the data. Researchers are careful to distinguish between events that are causally related and those that are only correlated. The topic of correlations is discussed further in the appendix at the end of this textbook.

Controlled Experiments

Learning Objective 2.4
Describe the specific components of a typical psychology experiment; explain what is meant by a *significant difference.*

When psychologists suggest that one situation causes another, they have to be sure that several specific conditions are met. They pay close attention to how the data are collected and to whether the results of the study are repeatable in additional experiments. To make meaningful causal inferences, psychologists must create situations in which they can limit the likelihood of obtaining a result that is simply a chance occurrence or due to other irrelevant factors. Only by using carefully formulated experiments can psychologists make sound interpretations of their results and cautiously extend them to other (sometimes therapeutic) situations. The primary technique they use to explore cause-and-effect relationships is the controlled experiment.

An **experiment** is a procedure in which a researcher systematically manipulates and observes elements of a situation in order to discover and describe the relationship between these elements. For example, if a researcher wanted to determine the relationship between a person's eating behavior and his or her weight gains or losses, the researcher could systematically vary (manipulate) how much the person ate and then weigh (observe) the person each day. Experiments have specific components and requirements, including *variables, experimental* and *control groups, operational definitions,* and guidelines for *sample sizes.*

Variables. A **variable** is a characteristic of a situation or of a person that is subject to change, either within or across individuals. Researchers manipulate variables in order to measure how changes in these variables affect behavior. For example, a characteristic of a situation that might change is temperature. A characteristic of a person that might change within an individual is his or her health; a characteristic that might change across individuals is place of birth. The variable directly and purposely manipulated by the experimenter in a controlled experiment is the **independent variable** (e.g., the temperature level, a drug dosage level, or an amount of food eaten). The independent variable is varied to see what effect it has on behavior. The person's (or organism's) behavior (or change) being measured is the **dependent variable** (e.g., the activity level of a person who is exposed to hot or cold temperatures, to a particular dose of a drug, or to a stressful film).

To see more clearly how variables come into play in an experiment, imagine a simple experiment to determine the effects of sleep loss on behavior. The independent variable (the variable being manipulated) might be the number of hours that college students were allowed to sleep. The dependent variable could be the students' reaction times to a stimulus, such as how quickly they push a button when a light is flashed. The subjects (or participants) in the study might be a large group of college students who normally sleep about 7 hours per night.

Hypotheses. A **hypothesis** is a tentative idea that expresses a proposed causal relationship between two events or variables. For example, the tentative idea, or hypothesis, of the sleep experiment might be that students deprived of sleep will do less well on the reaction-time task than those who are allowed to sleep their regular 7 hours. Suppose that the subjects sleep in the laboratory on four successive nights and are tested each morning in a reaction time task. The subjects sleep 7 hours on each of three nights, but only 4 hours on the fourth. If the response times after three nights of 7 hours of sleep are constant, the researcher can infer that any slowing of reaction time on the fourth test (following the night of 4 hours of sleep) is the result of depriving the subjects of sleep.

If all other factors are held equal, any observed differences in reaction time can be attributed to the independent variable (number of hours of sleep). That is, changes in the independent variable (numbers of hours of sleep) will produce changes in the dependent variable (reaction time). Also, if the results show that students deprived of sleep respond on the reaction time task one-half second slower than they did after normal sleep, the researcher could feel justified in concluding that sleep deprivation acts to slow down reaction time. The researcher's initial idea would have been affirmed by the experiment.

Control and Experimental Groups. Researchers must determine whether it is actually changes in the manipulated variable and not in some unknown extraneous factor that cause a change in the dependent variable. One way to do this is to have at least two groups of subjects who are identical in important ways before the experiment begins. The attributes they must have in common depend on what the experimenter is testing. For example, in a sleep experiment, because reflexes slow down as a person grows older, a researcher doing an experiment on reaction times would ensure that the two groups comprised subjects who are the same age.

experiment: A procedure in which a researcher systematically manipulates some variables to describe objectively the relation between the variables of concern and the resulting behavior; well-designed experiments permit inferences about cause and effect, and they test hypotheses.

variables: Conditions or characteristics of a situation (or experiment) that can change or that can vary across individuals or across situations.

independent variable: The variable in an experiment that is directly and purposefully manipulated by the experimenter to see how the manipulation will affect the variables under study.

dependent variable: The behavior measured by an experimenter to assess whether changes in the independent variable affect the behavior being studied.

hypothesis: A tentative statement about a causal relationship between two variables or conditions to be evaluated in an experiment.

Once the subjects are known to be identical on important attributes that might affect the results, they are assigned randomly to either the experimental or the control group. *Random assignment* means that individuals are assigned to groups by chance rather than on the basis of any particular characteristic, trait, preference, or situation that might have a remote possibility of influencing the outcome. An **experimental group** consists of subjects for whom the independent variable is manipulated. A **control group** consists of subjects tested on the dependent variable in the same way as the experimental group but for whom the independent variable is not manipulated; it is a comparison group. In the reaction time experiment, the students who sleep a full 7 hours are members of the control group. Those who are only allowed to sleep fewer hours are members of the experimental group. By comparing reaction time (the dependent variable) for the experimental and control groups, a researcher can determine whether the independent variable is responsible for any differences in the dependent variable between the groups.

Significant Differences. Researchers want to be sure that the differences they find could not have occurred just by chance. For psychologists, the statistically determined likelihood that a behavior has not occurred because of chance alone is called a **significant difference.** The results are only *significant* if they could not have occurred by chance, by one or two subjects, or by a unique collection of subjects. In the sleep experiment, statistical significance would assess the likelihood that the differences in reaction times between the experimental and control subjects could have occurred by chance. If an experiment's results do not show statistical significance, the results really could have occurred by chance, so they are not considered to have affirmed the hypothesis.

Operational Definitions. Another key component of successful scientific research is that all terms used in describing the variables and the experimental procedure must be given operational definitions. An **operational definition** is the set of methods or procedures used to define a variable. When a researcher manipulates an organism's state of hunger, the concept *hunger* must be defined in terms of the procedures necessary to produce hunger. For example, a researcher might be interested in the effects of hunger (independent variable) on exploratory behavior (dependent variable) in mice. The researcher might deprive mice of food for 6, 10, 12, or 24 hours and might record the exploratory behavior of the mice before and during each of the conditions of food deprivation. The researcher would operationally define hunger in terms of the number of hours of food deprivation; the dependent variable, exploratory behavior, would be operationally defined in terms of the number of times the mice walked down an alley farther than 2 feet.

Sample Size. Another important factor in an experiment is the size of the sample. A **sample** refers to the group of subjects who are examined by the researcher, and who are generally assumed to be representative of the population about which an inference is being made. Suppose, for example, there is a one quarter of a second difference between the reaction times of the control and the experimental groups in a reaction-time study. An experimenter who tested only three students could not be certain that the quarter-second difference in reaction time is significant. An experimenter who tested 100 students in both the control and experimental groups, on the other hand, can be more certain that the difference is unlikely to have occurred by chance.

The number of subjects in a sample is very important. If an effect is obtained consistently with a large enough number of subjects, a researcher can reasonably

experimental group: In an experiment, the group of subjects that receives the treatment under investigation and for whom the independent variable has been manipulated.

control group: The experimental subjects who do not receive the treatment under investigation; it is used for comparison purposes, so that the observed effects can be traced to the treatment being studied.

significant difference: A statistically determined likelihood that a behavior has not occurred due to chance alone.

operational definition: The set of methods or procedures used to define a variable within the context of a research study.

sample: A group of subjects or participants who are generally representative of the population about which an inference is being made.

rule out individual differences and chance as causes. The assumption is that a large sample better represents the population to which the researcher wishes to generalize his or her results.

Learning Objective 2.5
Explain how researchers can avoid problems created by the self-fulfilling prophecy and the Hawthorne effect.

Designing Successful Experiments: Avoiding Pitfalls. Frequently, things turn out just the way a researcher expects. Researchers are aware that their expectations about results might influence their findings, particularly regarding expectations of human behaviors. They fear that they may unwittingly create situations that lead to specific results: Such an event is a **self-fulfilling prophecy.** For example, teachers may develop expectations regarding their students' performance early in the year, and students usually confirm those expectations, even when those expectations may not reflect students' potential abilities (Jussim, 1989). In these instances, the students' performance fulfilled the teachers' prophecies regarding their performance, regardless of other factors, such as potential ability.

self-fulfilling prophecy: The finding that people frequently behave just the way a person expects that they will; researchers may unwittingly create situations that lead to specific (prophesied) results.

To avoid self-fulfilling prophecies, researchers often use a **double-blind technique** in which neither the experimenter nor the subjects know who is in the control or the experimental group. This is done by having some third individual, such as another researcher who is not connected with the research project, keep track of which subjects are assigned to which group. This technique minimizes the effect that a researcher's subtle, but nevertheless potent, cues might have on subjects. (In a normal, single-blind experiment, the researcher knows who is in the experimental group and who is in the control group, but the subjects do not know who is assigned to which group or whether they are being presented with a treatment.)

double-blind technique: A research technique in which neither the experimenter nor the subjects know who is in the control or the experimental group, thus minimizing the effects of self-fulfilling prophecies.

Even when a double-blind procedure is used, participants behave differently when they are in a research study. This finding is called the **Hawthorne effect.** Researchers are aware of these effects and attempt to make subjects feel comfortable and natural, and to create experimental situations that minimize the effects of participation. They often do not collect data until after subjects have adapted to the experimental situation and have become less excited about their participation in the research study.

Hawthorne effect: The finding that people behave differently (usually what they believe to be more appropriate or more desirable) when they know they are being observed.

Alternative Methods of Investigation

Experiments are not the only way to collect data about human behavior, however. Techniques providing information other than cause-and-effect relations also are important. These techniques include *questionnaires, interviews, naturalistic observation,* and *case studies.*

questionnaire: A printed form with questions, usually given to a large group of people; a means of gathering a substantial amount of data in a short time.

Learning Objective 2.6
Describe four nonexperimental research methods, and identify the strengths and weaknesses of each.

Questionnaires. A **questionnaire,** sometimes called a survey, is used by researchers to gather a large amount of information from many people in a short time. A survey might be used to learn the typical characteristics of psychology students. Such a survey could be sent to students enrolled in an introductory psychology course.

The questionnaire might ask each student to list his or her age, sex, height, weight, previous courses taken, grades in high school, SAT scores, number of brothers and sisters, and parents' financial status. There might also be questions regarding sexual relations, career goals, and personal preferences on topics such as TV shows, clothing styles, and music.

An aim of surveys and questionnaires is to discover relationships among variables. For example, a questionnaire designed to assess aggressiveness may ask respondents to list their gender, the number of fights they might have had in the past, their feelings of anger, and what types of sports they enjoy. When analyzing

UNDERSTANDING THE RESEARCH PROCESS

Evaluating Psychological Research

A psychologist, like all scientists, is trained to think and to evaluate research critically and to put it into a meaningful framework. Whatever the method used to ask questions and to answer research hypotheses, the researcher thinks critically about the question, the methods, and the results. Psychologists follow a traditional approach to evaluating research. To really benefit from this textbook, you may find it helpful to use the same critical thinking skills used by psychologists in order to follow their logic, to understand their approach, and to judge their research, using a psychological mental framework.

Critical thinking means evaluating evidence, sifting through choices, assessing outcomes, and deciding whether conclusions make sense. When you think critically, you are being evaluative; you are not accepting glib generalizations, you are determining the relevancy of facts; and you are looking for biases and imbalances, as well as for objectivity and testable repeatable results. A critical thinker identifies central issues and is careful not to reach cause-and-effect conclusions from correlations.

Whenever you think critically about research, you become a detective sorting through the facts. You look objectively at the facts, question the hypotheses and conclusions, avoid oversimplifications, and consider all of the arguments, objections, and counterarguments. You revise your opinions when the data and conclusions call for revisions.

As a critical thinker, whenever you have to evaluate a research study in this text, in the popular press, or in a psychological publication, it is helpful to focus on five research criteria: *purpose, methodology, subjects, repeatability,* and *conclusions.*

1. **Purpose**—What is the purpose of this research? What is the researcher trying to test, demonstrate, or prove? Has the problem been clearly defined? Is this researcher qualified to conduct this research?
2. **Methodology**—Is the methodology appropriate and carefully executed? Has the researcher used an appropriate method of investigation? For example, is the method used the most appropriate one for the topic (e.g., case study, survey, experiment). In addition, has the method been used properly? Is there a control group? Have variables been carefully (operationally) defined? Has the researcher followed ethical guidelines?
3. **Subjects**—Is the sample of subjects properly chosen and carefully described? How is the sample selected? Does the sample accurately reflect the characteristics of the population of individuals about which the researcher would like to make generalizations? Will any generalizations be possible from this study?
4. **Repeatability**—Are the results repeatable? Has the

the questionnaire results, a researcher will check to see whether the gender and personality traits of the respondents are related—that is, whether men and women tend to differ in aggressive behaviors.

The strength of a questionnaire is that it gathers a large amount of information in a short time. Its weaknesses are that it's impersonal, it gathers only the information asked by the questions, it limits the subjects' range of responses, it cannot prevent respondents from leaving some questions unanswered or from being untruthful in their responses, and it does not provide a structure from which cause-and-effect relationships can be inferred (although correlations may be found).

interview: A series of open-ended questions used to gather detailed information about a person; though time-consuming, this technique allows in-depth probing of potentially important issues or problems.

Interviews. An **interview** is a face-to-face meeting in which an interviewer asks an individual a series of standardized questions. The subject's responses are usually tape recorded or written by the interviewer. The advantage of an interview over a questionnaire is that it allows the interviewer to ask questions other than the standard ones. If the interviewer notes an exaggerated response, for example, instead of recording a simple answer, he or she may decide to ask related questions and thus explore more fully an area that seems important to the

researcher shown the same finding more than once? Have other investigators made similar findings? Are the results clear and unambiguous—that is, not open to criticism based on poor methodology? What additional evidence will be necessary for a psychologist to support the conclusions?

5. **Conclusions**—Are the conclusions, implications, and applications suggested by the study logical? Are they supported by the researcher's data? Has the researcher gone beyond his or her data and drawn conclusions that might fit a predisposed view rather than conclusions that follow logically from the facts of the study? In what ways do the data have implications for psychology as a science, as a profession, and potentially for you as an individual? Has the researcher considered alternative explanations?

Think back to the sleep-deprivation experiment described earlier (p. 23). Use the five criteria to evaluate this research. The subjects were college students deprived of sleep and tested on a reaction-time task. Think about purpose, methodology, subjects, repeatability, and conclusions. Was the purpose of the study clear? The purpose was to assess the effect of sleep loss on reaction time. Was the methodology appropriate? The method involved depriving subjects of sleep after they had grown used to sleeping in a controlled environment; subjects were tested each morning. The task was carefully operationally defined.

What about the subjects? The subjects were college students who were in good health. Reasonable generalizations might be possible from their reaction times to the reaction times of other similarly aged people. What about repeatability? If the results obtained were found with several groups of subjects, and if the results were consistent within each of those groups, the repeatability of the results seems assured.

Last, what about conclusions? Limited conclusions can be drawn from such a research study; there was only one age group—college students; there were no controls on other factors in the students' environment, such as work loads, school pressure, energy expenditures, and history of sleep loss. Simple limited conclusions about sleep deprivation still could be drawn, such as, "Among college students, in controlled research studies, sleep deprivation tends to slow down reaction time." However, based on the limited study, not much more could be said, and few or no generalizations could be applied to chldren, older adults, or populations of the chronically mentally ill. The results of the study do not contradict common sense, but they add little to our overall understanding of reaction time.

A key to thinking critically about research is to be *evaluative,* to question all aspects of the study. Think about the advantages as well as the limitations of the research method. As you read this text, evaluate the research findings contained herein. Thinking critically requires you to evalute facts and shed preconceived ideas.

- ***What are the implications of a study that is poorly conducted or has a flawed methodology?***
- ***When evidence has been presented in a biased manner, how must a critical thinker evaluate the results?***
- ***What evidence suggests that a well-meaning researcher may draw illogical conclusions?***

subject. However, the interview technique is very time-consuming and, again, no cause-and-effect relationships can be inferred.

Naturalistic Observation. A seemingly simple way to find out about behavior is to observe it. However, people who are told that they are going to be observed tend to become self-conscious and to alter their natural behavior. Therefore, psychologists use the technique of **naturalistic observation** by trying to observe from a distance how people or animals behave in their natural settings—the way that bird watchers watch birds—thereby minimizing the effects of their presence on the behavior being observed.

A psychologist conducting research on persuasion may act like a browsing shopper at car lots, furniture stores, and appliance centers, to discover how salespeople convince customers to buy expensive products. For example, the researcher may observe that one particularly successful car salesperson tends to show budget-minded customers the most expensive automobiles first; midpriced models then seem more affordable by comparison. A researcher might also simulate naturalistic observation by watching a salesperson through a one-way mirror or through videotapes, such as the kind used to detect thefts in supermarkets.

naturalistic observation: Careful and objective observation of events as they occur in nature, without observer intervention.

case study: A method of interviewing a subject to gain information about his or her background, including data on such things as childhood, family, education, and social and sexual interactions.

The strength of naturalistic observation is that the data collected are largely free of being contaminated by the researcher's presence or by the laboratory setting. The weakness is that the behavior the psychologist might wish to examine may not be exhibited. For example, animals sometimes do not show mating behavior, or groups of people or animals might not migrate, act persuasively, or become aggressive. Naturalistic observation is also very time-consuming.

Naturalistic observers take their data where and how they find them. They cannot manipulate the environment because this might interfere with the behavior they are observing. Because variables cannot be manipulated, data from naturalistic observation, like those from questionnaires and interviews, do not permit cause-and-effect conclusions.

Case Studies. The **case study** method involves interviewing subjects to gain information about their background, including data on such things as childhood, family, education, and social and sexual interactions. The information in a case study, or client history, describes in detail a specific person's responses to the world and can be used to determine a method of treatment for that person.

The strength of a case history is that the information it provides is complete. A weakness is that the information describes only one individual and his or her unique problem. Because the behavior of one person may be like that of others or may be unique, researchers cannot generalize from one individual to an entire population. Psychologists must be cautious even when generalizing from a large number of similar case histories.

See Table 2.2 for a summary of the major approaches psychologists use in conducting research.

Applying Research Findings

Learning Objective 2.7
Explain why the evaluation of research findings and subsequent application of those findings requires time and caution.

Psychologists from various fields and perspectives are often both scientists and practitioners. As scientists, they gather basic information about behavior and mental processes; as practitioners, they apply their findings in various disciplines, such as law. For example, psychologists influence legal decisions, serve on the faculties of law schools, and are cited in legal case books. Psychologically relevant legal issues include child development, custody, maladjustment, perception of fair-

Industrial/organizational psychologists use psychological research to help employers select, evaluate, and motivate workers.

TABLE 2.2 Five approaches to research: Major strengths and weaknesses

Approach	Strengths	Weaknesses
Experiment	Manipulation of variables to control extraneous influences; best method for identifying causal relationships	Artificiality of laboratory environment; limited generalizability of findings; unethicalness or impracticality of manipulation of some variables
Correlational study	Measurement of degree of association among variables; good basis for prediction	Limited opportunity to control third or additional factors; inability to draw conclusions about causal relationships
Questionnaire	Effective means of measuring actions, attitudes, opinions, preferences, and intentions of a large number of people	Lack of explanatory power: validity of findings may be limited by sample; reliability may be difficult to determine; self-report may be inaccurate or biased
Naturalistic observation	Observation of behavior in its natural context	Little opportunity to control variables; time-consuming
Case study	Study of rare events; extensive evidence gathered on a single person	Lack of generalizability of findings; time-consuming

ness, stereotyping and prejudice, and the accountability of potentially insane criminals (Davis, 1989; Melton, 1987).

Psychology is also applied in public-service sectors, and it helps formulate public policy. Psychologists are doing research and serving as consultants on issues that affect the quality of life for people everywhere. They are especially interested in the elderly, in health and nursing care, in education and learning, and in mental health issues (DeLeon, 1988). Psychologists do both laboratory and field-based research to investigate the effects of child care on emotional development, of aging on intelligence, of preparation courses on intelligence tests and the SAT, of drugs such as cocaine on memory, and of therapy on mental disorders.

The application of research results requires time and caution. As we have already indicated, psychologists do not have all the answers to questions about human behavior; they have not even defined all the questions that need to be asked. Moreover, before solving actual problems in meaningful ways, researchers must repeat successful experiments to ensure that their findings are **reliable** (i.e., they can be found by other experimenters, given the same experimental conditions). Even after publication and review by professionals, research should be applied cautiously at first. Then after cautious application, more research is usually conducted before considering wider application.

Both researchers in laboratories and health-care providers look at behavior and mental processes with the aim of understanding them and helping people lead more fulfilling, worthwhile, and productive lives. Sometimes, this may mean persuading others to accept the efficacy of a position—that is, convincing an agency, a client, or even another group of psychologists that a particular conclusion is well founded. For example, psychologists can help promote safety-belt usage by integrating knowledge about safety belts and commitment on the part of the public and by offering useful incentives (Geller, Kalsher, Rudd, & Lehman, 1989). Thus, today, psychologists must do more than just prove a truth, they must deliver the information in a way that will make it accessible to people so that it might be used (Levy-Leboyer, 1988).

reliable (experimental results): Observed in an experiment in which the conditions were clearly operationally defined and the manipulation of the independent variable produced consistent changes in the dependent variable, which could be repeated given the same operationally defined conditions.

Progress Check 2.2

Complete the following sentences with one of the options provided.

(L.O. 2.2) a. Animal studies account for about ________ of all the research published in psychological journals. (7% / 32% / 63%)

(L.O. 2.3) b. When the presence of one variable is regularly *associated* with the presence of another variable, we can confidently say that a ________ exists. (correlation / causal relationship)

(L.O. 2.4) c. A researcher has found a ________ when it is unlikely that the outcome on the dependent variable could have occurred by chance alone. (representative sample / significant difference)

(L.O. 2.4) d. The ________ variable is directly and purposefully manipulated by the experimenter; it can be thought of as the "cause" in a cause–effect relationship. (dependent / independent)

(L.O. 2.4) e. ________ is a tentative idea that expresses a causal relationship between two variables. (A hypothesis / An operational definition)

(L.O. 2.4) f. The ________ group is used for comparison purposes in an experiment. The subjects in this group are not exposed to the independent variable, but they are tested on the dependent variable. (experimental / control)

(L.O. 2.5) g. When an experimenter unwittingly creates a situation in which the desired research results are obtained, we say that ________ has occurred. (a self-fulfilling prophecy / the Hawthorne effect)

(L.O. 2.5) h. When neither the experimenter nor the subjects know who is in the experimental group and who is in the control group, a ________ technique has been used. (careless experimental / double-blind)

(L.O. 2.6) i. The advantage of an interview over a questionnaire as a means for collecting data is that the interview allows the researcher to ________. (save time / ask additional questions / detect lying)

(L.O. 2.6) j. One disadvantage of the naturalistic observation approach to collecting data is ________. (the researcher's presence / that the target behavior may not be exhibited)

(L.O. 2.7) k. The main reason that psychologists repeat successful experiments is to determine whether the research findings are ________. (reliable / significant)

Module Summary

A History of Psychology

- Psychology became a field of study in the mid-1800s; since then, it has developed into several schools, each with a specific interest or research focus. *Structuralism,* founded by Wundt, focused on the contents of consciousness and was the first true school of psychology. *Functionalism,* with James and others as its spokespersons, emphasized *how* and *why* the mind works. *Gestalt psychology* was a reaction to the narrow foci of structuralism and functionalism; the early Gestalt psychologists studied perception. John B. Watson led the revolt against subjective approaches to psychology, calling the revolutionary approach *behaviorism.* Watson argued that the proper subject of psychological study was observable behavior. *Psychoanalysis,* developed by Freud, was both a theory of personality and a treatment procedure to help people cope with their problems (pp. 16–17).
- Psychologists with a *biological perspective* tend to examine psychological issues based on how heredity and biological structures affect the process under discussion. The *behavioral perspective* concerns how observable responses are learned, modified, and forgotten. The *psychodynamic perspective* assumes that behavior arises because of unconscious conflicts and urges that originated early in life. *Humanistic perspectives* arose in response to the psychodynamic views and stress the ongoing nature of development. The *cognitive perspective* asserts that human beings engage in both worthwhile and maladjusted behaviors because of ideas and thoughts (pp. 18–20).

Techniques Used to Study Behavior

- An *experiment* is a procedure in which a researcher systematically strives to discover and describe the relationship between variables. A *variable* is a characteristic of a situation or person that is subject to change or that varies across persons or situations. The *independent variable* is directly and purposefully manipulated by the experimenter. The *dependent variable* is observed by the experimenter to see whether it is affected by changes in the independent variable (pp. 22–23).
- To investigate behavior, psychologists use a number of techniques, including case studies, naturalistic observation, interviews, questionnaires, and controlled experiments. Each has strengths and weaknesses, but only the controlled experiment allows for conclusions about cause and effect (pp. 25–28).

Applying Research Findings

- Psychologists are both scientists and practitioners. Psychology is applied in public service sectors to help formulate public policy (p. 28).
- Whether a researcher in a laboratory or a health-care provider, a psychologist looks at behavior with the aim of understanding it and thereby helping people to lead more fulfilling, worthwhile, and productive lives (p. 29).

KEY TERMS

behaviorism, p. 19
biological perspective, p. 19
case study, p. 28
cognitive psychology, p. 19
control group, p. 24
dependent variable, p. 23
double-blind technique, p. 25
eclectic, p. 19
experiment, p. 23
experimental group, p. 24
functionalism, p. 17
Gestalt psychology, p. 17
Hawthorne effect, p. 25
humanistic psychology, p. 19
hypothesis, p. 23
independent variable, p. 23
interview, p. 26
introspection, p. 16
naturalistic observation, p. 27
operational definition, p. 24
psychoanalytic approach, p. 18
questionnaire, p. 25
reliable, p. 29
sample, p. 24
self-actualization, p. 19
self-fulfilling prophecy, p. 25
significant difference, p. 24
structuralism, p. 16
subject, p. 21
variables, p. 23

SELF-TEST

Module 2

- Before taking the self-test, **recite** and **review.**
- Use the key at the back of the text to *correct* your answers.
- *Restudy* pages that correspond to any questions you answered incorrectly.

1. One weakness of the early structuralist school of thought was that it
   a. ignored conscious experience.
   b. produced results that could not be accurately generalized from one human subject to people in general.
   c. made use of animal, rather than human, subjects.
   d. focused on theology rather than psychology.
2. Cross out the statement that is *false* concerning the psychoanalytic approach.
   a. The unconscious is studied through techniques such as free association and dream analysis.
   b. Sexual energy fuels day-to-day behavior.
   c. Its focus is on emotional wellness, rather than the causes of emotional disturbance.
   d. Childhood experiences influence adult personality patterns and behaviors.
3. Behaviorism is primarily concerned with
   a. how behavior is learned and how it can be modified.
   b. the influences of early childhood experiences on behavior.
   c. inherited characteristics.
   d. fulfillment of the human potential.
4. Which of the following statements is most correct about the humanistic school of psychology?
   a. To be a clinical psychologist means that one adopts the humanistic perspective.
   b. Humanistic psychologists believe that many people require extensive therapeutic guidance in order to adapt to externally determined reality.
   c. Two important humanistic psychologists were Abraham Maslow and Carl Rogers.
   d. Humanists believe that human beings must be taught to want to self-actualize.
5. Animal studies allow researchers to do all of the following *except:*
   a. Study several generations in a relatively short period of time.
   b. Eliminate complex distractions and variables that often complicate studies involving humans.
   c. Control the life history of the organism being studied.
   d. Conduct research without concerning themselves over ethical issues.
6. Statements about cause-and-effect relationships among variables can be made from
   a. controlled laboratory experiments.
   b. naturalistic observations.
   c. any well-planned research technique.
   d. experiments and naturalistic observations, but not from interviews, questionnaires, or case studies.
7. Which of the following should researchers keep in mind when they select subjects for a scientific study?
   a. A small number of subjects should be used so that the recording of data is manageable.
   b. To rule out individual differences and chance occurrences, a relatively large sample of subjects should be used.
   c. Sample size is not important as long as subjects have been randomly assigned to groups.
   d. Sample size is important only when the experiment is conducted without a control group.

8. One way that experimenters can overcome the problem of the Hawthorne effect is to
   a. use a double-blind technique.
   b. postpone data collection until the subjects have adapted to the idea of being in a research study.
   c. have a neutral person keep track of subjects assigned to the control and experimental groups.
   d. be honest with the subjects, by telling them they are being observed as a part of a scientific study.
9. Data gathered from case studies
   a. can be generalized from one individual to an entire population.
   b. minimize the effects of experimental bias.
   c. provide detailed information that can be used to plan a method of treatment for a particular individual.
   d. are useful for experimental psychologists, but not for psychologists working in human service fields.
10. Research findings in psychology should be applied
    a. to mentally ill people first and maladjusted people second.
    b. only when medical treatment is ineffective.
    c. immediately, if the results indicate some application that could benefit people in need.
    d. with caution and only to small numbers of people at first.

Connections

If you are interested in . . .	Turn to . . .	To learn more about . . .
The various schools of psychology and their influence on theory and research	◆ Chapter 3, p. 95	How Gestalt psychology influences the study of perception
	◆ Chapter 9, p. 372	Cognitive psychology's explanations of motivation
	◆ Chapter 10, p. 398	How Freud's psychoanalytic theory explains personality development
	◆ Chapter 14, p. 565	Humanistic theory's influence on therapy techniques
Careers in the human service subfields of clinical, counseling, community, or school psychology	◆ Chapter 11, pp. 443–449	The administration and interpretation of tests
	◆ Chapter 12, p. 504	How psychologists help communities meet challenges and prepare for emergencies, such as hurricanes
	◆ Chapter 14, p. 579	How clinical psychologists help people develop effective coping strategies to deal with stress
How psychologists use research methods	◆ Chapter 5, p. 168	How the experimental method is used to study phenomena such as learning to avoid poisonous foods
	◆ Chapter 8, p. 289	How the correlational method is used to study the relationship between fathers and their children
	◆ Chapter 9, p. 352	How the experimental method is used to examine the causes of overeating

In this section, we would like to encourage you to begin thinking as psychologists do, by making connections among concepts that you learn. At the end of each chapter of this book, we point out to you some of the ways in which you can make connections among the topics and themes that are discussed in various chapters throughout the book. Connecting ideas involves taking the final leap in understanding new material. It means that you are going beyond the bits and pieces of factual information and that you are thinking critically. In the early chapters of the book, you may want to jump ahead from time to time to read more about a specific topic so that you can begin making connections that will make that topic more meaningful to you. In later chapters, many of the suggestions we give for making connections will encourage you to look back and to refresh your memory about material learned in earlier chapters. If you use these suggestions, you may begin to see how the broad and diversified field of psychology represents a unified science that has many applications for helping to improve the quality of life for all people.

When psychologists look at the history of their discipline, they see patterns of activities and are able to plot historical trends. They make connections from one theoretical perspective and era of research to the next. By seeing patterns and making connections, they can see the whole picture, and they can understand better where psychology came from, where it is now, and where it needs to go in the future. Like practicing psychologists, you can begin linking ideas as you continue learning from this book.

One thing that you learned while reading Chapter 1 is that psychologists' interest in "the contents of consciousness" subsided during the "stimulus–response" behaviorism era, but it recently reemerged as an interest with the rise of cognitive psychology and studies that focus on thinking. Several other ideas introduced in this chapter are discussed in later chapters, in relation to other topics in psychology. For example, *cognitive psychology* is discussed again later, with regard to learning (Chapter 5, p. 190), to intelligence (Chapter 11, p. 494), and to social psychology (Chapter 15, p. 602). *Behaviorism* (which is also called learning theory) is important for understanding motivation (Chapter 9, p. 351), human development throughout the life span (Chapter 8, p. 301), and psychological disorders (Chapter 13, p. 521). Also, the *biological perspective* is important in understanding the interests of physiological psychologists (Chapter 2, p. 39), clinical psychologists who study schizophrenia (Chapter 13, p. 547), and researchers who study motivation and hunger (Chapter 9, p. 352). Finally, the *research design and methods* discussed in Chapter 1 are used in research studies cited in every chapter of this book. The connections that can be made within chapters and from chapter to chapter when studying psychology are extensive, and realizing that the connections exist will enrich your understanding of psychology as a unified discipline.

Module 3 ► FOUNDATIONS OF THE NERVOUS SYSTEM 38

Module 4 ► THE BRAIN AND BEHAVIOR 56

Chapter 2

The Biological Basis of Behavior

The biological basis of behavior is especially important because the way our bodies interpret signals, convert them, and convey information to the muscles and glands is a principal determinant of day-to-day behavior. In the first module of this chapter we show how small changes in the environment can bring about enormous changes in the body's response. The role of nature and nurture is examined, the role of hormones is highlighted, and the relationship between these topics is examined. For example, it is shown how a frightful event can initiate changes in the autonomic nervous system which trigger the release of adrenalin. A consequence of the release of this hormone may be both a readying of the muscles for "fight or flight" and a change in a person's ability to concentrate. The module also examines the complex communication system on which our nervous system relies.

The second module of this chapter shows how the entire nervous system acts in an integrated manner. Signals that are presented to sense organs, such as the eyes or the ears or through the touch system of the fingers, send signals to various processing centers in the brain and the spinal cord. This complex processing of billions of neurons takes place effortlessly and at lightning speed. Psychologists study changes in single neurons, through computerized measuring devices, and they observe overt behavior that results from such changes. Thus, a topic such as sleep and dreams is often studied at the behavioral level, the neural level, and even the biochemical level. Only through an analysis of the biological basis of behavior can a complete understanding of even seemingly simple and automatic processes such as sleep take place. Thus, the module examines the organization of the nervous system, including the ways that researchers monitor nervous activity, as well as key brain structures.

Module 3

Foundations of the Nervous System

LEARNING OBJECTIVES

When you have mastered the material in this module, you will be able to

Nature Versus Nurture (pp. 39–42).

3.1 Discuss the ways that nature and nurture influence behavior and mental processes (p. 39).

3.2 Explain how both physical traits and basic behavioral traits are genetically transmitted from parents to their children (p. 40).

3.3 Explain how twins develop and why twin studies are important to psychologists (p. 41).

3.4 Describe some of the effects of genetic abnormalities on both physical development and behavior (p. 42).

Hormones and Glands (pp. 42–47).

3.5 Discuss the effects of hormones on both physiological functioning and behavior. (p. 43).

3.6 List the symptoms of premenstrual syndrome (PMS), and use PMS to explain the link between psychology and biology (p. 46).

Communication in the Nervous System (p. 47–53).

3.7 Name three types of neurons, identify the parts of a neuron, and explain how neurons transfer signals (p. 48).

3.8 Describe how neurotransmitters are involved in the transmission of electrochemical signals, and identify some of their effects on physiological functioning and behavior (p. 51).

SQ3R

- ▲ **Survey** to set goals for studying.
- ▲ Ask **questions** as you **read.**
- ▲ Stop occasionally to **recite** and **review.**

plus

- ▲ **Write** a summary of key points.
- ▲ **Reflect** on the hypotheses, evidence, and implications of this material and on the relevance it has to *your* life.

Lucy and Max Newman are fraternal twins who attend the same college but have distinctly different talents and interests. Lucy excels at athletics and Max is a gifted scholar. Lucy is leading her team to the state basketball championships and her admiring coaches claim she is a genius on the court. But Lucy is no genius in the classroom, even though she studies constantly. Max is a straight-A student whose professors predict he will graduate summa cum laude. But Max Newman does not share his twin sister's interest or talent in sports.

Why do the twins differ so much? Their father thinks it's because Lucy has enjoyed sports since she began walking and Max began reading at a very early age. He reasons that Lucy would be just as good a student as Max, and Max just as athletic as Lucy, if their early experiences and interests had been reversed. However, their mother argues that each child was born as either an athlete or scholar, and each is making the most of his or her gifts. The parental debate illustrates a major question in psychology: what is the relationship between biological mechanisms and environmental mechanisms—nature versus nurture? In this chapter, we examine the issue of nature versus nurture and then focus on the biological processes that underlie all human behavior and mental processes. First with genetics, then with neurons (the building blocks of behavior), we explore the structure and the functioning of the brain. We look at how scientists study brain activity, and how various chemical substances affect our behavior.

Nature Versus Nurture

Learning Objective 3.1 Discuss the ways that nature and nurture influence behavior and mental processes.

The impact of biological structures on behavior is profound. With advances in technology, scientists have the potential to alter a person's biology to enhance the quality of life. Biology, particularly genetics, plays a crucial role in shaping our psychological characteristics. In fact, many behavioral, psychological, and physical disorders actually stem from biological factors. A child who acts out in class may have a neurological problem. A person with severe depression may have a chemical imbalance. Recognizing the importance of such factors, psychologists have studied them closely to discover how the biological bases of behavior can be manipulated or controlled. Researchers are working to answer such questions as: Can people intentionally control their own physiological processes? What is the relationship between biological mechanisms and psychological mechanisms? Can diet affect day-to-day behavior?

A complex interplay exists between experience and biology, between conscious voluntary decision making and inherited traits—that is, between *nature* and *nurture*. **Nature** refers to a person's inherited characteristics, determined by genetics; **nurture** refers to a person's experiences in the environment. For example, you can lift weights in a gym for years, trying to build up physical strength, but your capabilities will always be limited by your inherited body structure. Similarly, people try to maximize their intellectual skills through education, yet not everyone can become a highly skilled brain surgeon.

nature: An individual's genetically inherited characteristics.

nurture: An individual's experiences in his or her environment.

The debate over what determines our abilities and behavior is actually a debate over the relative contributions of biological and environmental variables. How much of who we are is related to the genes we inherited from our parents? How much is related to the environment in which we were raised? Can the environment interact with and modify biological makeup? Valid answers to this question must take into account the idea that both nature and nurture affect the expression of traits. Further, the surrounding environment must make it possible for an inherited trait to be expressed in behavior. Last, the complex and constantly changing relationship between biology and environment affects behaviors directly. The truth is that genetic traits (inherited abilities) provide the framework for behavior; within that framework, experiences ultimately shape what a person feels, thinks, and does.

Genetics

Learning Objective 3.2
Explain how both physical traits and basic behavioral traits are genetically transmitted from parents to their children.

Genetics is the study of *heredity,* the biological transmission of traits and characteristics. Biologists examine such things as how blue eyes, brown hair, height, and blood pressure problems are transmitted from one generation to the next. Behavioral traits, aspects of personality, and intelligence can also be genetically transmitted, and this is why psychologists are especially interested in heredity. With the exception of identical twins (discussed on the next page), every human being is genetically unique. Although each of us shares traits with our brothers, sisters, and parents, none of us is identical to them or to anyone else. This occurs because of the large number of genes that determine characteristics.

Chromosomes, which are strands of deoxyribonucleic acid (DNA), carry genetic information in their basic functional units—**genes.** Genes are lined up on the chromosomes in the nucleus (or center) of a cell. Each human cell normally contains 23 pairs of chromosomes (46 chromosomes total), and genes control various aspects of a person's body structure, including eye color, hair color, height, and basic intellectual potential.

Traits are determined by pairs of genes, which are located in corresponding positions on the chromosome pairs. These corresponding genes both influence the same trait, but they often carry a different or alternative form of the genetic code for that trait, one of which may be dominant over the other. A different alternative form of the gene that occupies a particular place on the chromosomes is an **allele.** Each allele of a chromosome has a corresponding allele on the corresponding chromosome of the chromosome pair.

Sperm and ova each contain half of the final pairings of genes. The first 22 pairs of chromosomes are the same in both males and females. The 23rd pair, however, differs. This pair of chromosomes determines a person's sex. In females, the 23rd pair contains two X-type chromosomes; in males, it contains one X- and one Y-type chromosome (see Figure 3.1). In males, when sperm are formed, the pair of chromosomes divides, and the 23rd produces one X-type and one Y-type

genetics: The study of the potential transmitted from parents to offspring through genes.

chromosome: [KRO-muh-som] Strand in the nuclei of cells that carries genes. Composed of a DNA core, these are responsible for the hereditary transmission of traits. Found in pairs, they represent the genetic contribution of both parents.

gene: The unit of heredity transmission carried in chromosomes and consisting of deoxyribonucleic acid (DNA) and protein.

allele: [uh-LEEL] A single gene (member of a gene pair) that carries a different or alternative genetic code for a particular trait.

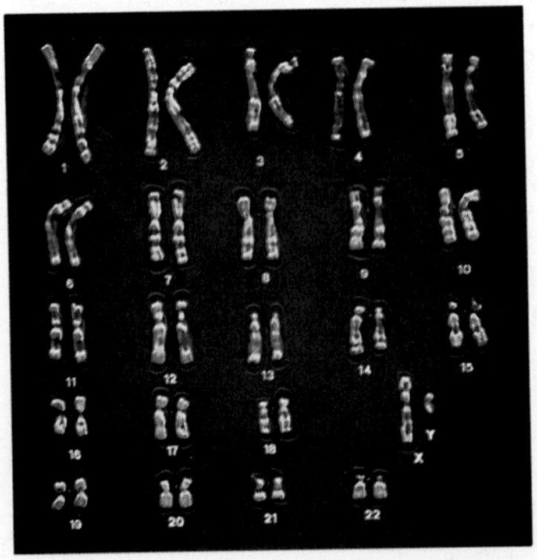

Figure 3.1

Each human cell contains 23 pairs of chromosomes. The first 22 pairs are alike and transmit similar characteristics in both males and females. The 23rd pair determines gender. In males, the 23rd pair contains one X and one Y chromosome (as shown here); in females, the 23rd pair contains two X chromosomes.

Fraternal twins (left) occur when two sperm fertilize two ova and both zygotes develop alongside each other in the uterus; they are genetically similar as any two siblings. Identical twins (right) occur when one zygote separates into two identical cells; their genetic make up is the same.

sperm cell. In females, the 23rd cell produces an X-type chromosome in each cell. If an X-sperm fertilizes an ovum, the result is a female—XX. If a Y-sperm fertilizes an ovum, the result is a male—XY.

At the moment of conception, a sperm and an ovum (each containing half of each pair of each parent's chromosomes) combine to form a new organism, and the chromosomes join to form new pairs. There are 8,388,608 possible recombinations of the 23 pairs of chromosomes, with a colossal 70,368,744,000,000 possible combinations of genes. You can see that the chances of any two individuals being exactly alike is exceedingly slim.

In an exciting research revolution that has been taking place since the early 1980s, biological researchers have been trying to map the traits associated with specific chromosomes. They have been trying to map the human *genome,* the DNA blueprint of heritable traits contained in every cell of the body. They have been modestly successful: More than 400 genetic "markers" or signposts have been discovered on all 46 chromosomes. Researchers have mapped the exact location of markers for muscular dystrophy, Huntington's disease, some cancers, and some psychological disorders. By understanding the basic biological mechanisms and their relationship to behavior, psychologists can better predict the situations in which maladjustment and some specific behavior disorders might occur.

fraternal twins: Double births resulting from the release of two ova in the female which are then fertilized by two sperms. Fraternal twins are no more or less genetically similar than nontwin siblings.

identical twins: Double births resulting from the splitting of a zygote into two identical cells that then separate and develop independently. Identical twins have exactly the same genetic makeup.

Twins

Learning Objective 3.3
Explain how twins develop and why twin studies are important to psychologists.

Psychologists often rely on studies of twins to assess the contributions of nature and nurture to a person's behavior. Twins make good subjects for these experiments because they begin life in the same uterine environment and share the same nutrition and other prenatal influences. There are two types of twins. **Fraternal twins** occur when two sperms fertilize two ova, and the two zygotes (fertilized eggs) implant in the uterus and grow alongside each other. Fraternal twins may be both male, both female, or one male and one female. Their genes are not identical, making them as genetically similar as other brothers and sisters. Only about 12 sets of fraternal twins occur in every 1000 births. **Identical twins** occur when one zygote (fertilized egg) separates into two identical cells. The multiplication of these cells then proceeds normally, and the cells become two genetically identical organisms If the two cells should also split, the result would be identical quadruplets. Identical twins are rarer than fraternal twins: Only 4 sets occur in every 1000 births. Of course, identical twins can only be both boys or both girls: They share exactly the same genetic heritage.

Twins' genetic factors (nature) are fixed, but if they are reared apart, their environments (nurture) are different—that is, they will grow up with different families and homes. By comparing psychological characteristics of identical twins who have been reared apart, researchers can assess the extent to which environment affects behavior, perhaps unraveling the nature–nurture puzzle a bit more. Researchers have concluded that significant psychological similarities between identical twins are probably due to biological variables, and significant differences are probably due to environmental variables.

Our genetic heritage is unaffected by day-to-day experiences. However, over tens of thousands of years, we humans have evolved a highly organized brain that allows learning to affect our behavior. Our brains act as libraries of information. Each new enriching experience affects our later behavior. Some who consider nurture more important than nature suggest that people are not limited by their genetic heritage because experience, training, and hard work can stretch their potential to amazing lengths. In the end, though, a person's genetic makeup is the foundation on which all his or her behaviors are built.

Genetic Defects

Learning Objective 3.4
Describe some of the effects of genetic abnormalities on both physical development and behavior.

Some scientists are involved in genetic research, attempting to crack the genetic code, manipulate cell structure, and control the transmission of genetic traits. One goal of genetic research is to prevent *genetic defects*—genetically transmitted diseases and behavioral abnormalities. When a person is born with the genetic defect of too few or too many chromosomes, the result is usually dramatic. **Down syndrome** occurs when every cell in the body has more than exactly two copies of chromosome number 21, either an entire extra copy or a piece of one chromosome number 21 that breaks off and is joined to another chromosome. This genetic accident occurs in 1 out of every 660 live births. Most people afflicted with Down syndrome have distinctive physical features (a short, stocky build, flattened face, and almond shaped eyes). Many are born with congenital problems, such as heart defects, eye problems, and respiratory disorders. People with Down syndrome also have some degree of mental retardation.

Another genetic disorder, **phenylketonuria** (PKU), is caused by the presence of a recessive gene that prevents the individual from processing the amino acid phenylanine. Unless the disorder is detected soon after birth and the newborn is put on a diet containing low levels of phenylanine, PKU can cause irreparable mental retardation. Accordingly, in the United States all newborns are given a PKU test. In this case, manipulating the physical environment (through diet) can help control the harmful consequences of a genetic disorder. Through genetic research, psychologists may eventually be able to understand and manage severe disorders such as schizophrenia.

Down syndrome: A human genetic defect in which more than two whole chromosomes are present for the 21st pair. Usually accompanied by characteristic physical abnormalities and mental retardation.

phenylketonuria (PKU): [fee-nil-key-ton-NYEW-ree-uh] A disorder that prevents an individual from metabolizing the amino acid phenylanine. Usually treatable with a special diet.

Hormones and Glands

In 1978, Dan White fatally shot both San Francisco Mayor George Moscone and supervisor/gay activist Harvey Milk. In court, White's attorney successfully argued that a diet of junk food had addled his client's brain and reduced his capacity for moral behavior. White spent only 3 years in prison for committing a double

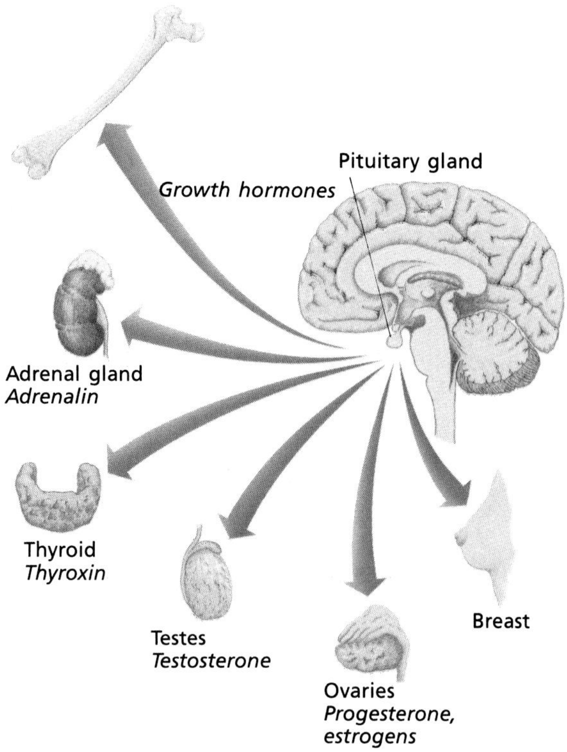

Figure 3.2

The pituitary is a small gland that directly affects behavior both through the control of other glands and through the release of hormones into the bloodstream.

homicide. Although the "Twinkie defense" is no longer a legal defense in California, White's lawyer capitalized on the fact that a person's body chemistry—even an imbalance in blood-sugar levels—can have a dramatic impact on behavior. In fact, body chemistry, hormones, and learned experiences *can* work together to influence a person, but does this render us unaccountable for our own actions, as Dan White's lawyer claimed? Combinations of factors are usually the answer to many complex psychological problems, but research shows that some abilities and behaviors have a direct hormonal link, as is shown by studies of endocrine glands.

Learning Objective 3.5
Discuss the effects of hormones on both physiological functioning and behavior.

Endocrine Glands

A group of cells that forms a bodily structure and secretes a substance is a *gland.* There are two types of glands in the human body: those with ducts (such as the tear and sweat glands) and those without ducts—the **endocrine glands.** Psychologists are particularly interested in the endocrine glands, which secrete **hormones** (chemicals) directly into the bloodstream and thereby can influence a person's behavior dramatically. The hormones travel through the bloodstream to target organs that contain cells that respond specifically to particular hormones.

endocrine glands: [END-oh-krin] Ductless glands that secrete hormones directly into the bloodstream.

hormones: Chemicals that regulate the activities of specific organs or cells. Hormones are produced by the endocrine glands and are transported by the bloodstream to their site of action.

The most important endocrine gland is the *pituitary gland,* sometimes referred to as the body's master gland because it regulates the actions of other endocrine glands. A major function of the pituitary is its control of growth hormones. That's why, when teenagers have extreme height or weight problems, the pituitary gland is often suspected (see Figure 3.2). The pituitary gland is divided into two lobes, the anterior (front) and the posterior (back). In addition to producing direct changes in bodily functions (e.g., growth), secretions from the lobes of the pituitary affect other glands.

APPLYING PSYCHOLOGY

Are We What We Eat?

We all know that foods affect us in various ways. A large Thanksgiving meal may make us sleepy. Hungry people feel weak and may cut back on their activities. Parents often say that their children are "off-the-wall" after consuming candy bars or other high-sugar foods, implying that sugar makes their children hyperactive. Most people agree that food affects behavior. Do some foods affect us more than others? Can some foods be used to help people change their behavior? In the end, are we what we eat?

The possibility of diet as an important variable in shaping children's behavior first emerged in the 1970s, when parents, educators, psychologists, and physicians began seeking new and better ways to treat *attention-deficit hyperactivity disorder,* a disorder that is estimated to affect 1–15% of school-age children. Some researchers initially thought hyperactivity was caused by specific food substances (e.g., Feingold, 1976). Since then, however, studies provided only modest support for dietary modifications. In the process of conducting these studies, researchers learned that there are problems inherent in studies of diet and behavior (e.g., Prinz & Riddle, 1986). From this beginning, further studies of diet and behavior emerged. Many focused on foods such as breads, pastas, and candy—foods made up mostly of *carbohydrates* (simple and complex sugars and starches).

Research on the effects of diet has been both correlational and experimental. Tests administered by Prinz and Riddle (1986) showed that children who ate large quantities of sugar demonstrated attention deficients when compared to children consuming low amounts of sugar. This was a correlational study, however, and we cannot draw causal conclusions from it. In an experimental study that attempted to state causality, Ferguson, Stoddart, and Simeon (1986) gave children sugar and compared their behavior to a control group of children, expecting adverse reactions to the sugar. Surprisingly, they found *no* differences between the groups regarding activity levels, behavior ratings made by trained observers, or cognitive activity (such as thinking, learning, and attending).

Critical evaluations have led researchers to argue that, in general, carbohydrates appear to have no immediate effect on children's behavior and may even cause a decrease in activity (Behar, Rappoport, Adams, Berg, & Cornblath, 1984; Wolraich, Milich, Stumbo, Schultz, 1985). So it is generally conceded that carbohydrates are not a cause of hyperactivity. However, many people seem to crave carbohydrates, especially snack foods, to elevate their mood. Foods high in carbohydrates are quick-energy sources and provide glucose easily; the brain thrives on and requires glucose (sugar) for neural activity.

Carbohydrates are found in table sugar, candy bars, and fruit juices, as well as in potatoes, vegetables, and breads. People who are obese, suffering from nicotine withdrawal, or experiencing postpartum depression are more likely to seek carbohydrates than those who aren't. Are these people practicing a form of self-

insulin: A hormone produced by the pancreas, necessary for the transport of sugar from the blood into body cells so that it can be metabolized.

diabetes mellitus: A condition in which too little insulin is present in the blood, so that insufficient quantities of sugar are transported into body cells.

Another gland, the *pancreas,* is involved in regulating the body's sugar levels. Sugar substances in the blood determine a person's energy level: When blood sugar is high, people are energetic; when it is low, they feel weak and tired. Cells in the pancreas—the islets of Langerhans—control the production of **insulin,** which facilitates the transportation of sugar to the body cells where it is metabolized. When an insufficient amount of insulin is produced, the sugar is inefficiently transported out of the bloodstream to the cells, too much sugar accumulates in the blood, and **diabetes mellitus** occurs. Excess sugar in the blood (or as it is more technically known, **hyperglycemia**) can lead to coma and death if left untreated. Nearly 10 million Americans have diabetes and must take daily doses of insulin to ensure that the sugar in their blood can be transported to the cells and metabolized properly. Researchers today expect that within a decade, diabetes may be preventable (Atkinson & Maclaren, 1990).

medication, providing their bodies with needed foods? After conducting a number of studies, researchers developed the hypothesis that carbohydrates contain substances that end up affecting people's moods. First, they noted that substances in carbohydrates alter the body's level of *tryptophan*, an amino acid from which the body makes serotonin. *Serotonin* is a specialized hormone known as a neurotransmitter (neurotransmitters are defined later in this module). When serotonin and tryptophan are released in the brain, people often feel calmer and in a better mood, and this ultimately affects their behavior. With this hypothesis, researchers began to test the idea that carbohydrate-rich diets alter levels of tryptophan and therefore affect behavior.

The research shows that when people limit their intake of protein (for example, meat) and increase their intake of carbohydrates (for example, pasta), their serotonin production increases, and their mood elevates. Research shows that people who fast after breakfast and then eat a carbohydrate-rich lunch show marked increases in tryptophan. However, for a test meal to reliably elevate tryptophan, it has to be carbohydrate rich *and* protein poor. After reviewing experimental studies of carbohydrate intake and behavior, Spring, Chiodo, and Bowen (1987) argued that carbohydrates can function as a drug. They can modify brain chemistry and, consequently, mood and behavior. They assert that "as individuals administer drugs so may they learn to select foods to achieve the same result" (p. 254). An anxious or depressed person may learn that snacking on high-carbohydrate, low-protein foods causes mood enhancement. As little as a piece of toast, a cookie, or a small bowl of pasta provides enough tryptophan to stimulate production of serotonin. With more research, researchers may eventually determine dietary plans in which selective snacking may be used to improve a person's disposition—sometimes for physical reasons and sometimes for psychological ones.

Researchers continue to ask critical questions about the effects of carbohydrates on behavior: Are there alternative explanations to the current results? Could the effects of carbohydrates and tryptophan be lessened by other foods? Could the behavior being evaluated by the wrong one—that is, would the effects be different if other behaviors were observed? What are the effects of long-term heavy dosages of sugar or carbohydrate consumption?

Evaluating the effects of food on behavior is one of the most formidable tasks that researchers face because it is difficult to target a specific behavior and draw a causal link to a specific food. Researchers must refine their methods and develop procedures that might remove (or perhaps add) one specific food substance from (or to) a person's diet and then see whether behavior changes. The use of the experimental method is essential if psychologists are to make causal inferences. Research in this controversial area continues, cutting across the disciplines of nutrition, medicine, nursing, and psychology.

- ***Early research on carbohydrates was correlational; why did researchers have problems with this research?***
- ***What was the evidence that led researchers to develop the hypothesis that carbohydrates can function as a drug?***
- ***Are there alternative explanations to the results that researchers have found, which could alter the implications that they have drawn?***

If the pancreas errs in the opposite direction and produces too much insulin, the result is **hypoglycemia,** or very low blood sugar. Hypoglycemic patients have no energy and often feel faint. This condition can usually be controlled through a diet that carefully monitors daily consumption of calories and types of food.

The *adrenal gland,* located near the kidneys, is also involved with behavior. This gland produces epinephrine (adrenaline), a substance that dramatically alters energy levels and can greatly affect a person's reactions to stress through changes in neuronal firing. Imagine you are being chased through a dark alley. The release of epinephrine causes your heart to pound and gives you a burst of energy to help you outdistance your pursuer. Hormones affect specific behaviors and affect one another. The glands, the hormones, and the target organs are interactive; the brain initiates the release of hormones, which affects the target organs, which affects behavior, which in turn affects the brain, and so on.

hyperglycemia: [hi-purr-gly-SEE-me-uh] A condition in which too much sugar is present in the blood.

hypoglycemia: [hi-po-gly-SEE-me-uh] A condition usually resulting from the overproduction of insulin, causing very low blood sugar levels. It is usually characterized by a lack of energy, and often by faintness and dizziness.

Psychology in the Biological Sciences: Premenstrual Syndrome

Learning Objective 3.6
List the symptoms of premenstrual syndrome (PMS) and use PMS to explain the link between psychology and biology.

The relationship between psychology and biology is the focus of this chapter. You can see the interplay of brain–behavior relationships when you observe changes in behavior as a result of regulating hormones, food substances (see the Applying Psychology box on pages 44–45), and drugs. Researchers who study behavior must study biology because the two are so closely connected; for example, the child who is hyperactive may have a glandular disorder; a drug addict is often physiologically as well as psychologically addicted; and a person suffering from migraine headaches can learn to alleviate pain through self-help procedures, in addition to taking prescribed drugs.

There has been an especially dynamic melding between psychology and biology. Psychologists work in biology and chemistry departments studying neuroscience, and whole new departments of neuroscience and brain science are emerging. These researchers are studying how the brain affects behavior and how behavior affects the brain.

The merging of the disciplines is especially apparent in the study of *premenstrual syndrome* (PMS). First described in the medical literature in 1931, PMS is a recurrent, cyclic condition characterized by one or more symptoms that develop during the 7–14 days before the onset of menstruation, subside when menstruation occurs, and are then absent for 2 weeks. The absence of symptoms during the postmenstrual phase is essential to a diagnosis. About one third of all premenopausal women, primarily those between 25 and 40 years of age, suffer from symptoms of PMS (Logue & Moos, 1986).

Women who have PMS may experience physical discomfort from water retention, weight gain, breast tenderness, dizziness, headaches, skin disorders, food cravings (including carbohydrates as mood elevators), fatigue, and swollen hands, feet, and ankles. These physical discomforts affect behavior; women suffering from PMS notice depression, irritability, anxiety, tension, mood swings, inability to concentrate, and confusion. As many as 150 different symptoms have been linked to the menstrual cycle (York, Freeman, Lowery, & Strauss, 1989). The severity of discomfort caused by PMS varies from woman to woman and from month to month.

The relationship of PMS to psychological states and biological mechanisms is striking; researchers in both disciplines are working together more than ever before to better understand the disorder. Researchers are not certain what causes PMS, and considerable controversy exists as to the relationships among the symptoms, hormones, and behavior (Ainscough, 1990). PMS does not seem to be caused by excesses or deficiencies of a particular hormone, but rather by a change in the way the hormones work. Currently, biological researchers are investigating the possibility that estrogen and progesterone, two hormones produced by the ovaries, may act in combination with neurotransmitters in the brain before menstruation and may cause some of the symptoms (Dalton, 1984). Most women who have PMS function effectively despite their discomfort. Both understanding the disorder and its symptoms and being conscious of the physical effects seem to help (Norris & Sullivan, 1983). Practitioners, researchers, and physicians often report that some women experience physical symptoms without emotional or cognitive symptoms. The physical, emotional, and cognitive changes that take place seem to be somewhat independent—a woman may experience physical maladies without emotional ones, or just the opposite. This is making some researchers begin to consider the possibility of several premenstrual syndromes—not just one.

Issues such as PMS demonstrate the link between psychology and the biological sciences. Psychologists are relying on chemists and biologists to develop new drugs; these scientists are relying on psychologists to evaluate the effectiveness of the drugs on behavior. The cross-fertilization of ideas, theory, and research continues.

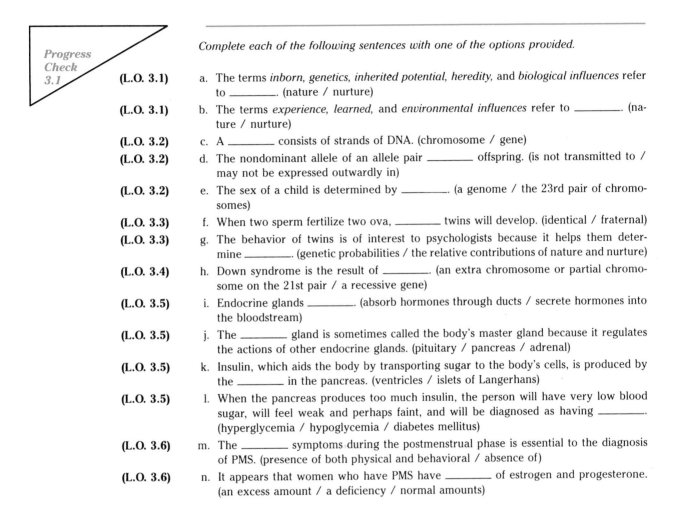

Progress Check 3.1

Complete each of the following sentences with one of the options provided.

(L.O. 3.1) a. The terms *inborn, genetics, inherited potential, heredity,* and *biological influences* refer to ________. (nature / nurture)

(L.O. 3.1) b. The terms *experience, learned,* and *environmental influences* refer to ________. (nature / nurture)

(L.O. 3.2) c. A ________ consists of strands of DNA. (chromosome / gene)

(L.O. 3.2) d. The nondominant allele of an allele pair ________ offspring. (is not transmitted to / may not be expressed outwardly in)

(L.O. 3.2) e. The sex of a child is determined by ________. (a genome / the 23rd pair of chromosomes)

(L.O. 3.3) f. When two sperm fertilize two ova, ________ twins will develop. (identical / fraternal)

(L.O. 3.3) g. The behavior of twins is of interest to psychologists because it helps them determine ________. (genetic probabilities / the relative contributions of nature and nurture)

(L.O. 3.4) h. Down syndrome is the result of ________. (an extra chromosome or partial chromosome on the 21st pair / a recessive gene)

(L.O. 3.5) i. Endocrine glands ________. (absorb hormones through ducts / secrete hormones into the bloodstream)

(L.O. 3.5) j. The ________ gland is sometimes called the body's master gland because it regulates the actions of other endocrine glands. (pituitary / pancreas / adrenal)

(L.O. 3.5) k. Insulin, which aids the body by transporting sugar to the body's cells, is produced by the ________ in the pancreas. (ventricles / islets of Langerhans)

(L.O. 3.5) l. When the pancreas produces too much insulin, the person will have very low blood sugar, will feel weak and perhaps faint, and will be diagnosed as having ________. (hyperglycemia / hypoglycemia / diabetes mellitus)

(L.O. 3.6) m. The ________ symptoms during the postmenstrual phase is essential to the diagnosis of PMS. (presence of both physical and behavioral / absence of)

(L.O. 3.6) n. It appears that women who have PMS have ________ of estrogen and progesterone. (an excess amount / a deficiency / normal amounts)

Communication in the Nervous System

Before we can fully understand the nature and diversity of human behavior, we must first examine the underlying biological structures of human beings. The nervous system underlies all of our day-to-day behavior; it allows us to drive cars, pull our hands away from hot fires, study for psychology examinations, eat when we are hungry, run in races, and so on. The nervous system acts like a busy air traffic control center, sending, receiving, processing, interpreting, and storing vital information. Many psychologists study how these electrical and chemical signals are used in the brain to represent and process information (Sejnowski, Koch, & Churchland, 1988).

nervous system: The structures and organs that act as the communication system for the body and allow for behavior and mental processes. It comprises the central and the peripheral nervous systems.

The **nervous system** is composed of structures that act as the communication system for the body and allows for both behavior and mental processes. The nervous system enables an organism to coordinate activities, including movement, thought processes, perception of pain, and the consistent beating of the heart. The nervous system is made up of two divisions—the *central nervous system* (consisting of the brain and spinal cord) and the *peripheral nervous system* (the rest of the nervous system, including sensory nerves inside the head but outside the brain). The peripheral and central nervous systems work in harmony. The central nervous system acts on information provided by the peripheral nervous system and sends out signals that sometimes modify it. The nervous system is composed of billions of cells, each of which receives information from thousands of other cells. The most elementary unit in the nervous system is the neuron, the building block of the entire system.

The Neuron

Learning Objective 3.7 Name three types of neurons, identify the parts of a neuron, and explain how neurons transfer signals.

The basic unit of the nervous system is the **neuron,** or nerve cell. Billions of neurons are found throughout the body, differing in shape, size, and function. (There are over 100 billion in the brain alone.) Some neurons operate quickly, some relatively slowly; some neurons are large, others are especially small. Often, neurons are grouped together in bundles; such groups of fibers are *nerves.*

Although all of the neurons in your body are alive and active, they are not all activated at once. Nonetheless, they are on alert, ready to convey information and signals to some part of the nervous system. Neuronal firing flows two ways: (1) to the brain and spinal cord from the sense organs and muscles, providing information, and (2) from the brain and spinal cord to the sense organs and muscles, with decisions and prompts to initiate new behavior.

Types of Neurons. There are three basic types of neurons:

1. *Sensory neurons* convey information inward from the body's outer tissues to the brain and spinal cord
2. *Motor neurons* carry information from the brain and spinal cord to the muscles and glands
3. *Interneurons* connect neurons together and combine activities of sensory and motor neurons.

There are many more interneurons than sensory or motor neurons, and they form the network that allows the neurons to interact with one another. The millions of neurons connected to one another are surrounded by a fourth type of cell, called glia. *Glial cells* (a) are small; (b) are 10 times more numerous than sensory, motor, or interneurons; and (c) act to nourish the neurons and to help hold them in place. In spite of their important function, they appear to play no direct role in behavior.

Each direction of the two-way flow of neuronal firing has a name: **Afferent** neuronal signals send the messages *to* the spinal cord and brain; **efferent** neuronal signals send messages *from* the brain and spinal cord to other structures in the body (see Figure 3.3). These signals are sent very rapidly and occur at all levels of the nervous system simultaneously.

neuron: [NEW-ron] The basic unit of the nervous system. This single cell comprises *dendrites* (receive neural signals), a *cell body* (generates electrical signals), and an *axon* (transmits neural signals).

afferent: Pathways and signals to the central nervous system.

efferent: Pathways and signals from the central nervous system to other structures in the body.

synapse: [SIN-apps] The small space between the axon terminals of one neuron and the receptor site (dendrite, cell body, or axon) of another neuron.

Parts of a Neuron. Typically, a neuron is composed of a cell body (containing a nucleus), dendrites, an axon, and axon terminals. *Dendrites* (from the Greek word *tree* because of their treelike appearance) are thin, widely branching fibers that get narrower as they spread away from the cell body. They receive information from neighboring neurons and carry it to the *cell body.* At the cell body, the signal is transformed and continues to travel along the long, slim *axon* to the *axon terminals* (the end points of the neuron). (See Figure 3.4.) Many axons, especially the longer ones, are *myelinated,* which means that they are coated with a

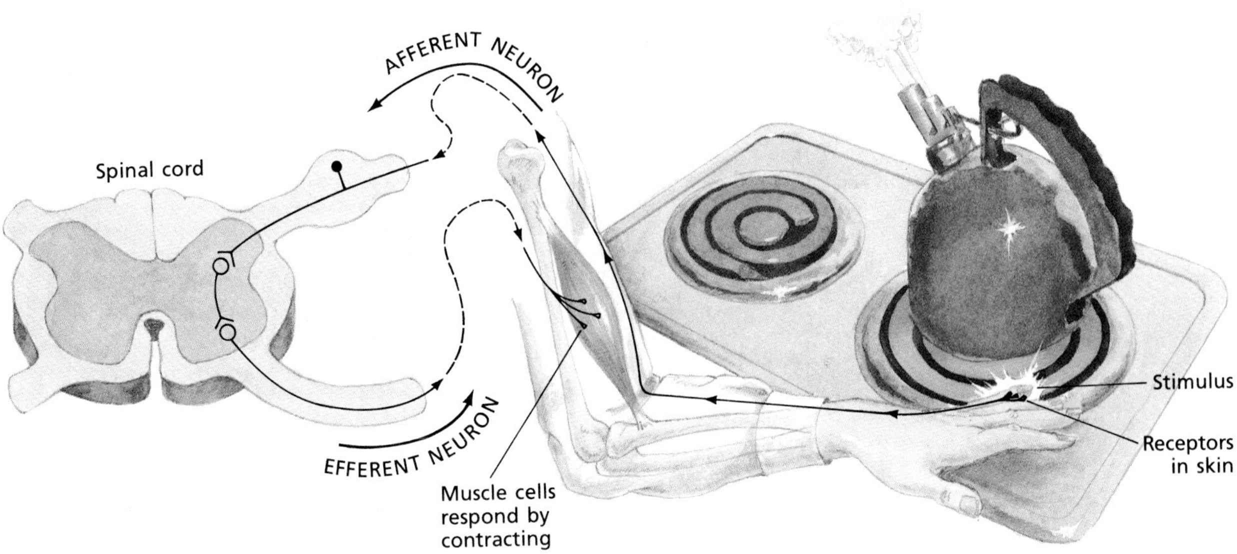

Figure 3.3

Afferent neurons carry signals from the muscles and glands to the spinal cord and brain; *efferent* neurons carry signals from the brain and spinal cord to the muscles and glands.

thin white substance (called a myelin sheath) that allows much faster conduction of the signal to the terminals. The *myelin sheath* is a form of glial cell and also serves to insulate one neuron from the next.

Neuronal Synapses. For almost all neurons, the axon terminals of one neuron are very close to the receptor site (i.e., dendrites or cell body) of another neuron. The microscopically small space between the axon terminals of one neuron and the receptor site of another is a **synapse** (Figure 3.5 on the next page). The signal from one neuron may leap across this synapse to go to another neuron. You can think of many neurons strung together in a long chain as a relay team sending signals, conveying information, or initiating action in a cell, muscle, or gland. Each neuron receives information from about 1000 neighboring neurons and may *synapse on* (transmit information to) 1000–10,000 other neurons.

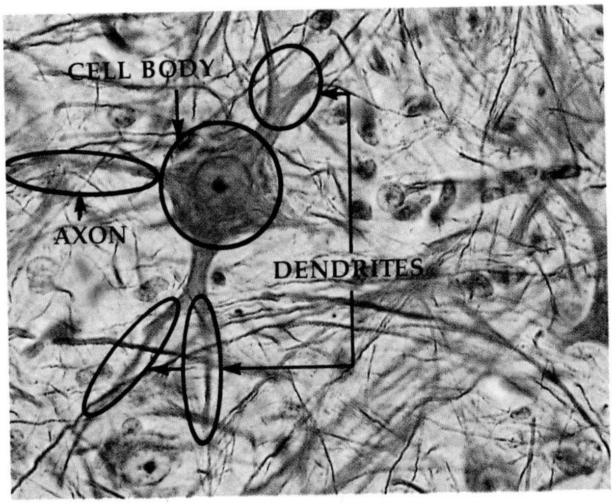

Figure 3.4

The basic components of a neuron: dendrites, cell body, and a long, slim axon.

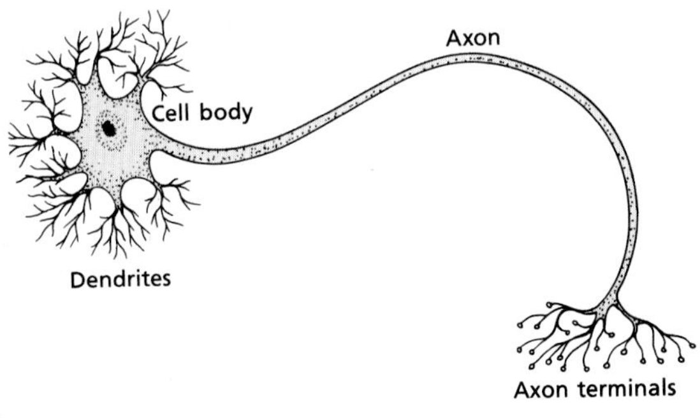

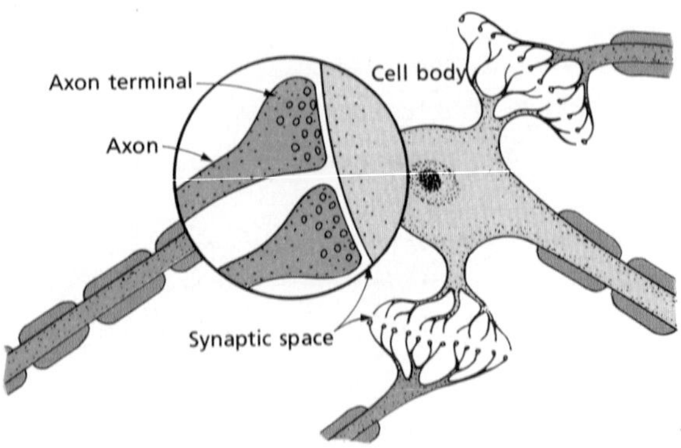

Figure 3.5

The synapse is very small. Chemicals released by the axon terminal cross the synapse to stimulate the cell body or dendrites of another neuron.

Action Potentials

How do neurons communicate with one another? Each year, scientists learn more about the nature of the neural impulse and how information is transmitted from cell to cell across synapses. The process, which involves both electrical and chemical changes, is termed *electrochemical.* Two types of electrochemical actions take place: the first involves electrochemical activity within a cell, the second involves transmitter substances (i.e., chemicals) released from the axons of one cell and acting on the cell body or dendrites of another cell.

Understanding electrochemical processes within a cell is essential to explaining the role of the neuron in behavior. The most widely accepted explanation of electrochemical processes is the following: Every cell (neuron) is surrounded by an extremely thin—less than 0.00001 millimeters (mm) thick—semipermeable membrane. *Semipermeable* means that some things can permeate (pass through) it—in this case, electrically charged ions and small particles in and around the neuron. Normally, the neuron is in a resting state, which is negatively charged inside and positively charged outside, creating a difference in electrical charge across the cell membrane. This difference in electrical charge is a state of *polarization:* that is, the internal state of the neuron (negatively charged) differs from its outside state (positively charged).

When the neuron has been stimulated such that it reaches a *threshold* (a level of stimulation intensity below which nothing happens), it reacts, triggering an *action potential,* which travels down the axon. The **action potential** is a rapid reversal of the electrical balance of the cell membrane. The rapid reversal of electrical polarity occurs when positively charged sodium ions move through the membrane into the neuron, and negatively charged ions simultaneously leave the neuron, thereby disturbing the resting level and causing the action potential (*spike discharge*).

A neuron does not necessarily fire every time it is stimulated. If the level of polarization across the cell membrane has not been disturbed enough to generate the action potential, the cell will not fire. Cells that are stimulated by many other neurons are more likely to fire than neurons that are less stimulated. When neurons fire, they generate action potentials (spikes) in an **all-or-none** fashion—that is, the firing of the neuron, like the firing of a gun, occurs at full strength or not at all. Action potentials are completed in 2–4 milliseconds; generally, neurons cannot fire more than 500 times per second (see Figure 3.6). After each firing, the cell needs time to recover, generally just a few thousandths of a second; the time needed for recovery is the neuron's **refractory period.** During this period, action potentials cannot occur, and the chemical balance between the axon and the area around it is reestablished. Action potentials also can be blocked at the synapse by

action potential: An all-or-none electrical current sent down the axon of a neuron, initiated by a rapid reversal of membrane potential. Also termed a *spike discharge.*

all-or-none: The principle by which a neuron will fire either at full strength or not at all.

refractory period: The recovery period of a neuron after it fires, during which time it cannot fire again. This period allows the neuron to reestablish electrical balance with its surroundings.

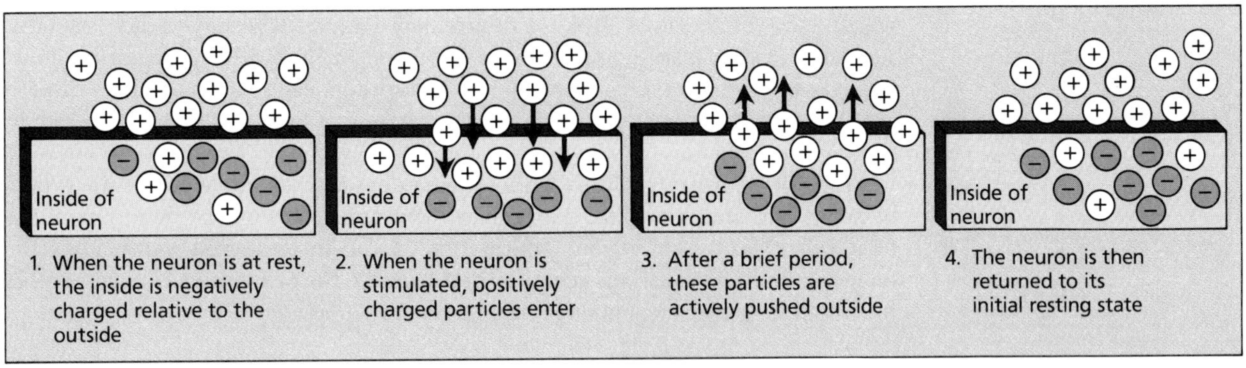
Inside of neuron
1. When the neuron is at rest, the inside is negatively charged relative to the outside
Inside of neuron
2. When the neuron is stimulated, positively charged particles enter
Inside of neuron
3. After a brief period, these particles are actively pushed outside
Inside of neuron
4. The neuron is then returned to its initial resting state

Figure 3.6

(1) When a neuron is at rest, there are more positively charged particles (sodium ions) outside it than inside. Thus, a tiny negative electric charge exists across the cell membrane. (2) When the cell is stimulated, positively charged particles enter. (3) A few milliseconds later, positively charged particles are actively pumped outside. (4) The previous potential is then restored, and the neuron is ready to fire once again.

a variety of chemicals; this chemical blocking is an important feature of drugs used to relive pain and depression.

Neurotransmitters

Neurotransmission. To transmit information from one cell to the next, neurons release neurotransmitters. When an action potential moves down the end of an axon, it stimulates chemicals—**neurotransmitters**—that reside in the axon terminal within *synaptic vesicles,* small storage structures in the axon terminal (Dunant & Israel, 1985). The neurotransmitter is released into the synapse, moves across the synaptic space, and binds to the dendrites of the next cell. (See Figure 3.7.)

Learning Objective 3.8 Describe how neurotransmitters are involved in the transmission of electrochemical signals, and identify some of their effects on physiological functioning and behavior.

Dozens of substances are known to be neurotransmitters, including serotonin, acetylcholine, norepinephrine, dopamine, and several *neuropeptides* (amino acid molecules that are produced in the body and that function in the nervous system). One neurotransmitter, serotonin, has been studied extensively and has been implicated in virtually every class of behavior (McGinty & Szymusiak, 1988). The most well known, however, is acetylcholine, which is found in neurons throughout the brain and spinal cord. Acetylcholine is crucial to exciting the skeletal muscles,

neurotransmitter: [NEW-roh-TRANS-mitt-er] A chemical substance released from the synaptic vesicles that crosses the synaptic space and affects postsynaptic dendrites by binding itself to the postsynaptic dendrite.

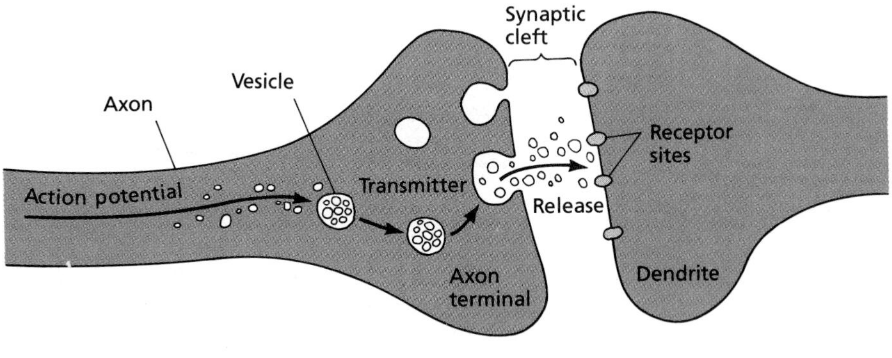
Synaptic cleft
Vesicle
Axon
Receptor sites
Action potential
Transmitter
Release
Axon terminal
Dendrite

Figure 3.7

A typical synapse.

which allow us to move. It is also extremely important in day-to-day functions such as memory, learning, and sexual behavior. Its involvement in normal functioning seems crucial, and many memory disorders such as Alzheimer's disease (discussed in Chapter 8) are evident when there is a loss of ability to produce it. (See Figure 3.8).

How do neurotransmitters work? Once released, they move across the synaptic space and attach or bind themselves to receptor sites on the dendrites of the next cell, thereby conveying information to the next neuron. Sometimes the neurotransmitters cause the receptor sites to make the cell more easily penetrable by creating an electrical change—a *postsynaptic potential (PSP).*

Excitatory and Inhibitory PSPs. The two kinds of postsynaptic potentials (PSPs) cause opposite effects: Excitatory PSPs make it more likely for the next cell to fire; inhibitory PSPs make it less likely that the next cell will fire. Because thousands of neurons may synapse onto a single cell, a single neuron can receive both excitatory and inhibitory PSPs. If it receives more excitatory ones, another action potential is likely to be generated. If it receives more inhibitory ones, further excitation along the nerve pathway may be ended. Some neurotransmitters appear to be involved in blocking pain; others seem to facilitate sensory experiences such as pain. Some may excite in some situations and inhibit in others. For example, when acetylcholine attaches to muscle cells, it has an excitatory effect. On the other hand, in some areas of the brain not related to the excitation of muscles, it can have inhibitory effects.

When neurotransmitters were first discovered, it was thought that only one type of neurotransmitter was found in each neuron and acted on one type of receptor. Today, however, we know that a neuron can hold more than one neurotransmitter, which may act on more than one receptor.

Neurotransmitters and Behavior. Although scientists have known about the existence of neurotransmitters for a long time, only recently have they realized their significance in the study of human behavior. For example, researchers have found that serotonin is involved in changes in motivation and mood (e.g., Young,

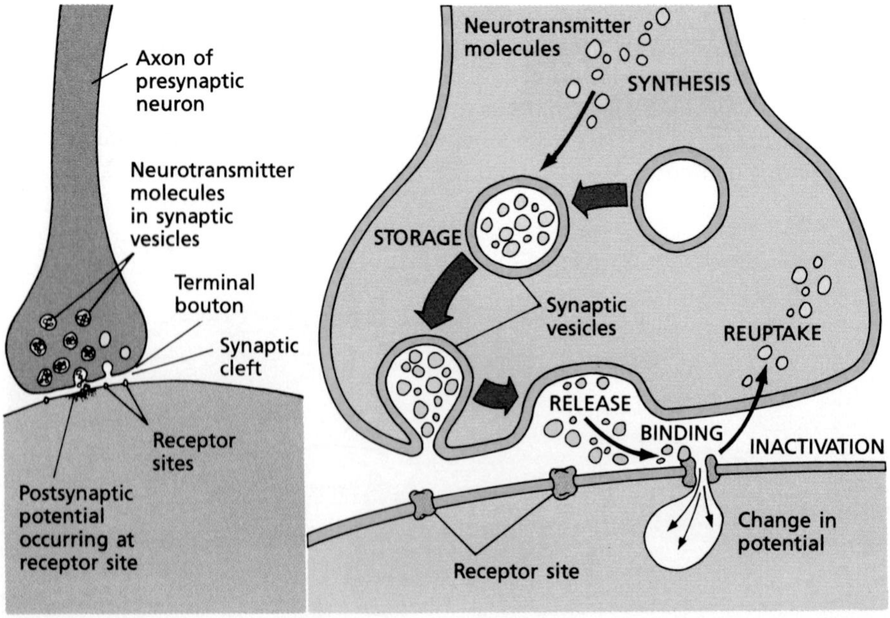

Figure 3.8

Synaptic transmission, (a) Neurons transmit information to each other by sending neurotransmitters across a synapse. (b) Following release, a neurotransmitter crosses the synapse, binding with a receptor and altering the electrical potential of the postsynaptic neuron. Most are then reabsorbed by the original neuron.

Smith, Pihl, & Ervin, 1985). Schizophrenia is thought to be associated with increased levels of some neurotransmitters. In addition, people with Parkinson's disease, whose symptoms include weakness and uncontrollable shaking, have been found to have low dopamine levels, and treatment with medication that has the same effects as dopamine (such as L-dopa) alleviates many of their symptoms. Although it is unlikely that one neurotransmitter alone can cause a disorder such as schizophrenia or depression, it may play an important role in the onset or maintenance of such an illness.

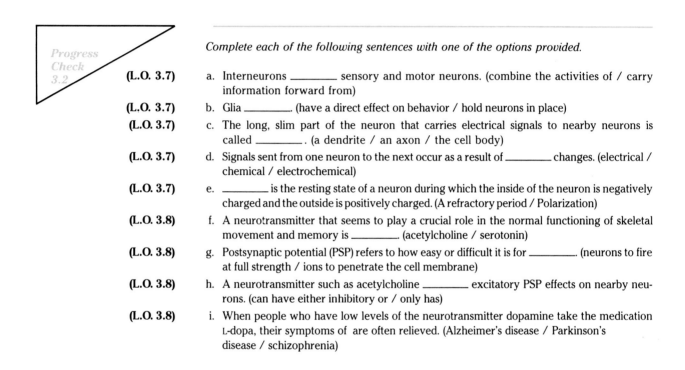

Progress Check 3.2

Complete each of the following sentences with one of the options provided.

(L.O. 3.7) a. Interneurons ________ sensory and motor neurons. (combine the activities of / carry information forward from)

(L.O. 3.7) b. Glia ________. (have a direct effect on behavior / hold neurons in place)

(L.O. 3.7) c. The long, slim part of the neuron that carries electrical signals to nearby neurons is called ________. (a dendrite / an axon / the cell body)

(L.O. 3.7) d. Signals sent from one neuron to the next occur as a result of ________ changes. (electrical / chemical / electrochemical)

(L.O. 3.7) e. ________ is the resting state of a neuron during which the inside of the neuron is negatively charged and the outside is positively charged. (A refractory period / Polarization)

(L.O. 3.8) f. A neurotransmitter that seems to play a crucial role in the normal functioning of skeletal movement and memory is ________. (acetylcholine / serotonin)

(L.O. 3.8) g. Postsynaptic potential (PSP) refers to how easy or difficult it is for ________. (neurons to fire at full strength / ions to penetrate the cell membrane)

(L.O. 3.8) h. A neurotransmitter such as acetylcholine ________ excitatory PSP effects on nearby neurons. (can have either inhibitory or / only has)

(L.O. 3.8) i. When people who have low levels of the neurotransmitter dopamine take the medication L-dopa, their symptoms of are often relieved. (Alzheimer's disease / Parkinson's disease / schizophrenia)

Module Summary

Nature Versus Nurture

- Psychologists generally assert that human behavior is influenced by both nature (heredity) and nurture (environment). Psychologists study the biological bases of behavior to understand better how these two variables interact (p. 39).
- Genetics is the study of heredity, the biological transmission of traits. Each person receives traits from his or her parents through the transmission of genes. The inherited potential of people is carried by chromosomes. Each chromosome contains thousands of genes made of DNA. The 23rd pair of chromosomes determines the gender of a fetus (p. 40).
- Identical twins share exactly the same genetic heritage; they come from one ovum and one sperm and are always the same sex. Fraternal twins are produced by two ova and two sperm and therefore can be either both males, both females, or one male and one female (p. 41).

Hormones and Glands

- The endocrine glands affect behavior by secreting hormones into the bloodstream. Each hormone controls a different aspect of behavior (p. 43).
- Studies of carbohydrate intake and behavior show that carbohydrates can function as a drug; they can modify brain chemistry and, consequently, mood and behavior (pp. 44–45).

Communication in the Nervous System

- The basic unit of the nervous system is the neuron. The neuron fires in an all-or-none manner and has a refractory period. The space between the axon terminals and the dendrite of another neuron is the synapse (pp. 48–49).
- Action potential stimulates the release of neurotransmitters that reside in the axon terminal and synaptic vesicles; neurotransmitters move across the synaptic space and attach themselves to receptor sites on the dendrites of the next cell (pp. 50–51).

KEY TERMS

action potential, p. 50
afferent, p. 48
all-or-none, p. 50
allele, p. 40
chromosomes, p. 40
diabetes mellitus, p. 44
Down syndrome, p. 42
efferent, p. 48
endocrine glands, p. 43
fraternal twins, p. 41
gene, p. 40
genetics, p. 40
hormones, p. 43
hyperglycemia, p. 45
hypoglycemia, p. 45
identical twins, p. 41
insulin, p. 44
nature, p. 39
nervous system, p. 47
neuron, p. 48
neurotransmitter, p. 51
nurture, p. 39
phenylketonuria (PKU), p. 42
refractory period, p. 50
synapse, p. 48

SELF-TEST

Module 3

- Before taking the self-test, **recite** and **review.**
- Use the key at the back of the text to *correct* your answers.
- *Restudy* pages that correspond to any questions you answered incorrectly.

1. The *primary* issue of concern in the nature versus nurture debate is
   a. which research method to use when studying genetic influences.
   b. which contributes more to behavior and mental processes—biological determinants or the environment?

   c. the assertion that inherited behavioral traits will not become evident unless the environment encourages them.
   d. the assertion that inherited traits provide a framework for behavior, and experiences ultimately shape behavior.
2. Cross out the statement concerning heredity that is *false*.
   a. If a sperm containing a Y chromosome fertilizes an ovum, the child will be female.
   b. An allele can be dominant.
   c. Each human cell contains 23 pairs of chromosomes.
   d. On some chromosomes, researchers have identified the exact location where certain traits are coded by specific genes.
3. Psychologists are able to assess the extent to which environment affects behavior by comparing psychological characteristics of
   a. fraternal twins who were reared apart, to identical twins who grew up in the same household.
   b. identical twins who were reared apart, to fraternal twins who grew up in the same household.
   c. identical twins who were reared apart.
   d. identical twins who grew up in the same household.
4. Phenylketonuria (PKU) provides a good example of
   a. a genetic disorder that can be controlled by careful management of the environment.
   b. what can happen if there are too many chromosomes present.
   c. how viral infections can modify inherited traits.
   d. an inherited trait that causes schizophrenic behavior.
5. A condition known as diabetes mellitus
   a. is also known as hyperglycemia.
   b. can lead to coma or death if left untreated.
   c. occurs when there is too little insulin, too much sugar in the blood, and too little sugar reaching body cells.
   d. all of the above
6. Some researchers think there may be several different types of PMS because
   a. men also show symptoms of the syndrome.
   b. the severity of the discomfort varies from month to month.
   c. some women show symptoms prior to menstruation, others after menstruation.
   d. some women have physical complaints, but no emotional symptoms, while other women's symptoms are just the opposite.
7. When catching a ball, your hand knows when to grasp because
   a. your parasympathetic nervous system is active.
   b. alpha waves are being generated by your brain.
   c. participating muscles receive efferent signals from the brain.
   d. afferent signals inform your hand that the ball is about to make contact.
8. The myelin sheath
   a. is a form of glial cell, and it insulates neurons from one another.
   b. is a thin, white substance covering the axon on some neurons.
   c. allows for faster conduction.
   d. all of the above
9. Neurons fire
   a. in an all-or-none fashion.
   b. as long as they have been stimulated by at least one other neuron.
   c. approximately 1000 times a second when they are in an active state.
   d. all of the above
10. Serotonin is
   a. a thinning of the skin caused by a genetic abnormality.
   b. a hormone that affects growth.
   c. an electrically charged ion that can penetrate cell membranes.
   d. a neurotransmitter that affects virtually every type of human behavior.

Module 4

The Brain and Behavior

LEARNING OBJECTIVES

When you have mastered the material in this module, you will be able to

Organization of the Central and the Peripheral Nervous Systems (pp. 57–61)

4.1 Describe the peripheral nervous system and its subsystems (p. 57).

4.2 Identify and describe the two main structures of the central nervous system (p. 59).

Monitoring Neural Activity (pp. 61–63)

4.3 Describe five techniques used to study electrical activity in the brain and give examples of how the data is being used (p. 61).

Brain Structures (pp. 63–69)

4.4 Describe the structure and functions of the brain, including the substructures of the hindbrain, midbrain, and forebrain (p. 63).

4.5 Discuss some of the ways that the brain changes over time and describe research that may lead to the treatment of learning problems and brain damage (p. 69).

SQ3R

- ▲ **Survey** to set goals for studying.
- ▲ Ask **questions** as you **read.**
- ▲ Stop occasionally to **recite** and **review.**

plus

- ▲ **Write** a summary of key points.
- ▲ **Reflect** on the hypotheses, evidence, and implications of this material and on the relevance it has to *your* life.

In 1976, a dangerously violent, mildly retarded mental patient became the first recipient of a brain "pacemaker" when doctors implanted tiny electrodes in the man's brain. The electrodes were wired to a human-palm-sized battery pack, which stimulated the limbic system (also known as the pleasure center) of his brain every few minutes. After the operation, the patient, who previously had to be tied to his bed because of his violent outbursts, became a calm man. The hospital sent him home, and all went well for several weeks. Then the man went berserk, tried to murder his parents, and seriously wounded his next-door neighbor. Hospital X-rays revealed the problem: The wires between the pacemaker and battery pack had become disconnected. The wires were reattached, and the patient's violent attacks ceased. The implanted electrical connections and their connection to the central nervous system was critical to this man's well-being.

Organization of the Central and the Peripheral Nervous Systems

Learning Objective 4.1 Describe the peripheral nervous system and its subsystems.

The nervous system, and especially the brain, controls behavior on a second-by-second basis. Psychologists must therefore understand the organization and functions of the nervous system and its mutually dependent systems and subsystems. Recall that the nervous system is made up of the central nervous system and the peripheral nervous system. The central nervous system comprises the brain and spinal cord; the peripheral nervous system connects the central nervous system to the rest of the body. We examine them both in detail, beginning with the peripheral nervous system.

peripheral nervous system: [puh-RIF-er-al] The part of the nervous system that carries information to and from the central nervous system through a network of spinal and cranial nerves that lie outside the brain and spinal cord. Its two functional subdivisions: the somatic and autonomic nervous systems.

somatic nervous system: [so-MAT-ick] The part of the peripheral nervous system that carries information to skeletal muscles and thereby affects bodily movement.

autonomic nervous system: [au-toe-NOM-ick] The part of the peripheral nervous system that controls the vital processes of the body, such as heart rate, digestive processes, blood pressure, and regulation of internal organs. (*Autonomic* means "self-regulating".) Its two main subdivisions are the sympathetic and parasympathetic systems.

The Peripheral Nervous System

The **peripheral nervous system** carries information to and from the spinal cord and the brain via spinal nerves attached to the spinal cord and by a system of 12 cranial nerves that carry signals directly to and from the brain (see Figure 4.1 on the next page). The peripheral nervous system contains all nerves that are not in the central nervous system; its nerves focus on the *periphery*, the outer parts of the body. The peripheral nervous system actually contains two major systems: the somatic nervous system and the autonomic nervous system.

The Somatic Nervous System. The **somatic nervous system,** which is generally under voluntary control, responds to and acts on the outside world. It is involved in *perceptual processing* (processing sensory information) and the control of movement and muscles that are under voluntary control. Consisting of both your sensory and your motor neurons, it carries information from your sense organs to your brain, and from your brain and spinal cord to your muscles that you consciously control. It is the somatic system that allows you to take off your jacket in the warm afternoon sun and facilitates a quick sprint to class before the instructor starts a lecture.

The Autonomic Nervous System. The **autonomic nervous system,** in contrast to the somatic nervous system, operates involuntarily (although the controversial technique of biofeedback, discussed in Chapter 4, has been proven effective in bringing some of these processes under voluntary control). The autonomic

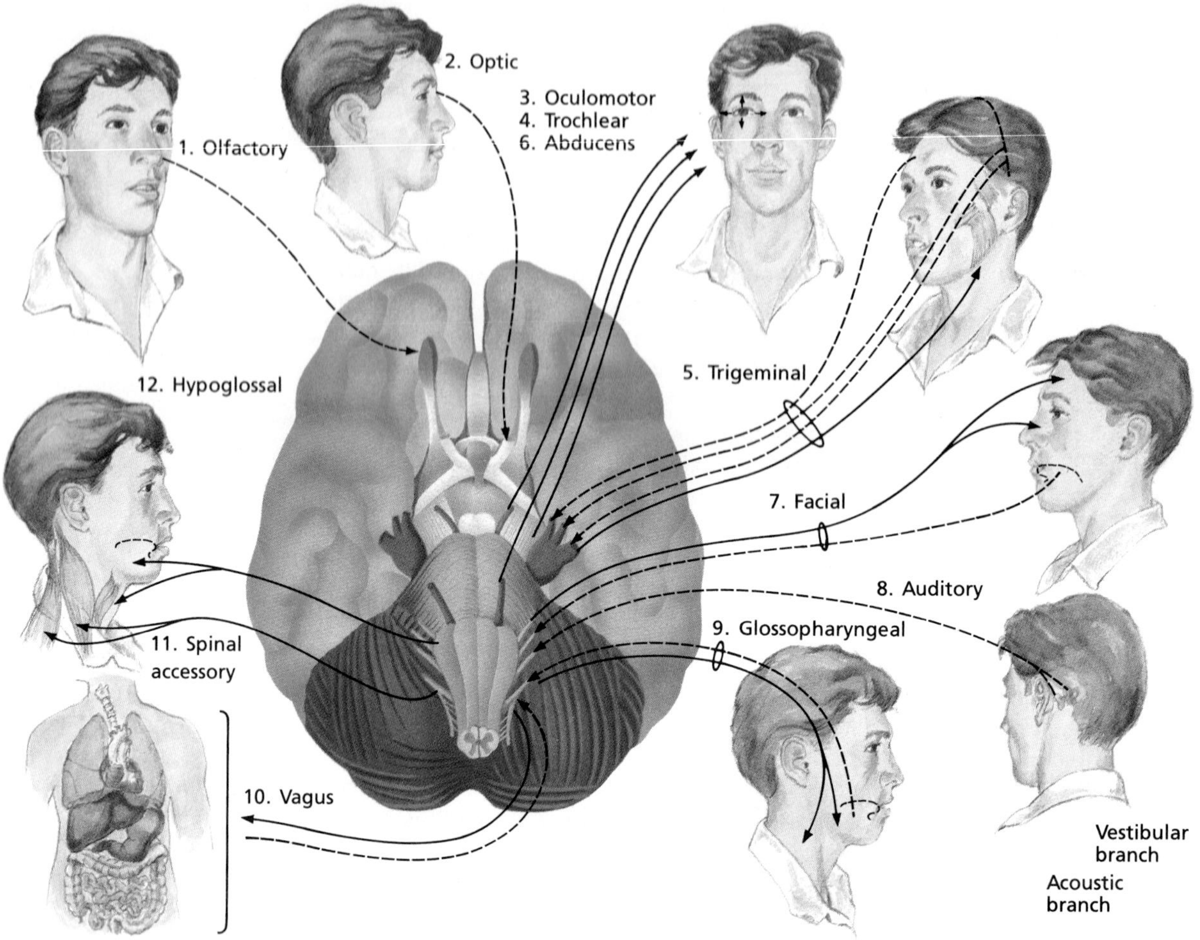

Figure 4.1

Each of the 12 cranial nerves sends information directly to its appropriate location in the brain.

sympathetic nervous system: The part of the autonomic nervous system that responds to emergency situations. Active only occasionally, it calls up bodily resources as needed for major energy expenditures.

parasympathetic nervous system: [PAIR-uh-sim-puh-THET-ick] The part of the peripheral nervous system that controls ongoing maintenance processes of the body such as heart rate, digestive processes, and blood pressure. It also involves building and maintaining energy stores.

nervous system regulates internal conditions such as heart rate, blood pressure, and even digestion; the system is called autonomic because many of its systems are self-regulating. It is made up of two divisions: the sympathetic nervous system and the parasympathetic nervous system (Figure 4.2), which work together in controlling the activities of the muscles and glands.

The activities of the **sympathetic nervous system** are easily observed and measured. Activation results in a sharp increase in heart rate and blood pressure, slowing of the digestive processes, dilation of the pupils, and general preparation for emergency—sometimes called the fight-or-flight reflex—usually accompanied by increased flow of epinephrine (adrenaline). The sympathetic nervous system makes your heart pound when you narrowly miss hitting an oncoming car.

In contrast, the **parasympathetic nervous system,** which is active most of the time, controls the normal operations of digestion, blood pressure, and heart rate, among other things. The parasympathetic nervous system calms everything down and regulates your heartbeat back to normal. In other words, it keeps the body running smoothly. Parasympathetic activity does not show sharp changes on a minute-by-minute basis.

When the sympathetic nervous system is activated and the organism is in a fight-or-flight posture, the somatic nervous system is also activated. For example, when a runner is chased by a large, growling dog and her adrenal glands are stimulated, the burst of energy produced by epinephrine affects the somatic system, making the runner's muscles respond strongly and rapidly. Thus, changes in the autonomic nervous system produce rapid changes in the organism; these changes are usually seen in stress reactions and emotional behavior, which is discussed more fully in Chapters 9 and 12. Even simple responses, such as blushing when a person is embarrassed, are regulated by the autonomic nervous system. For example, blushing occurs when a speaker realizes that his behavior is being observed and he has made a gaff, looks foolish, or is being scrutinized carefully and blushing occurs automatically.

central nervous system (CNS): One of the two major parts of the nervous system, consisting of the brain and spinal cord.

brain: The part of the central nervous system that regulates, monitors, processes, and guides other nervous system activity; located within the skull.

The Central Nervous System

The **central nervous system,** consisting of the brain and the spinal cord, serves as the main processing system for most information in the body (see Figure 4.3 on the next page). Recognizing that the **brain** plays a central role in controlling behavior, psychologists and physiologists are continually trying to understand it better. Some researchers study the brains of people who died of tumors, brain

Learning Objective 4.2
Identify and describe the two main structures of the central nervous system.

Figure 4.2

The activities of the two branches of the autonomic nervous system (ANS).

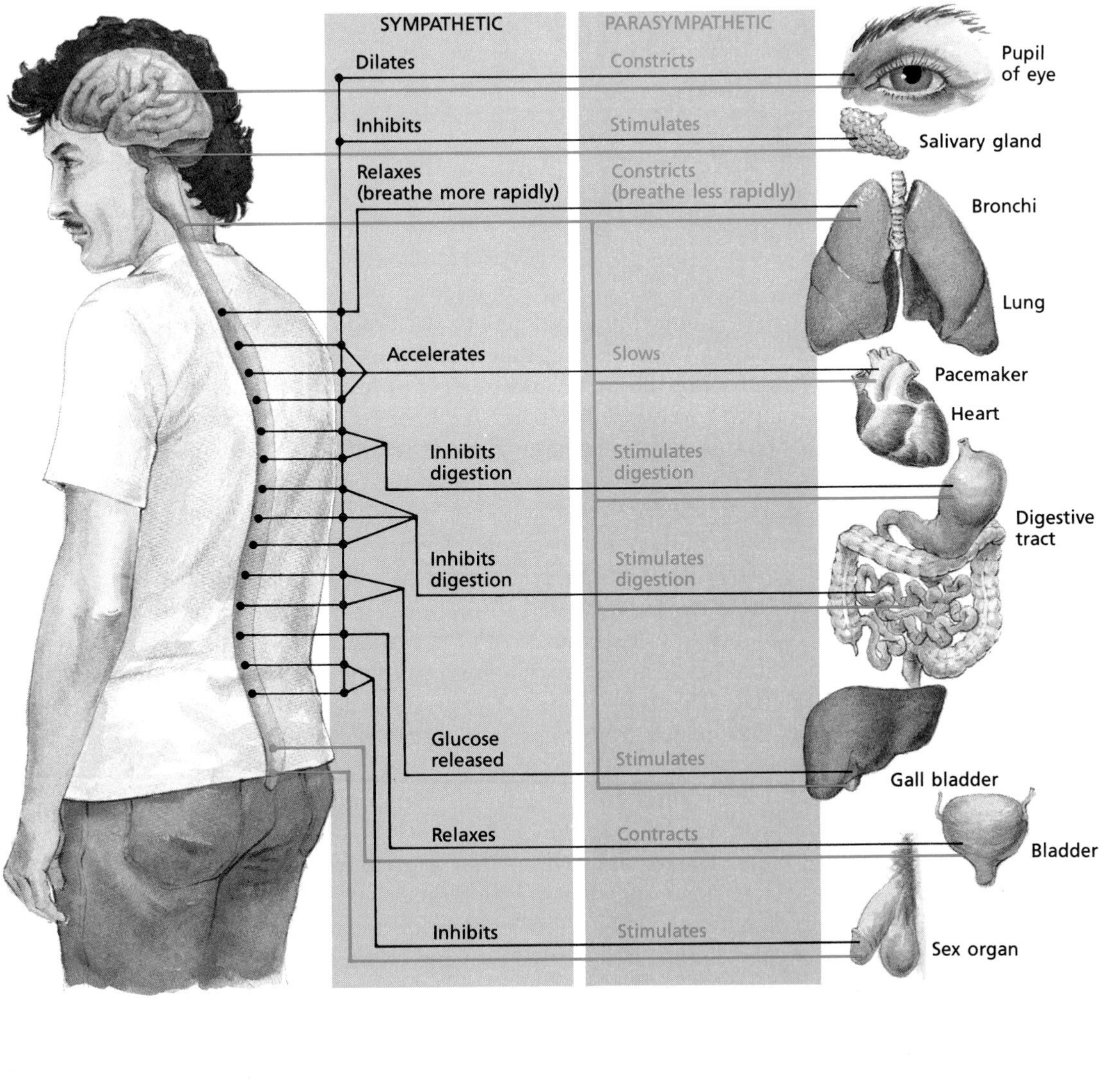

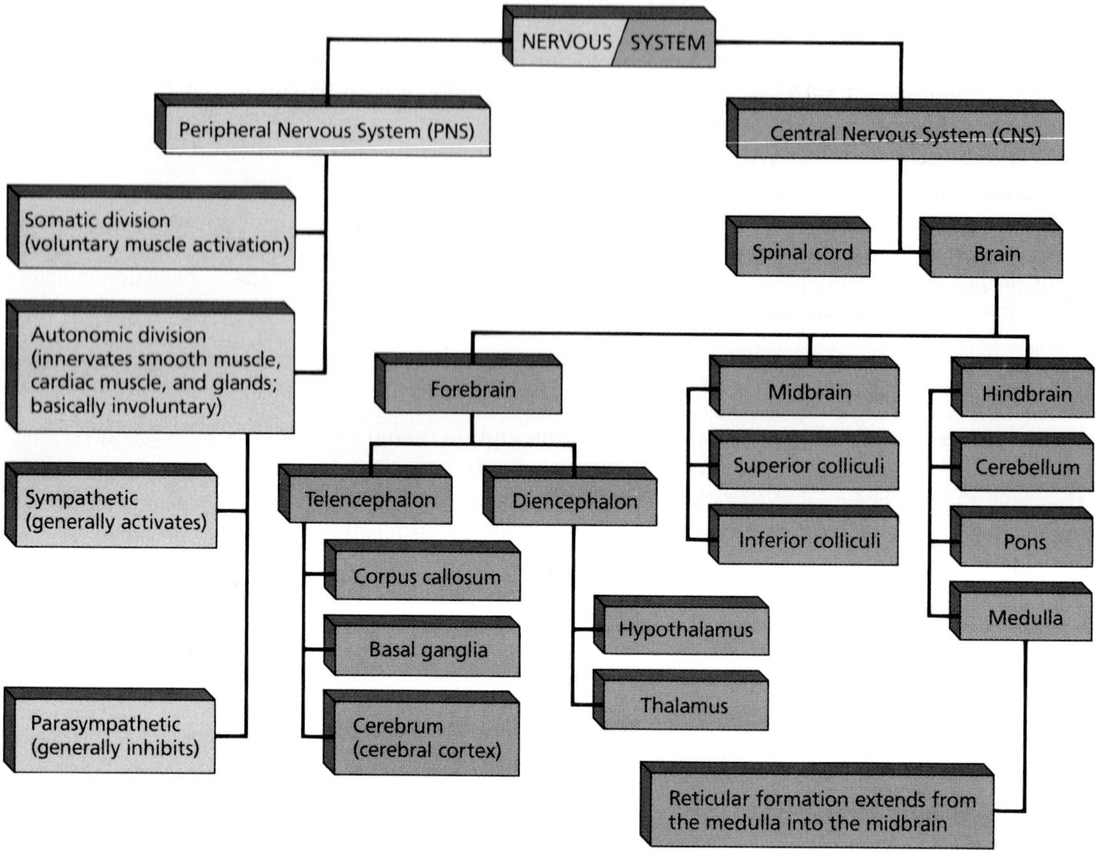

Figure 4.3

The basic divisions of the nervous system and their major subdivisions.

spinal cord: Portion of the central nervous system that is contained within the spinal column. It transmits signals from the senses to the brain, controls reflexive responses, and conveys signals from the brain to the muscles and glands.

diseases, and trauma (injury) to the brain, hoping to correlate the type of brain damage with the loss of specific abilities, such as seeing, reading, or writing. Others observe the behavioral effects of lesions (i.e., damage) to different areas of animals' brains. Still others study the brain–behavior relationships by watching both animals and children interact with their environment and solve problems.

Although our understanding of the brain's functions is far from complete, we know that it operates through many mutually dependent systems and subsystems to affect and control behavior. Thousands of brain cells are involved in the performance of even simple activities. When we walk, for example, the visual areas of the brain are activated so that our sight can guide us, the brain's motor areas help make our legs move, and the cerebellum helps us keep our balance. It is the central nervous system, communicating with the muscles and glands, that allows all these things to happen. The brain is the control center, but it receives most of its information from the spinal cord, the main communication line to the rest of the body.

The **spinal cord** receives signals from the senses, muscles, and glands and relays the signals to the brain. Some behaviors do not involve the brain directly: *Spinal reflexes* are actions that are controlled solely by the spinal cord and a system of neurons that create a reflexive response. When you touch a hot stove, a signal goes to the spinal cord, and the spinal cord initiates a hand-withdrawing signal to the muscles in the arm and hand. This is a *spinal reflex,* linking a sensory input to a motor response without passing through the brain. The *knee jerk,* elicited by a tap on the tendon below the kneecap, is another spinal reflex. Most signals eventually make their way up the spinal cord to the brain for further analysis, but the initial withdrawal of the hand happens at the level of the spinal cord, before your brain has had time to register and act on pain signals.

The spinal cord's importance cannot be overstated. When a person's spinal cord is severed, the information exchange between the brain and muscles and glands below the point of damage is halted. Spinal reflexes in such individuals still operate, and knee-jerk responses are evident. However, patients who suffer spinal cord damage lose voluntary control over muscles in the parts of their bodies below the spinal cord injury. The spinal cord thus serves a key communication function between the brain and the rest of the body; it is the chief trunk line for neuronal activity.

Monitoring Neuronal Activity

Learning Objective 4.3
Describe five techniques used to study electrical activity in the brain, and give examples of how the data is being used.

Though nonliving brains can be dissected easily, scientists are more interested in exploring the functions and interconnections of the active central nervous system, a more difficult task. Much of what scientists now know about physiology and behavior, specifically the electrical activity in the nervous system, comes from laboratory studies of abnormalities in brain structure and function. In conducting such studies, several basic procedures are used to measure the activity of the nervous system.

One technique for measuring the activity of the nervous system is *single-unit recording,* which involves placing a thin wire or needle (a microelectrode) in or next to a single neuron, to measure its electrical activity. The data are then recorded on an oscilloscope, which measures changes in electrical voltage. Because neurons fire extremely rapidly, the data are often fed into a computer, which averages the number of times the cell fires in 1 second or 1 minute. This technique is usually performed on cats, rats, or monkeys.

Another technique, *electroencephalography,* measures electrical activity in the nervous system. It produces a record (see Fig. 4.4) of brain-wave activity—an **electroencephalogram,** or **EEG** (*electro* = electrical; *encephalon* = brain; *gram*

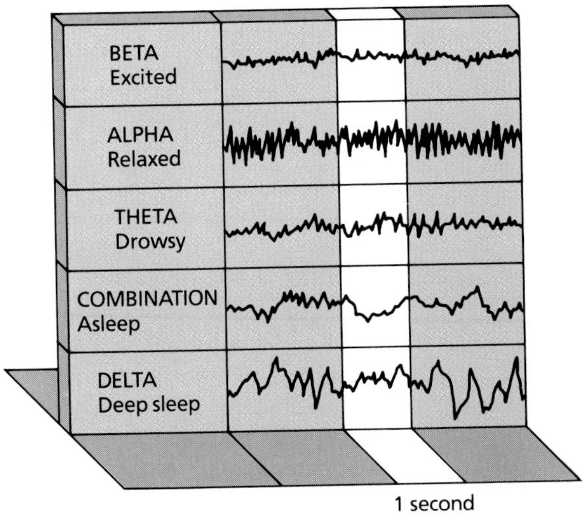

Figure 4.4

Characteristic electrical activity patterns in the EEGs of healthy humans in different states of excitation. High frequency is indicated by the occurrence of a large number of waves within a single unit or period of time.

electroencephalogram (EEG): [eel-ECK-tro-en-SEFF-uh-low-gram] Record of electrical-wave patterns obtained through electrodes placed on a subject's scalp.

= record). A small electrode placed on a subject's scalp records the activity of thousands of cells beneath the skull, thus producing an EEG. EEGs, which are generally computer analyzed, are used for a variety of purposes, including the assessment of brain damage, epilepsy, tumors, and other abnormalities.

In normal, healthy human beings, EEGs show a variety of characteristic brain-wave patterns, depending on the subject's *level* (such as degree of consciousness) and *kind* (such as listening to music versus talking) of mental activity. Brain waves are usually described in terms of their frequency and amplitude—that is, the number of waves in a unit of time and the height of waves. These brain waves are not yet fully understood, and it must be remembered that they reflect the activity of hundreds of thousands of cells that lie beneath an electrode.

If people are awake, relaxed, and not engaged in active thinking, their EEGs show *alpha waves,* which occur at a rate of 8–12 cycles per second and are of moderate amplitude. When people are excited, their brain waves change dramatically from alpha waves to high-frequency and low-amplitude waves—*beta* and *gamma waves.* At different times during sleep, people show patterns of high-frequency and low-frequency waves.

Three significant new techniques for measuring the activity of the nervous system have emerged. *CAT* (computerized axial tomography) *scans* are computer-assisted X-ray procedures used to visualize the brain in three dimensions; they especially help researchers locate specific lesions and tumors in the brain. They are essentially a computerized series of X-rays that show photographic slices of the brain. Another technique, *MRI* (magnetic resonance imaging) *scans,* are similar to CAT scans but do not use radiation, and they produce higher clarity and resolution. *PET* (positron emission tomography) *scans,* which use radiochemical procedures, enable researchers to watch metabolic changes taking place in an organism as they occur.

CAT scans are computer-assisted X-rays which allow researchers to view the brain in three dimensions.

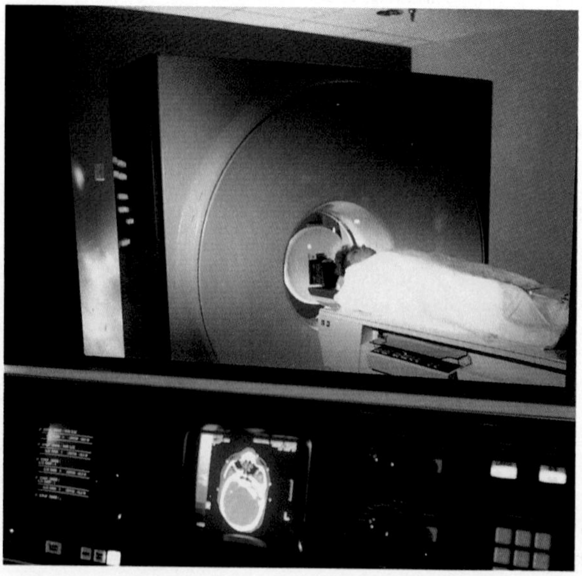

MRI scans are similar to CAT scans, but do not use radiation and produce higher clarity and resolution. This MRI scan reveals degeneration of the frontal lobe, a possible sign of Alzheimer's disease.

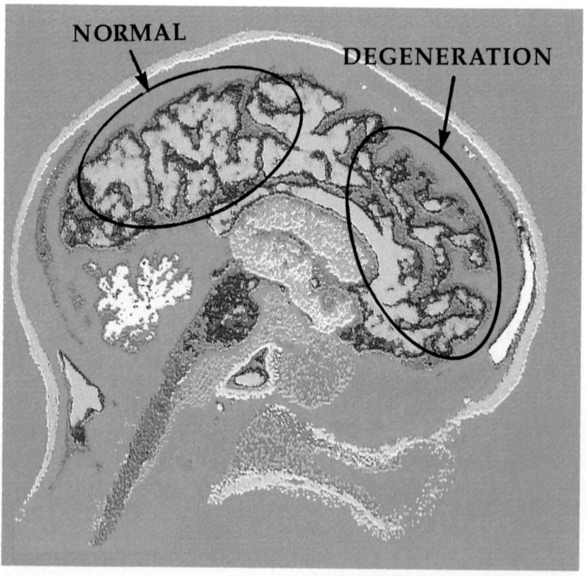

These three experimental techniques—CAT, MRI, and PET scans—make the examination of brain tissue and its processes easier and more precise, thereby providing more information about the brain and its workings. For example, researchers today are showing that small brain lesions are common in elderly people and are a natural part of aging. Further, a tentative link among brain lesions, illness, neurochemistry, and depression is being established (Nemeroff et al., 1988). Today, lawyers are using brain imaging as part of a defense in criminal trials; for example, attorneys now assert that PET scans can show that their client's brain may have damage that traditional neurological tests cannot find. In one California case, a diagnosis of a mental disorder was confirmed through a PET scan and kept a man from going to the gas chamber. The practical applications of such brain imaging techniques are rapidly being put to use by lawyers, but in the laboratory, researchers feel that brain scans not only allow better diagnoses of disease and malfunction, but also allow them to continue to examine, map, and study brain structures.

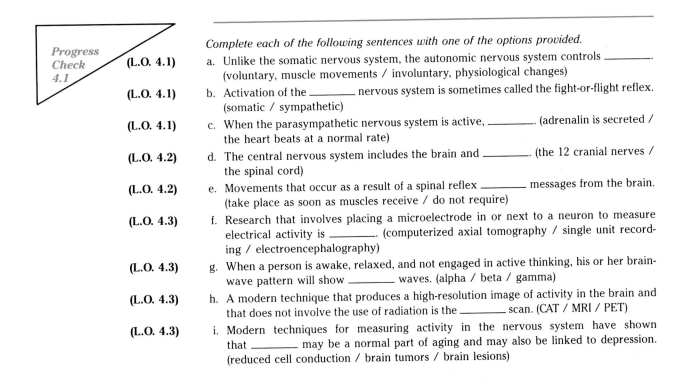

Progress Check 4.1

Complete each of the following sentences with one of the options provided.

(L.O. 4.1) a. Unlike the somatic nervous system, the autonomic nervous system controls ________. (voluntary, muscle movements / involuntary, physiological changes)

(L.O. 4.1) b. Activation of the ________ nervous system is sometimes called the fight-or-flight reflex. (somatic / sympathetic)

(L.O. 4.1) c. When the parasympathetic nervous system is active, ________. (adrenalin is secreted / the heart beats at a normal rate)

(L.O. 4.2) d. The central nervous system includes the brain and ________. (the 12 cranial nerves / the spinal cord)

(L.O. 4.2) e. Movements that occur as a result of a spinal reflex ________ messages from the brain. (take place as soon as muscles receive / do not require)

(L.O. 4.3) f. Research that involves placing a microelectrode in or next to a neuron to measure electrical activity is ________. (computerized axial tomography / single unit recording / electroencephalography)

(L.O. 4.3) g. When a person is awake, relaxed, and not engaged in active thinking, his or her brain-wave pattern will show ________ waves. (alpha / beta / gamma)

(L.O. 4.3) h. A modern technique that produces a high-resolution image of activity in the brain and that does not involve the use of radiation is the ________ scan. (CAT / MRI / PET)

(L.O. 4.3) i. Modern techniques for measuring activity in the nervous system have shown that ________ may be a normal part of aging and may also be linked to depression. (reduced cell conduction / brain tumors / brain lesions)

Brain Structures

Learning Objective 4.4
Describe the structure and functions of the brain, including the substructures of the hindbrain, midbrain, and forebrain.

The structure of the central nervous system and the organization of neurological pathways all seem to point toward the brain. There is no doubt that the brain is the central computing, processing, and storage mechanism that is intimately involved in day-to-day and minute-by-minute behavior. Our understanding of the brain and its relationship to behavior comes about in part through the study of neuroanatomy. *Neuroanatomy,* the study of the structures of the nervous system, uses a wide range of techniques. The principal method of early research was called ablation. In *ablation,* a portion of an animal's brain is removed and the animal's behavior is studied to determine which behaviors have been disrupted.

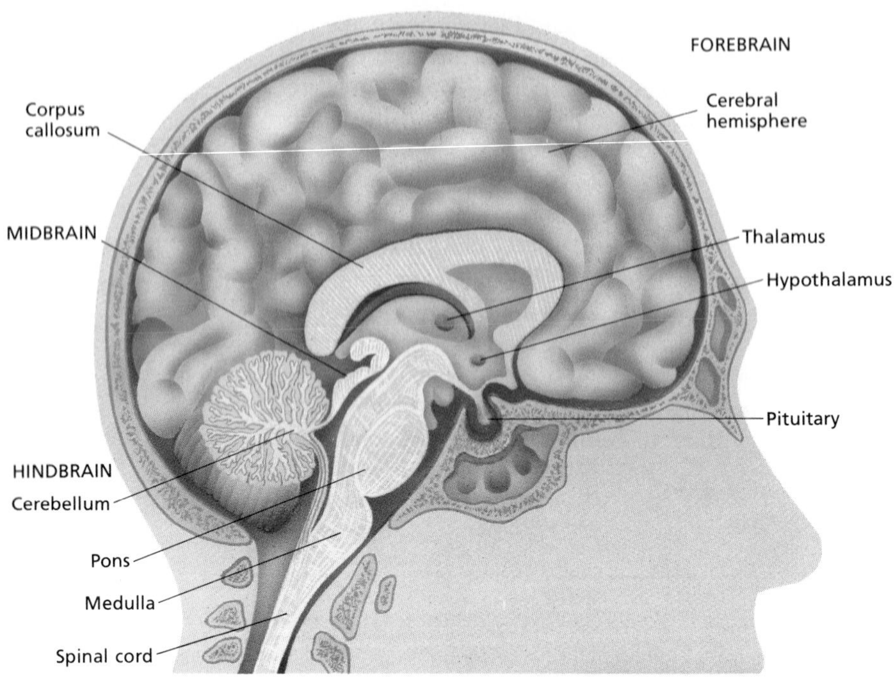

Figure 4.5

The three major sections of the brain: hindbrain, midbrain, and forebrain.

Today, in addition to ablation, electrical recording techniques (EEGs and CAT and PET scans) and neurochemical techniques are used.

We know a lot about the structure and functions of the brain, and we still have a great deal to learn. On first inspection, it is easy to see that the human brain weighs about three pounds and is relatively fragile. It is composed of two large *cerebral hemispheres,* one on the left side and one on the right side. A large, thick structure—the *corpus callosum*—connects the two cerebral hemispheres and permits the transfer of information between them. Besides being divided into right and left halves, the brain can be roughly divided into areas with special functions. Some parts are specialized for visual activities, while others are involved in hearing, sleeping, breathing, eating, and a number of other important functions. Some brain activities are localized: Most speech and language activity, for example, can be pinpointed to a specific area, usually in the left side of the brain. Other activities may occur in both hemispheres: Visual activity, for example, occurs in the visual cortex, which occupies both sides of the brain. Psychologists disagree on the extent to which functions are localized within the brain.

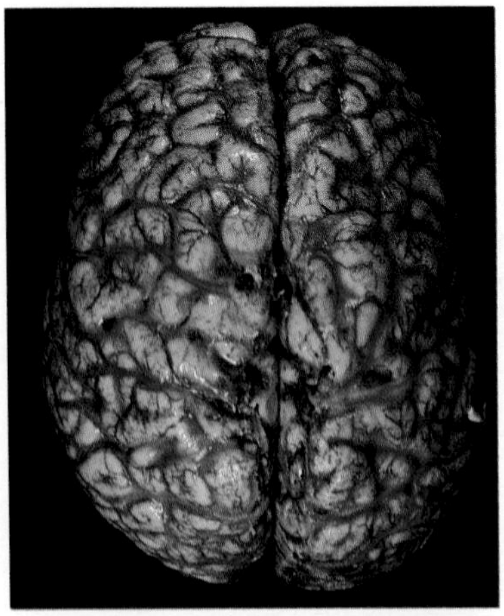

The human brain weighs about three pounds and is composed of two large cerebral hemispheres which are joined by the corpus collosum.

We examine the brain beginning where the spinal cord and brain meet. Many functions deep within the brain at its core are responsible for basic processes within the body, such as breathing, sleeping, and eating. As we move higher up through the brain, more complicated structures and functions are found. Organizationally, the brain is traditionally divided into three sections: the hindbrain, the midbrain, and the forebrain, which includes the cortex (see Figure 4.5). Structures found in the hindbrain and midbrain are often assumed to be organizationally more primitive and are responsible for more basic, reflexive actions. Structures in the lower portions of the forebrain are organizationally somewhat more complex and involve higher mental functions. Still higher is the cortex, which covers the cerebral hemispheres and serves as the basis for thought processes, a human being's most advanced ability.

Hindbrain

The *hindbrain* consists of three main structures: the cerebellum, the medulla, and the pons. The *cerebellum* is a large structure attached to the back surface of the brain stem. It influences balance, coordination, and movement, allowing you to do things such as walk in a straight line, type accurately on a keyboard, and coordinate the many movements involved in dancing. The cerebellum may also be involved in a number of cognitive or thought operations (Leiner, Leiner, & Dow, 1986).

The *medulla,* through which many afferent and efferent signals pass, lies just above the spinal cord and controls heartbeat and breathing. Within the medulla and extending out into the cortex is a latticelike network of nerve cells—the *reticular formation,* which directly controls a person's state of arousal, waking, and sleeping, as well as responsive bodily functions; damage to it can result in coma and death. The reticular formation extends into and through the pons and midbrain, with projections toward the cortex (see Figure 4.6). Like the reticular formation, portions of the *pons* are involved in sleep and dreaming.

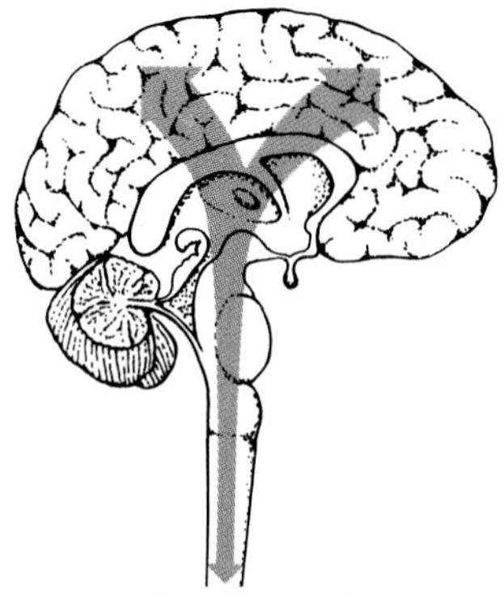

Figure 4.6

Many afferent and efferent signals pass through the reticular formation.

Midbrain

The *midbrain* is made up of nuclei (collections of cell bodies) that receive afferent signals from other parts of the brain and from the spinal cord; the nuclei then interpret the signals and either relay the information to a more complex part of the brain or cause the body to act at once. A portion of the midbrain has been shown to be involved in smoothness of movement and another in reflexive movements. Movements of the eyeball in its socket, for example, are controlled by the *superior colliculus,* which is a structure in the midbrain. The *reticular formation* system continues in the midbrain and is important in the regulation of attention, as well as sleep and arousal.

Forebrain

The *forebrain* is the largest and most complicated of the brain structures because of its many related parts: the thalamus and hypothalamus, the limbic system, the basal ganglia and corpus callosum, and the cortex.

Thalamus and Hypothalamus. The *thalamus* acts primarily as a routing station to send information to other parts of the brain, although it probably also performs some interpretive functions (see Figure 4.7). Nearly all sensory information proceeds through the thalamus before going to other areas of the brain. The *hypothalamus* has numerous connections with the rest of the forebrain and midbrain and is involved in many complex behaviors such as motivation, emotion, eating and drinking, and sexual behavior. The hypothalamus has long been known to play a crucial role in the regulation of food intake; disturbances in the hypothalamus often produce sharp eating and drinking behavior changes.

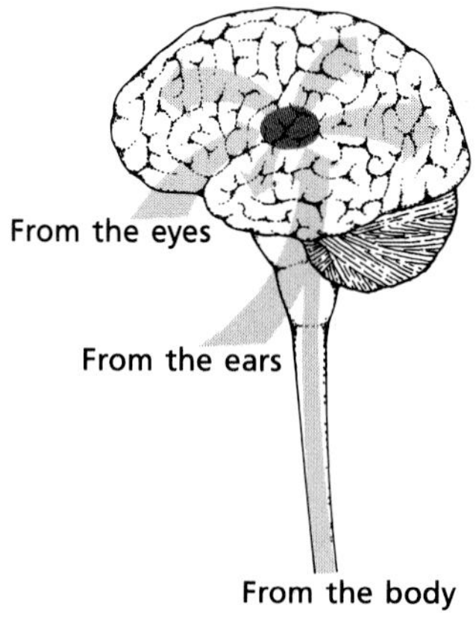

Figure 4.7

The thalamus acts as a relay station for sensory information and sends afferent input to the higher centers.

Limbic System. One of the most complex and least understood areas of the brain is the *limbic system.* This system is an interconnected group of structures (including parts of the cortex, thalamus, and hypothalamus) involved in emotional behavior, memory, social behavior, and brain disorders such as epilepsy. Within the limbic system are the hippocampus and the amygdala. In human beings, the *hippocampus* is closely involved in memory functions. The *amygdala* is thought to be involved in the control of emotional behavior. Stimulation of the amygdala

UNDERSTANDING THE RESEARCH PROCESS

Brain Specialization

The brain and the body clearly interact with one another continually. This two-way street is easily seen when psychoactive drugs (drugs that affect the nervous system, especially the brain) are taken: A person takes a drug, which affects the firing of neurons and the subsequent release of neurotransmitters (in the brain); this change makes the person feel different. The person responds (behavior) to the feeling and further brain changes take place. For example, cocaine addicts take the drug, which affects their neurotransmitters, then they feel a "high" and may then behave erratically. The essence is that the brain affects behavior *and* behavior affects the brain.

Are there specific places in the brain that control specific behaviors and thoughts? Does one side of the brain have more control than the other? Some of the most exciting work comes from studies that examine differences between the two cerebral hemispheres.

Studies of brain structure show that different areas of the brain are responsible for differing functions. Michael Gazzaniga has been at the forefront of research in brain organization and asserts that the human brain has a modular organization, that it is divided into discrete units that interact to produce mental activity (Gazzaniga, 1989). Studies by Sperry (1985) and Gazzaniga (1983) show that in most human beings, one cerebral hemisphere—usually the left—is specialized for processing speech and language; the other—usually the right—appears better able to handle spatial tasks and musical and artistic endeavors.

Some of this evidence comes from studies monitoring brain-wave activity in normal subjects exposed to different kinds of stimuli. For example, when normal subjects are asked to look at or think about letters or perhaps to rehearse a speech, some characteristic brain-wave activity can be detected on the left side of the brain. When they are asked to do creative tasks or are told to reorganize some spatial pattern, brain-wave activity is apparent on the right side of the brain.

What happens to behavior and mental processes when connections between the left and right sides are cut and communication between them ceases? A number of important studies have involved **split-brain patients.** In extreme cases, people with uncontrollable, life-threatening epilepsy have undergone an operation to sever the *corpus callosum* (the band of fibers that connects the left and right hemispheres of the brain) to prevent seizures from spreading across hemispheres. In such cases, there was little or no perceptual or cognitive interaction between the hemispheres, and the patients seemed to have two distinct, independent brains, each with its own abilities. Studies of split-brain patients have proven invaluable to scientists who seek to understand how the brain works and how the left and right sides function together. These studies have led to some startling results.

Each cerebral hemisphere is neurologically connected to the opposite side of the body; thus the left hemisphere normally controls the right side of the body. Split-brain patients are unable to use the speech and language capabilities of the left cerebral hemisphere to describe activities carried out by the right one. When stimulus information is presented exclusively to their left hemisphere, they can describe the stimulus, match it, and deal with it in essentially normal ways. However, when the same stimulus is presented to their right cerebral hemisphere, they can perform the matching tasks (saying that two items are identical) but are unable to verbally describe the stimuli (a left-hemisphere task). Although there seem to be specifically left-brain and right-brain activities, the two halves of our brain work together; although we have localization of functions, we have a unified conscious experience (we examine consciousness in Chapter 4).

Discovering how our modules of brain cells work together is the key to understanding brain activity. Gazzaniga believes that an *interpreter module* exists in the left side of the brain that takes both left- and right-brain experiences and unifies them, interprets them, and creates a conscious experience. This interpreter module serves an integrating function. Where and how this interpreter operates is yet to be determined.

There is no doubt that specificity of functions exist. There is also no doubt that the study of brain functions and the work of Sperry and Gazzaniga have been influ-

split-brain patients: Persons whose *corpus callosum*—which normally connects the two cerebral hemispheres—has been surgically severed.

in animals produces attack responses, and surgical removal of the amygdala in human beings was once a radical way of treating people who were extremely violent. Stimulation of several areas of the limbic system in rats also produces very pleasurable sensations. Olds and Milner (1954) discovered that rats, when

ential in developing our understanding of brain specificity. For example, people with a strong right-brain dominance who are generally left handed may in fact develop differently than right handers, and this may affect a number of important events in their lives, and perhaps even the length of their life (Coren and Halpern, 1991). Unfortunately, in the popular media, the specificity of functions has been oversimplified, and in some cases trivialized to account for school problems, marital problems, artistic abilities, and even baseball batting averages. The extent of hemispheric specialization is yet to be determined, and most scientists and critical thinkers maintain a healthy skepticism about the role of two minds in one.

- ***What is the evidence that led to the initial idea that there is brain specificity?***
- ***Split-brain patients provided data in the area of physiology which allowed researchers to make what conclusion?***
- ***Research is clear that brain specificity exists, but is there evidence to suggest that there are implications for practical applications of this knowledge?***

In most people, lateralization of brain functioning occurs by about age 13 years. The left hemisphere generally controls language and verbal abilities; the right hemisphere generally controls spatial, holistic abilities.

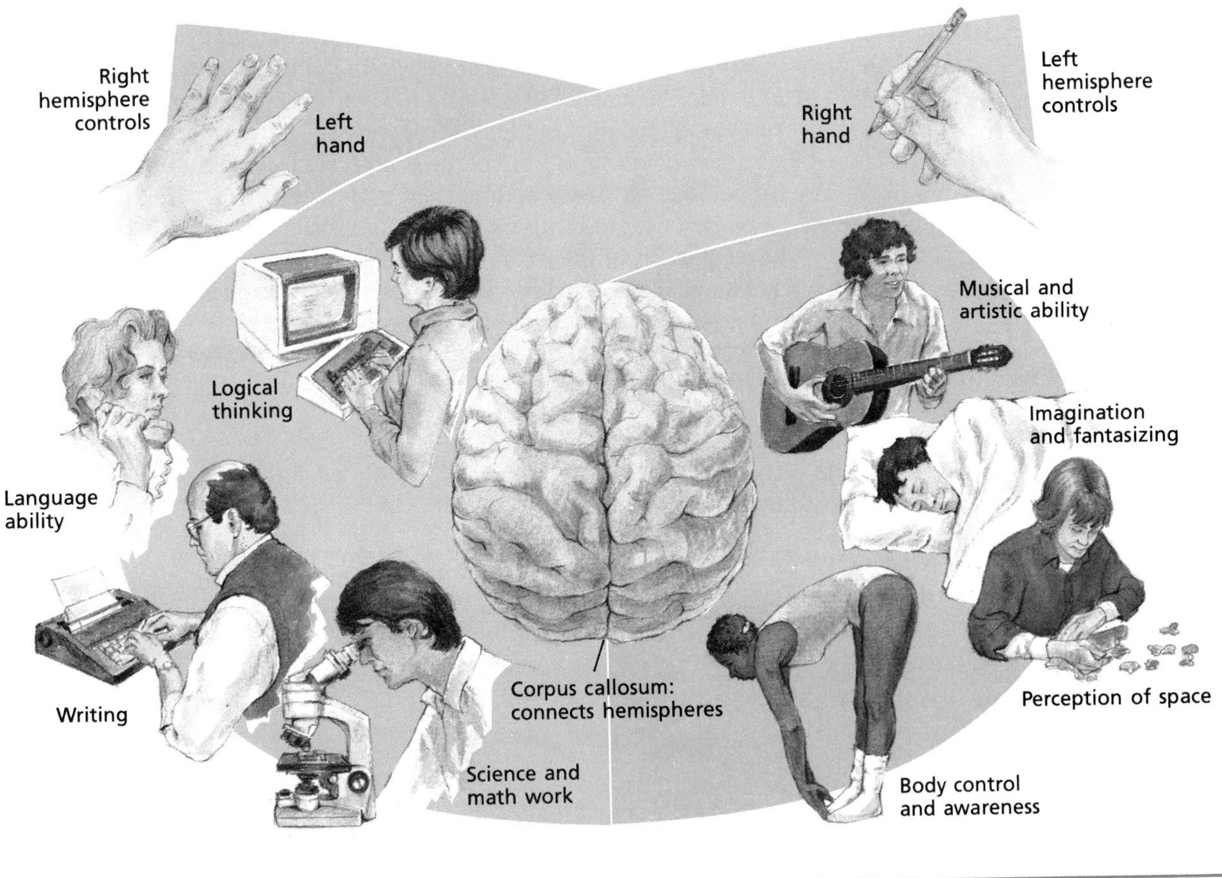

given small doses of electric current in some of the limbic areas as rewards for bar pressing, chose bar pressing over eating, even after having been deprived of food for long periods. They called the areas of the brain being stimulated pleasure centers.

convolutions: Characteristic folds in human tissues of the cerebral hemispheres and their overlying cortex.

The Basal Ganglia and Corpus Callosum. The *basal ganglia* are a series of nuclei located deep in the brain to the left and right of the thalamus. They control movements and posture and are also associated with Parkinson's disease (see Figure 4.8). Parts of the basal ganglia influence muscle tone and initiate commands to the cerebellum and to higher brain centers. The *corpus callosum* connects and conveys information between the cerebral hemispheres; damage to its results in essentially two separate brains. The corpus callosum is described in greater detail in subsequent paragraphs, and in the Understanding the Research Process box describing brain specialization on pages 66–67.

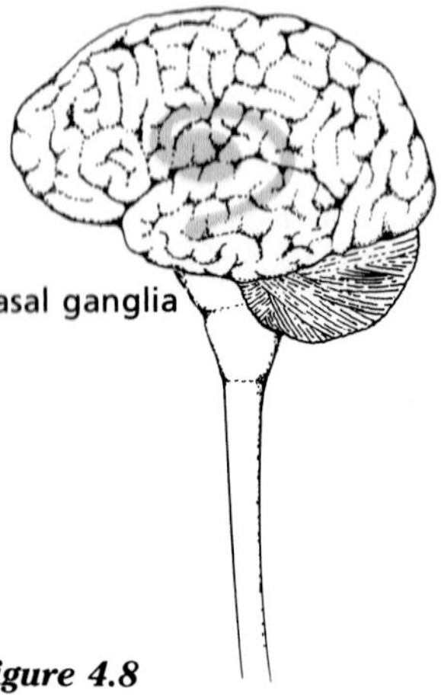

Figure 4.8

The basal ganglia, found deep within the brain, are involved in the regulation and control of gross movement. Damage to this important neurological center can have severe behavioral consequences.

Cortex. The brain is divided into two major portions, referred to as the left and the right hemispheres. The exterior covering of the cerebral hemispheres, called the *cortex* (or *neocortex*), is about 2 millimeters thick and consists of six thin layers of cells. A highly developed cortex is evident in human beings, but not all mammals show such specialization. The cortex plays a special role in behavior because it is so intimately involved in thought. The cortex is *convoluted,* or furrowed. These **convolutions** have the effect of creating more surface area within a small space: The overall surface area of the cortex is about 1.5 square feet.

A traditional way to divide the cortex is to consider it as a series of lobes, or areas, each with characteristic structures. The most prominent structures are the two deep *fissures* (very deep furrows or folds)—the *lateral fissure* and the *central fissure*—that divide the lobes. These easily recognizable fissures are like deep ravines that run among the convolutions, separating the various lobes. As shown in Figure 4.9, the *frontal lobe* is in front of the central fissure; behind it is the *parietal lobe.* The frontal lobe has some involvement with memory (Lewis, 1989); part of the frontal area is concerned with movement and is sometimes termed the *motor cortex.* A lower portion of the left frontal lobe, termed *Broca's area,* is involved in speech and language production. The parietal lobe is associated with activities involved in the sense of touch and of body position.

Below the lateral fissure and the parietal lobe is the *temporal lobe,* which is involved in speech, hearing, and the processing of some visual information. At

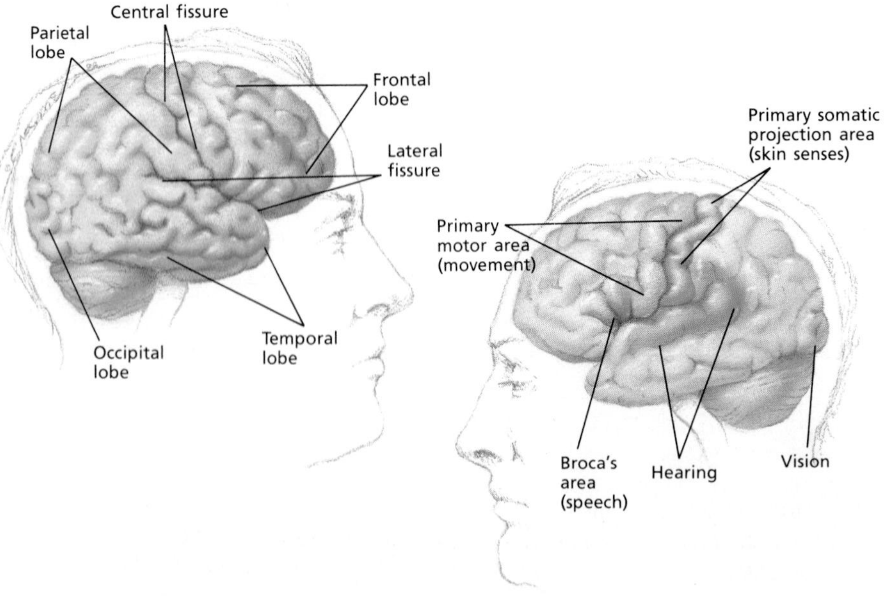

Figure 4.9

The cerebral cortex is divided into four major lobes (left). Specific areas are concerned with sensory and motor functions (right).

the back of the head, adjacent to the parietal and temporal lobes, is the *occipital lobe,* the principal responsibility of which is the visual sense. Other areas of the cortex have less-specific functions. For example, the *association cortex* is believed to be involved in complex behaviors that involve thinking *and* sensory processes. These activities may not be strictly visual, auditory, or motor. Instead, they involve the interaction of many different systems or areas.

Plasticity and Change

Learning Objective 4.5
Discuss some of the ways that the brain changes over time, and describe research that may lead to the treatment of learning problems and brain damage.

Do our brains stay the same from birth to death, or can they change, either through experience or simply the passage of time? The basic structure of brain organization is established well before birth and does not change in any substantial ways after birth, but details of its structure and functions, particularly in the cerebral cortex, are subject to change and modification (Kalil, 1989). Psychologists say that the brain is still *malleable* (capable of being shaped) or teachable during the formative years. Experience with some specific stimuli reinforces the development of neural structures. Aoki and Siekevitz (1988) liken the developing brain to a highway system that evolves with use: Less-traveled roads become abandoned, but popular ones are broadened and new ones added when needed; thus, when neural structures are used, reused, and constantly updated, they become faster and are more easily accessed.

Changes in the brain occur not only in young organisms, but in aging ones as well. As human beings grow older, their central nervous systems function differently, sometimes not as well as before. There are decreases in the number of receptors and cells, for example. Some learning tasks become more difficult for aging animals and human beings. Recent work has identified a drug that facilitates simple learning. When injected into aging rabbits, the drug Nimodipine helped them learn simple responses as well as young rabbits do. Nimodipine, used to improve blood flow in human stroke patients, may help learning by blocking calcium transmission to areas of the brain involved in memory. Nimodipine is only one of a large number of drugs that may be used for effective treatment of age-related learning problems (Deyo, Straube, & Disterhoft, 1989) or potential recovery of function after brain damage (LeVere, Brugler, Sandin, & Gray-Silva, 1989).

This work is speculative, new, and exciting; finding specific proteins, specific drugs, and new treatments that alter brain functioning may be a key to our overall understanding of brain development and how that development affects behavior. These issues become especially important when you consider the effects of a neural disease or trauma to the nervous system. Can damage done to the nervous system be repaired? Injury to the brain early in an organism's life is especially detrimental, but the extent and the permanence of the detriment depends on the nature of the injury, the age at which the injury takes place, and the presence of several helping factors, such as the availability of an enriching environment (Kolb, 1989).

Another new line of research is very exciting, although still somewhat speculative. In a series of studies done mainly with rats, researchers such as Fine (1986) have grafted (attached) brain tissue to the central nervous system of rats and other organisms. In some cases, the grafts are successful; new tissue grows and repairs old tissue. Someday these methods may be widely used with human beings and may offer therapeutic possibilities that exceed organ transplants. Victims of head injuries, brain diseases, and birth defects could all benefit. Research with human beings poses ethical problems, however. There are surgical risks; the techniques are dangerous and as yet unproven; and procedures must be established by physicians and researchers to decide who are the best candidates for such experimentation.

Progress Check 4.2

Complete each of the following sentences with one of the options provided.

(L.O. 4.4) a. Primitive and basic reflexive reactions are controlled primarily by the ________. (forebrain and limbic system / hindbrain and midbrain)

(L.O. 4.4) b. Two portions of the brain that are involved in sleep and dreaming are the ________. (reticular formation and pons / superior colliculus and thalamus)

(L.O. 4.4) c. The ________ is a part of the limbic system and participates in the control of emotional behavior. (hippocampus / amygdala)

(L.O. 4.4) d. The ________ a series of nuclei located deep in the brain that have control over movements and posture and also play a role in Parkinson's disease. (midbrain is made up of / basal ganglia are)

(L.O. 4.4) e. Information is transferred from one cerebral hemisphere to the other via the ________. (central fissure / lateral fissure / corpus callosum)

(L.O. 4.4) f. In a study involving the limbic system, Olds and Milner found that hungry rats chose ________ as a reward for pressing a bar. (food / exercising in a maze / electrical stimulation)

(L.O. 4.4) g. A major area of the cortex that is involved in body position and the sense of touch is the ________ lobe. (parietal / temporal)

(L.O. 4.4) h. Located on the left hemisphere, Broca's area plays a major role in ________. (speech and language production / hearing, vision, and movement)

(L.O. 4.5) i. It is thought that the drug Nimodipine may block the transmission of ________ to areas of the brain involved in memory. (neural coding for new learning / calcium / serotonin)

(L.O. 4.5) j. Researchers who have grafted healthy tissue to damaged tissue in the brains of rats have had ________ success in creating a situation where new tissue grows and repairs old, damaged tissue. (no / some / almost complete)

Module Summary

Organization of the Nervous System

- ▲ The nervous system is composed of two subsystems, the central and the peripheral nervous systems (p. 57).
- ▲ The central nervous system consists of the brain and the spinal cord (p. 59).
- ▲ The peripheral nervous system carries information to the spinal cord and brain through a series of nerve fibers. The peripheral nervous system is divided into somatic and autonomic nervous systems. The autonomic nervous system is made of the sympathetic and the parasympathetic nervous systems (pp. 57–59).

Monitoring Neuronal Activity

- ▲ One measure of the constant activity of the nervous system is the electroencephalogram, or EEG. The resulting records of brain-wave patterns can be used to assess neurological disorders (p. 61).
- ▲ CAT (computerized axial tomography) scans are computer-assisted X-ray procedures. MRI (magnetic resonance imaging) scans are similar to CAT scans but do not use radiation. PET (positron emission tomography) scans use radiochemical procedures and allow researchers to watch metabolic changes (p. 62).

Brain Structures

- ▲ Each cerebral hemisphere is neurologically connected to the opposite side of the body; in studies of split-brain patients, the patients are unable to use the speech and language abilities of the left hemisphere to describe activities carried out by the right hemisphere (with the left side of the body) (p. 64).
- ▲ The brain is usually divided into three sections: the hindbrain, the midbrain, and the forebrain, which includes the cortex (p. 65).
- ▲ The *hindbrain* consists of three main structures: the cerebellum, the medulla, and the pons (p. 65).
- ▲ The *midbrain* is made of nuclei that (1) receive afferent signals from other parts of the brain and from the spinal cord, (2) interpret the signals, and (3) either relay the information to other parts of the brain or cause the body to act at once (p. 65).
- ▲ The *forebrain* is the largest and most complicated of the brain structures and comprises the thalamus and hypothalamus, the limbic system, the basal ganglia and corpus callosum, and the cortex (p. 65).

KEY TERMS

autonomic nervous system, p. 57
brain, p. 59
central nervous system (CNS), p. 59
convolutions, p. 68
electroencephalogram (EEG), p. 61
parasympathetic nervous system, p. 58
peripheral nervous system, p. 57
somatic nervous system, p. 57
spinal cord, p. 60
split-brain patients, p. 66
sympathetic nervous system, p. 58

SELF-TEST

Module 4

- Before taking the self-test, **recite** and **review.**
- Use the key at the back of the text to *correct* your answers.
- *Restudy* pages that correspond to any questions you answered incorrectly.

1. Rapid changes in the autonomic nervous system are usually associated with
   a. sleep and dreaming.
   b. stress reactions and emotional behavior.
   c. increases in prolactin levels.
   d. the presence of alpha waves.
2. Which of the following phrases best describes the function of the spinal cord?
   a. control center
   b. fight-or-flight reflex
   c. main communication line
   d. system pacifier
3. Cross out the statement concerning the measurement of electrical activity in the brain that is *false.*
   a. Alpha, beta, and gamma waves are detected by EEGs.
   b. MRI scans describe brain activity in terms of number and height of waves.
   c. CAT scans produce a series of X-rays that slow photographic slices of the brain.
   d. PET scans allow researchers to observe metabolic changes in the brain as they take place.
4. The midbrain
   a. either relays information to a more complex part of the brain or causes the body to respond immediately.
   b. is the location of the thalamus and hypothalamus.
   c. regulates complex behaviors such as eating, drinking, and sex.
   d. has the sole function of transferring information from one cerebral hemisphere to the other.
5. The limbic system
   a. contains pleasure centers.
   b. is probably one of the most complex and least understood areas of the brain.
   c. is involved in emotional and social behavior, memory, and brain disorders such as epilepsy.
   d. all of the above
6. Two areas of the brain that are principally involved in the processing of sensory information are the
   a. thalamus and association cortex.
   b. reticular formation and basal ganglia.
   c. pons and amygdala.
   d. cerebellum and hippocampus.
7. Cross out the statement concerning the human brain that is *false.*
   a. An adult brain weighs about 3 pounds.
   b. Convolutions create a relatively large cortical surface area, measuring about 1.5 square feet.
   c. The cortex consists of six thin layers of cells and is about 2 millimeters thick.
   d. The lateral and central fissures separate and differentiate the hindbrain, midbrain, and forebrain structures.

8. Neural structures in the brain
   a. are established before birth and do not change.
   b. change with experience and time.
   c. heal rapidly if damaged.
   d. never reorganize to carry out functions for damaged neural structures.

Connections

If you are interested in . . .	**Turn to . . .**	**To learn more about . . .**
The nature versus nurture controversy	◆ Chapter 4, p. 148	The impact of a person's genetic heritage on the likelihood that he or she will become an alcoholic
	◆ Chapter 7, p. 266	How the study of communication in apes is helping to resolve the issue of nature versus nurture
	◆ Chapter 13, p. 547	The extent to which a person's home environment can increase the likelihood of developing schizophrenia
Communication between brain structures and the nervous system	◆ Chapter 3, p. 84	How the eyes communicate information to the brain
	◆ Chapter 9, p. 383	How emotional responses are affected by and in turn affect emotion
	◆ Chapter 12, p. 493	How our bodies' reaction to stressful situations is often arousal, followed by eventual exhaustion
Brain structures and how they affect behavior	◆ Chapter 4, p. 47	The extent to which alcohol affects higher brain functions
	◆ Chapter 8, p. 336	The profound effect of Alzheimer's disease on memory
	◆ Chapter 14, p. 587	The effects of electroconvulsive shock therapy when a person is suffering from depression

The relationship of a person's basic biological structures to day-to-day behavior is well established. Psychologists have long studied the relationship of nature and nurture in studies of intelligence (Chapter 11, p. 454), psychological disorders (Chapter 13, p. 548), and child development (Chapter 8, p. 277). They have taken a special interest in the biological underpinnings of specific behavior problems such as depression (Chapter 13, p. 539) and the treatment of schizophrenia (Chapter 14, p. 587). A person's motivation to eat, succeed, and seek happiness (Chapter 9, p. 352) has a biological basis, and many perceptual phenomena are clearly rooted in the basic neuroanatomy of the sensory systems (Chapter 3, p. 84). As we explore the complexity of human behavior, you will see that the underlying biological structures on which more complex behaviors are based often must first be studied in the laboratory, and then later studied in field settings. However, no picture of human behavior will be complete without an understanding of the biological basis of behavior.

Module 5 ► THE VISUAL SYSTEM 76

Module 6 ► HEARING, TASTE, SMELL, AND THE SKIN SENSES 104

Chapter 3

Sensation and Perception

Perception is the process by which people attach meaning to sensory stimuli by means of complex processing mechanisms. This chapter begins with a brief definition of perception but recognizes that a complete and accurate definition of perception must be sufficiently vague to account for all of the senses and all of the variables involved. The first module of this chapter more specifically defines perception and defines sensation. This module also shows how perceptual systems are organized so that we can take in a large amount of information and process it in meaningful ways in order to experience the world fully. Our perceptual systems are presented as adaptive systems, for without them we would be unable to cope with even the simple demands of life. For example, the visual system includes a complex processing system that enables us to handle the vast array of visual input, including the study of color vision, illusions, and subliminal perception. The structure of the visual system and its complex perceptual processes are discussed in the first module.

The second module of the chapter discusses the perceptual systems for hearing, tasting, smelling, and feeling through our skin (touch, pain, and so on). Our perceptual systems work together to achieve an integrated knowledge of the world. The interaction of our senses through our various experiences seems to be a critical variable. Although perceptual processing begins at the moment of birth, early experiences in the life of a newborn will determine how well his or her perceptual system will develop. Our auditory and tactile systems provide us with a wealth of information. They make our lives more varied and complete. As we discuss the structure and function of the remaining perceptual systems, we show their adaptive value in human functioning.

Module 5

The Visual System

LEARNING OBJECTIVES

When you have mastered the material in this module, you will be able to

Sensation Perception: Definitions (p. 78)

5.1 Explain why contemporary psychologists no longer make a distinction between the terms *sensation* and *perception* (p. 78).

5.2 Explain the basic process by which humans perceive the world around them (p. 78).

The Visual System (pp. 79–91)

5.3 List and describe the parts of the eye and explain how each part functions to process light (p. 79).

5.4 Describe how we are able to see in the light and in the dark, according to the duplicity theory (p. 80).

5.5 Describe the path that electrical impulses take as they leave the eye and enter the brain (p. 83).

5.6 Explain how photoreceptor cells are organized into receptive fields, allowing us to perceive form, shape, and color (p. 85).

5.7 Describe the relationship between the psychological and the physical properties of color (p. 87).

5.8 Explain the trichromatic theory and the opponent-process theory of color coding (p. 88).

5.9 Describe color blindness and its causes (p. 89).

Visual Perception (pp. 91–97)

5.10 Explain how we maintain an understanding of size and shape even when objects are presented at different distances or angles (p. 91).

5.11 Discuss how we perceive depth, using both monocular and binocular cues (p. 92).

5.12 Describe three illusions we experience and give some reasons for why these experiences are thought to occur (p. 94).

5.13 Discuss the Gestalt approach as it applies to perception and identify five Gestalt laws of organization (p. 95).

Attention (pp. 97–99)

5.14 Explain the limits of our visual and auditory systems and tell how we selectively extract information (p. 97).

SQ3R
- ▲ **Survey** to set goals for studying.
- ▲ Ask **questions** as you **read.**
- ▲ Stop occasionally to **recite** and **review.**

plus
- ▲ **Write** a summary of key points.
- ▲ **Reflect** on the hypotheses, evidence, and implications of this material and on the relevance it has to *your* life.

Highly trained chemists are cleaning the ceiling of the Sistine Chapel in the Palace of the Vatican in Rome. There are nearly five centuries of grime and dirt on Michelangelo's spectacular frescoes that cover the ceilings and walls. This ambitious art restoration begun in 1980 is being undertaken inch by inch; the cost of the cleaning will be about 3 million dollars and will take more than 12 years to complete. As it proceeds, the work is creating a furor in the art world.

Michelangelo's works have been described as dark, deep, and profound. That is, until the restoration began. The removal of 400 years of grime and of the soot from burning candles is showing a different Michelangelo. The colors are bright; the contrasts are striking and luminous. The ceiling, which rises 65 feet above the floor, is painted in azure, rose, lavender, and pink. The Sistine Chapel is neither dark nor ominous, but glowing with color and excitement. Researchers and art historians now have a new view of Michelangelo, and the restoration is showing his true colors.

Renovation of Michelangelo's paintings in the Sistine Chapel has drastically changed the world's perception of his art.

As a result of the restoration, Michelangelo's work must now be reinterpreted. Angels once viewed as haunting and austere are now seen as cherubic and lively. Older interpretations of Michelangelo are giving way to newer impressions; Michelangelo is seen with a new clarity. Imagine looking at television through a dirty window or trying to read an illustrated history of North America in a darkened theater. The television picture would be visible and the photographs would be seen, but both would be viewed with difficulty and with a loss of detail and visual clarity. Wearing sunglasses indoors would affect your perceptual experience similarly. What's more, when you first walk into a darkened theater, you may also have trouble seeing at all until your eyes have adjusted. Yet when you walk out of the darkened theater into the daylight, you may have trouble seeing until your eyes have readjusted. Similarly your hearing may be impaired for a few hours after a rock concert. Tasting the delicacy of a glass of wine may be nearly impossible after eating very spicy food. Our perception of the visual, auditory, and taste environment depends not only on light, sound, and food, but also on the intervening environmental events (such as soot and dirt) and intervening internal events (such as eating hot tamales).

Whenever you are exposed to a stimulus in the environment, it initiates an electrochemical change in the receptors in your body, which then initiates the processes of sensation and perception. Psychologists study sensation and perception because what people sense and perceive determines how they will understand and interpret the world. This interpretation depends on a combination of sensory stimulation, past experiences, and current interpretations.

Sensation and Perception: Definitions

Learning Objective 5.1
Explain why contemporary psychologists no longer make a distinction between the terms *sensation* and *perception*.

Traditionally, sensation and perception have been studied together as closely related fields. **Sensation** is defined as the process of stimulation of the sense organ receptor cells and the relaying of initial information to more complex nerve centers for further processing; **perception** is the selection and interpretation of sensory input that give meaning to the input. Thus, sensation provides the stimulus for further perceptual processing. Today, perceptual psychologists generally acknowledge that a strict distinction between sensation and perception is unnecessary. We now think in terms of *perceptual systems*—that is, the sets of structures, functions, and operations by means of which people perceive the world around them. Perception is not merely the firing of one group of neurons; it also involves sets of neurons and previous experience, as well as stimulation that occurs at the eyes, ears, or other sensory sites.

Learning Objective 5.2
Explain the basic process by which humans perceive the world around them.

Sensory and perceptual processes rely so closely on one another that many researchers think about the two processes together as perception. For them, *perception* is the process by which an organism interprets sensory information input (which has been converted into electrochemical energy) so that it acquires organization, form, and meaning. It is through perception that people explore the world and discover its rules (Gibson, 1988). This complex process involves the nervous system and one or more of the perceptual or sensory systems—that is, vision, hearing, taste, smell, or touch.

Although perceptual systems are different, they share common processes. In each case, an environmental stimulus creates an initial stimulation. Receptor cells translate that form of energy into a neuronal impulse, and these impulses are then sent to specific areas of the brain for further processing. Studies show that human beings (and animals for that matter) gather information, process it, and interpret it in an active, constructive manner. Studies of sensation and perception also show that past experiences affect interpretation and shape our perceptions.

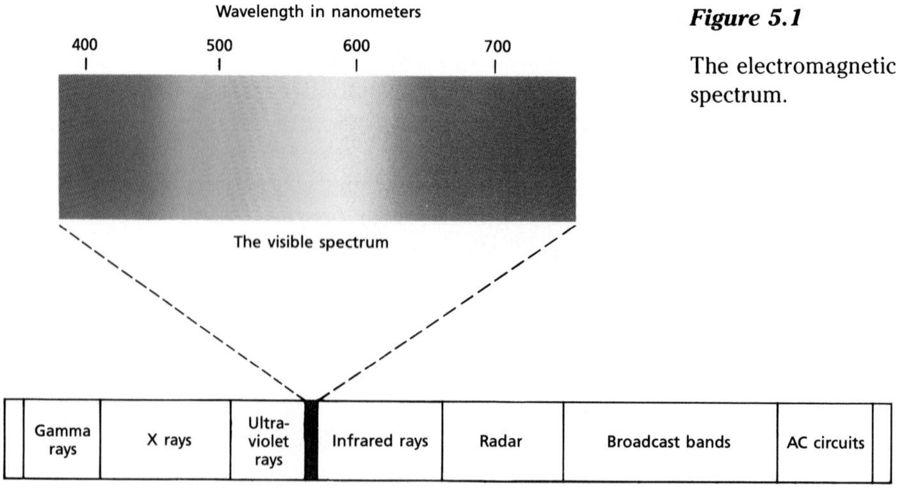

Figure 5.1

The electromagnetic spectrum.

sensation: The process in which sense organ receptor cells are stimulated and then transmit the stimulus data to nerve centers for more complex processing.

perception: The complex process by which an organism interprets sensory input so that it acquires meaning.

The Visual System

Imagine that you are in a house at night when the power goes out, and you are left in total darkness. You hear sounds but have no idea where they are coming from. You stub your toe on the coffee table, then frantically grope along the walls until you reach the kitchen, where you fumble through the drawers in search of a flashlight.

Human beings derive more information through sight than through any other sense. Although your eyes respond to pressure, the proper or appropriate stimulus for vision is **electromagnetic radiation.** Electromagnetic radiation includes visible light, cosmic rays, X-rays, and ultraviolet, infrared, and radar waves. **Light** is the very small portion of those wavelengths that is visible to the eye. It may either come directly from a source or be reflected from an object (see Figure 5.1).

electromagnetic radiation: [Ee-LEK-tro-mag-NET-ick] The entire spectrum of waves initiated by charged particles.

light: The portion of the electromagnetic spectrum visible to the eye.

The Structure of the Eye

Figure 5.2 shows the major parts of the human eye. Light first passes through the *cornea,* a small transparent bulge covering over both the *pupil* (the dark opening in the center of the eye) and the pigmented iris. The *iris* either constricts or dilates to make the pupil smaller or larger, respectively. Behind the pupil is the *crystalline*

Learning Objective 5.3
List and describe the parts of the eye, and explain how each part functions to process light.

Figure 5.2

The main structures of the eye. The fovea is the central portion of the retina. The photoreceptors of the retina connect to higher brain pathways through the optic nerve. Light filters through layers of retinal cells before hitting the receptors (rods and cones), located at the back of the eye and pointed away from the incoming light. The rods and cones pass an electrical impulse to bipolar cells. They relay the impulse to the ganglion cells. The axons of the ganglion cells form the fibers of the optic nerve.

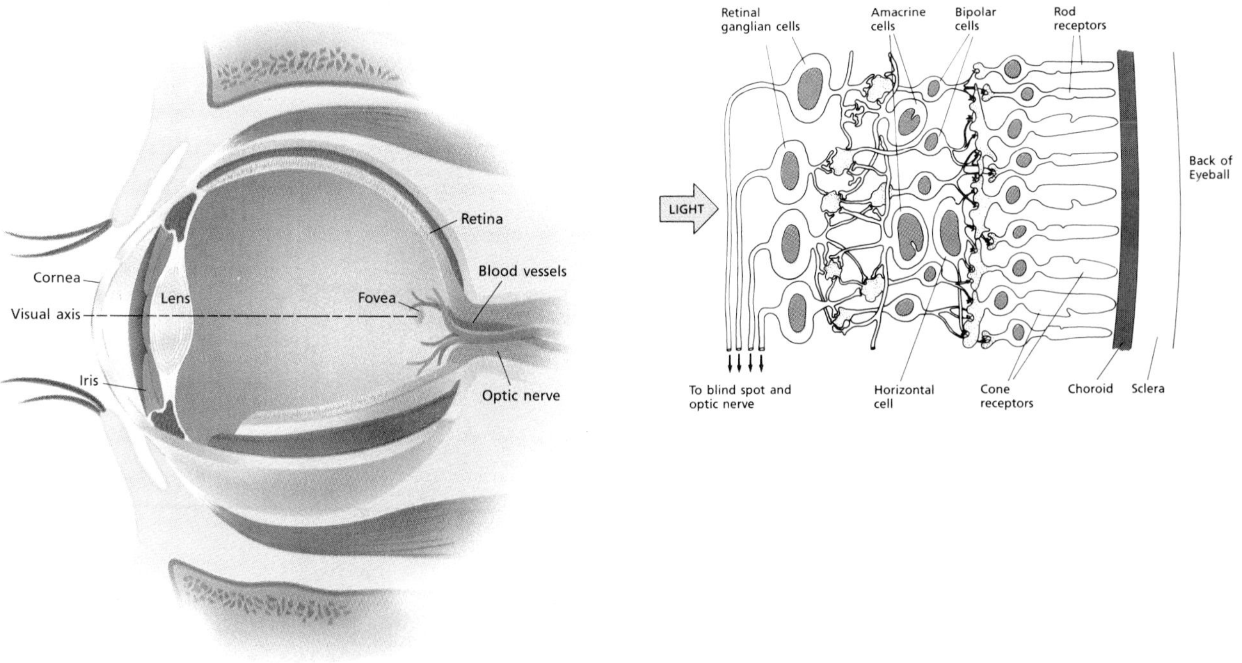

photoreceptors: The light-sensitive cells in the retina: rods and cones.

transduction: The process by which sensory systems analyze environmental stimuli and convert them into electrical impulses; in general, the conversion of one form of energy into another; also known as *coding*.

visual cortex: The first and most important layer of the occipital lobe, which receives information from the lateral geniculate nucleus; also known as *striate cortex*.

lens, which is about 4 millimeters (mm) thick. Together, the iris, the cornea, the pupil, and the lens form images in much the same way as a camera shutter and the inner and outer surfaces of the camera lens do. The *retina,* which lines the back of the eye, is like the film in a camera: It captures an image. Constriction of the iris makes the pupil smaller, improving the quality of the image on the retina and increasing the depth of focus—that is, the distance of the visual field that is in sharp focus. This constrictive action also helps control the amount of light entering the eye and reaching the retina.

The retina consists of 10 layers of cells; of these, the most important are (a) **photoreceptors** (light receptors), (b) bipolar cells, and (c) ganglion cells. After light passes through several layers of other kinds of cells, it strikes the photoreceptor layer, which consists of *rods* (rod-shaped receptors) and *cones* (cone-shaped receptors) (both types are described later). In this layer, the light breaks down *photopigments* (light-sensitive chemicals), which cause an electrochemical change in the rods and cones, and the electrical energy is transferred to the next major layer, the bipolar cells. The process by which the perceptual system analyzes stimuli and converts them into electrical impulses is generally known as *coding,* or more formally, **transduction.**

Each eye contains more than 120 million rods and 6 million cones (see Figure 5.3). These millions of photoreceptors do not have individual pathways to the higher visual centers in the brain. Instead, through the process of *convergence,* neural electrochemical energy from rods comes together onto a single bipolar cell. At the same time, hundreds of cones synapse and converge onto other bipolar cells. From the bipolar cells, electrochemical energy is transferred to the *ganglion cell* layer. A number of bipolar cells synapse and converge onto each ganglion cell (there are about 1 million ganglion cells). The axons of the ganglion cells make up the *optic nerve,* where information that was initially received by the rods and cones is carried via higher pathways in the nervous system, where still further coding takes place, at the **visual cortex** of the brain. (For an interesting note on the blind spot in human eyes, see Figure 5.4 on page 82.)

Learning Objective 5.4
Describe how we are able to see in the light and in the dark, according to the duplicity theory.

Rods and Cones. The *duplicity theory* of vision states that rods and cones are structurally different and are used to accomplish different tasks. Cones are tightly

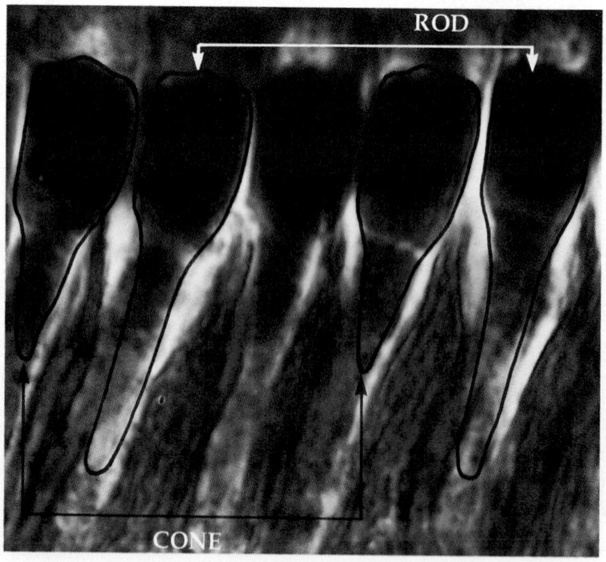

Rods assist in night vision; cones are necessary to day vision, color vision, and fine discrimination.

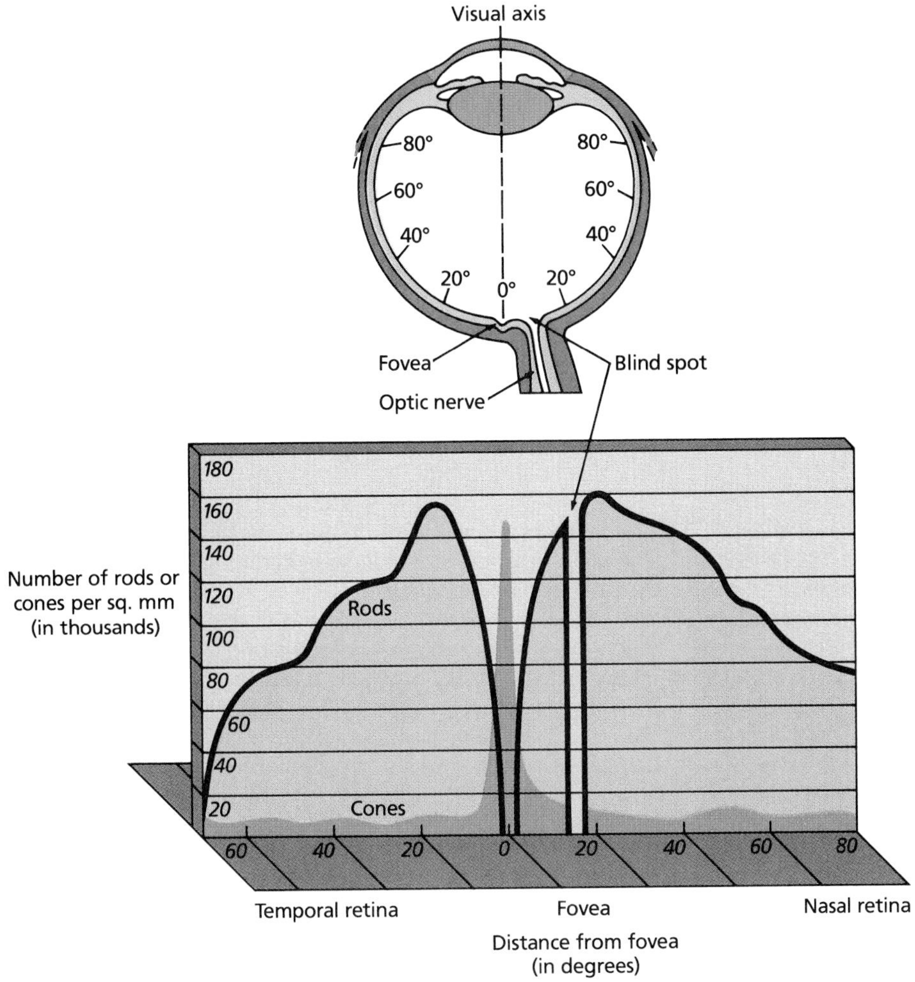

Figure 5.3

Top view of the left eye, with the corresponding densities of rods and cones across the retina. (Pirenne, 1967, p. 32)

packed in the center of the retina, or *fovea,* and are used for day vision, color vision, and fine discrimination. Rods (and some cones) are found on the rest of the retina, the *periphery,* which is used predominantly for night vision (see Figure 5.3).

The fact that cones are especially important in fine visual discrimination is shown in visual acuity tests you take when you apply for a driver's license. A *visual acuity test* measures the resolution capacity of the visual system—that is, the ability to see fine details. These abilities are especially mediated by cones. You do best on these tests in a well-lit room (cones operate at high light levels) and when the test is shown in your central (foveal) vision (again, cones occur in the center of your retina more than in any other place).

If you go from a well-lit lobby into a dark theater, you will experience a brief period of low light sensitivity, and you will be unable to distinguish empty seats. Within 30 minutes, you will have nearly fully adapted to the dark and will be far more light sensitive. Our eyes are always in some state of light or dark adaptation.

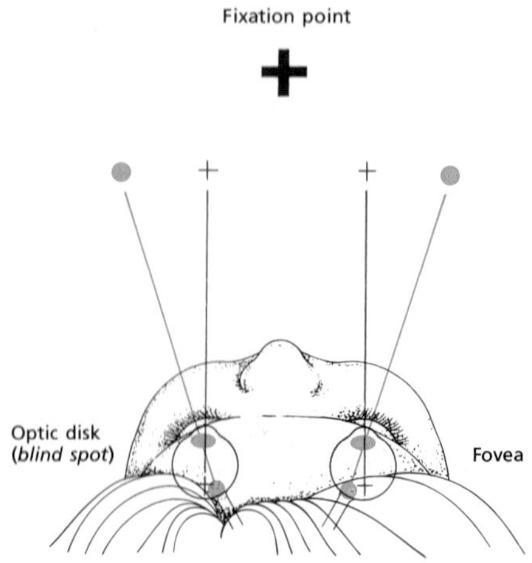

Figure 5.4

As shown in Figure 5.3, the center of the retina (the fovea) contains only cones. At about 18° of visual angle (a measure of the size of images on the retina) there are no receptors at all. This is the place where the optic nerve leaves the eye, called the blind spot. Because the blind spot for each eye is on the nasal side of the eyeball, there is no loss of vision—the two blind spots do not overlap. To demonstrate that you have a blind spot, close one eye and move the page in and out while staring at the point. The black spot will disappear when your eye is about four inches from the page. If you switch eyes, the blind spot for the other eye will be apparent. Once you have located the correct distance, move the tip of a pencil along the page until it reaches the blind spot and watch the tip disappear.

Rods and cones are sensitive to light, but in a well-lighted room, they are less sensitive than they are after having been in the dark. **Dark adaptation** is the increase in sensitivity that occurs when the illumination level changes from light to darkness. It is a process by which chemicals in the photoreceptors (rods and

dark adaptation: Increased sensitivity to light in a dark environment. When a person moves from a light environment to a dark one, chemicals in the photoreceptors regenerate and return to their inactive pre-light-adapted state, which results in an increase in sensitivity.

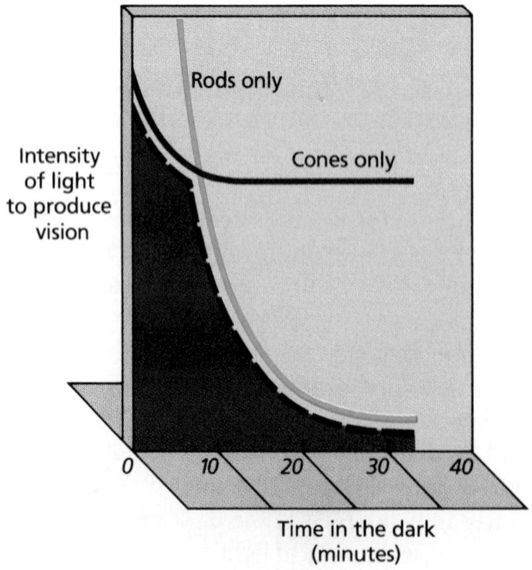

Figure 5.5

The dashed line represents a typical overall dark adaptation curve. The two solid lines represent the separate dark adaptation for rods and for cones. The process of light and dark adaptation occurs continually as people's eyes are exposed to different light intensities. The majority of dark adaptation takes place in the first 10 minutes after a change in light intensity.

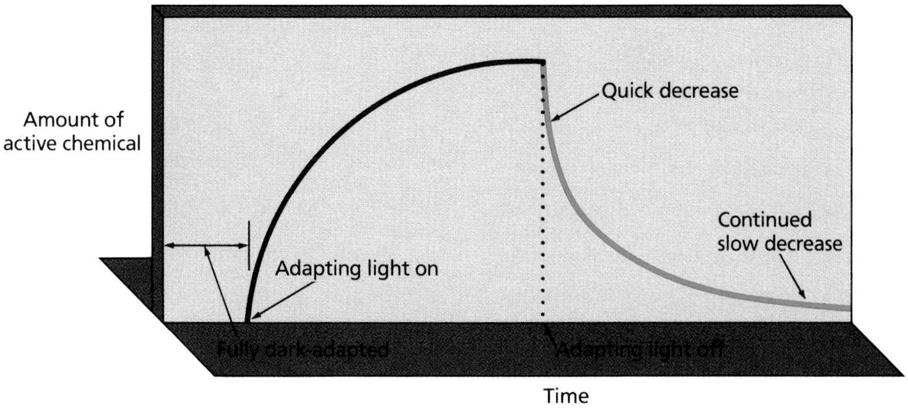

Figure 5.6

In the process of dark adaptation, chemicals in the photoreceptors return to a quiet, unactivated state. The fewer the active chemicals, the more sensitive the eye. When a light is turned on, the chemicals become very active; when the light is turned off, there is a quick drop in the amount of active chemical, and the eye becomes increasingly sensitive. (From Cornsweet, 1970, p. 132)

cones) regenerate and return to their inactive state, and the light sensitivity of the visual system increases (see Figure 5.5). Of course, after leaving a dark theater and returning to the afternoon sunlight, you must squint or shade your eyes until they become adapted to the light.

Look at Figure 5.5, which shows a dark-adaptation curve. The first part of the curve is determined by cones, the second part by rods. The data for such curves are obtained from experiments with subjects who possess only rods or cones. The speed at which the photochemicals in the rods and cones regenerate determines the shape of the two parts of the curve. This is why, when you are driving along a road at night, you may have trouble seeing clearly for a few minutes after a car drives toward you with its high beams on; the photochemicals in the rods take

Learning Objective 5.5
Describe the path that electrical impulses take as they leave the eye and enter the brain.

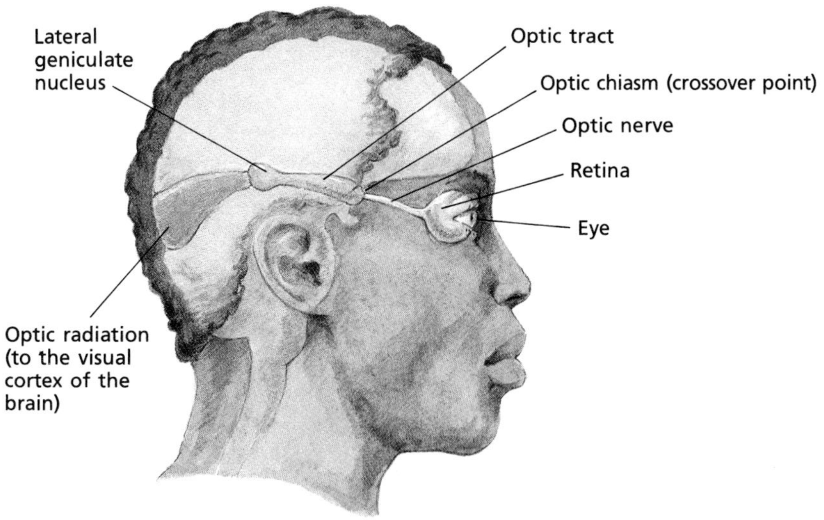

Figure 5.7

The major components of the visual system.

Figure 5.8

As this overhead view shows, some information from each eye crosses at the optic chiasm.

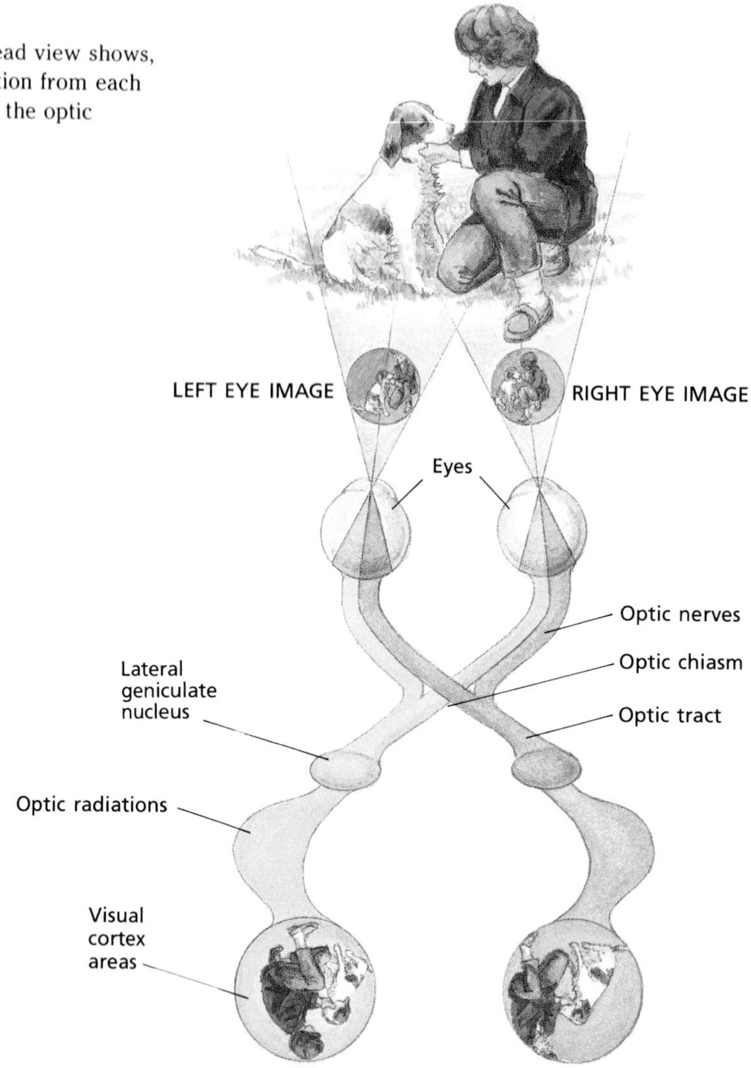

optic chiasm: [k-EYE-asm] Point at which optic nerve fibers from the nasal side of the eye cross over and project to the other side of the brain.

lateral geniculate nucleus: First major center at which impulses leaving the eye are processed; also known as the *lateral geniculate body.*

superior colliculus: A secondary part of the visual system, especially responsive to seeing movement.

striate cortex: The primary visual cortex to which projections are made in the visual system from the lateral geniculate nucleus.

some time to regenerate to their dark-adapted state. Figure 5.6 on the previous page shows both light- and dark-adaptation curves.

Higher Pathways. As electrical impulses leave the retina through the optic nerve, they proceed to higher centers of the brain (see Figure 5.7 on the previous page). Each eye is connected to both sides of the brain, with half of its impulses going to the left side of the brain and the other half crossing over to the right side. Half of the visual impulses from each eye cross over to the other side of the brain; the point at which the cross-over occurs is the **optic chiasm** (see Figure 5.8). This cross-over of impulses allows the brain to process two sets of signals from an image and helps human beings perceive form in three dimensions. If the optic nerves are severed at the optic chiasm, vision is sharply impaired. Normally, however, impulses proceed to higher brain structures, including the **lateral geniculate nucleus,** the **superior colliculus,** and the **striate cortex.** Of course, people are seldom, if ever, actively aware of the process.

The Electrical Connection

Learning Objective 5.6
Explain how photoreceptor cells are organized into receptive fields, allowing us to perceive form, shape, and color.

Vision and other perceptual processes are electrochemical in nature. When receptors in the perceptual systems are stimulated, the information is coded and sent to the brain for interpretation and further analysis. Psychologists are interested in understanding how electrical activity in the nervous system is transmitted and coded because such knowledge helps explain how the perceptual systems operate.

Measuring the electrical activity of the visual system by stimulating it with horizontal, vertical, and slanted lines is, in fact, one way to study how the visual system processes stimuli. Another way is by stimulating the photoreceptors with specific patterns of light, thereby causing a change in electrical activity at all levels of the visual system. Researchers measure this change in activity by means of

Figure 5.9

Hubel and Wiesel (1962) found cells that fire when stimulated in the center of their receptive field but do not fire (and instead produce suppression) when stimulated outside the center area. Receptive fields in the retina are often circular with a center–surround arrangement. Light striking the center of the field produces the opposite result of light striking the surround. Here, light in the center produces increased firing in the visual cell, and light in the surround produces decreased firing. The arrangement in other receptive fields may be just the opposite.

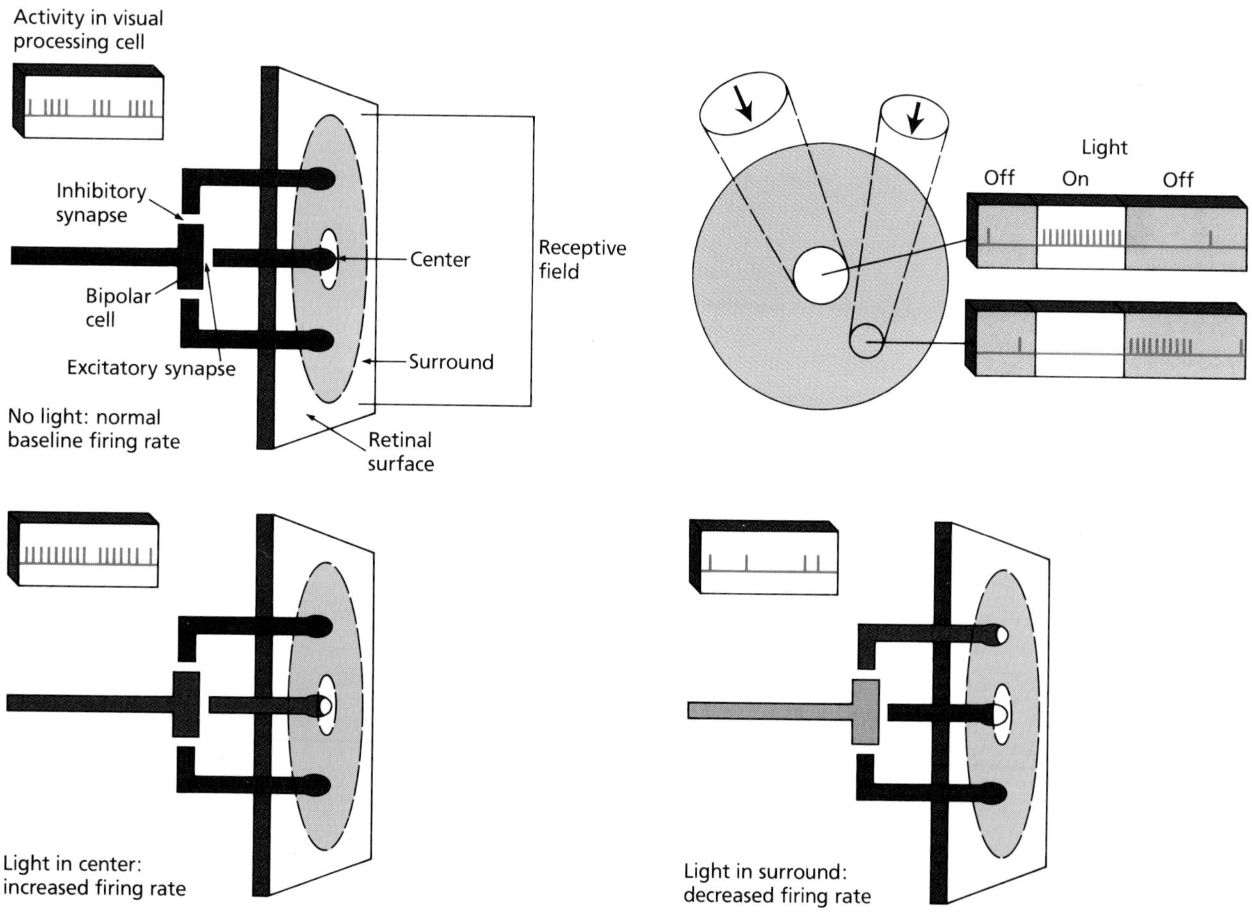

receptive fields: Areas of the retina that, when stimulated, affect the firing of a single cell in the visual system.

single-unit recording: They place an electrode in or next to a single cell and record its activity in response to stimuli of different sizes and shapes. This process has led to the identification of specific receptive fields involved in the perception of form, shape, and color.

Receptive fields are the areas on the retina that, when stimulated, produce a change in the firing of cells in the visual system. For example, specific cells will fire, or become active, if a vertical line is presented, but not if a horizontal line is presented. David Hubel and Torsten Wiesel (1962) found cells in the receptive fields that are sensitive to the position, length, movement, color, or intensity of a line. They characterized the cells as simple, complex, or hypercomplex. *Simple cells* respond to the shape and size of lights that stimulate the receptive field (see Figure 5.9 on the previous page). *Complex cells* respond most vigorously to movement of light in one direction. *Hypercomplex cells* are the most specific; they respond only to a line of the correct length and orientation that moves in the proper direction.

Hubel and Wiesel further learned that cells, especially those in the center of the visual cortex, are organized in columns; thus, lines with a single orientation or width will stimulate cells that cut across several, or even all, layers of the visual cortex. Coding becomes more complex as electrical information proceeds through the visual system to higher centers (Burr, Morrone, & Spinelli, 1989). The work of Hubel and Wiesel, which has been supported by other noted researchers (e.g., De Valois, Thorell, & Albrecht, 1985), earned them a Nobel prize in 1981.

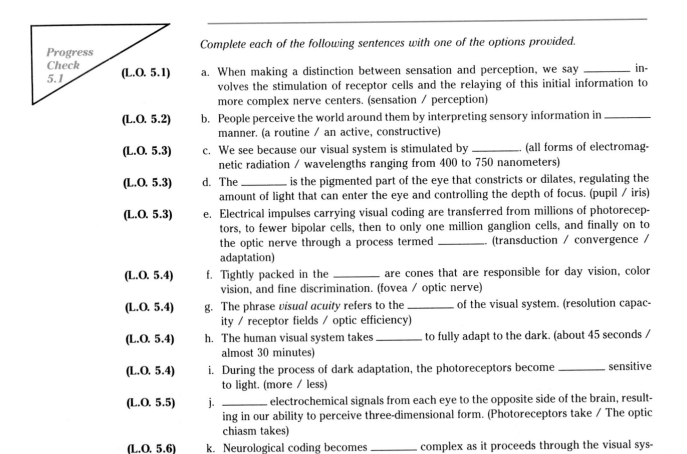

Progress Check 5.1

Complete each of the following sentences with one of the options provided.

(L.O. 5.1) a. When making a distinction between sensation and perception, we say ________ involves the stimulation of receptor cells and the relaying of this initial information to more complex nerve centers. (sensation / perception)

(L.O. 5.2) b. People perceive the world around them by interpreting sensory information in ________ manner. (a routine / an active, constructive)

(L.O. 5.3) c. We see because our visual system is stimulated by ________. (all forms of electromagnetic radiation / wavelengths ranging from 400 to 750 nanometers)

(L.O. 5.3) d. The ________ is the pigmented part of the eye that constricts or dilates, regulating the amount of light that can enter the eye and controlling the depth of focus. (pupil / iris)

(L.O. 5.3) e. Electrical impulses carrying visual coding are transferred from millions of photoreceptors, to fewer bipolar cells, then to only one million ganglion cells, and finally on to the optic nerve through a process termed ________. (transduction / convergence / adaptation)

(L.O. 5.4) f. Tightly packed in the ________ are cones that are responsible for day vision, color vision, and fine discrimination. (fovea / optic nerve)

(L.O. 5.4) g. The phrase *visual acuity* refers to the ________ of the visual system. (resolution capacity / receptor fields / optic efficiency)

(L.O. 5.4) h. The human visual system takes ________ to fully adapt to the dark. (about 45 seconds / almost 30 minutes)

(L.O. 5.4) i. During the process of dark adaptation, the photoreceptors become ________ sensitive to light. (more / less)

(L.O. 5.5) j. ________ electrochemical signals from each eye to the opposite side of the brain, resulting in our ability to perceive three-dimensional form. (Photoreceptors take / The optic chiasm takes)

(L.O. 5.6) k. Neurological coding becomes ________ complex as it proceeds through the visual system. (more / less)

Color Vision

Think of all the different shades of blue (navy blue, sky blue, baby blue, royal blue, turquoise, aqua) that are now apparent in Michelangelo's Sistine Chapel. If you are like most people, you have no trouble discriminating among a wide range of colors. Color depends on the wavelength of light particles that stimulate the photoreceptors. It has three psychological dimensions—*hue, brightness,* and *saturation*—that correspond to three physical properties of light—*wavelength, intensity,* and *purity.*

Learning Objective 5.7
Describe the relationship between the psychological and the physical properties of color.

When people speak of the color of an object, they are referring to its **hue**—that is, whether the light reflected from the object looks red, blue, orange, or some other color. *Hue* is a psychological term, because objects do not themselves possess color. Rather, people's perception of color is determined by how their eyes and brain interpret reflected wavelengths. In the visible spectrum, a different hue is associated with each wavelength. Light with a wavelength of 400 nanometers looks blue; light with a wavelength of 700 nanometers looks red. (See Figure 5.10.)

The second psychological dimension of color is **brightness.** This refers to how light or dark the hue of an object appears. It is affected by three variables: (1) The greater the intensity of reflected light, the brighter the object. (2) The longer the wavelength of reflected light, the less bright the object. (3) As shown in Figure 5.11 on page 88, the nearer the wavelengths are to the 500–600 nanometer range, the more sensitive the photoreceptors. This is why school buses and fire engines are usually painted yellow—to make them more visible.

The third psychological dimension of color is **saturation,** or purity. Few objects reflect light that is totally pure. Usually they reflect a mixture of wavelengths. Pure saturated light has a narrow band of wavelengths and, thus, a narrow range of perceived color. A saturated red light with no blue, yellow, or white in it, for example, appears as a very deep red. Unsaturated colors are produced by a wider band of wavelengths. Unsaturated red light can appear to be light pink or dark red. Or it can look muddy because its wider range of wavelengths makes it less pure.

hue: The psychological property of light referred to as color, determined by the wavelength reflected from an object.

brightness: The lightness or darkness of reflected light, determined in large part by a light's intensity.

saturation: The depth of hue of reflected light, as determined by the purity (homogeneity) of the wavelengths contained in the light.

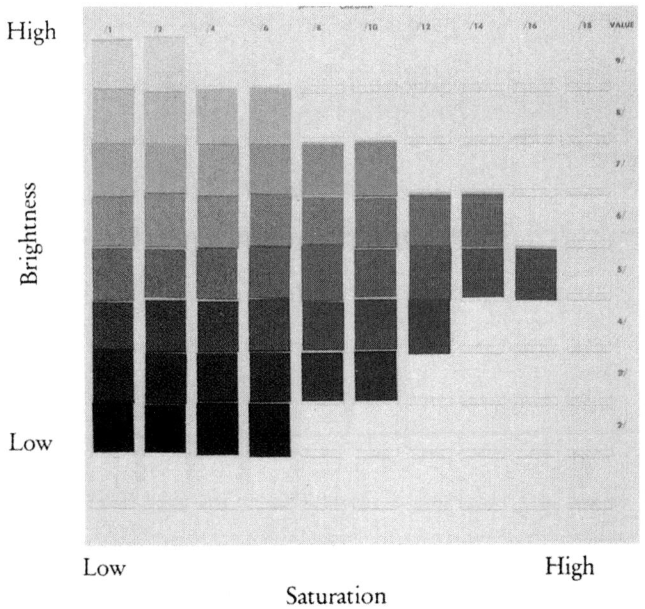

Figure 5.10

Hue, brightness, and saturation. These colors have the same dominant wavelength (hue) but different saturation and brightness. (Courtesy of Munsell Color Corporation.)

Figure 5.11

The average observer's sensitivity to visible light during daylight reaches a peak at 555 nanometers. Thus, the normal human eye is more sensitive to yellow wavelengths than to red or blue. Such a curve is called a spectral sensitivity curve.

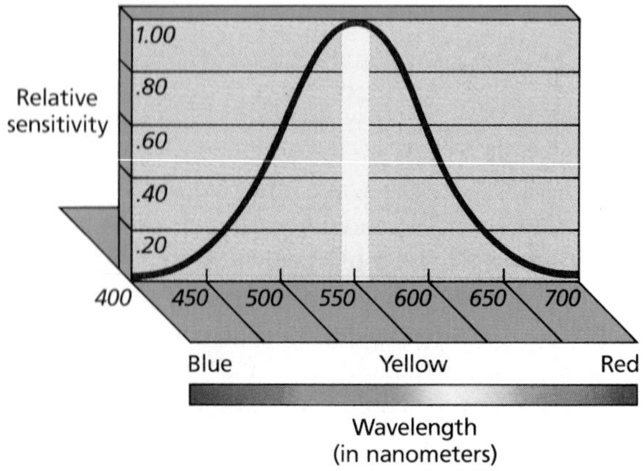

Learning Objective 5.8 Explain the trichromatic theory and the opponent-process theory of color coding.

trichromatic theory: [try-krom-AT-ick] A theory of color vision, which stated that all colors can be made by mixing three basic colors: red, blue, and green.

Color Coding. How does the brain code and process color? Two 19th-century scientists, Thomas Young and Hermann Von Helmholtz, working independently, proposed that different types of cones provide the basis for color coding in the visual system. *Color coding* is the ability to discriminate among colors based on differences in wavelength. According to the Young–Helmholtz theory, also termed the **trichromatic theory,** all colors can be made by mixing three basic colors: red, green, and blue. (*Trichromatic* means three colors; *tri* means three, and *chroma* means color.) All cones are assumed to respond to all wavelengths that stimulate them, but each type of cone—red, blue, or green—responds maximally to the red, blue, or green wavelength. The combined neural output of the three types of cones provides the information that enables a person to distinguish color. If the neural output of one type of cone is sufficiently greater than that of the others, a person's perception of color will be determined mainly by that type of color receptor. Because each person's neurons are unique, it is likely that each of us sees color somewhat differently.

Figure 5.12

Each of the three types of cones in the primate eye has peak sensitivity in a different area of the spectrum. Thus, certain cells are more responsive to some wavelengths than to others. (MacNichol, 1964)

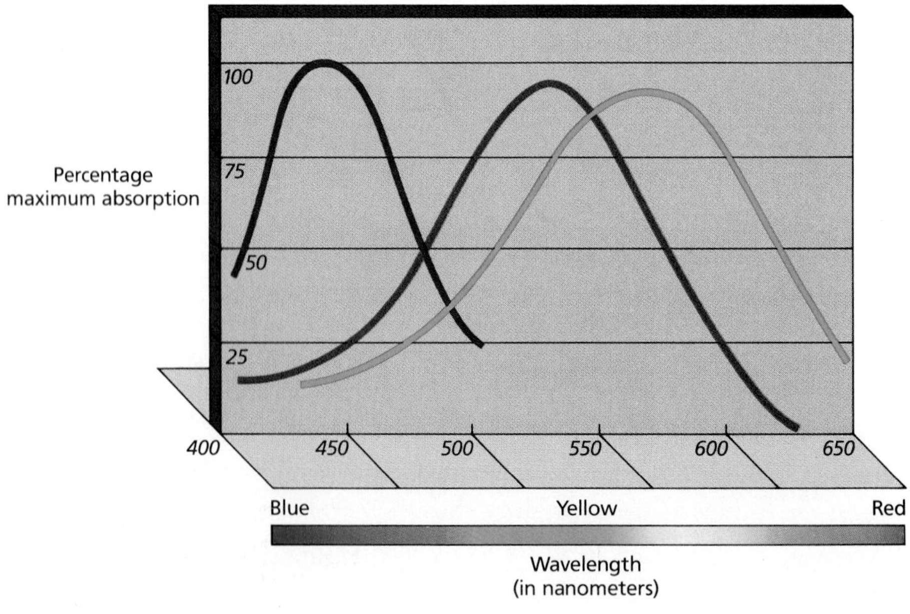

Unfortunately, the trichromatic theory does not explain some specific visual phenomena well. In response to some of the problems left unresolved, another theory of color vision, the **opponent-process theory,** was proposed by Ewald Herring in 1887. It assumes that there are six primary colors to which people respond, and three types of receptors: red–green, blue–yellow, and black–white. Every receptor fires in response to all wavelengths, but depending on the light entering the eye each receptor fires maximally to one wavelength. Maximum firing to red, for example, is accompanied by a low rate of firing to green (see Figures 5.12 and 5.13). Opponent-process theory explains color contrast better, and it also helps explain color blindness.

Both the trichromatic theory and the opponent-process theory have received support from research (e.g., Hurvich & Jameson, 1974). Studies of the chemical and absorptive properties of the retina show three classes of cones. Thus, the trichromatic theory seems to describe accurately the coding at the retina (Marks, Dobell, & MacNichol, 1964). Support for the opponent-process theory comes from microelectrode studies of the lateral geniculate nucleus in monkeys. (The lateral geniculate nucleus is one of the major visual projection areas in the visual system of both human beings and monkeys.) Cells in the lateral geniculate nucleus respond differently to various wavelengths. When the eye is stimulated with lights of a wavelength between 400 and 500 nanometers, some of the cells in the lateral geniculate nucleus decrease their rate of firing. If stimulated with a longer wavelength, firing rate increases (De Valois & Jacobs, 1968). This change is predicted by the opponent-process theory. Exactly how color information is transferred from the retina to the lateral geniculate nucleus remains to be discovered. Some of the data that helped test the trichromatic and opponent-process theories came from people with abnormal color vision.

opponent-process theory: Theory of color vision, which stated that color is coded by a series of receptors responding positively or negatively to different wavelengths of light.

trichromat: [TRY-kroe-mat] Person who experiences color vision in the most common way, and who requires only the three primary colors to see any color.

monochromat: [MON-o-kroe-MAT] Person whose retinas contain only rods and who therefore cannot perceive hue.

color blind: Unable to perceive one or more different hues.

Color Blindness. In 1794, John Dalton, founder of the atomic theory of matter, believed he had figured out why he couldn't distinguish his red stockings from his green ones. He reasoned that something blue in his eyeball absorbed red light and prevented him from seeing red. Dalton was not the first person to suffer from red–green color blindness, but he was the first to describe it scientifically.

Learning Objective 5.9 Describe color blindness and its causes.

Most human beings have normal color vision and are considered **trichromats.** A very few people (fewer than 1%) do not see any color. These **monochromats** are totally **color blind** and cannot discriminate among wavelengths, often because they lack cone receptors in their retinas (Boynton, 1988). The lack of a specific color-absorbing pigment or chemicals in the cones makes accurate color discriminations impossible. Fortunately, most people with color deficiencies (about 8% of men and 1% of women) are only partially color deficient (Nathans, 1989).

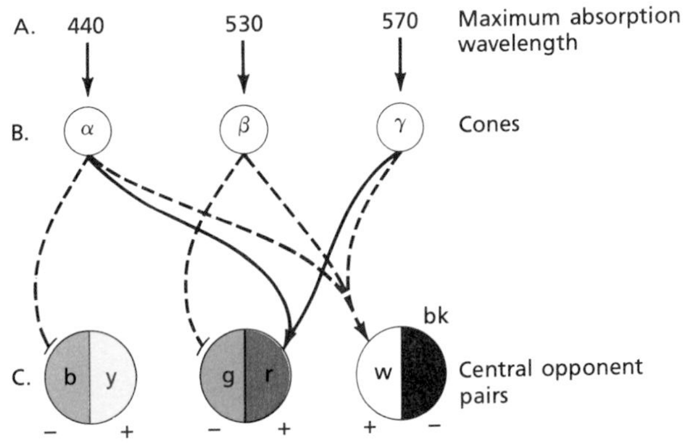

Figure 5.13

According to an opponent-process model proposed by Hurvich and Jameson (1974), three kinds of cones (alpha, beta, and gamma) respond maximally to light of different wavelengths, indicated at level A. These either stimulate (arrows) or inhibit (dotted lines) three kinds of central opponent pairs—cells that respond to either "blue" or "yellow" (a b/y pair), "green" or "red" (a g/r pair), or "white" or "black" (a w/b pair). This theory is influential because it is compatible with both color-blindness data and knowledge of physiology. (After Hurvich & Jameson, 1974. Copyright 1974 by the American Psychological Association. Reprinted by permission.)

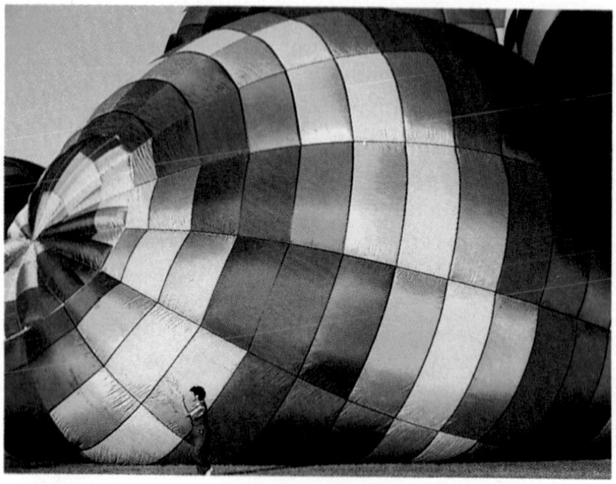

Color blindness, the inability to see certain colors, is a hereditary condition in which the proteins of one or more cones either do not function or are inadequate in number. The balloons on the right are shown as they might appear to a dichromat with a red-green deficiency.

dichromat: [DIE-kroe-mat] Person who can distinguish only two of the three basic hues.

Dichromats have deficiencies in either the red–green or the blue–yellow area. About 2% of men cannot discriminate between reds and greens (Wyszecki & Stiles, 1967). What does the world look like to a person who is a dichromat? People with color deficiencies see all the colors in a range of the electromagnetic spectrum as the same. For example, to a person with a blue deficiency, all greens, blues, and violets look the same; a person with a red–green deficiency may see red, green, and yellow, as yellow. Many color-blind individuals have distorted color responses in several areas of the electromagnetic spectrum—that is, they have trouble with several colors.

The precise role of genetics in color blindness is not clear, but we know that it is usually transmitted genetically from mothers to their male offspring. The high number of men who are color blind compared to women is due to the way the genetic information is coded and passed on to each generation. The genetic transmission occurs on the 23rd pair of chromosomes and results from inherited alterations in the genes that are responsible for cone pigments (Nathans, 1989).

Progress Check 5.2

Complete each of the following sentences with one of the options provided.

(L.O. 5.7) a. ________ is the psychological dimension of a color that indicates its lightness or darkness, its *intensity.* (Hue / Brightness / Saturation)

(L.O. 5.7) b. Objects ________ hue—what we usually call color. (possess and radiate / do not possess)

(L.O. 5.7) c. Long wavelengths are perceived as being ________ than short wavelengths. (brighter / duller)

(L.O. 5.7) d. A color such as gray is the result of a ________ band of wavelengths. (narrow / wide)

(L.O. 5.8) e. According to the trichromatic *and* the opponent-process theories, each cone is capable of producing neural output in response to ________ wavelengths. (all / a very limited range of)

(L.O. 5.8) f. According to the ________ theory, the retina contains three types of cones, each maximally sensitive to a different wavelength (red, green, or blue); the electrochemical signals received from each type of cone combine, enabling us to see all colors. (trichromatic / opponent-process)

(L.O. 5.8) g. According to the ________ theory, there are three types of photoreceptors, each responding to opposing wavelengths (red–green, blue–yellow, or black–white); each receptor fires maximally to one of the opposing colors and minimally to the other, depending on the wavelengths entering the eye. (trichromatic / opponent-process)

(L.O. 5.8) h. Studies concerning transduction at the ________ support the opponent-process theory. (retina / lateral geniculate nucleus / optic chiasm)

(L.O. 5.9) i. ________ have rods, but no cones, in their retinas and cannot perceive the hue of objects. (Monochromats / Dichromats / Trichromats)

(L.O. 5.9) j. People who are color deficient ________. (have fewer cones than normal / lack specific color-absorbing pigments)

(L.O. 5.9) k. Color blindness is usually transmitted genetically from ________. (the first to the sixth generation / mothers to their sons)

Visual Perception

Learning Objective 5.10 Explain how we maintain an understanding of size and shape even when objects are presented at different distances or angles.

The electrochemical processes that stimulate vision and the subsequent changes that take place in the pathways leading to higher visual centers are all crucial parts of the perceptual process. However, many perceptual experiences involve past events in addition to current stimulation. By integrating our previous experiences with new events, perceptual encounters become more meaningful. For example, it is only with experience that people know that an object stays the same size and shape when it is moved away from our immediate vision. We consider next a range of visual perceptual phenomena that are especially dependent on the integration of past experience with current experiences.

size constancy: The ability of the perceptual system to know that an object remains constant in size regardless of its distance or the size of its image on the retina.

Perception of Form: Constancy

Understanding how human beings perceive form and space helps architects to design buildings and designers to create furniture and clothes. Perception of form involves the interpretation of stimuli of different sizes, shapes, and depths to create a unit. Two important activities in form perception are (1) recognizing forms at a distance and (2) recognizing forms that appear to have changed size or shape.

At close range Seurat's paintings appear unintelligible; the forms and objects gain definition when seen as a whole from a distance.

Size Constancy. People can generally judge the size of an object, even if the size of its image on the retina changes. For example, you can estimate the height of a 6-foot tall man from 50 feet away, with a small image on the retina, as well as from only 5 feet away, with a much larger image on the retina. **Size constancy** is the ability of the perceptual system to recognize that an object remains constant in size regardless of its distance from the observer or the size of its image on the retina.

Three variables determine a person's ability to maintain size constancy: (1) previous experience with the true size of objects, (2) the distance between the object and the person, and (3) the presence of surrounding objects (Day & McKenzie, 1977). As an object is moved farther away, the size of its image on the retina decreases, while its perceived distance increases. These two processes always work together. Moreover, as an object is moved away, its perceived size does not change in relation to that of other stationary objects. This is why knowing the size of surrounding objects helps people determine their distance from an object as well as the object's actual size.

shape constancy: The ability to recognize a shape despite changes in the orientation or angle from which it is viewed.

Shape Constancy. Another important aspect of form perception is **shape constancy,** which is the ability to recognize a shape despite changes in the angle or position from which it is viewed. For example, even though you usually see trees perpendicular to the ground, you can recognize a tree when it has been chopped down and is lying on the ground. Similarly, an ice cream cone looks circular when you view it from above, yet you perceive it as an ice cream cone even when you view it from the side and it appears more triangular than circular.

Depth Perception

For centuries, artists have used the principles of perception to create illusions of depth in two-dimensional paintings. Although the artist can fool the eye, you are not fooled when you judge the distance of an object every day when you drive a car, catch a ball, or take a picture. You estimate your distance from the object and the distance between that object and another one. Closely associated with these two tasks is the ability to see in three dimensions—that is, in terms of height, width, and depth. Both *monocular* (one-eyed) and *binocular* (two-eyed) cues are used to perceive depth. Binocular cues predominate at close distances, and monocular cues are used for distance scenes and two-dimensional fields of view, such as paintings.

Monocular Depth Cues. Depth cues that do not depend on the use of both eyes are **monocular depth cues.** Two important monocular depth cues deal with the effects of motion on perception. The first, *motion parallax,* occurs when a moving observer stares at a fixed point. The objects behind that point appear to move in the same direction as the observer; the objects in front of that point appear to move in the opposite direction. For example, if you stare at a fence while riding in a moving car, the trees behind the fence rails seem to move in the same direction as the car (forward) and the bushes in front of the rails seem to

The illusion of space is well maintained in a Zen garden. What perceptual cues make this garden seem larger than it actually is?

move in the opposite direction (backward). Motion parallax also affects the speed at which objects appear to move. Objects at a greater distance from the moving observer appear to move more slowly than objects that are closer.

The second monocular depth cue derived from movement is the *kinetic depth effect.* Objects that look flat when they are stationary appear to be three-dimensional when they move. When two-dimensional projections, such as pictures of squares, cubes, or rods shown on a computer screen, are rotated, they appear to have three dimensions.

Other monocular depth cues come from the stimulus itself; they are often seen in photographs and paintings. For example, larger or taller objects are usually perceived to be closer than smaller ones, particularly in relation to surrounding objects. In addition, *linear perspective* affects perception; this is based on the principle that distant objects appear to be closer together than nearer objects. Two parallel lines in a painting will appear to converge as they recede into the distance (see Figure 5.14).

Another monocular cue for depth is *interposition.* When one object blocks out part of another, the first appears to be closer. A fourth monocular cue is *texture.* Surfaces that have little texture or detail seem to be in the distance. Artists often use the clues of *highlighting* and *shadowing.* Highlighted or light (bright) objects appear close; objects that are shadowed or dark appear to be farther away. In addition, the perceptual system picks up other information from shadowing, including the curvature of surfaces (Cavanagh & Leclerc, 1989).

Still another monocular depth cue is atmospheric perspective, which relates to the wavelengths themselves. Distant mountains often look blue, for example, because long (red) wavelengths are more easily scattered as they pass through the air, allowing more short (blue) wavelengths to reach our eyes. Leonardo da Vinci used this phenomenon in his paintings; he even developed an equation for how much blue pigment should be mixed with the normal color of an object so that it would appear as close or far away as he wished. Michelangelo's angels seem to float off the ceiling of the Sistine Chapel because he used color so effectively to portray depth.

The preceding monocular depth cues are derived from the stimulus. Accommodation, however, is not derived from the stimulus. If a person looks from one object to another one at a different distance, the lenses will accommodate—that is, change shape to adapt to the depth of focus. This cue is available from each of the eyes separately. **Accommodation** is the change in the shape of the lens that enables the observer to keep an object in focus on the retina when the object is moved or when the choice of object for focus changes. It is controlled by muscles attached to the lens, which provide information about the shape of the lens to the higher processing systems in the brain.

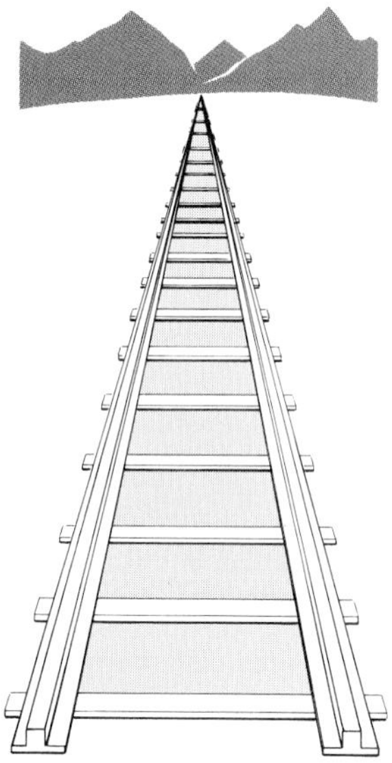

Figure 5.14

In a common illusion, parallel railroad tracks appear closer together when they are farther away.

monocular depth cues: [mah-NAHK-you-lur] Depth cues that do not require the use of two eyes.

accommodation: The change in shape of the lens of the eye to keep an object in focus on the retina when the object moves closer to or farther from the observer.

retinal disparity: The slight difference in the visual image cast on each eye; a principal binocular cue.

Binocular Depth Cues. Most people, even infants, use binocular as well as monocular depth cues. One important binocular depth cue is **retinal disparity**—that is, a slight difference in the image projected onto each retina. Retinal disparity occurs because the eyes are physically separated (by the bridge of the nose), causing them to see an object from slightly different angles.

To see how retinal disparity works, hold a finger up in front of some distant object. Examine the object first with one eye and then with the other eye. The finger will appear in different positions relative to the object. The closer that objects are to the eyes, the farther apart their images on the retinas will be, and the greater the retinal disparity. Objects at a great distance produce little retinal disparity.

Another binocular depth cue is **convergence.** As an object moves closer to a viewer, the viewer's eyes move toward each other (*converge*) in order to keep information at corresponding points on the retina. Like accommodation, convergence is controlled by muscles in the eye that convey information to the brain and thus provide a potent physiological depth cue for stimuli close to observers. Beyond 20 or 30 feet, the eyes are aimed pretty much in parallel, and the effect of this cue diminishes.

Learning Objective 5.12 Describe three illusions we experience, and give some reasons for why these experiences are thought to occur.

Illusions

When a person's normal visual process and depth cues seem to break down, he or she experiences an optical illusion. An **illusion** is the perception of a physical stimulus that differs from the commonly expected perception; many consider it a misperception of sensory stimulation.

A common illusion is the *Müller-Lyer illusion,* in which two equal-length lines with arrows attached to their ends appear to be of different lengths (see Figure 5.15). A similar illusion is the *Ponzo illusion,* in which two horizontal lines of the same length surrounded by slanted lines appear to be of different lengths (see Figure 5.15). A natural illusion is the *moon illusion.* Although the actual size of the moon and the size of its image on the retina do not change, the moon appears about 30% larger when it is over the horizon than when it is overhead. The moon illusion is quite striking. In just a few minutes, the size of the moon appears to change from quite large to quite small.

How do visual illusions work? No completely satisfactory explanations have been found. Recent theories account for them in terms of the backgrounds against which the objects are seen. These explanations are based on the observer's previous experiences and well-developed perceptual constancies.

The moon illusion, for example, is explained by the fact that when seen overhead, the moon has a featureless background, whereas at the horizon, objects are close to it. Objects in the landscape provide cues about distance that change the observer's perception of the size of the moon (Restle, 1970). To see how the moon illusion depends on landscape cues, try this: When the moon is at the horizon, bend over and look at it from between your legs. Because that position screens out some of the horizon cues, the magnitude of the illusion will be reduced. The moon illusion continues to be of interest to researchers, and newer theories emerge every year adding new variables and concepts (e.g., Baird, Wagner, & Fuld, 1990).

The Ponzo illusion is similarly accounted for by the linear perspective provided by the slanted background lines. The Müller–Lyer illusion occurs because of the angle and shape of the arrows attached to the ends of the lines. Lines angled inward are often interpreted as far corners—those that are distant from the observer. Lines angled outward are commonly interpreted as near corners—those that are close to the observer (see Figure 5.15). Therefore, lines with far-corner angles attached to them appear longer because their length is judged in a context of distance.

These are not the only ways of explaining illusions. Some researchers assert that people see the moon as a different size on the horizon than overhead because they judge it as they would judge other moving objects that pass through space. Because the moon does not get closer to them, they assume that it is moving away. Objects that move away get smaller; hence the illusion of a change in the size of the moon (Reed, 1984). This explanation focuses on constancies but also takes account of movement, space, and the atmosphere.

convergence: The movement of the eyes toward each other to keep corresponding points on the retina as an object moves closer to the observer; a binocular depth cue.

illusion: A perception of a stimulus that differs from normal expectations about its appearance.

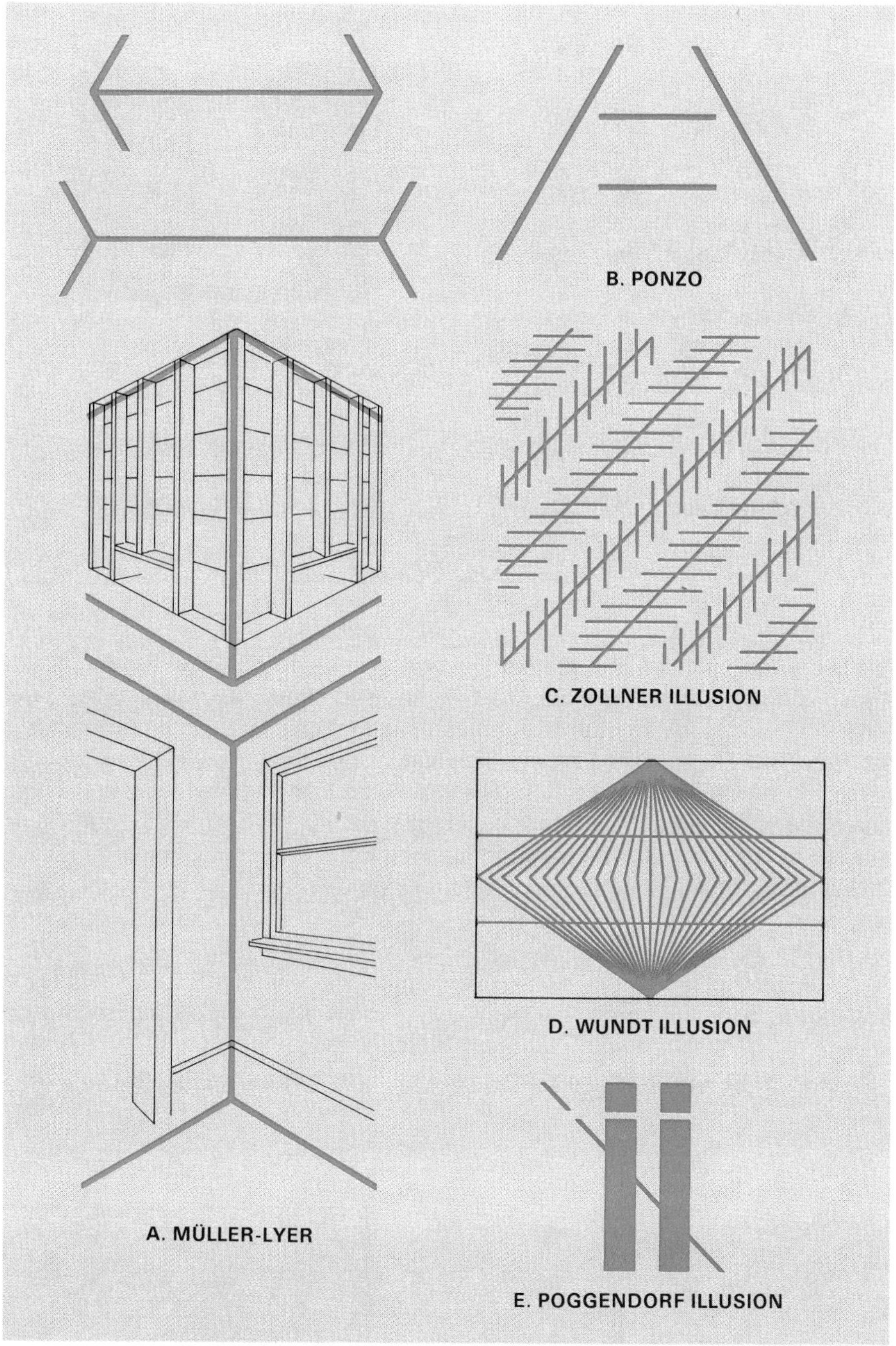

Figure 5.15

In the Müller-Lyer and Ponzo illusions at the top, lines of equal length appear different in length. The center and bottom Müller-Lyer illusions show how the arrows usually represent "near corners" and "far corners." In the Zollner illusion, the short lines make the longer ones not seem parallel, even though they are. In the Wundt illusion, the center horizontal lines are parallel, even though they appear bent. In the Poggendorf illusion, the line disappears behind a solid and reappears in a position that seems wrong.

Gestalt Laws of Organization

Learning Objective 5.13
Discuss the Gestalt approach as it applies to perception, and identify five Gestalt laws of organization.

Gestalt psychologists (see Chapter 1) suggest that conscious experience is more than the sum of its parts. They argue that the mind takes the elements of experience and organizes them to form something unique; they thus analyze the world in terms of perceptual frameworks. Analyzed as a whole experience, the patterns of a person's perceptions make sense. Gestalt psychologists such as Wertheimer,

Law of Prägnanz: The Gestalt principle that when items or stimuli can be grouped together and seen as a whole, they will be.

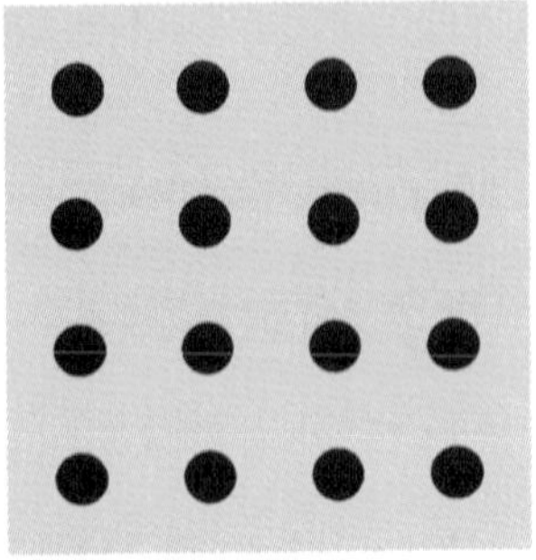

Figure 5.16

The *Law of Prägnanz:* The Gestalt principle that items or stimuli that can be grouped together as a whole will be. These 16 dots are typically perceived as a square.

Figure 5.17

A drawing in which figure and ground can be reversed. You can see either two faces against a white background or a goblet against a dark background.

Koffka, and Kohler greatly influenced early theories of form perception. These psychologists assumed (wrongly) that human perceptual processes reflect brain organization and that by studying perception, they could learn about the workings of the brain. They focused their perceptual studies on the way in which people experience form and organization. The early Gestaltists believed that people organize a complex visual field into a coherent whole rather than seeing individual, unrelated elements. We see groups of elements, not fragmented parts. According to this idea—the **Law of Prägnanz**—items or stimuli that can be grouped together and seen as a whole, or a form, will be seen that way. Figure 5.16 shows a series of 16 dots that people tend to see as a square.

The Law of Prägnanz as an organizing idea was based on principles of organization for the perception of figures. Gestalt psychologists focused on the nature of *figure-and-ground relationships,* contending that *figures* (i.e., the main object of sensory attention) are perceived as distinct from the *grounds* (i.e., back-

Figure 5.18

Two ambiguous figures: (A) a rabbit facing toward the right or a duck facing toward the left; (B) either an old woman in profile or a young woman whose head is turned slightly away.

A

B

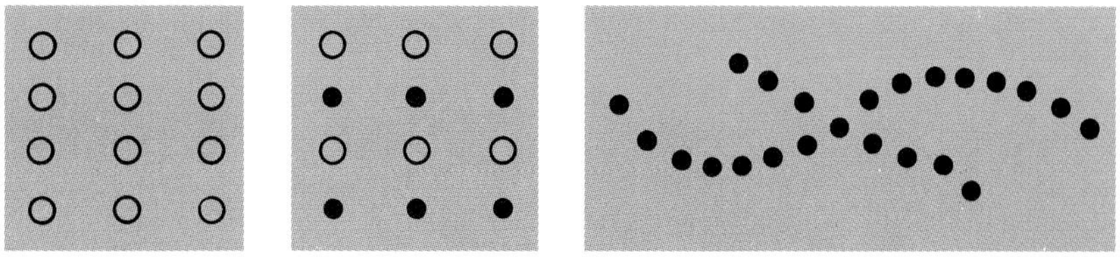

Figure 5.19

According to the Gestalt law of continuity, an observer will predict where the next item should occur (far right) because the group of items projects into space. According to the Gestalt law of similarity, the filled and empty circles (middle) appear to be arranged in horizontal rows because similar items tend to be perceived in groups. According to the Gestalt law of proximity, the circles (far left) appear to be arranged in vertical columns because items that are close together tend to be perceived as a unit.

grounds) on which they are presented (see Figures 5.17 and 5.18). Gestalt psychologists developed the following series of laws for predicting which areas of an ambiguous pattern would be seen as the figure (foreground) and which as the ground (background) (Hochberg, 1974, 1979):

- ▲ The *law of proximity:* Elements close to one another in space or time will be perceived as groups (see Figure 5.19).
- ▲ The *law of similarity:* Similar items will be perceived in groups (see Figure 5.19).
- ▲ The *law of continuity:* A string of items will indicate where the next item in the string will be found (see Figure 5.19).
- ▲ *Common fate principles:* Items that move or change together will be seen as whole.
- ▲ The *law of closure:* Parts of a figure that are not presented will be filled in by the perceptual system.

Research shows that the Gestalt laws are vague. Gestalt laws are not always obeyed, nor are they consistent with our current knowledge of brain organization. Nevertheless, these early investigations continue to influence perceptual psychologists. Attention is another area that has received special attention from perceptual psychologists, an area that often focused on the study of subliminal perception which is considered in the Understanding the Research Process box on page 99.

Attention

Learning Objective 5.14
Explain the limits of our visual and auditory systems, and tell how we selectively extract information.

People constantly extract signals from the world around them. Although they receive many different messages at once, they can watch, listen, and pay attention only to a selected message. In fact a person's selective attention is often called the cocktail party problem. An associated phenomenon inhibits our ability to remember names when being introduced. People often fail to catch the name of

Attending a three-ring circus is a visual selective attention task. Would you choose one act to concentrate on or be able to pay equal attention to all three acts?

someone they are introduced to because they are too preoccupied with thinking of something to say or with appraising the new person.

Perceptual psychologists are concerned with the complex processes involved in extracting information from the environment. They hope to answer the question, "Which stimuli do people choose to listen to?" In selective-listening experiments, subjects wear a pair of headphones and receive different messages simultaneously in each ear. Their task is often to *shadow,* or repeat a message heard in one ear. Typically, they report that they are able to listen to a speaker in either the left or the right ear and can provide information about the content and quality of that speaker's voice. The task of following one message and not the other is easier if (a) the voice in one ear is male and the voice in the other is female, (b) the pitch of each of two male voices is different, or (c) the content of the messages is different. If voice, pitch, intensity, quality, and content are similar in both ears, subjects often shift their attention from one ear to the other. Thus, the more discriminable the two auditory channels, the better the selective attention.

Of the several theories about how people are able to attend selectively, the two described here are the filter theory and the attenuation theory. The *filter theory* suggests that human beings possess a limited capacity to process information and that perceptual filters must choose between information presented to the left and the right ears. The *attenuation theory* states that all the information is analyzed but that intervening factors inhibit (i.e., attenuate) attention so that only selected information reaches the highest centers of processing.

Hundreds of selective-listening studies have examined the claims of filter versus attenuation theory (e.g., Cherry, 1953; Treisman, 1969). Regardless of whether people filter or attenuate information, selective-attention studies show that human beings must select one of the available stimuli (Duncan, 1980). It is impossible, for example, to pay attention to four lectures at once. A listener can extract information from only one speaker at a time. Admittedly, you can do more than one task at a time, such as drive a car and listen to the radio, but you cannot use the same sensory channel, such as vision, for several tasks simultaneously (e.g., drive a car, read a book, and inspect photographs all at once). Both the auditory and visual systems have limited capacities. People have limited ability to divide their atten-

UNDERSTANDING THE RESEARCH PROCESS

Subliminal Perception

If a visual or auditory stimulus is presented so quickly or at such a low intensity or volume that you cannot consciously perceive it, can it affect your behavior? Modern studies of subliminal perception (*subliminal* means below the threshold of awareness) began in the 1950s with an innovative advertising ploy. A marketing executive superimposed verbal messages that said things like "buy popcorn" on a regular movie. According to some advertising agents, movie theaters could induce audiences to buy more popcorn by flashing—at speeds too fast to be consciously observed—advertisements on the screen. Many psychologists dismissed the popcorn marketing campaign as nonsense, but it created a sensation.

Subliminal perception is possible, and many cognitive scientists take unconscious perception for granted. However, subliminal perception has not always been seen as valid; it has had a controversial history.

In the 1950s, when psychologists began to study subliminal perception, they defined it in terms of a threshold below which subjects are unaware of a stimulus at least 50% of the time. Many of the early 1960s studies lacked control groups and did not specify what variables were being manipulated. Some presented stimuli for durations in which several words might easily be seen by one subject and no words by another. Other studies presented "dirty" or taboo words to see if they affected responses more than neutral or emotionally uncharged words did. Unfortunately for the researchers, portions of results of the taboo word studies could be accounted for by the fact that some subjects were embarrassed to repeat the noxious words to the experimenter (often a person of the opposite sex) and denied having seen them.

To avoid some of these methodological problems, later experiments presented subjects with both threatening and neutral stimuli for very brief durations. The subjects responded by repeating the word or by pressing a button as soon as they saw it. In these experiments, threatening stimuli had to be presented for a longer time or at a greater intensity level than the nonthreatening stimuli, to be identified.

If a researcher presents a threatening stimulus, such as a dirty word, it may raise the perceptual threshold above normal levels, making it harder for the subject to perceive subsequent subliminal words. Some researchers suggest that the unconscious or some other personality variable acts as a censor. They maintain that subliminal perception can be explained in terms of such nonperceptual variables as motivation, previous experience, and unconscious or critical censoring processes that influence perceptual thresholds.

In some controlled situations, subliminal stimuli probably can influence behavior. In the real world, however, we are constantly faced with many competing sensory stimuli, and what grabs our attention depends on many variables, such as importance, prominence, and interest. Should we fear mind control by advertisers or other unsolicited outside stimuli? Should we buy tapes that offer help through subliminal perception? The answer is probably no (Greenwald, Spangenberg, Pratkanis, & Eskenazi, 1990). In the end, subliminal perception and any learning that results from it are greatly affected by such nonperceptual variables as motivation, previous experience, personality, and other learned behaviors. However, more research is needed to determine exactly what is taking place when subliminal perception occurs and to what degree subliminal stimuli can influence us, if at all.

- ***What was the initial hypothesis of both researchers and advertisers regarding unconscious perception?***
- ***Early research studies had serious methodology problems that limited the applicability of their results; what were two of those flaws?***
- ***What other variables and evidence must be brought to bear on studies of subliminal perception before a complete understanding of the processes is available?***

tion between tasks and must allocate their perceptual resources for greatest efficiency (Eriksen, Webb, & Fournier, 1990).

An interesting twist on the study of attention intrigued researchers in the 1950s, when some psychologists began to study subliminal perception, considered in the Understanding the Research Process box above.

Progress Check 5.3

Complete each of the following sentences with one of the options provided.

(L.O. 5.10) a. One reason we are able to maintain size constancy, even though the distance between ourselves and an object changes, is that ________. (the retinal image remains the same size / surrounding objects give us perceptual cues)

(L.O. 5.11) b. When viewing objects at a distance or when viewing two-dimensional fields, such as a painting, ________ depth cues predominate. (monocular / binocular)

(L.O. 5.11) c. Two monocular depth cues that occur because of the way an object moves are motion parallax and ________. (interposition / kinetic depth effect / linear perspective)

(L.O. 5.11) d. A monocular depth cue that occurs because the shape of the crystalline lens changes when an object is moved, allowing the object to stay in focus on the retina is ________. (accommodation / retinal disparity / convergence)

(L.O. 5.12) e. When two horizontal lines of the same length are enclosed by two slanted lines and are perceived as different in length, an individual is experiencing the ________ illusion. (Ponzo / Müller-Lyer)

(L.O. 5.12) f. One explanation for why we sometimes experience illusions has to do with visual stimuli ________. (that are not normally perceived / in the background)

(L.O. 5.13) g. Although early Gestalt psychologists were correct with their prediction of the Law of Prägnanz, their assumption that ________ is inaccurate, according to current knowledge. (it could be used as an organizing principle / perceptual processes reflect brain organization)

(L.O. 5.13) h. The Gestalt law of ________ states that a string of items indicates where the next item in the string will be found. (closure / common fate / continuity)

(L.O. 5.14) i. When subjects listen to two conversations at once, they find it easier to follow one of the conversations if the voices, pitches, intensity, quality, and content are ________. (of interest / different / similar)

(L.O. 5.14) j. The ________ suggests that people attend selectively because, although all information is analyzed at some level, other factors affect which information is selected and proceeds toward higher processing centers in the brain. (cocktail party problem / filter theory / attenuation theory)

(L.O. 5.14) k. Selective attention studies have shown that people have a ________ within and between the visual and auditory perceptual systems. (limited capacity / variated process / repetitious processing cycle)

Module Summary

Sensation and Perception: A Definition

- *Perception* is the process through which people attach meaning to sensory stimuli by means of complex processing mechanisms (p. 78).

The Visual System

- The main structures of the eye are the cornea, iris, pupil, crystalline lens, and retina. The retina is made up of 10 layers, of which the most important are the rods and cones, the bipolar layer, and the ganglion cell layer. The ganglion cells make up the nuclei of the long axons that form the optic nerve (pp. 79–80).
- *Receptive fields* are areas on the retina that, when stimulated, produce changes in the firing of cells in the visual system. After information leaves the retina, it proceeds to higher centers of analysis through the optic chiasm, the lateral geniculate nucleus, and the striate cortex (pp. 85–86).
- The three main psychological characteristics of color—hue, brightness, and saturation—are equivalent to three physical characteristics: wavelength, intensity, and purity (pp. 87–90).

Visual Perception

- Monocular cues for depth perception include linear perspective, texture, and accommodation. The primary binocular cue is retinal disparity (pp. 92–93).
- The term *illusion* refers to the perception of a stimulus that differs from the way people normally expect it to appear (pp. 95–97).
- Using the Law of Prägnanz as an organizing idea, Gestalt psychologists developed principles of organization for the perception of figures (pp. 96–97).

Attention

- If a visual or auditory stimulus is presented so quickly or at such a low intensity that you cannot consciously perceive it, it is presented *subliminally* (pp. 97–99).

KEY TERMS

accommodation, p. 93
brightness, p. 87
color blind, p. 89
convergence, p. 94
dark adaptation, p. 82
dichromat, p. 90
electromagnetic radiation, p. 79
hue, p. 87
illusion, p. 94
lateral geniculate nucleus, p. 84
Law of Prägnanz, p. 96
light, p. 79
monochromat, p. 89
monocular depth cues, p. 93
opponent-process theory, p. 89
optic chiasm, p. 84
perception, p. 78
photoreceptors, p. 80
receptive fields, p. 86
retinal disparity, p. 93
saturation, p. 87
sensation, p. 78
shape constancy, p. 92
size constancy, p. 91
striate cortex, p. 84
superior colliculus, p. 84
transduction, p. 80
trichromat, p. 89
trichromatic theory, p. 88
visual cortex, p. 80

SELF-TEST

Module 5

- Before taking the self-test, **recite** and **review.**
- Use the key at the back of the text to *correct* your answers.
- *Restudy* pages that correspond to any questions you answered incorrectly.

1. The process by which an organism interprets and evaluates sensory input so that it acquires meaning is
   a. sensation.
   b. feature extraction.
   c. perception.
   d. selective attention.
2. What is represented by this list of phrases: outside stimulus, receptor stimulation, receptor transduction, convergence to higher neural and brain pathways?
   a. The function of all rods and some cones.
   b. The function of some rods and all cones.
   c. The process that enables humans to perceive X-rays, ultraviolet rays, and infrared rays.
   d. The order of processing common to all perceptual systems.
3. The part of the eye that specifically functions to improve the quality and depth of focus of the image cast on the retina is the
   a. iris, when it constricts to make the pupil smaller.
   b. crystalline lens.
   c. cornea.
   d. the eyeball itself.
4. Each human eye contains
   a. more than 120 million rods and 6 million cones
   b. an equal distribution of rods and cones.
   c. more cones than rods; it appears there are at least 100,000 cones, but they are so small that it is impossible to determine the number.
   d. rods and cones that are distributed in a random and unequal fashion across the retina.
5. The photoreceptors located on the periphery of the retina and responsible for night vision are
   a. cones.
   b. rods.
   c. ganglion cells.
   d. bipolar cells.
6. During the process of dark adaptation, chemicals in the photoreceptors ______________ and then return to their inactive state.
   a. stimulate rods
   b. regenerate
   c. consolidate
   d. converge
7. Humans are able to perceive form in three dimensions because
   a. complex cells fire in the retina.
   b. the superior colliculus adjusts for flatness.
   c. the brain receives two sets of signals from a single image.
   d. we see things as they truly are in their natural form.
8. Cells on the retina that respond vigorously as light moves across them in one direction are called ______________ cells.
   a. simple
   b. complex

c. hypercomplex
d. linear perspective

9. Photoreceptors are most sensitive to wavelengths between
   a. 400–500 nanometers; blue
   b. 500–600 nanometers; yellow
   c. 600–700 nanometers; red
   d. a pure mixture of the nanometer spectrum; white light
10. The Young–Helmholtz (trichromatic) theory of color coding seems to accurately describe
   a. color contrast
   b. color blindness
   c. coding at the retina
   d. our tendency to name more than three basic colors
11. Color blindness is usually the result of
   a. damage to the photoreceptors in the retina.
   b. deterioration of neurons in the striate cortex.
   c. inherited alterations in the genes of the X (female) chromosomes of the 23rd pair.
   d. None of the above; the cause is not understood.
12. Cross out the statement that is *not* a variable that contributes to our ability to maintain size constancy.
   a. Having previous experience with the true size of objects.
   b. The image on the retina remains a constant size when objects move closer or further away.
   c. The distance between the object and the person plays a role in size constancy.
   d. The presence of surrounding objects plays a role in size constancy.
13. Two physiological depth cues involving muscles attached to the eye that convey information to the brain about the distance of an object are
   a. motion parallax and kinetic depth effect.
   b. retinal disparity and convergence.
   c. kinetic depth effect and retinal disparity.
   d. accommodation and convergence.
14. Perceptual psychologists sometimes consider an illusion to be a
   a. figment of one's imagination.
   b. misperception of sensory stimulation.
   c. hallucination.
   d. superstition.
15. Which of the following are the words and phrases that Gestalt psychologists use to describe the way we perceive our surroundings?
   a. organization, unique form, patterns, group, whole, perceptual framework, figure–ground
   b. separation, unrelated elements, fragmented, individual, parts, perceptual puzzle, bits-and-pieces
   c. categorize, unpredictable configuration, complementary sections, visible, fuzzy to clear
   d. materialize, energize, itemize, prioritize, organize, finalize
16. Jim often boasts about how he can do many things at one time. From selective attention studies, one thing we know is that Jim cannot effectively ________________ at the same time.
   a. listen to his wife and a female radio sports announcer
   b. read from a book and walk to the kitchen
   c. listen to a lecture and observe blackboard notations
   d. think and talk

Module 6

Hearing, Taste, Smell, and the Skin Senses

LEARNING OBJECTIVES

When you have mastered the material in this module, you will be able to

Sensory Experience (pp. 106–108)

6.1 Discuss what researchers have found about the factors necessary for normal perceptual development (p. 106).

6.2 Explain why psychologists study sensory deprivation and discuss some of its diverse effects on animals and people (p. 107).

Hearing (pp. 108–112)

6.3 Describe the physical and psychological properties of sound (p. 108).

6.4 List and describe the parts of the ear and explain how each part functions to process sound waves (p. 110).

6.5 Explain how sound perception occurs, according to both place and frequency theories, and discuss how modern researchers explain our ability to hear (p. 110).

6.6 Describe two types of hearing impairments and some of the problems they can create for people (p. 111).

Taste and Smell (pp. 113–117)

6.7 Explain how our taste and olfactory perceptual systems code chemical stimuli (p. 113).

The Skin Senses (pp. 115–119)

6.8 Describe the structure and functions of the skin and explain how various sensations are perceived through the skin (p. 116).

6.9 Discuss pain as a perceptual system, the gate control theory, and the effects of drug treatment for the relief of pain (p. 116).

Kinesthesis and Vestibular Sensitivity (p. 119)

6.10. Define *kinesthesis* and describe the vestibular sense (p. 119).

Extrasensory Perception (pp. 119–120)

6.11 Discuss extrasensory perception as it fits into the field of contemporary psychology (p. 119).

SQ3R
- ▲ **Survey** to set goals for studying.
- ▲ Ask **questions** as you **read.**
- ▲ Stop occasionally to **recite** and **review.**

plus
- ▲ **Write** a summary of key points.
- ▲ **Reflect** on the hypotheses, evidence, and implications of this material and on the relevance it has to *your* life.

With weights hanging from her feet, Ruth Lerner was feeling somewhat better, but the pain was still with her. She had never had more than a cold, and at age 63, this was her first hospitalization (except for childbirth). She always told people she was as healthy as a horse. Nonetheless, she had developed a back problem over the past 2 years, and it had become serious.

Initially, Ruth felt some lower back pain after walking through shopping malls. A few months later, she was beginning to feel the pain most of the time. Aspirin and a heating pad seemed to take care of her discomfort. Then, on a trip to Europe, where she did a great deal of walking, Ruth started to feel numbness in her feet. It was at that point, as she told her doctors, that things started to go downhill. The pain became worse, the numbness was constant, and the severity of her condition seemed to get worse each week. Even though she had a high threshold of pain, she was really hurting. She took heavy doses of pain killers every 4 hours and could not sleep. Finally, she wound up in the hospital in traction—the pain was so bad that she could not walk.

Her doctors were in disagreement over her disorder. She saw six different physicians—each one a renowned specialist: an internist, a neurosurgeon, an orthopedic specialist, a chiropractor, a neurologist, and a pain specialist. The diagnoses varied—one claimed that she had a slipped disk, another diagnosed damaged cartilage. A third said it was both a misaligned disk and damaged cartilage. The fourth said she would have to live with a degenerating nervous system. The fifth said he had no idea. Her most recent physician, Dr. Sullivan, wanted her to enter a pain clinic. At his clinic, he claimed he would help her lose weight, learn appropriate exercises to strengthen her back muscles, and teach her to live with her discomfort. Dr. Sullivan wanted to avoid surgery, especially with an overweight 63-year-old, otherwise healthy woman.

Dr. Sullivan claimed that his pain clinic would help treat Ruth's symptoms, teach her psychological techniques for dealing with pain, and help her to strengthen her body. He joked with her that she would become "a lean mean fighting machine" who could deal with her situation and, most important, avoid surgical intervention. Part of his treatment involved teaching her about pain, about how people perceive pain, and about how the human body deals with pain and medications. In addition, Dr. Sullivan knew how to help people learn to cope by using biofeedback, meditation, and self-hypnosis. Dr. Sullivan was as much a psychologist as he was a physician.

Ruth Lerner agreed with his view. She had to make her decision while lying in a hospital bed, but she argued that she wanted to use every nonsurgical technique possible before "going under the knife." Learning to live with her pain did not excite her, and studying pain physiology and pain perception did not delight her—but neither did traction. She was transferred to Dr. Sullivan's clinic the next day.

Often, people's pain is intensified because of the situation in which they find themselves. A person's headache will seem worse if they are in a stressful situation, and their toothache intensifies when their children misbehave. Psychological factors play a key role in our perception of pain. As with emotions and many other human responses, pain is not solely a physical phenomenon. All of our perceptual systems are affected by a number of different variables, yet these systems interact simultaneously to allow us multiple perceptions, even as we respond to these perceptions. For example, we can read verses and sing at the same time. We walk, talk, eat, and experience pleasure and/or pain simultaneously. To appreciate the complexity of the perceptual process, we next examine how sensory experiences are integrated.

Sensory Experience

A fast-paced indoor racquetball game provides an exhilarating example of the interaction of perceptual systems. Your opponent's serve ricochets off the front wall and whizzes overhead. By the loud smack on the wall behind you, you know instantly that the ball has rebounded too fast to be intercepted at the back of the court. You run to the front of the court, turn, and swat the ball, sending it flying into the left corner. Your opponent raises his racquet in response but is too slow, and the ball thumps into his chest. As you play, you must coordinate your hearing, eyesight, motor systems, sense of balance, and posture all at once in order to react effectively to the speeding ball as it bounces off the walls and floor of the court.

Interacting Perceptual Systems

Learning Objective 6.1 Discuss what researchers have found about the factors necessary for normal perceptual development.

An organism is a unitary system that acts on a mixture of perceptual information. Researchers who study the active integration of the perceptual systems find that for the systems to develop fully, they must have varied experiences, as well as a way to interact. In a classic study of visual and motor coordination in kittens, Held and Hein (1963) demonstrated the need for the perceptual systems to act together. Pairs of kittens were placed in a circular enclosure, and one of each pair was equipped with a harness and collar that let it move actively as it explored the environment (see Figure 6.1). The other kitten was restrained so that it moved only in response to the movements of the first kitten. Active, voluntary movement initiated by the first kitten caused identical, but involuntary, movement by the second kitten. After observing many pairs of kittens, Held and Hein noted that only the kittens who were allowed to *initiate* voluntary movements were later able to make good visually guided motor movements; the others had deficits in their perceptual abilities. In related investigations, the effects of limiting stimulation have been followed up with animal and human subjects in studies of restricted environmental stimulation.

Figure 6.1

Held and Hein (1963) raised kittens in a circular enclosure and allowed one kitten active movement, the other only passive movement. Both kittens saw the same view of the world but showed dramatically different types of responses when tested for sensorimotor coordination. (Copyright 1963 by the American Psychological Association. Reprinted by permission.)

Restricted Environmental Stimulation

Learning Objective 6.2
Explain why psychologists study sensory deprivation, and discuss some of its diverse effects on animals and people.

Throughout the ages, mystics of all kinds have claimed to obtain special trance states by taking vows of silence, adhering to austere life-styles, meditating while sitting as still as stone for hours, and so on, thereby purposely limiting their sensory experiences. In 1954, neurophysiologist John Lilly enlisted modern technology to find out what would happen if the brain were deprived of all sensory input (Lilly, 1956). He constructed an isolation tank that excluded all light and sound and was filled with heavily salted water, which allows for easy floating. In this human-made sea, deprived of all external stimuli, Lilly reported experiencing dreams, reveries, hallucinations, and other altered states. Ten years later, Lilly began enhancing his isolation-tank trips by taking drugs such as LSD (lysergic acid diethylamide, a hallucinogenic psychotropic drug). During the 1970s, many people said that they could "expand their consciousness" via immersion in an isolation tank. By this, they meant that they could consciously experience sensations not normally experienced in unaltered states of consciousness.

The benefits of sensory restriction—isolation from sights, sounds, smells, tastes, and feeling—have been greatly exaggerated, but it can have profound effects on developing animals and humans. Psychologists have used sensory deprivation experiments to test whether some animal perceptions are innate or learned. In some studies, for example, animals are deprived of a sensory stimulant, such as light, from birth to age 6 months and then tested on skills that require using the deprived sense—in this case, sight. If the animal performs at the same level as animals that have not been deprived of the stimulus, the experimenters may conclude that the perceptual system is inborn. If the animal does not perform as well, experimenters may conclude that experience is important for the normal development of that perceptual system. Sensory deprivation studies of kittens show that their experiences with their environment must occur during crucial periods (times during which a particular development must occur and after which it cannot occur) if their inborn perceptual structures are to develop properly. For example, if a newborn animal is deprived of light or patterned vision, its visual apparatus does not develop properly.

Heron studied the effects of sensory restriction in human beings. College students were confined to a comfortable but dull room. To limit their auditory experiences, they heard only the continuous hum of an air conditioner; they wore translucent plastic visors to limit their vision; and they wore tubes lined with cotton surrounding their hands and arms to limit their skin's sensory input. The results were dramatic. Within a few hours, the subjects' performance on tests of mental ability was impaired. They became bored and irritable, and many said they saw "images" (Bexton, Heron, & Scott, 1954).

Other studies of sensory restriction placed subjects in identical conditions to those of the Bexton et al. study *except* that they were told that their deprivation would serve as an aid to meditation. These subjects did not hallucinate or become irritable; in fact, their mental ability improved (Lilly, 1956; Zuckerman, 1969). This study suggests that people do not necessarily become bored because of lack of stimulation. Rather, when people *feel* that their situation is monotonous, they become bored. When given the opportunity to relax in a quiet place for a long time, many people meditate, and they find such deprivation relaxing. Such findings indicate the need for caution in interpreting data from sensory deprivation studies involving human beings, particularly because subjects approach these situations with powerful expectations (recall the effects of self-fulfilling prophecies, mentioned in Chapter 1).

Sensory restriction has proven to have positive effects with some people. Because of the profound relaxation that occurs in an extreme sensory-restricted environment, it can be highly effective in helping both to modify some habits, such as smoking reduction, and to treat behavior problems such as obesity and insomnia (Suedfeld & Coren, 1989). Research shows that sensory restriction does not necessarily produce hallucinations or cognitive impairment; instead, it can be facilitative. Research on sensory restriction is exceedingly complicated because so many variables might affect the results. Some subjects may be more likely to benefit than others (e.g., men, young persons, and the nonreligious may benefit more than women, older individuals, and persons with religious backgrounds), and some subjects may be adversely affected. Further, previous experience with sensory restriction may produce a cumulative effect, so that each time a person undergoes restriction, it has a greater effect.

Hearing

Learning Objective 6.3
Describe the physical and psychological properties of sound.

Listening to a Beethoven symphony is delightful and intriguing, but it is difficult because so much is going on at once. With more than 20 instruments playing, the listener must process many sounds, rhythms, and intensities simultaneously. Not all hearing is this difficult, but it is still a complex process. As in seeing, hearing involves converting physical stimuli into a psychological experience.

For example, suppose that a tuning fork is struck or a stereo system booms out a bass note. In both cases, sound waves are being created, and air is being moved. The movement of the air and the accompanying changes in air pressure (i.e., physical stimuli) cause the eardrum to move back and forth rapidly. The movement of the eardrum sets in motion a series of mechanical and electrochemical changes that people psychologically experience as sound.

Sound

When any object is set in motion, be it a tuning fork, the reed of a clarinet, or a person's vocal cords, its vibrations cause sound waves. You can place your hand in front of a stereo speaker (or over your throat) and feel the displacement of sound waves when the volume is turned up (or when you sing). **Sound** is often thought of in terms of two psychological aspects, pitch and loudness, which correspond to several physical attributes, especially frequency and amplitude. **Frequency** is the number of times a complete change in air pressure occurs during a given unit of time. Within 1 second, for example, there may be 50 complete changes (50 cycles per second) or 10,000 complete changes (10,000 cycles per second). Frequency determines the *pitch,* or tone, of a sound; high-pitched tones usually have high frequencies. Frequency is usually measured in hertz (Hz); 1 Hz equals 1 cycle per second. Middle C on a piano has a frequency of 262 cycles per second (or 262 Hz). When a piano hammer strikes a short string on a piano (at the far right), the string vibrates at a high frequency and sounds high in pitch; when long strings (at the far left) are struck, they vibrate less frequently and sound low in pitch.

The **amplitude,** or intensity, of a sound wave determines its perceived loudness. High-amplitude sound waves have more energy; they apply greater force to the ear (see Figure 6.2). Amplitude is measured in decibels. Every increase of 20 decibels corresponds to a 10-fold increase in intensity. (Decibels are a *logarithmic* scale which means that the increases are exponential, not linear, so the increases in sound intensity measured in decibels are really quite steep.) Normal speech occurs at about 60 decibels, and painful sounds occur at about 120 decibels.

Amplitude and frequency are not correlated. A low-frequency sound can be very loud or very soft—that is, it can have either high or low amplitude. Middle C on a piano, for example, can be loud or soft. The frequency (pitch) of the sound stays the same—it is still middle C; only its amplitude (loudness) varies. It is important to note that our psychological experience (i.e., the perception of loudness) depends on other factors, such as background noise and whether we are paying

sound: A psychological term describing changes in pressure through a medium.

frequency: A measure of the number of complete pressure waves per unit of time, expressed in hertz (Hz), cycles per second.

amplitude: The intensity or total energy of a sound wave, which determines the loudness of a sound; usually measured in decibels.

High amplitude sound waves, such as those generated by this jazz fusion band, have greater energy and a greater impact on the sensitive structure of our ears.

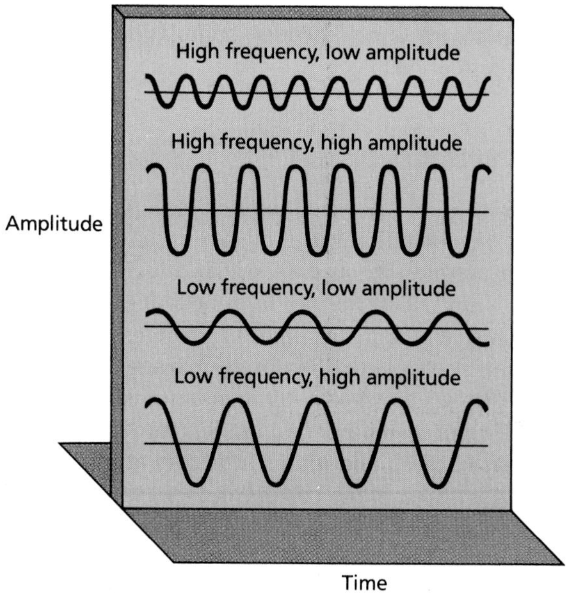

Figure 6.2

Frequency and amplitude are independent. High-frequency waves can be of high amplitude (and sound loud) or of low amplitude (and sound quiet). The top row of vibrations would sound high-pitched and quiet; the second row would be high-pitched and loud. The third row would sound low-pitched and quiet, and the fourth row would be low-pitched and loud.

attention to the sound. Another psychological dimension, *timbre,* refers to the quality of a sound—the different mixture of amplitudes and frequencies that make up a sound. Our perception of all these sound qualities depends on the physical structures of our ears.

Structure of the Ear

Learning Objective 6.4
List and describe the parts of the ear, and explain how each part functions to process sound waves.

The ear is the receptive organ for *audition,* or hearing. It translates physical stimuli (sound waves) into electrical impulses that the brain can interpret. The ear has three major parts: the outer ear, the middle ear, and the inner ear. The tissue on the outside of the head is part of the outer ear. The eardrum (*tympanic membrane*) is the boundary between the outer and middle ear. When sound waves enter the ear, they produce changes in the pressure of the air on the eardrum. The eardrum responds to these changes by vibrating (just as musical drums vibrate in response to pressure from a drumstick).

The middle ear is quite small. Within it, tiny bones known as *ossicles* help to convert the large forces that are striking the eardrum into a small force that proceeds to the next structure of the ear. When the sound is extremely loud (such as when a person vocalizes loudly or is exposed to an annoying loud noise), two small muscles attached to the ossicles contract involuntarily. They help protect humans from the damaging effects of a loud noise that could overstimulate the delicate mechanisms of the inner ear (Borg & Counter, 1989). Ultimately, the ossicles stimulate the *basilar membrane,* which runs down the middle of the length of the *cochlea,* a spiral tube in the inner ear. Figure 6.3 shows the major structures in the middle and inner ear.

In the cochlea, which is shaped like a snail's shell and comprises three chambers, sound waves of different frequencies stimulate different areas of the basilar membrane. These areas, in turn, stimulate hair cells that bring about the initial electrical coding of sound waves. These electrical impulses make their way through the brain's auditory nervous system in much the same way that visual information proceeds through the visual nervous system. The electrochemical neuronal impulses proceed through the auditory nerve to the midbrain and finally to the auditory cortex. Studies of single cells in the auditory areas of the brain show that some cells are more responsive to certain frequencies than to others. Such results are analogous to those reported by Hubel and Wiesel, who found receptive visual fields in which proper stimulation brought about dramatic changes in the firing of a cell.

Theories of Hearing

Learning Objective 6.5
Explain how sound perception occurs, according to both place and frequency theories, and discuss how modern researchers explain our ability to hear.

Most theories of hearing fall into two major classes: place theories and frequency theories. *Place theories* claim that the analysis of sound occurs in the basilar membrane, with different frequencies and intensities affecting different parts of (places on) the membrane. They assert that each sound wave causes a traveling wave on the basilar membrane, which in turn causes changes in the basilar membrane's displacement. The hair cells on the basilar membrane are displaced by the traveling wave, and the displacement of individual hair cells triggers specific information about pitch (see Figure 6.4 on page 112). By contrast, *frequency theories* maintain that the analysis of pitch and intensity occurs at higher levels of processing (perhaps in the auditory area of the cortex) and that the basilar membrane merely transfers information to those higher centers. Frequency theory suggests that the entire basilar membrane is stimulated, and its overall rate of responding is transferred to the auditory nerve and beyond, where analysis takes place.

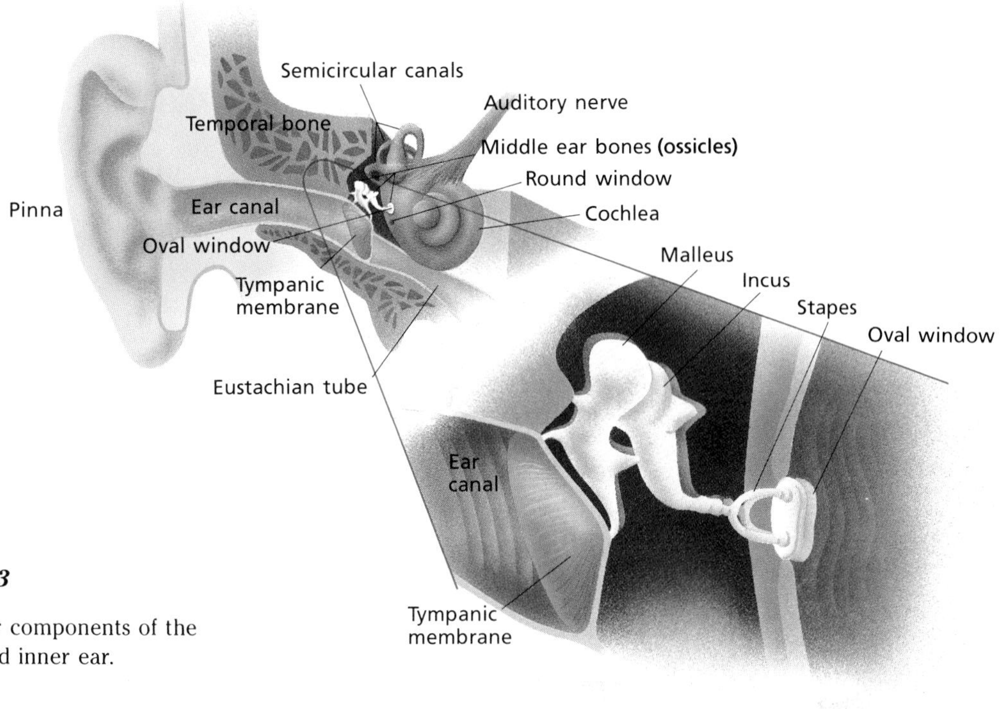

Figure 6.3

The major components of the middle and inner ear.

Both types of theories present theoretical problems, and neither explains all the data about pitch and loudness. For example, the hair cells do not act independently (as place theory suggests) but together (as frequency theory suggests). Further, the rate at which hair cells fire is not fast enough to keep up with sound waves (e.g., 1000 cycles per second), as frequency theory suggests. To get around the difficulties, modern researchers have developed theories of auditory information processing that attempt to explain pitch both in terms of specific action in parts of the basilar membrane *and* in terms of complex frequency analyses at higher levels. Theories that seem at odds with one another can work together to explain pitch and loudness when the best of both theories is combined. (Does this remind you of the debate between the trichromatic theory and the opponent-process theory of color coding?)

conduction deafness: Deafness resulting from interference with the transmission of sound to the neural mechanism of the inner ear.

sensorineural deafness: Impairment in hearing as a result of damage to the cochlea, the auditory nerve, or higher auditory processing centers.

Hearing Impairment

Learning Objective 6.6 Describe two types of hearing impairments and some of the problems they can create for people.

Not everyone has perfect hearing. About 13 million people in the United States have hearing impairments, which range from minor hearing losses to total deafness. The causes of the impairments are various and lead to varying degrees of conduction deafness, sensorineural deafness, or a combination of conduction and sensorineural deafness.

Conduction deafness results from interference in transmitting the sound to the neural mechanism of the inner ear. The interference may be caused by something simple, such as a head cold or a buildup of wax in the outer ear canal. Far more serious, it may be caused by hardening of the tympanic membrane, destruction of the tiny bones (ossicles) within the ear, or diseases that create pressure in the middle ear. If the person can be aided in transmitting the sound past the point of the conduction problem, hearing can be improved.

Sensorineural deafness results from damage to the cochlea, the auditory nerve, or higher centers in the brain. The most common cause is exposure to

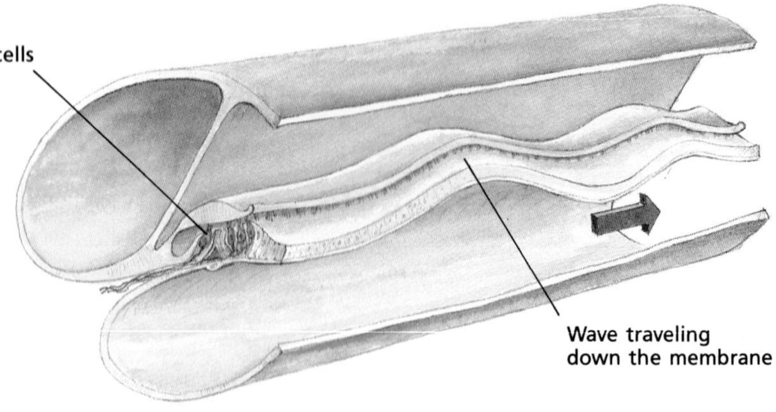

Figure 6.4

The basilar membrane. The cochlea has been unwound and cut open to reveal the basilar membrane, which is covered with thousands of hair cells. Pressure waves in the fluid filling the cochlea cause oscillations to travel in waves down the basilar membrane, stimulating the hair cells.

very high-intensity sound, such as a rock band or jet planes. Listening to even moderately loud music for longer than 15 minutes per day can cause permanent damage. The normal exposure to sound during a lifetime explains the common hearing difficulties of old age, particularly in terms of high-frequency sound, which is above the normal frequency range for speech (1000–5000 Hz).

Hearing impairments can create special problems for children. Too many schoolchildren have been diagnosed as having low intelligence and have been labeled as stupid by their classmates when they actually only suffer from hearing losses. Sometimes, children with partial hearing do not even realize that they are missing much of what is said to them. You can easily see that hearing and vision have many similarities in their perceptual mechanisms. In both perceptual systems, physical energy is transduced into electrochemical energy. Coding takes place at several locations in the brain, and people can have impairments in either visual or auditory abilities. As we study taste and smell, watch again for similarities among the perceptual systems.

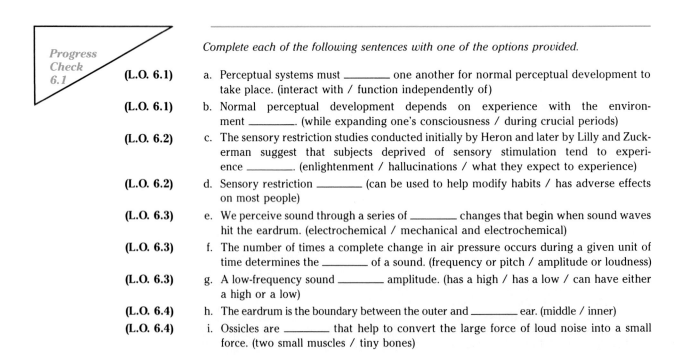

Progress Check 6.1

Complete each of the following sentences with one of the options provided.

(L.O. 6.1) a. Perceptual systems must ________ one another for normal perceptual development to take place. (interact with / function independently of)

(L.O. 6.1) b. Normal perceptual development depends on experience with the environment ________. (while expanding one's consciousness / during crucial periods)

(L.O. 6.2) c. The sensory restriction studies conducted initially by Heron and later by Lilly and Zuckerman suggest that subjects deprived of sensory stimulation tend to experience ________. (enlightenment / hallucinations / what they expect to experience)

(L.O. 6.2) d. Sensory restriction ________ (can be used to help modify habits / has adverse effects on most people)

(L.O. 6.3) e. We perceive sound through a series of ________ changes that begin when sound waves hit the eardrum. (electrochemical / mechanical and electrochemical)

(L.O. 6.3) f. The number of times a complete change in air pressure occurs during a given unit of time determines the ________ of a sound. (frequency or pitch / amplitude or loudness)

(L.O. 6.3) g. A low-frequency sound ________ amplitude. (has a high / has a low / can have either a high or a low)

(L.O. 6.4) h. The eardrum is the boundary between the outer and ________ ear. (middle / inner)

(L.O. 6.4) i. Ossicles are ________ that help to convert the large force of loud noise into a small force. (two small muscles / tiny bones)

(L.O. 6.5) j. Place theories suggest that the ________ on the basilar membrane codes specific information about pitch. (displacement of hair cells / movement of muscles)

(L.O. 6.5) k. Modern researchers ________ place and frequency theories to provide an explanation for how we perceive sound. (no longer use / combine the best of)

(L.O. 6.6) l. Damage to the cochlea or auditory nerve can lead to ________ deafness. (sensorineural / conduction)

(L.O. 6.6) m. As people age, they frequently develop hearing impairments that involve ________. (frequencies common to normal speech / sounds in the high-frequency range)

Taste and Smell

Learning Objective 6.7 Explain how our taste and olfactory perceptual systems code chemical stimuli.

Try the following experiment. Cut a fresh onion in half and inhale its odor while you have a piece of raw potato in your mouth. Now chew the potato. Does the potato taste like an onion? This experiment demonstrates that taste and smell are closely linked. Food contains substances that act as stimuli for both taste and smell.

Taste

I (LL) remember the first time I was in a cheese store. My father was supposed to buy some cheese and crackers because special company was coming for dinner. The store owner allowed me to sample a variety of cheeses: Swiss, blue, cheddar, Gruyère, Gorgonzola, and Brie. The cheddar was too sharp; the blue cheese tasted bitter; and the Swiss was bland in comparison. We finally decided on a large slice of Brie; it was soft and creamy, with a slightly sweet, mild flavor. I was overwhelmed by the quantity of cheeses and their different tastes and smells.

Taste is a chemical sense and refers to the flavor of a substance. Food placed in the mouth is partially dissolved in saliva and stimulates *taste buds,* the primary receptors for taste stimuli. When substances contact taste buds, we experience taste. The taste buds are found on small bumps on the tongue—*papillae.* Each hill-like papilla is separated from the next by a trenchlike moat, on the walls of which are located the taste buds, which can be seen only under a microscope. Each taste bud (human beings have about 10,000 of them) consists of several *taste cells.* Taste cells last only about 10 days and are constantly being renewed.

Although psychologists still do not know exactly how many tastes there are, most agree that there are four basic ones: sweet, sour, salty, and bitter. Most foods contain more than one primary taste; foods such as veal parmigiana, for example, offer a complicated stimulus to the tongue, and they also stimulate the sense of smell (described in the following subsection). All taste cells are sensitive to all taste stimuli, but certain cells are more sensitive to some stimuli than to others. (In this regard, they are much like the cones in the retina, which are sensitive to all wavelengths, but which are especially sensitive to a specific range of wavelengths.) By isolating stimuli that initiate only one taste sensation, psychologists have found that certain regions of the tongue seem to be more sensitive to particular taste stimuli than others. The tip of the tongue, for example, is more sensitive to sweet tastes than the back of the tongue, and the sides are especially sensitive to sour tastes (see Figure 6.5 on the next page).

The taste of a particular food or liquid depends on its chemical makeup, but it also depends on our past experiences with this or similar foods, how much saliva is being mixed into the food as we chew, and how long we chew the food. A food that is chewed well has a stronger taste than one that is chewed quickly and swallowed. A food that rests on the tongue for a long time will even lose its

olfaction: [ole-FAK-shun] The sense of smell.

flavor—in this case, *sensory adaptation* has occurred. Further, a food that loses its texture by being mashed up, blended, or mixed with other foods has less taste and is less appealing to most adults. Thus a flavor or taste experience, much like our other perceptual systems, depends not only on a sensory event, but also on past experience and other sensory and perceptual variables.

Smell

Like the sense of taste, **olfaction** (smell) is a chemical sense. That is, the stimulus for smell is a chemical in the air. The olfactory system in human beings is remarkably sensitive and can recognize a smell from as few as 40 or 50 molecules of a chemical. For the sensation of smell to occur, chemicals must move toward the receptor cells located on the walls of the nasal passage. This happens when we breathe them in through our nostrils or take them in via the back of the throat when we chew and swallow. When a chemical substance in the air moves past these receptor cells, it is partially absorbed into the mucus that covers the cells, thereby initiating the process of smell. (See Figure 6.6.)

For human beings to perceive smell, information must be sent to the brain. At the top of the nasal cavity is the *olfactory epithelium,* which contains the olfactory rods, the nerve fibers that transmit information about smell to the brain. There can be as many as 30 million olfactory rods in each nostril, making the olfactory system very sensitive.

Theories of smell involve both the stimulus for smell and the structure of the receptor system. Some theories posit a few basic smells; others suggest many, including flowery, foul, fruity, resinous, spicy, and burnt. Psychologists are not unanimous on a single classification system for smells, nor do they completely understand how odors affect the receptor cells. Research into the coding of smell is intense, and physiological psychologists make headway each year. Another area in which important progress has been made is about how and whether odors affect human behavior. We consider this issue in the Understanding the Research Process box on page 116.

Figure 6.5

The taste buds sensitive to specific basic tastes are distributed unevenly across the tongue. A blowup of a vertical cross-section of one of the tiny bumps (papillae) on the tongue shows that taste buds are found in the little trenches around the papillae.

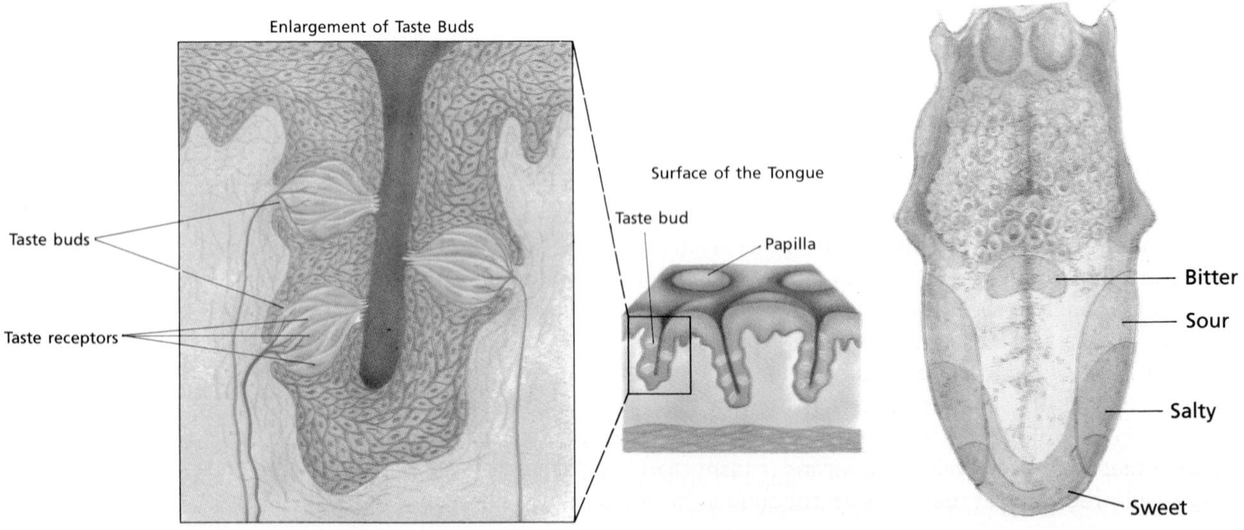

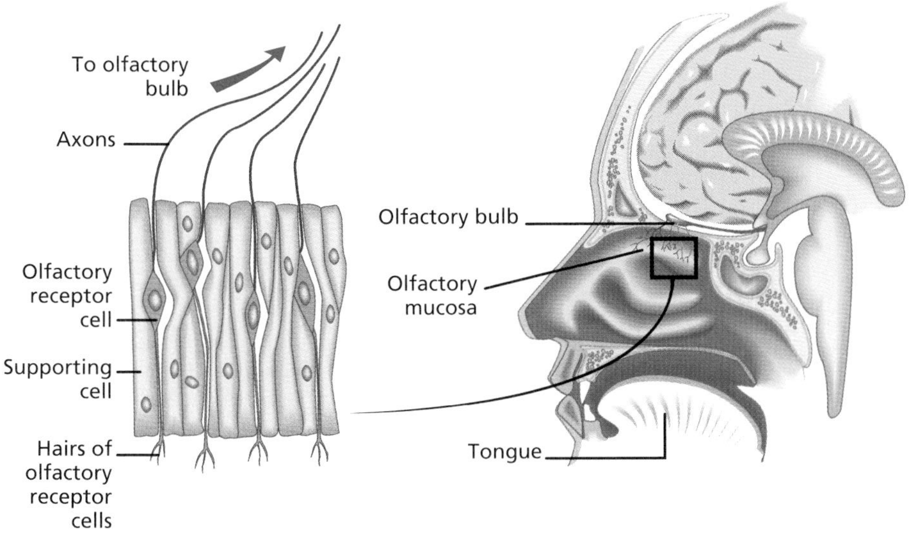

Figure 6.6

The olfactory system.

The Skin Senses

Learning Objective 6.8 Describe the structure and functions of the skin, and explain how various sensations are perceived through the skin.

Our skin, an organ of our body, contains a wide range of receptors that convey information about touch, pressure, warmth, cold, and pain. In each case, a stimulus is converted into neural energy, and then the brain interprets that neural energy into a psychological experience. Skin receptors ultimately send information to the somatosensory cortex of the brain.

Touch

The skin acts as the housing for our *sense of touch,* our *tactile system.* The skin is more than just a binding that holds a person together. The skin of an adult human being measures roughly two square yards and comprises three major layers:

1. The top layer, or *epidermis* (*epi* means "outer," among other things), consists primarily of dead cells and varies in thickness. On the face, it is thin; on the elbows and heels of the feet, it is quite thick. The epidermis is constantly regenerating; in fact, every 28 days or so, all of its cells are replaced.
2. The layer underneath the epidermis—the *dermis*—contains live cells as well as a supply of nerve endings, blood, hair cells, and oil-producing (*sebaceous*) glands. The dermis and epidermis, which are resilient, flexible, and quite thick, protect the body against quick changes in temperature and pressure. In particular, the epidermis guards against pain from small scratches and bumps.
3. The deepest layer, the *hypodermis* (*hypo* generally means "under"), is a thick insulating cushion.

Specialized receptors are responsible for relaying information about the *skin senses*—pain, touch, and temperature (warmth and cold). The receptors for each of these different senses vary in shape, size, number, and distribution. For example, the body has many more cold receptors than heat receptors; it has more pain receptors behind the knee than on the top of the nose. In the most sensitive areas of the hand, there are as many as 1300 nerve endings per square inch.

The skin sense receptors appear to interact with one another; sometimes, one sensation seems to combine with or change to another. Thus, increasing pressure can become pain. Similarly, an itch seems to result from a low level of irritation

UNDERSTANDING THE RESEARCH PROCESS

Smell and Communication

Although human beings have a good sense of smell, it pales by comparison to that of some animals. For example, dogs have 100 times as many olfactory receptors as human beings. Dogs use their sense of smell to recognize objects and other animals. Dogs use their acute smell abilities to sniff out marijuana, cocaine, natural-gas leaks, and bombs (Gibbons, 1986). Dogs can even discriminate among dog, cat, and squirrel urine, and through their sense of smell, they can know whether another dog is interested in or ready for a sexual encounter.

Animals secrete pheromones (pronounced "FER-uh-moans"), scented chemical substances which are then detected by other animals. Thus, pheromones act as means of communication: In fact, the scents released by one animal influence the physiology of another animal. There are two major kinds of pheromones: primary and releaser. *Primary pheromones* alter an organism's physiology by releasing hormones that change the way the organism will respond in the future, perhaps in 2 hours or a day later. *Releaser pheromones* usually trigger a relatively immediate behavioral response.

Pheromones are widely recognized as initiators of sexual activity. For example, female silkworms release a pheromone that can attract a male silkworm from miles away. Similarly, when female hamsters are sexually receptive, they emit a highly odorous substance that attracts males (Montgomery-St. Laurent, Fullenkamp, & Fischer, 1988) and mice are similarly equipped (Coppola & O'Connell, 1988). The impact of the release of a pheromone can be extreme: Early in pregnancy, if mice detect the odor of a strange mouse, they will abort their fetuses in order to keep them from being attacked.

Many animals emit pheromones to elicit specific behavioral reactions; others, notably dogs, use scents from their feces and urine simply to maintain territories and identify one another. Beavers attempt to keep strangers out of their territory by depositing foul-smelling substances emitted by sacs near the anus. Reindeer have scent glands between their toes that leave a trail for the rest of the herd. Communication through pheromones is found throughout the animal world, but do human beings share this ability?

Researchers have long known that the sexual and aggressive behavior of hamsters is under control of cues from the sense of smell. One study showed that adult male rats who were raised by lemon-scented mothers copulate more effectively with rats that smell of lemons (Fillion & Blass, 1986). Though people have always said that a kind of chemistry exists between close friends, few really believed that one person's secretions might alter another person's behavior, and it was generally thought that human beings do not communicate through smell; however, groundbreaking research in the 1970s began to change psychologists' thinking about smell and communication. McClintock (1971) found that menstrual periods of women who were either roommates or close friends in a college dormitory become roughly *synchronous*. That is, after they lived together for several months, their menstrual cycles began and ended at about the same time. McClintock and others began to

of nerve endings in the skin; however, a tickle can be caused by the same stimulus and produce a reflexlike response. Further, we are far more sensitive to pressure in some parts of our bodies than in other parts (compare your fingers to your thigh); the more sensitive areas have more receptors than do less sensitive areas.

Pain

Learning Objective 6.9
Discuss pain as a perceptual system, the gate control theory, and the effects of drug treatment for the relief of pain.

Generally, people look forward to sensory experiences. One exception is the sensation of pain. Pain is the most common symptom found in medical settings; nevertheless, pain is adaptive and necessary. In rare cases, children have been born without the ability to feel pain, which places them in constant danger because encounters with caustic substances, violent collisions, and deep cuts elicit no painful cautions to avoid such experiences. Further, they do not recognize conditions such as broken bones, serious burns, or the sharp pains that signal appendicitis, which would send most of us to the doctor to seek attention.

question whether the synchronization of the menstrual cycles was due to some type of chemical message.

In the mid-1980s, two studies stirred up the pheromone debate. These studies were conducted by two scientists, Cutler and Preti, and they focused on a specific issue: Could chemical signals from other people—both men and women—alter women's menstrual cycles? They sought to test McClintock's idea that synchronization of the menstrual cycles was caused by some type of chemical message—pheromones. They used a fascinating technique. They swabbed underarm secretions on the lips of women to see whether these chemicals affected their menstrual cycles.

In the first study, underarm secretions from men were gathered on swabs that they wore under their armpits (Cutler, Preti, Krieger, Huggins, Garcia, & Lawley, 1986). This male smell was then swabbed on the upper lips of seven women whose menstrual cycles were either short (under 26 days) or long (over 33 days). The female subjects were told that they were receiving a "natural fragrance" that was injected into alcohol. The study was double-blind—neither the subjects nor the experimenter knew which of the subjects were receiving the underarm smell and which were receiving the control smell that had nothing other than alcohol.

Within 3 months, the menstrual cycles of the experimental subjects became similar and approached the norm of 29.5 days. The researchers did a similar study, also double-blind, with secretions from other women (Preti, Cutler, Garcia, Huggins, & Lawley, 1986). As in the first study, women were swabbed on their upper lip either with underarm secretions or with the alcohol (control) substance. Results were again similar. The times of menstruation all became similar and approached the norm. The smell affected the womens' menstrual cycles; pheromones were causing the change.

A problem with the Cutler and Preti research is that they used a limited number of subjects; in the first study, there were 15 subjects, and in the second, 19 subjects. Because of this, the researchers were cautious in making generalizations. However, the study was well designed; its results were highly regarded because it was double-blind, used an experimental method with control groups, and produced results that were statistically analyzed as being significant.

These data suggest that the smell of other human beings affects physiological processes in women. The Cutler and Preti studies also suggest that pheromones emitted by a man may also alter a woman's menstrual cycle. The data suggest that women who live with men may have more regular cycles and thus may be more fertile than those who live alone (see Cutler et al., 1986).

Other people's physiological processes may affect us, but the evidence that smell affects human behavior is still suggestive. The effects of pheromones in animals is profound, but the role of pheromones in human beings still remains controversial and is being studied in a wide number of situations. Nevertheless, perfume makers have been sent into a frenzy of activity trying to make a perfume with pheromonelike abilities.

- ▲ ***What evidence existed to make researchers speculate and then hypothesize that human beings might have pheromones?***
- ▲ ***What was the importance of using a double-blind procedure in the Cutler and Preti study of underarm secretions?***
- ▲ ***What is a serious limitation of the Cutler and Preti study, which limits the researchers' ability to generalize their results?***

Studying pain is difficult because it can be elicited in so many ways. Stomach pains may be caused by hunger or the flu, toothaches by a cavity or an abscess, and headaches by stress, eye strain, or any number of different causes. Myriad kinds of pain exist, including sunburn pain, pain from terminal cancer, labor pains, frostbite, and even pain when a limb is lost as a result of trauma or surgery (Melzack & Loeser, 1978). Psychologists use several kinds of stimuli to study pain. Among them are chemicals, extreme heat and cold, and electrical shock (Flor & Turk, 1989). Most researchers believe that the receptors for pain are free nerve endings located throughout the body.

Some areas of the body are more sensitive to pain than others. For example, the sole of the foot and the ball of the thumb are less sensitive than the back of the knee and the neck. Also, though an individual's pain threshold remains fairly constant, different individuals possess different reactions to pain. Some people have a low threshold for pain; they will report a comparatively low-level stimulus as being painful. Others have fairly high pain thresholds. However, pain is partly

Pain is a complex experience both physically and psychologically.

psychological, and much depends on a person's experience and attitude and the situation in which the pain occurs. For example, athletes often report not feeling the pain of an injury until after the competition has ended. What allows pain suppression? How does the body process, interpret, and stop pain? Gate control theory may offer an answer.

Gate Control Theory. A widely accepted explanation of how the body processes pain is the Melzack–Wall gate control theory (Melzack & Wall, 1970). The theory is complex, taking into account the sizes of nerve fibers, their level of development, and the interplay of excitatory and inhibitory cells that can diminish painful sensations. The theory contends that when a signal that might normally indicate a painful stimulus is sent to the brain, it goes through a series of gates. These gates can be opened or closed either fully or partially. How far they open determines how much of the original pain signal gets through. A chemical called substance-P (P stands for pain), which is released by the sensory nerve fibers, transmits pain impulses across the gates. A variety of drugs, as well as electrical stimulation and acupuncture needles (Omura, 1977), are thought to close the gates partially or fully, making the original painful stimulus less potent.

Many people who suffer chronic, unrelieved pain have sought help from acupuncture. Initially developed in China thousands of years ago, *acupuncture* is a technique in which long, fine (slender) needles are inserted into the body at specific locations in order to relieve particular kinds and locations of pain. Controlled studies of acupuncture have yielded varying results, from the finding of the National Institutes of Health that reported acupuncture no more effective than sugar pills, to a few studies suggesting that it helps with mild back pain (Price et al., 1984). The controlled research and results on acupuncture are still inconclusive.

Endorphins. There have been some exciting breakthroughs in research on pain receptors and the nature of pain; consider the study of endorphins. **Endorphins** (from *endogenous,* meaning naturally occurring, and *morphine,* an opiate—that is, a painkiller, usually derived from opium) are painkillers that are naturally produced in the brain and pituitary gland. There are many kinds of endorphins, and many help regulate several bodily functions, including the control of blood pressure and body temperature (Bloom, 1981). Endorphins also can produce euphoria and a sense of well-being in the way that morphine does, but to an even greater extent. Stress, anticipated pain, and activities such as running bring about an increased endorphin level. During or after running, runners often report feeling "high," a sensation that many believe is directly related to their increased endorphin level.

Endorphins bind themselves to receptor sites in the brain and spinal cord, thereby preventing pain signals from going to higher levels of the nervous system. Naturally produced endorphins include some that increase tolerance to pain and others that actually reduce pain. *Enkephalin,* for example, is an innate brain endorphin that blocks pain signals (Snyder, 1980). Physicians prescribe synthetic endorphins or endorphinlike substances, such as morphine, to block pain.

Pain Management. Usually, the pain resulting from a headache, toothache, or small cut is temporary and can be alleviated with a simple pain medication such as aspirin. For millions of people, however, aspirin is not enough. For those who suffer from constant pain caused by back injury, arthritis, or cancer, drug treatment either is not effective, is dangerous because of the high dosages required, or is not prescribed because of fear of addiction—a fear that is often overstated in the case of pain relief (Melzack, 1990). Further, each type of pain may require a different treatment (Flor & Turk, 1989). Psychologists who deal with pain recognize that it can have both physical and psychological sources. Although pain may

endorphin: [en-DOOR-fin] Painkiller produced naturally in the brain and pituitary gland.

initially arise from physical complaints, it can continue even after the physical cause abates because it provides other benefits to the sufferer. For example, pain may provide the sufferer with attention that is reinforcing to the sufferer, or the pain may provide a distraction from other problems. Psychological treatment focuses on helping people cope with pain regardless of its origins; for example, psychologists help pain suffers through hypnosis (Chapter 4) or through cognitive coping strategies. With cognitive coping strategies, psychologists teach people to have a better attitude toward their pain. In these approaches, people learn to talk to themselves in positive direct ways, to divert attention to pleasant images, and to take an active role in managing their pain and transcending the experience.

Many new technologies are emerging to help people manage pain. Solomon Snyder, a leader in pain research, reasons that something must happen at the site of an injury to trigger endorphin production. What if a drug could stop the whole pain perception process at the actual place where an injury occurs? Solomon, Innis, and Manning are studying the receptor sites in skin tissue and observing how chemicals bind to them (Bishop, 1986). They hope to find compounds that will stop the entire pain perception process, even before endorphin production starts. The compounds they discover may not completely relieve all pain, but in combination with other mild pain medications, such as aspirin, they may be very effective.

kinesthesis: [kin-iss-THEE-sis] The awareness aroused by movements of the muscles, tendons, and joints; a form of *proprioception.*

vestibular sense: [ves-TIB-you-lar] The sense of bodily orientation and postural adjustment; another form of *proprioception.*

Kinesthesis and Vestibular Sensitivity

Learning Objective 6.10 Define *kinesthesis,* and describe the vestibular sense.

Kinesthesis refers to awareness aroused by movements of the muscles, tendons, and joints. It is what allows you to touch your finger to your nose with your eyes closed, to leap over hurdles during a track-and-field event, to dance without stepping on your partner's feet, and so on. The study of kinethesis provides information about bodily movements. The movements of muscles around your eye, for example, help to let you know how far away objects are. Kinesthesia and your other internal sensations such as a stomach upset) are *proprioception,* which means the sensations that you experience coming from within your body.

The **vestibular sense** is the sense of bodily orientation and postural adjustment; it helps us keep our balance and sense of equilibrium. The structures essential to these functions are in the ear. Vestibular sacs and semicircular canals, which are associated with the body wall of the cochlea, provide information about the orientations of the head and body relative to the eye-movement and posture systems (Parker, 1980). The vestibular sense allows you to walk on a balance beam without falling off, to know which way is up after diving into the water, and to sense that you are turning a corner on a ride even when your eyes are closed.

Rapid movements of the head bring about changes in the semicircular canals. These changes induce eye movements to help compensate for head changes and changes in body orientation. They may also be accompanied by physical sensations ranging from pleasant dizziness to unbearable motion sickness. Studies of the vestibular sense help scientists understand what happens to people during space travel and under conditions of weightlessness.

Extrasensory Perception

Learning Objective 6.11 Discuss extrasensory perception as it fits into the field of contemporary psychology.

Vision, hearing, taste, smell, touch, and even pain are all part of the normal sensory experience of human beings. Some people, however, claim that there are other perceptual experiences that not all normal human beings recognize as such. People have been fascinated by *extrasensory perception,* or ESP, for hundreds of years. The British Society for the Study of Psychic Phenomena has investigated reports of ESP since the 19th century. Early experimenters tested for ESP by asking subjects to guess the symbols on what are now called ESP cards, each marked with a star, a cross, a circle, a square, or a set of wavy lines. One of the most consistently successful guessers once guessed 25 cards in a row, an event with the odds of nearly 300 quadrillion to one of happening by chance.

ESP includes several different phenomena. *Telepathy* is the transfer of thought from one person to another. *Clairvoyance* is the ability to recognize objects or events, such as the contents of a message in a sealed envelope, that are not present to normal sensory receptors. *Precognition* is unexplained knowledge about future events, such as knowing when the phone is about to ring. *Psychokinesis* refers to the ability to move objects by using only one's mental powers.

Support for the existence of ESP is generally weak and has not been repeated very often. Moreover, ESP phenomena such as bending a spoon through mental manipulation and "reading people's minds" are not affected by experimental manipulations in the way that other perceptual events are. In addition, the National Research Council has denounced the scientific merit of most of these experiments. None of these criticisms means that ESP does not exist, and active research using scientific methods continues. However, as Child (1985) suggests, psychologists see so much trickery and falsification of data and so many design errors in experiments on this subject that they remain skeptical.

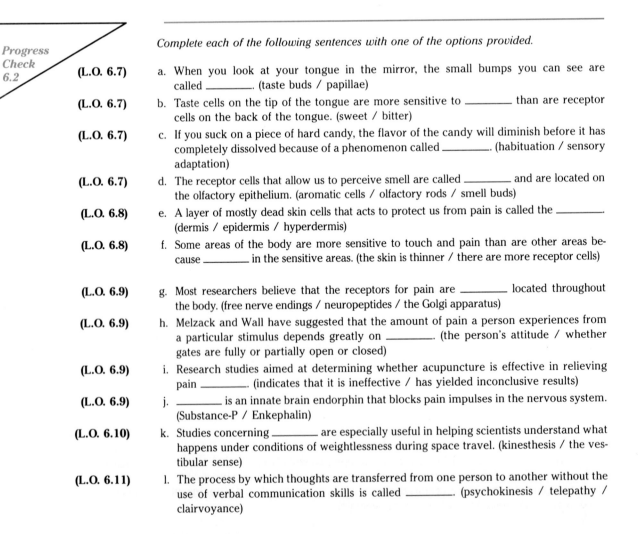

Progress Check 6.2

Complete each of the following sentences with one of the options provided.

(L.O. 6.7) a. When you look at your tongue in the mirror, the small bumps you can see are called ________. (taste buds / papillae)

(L.O. 6.7) b. Taste cells on the tip of the tongue are more sensitive to ________ than are receptor cells on the back of the tongue. (sweet / bitter)

(L.O. 6.7) c. If you suck on a piece of hard candy, the flavor of the candy will diminish before it has completely dissolved because of a phenomenon called ________. (habituation / sensory adaptation)

(L.O. 6.7) d. The receptor cells that allow us to perceive smell are called ________ and are located on the olfactory epithelium. (aromatic cells / olfactory rods / smell buds)

(L.O. 6.8) e. A layer of mostly dead skin cells that acts to protect us from pain is called the ________. (dermis / epidermis / hyperdermis)

(L.O. 6.8) f. Some areas of the body are more sensitive to touch and pain than are other areas because ________ in the sensitive areas. (the skin is thinner / there are more receptor cells)

(L.O. 6.9) g. Most researchers believe that the receptors for pain are ________ located throughout the body. (free nerve endings / neuropeptides / the Golgi apparatus)

(L.O. 6.9) h. Melzack and Wall have suggested that the amount of pain a person experiences from a particular stimulus depends greatly on ________. (the person's attitude / whether gates are fully or partially open or closed)

(L.O. 6.9) i. Research studies aimed at determining whether acupuncture is effective in relieving pain ________. (indicates that it is ineffective / has yielded inconclusive results)

(L.O. 6.9) j. ________ is an innate brain endorphin that blocks pain impulses in the nervous system. (Substance-P / Enkephalin)

(L.O. 6.10) k. Studies concerning ________ are especially useful in helping scientists understand what happens under conditions of weightlessness during space travel. (kinesthesis / the vestibular sense)

(L.O. 6.11) l. The process by which thoughts are transferred from one person to another without the use of verbal communication skills is called ________. (psychokinesis / telepathy / clairvoyance)

Module Summary

Sensory Experience

- Studies of sensory deprivation have shown that an organism's early experience is important in the development and proper functioning of its perceptual systems (pp. 106–107).

Hearing

- *Sound* is a psychological term. The frequency and amplitude of a sound wave determine how it will be experienced by a listener (p. 109).
- The ear has three main parts: the outer ear, the middle ear, and the inner ear. Place theories of hearing claim that the analysis of sound takes place in the inner ear; frequency theories claim that the analysis of pitch and intensity takes place at higher levels of processing (p. 110).

Taste and Smell

- The tongue contains thousands of bumps, or *papillae,* each of which is separated from the next by a trenchlike moat. The taste buds are located on the walls of the moats. Each taste bud consists of several *taste cells* (p. 113).
- The *olfactory epithelium* contains the *olfactory rods,* the nerve fibers that process odors (p. 113).

The Skin Senses

- The skin is made up of three layers: The top layer is the *epidermis,* the layer underneath the epidermis is the *dermis,* and the deepest layer, the *hypodermis,* is a thick insulating cushion (p. 115).

Kinesthesis and Vestibular Sensitivity

- *Kinesthesis* refers to the feelings aroused by movements of the muscles, tendons, and joints. The *vestibular sense* is the sense of bodily orientation and postural adjustment (p. 119).

Extrasensory Perception

- ESP includes several different phenomena: telepathy, clairvoyance, precognition, and psychokinesis. Support for the existence of ESP is generally weak (p. 119).

KEY TERMS

amplitude, p. 109
conduction deafness, p. 111
endorphins, p. 118
frequency, p. 109
kinesthesis, p. 119
olfaction, p. 114
sensorineural deafness, p. 111
sound, p. 109
vestibular sense, p. 119

SELF-TEST

Module 6

- Before taking the self-test, **recite** and **review.**
- Use the key at the back of the text to *correct* your answers.
- *Restudy* pages that correspond to any questions you answered incorrectly.

1. In their study of visual–motor coordination with kittens, Held and Hein found that ________________ in the kittens that were prevented from experiencing normal interaction of perceptual systems.
   a. visually guided motor movements lacked coordination
   b. visual perception was distorted, but motor coordination was normal
   c. one system became the dominant system, while the others showed impairment
   d. visual and motor systems developed separately

2. Human sensory restriction studies conducted initially by Heron and later by Lilly and Zuckerman
   a. illustrate the importance of being cautious when interpreting experimental data.
   b. provide convincing evidence that humans become bored and irritable if deprived of sensory stimulation for long periods of time.
   c. show that humans automatically relax and meditate when they are not distracted by outside stimuli.
   d. prove that immersion in a salt-water isolation tank is a constructive way to expand one's consciousness.
3. Cross out the characteristics that are *not* psychological aspects of sound.
   a. background noise and attention
   b. pitch and loudness
   c. frequency and amplitude
   d. timbre or quality
4. The technical term used in reference to the *eardrum* is
   a. tympanic membrane.
   b. basilar membrane.
   c. cochlea.
   d. ossicle.
5. Frequency theories of hearing maintain that the analysis of sound takes place
   a. at higher processing levels, such as in the auditory area of the cortex.
   b. in the basilar membrane of the inner ear.
   c. when air pressure changes stimulate the eardrum.
   d. when tiny bones and small muscles in the middle ear move.
6. Conduction deafness can be caused by all of the following *except*
   a. a hardening of the tympanic membrane.
   b. a severe head cold or a buildup of wax in the outer ear canal.
   c. diseases that create pressure in the middle ear.
   d. exposure to very high-intensity sound.
7. Genie enjoys anchovies on her pizza; Joe says he hates them. This difference is probably the result of
   a. Genie and Joe's past experience with eating anchovies or other exotic foods.
   b. how long Joe and Genie tend to chew their food.
   c. the amount of saliva that is secreted into their mouths when they eat pizza.
   d. a is correct; b and c also could be true explanations.
8. Cross out the statement concerning smell that is *false.*
   a. Dogs have 100 times as many olfactory receptors as humans.
   b. When compared to other perceptual systems, the olfactory sense in humans is probably the least sensitive.
   c. Our sense of smell affects our perception of taste.
   d. Like taste, smell is a chemical sense.
9. If you get a great summer tan while on vacation, when you return home to your more indoor, daily routine, you will notice that your tan fades rather quickly. This is because
   a. dermis cells cannot hold pigment.
   b. epidermis cells are completely replaced about every 28 days.
   c. hypodermis cells absorb the tanned cells.
   d. Both a and c
10. Natural painkillers that are produced by the brain and pituitary gland include
   a. morphine and substance-P.
   b. endorphins.
   c. opiate sedatives.
   d. all of the above
11. Which of the following occurs primarily because of the vestibular sense?
   a. Knowing the driver of the car you are in is making a turn even though your eyes are closed.
   b. Walking across a narrow beam without losing our balance and falling.
   c. Knowing which way is up after diving into a pool.
   d. all of the above

12. Psychologists find that research supporting the existence of extrasensory perception (ESP)
    a. describes behaviors that are not affected by experimental manipulations in the way that other, ordinary perceptual events are affected.
    b. actually disproves its existence, when evaluated carefully.
    c. shows that ESP must exist, but the studies give no explanation for how it works.
    d. has fairly strong scientific merit and should be taken more seriously by contemporary researchers.

Connections

If you are interested in . . .	Turn to . . .	To learn more about . . .
Sensory experiences in human beings	◆ Chapter 4, p. 142	How altered states of consciousness affect perception in both positive and negative ways
	◆ Chapter 15, p. 640	The impact of too much sensory experience, such as noise
The operation of our perceptual systems	◆ Chapter 4, p. 142	How feedback from our sensory systems can help manage certain bodily complaints
	◆ Chapter 6, p. 208	How the initial coding of the visual and auditory world lasts only for a brief time in the sensory register
	◆ Chapter 15, p. 602	How our perceptions of other people often come from nonverbal visual cues in the environment
The development of perception	◆ Chapter 7, p. 264	The unfolding of language and thought processes as an individual matures in the environment
	◆ Chapter 8, p. 283	How the inborn perceptual abilities of children develop over time and through experience
	◆ Chapter 8, p. 333	How sensory and perceptual abilities decline with advancing age

Our perceptual world has a biological basis that is rooted in neuroanatomy (Chapter 2, p. 57) and becomes important for most day-to-day behaviors. Our ability to learn (discussed in Chapter 5, p. 161), remember (discussed in Chapter 6, p. 203) and think (discussed in Chapter 7, p. 242) all suppose that a person has accurately perceived the world. A person's emotional response to a situation (discussed in Chapter 9, p. 381) depends on accurate perceptions, and when people develop psychological disorders (discussed in Chapter 13, p. 542), it often requires a treatment procedure (discussed in Chapter 14, p. 579) that teaches them new ways to look at and perceive the world.

Artists and designers rely on perceptual theory; they rely on environmental psychologists and industrial/organizational psychologists (discussed in Chapter 15, p. 640) to help create pleasing environments. The early Gestalt psychologists (discussed in Chapter 1, p. 17) based their entire theories on perceptual phenomena. Thus, in important ways, perceptual factors underlie a broad array of psychological phenomena, data, and theory.

Module 7 ► CONSCIOUSNESS AND SLEEP 126

Module 8 ► ALTERED STATES OF CONSCIOUSNESS 140

Chapter 4

Consciousness

Consciousness has been a controversial topic of research throughout the history of psychology. Contemporary researchers heavily emphasize the study of altered states of consciousness, such as hypnosis, sleep, and drug states. Their study may help psychologists understand how to alter behavior directly by using simple techniques. This chapter discusses theories of consciousness and how consciousness is affected by hypnosis, sleep, meditation, and drugs. Psychologists study altered states of consciousness to gain insight into normal consciousness. By comparing normal and altered states, researchers hope to understand human thought processes.

In Module 7, sleep is examined and shown to be a regularly occurring altered state of consciousness. Two kinds of sleep are discussed. It has been shown that people who have been deprived of sleep need extra sleep periods on subsequent nights. Psychologists are not certain why sleep is important; they do know that without sleep, behavior often becomes disturbed. The second part of the module presents studies of dreams. It is shown that dreams normally occur during key stages of sleep. Although people may not remember all their dreams, they dream intermittently throughout the night, and their dreams are often bizarre in imagery, characterization, and content; theories of dreaming are also presented.

The second module of this chapter, Module 8, presents altered states of consciousness other than sleep. An altered state of consciousness is a pattern of functioning that is dramatically different from that of ordinary awareness and responsiveness. An altered state of consciousness seems to occur during hypnosis, which uses trance-induction procedures. Hypnotized subjects perform tasks that they might not normally perform. They may even display rather spectacular abilities. However, studies show that other techniques, including meditation, produce effects resembling those of hypnosis.

In the 1980s and 1990s, the study of drugs and their effects on behavior has come under close scrutiny. Drugs alter behavior even more dramatically than sleep deprivation. People addicted to narcotic drugs such as heroin suffer from withdrawal symptoms if they are denied the drug and often engage in specific antisocial behaviors to maintain their drug habit. Methadone programs have helped many heroin addicts lead relatively normal lives. Other drugs are illegal but not addictive. However, even drugs that are not addictive can be abused by the people who use them. Alcoholism and its treatment are discussed at length in this module.

Module 7

Consciousness and Sleep

LEARNING OBJECTIVES

When you have mastered the material in this module, you will be able to

Consciousness (pp. 127–128)

7.1 Make distinctions both between *consciousness* and *altered state of consciousness* and between *levels* and *states* of consciousness (p. 127).

7.2 Describe Jaynes and Ornstein's theories of consciousness (p. 128).

Sleep (pp. 128–135)

7.3 Describe circadian rhythms in humans and tell how they correspond to 24-hour clock time (p. 129).

7.4 Describe the amount of sleep humans need, how sleep activity is measured, and the stages of NREM sleep and REM sleep (p. 130).

7.5 Describe the effects of sleep deprivation on behavior and on subsequent sleep patterns (p. 133).

Dreams (pp. 135–137)

7.6 Discuss the biological signs of dreaming, the frequency of dreaming and remembering dreams, and the types of dreams people have (p. 135).

7.7 Explain why we dream, according to Freud, Jung, and the activation–synthesis model (p. 136).

SQ3R
- ▲ **Survey** to set goals for studying.
- ▲ Ask **questions** as you **read**.
- ▲ Stop occasionally to **recite** and **review**.

plus
- ▲ **Write** a summary of key points.
- ▲ **Reflect** on the hypotheses, evidence, and implications of this material and on the relevance it has to *your* life.

"Had a date with Allison last night, huh?" asked Phil as he climbed into the passenger seat. "Your car smells like the inside of a perfume bottle."

"Phil, you dislike that perfume because Allison stopped dating you after she met me," retorted Frank, flicking on the headlights and nosing the car onto the highway. "I find the fragrance very sexy."

"Not to change the subject, but we better hurry if we're going to make the concert on time," said Phil, inserting a tape into the car stereo. "We should prep ourselves by listening to some old Vinyls."

"Anything but their first release," pleaded Frank, "It reminds me of the time I was in bed for a week with mono while you played Heart of Plastic incessantly."

"That was a great summer! Remember when. . . . Wow! I can't believe my eyes!"

"What? Where?" demanded Frank.

"Up there! Can't you see it? It's just like they describe it in the UFO book I'm reading."

"What? That big thing with all the flashing lights?"

"Yeah, isn't it incredible! My first UFO sighting."

"Look again, genius," sneered Frank. "That's the promotional blimp for the concert."

Phil and Frank illustrate a crucial fact of consciousness: although people see, hear, smell, feel, and taste by the same perceptual processes, their conscious experiences are also colored by individual psychological factors. This module focuses on consciousness and begins with a definition.

Consciousness

Overview

Learning Objective 7.1 Make distinctions both between *consciousness* and *altered state of consciousness* and between *levels* and *states* of consciousness.

Almost all psychologists agree that a person who is conscious is aware of the environment; for example, we are conscious when we listen to a lecture. However, being conscious also refers to inner awareness—that is, knowledge of our own thoughts, feelings, and memories. The word *conscious* describes a state of being; we say "I am conscious" or "he was conscious." The word *consciousness* also refers to the state of being conscious. So we say that "we are studying consciousness" or "he was in an altered state of consciousness."

Consciousness is the general state of being aware of and responsive to the environment and to our own mental processes. Consciousness can range from alert attention to dreaming, hypnotic trance, or drug-induced states. We say that a person in a state of consciousness that is different from the usual waking state is in an **altered state of consciousness**. Consciousness and the ongoing biological processes in our bodies are closely linked; our biological processes influence how incoming stimuli affect us and our degree of awareness about the world.

consciousness: [CON-shus-ness] The general state of being aware of and responsive to events in the environment and their own mental processes; a defining characteristic of being human.

The idea of a continuum guides many researchers who believe that consciousness is made up of several *levels* of awareness, from alertness to total unresponsiveness. Researchers who favor this view suggest, for example, that a person who is drinking heavily temporarily enters a lower (or deeper) *level* of his or her range of conscious levels—that of intoxication. Other researchers believe that distinctly different conscious *states* explain specific behaviors and attention patterns. Researchers who favor this interpretation believe that a heavy drinker has entered a totally different *state* of consciousness. This issue of levels versus states is far from resolved.

Theories of Consciousness

Learning Objective 7.2 Describe Jaynes and Ornstein's theories of consciousness.

As in other areas of psychology, theory guides research in the study of consciousness and its altered states. Several researchers have proposed biologically based theories of consciousness. Julian Jaynes (1976) suggests that understanding the evolution of the human brain is the key to understanding altered states. He believes that consciousness originates in differences in the function and physiology of the two hemispheres of the brain. Thus, when one of the two structures of the brain is operating, one specific level of consciousness will be revealed; when another structure is operating, other levels will be activated.

Robert Ornstein (1977) suggests that two modes of consciousness exist, each controlled by a different side of the brain: the active–verbal–rational mode (called the active mode) and the receptive–spatial–intuitive–holistic mode (called the receptive mode). Ornstein believes that evolution has made the active mode automatic: Human beings limit their awareness automatically in order to shut out experiences, events, and stimuli that do not directly relate to their ability to survive. When people need to gain perspective and judgment about what they are doing, they expand their normal awareness by using the receptive mode. Ornstein believes that techniques such as meditation, biofeedback, hypnosis, and even the use of some specific drugs can help people learn to use the receptive mode of their consciousness to balance the more active mode.

Being conscious means being aware, and because human beings are aware, we can tell researchers about our experiences. Psychologists can also study a person's consciousness by measuring some specific physiological functions. Much of the remainder of this chapter focuses on a wide array of states of consciousness. Some of the research techniques used are physiological; others are self-report. Some of these conscious states are desirable and normal; others alter human behavior in less positive ways. We begin with an altered state of awareness with which all of us are familiar—sleep.

Sleep

In January 1964, at age 17 years, Randy Gardner hoped to make history, and he did. He decided that he was going to break a world's record by staying awake for more than 260 hours—just short of 11 days. Physically and mentally healthy, Gardner was assured and self-confident. A science fair near his San Diego home was to be the location of his experiment. He enlisted two friends to help keep him awake, and he took no stimulants such as coffee.

altered state of consciousness: A pattern of functioning that is dramatically different from that of ordinary awareness and responsiveness.

After six days, a local physician came to supervise his progress, much to the relief of Gardner's parents. Although he did not suffer any serious physical symptoms, there were marked psychological effects. On Day 2, he had trouble focusing his eyes; on Day 3, there were mood changes; on Day 4, he was irritable and uncooperative. He also began to see images. By Day 6, Gardner had speech difficulties and memory lapses. By Day 9, his thoughts and speech were incoherent. On Day 10, blurred vision became more of a problem, and he was regularly forgetting things. Mornings were his most difficult time, but at no time did he behave in a socially deviant manner. Randy Gardner's record is the longest documented account of continuous sleep loss.

One of the most interesting aspects of Randy Gardner's adventure is what happened to his sleep after his deprivation. Sleep researcher William Dement followed Gardner's sleep, mental health, physical recovery, and electroencephalogram for days afterward to see how his subject recovered, what happened to his sleep patterns, and whether he made up for lost sleep. Dement found that for the three nights following his deprivation, Gardner slept an extra 6.5 hours, and on the fourth night, an extra 2.5 hours (Johnson, Slye, Dement, 1965).

Following Randy Gardner's sleep loss and his subsequent recovery is part of the history of the study of sleep. Early researchers such as Dement were just beginning to ask interesting questions; they were beginning to realize that sleep and wakefulness follow specific patterns that can be tracked and predicted. They noted that as you move through the day, your general awareness—responsiveness, thought processes, and physiological responses—changes. On first waking, you may not be fully aware and responsive. You move sluggishly and are slow to realize that the coffee is perking and your toast is burning. Later, at a job or in class, you are probably very alert. However, as the day wears on, you find your awareness decreasing, and in the evening, you may fall asleep in front of the television. Research on sleep is a part of the puzzle of human behavior and its biological basis.

The Sleep–Wakefulness Cycle: Circadian Rhythms

Learning Objective 7.3 Describe circadian rhythms in humans, and tell how they correspond to 24-hour clock time.

In the casinos of Las Vegas, it is difficult to tell night from day. There are no windows, activity is at fever pitch 24 hours a day, and there are few clocks. People never seem to sleep; it is as if there were no day or night. Nonetheless, people do sleep, and unlike Randy Gardner, people give in to their bodily urges to rejuvenate themselves. Our bodies tell us we are tired without a clock on the wall to remind us.

We are not at the mercy of light and darkness to control our activities. There seems to be a biological clock that ticks within us to control our sleep–wakefulness cycle. Some researchers argue that there are two clocks, one controlling a sleep–wakefulness cycle and one controlling various other aspects of our physiology. The second clock is supposed to control body temperature, which fluctuates by 1.5 degrees during the day, the lowest temperature occurring while we are sleeping. Whether there is one clock or two, neither seems to run on an exactly 24-hour day, and thus the term *circadian* was born—*circadian* comes from the Latin *circa diem* (around a day).

Circadian rhythms are internally generated and help control our bodily rhythms, sleep patterns, and body temperature. When time cues are removed from the environment (clocks, windows, temperature changes as the sun goes down) an interesting finding occurs—our circadian rhythm runs a bit slow. When placed in artificial environments and allowed to sleep, eat, and read whenever they want, human beings sleep a constant amount, but each "day," they go to sleep a bit later; the full sleep–wakefulness cycle runs at about 24.5 to 25.5 hours. Body temperature and other bodily functions tend to follow a similar circadian rhythm.

Daylight, clocks, and arbitrary schedules do not allow people's circadian rhythms to control their sleep or wakefulness. However, you can see that if this rhythm is thrown off by your having to work through the night, then sleep, then rise, and so

Figure 7.1

Most people complete about five sleep cycles per night. With each cycle, they spend progressively more time in REM sleep. (From *Some Must Watch While Some Must Sleep* by William C. Dement. Copyright William C. Dement and the Stanford Alumni Association. Stanford, California.)

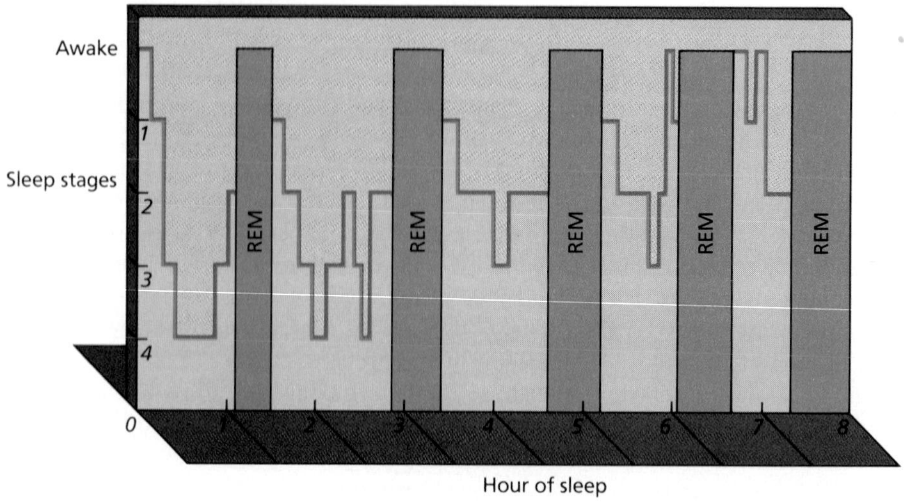

forth, your body's clock may not match your work clock. This becomes especially difficult if you are an airline pilot, a surgeon, or a firefighter.

Learning Objective 7.4 Describe the amount of sleep humans need, how sleep activity is measured, and the stages of NREM sleep and REM sleep.

Sleep Cycles and Stages: REM and NREM Sleep

Everyone needs some amount of **sleep.** Most of us require about 8 hours, but some people can function with only 4 or 5 hours, and others need as many as 9 or 10. Young teenagers tend to sleep longer than college students, and elderly people tend to sleep somewhat less than young people. Most young adults (65%) sleep between 6.5 and 8.5 hours a night, and about 95% of all people sleep between 5.5 and 9.5 hours (Horne, 1988). Although you might think that people who are active and energetic would require more sleep than those who are less active, this is not always the case. Bedridden hospital patients, for example, sleep about the same amount of time as people who are on their feet all day.

Our sleep–wakefulness cycle is repetitive, determined in part by circadian rhythms, work schedules, and a host of other events. When early sleep researchers such as Nathaniel Kleitman and William Dement studied the sleep–wakefulness cycle, they found stages within sleep that could be characterized through EEGs (**electroencephalograms**) and by eye movements that occurred during sleep. Researchers working in sleep laboratories use the EEG to study the brain's electrical activity during sleep by attaching electrodes to a subject's scalp and forehead and monitoring his or her brain-wave pattern throughout the night. Experimenters also record eye movements by using an electrooculogram and record muscle tension in the face by using an electromyogram.

Recordings of sleeping subjects' EEGs have revealed that in an 8-hour period, people typically progress through five full cycles of sleep, with each cycle having four stages (see Figure 7.1) and REM sleep. When people first fall asleep, they are in Stage 1; their sleep is rather light, and they can be wakened easily. Within the next 30–40 minutes, they pass through stages 2, 3, and 4. Stage 4 is very deep sleep; when subjects leave Stage 4 sleep, they pass again through Stages 3 and then 2 (both are described in the following paragraph). A full sleep cycle lasts approximately 90 minutes. We characterize the first four stages as **no rapid eye movements (NREM) sleep states;** the fifth pattern is called **rapid eye movement (REM) sleep**. Only during REM sleep do rapid and systematic eye movements occur.

sleep: A nonwaking state of consciousness characterized by general unresponsiveness to the environment and general physical immobility.

electroencephalogram (EEG): [eel-ECK-tro-en-SEFF-uh-low-gram] The record of an organism's electrical brain patterns, obtained through electrodes placed on a subject's scalp.

NREM (no rapid eye movements) sleep: Four distinct stages of sleep during which no rapid eye movements occur.

REM (rapid eye movements) sleep: A stage of sleep characterized by high-frequency, low-voltage brain-wave activity, rapid and systematic eye movements, and dreams.

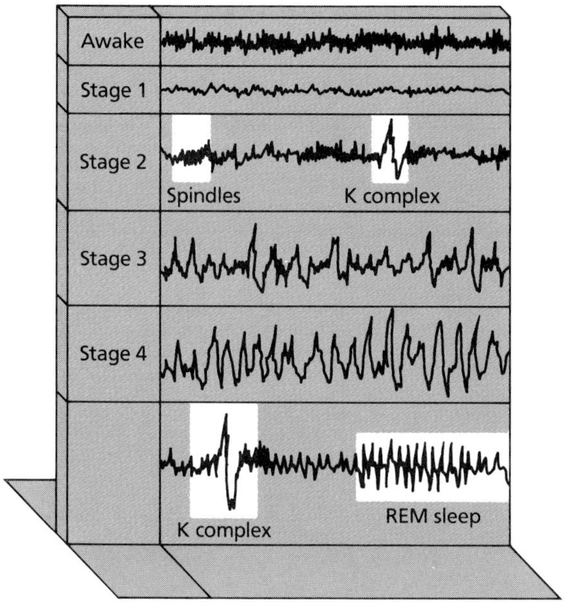

Figure 7.2

EEGs show distinctive characteristic patterns for a wakeful state, REM sleep, and each of the four NREM sleep stages. After sleep onset, the EEG changes progressively from a pattern of low voltage and high frequency to one of high voltage and low frequency. (From *Some Must Watch While Some Must Sleep* by William C. Dement. Copyright William C. Dement and the Stanford Alumni Association. Stanford, California.)

People experience REM sleep for the first time after they have left Stage 4 sleep and have passed again through Stages 3 and then 2. Thus, the longer they sleep (and the more sleep cycles they go through), the more REM sleep they experience. Figure 7.2 shows the distinctive brain-wave patterns of wakefulness, the four stages of NREM sleep, and REM sleep in a normal adult. The waking pattern exhibits a fast, regular rhythm. In Stage 1, sleep is light, and the brain waves are of low amplitude (height) but are relatively fast, with mixed frequencies. Sleepers in Stage 1 can be wakened easily. Stage 2 sleep shows low-amplitude, nonrhythmic activity combined with special patterns called "sleep spindles" and "K complexes." A *sleep spindle* is a rhythmic burst of waves that wax and wane for 1 or 2 seconds. A *K complex* is a higher-amplitude burst of activity seen in the last third of Stage 2. Sleep spindles and K complexes appear only during NREM sleep. Sleepers in Stage 2 are in deeper sleep than in Stage 1 but can still be easily awakened.

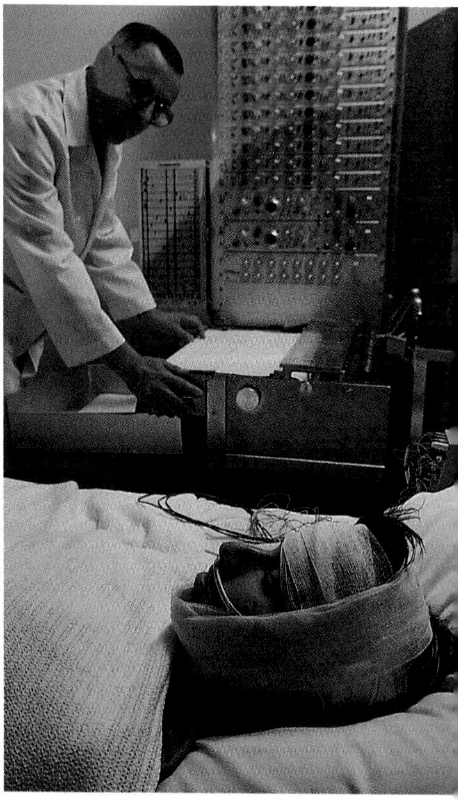

The exact role of sleep in maintaining our physical and mental well-being is still not well understood and scientists continue to study this complex state of consciousness.

Stage 3 sleep is a transitional stage between Stages 2 and 4, with slower but higher-amplitude activity than at stage 2. Stage 4 sleep, the deepest sleep stage, has even higher-amplitude brain-wave traces, called delta waves. During this stage, people breathe deeply and have slowed heart rate and lowered blood pressure. Stage 4 sleep has two well-documented behavioral characteristics. First, subjects are difficult to awaken; subjects wakened from Stage 4 often appear confused and disturbed and take several seconds to rouse themselves fully. Second, subjects in Stage 4 sleep generally do not dream, although they may report some vague mental activity.

In contrast to Stage 4 sleep, subjects who are awakened during REM sleep can report in great detail the imagery and activity characteristic of a dream state. Because REM sleep is considered necessary to normal physiological functioning and behavior, it might be expected to be a deep sleep; however, it is an active sleep during which the EEG resembles that of an aware person. For this reason, REM sleep is often called *paradoxical sleep.* In REM sleep, subjects seem agitated; their eyes move, and their heart rate and breathing are variable. Subjects are difficult to awaken during REM sleep.

TABLE 7.1 Minutes of REM sleep, ages 3–15 years

REM period	Age (in years)			
	3–5	6–9	10–15	13–15
1	18	18	18	20
2	24	26	29	29
3	27	32	35	30
4	35	35	37	35
5	31	34	32	27
6	29	34	32	27
7	28	58	—	—
8	25	—	—	—
9	38	—	—	—

Source: Williams, Karacan, & Hursch, 1974.

The bottom pattern of Figure 7.2 shows an EEG transition from NREM Stage 2 to REM sleep. The first part of the tracing shows a clear K complex, indicating Stage 2 sleep; the last part shows waves characteristic of REM sleep. During periods of sleep in which the high-frequency, low-amplitude waves are apparent, subjects experience rapid eye movements (REMs) and typically report dreaming. Researchers can identify the stage in which an individual is sleeping by watching an EEG recording. If delta waves are present, the subject is in Stage 4 sleep. To confirm this, the experimenters may waken the subject and ask whether he or she was dreaming.

Sleep cycles develop from before birth and continue to change into adulthood with elderly people showing less total sleep and less Stage 3 and Stage 4 sleep. Initially, fetuses show no eye movements. Later they show eye, facial, and body movements. Newborns spend about 50% of their sleep time in REM sleep. From age 1 year on, the proportion of REM sleep to Stage 4 sleep decreases dramatically (Ellingson, 1975) (see Table 7.1 and Figure 7.3).

Workers on swing shifts may suffer from decreased attentiveness due to the disruption of their circadian rhythms and sleep patterns.

Sleep Deprivation: Doing Without REM

The need for sleep is painfully obvious to anyone who has been deprived of it. Just ask Randy Gardner (introduced at the beginning of the chapter), who went without sleep for close to 11 days. When people who normally sleep 8 hours miss a few hours on a particular night, they may be tired the following day but can function quite well. However, when people lose a couple of hours of sleep for several nights in a row, they usually look tired, feel lethargic, and act irritable.

Researchers have investigated what happens to people who are totally or partially deprived of sleep for various amounts of time. The research is generally conducted on laboratory subjects who sleep in a sleep laboratory, where their EEGs and eye movements are recorded for several nights. For the first three or four nights, they are allowed to have their normal amount of sleep; the recordings taken during this time provide *baseline data* (that is, information about their normal behaviors and physiology, before the experimental treatment is implemented). Once baseline data are established, the subjects are deprived of sleep.

What happens to subjects who are regularly deprived of REM sleep? They become anxious and irritable, report difficulty concentrating, and do worse on tests that involve attention and original responses (May & Kline, 1987). The longer a person is deprived of sleep, the more sleepy, the worse the mood, and the more cognitive difficulties subjects will report (Mikulincer, Babkoff, Caspy, & Sing, 1989). As soon as they are allowed to have REM sleep again, however, the psychological changes disappear (e.g., Roehrs, Timms, Zwyghuizen-Doorenbos, & Roth, 1989), and they spend a greater amount of time in REM and Stage 4 sleep than usual (Kales et al., 1970; see also Webb & Agnew, 1975).

Learning Objective 7.5
Describe the effects of sleep deprivation on behavior and on subsequent sleep patterns.

As many as 20–30 million American workers have nontraditional work schedules, and they must alter their sleep patterns regularly. Studies of circadian rhythms (discussed earlier) generally show that when people put in long hours that stretch through the night and into the dawn, and when these hours are non-

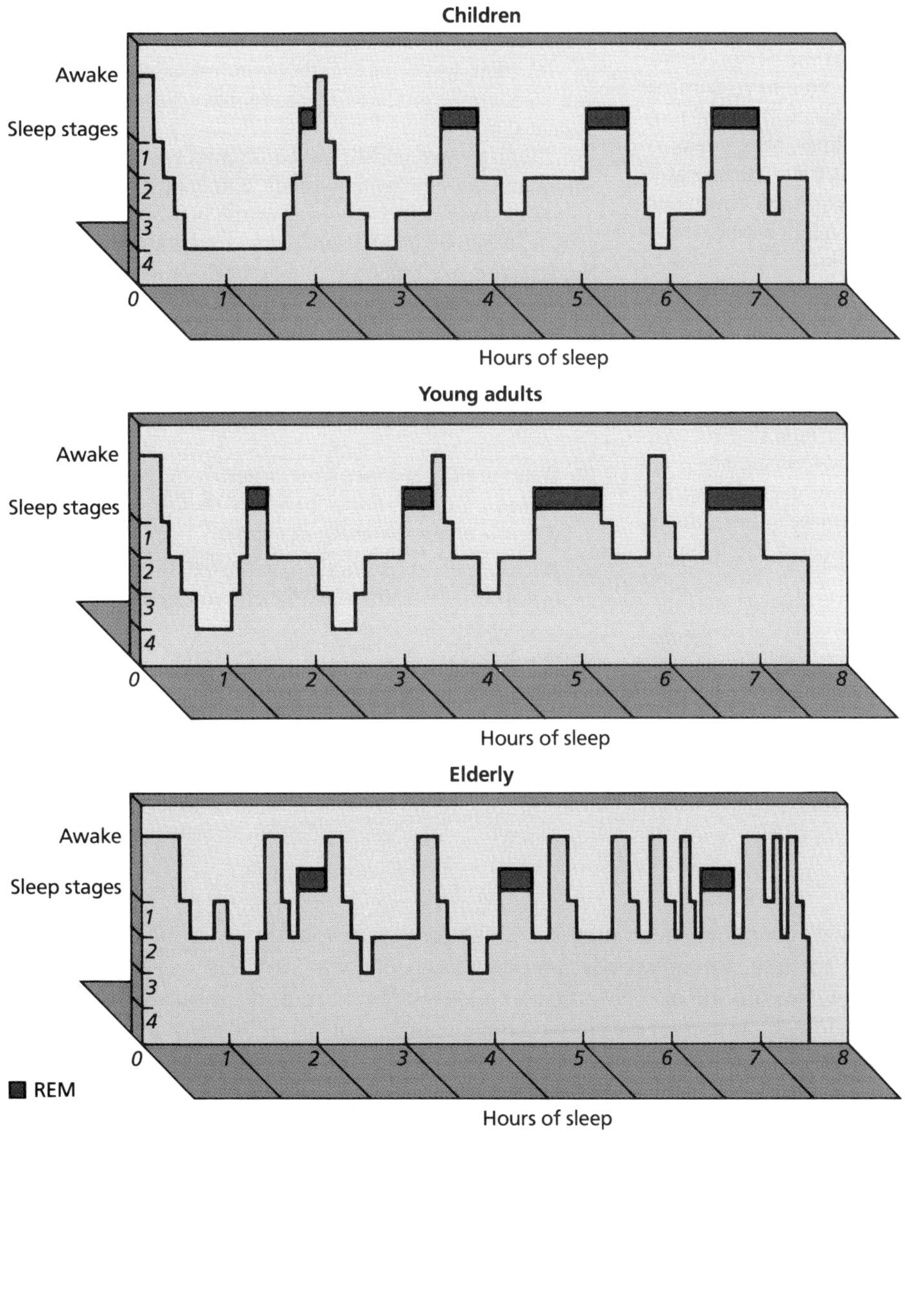

Figure 7.3

REM sleep (darker areas) occurs cyclically throughout the night at about 90-minute intervals in all age groups. However, Stage 4 sleep decreases with age. In addition, elderly people awaken more often and spend more time awake. (From *Some Must Watch While Some Must Sleep* by William C. Dement. Copyright William C. Dement and the Stanford Alumni Association. Stanford, California.)

APPLYING PSYCHOLOGY

Sleep Disorders

You may have a sleep disorder if you snore loudly, sleepwalk, or fall asleep at inappropriate times, such as when driving a car. People who fall asleep suddenly and unexpectedly (or at least when they do not want to) have a disorder known as *narcolepsy.* Narcolepsy is probably a symptom of an autonomic nervous system disturbance and of lowered arousal.

Another sleep disorder, *sleep apnea,* causes airflow to stop for at least 15 seconds so that the person ceases breathing. People with this disorder often have as many as 100 apnea episodes in a night; during the day, they are exceedingly sleepy and sometimes have memory losses. People with severe apnea may have work-related accidents and severe headaches and may fall asleep during the day. Drug therapy and some minor surgical techniques for creating better airflow have been used to treat those with sleep apnea. Monitoring equipment for prolonged breathing pauses has also been used to waken the sleeper (Sheridan, 1985). Males are more likely than females to have sleep apnea (Ingbar & Gee, 1985), and sleep apnea is a major hypothesis used to explain the causes of SIDS, sudden infant death syndrome, in which infants die suddenly during sleep for no obvious reason. Alcohol and other central-nervous-system-depressant drugs often contribute to sleep apnea in adults. (Alcohol and other drugs area discussed in Module 8.)

Insomnia, a prolonged inability to sleep, is a common sleep disorder often caused by anxiety or depression. One in 10 people report insomnia; they tend to be listless and tired during the day and may use sleeping pills or other drugs to induce sleep at night. Ironically, researchers have found that these drugs do not induce natural sleep: Instead, they *reduce* the proportion of REM sleep after a period of sleep deprivation (Webb & Agnew, 1975). Recall that the body's normal response to sleep deprivation is to increase REM sleep, and researchers such as Dement found that lack of REM sleep may alter normal behavior. Thus, people with chronic insomnia should not regularly use drugs that force sleep. This is especially true of the elderly, who are regularly prescribed medications to help them sleep (Prinz, Vitiello, Raskin, & Thorpy, 1990). Various researchers have proposed alternative behavioral methods that do not rely on drugs to help insomniacs (e.g., Woolfolk & McNulty, 1983), including relaxation training and self-hypnosis. Other researchers such as Vitiello (1989) assert that diet affects sleep because diet affects sympathetic nervous system activity, which may stimulate people in the middle of the night. Such research is still in its early stages but is very exciting, and as was shown in Chapter 2 (p. 44), diet (especially carbohydrates) affects mood and sleepiness, so these ideas do have other experimental support.

Night terrors consist of panic attacks that occur within an hour after falling asleep. Sitting up abruptly in a state of sheer panic, a person with a night terror may scream, breathe quickly, and be in a total state of fright. Night terrors are especially apparent in young children between ages 3 and 8 years. They usually disappear as a child grows older and do not seem to be a symptom of any psychological disorder. The cause of night terrors is not fully established but may be due to electrochemical processes overloading during NREM sleep.

- ▲ ***What is the evidence that suggests that there are serious implications for day-to-day behavior when a sleep disorder develops?***
- ▲ ***Why have researchers speculated that sudden infant death syndrome (SIDS) may be related to a sleeping disorder?***
- ▲ ***What evidence suggests that people should not take pills or alcohol to induce sleep when they suffer from a sleep disorder?***

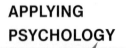

regular, people are less attentive, think less clearly, and may even nod off from time to time. Circadian rhythms and sleep patterns are closely related to and dependent on one another; thus, employers, workers, and consumers need to be aware of the potential decreased efficiency of night workers, such as airline pilots and medical interns, who often vary their schedules. The decreased efficiency of night workers can be explained by their irregular schedules, but some people exhibit far more serious alterations in their sleep–wakefulness cycle—they exhibit sleep disorders, which are discussed in the Applying Psychology box above.

insomnia: [in-SOM-nee-uh] Prolonged inability to sleep.

Progress Check 7.1

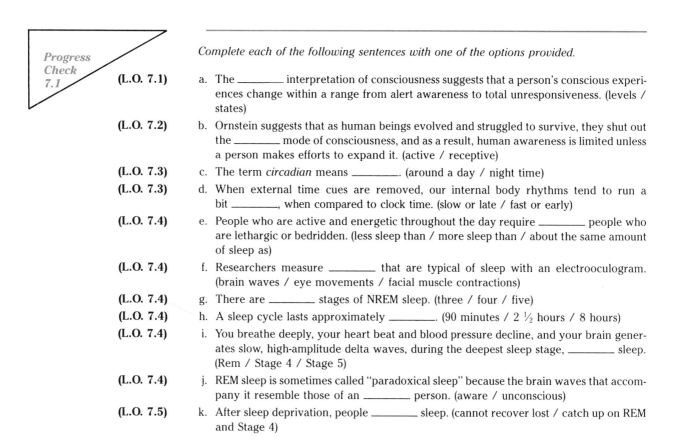

Complete each of the following sentences with one of the options provided.

(L.O. 7.1) a. The ________ interpretation of consciousness suggests that a person's conscious experiences change within a range from alert awareness to total unresponsiveness. (levels / states)

(L.O. 7.2) b. Ornstein suggests that as human beings evolved and struggled to survive, they shut out the ________ mode of consciousness, and as a result, human awareness is limited unless a person makes efforts to expand it. (active / receptive)

(L.O. 7.3) c. The term *circadian* means ________. (around a day / night time)

(L.O. 7.3) d. When external time cues are removed, our internal body rhythms tend to run a bit ________, when compared to clock time. (slow or late / fast or early)

(L.O. 7.4) e. People who are active and energetic throughout the day require ________ people who are lethargic or bedridden. (less sleep than / more sleep than / about the same amount of sleep as)

(L.O. 7.4) f. Researchers measure ________ that are typical of sleep with an electrooculogram. (brain waves / eye movements / facial muscle contractions)

(L.O. 7.4) g. There are ________ stages of NREM sleep. (three / four / five)

(L.O. 7.4) h. A sleep cycle lasts approximately ________. (90 minutes / 2 ½ hours / 8 hours)

(L.O. 7.4) i. You breathe deeply, your heart beat and blood pressure decline, and your brain generates slow, high-amplitude delta waves, during the deepest sleep stage, ________ sleep. (Rem / Stage 4 / Stage 5)

(L.O. 7.4) j. REM sleep is sometimes called "paradoxical sleep" because the brain waves that accompany it resemble those of an ________ person. (aware / unconscious)

(L.O. 7.5) k. After sleep deprivation, people ________ sleep. (cannot recover lost / catch up on REM and Stage 4)

Dreams

Learning Objective 7.6
Discuss the biological signs of dreaming, the frequency of dreaming and remembering dreams, and the types of dreams people have.

Why do some people rarely remember their dreams while other people can recall theirs in vivid detail? Do our dreams have hidden meanings and mysterious symbols to be uncovered? Sometimes lifelike, sometimes chaotic, and sometimes incoherent, dreams may replay a person's life history or may venture into the unknown. Dreams have long occupied an important place in psychology, but only since the 1950s have they come under close scientific scrutiny. Dream research is difficult to conduct; in addition, the data from dream research are always memories of past events and this sometimes is difficult to verify and quantify (Koulack, 1991).

What Is a Dream?

A **dream** is a state of consciousness that occurs largely during REM sleep and is usually accompanied by vivid visual imagery, although the imagery may be tactile or auditory. During a dream, there is an increase in heart rate, the appearance of REMs, a characteristic brain-wave pattern, and a lack of body movements. Although dreams occur most often during REM sleep, they can also occur during NREM sleep, but they tend to be less visual and more thinking-oriented during NREM sleep. REM sleep dreams are intensely visual, may be action-oriented, and are more likely to be emotional than NREM dreams.

dream: A state of consciousness that occurs largely during REM sleep and is usually accompanied by vivid visual, tactile, and auditory experiences.

Most people dream four or five times a night. Dreams last from a few seconds to several minutes. The first dream of a typical night occurs about 90 minutes after

lucid dream: A dream in which people are aware of their dreaming while it is happening.

manifest content: Overt storyline, characters, and setting of a dream; the overt, obvious, clearly discernible events of a dream.

latent content: Deeper meaning, usually involving symbolism, hidden content, and repressed or obscured ideas and wishes of a dream.

you have fallen asleep and lasts for about 10 minutes. With about four dreams per night and 365 days per year, a person dreams more than 100,000 dreams in a lifetime. However, we remember only a few; people usually recall a dream because they woke in the middle of it or because a specific dream had extremely powerful imagery.

Content of Dreams

Sometimes, the content of a dream is related to day-to-day events, to a desire that a person wishes would be fulfilled, or to reliving an unpleasant experience. Sometimes, a person experiences the same dream over and over again, or a sequence of related dreams. Most dreams are commonplace and focus on people and events with whom we come into contact frequently—family, friends, or coworkers. Common themes include sex, aggressive incidents, and misfortunes. Sounds and other sensations from the environment that do not waken a sleeper are often incorporated into a dream. For example, when a researcher sprayed water on the hands of sleepers, 42% of those who did not waken later reported dreaming about swimming pools, baths, or rain (Dement & Wolpert, 1958).

Dreams are mostly visual, and they occur mostly in color. Dement and Kleitman (1957) found that subjects' patterns of REMs related to the visual imagery of their dreams. When a subject dreamed about climbing a series of ladders, eye movements were vertical; when a subject dreamed about two people throwing tomatoes at each other, eye movements were horizontal. Blind individuals who lost their sight before age 5 years, tend to have dream imagery that is mostly auditory.

Sometimes, people report that they are aware of dreaming while it is happening; this is a **lucid dream.** Most people have had a lucid dream at one time or another. People are often overpowered by the compelling imagery of lucid dreams. Gackenbach and Bosveld (1989) assert that such events are quite spectacular and exciting.

When people experience a lucid dream, they often report later that they were inside and outside the dream at the same time. For some people, this is upsetting and they often waken from the dream. Some people attempt to navigate or control their lucid dreams. They tell themselves before going to sleep that they will remember their dreams, they lie quietly after waking up, and they let their thoughts wander—this helps them to recall all of their dreaming.

Dream Theories

Learning Objective 7.7 Explain why we dream, according to Freud, Jung, and the activation–synthesis model.

Some psychologists assume that dreams express desires and thoughts that may be unacceptable; therapists who interpret and analyze dreams assume that dreams represent some element of a person that is seeking expression. The suggested meaning of a dream will depend on a psychologist's orientation. Some see much symbolism in dreams and assert that the overt content of the dream hides the true meaning. Other psychologists find dreams meaningless.

Freud. Sigmund Freud made his position on dreams very clear: He described dreams as "the royal road to the unconscious." For Freud, a dream expressed desires, wishes, and unfulfilled needs that exist in the unconscious. In his book *The Interpretation of Dreams* (1900/1953), Freud spoke about the manifest and the latent content of dreams. The **manifest content** of a dream is its overt storyline, characters, and setting; it is the obvious, clearly discernible events of a dream. The **latent content** of a dream is its deeper meaning, usually involving symbolism, hidden content, and repressed or obscured ideas and wishes—often uncomfortable ones. Many contemporary therapists use patients' dreams to understand current problems and may see the dream only as a jumping-off point. They see the overt content of a dream, the part that is easily remembered, as only a topic not fully analyzed in day-to-day experience, which needs to be addressed.

Jung. Carl G. Jung (1875–1961) was trained in Freudian approaches to therapy and personality analysis, and he too considered the dream a crucial way to understand human nature. However, Jung, more than Freud, focused on the meaning of dreams and took for granted the idea that a dream was nature's way of communicating with the unconscious. Each thing a person dreams has a meaning, so dreams are the language through which an individual expresses his or her deepest feelings in an uncensored form. The dream gives visual expression to a person's instinct. Jungian therapy focuses on dream analysis as an approach to understanding the human condition. We consider Jung's ideas in more detail in Chapter 10.

Activation–Synthesis. Two researchers from Harvard Medical School, Allan Hobson and Robert McCarley, believe that dreams have a physiological basis (1977). They argue that during periods of REM sleep, the parts of the brain responsible for long-term memory, vision, audition, and perhaps even emotion, are spontaneously *activated* (stimulated) from cells in the hindbrain, especially the pons. The cortex tries to synthesize (integrate to make some sense out of) the messages. Because this activity is not organized by any coherent external stimuli, the resulting dream is often fragmented and incoherent (Hobson, 1989).

The activation–synthesis model necessitates the involvement of the cortex in dreams. The theory is supported by researchers who assert that during sleep, the brain (especially the cortex) scans previous memories, refreshes old storage mechanisms, and maintains the active memory. However, other researchers point out that dreamlike activity occurs even when cells in the pons are not active. This controversial approach is still being actively researched.

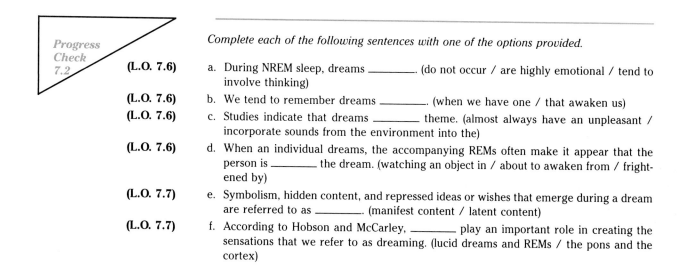

Progress Check 7.2

Complete each of the following sentences with one of the options provided.

(L.O. 7.6) a. During NREM sleep, dreams ________. (do not occur / are highly emotional / tend to involve thinking)

(L.O. 7.6) b. We tend to remember dreams ________. (when we have one / that awaken us)

(L.O. 7.6) c. Studies indicate that dreams ________ theme. (almost always have an unpleasant / incorporate sounds from the environment into the)

(L.O. 7.6) d. When an individual dreams, the accompanying REMs often make it appear that the person is ________ the dream. (watching an object in / about to awaken from / frightened by)

(L.O. 7.7) e. Symbolism, hidden content, and repressed ideas or wishes that emerge during a dream are referred to as ________. (manifest content / latent content)

(L.O. 7.7) f. According to Hobson and McCarley, ________ play an important role in creating the sensations that we refer to as dreaming. (lucid dreams and REMs / the pons and the cortex)

Module Summary

Consciousness

- Consciousness is the general state of being aware of and responsive to the environment. Consciousness can range from alert attention to altered states such as dreaming, hypnosis, or drug-induced conditions (p. 127).
- Normal consciousness and altered states are linked to the ongoing biological processes in our bodies (p. 128).

Sleep

- Circadian rhythms are internally generated and help control our bodily rhythms and sleep patterns (p. 129).
- Recordings of sleeping subjects' EEGs have revealed five distinct patterns of electrical activity. Four are called no rapid eye movement (NREM) sleep states; the other pattern is called rapid eye movement (REM) sleep. During REM sleep, rapid and systematic eye movements occur (p. 130).
- A full sleep cycle takes about 90 minutes, so five complete sleep cycles occur in an average night's sleep. Subjects deprived of REM sleep tend to catch up on REM sleep in subsequent nights (p. 133).

Dreams

- A *dream* is a state of consciousness that occurs largely during REM sleep and is usually accompanied by vivid visual imagery, although the imagery also may be tactile or auditory (p. 135).
- Most people dream four or five times a night. The first dream of a typical night occurs 90 minutes after you fall asleep and lasts for 10 minutes (p. 135).

KEY TERMS

altered state of consciousness, p. 128
consciousness, p. 127
dream, p. 135
electroencephalogram (EEG), p. 130
insomnia, p. 134
latent content, p. 136
lucid dream, p. 136
manifest content, p. 136
NREM sleep, p. 130
REM sleep, p. 130
sleep, p. 130

SELF-TEST

Module 7

- Before taking the self-test, **recite** and **review**.
- Use the key at the back of the text to *correct* your answers.
- *Restudy* pages that correspond to any questions you answered incorrectly.

1. Dreaming, hypnotic trance, and drug-induced states are called altered states of consciousness because
   a. some people do not experience them.
   b. they are different from the usual waking state.
   c. it can be shown that each one of them is the result of responses to unusual stimuli.
   d. they are not true states of consciousness.
2. The theories of consciousness put forth by Jaynes and by Ornstein are similar, in that both suggest that consciousness
   a. is a product of human evolution.
   b. is active, verbal, and rational.
   c. develops gradually as we mature.
   d. fluctuates from alert to drowsy, depending on moods.
3. In humans, the circadian sleep–wakefulness cycle
   a. runs about 24.5–25.5 hours.
   b. is influenced by sunlight and darkness.
   c. changes as circadian temperature rhythms change.
   d. all of the above
4. Which of the following describes the sequence of the first sleep cycle?
   a. Stage 1, Stage 2, Stage 3, Stage 4, REM
   b. REM, Stage 1, Stage 2, Stage 3, Stage 4
   c. Stage 1, Stage 2, REM, Stage 3, Stage 4
   d. Stage 1, Stage 2, Stage 3, Stage 4, Stage 3, Stage 2, REM
5. Prolonged sleep deprivation
   a. can lead to irreversible maladjustments in behavior.
   b. seems to have little or no effect on most bodily functions.
   c. interferes with a person's ability to concentrate on test questions and to give original responses to them.
   d. has little effect on people who are accustomed to losing sleep on a regular basis because of their nontraditional work schedules.
6. Who is most likely to experience dream imagery that is mostly auditory? A person who
   a. has been blind most of his or her life.
   b. is dreaming about being the lead singer in an opera.
   c. is oversensitive to noise.
   d. is an auditory learner.
7. When a person is very much aware of dreaming while it is happening and feels as if she is both inside and outside the dream, the person is having ________ dream.
   a. a manifest
   b. a latent
   c. an activation–synthesis
   d. a lucid
8. According to Sigmund Freud, dreams are
   a. a biological product of the cortex, synthesizing new learnings after being exposed to new stimuli during waking hours.
   b. psychic events that interfere with psychoanalysis.
   c. nature's way of communicating with the unconscious.
   d. "the royal road to the unconscious."

Module 8

Altered States of Consciousness

LEARNING OBJECTIVES

When you have mastered the material in this module, you will be able to

Controlling Consciousness: Biofeedback, Hypnosis, and Meditation (pp. 142–144)

8.1 Explain how biofeedback is used to control body functions and state questions that need to be answered concerning its effectiveness (p. 142).

8.2 Describe hypnotic induction, the effects and uses of hypnosis, and Barber's alternative explanation for hypnosis (p. 143).

8.3 Describe the consciousness-altering technique called "meditation" and some of its effects (p. 144)

Substance Abuse (pp. 145–146)

8.4 List the criteria used to diagnose a substance abuser and describe the potential biological, psychological, and behavioral effects of alcohol and other drugs (p. 145).

Altered Consciousness with Drugs (pp. 147–153)

8.5 Identify reasons why drug abuse is dangerous and the most effective approach for preventing it (p. 147).

8.6 Explain why alcohol is considered a drug, give statistics regarding its use, and describe how it affects the body and behavior (p. 147).

8.7 Make a distinction between a problem drinker and an alcoholic (pp. 148–149).

8.8 Identify some of the causes of alcoholism and describe two approaches for treating it (p. 149).

8.9 State how barbiturates and tranquilizers affect the body and explain who is a potential tranquilizer abuser (p. 150).

8.10 Describe the physical and psychological effects of heroin and the typical heroin user; also describe methadone treatment (p. 150).

8.11 State statistics concerning the use of marijuana and discuss its physical and psychological effects on the user (p. 151).

8.12 State statistics concerning the use of amphetamines and cocaine and discuss their physical and psychological effects on users (p.152).

SQ3R
- ▲ **Survey** to set goals for studying.
- ▲ Ask **questions** as you **read**.
- ▲ Stop occasionally to **recite** and **review**.

plus
- ▲ **Write** a summary of key points.
- ▲ **Reflect** on the hypotheses, evidence, and implications of this material and on the relevance it has to *your* life.

Larry Hagen had always been a straight-arrow sort of fellow—good parents, good family life, honor society in high school. He followed the fads, listened to the "in" music, and always had a nice group of friends. Initially a liberal arts major, Larry looked as if he were headed for a career in journalism. While he worked as a copyboy at the local newspaper, he occasionally talked about law school, but something was wrong. His friends noticed it first. Larry was drinking more than he used to. His closest friends knew he was using other drugs and also using them too often. In Larry's crowd, too often meant more than once a week. Larry was smoking pot (marijuana) nearly every day. Weekends were turning into one long drug scene.

Gradually, what started off as a good time with the gang turned into a daily drug dependence. Larry was losing it. He was "foggy" more often than not, and his school work was slipping. He missed work several times. His friends were beginning to think of him as a "druggie." Larry thought they were nerds. Spending more of his time drugged than not, Larry's behavior started to change noticeably. He became moody and argumentative, and school became a low priority for him. While Larry initially found that drugs gave him a high, he was now drugged so often that his normal state of functioning was a drugged state. As Larry grew used to using a number of drugs, he became unsure as to when he had taken something and when he hadn't. Larry's behavior seemed bizarre; it became difficult for him to describe what he was doing or how he was feeling. His life had become unmanageable, and his self-esteem had hit bottom. Unfortunately, Larry Hagen is but one of thousands of high school and college students who seek to escape normal consciousness and reality through the use of drugs.

Awake and aware human beings are conscious. Their thought is rational. However, people can alter this ordinary state of functioning in several ways. A junkie (heroin addict) who is physiologically dependent on heroin is an extreme example. A corporate executive developing a dependence on alcohol is another. However, drugs are not the only means of altering normal thinking states. People under hypnosis may be willing to think, say, and do things they might otherwise not do. Sleep also changes people's consciousness, perhaps with dreams and bizarre thoughts. Hypnosis, sleep, meditation, and drug states alter individuals' normal thought processes and normal patterns of behavior.

Controlling Consciousness: Biofeedback, Hypnosis, and Meditation

biofeedback: The general technique by which individuals can monitor and learn to control the involuntary activity of some bodily organs and functions.

Though studying altered states of consciousness does not answer all the questions scientists have about how and why people think and behave as they do, psychologists argue that it provides insight into how consciousness works. Although the task of understanding and controlling consciousness is by no means complete, progress has been made.

Can people actually control their consciousness? Can they manipulate their mental states to achieve certain bodily reactions? Research and anecdotal data suggest that they can. People have long been taught to relax and breathe deeply when they are in pain. Races have been won through intense concentration that allowed contestants to endure especially difficult circumstances. Laboratory research also shows that people can bring some otherwise autonomic (see Chapter 2) bodily states under conscious control through a technique called biofeedback.

Psychology and Medicine: Biofeedback

Learning Objective 8.1
Explain how biofeedback is used to control body functions, and state questions that need to be answered concerning its effectiveness.

Imagine a special clinic that teaches people to treat themselves for such ailments as headaches, nearsightedness, high blood pressure, and stress-related illness. By learning to influence consciously what are normally involuntary actions, patients can cure themselves. Such psychological–medical clinics exist in some communities and may prove biofeedback to be the healing tool some researchers predict that it will be.

Physicians and psychologists have traditionally assumed that most biological functions, especially those involving the autonomic nervous system, cannot be voluntarily controlled except through drugs or surgery. Since the late 1960s, however, studies with **biofeedback**, have explored the extent to which subjects can learn to control their bodily functions—and thus their autonomic behavior—by monitoring their neuronal (brain-wave) activity and other physiological responses. A well-known psychologist, Neal Miller, was one of the first researchers to train rats to control certain glandular responses. Miller (1969) suggested that the same techniques could be used to help human beings manage their bodies and behavior. Since then, studies have shown that human beings can manipulate the electrical activity of their bodies by changing their level of excitation.

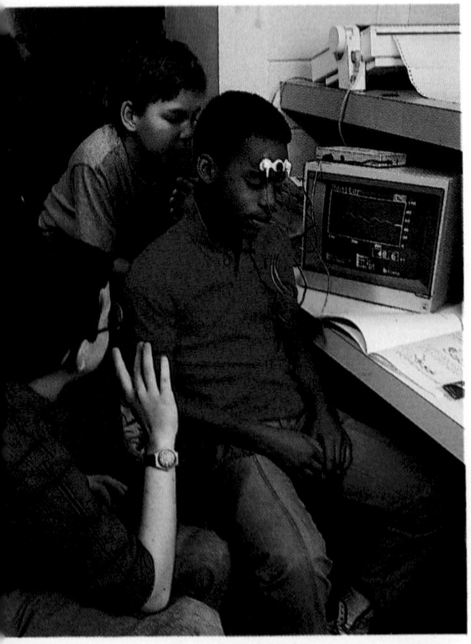

Through biofeedback, people attempt to learn how to control what are normally involuntary actions.

A relaxed person viewing alpha waves on an oscilloscope, for example, can change those alpha waves to high-frequency waves by becoming more alert and by paying attention. Similarly, a subject whose heart rate is displayed on an oscilloscope can watch the rate decrease as he or she relaxes, thereby learning what physiological states allow the body to work easily and efficiently. The person can learn which behaviors relax the heart muscles and lower blood pressure and in time can learn to control them by reproducing behaviors associated with reduced heart rate.

Although a number of laboratory studies have demonstrated biofeedback's effectiveness in helping people manage a wide range of physiological problems, only carefully controlled research will ultimately answer persistent questions about its long-term effects. Few physicians use biofeedback regularly in their practices today, but biofeedback may be more fully incorporated into medical and mental health plans in the future. There are still many issues that need to be resolved in biofeedback. For example, under what conditions, with what kind of problems, and with what kinds of clients is biofeedback effective? Methodological issues, such as those described in Chapter 1 (Hawthorne effects, for example) make this a challenging research area.

Hypnosis

Learning Objective 8.2
Describe hypnotic induction, the effects and uses of hypnosis, and Barber's alternative explanation for hypnosis.

"You are falling asleep. Your eyelids are becoming heavy. The strain on your eyes is becoming greater and greater. Your muscles are relaxing. You are feeling sleepier and sleepier. You are feeling very relaxed."

These instructions are typical of those used in *hypnotic induction*—that is, the process used to hypnotize people. The generally accepted view of **hypnosis** is that individuals are in a semimystical or altered state of consciousness and no longer have control over their behavior. They are aware of their surroundings and are conscious, but their level of awareness and willingness to follow instructions are altered. A person's willingness to follow unconventional instructions given by the hypnotist, such as acting out or making funny noises, is **hypnotic susceptibility** or **suggestibility.** Most people can be hypnotized to some extent; children between ages 7 and 14 years are the most susceptible; those who daydream for recreation are also especially susceptible (Hoyt et al., 1989).

Effects of Hypnosis. People who have been hypnotized report that they know they have been hypnotized and are aware of their surroundings. Some report a special, almost mystical state, and most report a sense of time distortion. A time distortion effect of hypnosis is **age regression,** the ability to report details about an experience that took place many years earlier, or to act and feel like a child. Because few studies that report age regression during hypnosis have been controlled for accuracy of recall, the authenticity of age regression has been questioned (Nash, 1987). *Heightened memory* is another effect of hypnosis. Evidence indicates that hypnosis helps subjects to recall information that may otherwise be difficult to retrieve (e.g., McConkey & Kinoshita, 1988). However, techniques that do not involve hypnosis may work just as well for this purpose.

A third effect of hypnosis is pain reduction. In a case reported by E. F. Siegel (1979), hypnosis successfully reduced lower-leg pain in a woman who had undergone an above-the-knee amputation. (This phenomenon, called *phantom pain,* occurs in some amputees). Hypnosis has also been used to reduce pain from heat, pressure, and childbirth. Few studies of pain management, however, are conducted with adequate experimental rigor. Most patients showed signs of pain even when hypnotized. Also in many cases, analgesic drugs (pain relievers) were used along with the hypnotism. Some researchers (especially Barber, considered next) challenge the ability of hypnosis to reduce pain and reason that relaxation and a subject's positive attitude and lowered anxiety account for reported reductions in pain.

Cognitive-Behavioral Viewpoint. Theodore Xenophon Barber, one of the major skeptics of traditional theories of hypnotism, contends that the concepts of hypnosis and the hypnotic trance are meaningless and misleading. According to Barber, behaviors of hypnotized subjects are no different from behaviors of subjects willing to think about and imagine themes suggested to them. If subjects' attitudes toward the situation lead them to expect certain effects, those effects will be more likely to occur. Barber's approach is called the *cognitive-behavioral viewpoint.*

Barber's studies show that subjects given task-motivating instructions perform similarly to subjects undergoing hypnotic induction. Barber has concluded that task-motivation instructions are almost as effective as hypnotic-induction procedures in increasing subjects' responsiveness to task suggestions. The evidence showing that hypnosislike effects can be achieved in various ways (e.g., Bryant & McConkey, 1989) does not mean that psychologists must discard the concept or

hypnosis: An altered state of consciousness brought about by trance-induction procedures.

hypnotic susceptibility: The willingness to follow unconventional instructions while under hypnosis.

age regression: The ability, sometimes induced by hypnosis, to return to an earlier time in one's life and report events that occurred many years earlier.

use of hypnosis. It means that they should reconsider their traditional assumptions.

Hypnosis continues to be widely used as an aid in psychotherapy. Most clients report that it is a pleasant experience; therapists assert that in some cases it can (a) help focus clients' energy on a specific topic, (b) aid memory, and (c) help children to cope with the aftereffects of child abuse. Many therapists use hypnosis to help patients to change their behavior, including relaxation, memory enhancement, stress and anxiety reduction, weight loss, and cessation of smoking. Research into the process of hypnosis and its effects continues, with an emphasis on defining critical variables, both in hypnosis and in subjects who are the most and the least easily hypnotized (e.g., Spanos, Perlini, & Robertson, 1989), as well as ascertaining potential negative effects (e.g., Owens, Bliss, Koester, & Jeppsen, 1989). Psychologists who are skeptical about hypnosis may have the same attitude toward another closely related practice, meditation.

Meditation

Learning Objective 8.3
Describe the consciousness-altering technique called meditation and some of its effects.

Meditation has become an important part of Carolyn's life. Previously, searing migraines, stomach pains, and high blood pressure had afflicted Carolyn during stressful periods. Despite prescription drugs and frequent doctor visits, she had found little relief. Then, in a stress-management clinic, Carolyn discovered how to ease her tensions through meditation. Now, instead of popping a pill, she meditates at the onset of a headache.

Meditation involves intense concentration, restriction of incoming stimuli, and deep relaxation to produce a sense of detachment. Meditation has been used for centuries to alter consciousness and help relieve health problems. Practitioners report that it can reduce anxiety, tension headaches, backaches, asthma, and the need for sleep. It can also increase self-awareness and feelings of inner peace (West, 1982).

There are several forms of meditation, each using different techniques to induce an altered state of awareness. They all direct the focus of attention away from the outside world by using intense concentration. The forms of meditation now practiced in the Western world derive from the Eastern religions of Buddhism and Hinduism. Zen, yoga, and transcendental meditation are especially popular among people interested in holistic health.

People using *Zen Buddhist* techniques concentrate on their breathing and count their breaths, with the aim of focusing attention very carefully on a specific stimulus. People using yoga focus their attention by gazing at a fixed visual stimulus. *Yoga* also involves special physical and breathing exercises, with attempts to control autonomic physiological processes such as heart rate and blood pressure; yoga may also require a special seating position. Those using *transcendental meditation* use techniques similar to those of yoga and may repeat a phrase over and over to themselves, although they do not have to meditate while in a specific posture.

Although most theories that explain the nature of meditation and its effects rely on concepts that are not scientifically measurable or observable, some controlled studies have been done. The data from these studies have shown that meditators can alter physiological responses, including oxygen consumption, brain-wave activity, and sleep patterns (Pagano, Rose, Stivers, & Warrenburg, 1976). Follow-up studies of those who use self-hypnosis or meditation to relieve stress found that it continues to exert beneficial effects among those who continue its practice (Soskis, Orne, Orne, & Dinges, 1989). Such evidence encourages some scientists to continue to investigate meditation for relieving tension, anxiety, and arousal.

meditation: A state of consciousness induced by a variety of techniques and characterized by concentration, restriction of sensory stimuli, and deep relaxation.

Substance Abuse

Substances

Each year during the 1980s, physicians wrote more than 2 billion prescriptions for drugs. Of these, almost 50 million prescriptions were written yearly for the tranquilizer diazepam (Valium®). At least one third of all U.S. citizens between the ages of 18 and 74 years regularly use some kind of consciousness-altering drug that changes both brain activity and daily behavior.

In the United States, people consume caffeine-laden coffee and cola drinks, inhale nicotine, and drink beer, wine, and other alcoholic beverages daily. Although many of these drugs are not considered dangerous, they are far more potent than you may realize. A **drug** is any chemical substance that alters normal biological processes. Many widely used drugs are both psychoactive and **addictive.** A **psychoactive drug** is one that alters behavior, thought, or emotions; such drugs affect behavior by altering biochemical reactions in the nervous system, and this affects consciousness.

Whenever a behavior is a repetitive action or habit that increases the risk of disease or social or personal problems, psychologists consider it an **addictive behavior.** This includes a whole array of behaviors such as gambling, overeating, sexual obsessions, and especially substance abuse. Substance abuse usually involves a loss of control despite a person's attempt to control it. There are often short-term rewards (such as feeling euphoric or stimulated), followed by long-term deleterious effects (such as memory loss or kidney damage).

Learning Objective 8.4
List the criteria used to diagnose a substance abuser, and describe the potential biological, psychological, and behavioral effects of alcohol and other drugs.

drug: Any chemical substance that alters normal biological processes.

addictive: Causing a compulsive physiological need. Addictive drugs usually produce tolerance, and abstinence from them initially produces withdrawal symptoms.

psychoactive drug: [SIE-koh-AK-tiv] A drug that alters behavior, thought, or emotions, by altering biochemical reactions in the nervous system.

addictive behavior: A repetitive action or habit that increases the risk of disease or social or personal problems.

Use and Abuse

There is no doubt that the United States is a drug-using culture. We use drugs to help us wake up in the morning, to get us through stresses in the day, and to help us sleep. Complex reasons determine why people overuse and rely on drugs; when people do so, they are **substance abusers.** Most of these people turn to alcohol and other readily available drugs such as cocaine and marijuana, but substance abuse is not confined to these drugs. Psychologists are seeing a growing number of people abusing legal drugs, such as tranquilizers and diet pills, as well as illegal drugs, such as amphetamines and heroin. A person is a substance abuser if

- the substance has been used for at least 1 month
- the substance use has caused legal difficulties or social (such as familial) or vocational problems
- there is recurrent use in hazardous situations such as driving a car

Substance abuse can lead to psychological dependence, pathological use, or both. **Psychological dependence** is a compelling desire to use the drug, along with an inability to inhibit that desire. **Pathological use** refers to out-of-control episodes of use, such as an alcohol binge. Most drugs produce a physiological reaction when they are no longer administered; in general, this reaction is **dependence.** A person who is dependent and without the drug suffers from **withdrawal symptoms**—that is, physical reactions, which may include headaches, nausea, and an intense craving for the absent drug.

In addition, addictive drugs usually produce **tolerance**, a progressive insensitivity to repeated use of the drug in the same dosage and at the same degree of frequency. Because of tolerance, an addict must use increasing amounts of the drug and/or must use the drug with increasing frequency to achieve the same

substance abuser: Person who overuses and relies on drugs to deal with stress and anxiety.

psychological dependence: A compelling desire to use a drug, along with an inability to inhibit that desire.

pathological use: Out-of-control episodes of use, such as extensive periods of substance abuse, perhaps for days on end.

dependence: The state that occurs when there is a reliance on regular use of a drug, without which the individual suffers a psychological and/or a physiological reaction.

withdrawal symptoms: A variety of physiological reactions that occur when an addictive drug is no longer administered to an addict.

tolerance: The state that occurs when there is a progressive insensitivity to the effects of a specific drug and dosage when that drug is administered repeatedly.

substance dependence: The state that occurs when there is evidence of substance abuse, as well as withdrawal symptoms (at initial abstinence) or drug tolerance.

effect. For example, alcoholics must consume increasingly large amounts of alcohol to become drunk. Most addictive drugs produce both withdrawal symptoms and tolerance. When a person shows evidence of substance abuse and withdrawal symptoms or tolerance, the person is exhibiting **substance dependence.**

Each time that persons take psychoactive drugs, they change their ability to function normally. Specifically, psychoactive drugs change behavior by altering their physiology and their normal state of consciousness. Some drugs increase alertness and performance; others relax people and relieve high levels of arousal and tension. Some produce physical and psychological dependence. All psychoactive drugs alter a person's thoughts and moods, and they are all considered to be consciousness altering. Illicit use of drugs dropped during the late 1980s for most drugs except for use of cocaine and use by some special populations (Oetting & Beauvais, 1990). This is probably in response to national media campaigns, school- and community-based drug programs, and interventions in the workplace.

Both physiological and psychological factors cause drug abuse. For example, some people are considered high-risk individuals—they are more likely to develop a substance abuse problem for physiological and genetic reasons. For numerous others, boredom, loneliness, despair, anxiety—the emotional problems caused by stress—contribute to their abuse. Most researchers argue that no single explanation can account for drug use and abuse (Marlatt, Baer, Donovan, & Kivlahan, 1988). Few substance abusers have similar abuse patterns. Some people use only alcohol or only one other drug. Others are *polydrug* abusers and take several drugs. A polydrug abuser who is a heroin addict, for example, might also take amphetamines. When amphetamines are difficult to obtain, he or she might switch to barbiturates.

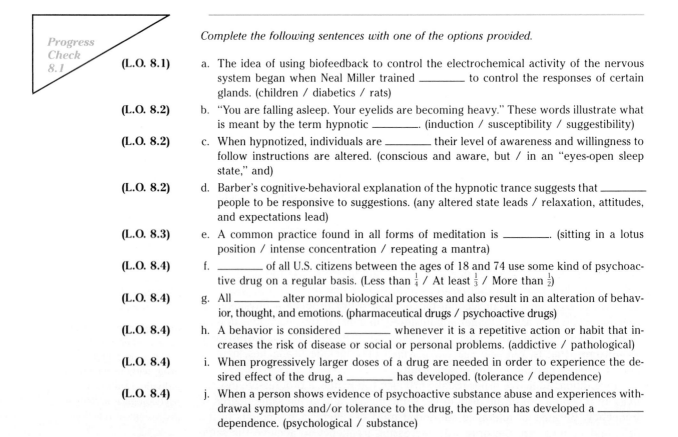

Progress Check 8.1

Complete the following sentences with one of the options provided.

(L.O. 8.1) a. The idea of using biofeedback to control the electrochemical activity of the nervous system began when Neal Miller trained ________ to control the responses of certain glands. (children / diabetics / rats)

(L.O. 8.2) b. "You are falling asleep. Your eyelids are becoming heavy." These words illustrate what is meant by the term hypnotic ________. (induction / susceptibility / suggestibility)

(L.O. 8.2) c. When hypnotized, individuals are ________ their level of awareness and willingness to follow instructions are altered. (conscious and aware, but / in an "eyes-open sleep state," and)

(L.O. 8.2) d. Barber's cognitive-behavioral explanation of the hypnotic trance suggests that ________ people to be responsive to suggestions. (any altered state leads / relaxation, attitudes, and expectations lead)

(L.O. 8.3) e. A common practice found in all forms of meditation is ________. (sitting in a lotus position / intense concentration / repeating a mantra)

(L.O. 8.4) f. ________ of all U.S. citizens between the ages of 18 and 74 use some kind of psychoactive drug on a regular basis. (Less than $\frac{1}{4}$ / At least $\frac{1}{3}$ / More than $\frac{1}{2}$)

(L.O. 8.4) g. All ________ alter normal biological processes and also result in an alteration of behavior, thought, and emotions. (pharmaceutical drugs / psychoactive drugs)

(L.O. 8.4) h. A behavior is considered ________ whenever it is a repetitive action or habit that increases the risk of disease or social or personal problems. (addictive / pathological)

(L.O. 8.4) i. When progressively larger doses of a drug are needed in order to experience the desired effect of the drug, a ________ has developed. (tolerance / dependence)

(L.O. 8.4) j. When a person shows evidence of psychoactive substance abuse and experiences withdrawal symptoms and/or tolerance to the drug, the person has developed a ________ dependence. (psychological / substance)

Altered Consciousness with Drugs

Drugs are often categorized by their effects on human behavior and by their chemical makeup. A wide range of substances are abused, and their effects and chemical compositions vary extensively. To understand drug abuse and its relationship to consciousness, researchers must consider the physiological effects of the drug, the social setting, and the personal factors and physiological makeup of the addict.

All the drugs discussed here are capable of creating a dependence that can not only alter the course of a person's life but also dismantle a normal family structure. Drug abuse has been under the critical eye of psychologists, physicians, politicians, and law enforcement officials for many years. Education programs for young people, designed to prevent drug abuse, are generally thought to be the most effective solution, and communication training and family therapy are often important adjuncts.

Learning Objective 8.5
Identify reasons why drug abuse is dangerous and the most effective approach for preventing it.

Alcohol Use and Abuse

Sedatives–hypnotics are drugs that relax and calm people, and in higher doses, they induce sleep. The most widely used sedative–hypnotic is alcohol. Even conservative people who do not think of themselves as drug users often use alcohol. Alcohol is used by thousands of people to help relieve stress. As a depressant, alcohol helps people rid themselves of tension and anxiety, to move from a state of active consciousness to one in which they do not have tension but are also less aware and alert. After several drinks, they may behave in erratic, irrational ways that are dangerous both for the drinkers and for those around them.

Learning Objective 8.6
Explain why alcohol is considered a drug, give statistics regarding its use, and describe how it affects the body and behavior.

sedatives–hypnotics: A class of drugs that relax and calm people and that in high doses, induce sleep.

Statistics. Alcohol consumption in the United States has been at an all-time high for more than a decade. According to the U.S. Department of Health and Human Services, about 80% of urban U.S. adults report having consumed alcohol at some time. It is estimated that 10 million people in the United States over age 18 years are problem drinkers or alcoholics (Barnes, 1988).

Effects. Alcohol is absorbed into the bloodstream from the stomach and small intestines. In general, alcohol, which is a central nervous system depressant, decreases inhibitions and thus increases some behaviors that are normally under tight control. For example, it may diminish people's fears, particularly their social inhibitions or their awareness of their own mortality, and it may make them less likely to restrain their aggressive impulses (Bushman & Cooper, 1990). The physiological effects of alcohol vary, depending on the amount of alcohol in the bloodstream and the weight and gender of the user. After equal amounts of alcohol consumption, women have higher blood alcohol levels than do men, even with allowance for differences in body weight (Frezza, et. al., 1990).

With increasing amounts of alcohol in the bloodstream, people typically exhibit progressively slowed behavior; often they exhibit severe motor disturbances such as staggering. Blood alcohol levels greater than 0.10% usually indicate that the person has consumed too much alcohol to function responsibly. In most states, a 0.10% blood alcohol level (i.e., 0.1 *milligrams* of alcohol per 100 *milliliters* of blood) legally defines intoxication; police officers may arrest drivers who have this level of blood alcohol. The nervous system becomes less sensitive, or accommodates, to alcohol with its increased usage. After months or years of drinking, drug tolerance develops, and a person has to consume ever increasing amounts of alcohol to achieve the same effect. Thus, when not in an alcoholic state, a

The liver at the top is normal. Excessive alcohol consumption has caused the middle liver to be fatty and unhealthy and the liver at the bottom to be cirrhotic.

APPLYING PSYCHOLOGY

Who Is at Risk for Alcholism?

Are some people more likely to develop substance abuse problems such as alcoholism than other people? The answer is "yes" according to researchers who study the biological side of alcoholism. Researchers have long asserted that genetics, blood and brain chemistry, and some specific brain structures predispose some people to alcoholism.

Studies have shown that alcoholics, more than nonalcoholics, tend to respond with physiological arousal to stress and other aversive stimulation. Finn and Pihl (1987), two McGill University researchers, decided to test the hypothesis that men with extensive family histories of alcoholism were more reactive physiologically to aversive stimulation than were control subjects. Further, they attempted to see whether alcohol reduces physiological responses more for men with a family history of alcoholism than for control subjects. Their overall aim was to find out whether some people are at high risk for alcoholism.

They divided men up into three groups based on family history: high, moderate, and low risk for alcoholism. The high-risk subjects had alcoholic fathers and grandfathers, and at least one other male alcoholic in the family. The moderate-risk subjects had one alcoholic parent, and no other close alcoholic relative. The low-risk subjects had no identifiable alcoholics in the present or the two previous generations of their family trees.

Finn and Pihl investigated two physiological responses, heart rate and blood volume, of subjects who knew they were going to receive mild electrical shocks. Anticipating a shock induces a physiological response in nearly everybody, but are the responses more pronounced in high-risk subjects? The results showed that sober high-risk subjects were more cardiovascularly reactive than sober moderate-risk subjects. In addition, alcohol consumption led to a reduction in physiological response in the high-risk group only. In the moderate- and low-risk groups, alcohol consumption increased physiological responses. Research following up on Finn and Pihl's work shows that sensitivity is especially acute after initially ingesting the alcohol (Newlin & Thomson, 1990).

According to Finn and Pihl, when a strict criterion for selecting high-risk subjects is used, a different pattern of alcohol sensitivity may result than when only a one-generation-alcoholic-father criterion is used. Men at high genetic risk for alcoholism in stressful situations show a consistent reduction in physiological responses when they consume alcohol. This finding suggests a genetic predisposition to be calmed by alcohol when faced with stressful or aversive stimulation. The researchers assert that a high-risk label should be assigned to an individual only if two prior generations have been considered. They were able to show a difference between the high-risk (two generations) and the moderate risk (one generation) subjects when comparing them to control low-risk subjects. Place a man who is genetically at high risk for alcoholism in a stressful situation, provide that man with alcohol, and the reinforcing effects of stress reduction are likely to make alcohol a highly rewarding substance (Pihl, Peterson, & Finn, 1990). The research continues; this study is just one of hundreds that examine the genetic and other risk factors of alcoholism.

- ***Why would dividing subjects into high, moderate, or low risk for alcoholism, based on the number of relatives who were alcoholics, help test the hypothesis that alcoholism may have genetic components?***
- ***What evidence did the researchers find that suggest a genetic predisposition to alcoholism among some of their subjects?***
- ***What are the implications of the findings of the Finn and Pihl study for men who have a father who is an alcoholic? Are the implications the same when a man is raised in a warm, nonstressful household?***

person who is a heavy drinker develops heightened anxiety, cravings, and other withdrawal symptoms (Levin, 1990).

Learning Objective 8.7
Make a distinction between a problem drinker and an alcoholic.

Problem Drinkers Versus Alcoholics. From both a medical and a psychological standpoint, alcohol abuse is one of the greatest social problems in the United States. Alcohol-related problems are medical, social, or psychological problems associated with alcohol use. A person who shows an alcohol-related problem, such as missing work occasionally, spending a paycheck to buy drinks for friends, or

TABLE 8.1 Warning signals of alcoholism

The following are some of the warning signals that a drinking problem is developing or has developed:
You drink more than you did when you first started to drink, and you tend to gulp your drinks.
You try to have a few extra drinks before or after drinking with others.
You occasionally or often drink alone.
You are noticeably drunk on important occasions.
You drink the "morning after" to overcome the effects of the previous day's drinking.
You drink to relieve feelings of boredom, depression, anxiety, or inadequacy.
You drink at regularly anticipated times, to get through difficult situations, or when you have problems.
You have weekend drinking bouts and Monday hangovers.
You suspect that you are losing control of your drinking: You drink more than you planned and get drunk when you did not want to.
You promise to drink less but do not.
You often regret what you have said or done while drinking.
You occasionally or often feel guilty about your drinking.
You are sensitive when others mention your drinking.
You occasionally or often deny your drinking or lie about it.
You have memory blackouts or pass out while drinking.
Your drinking is affecting your relationship with friends or family.
You have lost time at work or school because of drinking.
You occasionally or often stay away from people who do not drink.

From F. P. Rio, *The Adolescent: Development, relationships, and culture.* Boston: Allyn and Bacon, 1987.

losing his or her driver's license because of drunk driving, exhibits alcohol abuse. Alcohol-related problems due to *chronic* (i.e., repeated or continual) use may include a deteriorating liver condition, memory loss, and significant mood swings (Nace, 1987).

A person with alcohol-related problems who also has a physiological and psychological need to consume alcohol is an **alcoholic.** All alcoholics are problem drinkers, but not all problem drinkers are alcoholics. Without alcohol, alcoholics develop physiological withdrawal symptoms. In addition, they often develop tolerance, whereby a single drink or even a few will not affect them. Active alcoholics are often unable to face the world without alcohol. Table 8.1 lists the warning signs of alcoholism.

Learning Objective 8.8 Identify some of the causes of alcoholism, and describe two approaches for treating it.

Causes. The causes of alcoholism are complex; heredity (Blum 1990), alcohol abuse in parents, societal pressures, and antisocial behavior are only some. There is no single personality type for all alcoholics, and alcoholism cuts across socioeconomic lines (Graham & Strenger, 1988). Researchers do know, however, that alcoholism runs in families; this issue is discussed in the Applying Psychology box on the preceding page. A son of an alcoholic parent is four times more likely to develop alcoholism than a son of nonalcoholic parents. If that son is involved in criminal behavior as well, he is far more likely to become an alcoholic himself. Nevertheless, about 60% of alcohol abusers are from families in which no other member shows signs of abuse (Cadoret, Troughton, & O'Gorman, 1987).

alcoholic: A problem drinker who has both a physiological and a psychological need to consume alcohol products and to experience their effects.

Treatment. For some alcoholics, psychological and medical treatment is successful. The most widely known program is Alcoholics Anonymous, which helps

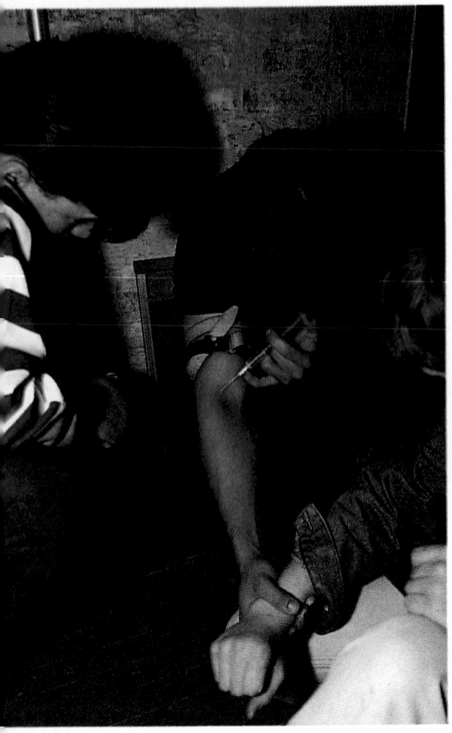

Peer pressure and unsatisfactory social and economic conditions often contribute to heroin use.

individuals abstain from alcohol by providing a therapeutic and emotionally nurturing environment. Begun in 1935, Alcoholics Anonymous includes 600,000 members, and its success rate is considerably better than that of many other treatment programs. Programs such as Alcoholics Anonymous make abstinence their goal. The fundamental assumptions, based on the difficulty of alcoholics to control their drinking, are that an alcoholic is an alcoholic forever and that alcoholism should be considered diseaselike in nature and thus incurable (Peele, 1984).

Some practitioners, on the other hand, believe that limited, non–problem drinking should be the goal of treatment programs (Vaillant & Milofsky, 1982). This view assumes that alcohol abuse is a learned behavior and can therefore be unlearned. It also assumes that abstinence is an unattainable goal. Those who prefer controlled use claim that alcohol abuse is merely a symptom of a larger underlying problem such as poor self-esteem and family instability (Sobell & Sobell, 1982). However, most researchers hold that controlled drinking is not a reliable answer for most alcoholics (Hall, Havassy, & Wasserman, 1990), although it might be a reasonable alternative for young, heavy drinkers who are not yet alcoholics (Nathan & Skinstad, 1987).

Family therapy is generally considered an important part of treatment for alcoholism because one family member's problem with alcohol becomes a problem for the entire family. Combined with individual or group therapy and Alcoholics Anonymous or some other self-help group, a multimodal (i.e., involving various modes of treatment) approach is often the best treatment plan (Levin, 1990).

Barbiturates and Tranquilizers

Learning Objective 8.9
State how barbiturates and tranquilizers affect the body, and explain who is a potential tranquilizer abuser.

Like alcohol, most barbiturates and tranquilizers are considered to be in the sedatives–hypnotics class of drugs, which relax and calm individuals, and often when taken in higher doses, induce sleep. *Barbiturates* decrease the excitability of neurons throughout the nervous system. They calm an individual by depressing the central nervous system. Used as sedatives, drugs such as phenobarbital have largely been replaced by another class of drugs, often called *tranquilizers.*

Tranquilizers are a chemical class of drugs (technically, benzodiazepines) that sedate, calm, and relax people. With a somewhat lower potential for abuse and for central-nervous-system-drepressing effects, they are sometimes called minor tranquilizers. Valium® and Librium® are two of the most widely used tranquilizers prescribed by physicians for relief of mild stress. Such drugs have been widely abused by all segments of society because of their availability.

Opiates: Heroin

Learning Objective 8.10
Describe the physical and psychological effects of heroin and the typical heroin user; also describe methadone treatment.

Heroin is the most widely known *opiate* (derivative of opium, which dulls the senses, relieves pain, tranquilizes, and induces euphoria). Most opiates are **narcotic drugs,** which generally have sedative properties, are addictive, and produce tolerance. Like many other addictive drugs, heroin is considered biologically reinforcing; many researchers feel that it is this reinforcing property that keeps people addicted (Wise & Bozarth, 1987).

narcotic drugs: Drugs with sedative properties that are addictive and produce tolerance.

In the past, opium has been used for everything from relieving children's crying to reducing pain from headaches, surgery, childbirth, and menstruation. Today, opium is illegal, but heroin and other opiates such as morphine (which is illegal when not prescribed by a physician) are readily available "on the street" from dealers of illegal drugs. The high cost of the drugs has led many addicts to engage in crime to support their habits.

Heroin can be smoked or eaten, but typically it is injected into a vein. Heroin addicts tend to be young, poor, and undereducated. Most become addicts as a result of peer pressure and a desire for upward mobility among their peers. Estimates of the number of heroin addicts range dramatically from half a million to 13 million active users. Heroin users often use other drugs, including alcohol, amphetamines, barbiturates, and cocaine, in combination with heroin. This *polydrug* use makes it difficult to classify heroin users as addicts of one drug or another. Moreover, even when classification is possible, treatment is complicated by the medical, psychological, and social problems associated with using many drugs simultaneously.

The major physiological effect of heroin is impaired functioning of the respiratory system. Other effects are some deleterious changes in the heart, arteries, and veins, as well as possible constipation and loss of appetite. Few heroin addicts die of overdoses. A lethal dose of the drug would be much larger than that injected even by heavy users. More often than not, heroin addicts die from taking a mixture of drugs (such as heroin and alcohol) or from disease, especially AIDS, contracted from nonsterile needles and other paraphernalia used in injecting the substance into the bloodstream. Some lawmakers are advocating community programs to distribute sterile needles to drug users to prevent the spread of AIDS, but, as you might expect, such programs are extremely controversial.

The only major successful heroin treatment program for heroin addiction is methadone maintenance. Like heroin, methadone is an addictive drug and must be consumed daily or withdrawal symptoms will occur. Unlike heroin, however, methadone does not produce euphoria or tolerance in the user, and daily dosages do not need to be increased. Because methadone blocks the effect of heroin, a normal injection of heroin has no effect on individuals on a methadone maintenance program. As a result, many methadone-treatment patients (there are about 100,000 such individuals) who might be tempted to use heroin to achieve a high do not do so. Moreover, because methadone is legal, many of the patients are able to hold jobs to support themselves and stay out of jail.

Smoking marijuana interferes with mental processes.

Marijuana

Learning Objective 8.11
State statistics concerning the use of marijuana, and discuss its physical and psychological effects on the user.

Consciousness-altering drugs that affect moods, thoughts, memory, and perception are *psychedelics* (or *hallucinogens*). Perhaps the most widely used of these drugs is marijuana (nearly 20% of the adult population has tried it).

The marijuana that is used is the dried leaves and flowering tops of the *cannabis sativa* plant, the active ingredient of which is **THC**, tetrahydrocannabinol. Marijuana can be ingested (eaten), but in the United States, it is most commonly smoked. It is interesting to note that smoking marijuana is inefficient because 20–80% of the active ingredient, THC, is lost in the smoke.

People smoke marijuana to alter their consciousness, to alleviate depression, or just to be distracted. Most users report a sense of elation and well-being, but others assert that it makes them feel fearful and induces psychoses. Also, some report other adverse reactions, such as sleeplessness, bad dreams, and nausea. Marijuana's effects are felt about 1 minute after smoking, begin to diminish within an hour, and disappear almost completely after 3–5 hours, although traces of THC can be detected in the body for weeks afterward.

Individuals under the influence of marijuana demonstrate impaired performance on simple intellectual and psychomotor tasks. They become less task-oriented and have slower reaction times. Marijuana also interferes with memory. Little is known about how marijuana affects fetal development or its long-term effects on people who use it from early adolescence until middle age.

THC (tetrahydrocannabinol): The psychoactive ingredient in marijuana.

Although researchers agree that marijuana is not physiologically addictive like heroin, many argue that it produces psychological dependence. People become dependent on marijuana for a variety of reasons. One is that it is more easily available than substances such as barbiturates and cocaine. Another is the desired relief of tension that marijuana users experience. Further, most people believe that the drug has few or no long-lasting side effects, though this is untrue. For example, marijuana has up to 50% more tar than an equivalent weight of tobacco cigarettes and because of the way that marijuana is usually inhaled, much of it is deposited in the lungs. Like tobacco tar, marijuana tar causes cancer. Also, smoking marijuana almost every day for 6 weeks can impair the lungs, causing asthmalike conditions. Marijuana may also have lasting effects on the cardiovascular, immune, and reproductive systems.

Amphetamines and Cocaine

Learning Objective 8.12
State statistics concerning the use of amphetamines and cocaine, and discuss their physical and psychological effects on users.

Amphetamines and cocaine are considered psychostimulants and are highly addictive. A **psychostimulant** is a drug that increases alertness, reduces fatigue, and elevates mood when taken in low-to-moderate doses. Acting on the central nervous system, *amphetamines* are a chemical grouping of drugs (such as Dexedrine®) that increase excitability, depress appetite, and increase alertness and talkativeness. They also increase blood pressure and heart rate. After long-term use, individuals have cravings for the drug and experience exhaustion, lethargy, and depression.

Cocaine was widely abused in the 1980s. At least 15% of high school seniors have used cocaine at least once. Admissions to cocaine treatment centers have increased sharply, as have deaths associated with cocaine abuse. *Crack,* the processed and smokable form of cocaine, is also in wide use; it is potent and readily available (especially in the schools).

Cocaine, a central nervous system stimulant and an anesthetic, increases heartbeat, decreases appetite, and raises blood pressure. It can be smoked, sniffed, or injected; when sniffed, it temporarily numbs the user's nasal passage. Sniffing it up the nostrils—snorting—is the most popular method of using cocaine. Once inhaled, it is absorbed into the tiny blood vessels that line the nose. Within 5 minutes, a user starts to feel the effects; the peak effect is in 15 minutes and may last 20–30 minutes. The smokable form of cocaine, crack, delivers an unusually large dose and induces euphoria in a matter of seconds. An even more dangerous form of cocaine, called "ice," is the combination of cocaine with heroin; when smoked, it is especially potent and dangerous. Cocaine produces an exceptional high, but it is short lived, and the user's mood drops rapidly. Because cocaine is soluble in water, it can also be injected; however, due to the concern about contracting AIDS through infected needles, such intravenous injections are now less common (Washton, 1989).

Cocaine acts on neurotransmitters in the brain such as norepinephrine (noradrenalin) and dopamine. It also stimulates sympathetic activity in the peripheral nervous system, giving rise to increases in heart rate, blood pressure, and blood sugar, and dilation of the pupils. It produces a light-headed feeling, a sense of alertness, increased energy, and sometimes a sense of infallibility. People who use cocaine report feeling a sense of new confidence and self-worth, increased energy, increased awareness, and sexual arousal.

psychostimulant: A drug that, in low-to-moderate doses, increases alertness, reduces fatigue, and elevates mood.

Why is cocaine use so prevalent in our society? *First,* cocaine acts as a powerful reward. For example, animals will work incessantly, even to the point of exhaustion, to obtain cocaine. A cocaine high is pleasurable, but also brief—users wish to repeat the sensation. When the cocaine wears off, it is replaced by unpleasant feelings (known as crashing). When people have these unpleasant feelings, they can alleviate them through more cocaine. *Second,* cocaine produces tolerance and potent urges and cravings. *Third,* in our pleasure-now, pay-later society, to some people, instant gratification through drug use seems appropriate (Washton, 1989).

Cocaine is considered a drug with high abuse potential and little medical value. The drug causes problems due to overdoses (heart attacks, hemorrhage, and heat stroke), complications associated with its administration (nose sores, lung damage, infection at injection sites, and AIDS), and use during pregnancy (premature birth, malformations of the fetus, and spontaneous abortions). At a minimum, the drug is addictive, produces irritability, and eating and sleeping disturbances. It also seems to precipitate other disturbances, such as panic attacks. Further, cocaine can produce serious mental disorders, including paranoia, agitation, and suicidal behavior.

Treatment for cocaine addiction first requires getting the cocaine addict into therapy, providing a structured program, and making sure that the addict refrains from all mood-altering addictive drugs, including alcohol. Blocking the pleasure centers with a drug such as methadone is not realistic because cocaine works through most of the major neurotransmitter systems. Even if such a drug could be found, it would probably make the person spiritless. Because a drug treatment for this addiction is so hard to achieve, this places even more of a burden on psychological therapy. Treatment usually means a strong educational involvement, family involvement, group and individual therapy, and long-term follow-up—and it is time intensive and expensive.

Progress Check 8.2

Complete each of the following with one of the options provided.

(L.O. 8.5) a. *Most* drugs that are capable of creating a dependence ________. (are not dangerous / can destroy a person's life and family structure)

(L.O. 8.6) b. Alcohol is a central nervous system ________. (stimulant / depressant)

(L.O. 8.6) c. If a male and female of equal height and weight consume an equal amount of alcohol ________ blood alcohol level. (they will have an equal / the female will have a greater)

(L.O. 8.6) d. A blood alcohol level of ________ is used as the legal definition of intoxication in most states. (0.10% / 1% / 10%)

(L.O. 8.7) e. Alcohol abuse ________. (is a behavior found only in alcoholics / creates medical, social, and psychological problems)

(L.O. 8.8) f. The son of an alcoholic parent is ________ times more likely to develop alcoholism than a son of nonalcoholic parents. (two / four / ten)

(L.O. 8.8) g. Alcoholics Anonymous is based on the assumption that ________. (once an alcoholic, always an alcoholic / alcoholism is curable)

(L.O. 8.9) h. Valium® and other prescribed mild tranquilizers that sedate, calm, and relax people have ________ substance abuse problems in the United States. (decreased / added to)

(L.O. 8.10) i. The major physiological effect of heroin use is impaired functioning of the ________ system. (respiratory / circulatory / central nervous)

(L.O. 8.10) j. Most heroin users who die from their use of the drug do so because they ________. (inject a lethal dose / are polydrug users)

(L.O. 8.10) k. Methadone ________ heroin. (blocks the effect of / induces nausea if a person uses)

(L.O. 8.11) l. Marijuana ________ memory. (enhances / interferes with)

(L.O. 8.12) m. Amphetamines and cocaine ________ addictive. (produce a psychological dependence, but are not / are highly)

(L.O. 8.12) n. Cocaine is a central nervous system ________ and an anesthetic. (depressant / stimulant)

(L.O. 8.12) o. A combination of cocaine and heroin that is smoked by users is called ________. (crack / PCP / ice)

Module Summary

Controlling Consciousness: Biofeedback, Hypnosis, and Meditation

- ▲ Biofeedback studies have explored the extent to which subjects can learn to control their body functions and behavior by monitoring their neuronal activity (p. 142).
- ▲ The traditional view of hypnosis is that it is a special state of consciousness brought about by trance-induction methods. Hypnosis can produce special effects such as age regression, increased memory, and insensitivity to pain (p. 143).
- ▲ Meditation has its roots in the Eastern religions of Buddhism and Hinduism. Its popular forms (Zen, yoga, and transcendental meditation) have been practiced only recently in the Western world (p. 144).

Substance Abuse

- ▲ Whenever a behavior is a repetitive action or habit that increases the risk of disease or social or personal problems, psychologists consider it an addictive behavior (p. 145).
- ▲ A person is a *substance abuser* if (1) the substance has been used for at least 1 month; (2) the substance use has caused legal difficulties or social or vocational problems; and (3) there is recurrent use in hazardous situations (p. 145).

Altered Consciousness with Drugs

- ▲ Alcohol affects behavior in proportion to its level in the bloodstream. Alcohol can become physiologically addictive, and many people are psychologically dependent on the drug (p. 147).
- ▲ Barbiturates and tranquilizers are in the class of drugs that relax and calm individuals and often, when taken in higher doses, induce sleep (p. 150).
- ▲ Although heroin is addicting, its use, in and of itself, is not usually lethal. Although addictive, methadone is legal, medically safe, and does not induce tolerance (p. 150).
- ▲ A *psychostimulant* is a drug that increases alertness, reduces fatigue, and elevates mood when taken in low-to-moderate doses. Cocaine is such a drug, with high abuse potential and little medical value (pp. 151–153).

KEY TERMS

addictive, p. 145
addictive behavior, p. 145
age regression, p. 143
alcoholic, p. 149
biofeedback, p. 142
dependence, p. 145
drug, p. 145
hypnosis, p. 143
hypnotic susceptibility, p. 143
meditation, p. 144
narcotic drugs, p. 150
pathological use, p. 145
psychoactive drug, p. 145
psychological dependence, p. 145
psychostimulant, p. 152
sedatives–hypnotics, p. 147
substance abuser, p. 145
substance dependence, p. 146
THC (tetrahydrocannabinol), p. 151
tolerance, p. 146
withdrawal symptoms, p. 146

SELF-TEST

Module 8

- Before taking the self-test, **recite** and **review**.
- Use the key at the back of the text to *correct* your answers.
- *Restudy* pages that correspond to any questions you answered incorrectly.

1. Biofeedback involves techniques that enable people to gain control over the ________ activity of some organs and body functions.
   a. subliminal
   b. erratic
   c. voluntary
   d. involuntary
2. Which of the following is a true statement concerning susceptibility to hypnosis?
   a. Most people can be hypnotized.
   b. Children between the ages of 7 and 14 are the most susceptible subjects for hypnosis.
   c. People who daydream about recreational activities have a high susceptibility to hypnotic induction.
   d. all of the above
3. Dory sits on the floor in a relaxed, straight-posture, crossed-leg position. She gazes at light reflecting from a glass bowl containing water, and maintains a deep, steady breathing pattern. Most likely, Dory is involved in a technique called
   a. self-hypnosis
   b. sitting
   c. yoga
   d. transcendental meditation
4. Which of the following is considered an addictive behavior?
   a. sexual obsession
   b. overeating
   c. substance abuse
   d. all of the above
5. "Pathological use" of a drug means that a person has
   a. physical reactions such as headaches, nausea, dizziness, sneezing, and stomach pain when the drug is withheld.
   b. abused a drug on a regular basis for at least 1 month and has experienced problems as a result.
   c. a compelling desire to use a drug, along with an inability to inhibit that desire.
   d. episodes of being completely out-of-control with the use of a drug.
6. Currently, it is thought that the most effective way to prevent substance abuse is to
   a. conduct educational programs about drugs for young people.
   b. develop more lenient laws to eliminate the "forbidden fruit" attraction.
   c. restrict the use of legal and illegal drugs in public places.
   d. run a national campaign advocating the controlled use of drugs.
7. What percentage of adults in the United States have consumed alcohol at some time?
   a. 25%
   b. 48%
   c. 67%
   d. 80%

8. An alcoholic is a person who
   a. drinks alcohol every day.
   b. gets rowdy as a result of consuming alcohol.
   c. gets a DWI (driving while intoxicated) citation.
   d. cannot control drinking or must drink alcohol to prevent psychological and physical withdrawal symptoms from occurring.
9. The goal of controlled drinking
   a. may be a reasonable goal for young, heavy drinkers who are not yet alcoholics.
   b. is an effective treatment alternative for most alcoholics.
   c. is an important goal because total abstinence is unobtainable for most alcoholics.
   d. will work if the alcoholic also attends Alcoholics Anonymous meetings.
10. When comparing the effects of minor tranquilizers to barbiturates, we find that
    a. barbiturates are narcotic drugs, and tranquilizers are psychostimulants.
    b. tranquilizers tend to depress activity in the central nervous system to a lesser degree than barbiturates.
    c. barbiturates are prescribed by physicians more frequently than are tranquilizers.
    d. tranquilizers calm and relax people; barbiturates excite and energize people.
11. Cross out the statement concerning methadone that is *false.*
    a. Methadone is used as a treatment for heroin addiction.
    b. Methadone is a legal, addictive drug.
    c. If not used daily, a person taking methadone will experience withdrawal symptoms.
    d. Methadone produces drug tolerance.
12. When a person uses marijuana, traces of THC remain in the body for
    a. about 1 hour.
    b. 3–5 hours.
    c. weeks.
    d. life.
13. Which of the following is *not* a known effect of cocaine use? Cocaine
    a. sedates patients who are in extreme pain.
    b. has the potential for fatal overdose.
    c. can cause malformations in developing fetuses.
    d. can cause panic attacks and mental disorders.
14. Two drugs that are associated with AIDS are
    a. marijuana and ice.
    b. ice and crack.
    c. cocaine and heroin.
    d. heroin and marijuana.
15. One reason that people abuse and become addicted to psychoactive drugs is that, in general, psychoactive drugs
    a. are psychedelics.
    b. have narcotic qualities.
    c. can be obtained with a physician's prescription.
    d. have reinforcing effects because they temporarily reduce or eliminate unpleasant emotional and physical feelings.

Connections

If you are interested in . . .	Turn to . . .	To learn more about . . .
Sleep and dreaming	◆ Chapter 10, p. 406	How personality researchers use dreaming as an important part of their personality theories
	◆ Chapter 12, p. 502	How stress affects sleep and dreams
	◆ Chapter 13, p. 540	The impact of depression on sleep
	◆ Chapter 14, p. 560	Why Freud's interpretation of dreams is used as a therapeutic technique by many therapists
Consciousness	◆ Chapter 12, p. 481	How biological underpinnings of normal everyday awareness depend on normal consciousness
	◆ Chapter 12, p. 488	How everyday awareness is affected in adverse ways when people are under stress
	◆ Chapter 14, p. 562	How treatment procedures of maladjustment sometimes rely on the notion of an *un*conscious to direct day-to-day behavior
Substance abuse	◆ Chapter 8, p. 281	How drug use by pregnant women affects their unborn children
	◆ Chapter 12, p. 498	Why people turn to substances such as alcohol to help relieve stress
	◆ Chapter 15, p. 598	How people's attitudes about life-styles, including substance use and abuse, are influenced by parents and peers

Because human beings are aware of their surroundings and can report how they feel and how they have felt, researchers can ask them to describe, measure, and compare their conscious states to other times when they have been in an altered state of consciousness. Not only can researchers take self-reports, but they also can measure physiological changes that take place in various states of consciousness. Thus physiological psychologists (Chapter 2, p. 51) measure changes in brain functions during sleep, and psychopharmacologists study behavior changes after an organism has consumed drugs. Learning theorists (Chapter 5) study how the brain stores information that has recently been learned in drugged or nondrugged states. Is intellectual functioning effected by altered states of consciousness? Chapter 11, p. 454 discusses the nature of intelligence and the biological and environmental influences on intelligence. Can altered states of consciousness help in therapy? Researchers address those issues in treatment studies discussed in Chapter 14 (p. 561). Last, people's motivation to succeed and their emotional responses are affected by their level of consciousness, topics discussed in Chapter 9 (p. 381).

Because human beings are aware of their consciousness, it is especially interesting to study. Yet, as in so many areas of psychology, it is not easy to study. So many variables affect consciousness that researchers must be especially sensitive to experimental controls, such as those discussed in Chapter 1 (p. 22). Nonetheless, after well-designed studies are conducted, inferences can be made (Statistical appendix, p. 654) about how people interact with others in our social world (Chapter 15, p. 613).

Module 9 ► CLASSICAL CONDITIONING 160

Module 10 ► OPERANT CONDITIONING AND COGNITIVE LEARNING 174

Chapter 5

Learning

More than any topic in psychology, the study of learning has undergone intense scrutiny because learning is involved in most behaviors that psychologists study. The study of learning began with studies of conditioning. Those early studies by Pavlov, which are now widely-known, are a part of the vocabulary of day-to-day life. As many people know, Pavlov conditioned his dogs to salivate when they heard a bell. This process of conditioning is neither simple nor isolated to dogs, bells, and laboratories. Classical conditioning is a process that occurs in animals and human beings and accounts for a wide array of behaviors, including our well-known fears of dentists, German shepherd dogs, and even state troopers. This chapter's first module presents the basic findings of studies of classical conditioning, the key variables that affect it, and the applications of classical conditioning to everyday life.

Learning involves more than the mere association of bells and food, and although classical conditioning helps explain well some behavioral phenomena, it is not comprehensive enough to explain why people work in factories, develop a love of money, or use polished table manners. The chapter's second module presents an introduction to operant conditioning and cognitive learning. Operant conditioning explains especially well the role that reinforcers and punishers play in our lives. It helps explain why children develop some specific behaviors and, when combined with the more cognitive learning theories, can explain a host of behaviors that classical conditioning can not explain. The last part of the chapter focuses on four types of cognitive learning: insight, latent, generative, and observational learning. Together, the theories discussed in this chapter explain a range of learned behaviors.

Module 9

Classical Conditioning

LEARNING OBJECTIVES

When you have mastered the material in this module, you will be able to

Introduction (p. 161)

9.1 Define learning and explain how psychologists study it (p. 161).

Classical Conditioning (pp. 161–165)

9.2 Explain how conditioned responses compare and contrast with reflexes (p. 161).

9.3 Describe classical conditioning and the types of stimuli and responses involved (p. 162).

9.4 Give examples of responses learned through classical conditioning (p. 164).

9.5 Describe higher-order conditioning (p. 165).

Key Variables in Classical Conditioning (pp. 165–171)

9.6 Explain how the strength, timing, frequency, and predictability of the unconditioned stimulus affect classical conditioning (p. 165).

9.7 Describe extinction and spontaneous recovery in classical conditioning (p. 167).

9.8 Discuss stimulus generalization and stimulus discrimination in classical conditioning (p. 167).

SQ3R

- ▲ **Survey** to set goals for studying.
- ▲ Ask **questions** as you **read.**
- ▲ Stop occasionally to **recite** and **review.**

plus

- ▲ **Write** a summary of key points.
- ▲ **Reflect** on the hypotheses, evidence, and implications of this material and on the relevance it has to *your* life.

learning: A relatively permanent change in an organism that occurs as a result of experiences in the environment, often seen in overt behavior.

conditioning: A systematic procedure through which new responses are learned.

A former Marine made a surprising public demonstration of the power of conditioning. This Marine had been a sniper in Vietnam, where he learned to dive for cover at the sound of gunfire. Gunfire was a stimulus followed by death and destruction, and soldiers quickly learned to seek cover on hearing it. While on leave in Houston, this Marine heard a car backfire as he walked down a sidewalk. He instantly dove for cover—right through a storefront window. Fortunately, he wasn't seriously injured, but he certainly startled those around him. He had been conditioned to seek cover at the sound of gunfire (and by association, cars backfiring).

By the time we're adults, experience has taught us a large number of simple, predictable associations. We know, for example, that a day at the beach without sunblock will result in a painful sunburn, that staying up late the night before an exam will not help our grades, and that a gas station should be our next stop when the fuel gauge reads empty. We have also learned complicated processes, such as how to drive a car, play baseball, use a computer, and appreciate music—from Bach to Springsteen. Some people also learn socially unproductive behaviors, such as stealing and drug abuse. We also learn how others view us and how they respond to our actions.

Learning Objective 9.1
Define learning, and explain how psychologists study it.

Psychologists define **learning** as a relatively permanent change in the organism that occurs as a result of experience; this change is often seen in overt or observed behavior, but not always. For example, a teenager may learn good driving skills but may show them only rarely. The definition of learning has three important parts: Experience in the environment, change in the organism, and permanence.

First, in order for learning to occur, the organism must experience something in the environment. Second, some measurable change in the organism must be evident. The third component, permanence, means that this measurable change does not quickly disappear.

Because the internal processes of learning cannot be seen, psychologists study the *results* of learning, usually seen in overt behavior, which may include solving an algebra problem or throwing a ball. They also measure physiological changes, such as brainwave activity, heartbeat, and temperature. It is important to remember that practice and repeated experiences sharpen our skills and ensure that newly acquired learning, information, and skills are recalled and easily exhibited. When learning has occurred, some process within us has changed, and a physiological change has occurred as well. Most psychologists agree that learning results from one of three basic processes: classical conditioning, operant conditioning, and cognitive learning.

Classical Conditioning

Learning Objective 9.2
Explain how conditioned responses compare and contrast with reflexes.

Imagine you are in a dark movie theater when sinister music begins to play. Do you slump down into your seat? Cover your eyes? Hold your breath? People generally experience suspense or fear when they hear sinister music during a horror movie. Such a response has been learned. Psychologists say that this type of learned response has been *conditioned;* it is termed a *conditioned response.*

In a general sense, psychologists use the term *conditioning* to mean *learning.* **Conditioning** is a systematic procedure through which associations and responses to specific stimuli are learned. Consider what generally happens when sinister music is played during a horror movie. We know that something evil will soon happen, and we become fearful. We have been conditioned to feel that way toward the music. In the terminology used by psychologists, the sinister music is the *stimulus*, and fear is the *response*. Psychologists who first studied conditioning found definite relationships between specific stimuli and specific responses. Each time the stimulus occurred, the same reflexive response, or behavior, followed. These responses are not learned; they are automatic and are termed **reflexes.** For example, if a dentist sticks a needle into your gum, your muscles will probably tense, and you may try to pull away. In this case, the pain caused by the needle is the stimulus, and muscles tensing and trying to pull away are automatic reflex responses. Many people have *learned* the response of fear to the stimulus of sitting in a dentist's chair; they have learned to associate the chair with needles, drilling, and pain. A chair by itself does not elicit fear, but when associated with pain, it becomes a stimulus that can elicit fear. This is an example of conditioning—the procedure by which a person learns an association and a response (such as fear) to a neutral stimulus (such as a dentist's chair). Some conditioned behaviors occur so automatically that they appear to be reflexive. Like reflexes, these conditioned responses are involuntary, but unlike relexes, they are learned.

Learning Objective 9.3
Describe classical conditioning and the types of stimuli and responses involved.

Pavlovian or Classical Conditioning

In 1927, Ivan Pavlov (1849–1936), a Russian physiologist, summarized a now-famous series of experiments. His research began quite by accident in a series of studies on how saliva and gastric secretions work in the digestive processes of dogs. He knew that it is normal for dogs to salivate when they eat—salivation is a reflexive behavior that aids digestion—but the dogs were salivating *before* they tasted food. Pavlov reasoned that this might be happening because the dogs had learned to associate the trainers, who brought them food, with the food itself.

What Pavlov discovered was **classical conditioning,** now also called *Pavlovian conditioning.* In classical conditioning, a stimulus can bring about a response that was initially evoked by another stimulus. The process happens in this way: When a neutral stimulus (such as a bell) is associated with a stimulus that naturally brings about a response (such as food), the neutral stimulus (the bell) over time will bring about the same response as the natural stimulus. Pavlov termed the natural stimulus (e.g., food) an **unconditioned stimulus** and the natural response (e.g., salivating) an **unconditioned response.** The unconditioned response occurs naturally, without learning, to the unconditioned stimulus.

Pavlov started with a relatively simple experiment to teach dogs to salivate in response to a bell. First, he attached tubes inside the dogs' mouths to measure the amount of saliva produced by the unconditioned stimulus, food. He then introduced the new stimulus, a bell (see Figure 9.1). He called this a *neutral stimulus,* because the sound of a bell is not related to salivation.

Pavlov measured the amount of saliva the dogs produced when a bell was rung by itself; the amount was negligible. He began the conditioning process by ringing the bell and *immediately* placing food in the dogs' mouths. After this was done several times, the dogs salivated in response to the sound of the bell alone. Pavlov reasoned that the dogs had learned that the bell meant that food was coming. Pavlov termed the bell, which elicited salivation as a result of learning, a **conditioned stimulus.** He termed salivation, the learned response to the sound of the bell, a **conditioned response.** From his experiments, Pavlov discovered that the conditioned stimulus (the bell) brought about a similar but somewhat weaker response than the unconditioned stimulus (the food). The process of classical conditioning is outlined in Figure 9.2.

reflex: An involuntary, automatic behavior in response to stimuli that occurs without prior learning; such behaviors usually show little variability from instance to instance.

classical conditioning: A conditioning process in which an originally neutral stimulus, through repeated pairing with a stimulus that naturally elicits a response, comes to elicit a similar or even identical response; sometimes called *Pavlovian conditioning.*

unconditioned stimulus: A stimulus that normally produces an involuntary, measurable response.

unconditioned response: The unlearned or involuntary response to an unconditioned stimulus.

conditioned stimulus: A neutral stimulus that, through repeated association with an unconditioned stimulus, becomes capable of eliciting a conditioned response.

conditioned response: The response elicited by a conditioned stimulus.

Figure 9.1

Pavlov attached a tube to a dog's cheek and measured the number of drops of saliva produced in response to food paired with the sound of a bell and to the sound of the bell alone. The dog learned to associate the ringing of the bell with the presentation of food. This kind of association is a fundamental component of classical conditioning.

The key characteristic of classical conditioning is the use of an originally neutral stimulus (a bell) to elicit a response (salivation) through repeated pairing of the neutral stimulus with an unconditioned stimulus (food) that elicits the response naturally. On the first few trials or pairings, conditioning is unlikely to occur. With additional trials, there is a greater likelihood that conditioning will occur. After dozens or even hundreds of pairings, the neutral stimulus will yield a conditioned response. We generally refer to this as the acquisition process; we say that an

Figure 9.2

In classical conditioning, there are three basic stages by which a neutral stimulus eventually leads to a conditioned response such as salivating.

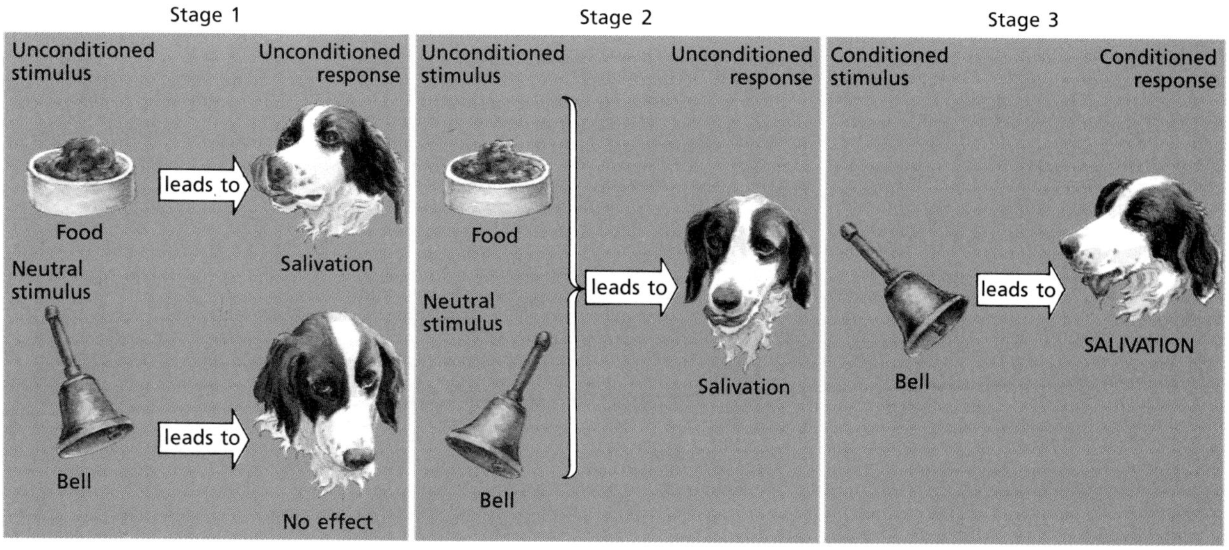

Ivan Pavlov (center), shown here at the 1932 International Congress of Psychology, reported some of the first systematic studies of classical conditioning.

organism has acquired or learned a response. Figure 9.3 shows a typical acquisition curve.

Conditioning in Human Beings

Learning Objective 9.4
Give examples of responses learned through classical conditioning.

Newborns show reflexive responses to loud noises, pain, falling, and even strange people or surroundings (we examine newborns' reflexes in Chapter 8). For example, a loud noise naturally elicits a startle response—an outstretching of the arms and legs, associated with changes in heart rate, blood pressure, and breathing. All kinds of neutral stimuli can become conditioned stimuli that elicit either pleasant

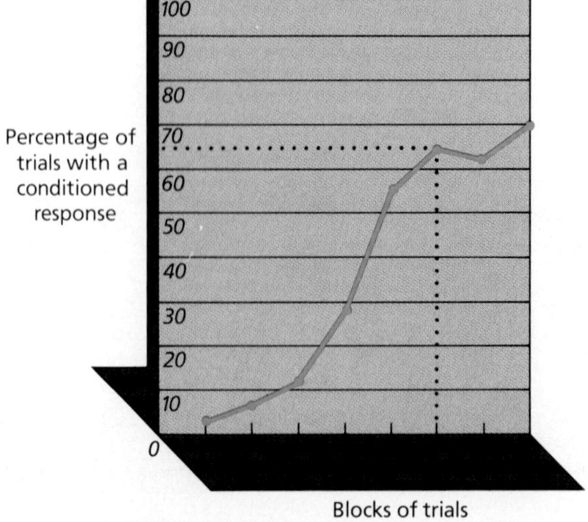

Figure 9.3

This acquisition curve plots the development of a conditioned eye-blink response in a rabbit in a series of eight blocks of trials. By the sixth block, eye-blinks occur 65% of the time. (Data from Schneiderman, Fuentes, & Gormezano, 1962. Copyright 1962 by the AAAS.)

or defensive reactions. A puff of air delivered to the eye, for example, produces an unconditioned response: an eye blink. When a buzzer is paired with puffs of air to the eye, it will eventually elicit the eye blink by itself. This effect can be produced in many animals as well as in human adults and infants.

higher-order conditioning: The process by which a neutral stimulus takes on conditioned properties through pairing with a conditioned stimulus.

Both pleasant and unpleasant emotional responses can be classically conditioned. Consider the following: If a child who is playing with a favorite toy is repeatedly frightened by a sudden loud noise, the child may be conditioned to be afraid each time he or she sees the toy. Think about the well-known relationship between letter carriers and dogs. Dogs deliver an unconditioned stimulus (a bite) that elicits an unconditioned response (pain). Through repeated *pairings* of stimulus and response, dogs can become conditioned stimuli. At that point, the mere sight of a dog will elicit in the letter carrier a series of defensive reactions associated with fear, including increased heart and respiration rates.

Higher-Order Conditioning

Learning Objective 9.5 Describe higher-order conditioning.

After a neutral stimulus becomes a conditioned stimulus, it is likely to elicit the conditioned response whenever it is presented. Moreover, through the process of **higher-order conditioning,** when another neutral stimulus is associated with a well-established conditioned stimulus, it can also take on conditioning properties. Thus, higher-order conditioning permits increasingly remote associations, which can result in a complex network of conditioned stimuli, all of which lead to the same basic conditioned response.

Consider the following example of higher-order conditioning: A light is paired with mild electric shocks so that on seeing the light, a dog exhibits fear; the light has thus become a conditioned stimulus that elicits a set of fear responses. If, after repeated pairings of the light and the electric shock, a bell is presented with or before the light, the new stimulus (the bell) can also take on properties of the conditioned stimulus (the light). After repeated pairings, the dog will learn to associate the two events, the light and the bell, and either event by itself will elicit a fear response. When a third stimulus—say, an experimenter in a white lab coat—is introduced, the dog may learn to associate the experimenter with the bell or light. After enough trials, the dog may have conditioned fear responses to each of the three stimuli: the light, the bell, and the experimenter (Pavlov, 1927; Rescorla, 1977). We next discuss those key variables in classical conditioning which alter the likelihood of conditioning.

Key Variables in Classical Conditioning

Classical conditioning is a multistage process that occurs only when certain criteria are met. How loud does the buzzer have to be? How long does the bell have to ring? How sinister must the movie's scary music be? Some of the most important variables in classical conditioning are the strength, timing, frequency, and predictability of the unconditioned stimulus. When these variables are optimal, conditioning occurs easily.

Learning Objective 9.6. Explain how the strength, timing, frequency, and predictability of the unconditioned stimulus affect classical conditioning.

Variables That Affect Conditioning

Strength of the Unconditioned Stimulus. A puff of air delivered to the eye will easily elicit an unconditioned response, but only if the puff of air (i.e., the unconditioned stimulus) is sufficiently strong. Research shows that when the unconditioned stimulus is strong and elicits a quick and regular reflexive (unconditioned) response, conditioning of the neutral stimulus is likely to occur. On the other hand, if the unconditioned stimulus is weak, it is unlikely to elicit an unconditioned response, and conditioning of the neutral stimulus is unlikely to occur.

Timing of the Unconditioned Stimulus. For conditioning to occur, an unconditioned stimulus must usually be paired with a neutral stimulus close enough in time for the two to become associated. For example, in Pavlov's experiment, conditioning would not have occurred if the bell and the food had been presented an hour apart. The two stimuli may be presented together or separated by a brief interval; the timing varies from one study to another. Some types of conditioning can occur with fairly long delays, but a general guideline for achieving a strong conditioned response is that the neutral stimulus should occur about half a second before the unconditioned stimulus and should overlap with it.

Frequency of Pairings. Occasional or rare pairings of a neutral stimulus with an unconditioned stimulus at a close interval does not usually result in conditioning; frequent pairings are usually necessary to establish a relationship between the unconditioned and the conditioned stimuli. If, for example, food and the sound of a bell are paired on every trial, a dog is conditioned more quickly than if the stimuli were paired on every other trial.

Predictability. A key determining factor in whether conditioning will occur is the predictability of the association of the unconditioned and conditioned stimulus. Closeness in time and a regular frequency of pairings promotes conditioning, but these are not enough. Predictability facilitates and turns out to be a central factor in conditioning (Rescorla, 1988).

Pavlov thought that classical conditioning was based on timing. However, research now shows that if the unconditioned stimulus (such as the food) can be predicted by the conditioned stimulus (such as the bell), then conditioning is rapidly achieved. In other words, conditioning is not achieved solely because of the number of times the two events have occurred together, but rather because of the reliability with which the conditioned stimulus *predicts* the occurrence of the unconditioned stimulus. Thus, if one event predicts another very well, the number of times they have occurred together is not especially important. Although not all researchers agree (Papini & Bitterman, 1990), the predictability of events is important in learned behaviors such as food aversions, considered in the Understanding the Research Process box on page 168.

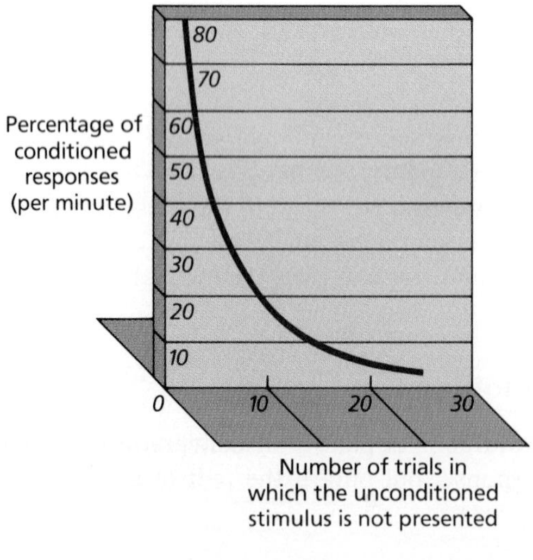

Figure 9.4

In the process of extinction, the percentage of times an organism will display a conditioned response decreases when the unconditioned stimulus (such as food) is no longer presented.

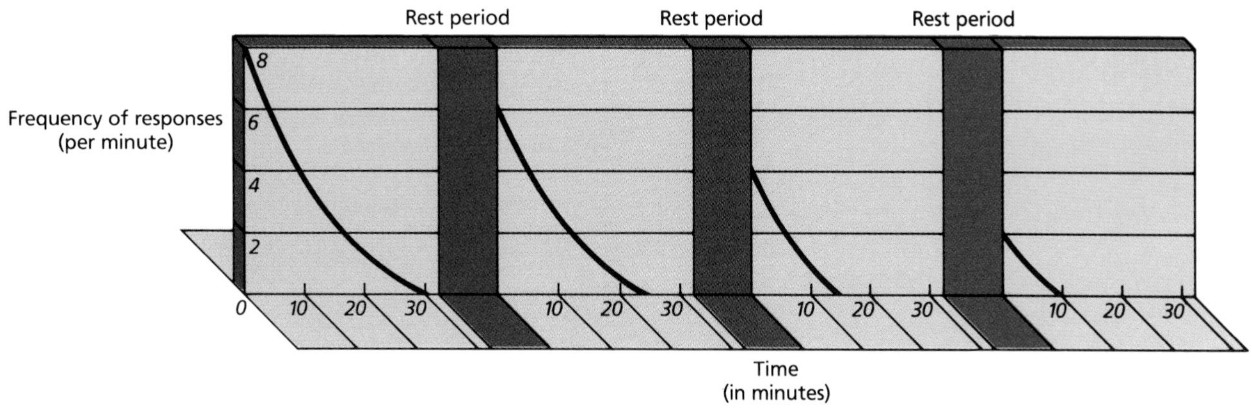

Figure 9.5

Once a conditioned response extinguishes, an organism will show the response again after a rest interval. This recurrence of a conditioned response is called *spontaneous recovery.* After each successive rest interval, the rate of response decreases, and extinction occurs more quickly.

Extinction and Spontaneous Recovery

Learning Objective 9.7 Describe extinction and spontaneous recovery in classical conditioning.

What would have happened to Pavlov's dogs if he had rung the bell each day but no longer followed the bell with food? If a researcher continues Pavlov's experiment by presenting the conditioned stimulus (bell) but no unconditioned stimulus (food), the likelihood of a conditioned response decreases with every trial. In classical conditioning, the term **extinction** refers to the process by which withholding the unconditioned stimulus gradually reduces the probability (and often the strength) of a conditioned response. Imagine a different study, in which a puff of air is associated with a buzzer that consistently elicits the conditioned eye blink response. If the unconditioned stimulus (the puff of air) is no longer delivered in association with the buzzer, the likelihood that the buzzer will continue to elicit the eye blink response decreases over time (see Figure 9.4). When presentation of the buzzer alone no longer elicits the conditioned response, we say that the conditioned response has been extinguished.

A conditioned response that has undergone extinction can recur, especially after a rest period; in classical conditioning, this phenomenon is **spontaneous recovery.** For example, when a dog has been conditioned to salivate in response to the sound of a bell and then experiences a long series of trials in which food is not paired with the bell, the dog makes few or no responses to the bell: The behavior has been extinguished. (see Figure 9.5). If the dog is placed in the experimental situation again after a rest period of 20 minutes, its salivary response to the bell will recur briefly (although less strongly than before). This behavior shows that the effects of extinction are not permanent and that the learned association is not totally forgotten (see Figure 9.6 on page 169).

extinction: [Egg-STINCK-shun] In classical conditioning, the process of reducing the likelihood of a conditioned response to a conditioned stimulus by not pairing the unconditioned and conditioned stimuli.

spontaneous recovery: The recurrence of a conditioned response following a rest period after extinction.

Stimulus Generalization and Stimulus Discrimination

Learning Objective 9.8 Discuss stimulus generalization and stimulus discrimination in classical conditioning.

Imagine that a 3-year-old child pulls a cat's tail and receives a painful scratch. It would not be surprising if the child developed a fear of that cat, or even of all cats. It is possible that she or he might even develop a fear of dogs and other four-legged animals. People may respond in the same way to similar stimuli, a phenomenon that psychologists call stimulus generalization.

UNDERSTANDING THE RESEARCH PROCESS

Taste Aversion Studies

My daughter, Sarah Lefton, has hated mustard every since her sixth birthday party. After her friends and their mothers left the party, we sat down for a ham sandwich with lettuce and mustard. Two hours later, she was ill—fever, vomiting, chills, and swollen glands. It was the flu, but as far as Sarah was concerned, it was the mustard that made her sick. To this day, she refuses to eat mustard.

Sarah's association of mustard and nausea is an example of conditioned taste aversion. John Garcia has studied conditioned taste aversion by giving animals some specific foods and then inducing illness (usually by injecting a drug or by providing irradiated water to drink). He found that after only *one* pairing of a food (the conditioned stimulus) and the drug or irradiated water (the unconditioned stimulus), the animals avoided the food or drink that preceded the nausea (see, for example, Garcia & Koelling, 1971).

Two aspects of Garcia's work startled the psychological community. First, Garcia showed that conditioned taste aversion could be obtained even if the nausea was induced several hours after the food had been consumed. This contradicted the previously held assumption that the time interval between the unconditioned stimulus and the conditioned stimulus had to be short, especially if conditioning was to occur quickly. Second, Garcia proved that not all stimuli can serve as conditioned stimuli, in contrast to what most learning psychologists believed. He tried to pair bells and lights with nausea to produce aversion in rats, but he was unable to do so. These two findings led Garcia to conclude, "Strong aversions to the smell or taste of food can develop even when illness is delayed for hours after consumption [but] avoidance reactions do not develop for visual, auditory, or tactile stimuli associated with food" (Garcia & Koelling, 1971, p. 461). Garcia's research had disproved two accepted principles of learning.

Conditioned taste aversion, sometimes called the *Garcia effect,* has adaptive value. Anyone who has had food poisoning will attest to the lasting memory of the food or meal that caused it! Human beings quickly learn to associate rancid smells with the illness caused by spoiled food. In one trial or instance, animals and humans learn to avoid foods that make them sick by associating the smells of poisonous food with the foods themselves. Conditioned taste aversion is unaffected by intervening events during the delay between the taste and the illness (Holder, Yirmiya, Garcia, & Raizer, 1989).

In addition to its survival value, conditioned taste aversion has practical uses. For instance, coyotes often attack sheep and lambs, destroying entire flocks. In a fascinating study, Garcia laced lamb meat with a substance that causes a short-term illness and put the food on the outskirts of a sheep ranch. Coyotes who ate the lamb became sick and subsequently developed an aversion to lamb meat. After this experience, they approached the sheep as if ready to attack, but they nearly always backed off (Garcia, Gustavson, Kelly, & Sweeney, 1976). By using conditioned taste aversion, Garcia deterred coyotes from eating sheep.

Conditioned taste aversion has implications for humans as well. Patients who have cancer often undergo chemotherapy, which has unfortunate side effects, including vomiting and nausea. Such people often lose weight during treatments. Is it possible that cancer patients lose weight during their treatments because of conditioned taste aversion? According to researcher Ilene Bernstein (1988), cancer patients become conditioned to avoid food. They often check into a hospital, have a meal, are given chemotherapy, become sick, and then avoid the food that preceded the chemotherapy. Moreover, patients develop food aversions even when they know that it is the chemotherapy that induces nausea, not the food. As a result of her research, Bernstein suggests that cancer patients could be given "scapegoat" food just before chemotherapy so that their conditioned taste aversion develops to a low frequency, nutritionally unimportant food, rather than to proteins, carbohydrates, or other nutritious foods. When implemented, Bernstein's procedure was successful.

- ***What is the evidence that led Garcia to conclude that taste aversion can happen in one trial or one instance?***
- ***Garcia's research challenged what assumptions about learning processes?***
- ***What practical uses could be derived from knowledge of the Garcia effect?***

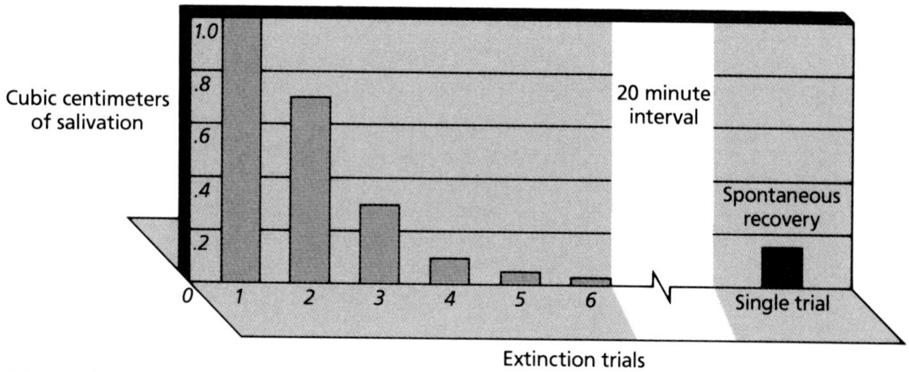

Figure 9.6

In a series of trials at 3-minute intervals, Pavlov extinguished a conditioned salivary response by omitting presentation of the unconditioned stimulus (food). After a rest interval of 20 minutes, the salivary response recurred, but it was not as strong as in earlier trials. (Data from Pavlov, 1927, p. 58)

stimulus generalization: The occurrence of a conditioned response to stimuli similar to, but not the same as, the training stimulus.

stimulus discrimination: The process by which an organism learns to respond only to a specific reinforced stimulus; the complementary process to stimulus generalization.

Stimulus generalization occurs when an organism exhibits a conditioned response to a stimulus that is similar, but not identical to, the original conditioned stimulus. The extent to which an organism responds to a stimulus similar to the original one depends on how alike are the two stimuli. If, for example, a loud tone is the conditioned stimulus for an eye-blink response, somewhat lower but similar tones will also produce the eye-blink response. A totally dissimilar tone will produce little or no response. Likewise, the aforementioned Marine responded to the sound of a car backfiring because it was similar to the sound of gunfire.

Stimulus discrimination is the process by which an organism responds differently to dissimilar stimuli (see Figure 9.7). (See Table 9.1 on the next page for a summary of important properties of classical conditioning.) Pavlov showed that

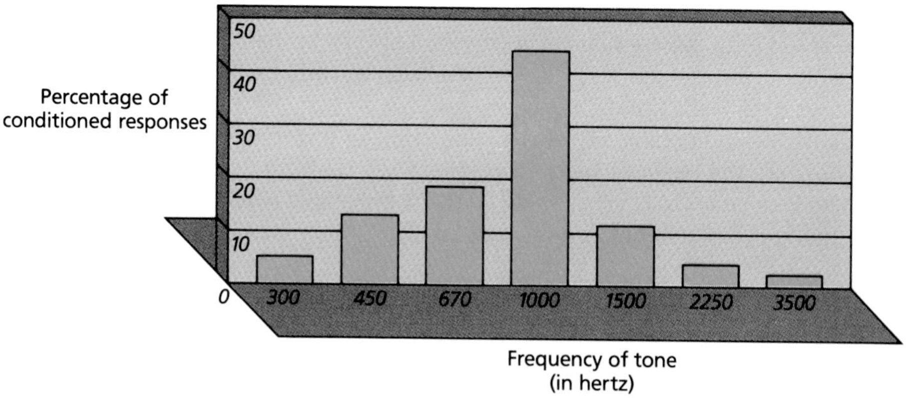

Figure 9.7

Stimulus generalization occurs when an organism emits a conditioned response to stimuli similar to but not identical to the conditioned stimulus. The bar graph shows the responses of an organism trained with a 1,000-hertz tone. When the organism was later presented with tones of different frequencies, its percentage of responses decreased as the tone's frequency became increasingly different. (Data from Jenkins & Harrison, 1960)

TABLE 9.1 Four important properties of classical conditioning

Property	Definition	Example
Extinction	The process of reducing the probability of a conditioned response by withholding the unconditioned stimulus (the reinforcer)	An infant conditioned to suck in response to a light is no longer given the unconditioned stimulus of stroking the lips; the infant stops sucking in response to the conditioned stimulus.
Spontaneous recovery	The reoccurrence of a conditioned response following a rest period after extinction	A dog's conditioned salivary response has undergone extinction; after a rest period, the dog again salivates in response to the conditioned stimulus, though less than it did before.
Stimulus generalization	The process by which an organism learns to respond to stimuli that are similar to but not identical to the training stimulus.	A dog conditioned to salivate in response to a high-pitched tone also salivates to a lower-pitched tone.
Stimulus discrimination	The process by which an organism learns to respond to a specific stimulus and then to no other similar stimulus; the complementary process to stimulus generalization	A goat is conditioned to salivate only in response to lights of high intensity and not to lights of low intensity.

animals that have learned to differentiate between pairs of stimuli display frustration or even aggression when discrimination is made difficult or impossible. He trained a dog to discriminate between a circle and an ellipse and then changed the shape of the ellipse on successive trials to look more and more like the circle. Eventually, the animal was unable to discriminate between the shapes; it randomly chose one or the other and also became aggressive.

Human beings exhibit similar disorganization in behavior when placed in situations in which they feel compelled to make a response but do not know how to respond correctly. In such situations, where discrimination becomes impossible, behavior can become stereotyped and limited in scope; people may choose either not to respond to the stimulus or to respond always in the same way. Often psychotherapists must teach maladjusted people to learn to be more flexible in their responses to difficult situations.

Classical conditioning explains a wide range of phenomena, but not all of our behaviors are the result of such associations (see Building Table 9.1). As we indicated in the chapter overview, many complex behaviors result from another form of learning, called operant conditioning, which is discussed in the next module.

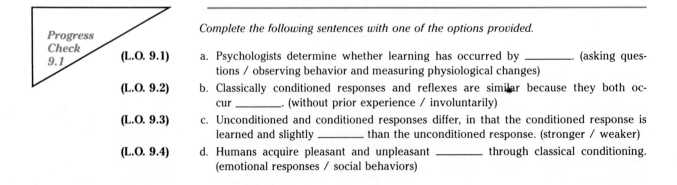

Progress Check 9.1

Complete the following sentences with one of the options provided.

(L.O. 9.1) a. Psychologists determine whether learning has occurred by ________. (asking questions / observing behavior and measuring physiological changes)

(L.O. 9.2) b. Classically conditioned responses and reflexes are similar because they both occur ________. (without prior experience / involuntarily)

(L.O. 9.3) c. Unconditioned and conditioned responses differ, in that the conditioned response is learned and slightly ________ than the unconditioned response. (stronger / weaker)

(L.O. 9.4) d. Humans acquire pleasant and unpleasant ________ through classical conditioning. (emotional responses / social behaviors)

(L.O. 9.5) e. In higher-order conditioning, ________ stimuli lead to the same basic conditioned response. (unconditioned / a complex network of conditioned)

(L.O. 9.6) f. If the strength of the ________ stimulus is strong, conditioning is much more likely to occur than if the strength is weak. (unconditioned / neutral)

(L.O. 9.6) g. When timing the presentation of neutral and unconditioned stimuli, the general guideline is that the neutral stimulus should be presented ________ the unconditioned stimulus. (half a second before and should overlap with / immediately after)

(L.O. 9.6) h. The ________ of the unconditioned stimulus seems to be the most important factor in determining how quickly classical conditioning will occur. (frequency / predictability)

(L.O. 9.7) i. Extinction occurs in classical conditioning because the unconditioned stimulus is ________. (too weak / no longer paired with the conditioned stimulus)

(L.O. 9.7) j. The reoccurrence of a conditioned response following a rest period after extinction is called ________. (spontaneous recovery / relearning)

(L.O. 9.8) k. Stimulus ________ is the process by which an organism learns to make a particular response to a specific stimulus and to no other similar or dissimilar stimulus. (generalization / discrimination)

Types of Learning: Classical Conditioning

Building Table 9.1

Type of learning	Procedure	Result	Example
Classical conditioning	A neutral stimulus (such as a bell) is paired with an unconditioned stimulus (such as food).	The neutral stimulus becomes a conditioned stimulus—it *elicits* the conditioned response.	A bell elicits a salivary response in a dog.
Operant conditioning			

Module Summary

Classical Conditioning

- *Learning* is a relatively permanent and stable change in an organism that usually, but not always, can be seen in behavior; it occurs as a result of experience with the environment (p. 161).
- Both animals and humans exhibit behaviors that are always associated with specific stimuli. These are reflexes; that is, they occur involuntarily, quickly, and *without learning* in response to some stimulus (pp. 161–162).
- *Classical conditioning* involves the pairing of a neutral stimulus (e.g., a bell) with an unconditioned stimulus (e.g., food). The neutral stimulus eventually becomes a conditioned stimulus that is capable of eliciting a conditioned response similar to the unconditioned response. In higher-order conditioning, a second neutral stimulus takes on reinforcing properties by being associated with the conditioned stimulus (p. 162).

Key Variables in Classical Conditioning

- For conditioning to occur, the *unconditioned stimulus* and the *conditioned stimulus* must be presented in rapid sequence, and the conditioned stimulus must predict the occurrence of the unconditioned stimulus. The appropriate interval is generally half a second, but it may vary, depending on the response being conditioned (p. 166).
- *Extinction* is the process of reducing the probability that a conditioned response will recur. *Spontaneous recovery* is the recurrence, after a rest period, of a conditioned response that has undergone extinction (p. 167).
- The most important variables in classical conditioning are the strength, timing, and frequency of the unconditioned stimulus. When these variables are optimal, the conditioned stimulus will predict the likelihood of an unconditioned stimulus, and conditioning can easily occur. (pp 165–167).

KEY TERMS

classical conditioning, p. 162
conditioned response, p. 162
conditioned stimulus, p. 162
conditioning, p. 161
extinction, p. 167
higher-order conditioning, p. 165
learning, p. 161
reflex, p. 162
spontaneous recovery, p. 167
stimulus discrimination, p. 169
stimulus generalization, p. 169
unconditioned response, p. 162
unconditioned stimulus, p. 162

SELF-TEST

Module 9

- Before taking the self-test, **recite** and **review.**
- Use the key at the back of the text to *correct* your answers.
- *Restudy* pages that correspond to any questions you answered incorrectly.

1. Learning is defined as
   a. a systematic procedure through which new responses to stimuli are acquired.
   b. the ability to recall past events, information, and skills.
   c. a relatively permanent change in behavior that occurs as a result of experience in the environment.
   d. the process by which a neutral stimulus takes on conditioned properties.
2. When comparing reflexes to classically conditioned responses, the main difference between the two is that only reflexes are
   a. elicited.
   b. emitted.
   c. natural and unlearned.
   d. tied to specific stimuli.
3. In Pavlov's classic experiment, the conditioned stimulus was the
   a. food.
   b. salivation.
   c. bell.
   d. dog.
4. Some psychologists believe that ________ are conditioned behaviors learned through classical conditioning.
   a. walking and talking
   b. eating and sleeping
   c. thinking and problem solving
   d. emotions and defensive reactions
5. Ginny acquired a conditioned fear response to red balloons. Later, she saw a clown holding a red balloon, and still later, she saw the clown on a skateboard. As a result of this, Ginny now has conditioned fear responses to red balloons, clowns, and skateboards. This represents
   a. stimulus generalization.
   b. higher-order conditioning.
   c. the importance of timing in classical conditioning.
   d. the importance of predictability in classical conditioning.
6. A researcher conducts a conditioning experiment in which she sounds a buzzer and immediately follows the sound with a flash of a light located 5 feet away from the subject. Her goal, to establish a conditioned eye-blink response to the buzzer, is not achieved. We can assume that the conditioned response failed to occur because
   a. the strength of the unconditioned stimulus (light) was too weak.
   b. the researcher neglected to use a neutral stimulus.
   c. the light should have been presented before the buzzer.
   d. conditioned stimulus discrimination occurred instead.
7. Because spontaneous recovery occurs after a rest period, we can conclude that
   a. conditioned responses are bad habits.
   b. animals cannot be completely retrained because they do not think as humans do.
   c. learned associations are not totally forgotten.
   d. maladjusted behaviors occur when extinction works too well.
8. When animals or humans are in a situation where they cannot discriminate between pairs of stimuli and therefore cannot predict the outcome of their responses, their behavior may become
   a. aggressive.
   b. disorganized or they may not respond at all.
   c. stereotyped and limited in scope.
   d. all of the above

Module 10

Operant Conditioning and Cognitive Learning

LEARNING OBJECTIVES

When you have mastered the material in this module, you will be able to

Operant Conditioning (pp. 175–182)

10.1 Describe operant conditioning and identify two American psychologists who pioneered research for this type of learning (p. 175).

10.2 Describe two devices that psychologists used in early operant conditioning research and explain how they measure operant behaviors today (p. 176).

10.3 Explain how shaping is used in operant conditioning (p. 177).

10.4 Describe both positive and negative reinforcement and explain how both escape and avoidance behaviors are learned (p. 178).

10.5 Describe the types of behavioral consequences that can act as reinforcers (p. 179).

10.6 Explain what is meant by superstitious behavior and tell how it is learned (p. 179).

10.7 Describe the types of behavioral consequences that can act as punishers and discuss the limitations of punishment (p. 180).

Key Variables in Operant Conditioning (pp. 182–189)

10.8 Discuss the strength, timing, and frequency of consequences and describe continuous, interval, and ratio schedules (p. 182).

10.9 Describe stimulus generalization, stimulus discrimination, extinction, and spontaneous recovery in operant conditioning (p. 186).

10.10 Describe how electrical brain stimulation experiments are conducted and identify some behaviors that animals exhibit to receive brain stimulation (p. 188).

Cognitive Learning (pp. 190–193)

10.11 Describe insight, latent learning, and generative learning (p. 190).

Observational Learning (pp. 193–195)

10.12 Describe observational learning and the variables that affect it (p. 193).

SQ3R
- ▲ **Survey** to set goals for studying.
- ▲ Ask **questions** as you **read.**
- ▲ Stop occasionally to **recite** and **review.**

plus
- ▲ **Write** a summary of key points.
- ▲ **Reflect** on the hypotheses, evidence, and implications of this material and on the relevance it has to *your* life.

When I (LV) was a sophomore in high school, I developed a particular affection for a blue argyle sweater. The sweater became my favorite after I was complimented on it by several friends. By wearing the blue argyle sweater, I demonstrated another type of conditioning that involves associations: operant conditioning. My decision to wear that sweater on many occasions can be explained by reinforcement principles integral to instrumental or operant conditioning.

Operant Conditioning

The process by which I was conditioned to wear my sweater was described in the 1930s by B. F. Skinner (1904–1990), who challenged and began to change the way in which psychologists think about conditioning and learning. In fact, Skinner questioned whether Pavlovian (classical) conditioning should be studied at all. Like Pavlov, Skinner also focused only on an organism's *observable* behavior; thought processes, consciousness, brain-behavior relationships, and the mind were not then considered the proper subject matter of psychology. Skinner's early work was in the tradition of strict behaviorists such as Watson, although ultimately Skinner modified some of his most extreme positions. Skinner is arguably the most influential psychologist the United States has ever produced. His theories about using principles of operant conditioning to design a utopian society brought him lasting fame. Skinner died in 1990, shortly after receiving an award from the American Psychological Association for his lifetime contributions to psychology.

Learning Objective 10.1 Describe operant conditioning, and identify two American psychologists who pioneered research for this type of learning.

operant conditioning: [OP-er-ant] A conditioning procedure in which the probability that an organism will emit a response is increased or decreased by the subsequent delivery of a reinforcer or punisher; sometimes called *instrumental conditioning.*

Pioneers: B. F. Skinner and E. L. Thorndike

According to Skinner, many behaviors are acquired and maintained through what he called operant conditioning. He used the term *operant conditioning* because the organism *operates* on the environment, with every action followed by a specific event or consequence. In **operant conditioning,** an increase or decrease in

Skinner box: Named (by others) for its developer, B. F. Skinner, the box contains a responding mechanism (usually a lever) capable of delivering a reinforcer (often food or water) to an organism.

the likelihood that a behavior will recur is affected by the delivery of a rewarding or punishing event as a consequence of the behavior. Moreover, the conditioned behavior is usually voluntary, not reflexlike, as in classical conditioning. Consider what happens when a boss rewards and encourages her overworked employees by given them unexpected cash bonuses. If the bonuses improve the employee morale and induce them to work harder, then the employer's conditioning efforts are successful. In turn, the employees could condition the boss by rewarding her bonus-paying behavior through further increasing their productivity, thereby encouraging her to continue paying bonuses.

In the laboratory, researchers have studied similar sequences of behaviors followed by rewards. One of the most famous experiments was conducted by the American psychologist E. L. Thorndike (1874–1949), who pioneered the study of operant conditioning during the 1890s and first reported his work in 1898. Thorndike placed hungry cats in boxes and put food outside the boxes. The cats could escape from the boxes and get food by hitting a lever that opened a door in the box. The cats quickly performed the behavior Thorndike was trying to condition (hitting the lever) because hitting the lever (at first by accident and then deliberately) gave them access to food. Because the response (hitting the lever) was important (i.e., instrumental) in obtaining the reward, Thorndike used the term *instrumental conditioning* and termed the behaviors *instrumental behaviors.* Although Skinner spoke of operant conditioning and Thorndike of instrumental conditioning, the two terms are often used interchangeably. What is important is that both Skinner and Thorndike acknowledged that first the behavior is *emitted* or displayed, and then a consequence (e.g., a reward) follows. This is unlike classical (Pavlovian) conditioning, in which first there is a change in the environment (e.g., bells and food are paired) and then the conditioned behavior (usually a reflexive response) is *elicited* (see Figure 10.1).

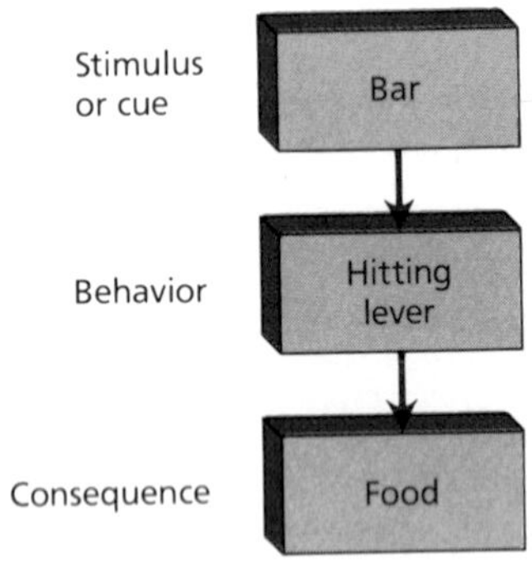

Figure 10.1

In instrumental conditioning—unlike classical conditioning—the behavior to be conditioned (such as hitting a lever) is reinforced or punished *after* it occurs.

In operant conditioning, such as in Thorndike's experiment with cats, an organism emits a behavior, and then a consequence follows. The *type* of consequence that follows the behavior is a crucial component of the conditioning because it determines whether the behavior is likely to recur. Principally, the consequence can be a *reinforcer* or a *punisher.* A reward acts as a reinforcer, increasing the likelihood that the behavior targeted for conditioning will recur; in Thorndike's experiment, food was the reinforcer for hitting the lever. A punisher, on the other hand, decreases the likelihood that the targeted behavior will recur. If an electric shock is delivered to the feet of a cat each time the cat touches a lever, the cat quickly learns not to touch the lever. Parents use reinforcers and punishers when they link the behavior of their teenaged children to the use of the family car.

The Skinner Box and Shaping

Learning Objective 10.2 Describe two devices that psychologists used in early operant conditioning research, and explain how they measure operant behaviors today.

Much of the research on operant conditioning has used an apparatus that most psychologists call a Skinner box. The apparatus is named after pioneering researcher B. F. Skinner—even though he never liked or approved of the idea of naming it after him. A **Skinner box** usually contains a mechanism for delivering a consequence whenever the animal in the box makes a readily identifiable response that the experimenter has decided to reinforce or punish. In studies that involve rewards, the delivery mechanism if often a small lever or bar in the side of the box; whenever the animal presses it, the behavior is rewarded. Punishment in a Skinner box often takes the form of electric shocks delivered through a grid on the floor of the box.

In a traditional operant conditioning experiment, a rat that has been deprived of food is placed in a Skinner box. The rat moves around the box, often seeking

In the Skinner box, behavior is punished or rewarded after an animal makes a response.

to escape; eventually, it stumbles on the lever and presses it. With that action, the experimenter delivers a pellet of food into cup. The rat moves about some more and happens to press the lever again; another pellet of food is delivered. After a few trials, the rat learns that pressing the lever brings food. A hungry rat will learn to press the lever many times in rapid succession to obtain food.

Counting the lever presses or measuring the salivary responses is a tedious but necessary part of studying conditioning. Psychologists have developed a practical and simple device, called a *cumulative recorder,* to measure animal behavior (see Figure 10.2 on the next page). These devices were essential for the early progress made in animal learning laboratories. Today, psychologists use computerized devices to quantify behavior such as bar pressing and to track the progress that an organism makes in learning a response. Teaching an organism a complex response takes many trials because most organisms need to be taught in small steps through the process of *shaping.*

Learning Objective 10.3
Explain how shaping is used in operant conditioning.

Shaping Simple Behaviors. **Shaping** is the process of reinforcing behavior that *approximates* (comes close to) a desired behavior. To teach a hungry rat to press a bar in a Skinner box, for example, a researcher begins by giving the rat a pellet of food each time it enters the side of the box in which the bar is located. Once this behavior is established, the rat receives food only when it touches the wall where the bar is located. It then receives food only when it approaches the lever, and so on until it receives food only when it actually presses the bar. At each stage, the reinforced behavior (entering the half of the box nearest the lever, touching the wall that houses the lever, etc.) more closely approximates the desired behavior (i.e., pressing the lever). (This sequence of increasingly closer approximations of the desired behavior is sometimes called "successive approximations," which means approximately the same thing as *shaping.*)

shaping: The gradual training of an organism to give the proper responses by selectively reinforcing behaviors as they approach the desired response.

Shaping is effective for teaching animals new behaviors; for example, you use shaping to train a dog to sit on command. This generally is done by pairing food with a push on the dog's rear while verbally commanding "Sit!" With reinforcement following sitting, the dog begins to sit with less and less pressure applied to its rear, and eventually the dog sits on command. Shaping is also helpful in teaching people new behaviors. For example, were you taught how to play baseball?

If so, first, you were taught how to hold the bat correctly, then how to swing it, then simply how to make contact with the ball, and finally how to hit the ball for a base hit.

Reinforcement

Learning Objective 10.4
Describe both positive and negative reinforcement, and explain how both escape and avoidance behaviors are learned.

To really understand operant conditioning you need to study the basic principles of reinforcement. To psychologists, a **reinforcer** is any event that increases the probability of the recurrence of a response that preceded it. Thus, a behavior followed by a desirable event is likely to recur. Examples of reinforcement in our lives abound: A person works hard in a factory and is rewarded with high pay; a student studies long hours for an examination and is rewarded with a top grade; sales agents call on hundreds of clients and sell lots of their products; young children behave appropriately, and their parents reward them with affection and praise. Such behaviors can be taught by using either or both of two kinds of reinforcers: positive and negative.

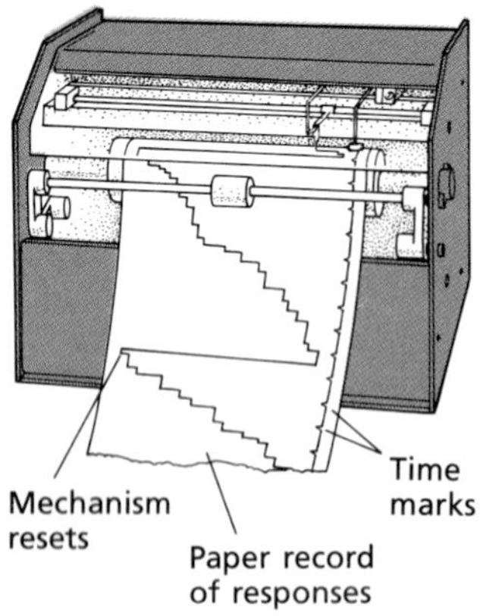

The cumulative recorder marks each time an organism makes a response. The paper in the device moves constantly; if the organism does not respond, the pen makes a straight line.

Positive Reinforcement. Most people have used **positive reinforcement** at one time or another. When teaching your dog tricks, you reward it with food or a pat on the head. When toilet training a 2-year-old, a parent often applauds, smiles, or gives praise when the child successfully completes a bowel movement; the applause, smile, or praise is a reinforcer. Both the dog and the child continue the behaviors because they have been given something. They have been rewarded with something that is important or desired; their behaviors have been positively reinforced.

Some reinforcers are more powerful than others, and a reinforcer for one person may not have reinforcing value for another. Praise from an approving parent may be a powerful reinforcer for a 2-year-old. A smile of approval from a teacher may reinforce a grade school student, but high grades may be the most effective reinforcer for a high school student. Money may be effective for one adult, position or status for another. At many corporations, bonuses for effective performance may include color televisions, cassette tape recorders, or trips to Hawaii (e.g., Gorham, 1988).

Negative Reinforcement. Whereas positive reinforcement increases the probability of a response through delivery of a reward, **negative reinforcement** increases the probability of a response through removal of an unpleasant, aversive, or noxious stimulus. Negative reinforcement is still *reinforcement* because it strengthens or increases the likelihood of a response, but it is called negative because instead of adding a positive experience, it removes a negative one. For example, suppose a rat is placed in a maze with an electrified grid that delivers a shock every 50 seconds, and the rat can escape the shock by turning to the left in the maze. The behavior to be conditioned is going left in the maze; the reinforcement is termination of the painful stimulus. In this case, negative reinforcement—termination of the painful stimulus—increases the probability of the response (going left) because that is the way to turn off the unpleasant stimulus.

Noxious or unpleasant stimuli are often used in animal studies of escape and avoidance. In *escape conditioning,* a rat in a Skinner box receives a shock just strong enough to cause it to thrash around until it bumps against the bar, thereby stopping the shock. In just a few trials, the rat learns to press the bar to *escape* being shocked, to bring an unpleasant situation to an end. In *avoidance conditioning,* the same apparatus is used, but a buzzer or some other cue precedes the shock by a few seconds. In this case, the rat learns that when presented with a stimulus or cue such as a buzzer, it should press the bar to *avoid* or prevent the shock from occurring. Pressing the bar allows it to avoid the unpleasant experience.

reinforcer: Any event that increases the probability of the recurrence of the response that precedes it.

positive reinforcement: Presentation of a rewarding or pleasant stimulus after a particular response, to increase the likelihood that the response will recur.

negative reinforcement: Removal of an aversive stimulus after a particular response, to increase the likelihood that the response will recur.

Avoidance conditioning generally also involves escape conditioning: First, the animal learns how to escape the shock by pressing the bar. Then it learns how to avoid the shock by pressing the bar when it hears the buzzer that signals the oncoming shock. In avoidance conditioning, the organism learns to respond so that the noxious stimulus is never delivered. For example, to avoid a bad grade on an English quiz, a student may study before an examination, and when people develop irrational fears (e.g., of airplanes or trains), they may avoid the object of the fear (e.g., those vehicles).

Learning Objective 10.5 Describe the types of behavioral consequences that can act as reinforcers.

The Nature of Reinforcers. The precise nature of reinforcers is a murky issue. Early researchers recognized events that satisfy biological needs as powerful reinforcers. Later researchers included events that decrease a person's need to meet specific goals, such as conversation that would relieve boredom, sounds that would relieve sensory deprivation, and money that would relieve housing congestion. Then, in the 1960s, researchers acknowledged that an array of events can be reinforcers. *Probable behaviors* (that is, behaviors likely to happen, including biological behaviors such as eating and social behaviors such as playing tennis, writing letters, or talking) can reinforce less probable or more unlikely behaviors such as cleaning closets, studying calculus, or pressing levers (by rodents). Researchers call this idea the *Premack principle,* after David Premack, whose influential writings and research fostered the idea (Premack, 1962, 1965). Parents employ the Premack principle when they tell their children that they can go outside and play after they clean up their rooms.

Primary reinforcers are those that have survival value for the organism, such as food, water, or termination of pain; their value does not have to be learned. Food can be a primary reinforcer for a hungry rat, water for a thirsty one. **Secondary reinforcers** are neutral stimuli (such as money or grades) that initially have no intrinsic value for the organism but when linked with a primary reinforcer, they too can become rewarding. Many human pleasures are secondary reinforcers that have acquired value, such as leather coats that keep people no warmer than cloth ones and racy sports cars that take people around town no faster than four-door sedans.

Secondary reinforcers are generally used to modify human behavior. An approving nod, unlimited use of the family car, and a job promotion are secondary reinforcers that act to establish and maintain a wide spectrum of behavior. People will work long hours when the rewards are significant; successful salespeople may even work 72 hours per week to reach their sales objectives. This can happen when managers, using basic psychology, offer salespeople bonuses for increasing their sales by a certain percentage during a slow month. They reason that by increasing the amount of a reinforcer (money), they may be able to get better performance (higher sales). Research shows that changing the amount of a reinforcer (by increasing it or decreasing it) can significantly alter an organism's behavior.

primary reinforcer: Any stimulus or event that follows a particular response and, by its mere delivery (if pleasant) or removal (if unpleasant), acts naturally (without learning) to increase the likelihood that the response will recur.

secondary reinforcer: A neutral stimulus with no intrinsic value to the organism that acquires reinforcement value through repeated pairing with a reinforcing stimulus.

superstitious behavior: Behavior learned through coincidental association with reinforcement.

Learning Objective 10.6 Explain what is meant by superstitious behavior, and tell how it is learned.

Superstitious Behaviors. Because reinforcement plays a key role in learning new behaviors, parents and educators try to reinforce children and students on a regular basis. However, what happens when a person or animal is unintentionally rewarded for a behavior? What happens when a reward has nothing to do with the behavior that immediately preceded it? Under such conditions, people and animals may develop **superstitious behavior.** For example, a baseball player tries to extend his hitting streak by using the same "lucky" bat. A student may study at the same table in the library because she earned an A after studying there for the last exam. Thus, a person who happens to wear the same pair of shoes in three bicycle races and wins all three races may come to believe that there is a causal relationship between wearing that pair of shoes and winning a bicycle race.

For centuries people have tried to influence the events affecting their lives. The belief that repeating a certain random action such as lighting joss sticks may elicit a positive outcome is known as superstition.

Punishment

Learning Objective 10.7 Describe the types of behavioral consequences that can act as punishers, and discuss the limitations of punishment.

You already know that the consequences of an action, be they rewards or punishment affect behavior. Clearly, rewards can establish new behaviors and maintain them for long periods. How effective is punishment as a way to manipulate behavior? **Punishment,** unlike reinforcement, *decreases* the probability of a particular response. As such, it is one of the most commonly used techniques for teaching children and pets to control their behavior. For example, when a dog growls at visitors, its owner chastises it or chains it to a post. When children write on the walls with crayons, their parents may scold them harshly or make them scrub the walls clean. In both cases, people indicate displeasure by the delivery of an action in order to suppress an undesirable behavior.

Another form of punishment involves removal of a pleasant stimulus. For example, if a teenager stays out past her curfew, she may be grounded for a week. A child may be forbidden to watch television if he misbehaves. One punishment procedure that has proven effective is *time out,* in which a person is removed from an environment containing positive events or reinforcers. For example, a child who hits and kicks may be put in a room in which there are no toys, television, or people. Thus, punishment can involve either adding a noxious event, such as a scolding, or subtracting a positive event, such as television watching. In both cases, the aim is to decrease the likelihood of a behavior (see Table 10.1).

punishment: The process of presenting an undesirable or noxious stimulus, or the removal of a positive desirable stimulus, to decrease the probability that a particular preceding response will recur.

primary punisher: Any stimulus or event that follows a particular response and, by its delivery (pleasant) or removal (unpleasant) acts unnaturally (without learning) to decrease the likelihood that the response will recur.

secondary punisher: A neutral stimulus with no intrinsic value to the organism that acquires punishment value through repeated pairing with a punishing stimulus.

The Nature of Punishers. Just as reinforcers are used for reinforcement, *punishers* are used for punishment. Punishers can be **primary**—stimuli that are naturally painful to an organism, such as an electric shock to an animal or a spanking to a child—or **secondary**—neutral stimuli that take on punishing qualities, such as a verbal "no," a frown, or indifference. Secondary punishers can be effective means of controlling behavior, especially when used in combination with reinforcers for desired behaviors.

Limitations of Punishment. Punishment by itself is not an effective way to control or eliminate behavior. Punishment can suppress simple behavior patterns, but once the punishment ceases, animals (and humans) often return to their previous behavior. To be effective, punishment must be continuous, and the desired alternative behavior should be reinforced. Therefore, those who study children in classrooms urge the combination of punishment for antisocial behavior and

TABLE 10.1 Effects of reinforcement and punishment

Addition of a stimulus	Subtraction or withholding of a stimulus	Effect
Positive reinforcement Delivery of food, money, or some other reward	*Negative reinforcement* Removal of shock or some other aversive stimulus	Establishes or increases a specific behavior
Punishment Delivery of electric shock, a slap on the hand, or some other aversive stimulus	*Punishment* Removal of automobile, television, or some other pleasant stimulus	Suppresses or decreases a specific behavior

reinforcement for prosocial, worthwhile behaviors. A combination of reprimands for disruptive behaviors and praise for good behaviors is often the most effective method for controlling classroom behavior.

A serious limitation of punishment as a behavior-shaping device is that it will suppress only existing behaviors. It cannot be used to establish new, desired behaviors. Punishment also has serious social consequences (Azrin & Holtz, 1966). If parents use excessive punishment to control a child's behavior, for example, the child may try to escape from the home so that punishment cannot be delivered. Further, children who receive frequent physical punishment demonstrate increased levels of aggression when away from the punisher. Punishment may control the child's behavior while the parents are nearby, but it may also alienate the child from the parents. Further, if punishment is ineffectively or inconsistently delivered, it may lead to learned helplessness, in which a person or animal feels powerless to control the punishment and stops making any response at all. We discuss learned helplessness in detail in Chapter 15.

Punishment does not always succeed as a behavior shaping device. Punishment can lead to aggressive behavior such as prison riots.

Progress Check 10.1

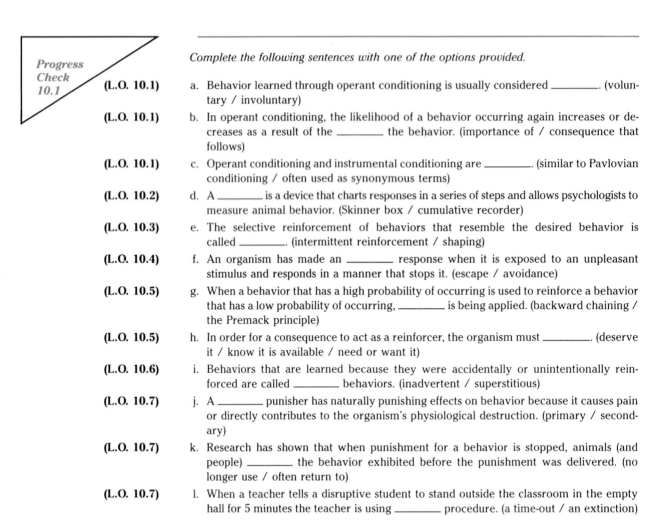

Complete the following sentences with one of the options provided.

(L.O. 10.1) a. Behavior learned through operant conditioning is usually considered ________. (voluntary / involuntary)

(L.O. 10.1) b. In operant conditioning, the likelihood of a behavior occurring again increases or decreases as a result of the ________ the behavior. (importance of / consequence that follows)

(L.O. 10.1) c. Operant conditioning and instrumental conditioning are ________. (similar to Pavlovian conditioning / often used as synonymous terms)

(L.O. 10.2) d. A ________ is a device that charts responses in a series of steps and allows psychologists to measure animal behavior. (Skinner box / cumulative recorder)

(L.O. 10.3) e. The selective reinforcement of behaviors that resemble the desired behavior is called ________. (intermittent reinforcement / shaping)

(L.O. 10.4) f. An organism has made an ________ response when it is exposed to an unpleasant stimulus and responds in a manner that stops it. (escape / avoidance)

(L.O. 10.5) g. When a behavior that has a high probability of occurring is used to reinforce a behavior that has a low probability of occurring, ________ is being applied. (backward chaining / the Premack principle)

(L.O. 10.5) h. In order for a consequence to act as a reinforcer, the organism must ________. (deserve it / know it is available / need or want it)

(L.O. 10.6) i. Behaviors that are learned because they were accidentally or unintentionally reinforced are called ________ behaviors. (inadvertent / superstitious)

(L.O. 10.7) j. A ________ punisher has naturally punishing effects on behavior because it causes pain or directly contributes to the organism's physiological destruction. (primary / secondary)

(L.O. 10.7) k. Research has shown that when punishment for a behavior is stopped, animals (and people) ________ the behavior exhibited before the punishment was delivered. (no longer use / often return to)

(L.O. 10.7) l. When a teacher tells a disruptive student to stand outside the classroom in the empty hall for 5 minutes the teacher is using ________ procedure. (a time-out / an extinction)

Key Variables in Operant Conditioning

As with classical conditioning, many variables affect operant conditioning. Most important are the strength, timing, and frequency of the consequences (either reinforcement or punishment).

Consequences

Learning Objective 10.8
Discuss the strength, timing, and frequency of consequences, and describe continuous, interval, and ratio schedules.

Strength of Consequences. Studies comparing productivity with varying amounts of reinforcement show that the greater the reward, the harder, longer, and faster a person will work to complete a task (see Figure 10.3). For example, if you were a gardener, the more money you received for mowing lawns, the more lawns you would want to mow. Similarly, the stronger the punishment, the more quickly and longer the behavior can be suppressed.

The strength of a consequence can be measured in terms of either time or degree. For example, the length of time a child stays in a time-out room without

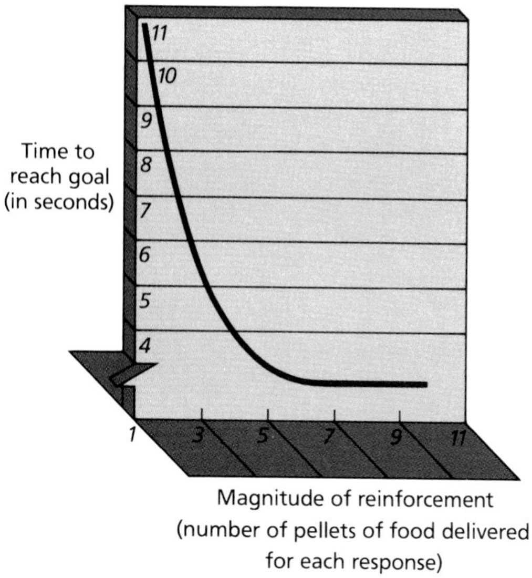

Figure 10.3

As the amount of the reinforcer (such as food) increases, an organism's time to reach a goal usually decreases.

positive reinforcements affects how soon and for how long an unacceptable behavior will be suppressed. Thus, theoretically, a 2-minute stay would not be as effective as a 10-minute stay. However, adults should keep the amount of time they set for time-out relatively short because the procedure is used only to suppress behavior and does not provide opportunities for the child to practice and learn desired behavior. Likewise, a tentative "Please do not do that, sweetiepie," is not as effective as a firm "Don't do that again."

Timing of Consequences. The interval between a desired behavior and the delivery of the consequence (reward or punishment) is important in operant conditioning. Generally, the shorter the interval, the greater the likelihood that the behavior will be learned (see Figure 10.4). If you punish your dog for chewing up the newspaper several hours after the behavior, it is unlikely that the punishment will be effective. Similarly, if you reward a child on Wednesday for eating her

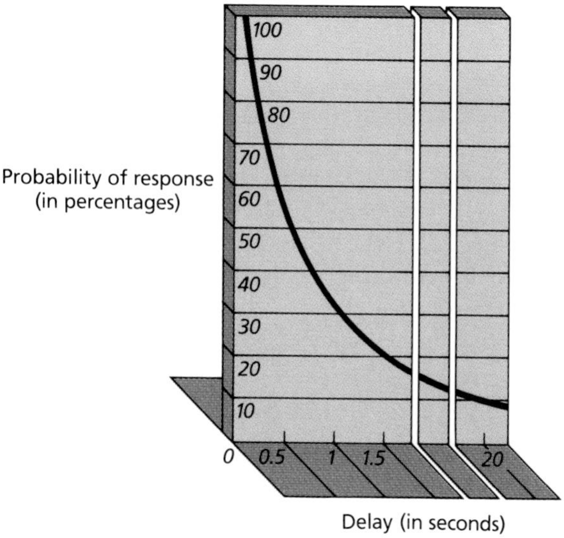

Figure 10.4

A delay between a response and reinforcement reduces the probability that the behavior will recur. Short delays (or no delays) between a response and reinforcement maximize the chances that the behavior will recur.

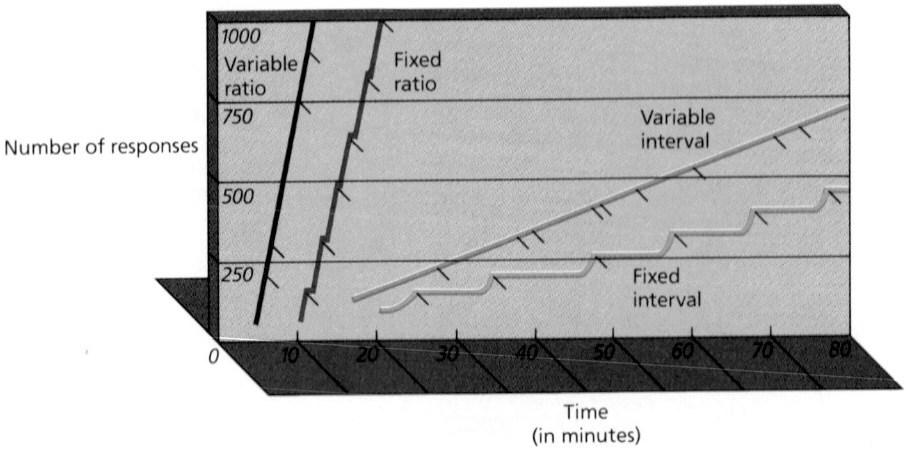

Figure 10.5

The four basic types of reinforcement schedules. The fixed-interval schedule produces a scalloping pattern of responses; the variable-ratio schedule produces a higher performance rate. Steep slopes represent high frequency of desired responses (called work rates). In general, the rate of responding is higher under ratio schedules than under interval schedules. It is also higher under variable schedules than under fixed schedules.

green beans the preceding Monday, her repetition of the good behavior is less likely.

Frequency of Consequences. How often do people want to be reinforced? Is a paycheck once a month sufficient? Will people work better if they receive reinforcement regularly or if they receive it at unpredictable times? In the studies discussed so far, we have assumed that a consequence follows each response.

What if people are reinforced only some of the time, not continually? When a researcher varies the frequency with which an organism is to be reinforced, the researcher is said to manipulate *schedules of reinforcement* or the pattern of presentation of the reinforcer over time. The simplest and easiest reinforcement pattern is *continuous reinforcement.* This is reinforcement for every occurrence of the targeted behavior. However, most researchers, or parents for that matter, do not reinforce a behavior every time it occurs; rather, they reinforce occasionally, or intermittently. What causes the occurrence of reinforcement? Schedules of reinforcement generally are based on either frequency of response or on intervals of time. Some schedules establish a behavior quickly; you will also see that those that help establish it quickly are more quickly extinguished than those that are slower to be established. (We will discuss extinction further in a few paragraphs.) Researchers have devised four basic schedules of reinforcement: two *interval schedules,* which deal with time periods, and two that are *ratio schedules,* which deal with frequency of response (usually work output).

The interval schedules can be either fixed or variable. Imagine that a rat in a Skinner box is being trained to press a bar in order to obtain food. If the experiment is on a fixed-interval schedule, the reward will follow the first response that occurs after a specified interval of time. That is, regardless of whether the rat works a great deal or just a little, it will be given a reinforcer if it presses the bar at least once after a specified interval. The reinforcement schedule is fixed. As Figure 10.5 shows, output on a **fixed-interval** schedule follows a scalloping pattern: Just after reinforcement, both animals and human beings typically respond slowly; on the other hand, just before the reinforcer is due, there is an increase in performance.

With a **variable-interval** schedule, a person or an animal is reinforced after varying amounts of time, as long as an appropriate response is made after the variable interval has elapsed. The organism may be reinforced if it makes a response after 40 seconds, after 60 seconds, and then 25 seconds. For example, if

fixed interval: A reinforcement schedule in which a reinforcer is delivered after a specified interval of time, provided that the required response has occurred at least once after the interval had elapsed.

variable interval: A reinforcement schedule in which a reinforcer is delivered after a varying interval of time, provided that the required response has occurred at least once after the interval.

grades are posted at various unpredictable intervals during a semester, you probably will check the bulletin board at a fairly steady rate.

Rats reinforced on a variable-interval schedule work at a slow, steady rate without showing the scalloping effect of those on a fixed-interval schedule. The delivery of a reinforcer is tied to time intervals rather than work to output, so the work rate is relatively slow. Nevertheless, rats on a variable-interval schedule have a better overall rate of response than those on a fixed-interval schedule.

Ratio schedules, which can also be either fixed or variable, deal with output instead of time. In a **fixed-ratio** schedule, the subject is reinforced for a specific amount of work. For example, a rat in a Skinner Box might be reinforced after every tenth bar press. In this case, the rat will work at a fast, steady, regular rate. It has learned that hard work brings the delivery of a reinforcer on a regular basis. The work rate of a rat on a fixed-ratio schedule is much higher than that of a rat on an interval schedule. In the same way, a teenager who is paid by the job (i.e., for the amount of work completed) will probably mow more lawns than one who is paid by the hour. See Figure 10.5.

Variable-ratio schedules can achieve very high rates of response. In contrast to a fixed-ratio schedule, a variable-ratio system reinforces the subject after various amounts of work have been completed. Thus, a rat learns that hard work produces a reinforcer, but it cannot predict when the reinforcer will be delivered. Therefore, the rat's best bet is to work at an even, steady, high rate, thereby generating the highest available rate of response. Sales agents for insurance companies know that the more individuals they approach, the more insurance they will sell. They may not know who will buy, but they do know that a greater number of selling opportunities will result in more sales. Table 10.2 lists the four basic reinforcement schedules and their effects. Note that when an experimenter implements a *variable*-ratio or a *variable*-interval schedule, the frequency for each ratio or the length of each interval is predetermined, though it will not appear to be so in the view of the subject.

Lottery participants always hope to be the one lucky person reinforced for having participated.

Using Schedules of Consequences. The study of reinforcement has many practical implications. Psychologists use the principles of reinforcement to study

TABLE 10.2 Schedules of reinforcement

Schedule	Description	Effect
Fixed interval	Reinforcement is given for any number of responses after a fixed time.	Response rate drops right after reinforcement but increases near the end of the interval.
Variable interval	Reinforcement is given for any number of responses after a predetermined but variable interval.	Response rate is relatively slow but steady.
Fixed ratio	Reinforcement is given after a fixed number of responses.	Response rate is rapid.
Variable ratio	Reinforcement is given after a predetermined variable number of responses.	Response rate is high and steady.

fixed ratio: A reinforcement schedule in which a reinforcer is delivered after a specific number of responses has occurred.

variable ratio: A reinforcement schedule in which a reinforcer is delivered after a specific but variable number of responses has occurred.

frequently asked questions such as "How can I change my little brother's rotten attitude?" "How can I get more work out of my employees?" "How do I learn to say no?" "How do I get my dog to stop biting my ankles?" or even "How can I get people to do more exercise?" (De Luca & Holborn, 1990).

To get your brother to shape up, you can shape his behavior. Each time he acts in a way that you like, however slight the action, reward him with praise or affection. When he acts poorly, use an extinction procedure—that is, withhold attention or rewards, and ignore him. (We will discuss extinction in more detail in a few paragraphs.) Continue this pattern for a few weeks, and as he becomes more pleasant, show him more attention. Remember, reinforced behaviors tend to recur.

Stimulus Generalization and Stimulus Discrimination

Learning Objective 10.9 Describe stimulus generalization, stimulus discrimination, extinction, and spontaneous recovery in operant conditioning.

Operant conditioning focuses on the relationship between stimuli and responses, and specifying those relationships is a key task of theorists and practitioners. However, sometimes this task is difficult. Consider what it means when your friend says, "The holidays make me depressed." Does she mean that the holidays act as a stimulus for the depression, or does she really mean that her concern for family, money, and homeless people, which she associates with the holidays, causes the depression? It is more likely that some event, some stimulus associated with the holidays actually initiates the depression.

Stimulus generalization and **stimulus discrimination** occur in operant conditioning much as they do in classical conditioning. The difference is that in operant conditioning, the reinforcement is delivered only after the animal makes a correct response, such as discriminating between two stimuli. For example, suppose that an animal in a laboratory is given either a vertical or a horizontal line and two keys, one to be pressed if the line is vertical, the other if the line is horizontal. The animal is reinforced for correct responses. The animal will usually make errors at first, but after repeated presentations of the vertical and horizontal lines, with reinforcements given only for correct responses, discrimination will occur. Stimulus discrimination can also be established with colors, tones, and more complex stimuli.

stimulus discrimination: The process by which an organism learns a specific response to a specific reinforced stimulus and to no other stimulus.

stimulus generalization: Responding to stimuli that are similar to, but not the same as, the stimulus involved in learning the response.

extinction: In operant conditioning, the process in which the probability of an organism emitting a conditioned response is reduced when reinforcement no longer follows the response.

spontaneous recovery: The recurrence of a conditioned response, following a rest period, after extinction.

Extinction and Spontaneous Recovery

In operant conditioning, if a reinforcer or punisher is no longer delivered—that is, if a consequence does not follow an instrumentally conditioned behavior—the behavior will not be well established and if it is established it will undergo **extinction** (see Figure 10.6). Suppose, for example, that a pigeon is trained to peck a key whenever it hears a high-pitched tone. Pecking in response to a high-pitched tone brings reinforcement, but pecking in response to a low-pitched tone does not. If the reinforcement process ceases entirely, the pigeon will eventually stop working. If the pigeon has been on a variable-ratio schedule and thus expects to work for long periods before reinforcement occurs, it will probably work for a very long time before stopping. If it is on a fixed-interval schedule and expects reinforcement within a short time, it will stop pecking after just a few nonreinforced trials.

As in classical conditioning, **spontaneous recovery** also occurs in operant conditioning. If an organism's conditioned behavior has undergone extinction, is given a rest period, and is then retested, it will show spontaneous recovery. If the organism is put through this sequence several times, its work rate in each

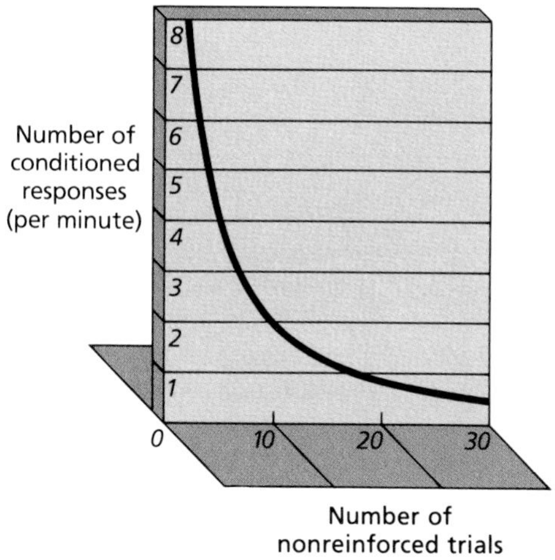

Figure 10.6

When an animal's conditioned behavior is not reinforced over several trials, the likelihood of the conditioned response decreases. After many such trials, the behavior undergoes extinction.

spontaneous-recovery session decreases. After one rest period, the organism's work rate almost equals what it was when the conditioned response was reinforced. However, after a dozen or so rest periods (with no reinforcements) the organism may make only one or two responses; the level of spontaneous recovery will have decreased markedly. Eventually, the behavior will disappear completely (see Figure 10.7), although it may not be completely forgotten.

People also show spontaneous recovery. When you answer a question in class, reinforcement usually follows. The instructor praises you for your extraordinary intelligence or berates you for your ignorance. However, if the instructor stops reinforcing correct answers or does not call on you when you raise your hand, you will probably stop responding (i.e., your behavior will be extinguished). After a vacation, however, you may start raising your hand again (spontaneous recovery), but you will quickly stop if your behavior again is not reinforced (see Table 10.3 on the next page). Instructors learn early in their careers that if they want to have a lively class, they need to reinforce not just correct answers, but

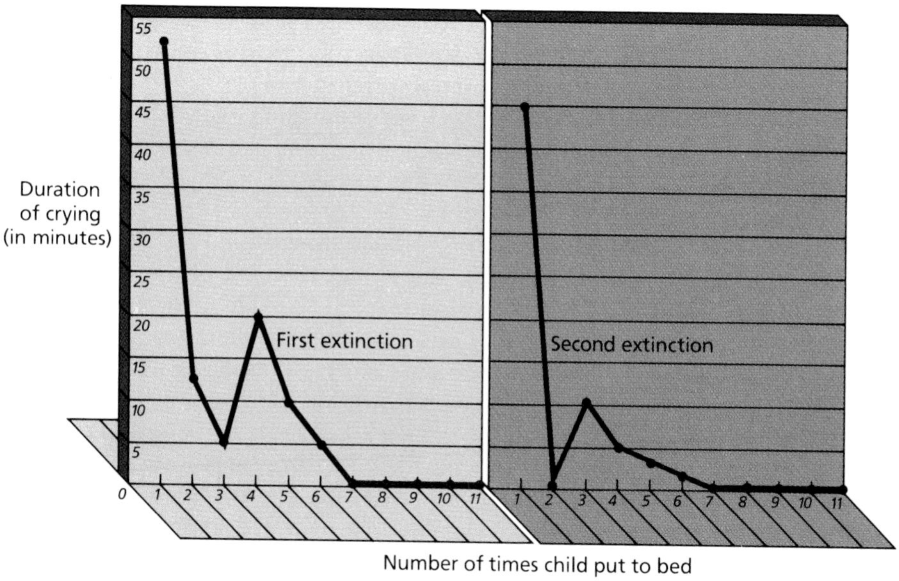

Figure 10.7

A child emitted tantrums at bedtime to gain attention. Williams counted the number of minutes the child cried and instructed the parents not to pay attention to the tantrums. After several days, the number of minutes the child cried decreased to zero. A week later, an aunt put the child to bed; when the child made a fuss (spontaneous recovery), the aunt reinforced the child with attention. The child then had to go through a second series of extinction trials. (Data from C. D. Williams, 1959, p. 269)

TABLE 10.3 Four important properties of operant conditioning

Property	Definition	Example
Extinction	The process of reducing the probability of a conditioned response by withholding the reinforcer	A rat trained to press a bar stops pressing when it is no longer reinforced.
Spontaneous recovery	The reoccurrence of a conditioned response following a rest period after extinction	A rat's continued bar-pressing behavior has undergone extinction; after a rest interval, the rat again presses the bar.
Stimulus generalization	The process by which an organism learns to respond to stimuli that are similar to but not identical to the training stimulus	A cat presses a bar when presented with either an ellipse or a circle.
Stimulus discrimination	The process by which an organism learns to respond to a specific stimulus and then to no other similar stimulus; the complementary process to stimulus generalization	A pigeon presses a key only in response to red lights, not to blue or green ones.

also attempts at correct answers. In doing so, they help shape or manage their student's behavior. Managing behavior is a central concern of both parent and teachers; effective behavior management usually relies on applying principles of psychology.

Electrical Brain Stimulation

Learning Objective 10.10 Describe how electrical brain stimulation experiments are conducted, and identify some behaviors that animals exhibit to receive brain stimulation.

Until the 1950s, researchers assumed that reinforcers are effective because they satisfy some need or drive in an organism. Then James Olds (1955, 1969) found an apparent exception to this assumption: He discovered that rats find electrical stimulation of certain areas of the brain to be rewarding.

Olds implanted an electrode in the hypothalamus of rats and attached the electrodes to a stimulator that provided a small voltage. The stimulator was activated only when the rats pressed a lever in a Skinner box. Olds found that the rats pressed the lever thousands of times in order to continue the self-stimulation. In one study, they pressed it at a rate of 1920 times per hour (Olds & Milner, 1954). Rats will even cross an electrified grid to obtain this reward. Animals who were rewarded with brain stimulation performed better in a maze, running faster with fewer errors. Also, hungry rats often chose self-stimulation over food. Stimulation of certain areas of the brain initiates different drives and activities. In some cases, it reinforces behaviors such as lever pressing; in others, it increases eating, drinking, or sexual behavior.

Psychologists are still not sure how electrical stimulation reinforces a behavior such as lever pressing, but they do know that the area of the brain that is stimulated, the state of the organism, and its particular physiological needs are important. A hungry rat, for example, will self-stimulate faster than a rat that is not hungry. In addition, a hungry rat will generally choose electrical brain stimulation over food but will *not* starve to death by always making this choice.

Operant conditioning has a great influence on how we behave on a daily basis, but human beings are decision makers; they can evaluate alternatives and decide how they will behave. This decision process and the interest in thought processes is clearly seen in studies of cognitive learning, considered next. Building Table 10.1 presents a comparison of the theories presented in this chapter.

Progress Check 10.2

Complete the following sentences with one of the options provided.

(L.O. 10.8) a. The number of responses an organism makes is of little importance in determining when a reinforcer will be delivered in ________ schedule of reinforcement. (a ratio / an interval)

(L.O. 10.8) b. Among all schedules of reinforcement, the highest overall response rate is produced by a ________ schedule of reinforcement. (fixed-interval / variable-ratio)

(L.O. 10.9) c. Stimulus ________ means that an organism responds to stimuli that are similar to, but not the same as, the training stimulus. (generalization / discrimination)

(L.O. 10.9) d. In operant conditioning, if a reinforcer is withheld following a behavior that at one time was followed by the reinforcer, and as a result the behavior decreases, we would say that ________ is occurring. (negative reinforcement / extinction)

(L.O. 10.9) e. In operant conditioning, behavior that is affected by the phenomenon known as spontaneous recovery ________ if it is no longer followed by reinforcers. (strengthens on its own / eventually disappears completely)

(L.O. 10.10) f. James Olds found that rats will ________ electrical brain stimulation. (avoid / cross an electrified grid to receive)

Building Table 10.1

Types of Learning: Classical Conditioning and Operant Conditioning

Type of learning	Procedure	Result	Example
Classical conditioning	A neutral stimulus (such as a bell) is paired with an unconditioned stimulus (such as food).	The neutral stimulus becomes a conditioned stimulus—it *elicits* the conditioned response.	A bell elicits a salivary response in a dog.
Operant conditioning	A behavior is followed by a consequence of reinforcement or punishment.	The behavior increases or decreases in frequency.	A pigeon will peck on a key 20 times per hour to achieve a reward or to avoid punishment.
Observational learning			

Cognitive Learning

"Enough!" shouted Bernie after 4 grueling hours of trying to program his personal computer. Errors were rampant in his program, and they all resulted from the same basic problem, but he didn't know what the problem was. After dozens of trial-and-error manipulations, Bernie turned off the computer and went on to study for his history exam. Then, while staring at a page in the text, he saw a difficult phrase that was set off by commas; he thought about it and suddenly realized his programming mistake. His program's "if–then" statements were missing a necessary comma. After placing the missing comma in all the statements, the program ran flawlessly.

Bernie solved his problem by thinking. His learning was not a matter of simple conditioning of a simple response with a simple reinforcer. Learning researchers have actively focused on learning that involves reinforcement. Many studies suggest that a reinforcer is crucial if behavior is to be maintained. Much of the learning literature has focused on stimuli and responses and their relationships, timing, and frequency. However, is an external (ie., outside of the learner) reinforcer always necessary for learning? Can a person learn new behaviors just by thinking or using his or her imagination? These questions are problematic for traditional learning researchers, but not for cognitive psychologists or learning researchers who have a cognitive emphasis on learning.

Learning Objective 10.11
Describe insight, latent learning, and generative learning.

Thinking about a problem allows you to solve the problem and makes other behaviors possible; this thinking becomes crucial to learning and problem solving (Skinner, 1989). The emphasis of cognitive research, evident even in early learning studies, will be shown over and over again as we examine areas of psychology such as motivation, maladjustment, and therapy. Some of the most famous psychologists of the early part of the century examined learning when reinforcement was not evident and behavior was not shown. These early studies focused on *insight* and on *latent learning* (discussed in this section). Some of these studies gave birth to modern studies of *generative learning.* Other recent research has focused on *observational learning* (these two forms of learning are also discussed in this section). Still other cognitive research has focused on problem solving, creativity, and concept formation, which are covered in Chapter 7 and Learning to Learn is examined in the Applying Psychology box on page 192.

Insight

When you discover a relationship between a series of events, you may say that you had an *insight.* Insights are usually not taught to people, but rather are discovered after a series of events have occurred. Like Bernie's discovery of his missing comma, many types of learning involve sustained thought and insight.

Discovering the causes of insight was the goal of researchers working with animals in the 1920s. Wolfgang Köhler, a Gestalt researcher, showed that chimps developed insights into methods of retrieving food that was beyond their reach. The chimps discovered that they could pile boxes on top of one another to reach food, or they could attach poles together, making a long stick with which to grab bananas. They were never reinforced for the specific behavior, but they learned how to get their food through insight. Once a chimp learns how to pile boxes, or once Bernie realizes his comma error, the insight is not forgotten. The insight occurs through thought, without direct reinforcement. Once the insight occurs, no further instruction, investigation, or training is necessary.

Latent Learning

After a person has an insight, learns a task, or solves a problem (or elements of a problem), the new learning is not necessarily evident. Early researchers were baffled by rats that ran mazes for them and showed the phenomenon of **latent learning.**

latent learning: Learning that occurs in the absence of any direct reinforcement and that is not necessarily demonstrated in observable behavior, though it has occurred and has the *potential* of being exhibited.

Researchers in the 1920s placed hungry rats in mazes and recorded how many trials it took the rats to reach a goal where food was found. It took many days and many trials, but hungry rats learned the mazes well. Other rats were put into the mazes but were not reinforced with food on reaching the goal; instead, they were merely removed from the maze. A third group of rats, like the second group, was not reinforced, but after 10 days was given food on reaching the goal. Surprisingly, in one day, these rats were reaching the goal with few errors. During the first 10 days of maze running, they must have been learning something but not showing it. After being given a reward, they had a reason to reach the goal quickly. Researchers such as E. C. Tolman argued that their learning was *latent*—that is, it was not demonstrated when it occurred. We call this latent learning.

Tolman showed that when a rat is given a reason (such as food) to show learning, the behavior will be evident. In other words, a rat—or a person—without motivation may not show learning, even if it exists. Tolman's work with rats led him to propose the idea that animals and humans develop (or "generate") a kind of mental map of their world, which allows them to navigate a maze, a city route, or even mental associations between past and present life events. His early work laid the foundation for more modern studies of generative learning.

Generative Learning

Modern cognitive psychology is changing the way in which educational psychologists think about learning that occurs in school. In addition to realizing that people organize new information in neural structures resembling maps, most cognitive psychologists are suggesting that each individual also places a unique meaning on the information being learned because each uses existing individually customized cognitive maps to interpret new information. These psychologists see learning as a *generative* process—that is, the learner *generates* (constructs) meaning by building relationships between familiar and unfamiliar events (Wittrock, 1987). According to this model, when we are exposed to new experiences or information, we perceive the new event according to our own previous experiences, and we interpret the event (generate meaning about it) in ways that are consistent with our prior learning experiences and with our memories of those experiences. In other words, we access existing ideas and link new ideas and experiences to them and, as a result, alter our brain structures. These modified structures are then encoded in memory and can be accessed later to interpret more new information. The generative learning model asserts that learning with comprehension occurs when a person actively transfers previously learned ideas to new information. As a result of this process, learning is seen as a generative or constructive process, a process of constantly remodeling and building upon existing knowledge.

According to the generative learning model, learning in the classroom is not so much a matter of engaging in activities that receive external reinforcement from the teacher or even of receiving thoughts that are transferred from the teacher to the learner. Rather, it is the result of an active process in which the learner plays a critical role in generating meaning and learning. This is because no one other than the learner can build relationships between what is already

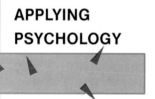

APPLYING PSYCHOLOGY

Learning to Learn

Most college seniors feel they are much better students now than they were as freshmen. What makes the difference? How do students learn to learn better? Today, educators and cognitive researchers are focusing on *how* information is learned, as opposed to *what* is learned. To learn new information, students generate hypotheses, make interpretations, make predictions, and revise earlier ideas. They are active learners (Wittrock, 1987).

Human beings learn how to learn; they learn special strategies for special topics, and they devise general rules that depend on their goals (McKeachie, 1988). The techniques for learning foreign languages differ from those needed to learn mathematics. Are there general cognitive techniques that students can use to learn better? McKeachie, Pintrich, and Lin (1985) argued that lack of effective learning strategies is a major cause of low achievement by university students. They conducted a study to see whether overall grades improved when rote learning, repetition, and memorization were replaced by more efficient cognitive strategies.

To help students become better learners, McKeachie, Pintrich, and Lin developed a course on learning to learn that provided practical suggestions for studying and a theoretical basis for understanding learning. It made students aware of the processes used in learning and remembering. This awareness (thinking about thinking, learning about learning) is called "metacognition." Learning-skills practice, development of motivation, and development of a positive attitude were also included. Among specifics topics were learning from lectures, learning from textbooks, taking tests, self-monitoring, reduction of test anxiety, discovering personal learning styles, and traditional strategies such as SQ3R plus (**S**urvey, **Q**uestion, **R**ead, **R**ecite, **R**eview, *plus,* write and reflect). The course focused on learning in general, not on specific courses such as history or chemistry. The goal was to develop generalized strategies or plans to facilitate learning.

One hundred eighty students were enrolled in a voluntary learning-to-learn course and were tested at the beginning and end of the semester; their test scores were compared with control groups enrolled in other psychology classes. Various measures were used to assess whether the course had any impact on SAT scores, reading test scores, anxiety test scores, and—especially—academic grades.

The results showed that learning-to-learn students made gains in a number of areas, including grades and motivation. In later semesters, the students continued to improve. This straightforward study tells an important story about psychology in general, and about cognitive psychology in particular. First, it shows that psychologists are engaged in activities that help people, not just esoteric laboratory studies. Second, it shows a shift in emphasis from studies of learning specific facts or specific stimuli and responses, to studies of learning strategies. Third, it shows that research into thought processes can lead to more effective thought and, subsequently, to high levels of motivation. Last, this simple study shows that people can be taught to be more efficient learners.

McKeachie, Pintrich, and Lin argued that "the cognitive approach has generated a richer, deeper analysis of what goes on in learning and memory, increasing our understanding and improving our ability to facilitate retrieval and use of learning . . . we need to be aware of several kinds of outcomes—not just *how much knowledge* was learned, but as *what kinds of learning* took place" (p. 602). Students can better grasp history, chemistry, or economics if they understand *how* to go about studying these topics. Law, psychology, and medicine require different learning strategies. After we learn how to learn, the differences come into sharp focus; indeed, some researchers think of creativity as a metacognitive process involving thinking about our own thoughts (Pesut, 1990). Individuals can learn to learn, reason, and make better choices accross a variety of domains (Larrick, Morgan, and Nisbett, 1990).

- ▲ ***Identify the hypothesis made by McKeachie, Pintrich, and Lin.***
- ▲ ***What was the evidence used to support the claim that students who were taught how to learn made gains in a number of areas, including grades and motivation?***
- ▲ ***What are the implications of this study for cognitive psychologists and for teachers in the public schools?***

known by the learner and what he or she is currently learning. As a result, what a person actually learns is unique to the person.

Observational Learning

Learning Objective 10.12 Describe observational learning and the variables that affect it.

observational learning theory: The process by which organisms learn new responses by observing the behavior of a model and then imitating it; also called *social learning theory.*

A truly comprehensive learning theory of behavior must be able to explain how people learn behaviors that are not taught. Everyone knows that smoking cigarettes is unhealthy; smokers regularly try to stop smoking, and for most people, the first experience with smoking is unpleasant. Nonetheless, 12-year-olds light up anyway. They inhale the smoke, cough for several minutes, and feel nauseated. There is no doubt that it is a punishing experience for them, but they try again. Over time, they master the technique of inhaling and, in their view, look "cool" with a cigarette. That's the key to the whole situation: The 12-year-olds observed other people with cigarettes, thought they looked cool, wanted to look cool themselves, and therefore imitated the smoking behavior.

Such situations present a problem for traditional learning theorists. There is little reinforcement to establish smoking behavior; instead, there is punishment (coughing and nausea). Nonetheless, the behavior recurs. To explain this type of learning, Stanford University psychologist Albert Bandura contends that the principles of classical and operant conditioning are just two ways in which people learn; another way is by observing other people.

During the past 25 years, Bandura's ideas, expressed through **observational learning theory** (also called *social learning theory*), have expanded the range of behaviors that can be explained by learning theory (Woodward, 1982). The theory focuses on the role of thought in establishing and maintaining behavior. Bandura and his colleagues conducted important research to confirm their idea that people can learn by observing and then imitating the behavior of others (Bandura 1969, 1977b; Bandura, Ross, & Ross, 1963). In their early studies, they showed one group of children some films with aggressive content in which an adult punched an inflated doll, and they showed another group some films that had neither aggressive nor passive content. They then compared the play behavior of both groups. The researchers found that the children who had viewed aggressive, violent films tended to be aggressive and violent afterward, whereas the other children showed no change in behavior (Bandura, Ross, & Ross, 1963; Bandura & Walters, 1963). Bandura's research and many subsequent studies have shown that observing aggression creates aggression in children, but children do not imitate aggressiveness when the person they observe is punished for aggressive behavior.

These young boys have learned to mimic the traits of the adults around them simply by observing on-going behavior mannerisms in their community.

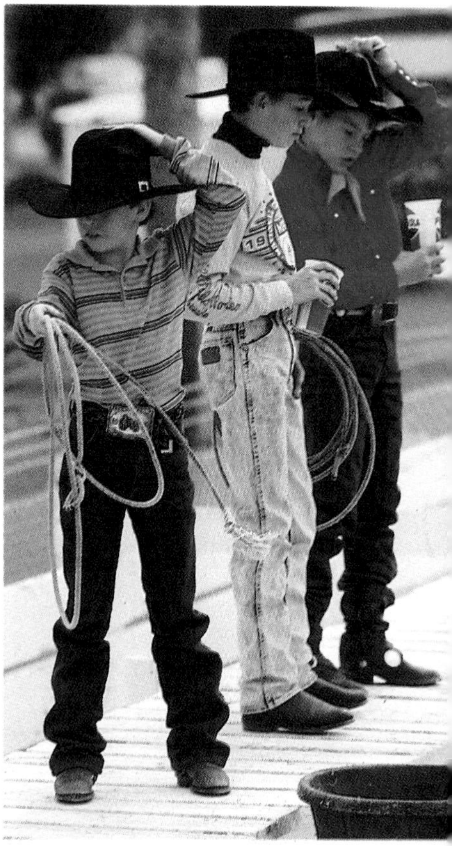

Everyday experience also shows that people imitate the behavior of others, especially those whom they hold in high esteem. Children emulate Rambo, dress in army fatigues, carry toy machine guns and pretend to launch patriot missiles. You may buy a particular brand of shampoo because your favorite television star claims to use it. Scores of young girls became interested either in gymnastics after watching Olympic star Mary Lou Retton or in track events after watching Florence Griffith Joyner. Unfortunately, not all observational learning is positive: Alcohol and other drug use often begins when children and teenagers imitate people they admire.

A key point to remember is that if a person observes an action that is not reinforced, but rather punished, it will not be imitated. Children who observe aggression that is punished do not immediately behave aggressively; nevertheless, they may learn aggressive responses that might be evident in the future. Learning may take place through observation, but performance of specific learning may depend on a specific setting and a person's perceived expectations about the effect of exhibiting those behaviors. Observational learning, like latent learning, is not always immediately exhibited in behavior.

Variables That Affect Observational Learning

Observational learning theory has several important elements. One is the *type and power of the model* employed. Nurturing, warm, and caring models, for example, are more likely to be imitated than nonnurturing, angry ones; dominant parents are more likely to be imitated than relatively passive ones. In a classroom, children are more likely to imitate peers whom they see as powerful and dominant.

Another element is the *learner's personality and degree of independence.* Dependent children are more likely to imitate models than are independent children. Generally, the less self-confidence a person has, the more likely he or she is to imitate a model. A third factor is the *situation.* People are more likely to imitate

Types of Learning: Classical Conditioning, Operant Conditioning, and Observational Learning

Building Table 10.2

Type of learning	Procedure	Result	Example
Classical conditioning	A neutral stimulus (such as a bell) is paired with an unconditioned stimulus (such as food).	The neutral stimulus becomes a conditioned stimulus—it *elicits* the conditioned response.	A bell elicits a salivary response in a dog.
Operant conditioning	A behavior is followed by a consequence of reinforcement or punishment.	The behavior increases or decreases in frequency.	A pigeon will peck on a key 20 times per hour to achieve a reward or to avoid punishment.
Observational learning	An observer attends to a model to learn a behavior.	The observer learns the sequence of behaviors and becomes able to perform it at will.	After watching television violence, children are more likely to show aggressive behaviors.

others when there is uncertainty about correct behavior. For example, a teenager going on his or her first date, for example, takes cues from peers about dress and imitates their behavior. When a person who has never been exposed to death loses someone close, he or she may not know what to say or how to express feelings. Watching other people express their grief provides a model for behavior.

Traditional and Cognitive Learning

Cognitive approaches to understanding learning are gaining an ever more important role in learning theory. Generative, insight, and latent learning are all being placed in new frameworks for learning. For example, even die-hard learning researchers who have been doing work on operant conditioning for years acknowledge that some learning takes place through thought processes involving observation. Observational learning theorists are not interested in replacing traditional learning theory; rather, they want observational learning to stand alongside classical and operant conditioning as another way of explaining human learning and behavior. Psychologists are concluding that cognitive learning in combination with classical and operant conditioning can account for nearly all learned behavior (see Building Table 10.2).

Bandura's explanation of learning through observation (1977b) has filled a large gap in psychologists' understanding of the role of thought in how learning occurs, but it has also raised questions. Psychologists must identify the variables involved in observational learning and understand what people think about the events they observe. In Chapter 15 we discuss more fully Bandura's research on observational learning and its effects on social behaviors.

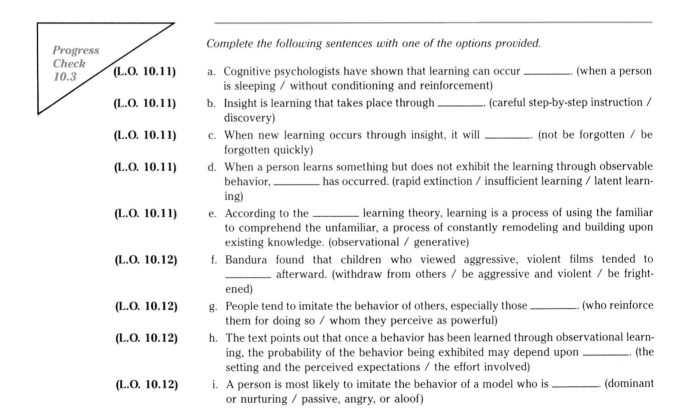

Progress Check 10.3

Complete the following sentences with one of the options provided.

(L.O. 10.11) a. Cognitive psychologists have shown that learning can occur ________. (when a person is sleeping / without conditioning and reinforcement)

(L.O. 10.11) b. Insight is learning that takes place through ________. (careful step-by-step instruction / discovery)

(L.O. 10.11) c. When new learning occurs through insight, it will ________. (not be forgotten / be forgotten quickly)

(L.O. 10.11) d. When a person learns something but does not exhibit the learning through observable behavior, ________ has occurred. (rapid extinction / insufficient learning / latent learning)

(L.O. 10.11) e. According to the ________ learning theory, learning is a process of using the familiar to comprehend the unfamiliar, a process of constantly remodeling and building upon existing knowledge. (observational / generative)

(L.O. 10.12) f. Bandura found that children who viewed aggressive, violent films tended to ________ afterward. (withdraw from others / be aggressive and violent / be frightened)

(L.O. 10.12) g. People tend to imitate the behavior of others, especially those ________. (who reinforce them for doing so / whom they perceive as powerful)

(L.O. 10.12) h. The text points out that once a behavior has been learned through observational learning, the probability of the behavior being exhibited may depend upon ________. (the setting and the perceived expectations / the effort involved)

(L.O. 10.12) i. A person is most likely to imitate the behavior of a model who is ________. (dominant or nurturing / passive, angry, or aloof)

Module Summary

Operant Conditioning

- In *operant conditioning,* an organism emits or shows a particular behavior, which is then followed by a consequence (reward or punishment). The term *reinforcer* refers to any consequence that increases the probability that the response that preceded it will recur. *Shaping* is the process of reinforcing behavior that approximates a desired behavior (pp. 175–176).
- *Positive reinforcement* increases the probability that a desired response will occur by introducing a rewarding or pleasant stimulus. *Negative reinforcement* increases the probability that a desired behavior will occur by removing an aversive stimulus (p. 178).
- *Primary reinforcers* are those that have survival value for the organism; their value does not have to be learned. *Secondary reinforcers* are neutral stimuli that initially have no intrinsic value for the organism, but when paired, coupled, or linked with a primary reinforcer, they too become rewards (p. 179).

Key Variables in Operant Conditioning

- The most important variables affecting operant conditioning are the strength, timing, and frequency of consequences (p. 183–186).
- Schedules of reinforcement may be of two types: interval schedules and ratio schedules. Interval schedules provide reinforcement after fixed or variable time periods; ratio schedules provide reinforcement after fixed or variable amounts of work (p. 185).

Cognitive Learning

- Cognitive learning psychologists focus on thinking processes and on thought that helps process, establish, and maintain learning (p. 190).
- Some of the early studies focused on insight and latent learning and gave birth to modern studies of cognitive mapping (p. 190).

Observational Learning

- Observational learning, also called social learning, is the process of learning new responses by observing and then imitating the behavior of a model (p. 193).
- Some of the key elements of social learning theory are the characteristics and power of the model, the learner's own personality and independence, and the learner's present situation (p. 193).

KEY TERMS

extinction, p. 186
fixed interval, p. 184
fixed ratio, p. 185
latent learning, p. 191
negative reinforcement, p. 178
observational learning theory, p. 193
operant conditioning, p. 173
positive reinforcement, p. 178
primary punisher, p. 180
primary reinforcer, p. 179
punishment, p. 180
reinforcer, p. 178
secondary punisher, p. 180
secondary reinforcer, p. 179
shaping, p. 177
Skinner box, p. 176
spontaneous recovery, p. 186
stimulus discrimination, p. 186
stimulus generalization, p. 186
superstitious behavior, p. 179
variable interval, p. 184
variable ratio, p. 185

SELF-TEST

Module 10

- Before taking the self-test, **recite** and **review.**
- Use the key at the back of the text to *correct* your answers.
- *Restudy* pages that correspond to any questions you answered incorrectly.

1. E. L. Thorndike pioneered instrumental conditioning research by
   a. making food available to cats who hit a lever.
   b. conditioning infants to suck in response to a sound.
   c. teaching pigeons to discriminate between a circle and an ellipse.
   d. toilet training his 2-year-old.
2. A device that allows researchers to control when an organism will receive reinforcement or punishment is a
   a. cumulative recorder.
   b. Skinner box.
   c. conditioning maze.
   d. differential apparatus.
3. Joe's dad is teaching him to play golf. Each time Joe makes progress toward perfecting his swing, his dad tells him he did a good job. When Joe does not show an improved swing, his dad says nothing. Joe's dad is using________to teach his son how to hit a golf ball.
   a. primary reinforcement.
   b. a variable-interval schedule.
   c. shaping.
   d. all of the above
4. Which of the following illustrates a behavior that is receiving negative reinforcement?
   a. Sue accuses Jim of being lazy, so he hangs up on her.
   b. Ollie lies when her teacher confronts her about cheating on an exam; the lie works because the teacher drops the issue and Ollie avoids further punishment.
   c. Pete gets caught while cheating on an exam and is expelled.
   d. Eric did not join his friends for pizza so that he could study for his exam.
5. Which of the following is a primary reinforcer?
   a. money
   b. food and water
   c. termination of pain
   d. both b and c
6. Superstitious behavior is learned
   a. through negative reinforcement.
   b. as a result of coincidental association with reinforcers.
   c. by decreasing the number of times the behavior is reinforced.
   d. when a person pays attention to the unlucky aspects of life more than to the rewarding aspects.
7. Cross out the statement that is *false* concerning punishment.
   a. Punishment can be used to teach new, desired behaviors such as putting toys away.
   b. Punishment suppresses learned behaviors.
   c. Punishment can set up the conditions for escape and avoidance behaviors, such as running away or lying about a mistake.
   d. Punishment can result in learned helplessness, in which a person feels powerless and stops trying.

8. Ratio schedules of reinforcement are based on
   a. time passing between responses.
   b. time passing between the response and the consequence.
   c. the number of consequences that are given for one response.
   d. work output, which is determined by the number of response made.
9. Sue has decided to use an extinction procedure with the hope of eliminating her son's habit of begging for treats at the grocery store. In order to be successful with this procedure, Sue needs to
   a. ignore her son's pleas for treats.
   b. wait until the shopping is almost complete before agreeing to buy a treat.
   c. scold or spank her son if he begs for a treat after being asked not to beg.
   d. promise her son a special treat if he can make it through shopping without begging.
10. In his studies investigating electrical brain stimulation, Olds found that rats
   a. pressed a lever up to 1920 times in 1 hour to receive brain stimulation.
   b. could not successfully find their way through a maze.
   c. could find their way through a maze, but did so at a much slower pace than rats that were not receiving brain stimulation.
   d. could make their way through a maze, but made more errors than rats who were not receiving brain stimulation.
11. The generative learning model emphasizes the critical role of ________ in generating meaning so that learning with comprehension will occur.
   a. the teacher
   b. the learner
   c. reinforcers
   d. powerful models
12. Cross out the statement that is *false* concerning the imitation of observed aggressive behavior.
   a. Children who observe aggressive, violent films behave with aggression and violence afterward.
   b. Children do not imitate aggressive behavior if the observed aggressor is punished for being aggressive.
   c. Viewing aggression and violence in films has no significant effect on the behavior of children.
   d. Although children may not exhibit aggressive behavior after observing it, they may have learned these behaviors through observation and may exhibit them at some future time.

Connections

If you are interested in . . .	Turn to . . .	To learn more about . . .
Classical conditioning	◆ Chapter 10, p. 429	Why behavioral theories of personality depend on the idea that predictability in the environment determines personality
	◆ Chapter 12, p. 505	How a person's physical responses to the stresses in his or her life can be conditioned and reversed
	◆ Chapter 14, p. 577	How treatment for phobias relies on reconditioning of individuals
Operant conditioning	◆ Chapter 7, p. 265	How conditioning has played a crucial role in the development of theories of how people learn language
	◆ Chapter 9, p. 372	The impact of providing reinforcement to people when they already find a behavior rewarding
	◆ Chapter 15, p. 625	When, and under what conditions, attitudes such as prejudice are shaped by a parent's use of reinforcement
Cognitive learning	◆ Chapter 7, p. 247	How people develop reasoning processes and gain insight into problem-solving tasks
	◆ Chapter 10, p. 426	Why behavior this is observed, imitated, and then reinforced becomes part of an individual's personality
	◆ Chapter 15, p. 632	How aggression researchers have used observational learning theory to show that watching television violence has a deleterious influence on children's behavior

There is probably no more well-researched area in psychology than learning. Thousands of research studies have investigated its many variables, and yet there are still many unanswered questions. Part of the reason for the depth of research has been its fundamental link to other areas of psychology. The whole nature versus nurture issue raised in Chapter 2 (Biology, p. 39), depends on the study of learning. The study of many disorders such as schizophrenia and depression (Chapter 13, p. 547) and their causes often focuses on learning theory. Psychologists are applying learning research to issues such as how to raise children in studies of development (Chapter 8, p. 307) and in how to motivate students and workers (Chapter 9, p. 368). Personality theorists (discussed in Chapter 10, p. 422) rely on studies of learning, as do behavior therapists (Chapter 14, p. 542) when they examine learning, behavior modification, and cognitive approaches to therapy. If there were one area more than any other that pervades psychological inquiry—it would be the study of learning. In the next chapter, we study memory, how learned behavior is stored and accessed for continued use.

Module 11 ► BASIC MECHANISMS OF MEMORY 202

Module 12 ► FORGETTING AND THE BIOLOGY OF MEMORY 222

Chapter 6

Memory

Once an organism learns something, psychologists can study its memory. With humans, studying memory is fairly easy because they can report what they remember; with animals, psychologists must study observable learned behaviors and how long the animal continues to express them before they appear to have been forgotten. Chapter 6 presents an overview of research and applications of memory studies.

Module 11 begins with a definition of memory and a review of early studies. It continues with a presentation of contemporary formulations of memory, especially the information-processing approach. The three basic mechanisms of memory are presented: (1) The sensory register performs initial coding of stimuli. This information must be transferred immediately to short-term memory or be lost. (2) Short-term memory performs additional coding for about 30 seconds; after that, interference or decay may cause the loss of information. Short-term memory can effectively code only five to nine items of information at a time. Information rehearsed in short-term memory will be retained and, if considered important enough by the organism, (3) information can be stored in long-term memory.

If information that is stored in memory is not important, used often, or rehearsed, it is likely to be forgotten; this is the focus of Module 12. The processes of forgetting have been studied extensively by psychologists. Decay, interference, and special considerations such as state-dependent learning are presented. The module ends with a discussion of how psychologists are just beginning to understand the physiological processes, such as consolidation, that allow for memory. Consolidation and the location of memory are considered. It is concluded that with further insight into learning and memory processes, psychologists can maximize people's abilities to deal with the world effectively and to cope ingeniously with its complexities.

Module 11

Basic Mechanisms of Memory

LEARNING OBJECTIVES

When you have mastered the material in this module, you will be able to

Introduction (p. 203)

11.1 State the relationship between learning and memory (p. 203).

Memory: Retaining Information (pp. 203–207)

11.2 Discuss the research findings of early memory studies concerning relearning, massed and distributed practice, and the von Restorff effect (p. 203).

11.3 Describe the recall, recognition, reconstruction, and picture memory techniques used by psychologists to study retention (p. 204).

The Information—Processing Approach to Memory (p. 207)

11.4 List the stages involved in information processing and describe how encoding, storage, and retrieval are involved (p. 207).

The Sensory Register (pp. 207–208)

11.5 Describe the encoding, storage, and retrieval processes that take place at the sensory register and explain the function of the sensory register (p. 207).

Short-Term Memory (pp. 209–212)

11.6 Describe the encoding, storage, and retrieval processes; the concept of working memory; and the duration, capacity, and types of rehearsal that are characteristic of short-term memory (p. 209).

Long-Term Memory (pp. 212–218)

11.7 Describe the encoding, storage, and retrieval processes characteristic of long-term memory and distinguish procedural from declarative memories (p. 212).

11.8 Describe the nature of imagery, the research that has examined it, and the reason it is an important memory aid (p. 215).

11.9 Describe state-dependent learning and explain how it affects memory (p. 217).

SQ3R
- **Survey** to set goals for studying.
- Ask **questions** as you READ.
- Stop occasionally to **recite** and **review**.

plus
- **Write** a summary of key points
- **Reflect** on the hypotheses, evidence, and implications of this material and on the relevance it has to *your* life.

It was afternoon, and 12-year-old Martha stood in the kitchen stirring cookie dough while her mother greased a baking sheet. Her father was in the living room, listening to a televised broadcast of a concert. Suddenly, the music stopped, and an announcer, his voice charged with excitement, told listeners that Neil Armstrong in Apollo 11 had just landed on the moon. Her mother rushed to her father's side; Martha followed, still holding onto the bowl of batter as she knelt down by the television to watch the news.

memory: The ability to recall or remember past events, images, ideas, or previously learned information or skills; the storage system that allows for retention and retrieval.

Those childhood images recalled from events that happened more than 20 years before, flashed in Martha's mind as she rewrote modern American history class lecture notes. In class, she had been the center of attention because she was the only person, other than the professor, old enough to remember the day United States astronauts landed on the moon. Although Martha could remember an event that occurred two decades earlier, she often had to make a concerted effort to memorize important lecture points heard only hours before.

Learning Objective 11.1
State the relationship between learning and memory.

Psychologists have long recognized that recalling well-learned facts can be easy or difficult. Even though something has been *learned,* it may not always be *remembered.* A person may easily remember the Pledge of Allegiance, but forget the chemical formula for sugar. That's because learning and memory are two separate processes. From Chapter 5, recall that *learning* is a relatively permanent change in the organism that occurs as a result of experience; this change is often seen in overt or observed behavior, but not always. *Memory* is the ability to remember past events or previously learned information or skills; memory is also the storage system that allows for retaining and retrieving of previously learned information.

Memory: Retaining Information

Learning Objective 11.2
Discuss the research findings of early memory studies concerning relearning, massed and distributed practice, and the von Restorff effect.

Some of the first experiments in psychology studied learning, memory, and forgetting. Sometimes, these tasks involved paper and pencil, but more often they merely involved a subject and an experimenter and some information to be learned. Computers were unheard of, and techniques that psychologists use today, such as the lexical decision task which we examine later in this chapter, would not have been understood. We now follow the development of memory studies through its relatively recent history.

Early Studies: Focus on Forgetting

Through the technique of *relearning,* Hermann Ebbinghaus (1850–1909) studied how well people learn stored information. Ebbinghaus earnestly believed that the

Hermann Ebbinghaus was the first person to scientifically investigate how people store information.

contents of consciousness could be studied by scientific principles. He tried to quantify how quickly subjects could learn, forget, and relearn information. Ebbinghaus was the first person to investigate memory scientifically and systematically, making his technique as important as his findings.

In his early studies, in which he was both researcher and subject, Ebbinghaus assigned himself the task of learning lists of letters in order of presentation. First, he strung together groups of three letters to make nonsense syllables such as *nak, dib, mip,* and *daf.* He then recorded how many times he had to present the lists to himself before he could remember them perfectly. Ebbinghaus found that when the lists were short, learning was nearly perfect in one or two trials. When they contained more than seven items, however, he had to present them over and over for accurate recall.

Later, Ebbinghaus did learning experiments with other subjects. He had them learn lists of words and then, after varying amounts of time, measured how quickly they relearned the original list. If a subject relearned the list quickly, Ebbinghaus concluded that he or she still had some memory of it. He called this learning technique the *saving method* because what was initially learned was not totally forgotten (see Figure 11.1).

Following Ebbinghaus's lead, from the 1930s through the 1960s many researchers investigated the best ways for people to learn new material and relearn forgotten skills. For example, they examined how intensive practice at one time as opposed to practice over several intervals—that is, *massed* (all at once) versus *distributed* (spread out) *practice*—affected learning and retention. Generally speaking, distributed practice is most effective. Researchers have learned that the effectiveness of distributed practice depends on several variables, including the method, order and speed of presentation. Distributed practice is especially effective in perceptual-motor skills where eye–hand coordination is important.

In the 1970s, researchers began to study the best way to present information to be learned. (This interest paralleled the innovations being carried out in public schools, including open classrooms, new math, and cooperative learning.) For example, researchers found that if one item in a list differs from the others (such as a list of 10 animal names and 1 plant name), the one item that is different is recalled more easily. This phenomenon is called the *von Restorff effect.*

Measures of Retention

Learning Objective 11.3 Describe the recall, recognition, reconstruction, and picture memory techniques used by psychologists to study retention.

Psychologists study retention by measuring people's ability to learn information through several techniques: recall, recognition, reconstruction, and pictorial memory. The most widely investigated techniques have been recall and recognition. *Recall* involves remembering the details of a situation or idea and placing them together in a meaningful framework (usually without any cues or aids). Asking someone to name the craft in which United States astronauts first landed on the moon is a test of recall. *Recognition* involves remembering whether one has seen a stimulus before—that is, whether the stimulus is familiar. Asking someone whether Neil Armstrong landed on the moon in 1969 is a test of recognition.

Recall. In recall tasks, subjects have to remember previously presented information. (Essay exams require you to recall information.) Usually, in experiments, the information comprises strings (i.e., lists) of digits or letters. For example, a typical study might ask subjects to remember 10 nonsense syllables, each of which was presented on a screen every $\frac{1}{2}$ second. They would then have to repeat the list at the end of the 5-second presentation period.

Three widely used recall tasks are free recall, serial recall, and paired associates. In *free-recall tasks,* subjects can recall items in any order, much as you might recall the items on a grocery list. *Serial-recall* tasks are more difficult because the

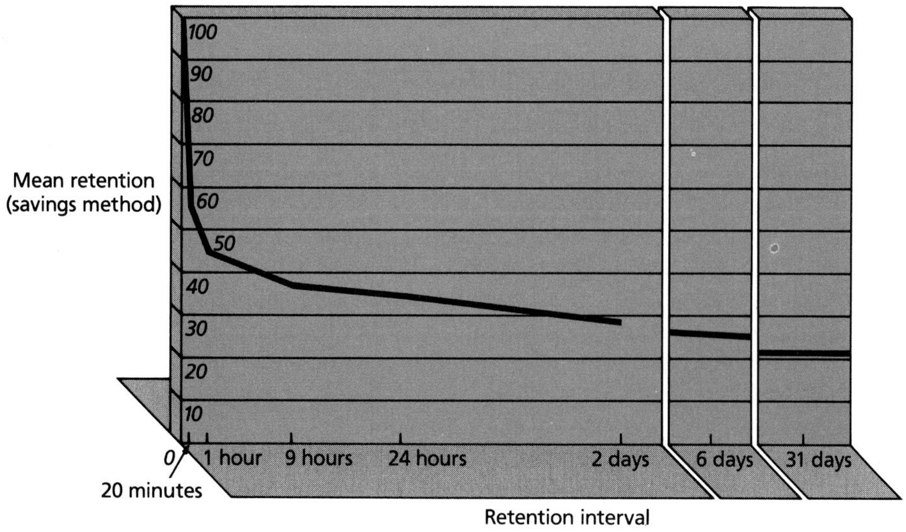

Figure 11.1

Ebbinghaus's forgetting curve: Ebbinghaus found that most forgetting occurs during the first 9 hours after learning.

items must be recalled in the order in which they were presented, just as you would a telephone number. In *paired-associate tasks,* subjects are given a cue to help them recall the second half of a pair of items. In the learning phase of a study the experimenter would pair the words "tree" and "shoe." In the testing phase, subjects would be presented with the word "tree" and have to respond with the correct answer, "shoe." Table 11.1 lists typical items and requirements used in the three main types of recall tasks.

Recognition. In a multiple-choice test, you are asked to recognize relevant information. Psychologists have found that recognition tasks can help them measure differences in memory ability better than recall tasks. That's because al-

TABLE 11.1 Three types of traditional list-learning tasks, materials, and requirements

Type of task	Material	Example	Requirement
Serial recall	Nonsense syllables	GIP MAG DEC LIG DEL VEH	Subject learns the items in the order in which they were presented; often items are nonsense syllables, but not always.
Free recall	Words	ghoul vanquish painless telephone burp	Subject learns the items in any order.
Paired associate	Nonsense syllables or words	GIP/MAG LIG/ZEP hall/pencil coffee/plant	Subject learns to associate the second item of the pair with the first.

Note: Based on Hall, 1982, p. 153.

schema: [SKEEM-uh] Conceptual framework that organizes information and makes sense out of the world by laying out a general framework in which events can be coded.

though a person may recognize a previously studied fact, he or she may be unable to recall the associated details contained in the fact. Asked to name the state capital of Maine, you would probably have a better chance of answering correctly if given four items to choose from: Columbus, Annapolis, Helena, or Augusta.

Reconstruction. Here's a test of your memory: What did Neil Armstrong say when he first landed on the moon (his "one small step for a man" statement)? Few of us can recall Armstrong's words exactly, but most can probably recognize them, or reconstruct them approximately. Researchers have shown that people often construct memories of past events that are close approximations but not exact memories. For example, you might construct the gist of the speech by saying that Armstrong said something about man's first steps on the moon being important for all mankind. (Just for the record, his exact words were "That's one small step for a man, one giant leap for mankind.")

Contemporary explanations of *reconstructive memory* have focused on the constructive nature of the memory process and how people develop a **schema,** or conceptual framework, that organizes and make sense of the world. Because we cannot remember *all* the details of an event or situation, we keep key facts and lose minor details. By developing schemas, we group key pieces of information together. In general, we try to fit the entire memory into some schematic that will be available for later recall. For example, Martha's schema for life in the United States during 1969, the year the United States landed on the moon, might include memories of such events as watching Walter Cronkite's news reports, listening to the Beatles, and reading about urban unrest. Martha can access this schema to recall events that occurred in 1969; she can also access it to generate meaning, in order to comprehend and learn about events occurring in her present life. As with learning, our memories develop through a generative or constructive remodeling and building process.

Picture Memory. Related to reconstruction is the study of *picture memory,* whereby researchers can see how well people can remember pictures. The results of these studies show that people are amazingly good at recognizing pictures they have previously seen. Haber (1979) found that subjects can recognize hundreds or even thousands of pictures with almost 100% accuracy. Picture memory studies suggest that pictorial information may be coded, stored, and retrieved differently from other information; this is why recognition memory may be so good. The processes of coding, storing, and retrieving information are important in the information-processing approach examined next.

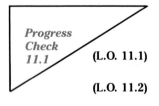

Progress Check 11.1

Complete the following sentences with one of the options provided.

(L.O. 11.1) a. Memory and learning are ________ processes. (basically identical / separate, but interdependent)

(L.O. 11.2) b. Ebbinghaus studied how well subjects had initially learned a list of words by measuring how quickly the subjects ________ the list of words. (forgot / could relearn)

(L.O. 11.2) c. ________ practice is generally the most effective type of practice when learning anything new, but when skills involving eye–hand coordination are being learned, it is especially effective. (Massed / Distributed)

(L.O. 11.2) d. The ________ describes a phenomenon where we find it easier to remember one item in a group that differs from all the other items in that group. (Ebbinghaus method / von Restorff effect / lexical decision task)

(L.O. 11.3) e. When recall and recognition tasks are compared, we find that ________ requires more information to be remembered by an individual. (recognition / recall)

(L.O. 11.3) f. When a subject is shown two words at the same time and then later shown only one of the words as a cue for remembering the second word a ________ task is being used. (serial / paired-associate / matching)

(L.O. 11.3) g. We group pieces of information together in memory by ________. (memorizing ideas / developing schemas)

(L.O. 11.3) h. Picture-memory studies have shown that people are ________ when it comes to identifying pictures that they have seen before. (amazingly accurate / not very accurate)

The Information-Processing Approach to Memory

Human brains are not computers, nor do they work exactly the way computers do. They make mistakes and are affected by biological, environmental, and interpersonal events. Nevertheless, enough similarities exist between human brains and computers for psychologists to discuss learning and memory in terms of information processing. The *information-processing approach* typically describes three stages (sensory register, short-term memory, and long-term memory) in learning and memory, and it assumes that each stage is separate, although related, and analyzable by scientific methods. Within each stage, three processes occur: encoding, storage, and retrieval (see Figure 11.2 on the next page).

Learning Objective 11.4
List the stages involved in information processing, and describe how encoding, storage, and retrieval are involved.

Encoding involves organizing information so that the nervous system can process it. Encoding can be visual or acoustic, or it can even include taste, touch, temperature, or other sensory information; encoding is the first step in establishing a memory. **Storage** is the process of maintaining information in memory, for a few seconds or for many years. **Retrieval** is the process by which stored information is recovered from memory. Recalling your Social Security number, the details of a phone call, or the names of the U2 band members are all retrieval tasks. Think of information stored in the brain as books in a library. Books can be checked out and new ones added. Similarly, the books can deteriorate with age, be misplaced, or be difficult to locate. Books that are used frequently will often be easier to find—you'll know exactly where to look—than those used infrequently. Sometimes, you may reorganize the books and store them differently. To better understand how the information-processing approach views encoding storage and retrieval, we examine the three main stages of memory.

encoding: The process by which information is transferred into memory, through the transduction of an experience into electrochemical energy, for neural representations.

storage: The process of maintaining information in memory.

retrieval: The process by which information is recovered from memory after it has been stored.

sensory register: The mechanism that performs initial coding and brief storage of stimuli.

The Sensory Register

Learning Objective 11.5
Describe the encoding, storage, and retrieval processes that take place at the sensory register, and explain the function of the sensory register.

The three stages in memory—the sensory register, short-term memory, and long-term memory—are each responsible for different functions. The **sensory register** provides initial encoding of information and instantaneous, fleeting, storage and retrieval. Later, short-term memory provides coding and temporary storage for about 30 seconds. Long-term memory may preserve information for a lifetime. (see Figure 11.3 on the next page). Within each of these three stages, encoding, storage, and retrieval are possible.

As demonstrated by George Sperling in the early 1960s, the purpose of the sensory register is to perform initial encoding and brief storage from which human beings can retrieve information. Sperling and other researchers visually pre-

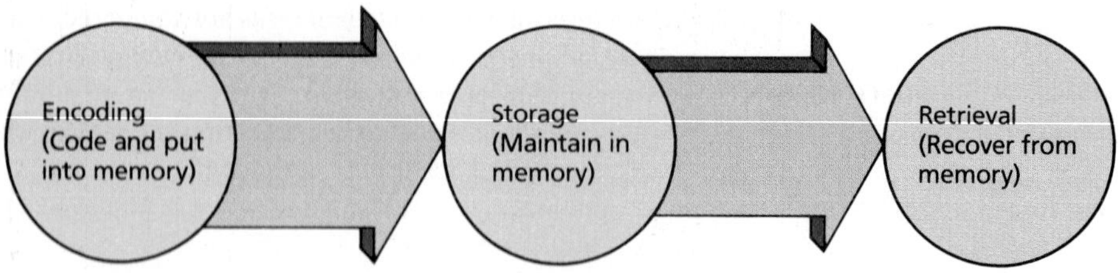

Figure 11.2

Basic memory processes.

sented letters to subjects briefly and found they were able to recall more than three items from just a 50-millisecond presentation. From his studies and others that followed, researchers claimed the existence of a brief (250 milliseconds), rapidly decaying sensory store (see Figure 11.4). This brief image of a stimulus appears the way lightning does on a dark evening; the lightning occurs, and you have a brief (250 milliseconds) continuing image of it.

Encoding and Storage

The sensory register transforms a visual, auditory, or chemical stimulus into a form the brain can interpret. Consider the visual system. The initial coding usually contains information in a picturelike representation. The sensory register establishes the visual stimulus in an electrical or neural form and stores it for 0.25 seconds (250 milliseconds) with little interpretation, still in an almost photographic manner. This visual sensory register is sometimes called the *icon,* and the storage mechanism is called *iconic storage.* The storage mechanism for the auditory system is called *echoic storage;* it stores an auditory representation for about 3 seconds.

The sensory register is temporary and fragile. Once information is established there, it must be transferred elsewhere for additional coding, or it will be lost. For example, when you look up an address in a telephone book, it is established in the visual sensory register, but unless you quickly transfer it to short-term memory (e.g., by repeating it over and over to yourself), you will forget it.

Retrieval

After encoding, retrieval is possible from the sensory register. How this storage is used remains controversial. Loftus (Loftus, Shimamura, & Johnson, 1985) and Cowan (1988) argue that perhaps the first 100 milliseconds may be crucial for proper encoding and retrieval. This debate is continuing, with new theories and interpretations being offered regularly.

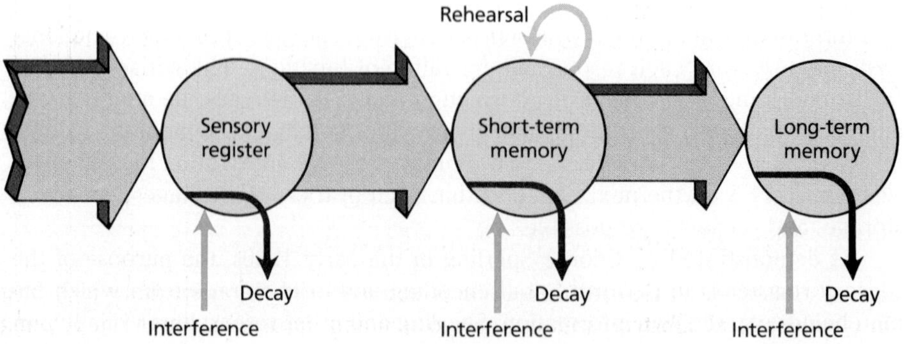

Figure 11.3

The information-processing approach emphasizes analysis by stages in which each level can be examined separately. When information enters the memory-processing system, it proceeds from the sensory register to short-term memory and then to long-term memory. At each stage, decay or interference may be operative.

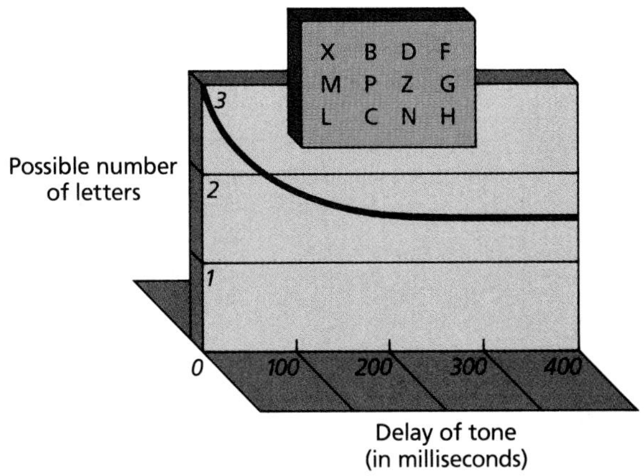

Figure 11.4

This graph plots Sperling's subjects' accuracy in reporting 1 four-letter row of letters as a function of the delay of the tone that told subjects which row to report. Note that there are no further decreases in accuracy after 250 milliseconds. (Data from Sperling, 1960, p. 11)

Short-term Memory

Learning Objective 11.6
Describe the encoding, storage, and retrieval processes; the concept of working memory; and the duration, capacity, and types of rehearsal that are characteristic of short-term memory.

After the sensory register, stimuli either decay and are lost or they are transferred to a second stage, called short-term memory. In **short-term memory,** information is further encoded, then stored or maintained for about 20–30 seconds. In short-term memory, active processing takes place. A person may decide that a specific piece of information is important. If it is complicated or lengthy, it needs to be actively repeated or rehearsed. **Rehearsal** is the process of repeatedly verbalizing, thinking about, or otherwise acting on information. Generally, researchers agree that the more rehearsal, the greater a person's memory for the item to be recalled, and not all items are recalled equally well.

Short-term Memory Is Discovered

For decades, researchers had been studying memory and retrieval, but it was not until 1959 that Margaret and Lloyd Peterson presented evidence for the existence of short-term memory. The Petersons asked subjects to recall a three-consonant sequence, such as *xbd,* after varying time intervals. During a time that ranged from no delay to 18 seconds, the subjects were required to count backward by threes. The aim of counting backwards was to prevent the subjects from repeating or rehearsing the sequence.

The Petersons' aim was to examine recall when rehearsal was not possible. Figure 11.5 (on the next page) presents their results. As the interval between presentation and recall increased, accuracy of recall decreased. The Petersons interpreted these results as evidence for the existence of a short-term memory. Using the library analogy, short-term memory could be likened to books that are on loan for a very brief period, then removed unless they are transferred to the library's permanent collection.

Short-term memory, as a brief repository, a way station for memory, has intuitive appeal. However, in everyday life, more tasks, more competing events, and much more processing occur than in laboratory studies. Thus, in terms of your awareness of memory, you might find the working memory conception of short-term memory, discussed next, appealing.

short-term memory: The memory storage system and process that temporarily (up to 30 seconds) holds up 5–9 items of current or recently sensed information.

rehearsal: Repetitive review through verbalizing or thinking about previously learned information; the goal is to keep the information in memory.

working memory: A new and broader conception of short-term memory that focuses on the executive processing capacities of memory and conceives of memory as a blackboard or scratch pad, holding information while other information is being manipulated.

Short-term Memory as Working Memory

Baddeley and Hitch (1974) think of short-term memory as a **working memory** in which several substructures operate to maintain information while it is being

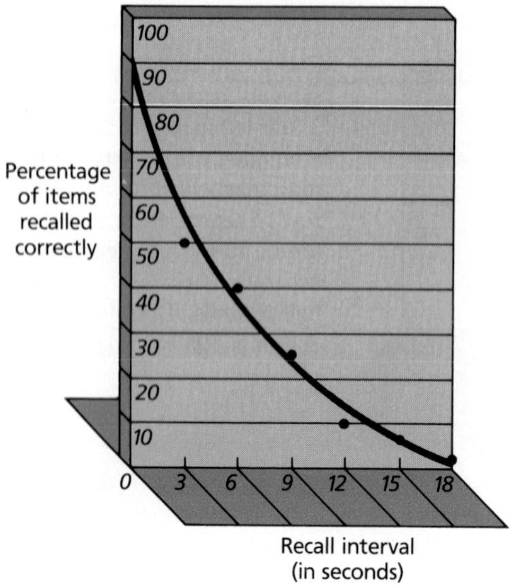

Figure 11.5

Peterson and Peterson found that when they delayed the report of three-letter syllables by having subjects count backward, accuracy of recall decreased over the first 18 seconds. They interpreted these results as evidence for the existence of short-term memory.

processed. One subsystem may code auditory information; another may be a visual–spatial scratch pad or blackboard that stores information for a brief time and then is erased, and new information is stored; this occurs over and over. Baddeley demonstrated the several components of working memory by having subjects recall digits while doing some other type of reasoning task. He showed that people have limited capacities. If one mental task is demanding, performance on the other will suffer.

Baddeley's introduction of a working memory expanded the concept of short-term memory, focusing on its complexity and how single components analyze only single tasks of a multistage system. Psychologists often focus on those single tasks, trying to understand each of the components in encoding, storage, and retrieval. However, Baddeley's conception of working memory goes beyond individual stages and describes the active integration of both conscious processes (such as repetition) and unconscious processes that is, processes a person is unaware of, such as retrieval of general knowledge about mathematical relationships from existing schema. Repetition or practice turns out to be an important component of developing some type of working memory (Carlson, Sullivan, & Schneider, 1989).

Baddeley and other researchers argue that within working memory, there is a central processing mechanism, like an executive, that controls the work flow, and the distinction between short-term memory and long-term memory is blurred (Cowan, 1988). This notion of an executive suggests that people can control the processing flow of information and adjust it when necessary.

Encoding and Storage

As we said earlier, storage of information in the sensory register is temporary, and the information is either lost through decay or transferred to the second stage—short-term memory. In short-term memory, semipermanent storage exists in which information is actively processed, that is, further encoded and stored for a bit longer—about 20–30 seconds. At this stage, people rehearse important information to make sure they remember it, because if they do not, it will be lost.

To understand the encoding that takes place in short-term memory, imagine a waiter who is given a lengthy and complex order. When the order is no longer in short-term memory, it is unlikely that the waiter will remember it. Thus, he might repeat the order over and over, rehearsing it until he is able to write it down or give it to the chef. Because of the limitations of short-term memory, rehearsal of information is crucial for encoding and keeping the information active. Thousands of research studies have been done on the components and characteristics of storage in short-term memory. They led researchers to conclusions that focus on duration, capacity, and rehearsal in short-term memory.

Duration. The Peterson's experiment showed that information contained in short-term memory is available for no more than 30 seconds. After that, it must either be transferred and stored in long-term memory, or it is lost. (Of course, it could be maintained indefinitely if a person were to rehearse it over and over again until recall was necessary.)

Capacity. In 1956, George Miller argued that human beings can retain about seven (plus or minus two) items in short-term memory. Subsequent research confirmed that claim. The brief and limited number of items that can easily be reproduced after presentation is called the immediate **memory span.** The immediate memory span usually contains a single **chunk**—that is, a manageable and meaningful unit of information. A chunk can be a letter, a group of numbers and words, or even sentences organized in a familiar way for easy coding, storage, and retrieval. Many people remember their Social Security number in three chunks, and their telephone number in two chunks. Chunks can be made up of groupings based on meaning, experiential or schematic associations, perception, rhythm, (e.g., the rhythm of how you say your phone number), or some arbitrary strategy devised by a learner to help code large amounts of data (Schweickert & Boruff, 1986).

Rehearsal. *Rehearsal* is the process of actively repeating, reviewing, or thinking about items to be remembered. People will quickly forget a list of meaningless letters and symbols, such as *xbdfmpg,* unless they use rehearsal to maintain the list in short-term memory. Actively rehearsed items can be maintained in short-term memory almost indefinitely. In general, however, the information entered in short-term memory either is transferred to long-term memory or is lost (see Figure 11.6).

There are two types of rehearsal: maintenance and elaborative. **Maintenance rehearsal** is repetitive review with little or no interpretation; this shallow form of rehearsal involves the physical stimulus, not its underlying meaning. It is the type of rehearsal that goes on principally in short-term memory, for example, when repeating a list of meaningless numbers to be recalled. A more complex **elaborative rehearsal** involves repetition in which the stimulus may be associated with other events and further processed; this type of rehearsal is more typical of long-term memory and the processes of encoding information into long-term

memory span: The brief and limited number of items that can be easily reproduced after presentation in short-term memory, usually confined to a chunk of information.

chunk: A manageable, familiar, and meaningful unit of information, which allows for groupings to be easily coded, stored. and retrieved.

maintenance rehearsal: Repetitive review of information in short-term memory with little or no interpretation; typically does not involve the stimulus' underlying meaning.

elaborative rehearsal: Rehearsal involving repetition in which the stimulus may be associated with other events and further processed; more typical of long-term memory and its processes

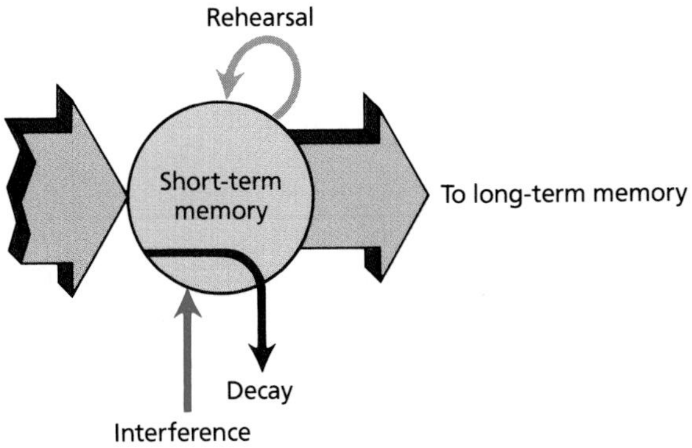

Figure 11.6

Information maintained in short-term memory can be transferred into more permanent long-term memory. Transfer to long-term memory is subject to both decay and interference.

Lengthy information, such as a script, must be rehearsed repeatedly in order to pass beyond short-term memory.

memory. Maintenance rehearsal alone is usually not sufficient for items to be transferred into long-term memory and permanently stored (exceptions include highly practiced data such as phone numbers that are often written or dialed).

Retrieval

As in the sensory register, short-term memory retrieval is the process by which something previously learned is recalled, recognized, or reproduced. When a person has to retrieve a piece of information from memory, there are vast amounts to search through. Using the library analogy, the stacks of books seem endless. One way of retrieving an item in short-term memory is to search through memory *exhaustively,* looking at all the items stored there and then choosing the desired one. Another type of retrieval search is *self-terminating;* that is, searching for something and ending the search as soon as the needed item item is found. These two approaches to memory retrieval are being actively examined; understanding the differences between exhaustive and self-terminating searches helps researchers comprehend how retrieving information from memory can be done so rapidly.

We examine the loss of information from short-term memory in a later section on forgetting, and we have much more to say about these processes when we look at long-term memory, considered next.

Long-term Memory

Learning Objective 11.7
Describe the encoding, storage, and retrieval processes characteristic of long-term memory, and distinguish procedural from declarative memories.

Information stored in **long-term memory,** such as names, faces, dates, places, smells, and events (both important and trivial ones), is encoded in a relatively permanent form. The duration of long-term memory is indefinite—much of the information in long-term memory lasts for a lifetime. The capacity for long-term memory is seemingly infinite; the more information we acquire, the easier it is to learn. Using the library analogy again, long-term storage includes all the books that are part of the library's permanent collection.

Encoding and Storage

The information that is typically encoded and stored in long-term memory either is important, such as a friend's birthday, or is used frequently, such as your telephone number. A fact such as the price of bananas will probably not be entered into long-term memory. Encoding information into long-term memory often involves rehearsal or repetition, but sometimes a salient or important event is immediately etched into long-term memory.

Several types of information are stored in long-term memory. For example, a person may remember the words to a Billy Joel song, the meaning of the word sanguine, and the way to operate a tape deck. Each of these types of information seems to be stored and called on in a different way. Psychologists categorize the different types of long-term memory into procedural and declarative kinds of memory.

long-term memory: The memory storage system and process that keeps a relatively permanent record of information.

procedural memory: Storage for the perceptual, motor, and cognitive skills required to complete a task.

Procedural memory is storage for the perceptual, motor, and cognitive skills necessary to complete a task (see Figure 11.7). Learning how to drive an automobile, wash the dishes, and swim involves a series of steps that include perceptual, motor and cognitive skills, and thus procedural memory. Acquiring such skills is usually time consuming and difficult at first, but once the skills are learned, they are relatively permanent. Coding of procedural information and its retrieval is

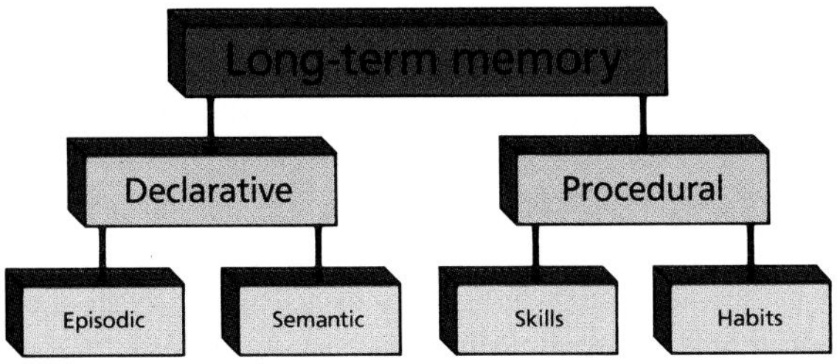

Figure 11.7

A tentative model of memory: *Declarative memory* includes what can be declared or brought to mind as a fact. *Procedural memory* includes motor skills and cognitive skills.

indirect; it is not stored all together and must be assembled (Richardson-Klavenhn & Bjork, 1988).

Declarative memory is memory for specific facts, such as "Jimmy Carter was President" or "Neil Armstrong was accompanied to the moon by Edwin Aldrin and Michael Collins." The memory is established quickly, and the information is more likely to be forgotten than that in procedural memory. It is easier to examine declarative memory than procedural memory because people can quickly relate a specific fact but have more trouble explaining how to do something, such as how to swim. We consider declarative memory in more detail next.

declarative memory: Memory for specific facts; distinct from memory for skills to complete tasks.

episodic memory: [ep-ih-SAHD-ick] Memory for specific events, objects and situations; time and place of events is often coded.

Declarative Memory: Episodic and Semantic Memory

In 1972, Tulving suggested that there are two kinds of declarative long-term memory: episodic and semantic. **Episodic memory** covers specific events, objects, and situations, such as what you had for breakfast, the movie you saw last night, or what you did on vacation last summer. Studies of memory for events long past show that people remember them well, especially information about themselves (Barclay & Wellman, 1986). Episodic memory is often specific; a person can say when an event happened, where it happened, and the circumstances surrounding it. It may deal with an individual's personal experiences or his or her memory about other people's experiences.

Declarative memory, the ability to recall specific facts, allows these players to challenge each other at a game of Trivial Pursuit.

Is it easier to remember what Neil Armstrong said when he first landed on the moon, or the details of the exact date and time?

When researchers have examined people's ability to remember real-world events (rather than artificially created laboratory situations), results show amazingly good recognition memory. These studies often come under the general topic of *autobiographical memory studies* because they often have examined people's memory for their own past (Conway, 1991). People can recognize with good accuracy a person, situation, or event for years after its occurrence. However, recall performance is not as accurate. Studies of autobiographical memory suggest that long-term memory is especially durable and fairly easy to access if a retrieval cue is available (as in a recognition task). The more clearly and sharply defined our memory cues are, the more vivid are the memories, and the less likely that the person will experience retrieval failures. We discuss this issue later in this chapter when we examine forgetting.

Semantic memory covers the memory of ideas, rules, and general concepts about the world. Semantic memory must be based on a set of generalizations relying on an array of previous events, experiences, and learned knowledge. Thus, it develops based on existing episodic and semantic memory and is more global. It is not time specific and refers to knowledge that may have been gathered over days or weeks and continues to be modified and expanded over a lifetime (Bahrick & Hall 1991).

Semantic memory seems to be stored at different *levels* of memory, like sections or floors of a library, so that a person needing information must go to different levels to access it. At superficial levels of processing, the immediate sensory cues are interpreted. At deeper levels of processing, the cues are coded and categorized according to the kind of information they give and the meanings for each cue. At still deeper levels, the meanings are analyzed and synthesized. For example, is the following sentence true or false? "U.S. astronauts Armstrong, Collins, and Aldrin were the first to land on the moon and did so on July 20, 1969, at 4:18 P.M. eastern standard time." You would need to access several classes of information, including interrelations among times, dates, people, and historical events, which may be complex. The time and effort you need in order to respond will depend in part of the number of levels of processing required (Tilley & Warren, 1983) and the complexity of the information. The idea that there are levels of processing became very popular in the 1970s. In Chapter 7 (on p. 241), we examine the *levels-of-processing* idea more fully.

The semantic–episodic distinction becomes blurred in situations where you expect people to use episodic information, but they use semantic information. For example, if you ask people about the last time they saw a doctor and you expect them to tell you about an episode—a specific time. Instead, most people will tell you about what happens in general, for example, by saying things such as "I usually get a cold once or twice a year, and if it's really bad, I take a day off." Such responses suggest that people are drawing on semantic memory and reconstructing or creating what *might* have happened. They are using schemas, or conceptual frameworks, that organize and make sense of the world (Means et al., 1989).

Retrieval

Encoding and storing information in long-term memory are primary tasks for a person learning a new skill, language, or set of facts. However, all the study time and rehearsal is wasted if the information cannot be retrieved. Some interesting findings about retrieval from long-term memory have emerged.

semantic memory: Memory for ideas, rules, and general concepts about the world; contains the meaning of words; not time or date specific.

Primacy and Recency Effects. Generally, psychologists researching memory study people of normal intelligence and behavior, such as college students. In a typical experiment a subject may be asked to study a list of 30 or 40 words, one presented every 2 seconds. A few minutes later, the subject is asked to recall the list, to see whether the information was transferred from short-term to long-term memory. Such experiments typically show an overall recall of 20%. However, recall is higher for words at the beginning of a list than for those at the middle, a phenomenon termed the **primacy effect.** This occurs when no information is being stored in short-term memory; at the moment a new task is assigned, the subject's attention to a new stimuli is at its peak. Recall is even higher for words at the end of a list (see Figure 11.8), a tendency termed the **recency effect.** This is due to the active rehearsal of the information in short-term memory and its subsequent coding into long-term memory.

Campaign managers attempt to capitalize on the primacy and recency effects in speeches. For example, they urge their candidate to speak both very early in the campaign and late, just before people vote. If several candidates are to speak back-to-back, campaign managers will try to schedule their candidate either first or last; primacy effects suggest that attention is at its peak at the beginning; recency effects suggest that speaking last will be effective because such a speech is more likely to be remembered with no one following the speaker. That is, other speakers won't interfere with the transfer of information from short-term to long-term memory.

primacy effect: The more accurate recall of items that were presented first in a list.

recency effect: The more accurate recall of items that were presented at the end of a list.

imagery: Cognitive process in which a mental picture is created of a sensory event.

Imagery

Learning Objective 11.8 Describe the nature of imagery, the research that has examined it, and the reason it is an important memory aid.

People use perceptual **imagery** every day as a long-term memory aid. In imagery, people create, re-create, or conjure up a mental picture of a sensory or perceptual experience to be remembered. They constantly invoke images to recall things they did, said, read, or saw. People's imagery systems can be accessed by visual, auditory, olfactory, and emotional memories, as well as memories stored by other perceptual systems. Even lack of sensory stimulation can produce vivid imagery. Your imagery helps you answer questions such as: Which is darker, a pea or a Christmas tree? Which is bigger, a tennis ball or an orange?

Measuring Imagery. One technique to measure imagery, used extensively by Stephen Kosslyn of Harvard University, is to ask subjects to imagine objects of various sizes (for example, an animal such as a rabbit next to either an elephant or a fly). In a 1975 study, subjects reported that when they imagined a fly, plenty of room remained in their mental image for a rabbit. However, when they imagined an elephant, it took up most of their mental space. One particularly interesting result was that the subjects required more time and found it harder to "see" the nose of the rabbit when it was next to an elephant than when it was next to a fly because it appeared so small (see Figure 11.9 on the next page).

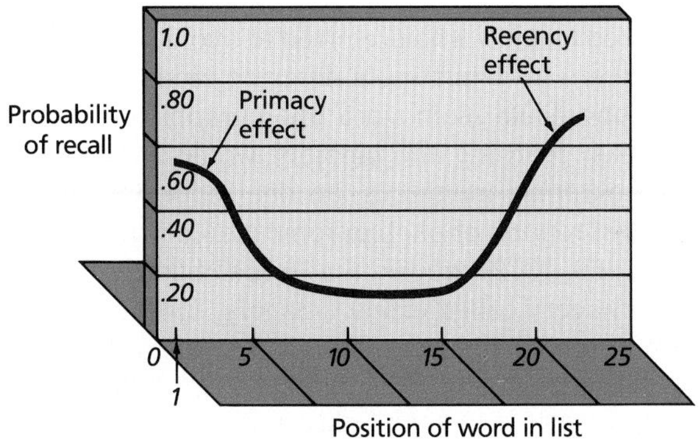

Figure 11.8

A serial-position curve: the probability of recalling an item is plotted as a function of its serial position on a list of items. Generally, the first several items are likely to be recalled (the primacy effect), and the last several are recalled very well (the recency effect).

Figure 11.9

Kosslyn had subjects imagine elephants and flies; a rabbit that was subsequently imagined appeared small in size next to the elephant and large in size in relation to a fly. (Source: Kosslyn, 1975, after Solso, 1979.)

In another series of experiments, Kosslyn (1978) asked subjects first to imagine an object at a distance and then to imagine that they were moving toward the object. The subjects were next asked whether the object seemed larger to them than before and whether it overflowed their mental visual field so they could no longer see all of it. The subjects were instructed to stop mentally walking at the point at which the object seemed to overflow. By having the subjects estimate the size of the object and the distance at which the images seemed to overflow the mental image frame, Kosslyn was able to estimate the size of a visual image that people can imagine.

Using this mental walk technique, Kosslyn found a limited image space. Larger objects tended to overflow at greater imagined distances than smaller objects did. He also learned that images overflowed in all directions at about the same size. Perhaps the most important finding from Kosslyn's research is that images possess spatial properties. Although they are mental, not physical, phenomena, the images have photographlike edges—points beyond which visual information ceases to be represented (Kosslyn, 1987). People can construct mental images, transform them, and interpret what they look like (Finke, Pinker, & Farah, 1989). For example you may use your mental imagery ability to decide whether your new station wagon will fit into your single-car garage or to count the number of windows in your new apartment, and you do so in three dimensions regardless of the angle from which you view these objects (Roth & Kosslyn, 1988).

Imagery as a Memory Aid. Imagery is an important perceptual memory aid. In fact, a growing body of evidence suggests that it is a means of preserving perceptual information that might otherwise decay. According to Paivio (1971), a person told to remember two words may form an image combining those words. If someone is told to remember the words *house* and *hamburger,* for example, he or she might form an image of a house made of hamburgers or of a hamburger on top of a house. When later presented with the word *house,* the word *hamburger* will come to mind. Paivio suggests that words paired in this way are conceptually linked, with the mediation factor being the image.

We know that imagery is an important memory aid and that images can even be rotated in mental space (see Figure 11.10). How images facilitate recall and recognition is not yet fully understood; it's possible that an image adds another code to semantic memory. Thus, with two codes, semantic and image-based, a person has two ways to access previously learned information. Some researchers argue that imagery, verbal coding mechanisms, and semantic memory operate together to encode information and to aid in its retrieval (Marschark, Yuille, Richman, & Hunt, 1987).

Test for yourself the mnemonic effectiveness of imagery with this example: Suppose you park in section E-17 of an airport parking lot. Now memorize E-17 by visualizing an elephant sitting in your car and reading *Seventeen* magazine. Later in this chapter, you'll be asked where you parked.

Eidetic Imagery. In the 1960s, while Paivio was trying to make the study of imagery respectable to behavioral colleagues who preferred to avoid such mentalistic concepts, other researchers were investigating a different kind of imagery: *photographlike imagery.* If everyone could maintain a photographlike image of each glimpse of the world, how easy learning and memory would be. Although many people say they have photographic memories, no one reports having an image of everything ever seen. Most reports of photographic memory are normal vivid imagery. However, Haber (1969, 1979) showed that some children do have a special kind of photographlike imagery called eidetic imagery. *Eidetic imagery,* which is found in fewer than 4% of school-age children, is vivid, long-lasting, and complete.

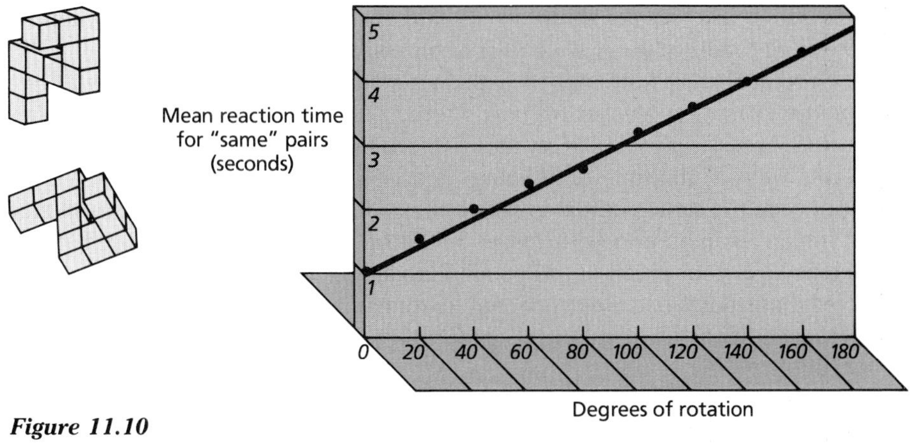

Figure 11.10

In exploring the nature of imagery, researchers such as Roger Shepard have drawn pairs of visual stimuli like those shown on the left so that one appears to have been rotated in space. Shepard and Metzler asked subjects to say as quickly as possible whether such stimuli were in fact the same stimuli, which were rotated, or different stimuli altogether. Sometimes, the stimuli were drawn rotated in space only slightly; at other times, the rotations were as much as 180°. Subjects' reaction times to respond correctly varied with the amount of rotation involved. The graph at the right plots the reaction time for "same" pairs as a function of degrees of rotation. This was one of the first of several studies in the 1970s that began to explore visual image ability in a systematic and carefully controlled way. (Roger Shepard, "Mental Rotation of Three-Dimensional Objects," *Science* 171 [19 Feb. 1971]: 701–3. Copyright 1971 by the AAAS.)

State-Dependent Learning

Distinguished psychologist Gordon Bower used the following example to describe a phenomenon known as *state-dependent learning* (Bower, 1981, p 129):

Learning Objective 11.9
Describe state-dependent learning, and explain how it affects memory.

> When I was a kid I saw the movie *City Lights* in which Charlie Chaplin plays the little tramp. In one very funny sequence, Charlie saves a drunk from leaping to his death. The drunk turns out to be a millionaire who befriends Charlie, and the two spend the evening together drinking and carousing. The next day, when sober, the millionaire does not recognize Charlie and even snubs him. Later, the millionaire gets drunk again, and when he spots Charlie treats him as his long-lost companion. So the two of them spend another evening together carousing and drinking and then stagger back to the millionaire's mansion to sleep. In the morning, of course, the sober millionaire again does not recognize Charlie, treats him as an intruder, and has the butler kick him out by the seat of his pants.

The millionaire remembers Charlie only when he is intoxicated, the same state in which he originally met him. Psychologists find that information learned while a person is in a particular physiological state is recalled better when the subject is again in that physiological state. The phenomenon, known as **state-dependent learning,** is associated with drugs, time of day, mental illness, and electroconvulsive shock.

state-dependent learning: The tendency to recall information learned in a particular physiological state more accurately when one is again in that physiological state.

In a typical state-dependent learning study, Weingartner, Adefris, Eich, and Murphy (1976) had four groups of subjects learn lists of high- and low-imagery words. To induce intoxication, all subjects except those in the control group drank vodka and fruit juice. The control group learned and recalled while sober; a second group learned and recalled while intoxicated; a third learned while sober and recalled while intoxicated; and a fourth learned while intoxicated and recalled while sober. The results showed that subjects recalled the lists best when they were in the same state in which they had learned the lists.

Several theories attempt to explain state-dependent learning. A widely accepted explanation focuses on how altered or drugged states affect the storage process. According to this view, part of learning involves the coding of stimuli in specific ways at the time of learning; to access the stored information, a person must evoke the same context in which the coding occurred. When you are studying for an examination with music in the background, but are tested in quiet conditions, is your recall not as good? The answer to this question is as yet unresolved, but studies of state-dependent learning may hold the key, and recent studies of mood-dependent memory suggest that the answer may be "yes" (Eich & Metcalfe, 1989).

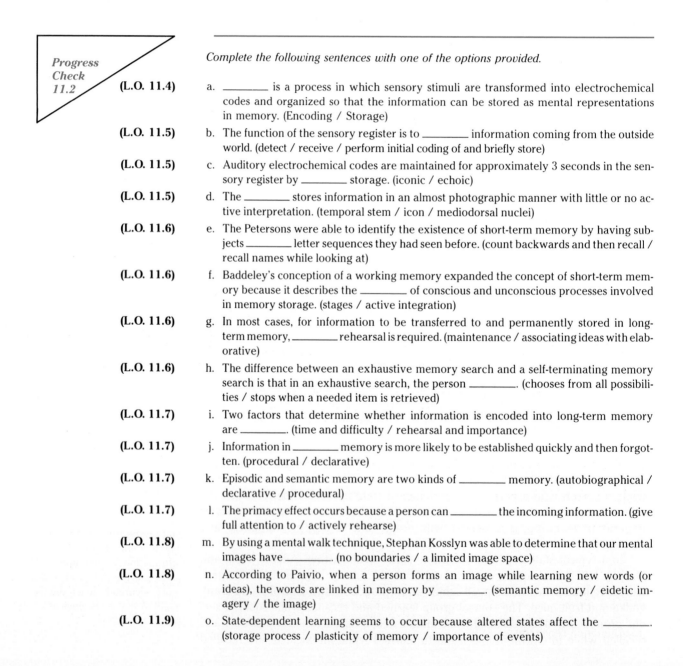

Progress Check 11.2

Complete the following sentences with one of the options provided.

(L.O. 11.4) a. ________ is a process in which sensory stimuli are transformed into electrochemical codes and organized so that the information can be stored as mental representations in memory. (Encoding / Storage)

(L.O. 11.5) b. The function of the sensory register is to ________ information coming from the outside world. (detect / receive / perform initial coding of and briefly store)

(L.O. 11.5) c. Auditory electrochemical codes are maintained for approximately 3 seconds in the sensory register by ________ storage. (iconic / echoic)

(L.O. 11.5) d. The ________ stores information in an almost photographic manner with little or no active interpretation. (temporal stem / icon / mediodorsal nuclei)

(L.O. 11.6) e. The Petersons were able to identify the existence of short-term memory by having subjects ________ letter sequences they had seen before. (count backwards and then recall / recall names while looking at)

(L.O. 11.6) f. Baddeley's conception of a working memory expanded the concept of short-term memory because it describes the ________ of conscious and unconscious processes involved in memory storage. (stages / active integration)

(L.O. 11.6) g. In most cases, for information to be transferred to and permanently stored in long-term memory, ________ rehearsal is required. (maintenance / associating ideas with elaborative)

(L.O. 11.6) h. The difference between an exhaustive memory search and a self-terminating memory search is that in an exhaustive search, the person ________. (chooses from all possibilities / stops when a needed item is retrieved)

(L.O. 11.7) i. Two factors that determine whether information is encoded into long-term memory are ________. (time and difficulty / rehearsal and importance)

(L.O. 11.7) j. Information in ________ memory is more likely to be established quickly and then forgotten. (procedural / declarative)

(L.O. 11.7) k. Episodic and semantic memory are two kinds of ________ memory. (autobiographical / declarative / procedural)

(L.O. 11.7) l. The primacy effect occurs because a person can ________ the incoming information. (give full attention to / actively rehearse)

(L.O. 11.8) m. By using a mental walk technique, Stephan Kosslyn was able to determine that our mental images have ________. (no boundaries / a limited image space)

(L.O. 11.8) n. According to Paivio, when a person forms an image while learning new words (or ideas), the words are linked in memory by ________. (semantic memory / eidetic imagery / the image)

(L.O. 11.9) o. State-dependent learning seems to occur because altered states affect the ________. (storage process / plasticity of memory / importance of events)

Module Summary

Memory: Retaining Information

- *Memory* is the ability to remember past events or previously learned information or skills; memory is also the storage system that allows retention and retrieval (p. 203).
- *Recall* involves remembering the details of a situation or idea and placing them together in a meaningful framework; *recognition* involves remembering whether one has seen a stimulus before; *reconstructive memory* focuses on the constructive nature of the memory process and how people develop a *schema* (pp. 204–206).

The Information-Processing Approach to Memory

- The *information-processing approach* assumes that each stage of learning and memory is separate, although related, and analyzable by scientific methods (p. 207).
- *Encoding* involves organizing information so that the nervous system can process it. *Storage* is the process of maintaining information in memory for a few seconds or for many years. *Retrieval* is the process by which stored information is recovered from memory (p. 207).

The Sensory Register

- The visual sensory register is sometimes termed the *icon,* and the storage mechanism is *iconic storage* (p. 209).
- The storage mechanism for the auditory system is *echoic storage,* (p. 209).
- Once information is established in the sensory register, it must be transferred elsewhere for additional coding, or it will be lost (p. 209).

Short-term Memory

- In short-term memory, information is further encoded, then stored or maintained for about 20–30 seconds; short-term memory is an active processing stage. Working memory is a new and broader conception of short-term memory (pp. 209–210).
- *Rehearsal* is the process of actively repeating and reviewing items to be remembered. *Maintenance rehearsal* is repetitive review with little or no interpretation; this shallow form of rehearsal involves the physical stimulus, not its underlying meaning. *Elaborative rehearsal* involves repetition in which the stimulus may be associated with other events and further processed; this type of rehearsal is more typical of long-term memory (p. 211).
- A *primacy effect* is the more accurate recall of items presented first in a list; a *recency effect* is the more accurate recall of items presented at the end of a list. (p. 212).

Long-term Memory

- *Procedural memory* is storage for the perceptual, motor, and cognitive skills necessary to complete a task; *declarative memory* is memory for specific facts (pp. 212–213).
- Within declarative memory, *episodic memory* covers specific events, objects, and situations; *semantic memory* covers ideas, rules, and general concepts about the world (pp. 213–214).

KEY TERMS

chunk, p. 211
declarative memory, p. 213
elaborative rehearsal, p. 211
encoding, p. 207
episodic memory, p 213.
imagery, p. 215
long-term memory, p. 212
maintenance rehearsal, p. 211
memory, p. 203
memory span, p. 211
procedural memory, p. 212
primacy effect, p. 215
recency effect, p. 215
rehearsal, p. 209
retrieval, p. 207
schema, p. 206
semantic memory, p. 214
sensory register, p. 207
short-term memory, p. 209
state-dependent learning, p. 217
storage, p. 207
working memory, p. 209

SELF-TEST

Module 11

- Before taking the self-test, **recite** and **review.**
- Use the key at the back of the text to *correct* your answers.
- *Restudy* pages that correspond to any questions you answered incorrectly.

1. This text defines memory as
   a. the storage system from which we retain and retrieve previously learned information.
   b. the ability to recall past events or previously learned information.
   c. a relatively permanent change in behavior that occurs as a result of experience.
   d. Both a and b.
2. Based on research concerning massed versus distributed practice, the most effective study schedule you could follow when studying for your next psychology test would be to study
   a. 1 or 2 hours a day, every day before the test.
   b. a week prior to the test with a quick review the day before the test.
   c. for as long as you need to, the day before the test.
   d. in a cram session right before the test.
3. Research on memory shows that people
   a. have amazingly accurate memories of *everything* they learn.
   b. construct memories of events that are close approximations, but not exact memories.
   c. find it easier to recall details and harder to recall key facts.
   d. forget events that have been remodeled during memory storage.
4. The ________ approach suggests that memory coding and storage involves three separate but related stages.
   a. information-processing
   b. levels-of-processing
   c. executive-processing
   d. central-processing stages
5. Information stored in the sensory register
   a. is always visual information.
   b. is preserved in schema for a lifetime.
   c. is important for perception, but not for memory.
   d. will be forgotten quickly if not transferred to short-term memory.
6. The concept of a *working memory* suggests that
   a. previously stored conceptions are rearranged.
   b. rehearsal is not necessary for some types of memory storage.
   c. several substructures maintain information while it is being processed.
   d. all of the above
7. The phrase ________ is used to describe the limited duration and capacity of items that can be recalled from short-term memory.
   a. one-track storage
   b. immediate memory span
   c. fixed attention span
   d. maintenance rehearsal
8. If you rehearse a poem on Sunday evening for a speech you must give on Monday morning, you are relying on ________ to enable you to recite the poem with no errors.
   a. short-term memory
   b. long-term memory
   c. a recency effect
   d. Both a and c

9. Semantic memory
   a. appears to be stored on different *levels* of memory.
   b. contains, for the most part, memories about one's self and one's personal experience.
   c. includes the memories of specific events, objects, and situations.
   d. stores perceptual, motor, and cognitive memories needed to complete a task involving skill.
10. Mental images
    a. are fixed images located in memory schema that are like photographs.
    b. are available only to people who are highly sensitive or emotional.
    c. can be transformed and interpreted by the person who constructs them.
    d. are daydreams that interfere with learning and memory.
11. Eidetic imagery
    a. begins once an image has overflowed the mental visual field.
    b. is available to most people if they use Kosslyn's technique of mental walking.
    c. interferes with a person's ability to see the smaller details of a whole image.
    d. is a rare ability available to a few school-age children and perhaps some young adults.
12. State-dependent learning has been linked to
    a. time of day, mental illness, drugs, and electroconvulsive shock.
    b. intelligence, self-esteem, and personality.
    c. sleep, dreams, and unconscious libido motivations.
    d. forgetfulness, attentiveness, and inventiveness.

Module 12

Forgetting and the Biology of Memory

LEARNING OBJECTIVES

When you have mastered the material in this module, you will be able to

Forgetting (pp. 223–227)

12.1 Explain how memory is lost or forgotten through decay, interference, and retrieval failure (p. 223).
12.2 Explain what is meant by motivated forgetting (repression) and describe two types of amnesia (p. 225).
12.3 Discuss the contradictory research findings concerning the accuracy of eyewitness testimony (p. 226).

The Physiology of Memory (pp. 227–232)

12.4 Explain how consolidation and biochemical changes in the brain play a role in the physiological basis of memory (p. 227).
12.5 Discuss what researchers know about where memories are stored in the brain (p. 230).

SQ3R

- ▲ **Survey** to set goals for studying
- ▲ Ask **questions** as you **read.**
- ▲ Stop occasionally to **recite** and **review.**

plus

- ▲ **Write** a summary of key points.
- ▲ **Reflect** on the hypotheses, evidence, and implications of this material and on the relevance it has to *your* life.

"Ready, go!" Marcia Rothstein had said that phrase about a million times in the last year—or so it seemed. Each time she was about to test her students for reading comprehension, she began with the same phrase. Marcia is a school psychologist who works in a program for developing reading and memory skills in the Boston, Massachusetts city schools. Trained first with a master's degree in experimental psychology, Marcia realized that her interest in animal learning and memory could be applied to real life, to people, and especially to disadvantaged children. Marcia studied for an extra year and a half and obtained a second master's degree—this time in school psychology. In her studies, she focused on memory processes in adolescents; she knew exactly what she wanted to do. She was interested in helping youngsters develop their reading comprehension, study, and memory skills. Marcia's background in experimental and then school psychology uniquely qualified her for the task. She was an expert in learning and memory. She knew why people remembered and forgot. She knew how to help people develop the skills to do well in school.

Think about a time you prepared for an examination yet still did poorly. Perhaps you didn't study enough, or you learned the material but then forgot it. Maybe, for some reason, you were simply unable to show what you had learned on the test. Psychologists like Marcia Rothstein have long recognized that recalling supposedly well learned facts is not easy. For one thing, learning and remembering involve different processes. Our ability to remember is not limitless: People forget past experiences and previously learned information.

Quick! Name your first-grade teacher . . . your Social Security number . . . your telephone number . . . your mother's birthdate . . . and where you went on your last vacation. In general, our memories serve us amazingly well. Nevertheless, at times, you may have trouble recalling the name of someone you know well, where you read an interesting article, or the phone number of a close friend. Have you ever begun an examination only to suddenly have your mind "go blank"? Each of these cases involves a memory failure.

Forgetting

There are many causes of forgetting, such as not rehearsing information well enough, or not using it for a long time. Forgetting also occurs because of interference from newly learned information, because the information is unpleasant, or because of physiological problems. Moreover, forgetting occurs in both short- and long-term memory.

Learning Objective 12.1 Explain how memory is lost or forgotten through decay, interference, and retrieval failure.

Reasons for Memory Loss

Researchers recognize that data are lost from both short- and long-term memory. They want to find out how and why that loss happens. Among other factors, they found that two concepts, decay and interference, help explain the loss (see Figure 12.1 on the next page).

decay: The loss of information from memory as a result of the passage of time and/or disuse.

Decay of Information. According to the **decay** theory, information is lost through *disuse* over time. Unimportant events fade from memory; details become lost, confused, or fuzzy. Another way to look at the decay theory is that memory

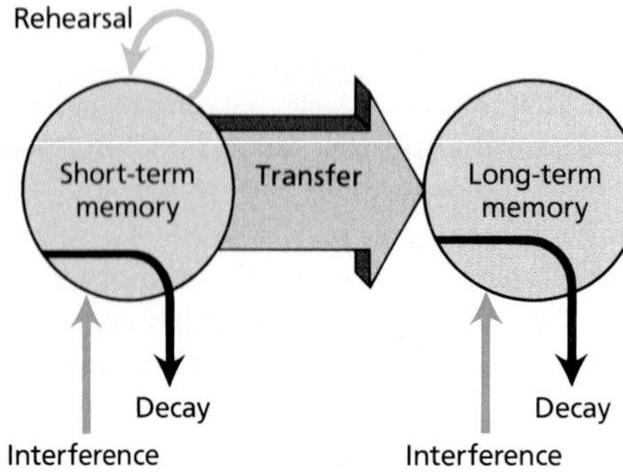

Figure 12.1

When information enters short-term memory, it is subject to decay, interference, rehersal, or transfer into long-term memory.

exists in the brain in a physiological form known as a *memory trace.* With the passage of time and a lack of active use, the trace disintegrates, fades, and is lost.

The decay hypothesis was popular for many years but is not widely accepted today. Many early studies did not consider several important variables that affect memory processes, such as rate and mode of stimulus presentation. Although decay forms a small part of the final explanation of forgetting, it is probably less important than other factors, such as interference.

Interference in Memory. According to the **interference,** theory the limited capacity of short-term memory makes it susceptible to interference from or confusion among learned items. That is, when competing information is stored in short-term memory, the resulting crowding affects a person's memory for particular items. For example, if someone looks up a telephone number and is then given another number to remember, the second number will probably interfere with the ability to remember the first one. Moreover, interference in memory is more likely to occur when a person is presented with a great deal of new information.

Research on interference theory shows that the extent and nature of a person's experiences both before and after learning are important. For example, a subject given a list of nonsense syllables may recall 75% of the items correctly. However, if the subject was given 20 similar lists to learn earlier, the number of items correctly recalled will be lower; the previous lists will interfere with recall. If the subject is given additional lists to learn, recall will be even lower. Psychologists call these interference effects proactive and retroactive inhibition. **Proactive inhibition** is the decrease in accurate recall as a result of previous experiences interfering with a to-be-remembered one. **Retroactive inhibition** is the decrease in accurate recall of information as a result of later presentation of other information (see Figure 12.2).

To understand proactive and retroactive inhibition, suppose you were to hear a series of lectures, each 5 minutes long. According to psychological research, the proactive and retroactive inhibition (interference) effects would make you most likely to remember the first and last speeches. There would be no proactive inhibition on the first speech and no retroactive interference on the last speech. All the middle speeches would have both proactive and retroactive inhibition; thus, the first and last speeches would be remembered best. (Don't forget that primacy and recency effects also will aid in your recall, see page 214).

interference: The suppression or confusion of one bit of information with another that was received either earlier or later.

proactive inhibition: [pro-AK-tiv] The decrease in accurate recall of a target list as a result of previous events that interfere with recall of the target list.

retroactive inhibition: [RET-ro-AK-tiv] The decrease in accurate recall of a target list as a result of subsequent presentation of material.

Retrieval Failure. Some contemporary researchers assert that every memory is retained and available, but that some information is just less accessible than others. Think of the library analogy; all the books in the library are there, but some cannot be found, or perhaps are misshelved, making retrieval difficult or impossible.

Research on retrieval failures focuses on how people code information, and what cues act to help in retrieval. If you are given a cue for retrieval and the originally stored information contains that cue, retrieval is easier, faster, and more accurate. The value of a specific retrieval cue depends on how well it compares with the original memory code; this notion is referred to as the *encoding-specificity* hypothesis. The more clearly and sharply your memory cues are defined, the better your recall will be, and the less likely that you will experience retrieval failures. To increase your access to information stored in memory, you should match the test situation to the original learning situation as much as possible. (Recall also the state-dependent learning effects mentioned on page 217).

amnesia: A loss of memory, usually due to traumatic injury.

Motivated Forgetting and Amnesia. Freud (1933) was the first to formally suggest the idea of *motivated forgetting*—that unwanted or unpleasant events might be lost in memory simply because people wanted to forget them. He stated that such loss occurs through repression, the burying of unpleasant ideas in the unconscious, where they remain inaccessible. Although most researchers agree that motivated forgetting probably exists in some form, they have found it hard to measure and are thus far unsuccessful in demonstrating it experimentally, though anecdotal clinical evidence abounds. Motivated forgetting is hard or impossible to produce in the laboratory, but a related phenomenon, amnesia, can be examined in the laboratory.

Learning Objective 12.2 Explain what is meant by motivated forgetting (repression), and describe two types of amnesia.

Television soap operas frequently portray people with **amnesia,** but in fact the condition is relatively rare. Amnesia is the inability to remember events from the past, usually because of physiological trauma (such as an auto accident, a blow to the head, or a fall from a height). Typically, it involves loss of memory for all events within a specific period. There are two basic kinds of amnesia: retrograde and anterograde.

Figure 12.2

Proactive and retroactive inhibition or interference occur in memory when old or new information interferes with (or inhibits recall of) to-be-learned material. *Proactive inhibition* refers to the finding that old information interferes with learning new information. *Retroactive inhibition* occurs when new information inhibits (interferes with) the recall of previously learned information. Thus, studying French, followed by studying psychology, may interfere with your recall of psychology—proactive inhibition. Also, studying French, followed by studying psychology, may interfere with or inhibit you recall of French—retroactive inhibition.

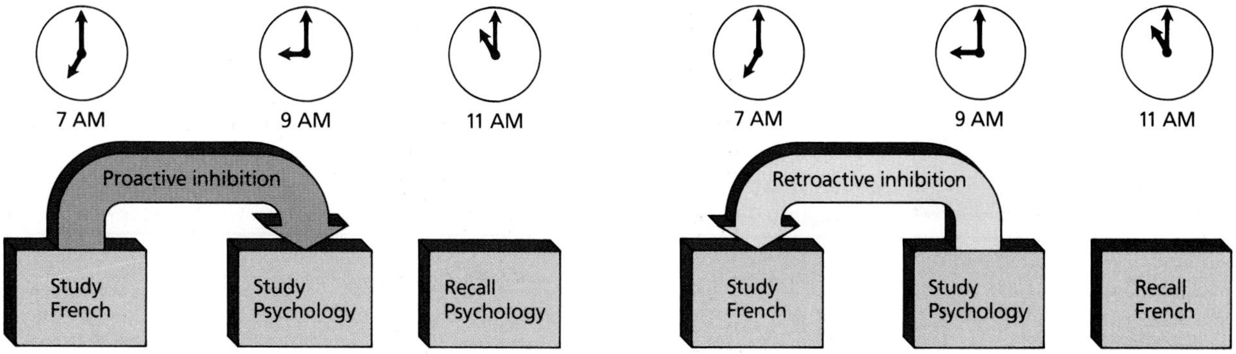

retrograde amnesia: [RET-ro-grade] Loss of memory for events and experiences occurring in a period preceding the amnesia-causing events.

anterograde amnesia: Loss of memory for events and experiences occurring after the amnesia-causing event.

Retrograde amnesia is the inability to remember events that preceded a traumatizing event (what might be called "soap opera loss"). The loss of memory can cover only the period just before the accident or it can cover several years. Retrograde amnesia can be caused by injuries to the head, carbon monoxide poisoning, or several kinds of shock therapy in patients with depressive problems. Recovery is generally gradual, with earlier events remembered before more recent ones.

Anterograde amnesia is the inability to remember events after an injury or brain damage. People suffering from anterograde amnesia appear stuck in the lives they led before being injured; new events are often utterly forgotten. For example, if the onset of the amnesia occurred in 1991, the sufferer may be able to remember clearly events in 1990 or earlier, but have a difficult time recalling what he or she did only half an hour before. The victim may meet someone for the hundredth time (after the injury), yet think he is being introduced to a perfect stranger. The ability to remember past events seems to depend on brain mechanisms that are separate from those required for new learning of recent events (Shimamura & Squire, 1986). The ability to remember remote events seems particularly important in studies of eyewitness testimony, in which people try to remember real-life past events.

Learning Objective 12.3 Discuss the contradictory research findings concerning the accuracy of eyewitness testimony.

Psychology and Law: Eyewitness Testimony

Subjects sometimes construct and alter their memories. The constructive nature of memory can have serious consequences for real-life situations, especially for eyewitness testimony. If someone sees an accident or a crime, for example, can he or she accurately report the facts of the situation to the police or the court? The answer is both yes and no. The police and the courts have generally accepted *eyewitness testimony* as some of the best evidence that can be presented. They are hearing from people who saw the crime, have no bias or grudge, and are sworn to tell the truth—but do they?

Some studies of eyewitnesses show that witnesses often recall events incorrectly and identify the wrong people as being involved in the events (Bekerian & Bowers, 1983). In fact, eyewitnesses of the same event often report seeing different things. Langman and Cockburn (1975) recorded the eyewitness testimony of people who reported seeing Sirhan Sirhan shoot Senator Robert F. Kennedy (brother of President John F. Kennedy) in 1968. Even though many of the eyewitnesses were standing next to each other, they reported seeing different things. Identification even in a line-up is prone to significant mistakes (Navon, 1990).

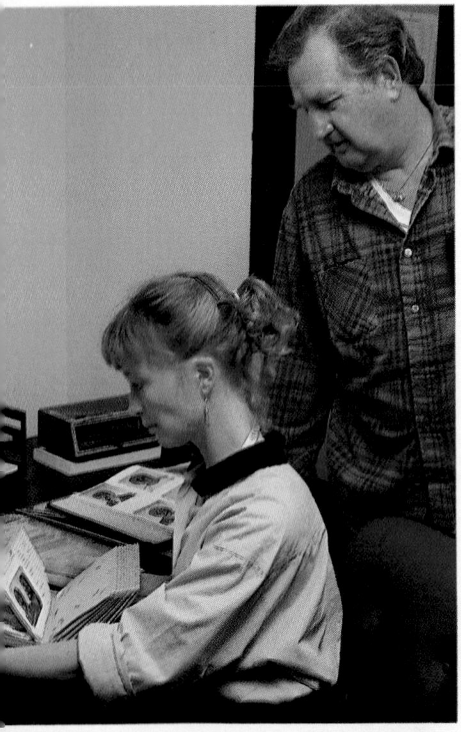

Both field-based research and laboratory simulations are needed in order to determine the accuracy of eyewitness recollections.

To complicate the matter, eyewitnesses often enhance their memories over time. Harvard law professor Alan Dershowitz asserts that the memories of witnesses—particularly those of witnesses with a stake in the eventual outcome—tend to get better with the passage of time. Dershowitz calls this process memory enhancement and argues that it occurs when people fit their hazy memories into a coherent theory and pattern of other results. A witness's initial recollections of an event may be vague, for example. However, as a trial approaches, he or she is coached and rehearsed and tends to remember better, with more clarity and less ambiguity. According to Dershowitz, "what began as a hazy recollection becomes frozen into crystalline clarity." The result in the courtroom, however, may be slightly inaccurate, seriously biased, or even largely untrue testimony (Dershowitz, 1986); that is, it may be constructed testimony.

Despite the strong evidence of errors in eyewitness testimony, two researchers from the University of British Columbia assert that eyewitness testimony is accurate and that it is the laboratory studies of eyewitness testimony that may be inaccurate. Yuille and Cutshall (1986) argue that laboratory studies generally use simulated events, films of events, television presentations, and slide shows to study eyewitness testimony, which is not the same as actually having seen a crime or accident. They further state that real events are well remembered and that researchers who study eyewitness testimony have to do fieldwork before they make further claims. This idea is being echoed by other prominent memory researchers (e.g., Klatzky, 1991.) Studying real-life everyday memories may turn out to be crucial to the study of learning and memory (Ceci and Bronfen-Brenner, 1991).

Yuille and Cutshall's work is important because it questions laboratory research on eyewitness testimony. Generalizing from field-based situations is hard because of all of the uncontrolled variables; generalizing from laboratory situations is difficult because of the artificial nature of the situation (Banaji & Crowder, 1989). Today, researchers are insisting on both. Before the issue is resolved, however, more field-based research *and* further laboratory simulation studies are needed before researchers can apply psychology in this area.

consolidation: [kon-SOL-ih-DAY-shun] The evolution of a temporary neural circuit into a more permanent circuit.

coding: The organization of information and the rules for organization by which the initial stimulus is transformed.

The Physiology of Memory

Memories are stored in electrochemical form in the brain. Many psychologists who study the biological bases of behavior now believe that most, if not all, memories are retained at least in some manner. Today, researchers are exploring the neurobiological basis of memory. How does the brain store memories? Where are memories stored?

Learning Objective 12.4
Explain how consolidation and biochemical changes in the brain play a role in the physiological basis of memory.

Consolidation Theory and Coding

Memories are not physical *things;* rather, most researchers believe that memories are made up of unique groupings of and connections among neurons in the brain. Based on this fact, in 1949, Canadian psychologist Donald Hebb (1904–1985) presented one of the major psychological and physiological theories of memory. Hebb suggested that when groups of neurons are stimulated, they form patterns of activity. If this pattern of neural activity fires frequently, a reverberating and regular neural circuit is established. This evolution of a temporary neural circuit into a more permanent structure is **consolidation.**

According to Hebb, consolidation serves as the basis of short-term memory and permits **coding** of information into long-term memory. If Hebb is correct, when people first sense a new stimulus, only temporary changes in neurons take place; with repetition, consolidation occurs and the temporary circuit becomes a permanent one.

Many psychologists believe that the consolidation process provides the key to understanding both learning and memory—that individual differences in ability to learn or remember may be due to differing abilities to consolidate new information properly. Confirmation of the notion comes from studies using electroconvulsive shock to disrupt consolidation, which results in impaired memory, both in human beings and in animals. Further support comes from studies showing that recent memories are more susceptible to amnesic loss than older memories (Milner, 1989).

The consolidation process may even play a role in the physiological development of the brain. Researchers have studied the brains of animals raised in enriched environments compared with animals raised in deprived environments. In enriched environment, toys and objects are available for the animals to play with and to learn from. Enriched environments may create more opportunities for brain stimulation and growth. The brains of animals raised in such environments

To improve your memory, prepare your environment. Limit interruptions, study in quiet, create an uncluttered workplace, and focus.

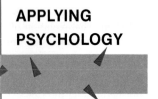

APPLYING PSYCHOLOGY

Improving Memory

Here are some ways you can use what you have learned in this chapter to improve your own learning and memory.

Rehearse, Rehearse, Rehearse

We defined rehearsal as the repetitive review of previously learned information through verbalizing or thinking about the information. If you want to remember something, there is no substitute for rehearsal. Maintenance rehearsal, in which you simply memorize words without giving any meaning to them will facilitate recognition or rote recall if you do not have to remember the words for very long. However, if you really want to remember ideas for a long time, you need to understand them, and this requires the use of elaborative rehearsal (see p. 211). With this kind of rehearsal, you generate meaning as you repeat and think about the information you are learning. Active learning techniques such as the "Question" step of *SQ3R* plus are designed to encourage elaborative rehearsal of information.

Distribute Practice over Time

Earlier, we discussed massed versus distributed practice (p. 204) and showed that distributed practice is especially effective, but students and teachers often do not optimize the use of this principle. Further, this does not mean that massed practice should never be used. There are times when it is beneficial to do so. For example, if you review newly presented information as soon as possible after you have first been exposed to it, you are more likely to organize it and remember it. Thus you can benefit from massed practice if you review your class notes soon after class, or you write a summary of an article, soon after reading it. However, when you plan to hit the books and study, distributed practice becomes important. Distributed practice means to study a particular subject for a relatively short time every day or every other day instead of trying to cram all your studying into one long marathon study session. If you stick with a schedule for doing school work so that you can avoid cramming, you can make use of the distributed practice principle, and you will increase the amount of material you learn and remember within the same total amount of time.

Plan on Relearning

Ebbinghaus's early studies of memory showed us that most forgetting occurs right after we have learned something. He also showed that if we go back and relearn (rehearse again) the same material, we learn it more quickly and forget less of it (p. 203). Ebbinghaus's studies on relearning provide us with additional evidence that distributed practice and repeated rehearsal is important for encoding information into long-term memory. To apply this, whenever you return to one of the subjects you are studying, go back and review what you already studied before you move forward to learn more. In this way, you will be making use of the relearning principle.

Take Advantage of Primacy and Recency Effects

Research concerning the primacy and recency effects (p. 214) show us that we are most likely to remember information at the beginning and at the end of a study session or lecture. So, instead of forcing yourself to have long, drawn-out study sessions, after you have studied for 20–30 minutes, take a short (5–10 minute) break. Taking breaks will enhance your learning and memory because they will increase the number of times that the primacy and recency effects can influence you. Breaks will also allow you to lessen the interference effects of proactive and retroactive inhibition (unless your breaks are also cognitively demanding).

Focus, to Prevent Interference

Because we have so much to learn when we are in college and we have so little time in which to learn it, it is not surprising that we sometimes experience confusion. We all know that it makes sense not to take Introductory French and Introductory Spanish at the same time. You can facilitate memory storage by doing whatever you can do to avoid unnecessary interference. For example when studying, focus on one course or one learning task at a time. If you are studying for a big Shakespeare test, stick with that subject until you feel confident that you have learned a discrete "chunk" of the material and have encoded it into memory. Distributed practice remains important, and switching from one subject to another is sometimes unavoidable. As a guiding principle, try the following:

1. Study every subject often.
2. Focus on and give added time to subjects as their due dates or test dates approach.
3. Avoid unnecessary interference, such as the social interruptions you are likely to get if you study in the cafeteria or the partial attention you will give to a subject if you study while the television or the stereo is on.

Make Use of Chunking

In Module 11, we talked about immediate memory span and how our working, short-term, memories have a limited capacity of retaining only five to nine items. Just think how long it would take you to learn everything you need to learn if you were bound to this limited memory capcity. Chunking allows us to increase the capacity of our working memory store. For instance, consider this word, *psychoneuroendocrinology*. This long word refers to a field of psychology ("psycho- . . . -ology") that investigates the influence of hormones ("-endocrino-") on the nervous system ("-neuro-"), which affect stress, emotions, and behavior. What if you had to learn to say this word so you could spell it on an essay exam? How would you do it with the limited capacity of short-term memory? The answer is that you would use *chunking*. To remember the word, you would break it into small chunks and remember *psycho-neuro-endo-crin-ology*. These five chunks would make it easier for you to learn to say and spell the 24-letter word. What's more, you've probably already learned the "psycho-" the "neuro-," and the "-ology" chunks, so you really only have two chunks to learn. Another way to chunk material is to group ideas together in organized ways. For example, list factors that increase recall as one chunk of things to remember and factors that contribute to forgetting as another chunk.

Use Mnemonics

If you transform information that is abstract, difficult, or still unlearned into information that is personally meaningful, it will be easier to remember. Using mnemonics allows you to combine seemingly unrelated items into an organized format, rhyme, or jingle so that you can easily remember all of the items. For example, as a child, you may have learned the notes of the treble-clef muscial scale EGBDF by using a mnemonic jingle, such as "Every Good Boy Does Fine." You also may have learned to spell and know the meaning of the word *principal* with the ending *pal* because the *principal* is your *pal*. The more you can relate unfamiliar information that you want to recall to familiar information that you already know, the easier it will be for your to learn and remember it.

Use Mediation

Mediation is a bridging technique that allows you to link two items to be remembered with a third item (or image) that ties them together and serves as a cue for retrieval. Cermak (1975) uses the names John and Tillie as an example. John reminds someone of a bathroom, which can be associated with the image of tiles, which sounds and is spelled somewhat like Tillie. Therefore, remembering a tiled bathroom helps the person remember the two names John and Tillie.

Make Use of the von Restorff Effect

The von Restorff effect (p. 204) tells us that if one item in a group of things to be learned stands out because it differs from the other items, it will be easier to learn and remember. You can make use of the von Restorff effect by deliberately making an idea you want to remember stand out. Do this by using bold or colored highlighting on printing in your notes, by exaggerating the meaning of the idea you want to remember, by making the idea somehow funny or bizarre in your mind, or by emphasizing the distinctiveness of the idea in your mind as you think about it. Underlining of key ideas in texts is a common way to use the von Restorff effect to make ideas stand out.

Review in Different Contexts and Modalities

The place where you learned something can be an important retrieval cue. (For example, when you see your favorite bank teller in a gymnasium, you may not be able to remember who he or she is.) Try to review and rehearse in different settings. Also, try learning and studying through more than one sensory modalities. For example, if you heard (auditory) a lecture, write down (tactile–kinesthetic and visual) what you heard. If you have been developing mnemonics on paper, try saying them out loud. If you have been outlining a chapter aloud write down or draw a map of the key ideas.

Use Effective Strategies Such as SQ3R Plus

Throughout this book you are encouraged to use the SQ3R plus active reading study method. These methods make use of what psychologists have learned about how we learn and remember. Although no single studying strategy works for all people, this approach helps a learner focus his or her attention and directs studying in a clear organized manner (Sherman, 1985).

- ▲ ***What is a fundamental assumption that memory researchers have taken from studies of short-term memory and have applied to help people improve memory?***
- ▲ ***What evidence exists to support the idea that primacy and recency effects help people remember new information?***
- ▲ ***What are the implications of the finding that people can learn and remember through many different sensory modalities?***

When an animal is raised in an environment that offers novelty and stimulation, the cortical neurons increase in number.

have more elaborate networks of nerve cells, which have more dendrites and more synapses with other neurons (Turner & Greenough, 1985). This means that when a neuron is stimulated over and over again, it is enriched and may branch out and become more easily accessible.

If a neuron is stimulated, the biochemical processes that are involved make it more likely to respond again later, when compared with nonstimulated neurons; further, the number of dendrites of that cell increases because of previous stimulation (Lynch & Baudry, 1984). This suggests that biochemical actions and repeated use may make learning and memory easier, a conception that fits perfectly with Hebb's suggestions. In addition, clear evidence exists that specific protein synthesis occurs just after learning and that long-term memory depends on this protein synthesis (Matthies, 1989). Psychologists now generally accept the idea that the structure of brain organization changes after learning, and especially after repeated learning experiences. As Hebb said in 1949, "some memories are both instantaneously established and permanent. To account for the permanence, some structural change seems necessary" (p. 62).

Consolidation theory has been refined, extended, and supported by research. For example, we know that a single neuron has many synaptic sites on its dendrites; Alkon (1989) showed that there is extensive interaction among those sites and with sites of other neurons. He asserts that on a given neuron, a huge number of different incoming signals can be received and stored. Alkon has been developing mathematical and computer models to simulate neuronal coding for memory and to study animal memory. This exciting work extends Hebb's ideas one step further.

Location of Memory in the Brain

Learning Objective 12.5
Discuss what researchers know about where memories are stored in the brain.

The search for the location of memory—that is, the memory trace—has been longstanding. Early researchers such as Penfield (1958) looked for a single place in the brain; later researchers discovered that memory resides in many areas. Some areas might involve every memory; others are used to remember only one type of memory, such as sensorimotor visual or auditory memories. In addition, because of the many steps involved and the many features involved, procedural information is probably stored in many more locations than is declarative information. For example, when loading a videocassette into a videocassette recorder (VCR), you must coordinate your hand and eye to insert the cassette, and you probably unconsciously listen and feel (kinesthetically) to sense when the cassette has been inserted far enough. This requires a great deal of neural interconnections for a relatively simple procedure.

Studies focusing on a distinction between short-term and long-term memory provide anatomical evidence about the locations of memory. Baddeley and Warrington (1970), for example, conducted memory experiments comparing normal subjects with amnesic subjects who had various types of brain damage. Their results showed that amnesiacs had intact short-term memories but grossly defective long-term memories.

Milner (1966) reported the case of a brain-damaged adult whose short-term memory was intact but who was unable to form new long-term memories. As long as the subject was able to rehearse information and keep it in short-term memory, his recall performance was normal. However, as soon as he could no longer rehearse and had to use long-term memory, his recall was very poor. Milner's data provide neurological support for a distinction between short- and long-term memory. They also focus researchers' attention on the action of specific brain centers and cells, and on how cells might change through time and experience.

UNDERSTANDING THE RESEARCH PROCESS

Where Does Memory Reside?

Early researchers tried in vain to determine exactly where memory resides in the brain. They hoped to find the location of the memory trace or, as it was sometimes called, the engram. Although the ultimate goal was not achieved, the research took some important and fascinating turns. Wilder Penfield, a surgeon, was one of the principal players in the memory-trace hunt.

During brain surgery on patients suffering from epilepsy, Penfield and his colleagues were able to explore the cortex with electrodes. Electrodes were used to stimulate specific cortical neurons. The patients received only local anesthetic because the brain contains no pain receptors, so the patients were not sedated, and were conscious during surgery. When Penfield stimulated the temporal lobe cortex (either the left or the right side), patients reported seeing images, coherent perceptions of experiences. They also reported visual and auditory perceptions that included speech or music. Familiar and unfamiliar experiences were often intermixed with unrealistic and even strange circumstances (Penfield, 1958; Penfield & Perot, 1963).

Penfield interpreted these reports as true perceptions of past events. His patients were reporting memories elicited by the stimulation (Squire, 1987). Penfield concluded that temporal lobe stimulation triggered the memory retrievals. The concept that specific brain locations stored specific memories that could be accessed through stimulation was revolutionary.

The initial excitement soon dissipated, however. Penfield's patients may not have been retrieving memories at all. Even Penfield acknowledged that the reported memories were dreamlike. Experiences were said to seem familiar, but were not necessarily specific past occurrences. Further, stimulation of different brain sites often brought about the same perception. In addition, removal of specific sites (due to surgery) failed to destroy the memory for the experience (Squire, 1987).

More recent research using similar techniques has shown that patients report mental images when stimulated with small electrical charges, and they are more likely to report these images with greater stimulation or repeated stimulation. However, when the same site is stimulated repeatedly, different mental images are reported. No consistent mental image has been associated with specific anatomical locations (see Halgren, Walter, Cherlow, & Crandall, 1978). One study found that reports of visual effects occurred only when stimulation of the cortex was great enough to spread to visual areas of the brain (Gloor et al. 1982). Perceptual experiences seemed to be reported only when structures deep within the brain, in the limbic system, were also stimulated. (Remember that Penfield searched *only* through the temporal cortex.)

Penfield's conclusion that the temporal lobe holds the memory trace has been contested for several reasons. First, destruction of tissue at these locations did not destroy the memory. Second, nearly half the reported visual images occurred when stimulation spread from the cortex to other areas of the brain. Third, structures in other parts of the brain, especially the limbic system, seem to be involved in producing mental images.

Nonetheless, Penfield's work was a landmark. It gave impetus to additional research, speculation, controversy, and excitement. Subsequent work has shown that many brain areas other than the cortex are involved in memory, especially the limbic system. No one area holds the memory trace. As is often the case with scientific research, though Wilder Penfield's conclusions were wrong, his work was significant and important.

- ▲ ***What was the initial evidence that led Penfield to hypothesize that the location of memory could be found?***
- ▲ ***What are two reasons that Penfield's conclusions are scientifically flawed?***
- ▲ ***Penfield's conclusion and suggestions about the location of memory were wrong, but what did it show researchers that made it an important contribution in the history of psychology?***

Until recently, psychologists only asked questions about how cells and synapses changed in response to environmental changes, such as deprivation of sound or light. Now, however, researchers use a variety of techniques to investigate the physiological basis of memory (Zola-Morgan, 1982). For example, McGaugh (1983) contends that *hormones* (chemicals in the bloodstream) may affect the way in which memories are stored, pointing out that newly established memories are particularly sensitive to chemical and electrical stimulation of the brain. Gevins and his colleagues (Gevins et al., 1987, 1990) focused new research on the spatial location of brain activity and found gross patterns of activity that reflect later human performance and memory. (We examined research on the location of memory in the Understanding the Research Process box on the previous page.) Quickly test your memory. Can you recall the letter and number of the airport parking section described earlier? Did the suggested image help you?

Progress Check 12.1

Complete the following sentences with one of the options provided.

(L.O. 12.1) a. The term ________ is used to describe the idea that each memory exists in the brain in a physiological form. *(neuron / memory trace / icon)*

(L.O. 12.1) b. Decay theory, as a chief explanation for why we forget, ________ widely accepted today. (is / is not)

(L.O. 12.1) c. The interference explanation suggests that we forget because ________. (memories fade and disintegrate / of crowding of information)

(L.O. 12.1) d. ________ is the decrease in accurate recall of information because other information was presented prior to the target list of information. (Proactive inhibition / Retroactive inhibition)

(L.O. 12.1) e. The ________ hypothesis predicts that retrieval of a memory will be easier, faster, and more accurate when a cue presented to activate retrieval compares closely with original memory codes. (memory-enhancement / encoding-specificity)

(L.O. 12.2) f. Because the memories are inaccessible due to their unpleasantness and their dismissal to the unconscious, ________ is hard, if not impossible, to research. (amnesia / motivated forgetting)

(L.O. 12.2) g. ________ amnesia is the inability to remember events that occurred *after* a traumatizing event. (Retrograde / Anterograde)

(L.O. 12.3) h. Dershowitz says that witnesses tend to give inaccurate or even untrue accounts in the courtroom because of a process called ________. (eyewitness anxiety / memory enhancement)

(L.O. 12.4) i. When a temporary neural circuit evolves into a more permanent neural structure, ________ has occurred. (cell assembly / consolidation / mediation)

(L.O. 12.4) j. Studies of animals raised in enriched environments suggest that neurons used repeatedly ________ and as a result, become more accessible for future learning. (condense and solidify / branch out with new dendrites and synapses)

(L.O. 12.5) k. Studies investigating the physiological basis of memory provide evidence that there ________ neurological distinction between short-term and long-term memory. (is no / is a)

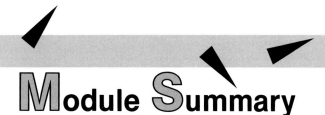

Module Summary

Forgetting

- According to the *interference explanation,* the limited capacity of short-term memory makes it susceptible to interference or confusion. *Proactive inhibition* is the decrease in accurate recall as a result of previous presentation of material. *Retroactive inhibition* is the decrease in accurate recall as a result of subsequent presentation of material (p. 224).

- *Amnesia* is the inability to remember events from the past, usually because of physiological *trauma* (such as an auto accident, a blow to the head, or a fall from a height). *Retrograde amnesia* is the inability to remember events that preceded a traumatizing event; *anterograde amnesia* is the inability to remember events that occur after an injury or brain damage (p. 225).

The Physiology of Memory

- *Consolidation* is the evolution of a temporary neural circuit into a more permanent circuit. If a neuron is stimulated, the biochemical processes involved make it more likely to respond later than would nonstimulated neurons; further, the cell's number of dendrites increases because of previous stimulation (p. 227).

- When Penfield stimulated the temporal lobe cortex, patients reported seeing images, coherent perceptions of experiences. More recent research shows, however, that no consistent mental images are associated with specific anatomical locations. Further research has proven that *no* single area holds the memory trace (p. 230).

KEY TERMS

amnesia, p. 225
anterograde amnesia, p. 226
coding, p. 227
consolidation, p. 227
decay, p. 223
interference, p. 224
proactive inhibition, p. 224
retroactive inhibition, p. 224
retrograde amnesia, p. 226

SELF-TEST — Module 12

- Before taking the self-test, **recite** and **review.**
- Use the key at the back of the text to *correct* your answers.
- *Restudy* pages that correspond to any questions you answered incorrectly.

1. As the class dismissed, three students spoke to Professor White. Sue said, "I will miss class Tuesday." Dave said, "My make-up exam is in the lab, ready for you to grade." Al said, "Don't forget, I have an appointment with you at noon on Thursday." If Dr. White forgets Sue and Dave's messages, it probably will be because of
   a. proactive inhibition.
   b. retroactive inhibition.
   c. an unusually short memory span.
   d. anterograde decay.
2. Sigmund Freud used the term ________ to describe motivated forgetting.
   a. denial
   b. repression
   c. rationalization
   d. lying
3. The contradictory research findings concerning the accuracy of eyewitness testimony provides a good example of
   a. the mixed effects of interference and decay.
   b. memory enhancement and motivated forgetting.
   c. what can happen if researchers use haphazard experimental designs.
   d. why psychologists need to use both field-based and laboratory research findings to fully understand human behavior.
4. Memory enhancement occurs because
   a. no one has a perfect memory, so most people practice memory techniques.
   b. people standing next to one another see things differently, and when put together, their testimonies provide an enhanced picture of the incident.
   c. juries are not allowed to take notes during their deliberations.
   d. of the constructive nature of memory.
5. Many psychologists believe that individual differences in ability to learn and remember may be the result of
   a. the location of engrams.
   b. the number of neurons in a person's brain.
   c. the size of a person's brain.
   d. the way in which a person consolidates new information.
6. Which of the following is considered a valid physiological explanation of memory.
   a. Memory involves a biochemical process of consolidation, which causes changes in the structure of neurons.
   b. Protein synthesis and the release of hormones appear to affect memory storage.
   c. Memories are stored in a specific and identifiable location of the brain.
   d. Both a and b.

Connections

If you are interested in ...	Turn to ...	To learn more about ...
The role of memory in everyday life	◆ Chapter 3, p. 95	How Gestalt psychologists developed theories of perception based on past experiences
	◆ Chapter 4, p. 147	The effects of drug abuse on long-term memory
	◆ Chapter 10, p. 398	How personality theorists such as Freud suggested that everyday memories are buried deep within the unconscious
Forgetting	◆ Chapter 8, p. 336	How Alzheimer's disease has such a profound effect on people's ability to remember past events
	◆ Chapter 14, p. 562	Why certain personality approaches to treatment rely on the ability to recall events that were forgotten and perhaps dismissed to the unconscious
The biological basis of memory	◆ Chapter 2, p. 51	How psychobiologists study the biochemical bases of behavior, including memory, to understand the role of biology in memory
	◆ Chapter 9, p. 381	How theories of emotion depend, in part, on a person's memory for past events and the subsequent interpretation of new events
	◆ Chapter 14, p. 587	How electroconvulsive shock therapy has been used to treat people who have been seriously depressed and at the same time wipes out many past memories

So much of our everyday behavior is dependent upon our learning and subsequent memory of past events that its is not surprising that the study of memory is connected extensively with many areas of psychological investigation. Personality, discussed in Chapter 10, p. 398, depends upon our past events; similarly, our abilities to deal with stress (Chapter 12, p. 504) depends upon how we perceive and remember previously stressful situations. When we look back and look to the future in our personal development (Chapter 8, pp. 298, 336) memory is involved. Our memory is implicated in the way we perceive the visual world (Chapter 3, p. 92) and in how we perceive people in their social world (Chapter 15, p. 603). Our memory and our ability to recall underlies so much of the behavior of human beings that it has been a classical area of study and of high interest to psychologists and students of psychology for decades.

Module 13 ► PROBLEM SOLVING AND CONCEPT FORMATION 238

Module 14 ► LANGUAGE 258

Chapter 7

Thought and Language

This chapter focuses on the study of thought (cognition) and language. In Module 13, it is shown that the study of human thought processes helps psychologists discover the best methods of teaching individuals to think. One aspect of thought that is available to study are the responses used to conceptualize and solve problems. Psychologists have learned that people adopt specific hypothesis-testing strategies and use *conservative focusing* techniques and memory to solve problems. (Conservative focusing means progressively narrowing the possible solutions, from a limited set of options, such as you might do when trying to guess a person's age or weight.) Psychologists know that people who use *divergent thinking* (considering a wide variety of options—*diverging* from one to many) solve problems better than people who are functionally fixed. However, the basic nature of concept formation remains to be discovered. It is easier to test people's basic mental abilities or their language development than it is to examine and describe the processes by which people think.

One of the most complex cognitive processes is language, the focus of Module 14. Studying language, and especially how language is acquired, is one way to study how people think and communicate. The module shows how the study of chimps and their use of language allows psychologists to study thought and the conditions in which language develops in nonhumans. Most psychologists agree that language has a biological component. Children develop language in a relatively orderly and meaningful way, although the age at which specific patterns develop varies among individuals. Furthermore, most people have the ability to generate an infinite number of correctly formed sentences in their language. Because this ability cannot be acquired through mere imitation or instruction, it suggests the presence of an innate grammar or language ability. Nonetheless, children also learn language by imitating their parents and peers. Further, children whose parents reinforce their verbalizations use language more than children whose parents do not. The module concludes with the basic idea that a comprehensive theory of language development will probably take into account both biological and environmental factors.

Module 13

Problem Solving and Concept Formation

LEARNING OBJECTIVES

When you have mastered the material in this module, you will be able to

Cognitive Psychology Overview (pp. 240–242)

13.1 Describe the field of cognitive psychology and state some of its basic assumptions (p. 240).

13.2 Describe the levels-of-processing explanation for memory storage (p. 241).

Concept Formation (pp. 242–244)

13.3 Describe the elements involved in concept formation and discuss how psychologists study it (p. 242).

13.4 Describe the mediation and hypothesis-testing theories of concept formation (p. 244).

Decision Making (pp. 245–247)

13.5 Define the terms *thinking, reasoning, logic,* and *decision making* and discuss how people make decisions by means of formal reasoning, logic, and estimation of probabilities (p. 245).

Problem Solving (pp. 247–254)

13.6 List the four stages involved in effective problem solving (p. 247).

13.7 Explain how functional fixedness and psychological set can interfere with problem-solving abilities (p. 248).

13.8 Describe how brainstorming can affect problem solving (p. 249).

13.9 Identify important attributes of creative thought and distinguish between convergent and divergent thinking (p. 249).

13.10 Discuss the impact that computer simulations of the brain have had on psychology and describe the nature of heuristics and algorithms (p. 250).

SQ3R
- ▲ **Survey** to set goals for studying.
- ▲ Ask **questions** as you **read.**
- ▲ Stop occasionally to **recite** and **review.**

plus
- ▲ **Write** a summary of key points.
- ▲ **Reflect** on the hypotheses, evidence, and implications of this material and on the relevance it has to *your* life.

Blindfolded, facing 12–16 opponents at one time, Harry Pillsbury played chess. He was able to remember all of his moves and to play skillfully. George Koltanowski once played 50 opponents at once while he was blindfolded—in this instance, he played with a limit of 10 seconds per move—and he won 43 of the games. Pillsbury was the United States chess champion from 1897 to 1906; in the 1950s, Koltanowski was a master chess player; both regularly played chess blindfolded, and both had memorized all the moves at each phase of the game. Each blindfolded player was not permitted to see the board, the pieces, or the opponent, but rather was told his opponent's moves by a third person. This amazing ability is a testament to these players' skill at chess and their extraordinary memory.

Chess is a game of skill, knowledge, and imagination. It requires a player to think not only of his or her own moves, but also of the opponent's completed and potential moves and responses. The game is usually divided into three parts, the opening moves, the middle game in which strategies are played out, and the end game when a skillful player can use his or her few remaining pieces to win.

Chess was one of the first games that human beings played against a computer. It was a logical choice: Chess has a finite number of rules; there is a clear playing field (the chessboard); the game is extremely complex (so that the computer doesn't always win); and the rules are rational. Human beings often lose to computers. Whenever I (LL) play computer chess, I invariably lose, even on the lowest difficulty level. Nonetheless, through playing computer chess and studying the computer's responses, I have learned a great deal. One thing I have learned is that I usually have not looked at all the alternatives before making a move. The computerized chess game that I own allows me to peek at the computer's logic by showing me its first, second, and third choice moves. This allows me to trace the logic of the computer program—exactly what psychologists attempt to do when they study thought, reasoning, and language. They try to peek inside the human brain by devising tasks that will reveal human logic and reasoning. They try to map human strategies and listen to human speech, with the aim of getting a glimpse inside the mind.

Thought and language are two separate processes, but they are closely related. Thoughts are usually expressed in language. Language gives human beings a unique vehicle for planning for the future and analyzing the past. This chapter covers thought—especially cognition related to learning, perceiving, remembering, and using information—and *language,* the symbolic system people use to communicate their thoughts verbally.

Understanding how the brain comprehends a game of chess gives psychologists one window into its overall workings.

Cognitive Psychology

Learning Objective 13.1 Describe the field of cognitive psychology, and state some of its basic assumptions.

How are a tiger and a domestic cat physically similar? Who is the U.S. Secretary of State? How do you make an omelette?

Answering each of these questions requires a different mental procedure. To answer the first question, you probably drew mental images of both felines and then compared the images. In answering the second question, you may simply have known the right name or called forth a list of cabinet members and chosen from the list. The third question may have required you to mentally walk through the procedure of preparing an omelette and describe each step out loud. The thinking you used to answer all the questions required the use of knowledge, language, and images.

Overview

cognitive psychology: [COG-nih-tiv] The study of how we perceive, analyze, remember, and construct meaning about our world and ourselves. This broad field focuses on thought and knowledge. It is influencing contemporary theories of learning, personality, social psychology, and maladjusted behavior.

Cognitive psychology is the study of complex mental processes that involve perception, learning, thinking, reasoning, memory storage and retrieval, comprehension, problem solving, decision making, and creativity. The word *cognition* means "to know," and cognitive psychologists are primarily interested in mental processes that influence our acquisition and use of knowledge.

Cognitive psychologists study thinking; cognitive researchers assume that mental processes exist, that we are active processors, and that we can study cognitive processes through time and accuracy measures (Ashcraft, 1989). A cognitive psychologist assumes that *mental processes* are systematic, and that they can be studied scientifically. Cognitive psychologists also believe that we are *active participants* in analyzing our world. We do not sit back passively and have the world impose order on us, but rather, we actively construct reality by making associations and generalizations. They also believe that through measures of performance such as *time and accuracy,* a researcher can learn about mental processing.

This might mean measuring how long it takes someone to perform a task, how accurately the person does it, and what other factors affect mental activity.

Contemporary cognitive psychologists do research in areas such as memory, maladjustment, computers, and personality, to name just a few. This chapter concentrates on a series of cognitive topics that show the breadth of cognitive psychology—the diversity of thought processes being examined and the topics emerging in the 1990s. Some of today's research questions have their roots in studies of levels of processing; other foci of cognitive psychology examine related areas, concentrating on storage and retrieval of thoughts. Because the levels-of-processing idea has generated so much research and so many new ideas, let's examine it before we go any further.

encoding elaboration: Mental processes that involve making associations among items and/or analyzing the special features of a new item.

Levels of Processing and Encoding Elaboration

Learning Objective 13.2 Describe the levels-of-processing explanation for memory storage.

Does the human brain process some information at a deeper, more complex level than other information? Is our ability to recall and use stored knowledge dependent on how we encoded it into memory in the first place? Researchers Craik and Lockhart (1972) argued that a person can process a stimulus in different ways, to different extents, and at different levels. For example, if presented with a display flashed on a computer screen that says "Cast your vote for Smith, the candidate of distinction," a person can analyze the display on several levels. The lines and angles of the letters are coded at one level (this is considered *shallow* depth-of-processing); the words can be analyzed for basic meaning and are categorized and coded at another level (this is *intermediate* processing); and the meaning of the sentence can be analyzed, stored, and coded (this is *deep* processing). Craik and Lockhart found that subjects' performance on subsequent recognition and recall memory tests depended on how deeply they had processed the information during the learning stage. Deep processing enhanced recall ability.

Based on experimental studies, Craik and Tulving (1975) revised the levels-of-processing model and stated that it was not just depth-of-processing that leads to long-lasting, durable, memory traces, but rather that spread of processing also is important. *Spread* refers to the number of features or characteristics of a new item that are encoded and the extent of elaboration that takes place during encoding. Their studies showed that **encoding elaboration** is the critical factor in determining what will be retained at any level of processing. Encoding elaboration involves mental processes such as making associations between new information and existing memories, making associations among two or more new items, and/or analyzing the special features of the new item. The quality of elaborations, as well as the number of elaborations, are considered to be important to retention.

This revised model showed that elaborations (spread) at any level (depth) would improve memory. On a practical level, what this means is when trying to learn something, such as memorizing a poem, you will be more likely to remember it for a long time if you process it on several levels and elaborate at each level. This could be done by paying attention to the sounds of words and patterns of rhythm in the poem (elaboration at the shallow level), the imagery elicited by the words (intermediate-level elaboration), as well as what the poem means to you and how it relates to something you already know (deep-level elaboration).

For Olympic skater Brian Boitano, performing triple jumps has become nearly automatic, but a quadruple jump still takes great concentration and practice.

The levels-of-processing approach suggests that distinctions in memory stores such as short-term and long-term memory may not be as important to understanding how we remember as are the *operations* involved in storing thoughts and perceptions (Lockhart & Craik, 1990). It also suggests that information processing does not always follow a fixed sequence. Craik and Tulving assert that factors such as intention to learn, effort, difficulty of the task, and the time spent learning

concept: A classification of objects or ideas that distinguishes them from others on the basis of some common feature.

or rehearsing items are less important to successful retention than the quality and number of operations performed during encoding. Shallow and narrow encoding operations do not facilitate recall, while deep and elaborate encoding operations enhance recall ability. As discussed in Module 11, researchers are finding memory to be a constructive process. The coding of information becomes crucial when a person has to form a concept in order to make a decision, the topic we consider next.

Concept Formation

Learning Objective 13.3 Describe the elements involved in concept formation, and discuss how psychologists study it.

Each day people make hundreds of decisions, solve problems, and behave quite logically; the steps in decision making and problem solving are complicated but orderly. Before we can better understand these more complex forms of reasoning, we have to realize that every decision involves our ability to form, manipulate, transform, and relate concepts. **Concepts** are the mental categories we use to classify events and objects with respect to common properties. The study of *concept formation* is the examination of the way people organize and classify events and objects, in order to solve problems. How do you plan a winning strategy in a game of chess? How do you decide whether you are for or against the death penalty?

Concepts help people organize their thinking and thus make events in the world more meaningful. People develop progressively more complex concepts throughout life. Infants learn the difference between parents and strangers very early. Within a year, they can discriminate among objects, colors, and people, and they comprehend simple concepts such as animals and flowers. By age 2 years, they can verbalize these differences.

Much of what we teach young children involves classification, because this is the key to organizing and understanding our complex world (see Figure 13.1).

Figure 13.1

In a typical classification task given to first- or second-graders, the task is to circle the picture that is most like the sample.

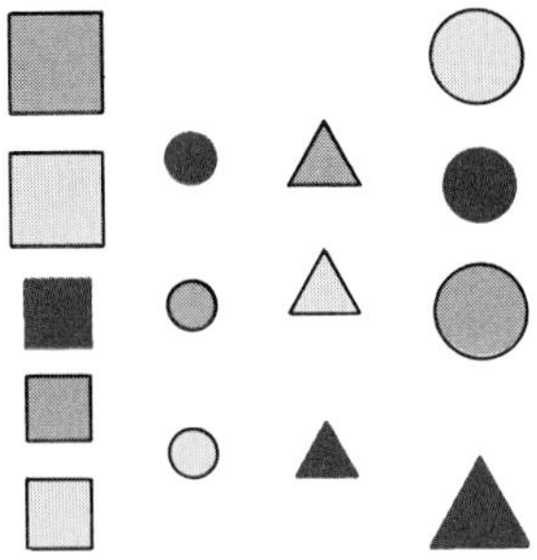

Figure 13.2

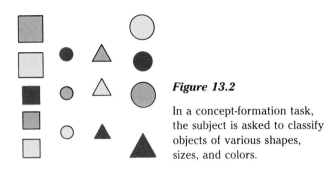

In a concept-formation task, the subject is asked to classify objects of various shapes, sizes, and colors.

Think back to your early school years, and think about current educational television shows such as "Sesame Street." You were taught to classify the range of colors; different farm animals (and their sounds); shapes such as triangles, circles, and squares; and the letters in the alphabet. You learned to organize the people in your house—mother, father, sister, brother—into a group called a family. You learned that the world is made up of a multitude of countries, states, and towns, and that you can do both "bad things" and "good things." The process of concept formation is lifelong and always changing. It involves separating dissimilar events and finding commonalities (Medin, 1989). But what is the best way to study the processes by which children or adults classify and organize information?

Studying Concept Formation

To study concept formation in a carefully controlled environment, psychologists design laboratory studies in which the subject's task is to form a concept using a wide range of tasks. Suppose you are the subject in a laboratory experiment. You might be asked to make judgments of "Who belongs to this category?" or "Is a bicycle a toy or a vehicle?" A concept formation task might ask you to classify colors: "Is aqua more blue or more green?" "Do you place yellow next to blue or next to red?"

Here is a common task used in laboratory investigations of concept formation: An experimenter presents you with objects of different shapes, sizes, and colors and says that some characteristic of some of those objects makes them similar. You are asked to identify this characteristic. Each time the researcher presents a stimulus, you ask whether it has the property (characteristic) being targeted, and the experimenter answers yes or no.

Suppose, for example, the first stimulus is a large red triangle. The experimenter tells you that it is a **positive instance** (an example of the concept being sought). You now know that the concept may be largeness, redness, or triangularity. The second stimulus is a small red triangle; the experimenter says that this too is a positive instance. You now know that size is not important. The third stimulus is a large blue triangle; it too is a positive instance. You surmise that the relevant dimension is triangularity. When, on the fourth trial, the stimulus is a large blue circle and the experimenter responds that it is a **negative instance** (a stimulus that is not an example of the concept), you can say with conviction that triangularity is the concept.

Stimuli also vary along dimensions. A **dimension** is one of many categories of features (characteristics) that distinguish objects from one another. For example, a large red triangle has three dimensions: size, shape, and color (see Figure 13.2). Within each dimension, there are different *values* or *attributes* (characteristics). The color dimension may have red, blue, and green attributes. The size dimension may have large, medium, and small attributes. The shape dimension may have

positive instance: A stimulus that is an example of the concept under study.

negative instance: A stimulus that is not an example of the concept under study.

dimension: A conceptual category of features (or attributes) that distinguish objects or phenomena from one another.

triangular, circular, and square attributes. In the given example, you had to learn that the relevant dimension was *shape.*

Concept-Formation Theories

Learning Objective 13.4
Describe the mediation and hypothesis-testing theories of concept formation.

As in other areas of psychology, theory has guided research. Over the past 50 years, theories of concept formation have changed substantially, from mediation theories to hypothesis-testing theories.

Mediation Theory. Can people form concepts about situations without much effort, simply by absorbing new ideas? If so, then concept formation is simply the association of certain stimuli and responses. According to **mediation** theory, people use internal bridging thought processes to connect a stimulus (for example, a German shepherd) to a concept response (dog). Mediation theory thus suggests that a link exists between specific instances of a category and the general category. Mediation theory was very popular in the 1950s and 1960s, but it has been replaced by the more sophisticated hypothesis-testing theory.

Hypothesis-Testing Theory. The hypothesis-testing theory views concept formation as an active rather than an automatic process. It assumes that people acquire new information by generating hypotheses about stimuli, testing those hypotheses, discarding old hypotheses if necessary, and making an inference regarding the stimuli. Levine (1975) identified three hypothesis-testing strategies in adults: (1) In *hypothesis checking,* an unsophisticated strategy that resembles gambling, subjects test one hypothesis at a time. (2) In *dimension checking,* subjects test the hypotheses of a single dimension. (3) In **global focusing,** the most consistently efficient strategy, subjects keep all possible hypotheses in mind but focus on one at a time, ruling out alternatives as they are given feedback. To be an efficient global focuser, a person has to be actively involved in seeking solutions and in forming concepts.

Another type of hypothesis-testing strategy, **conservative focusing,** is the successive elimination of possible solutions. It is efficient for a limited range of concepts. If you are asked to identify a whole number from 1 to 10, for example, the best strategy is first to ask whether the number is greater than 5. The answer eliminates half the possibilities. If the answer is yes, the next question could be, "Is the number greater than 8?" which would eliminate about half of the remaining possibilities. If the response is yes, only one other question is necessary: "Is the number 9?" By narrowing the choices in this way, the number can be guessed in three or four tries. A less efficient approach is to guess each number: "Is the number 6? Is the number 7? Is the number 2?" and so on. Of course, this entire process is part of thinking and decision making.

mediation: The process of finding a connection between previously unconnected things.

global focusing: A problem-solving strategy that involves considering a wide range of solutions and testing the solutions one by one.

conservative focusing: A problem-solving strategy that involves the elimination of alternative possibilities from a narrow range of options.

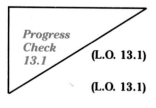

Progress Check 13.1

Complete the following sentences with one of the options provided.

(L.O. 13.1) a. Cognitive psychologists believe that ______. (reality is imposed upon us by the world / we actively construct our reality)

(L.O. 13.1) b. Cognitive psychology differs from traditional behavioral psychology, in that cognitive psychology assumes that mental processes ______ measured with regard to performance. (do not have to be / can be)

(L.O. 13.2) c. The levels-of-processing model suggests that the ______ of processing at the time of encoding determines how well we will remember new information. (sequence / depth and spread)

(L.O. 13.3) d. A ________ refers to the mental categories we use to organize and classify events, objects, and ideas. (thought / concept / psychological set)

(L.O. 13.3) e. Concept formation involves determining positive and negative instances among various ________ of a stimulus. (levels / dimensions)

(L.O. 13.4) f. According to mediation theory, people form concepts because an ________ thought process links specific instances of a category to the general category. (active / constructive / internal bridging)

(L.O. 13.4) g. When explaining concept formation, psychologists today tend to favor the ________ theory. (mediation / hypothesis-testing)

(L.O. 13.4) h. A hypothesis-testing strategy that involves keeping all possible hypotheses in mind and then ruling out alternatives one at a time is ________. (global focusing / conservative focusing)

Decision Making

Learning Objective 13.5 Define the terms *thinking, reasoning, logic,* and *decision making,* and discuss how people make decisions by means of formal reasoning, logic, and estimation of probabilities.

We are generally unaware of our cognitive processes; we don't usually think about thinking. And yet we are thinking all the time, sorting through choices, deciding where to go, what to do, and when to do it. In general, *thinking* refers to reasoning, decision making, and problem solving (Galotti, 1989). **Reasoning** is the process by which we generate and evaluate arguments and reach conclusions; the procedure that we use to reach a *valid* conclusion is **logic. Decision making** is the assessment of and choice among alternatives; we make decisions that sometimes involve the probability of occurrence of some event (will my friends want to go on this trip with me) and expected value (how important is this trip, rather than some other one). Our decisions vary from the trivial to the complex: what to eat for breakfast, which courses to take in a semester, what career to pursue, what birthday present to buy for a friend, which jacket to wear, and whether to marry. The trivial decisions are usually made quickly, without much effort, and usually unconsciously. The complicated ones require conscious thought and effort. Often, our reasoning, thought, and decision making is logical, but at other times, our decisions are uncertain; we are not sure how things will work out or whether our reasoning is valid. Part of these differences rely on how much we know about the problem at hand; a good thinker (one who reasons well, a critical thinker) who has little overall knowledge of the subject matter will be at a disadvantage, compared to a person with a wealth of knowledge about a topic (Glaser, 1989).

Psychologists have devised many techniques for looking inside the thought processes of individuals, especially reasoning. We examine two of these techniques: (1) formal reasoning for which there is a single correct answer; and (2) situations in which the answer or decision is less certain, which involves estimating probabilities.

reasoning: The process by which we generate and evaluate arguments, and reach conclusions.

logic: The procedure that we use to reach a valid conclusion.

decision making: The assessment of and choice among alternatives sometimes involves the probability of occurrence of some event and expected value.

Syllogisms: Formal Reasoning

One of the traditional ways to study reasoning, decision making, and thinking processes is to provide subjects with deduction tasks such as syllogisms. *Syllogisms* are a sequence of statements (usually two), or premises, followed by a conclusion; the task is to decide (deduce) whether the conclusion is warranted. By asking subjects to describe their thinking and decision-making processes while they contemplate syllogisms, a psychologist can trace people's cognitive processes. The psychologist can analyze each decision in the process and thus trace the subjects' thoughts. People are not especially good at solving syllogisms, especially those in an abstract form, but when made more concrete, syllogisms are easier to follow. Consider the following:

Premise 1: All poodles are dogs.
Premise 2: All dogs are animals.
Conclusion: All poodles are animals.

Is the conclusion a logical statement? Do the two premises (in logic, you assume that the premises are true) allow someone to conclude that poodles are animals? When researchers study syllogisms, they trace a person's logical steps. In the preceding example, it is easy to see that the conclusion is accurate. Because logic assumes that the premises are true, you can devise a syllogism where the logic follows—that is, the conclusion validly follows from the premises, but the conclusion is really false because the premises are false. For example, if you changed Premise 1 to "All flowers are dogs," you could logically come to the valid (but false) conclusion that "All flowers are animals."

People can learn how to use logic and how to be critical thinkers and decision makers. One way is to be skeptical about the logic of the conclusions, based on the premises; a second is to systematically evaluate premises for truth. Another way to engage in critical thinking is to think the way a detective does, eliminating possibilities one by one, thus using logical decision-making skills.

Logical Decision Making

When making a decision, people are often faced with outcomes that have various attributes, pro and con. On the simplest level, decision-making entails adding up the positive attributes of the alternatives and then making a decision. For example, each breakfast meal involves a cereal decision for me (LV). Wheaties® versus Fruit Loops®. (This is hardly a major life decision, but it shows the process.) Wheaties have more protein and less sugar than Fruit Loops, but I don't like the taste of Wheaties as much as I like Fruit Loops. If the taste issue is more important to me than the nutrition issue, I'll eat the better-tasting Fruit Loops. If I feel the need for more protein, I'll eat the Wheaties.

Most decisions involve more complicated variables than my cereal dilemma. For example, when I buy a bicycle, I have to consider cost, weight, look, use, and safety, as well as preference for a specific brand. Each of these factors must be considered and weighed for its relative importance to me. If you were buying the bicycle, you might consider different variables, and you'd give each variable a different weight in terms of its importance to you.

A decision-making approach in which some variables or characteristics take on more importance than others is called a *compensatory model.* In the bicycle example, you might do the following:

1. Assign a relative importance to each of the several factors you chose.
2. Evaluate the factors for each bicycle you were considering.
3. Determine which bicycle has the greatest overall positive score, according to your assessment.

Another approach to decision making involves ruling out alternatives that do not meet minimum criteria. For example, if you are interested in purchasing a mountain bike, you need not consider a high-performance racing bike. Alternatively, if you cannot spend more than $250 for the bicycle, you can rule out all the higher-priced models. This approach, called *elimination by aspects,* is generally a fast and efficient way to make decisions. It is logical, and it helps people reduce many of their uncertainties about a pending decision.

Uncertainty: Estimating Probabilities

How do we decide what to wear, where to go, or how to answer a test item on the SAT? How do we decide when something is bigger, longer, or more difficult? Many decisions are based on formal logic, some on carefully tested hypotheses, and some on educated guesses. Making an educated guess implies being educated (i.e., knowing something), based on past experiences. When you see rain clouds, for example, you may guess—but you cannot be 100% sure—it will rain. The likelihood of rain is expressed as a percentage—that is, as a probability.

Psychological factors, especially previous events, affect how people estimate probabilities. People make probability estimates of all types of behaviors and events. In election years, people guess about the likelihood of a Democratic or Republican victory; each spring, people bet on the likelihood that a particular team will win the World Series; you probably evaluate the chances of getting an "A" on your next exam. Based on our past experiences, we estimate the probability of staying on a study schedule, an exercise regime, or a diet. We can judge that a particular event increases or decreases the probability of another event. When several factors are involved, their compounding or mitigating effects alter the probability. For example, the probability that there will be rain, given that there are thunder clouds, high winds, and low barometric pressure, is much higher than the probability of rain when there are only a few thunder clouds.

When subjects are asked to make probability judgments about events in the real world, they are more likely to fail on the task than in making laboratory task judgments. We human beings make mistakes and errors in judgment, and we may act irrationally. However, cognitive psychologists suggest ways for us to become the most efficient learners and thinkers we can be—by focusing on learning how to learn, a topic discussed in Chapter 5, p. 192.

In order to succeed in the stock market, analysts must learn to estimate probability with the least chance of error.

Problem Solving

Learning Objective 13.6
List the four stages involved in effective problem solving.

How do you study for your psychology exam when you have an English paper due tomorrow? How should you handle a friend whose feelings were hurt by something you said? How can you arrange your minuscule closet so that all of your clothes and other belongings will fit? Your car gets a flat tire; what should you do? These are problems to be solved. In important ways, they represent some of the highest levels of cognitive functioning.

We human beings are wonderful at **problem solving;** we excel at confronting a situation that requires insight to solve it. Because we can form concepts and group things together in logical ways, we are able to organize our thoughts and attack a problem to be solved. Psychologists believe that there are four stages to problem solving: *First,* you have to realize that a problem exists. *Second,* you have to assess its complexity. *Third,* you have to devise ways of solving the problem (which might include a number of strategies leading to an insight and then actually implementing the problem-solving strategy). *Fourth,* you have to assess whether your problem-solving approach has been successful.

Huge differences exist in people's problem-solving abilities, but understanding the processes of thought, problem solving, and thinking enables psychologists to help everyone become more effective problem solvers. Although our problem-solving abilities are usually quite good, we may create our own limitations to problem solving, such as functional fixedness and psychological set, which are discussed next. Researchers study these hindrances, to gain a better understanding of the processes of problem solving.

problem solving: The behavior of individuals when confronted with a situation or task that requires some insight to solve.

Functional Fixedness: Cognition with Constraints

Learning Objective 13.7 Explain how functional fixedness and psychological set can interfere with problem-solving abilities.

When my (LL's) daughter Jesse was 4 years old, she observed me taking her raincoat out of the closet before our trip to the zoo. Jesse insisted that it was not raining outside, and that raincoats are for rain. I explained that the coat could also be used as a windbreaker or a light spring jacket. Reluctantly, she put on the coat. In this exchange, Jesse exhibited a basic characteristic of most people: functional fixedness. **Functional fixedness** is the inability to see that an object can have a function other than its stated or usual one. When people are functionally fixed, they have limited their choices and their conceptual framework.

Studies of functional fixedness show that the name given to a tool often limits its function. A typical study presents a subject with a task and provides tools that can be used in various ways. When an object is used for a specific function, the probability of its being considered for use in another way is decreased.

Functional fixedness can also limit, through labeling, people's flexibility in responding to other people and situations. Labeling often leads to stereotyped ideas about social conditions. For example, people may see poverty as a human condition that cannot be changed because it has always existed. Or they may think that mentally retarded people are beyond help. Avoiding the trap of functional fixedness requires thinking about objects and people in new ways, which can reap surprising benefits. For example, Arm & Hammer dramatically increased sales of its baking soda by showing consumers that the product can be used for more than baking, such as to absorb refrigerator odors, brighten teeth, freshen laundry, and diminish the odor of cat litter boxes.

Psychological Set

Psychologists have found that most individuals are flexible in their approach to solving a problem. In other words, they do not use preconceived or "set" solutions or strategies. However, thinking about objects, people, and situations in new ways becomes especially important when we realize that people sometimes develop a

Brainstorming can be an effective problem solving process for groups in diverse settings.

functional fixedness: The inability to see that an object can have a function other than the one normally associated with it.

rigid strategy or approach to certain types of problems. Avoiding a rigid, fixed approach or strategy allows a painter to work in charcoal, pastels, latex, and oils all at once. A flexible scientist will rely on existing technology, technology that needs to be developed, and even technology beyond the realm of modern science. Politicians such as John F. Kennedy could conceive of new innovative solutions to complex problems, such as the Peace Corps. All of these solutions require limber thought processes.

Creative thinking requires that people break out of their *psychological set*—that is, their limited ways of thinking about possibilities. Having a psychological set is the opposite of being creative. According to the principle underlying the psychological set, prior experience predisposes a person to make a particular response. Most of the time, this predisposition or readiness is useful and adaptive; for the most part, what worked in the past will work in the future. Sometimes, however, the biasing effect of a set is not productive. It limits innovation and prevents a person from solving new and complex problems. In an increasingly complex and changing world, these limitations are increasingly problematic.

Here's a problem that is difficult because of a psychological set. In Figure 13.3, draw no more than four lines that will run through all nine dots without lifting your pen from the paper. The answer is provided later in this chapter.

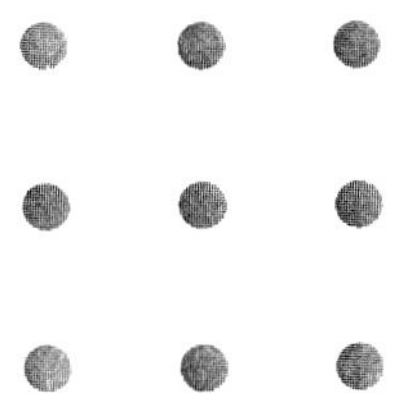

Figure 13.3

The nine-dot problem: In this problem, try to connect all nine dots with no more than four lines running through them, and do it without lifting your pen from the paper.

Brainstorming: Thinking without Barriers

Committees formed to evaluate problems and recommend solutions are often composed of people with different viewpoints. After the committee members define the problem, they may write down all possible solutions, rank-order them, and evaluate the possibilities. They have used an effective problem-solving tool called brainstorming. **Brainstorming** is a problem-solving technique whereby people consider all possible solutions without making any initial judgments about the worth of those solutions. As a technique, brainstorming can be used to illuminate alternative solutions to problems as diverse as a city's waste disposal or a topic for a group project. The rationale behind brainstorming is that people will produce more high-quality ideas if they feel unrestrained and do not have to evaluate the suggestions immediately. Brainstorming is a cognitive technique to release the potential of the brainstormer, to free the person from a potential functional fixedness or psychological set, to increase the diversity of ideas, and to promote creativity.

Learning Objective 13.8
Describe how brainstorming can affect problem solving.

brainstorming: A technique for problem solving that involves considering all possible solutions without making prior evaluative judgments.

creativity: A characteristic of thought and problem solving, generally considered to include originality, novelty, and appropriateness.

Creative Problem Solving

The owners of a high-rise professional building were deluged with complaints that the building's elevators were too slow. The owners called in a consultant who researched the problem and discovered that tenants often had to wait several minutes for an elevator. Putting in new, faster elevators would cost tens of thousands of dollars, which exceeded the owner's budget. Eventually, the consultant devised a creative solution that ended the complaints but cost only a few hundred dollars—he installed wall mirrors by each elevator stop so that people could look at themselves while waiting.

Learning Objective 13.9
Identify important attributes of creative thought, and distinguish between convergent and divergent thinking.

Creativity has a wide range of definitions that can refer to the environment in which a person creates, the product of the creativity, the creative person, or the creative process (Taylor, 1988). Here, we focus on the process. **Creativity** is the process of developing original, novel, and appropriate responses to a problem. An *original response* means a response that was not copied from or imitative of another person's response; that is, the respondent *originated* the idea. In this discussion, it simply means one that is not usually given. A *novel response* is one

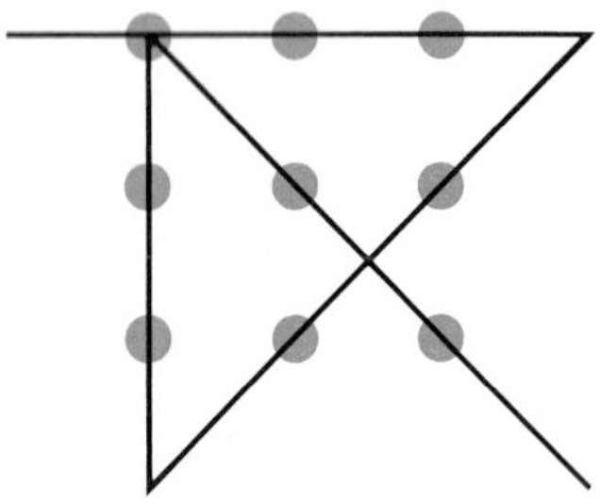

Figure 13.4

Here is a creative solution to the nine-dot problem found on p. 249. Notice that you have to think beyond your normal psychological set and not see the nine dots as a square. (Remember the discussion on Gestalt psychology, regarding our tendency to form a whole from the parts we perceive—See Module 2 of Chapter 1.)

convergent thinking: Process by which possible options are selectively narrowed until converging onto one answer.

Learning Objective 13.10 Discuss the impact that computer simulations of the brain have had on psychology, and describe the nature of heuristics and algorithms.

divergent thinking: According to Guilford, the production of new information from known information, or the generation of logical possibilities, which serves as the basis of creativity.

that is new or that has no precedent. Unless an original and novel solution is also appropriate, however, psychologists do not consider it creative. An *appropriate response* is one that is deemed reasonable in terms of the situation. Building your home out of soap bubbles may be an original and novel idea, but it is clearly not appropriate. A key issue in creativity is how people become more creative in their thinking (Greeno, 1989).

A person does not have to be an Einstein or a Picasso to be creative, as the building consultant demonstrated. To make sure that a solution is appropriate, effective problem solvers form a hypothesis and then test it to evaluate potential solutions. For a particularly difficult problem, they may arrive at a creative solution, one that makes others say, "Why didn't I think of that?" Creativity is a different way of thinking. Not all problems demand creative solutions. The question "How much is 75 plus 25?" has only one correct answer. However, an architect who has to design a new museum for a community can produce a variety of solutions, most of which are creative.

When people sort through alternatives or try to solve a problem, they attempt to focus their thinking, discarding inappropriate solutions until a single appropriate option is left. To do so, they *converge* on an answer, or they use *convergent* thinking skills. **Convergent thinking** involves narrowing down choices and alternatives to arrive at a suitable answer. **Divergent thinking,** in contrast, is the approach in which a person widens the range of possibilities and expands his or her options for solutions; this lessens the likelihood of functional fixedness or psychological sets.

Guilford (1967) defined creative thinking as divergent thinking. According to other psychologists, any solution to a problem that can be worked out only with time and practice is not a creative solution. (For example, Figure 13.4 shows a creative solution to the problem shown in Figure 13.3.) To foster creativity, people need to rethink their whole approach to a task (Greeno, 1989). Successful entrepreneurs know this to be the case (McClelland, 1987), and those who develop new technologies, products, and services are often well rewarded for their creativity. Schools of business are paying closer attention to developing creativity in marketing courses, and researchers are examining the role of creativity and insight in solving problems (Kaplan & Simon, 1990).

Problem Solving and Computers

Human beings determine the ways in which computers accept, store, process, and retrieve data; it is not surprising that computers handle information in much the same manner as the human brain, though the brain has far more options and strategies for information processing than a computer does. By simulating specific models of the human brain, computers help psychologists understand human thought processes. Specifically, computers help shape theoretical development (as in hypotheses about information processing and about perception), assist researchers in investigating how people solve problems, and enable psychologists to test models of aspects of behavior, such as memory. Researchers who program computers to work like a human brain are designing *computer simulations.* When computer programs implement some types of human activities, they are said to involve *artificial intelligence (AI),* particularly if the program is designed to optimize the efficiency of implementing the activity. Their task is formidable because, as Chapter 2 showed, the brain is exceedingly complex, with billions of interconnections. Chapters 3 and 6 showed that researchers break down many perception and memory problems into small steps, using the information-processing approach.

Information Processing. The information-processing approach to perception, memory, and problem solving is a direct outgrowth of computer simulations. Flowcharts showing how information from the sensory register reaches short- and long-term memory rely implicitly on a computer analogy. Those who study memory extend the computer analogy further by referring to storage areas as buffers and information processing mechanisms as "central processors."

In addition, computers have been programmed to understand and produce human language. These programs store information in their memories about the rules for generating English sentences and even speech. For example, programs exist for blind people, in which information can be typed at a keyboard, and the computer vocalizes what has been typed. The information-processing approach is widely used, although it has come under attack as reducing everything to its smallest element to too great an extent (Bruner, 1990).

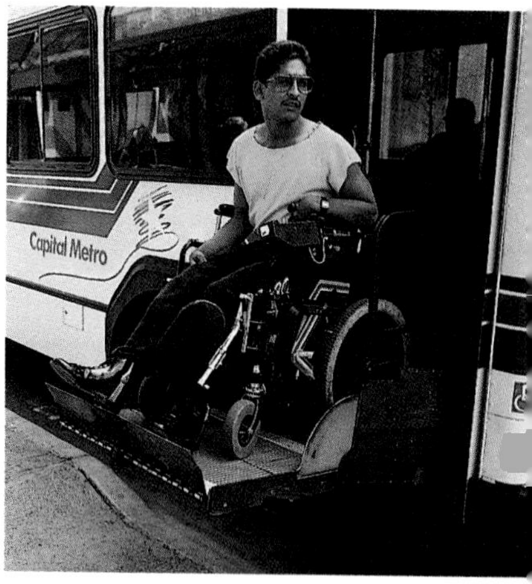

Providing public transportation for people with wheelchairs required creative problem solving skills. The solution—kneeling buses!

Computer Programs. The most widely investigated aspect of computer simulation and artificial intelligence is problem solving. As we saw at the beginning of this chapter, chess was one of the first problems attacked by computers. Computers have been taught to play other games, such as checkers and backgammon, and to solve simple number-completion tasks. They also solve complicated problems involving large amounts of memory. The most sophisticated programs attempt to incorporate aspects of human memory systems into computer programs.

Problem-solving programs use two basic approaches: algorithms and heuristics. **Algorithms** involve reaching a solution to a problem by using a set of rules to implement a particular procedure's steps over and over again until the problem is solved. Many mathematics problems involve using algorithms (e.g., finding a square root). Algorithms are precise and are usually implemented exhaustively until the solution is reached. For example, in a chess game, a particular chess algorithm might involve having the computer use a procedure to examine every permutation and combination of possible plays before choosing the one move that has the highest probability of success. Algorithms are used in a wide variety of real-life problems, from increasing the output of a recipe (e.g., doubling each ingredient), to writing a computer program (which would involve incorporating a number of algorithms for even a relatively simple program). To implement the algorithm, you follow the rules regarding which task to implement at what point in the procedure. For example, an algorithm for doubling a recipe might be, "Find the list of ingredients. For each ingredient, find the measured amount of the ingredient, multiply that amount by 2, and use the product as the new amount for the ingredient. Repeat this procedure until there are no more ingredients listed in the recipe." It's tedious, monotonous, and uninspired, but it works.

However, because algorithms are a set of rules and procedures that *must* be followed, they are often impractical. Human problem solvers, such as chess master Harry Pillsbury, often know things that help them not have to follow a rigidly routine set of rules and procedures to solve a problem; they have rules-of-thumb that facilitate their work. These rules-of-thumb are integral to heuristic strategies.

algorithms: [AL-go-rith-ums] Simple, specific, exhaustive procedures that provide a solution to a problem after a step-by-step analysis.

heuristics: [hyu-RISS-tiks] Sets of selective strategies that act as guidelines for decision making, but are not strict rules.

Heuristics are sets of strategies that act as flexible guidelines—not strict rules and procedures—for discovery-oriented problem solving. Heuristic procedures reflect the processes used by the human brain; they involve making rough estimates, guesses, and subjective evaluations that might be called hunches or intuitions. To contrast heuristics with algorithms, we return to the chess example. When deciding on a move, an algorithm strategy would iteratively consider *every* possible move in terms of its probability for success, then would choose the one with the highest calculated likelihood of success. A heuristic strategy would consider only the moves believed most likely to be successful. These moves would not be given statistical probabilities of outcomes; instead, the heuristic strategist

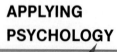

APPLYING PSYCHOLOGY

Improve Your Problem-Solving Abilities

Each of us solves problems each day; it makes sense to be the best problem solver possible. Problem solving is deliberate and time-consuming and affects day-to-day decisions. Ashcraft (1989) has suggested ways for people to improve their problem-solving abilities.

Increase Your Knowledge

A person with limited knowledge about a topic is far less able to solve problems than a well-informed problem solver. For example, learn about bicycles if you are going to buy one. Study computer programming if you are going to program a computer.

Automate Some Tasks

Become an expert at some simple tasks involved in solving your problem. Because you have limited capacities of attention (see Chapter 3), you should free mental resources to solve more complex aspects of a problem by automatically solving smaller goals. In chess, have a couple of opening moves prepared; in studying, plan always to make an outline first—these tasks will then be routine and automatic.

Follow a Plan

Have a plan of action. If your problem is remembering material for an exam, use the SQ3R-plus approach (see To the Student 6, p. xiv). Identify the problem, explore alternative approaches, look at the effects, think critically (see Chapter 1, p. 26).

Draw Inferences, and Develop Subgoals

Try to draw inferences about the facts that are known and possible ways to solve the problem. Then break down (analyze) large problems into smaller, more manageable tasks. In planning a Thanksgiving dinner, think first about the appetizers, then about the main course, and last about the desserts.

Work Backward

Trace a solution in reverse order, working backward toward the fact that you know. In writing a computer program, decide what the output should look like first, and then decide what steps would produce that output.

Search for Contradictions and Relations

Are these possibilities that can be ruled out right away because they violate basic rules, guidelines, or assumptions? Actively consider things you already know to help you rule out inconsistencies. This means using your existing framework of knowledge to help you solve new problems.

Reformulate the Problem, and Represent It Physically

Go back to the beginning of the problem and try to restate it; rethink it in different terms. For example, if you have been thinking in terms of building with wood, think about other materials to achieve a fresh look. Draw, build, or in some way represent the problem physically—make it tangible and concrete instead of abstract and ethereal. Don't use just your brain to solve a problem. Some of the most creative solutions have been sketched out on napkins by problem solvers attempting to represent the problem in some new way.

Practice

To be good at problem solving, practice doing it. Practice makes perfect—or at least makes you better. The more often you solve algebra word problems that focus on solving two unknowns, the better you will be at solving them.

- ▲ ***Identify at least one strategy to improve your problem-solving skills that has a distinctly cognitive emphasis.***
- ▲ ***What evidence exists to suggest that people should try to reformulate problems and rethink them in different terms?***

would ask, "Which move has usually enhanced my strategic position in the game?" Attacking a queen and castling a king are generally perceived to be important heuristic strategies because they usually work to the player's strategic advantage. Thus, a heuristic rule-of-thumb might be, "When in doubt as to a good move, castle your king or attack your opponent's queen."

A number of heuristic approaches exist, most of which center on the goal that the problem's solution should achieve. For example, in **subgoal analysis,** a problem is *analyzed* (taken apart or broken down) into several smaller steps (each of which have a *subgoal*). In **means–ends analysis,** the current situation or position is compared with the desired *end* (the goal), in order to determine the most efficient *means* for getting from one (present) to the other (goal). The objective is to reduce the number of steps needed to reach the goal. A **backward search** involves working *backward* from the goal or end point to the current position, both to analyze the problem and to reduce the steps needed to get from the goal to the current position.

Human beings often use all three of these heuristic approaches, but human beings can be bounded by a psychological set. They may use only one approach or problem-solving set. Human beings are also hampered by their limited attention span and limited ability to work on a number of tasks at one time. In contrast, computers can have hundreds or even thousands of processors operating at once. Today's supercomputers are made up of many powerful computers that operate simultaneously (in parallel) to solve problems. Table 13.1 summarizes the major advantages and disadvantages of algorithms and heuristics.

subgoal analysis: A heuristic procedure in which a task is broken down into smaller, more manageable parts.

means–ends analysis: A heuristic procedure in which efforts are made to move the problem solver closer to a solution by finding the interviewing steps and making changes that will bring about the solution as efficiently as possible.

backward search: A heuristic procedure in which a problem solver starts at the end of a problem and systematically works in reverse steps to discover the subparts necessary to achieve a solution.

TABLE 13.1 Comparison and contrast of algorithms and heuristics

Strategy	Procedure	Advantages	Disadvantages	Example
Algorithms	Implement one or more procedures, according to a set of rules	The single, most probably accurate solution is guaranteed if the rules and procedures are appropriate and are implemented appropriately	Very time-consuming, tedious, and inefficient	Computerized diagnostic equipment for car mechanics often use algorithms to iteratively check a series of mechanical systems in the car
Heuristics	Determine the optimal strategy, based on rules-of-thumb that generally have worked pretty well in the past	Efficient; saves time and effort; adds to existing experience to enhance future heuristic strategies	Solution isn't guaranteed to work, even if the rules-of-thumb are followed closely	Car mechanic who uses past experience to rule in or out an array of potential problems, to determine the most probable problems

Progress Check 13.2

Complete the following sentences with one of the options provided.

(L.O. 13.5) a. The cognitive process called ________ refers to reaching a valid conclusion. (decision making / logic)

(L.O. 13.5) b. Before deciding whether a conclusion is valid, you must first evaluate the ________ of the premises. (logic / truth)

(L.O. 13.5) c. ________ is a decision-making strategy that involves giving importance to some aspects involved in making the decision and then determining which alternative has the greatest overall score. (The compensatory model / Elimination by aspects)

(L.O. 13.5) d. When making decisions that involve uncertain outcomes, a good approach to use is ________. (formal reasoning / estimating probabilities)

(L.O. 13.5) e. Probability decision making ________. (is mathematical and very accurate / can be influenced by psychological factors)

(L.O. 13.6) f. The first step in being able to solve a problem effectively is to ________. (recognize that a problem exists / identify the dimensions of the problem)

(L.O. 13.7) g. When a person uses a fixed and rigid strategy to solve certain types of problems, the person is bound ________. (by functional fixedness / to a psychological set)

(L.O. 13.8) h. Brainstorming is thought to produce ________ ideas because a brainstormer does not have to judge the ideas' value while generating them. (low-quality / high-quality)

(L.O. 13.9) i. When a person widens and expands options for solutions by generating logical possibilities, the person is using ________ and is involved in creative thinking. (convergent thinking / divergent thinking)

(L.O. 13.10) j. Computer simulations that work optimally to produce human language or to solve problems in ways that humans would solve them make use of ________ programs. (computelligence / artificial intelligence)

(L.O. 13.10) k. ________ are problem-solving strategies that make use of general guidelines or "rules-of-thumb." (Algorithms / Heuristics)

(L.O. 13.10) l. A ________ is a problem-solving approach in which a problem is broken down into smaller steps so that it can be solved more easily. (subgoal analysis / means–ends analysis / backward-search)

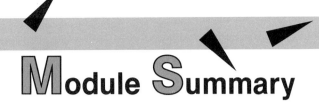

Module Summary

Cognitive Psychology

- ▲ Cognitive psychologists study thinking; they assume that mental processes exist, that they are systematic, and that they can be studied scientifically (p. 240).
- ▲ Cognitive psychologists believe that we are active participants in analyzing our world and that through measures of performance, such as rate of responding and response accuracy, a researcher can learn about mental processing (p. 240).

Concept Formation

- ▲ In concept formation, people try to classify objects by grouping them with or by isolating them from others on the basis of a common feature (p. 242).
- ▲ The hypothesis-testing view considers concept formation to be an active process (p. 244).

Decision Making

- ▲ *Reasoning* is the process by which we evaluate and generate arguments, and reach conclusions; the procedure we use to reach a valid conclusion is *logic* (p. 245).
- ▲ *Decision making* is the assessment of and choice among alternatives; we make decisions that sometimes involve the probability of occurrence of some event and its expected value (p. 245).
- ▲ A decision-making approach in which some variables or characteristics take on more importance and can make up for others is a *compensatory model.* In another approach, people rule out alternatives that do not meet minimum criteria; this approach—*elimination by aspects*—is generally a fast and efficient way to make decisions (p. 246).

Problem Solving

- ▲ *Functional fixedness* is an inability to see that an object can serve more than its stated or usual purpose. Functional fixedness has proven detrimental in problem solving and is closely associated with verbal labels. In contrast, *brainstorming* is a problem-solving technique whereby people consider all possible solutions without making any initial judgments about the worth of those solutions (p. 248).
- ▲ *Algorithms* are procedures that provide a solution to a problem by routinely following a set of rules and implementing a specific set of procedures, in accordance with the rules. *Heuristics* are sets of strategies that act as guidelines, not strict rules, for decision making (p. 251).

KEY TERMS

algorithm, p. 251
backward search, p. 253
brainstorming, p. 249
cognitive psychology, p. 240
concept, p. 242
conservative focusing, p. 244
convergent thinking, p. 250
creativity, p. 249
decision making, p. 245
dimension, p. 243
divergent thinking, p. 250
encoding elaboration, p. 241
functional fixedness, p. 248
global focusing, p. 244
heuristic, p. 251
logic, p. 245
means–ends analysis, p. 253
mediation, p. 244
negative instance, p. 243
positive instance, p. 243
problem solving, p. 247
reasoning, p. 245
subgoal analysis, p. 253

SELF-TEST

Module 13

- Before taking the self-test, **recite** and **review.**
- Use the key at the back of the test to *correct* your answers.
- *Restudy* pages that correspond to any questions you answered incorrectly.

1. Which of the following is *not* of particular interest to a cognitive psychologist?
   a. perception
   b. attraction
   c. thinking
   d. creativity
2. The levels-of-processing model suggests that the best way to understand effective memory storage is to look at
   a. how long a code stayed in short-term memory before being transferred to long-term memory.
   b. the sequence of information processing.
   c. the encoding operations that are involved in storing thoughts and perceptions.
   d. the amount of time a person spends rehearsing new information.
3. To prepare for his psychology quiz, Paul scanned his textbook's bold-print words and definitions. Then, while taking the quiz, he found he did not know some of the answers. Based on what is known about levels of processing, Paul probably had trouble with the quiz because
   a. it failed to provide him with positive instances of important concepts.
   b. he used a shallow and sparse encoding process.
   c. to answer the questions, novel responses were required.
   d. he had studied attributes, but had not become familiar with dimensions.
4. Psychologists study concept formation by
   a. giving conceptual pencil-and-paper tests to subjects.
   b. asking subjects to explain how they know that a particular concept is true.
   c. telling subjects whether a stimulus represents a positive or negative instance of the concept being taught.
   d. watching subjects as they try to solve complex conceptual problems.
5. A hypothesis-testing strategy that resembles gambling is
   a. hypothesis checking.
   b. dimension checking.
   c. global focusing.
   d. conservative focusing.
6. A syllogism is a
   a. general guideline for problem solving.
   b. strict rule for problem solving.
   c. set of premises followed by a conclusion.
   d. procedure that provides a solution to a problem by examining every possible outcome.
7. Problem solving always requires
   a. mathematical skills.
   b. a good vocabulary.
   c. the ability to use formal logic.
   d. insight.
8. If a person is unable to see that a brick could be used as a paperweight we say the person is limited because of
   a. illiteracy.
   b. a mediating process.
   c. conservative focus.
   d. functional fixedness.

9. Which cognitive technique can be used to generate a list of creative and diverse ideas that are then ranked and evaluated to solve a problem?
   a. convergent thinking
   b. heuristics
   c. brainstorming
   d. probability estimation
10. Creative thought is characterized by all of the following *except:*
    a. psychological sets.
    b. novel responses.
    c. original responses.
    d. appropriate responses.
11. Computers have been programmed by psychologists to do all of the following *except:*
    a. shape and develop theories about human information processing and perception.
    b. investigate human problem-solving processes.
    c. test hypotheses about how people remember.
    d. think like humans think.
12. Which of the following would be attributed to heuristics?
    a. precise
    b. exhaustive
    c. often impractical
    d. means–ends analysis

Module 14

Language

LEARNING OBJECTIVES

When you have mastered the material in this module, you will be able to

Language (pp. 259–264)

14.1 Discuss the relationship between thought and language (p. 259).

14.2 Describe the linguistic structures that linguists and psycholinguists study (p. 260).

14.3 Explain how transformational grammar allows humans to generate an infinite number of sentences (p. 263).

Language Acquisition: Nature Versus Nurture (pp. 264–269)

14.4 Explain how psychologists evaluate the relative influences of nature and nurture on language development and discuss the biological (nature) and learning (nurture) explanations of language acquisition (p. 264).

14.5 Discuss the research on language development in chimpanzees and describe how chimp language differs from human language (p. 265).

SQ3R

- ▲ **Survey** to set goals for studying.
- ▲ Ask **questions** as you **read.**
- ▲ Stop occasionally to **recite** and **review.**

plus

- ▲ **Write** a summary of key points.
- ▲ **Reflect** on the hypotheses, evidence, and implications of this material and on the relevance it has to *your* life.

Susan and Al were former psychology students who married, had many friends with children, and were used to infants, toddlers, and preschoolers. Like most parents, they thought their own child was special. They knew their son Lee was active and alert, but they did not fully realize how bright he was until Lee was about $3\frac{1}{2}$ years old. Until then, like other toddlers, Lee had used simple words and short sentences to communicate. Suddenly, though, he was speaking in longer sentences, asking questions, and answering questions with sentences that involved structures not usually used until children are 7 years old. Initially, Lee's sudden abilities were surprising. Later, it was exciting. Then, Susan and Al began to find Lee's language abilities scary. By age 4 years, Lee was reading; at $4\frac{1}{2}$, he was reading third-grade books to himself. Al spoke to a reading specialist and then to an educational psychologist. Both recommended that Lee be evaluated by a school psychologist to determine his potential—linguistic and otherwise.

Language

Learning Objective 14.1 Discuss the relationship between thought and language.

The doorbell rings. You open the door and see someone wearing sunglasses, a T-shirt, and pink-and-green neoprene (rubbery) swim trunks. The person says, "Tell your roommate to get her stick. It's 6 foot and glassy." Some people might interpret this to mean that they'd better arm themselves with a club because a shiny 6-foot monster is running loose. However, a surfer would grab his surfboard ("stick") and head out to the beach, where 6-foot-high waves ("It") are breaking on a beautiful, windless day (making the ocean's surface "glassy"). Although the words sound the same to surfer and nonsurfer alike, the interpretation made by each is radically different because surfers use special expressions when talking about their sport. If a surfer and nonsurfer who speak the same language use different expressions to describe surf conditions, does this mean they think about the ocean in different ways? Does language determine thought, or do all people think alike, regardless of their language?

Thought and Language

When researchers discovered that Eskimo languages have many more nouns to describe snow than English does, anthropologist and linguist Benjamin Whorf hypothesized that verbal and language abilities affect thought directly. In Whorf's view, the structure of the language that people speak determines their thoughts and perceptions (Whorf, 1956).

To investigate Whorf's claim, cognitive psychologist Eleanor Heider Rosch studied the language structure and color-naming properties of two cultures with different languages (Heider, 1971; Rosch, 1973). Every language has ways of classifying colors, although no language includes more than 11 basic colors (Berlin & Kay, 1969). Rosch's subjects were native English-speaking Americans and native speakers of the Dani, the language of a primitive Stone Age tribe (the Dani) in Indonesian New Guinea. In Dani, there are only two basic color names: *mola* for bright colors and *mili* for dark colors. In English, there are many ways of classifying color, usually based on hues (e.g., red, blue, yellow, green, turquoise, pink, brown). If language determines thought, as Whorf claimed, then the English speakers and the Dani would show two different ways of thinking about color.

Rosch showed both groups of subjects single-color chips for 5 seconds. After 30 seconds, she asked the subjects to pick the same color from a group of 40 color chips. Whorf's hypothesis predicted that because the Dani have only two basic color-naming words, they would confuse colors within a group. Two different hues from the *mola* category of color would be considered the same basic color, *mola*. Neither the Dani nor the English-speaking subjects, however, confused colors within categories. The Dani's two-color language structure did not limit their ability to discriminate, remember, or think about colors.

Rosch's studies showed that language does not directly determine thought. Although various languages have developed specific grammars and thought processes, they have probably done so in response to specific environments, events, and cultures. It is adaptive for Eskimos to discriminate among many kinds of snow, but their language does not determine their thoughts. Rather, their thoughts about snow help shape and mold their language and the words in it.

In the same manner, even though human beings are sensitive to odors, they have a rather impoverished language structure to describe them. Research shows that although odors are easily detected, descriptions are difficult, often based on personal experiences and sometimes coded in terms of a personal biographical event (for example, grandad's pipe tobacco, mother's perfume, Aunt Bea's upstairs attic) (Richardson & Zucco, 1989). Linguistic processes play a limited role in the processing of smell, and like the description of snow, our language of odors is determined by other factors. Nonetheless, linguistic processes are far from simple and have undergone much careful research and study, as the following sections show.

Linguistics

Learning Objective 14.2 Describe the linguistic structures that linguists and psycholinguists study.

Tens of thousands of years go, our cave-dwelling ancestors used to put their thoughts into words to organize hunting parties. Several millennia later, Egyptian scribes used hieroglyphics to represent the spoken word. Still later, Socrates was sentenced to drink hemlock for preaching corrupting ideas to the youth of ancient Greece. Today, world leaders such as Pope John Paul II and Mikhail Gorbachev employ oratory to rouse their constituencies to moral behavior and social progress; professors verbally instruct students in the various fields of human knowledge; and people from all walks of life use language to exchange ideas with others or to mentally solve problems. Throughout the ages and in every culture, human beings have rendered their thoughts into language and have employed words to order their thoughts. Without this ability, human civilization could never exist. In many ways, language and thinking define humanity.

We learn language as children; children are astonishingly adept at understanding and utilizing the basic rules of language. A 3-year-old, noticing that many nouns can be turned into verbs by adding a suffix, may say "It sunned today" to mean it was a sunny day. The miracle of language acquisition in children has long puzzled linguists and psycholinguists.

linguistics: [ling-WIST-icks] The study of language including speech sounds, meaning, and grammar.

psycholinguistics: [SIE-ko-ling-WIST-icks] The study of how language is acquired, perceived, comprehended, and produced.

Linguistics is the study of language, including speech, sounds, meaning, and grammar. **Psycholinguistics** is the study of how language is acquired, perceived, understood, and produced; psycholinguists such as Noam Chomsky seek to discover how children learn the complicated rules necessary to speak correctly. Psycholinguistic studies since the early 1970s show that children acquire the simple aspects of language first, followed by progressively more complex elements and capabilities.

Studies have also revealed *linguistic structures,* the rules and orderly regularities that exist in and make it possible to learn a language. This section examines the study of three major areas of linguistics: *phonology,* the study of the sounds of language; *semantics,* the study of the meanings of words and sentences; and *syntax,* the study of the relationships among words and how they combine to form sentences.

phonemes: [FOE-neems] The basic units of sound in a language.

morphemes: [MORE-feems] The basic units of meaning in a language.

Phonology

The gurgling, spitting, and burping noises infants first make are caused by air passing through the vocal apparatus. At about 6 weeks, infants begin to make speechlike cooing sounds. During their first 12 months, infant vocalizations become more varied and frequent. Eventually, they combine sounds into pronounceable units.

Phonemes. The basic units of sound that compose the words in a language are **phonemes.** In English, phonemes are the sounds of single letters, such as *b, p, f,* and *v,* and of combinations of letters, such as *t* and *h* in *th*ese. Forty-five phonemes express all the sounds in the English language; of those, just nine make up nearly half of all words.

Morphemes. At about 1 year of age, children make the first sounds that psychologists classify as real speech. Initially, they utter only one word, but soon they are saying as many as four or five words. Words consist of **morphemes,** the basic units of meaning in a language. A morpheme consists of one or more phonemes combined into a meaningful unit. The morpheme *do,* for example, consists of two phonemes, the sounds of the letters *d* and *o.* Other words can be formed by adding prefixes and suffixes to morphemes. Adding *un* or *er* to the morpheme *do,* for example, gives *undo* or *doer. Morphology* is the study of these meaningful sound units.

It is interesting to note that no matter what language people speak, one of their first meaningful utterances is the morpheme *ma.* It is coincidental that *ma* is a word in English. Other frequently heard words of English-speaking people are *bye-bye, mama,* and *bebe.* In any language, the first words often refer to a specific object or person, especially food, toys, and animals. In the second year, children's

A child's acquisition of language is a marvel to families and scientists alike.

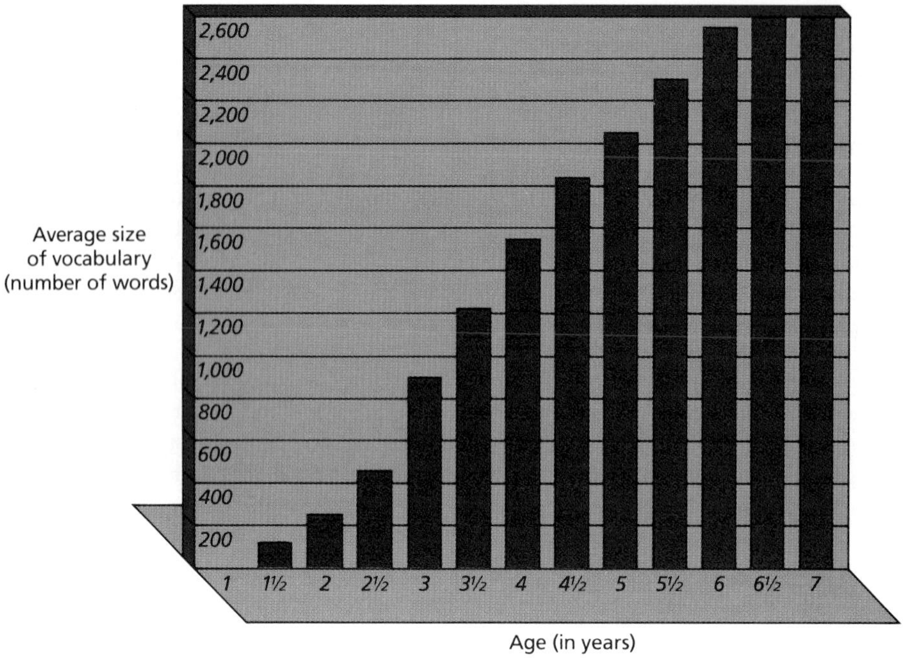

Figure 14.1

Children's average vocabulary increases rapidly from age $1\frac{1}{2}$ to $6\frac{1}{2}$. (Adapted from "The Acquisition of Language," by Barbara A. Moskowitz [on work by Smith]. Copyright © 1978 by Scientific American, Inc. All rights reserved.)

vocabulary increases to about 50 words and in the third year to as many as 1000 words (see Figure 14.1).

Semantics

At first, infants do not fully understand what their parents' utterances mean. However, as more words take on meaning, they develop semantic capability. **Semantics** is the analysis of the meaning of individual words, the relationships among words, and the placement of words in a context that generates thought.

Consider how a 4-year-old child might misconstrue her father when he says to her mother, "I've had a terrible day. First, the morning traffic made me a nervous wreck. Then, I got into an argument with my boss, who became so furious he almost fired me." The child might think her dad got into a car accident and was nearly set on fire. In trying to understand the meaning of utterances, a child is faced with understanding not only the meanings of single words, but also their relationships to other words. As everyone who has attempted to learn a new language knows, the meaning of a sentence is not the same as the definitions of the individual words added together. Words mean different things, depending on their sentence context. For example, a Chinese student studying English at a California college needed a light for his cigarette and followed these directions printed on a red box: "PULL FOR FIRE." He was astonished to hear a clanging alarm!

semantics: The study of the meaning of language components.

syntax: [SIN-taks] The relation between groups of words and how those words are arranged in phrases and sentences.

Syntax

Once children can use words that have distinct meanings, they begin to combine those words into short sentences such as "Mama look" or "Bye-bye, mama." That is, they develop a syntactic capability. **Syntax** is the study of how words and groups of words combine to form phrases, clauses, and sentences. Syntactic capability enables children to convey more meaning. For example, children acquire a powerful new way of making their demands known when they learn to combine the words "I want" or "give me" with appropriate nouns. Suddenly, they can ask for cookies, toys, or mommy, without any of those things being within pointing range. The rewards that such linguistic behavior provide to children are powerful incentives for them to learn more language. (Children don't really need external rewards to want to learn language, though; this is discussed later in this chapter, when comparing chimpanzees with humans.) Children begin to use sentences at different ages, but once they begin, they tend to develop at similar rates (Brown, 1970), though children like Lee pop up from time to time. Moreover, the average length of sentences increases at a fairly regular rate as children grow older.

Early studies of children's short sentences suggested that a description of the position of the words and their types could characterize early speech, but later analyses showed these descriptions to be inadequate. Later investigations suggested that young children possess an innate grammar and that they use grammatical relationships in much the same ways that adults do. **Grammar** is the linguistic description of a language in terms of the rules and patterns for how a language works. Table 14.1 presents some of the major linguistic milestones in a child's life.

Does this sign really mean that the children are slow? Common usage can change the meaning of words and word groupings.

Transformational Grammar

Learning Objective 14.3
Explain how transformational grammar allows humans to generate an infinite number of sentences.

In 1957, linguist Noam Chomsky described a radical approach to grammar that changed many psychologists' views of language development. Chomsky claimed that each person is born with the ability to transform a particular kernel of meaning into an infinite number of meaningful sentences. In Chomsky's grammar, the meaningful message of a sentence is stored differently from the words used to compose it. Psychologists are especially interested in transformational grammar because it helps explain unique features of human language.

The fundamental idea of Chomsky's **transformational grammar** is that each sentence has both a surface structure and a deep structure. The **surface structure** is the actual sentence, such as "Alex gave Mary a dog." The surface structure shows the words and phrases that can be analyzed through the diagramming procedures that are often taught in junior high school. The **deep structure** is the

grammar: The linguistic description of how a language functions, especially the patterns for generating appropriate comprehensible sentences.

transformational grammar: Developed by Chomsky, an approach to the study of language that assumes that each surface structure of a sentence has a deep structure associated with it. This grammar includes transformational rules for generating surface structures from deep structures.

surface structure: The organization of a sentence that is closest to its written or spoken form.

TABLE 14.1 Language milestones

Age	Language activity
12 weeks	Smiles when talked to; makes cooing sounds spontaneously
16 weeks	Turns head in response to human voices
20 weeks	Makes vowel and consonant sounds while cooing
6 months	Changes from cooing to babbling
12 months	Imitates sounds; understands some words
18 months	Uses from 3 to 50 words; understands basic speech
24 months	Uses more than 50 words; uses two-word phrases
30 months	Uses new words daily; has very good comprehension of speech
36 months	Has vocabulary of over 1000 words; makes grammatical mistakes, but the number of grammatical mistakes decreases significantly with each passing week

deep structure: The organization of a sentence that is closest to its underlying meaning.

underlying pattern of the words that helps to convey meaning. Thus, the sentences "Alex gave Mary a dog" and "Alex gave a dog to Mary" have different surface structures, but they have the same deep structure.

To understand transformational grammar more clearly, consider the simple sentence, "Visiting relatives can be a pain." Although simple, the sentence can have two distinct meanings. It might mean that relatives who visit can be annoying guests or, alternatively, that going to visit relatives is an annoying chore. Transformational grammar accounts for these two meanings by showing that for the same surface structure, there are two possible deep structures. To a great extent, the meaning of a word or a sentence is far more important than its form or structure. There is no doubt that the structure of a sentence conveys meaning, but semantic (meaning) factors help convey the abstract significance of a word or sentence.

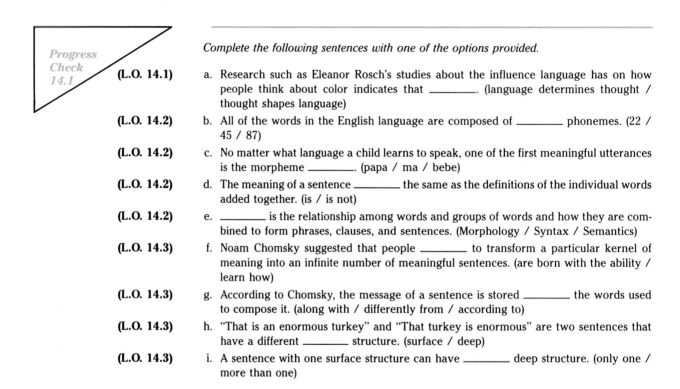

Progress Check 14.1

Complete the following sentences with one of the options provided.

(L.O. 14.1) a. Research such as Eleanor Rosch's studies about the influence language has on how people think about color indicates that ______. (language determines thought / thought shapes language)

(L.O. 14.2) b. All of the words in the English language are composed of ______ phonemes. (22 / 45 / 87)

(L.O. 14.2) c. No matter what language a child learns to speak, one of the first meaningful utterances is the morpheme ______. (papa / ma / bebe)

(L.O. 14.2) d. The meaning of a sentence ______ the same as the definitions of the individual words added together. (is / is not)

(L.O. 14.2) e. ______ is the relationship among words and groups of words and how they are combined to form phrases, clauses, and sentences. (Morphology / Syntax / Semantics)

(L.O. 14.3) f. Noam Chomsky suggested that people ______ to transform a particular kernel of meaning into an infinite number of meaningful sentences. (are born with the ability / learn how)

(L.O. 14.3) g. According to Chomsky, the message of a sentence is stored ______ the words used to compose it. (along with / differently from / according to)

(L.O. 14.3) h. "That is an enormous turkey" and "That turkey is enormous" are two sentences that have a different ______ structure. (surface / deep)

(L.O. 14.3) i. A sentence with one surface structure can have ______ deep structure. (only one / more than one)

Language Acquisition: Nature Versus Nurture

Learning Objective 14.4
Explain how psychologists evaluate the relative influences of nature and nurture on language development, and discuss the biological (nature) and learning (nurture) explanations of language acquisition.

Research shows that language and thought are sensitive to both experience (nurture) and genetic inheritance (nature). As in other areas of human behavior, the debate continues about the relative contribution of each factor. If language is based on biology, two things should be true: (1) Many aspects of language ability should be evident early in life. (2) All children, regardless of their culture or language, should develop a *grammar* (that is, an understanding of a language's patterns) in a similar way. On the other hand, if environmental factors account for language acquisition, the role of learning should be preeminent.

Consider what happens when people take their first course in Spanish, French, or Latin. They recognize that there will be a new language in which they will learn to communicate, which includes a new grammar, new written forms, and new pronunciation. Students may buy study aids: books, dictionaries, and tapes. They may read about the country of the new tongue, talk to someone who speaks the language, and rely on foreign language teachers. In general, a student prepares to acquire the new language. When you learned your very first language, how were you prepared to learn language? Were you prepared at all? When trying to resolve this nature–nurture debate over language acquisition, researchers study the development of language through observational studies of infants and children, case histories of sensory-deprived infants, studies of reading-disabled or brain-damaged individuals, and experiments with chimpanzees.

Learning Theories

Learning theories emphasize the role of environmental influences, or nurture, in language acquisition. The basic idea is that language is not a magic process but a natural unfolding of traditional learning.

One learning theory, the *conditioning approach,* highlights the importance of language experiences during the formative years. According to this theory, both other-person reinforcement (in the form of parental approval) and self-reinforcement (in the form of speech) increase the probability that children will emit words and sentences. As the sole explanation of language, the conditioning approach has one serious weakness. Slobin says, "A mother is too engaged in interacting with a child to pay attention to the linguistic form of his utterances" (1975, p. 290). Despite parental inattention to reinforcing language structure, children eventually learn to form sentences.

Another learning theory claims that children acquire language through *imitation*—that is, by copying adult speech. Through imitation, children learn to use the proper forms of language. An example of learning by imitation is picking up regional terminology, such as "*Y'all come back, now.*"

Learning approaches have several weaknesses, however. They do not explain how children, who learn grammar in a short period of time, using the small sample of sentences they've heard, are able to generate an infinite number of new sentences. Additionally, learning approaches do not consider biological or maturational readiness. If readiness were not to some extent biologically determined, parents could teach their child to speak, read, and write soon after birth. Thus, psycholinguists speak of *acquiring* your first language, not *learning* it.

Biological Theories

Psychologist George Miller (1965) asserts that human beings have an innate, unique capacity to acquire and develop language. Although he does not exclude experience as a factor in shaping children's language, Miller claims that it is human nature itself that allows children to pay attention to language in their environment and ultimately to use it.

Nonetheless, even the strongest proponents of the nature (biological) argument do not contend that a specific language is inborn. Rather, they agree that a predisposition toward language exists and that a blueprint for language is preprinted. As a child matures, this blueprint provides the framework through which the child learn a language and its rules. Three major sources of evidence support the biological side of the nature-versus-nurture debate: (1) studies of brain structure and lateralization, (2) studies of readiness, and (3) language acquisition in children and chimpanzees.

Studies with chimps such as Nim Chimpsky have raised questions concerning the chimp's ability to truly learn language as opposed to merely mimicking words.

Brain Structure and Lateralization. As early as the 1800s, researchers knew that the brain of a human being is specialized for different functions. At that time researchers began mapping the brain and discovered that if certain areas were damaged (usually through accidents), the person had severe disorders in language abilities. Later work led to the idea of **lateralization,** the localization of a particular brain function primarily in one of the two hemispheres.

As Chapter 2 showed, considerable evidence suggests that the left and right sides of the brain handle distinctly different functions. Some researchers argue that studies of laterality show that the brain has unique processing abilities in each hemisphere. For example, language functions are predominantly, but not exclusively, left-hemisphere functions. However, the available data do not make an airtight case; each hemisphere seems to play a dominant role in some functions and to interact in the performance of others.

Learning Readiness. Researchers such as Erik Lenneberg (1921–1975) claim that human beings are born with a grammatical capacity and a readiness to produce language (Lenneberg, 1967). They claim that language simply develops as people interact with their environment. One important aspect of this theory is that a child's capacity to learn language depends on maturation of specific neurological capacities. Lenneberg's view derives in part from observations that most children learn the rules of grammar at a very early age, and they develop specific aspects of language at about the same ages.

Lenneberg believes that the brain continues to develop from birth until about age 13 years, with optimal development at age 2 years. During this period, children develop grammar and learn the rules for language. After age 13, there is little room for improvement or change in their neurological structure. Lenneberg supports his argument with the observation that brain-damaged children can relearn some speech and language, whereas brain-damaged adults or adolescents who lose language and speech are unable to completely regain the lost ability.

Lenneberg's view is persuasive, but some of his original claims have been seriously criticized, particularly his idea of the role of a critical readiness period in language development. Some researchers claim that not only human beings but also other organisms are born with a grammatical capacity and a readiness for language, such as chimpanzees.

Studies with Chimpanzees

Learning Objective 14.5 Discuss the research on language development in chimpanzees, and describe how chimp language differs from human language.

Do animals communicate with one another through language? If they do, is that language the same as, similar to, or totally different from the language of human beings? Most important, what can human beings learn from animals about the inborn aspects of language?

The biological approach to language suggests that human beings are prewired, born with a capacity for language. Experience is the key that unlocks this existing capacity and makes it available for expression. The arguments for and against the biological approach to language acquisition use studies showing that chimpanzees naturally develop some language abilities. Researchers can control and shape the environment in which language learning occurs with chimps, something they cannot do in studies involving human subjects.

Chimpanzees are generally considered among the most intelligent animals; in addition, they resemble human beings more closely than any other animal. Playful and curious, chimps share many common physical and mental abilities with human beings. For these reasons, they have been the species of choice when psychologists have studied language in animals.

lateralization: The concentration of a particular brain function in one hemisphere.

However, all attempts to teach animals to talk have failed, which led most psycholinguists to conclude that only human beings have the capacity to acquire language. Two decades ago, however, some major research projects show that even though chimpanzees lack the necessary vocal apparatus to speak, they can learn to use different methods of communication (Rumbaugh & Savage-Rumbaugh, 1978).

Figure 14.2

Sarah learned to construct sentences by using pieces of plastic that varied in color, size, and shape. (Premack 1971; copyright 1971 by the AAAS.)

Washoe. From age 1 year, the chimpanzee Washoe was raised like a human child in the home of Allen and Beatrice Gardner (1969). During the day, Washoe was in the house or the large fenced yard. At night, she slept in a trailer. The Gardners and their research assistants did not speak to Washoe. Instead, they used Ameslan (American Sign Language). Rather than being taught to speak words, Washoe was taught to make signs that stood for words, as well as for simple commands and concepts such as *more, come, give me, flower, tickle,* and *open.*

Within 7 months, Washoe learned four signs; after 12 months, she had learned 12. At 22 months, she had a vocabulary of 34 signs; by age 4 years, she knew 85 signs; and by the end of her fifth year, Washoe had accumulated 160 signs (Fleming, 1974). Washoe learned a large number of signs that refer to specific objects or events. She was able to generalize these signs and to combine them in a meaningful order to make sentences. There is no proof, however, that Washoe used a systematic grammar (with rules to transform and generate novel sentences).

Sarah. The chimp Sarah was raised in a cage, with more limited contact with human beings than Washoe had. Psychologist David Premack (1971) used magnetized plastic symbols and instrumental training methods to teach Sarah words and sentences (see Figure 14.2). Initially, Premack placed several plastic symbols on a board in front of Sarah and placed a banana slightly out of reach. Each time Sarah chose the appropriate symbol, he would give her the banana as a reward. Eventually (through *shaping;* see Chapter 5, Module 10), Sarah came to associate a specific symbol with a banana, and learned to place the token on the board when she wanted a banana.

Gradually, Sarah developed a small but impressive vocabulary. She learned to make compound sentences, to answer simple questions, and to substitute words in a sentence construction, such as "*Place banana dish,*" "*Place apple dish,*" and "*Place orange dish.*" There is no evidence, however, that she could generate a new sentence, such as, "*Is the apple in the dish*?" or "*Where are the apples*?"

Lana. Lana the chimp learned to interact with a computer at the Yerkes Primate Research Center. Researchers Rumbaugh, Gill, and Von Glaserfeld (1973) gave Lana 6 months of computer-controlled language training. Lana learned to press a series of keys with imprinted geometric symbols. Each symbol represented a word in an artificial language called Yerkish. The computer varied the location of each Yerkish word and the color and brightness of the keys. Through instrumental conditioning, Lana was able to demonstrate some of the rudiments of language acquisition. However, like Washoe and Sarah, Lana did not show that she could manipulate grammatical relations in meaningful and regular ways.

So far, most studies of chimps show that their language is similar to that of young children: It is concrete, specific, and limited. However, chimps do not show the ability to generate an infinite number of grammatically correct sentences, an ability that human beings acquire with age.

Nim. A Columbia University psychologist, H. S. Terrace (1980), claims that even the limited results with chimps are greatly overvalued. He suggests that chimps do not have language abilities and that the data reported so far with chimps show only that they were mimicking their teachers' signs.

Terrace reports significant differences between chimp language and that of young children. In raising his chimp, Nim Chimpsky (named after famous linguist Noam Chomsky), he found that Nim's utterances did not increase in length as young children's do. Nim acquired many words, but she did not use them in longer and longer sentences as time passed. In addition, only 12% of Nim's utterances were spontaneous; the remaining 88% were responses to her teacher. Terrace points out that a significantly greater percentage of children's utterances are spontaneous. Terrace also found no evidence of grammatical competence either in his own data or in those of other researchers.

Kanzi. Recent work with a little-known species of ape, the pygmy chimpanzee, shows that chimps can acquire symbols without training. According to well-known language researcher Sue Savage-Rumbaugh, these chimps comprehend symbols before they produce them, and they also comprehend human speech. In Savage-Rumbaugh's view (1987), they have the ability to construct a rudimentary grammar.

Kanzi, a pygmy chimp, was provided a keyboard to talk to his human trainers. His keyboard has 256 symbols, and he has mastery of more than 150. Records of interactions with Kanzi have shown that he comprehends both individual words and sentences and responds appropriately. He learned his language by being enmeshed in a language environment, not through training procedures. His unique contribution is that he understands human speech and syntax and has learned to do so without training. He learned his languages steadily and rapidly, and Savage-Rumbaugh feels that this sets him apart from all other apes who have learned (not acquired) language and have shown that learning through production of language (e.g., moving symbols) (Greenfield & Savage-Rumbaugh, 1990).

Chimp Language? Terrace's work challenged the findings of previous investigators and made them think about language in new ways. Other researchers, at the Yerkes Regional Primate Center at Emory University, have presented additional challenges to primate language acquisition (Savage-Rumbaugh, Pate, Lawson, Smith, & Rosenbaum, 1983), claiming that not only is chimp language different from that of human beings, but also that the purpose of chimp language is different.

Unlike young children, who spontaneously learn to name and point to objects (often called *referential naming*), chimps do not spontaneously develop such communication skills. For Savage-Rumbaugh and her colleagues, such skills are crucial components of human language. Terrace (1985) agrees that the ability to name is a basic part of human consciousness. He argues that as part of our socialization, we learn to refer to our various inner states: our feelings, thoughts, and emotions.

Chimps can be taught some naming skills, but the procedure is long and tedious. Children, on the other hand, develop this skill easily and spontaneously at a young age. Accordingly, researchers such as Sanders (1985) assert that chimps do not interpret the symbols they use in the same way that children do. These researchers question the comparability of human and chimp language.

Although few psychologists are completely convinced about the role of language in chimps, their criticisms do not diminish the chimps' language abilities or their accomplishments in other areas such as mathematics (Boysen & Berntson, 1989, 1990) and guessing (Povinelli, Nelson, & Boysen, 1990). Most also do not rule out language and speech processing in some chimps (Savage-Rumbaugh, 1987). Chimp language remains an emerging part of psychology about which the answers are far from complete, but the quest is exciting.

Progress Check 14.2

Complete the following sentences with one of the options provided.

(L.O. 14.4) a. If language acquisition is based primarily on *nature*, ________ would prove to be the most relevant contributing factors. (experience in the environment / genetic inheritance)

(L.O. 14.4) b. The ________ explanation of how language is learned suggests that parental approval and speech itself act as reinforcers. (conditioning / imitation)

(L.O. 14.4) c. Learning theories of language acquisition fail to explain ________. (regional dialects / how we generate an infinite number of sentences)

(L.O. 14.4) d. From a biological point of view, language development is the result of ________. (a genetic blueprint / nurture)

(L.O. 14.4) e. Biological theories rely heavily on the ideas of ________ when explaining language acquisition. (syntactical combinations / brain lateralization)

(L.O. 14.4) f. According to the learning readiness theory of language acquisition, a child's capacity to learn language depends on ________. (the child's motivation / maturation of neurological capacities)

(L.O. 14.5) g. At age 5 years, Washoe had learned ________ Ameslan signs. (4 / 34 / 160)

(L.O. 14.5) h. Both Washoe and Sarah ________ to combine symbols to make sentences. (were unable / learned)

(L.O. 14.5) i. Chimp language is similar to the language of a young child, in that it is ________. (difficult to understand / concrete, specific, and limited)

Module Summary

Language

- *Psycholinguistics* is the study of how people acquire, perceive, comprehend, and produce language. *Grammar* is the linguistic description of a language in terms of patterns for generating appropriate (i.e., comprehensible) sentences in the language (p. 260).
- *Phonemes* are the basic units of sounds in a language. *Morphemes* are the basic units of meaning. *Semantics* is the study of the meaning of components (such as words) of language. *Syntax* is the study of the relationships among groups of words and the way in which words are arranged into phrases and sentences (p. 261).
- Transformational grammar, developed by Chomsky, is an approach to studying the structure of a language. It assumes that each surface structure of a sentence is associated with at least one deep structure (p. 263).

Language Acquisition: Nature Versus Nurture

- Although learning studies have used different methods and children of different ages, each learning study supports the idea that learning plays an important part in language acquisition, but that acquisition of a first language differs from language learning (p. 265).
- People have the ability to generate an infinite number of correctly formed sentences in their language. Because this ability cannot be acquired through mere imitation or instruction, it suggests the presence of an innate grammar, or language acquiring ability (p. 266).
- Few psychologists are completely convinced about the ways in which chimps use language, but their criticisms do not diminish the chimps' language abilities or accomplishments in other areas such as mathematics; language and speech processing in some chimps is not ruled out, but a healthy skepticism still exists among most psychologists (p. 266).

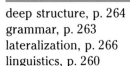

KEY TERMS

deep structure, p. 264
grammar, p. 263
lateralization, p. 266
linguistics, p. 260
morphemes, p. 261
phonemes, p. 261
psycholinguistics, p. 260
semantics, p. 262
surface structure, p. 263
syntax, p. 262
transformational grammar, p. 263

SELF-TEST

Module 14

- Before taking the self-test, **recite** and **review.**
- Use the key at the back of the text to *correct* your answers.
- *Restudy* pages that correspond to any questions you answered incorrectly.

1. Based on studies such as those of Eleanor Rosch, a logical explanation for why Eskimos have so many different words to describe snow is that
   a. language determines thought and perception.
   b. it is adaptive for Eskimos to discriminate among many kinds of snow.
   c. Eskimos have more phonemes in their language structure.
   d. Eskimos have better perceptual abilities than most English-speaking people.

2. Which of the following statements concerning language development is false?
   a. Infants begin cooing within hours after birth.
   b. Two-year-olds have about 50 words in their vocabulary.
   c. Most babies utter their first word when they are about 1 year old.
   d. Three-year-olds have as many as 1,000 words in their vocabulary.

3. A person who examines the meaning of the word *love* in the sentence "I love roses" is concerned with
   a. grammar.
   b. semantics.
   c. syntax.
   d. phonology.

4. Which of the following sentences is a transformation of the deep structure of the sentence "Clowns make me laugh"?
   a. "Clowns have funny faces."
   b. "I laugh when I see clowns."
   c. "Most clowns laugh."
   d. "Some clowns frown."

5. Based on all the data available concerning brain lateralization and the processing of language, it appears that
   a. language is controlled by the right hemisphere of the brain.
   b. language is controlled by the left hemisphere of the brain.
   c. the left hemisphere plays a dominant role, and the right hemisphere plays a minor role in the production of language.
   d. both hemispheres interact, and both play a dominant role in some functions of the production of language.

6. Although chimpanzees have been taught languagelike abilities, there is no proof that they can
   a. attach meaning to symbols.
   b. use grammatical rules to generate new and meaningful sentences.
   c. acquire and communicate with a vocabulary of words or symbols.
   d. learn to communicate ideas to humans.

7. Terrace suggests that the language development reported in chimps is overrated because
   a. chimpanzees do not increase the length of their sentences over time as humans do.
   b. the language used by chimpanzees lacks the spontaneity of human language.
   c. chimps only mimic their teachers' signs in much the same way that parrots mimic human speech.
   d. all of the above

8. What is a critical aspect of human language that is *not* found in language-trained chimpanzees?
   a. Humans can point, name, and interpret, and they can to refer to inner states.
   b. Humans learn languages that make use of different symbols.
   c. Humans think mathematically.
   d. Humans communicate in concrete and specific terms.

Connections

If you are interested in . . .	**Turn to . . .**	**To learn more about . . .**
Thought processes	◆ Chapter 9, p. 372	How motivational researchers are considering the role of thought in determining a person's day-to-day decision making.
	◆ Chapter 12, p. 493	Why stress is considered an interpreted state.
	◆ Chapter 15, p. 646	How business managers and personnel officers are taking into account the way people remember, code, and interpret information.
Decision making and problem solving	◆ Chapter 9, p. 372	How reinforcement for problem solving can get in the way of a person's intrinsic enjoyment of a task.
	◆ Chapter 11, p. 451	How psychologists use problem solving to help determine intelligence.
	◆ Chapter 14, p. 579	How psychologists consider many maladjustments as a series of problems to be solved.
The role of language in everyday life	◆ Chapter 5, p. 175	How operant learning principles can be used to explain some aspects of language acquisition.
	◆ Chapter 11, p. 450	The crucial role of language in determining a person's intelligence.
	◆ Chapter 15, p. 602	The various ways of communicating without overt vocalizations.

Thought and language underlie so many behaviors that human beings exhibit that they have become topics of study themselves. The connections of the study of language and thought to other subspecialties of psychology are very direct; today, researchers often consider themselves cognitive researchers in personality, social psychology, or learning. The study of thought is dominating the discipline. For example, when studying learning, the role of thought is preeminent—How can a researcher study human learning without studying human thought (Chapter 5, p. 195)? Similarly, the study of memory is the study of thought and its relationships to language—That is, how are previous thoughts and experiences coded and recalled (Chapter 6, p. 207)? This book's study of the biological basis of behavior examined how memories and thoughts were coded (Chapter 6, p. 227); further, Chapter 8 (p. 296) examines carefully the intellectual development of thought in children. Our thoughts affect our personalities (Chapter 10, p. 426), our ability to adjust in a stress-filled world (Chapter 12, p. 504), and our view of other people (Chapter 15, p. 603).

Module 15 ► PRENATAL DEVELOPMENT AND INFANCY 276

Module 16 ► CHILDREN'S INTELLECTUAL, MORAL, AND SOCIAL DEVELOPMENT 294

Module 17 ► ADOLESCENCE, ADULTHOOD, AND AGING 314

Chapter 8

Development

During their lives, people experience enormous physical, intellectual, and social growth. This chapter describes the psychological changes that accompany that growth. It comprises three modules. The first module, Module 15, focuses on prenatal development and infancy. At conception, people have only the potential that is passed to them by their parents' genes. It is highlighted in this module that from then on, development depends not only on genetic endowment but also on interactions with the environment, particularly the social and intellectual interactions that occur after birth. Early interactions with the world determine when and how people develop intellectually and socially. The module examines inborn systems and subsequent changes that occur in attachment, temperament, and early social development as a function of childrearing.

Module 16 focuses on children's intellectual, social, and moral development. Piaget's theory is covered in detail. Piaget has shown that all children pass through a series of social and intellectual stages. They are ready for specific types of interactions at different ages. A 4-year-old is markedly dependent on parents, whereas a 12-year-old is increasingly dependent on a peer group. The older children become, the more their interactions with peers and others influence their development.

Parents are the primary and crucial influences on children's social development, but other people and experiences may also have significant impact. Either a parent or sensitive caregivers outside the home can provide a stimulating, varied environment that encourages growth—both parental and day care situations are examined. One of the types of growth on which the module focuses is moral growth and development and how to promote it in both boys and girls.

The foundations laid during childhood affect people's development through adolescence, adulthood, and old age—this is the focus of the third module, Module 17. Eventually, the stresses of adolescence give way to the rewards and challenges of adulthood. Several stage theories have been developed to describe this development: Piaget's theory describes intellectual development from infancy through adolescence, Kohlberg's describes moral development from childhood through adulthood, Erikson's describes psychosocial development throughout life, Levinson's focuses on adult males, and Kubler-Ross's on the process of preparing for death. All these theories emphasize the gradual development of complex feelings, beliefs, and experiences, usually through successful completion of one stage at a time.

Module 15

Prenatal Development and Infancy

LEARNING OBJECTIVES

When you have mastered the material in this module, you will be able to

The First Nine Months (pp. 278–282)

15.1 Discuss what developmental psychologists hope to discover through their research and describe two common research methods (p. 278).

15.2 Describe human development during the prenatal stage of life (p. 279).

15.3 Identify environmental factors that affect prenatal development and consider the risks of ingesting teratogens during pregnancy (p. 281).

Newborns, Infancy, and Early Childhood (pp. 282–290)

15.4 Describe the sensory abilities and five primary reflexes found in newborns (p. 282).

15.5 Describe depth and other visual perceptual abilities of infants and identify one key source of information for infants (p. 283).

15.6 Discuss some physical, behavioral, and emotional changes that take place during the first 2 years of life; describe bonding (p. 285).

15.7 Discuss the influence of infant attractiveness and the importance of early parent-infant attachments (p. 286).

15.8 Discuss how inborn temperaments may influence personality development (p. 288).

SQ3R
- **Survey** to set goals for studying.
- Ask **questions** as you **read.**
- Stop occasionally to **recite** and **review.**

plus
- **Write** a summary of key points.
- **Reflect** on the hypotheses, evidence, and implications of this material and on the relevance it has to *your* life.

Donna and Peter Bell, and their neighbors BethAnn and Jim Green and Judy and Miguel Guerrera, each have a 4-year-old child, but the parents differ radically in their approaches to childhood education. Donna and Peter enrolled their daughter in a preschool that teaches 3- to 5-year-olds discipline and academic skills, and they expect her to attend a private school for gifted children in 2 or 3 years; after her 4-hour school day, she attends ballet classes. Donna and Peter argue that an accelerated education will provide their daughter with special advantages and help her become a more successful and capable adult.

In contrast, BethAnn and Jim Green believe that nature has set a timetable for childhood, and parents should not try to rush it. Accordingly, BethAnn and Jim expect the public school system to provide the early education that their child needs.

Like the Greens, Judy and Miguel Guerrera believe that childhood development occurs in stages set by nature. However, like the Bells, Judy and Miguel also believe that special education and other environmental influences will help their child realize his maximum potential. They enrolled their child in a preschool that emphasizes playful interaction among the students and is less achievement-oriented than the one the Bell's child attends. Judy and Miguel plan to send their son to a private school when he is 6 years old.

Which parents are helping their child the most? Will the Bell's child realize lifelong advantages because of her parents' efforts? Will the Greens' and the Guerreras' children find themselves saddled with disadvantages because their parents weren't "tough" enough on them?

Parents want their children to do well in school and ultimately in life. Often, however, they push them too fast and too far. According to David Elkind (1987), a well-known psychologist and professor of child development, this pushing can have adverse consequences. Elkind asserts that parents sometimes take a "superkid" approach to childrearing. They hurry their children, expecting them to think, feel, and act much older than they are. Elkind's ideas about hurried children are based on the recognition of individual differences among children and their abilities. Some develop slowly; others develop rapidly. Some are cognitively advanced; others are average or slow. In this chapter, we discuss the processes of human development as it occurs in richly diverse individuals.

Regardless of the technique used, most psychologists have a point of view; as each psychologist's view of child development is presented, the reasoning underlying each of these approaches is shown. We begin by looking at events that happened to each of us long before we can remember them.

The First 9 Months

Learning Objective 15.1
Discuss what developmental psychologists hope to discover through their research, and describe two common research methods.

Psychologists study development to find out how people change throughout their lives and to learn what causes those changes. They are especially interested in discovering whether the developing infant's abilities, interests, and personality are determined by *nature* (at or before birth) or by *nurture* (by their experiences after they are born). Separating biological from environmental causes of behavior is complicated, and the answer to any specific question about human behavior often involves the interaction of both nature and nurture.

To unravel the causes of behavior, psychologists adopt various methods and viewpoints in their study of development. Two widely used methods are the cross-sectional method and the longitudinal method. In the *cross-sectional* method, subjects of different ages are compared to determine whether they differ on some important dimension. In the *longitudinal method,* a single group of people is compared at different ages to determine whether changes have occurred over time. Each method has some problems, however. For example, the cross-sectional method suffers from the fact that the subjects' backgrounds (parents, family income, nutrition) differ and they may have learned various things in different ways. Further, the subjects' behavior or performance in a specific task or ability might

Figure 15.1

In *cross-sectional* research, subjects of different ages (for example, ages 2, 4, 6, and 8 years) are examined to determine whether they differ on some specific dimension. In *longitudinal* research, a single group of subjects is examined over time.

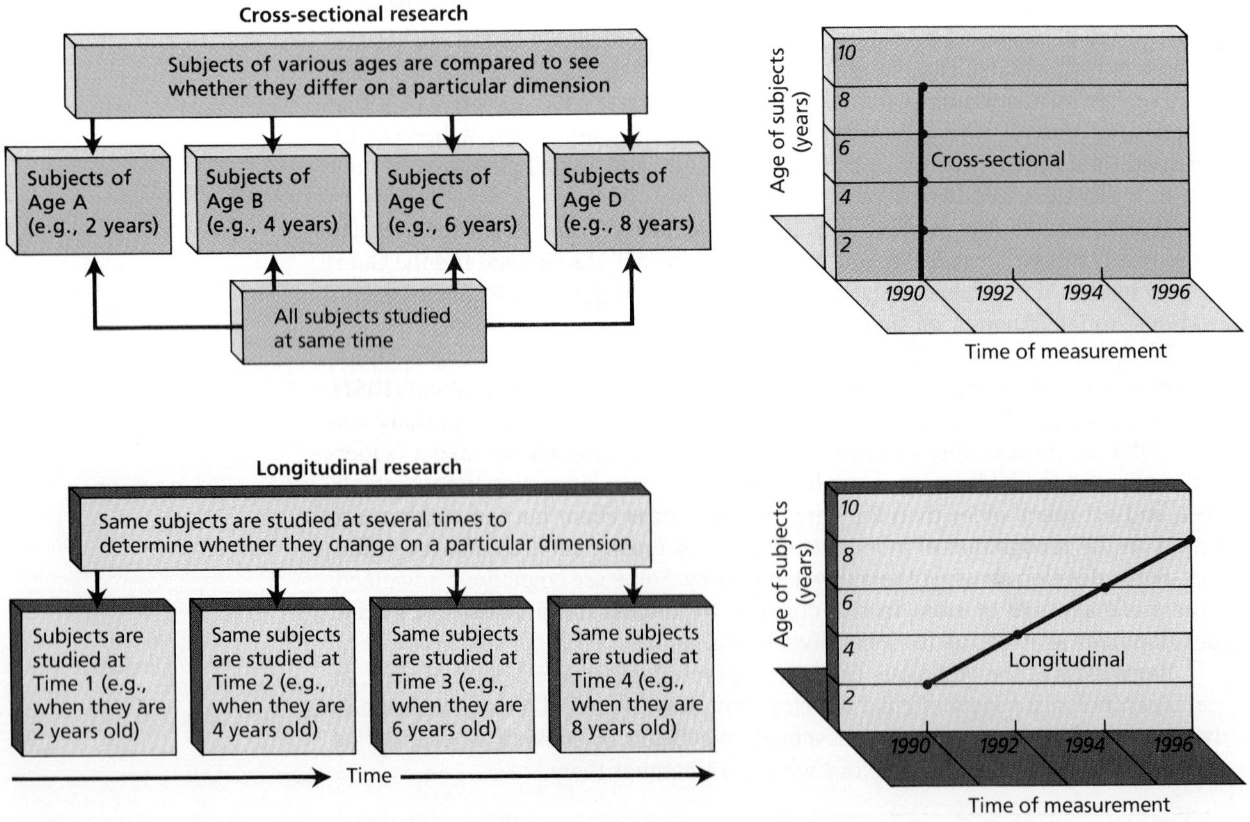

reflect their predisposition, liking of the task, or some other variable unrelated to changes due to development or aging. Using this method, individual differences are impossible to assess. The longitudinal method also has problems; it requires repeated access to the same subjects. Some subjects may move, withdraw from the study, even die. Also, after repeated testing on the same task (even though months or years apart), subjects may do better because of practice. Further, longitudinal research sometimes takes years to complete and there may be important changes in the environment and the social world of subjects; still further, it is time-consuming and expensive. See Figure 15.1 for a comparison of cross-sectional and longitudinal approaches.

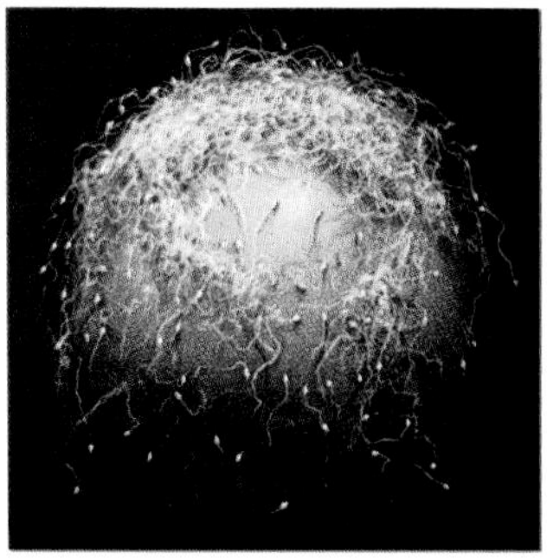

Conception occurs when an ovum and sperm join.

The Three Trimesters

Learning Objective 15.2 Describe human development during the prenatal stage of life.

Conception occurs when an ovum and a sperm join in the fallopian tube to form a **zygote,** or fertilized egg. During the next 5–7 days, the zygote descends through the Fallopian tube and implants itself in the blood-lined wall of the uterus. From that time until the 49th day after conception, the organism is an **embryo.** Then, from the eighth week until birth, the organism is a **fetus.** On the average, maturation and development take 266 days; for descriptive purposes, these 9 months are divided into three trimesters (3-month periods) (see Table 15.1).

The *first trimester* begins at conception. Within minutes after the zygote is formed, basic characteristics—including hair, skin, and eye color; sex (gender); likelihood of being tall or short, fat or lean; and perhaps basic intellectual gifts and personality traits—are established. Within 10 hours, the zygote divides into four cells. During the first week, about a dozen cells descend from the fallopian tube to the uterus, where they begin the process of *differentiation* (organs and parts of the body begin to form). Some cells form the *umbilical cord,* a group of blood vessels and tissues that connect the zygote to the placenta. The **placenta** is a mass of tissue in the uterus that acts as the life-support system for the fetus by supplying it with oxygen, food, and antibodies from the mother, and by eliminating wastes out to the mother. By the end of the first week, the developing organism is an embryo made up of as many as 100 cells that are attached to the wall of the uterus.

zygote: A fertilized egg.

embryo: [EM-bree-o] The term used to refer to the human organism from the 5th through the 49th day after conception.

fetus: The term used to refer to the human organism from the 49th day after the conception until birth.

placenta: [pluh-SENT-uh] A group of blood vessels and membranes in the uterus connected to a fetus by the umbilical cord and serving as the mechanism for the exchange of nutrients and waste products.

TABLE 15.1 General stages and age spans of development

Life stage	Approximate age
Prenatal period	
Zygote	Conception to Day 5 or 6
Embryo	Day 5 to Day 49
Fetus	Week 8 to birth
Postnatal period	
Infancy	Birth to age 2
Toddlerhood	Age 2 to 3
Early childhood	Age 3 to 6
Middle childhood	Age 6 to 12
Adolescence	Age 13 to 19
Young adulthood	Age 20 to 40
Middle adulthood	Age 40 to 65
Late adulthood	Age 65 on

By the time it is five to six weeks old, the embryo has begun to resemble a human being. The heart begins to beat at about four weeks.

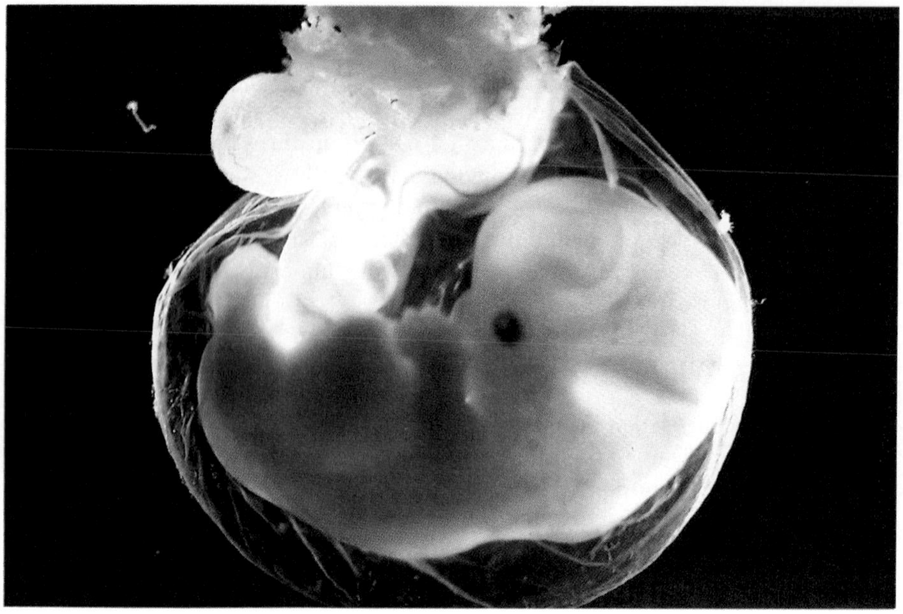

During the first month, the embryo begins to take shape. By the 25th day, a primitive version of the heart is beating. During the second month, the embryo begins to resemble a human being. Each day it grows about a millimeter, and new parts begin to take shape. In the third month, growth continues, features become more defined, and sex characteristics begin to appear. At the end of the third month, the fetus is about 3 inches long and weighs 1 ounce.

During the second 3 months, the *second trimester,* the fetus consumes a lot of food, oxygen, and water through the placenta, increasing in weight and strength. In the fourth month, it can be up to 10 inches long. In the early part of

By the fifth month, the fetus has a significant heartbeat and has begun to kick.

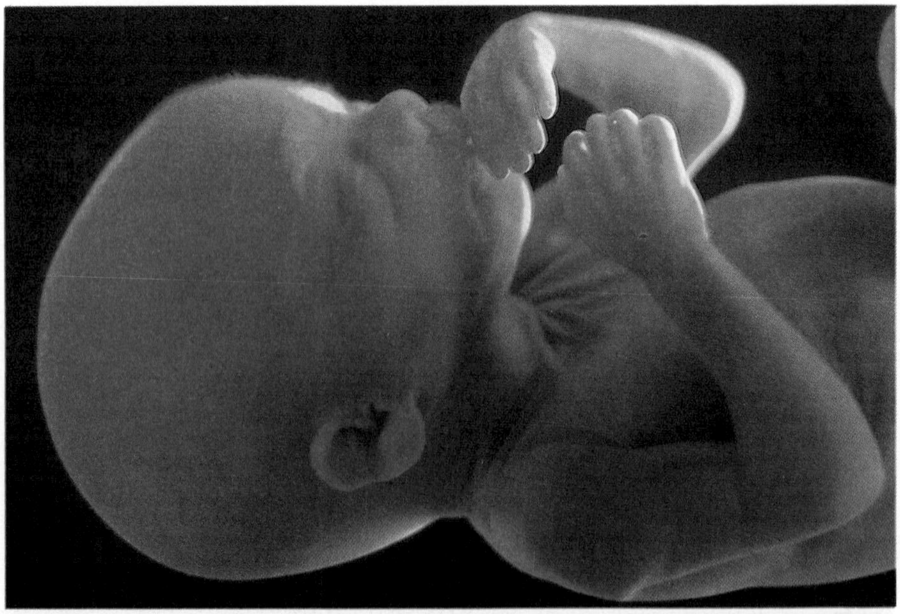

the fourth month, the mother may begin to feel the movement of the fetus. In the fifth and sixth months, the fetus grows about 2 inches per month. At the end of the second trimester (about 28 weeks), it is about 14 inches long, and its respiratory system is mature enough to enable it to live outside the uterus, increasing the chances of survival if it is born prematurely.

In the *last trimester*, the fetus gains weight rapidly—usually a pound in the seventh month, 2 pounds in the eighth, and a pound a week in the ninth. Its respiratory system and internal organs continue to develop, and the muscles mature significantly. The mother can feel strong kicking and movement. Table 15.2 summarizes the major physical developments during the prenatal period.

teratogen: [ter-AT-oh-jen] A substance that can produce developmental malformations in a fetus; such substances are *teratogenic* and have *teratogenic effects.*

Pregnancy and Birth: Early Influences

Learning Objective 15.3 Identify environmental factors that affect prenatal development, and consider the risks of ingesting teratogens during pregnancy.

People have long assumed that the behavior of a pregnant woman affected her unborn child's development. Medieval European doctors advised pregnant women that uplifting thoughts would help the baby develop into a good, happy person, while fright, despondency, and negative emotions might disrupt the pregnancy and possibly influence the infant to become sad or mean-spirited. Today, some pregnant women wear fetal belts that play soothing music to their unborn children, who can listen and thereby gain a benevolent perspective of the outside world.

While a fetus may not be affected by the mother's condition to the extent suggested by medieval doctors, it is known that from conception until birth, the environment and life-support systems provided by the mother influence the fetus. Environmental factors such as diet, infection, radiation, and drugs affect both the mother and the fetus. A **teratogen** is a substance that can produce developmental malformations in a fetus. For example, if the mother drinks alcoholic beverages

TABLE 15.2 Major developments during the prenatal period

Age	Size	Characteristics
1 week	150 cells	Ovum attaches to uterine lining.
2 weeks	several thousand cells	Placental circulation established.
3 weeks	1/10 inch	Heart and blood vessels begin to develop. Basics of brain and central nervous system form.
4 weeks	1/4 inch	Kidneys and digestive tract begin to form. Rudiments of ears, nose, eyes are present.
6 weeks	1/2 inch	Arms and legs develop. Jaws form around mouth.
8 weeks	1 inch, 1/30 oz.	Bones begin to develop in limbs. Sex organs begin to form.
12 weeks	3 inches, 1 oz.	Sex distinguished. Kidneys functioning, liver manufacturing red blood cells. Fetal movements.
16 weeks	6 1/2 inches, 4 oz.	Heartbeat may be detected by physician. Bones begin to calcify.
20 weeks	10 inches, 8 oz.	Mother feels movements.
24 weeks	12 inches, 1 1/2 lbs.	Vernix (white waxy substance) protects body. Eyes open, eyebrows and eyelashes form, skin wrinkled and red, respiratory system not mature enough to support life.
28 weeks	15 inches, 2 1/2 lbs.	Fully developed, but needs to gain in size, strength, and maturity of systems.
32 weeks	17 inches, 4 lbs.	Fat layer forms beneath skin to regulate body temperature.
36 weeks	19 inches, 6 lbs.	Settles into position for birth.
38 weeks	21 inches, 8 lbs.	Full term—266 days from conception.

in early and middle pregnancy, the baby is more likely to be born premature, to have a lower birth weight, and to suffer from mental retardation or hyperactivity (Streissguth, Barr, & Martin, 1983). One study showed that the use of more than 3 ounces of 100 proof liquor per day during pregnancy was significantly related to a small decrease in a 4-year-old's intelligence test scores (Streissguth, et al., 1989). Studies show that *any* drug can affect fetal development. The influence of drugs is especially important during the embryonic stage of development, when the mother may not realize that she is pregnant. Even a mother's mood during pregnancy or shortly thereafter *may* have an effect; one recent study (Dawsons, et al., 1991) showed that children of depressed mothers showed brainwave activity that was unusual. This study is just a first step in studying such relationships, and its results are likely to generate a great deal of debate and further research.

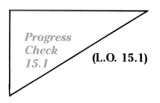

Progress Check 15.1

Complete the following sentences with one of the terms provided.

(L.O. 15.1) a. A developmental psychologist asks 3–7-year-olds, 8–11-year-olds, and 12–17-year-olds to describe their favorite hobby. The psychologist then compares the data to see whether there are any obvious differences in pastime interests among the different age groups. This psychologist is using a ________ research method. (cross-sectional / longitudinal)

(L.O. 15.2) b. In humans, conception generally occurs in ________. (the uterus / a Fallopian tube)

(L.O. 15.2) c. The umbilical cord and ________ can be thought of as providing a life-support system for the fetus. (placenta / uterus)

(L.O. 15.2) d. Basic characteristics such as hair color, height, and sex are established when the zygote ________ . (is formed / becomes an embryo)

(L.O. 15.2) e. The respiratory system of a fetus is mature enough by the end of the ________ that the child probably can continue living outside the uterus. (first trimester / 20th week / second trimester)

(L.O. 15.3) f. A study conducted in 1989 found a decrease in ________ 4-year-olds who were born to mothers who had consumed more than 3 ounces of alcohol per day during pregnancy. (active play among / the intelligence test scores of)

(L.O. 15.3) g. Alcohol or any other drug can have serious detrimental effects on the developing fetus ________. (only if they are taken in large doses / before the mother is even aware of being pregnant)

Newborns, Infancy, and Early Childhood

Learning Objective 15.4 Describe the sensory abilities and five primary reflexes found in newborns.

Babinski reflex: A reflex in which an infant projects its toes outward and up when the soles of its feet are touched.

Newborns are not nearly as helpless as many people believe. At birth, they can hear, see, smell, and respond to the environment in adaptive ways—in other words, they have good sensory systems. They also are directly affected by experience. Psychologists are interested in finding out how experience affects the perception of infants and children, to help them develop in optimal ways.

Newborns' Reflexes

Touch the palm of a newborn baby, and chances are you'll find one of your fingers in the surprisingly firm grip of a tiny fist. The baby is exhibiting a reflexive reaction. Babies are born with *primary reflexes,* that is, unlearned responses to stimuli.

TABLE 15.3 Newborn reflexes

Reflex	Stimulus	Response	Duration
Eye blink	Flash a light in infant's eyes	Closes both eyes	Permanent
Babinski	Gently stroke the side of the infant's foot	Flexes the big toe; fans out the other toes	Usually disappears near the end of the first year
Withdrawal reflex	Prick the sole of the infant's foot	Flexes leg	Present during the first 10 days; present but less intense later
Plantar	Press finger against the ball of the infant's foot	Curls all toes under	Disappears between 8 and 12 months
Moro reflex	Make a sudden loud sound	Extends arms and legs and then brings arms toward each other in a convulsive manner	Begins to decline in third month, gone by fifth month
Rooting reflex	Stroke cheek of infant lightly with finger or nipple	Turns head toward finger, opens mouth, and tries to suck	Disappears at approximately 3 to 4 months
Sucking response	Insert finger into the baby's mouth	Sucks rhythmically	Sucking often less intense and less regular during the first 3 to 4 days

These reflexes are innate; some help ensure the baby's survival, and most disappear over the course of the first year of life. One primary reflex exhibited by infants is the **Babinski reflex,** a projection of the toes outward and up in response to a touch to the sole of the foot. Another is the **Moro reflex,** an outstretching of the arms and legs and crying in response to a loud noise or change in the environment. Infants also exhibit the **rooting** reflex, in which they turn their head toward a stimulus (such as a breast, or hand) that touches their cheek. They show a **sucking** reflex in response to objects that touch their lips and a **grasping** reflex in response to an object touching the palms of their hands. Physicians use the presence or absence of primary reflexes at birth to assess neurological damage and to evaluate an infant's rate of development. Table 15.3 summarizes the primary reflexes and the ages at which they normally disappear.

At first, an infant's abilities and reflexes are biologically determined through genetic transmission. Gradually, learned responses such as reaching for desired objects or grasping a cup replace reflex reactions such as rooting. New experiences in the environment become more important in determining behavior. These complex interactions between nature and nurture follow a developmental time course that continues throughout life (see Table 15.4 on page 285).

Moro reflex: A reflex in which an infant outstretches its arms and legs and cries when there is a loud noise or abrupt change in the environment.

rooting: A reflex in which an infant turns its head toward a mild stimulus applied to its lips or cheeks.

sucking: A reflex in which an infant makes sucking motions when presented with a stimulus to the lips, such as a nipple.

grasping: A reflex in which an infant grasps vigorously any object touching its palm or fingers or placed in its hand.

Infants' Perceptual Systems

Learning Objective 15.5
Describe depth and other visual perceptual abilities of infants, and identify one key source of information for infants.

Visual Preferences. An avalanche of research on infant perception shows that newborns have surprisingly well-developed perceptual systems. Some of the early work on infant perception was done by Robert Fantz. Fantz designed a viewing box in which he placed infants and had a hidden observer or camera record their responses to stimuli (see Figure 15.2 on the next page). By showing infants various pictures of faces and patterns and recording their eye movements, he

Figure 15.2

Using a viewing box to observe newborns' eye movements, Fantz recorded the total time they spent looking at various patterns. He found that they looked at faces or patterned material much more often than at homogeneous fields. (Source: Fantz, 1961; photo by David Linton)

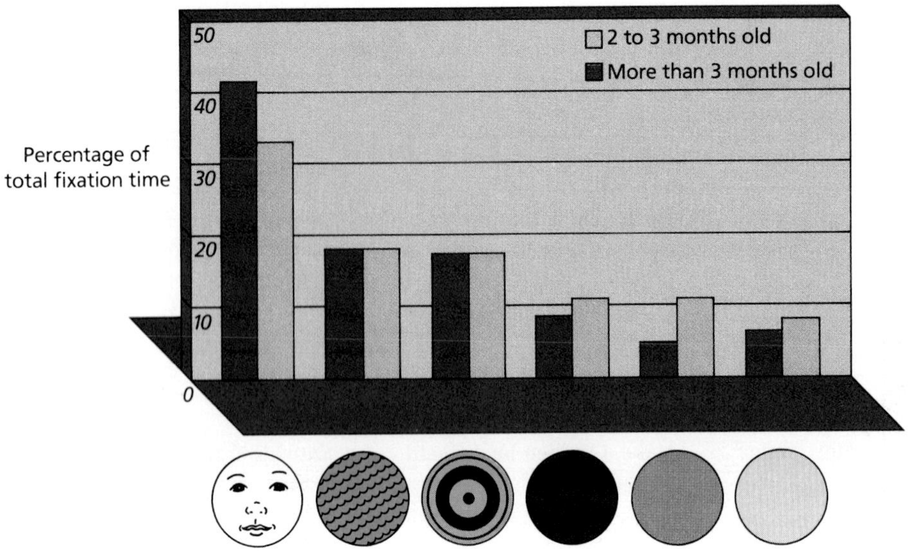

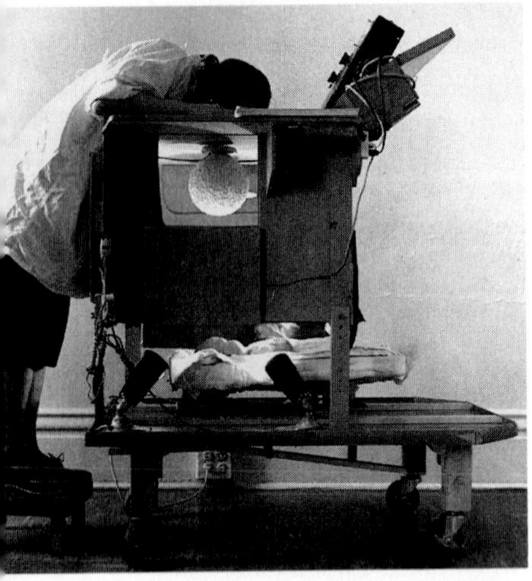

Fantz designed a viewing box which allowed him to record infants' responses to various types of visual stimuli.

Walk and Gibson's visual-cliff method tested whether infants of various ages possessed depth perception.

discovered the infants' visual preferences. He recorded how long and how often the infants looked at each picture and calculated the total time spent viewing each type of picture. Because they spent more time looking at pictures of faces than at random squiggles, Fantz concluded that they could see different patterns and that they preferred faces. They also prefer complex visual fields over simple ones, curved patterns over straight or angular ones, and human faces over random patterns or faces with mixed-up features (Haaf, Smith, & Smitley, 1983). We also know that babies respond to caregivers by imitating their facial gestures some of the time (Kaitz, Meschulach-Sorfaty, & Auerbach, 1988).

The Visual Cliff. One of the best-known developmental research studies was done by Walk and Gibson in 1961. They devised the *visual-cliff method* to determine the extent of infants' depth perception. The researcher places an infant on a glass surface, half of which is covered with a checkerboard pattern. The same pattern is placed several feet below the transparent half of the glass surface. Infants can crawl easily from the patterned area onto the transparent area. Infants who lack depth perception should be willing to crawl into the transparent side as often as onto the patterned side. Conversely, infants who have depth perception should refuse to crawl onto the transparent side, even when encouraged to do so by their mothers. Walk and Gibson found that infants who can crawl will show avoidance behavior, thus proving that they have depth perception. Interestingly, researchers have found that when the babies were uncertain about what to do at the visual cliff, they used their mother's facial expression to help them decide (Sorce, Emde, Campos, & Klinnert, 1985). If the mother looked fearful or angry, few babies crossed; if the mother smiled, most of the babies crossed. Sorce and his colleagues concluded that the mother's facial expression is a key source of information for infants. Babies are responsive to a mother's facial expression, and even to its attractiveness (Langlois, Roggman, & Rieser-Danner, 1990).

In sum, newborns enter the world with the ability to experience, respond to, and learn from the environment. In general, therefore, we can say that the sensory systems of newborns are well formed, but still developing. Babies develop in an order and on a rough timetable of developmental events during infancy and early childhood, the topics considered next.

TABLE 15.4 Perceptual-cognitive milestones of infants

First week:

- ◆ See patterns, light, dark
- ◆ Are sensitive to the location of sounds
- ◆ Can distinguish volume and pitch
- ◆ Prefer high voices
- ◆ Will grasp object if they touch it accidentally
- ◆ Stop sucking to look at a person momentarily

First month:

- ◆ Become excited at sight of person or toy
- ◆ Look at objects only if in their line of vision
- ◆ Prefer patterns to any color, brightness, or size
- ◆ Coordinate eyes sideways, up and down
- ◆ Can follow a toy from side to center of body

Second month:

- ◆ Prefer people to objects
- ◆ Stare at human face, become quiet to human voice
- ◆ Startle at sounds and make a facial response
- ◆ Reach out voluntarily instead of grasping reflexively
- ◆ Can perceive depth
- ◆ Can coordinate eye movements
- ◆ Discriminate voices, people, tastes, and objects

Third month:

- ◆ Follow moving object
- ◆ Glance from one object to another
- ◆ Distinguish near objects from distant ones
- ◆ Search with eyes for sound
- ◆ Become aware of self through exploration
- ◆ Show signs of memory

Four to 7 months:

- ◆ See world in color and with near-adult vision
- ◆ Can pull dangling objects toward self
- ◆ Follow dangling or moving objects
- ◆ Turn to follow sound, vanishing object
- ◆ Visually search out fast-moving or fallen objects
- ◆ Begin to anticipate a whole object by seeing only part
- ◆ Deliberately imitate sounds and movements
- ◆ Remember a segment representative of an entire situation
- ◆ Can recall short series of actions
- ◆ Look briefly for a toy that disappears

Eight to 12 months:

- ◆ Put small objects into and out of containers
- ◆ Search behind screen for an object if they see it hidden
- ◆ Can hold and manipulate one object while looking at a second
- ◆ Recognize dimensions of objects

One Year:

- ◆ Group objects by shape and color
- ◆ Have a clear perception of objects as detached and separate
- ◆ Can relate objects in time and space
- ◆ Search for object even if they have not seen it hidden
- ◆ Remember only where object was last seen
- ◆ Imitate absent models
- ◆ Solve simple problems

After Clarke-Stewart, Friedman, & Koch, 1985, p. 191.

Physical and Behavioral Changes: Infancy and Childhood

Learning Objective 15.6 Discuss some physical, behavioral, and emotional changes that take place during the first 2 years of life; describe bonding.

An infant who weighs $7\frac{1}{2}$ pounds at birth may weigh as much as 20 or 25 pounds by age 12 months. By age 18 months, the infant is usually walking and beginning to talk. For psychologists, infancy ends when the child begins to represent the world abstractly through language. Thus, *infancy* refers to the period from birth to age 18 months, and *childhood* is the period from 18 months to about age 13 years, the onset of adolescence.

In the minutes and hours immediately after birth, bonding occurs. **Bonding** is a special process of emotional attachment between parents and babies; it is

bonding: A special process of emotional attachment occurring between parent and child in the minutes and hours immediately after birth.

separation anxiety: The fear response in children from 8 to 15 months, displayed when a parent is absent.

neither a reflex nor a learned behavior, though some psychologists claim that it is inborn. Research has not especially supported claims for bonding, but many parents have welcomed the increased contact with their newborns that is reputed to facilitate bonding (Klaus & Kennell, 1983).

In the first weeks and months of life, the parent-infant attachment deepens as some of the infant's reflexes disappear and new behaviors appear. At about 4–8 weeks, infants may sleep for 4–6 hours during the night, uninterrupted by the need to eat (to the great relief of their weary parents). When awake, they smile at their mothers, stare intently at mobiles and other moving objects, listen attentively to human voices, and reach out to touch objects. At 4 months, they have greater control over head movements and posture, they can sit with support, and they play with toys for longer periods.

At about 7 months, infants begin to crawl, giving them more freedom to seek out favorite toys and people and to avoid threatening situations. The ability to crawl is accompanied by important changes in behavior. Infants now show strong preferences for their mothers or other caregivers. During the period from 8 to 15 months, attachment to the mother may become so strong that her departure from the room causes or the entry of strangers into the room will induce a fear response known as **separation anxiety.** Some researchers have found that infants who show strong attachment at this age tend to be more curious and self-directed later in life (Ainsworth, 1979).

At the end of the first and the beginning of the second year of life, children can walk, climb, and manipulate their environment—skills that often lead to the appearance of safety gates that block stairways, fasteners that lock cabinets, child-proof medicine bottles, and a variety of other safety features in the home. There is significant variability in the age at which a child begins to walk or climb; some babies mature early, while others are slow to develop these abilities. The age at which these specific behaviors occur seems unrelated to any other major developmental abilities. Figure 15.3 shows the major achievements in motor development for the first 15 months.

Emotional Changes

The extent to which infants focus on their caregivers increases significantly as they mature. Dialogues in the form of gestures, smiles, and vocalizations become more common. Mothers and fathers initiate these interactions as often as the infants do. This early play is stimulating for babies as long as the babies are not overstimulated and annoyed by too much tickling and excitement (Singer & Singer, 1990).

Interactions between parents and babies are important to the child's development. In an experiment in which mothers remained still and expressionless, their infants appeared sad and turned away from the mothers (Cohen & Tronick, 1983). The implication is that the mere presence of a parent is not enough; the parent must interact both physically and vocally with the infant (Sorce & Emde, 1981) and must pay attention to the infant (Jones & Raag, 1989). Table 15.5 on page 288 presents the approximate time at which various emotions emerge in infants.

Learning Objective 15.7 Discuss the influence of infant attractiveness and the importance of early parent-infant attachments.

Several important variables influence the type and amount of interaction between parents and infants. One is the baby's physical attractiveness, or cuteness; people judge especially beautiful babies as more competent, more likeable, and healthier than average or unattractive babies (Stephan & Langlois, 1984). They are more likely to play with, speak to, pinch, jiggle, or smile at attractive children. The baby's own behavior is also important; both are active participants in forming a relationship, an attachment.

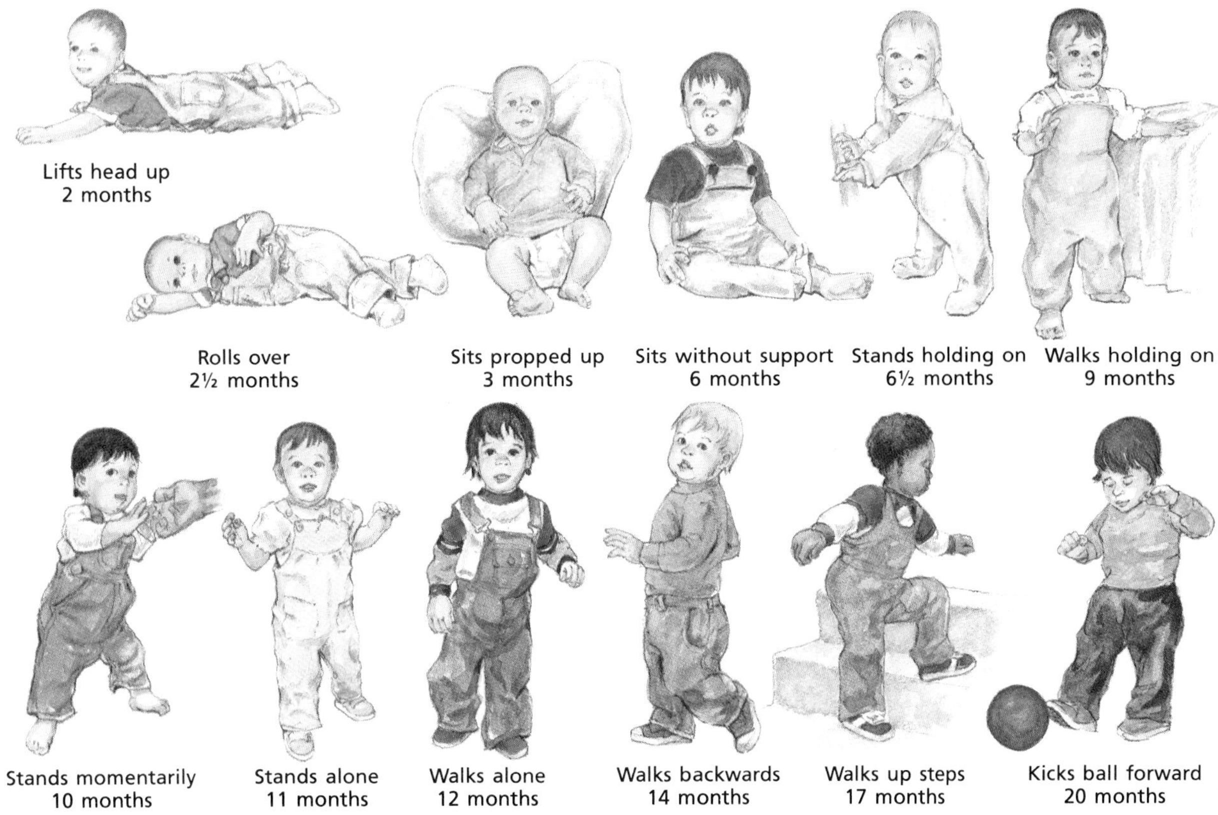

Figure 15.3

Of the 1036 normal Denver babies tested for motor skills in the Denver Development Screening Test, 50% had mastered them at the ages indicated. (Source: Frankenberg & Dodds, 1967)

Attachment

Some psychologists consider the establishment of a close and warm parent–child relationship one of the major accomplishments of the first year of life, and secure babies have mothers who are affectionate and especially responsive (Isabella, Belsky, & von Eye, 1989). Babies who are being cared for by those with whom they have close attachments are more likely to be happy (Singer & Singer, 1990). Experimental studies show that the quality and nature of the mutual closeness formed between newborns and their mothers can make a big difference in later life (Schwartz, 1983). Children who have not formed warm, close attachments early in life lack a sense of security and become anxious and overly dependent; as 6-year-olds, they are perceived as more aggressive and less competent than their more secure counterparts (Cohn, 1990). Those who have close attachments require less discipline and are less easily distracted from a task (Lewis & Feiring, 1989).

Once established, early attachment is fairly permanent. Brief separations from parents, as in child care centers, do not adversely affect it. Influential psychologists such as Mary Ainsworth (1979) assert that these early parental attachments affect the child's later friendships, relations with relatives, and any enduring adult relationship.

TABLE 15.5 Emergence of infants' emotional expressions

Emotions	Approximate age of emergence
Interest	Birth
Neonatal smile (a sort of half smile that appears spontaneously)	Birth
Distress	Birth
Disgust	Birth
Social smile	4–6 Weeks
Anger	3–4 Months
Surprise	3–4 Months
Sadness	3–4 Months
Fear	5–7 Months
Shame	6–8 Months
Guilt	Second year

Shyness and Temperament

Learning Objective 15.8 Discuss how inborn temperaments may influence personality development.

During the earliest months of life, some infants do smile or reach out to a new face and readily accept being held or cuddled; others are more inhibited. Still others exhibit extreme hesitation, even distress, in the presence of strangers. As adults, the xenophobic infants (those who fear strangers) are likely to be inhibited, meek, and wavering (Caspi, Elder, & Bem, 1988).

Some psychologists believe that each of us is born with a particular temperament: easygoing, willful, outgoing, shy, to name a few. Newborns, infants, and children, like the adults they will eventually grow to be, are all different from one another. Generalizations from one child to all children are impossible, and even generalizations from a sample of children must be made with caution. So many variables can affect a child's growth and development that researchers painstakingly try to separate all the important ones.

Many researchers contend that some specific personality traits, including shyness, are long-lasting. For example, Jerome Kagan and his colleagues found that 2- and 3-year-olds who were extremely cautious and shy tended to remain that way for 4 more years (the next age at which Kagan checked the same children) (Kagan, 1989; Kagan, Reznick, & Gibbons, 1990). They also found physiological evidence (increase in autonomic nervous system activity, for example) that these children may be less able to respond adaptively to change and unfamiliarity (Kagan, Reznick, & Snidman, 1987). Daniels and Plomin (1985) found adopted infants who had shy biological mothers showed significant signs of shyness at age 2 years. These findings, along with Kagan's and others (Broberg, Lamb, & Hwang, 1990), suggest that genetic factors also play a role in shyness. However, it is important to remember that shyness or any specific temperament can be changed; human behavior is the product of deliberative thought processes as well as biological or historical forces. Parents recognize that they affect a child's temperament and personality; that's why they often spend many hours talking with each other and with friends and relatives about childrearing practices. They assume that their childrearing practices will have important influences on development.

APPLYING PSYCHOLOGY

Fathers and Their Children

The American family is undergoing dramatic changes. During the past two decades, women have entered the work force in unprecedented numbers and in so doing have changed the shape, structure, and fabric of family life. Women are spending less time with their young children. Are fathers taking up the slack? Do fathers spend enough time with their children? Is it "quality" time?

Today's fathers are more interested in their newborns and may be involved in their children's upbringing from the first moments of the child's life, as evidenced by the fact that many more fathers are now present in the delivery room during their child's birth. They are affectionate and responsive caregivers. Two words often used in describing fathers' interactions with children are *quality* and *quantity.* Fathers sometimes assert that they spend limited time with their children, but that this time is quality time. Grossman, Pollack, and Golding (1988) looked at the quality and quantity of interactions between fathers and their firstborn 5-year-old children to determine whether this is true.

The researchers used 23 families participating in a Boston University pregnancy and parenthood project. They met with the parents during early pregnancy and within 2 weeks of the child's fifth birthday. On the first occasion, they measured a number of psychological, marital, and sociocultural variables. For example, they examined both the husband's and the wife's adaptation to life as an adult—their levels of anxiety, autonomy, marital adjustment, and age. At the 5-year follow-up, they measured both the quantity and the quality of time fathers spent with their children. To measure quantity, the father estimated the average amount of time he spent with his child on weekdays and weekends, with respect to both playtime and caregiving. To measure quality, the researchers had the subjects perform a task that involved both of the parents and the child in their home. The researchers recorded the quality of the interactions during play in terms of *warmth* (Was the parent critical or reinforcing?), *attention,* and *responsiveness.*

Quality and quantity of time were not directly related but were affected by numerous variables. Some fathers spent enormous amounts of time with their child, others very little. Some spent quality time; others did not. Men who had been well adjusted during their wife's pregnancy spent relatively more time with their 5-year-olds. Men who enjoyed and were involved in their work spent less time with their children. Interestingly, women played a key role in the amount of time fathers spent with their children. Self-sufficient and autonomous women tended to have husbands who spent less time with their children. These women tended to be very willing and able to do it all. (Of course, women who "do it all" may create situations that allow husbands to spend less time with their children.) On the quality issue, men who were happy, well-adjusted, and satisfied at work were supportive of their children and spent quality time with them. The same was true of men who valued their own independence.

A striking conclusion of the Grossman, Pollack, and Golding study is that the amount of time men spend with their children is directly affected by their wives. Men married to autonomous, self-sufficient, competent women spent less time with their children. The quality of their time seemed to be affected more by their own feelings of self-worth and adjustment. In sum, the quality and quantity of time men spend with their children cannot be analyzed in simple terms because it is affected by personal psychological variables as well as by marital factors and even the gender of the child (Ross & Taylor, 1989). Parents' interactions with their children must be described in the context of family relationships. There are still unanswered questions: Do some types of men marry autonomous women because they want little to do with their children? Why is it that their wives' autonomy keeps men from spending time with their children? Do the children seek out the more autonomous parent? The research continues.

- ***In formulating their research hypothesis, what did the scientists in this study want to learn?***
- ***What evidence did the researchers use to conclude that the quality and quantity of time spent with children depend on a number of different interrelated variables?***
- ***Do the researchers present enough evidence to allow the conclusion that fathers are spending enough quality time with their children and that quality makes up for quantity?***

Progress Check 15.2

Complete the following sentences with one of the terms provided.

(L.O. 15.4) a. At birth, the sensory abilities of newborns are ________. (fairly primitive / well developed)

(L.O. 15.4) b. When the soles of a newborn's feet are touched, the baby projects its toes outward and up because of a primary reflex known as the ________ reflex. (Moro / Babinski)

(L.O. 15.4) c. Most of the primary reflexes usually disappear by the age of ________ months and are replaced by learned behaviors. (6 / 9 / 12)

(L.O. 15.5) d. Newborns prefer to gaze at ________ visual fields. (simple / complex)

(L.O. 15.5) e. By using the ________ method, Walk and Gibson demonstrated that infants have depth perception at least by the time they have learned to crawl. (viewing box / sink-or-swim / visual cliff)

(L.O. 15.5) f. Babies who are old enough to crawl ________ their mothers' facial expressions. (do not yet understand / make decisions based on)

(L.O. 15.6) g. Psychologists say that infancy ends when a child ________. (begins to walk / begins to use language / is fully potty trained)

(L.O. 15.6) h. Infants begin to crawl at about ________ months. (4 / 7 / 10)

(L.O. 15.6) i. Some researchers have shown that infants who show separation anxiety in the first year of life tend to be more ________ later in life. (passive and dependent / curious and self-directed)

(L.O. 15.7) j. Bonding refers to a ________ that occurs between parents and babies in the minutes and hours immediately after birth. (secondary reflex / process of emotional attachment)

(L.O. 15.7) k. One important factor that influences the type and amount of interaction between parents and infants is ________. (who initiates the interaction / the physical attractiveness of the infant)

(L.O. 15.7) l. Close attachments between infant and parent are important because this early relationship influences other relationships ________. (for the first 7 years of life / throughout one's life)

(L.O. 15.8) m. Research concerning personality traits such as shyness indicate that ________ contribute to their development. (genetics and childrearing practices / an imbalance in hormones)

Module Summary

The First 9 Months

- Psychologists are especially interested in discovering whether a developing infant's abilities, interests, and personality are determined by *nature* (i.e., at or before birth) or by *nurture* (i.e., by their experiences after they are born) (p. 278).
- From the 5th through the 40th day after conception, an unborn human being is called an embryo; from then until birth, it is called a fetus. Throughout pregnancy, the umbilical cord and placenta serve as a mechanism for the exchange of nutrients and waste products (p. 279).
- During the first month, the embryo begins to take shape. During the second month, the embryo begins to resemble a human being. In the third month, growth continues, features become more defined, and sex characteristics begin to appear. During the second three months, the fetus consumes food, oxygen, and water through the placenta, increasing in weight and strength. In the fifth and sixth months, the fetus grows about 2 inches per month. In the last trimester, the fetus gains weight rapidly—usually a pound in the seventh month, 2 pounds in the eighth, and a pound a week in the ninth (p. 280).

Newborns, Infancy, and Early Childhood

- In a full-term baby, the sensory, motor, respiratory, and circulatory systems are fully functional. Human infants are born with a set of reflexes that include the rooting, sucking, Babinski, and Moro reflexes (p. 282).
- Newborns have surprisingly well-developed perceptual systems. They prefer complex visual fields over simple ones, curved patterns over straight or angular ones, and human faces over random patterns or faces with mixed-up features. Their nervous systems, however, will be further developed by experience (p. 283).
- *Infancy* refers to the period from birth to about 18 months, and *childhood* is the period from 18 months to about age 13 years, the onset of adolescence (p. 285).

KEY TERMS

Babinski reflex, p. 282
bonding, p. 286
embryo, p. 279
fetus, p. 279
grasping, p. 283
Moro reflex, p. 283
placenta, p. 279
rooting, p. 283
separation anxiety, p. 286
sucking, p. 283
teratogen, p. 281
zygote, p. 279

SELF-TEST

Module 15

- Before taking the self-test, **recite** and **review.**
- Use the key at the back of the text to *correct* your answers.
- *Restudy* pages that correspond to any questions you answered incorrectly.

1. Which of the following is considered a disadvantage of the *cross-sectional* research method?
   a. The subjects' backgrounds often differ significantly with regard to things such as family, economic status, education, and nutrition.
   b. The subjects may do better on tasks required in the study because of repeated practice.
   c. Some of the subjects may move, withdraw from the study, or even die.
   d. Such studies are often time-consuming and expensive because they can take years to complete.
2. A primitive version of the heart begins beating in the fetus at about the ________ day after conception.
   a. 25th
   b. 47th
   c. 60th
   d. 266th
3. Human mothers generally begin to feel their unborn babies moving in the early part of the ________ month.
   a. third
   b. fourth
   c. fifth
   d. sixth
4. The use of alcohol, other drugs, or other teratogens can be especially harmful to the developing child if consumed in the ________ of pregnancy.
   a. first 8 weeks of pregnancy
   b. middle to end of the first trimester
   c. second trimester
   d. third trimester
5. Two adaptive primary reflexes that contribute to a newborn's eating behavior are
   a. sucking and rooting.
   b. sucking and the Babinski reflex.
   c. grasping and rooting.
   d. rooting and the Moro reflex.
6. Fantz measured infants' visual preferences by
   a. asking mothers to report on what captures their babies' attention.
   b. placing babies in a viewing box and recording how long and how often they gazed at various visual patterns.
   c. putting babies on a visual cliff and recording the direction of their crawling.
   d. observing infants as they crawled freely in a room wallpapered with all kinds of pictures, patterns, and designs.
7. When considering the age at which children develop motor skills such as crawling, walking, and climbing, we can say that
   a. most children learn to climb before they learn to crawl.
   b. there is significant variability from child to child.
   c. parents should be concerned if their child is developing a month or 2 behind the average child.
   d. psychologists can use this information to predict how other abilities, such as language and intelligence, will develop.

8. Researchers have shown that normal emotional development in infants
   a. will occur as long as the parent is available and not abusive.
   b. cannot occur if the child experiences separation anxiety.
   c. requires the parent to pay attention and to interact physically and vocally with the infant.
   d. is undefinable because of the extreme variability in ages and types of emotions expressed during the first 2 years of life.
9. Which statement accurately describes early parent–child attachment?
   a. Brief separations, such as those created by leaving a child in a child care center, erode the parent–infant bond.
   b. Babies who feel secure in the first year of life tend to have an easier time with development later in life.
   c. When a close attachment is formed early in life, the child is likely to become overly dependent.
   d. Children who have close attachments tend to be aggressive and easily distracted.
10. Personality traits such as shyness are
    a. genetically determined and therefore not subject to change.
    b. learned in the first 6 months of life.
    c. short-term traits that usually disappear before the age of 3 years.
    d. the products of biological, historical, and environmental factors.

Module 16

Children's Intellectual, Moral, and Social Development

LEARNING OBJECTIVES

When you have mastered the material in this module, you will be able to

Intellectual Development (pp. 296–302)

16.1 Identify two strengths of Piaget's theory and explain the role of assimilation and accommodation in intellectual development (p. 296).

16.2 Name and describe Piaget's four stages of intellectual development (p. 296).

16.3 Describe what children need from parents for optimal intellectual and social development (p. 301).

16.4 Describe language development from birth to age 6 years (p. 301).

Moral Reasoning (pp. 302–305)

16.5 Discuss Piaget's and Kohlberg's views regarding the development of moral reasoning (p. 302).

16.6 Discuss Carol Gilligan's findings regarding moral reasoning and gender differences (p. 304).

16.7 Discuss how adults can help children to develop a mature sense of morality and state the benefits of having strong moral reasoning skills (p. 305).

Social Development (pp. 306–310)

16.8 Describe the nature of social interactions, sharing, and play in children (p. 306).

16.9 Characterize single-parent families (p. 308).

16.10 Discuss the research concerning the effects of child care on emotional, social, and intellectual development (p. 308).

16.11 Discuss what is currently known about the effects of latchkey child care arrangements (p. 310).

SQ3R
- ▲ **Survey** to set goals for studying.
- ▲ Ask **questions** as you **read.**
- ▲ Stop occasionally to **recite** and **review.**

plus
- ▲ **Write** a summary of key points.
- ▲ **Reflect** on the hypotheses, evidence, and implications of this material and on the relevance it has to *your* life.

Ron Clement is a friend of ours. He had never been much of a conformist. In fact, as he matured into adulthood, he found it rather rewarding to do the less obvious, and even the shocking. However, he was about to take on something bigger than he had ever done before. Ron was about to become a father and a househusband. He had decided that he would raise his soon-to-be-born child while his wife continued working.

In characteristic style, Ron announced to his wife that he would become father of the year and stay home for the next few years—until Sarah or Josh (depending on whether the baby was a girl or boy) was launched into a school setting. He argued that his child would have to be brought up properly and that to optimize his or her development, he was going to stay home with the baby. Their friends thought it was a great idea but that Ron was nuts—giving up his job had serious economic consequences. Ron's mother argued that he didn't know how to care for a child. He responded by indicating that his wife didn't know either.

With all of the passion and perhaps naïvete of a new father, Ron Clement declared that his child would be brought up in a loving, caring, intellectually stimulating home. He, like many parents before him, was going to enhance this child's development. He asserted, to anyone who would listen, that nobody would be able to do it the way he could. He had taken courses in child and developmental psychology in college, and he felt that he could meet the challenge. If it took being a househusband, so be it.

There are not many men like Ron Clement. Few men (and increasingly fewer women) are willing to give up active careers to pursue child-care activities. Nonetheless, Ron and his wife recognized that for optimum development, a child needs a great deal of loving care, attention, and thought. They sought to give their new child every opportunity, every chance to become everything that it might. They knew that Sarah or Josh was going to be the product of their genetics, their home and community environment, and a little luck. They knew that they would be providing good genes to their baby. They hoped that they'd have good fortune and their baby would be born healthy. The other important element in the equation was going to be a good environment.

The Clements will have quite a story to tell their child when he or she is grown about their househusband dad. They will recount how few men were as actively involved in raising their children. They will also probably tell their son or daughter stories about their own youth, stories that they hope will help shape and mold their child, especially the child's intellectual, moral, and social development.

Intellectual Development

Learning Objective 16.1
Identify two strengths of Piaget's theory, and explain the role of assimilation and accommodation in intellectual development.

Why do some automobiles have childproof locks and windows? Why do parents use both gates to guard stairs and gadgets to keep kitchen cabinets closed? Why are young children's toys made so that small parts cannot come off? The answer: Children are curious, inquisitive, and much more intelligent than many people give them credit for being.

Children are continually developing intellectually; the changes they experience center on their ability to cope with an ever-expanding world. Older children can determine the difference between external versus internal causes of behavior more easily than younger children. Much of this difference is intellectually based (Miller & Aloise, 1989). The noted Swiss psychologist Jean Piaget (1892–1980) believed that the fundamental development of all intellectual abilities takes place during the first 2 years of life; many psychologists and educators agree. Piaget's theory focuses on *how* people think (thought processes) instead of on *what* they think (content), making it applicable to people in all societies and cultures. However, perhaps Piaget's greatest strength is his description of how a person's inherited capacities interact with the environment to produce an intellectually functioning child and adult.

assimilation: According to Jean Piaget, the process by which new concepts and experiences are incorporated into existing mental frameworks so as to be used in a meaningful way.

accommodation: According to Jean Piaget, the process by which new concepts and experiences modify existing cognitive structures and behaviors.

sensorimotor stage: The first of Piaget's four major stages of intellectual development, covering roughly the first 2 years of life. During this period, the child begins to interact with the environment, and the rudiments of intelligence are established.

According to Piaget, both children and adults use two processes to deal with new ideas. One is **assimilation,** in which the person absorbs new ideas and experiences, incorporates them into existing cognitive structures (thought processes) and behaviors, and uses them later in similar situations. The second is **accommodation,** the process of modifying previously developed cognitive structures and behaviors so as to adapt them to a new concept.

For example, a child who learns to grasp a spoon, demonstrates assimilation by later grasping similar objects, such as forks, crayons, and sticks. This assimilated behavior then serves as a foundation for accommodation. The child can learn the new, more complex behavior of grasping a sphere (such as a ball) by modifying her earlier response and widening her grasp. People accommodate new information every day by learning new vocabulary and then assimilating it by using it in their language, only to be confronted with more new information. The two processes alternate in a never-ending cycle of intellectual and behavioral growth. Assimilation and accommodation occur throughout Piaget's four stages of development. Figure 16.1 shows activities typical of each stage.

Piaget's Four Stages

Learning Objective 16.2
Name and describe Piaget's four stages of intellectual development.

Stages are central to Piaget's theory. Piaget believed that just as standing must precede walking, some stages of intellectual development must precede others. For example, if a parent presents an idea that it too advanced, the child will not understand the new concept, and no real learning will take place. A 4-year-old who asks how babies are made will probably not understand his mother's biologically accurate explanation and will not learn or remember it. If the same child asks the question a few years later, the explanation will be more meaningful and more likely to be remembered. Piaget's stages are associated with approximate ages and in his views are biologically determined. Piaget's theory brings the biological component of behavior into sharp focus. Although he acknowledges the role of environmental influences, Piaget clearly has a strong biological bias, especially in referring to stages of development.

The Sensorimotor Stage. Piaget considered the **sensorimotor stage,** which extends from birth to about age 2 years, to be the most important because the foundation for all intellectual development is established during this period. At age 2 months, infants develop rudimentary memory for past events and predict future visual events (Haith & McCarty, 1990). According to Piaget, the acquisition of memory is a crucial foundation for further intellectual development.

By the age of 6–8 months, children seek new and more interesting kinds of stimulation. They can sit up and crawl. No longer willing just to watch what goes on around them, they begin to manipulate their environment, attempting what Piaget called "making interesting sights last." At about 8 months, children begin to develop a sense of their own intentions, and they attempt to overcome obstacles to reach goals. They can now crawl to the other side of a room to where the cat is lying or follow their mothers into the next room.

From about 9 months on, children develop *object permanence,* the ability to realize that objects continue to exist even when they are out of sight. Prior to object permanence, when a mother leaves the room and the child can't see or hear her, she no longer exists. After object permanence develops, the baby realizes that she is just out of view. Various aspects of object permanence evolve gradually throughout the sensorimotor stage (see Figure 16.2 on the next page).

In the second half of the sensorimotor stage (from about 12 to 24 months), children begin to walk, talk, and use simple forms of logic. Object permanence is more fully developed; the child can now follow a ball that rolls away and can search for her mother after she has left the room. Children also begin to use language to represent the world, an ability that takes them beyond the concrete world of visual imagery.

Throughout the sensorimotor stage, few demands are made on the child. Self-centeredness, or **egocentrism,** shapes all behavior, and the child is unable to understand that the world does not exist solely to satisfy his or her interests and needs. Children who are egocentric respond to questions such as "Why does it

Piaget studied thought processes in both children and adults, but his focus was on early intellectual development.

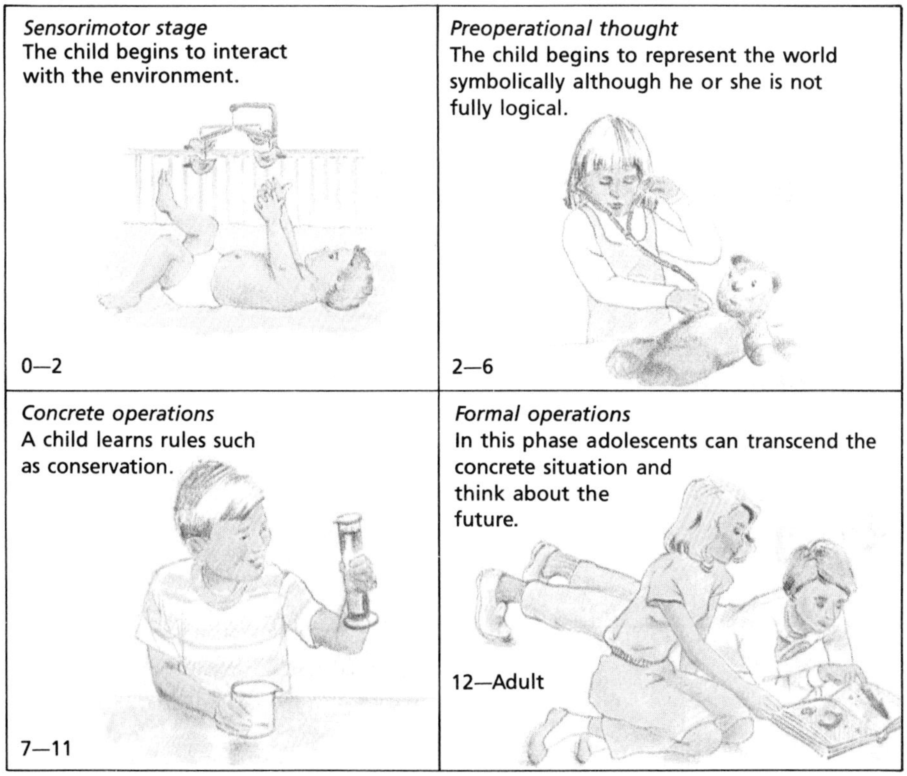

Sensorimotor stage
The child begins to interact with the environment.
0–2
Preoperational thought
The child begins to represent the world symbolically although he or she is not fully logical.
2–6
Concrete operations
A child learns rules such as conservation.
7–11
Formal operations
In this phase adolescents can transcend the concrete situation and think about the future.
12—Adult

Figure 16.1

Piaget's stages of intellectual development.

egocentrism: [ee-go-SENT-trism] The inability to perceive a situation or event except in relation to oneself; a characteristic of the sensorimotor stage. In infancy, it is the attitude that directs all concerns and behaviors to personal interests and needs.

decentration: The process, beginning at about age 2 years, of changing from a totally self-oriented point of view to one that recognizes other people's feelings, ideas, and viewpoints.

preoperational stage: Piaget's second major stage of intellectual development, lasting from about age 2 years to age 7, when initial symbolic thought is developed.

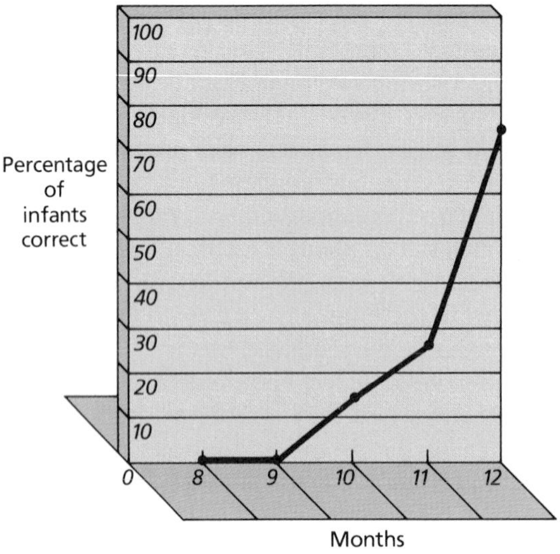

Figure 16.2

Object permanence is the ability to know that an object continues to exist even when out of view. Research shows that the ability to remember the location of an object that is subsequently hidden improves over time. Most 1-year-olds can remember where an object has been hidden even after a delay of 7 seconds. (Adapted from Fox, N., Kagan, J. & Weiskopf, S. The growth of memory during infancy. *Genetic Psychology Monograms* 99 (1979): 99–130. Reprinted with permission of the Helen Dwight Reid Educational Foundation. Published by Heldref Publications, 4000 Albemarle St., N. W., Washington, D.C. 20016. Copyright © 1979.)

snow?" with answers such as, "So I can play in it." For the next few years, the child will be unable to see situations from the point of view of another person. Children cannot usually put themselves in their mother's (or anyone else's) position.

The Preoperational Stage. At the end of Piaget's sensorimotor stage, children are just beginning to understand the difference between their interests and those of others. This process of **decentration** continues for several years. Simultaneously, children may also become manipulative, difficult to deal with, and belligerent. Parents often describe this stage as the terrible twos, characterized by the appearance of the ever-popular word "No!" The child's behavior vacillates between charming and awful. This vacillation and annoying new habits, such as being difficult to dress and bathe, are signs of normal development and mark the beginning of the stage of preoperational thought.

In the **preoperational stage,** which lasts from about age 2 years to age 6 or

According to Piaget, children develop object permanence at about nine months of age. At this stage they begin to understand that objects may be out of sight yet still exist.

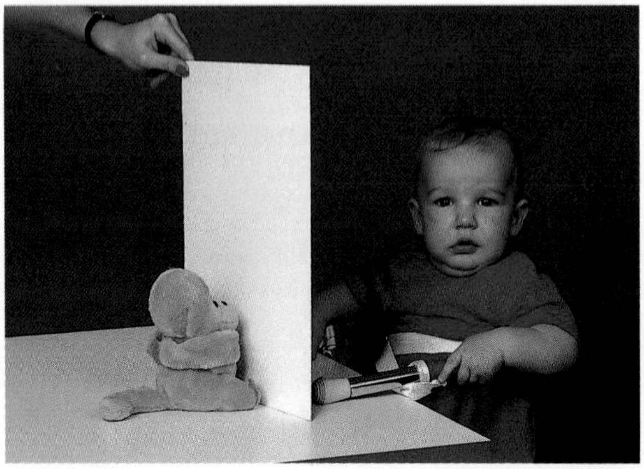

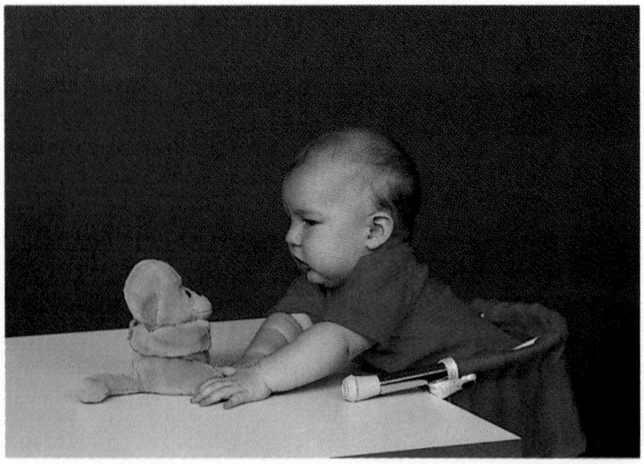

7, children begin to represent the world symbolically. As preschoolers, they play with objects in new ways and try, through let's-pretend games, to represent reality. Nonetheless, they remain somewhat egocentric, continue to think concretely, and cannot deal with abstract thoughts that are not easily represented. They make few attempts to make their speech more intelligible or to justify their reasoning, and they may develop behavior problems such as inattentiveness, belligerence, or temper tantrums. During this stage, adults begin to teach children how to interact with others, but major social and intellectual changes will not become fully apparent until the next stage of development.

The Stage of Concrete Operations. According to Piaget, the preoperational stage is followed by the **concrete operational stage,** which lasts from about age 7 years to age 11. Children in this stage attend school, have friends, can take care of themselves, and may take on many household responsibilities. They can look at a situation from more than one viewpoint and evaluate different aspects of it. This allows more complicated ways of thinking about situations and objects. The child has gained sufficient mental maturity to be able to distinguish between appearances and reality, as well as to think ahead one or two moves in checkers or other games. During this stage, children discover constancy in the world; they discover rules and understand the reasons for them. For example, a child learns to wear a raincoat on a cloudy morning, anticipating rain later in the day.

The hallmark of this stage is **conservation,** the ability to recognize that objects may be transformed visually or physically, yet still represent the same amount of weight or volume. This concept has been the subject of considerable research. In a typical conservation task, a child is shown two beakers. One beaker is short, squat, and half full of water; the other is tall, thin, and empty (see Figure 16.3). The experimenter pours the water from the short, squat beaker into the tall, narrow one and asks the child, "Which beaker has more water, the first or the second?" A child who does not understand the principles of conservation will claim that the taller beaker contains more water. A child who is able to conserve volume will recognize that the same amount of water was in both beakers and that therefore the amount in both is equal. A child who has mastered one type of conservation (e.g., conservation of volume) often cannot immediately transfer that knowledge to other conservation tasks (e.g., those involving weight).

Intellectual abilities continue to develop as a child matures, and slowly, in different ways, children grasp new and ever-more-difficult concepts (Flavell, Green, & Flavell, 1989). The development of conservation, in fact, is a necessary prelude to the fourth and final stage of intellectual development, the stage of formal operations.

The Stage of Formal Operations. Piaget's final stage of intellectual development, which starts at about age 12 years, is the **formal operational stage.** Unlike concrete-operational-stage children, whose thought is still tied to immediate situa-

concrete operational stage: Piaget's third stage of development, lasting from approximately ages 7 to 11 years. During this stage, the child develops the ability to understand constant factors in the environment, rules, and higher-order symbolism (such as arithmetic and geography).

conservation: The ability to recognize that something that is changed in some way (such as the "shape" of liquid in a container) still has the same weight, substance, or volume.

formal operational stage: Piaget's fourth and final stage of intellectual development, beginning at about age 12, when the individual can think hypothetically, can consider all future possibilities, and is capable of deductive logic.

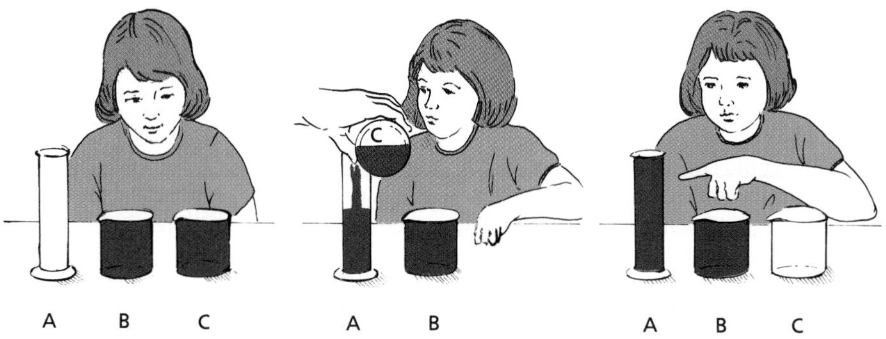

Figure 16.3

Conservation is the ability to recognize that an object remains the same object regardless of any changes it undergoes, such as a change in shape. When the contents of C are poured into A, young children, who have not yet learned the principle of conservation, will indicate that there is more water in A than in B.

UNDERSTANDING THE RESEARCH PROCESS

Did Project Head Start Work?

Project Head Start was initiated in the 1960s in an effort to break the poverty cycle by raising the social and educational competency of disadvantaged preschool children. Head Start has received federal support for more than two decades and is often referred to as a milestone in psychology. The multimillion-dollar project showed what can be done to provide remedial education, equal education, and proactive use of child development techniques, but did it really work?

During the past 30 years, there have been many reports documenting the success of Head Start. Preschool children score sharply higher at the end of their Head Start year than they did at the beginning (Haskins, 1989). Lee, Schnur, and Brooks-Gunn (1988) questioned whether Head Start actually closed the gap for disadvantaged children. Did it put them on an equal footing with other children?

The investigators reanalyzed the data from Head Start, focusing on intellectual differences. They compared gains made by three groups of economically disadvantaged children: (1) students in Head Start, (2) students who attended no preschool program, and (3) students who attended another preschool program. More than 78% of the 900 participants were members of ethnic minority groups. The aim was to determine whether the Head Start students made gains, and if so, whether those gains were equal to or better than those made by other students from low-income families.

The analysis showed clearly that children enrolled in Head Start programs made important gains and had an advantage over children who did not attend preschool and even over children who attended another preschool program.

However, although they made significant gains in cognitive abilities, Head Start children still did not do as well as children from advantaged homes. Head Start did not close the gap. Why? One reason is that Head Start children tended to be especially disadvantaged, even compared with other disadvantaged groups. The researchers suggest that 1 year of Head Start may not be enough to close the gap. They argue that their data should be seen "as a mandate for enhancing the program, suggesting that a second year would be likely to magnify and solidify the Head Start advantage" (Lee et al., 1988, p. 220).

Today, Head Start enrolls about 450,000 children, most of them from the neediest families—mostly black and from the lower socioeconomic classes. As children from other racial minorities and from single-parent homes enter the program, different kinds of gains may be seen. Socioeconomic class is a critical determinant in school success (Duyme, 1988). Many psychologists consider it imperative that programs such as Head Start and follow-up programs be expanded and funded at higher levels so that they may reach out to a wider community. For example, the school breakfast program that provides nutritious meals for low-income children also produces increases in academic performance (Meyers et al., 1989). As Zigler (1987) has written, "We simply cannot inoculate children in one year against the ravages of a life of deprivation" (p. 258). It is essential that economically disadvantaged children be given an equal educational start in life so that they are affected not only at the time of the intervention, but also throughout their childhood years (Woodhead, 1988).

- ▲ ***Identify the fundamental question that the researchers asked about Head Start.***
- ▲ ***What was the evidence that the researchers in this study used to show that Head Start is a worthwhile program?***
- ▲ ***What are some of the implications of the data from this study of Head Start children for social and educational policy in the United States?***

tions, adolescents can engage in abstract thought. They do this by forming hypotheses that allow them to think of different ways to represent situations, organizing them into all possible relationships and outcomes. Adolescents' intellectual worlds are full of informal theories of logic and ideas about themselves and life (Flavell, 1963). By age 12, the egocentrism of the sensorimotor and preoperational stages has, for the most part, disappeared. A summary of some important points about Piaget's theory is presented in Table 16.1.

TABLE 16.1

Important points about Piaget's theory
▲ Cognitive development is a process in which each stage builds on the previous one.
▲ The egocentrism of infants is reduced over a period of several years through the process of decentration.
▲ The exact age at which each stage of development appears differs from one child to another, but all children in all societies go through the same stages.
▲ The actual content of children's thoughts is less important to psychologists than the nature of their thinking. By discovering how children think, psychologists can find ways to facilitate learning.

Learning Objective 16.3
Describe what children need from parents for optimal intellectual and social development.

Implications and Criticisms of Piaget's Theory. Parents, educators, and psychologists can enhance children's intellectual development by understanding how cognitive abilities develop. For example, Piaget recognized that parental love and interaction are always important to a child's development, but he asserted that they are *essential* in the first 2 years of life. He also stressed the importance of providing a great deal of physical and intellectual stimulation, especially stimuli that move and change color, shape, and form.

While acknowledging that it is possible to accelerate children's development, Piaget emphasized that children should not be pushed too fast. Parents serve their children best by providing intellectual stimulation that is appropriate to their current developmental level. David Elkind (mentioned in Module 15) supports this view in his book *The Hurried Child* (1981b), in which he argues that overacceleration ultimately has deleterious effects. He holds that the real business of a preschooler is socialization, not education.

Piaget has not gone unchallenged, and researcher such as Rene Baillargeon assert that Piaget underestimated the abilities of infants. She holds that the infant abilities Piaget saw at 18 months, researchers now find evident at 6 months of age (e.g., Baillargeon & Garber, 1989; Miller & Baillargeon, 1990). We now know that cognitive maturity is impressive in 2-year-olds. Can such maturity, along with social maturity, be enhanced? Can the competency of young children be given a push, a leg-up, a head start? In the 1960s, the federal government thought it could, and as you will see in the Understanding the Research Process box on the facing page, the psychologists who advised the government were correct.

Language Development

Learning Objective 16.4
Describe language development from birth to age 6 years.

One of the most important aspects of children's development is the acquisition of language. Young children have ways of communicating their desires and needs nonverbally through facial expressions, hand motions, and other behaviors, but effective communication begins with the acquisition of language. The ability to use language produces dramatic changes in children's lives, allowing them to interact on a more mature level with other people and to represent the world in increasingly complex ways.

In the first few months of life, babies coo. By 6 months of age, the sounds they make may become differentiated and are called "babbling." Very often, 6- to 8-month-old babies repeat the same sounds for hours or days at a time. By the end of a year, they have learned a few simple words, perhaps including *mama* and *dada*. From this naming stage, the child goes on to develop simple two- and

morality: A system of learned attitudes about social practices, institutions, and individual behavior, used to evaluate events as being morally right or wrong.

three-word utterances that are often characterized as telegraphic because they use few words, as if the child is trying to be economical.

Through their telegraphic two-word utterances, young children can convey an amazingly large number of thoughts. Sentences such as "No peas," "More ice cream," and "Change diaper" are quite explicit and make the child's needs known. However, more important than these utterances themselves is the way they evolve into more complex statements as children learn grammar. Children learn grammar, or the rules and patterns for generating sentences in a langauge, at an early age. Although 5- and 6-year olds have not yet learned all the grammar of their language, their speech includes nouns, verbs, and adjectives in essentially the correct ways. Of course, we examined language and its development in more detail in Chapter 7.

Moral Reasoning

Learning Objective 16.5
Discuss Piaget's and Kohlberg's views regarding the development of moral reasoning.

The physical and intellectual development of childhood is paralleled by growth in the capacity for moral reasoning. From childhood on, people develop **morality,** a set of values that enables them to make decisions about what is right or wrong, good or bad. Morality lets people evaluate situations and behavior and act according to their beliefs.

Attitudes about morals develop and change throughout life. At an early age, children learn from their parents the behaviors, attitudes, and values considered appropriate and correct in their culture. Morality is aided by teachers and bolstered by church and community leaders, as well as by family and friends. As they mature, children acquire new attitudes that accommodate an increasingly complex view of the world and of reality. Your views of morality when you were 10 years old probably differ from your views today. Recognizing the differences in the moral maturity of adolescents and adults, the United States Supreme Court has restricted adolescents' rights to make important life decisions, in part because the court feels that adolescents lack moral maturity (Gardner, Scherer, & Tester, 1989). But do they? Are the reasoning and judgment of a child, a preteen, or an adolescent like that of an adult?

Piaget and Morality

Piaget examined children's ability to analyze questions of morality and found the results to be consistent with his ideas about intellectual development. Young children's ideas about morality are rigid and rule bound. When playing a game, for example, a young child will not allow the rules to be modified. Older children, on the other hand, recognize that rules are established by social convention and may need to be altered, depending on the situation. They have developed a sense of *moral relativity* that allows them to recognize that situational factors affect the way things are perceived (Piaget, 1932). According to Piaget, as children mature, they move from inflexibility toward relativity in their moral judgments; they develop new cognitive structures and assimilate and accommodate new ideas.

Kohlberg: Heinz's Dilemma

Piaget's theory of moral development was based on descriptions of how children respond to certain kinds of questions and at what age they switch and use other forms of answers. The research of Harvard psychologist Lawrence Kohlberg (1927–1987) grew out of Piaget's work. Kohlberg believed that moral development proceeds through a series of three levels, each of which is divided into two

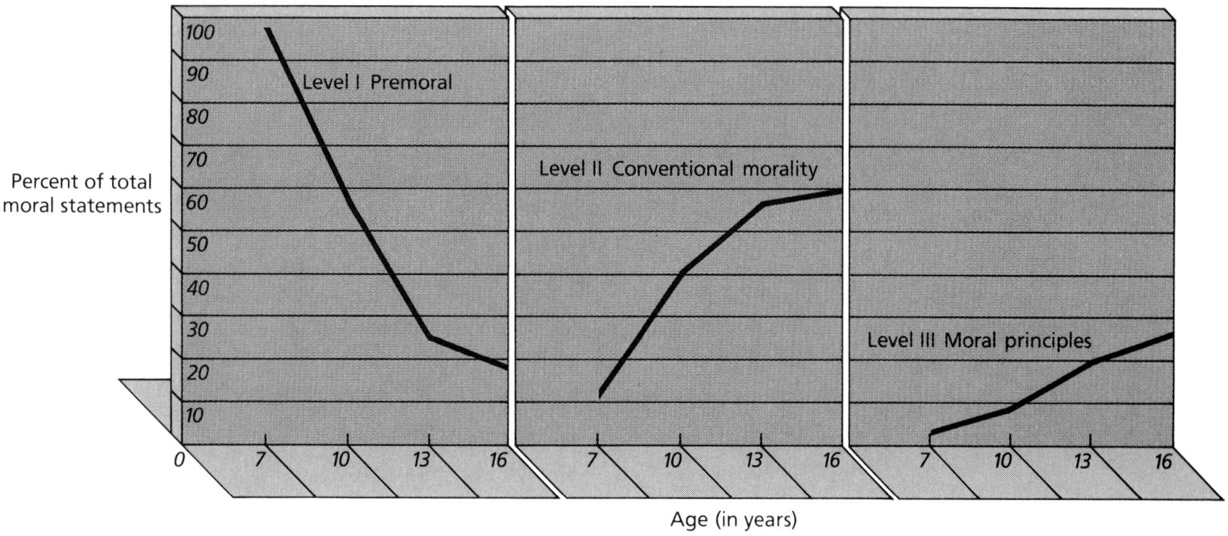

Figure 16.4

In Kohlberg's theory of moral development, there is a distinct progression from one stage of morality to another as age increases. Thus, Level 1 morality decreases with age and maturity, and Levels 2 and 3 continue to increase. (Source: Data from Kohlberg, 1963)

stages. The central concept in Kohlberg's theory is that of justice. In his studies of moral reasoning, Kohlberg presented different types of stories to people of various ages and asked them what the story meant to them and how they felt about it (Kohlberg, 1969). In one story, Heinz, a poor man, stole a drug for his wife, who would have died without it; Kohlberg asked his subjects about the morality and justice of Heinz's action: "Would a good husband steal for his wife?" "Was it actually wrong?" "Why?" Adults' interpretations of Heinz's plight differed from those of adolescents and 5-year-olds. Children had difficulty seeing that Heinz's circumstances might influence the way his action could be judged (Kohlberg, 1976). Adults focused on the special dilemma in which Heinz found himself and analyzed his predicament differently.

Kohlberg found that people's judgments of the behavior of others vary with their level of moral development. Presented with the story of Heinz, children at Level 1 morality either condemn Heinz's behavior, explaining that he should be punished because he stole, or justify it, explaining that Heinz was good because he tried to save his wife's life. People at Level 2 morality said that Heinz broke the law by stealing and should go to jail. Only people who have reached Level 3 can see that Heinz was justified in his action while noting the complexity of the ethical dilemma (see Figure 16.4).

Young children, at Level 1 or *preconventional,* morality, base their decisions about right or wrong on the likelihood of avoiding punishment and obtaining rewards. A child in this stage would say that it is "bad" to pull the cat's tail, "because mom will spank me." School-age children, who are at Level 2, adopt *conventional* ideas about morality. They conform in order to avoid the disapproval of other people. At this stage, a 10-year-old might choose not to try cigarettes because his parents and friends disapprove of smoking. Level 2, judgments are also governed by a process that considers the implications of a person's behavior. Why did he do it? What will be the consequences for him and for others?

Level 3, or *postconventional,* morality is concerned with contracts, laws, and moral conscience. In the first stage of Level 3 morality, people make judgments on the basis of their perception of the needs of society, with an end toward maintaining community welfare and legal order. In the second stage of Level 3, morality of conscience, people make judgments based on their personal moral beliefs and values rather than on those of society. Conscientious objection to legally sanctioned behaviors would be associated with this stage. For example, a person may

TABLE 16.2 A comparison of Piaget and Kohlberg on moral development

Piaget	Kohlberg
Sensorimotor and Preoperational (birth–7 years)	Level I—Preconventional *Stage 1:* Obedience and punishment orientation *Stage 2:* Naïvely egotistic orientation
Concrete operations (8–11 years)	Level II—Conventional *Stage 3:* Good-boy or -girl orientation *Stage 4:* Authority and social order maintenance orientation
Formal operations (12 years and after)	Level III—Postconventional *Stage 5:* Contractual-legalistic orientation *Stage 6:* Conscience or principle orientation

Lawrence Kohlberg

oppose capital punishment, even though it is legal in some states. Most adults reach at least the first stage of Level 3. A comparison of Piaget's and Kohlberg's theories on moral development is found in Table 16.2.

Research and Challenges

Piaget set the stage for two decades of research by Kohlberg, whose work was monumental in scope. Like other great thinkers, Kohlberg laid down a theory that he knew would be tested, evaluated, and revised, a firm foundation for the next generation of research.

Kohlberg and Piaget. Piaget and Kohlberg studied moral reasoning, not moral behavior. Both theorists focused on how people make decisions, not on the behavior that might result from those decisions. However, their theories differ, in that Piaget thought of the stages of moral development as discrete, whereas Kohlberg viewed them as overlapping. Kohlberg also went further than Piaget in systematizing the development of morality. He elaborated on ideas about how children's interactions with parents and friends may influence their conceptions of morality.

In Kohlberg's view, a child might use earlier levels of moral reasoning from time to time, even though he or she is capable of higher levels, a finding that has been substantiated by the work of DeVries and Walker (1986). Kohlberg's theory has not gone unchallenged. Some have suggested that his views are culturally bound and that he did not examine issues with which normal adults have to deal. For example, Yussen (1977) has shown that older children and teenagers consider other moral issues in their lives more important than the Heinz dilemma. This criticism does not make Kohlberg's work any less important, but it does raise some important questions.

Learning Objective 16.6
Discuss Carol Gilligan's findings regarding moral reasoning and gender differences.

Gilligan's Work: Gender Differences. A major addition to the study of morality has been the work of Carol Gilligan (1982), who found that people look at more than justice when reasoning moral conflicts. She found that people were also concerned with caring, with relationships, and with connections with other people. Gilligan focused her research on caring. The morality of caring focuses on the welfare of others and ourselves; it assumes that both are important.

Also, though Kohlberg and his colleagues had not generally reported any gender differences, Gilligan did. She examined differences between girls and boys with respect to their inclinations toward caring and justice. She found that girls were more concerned with care, relationships, and connections with other people. As younger children, girls gravitate toward a morality of caring, while boys gravitate to a morality of justice. Gilligan asserts that the difference between boys and girls is established by virtue of the child's gender and the child's relationship with the mother. Because of the gender difference between boys and their mothers, boys see that they are essentially different from other people, whereas girls develop a belief in their similarity (connectedness) with others. Gilligan shows that boys respond to the Heinz dilemma by indicating that sometimes people must act on their own to do the right thing. Girls, by contrast, are more likely to look for alternatives, for ways to talk out differences or to seek some compromise. Like Kohlberg, Gilligan argues that the development of caring follows a time course, with initial caring only toward oneself, later caring toward others as well, and ultimately (in some people) a more mature stage of caring for truth. Gilligan's work has been influential in psychologist's evaluations of morality. Some researchers assert that her approach fosters a continuation of sex-role stereotyping—women as caring, men as logical. Others point out that her work has been limited to white middle-class girls and needs a broader multicultural perspective.

Carol Gilligan

Learning Objective 16.7
Discuss how adults can help children to develop a mature sense of morality, and state the benefits of having strong moral reasoning skills.

Care and justice are not incompatible values; indeed, they go together. That boys and girls develop them differently need not be seen as negative. Recognizing the differences between boys and girls allows us to expand the horizons of each to the full limit of their human potential (Damon, 1988). Further, although parents are the main source of children's moral values, Kohlberg suggested that other people can also help promote the development of morality and conscience. This can be accomplished through *role-taking,* the ability to adopt perspectives different from one's own. According to Kohlberg, children who have opportunities in classrooms, churches, and at home to consider moral dilemmas from another person's point of view are more likely to develop a mature sense of morality (Kohlberg, 1971). Through such methods, people learn not only what society's values are, but also how to think independently. Moreover, they achieve higher levels of moral reasoning, thereby gaining greater flexibility and independence in both judgment and behavior. The study of morality and caring have gone beyond Kohlberg's original view. For example, Kitwood (1990) argues that only after people have developed a sense of themselves can they fully realize caring for others; he thus combines personality theory (discussed in Chapter 10) with studies of morality. Moral behavior, from Kitwood's view, has to be studied within the context of the total person—as in so many other areas of psychology, more research is needed.

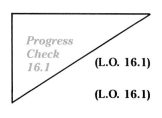

Progress Check 16.1

Complete the following sentences with one of the options provided.

(L.O. 16.1) a. Piaget's theory applies to people in all societies and cultures because it focuses on ________ people think. (thought processes or "how" / content or "what")

(L.O. 16.1) b. When a behavior that is already a part of an individual's collection of cognitive structures and then is easily applied, without modification, to another situation, the applied behavior is ________ into the existing cognitive structure. (assimilated / accommodated)

(L.O. 16.2) c. ________ is developing when an infant in the sensorimotor stage is able to overcome an obstacle in order to achieve a goal. (A sense of intention / Object permanence / Making interesting sights last)

(L.O. 16.2) d. Piaget thought the ________ stage was the most important because as the child learns to perceive and interact with the environment, the foundation for all future intellectual development is established. (sensorimotor / preoperational)

(L.O. 16.2) e. The process that begins around the age of 2 years, allowing children to move away from a totally self-oriented viewpoint to one that recognizes other people's feelings and ideas, is ______. (egocentrism / decentration)

(L.O. 16.2) f. A child moves from preoperations to concrete operations when he or she can ______. (form hypotheses / make appearance-reality distinctions)

(L.O. 16.2) g. During the ______ stage, thought processes develop that enable the child to understand constant factors in the environment (such as conservation), rules, and higher-order symbolism (such as arithmetic). (concrete operations / formal operations)

(L.O. 16.3) h. Piaget believed that parents could help their children's intellectual development along by ______ their current level of intellectual development. (pushing them to accelerate beyond / recognizing and providing stimuli for)

(L.O. 16.4) i. As a key part of their developing language abilities, 6- to 8-month-old babies tend to ______. (repeat the same sounds / use telegraphic speech / coo and babble)

(L.O. 16.5) j. Piaget found the moral reasoning of young children to be ______. (relative / flexible / rigid and rule bound)

(L.O. 16.5) k. When a person alters conventional rules and makes moral judgments based on situational factors, Piaget would say the person has developed a sense of ______. (moral relativity / immoral justification)

(L.O. 16.5) l. The central concept in Kohlberg's theory of morality is ______. (acceptance / justice / truth)

(L.O. 16.5) m. Kohlberg found that very young children make moral decisions based on ______. (approval and disapproval / reward and punishment)

(L.O. 16.5) n. The second stage of Kohlberg's postconventional stage of morality is called morality of ______. (community welfare / laws and contracts / conscience)

(L.O. 16.6) o. According to Gilligan, when making moral decisions, girls are more likely than boys to ______. (look for alternatives or a compromise / act on their own, based on what is right)

(L.O. 16.7) p. According to Kohlberg, children will be more likely to develop a mature sense of morality if they are provided with ______. (strict guidelines of right and wrong / opportunities for role-taking)

Social Development

As society changes, so do ideas and practices related to a child's social development. In a 1959 study of masculinity and father–son relationships, Paul Mussen and Luther Distler concluded that a father's importance and involvement in his son's life are crucial in determining the child's gender-based interests. A generation ago, when Mussen and Distler conducted their research, parents tended to encourage "masculine" traits such as athletic prowess in their sons and "feminine" traits such as shyness in their daughters. They accepted and promoted a gender-based social environment. Today, many parents deemphasize gender-based interests in their children, seeking to reduce and even eliminate society's tendency to stereotype people, their interests, and their occupations on the basis of gender.

Early Social Development

Learning Objective 16.8 Describe the nature of social interactions, sharing, and play in children.

Social development begins at birth, with the development of attachment between parents and their newborn. The nature of a child's beginning and early interactions with parents is a crucial part of personality development. Infants have a great need to be hugged and cuddled, nurtured, and made to feel good, but parents must also teach their children to interact with others and to become independent.

Once encouraged to share, children begin to understand that sharing can involve a reciprocal agreement.

In the first year of life, social interaction is limited because infants are largely egocentric. They seldom distinguish their needs and desires from those of others. At about the second half of the first year, children exhibit strong attachments and a fear of strangers. At 18–24 months, they have matured sufficiently to have specific desires and needs, but they lack the language skills to make those needs known. A child cannot tell her father, for example, that she wants the green bib, not the blue one, although she can indicate her displeasure, often quite loudly (Ames et al., 1979). As early as 9 months of age, infants show that they like to play games by indicating unhappiness when an adult stops playing with them. They play by themselves, but as they grow older, especially beyond 2 years of age, they engage in more social play with other children.

By the end of their second year, children have begun to understand that they are separate from their parents. They learn to differentiate themselves from others, to manipulate the world, and to interact with other people. As the child enters the preoperational stage, egocentrism gives way to increased social interaction. Two-year-olds generally play alone or alongside other children, but with little interaction. They prefer to play with an adult rather than with another 2-year-old. They are now better at controlling their emotional responses than they were at 18 months. Gradually, they begin to socialize with their peers.

Sharing. Benjamin Spock, noted pediatrician, once said that the only two things a child will share willingly are communicable diseases and her or his mother's age. Actually, from age 2 years until they begin school, children vacillate between quiet conformity and happy sharing, on the one hand, and making stubborn negative demands and exhibiting egocentric behavior on the other. Because sharing is a socially desirable behavior, children must learn to share when they enter child care, nursery school, or kindergarten.

Very young children do not understand the concept of sharing, particularly the idea that if you share with another child, he or she is more likely to share with you. In a laboratory study of sharing, researchers observed groups of two children separated by a gate. Initially, one child was given toys and the other wasn't; then the situation was reversed. The researchers found that none of the

As more women enter the workforce, more men are taking the time to develop an intimate relationship with their children.

children shared spontaneously, but 65% shared a toy when asked to do so by their mothers. Moreover, when deprived of a toy after having shared one, a child often approached another child who had the toy. One child even said, "I gave you a toy, why don't you give me one?" Children do not initiate sharing at a young age, but once they get older, they are more willing to share and seem to exhibit knowledge about reciprocal arrangements.

Gender Segregation in Play. Children at age 18 months display gender-stereotyped preferences for toys (Caldera, Huston, & O'Brien, 1989); these preferences are also evident in their choice of playmates. Starting at age 3 years and continuing for several years, they prefer same-gender play partners. According to Eleanor Maccoby and Carol Jacklin (1987), this finding is reliable, cuts across a variety of situations, and is difficult to change. Gender segregation probably does not happen because children have been given "boy" toys or "girl" toys, nor does it result solely from inborn temperamental differences that lead to rough-and-tumble play for boys and more sedate play for girls.

The reasons for sex segregation are not fully understood, but Maccoby and Jacklin argue that children know that they are members of one gender or the other. This knowledge binds members of each sex together and differentiates them from members of the other sex. Children with widely different personalities are drawn together solely on the basis of their shared gender. Research supports this idea (Skitka & Maslach, 1990) and throughout childhood, temperamental differences interact with social effects, and gender segregation becomes even more pronounced. Maccoby (1990) asserts that sex differences are minimal when children are observed individually but become more apparent in social situations. Although boys and girls don't have much to do with one another during early childhood, they both have opportunities to interact with parents, either together or singly.

Single Parenting

Learning Objective 16.9
Characterize single-parent families.

Today, more children than ever are being raised in single-parent homes. According to the U.S. Department of Commerce, in the decade between 1970 and 1980, the number of single parents raising children increased by at least 28%. This means that 15 million children in the United States live with only one parent; 24% of these children are under the age of 6 years (U.S. Bureau of the Census, 1989). Only 4% of American households fit the traditional description of a working father, a mother who stays at home, and two or more school-age children.

For the millions of divorced, widowed, or never-married parents who are rearing children alone, many of the traditional supports, such as the assistance of grandparents, are unavailable. Single parents tend to work longer hours than married parents, and their own parents and other relatives seldom live in the same community. Still, evidence exists that the effects of single parenthood are indirect and that single parents in some cases can do just as well as, if not better than, they did if and when they were married (Wilson, 1989). Researchers are just beginning to examine the effects of single parenting; only recently have they realized the extent to which school-age children are being raised by single parents and the extent to which younger children are being cared for in child-care centers, considered next.

Learning Objective 16.10
Discuss the research concerning the effects of child care on emotional, social, and intellectual development.

Child Care

According to the U.S. Bureau of the Census there has been an extremely sharp drop in the proportion of mothers who quit their jobs when their first child is born (1990) and now more than 29 million children under age 15 years have a mother who works outside the home. By 1995, it is expected that 34 million children will have working mothers. For families in which both parents work, as well as for single parents, child care can be a necessity; child-care centers provide care for about 23% of preschool children who have working mothers.

Child care situations are becoming increasingly diverse as parents seek alternative arrangements for their children. While their mothers work, most preschool children are cared for in their own or other people's homes, often by baby-sitters, relatives, friends, fathers, ex-spouses, or grandparents (Presser, 1989). Most Americans believe that when children are reared by people other than their parents, their development is less than optimal. Since the early 1980s, this issue has been the subject of intensive research.

As day care becomes increasingly necessary to the contemporary family, psychologists are studying its effects, both positive and negative.

Effects of Child Care. It isn't easy to determine the effects of child care because of a number of variables, including the child's age at entry into a child care program, the child's family background, the security of the child's attachment to parents, and the stability of the child's child care arrangements (Belsky, 1980). All these factors can affect a child's response to the child care experience (Clarke-Stewart, 1989). Psychologists are especially interested in the relationship of child care and attachment because they believe that a child's emotional security depends on a strong, loving bond with a parent or primary caregiver. Contrary to popular belief, most studies of attachment behaviors find that nonparental care does not reduce a child's emotional attachment to the mother (Etaugh, 1980). Moreover, there is no firm evidence that temporary separations, such as those caused by child care for preschool children, create later psychological trauma (Lamb et al., 1988).

Considerable evidence suggests that a stimulating, varied environment is necessary for optimal intellectual development and that high-quality child care centers provide a sufficiently stimulating environment. High-quality child care means one that has an experienced and highly qualified staff, a low staff-to-child ratio, and low staff turnover. Belsky and Steinberg (1978) found no differences in intellectual functioning between middle-class children enrolled in high-quality child care centers and children reared at home. In fact, high-quality child care centers may increase children's positive social interactions with peers (Schindler, Moely, & Frank, 1987).

However, recent research has questioned the conventional wisdom of child care, suggesting that child care centers may have negative effects on psychological development for children who spend more than 20 hours per week there. Jay Belsky, of Pennsylvania State University, asserts that extensive nonmaternal care in the first year of life is associated with insecurity in infants. Infants who received more than 20 hours of child care per week displayed more avoidance of their mothers when they were reunited than babies who spent only a couple of hours in child care (Belsky & Rovine, 1988). In related work with noninfant children, Clarke-Stewart (1989) argued that studies show that children who spend extensive periods of time in child care settings show increased disobedience, aggressiveness, bossiness, and brattiness, and that these children want their own way and do not know how to comfortably achieve it. Interestingly, this may be associated with the academic training of child care workers, which emphasizes children's independence and assertiveness. Clarke-Stewart suggests that this may be considered the "dark side" of children's social training. "In good or poor day-care programs, it seems children do not follow social rules or resolve social conflicts without resorting to aggression unless special efforts are made by their caregivers" (p. 271).

A child's home environment and socialization can, of course, moderate some of these negative consequences. First-class child-care centers do not necessarily produce negative effects. However, a short-staffed center, lengthy periods spent in child care, and parents who are not especially attentive to a child's needs may have deleterious effects. Belsky's and some of Clarke-Stewart's arguments contradict the findings of previous research, and as a result, most psychologists are maintaining an open mind regarding child care and its effects. As Scarr, Phillips, and McCartney (1990) assert, we must consider the facts about child care—the evidence—not just the fantasies and the hopes of parents and psychologists. The research is far from complete.

Learning Objective 16.11
Discuss what is currently known about the effects of latchkey child care arrangements.

Latchkey Children. Millions of children come home from school to empty homes where they take care of themselves until their parents arrive home from work. They are known as self-care, or latchkey, children. Most parents who leave their children in self-care arrangements establish rules for them to follow and maintain telephone contact with them in order to supervise even while they are not present in the home. Do these latchkey arrangements work? Are there behavioral consequences for children left to care for themselves?

Rodman and his colleagues compared self-care children with adult-supervised children. A self-care child is one between the ages of 6 and 13 years who spends time alone or with a younger sibling on a periodic basis (Rodman, Pratto, & Nelson, 1988). Rodman and others have found that among former latchkey children, college students do not seem to differ on personality or academic variables (Messer, Wuensch, & Diamond, 1989). For now, the overall developmental effects of self-care for children seem to be minimal or nonexistent (Vandell & Corasaniti, 1988) and those of child care are minimal.

Researchers who study topics such as single parenting, child care, and self-care focus on personality and academic differences between children raised in these environments and children raised in non–child care or non-self-care homes. Their aim is to discern whether differences exist, and if they exist, whether they bring about adverse effects.

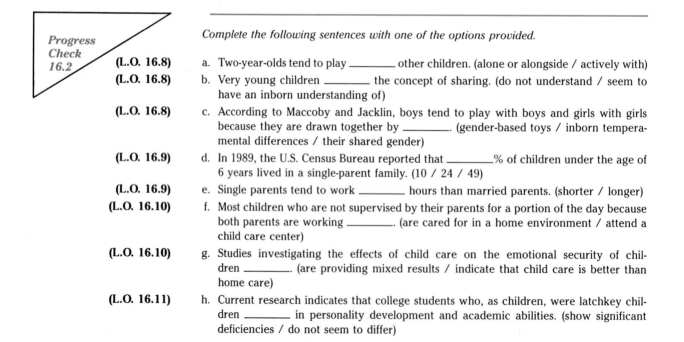

Progress Check 16.2

Complete the following sentences with one of the options provided.

(L.O. 16.8) a. Two-year-olds tend to play ________ other children. (alone or alongside / actively with)

(L.O. 16.8) b. Very young children ________ the concept of sharing. (do not understand / seem to have an inborn understanding of)

(L.O. 16.8) c. According to Maccoby and Jacklin, boys tend to play with boys and girls with girls because they are drawn together by ________. (gender-based toys / inborn temperamental differences / their shared gender)

(L.O. 16.9) d. In 1989, the U.S. Census Bureau reported that ________% of children under the age of 6 years lived in a single-parent family. (10 / 24 / 49)

(L.O. 16.9) e. Single parents tend to work ________ hours than married parents. (shorter / longer)

(L.O. 16.10) f. Most children who are not supervised by their parents for a portion of the day because both parents are working ________. (are cared for in a home environment / attend a child care center)

(L.O. 16.10) g. Studies investigating the effects of child care on the emotional security of children ________. (are providing mixed results / indicate that child care is better than home care)

(L.O. 16.11) h. Current research indicates that college students who, as children, were latchkey children ________ in personality development and academic abilities. (show significant deficiencies / do not seem to differ)

Module Summary

Intellectual Development

- Piaget believed that intellectual development occurs in a series of stages, each of which must be completed before the next stage begins. During the first stage, the *sensorimotor period,* intellectual behaviors are established and the child begins to interact with the environment and attempt to control it. The second stage in Piaget's theory is *preoperational thought,* in which the child tries to represent the world in symbolic ways, particularly through the use of language (p. 296).
- During the stage of *concrete operations,* children attend school and learn rules about the world. One of those rules is *conservation,* the ability to understand that objects may be transformed visually or physically yet still represent the same amount of weight or volume. The final stage of Piaget's theory of intellectual development is the stage of *formal operations;* During this stage, the adolescent becomes able to engage in abstract thought (p. 299).

Moral Reasoning

- Morality is a system of learned attitudes concerning ideal behavior. People exercise moral judgments about the rightness or wrongness of individual behavior and of social institutions and practices (p. 302).
- Whereas school-age children adopt conventional ideas of morality, adults adopt more mature views, opting initially for rights under contracts and laws, and ultimately for decisions made by conscience (p. 303).

Social Development

- Boys and girls don't have much to do with one another during middle childhood. Starting at age 3 years and continuing for several years, they prefer same-gender play partners (p. 308).
- As a result of the immense increase in the number of women in the labor force since the 1950s, significant changes have occurred in child care arrangements, and child care has become more common. Research shows that under optimal conditions, group child care centers and home rearing produce children with similar psychological profiles (p. 309).

KEY TERMS

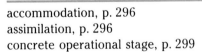

accommodation, p. 296
assimilation, p. 296
concrete operational stage, p. 299
conservation, p. 299
decentration, p. 298
egocentrism, p. 297
formal operational stage, p. 299
morality, p. 302
preoperational stage, p. 298
sensorimotor stage, p. 296

SELF-TEST

Module 16

- Before taking the self-test, **recite** and **review.**
- Use the key at the back of the text to *correct* your answers.
- *Restudy* pages that correspond to any questions you answered incorrectly.

1. Probably the greatest strength of Piaget's theory of intellectual development is that it
   a. originated from asking children of different ages different types of questions.
   b. focuses on the wealth of human knowledge.
   c. describes how inherited potentials interact with the environment to produce intellectual behaviors.
   d. provides a model for teaching advanced concepts to young children.
2. The process of ________ takes place when a person must modify previously developed cognitive structures and behaviors in order to adapt to a new concept or experience.
   a. conservation
   b. decentration
   c. accommodation
   d. assimilation
3. Which of the following is an accurate statement concerning assimilation and accommodation?
   a. They are separate and independent processes.
   b. Assimilation serves as a foundation for accommodation.
   c. Assimilation is found during the sensorimotor and preoperational stages, accommodation during the concrete and formal operations stages.
   d. All of the above are true.
4. From birth to about 9 months of age, the saying "out-of-sight, out-of-mind" can be used to describe an infant's awareness because it takes this long for ________ to develop.
   a. egocentrism
   b. object permanence
   c. concrete operations
   d. intentionality
5. Which of the following illustrates the ability of *conservation*? The child is able to
   a. represent the world symbolically.
   b. recognize that people have different feelings, ideas, and viewpoints.
   c. recognize that although things in the material world change in shape, their weight or volume remains the same.
   d. think of different ways to represent ideas by developing informal theories based on logic.
6. Psychologist David Elkind believes that ________ is of primary importance during the preschool years.
   a. education
   b. socialization
   c. developing the creative process
   d. accelerated learning
7. Five- and 6-year-old children
   a. speak telegraphically.
   b. parrot the words and sentences that they find interesting.
   c. have a good grammatical foundation and, for the most part, use nouns, verbs, and adjectives correctly.
   d. use verbs and nouns correctly, but do not yet understand the correct use of adjectives.

8. Moral judgments in Kohlberg's Level 2, conventional morality, are governed by a process that also considers
   a. an individual's personal values.
   b. good and bad or right and wrong.
   c. the implications of a person's behavior.
   d. the needs of society and ways of maintaining order.
9. Both Piaget and Kohlberg focused their studies of morality on
   a. defining moral and immoral behaviors.
   b. how people make moral decisions.
   c. gender differences between boys and girls.
   d. the relative importance of truth and honor.
10. Which of the following lists the correct order of the development of moral caring, according to Gilligan?
    a. logic, justice, caring.
    b. virtue, caring, connectedness.
    c. caring toward oneself, caring toward others, caring for truth.
    d. preconventional caring, conventional caring, postconventional caring.
11. People who achieve higher-level moral reasoning skills
    a. tend to behave in rebellious and nonconforming ways.
    b. are more likely to have flexibility and independence in the way they behave and the judgments they make.
    c. frequently lose touch with conventional values.
    d. Both b and c
12. Beginning around the age of 3 years and continuing for several years thereafter, children prefer playmates who are
    a. younger than 3 years.
    b. over the age of 5 years.
    c. of the same gender.
    d. of the opposite gender.
13. Your text points out that raising children today, especially in a single-parent family, can be difficult because
    a. children expect more from parents.
    b. many traditional support systems are not available.
    c. schools and child care have serious negative effects on children.
    d. parents cannot find effective role models.
14. Research suggests that quality day care centers may actually improve a child's opportunity to
    a. bond with parents.
    b. develop positive social interactions with peers.
    c. understand separation anxiety.
    d. develop a sense of basic trust.
15. A latchkey child is a child
    a. between the ages of 6 and 13 years who spends a significant amount of time alone at home.
    b. who is supervised by a number of different caregivers depending primarily on who is available when needed.
    c. skips school, "forgets" to come home on time, and retreats from family members while at home.
    d. has a special talent and lives away from home in an expert training environment so that the talent can be cultivated.

Module 17

Adolescence, Adulthood, and Aging

LEARNING OBJECTIVES

When you have mastered the material in this module, you will be able to

Adolescence (pp. 316–322)

17.1 Discuss the number of teenagers who experience psychological turmoil and explain why it is important to describe adolescence in a cultural context (p. 316).

17.2 Describe the physical changes that occur with puberty (p. 316).

17.3 Discuss the biological and environmental factors that influence the social development of an adolescent (p. 317).

17.4 Discuss gender differences in sex roles and in intellectual functioning (p. 318).

17.5 Discuss the rate of adolescent sexual behavior and pregnancy in the United States and explain why teenagers often fail to use contraceptives (p. 319).

17.6 Describe Erik Erikson's psychosocial stage theory of development (p. 320).

Adulthood (pp. 323–329)

17.7 Discuss some of the current research interests of developmental psychologists (p. 323).

17.8 Discuss the fitness, sexual, and sensory changes that occur during adulthood (p. 323).

17.9 Make a distinction between the terms *transition* and *crisis* and explain how these terms apply to a variety of life changes (p. 324).

17.10 Discuss some of the things researchers have discovered in recent years concerning adult personality development (p. 325).

17.11 Compare and contrast Levinson's and Erikson's stage theories and discuss Levinson's four eras of adult life (p. 326).

17.12 Explain why Levinson's theory receives some criticism and discuss a recent study that outlines the life transitions of women (p. 328).

Aging (pp. 330–338)

17.13 State some of the trends in the population of elderly people and discuss social conditions that make life difficult for some elderly people (p. 330).

17.14 Describe the heredity, external factors, and physiological–genetic theories of aging (p. 331).

17.15 Describe the biobehavioral approach to aging, various types of dementia, and other physiological changes that can accompany the aging process (p. 333).

17.16 Discuss changes in intellectual functioning and work performance that can accompany the aging process (p. 335).

Dying: The End of the Life Span (pp. 338–341)

17.17 Discuss Elisabeth Kübler-Ross's stage theory of accepting a loved one's or one's own death or dying and comment on Western society's view of death (p. 338).

SQ3R
- ▲ **Survey** to set goals for studying.
- ▲ Ask **questions** as you **read.**
- ▲ Stop occasionally to **recite** and **review.**

plus
- ▲ **Write** a summary of key points.
- ▲ **Reflect** on the hypotheses, evidence, and implications of this material and on the relevance it has to *your* life.

In the past year, Marlene has matured physically into a woman, yet her parents sometimes treat her like a child. She is eager to finish her senior year in high school but worries about leaving friends and family to start college. She constantly asks herself what sort of career she should have. Although she finds her life exciting, Marlene is looking forward to becoming an adult and leaving the uncertainty of adolescence behind.

Like Marlene, Luis is undergoing a transition in his life. Although still physically fit, the 39-year-old baseball star now needs to wear contact lenses in order to hit a fast pitch, and he finds it increasingly difficult to keep up with the younger players. Luis says he will retire as a baseball player next year and devote more time to coaching and to his family.

At age 75 years, Sierra finds life more rewarding now than ever before. Her youngest child left home to start his own family years ago, and since then Sierra has devoted most of her spare time to painting. She and her husband have opened a gallery in which they sell her artwork. However, Sierra is struggling with the physical challenges of old age, including arthritis, which threatens to end her painting career.

Every age—infancy, childhood, adolescence, early adulthood, and late adulthood—brings its own particular joys and difficulties. Psychologists see aging as a process of continued growth that is influenced by a person's biological inheri-

puberty: [PEW-burr-tee] The period during which the reproductive system matures; it occurs at (and signals) the end of childhood.

adolescence: [add-oh-LESS-since] The period extending from the onset of puberty to early adulthood.

tance, life experiences, frame of mind, and a certain amount of chance. For example, changing residences from one state to another changes people's lives; a divorce is unsettling; a death in the family can be devastating; winning the lottery can jolt a person from poverty to luxury and from anonymity to fame. So, in addition to normal predictable maturational and developmental changes, a once-in-a-lifetime happening can permanently alter physical, personality, and social development. In this module, we discuss some of the developmental changes that occur during adolescence and adulthood, and we trace the psychological processes that underlie these stages of development.

Learning Objective 17.1
Discuss the number of teenagers who experience psychological turmoil, and explain why it is important to describe adolescence in a cultural context.

Adolescence

In our culture, the transition from childhood to adulthood brings dramatic intellectual, social, emotional, and physical changes. Generally, this transition occurs between the ages of 12 and 20 years, a period known as *adolescence,* when children bridge the gap to adulthood. Although adolescents are in many ways like adults—they are nearly mature physically and mentally, and their moral development is fairly advanced, their emotional development may be far from complete.

Adolescence is often referred to as a time of storm and stress, and for some adolescents, this is indeed the case. Adolescence may be a challenging life period, just as adulthood is, but only 11% of adolescents have serious difficulties (Petersen, 1988). Thirty-two percent have only sporadic difficulties. Also, 57% of adolescents have basically positive, healthy development during these teenage years. The current consensus among psychologists is that adolescence is not ordinarily a time of great psychological turmoil (Powers, Hauser, & Kilner, 1989) and that adolescents have no more psychological disturbances than the rest of the population (Hauser & Bowlds, 1990).

Today, it is common for an American teenager to feel as if "no one understands me," but it's difficult to imagine a teenaged tribeswoman growing up in the jungles of New Guinea expressing the same sentiment. Thus, the problems of adolescence must be considered in a cultural context. Even when they grow up in the same country, adolescents experience life's joys and disappointments in different ways. Some come from disadvantaged cultural or economic groups, perhaps from a Chicago ghetto or an American Indian reservation; some grow up in luxury, perhaps in a wealthy suburb of Los Angeles; others are exposed to racial prejudice, alcohol and other drug abuse, nonsupportive families, or other stressful situations that lead them to feel powerless in controlling their own lives. Researchers now understand that the life experiences of whites, Navajos, Hispanics, African-Americans, Asian-Americans, and other groups are not all alike, and each year, more studies compare the experiences of different groups and sensitize both professionals and the public to cultural differences. Unfortunately, most of the research on adolescence has been conducted on white, middle-class American teenagers.

Unfortunately, research has concentrated on the life experiences of white, middle-class American teenagers.

Learning Objective 17.2
Describe the physical changes that occur with puberty.

Physical Development

The words *adolescence* and *puberty* are often used interchangeably, but in fact they mean different things. **Puberty** is the period during which the reproductive system matures; it begins with the increase in sex hormone production and occurs at (and signals) the end of childhood. **Adolescence** is the period extending from the onset of puberty to early adulthood. Psychologists observe this distinction when studying adolescence. See Figure 17.1.

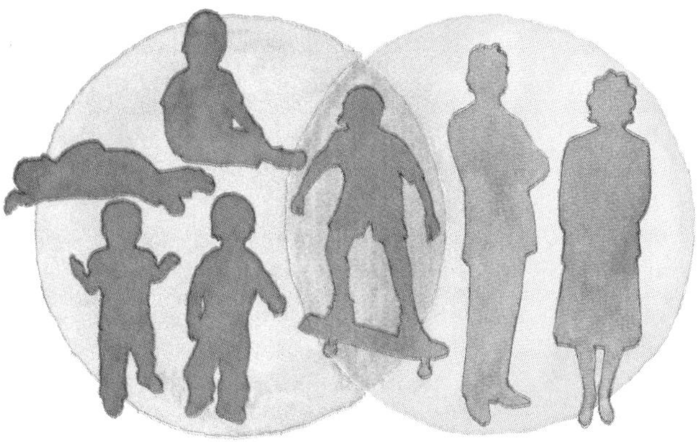

Figure 17.1

The world of the adolescent has sometimes been characterized as being between childhood and adulthood but belonging to neither.

The age of onset of puberty varies widely; some girls begin to mature physically as early as age 8 years, some boys at 9 or 10 years. The average age of puberty is 13 years, plus or minus a year or 2. Just before the onset of puberty, boys and girls experience significant growth spurts, gaining as much as 5 inches in a single year.

By the end of the first or second year of the growth spurt, body proportions, fat distribution, bones and muscles, and physical strength and agility change. In addition, the hormonal system produces secondary sex characteristics. **Secondary sex characteristics** are the physical features of a person's gender identity not directly involved with reproduction. Boys experience an increase in body mass, as well as growth of pubic, underarm, and facial hair. Girls experience an increase in the size of the breasts, widening of the hips, and growth of underarm and pubic hair. Puberty ends with maturation of the reproductive organs, at which time boys produce sperm and girls produce ova and begin to menstruate. These physical changes generally take several years to complete, and the maturing adolescent may find them both exciting and disturbing. Researchers assert that puberty itself does not create psychological maladjustment.

Social Development

Learning Objective 17.3
Discuss the biological and environmental factors that influence the social development of an adolescent.

Factors Affecting Development. The development of a teenager's personality is affected by both the timing of puberty, a biological factor, and how people react to that timing, an environmental factor. Parents and teachers can help adolescents with feelings about body image. Research shows that satisfying involvement with athletics can serve as a buffer against the negative feelings that arise during this period. Increased time spent in sports is associated with increased satisfaction and higher self-ratings of strength and attractiveness. Physical activity is associated with achievement, weight reduction, muscle tone, and stress reduction, all of which aid a positive self-image (Kirshnit, Richards, & Ham, 1988).

Environmental factors that influence adolescents' social development and self-image affect their later adult behavior. The two most important groups of people who influence the social behavior of adolescents are parents and peers. There is no question that adolescents are responsive to parental influence. If their views are sharply different from those of their parents, they put up serious resistance only in life-altering decisions, for example, medical decisions (Scherer & Reppucci, 1988). In comparing peer and parental influence, studies disagree, but most indicate that adolescents' attitudes fall somewhere between those of their parents and those of their peers (e.g., Kelly & Goodwin, 1983).

secondary sex characteristics: The physical features of a person's gender identity that are not directly involved with reproduction, such as pubic hair.

Peer Groups. The influence of peer groups is formidable; *peer groups* are people who identify with and compare themselves to each other. Peer groups often consist of people of the same age, sex, and race, although adolescents may change their peer group memberships and belong to more than one group. As adolescents spend more time away from parents and home, they experience increasing pressure to conform to the values of their peer group.

Peer groups are a source of information about society, educational aspirations, and group activities. Some peer groups are institutional (set up by school, church, or parents); others are formed spontaneously and set up by the teenagers themselves (B. B. Brown, 1990). Peers set standards for adolescents; they sometimes praise, sometimes cajole, and constantly pressure one another to conform to behavioral standards, including dress styles, social interaction, and forms of rebellion such as drug taking or shoplifting. Most important, they influence the adolescent's developing self-concept. Recognizing the importance of peer pressure among the young, the administrations of Presidents Reagan and Bush attempted to curb drug abuse among teenagers by instituting the "Just Say No" campaign. The goal of the campaign was to encourage teenagers to say no to peers who offered them drugs.

Gender Differences: Behavior and Mental Processes

Learning Objective 17.4
Discuss gender differences in sex roles and in intellectual functioning.

Gender differences are differences between males and females in behavior or mental processes. Research on the biological factors that affect gender differences has been extensive and has shown few if any important differences between the sexes. Although adolescent girls often reach milestones earlier than boys, the difference between the genders usually disappear by late adolescence (Cohn, 1991). Learning and experience, the way a person is raised and taught, have a far more profound impact on behaviors in which there seems to be a gender difference.

Gender Identity. As noted earlier, a key feature of adolescence is that it is a period of transition and change. Adolescents must develop their own *identities*, a sense of themselves as independent, mature individuals. One important aspect of identity is **gender identity,** a person's sense of being male or female. Children develop a sense of gender identity by age 3 years; by age 4 or 5, children realize that their identity is permanent; and by age 8, children know that alteration in their hair, clothes, or behavior does not alter their gender. Consider for example the experience that adolescents have when their bodies change in appearance very rapidly, sometimes in unpredictable ways. During the transition to adulthood, they often try out various types of behaviors, including those relating to male–female relationships and dating.

Many psychologists believe that once gender identity is firmly established, children and then adolescents attempt to bring their behavior and thoughts within generally accepted gender specific roles. Young children use gender as a social category. In doing so, appropriate and inappropriate gender behaviors are decided on. In fact, many children's and adolescents' self-esteem and feelings of worth become tied to their gender-based perceptions about themselves, many of which are determined by identification with the same-sex parent (Heilbrun, Wydra, & Friedberg, 1989).

gender differences: Differences between males and females in behavior or mental processes.

gender identity: A person's sense of being male or female.

sex roles: The full range of behaviors that are generally associated with one's gender; they help people establish who they are; also called *gender roles.*

sex-role stereotyping: The typical beliefs concerning the patterns of behavior that are expected of persons, depending on their gender.

Sex Roles. **Sex roles,** or gender roles, are the full range of behaviors generally associated with one's gender; these roles help people establish who they are. However, in the course of establishing a sexual identity, people sometimes adopt **sex-role stereotyping.** That is, they learn gender-based behaviors that are strongly expected, regulated, and reinforced by society. Men, for example, may learn to hide their emotions because society frowns on men who cry in public and reinforces men who appear strong and stoical when faced with sorrow or stress.

Parents are the first and most important sources of gender-based stereotyping; they influence a child in the earliest years. Peers and the schools are the second most important sources of information. Last but not least important, the media, especially television, has a profound impact on people's perceptions. Even today, television networks do not seem to be able to let a woman be "the" six o'clock news anchor.

Sex-role stereotypes are very difficult to change; even today, relatively few women plan to become firefighters and few men intend to teach in day care centers.

Androgyny. In earlier decades, women were expected to pursue marriage and homemaking, which were considered full-time careers. Today, women's plans often include a career outside the home, which may be interrupted for childbearing. Since the 1970s, however, many men and women have developed new attitudes about sex roles, encouraging *both* traditionally masculine and traditionally feminine traits. They have deliberately adopted **androgynous** behaviors, those that are shared by both sexes. Thus, both men and women fix cars, have careers, do housework, and help care for children. A number of studies have found that people who rate high in androgynous characteristics tend to feel more fulfilled and more competent when dealing with social and personal issues (Worell, 1978).

Differences in Abilities. Cognitive differences between boys and girls, and among male and female adolescents, are minimal, and in most cases nonexistent. Gender differences in verbal ability are so small that researchers should not say that they exist (Hyde & Linn, 1988) and when they exist in mathematical abilities, differences are very small (Hyde, Fennema, & Lamon, 1990). This does not mean that some differences are not apparent in certain tests (such as the SAT), but that when cultural variables are extracted, the differences are small, unimportant, and refer to overall group differences.

Biologically based mechanisms may account for some gender-based behaviors, but learning is far more potent in establishing and maintaining sex-role stereotypes and gender-specific attitudes (see Chapter 5, p. 193). Our society continues to reinforce gender-based activities (Pomerleau, Bolduc, Malcuit, & Cossette, 1990). This shapes the behavior of children and adolescents into sex roles. However, as our society's views change, so will gender-based activities, including some sexual behaviors, considered next.

Sexual Behavior

Learning Objective 17.5
Discuss the rate of adolescent sexual behavior and pregnancy in the United States and explain why teenagers often fail to use contraceptives.

In human beings, learned attitudes have a greater influence than biological factors in determining sexual behavior, and people first learn about such relationships at home. Children are affected by their parents' attitudes and behavior—whether, for instance, they hug and kiss openly, seem embarrassed by their bodies, or talk freely about sexual matters. A strong relationships exists between a mother's own sexual behavior and that of her daughter (Katchadourian, 1990).

Relaxed Attitudes. American adolescents view sexual intimacy as an important and normal part of growing up, and premarital heterosexual activity has become increasingly common among adolescents, especially 13- to 17-year-olds. One study found that 60% of white male teenagers had had intercourse by age 18, and 60% of white girls just a year later, by age 19 years. For blacks, 60% of males had had intercourse by age 16 years, and females, 60% by age 18. There are great individual differences in the age of first intercourse and its subsequent frequency; it is not uncommon for a first intercourse to occur at age 14 or 15, and

androgynous: The condition in which some typically male and some typically female characteristics are apparent in one individual.

then for the teenager not to have relations again for a year or 2 (Furstenberg, Brooks-Gunn, & Chase-Lansdale, 1989).

More relaxed attitudes about adolescent sexual behavior have brought about increased awareness of contraception and the problems of teenage pregnancy. Nevertheless, in the late 1980s, 1 in 10 teenage girls became pregnant—in fact, by the middle of the decade, 19% of white females and 41% of black females became pregnant by age 18 (Furstenberg et al., 1989). More than 1 million teenage girls become pregnant each year in the United States, and nearly 470,000 give birth. The consequences of childbearing for teen mothers are great; a young woman's chances for future education and employment become more limited, and many young women are forced to rely on public assistance.

Contraception. Not using contraception is the principal reason for teenage pregnancy. Morrison (1985) asserts that teenagers are still largely uninformed or ill-informed about reproductive physiology and contraception. Too many underestimate the likelihood of pregnancy and have negative attitudes toward contraception, although they have trouble explaining why. Low levels of self-esteem, and feelings of powerlessness and alienation are also associated with the personalities of those who fail to use contraceptives. However, as teenagers become older and more sexually active, they tend to use contraception more responsibly (Brooks-Gunn & Furstenberg, 1989).

Erik Erikson and the Search for Identity

Learning Objective 17.6
Describe Erik Erikson's psychosocial stage theory of development.

After years of being allowed to behave like children, suddenly adolescents are expected to behave like adults. Trying to achieve the freedom and responsibilities of adulthood, such as taking responsibility for contraception while giving up the security of childhood, can create stress. Marlene, introduced at the beginning of this module, is nervous about the enormous decisions she is facing as she prepares to leave high school, friends, and family to attend college and choose a career path.

Erikson believed in adolescence as a time of identity formation and explained how the "identity crisis" would shape the adult each adolescent would eventually become.

Erikson's Theory. Perhaps no one is more closely associated with the challenges of adolescence than Erik H. Erikson (1902–1990), who studied with Freud in Austria. Erikson's theory is noted for its integration of a person's disposition and environment with historical forces in shaping that person's life. With a logical, coherent approach to studying human behavior, Erik Erikson is a key figure in the history of psychology.

Erikson saw that environment–person relationships were interactive—it is thus often called a psychosocial theory. He asserted that people have to accept responsibility for their lives and their place in history. Nowhere is this idea more evident than in adolescence. According to Erikson, the growth and turmoil of adolescence creates an identity crisis, and the major task for adolescents is to resolve that crisis successfully by forming an *identity.* Failure to complete the process leaves the adolescent confused about adult roles and unable to cope with the demands of adulthood, including the development of mature relationships with members of the opposite sex (Erikson, 1968).

Erikson believed that people form self-images from their perceptions of themselves as well as from other people's perceptions of them (expressed through behavior). Membership in political, religious, or ideological groups, for example, helps adolescents discover what they believe in and what satisfies their needs. Erikson maintains that personality development continues throughout life.

Erikson's theory describes a continuum of stages, dilemmas, or crises through which all individuals must pass. Each stage can have either a positive or a nega-

TABLE 17.1 Erikson's eight stages of psychosocial development

Stages	Approximate age	Important event	Description
1. Basic trust vs. basic mistrust	Birth to 12–18 months	Feeding	The infant must form a first loving, trusting relationship with the caregiver, or develop a sense of mistrust.
2. Autonomy vs. shame/doubt	18 months to 3 years	Toilet training	The child's energies are directed toward the development of physical skills, including walking, grasping, and rectal sphincter control. The child learns control but may develop shame and doubt if not handled well.
3. Initiative vs. guilt	3 to 6 years	Independence	The child continues to become more assertive and to take more initiative, but may be too forceful, leading to guilt feelings.
4. Industry vs. inferiority	6 to 12 years	School	The child must deal with demands to learn new skills or risk a sense of inferiority, failure, and incompetence.
5. Identity vs. role confusion	Adolescence	Peer relationships	The teenager must achieve a sense of identity in occupation, sex roles, politics, and religion.
6. Intimacy vs. isolation	Young adulthood	Love relationships	The young adult must develop intimate relationships or suffer feelings of isolation.
7. Generativity vs. stagnation	Middle adulthood	Parenting	Each adult must find some way to satisfy and support the next generation.
8. Ego integrity vs. despair	Late adulthood	Reflection on and acceptance of one's life	The culmination is a sense of acceptance of oneself as one is and of feeling fulfilled.

tive outcome. New dilemmas emerge as a person grows older and faces new responsibilities, tasks, and social relationships. A person may experience a dilemma as an opportunity and face it positively or view the dilemma as a catastrophe and fail to cope with it effectively. For example, an adolescent may be pressured to engage in drug use or shoplifting; whether the teen succumbs to pressure or emerges as a victor able to withstand peer pressure affects his or her self-image. To emerge as a fully mature, stable adult, a person has to pass through each stage successfully. Table 17.1 lists the stages of Erikson's theory and the important events, crises, dilemmas, and opportunities associated with them. We take a closer look at each stage.

Erikson's Eight Stages of Development. Stages 1 through 4 of Erikson's theory cover birth through age 12 years. Stage 1 involves the development of *basic trust versus basic mistrust.* During their first months, infants make distinctions about the world and decide whether it is a comfortable, loving place in which they can feel basic trust. At this stage they develop beliefs about the essential truthfulness of other people. If their needs are adequately met, they learn that the world is a predictable and safe place. Infants whose needs are not met learn to distrust the world.

During the second stage, the toddler must resolve the crisis of *autonomy versus shame and doubt.* Success in toilet training and other tasks involving control leads to a sense of autonomy and more mature behavior. Difficulties dealing with autonomy during this stage result in fears and a sense of shame and doubt.

The third stage, which occurs at ages 4 and 5, is that of *initiative versus guilt,* when children develop the ability to use their own initiative. During this stage, they either gain a sense of independence and good feelings about themselves or develop a sense of guilt, lack of acceptance, and negative feelings about their sexuality. If children learn to dress themselves, clean their rooms, and develop friendships with other children, they can feel a sense of mastery; alternatively, they can be dependent or regretful. Next, in Stage 4, *industry versus inferiority,* children either develop feelings of competence and confidence in their abilities or experience failure, inferiority, and feelings of incompetence.

Erikson's Stage 5, *identity versus role confusion,* marks the end of childhood and the beginning of adolescence. At this time, adolescents must decide who they are and what they want to do in life. Otherwise, they will become confused and rebellious. The special problems of adolescence—including rebellion, suicide, and drug problems—must be dealt with. During Stage 6, *intimacy versus isolation,* young adults begin to select other people with whom they can form intimate relationships. They learn to relate on a warm, social basis with members of the opposite sex. The alternative is to become isolated.

In Stage 7, *generativity versus stagnation,* people hope to convey information, love, and warmth to others, particularly their children. As adults, they hope to influence their family and the world; otherwise, they will stagnate, feeling that life is unexciting. In Erikson's eighth stage, *ego integrity versus despair,* people decide whether their existence is meaningful, happy, and cohesive or wasteful and unproductive. Many individuals never complete Stage 8; those who do feel fulfilled, with a sense that they understand, at least partly, what life is about.

A key point of Erikson's theory is that people go through each stage, resolving the crises of that stage as best they can. Of course, people grow older whether or not they are ready for the next stage. A person may still have unresolved conflicts, opportunities, and dilemmas from the previous stage. This can cause anxiety and discomfort and may make resolution of advanced stages more difficult. Because adolescence is such a crucial stage for the formation of a firm identity, the environment surround an adolescent becomes especially important for the emerging adult.

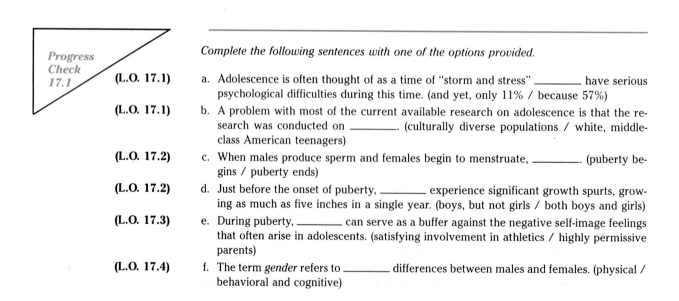

Progress Check 17.1

Complete the following sentences with one of the options provided.

(L.O. 17.1) a. Adolescence is often thought of as a time of "storm and stress" ________ have serious psychological difficulties during this time. (and yet, only 11% / because 57%)

(L.O. 17.1) b. A problem with most of the current available research on adolescence is that the research was conducted on ________. (culturally diverse populations / white, middle-class American teenagers)

(L.O. 17.2) c. When males produce sperm and females begin to menstruate, ________. (puberty begins / puberty ends)

(L.O. 17.2) d. Just before the onset of puberty, ________ experience significant growth spurts, growing as much as five inches in a single year. (boys, but not girls / both boys and girls)

(L.O. 17.3) e. During puberty, ________ can serve as a buffer against the negative self-image feelings that often arise in adolescents. (satisfying involvement in athletics / highly permissive parents)

(L.O. 17.4) f. The term *gender* refers to ________ differences between males and females. (physical / behavioral and cognitive)

(L.O. 17.4) g. ________ refers to a full range of behaviors that help us understand our identity as being male or female. (Sex roles / Gender identity)

(L.O. 17.4) h. Gender-based self-perceptions are strongly influenced by a child's identification with ________. (the parent of the same sex / brothers, sisters, and children of the same age)

(L.O. 17.5) i. A primary reason that premarital sexual behavior has become increasingly common among American adolescents is that teenagers today perceive sexual intimacy as ________. (a recreational activity / a normal part of growing up)

(L.O. 17.5) j. Adolescents frequently do not use contraceptives because ________. (parental permission is required / they are uninformed about reproduction)

(L.O. 17.6) k. According to Erikson, we each ________ from the perceptions we have of ourselves and from the way others behave toward us. (decide what developmental stage to tackle next / form our self-image)

(L.O. 17.6) l. Erikson believed that a person would remain confused and would be unable to cope with the demands of adulthood if the person ________ during adolescence. (experienced an identity crisis / failed to form an identity)

(L.O. 17.6) m. Resolution of conflict during Erikson's stages of development should be viewed ________. (in terms of "passing" or "failing" / on a continuum of doing one's best)

(L.O. 17.6) n. During Erikson's ________ stage, adults convey information, love, and warmth to others, or they find life boring and unexciting. (intimacy versus isolation / generativity versus stagnation)

Adulthood

Learning Objective 17.7 Discuss some of the current research interests of developmental psychologists.

Psychologists look at growing older and the process of development as a process of growth, not of deterioration. Psychologists recognize that at all times of life, people's biological inheritance, life experiences, and frame of mind affect their development. People do not follow predetermined paths to emotional turmoil or to mental or physical dependence upon others. Psychologists therefore focus on development throughout the entire life span, recognizing that new challenges are faced in every stage of a person's life. They study adult development by looking at the factors that contribute to stability or frustration, to a sense of accomplishment or feelings of despair, and to physical factors that may affect functioning. Researchers today are also examining the differences between men and women, with a special emphasis on the unique experiences of women in U.S. culture. Minorities are being studied, and theories now are recognizing and focusing on cultural diversity. Psychologists are now also recognizing that a person's career, not just his or her family or life stage, is a defining characteristic of adulthood. Adults spend an enormous amount of time and energy on their careers, topics which have been studied relatively little by psychologists.

Physical Development

Learning Objective 17.8 Discuss the fitness, sexual, and sensory changes that occur during adulthood.

Although physical development in adulthood is slower, less dramatic, and sometimes less visible than in childhood and adolescence, it does occur.

Fitness Changes. Fitness involves both a psychological and a physical sense of well-being. Physically, human beings are at their peak of agility, speed, and strength between ages 18 and 30. From 30 to 40, there is some loss of agility and speed. Between 40 and 60, much greater losses occur. In general, strength, muscle tone, and overall fitness deteriorate from age 30 on. People become more susceptible to disease; respiratory, circulatory, and blood pressure problems are more apparent; lung capacity and physical strength are significantly reduced.

Sexual Changes. In adulthood, sexual changes occur in adults of both sexes; for example, in women, there is often an increase in sexual desire; but in men, erections are less rapidly achieved. In these childbearing years, women and men's sexual desires are sometimes modulated by the stresses of raising a family and juggling a work schedule. For women, midlife changes in hormones lead to the cessation of ovulation and menstruation at about age 50 years, a process known as *menopause.* At about the same age, men's testosterone levels decrease, their ejaculations are weaker and briefer, and their desire for sexual intercourse decreases from adolescent levels.

Sensory Changes. In early adulthood, most sensory abilities remain fairly stable, and many women and men increase their involvement in fitness and better nutrition. As the years pass, however, adults must contend with inevitable sensory losses. Reaction time slows; visual acuity decreases; and the risks of glaucoma and retinal detachment increase. Hearing loss also occurs. By age 60 years, most people can no longer hear high-frequency sounds, and some are unable to hear ordinary speech.

Social Development: Midlife Crises

Learning Objective 17.9 Make a distinction between the terms *transition* and *crisis,* and explain how these terms apply to a variety of life changes.

If it hasn't happened already, some time in the future, you probably will have a crisis in your life—so goes the popular idea that people pass through predictable life crises. In the movies, a midlife crisis is seen as a time when people reevaluate their choices, change their life, reorient, become depressed in the process, buy a fast sports car, and perhaps throw over their spouse for another. The idea that people will have a life crisis is widely accepted and considered almost inevitable. It sounds depressing.

Are crises unavoidable, though? Does everyone go through a midlife crisis? We know that people go through transitions. At certain junctures, new decisions must be made, and people must reassess who they are, where they are going, and how they want to get there. But does this have to be a crisis?

A distinction should be drawn between the idea of a *transition* and a *crisis.* A transition suggests that a person has reached a time in life when old ways of coping no longer work, old tasks have been accomplished, and new methods of living are forthcoming. A person in transition must face new dilemmas, challenges, and responsibilities, which often require reassessment, reappraisal, and development of new skills. A *crisis,* by contrast, occurs when old ways of coping become ineffective and a person is helpless, not knowing what to do, and needing new, radically different coping strategies. Crises are often perceived as painful turning points and catastrophes in a person's life.

Not everyone experiences the infamous midlife crisis, but most people pass through a midlife transition, and some pass through two, three, or even more transitions. Often, a transition occurs at the beginning of adulthood when people must give up adolescent freedom and accept adult responsibilities. At around age 30 years, another transition may occur when career and relationships begun in a person's 20s are reevaluated and sometimes rejected. In the transitions of early and middle adulthood, people reorient their career and family choices—the midlife "crisis" at about age 40. Sometimes parents experience another transition when their children leave the home—often called the empty nest syndrome; the empty nest syndrome is less likely to occur, however, in people who are engaged in paid employment outside the home (Adelmann, Antonucci, Crohan, & Cole-

A mid-life transition, popularly believed to occur around age forty, may or may not be experienced as a crisis.

man, 1989). Transitions also occur at retirement, not only for the retiree, but for his or her spouse.

Consider Sarah. Sarah, a single 44-year-old, has operated her own greeting card distributing company for 20 years. Although the company earns her a comfortable living, it has yet to produce enough profits to enable Sarah to establish a retirement fund, and she worries about how she'll make ends meet in another 20 years. Moreover, Sarah would like to try another vocation, perhaps a career in interior decorating. Although she finds the idea of a career change exciting, Sarah questions whether she has the skill and energy to start over. Friends say Sarah is experiencing a midlife crisis. Nonetheless, Sarah may emerge from her situation a happier, wiser, and more secure adult.

People who experience midlife transitions show no evidence of increased maladjustment or increased suicides or alcoholism. In fact, suicide rates are at their lowest during midlife transitions. For some people, however, midlife changes can be difficult. The midlife change must be examined for each individual, rather than across all individuals. Like the adolescents in storm and stress, some adults face crises in their lives, while others merely go through transitions that are not perceived as difficult or painful. Adults, like adolescents, face new experiences, new task demands, and new dilemmas as they grow older. Their unique personalities and ways of coping with the world shape whether they will have a crisis or whether they will move from stage to stage in a relatively smooth manner. The term *midlife crisis* may be a misnomer; as Levinson (1980) suggests, it should more properly be called a midlife transition—a transition that may be more difficult for some individuals than others.

Personality Development

Learning Objective 17.10 Discuss some of the things researchers have discovered in recent years concerning adult personality development.

A basic tenet of traditional personality theory is that, regardless of day-to-day variations, an individual's personality remains stable over time. That is, despite the frequently observed deviations from their normal patterns or stages of development, the way people cope with life tends to remain fairly consistent throughout their lifetimes. While this may be true to a great extent, recent research is challenging traditional theory and shows that personality may be sensitive to the unique experiences of the individual, especially during the adult years. The data suggest that the adult years are filled with great personal challenges and opportunities and therefore are the years in which people need to be innovative, flexible, and adaptive.

Positive changes during adulthood—developing a sense of generativity, fulfilling yearnings for love and respect—usually depend on some degree of success at earlier life stages. Adults who continue to operate with youthful ideals and false assumptions are less likely to experience personality growth in later life.

Women have undergone special scrutiny since the early 1970s. Researchers now recognize that the male-dominated psychology profession of the 1950s generated a host of personality theories that failed to highlight adequately women's unique personality and development issues. Personality researchers now acknowledge that the life experiences of contemporary women are unique. Women face challenges in the work force and the home that were not conceived of three decades ago. Managing careers, creating homes, and developing a sense of personal satisfaction have given rise to the "supermom" phenomenon: women who are trying to do it all—home, family, career, personal satisfaction. Serious research into supermom and the psychological life of women is just beginning to emerge. We discuss personality development further in Chapter 11. Building Table 17.1 presents a summary of changes in important domains of adult functioning—for men and women.

Adult Stage Theories

Learning Objective 17.11 Compare and contrast Levinson's and Erikson's stage theories, and discuss Levinson's four eras of adult life.

Some people—perhaps the more poetic among us—think of life as a journey that each person takes along a road from birth to death. The concept of a journey through life is similar to Erik Erikson's stage theory, in which people move through a series of stages, resolving a different dilemma in each stage. An important aspect of Erikson's theory is that people progress in a specific direction from the beginning of life to the end.

One noted theorist, Daniel Levinson (mentioned previously in relation to transitions vs. crises), has also devised a stage theory of adult development. He agrees that people go through stages and that they have similar experiences at certain points in their lives. He also agrees that studying those shared experiences allows psychologists to help people manage their lives. However, unlike Erikson, Levinson does not see life as a journey toward some specific goal or objective. In Levinson's view, a valid theory of development is not a blueprint that everyone must follow. Rather, a theory of development should lay out the stages (or eras) during which individuals work out various developmental tasks.

Levinson's Four Eras. Levinson (1978) suggests that as people grow older, they adapt to the demands and tasks of life. He describes four basic eras in the adult life cycle, each with distinctive qualities and different life problems, tasks, and situations; each also brings with it different *life structures,* or unique patterns of behavior and ways of interacting with the world. However, because no two people have the same life situation, no two people adapt in exactly the same way. Each person develops a life structure to deal with each era. A young man in his early 30s, for example, may become involved in religious work and learn how groups function to achieve common goals; those skills may be less necessary during his 40s, when he concentrates more on his sales career.

During late adulthood family relationships again become very important.

In each era, people develop stable life structures that get them through the period successfully. They then enter a new era in which they encounter new life conditions, challenges, and dilemmas. Because the old life structures no longer work, they must go through a period of transition during which they adjust to their new situation. Sometimes the transition is difficult, characterized by anxiety and even depression. Thus, according to this theory, we can think of a person's life as alternating between stable periods and transitional periods. The four eras outlined by Levinson are

Major changes in important domains of adult functioning

Building Table 17.1

Period	Physical change	Cognitive change	Work roles	Personality development	Major tasks
Young adulthood 18–25	Peak functioning in most physical skills; optimum time for child-bearing	Cognitive skills high on most measures	Choose career, which may involve several job changes; low work satisfaction is common	Conformist; task of intimacy	Separate from family of origin; form partnership; begin new family; find job; create individual life pattern
Early adulthood 25–40	Still good physical functioning in most areas; health habits during this time establish later risks	Peak period of cognitive skills on most measures	Rising work satisfaction; major emphasis on career or work success; most career progress steps made	Task of generativity	Rear family; establish personal work pattern and strive for success
Middle adulthood 40–65					

- Ages 11–17—adolescence
- Ages 18–45—early adulthood
- Ages 46–65—middle adulthood
- Ages 65 on—late adulthood

Each of Levinson's eras is made up of several stages. During *adolescence,* young people enter the adult world but are still immature and vulnerable. During *early adulthood,* they make their first major life choices regarding family, occupation, and style of living. Throughout this period, adults move toward greater independence and senior positions in the community. They raise their children, strive to advance their careers, and launch their offspring into the adult world. Early adulthood is an era of striving for, gaining, and accepting responsibility. By the end of this era, at about age 45 years, people no longer have to care for their babies, but they may assume the responsibility of caring for their parents.

The much discussed midlife crisis occurs at the end of the early adulthood. During this era, people realize that their lives are half over—that if they are to change their lives, they must do so now. Some resign themselves to their original course, while others decide to change, grow, and strive to achieve new goals. (This era is equivalent to Erikson's stage of generativity versus stagnation.)

Middle adulthood spans the years from 46 to 65. Adults who have gone through a midlife crisis now live with the decisions they made during early adulthood. Career and family are usually well established. People experience either a sense of satisfaction, self-worth, and accomplishment or a sense that much of their life has been wasted. It is often during this period that a man or woman reaches his or her peak in creativity and achievement (Simonton, 1988). In the middle of this era, some people go through a crisis similar to that of early adulthood. Sometimes, it is a continuation of the earlier crisis; at other times, it is a new one.

The years after age 50 are ones of mellowing. People approaching their 60s begin to prepare for late adulthood, making whatever major career and family decisions are necessary before retirement. People in their early 60s generally learn to assess their lives, not in terms of money or day-to-day successes, but according to whether they have been meaningful, happy, and cohesive. At this time, people stop blaming others for their problems. They are less concerned about disputes with other people. They try to optimize their lives because they know that at least two thirds of it has passed, and they wish to make the most of their remaining years. Depending on how well they come to accept themselves, the next decade may be one of great fulfillment or great despair.

Levinson's fourth and final era, *late adulthood,* covers the years from age 65 on. During retirement, many people relax and enjoy the fruits of their labors. Children, grandchildren, and even great-grandchildren can become the focus of an older person's life.

Learning Objective 17.12
Explain why Levinson's theory receives some criticism, and discuss a recent study that outlines the life transitions of women.

Gender Differences. Levinson developed his theory by studying 40 men in detail over several years. His subjects were interviewed weekly for several months and were then interviewed again after 2 years. Spouses were interviewed, and extensive biographical data were collected. Levinson's theory has achieved wide acclaim, but it has also been challenged. Psychologists point out that it is based on information gathered from a small sample of middle-class men. It does not consider socioeconomic class or gender differences or the many variations in life-style such as postponing marriage and parenting to later years.

Women do not necessarily follow the same life stages or changes as men. As children, women are taught different values, goals, and approaches toward life, and these are often reflected later in their choices of vocations, hobbies, and intellectual pursuits (Kalichman, 1989). Women have traditionally sought different career opportunities, although this is changing. In the field of law, for example, women now compose nearly half of all law school students. However, female attorneys often choose careers that do not follow the traditional male associate–partnership ladder.

The developmental course of women, and especially of women's transitions, is similar to that of men, but women tend to experience transitions and life events at later ages and in more irregular sequences than those reported by Levinson. In a major study of women's transitions, Mercer, Nichols, and Doyle (1989) found a developmental progression for women. They especially considered the role of motherhood and how it influences the life courses of women. Mercer, Nichols, and Doyle broke the developmental progression into five eras at which there are important transitions:

- Ages 16–25—launching into adulthood
- Ages 26–30—leveling
- Ages 36–40—liberating
- Ages 61–65—regeneration/redirection
- Ages 65–80—creativity/destructiveness

In *launching into adulthood,* women break away from families to go to school, marry, or work. In *age 30—leveling,* many women readjust their life courses; this is often a time for marriage, separation, or divorce. In *age 40—liberating,* women focus their aspirations and grow personally. In *age 65—regeneration/redirection,* women, like men, adjust to their lifetime choices and prepare for retirement and a more leisurely life-style. In *age 80—creativity/destructiveness,* women are challenged to adapt to health changes and loss of spouses and friends, and this time is characterized by a surge of creativity, or sometimes depression. With a five-stage approach, this women's developmental life-stage theory is similar to Levinson's, but it has its own unique flavor and recognizes differences in the life courses of men and women.

Today many universities, recognizing that women have special issues that are different from those of men, are establishing departments of women's studies. Women still face discrimination in the work force, and society has vacillating expectations for women and for child care. Women still have the burden of family responsibilities, especially child care; in the aftermath of a divorce, the woman usually gets physical custody of the children. The assumption of child care after divorce has sharp economic consequences that alter the life-style and course of life stages for women. So the differences in the life stages of men and women, whether upper-, middle-, or lower-class, are evident.

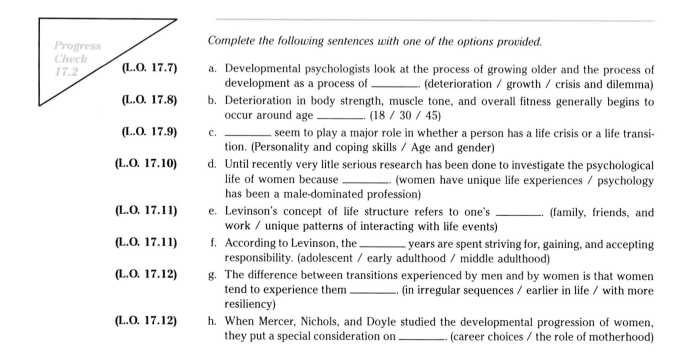

Progress Check 17.2

Complete the following sentences with one of the options provided.

(L.O. 17.7) a. Developmental psychologists look at the process of growing older and the process of development as a process of ________. (deterioration / growth / crisis and dilemma)

(L.O. 17.8) b. Deterioration in body strength, muscle tone, and overall fitness generally begins to occur around age ________. (18 / 30 / 45)

(L.O. 17.9) c. ________ seem to play a major role in whether a person has a life crisis or a life transition. (Personality and coping skills / Age and gender)

(L.O. 17.10) d. Until recently very litle serious research has been done to investigate the psychological life of women because ________. (women have unique life experiences / psychology has been a male-dominated profession)

(L.O. 17.11) e. Levinson's concept of life structure refers to one's ________. (family, friends, and work / unique patterns of interacting with life events)

(L.O. 17.11) f. According to Levinson, the ________ years are spent striving for, gaining, and accepting responsibility. (adolescent / early adulthood / middle adulthood)

(L.O. 17.12) g. The difference between transitions experienced by men and by women is that women tend to experience them ________. (in irregular sequences / earlier in life / with more resiliency)

(L.O. 17.12) h. When Mercer, Nichols, and Doyle studied the developmental progression of women, they put a special consideration on ________. (career choices / the role of motherhood)

Aging

As people grow older, they age experientially as well as physically; that is, they gather experiences and expand their worlds. Nevertheless, in Western society, growing older is not always easy, especially because of the negative stereotypes associated with the aging process in both men and women.

Although most older adults face aging from a mature and experienced vantage point, are in good health, and look forward to a fruitful retirement, they also face many challenges. Sometimes, failing health (their own or a spouse's) complicates life; sometimes society's negative attitudes complicate it. In general, being over age 65, like being over 21, brings with it new developmental tasks—retirement, health issues, and maintenance of a long-term standard of living.

An Aging Population

Learning Objective 17.13 State some of the trends in the population of elderly people, and discuss social conditions that make life difficult for some elderly people.

How older people view themselves depends, in part, on how society treats them. Many Asian cultures greatly respect the elderly for their wisdom and maturity; in such societies, gray hair is a mark of distinction, not embarrassment. In contrast, the United States is a youth-oriented society where people spend a fortune on everything from hair dyes to facelifts to make themselves look younger. However, because the average age of Americans is climbing, how we perceive the elderly and how they perceive themselves may be changing.

In the first 5 years of the 1990s, approximately 12% of the U.S. population—more than 30 million Americans—will be 65 or older. The proportion of elderly people is expected to increase substantially by 2030, and the number of Americans past 65 will exceed 60 million (see Figure 17.2). At present, the average life expectancy at birth in the United States is about 74.7 years. Note that life expectancy is different for men and women—women at age 65 live about 3 years longer

Figure 17.2

In the year 2030, the U.S. population will be distributed fairly evenly among 10-year age groups ranging from birth through 69 years old (U.S. Census Bureau).

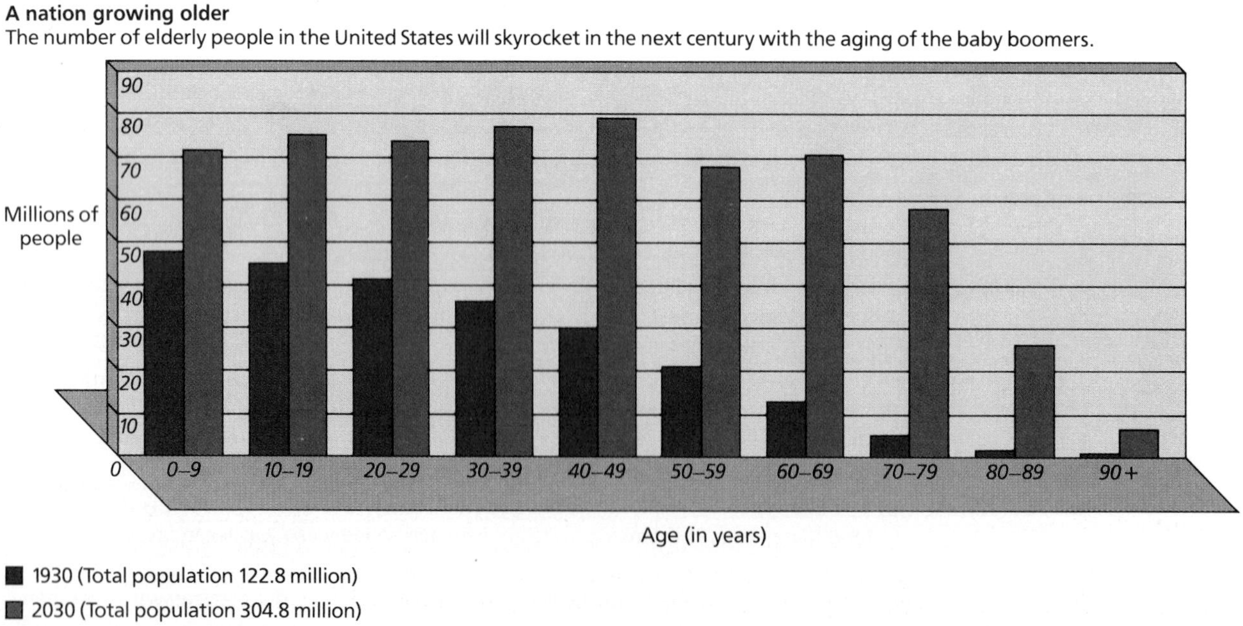

than men, on the average, and at birth, their life expectancy is now 7 years greater!

For many people, the years after age 60 are filled with excitement. Financially, two thirds of American workers are covered by pension plans provided by their employers. Socially, most maintain close friendships and stay in touch with family members. Some, however, experience financial problems, while others experience loneliness and isolation because many of their friends and relatives have died or they have lost touch with their families. In the United States, there are now as many people over the age of 60 as there are under the age of 7 years, yet funding for programs involving the health and psychological well-being of older people is relatively limited.

In an Asian household, elders are deeply respected.

Aging: Myths, Realities, and Stereotypes

There is a widely held myth that all older people are less intelligent, lacking in common sense, unable to care for themselves, financially insecure, inflexible, and environmental factors, these theories rely on both concepts. The *wear-and-tear* as they were in their earlier adulthood. They work, play golf, compete in races, socialize, and stay politically aware and active. Healthy elderly people maintain a good sex life (Bretschneider & McCoy, 1988), and if they were not depressed earlier, they are unlikely to become depressed. As grandparents, they may be seen as buffers between children and their parents, as wise advice givers, and as a link to the past. Children, in fact, may have difficulty understanding why older people are viewed so negatively. Building Table 17.2 summarizes important changes in adult functioning from young adulthood to late adulthood.

Stereotypes about the elderly have given rise to **ageism,** prejudice against the elderly and the discrimination that follows from it. Ageism is prevalent in the job market, in which older people are not given the same opportunities as their young coworkers, and in housing and health care. Ageism is exceptionally prevalent in the media—on television and in newspapers, cartoons, and magazines—and in everyday language. For example, *elder* statesman implies that a person is experienced, intelligent, or perhaps conservative. However, *old* statesman might suggest that a person is past his or her prime, tired, or useless. The term *old people* may allude to positive elements in older adults—for example, the perfect grandparent—or to negative qualities such as grouchiness or mental deficiencies. What does *old* mean?

People have a variety of ideas about older adults, and it follows that they may behave differently toward various kinds of older adults. People who are perceived to represent negative stereotypes are more likely to suffer discrimination than those who appear to represent more positive stereotypes. This means that an older person who appears healthy, bright, and alert is more likely to be treated with the same respect shown to younger people. By contrast, an older adult who *appears* less capable may not be given the same respect or treatment. Chapter 15 shows that first impressions have a potent effect on an individual's behavior. This seems to be particularly true for older people. An older person's physical appearance may invoke ageism and discrimination, whereas a younger person's appearance seems less likely to have such an immediate effect. In any case, ageism can be reduced if people recognize the diversity that exists among aging populations.

ageism: Discrimination on the basis of age, often resulting in the denial of rights and services to the elderly.

Theories of Aging

Learning Objective 17.14 Describe the heredity, external factors, and physiological–genetic theories of aging.

The quest for eternal youth has inspired extravagant attempts to slow, stop, or reverse the aging process. In recent years, scientists seem to have increased dra-

Major changes in important domains of adult functioning

Building Table 17.2

Period	Physical change	Cognitive change	Work roles	Personality development	Major tasks
Young adulthood 18–25	Peak functioning in most physical skills; optimum time for child-bearing	Cognitive skills high on most measures	Choose career, which may involve several job changes; low work satisfaction is common	Conformist; task of intimacy	Separate from family of origin; form partnership; begin new family; find job; create individual life pattern
Early adulthood 25–40	Still good physical functioning in most areas; health habits during this time establish later risks	Peak period of cognitive skills on most measures	Rising work satisfaction; major emphasis on career or work success; most career progress steps made	Task of generativity	Rear family; establish personal work pattern and strive for success
Middle adulthood 40–65	Beginning signs of physical decline in some areas—strength, elasticity of tissues, height, cardiovascular function	Some signs of loss of cognitive skill on timed, unexercised skills	Plateau on career steps, but higher work satisfaction	Increase in self-confidence, openness; lower use of immature defenses	Launch family; redefine life goals; redefine self outside of family and work roles; begin care for aging parents
Late adulthood 65–75	Significant physical decline on most measures	Small declines for virtually all adults on some skills	Retirement	Perhaps integrated level; perhaps more inferiority; or perhaps self-actualized; task of ego integrity	Cope with retirement; cope with declining health; redefine life goals and sense of self
Late, late adulthood 75+					

matically the life span of some laboratory animals by feeding them calorie-restricted diets. However, so far, the maximum life span attained by human beings is between 100 and 120 years.

Biobehavioral changes occur as the body ages. Years of hard work in the sun are evident in this elderly rancher's face.

Despite the centuries-long search for the secret of eternal youth, psychologists and physicians have been examining the behavioral and physiological changes that accompany aging only since the early 1970s. Three basic types of theories have developed to explain why people age. These theories are based on heredity, external factors, and physiology. Although each emphasizes a different cause for aging, it is most likely that aging results from a combination of all three.

Genes determine much of a person's physical makeup; thus, it is probable that *heredity,* to some extent, determines how long a person will live. There exists a strong genetic component to aging and much supporting evidence. For example, we know that long-lived parents tend to have long-lived offspring. However, researchers still do not know *how* heredity exerts its influence over the aging process.

Kimmel (1980) suggests that *external factors* affect how long a person will live. For example, people who live on farms live longer than those in cities; normal-weight people live longer than overweight people; and people who do not smoke cigarettes, who are not constantly tense, and who do not expose themselves to disease or radiation live longer than others. Because data on external factors are often obtained from correlational studies, one cannot base cause-and-effect statements on these data, but it is reasonable to assume that external factors such as disease, smoking, and obesity affect a person's life span.

Several theories use *physiological and genetic* explanations to account for aging. Because a person's physiological process depends on both hereditary and environmental factors, these theories rely on both concepts. The *wear-and-tear* theory of aging claims that the human organism simply wears out from overuse, much like the parts of a machine; although a commonsense notion, this view does not have much experimental support.

The *homeostatic theory* suggests that the body's ability to adjust to varying situations decreases with age. For example, as the ability to maintain a constant body temperature decreases, cellular and tissue damage occur and aging results. Similarly, when the body can no longer control the use of sugar through the output of insulin, signs of aging appear (Eisdorfer & Wilkie, 1977). On the other hand, aging may be the *cause* of deviations from homeostasis, rather than the result. Whatever the causes of aging, people go through a number of predictable changes as they age; these are often called biobehavioral changes, and we consider them next.

Biobehavioral Changes

Learning Objective 17.15 Describe the biobehavioral approach to aging, various types of dementia, and other physiological changes that can accompany the aging process.

Elderly people must contend with significant biological changes. These changes include alterations in calcium metabolism, which make the bones more brittle; increased susceptibility to diseases of the joints, such as arthritis and gum disease; decreased elasticity in the skin, creating folds and wrinkles. Some biological changes interact with behavioral ones. For example, people who live alone may not eat properly and may suffer vitamin deficiencies as a result. These changes that come about from the interaction of biology and behavior are *biobehavioral changes.* Figure 17.3 on the next page shows some changes seen in elderly people as a result of aging.

Brain Disorders. Many people wrongly assume that aging is inevitably accompanied by *senility,* a term once used to describe cognitive changes that occur in

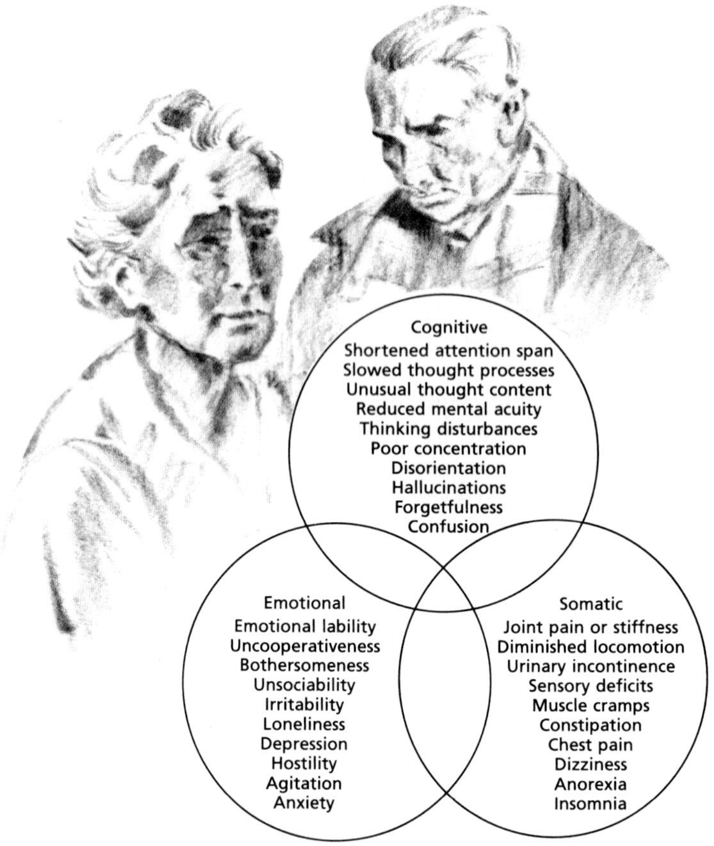

Figure 17.3

Symptoms commonly seen in elderly patients. (Source: Usdin & Hofling, 1978)

older people. Today, these cognitive deficits are known to be caused by brain disorders that occur only in *some* older people. Brain disorders, sometimes termed **dementias,** involve losses of cognitive or mental functioning; at a minimum, they are losses of memory. Many people can develop dementias; for example, we know that AIDS patients have a failing immune system that causes brain infections, which in turn lead to dementia. Practitioners, moreover, realize that some illnesses that cause dementia can be treated and that treatment often halts (but does not reverse) the dementia. Memory loss can occur for recent events (short-term memory) as well as for past events. Additional symptoms include loss of language skills, reduced capacity for abstract thinking, personality changes, and loss of a sense of time and place. Severe and disabling dementias affect about 1.5 million Americans; mild or moderate dementias affect an additional 1 to 5 million (U.S. Congress, 1987). With the increasing number of elderly citizens, these statistics are on the rise, and people are recognizing this as a serious national problem.

dementias: Impairment in mental functioning and global cognitive (thought) abilities of long-standing duration in an otherwise alert individual. Dementias cause a loss of memory and other related symptoms. The leading cause in the United States is Alzheimer's disease.

More than 70 conditions cause dementias. *Reversible dementias,* which are caused by malnutrition, alcoholism, or toxins (poisons), usually affect younger people. *Irreversible dementias* are of two types—multiple infarcts and Alzheimer's disease. Multiple-infarct dementia is usually caused by two or more small strokes (ruptures of small blood vessels in the brain); it results in a slow degeneration of the brain. In the Applying Psychology box on page 336 we examine in detail one of the major dementias—the impact of which is profound—that affect other people in our society: Alzheimer's disease.

Sensory Abilities. Older people are likely to experience decreased sensory abilities. Their vision, hearing, taste, and smell require a higher level of stimulation to respond the way younger people's senses do. Older people, for example, usually are unable to make fine visual discriminations without the aid of glasses, have limited capacity for dark adaptation, and often have some degree of hearing loss, especially in the high-frequency ranges.

Changes in the Nervous System. One change that can be seen easily in older individuals is a slowing of their reaction time in some situations. Although the sensory systems themselves may not be impaired, older people respond less quickly to events. In an emergency, for example, an elderly driver may be unable to stop a car as quickly as a younger driver could. Many explanations for this decreased response time have been suggested, but none has been proved conclusively. Other changes include alterations in brain-wave activity, as measured by an EEG, and in autonomic nervous system activity. Some researchers have suggested that older individuals appear to be underaroused. However, studies of autonomic nervous system responsiveness in old and young adults show little support for this once popular idea (Powell, Milligan, & Furchtgott, 1980).

Alzheimer's disease is increasingly prevalent in our society. Alzheimer's victims have difficulty functioning on a daily basis without assistance.

Overall Health. People's overall health deteriorates as they age. For men, the probability of dying doubles in each decade after midlife. Blood pressure rises, cardiac output decreases, and the likelihood of stroke increases. One impact of this deterioration is that cardiovascular disease influences intellectual functioning by decreasing blood flow to the brain.

Some individuals experience *terminal drop*—a rapid decline in intellectual functioning in the year before death. Some researchers attribute this change to cardiovascular disease, claiming that the decreased blood flow (and resulting decrease in oxygen) to the brain causes declining mental ability and, ultimately, failing health. However, although there is evidence for the terminal drop, no satisfactory method exists for predicting death on the basis of poor performance on intelligence or neuropsychological tests (Botwinick, 1984).

Intellectual Changes

Learning Objective 17.16
Discuss changes in intellectual functioning and work performance that can accompany the aging process.

Perhaps the most distressing change that occurs with aging is a decline in intellectual ability. Many researchers who once believed that general intellectual functioning remains stable throughout life now acknowledge that certain aspects of intelligence deteriorate with age. However, it is difficult to know exactly what and how much change occurs. The debate continues.

Many researchers have studied changes in intellectual functioning. A major problem, however, is defining it. Aged people are likely to do poorly on standardized intelligence tests, not because their intelligence is lower, but because the tests require the manipulation of objects during a timed interval, and older people have a slower reaction time or decreased manual dexterity (often because of arthritis). To overcome these disadvantages, researchers have devised different methodologies for studying intelligence in older people.

Although most research indicates that cognitive and intellectual abilities decrease with advancing age, many of the changes are of little importance for day-to-day functioning. For example, overall vocabulary decreases only slightly (Shneidman, 1989). Moreover, some of the changes observed in laboratory tasks (e.g., reaction time tasks) are either small or reversible (Baltes, Reese, & Lipsitt,

APPLYING PSYCHOLOGY

Alzheimer's Disease

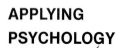

Alzheimer's disease is a degenerative disorder of the brain that could well be the most widespread neurological disorder of all time. As the population grows older, a result of advanced medical technology aiding more people to survive illness and injury, the number of cases of Alzheimer's disease increases. Currently, there are about 1.5 to 2 million diagnosed Alzheimer's patients in the United States; in addition, a large number of cases are undiagnosed. A recent estimate suggested that the numbers may be even greater than once thought: 1 in 10 people over age 65 may have the disease, and almost one half of those over age 85 may have the disease (Evans et al., 1989). Because it is a degenerative disease, its progression cannot be stopped; it is irreversible and ultimately ends in death. To date, there is no fully effective method of prevention, treatment, or cure. What causes this disease? What is its impact on our population? How will Alzheimer's disease affect health care delivery in the United States?

A definitive diagnosis of Alzheimer's disease can be made only by examining brain tissue, and "tangled neurons" is the typical explanation given to relatives. Brain scans usually confirm that explanation: The patient's neurons seem to be twisted, gnarled, and tangled and are coated with *plaque* (fibrous tissue that impedes neurotransmissions). Levels of neurotransmitter substances are usually lowered.

Correlational research shows that Alzheimer's disease tends to run in families, suggesting a genetic basis or at least a predisposition to the disorder. Some researchers posit a depletion of enzymes; others suggest an accumulation of toxins; and still others have focused on neurotransmitters and metabolic patterns. Blood supply problems, immune system factors, head injuries, and viruses have also been implicated in the disease. Proteins that accumulate in the brain of Alzheimer's patients are now being found elsewhere in the body, which makes the proteins easier to extract and study. This is a great advantage for Alzheimer's researchers.

Recent *experimental research* shows that certain drugs may halt the progress of Alzheimer's; unfortunately, research efforts remain inconclusive. No one yet knows the causes of Alzheimer's disease or has developed an effective treatment. Researchers are beginning to think that there are many types of Alzheimer's disease, some of which may be hereditary (Martin, 1990) and some of which may have been generated by early life events such as a head injury (Roberts, 1988).

The impact of Alzheimer's disease on the patient is enormous, severely damaging the quality of his or her life. Patients are not necessarily stripped of their vigor or strength, but they slowly become confused and helpless. Initially, they may forget to do things. Later, appointments, anniversaries, and dates for lunch may be forgotten. Such mistakes are often overlooked at first. Jokes and other coping strategies cover up for memory losses and lapses. The memory losses are not always apparent; some days are better than others. Ultimately, the disorder grows worse. Soon Alzheimer's patients have trouble finding their way home and remembering their own names and the names of their spouses or children. Within months, or sometimes years, they lose their speech and language functions. Eventually, the patient loses all control, especially of memory (e.g., Karlsson, Backman, Herlitz, Nilsson, Winblad, and Osterlind, 1989) and even of simple bodily functions. Patients' personalities also change; they may become abrupt, abusive, and hostile to family members.

In addition to studying the effects of Alzheimer's disease on patients, researchers are also studying the impact on the patient's family. Caring for the patient imposes great physical, emotional, and financial hardships. Because families cannot care for relatives with Alzheimer's indefinitely, hospitalization or at least day care is often necessary. The patient's loved ones "walk a tightrope between meeting the patient's needs and preserving their own well-being" (Heckler, 1985, p. 1241). Alzheimer's disease changes family life and finances in irreversible ways because most patients are placed in nursing homes after extensive and exhausting care at home. Researchers argue, "In the overwhelming majority of cases, nursing home placement occurs only after responsible family caregivers have endured prolonged, unrelenting caring (often for years) and no longer have the capacity to continue their caregiving efforts" (Brody, Lawton, & Liebowitz, 1984, p. 1331). It is estimated that by 1995, the cost of nursing home care for Alzheimer's patients may be as high as $41 billion per year.

- ***What are the implications of Alzheimer's disease on the financial and medical health plans for the people of this country?***
- ***Because large numbers of people are being affected by Alzheimer's disease, what are the implications for mental health practitioners?***
- ***If researchers are correct that there may be many types of Alzheimer's disease, what are the implications for finding treatments and a potential cure?***

TABLE 17.2 Summary of age changes in intellectual skills

Age 20–40 years	Age 40–65 years	Age 65 years and older
Peak intellectual ability between about 20 and 35	Maintenance of skill on measures of verbal, non-speed-related intelligence; little to no decline of skill on measures of performance or speed-related IQ; any decline is usually not functionally significant till age 60 or older	Some loss of verbal IQ; most noticeable in adults with poorer health, lower levels of activity, and less education
Optimal performance on memory tasks	Little change in performance on memory tasks, except perhaps some slowing later in this period.	Slowing of retrieval processes and other memory processes; less skillful use of coding strategies for new memories
Peak performance on laboratory tests of problem solving	Peak performance on real-life problem-solving tasks and many verbal abilities	Decline in problem-solving performance on both laboratory and real-life tests

Source: Adapted with permission of Macmillan Publishing Company from the Journey of Adulthood by Helen L. Bee. Copyright © 1987 by Macmillan Publishing Company.

1980). Finally, extreme variability in both the types and causes of intellectual deficits suggests that changes in health and family situation may produce the severe biological and psychological consequences that in turn affect intellectual functioning. See Table 17.2 for a summary of age changes in intellectual skills through adulthood.

Whatever the causes, deficits in intellectual functioning that occur with age and influence behavior and functioning are seldom devastating. Up to the ages of 60–65, there is little decline in learning or memory; motivation, interest, and lack of recent educational experience are probably more important in learning complex knowledge than is age. Learning may just take a bit longer for the elderly.

Despite evidence that old age takes a toll, there exist many remarkable examples of intellectual achievement by people 70 years old or more. Golda Meir, for example, became prime minister of Israel at age 70, Benjamin Franklin invented bifocal eyeglasses at age 74 and helped to frame the Constitution of the United States at 81, and Arthur Rubinstein, the Polish-born American concert pianist, gave one of his greatest recitals at New York's Carnegie Hall at age 89. Elderly people are found in the workplace, in the executive suite, on the road, and in small shops all around the country.

Alzheimer's disease: [ALTS-hy-merz] A chronic and progressive disorder that is a major cause of degenerative dementia, currently affecting about 2 million people in the United States. The disease may be a group of related disorders tied together loosely under one name.

Old age does not automatically relegate older people to their rocking chairs.

Psychology and Business: Elderly People in the Workplace

Because many employers believe that older adults are less efficient than their younger coworkers, there is widespread discrimination against older workers in industry, according to Ross Stagner (1985), a retired psychology professor at Wayne State University. Much of the following discussion is based on Stagner's analysis of elderly people in the workplace and how businesses treat the elderly.

Job Performance. Some researchers allege that older workers do not perform as well, are less flexible, and are slower to learn new technologies than younger workers. Stagner, however, reports that the work output and quality of older

Elderly workers can perform just as well as their younger counterparts in many jobs. Stability and experience are two important assets of older employees.

workers is just as good as that of younger workers. He says that the reports are biased because many of the individuals who evaluate the older workers have stereotyped ideas about them: They evaluated them negatively *regardless* of their actual work performance.

Some older workers do show declines in performance. As discussed earlier, older people experience sensory losses that can affect their performance on jobs that require excellent hearing, vision, or motor abilities. Also, in noisy environments in which verbal instructions are given, hearing loss can have important implications. On the other hand, even though older adults may experience decreased visual–motor coordination in complex tasks, drill operators over age 60 have been shown to be more accurate than their younger counterparts. Their years of training and perceptual skills make up for lost visual–motor coordination.

Job Satisfaction. Older adults tend to be more satisfied with their jobs than younger workers. They pay more attention to intrinsic characteristics of a job than to extrinsic values such as pay, vacation time, and work environment. Older workers may find more satisfaction in their work because they have had more time to find the right job for themselves. Moreover, research shows that their mental health tends to be superior to that of younger coworkers.

The motivation, performance, and satisfaction of older workers are much like those of their younger counterparts, and the psychological management principles examined in the laboratory are relevant for older workers, as well as for younger ones. Business schools are adjusting their curriculum to reflect this fact; businesses themselves are showing it by hiring older (and more experienced) workers. Building Table 17.3 summarizes important changes in adult functioning from young adulthood to late, late adulthood.

Dying: The End of the Life Span

Learning Objective 17.17 Discuss Elisabeth Kübler-Ross's stage theory of accepting a loved one's or one's own death or dying, and comment on Western society's view of death.

Everyone recognizes that death is inevitable, but in the 20th century, few people actually witness death. Before this century, most people died in bed at home, where other people were likely to be with them. Today, nearly 80% of people die in hospitals and nursing homes. About 8 million Americans experience the death of an immediate family member each year. Every year, there are about 2 million

Major changes in important domains of adult functioning

Building Table 17.3

Period	Physical change	Cognitive change	Work roles	Personality development	Major tasks
Young adulthood 18–25	Peak functioning in most physical skills; optimum time for childbearing	Cognitive skills high on most measures	Choose career, which may involve several job changes; low work satisfaction is common	Conformist; task of intimacy	Separate from family of origin; form partnership; begin new family; find job; create individual life pattern
Early adulthood 25–40	Still good physical functioning in most areas; health habits during this time establish later risks	Peak period of cognitive skills on most measures	Rising work satisfaction; major emphasis on career or work success; most career progress steps made	Task of generativity	Rear family; establish personal work pattern and strive for success
Middle adulthood 40–65	Beginning signs of physical decline in some areas—strength, elasticity of tissues, height, cardiovascular function	Some signs of loss of cognitive skill on timed, unexercised skills	Plateau on career steps, but higher work satisfaction	Increase in self-confidence, openness; lower use of immature defenses	Launch family; redefine life goals; redefine self outside of family and work roles; begin care for aging parents
Late adulthood 65–75	Significant physical decline on most measures	Small declines for virtually all adults on some skills	Retirement	Perhaps integrated level; perhaps more inferiority; or perhaps self-actualized; task of ego integrity	Cope with retirement; cope with declining health; redefine life goals and sense of self
Late, late adulthood 75+	Marked physical decline on virtually every measure, including speed, strength, work capacity, elasticity, system functioning	Often significant loss in many areas, including memory	Work roles now unimportant	Perhaps integrated or self-actualized, at least for some people	Come to terms with death

deaths and 800,000 new widows and widowers (Osterweis & Townsend, 1988); we are all affected by death, but most people avoid discussing it.

Coping with Death

Elisabeth Kübler-Ross has become famous for her studies of the way people respond psychologically to the death of a loved one and to people who are dying. Kübler-Ross believes that people in Western society fear death because it is unfamiliar, often hidden away in hospitals. She suggests that a way to reduce this fear is to involve members of a dying person's family more closely in what is, in fact, a very natural process. Kübler-Ross contends that it is better for people to die at home among people they love than in an unfamiliar hospital room, attached to machines and tubes.

Kübler-Ross's Stage Theory. Kübler-Ross was one of the first researchers to use a stage theory to discuss people's fear of their own death and that of loved ones. People who learn that they are terminally ill, from Kübler-Ross's view, typically go through five stages: *denial,* which serves as a buffer against the shocking news; *anger,* directed against family, friends, or medical staff; *bargaining,* in which a person tries to gain more time by "making a deal" with God, themselves, or their doctors; *depression,* often caused by the pain of their illness and guilt over inconveniencing their family; and finally, *acceptance,* in which the person stops fighting and accepts death.

Criticisms of Kübler-Ross's Theory. Kübler-Ross's theory has been subject to considerable criticism. Not all researchers find the same sequence of events in the dying process (Stephenson, 1985). They argue that the sequence outlined by Kübler-Ross does not work for all people and that the stages are not necessarily experienced in the order she suggested. However, Kübler-Ross contends that her theory was meant to be an overall outline, not a strict set of stages or steps.

Kübler-Ross has also been criticized for her research techniques—her interviews were not very systematic; she offers few statistics, and some of her ideas rely more on intuition than on facts established through scientific methods. Specifically, her data-gathering techniques were highly subjective. Schaie and Willis (1986) have suggested that Kübler-Ross's ideas should not be considered a theory but "an insightful discussion of some of the attitudes that are often displayed by people who are dying" (p. 483). Although Kübler-Ross's ideas about death and dying may not actually be true in every case, many practitioners find them useful in guiding new medical staff through the difficult task of helping the dying, especially those who are facing premature death because of illness such as cancer.

Whether or not one accepts Kübler-Ross's stages as typical, it is clear that, as in all areas of life, people approach death with different attitudes and behaviors. In general, people fear death, although they are more fearful of death in middle age than at any other time in the life cycle. Religious people fear death less than others; older women fear it less than older men; and financially stable people have less-negative attitudes toward death than do poor people. Moreover, most psychologists believe that the ways in which people have dealt with previous stresses in their lives largely predict how they will deal with death.

In addition to imposing emotional stresses on the terminally ill patient, impending death also causes stress for the patient's family. Kübler-Ross has drawn attention to the additional stresses on family members created by interactions with doctors, especially in traditional impersonal hospital settings. Like many other physicians and psychologists, she believes that a more homelike setting can help patients and their families deal better with death.

Progress Check 17.3

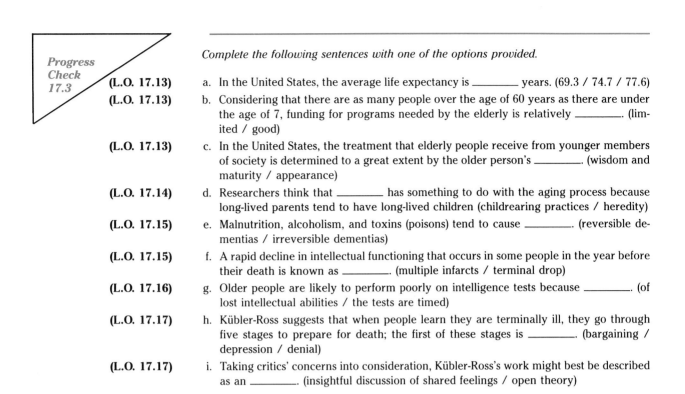

Complete the following sentences with one of the options provided.

(L.O. 17.13) a. In the United States, the average life expectancy is ________ years. (69.3 / 74.7 / 77.6)

(L.O. 17.13) b. Considering that there are as many people over the age of 60 years as there are under the age of 7, funding for programs needed by the elderly is relatively ________. (limited / good)

(L.O. 17.13) c. In the United States, the treatment that elderly people receive from younger members of society is determined to a great extent by the older person's ________. (wisdom and maturity / appearance)

(L.O. 17.14) d. Researchers think that ________ has something to do with the aging process because long-lived parents tend to have long-lived children (childrearing practices / heredity)

(L.O. 17.15) e. Malnutrition, alcoholism, and toxins (poisons) tend to cause ________. (reversible dementias / irreversible dementias)

(L.O. 17.15) f. A rapid decline in intellectual functioning that occurs in some people in the year before their death is known as ________. (multiple infarcts / terminal drop)

(L.O. 17.16) g. Older people are likely to perform poorly on intelligence tests because ________. (of lost intellectual abilities / the tests are timed)

(L.O. 17.17) h. Kübler-Ross suggests that when people learn they are terminally ill, they go through five stages to prepare for death; the first of these stages is ________. (bargaining / depression / denial)

(L.O. 17.17) i. Taking critics' concerns into consideration, Kübler-Ross's work might best be described as an ________. (insightful discussion of shared feelings / open theory)

Module Summary

Adolescence

- Changing intellectual abilities, body proportions, and sexual urges (together with parental expectations for more adult behavior) create the classic adolescent identity crisis of Western culture (p. 316).
- *Gender identity* is a person's sense of being male or female; *androgyny* is the condition in which some typically male and some typically female characteristics are apparent in one individual (p. 318).
- Erikson describes psychosocial development throughout life, focusing on life's dilemmas. His approach emphasizes the gradual development of complex feelings, beliefs, and experiences, usually through successful completion of one stage at a time (p. 320).

Adulthood

- A distinction should be drawn between the idea of transition and crisis. A *transition* suggests that a person has reached a time in life when new dilemmas, challenges, and responsibilities suggest reappraisal and new ways of coping. A *crisis* occurs when old ways of coping become ineffective and a person is helpless, not knowing what to do (p. 324).
- Daniel Levinson's stage theory of adulthood (which was generated from data on males) describes four basic eras: adolescence, early adulthood, middle adulthood, and late adulthood. Women do not necessarily follow the same life stages as men; consequently, Mercer, Nichols, and Doyle developed a developmental progression for women broken into five eras: launching into adulthood, age 30—leveling, age 40—liberating, regeneration/redirection, and age 80—creativity/destructiveness (p. 326).

Aging

- Changes in overall physical fitness and in sexual and sensory abilities occur in adulthood. Various theories of aging emphasize the roles of heredity, external factors, and physiology (p. 331).
- Individuals who suffer from Alzheimer's disease slowly lose their memories. Within months, or sometimes years, they lose their speech and language functions. Eventually, the patient loses all control, especially of memory (p. 337).

Dying: The End of the Life Span

- Elisabeth Kübler-Ross has described dying as a process involving five stages (p. 340).
- Although controversial and not widely accepted by the scientific community, Kübler-Ross's ideas have generated much interest (p. 340).

KEY TERMS

adolescence, p. 316
ageism, p. 331
Alzheimer's disease, p. 337
androgynous, p. 319
dementias, p. 334
gender differences, p. 318
gender identity, p. 318
puberty, p. 316
secondary sex characteristics, p. 317
sex roles, p. 318
sex-role stereotyping, p. 318

SELF-TEST Module 17

- Before taking the self-test, **recite** and **review.**
- Use the key at the back of the test to *correct* your answers.
- *Restudy* pages that correspond to any questions you answered incorrectly.

1. Which of the following characteristics is often *last* to mature in adolescents?
   a. physical growth
   b. intellectual and mental abilities
   c. moral reasoning
   d. emotional development
2. When studying physical changes that occur in adolescence, we find that
   a. puberty signals the end of childhood.
   b. *adolescence* and *puberty* are synonymous terms; they begin and end at the same time.
   c. it takes several years for the physical changes to occur.
   d. Both a and c
3. Studies comparing the degrees of peer and parental influence on adolescent attitudes indicate that
   a. peers have a greater influence.
   b. parents have a greater influence.
   c. adolescents' attitudes fall somewhere between those of their parents and their peers.
   d. a comparison cannot be made because influences such as these are too difficult to study scientifically.
4. A person who displays some behaviors that have traditionally been thought of as masculine and others that have traditionally been thought of as feminine
   a. is homosexual.
   b. is androgynous.
   c. has stereotyped behavior.
   d. lacks a sense of gender identity.
5. At least ________ of American adolescents have had experience with sexual intercourse by the age of 19.
   a. 10%
   b. 25%
   c. 37%
   d. 60%
6. Sexually active teenagers
   a. use contraceptives about 50% of the time.
   b. are generally well-informed about reproduction and contraception.
   c. seem to understand contraception but not reproduction.
   d. underestimate the likelihood of getting pregnant.
7. According to Erik Erikson,
   a. development is a biological process.
   b. new dilemmas emerge and need to be resolved as we move through specific developmental stages.
   c. personality development is basically complete by the age of 12 years.
   d. many people skip particular social developmental stages, but still mature successfully.

8. Toilet training and other behaviors involving control create a crisis for a child during Erikson's ________ stage.
   a. basic trust versus distrust
   b. autonomy versus shame and doubt
   c. initiative versus guilt
   d. industry versus inferiority
9. Psychological research investigating ________ is relatively new in the field of developmental psychology.
   a. women and minorities
   b. cultural differences
   c. differences between men and women
   d. all of the above
10. Most people who are 60 years of age
    a. have difficulty hearing high-frequency sounds.
    b. begin to experience dementia.
    c. are more physically fit than those who are 40 to 55 years old.
    d. experience frustration and despair over their physical condition.
11. Which of these statements about midlife is true?
    a. The experience of a life transition can be more difficult for some individuals than for others.
    b. Few people experience more than one significant life transition during their lifetime.
    c. People usually enter the midlife crises feeling happier, wiser, and more secure than they feel after the crises.
    d. Most people experience the infamous midlife crisis.
12. Contemporary personality theorists have found that adult personality
    a. remains fairly stable and consistent.
    b. is sensitive to the unique experiences of the individual.
    c. needs to be innovative, flexible, and adaptive if a person is to successfully cope with modern life.
    d. all of the above
13. Daniel Levinson suggests that when people enter a new era of life,
    a. crisis is inevitable.
    b. old life structures often no longer work.
    c. they have matured to a more advanced life stage.
    d. psychological growth subsides for a few years.
14. Men and women often reach their peak of creativity and achievement during Levinson's
    a. late adolescent years.
    b. early adult years.
    c. middle adult years.
    d. late adult years.
15. One problem with Levinson's theory is that it
    a. does not consider things such as socioeconomic class, gender differences, and variations in life-style.
    b. puts too much emphasis on the aging process.
    c. considers work life, but not home life.
    d. skips several important eras in adult life.
16. Based on Mercer, Nichols, and Doyle's study concerning the developmental progression of women, women tend to focus their aspirations and grow personally during the ________ era.
    a. launching
    b. leveling
    c. liberating
    d. regeneration/redirection

17. Many universities have established departments of women's studies so that
    a. women do not have to struggle with a male-dominated educational system.
    b. people can study the special issues of women.
    c. men and women can attend segregated classes.
    d. women can attend college without concern for child care.
18. The percentage of people over age 65 is expected to ______ by the year 2030.
    a. increase
    b. decrease
    c. stabilize
    d. remain about the same as it is today
19. Ageism is the result of
    a. the rising cost of health care.
    b. negative stereotyping in American society.
    c. having an increased number of older people in our society.
    d. personality characteristics commonly found in aging people.
20. The theory of aging that suggests that the body's ability to adjust to varying situations decreases with age is called the ______ theory.
    a. wear-and-tear
    b. cellular aging
    c. metabolic waste
    d. homeostatic
21. An irreversible dementia that is caused by ruptures of small blood vessels in the brain is
    a. Alzheimer's disease.
    b. Parkinson's disease.
    c. multiple-infarct dementia.
    d. sensory depreviation.
22. Although some older employees have experienced decreases in abilities such as sensorimotor coordination, they sometimes perform better than younger employees because
    a. they have years of experience with the necessary job skill.
    b. their mental health is superior to that of younger coworkers.
    c. they are more satisfied with their job than are younger workers.
    d. all of the above
23. Elisabeth Kübler-Ross believes that terminally ill people should
    a. never be left alone in the final stages of dying.
    b. be ignored or avoided when they become angry.
    c. be encouraged to cheer up when they become depressed.
    d. be allowed to die at home among the people they love.
24. Of the following categories of people, who is likely to have the greatest fear of death?
    a. middle-aged people
    b. older women
    c. religious people
    d. financially stable people

Connections

If you are interested in . . .	Turn to . . .	To learn more about . . .
The role of early childhood experiences in development	◆ Chapter 2, p. 69	The way the brain of a newborn is modifiable and continues to develop until age 13 years.
	◆ Chapter 7, p. 264	How language development proceeds very rapidly once it begins at about 18 months of age.
	◆ Chapter 15, p. 632	How viewing violence and sex situations on television proves to have long-lasting effects on children.
Social development in childhood and adulthood	◆ Chapter 5, p. 178	The way that operant conditioning, used by parents to reinforce certain ideas in their children, leads to long-lasting ideas and evaluations.
	◆ Chapter 9, p. 366	The way that children develop specific motives, such as to achieve, succeed, or be successful.
	◆ Chapter 10, p. 400	Freud's view that the first 6 years of a child's life are crucial for later personality development.
	◆ Chapter 12, p. 495	The way that people's health can be affected by their reactions to life-cycle events, as well as to other stressors in the environment.
	◆ Chapter 15, p. 598	How a child's early interactions with parents, peers, church, and school shape his or her attitudes.
Gender differences in development	◆ Chapter 11, p. 457	How psychologists have found that cognitive differences in development are, in most cases, overexaggerated.
	◆ Chapter 15, p. 630	The aggressive behaviors males and females exhibit and their different modes of expression.
	◆ Chapter 15, p. 621	The fact that people are attracted to those who share their attitudes and who like them.

Psychologists pay special attention to child development because by understanding it, they hope to better the human condition. The future generation depends on the development of today's young children. Whether they will be motivated (Chapter 9, p. 351), whether they will cope with stress and adjust to their demanding world (Chapter 12, p. 494), or whether they will develop psychological disorders as children and adults (Chapter 13, p. 523) depends on both biology and learning. For example, a child's biological structures (Chapter 2, p. 39) will determine their language abilities (Chapter 7, p. 259). However, learning in the environment (Chapter 5, p. 193) will have a profound effect on their emotional life (Chapter

9, p. 381) and their personality (Chapter 10, p. 422). Both biological structures and learning will affect children's developing intelligence and their abillity to interact in the social world (Chapter 15, p. 597). Many aspects of psychology are studied from the developmental point of view with the aim of assessing how developmental processes affect other psychological ones.

As adults, our ability to function effectively is determined by a wide range of factors in our lives. It is therefore not surprising that when psychologists study adolescents and adulthood, they see a wide range of connections that cut across the psychological spectrum. Clearly, a person's biological inheritance (Chapter 2, p. 40) affects a person's basic abilities. Some of these abilities are measured through achievement and intelligence tests (Chapter 11, p. 439). Biological influences, however, do not work alone; indeed, most psychologists feel that learning (Chapter 5, p. 161) and memory (Chapter 6, p. 203), along with a person's motivation (Chapter 9, p. 351), are likely to affect how a person copes with the stresses of his or her life (Chapter 12, p. 486) and even the type of psychological disorder that a person might develop when normal coping mechanisms break down (Chapter 13, p. 519). Even the treatment method of choice when a person is suffering some form of maladjustment depends on the person's stage of development (Chapter 14, p. 557). Thus, each adult's ability to interact with others (Chapter 15), to develop a normal personality (Chapter 10, p. 397), and to think about the world (Chapter 7, p. 246) all depend on one another. Normal adult development must consider the connections to all of these areas of psychology.

Module 18 ► BIOLOGICAL BASIS OF MOTIVATION 350

Module 19 ► BEHAVIORAL, EXPECTANCY, AND COGNITIVE MOTIVATION 364

Module 20 ► EMOTION 380

Chapter 9

Motivation and Emotion

Studies of motivation investigate the whys of behavior. When conducting such studies, psychologists recognize that people's behavior or performance is affected by their physiology, their emotional states (including arousal), their abilities and their thought processes. This chapter is divided into three modules discussing these topics. The first, Module 18, presents the biological basis of motivation—the biology of the "whys" of behavior. It focuses on the genetic, physiological, and biochemical reasons for behavior. The module begins with a definition of motivation and moves on to show that biological mechanisms account for many of the fundamental behaviors in which human beings engage—especially eating and drinking. Nonetheless, it is readily acknowledged that biology alone does not dictate behavior and that both learning and cognitive explanations for motivation are also important.

The second module, Module 19, explores the role of learning and thought in motivation. It shows that we humans learn to have expectancies for some specific events in life. These expectancies are based on our past experience, current activities, and thoughts about the future. Expectancy theories show that if we hold beliefs or expectations for success, we behave, operate, or cooperate in specific ways. Our expectancies help shape our personalities and mold our thoughts about when we should undertake specific behaviors. The cognitive theory of motivation asserts that we are actively and regularly involved in determining our goals and in deciding how to achieve them. The module shows that behavior, thoughts, learning, and expectancy are all integrated. Once we understand these integrated influences, we may understand why we behave as we do.

The third module, Module 20, presents the range of behaviors and theories that explain emotion. An emotion is a subjective response, accompanied by a physiological change, which is interpreted by the individual and readies the person toward some action, which is associated with a change in behavior. These changes are internal, sometimes overt, and affect the way people interact with one another. Some theories of emotion presume a biological basis for emotions, whereas others have a more cognitive (thought) orientation; contemporary researchers combine biological approaches with cognitive ones. Starting at birth, our ability to express emotion develops throughout our lives, and we can learn, quite effectively, to control our emotional responses—as can be seen in studies of so-called lie detectors, which measure our physiological responses to emotions.

Module 18

Biological Basis of Motivation

LEARNING OBJECTIVES

When you have mastered the material in this module, you will be able to

Definition of Motivation (pp. 351–352)

18.1 Describe the basic components of motivation (p. 351).

Biologically Based Motives (pp. 352–361)

18.2 Describe drive theory and the meaning of "a mechanistic view of behavior" (p. 352).

18.3 State three explanations for why we experience the sensation of hunger (p. 352).

18.4 Describe some of the physiological and psychological causes of obesity (p. 353).

18.5 Characterize anorexia nervosa and bulimia nervosa and identify possible causes of these disorders (p. 355).

18.6 Explain what causes the sensation of thirst (p. 358).

18.7 Explain how our need for sensory stimulation motivates behavior; discuss what is meant by arousal and explain how levels of arousal affect behavior (p. 359).

SQ3R
- ▲ **Survey** to set goals for studying.
- ▲ Ask **questions** as you **read.**
- ▲ Stop occasionally to **recite** and **review.**

plus
- ▲ **Write** a summary of key points.
- ▲ **Reflect** on the hypotheses, evidence, and implications of this material and on the relevance it has to *your* life.

As children, most of us have dreams about the future. We think about being athletes, airline pilots, or physicians. We set high goals about which we have little realistic understanding. Jim Abbott, too, had high goals—and he achieved them. Abbott was the star pitcher on his high school baseball team, he led the U.S. Olympic baseball team to a gold medal, and he has pitched a fastball clocked at 93 miles per hour. If these statistics are not enough to separate Jim Abbott from other athletes, the fact that he has only one hand ensures his distinction.

As a youngster, Abbott, whose right arm is ten inches shorter than his left, was never treated disabled; instead, he was encouraged to try harder. He was motivated by his parents and urged to work hard, and he developed a can-do attitude about life. He practiced, practiced, practiced—as do all superb athletes—and he is now practicing full time with an incredible degree of success as a starting pitcher for the California Angels.

Why do some people strive to achieve success, while others are content to enjoy life at a more relaxed pace? Why will one person spend a free afternoon watching soap operas and munching potato chips, while another will use the time for a five-mile run and a quick study session before dinner? Why do some people crave the excitement of competition while others seem to shy away from it? Many modern theories of motivation have been developed to explain the causes of people's behaviors, but no one theory of motivation can explain all behavior. In fact, most psychologists believe that both inborn motivation and learning cause people to behave in different ways. To understand these interacting forces, we first must define motivation.

Definition of Motivation

Learning Objective 18.1
Describe the basic components of motivation.

Motivation is any condition that is internal to an organism and that appears by influence to initiate, activate, or maintain goal-directed behavior. Note that this definition has four basic parts: (1) internal condition, (2) observed by inference, (3) initiation, activation, or maintenance, and (4) goal-directed behavior.

Motivation is usually understood to reflect an *internal condition.* It may develop from physiological needs and drives or from complex desires, such as the desire to help others, to obtain approval, or to earn a high income. Motivation is an *inferred* concept that links a person's internal conditions to external behavior; it cannot be observed directly, but we can infer its presence based on its behavioral effects. Motivation *initiates, activates,* or *maintains* behavior. For example, because Jim Abbott is motivated to become a good ball player, he initiated a regimen of practice, which he may maintain throughout the competitive season and may then reactivate next season.

Last, motivation generates *goal-directed* behavior. Goals vary widely across individuals and across situations. Some goals are very concrete and immediate, such as to get and eat food, to remove a painful stimulus, or even to win a specific diving match. Other goals are more abstract and long term; the behavior of someone who studies hard, for example, is to maximize learning and eventually to obtain good grades and get a good job.

motivation: An internal condition that appears by inference to initiate, activate, or maintain goal-directed behavior.

Drive-reduction theories have focused on an organism's motivation to act because of a need to establish, balance, or maintain some goal that helps with the survival of the organism or the species. For example, the behavior of a person who eats lunch quickly is directed toward reducing hunger quickly. Theories that focus on *learned motives* emphasize choices, especially how an individual's expectation of success or achievement is thought to affect how he or she will respond. *Cognitive theories* and *humanistic theory* focus on the role of human choice and personal expression. We examine each of these theories and then look at how motivation affects emotions.

Biologically Based Motives

Learning Objective 18.2
Describe drive theory and the meaning of "a mechanistic view of behavior."

drive theory: An explanation of behavior emphasizing internal factors that energize organisms to seek, attain, or maintain some goal. Often, the goal is to reestablish a state of physiological balance.

drive: An internal aroused condition that initiates behavior to satisfy physiological needs. Drives are inferred from behavior.

need: A physiological condition arising from an imbalance and usually accompanied by arousal.

Some of the most influential and best-researched motivation theories are forms of **drive theory.** Drive theories assume that an organism is motivated to act because of a need to attain, reestablish, balance, or maintain some goal that helps with the survival of the organism or the species. Physiological drives are thus said to be *mechanistic* because the organism is pushed, pulled, and energized almost like a machine. Thus, stimuli such as hunger pains create, energize, and initiate behavior. An organism deprived of food for 24 hours will spend most of its time looking for food; it is *driven* to seek food.

A **drive** is an internal condition of arousal that directs an organism to satisfy physiological needs. Drive theories focus on a state of physiological imbalance usually accompanied by arousal, a **need,** and they describe an organism that is motivated by a need as being in a *drive state.* Under conditions of drive, both animals and human beings show goal-directed behavior. For example, a thirsty animal will seek out water.

In examining the whys of behavior from a drive-reduction point of view, psychologists seek to understand simple behaviors such as eating and why people eat when they do. As Maslow suggested (1962, 1969), a person's physiological need for food and water must be satisfied before any others. Hunger and thirst, as well as a third important physiological drive—arousal, sometimes associated with sex—are motivated by both physiological and psychological factors.

Physiological Determinants of Hunger

Learning Objective 18.3
State three explanations for why we experience the sensation of hunger.

When you are hungry, you may feel stomach pains or become weak or dizzy—all sensations that cause you to seek food. What causes these sensations of hunger? Explanations of hunger focus on the glucostatic approach, the role of the brain, and hormones. The *glucostatic approach* argues that the principal physiological cause of hunger is the low blood-sugar level that accompanies food deprivation and its creation of a chemical imbalance. In the body, sugar is quickly broken down into glucose, which is crucial to cellular activity. When the blood-sugar level is low, the body sends warning signals to the brain, and the brain immediately responds by generating hunger pangs in the stomach. Hunger does not depend directly on the central nervous system but rather on blood-sugar levels.

Much of psychologists' understanding of hunger and eating behavior comes from studies of the brain, particularly the hypothalamus, a region of the forebrain (see p. 65). Researchers now know that two areas of the hypothalamus are partly responsible for eating behavior. When the stomach becomes full, when the blood-sugar level is high, or when stimulated electrically, the ventromedial hypothalamus, or the stop-eating center, is activated, and an organism stops eating. By contrast, when the lateral hypothalamus, the start-eating center, is activated, the organism is driven to start eating. As Figure 18.1 shows, researchers have also destroyed through lesioning techniques these same areas; destruction caused just the opposite effects of stimulation.

Researchers find that portions of the hypothalamus may influence eating by stimulating the hormonal and metabolic systems (Powley, 1977). As you recall from Chapter 2, insulin is a hormone secreted by the pancreas; it is released into the bloodstream when sugar (glucose), is present to allow the blood-sugar to be metabolized into the body's cells. When a person eats food that increases blood-sugar level quickly, this triggers the pancreas to release insulin quickly. The body then quickly metabolizes the blood-sugar and once again lowers the blood-sugar level. Thus, a person generally finds that after an initial feeling of relief from hunger, hunger will rapidly recur—blood-sugar level is now low again (often even lower than before eating). The rapid increase in insulin (often too much) allows metabolization of the sugar quickly. Thus, eating a sugar-laden candy bar relieves hunger, but it may bring a person to an even greater level of hunger within a half hour or so. What happens when a person's motivation for eating, hormonal system, or perhaps genetics lead them to overeating and its resulting condition, obesity?

Hunger and Obesity

Learning Objective 18.4
Describe some of the physiological and psychological causes of obesity.

In an address to the American Psychological Association, Yale University psychologist Judith Rodin (1981) summarized the plight of fat people, "obesity is unusual because being fat is one of the factors that may keep one fat. . . . the perverse fact is that it often does take fewer calories to keep people fat than it did to get them fat in the first place. This occurs because obesity itself changes the fat cells and body chemistry and alters level of energy expenditure" (Rodin, 1981, p. 361). Obesity, whatever its causes, has important health implications; for example, it puts people at risk for high blood pressure and heart disease.

The Pima Indians of Arizona have unusually low metabolisms, resulting in an inherited tendency toward being overweight.

Obesity: Genetic Explanations. Richard Nisbett (1972), a psychologist at the University of Michigan, proposed a *fat cell* explanation, asserting that the number of fat cells people are born with, which differs with each person, determines eating behavior and propensity toward obesity. Body fat is stored in fat cells, so people

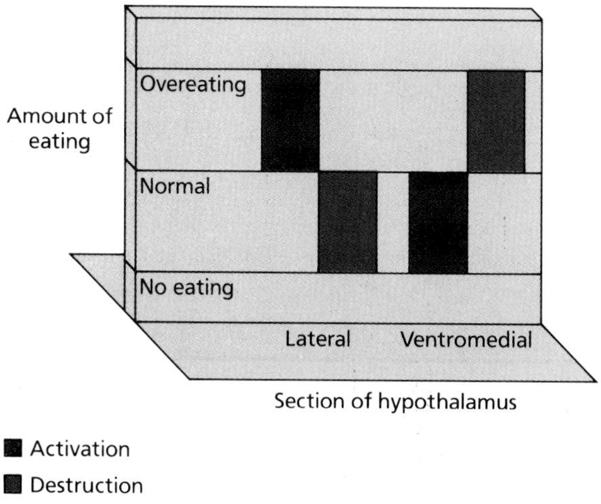

Figure 18.1

When the hypothalamus of an animal is either destroyed or activated, an animal's eating behavior is sharply affected.

born with many fat cells are more likely to be obese than are those born with few fat cells. The number of fat cells each person has is initially genetically determined, but the size of each cell is affected by nutritional experience early in life as well as genetics. Dieting decreases only the *size,* not the *number,* of fat cells. Moreover, the body tends to maintain the size of fat cells at a constant level, so people who have shrunk the normal size of their fat cells by dieting will experience a constant state of food deprivation.

In addition, significant weight gain may be adding new fat cells. Thus, permanent weight loss becomes extremely difficult. This accounts for the finding that most people who lose weight (about two thirds) will gain it back within 1 year. Adding to these problems is the finding that heavy people are more likely than thin people to gain fat rather than muscle mass when they overeat (Forbes, 1990). Closely associated with the fat cell explanation of eating and obesity is the view that each person has a *set point*—a level of body weight that is established and maintained by many factors, including genetics, early nutrition, current environment, and learned habits.

People don't have the luxury of choosing their genetic heritage, but that does not condemn those who inherit a predisposition toward obesity to become fat. Keesey and Powley (1986) agree that the body's natural predisposition is to maintain homeostasis—a steady state or stability—and therefore the individual's attempts to lose weight through intake regulation (such as dieting) are prone to failure. However, Keesey and Powley assert that weight control is achievable by increasing energy expenditure through exercise.

Obesity: Psychological Explanations. Physiological makeup isn't the only important factor in eating behavior; our experiences also teach us how to interact with food. The social environment is rampant with food-oriented messages that have little to do with nutritional needs. People use lunch to discuss business and attend dinner parties to celebrate special occasions. Advertisements proclaim that merriment can be found at a restaurant or a supermarket. Parents coax good behavior from their children by promising them desserts or fat-laden snacks. Thus, as you see in the Understanding the Research Process box on page 356, eating acquires a significance that far exceeds its role in satisfying physiological needs; it also serves as a rationale for social interaction, a means to reward good behavior, and a way to fend off unhappy thoughts.

What causes overeating? Some research suggests that overweight people are especially susceptible to external cues that trigger eating.

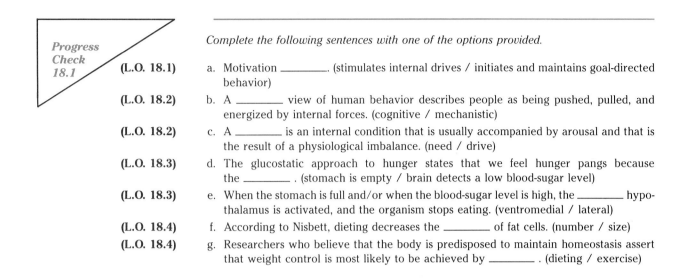

Progress Check 18.1

Complete the following sentences with one of the options provided.

(L.O. 18.1) a. Motivation ________. (stimulates internal drives / initiates and maintains goal-directed behavior)

(L.O. 18.2) b. A ________ view of human behavior describes people as being pushed, pulled, and energized by internal forces. (cognitive / mechanistic)

(L.O. 18.2) c. A ________ is an internal condition that is usually accompanied by arousal and that is the result of a physiological imbalance. (need / drive)

(L.O. 18.3) d. The glucostatic approach to hunger states that we feel hunger pangs because the ________ . (stomach is empty / brain detects a low blood-sugar level)

(L.O. 18.3) e. When the stomach is full and/or when the blood-sugar level is high, the ________ hypothalamus is activated, and the organism stops eating. (ventromedial / lateral)

(L.O. 18.4) f. According to Nisbett, dieting decreases the ________ of fat cells. (number / size)

(L.O. 18.4) g. Researchers who believe that the body is predisposed to maintain homeostasis assert that weight control is most likely to be achieved by ________ . (dieting / exercise)

Psychological Factors in Eating Disorders

Learning Objective 18.5 Characterize anorexia nervosa and bulimia nervosa, and identify possible causes of these disorders.

Although she had been fighting the urge all day, Arlene knew she was headed for another eating binge. When her roommates asked her to come with them to a party, Arlene declined, saying she had to study. As soon as her roommates left, Arlene dashed to her car, drove to the corner bakery, and bought a dozen doughnuts. Then she stopped at the grocery store for milk, crackers, ice cream, jam, and half a dozen candy bars. She rushed back home, locked the door, unplugged the phone, and began eating. Within 20 minutes she consumed nearly 7,000 calories. Her stomach painfully swollen, Arlene drank several glasses of water and made herself throw up. Then she swore, for the hundredth time, she would never binge again.

Eating, one of the great joys of life, has become the focus of a psychological disorder that is now widely recognized. **Eating disorders** are characterized by gross disturbances in eating behavior and the way in which individuals respond to food. Two such disorders are anorexia nervosa and bulimia nervosa, the disorder that affects Arlene.

Anorexia Nervosa. **Anorexia nervosa,** or starvation disease, is an eating disorder characterized by an obstinate and willful refusal to eat. Individuals with the disorder, usually young high-school girls from well-educated families, have a distorted body image, which oversensitizes them to perceiving themselves as being "fat" in response to any lack of muscle tone or deviation from their idealized body image. They intensely fear being fat and relentlessly pursue becoming thinner. As many as 40 out of 10,000 young women may develop the disorder; most come from middle- and upper-middle-class backgrounds, although these disorders cut across racial, ethnic, and socioeconomic groups (Schlundt & Johnson, 1990). The anorexic's refusal to eat eventually brings about emaciation and malnutrition (which may further diminish muscle tone and distort body image). Victims can sustain permanent damage to their heart muscle tissue, sometimes dying as a result.

Many therapists believe that anorexia nervosa has strictly psychological origins, citing family interactions and overprotective parents as the main causes. Others are exploring both the physiological and the psychological origins of the

eating disorders: A disorder characterized by gross disturbances in eating behavior and the way individuals respond to food.

anorexia nervosa: [an-uh-REX-see-uh ner-VOH-suh] An eating disorder characterized by an intense fear of becoming obese, dramatic weight loss, concern about weight, disturbances in body image, and an obstinate and willful refusal to eat.

UNDERSTANDING THE RESEARCH PROCESS

What Causes Overeating?

There are facts of nature that cannot be contradicted. Unfortunately, one fact is that calories not expended will be stored as fat, and a continued imbalance between food intake and calorie expenditure results in obesity. What causes people to eat more food than they expend in calories? Answers to this question have slowly evolved through research spanning three decades.

Stanley Schachter investigated the eating patterns of obese people. He disguised the true purpose of his experiments because people often alter their behavior when told they are being watched. In one experiment, some subjects were given roast beef sandwiches to eat and others were not. The subjects were then seated in front of bowls of crackers and presented with rating scales. They were told to eat as many of the crackers as necessary to judge whether each bowl contained crackers that were salty, cheesy, or garlicky. The researcher's actual goal was to observe how many crackers the subjects ate in making their judgments.

As Figure 18.2 shows, the normal-weight subjects ate far fewer crackers than they would have if they had not eaten the roast beef sandwiches. In contrast, the obese subjects ate even more than they normally would eat. Schachter concluded that the eating behavior of the obese subjects had little correlation with the actual state of their stomachs but was determined principally by external factors (Schachter, Goldman, & Gordon, 1968).

This evidence led Schachter to infer that the sight of food motivates overweight people to eat; he contended that the availability of food, its prominence, and other *external* cues tell obese subjects when to eat (too much, too fast, and too often). In contrast, normal-weight individuals eat more in response to *internal* physiological mechanisms, such as hunger.

Schachter's work set off wide-ranging research into the psychological variables that cause overeating. It forced psychologists to consider all the factors that motivate people to eat, overeat, and become obese. His work focused on external cues, but other researchers argue that obese people are not necessarily more responsive to external cues than normal-weight people. Stunkard and others suggest that differences between the eating habits of obese and normal-weight individuals are small and inconsistent (Rodin, 1981; Stunkard, Coll, Lundquist, & Meyers, 1980). Instead, they contend that the physiological responses of obese individuals may be triggered more quickly than those of normal-weight people. According to physicians Hirsch and Leibel (1988), people who have lost weight often have a lower caloric intake requirement for weight maintenance than those who have never been obese. This means that formerly obese people have a more difficult time keeping their weight down; other researchers agree and assert that a cycle of dieting and regaining weight makes permanent weight loss difficult (Heatherington, Polivy, & Herman, 1991).

disease, including the many physiological and psychological changes taking place at puberty that might influence its emergence (Attie & Brooks-Gunn, 1989).

Anorexia nervosa patients need a structured setting and are often hospitalized to help them regain weight. To ensure that the setting is reinforcing, hospital staff members are always present at meals, and individual and family therapy is provided. Clients are encouraged to eat and are rewarded for consuming specified quantities of food. Generally, psychotherapy is also necessary to help these young women maintain a healthy self-image and body weight. Even with treatment, however, as many as 50% suffer relapses within a year.

bulimia nervosa: [byoo-LEE-me-uh ner-VOH-suh] An eating disorder characterized by repeated episodes of binge eating and fear of not being able to stop eating, followed by purging.

Bulimia Nervosa. When Arlene made herself vomit, she was showing one of the symptoms of bulimia. **Bulimia nervosa,** another eating disorder, tends to occur in normal-weight women with no history of anorexia nervosa. It involves binge eating (recognized by the person to be abnormal) and a consequent fear of not being able to stop eating. Individuals who engage in binge eating become fearful of gaining weight. Therefore, they often purge themselves of unwanted

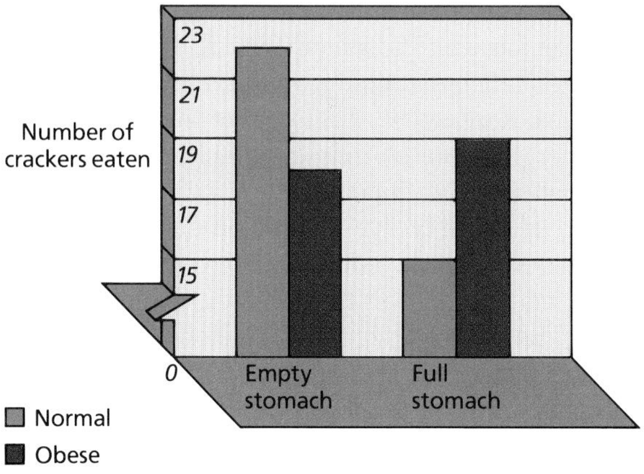

Figure 18.2

In an experiment involving normal-weight and obese subjects, normal-weight subjects ate fewer crackers when their stomachs were full, whereas obese subjects ate more when their stomachs were full. (Schachter, S. Some extraordinary facts about obese humans and rats. *American Psychologist* 26 (1971): 129–144. Copyright 1971 by the American Psychological Association. Reprinted by permission.)

In addition, Stunkard argues that genetics may play a stronger role than environmental influences and that disorders of the autonomic nervous system may keep obese people fat (Peterson, Seligman, & Vaillant, 1988).

The newest research and assertions force a critical evaluation of all previously collected data. They imply that physiological mechanisms may play a much larger role than psychological ones in determining eating behavior and resulting obesity. Today, there is no clear, convincing, simple answer to the nature and nurture of obesity, but the research continues. Some of the latest even suggests a relationship between socioeconomic status and obesity. Sobal and Stunkard (1989) report that in developed societies such as the United States, women of lower socioeconomic status are more likely to be obese than women of higher socioeconomic status. Research into the causes for this finding is just beginning.

▲ ***What is the evidence that the relationship between eating and obesity is explained by external cues?***

▲ ***With what evidence would a biologically based theorist respond to Schachter's studies?***

▲ ***Human beings do not always respond in the same manner; what variables might have affected Schachter's subjects so that they might not always behave the way they did in his experiments?***

calories. Methods of purging include vomiting, laxatives, diuretics, compulsive exercising, and weight-reduction drugs. Bulimics become depressed, and the medical complications are serious, including cardiovascular system changes, gastrointestinal changes, menstrual irregularities, blood and hormone dysfunctions, muscle and skeletal changes, and sharp swings in mood and personality (Kaplan & Woodside, 1987).

The ratio of female to male bulimics is 10 to 1. Researchers theorize that women more than men readily believe that fat is bad, and thin is beautiful. Women of higher socioeconomic classes are at greater risk of becoming bulimic, as are professionals whose weight is directly related to achievement, such as dancers, athletes, and models (Striegel-Moore, Silberstein, & Rodin, 1986); about 1.5% of adolescent girls are affected. Disharmonious family life or having maladjusted parents appears to increase the likelihood of bulimia (Strober & Humphrey, 1987). Bulimics also have lower self-esteem than people who eat normally (Laessle, Tuschl, Waadt, & Pirken, 1989); they perceive their families as having poor relationships and a high level of conflict; and they may have experienced some kind of clinical depression in the past (Walsh, et al., 1985). According to Johnson and Larson (1982), some women may eat as a means of lightening their mood swings and regulating their tension. After binging, however, they feel guilty. To lessen their guilt and the potential consequence of gaining weight, they "get away with something" by purging themselves. Researchers believe that their purges reduce postbinge anguish. Bulimic women become entirely involved in food-related behaviors to the exclusion of contact with other people.

If an adolescent girl is raised in a family that focuses on dieting, has parents with personality disorders, and is genetically predisposed to weight problems, her likelihood of developing bulimia may be greater than that of the general population (Strober & Humphrey, 1987). Efforts to reduce the likelihood that adolescents will develop the disorder continue, as does research into its potential biological causes. Researchers suggest that prevention programs be established at home, in schools and colleges, and in the community.

Thirst

Learning Objective 18.6 Explain what causes the sensation of thirst.

People have many basic needs, among them the need for water and other fluids. A human embryo is made up of more than 80% water, a newborn child is about 75% water, and a normal adult about 60–70% water. Like hunger, thirst serves as a strong drive mechanism in both animals and human beings. Although you can live for weeks without food, you can live only a few days without replenishing your supply of fluid.

Individuals suffering from anorexia nervosa are unable to see themselves realistically. They compulsively refuse food.

A delicate balance of fluid intake is necessary for proper physiological functioning; any imbalance results in a drive to restore the balance. When people experience fluid deprivation and the resulting cellular dehydration, their mouths and throats become dry, cuing them to drink. It is important to note that thirst is not a *result* of dryness in the throat or mouth, and simply placing water in the mouth will not reduce thirst.

Approximately two thirds of our body's fluid is contained within the cells, and the remaining one third is found between the cells. Regulation of fluid within cells is controlled primarily by the hypothalamus (an area of the forebrain, see p. 65); regulation of fluid between cells is controlled primarily by the kidneys and the pituitary. The human body thus is highly sensitive to water losses.

When the body does not have an adequate supply of fluid, cells in the hypothalamus and the pituitary respond. Consider fluid floss between cells: Recall from Chapter 2 (p. 43) that the pituitary initiates an antidiuretic hormone that acts on the kidneys to increase fluid absorption and to decrease the amount of urine produced by the body. Thus, when the pituitary is stimulated in this way, a person urinates less frequently. If a person consumes a great deal of sodium (found in table salt, soy sauce, and many common junk foods), the body responds by needing more fluids—the ratio of the chemical sodium to water content is too great. Again, the body responds by creating a need for fluid and with fewer trips to the bathroom.

A key point to remember is that thirst is a response on the part of the body to trigger fluid consumption—it is not the cause or initiator of fluid consumption. Cells in the brain (hypothalamus and pituitary) initiate fluid consumption and respond to cellular changes and ratios of chemicals to fluids in the body. We are motivated to drink because of internal processes. Of course, we can drink too much or too little. We develop many learned preferences, for example, quenching our thirst with Coke® versus Pepsi®, coffee or tea, or plain bottled water. The role of learning and preferences becomes especially important in more complex biologically motivated behaviors such as sex (which is considered in Chapter 13).

Sensory Stimulation and Arousal Theory

Learning Objective 18.7
Explain how our need for sensory stimulation motivates behavior; discuss what is meant by arousal, and explain how levels of arousal affect behavior.

In addition to hunger and thirst, people have complex physiological needs for sensory stimulation. Unlike hunger and thirst, lack of sensory experience does not result in physiological imbalance, yet both human beings and animals seek sensory stimulation. When deprived of a normal amount of visual, auditory, or tactile stimulation, some adults may become irritable and consider their situation or environment intolerable. Kittens like to explore their environment; young monkeys will investigate mechanical devices and play with puzzles; and people seem motivated or impelled toward seeking sensory stimulation. (However, in some situations people seek to avoid stimulation—for example, when they are sick or otherwise in need of rest.)

Neither a need for sensory stimulation nor the previously discussed drive-reduction theory explains many basic behaviors. *Arousal theory* attempts to bridge the gap by explaining the link between our behavior and our state of arousal. Think of some activity that you practice often and occasionally either compete in or perform publicly. For example, you may be a diver, an actor, or a member of a debating team. Chances are, you performed most poorly when you were either not interested in practicing or exceedingly nervous about your performance, such as during competition. Conversely, you probably did your best when you were eager to practice or when you were moderately excited by competition. This phenomenon explains why some baseball players perform exceptionally well at the beginning of the season, when pressure is only moderately high, and then commit numerous errors when pressure increases—for instance, in the final games of the World Series.

Arousal is generally thought of in terms of activation of the central nervous system, the autonomic nervous system, and the muscles and glands. The link between performance and arousal was first scientifically explored in 1908 by R. M. Yerkes and J. D. Dodson. They described a relationship, called the *Yerkes–Dodson law*, between avoidance learning and task difficulty in mice. Contemporary researchers have extended that relationship by suggesting that when a person's level of arousal and anxiety is too high or too low, performance will be poor,

The human body is extremely sensitive to any loss of water and will always seek to have the balance restored.

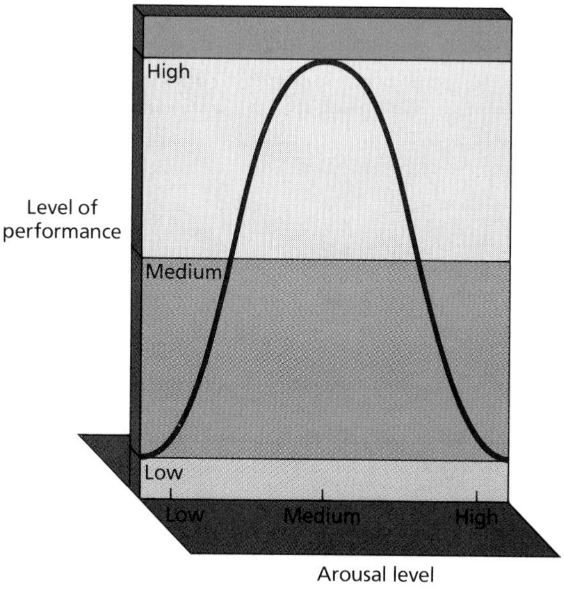

Figure 18.3

Performance is at its best when arousal is at a moderate level.

especially on complex tasks. Thus, people who do not care about what they are doing have little anxiety, but they also have little arousal and usually perform poorly in both work and play. If arousal increases to the point of high anxiety, though, they also perform poorly.

Researcher Donald Hebb (1904–1985) suggested that behavior varies from disorganized to effective, depending on a person's level of arousal. He argued that human functioning is most efficient when people are at an optimal level of arousal and, along with other researchers, assumed that people seek, and are most efficient at, specific arousal levels (Anderson, 1990). The inverted U-shaped curve in Figure 18.3 on the previous page shows the relationship between level of arousal and effectiveness of behavior and is useful in thinking about a broad range of behavioral phenomena.

Building Table 18.1

Drive theories of motivation

Theory	Theorist(s)	Principally explains	Key idea	View of behavior
Drive	a. Nisbett b. Schachter c. Hebb	a. Obesity b. Hunger and obesity c. Optimal arousal	a. Number of fat cells determines obesity. b. External cues energize eating behavior. c. Performance depends on level of arousal.	a. Mechanistic: obesity is biologically determined. b. Partially mechanistic but recognizes the role of learning. c. Mostly mechanistic: The efficiency of behavior is determined by level of physiological arousal.
Expectancy				

Fundamental to all arousal theories is the notion that it is not the stimulus itself but the organism's internal response to the stimulus that determines how the organism behaves. Hebb's idea shifted the focus from stimuli and drives or needs to people's response-determining behavior. Thus, for Hebb, arousal energizes behavior but does not direct it.

The development of optimal arousal theories helped psychologists explain the variation in people's responses to situations in terms of a state of internal arousal rather than solely in terms of the stimuli encountered (see Building Table 18.1). This shift in emphasis marked a subtle but important transition from solely mechanistic drive-reduction theory toward learning and more cognitive theories, in which a person's expectations, past experiences, and thought processes play a more important role.

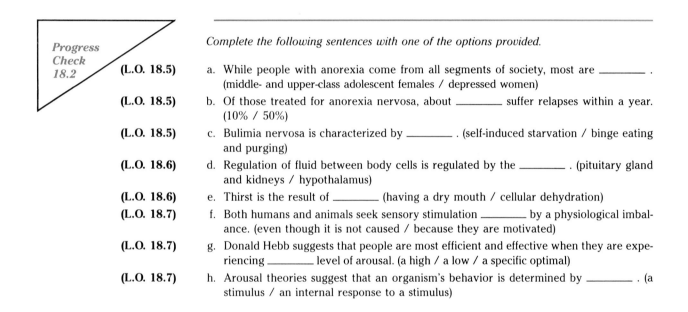

Progress Check 18.2

Complete the following sentences with one of the options provided.

(L.O. 18.5) a. While people with anorexia come from all segments of society, most are ________ . (middle- and upper-class adolescent females / depressed women)

(L.O. 18.5) b. Of those treated for anorexia nervosa, about ________ suffer relapses within a year. (10% / 50%)

(L.O. 18.5) c. Bulimia nervosa is characterized by ________ . (self-induced starvation / binge eating and purging)

(L.O. 18.6) d. Regulation of fluid between body cells is regulated by the ________ . (pituitary gland and kidneys / hypothalamus)

(L.O. 18.6) e. Thirst is the result of ________ (having a dry mouth / cellular dehydration)

(L.O. 18.7) f. Both humans and animals seek sensory stimulation ________ by a physiological imbalance. (even though it is not caused / because they are motivated)

(L.O. 18.7) g. Donald Hebb suggests that people are most efficient and effective when they are experiencing ________ level of arousal. (a high / a low / a specific optimal)

(L.O. 18.7) h. Arousal theories suggest that an organism's behavior is determined by ________ . (a stimulus / an internal response to a stimulus)

Module Summary

Definition of Motivation

- *Motivation* produces goal-directed behavior. It is inferred from behavior and initiated by drives, needs, or desires. A *need* is an aroused physiological condition involving an imbalance (p. 351).
- People's motivated behavior is affected by (1) physiology, (2) emotional state (including arousal), (3) ability, and (4) thought processes. High motivation without ability will not yield high performance, nor will high ability with no motivation (p. 352).

Biologically Based Motives

- The glucostatic approach to hunger argues that the principal physiological cause of hunger is the low blood-sugar level that accompanies food deprivation. Researchers know that two areas of the hypothalamus, lateral and ventromedial, are primarily responsible for the brain's control of eating behavior, but hormones, especially insulin, play a regulatory role influencing the brain and behavior (p. 352).
- Physiological makeup isn't the only important factor in eating behavior; our experiences also teach us how to interact with food. Schachter showed that obese adults tend to eat not only when they are hungry but also whenever food is present. Still, genetics and disorders of the autonomic nervous system may play a strong role (p. 352).
- Although humans can live for weeks without food, we can live only a few days without replenishing our supply of fluid. Any imbalance in fluid is reflected in a drive to restore the balance (p. 358).
- According to optimal arousal theories, individuals seek an optimal level of stimulation. Behavior varies from disorganized to effective to optimal, depending on the person's level of arousal (p. 359).

KEY TERMS

SELF-TEST

Module 18

- ▲ Before taking the self-test, **recite** and **review.**
- ▲ Use the key at the back of the text to *correct* your answers.
- ▲ *Restudy* pages that correspond to any questions you answered incorrectly.

1. The concept of motivation assumes that
   a. all behavior is learned.
   b. humans are procrastinators by nature and must learn to become active doers.
   c. some people are motivated and other people are not motivated.
   d. observed behavior is linked to internal conditions.
2. Drive theories of motivation focus on
   a. impulsive and spontaneous behaviors.
   b. overachievers and how they perceive goals.
   c. what organisms do when they are in a state of physiological imbalance.
   d. what motivates people to stay with a task until a goal has been achieved.
3. We feel hungry when
   a. our blood-sugar level is low.
   b. insulin is secreted by the pancreas.
   c. there is a high level of glucose in the bloodstream.
   d. the ventromedial hypothalamus is activated.
4. Blood-sugar is metabolized by ________ , a hormone secreted by the pancreas.
   a. glucose
   b. insulin
   c. thyroxin
   d. thyrotrophin
5. The *set-point* explanation of body weight suggests that each person
   a. has an ideal body weight.
   b. has a body weight that is maintained by the body and is determined by many factors
   c. can control body weight by eating the number of calories needed to achieve the desired weight.
   d. both a and c
6. People with bulimia nervosa
   a. show an obstinate and willful refusal to eat.
   b. become entirely involved in food-related behavior to the exclusion of wanting to be with other people.
   c. are usually obese and resort to purging in a desperate attempt to lose weight.
   d. generally have a history of anorexia nervosa.
7. Which structures in the brain detect cell dehydration and initiate the thirst drive?
   a. hypothalamus and pituitary gland
   b. medulla and thalamus
   c. pons and cerebellum
   d. colliculi and corpus callosum
8. Optimal arousal theories helped psychologists explain
   a. reactions to sex-related stimuli.
   b. variations in performance, based on anxiety and other arousal states.
   c. the peak hours for productive work.
   d. why some people are lethargic.

Module 19

Behavioral, Expectancy, and Cognitive Motivation

LEARNING OBJECTIVES

When you have mastered the material in this module, you will be able to

Learned Motives (pp. 365–371)

19.1 Describe expectancy theory and define the terms *motive, social motive,* and *social need* (p. 365).

19.2 Describe the need for achievement and identify factors that lead some people to have high achievement needs (p. 366).

19.3 Explain both how people are motivated by the attributions they make and how personality affects motivation (p. 369).

19.4 Identify the mechanistic and cognitive elements of expectancy theories and explain how expectancy theories are used to predict behavior (p. 370).

Cognitive Theory (pp. 372–374)

19.5 Describe the cognitive theory of motivation and cite the results of a study that investigated the degree of cognitive control we have over physiological reactions (p. 372).

19.6 Describe intrinsically motivated behavior and explain how extrinsic rewards affect these behaviors (p. 372).

Humanistic Theory (pp. 375–377)

19.7 Describe Abraham Maslow's theory of human motivation (p. 375).

SQ3R
- ▲ **Survey** to set goals for studying.
- ▲ Ask **questions** as you **read.**
- ▲ Stop occasionally to **recite** and **review.**

plus
- ▲ **Write** a summary of key points.
- ▲ **Reflect** on the hypotheses, evidence, and implications of this material and on the relevance it has to *your* life.

Beverly Stanton was married when she was 18, had a child when she was 19, and was divorced at 20. At 25, she was just trying to hang on. By working as an advertising copywriter, she was lucky. She had flexible hours and a boss who gave her a job that usually goes to college graduates, though Beverly was just now completing her third year of college. It was tough—working during the day, going to school at night, and playing with her child whenever she had a spare moment. She didn't have much time for herself, friends, social causes, or fashion. She just tried to get by, day-by-day.

Beverly described herself as just doing what she had to, but many of her friends questioned her reasons. Her parents were wealthy; on many occasions, they had volunteered to help her financially. She could have gone to school full-time and not worked. She could have lived in a nicer apartment, had help with her daughter, and had a few minutes to herself each week.

However, Beverly Stanton was an individualist, and she refused help. She argued that she had to do it herself to make it worthwhile. Her mother argued that she was trying to prove something to herself. Her father called her a fool, and her friends could not figure out why she was wearing herself out. Nonetheless, Beverly argued vehemently that if she was to make it in this world, she needed a sense of accomplishment and independence. Beverly Stanton was quite a young woman. She had courage, stick-to-itiveness, and determination. Her friends and family may have been correct that there was an easier way for her to get through school and to make a mark for herself in life, but it wasn't Beverly's way. She was neither crusader nor hero, she just had to do it her way—and that meant without financial help from her family. Her mother regularly questioned her about her situation and kept asking her why she refused help. Beverly kept giving her the same answer, "Mother, I have to do it on my own." The conversation had taken place so many times it seemed to be like a recording.

The drive and determination that Beverly drew upon was deep within her. She had always been single-minded and driven as a child. It should not have surprised her parents that she would carry the same approach to her adult life that she had as a child. Her mother should have realized that she was instrumental in teaching Beverly to be as independent. Beverly was encouraged to walk early, talk early, ride bikes before other kids. With her parents' encouragement, she was always the first one to complete science fair projects. Why should her mother wonder why Beverly was so eager to do it her way, independently?

Learned Motives

The whys of people's behavior aren't always easily understood, and looking back into our childhood doesn't always yield a clear picture. People act the way they do for many complex reasons. Sometimes, their motivation is biological; at other times, it is learned in childhood; and at other times, behaviors are acquired or learned as adults. If you trace the history of motivation theory, you find distinct shifts from one to another concept. For example, many early researchers focused on internal conditions—needs—that impel organisms to action. However, contemporary researchers recognize and embrace the idea that some motives are physiological, others are learned, and others result from human beings thinking about and evaluating their motivations and their behaviors. This third idea is most aptly expressed in expectancy theory, which connects thought and motivation.

Learning Objective 19.1
Describe expectancy theory, and define the terms *motive, social motive,* and *social need.*

expectancy theory: An explanation of behavior that emphasizes a person's expectation of success and need for achievement as energizing factors.

motive: A specific internal condition directing an organism's behavior toward a goal.

social motive: An internal condition that directs people toward establishing or maintaining relationships with other people and toward establishing feelings about themselves.

social need: An aroused condition involving feelings about self, others, and relationships.

need for achievement: A social need that directs a person to strive constantly for excellence and success.

Expectancy theory focuses on our human need for achievement and success; it suggests that our expectations of success and our valuation of it may direct our behavior. A key element of expectancy theory is that our thoughts guide our behaviors. The social motives and needs that we develop are not physiological in origin; they are not initiated because of some physiological imbalance. Rather, we learn through our interactions in the environment to have needs for mastery, affiliation, or competition. These needs lead to expectations about the future and about how various efforts will lead to various outcomes.

The expression *self-fulfilling prophecy* suggests that those who expect to succeed will do so; those who don't won't (see Chapter 1, p. 25). Expectations for success and failure can influence the outcome of an effort if those expectations help shape the person's behavior. Thus, a teacher who expects a student to fail may treat the student in ways that increase the likelihood of the student's failure; things tend to turn out just the way the teacher expected (or prophesied) they would. Expectancy thus becomes a key component of the whys of behavior.

Motives and Social Needs

A **motive** is a specific internal condition that usually involves some form of arousal that directs or impels a person (or animal) toward a goal. Unlike a drive, which has a physiological origin, a **social motive** does not have to have a physiological explanation. Thus, although a person may be driven to be among the best, there is usually no urgent physiological need for him or her to do so.

A **social need** is an aroused condition involving feelings about self, others, and relationships. A person's social needs, for example, may include winning approval from family, friends, and associates. These needs for achievement, affiliation, and good feelings about oneself are affected by many factors, including socioeconomic status and race and experiences from birth onward.

Social Need for Achievement

Learning Objective 19.2 Describe the need for achievement, and identify factors that lead some people to have high achievement needs.

The most notable expectancy theories focus on the social **need for achievement.** According to achievement theories, people engage in behaviors that satisfy their desires for success, mastery, and fulfillment. Tasks not oriented toward these goals are not motivating and are either not undertaken or are only done without energy and commitment.

McClelland. One of the early leaders in studies of achievement motivation was David C. McClelland (1917–), whose studies were cited in 1988 by the American Psychological Association for their innovation. McClelland's early research focused on the idea that people have strong social motives for achievement. Ultimately, he showed that achievement motivation is learned in a person's home environment during childhood. Adults with high needs for achievement had parents who stressed excellence and who provided physical affection and emotional rewards for high achievement. These adults also generally walked early, talked early, and had high needs for achievement even in elementary school (e.g., Teevan & McGhee, 1972). High achievement needs are most pronounced in firstborn children, perhaps because parents typically have more time to give them direction and praise. Achievement motives are often measured through scores derived from coding the thought content of imaginative stories, such as the Thematic Apperception Test (TAT). During this test, subjects are shown scenes with no captions and only vague themes, which are thus open to interpretation. They are instructed not to think in terms of right or wrong answers but to answer basic questions for each picture:

- What is happening?
- What has led up to this situation?
- What is being thought?
- What will happen?

Using a complex scoring system, researchers analyze subjects' descriptions of each scene and find that subjects with high needs for achievement tell stories that stress success, getting ahead, and competition.

A person's learned need to succeed can be enhanced through competition.

High Versus Low Need for Achievement. In tests such as the TAT, a researcher can quickly discern high- versus low-need achievement subjects. Lowell (1952), for example, found that when he asked subjects to rearrange scrambled letters (such as *wtse*) to construct a meaningful word (such as *west*), subjects with low needs for achievement improved only slightly over successive testing periods. In contrast, subjects who scored high in need for achievement showed heightened regular improvement over several periods of testing (see Figure 19.1). The researchers concluded that when presented with a complex task, subjects with high needs for achievement find new and better ways of performing the task as they practice it, whereas subjects with low needs for achievement try no new methods. High-need achievers constantly strive toward excellence and better performance (McClelland, 1961).

Risk and Achievement. People's need for achievement seems closely related to the amount of risk they are willing to take. Some researchers claim that children exposed to praise are likely to be more achievement oriented and thus willing to take on higher levels of risk. The goals people set and the amount of risk they are willing to take are also affected by the kind of needs that motivate them, their experiences, and even their moods (Hom & Arbuckle, 1988). For example, a person heavily pushed toward success by parents, drama instructors, or sports coaches may develop a high need for achievement; after positive experiences, such an individual will typically set challenging but attainable goals. Thus, those with high needs for power and public recognition take high risks; in contrast, those with high needs for affiliation take low risks. Even people's voting strategies are affected by their achievement motivations and personalities (Wilcox, 1989).

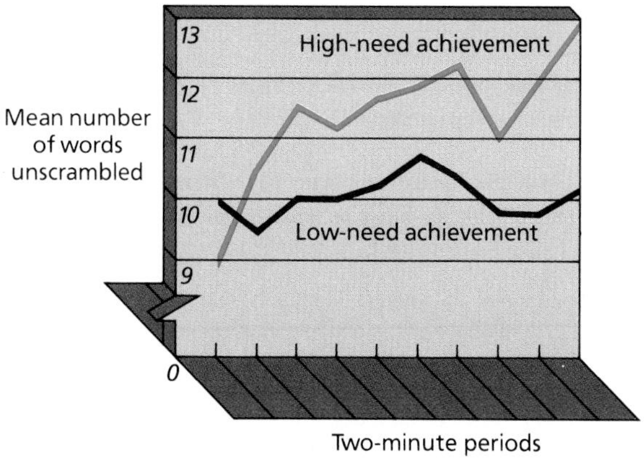

Figure 19.1

On scrambled-letter tasks, over successive 2-minute periods, low-need achievers improved overall, but high-need achievers improved even more.

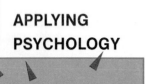

APPLYING PSYCHOLOGY

Cooperative Learning

Most American classrooms set students against each other by having them compete; when students help each other, it's often called cheating. However, research from the University of Minnesota, Johns Hopkins University, and the University of California shows that the interactions among students—not just between student and teacher or student and books—play a significant role in real learning. Teachers who overlook student-to-student teaching may be failing their own courses (Kohn, 1986).

Studies show that forming teams of students in which no one gets credit until everyone understands the material is far more effective than competitive or individualized learning. Preschoolers or college students, in English or physics—students have more fun, enjoy the subject matter more, and learn more when they work together.

What's the secret? Learning stems more from providing explanations than from receiving them. In a cooperative group, everyone has an incentive to help everyone else. The result is that high-, medium-, and low-ability students all benefit from a sharing of skills.

Our society associates excellence with being Number One. However, the data show that competition—one student can succeed only if others fail—actually impedes learning. David Johnson, a social psychologist and education professor at the University of Minnesota, noted the effectiveness of team learning: "There's almost nothing that American education has seen with [the] level of empirical support [shown for team learning]. None of us is as smart as all of us" (Kohn, 1986).

Cooperative education isn't as simple as grouping students around a table and telling them to work together. It means carefully establishing a positive interdependence that makes each student dependent on and accountable to others in the group. The students start to think of themselves as a team. Knowing that they will sink or swim together, they start swimming.

There are several ways to put this theory into practice. One approach, called the *jigsaw method,* was invented by Elliot Aronson, a social psychologist at the University of California, Santa Cruz. He divided a study project into parts and gave one piece to each student in a group. Then he told them that everyone would be responsible for all the material.

Students had to learn from each other, and they did. In addition, Aronson found other results. Self-esteem went up as each child saw that others were depending on him or her. Also, each child realized that being a good student didn't depend on besting others. Students in the groups also grew to like each other more, including those of different races and ability levels.

When Aronson's experiment was finished, an interesting thing happened. Even though they were free to resume standard teaching methods, some teachers whose classes were used in the study retained the cooperative learning method. It had worked so well that they decided to keep it.

According to Kohn (1986), competition gets in the way of real learning by making students anxious. It also makes them doubt their own abilities and become nasty toward losers, envious of winners, more prejudiced toward those from other ethnic groups, and suspicious of just about everyone. In a book on competition, Kohn documented the case against competitive learning and asserted that we should move toward cooperative ventures. Cooperation works in a variety of forums; for example, cooperative ventures are better than competitive ones when workers and managers are involved (Tjosvold and Chia, 1989), but such ventures depend on the makeup of each group, including variables such as gender (Garza & Borchert, 1990).

Psychologists and educators continue to fine-tune the techniques of cooperative learning. In fact, some of them formed an organization, the International Association for the Study of Cooperation in Education (IASCE). The group conducts research and tries to spread the message that cooperation works better than competition in the classroom.

- ▲ ***What do the researchers mean when they use the term* cooperative interdependence?**
- ▲ ***What is the evidence that Kohn uses to support the idea of cooperative learning?***
- ▲ ***What are the implications for classroom instruction if the studies of cooperative learning prove to be supported by additional research?***

As theories about motivation move away from simple mechanistic explanations, it becomes harder to specify all the potent variables that affect motivation. For example, what happens to people's motivation when they cooperate rather than compete? This topic is considered in the Applying Psychology box on the facing page.

Attributions and Motivation

Learning Objective 19.3
Explain both how people are motivated by the attributions they make and how personality affects motivation.

Expectancy theories show that if people hold beliefs or expectations for success, they will behave in specific ways that lead to success. However, people's beliefs and expectations are partly determined by how they perceive the causes of success or failure. If a person believes that a task is impossible, for example, then that person will probably fail and will attribute the failure to the impossibility of the task. Similarly, if a person believes that a task is so simple that anyone can do it properly, then success at the task will provide little reward or satisfaction.

Human beings not only have expectancies about their success and failure, but they also hold causal beliefs. They may believe that some tasks are especially easy, that they are especially lucky persons, or that they are destined to be successful. Such dispositions toward tasks affect behavior directly. Such general views about the causes of behavior are *attributions.* People make attributions, or interpretations, about the causes of behavior. Attribution theory, examined in more detail in Chapter 15, can be used here to explain motivation. People often make attributions about the reasons things turn out the way they do, and these attributions affect their day-to-day thoughts and feelings, as well as their specific behaviors.

For example, a person who feels destined to win a state lottery may spend hundreds of dollars buying tickets; if he does not win, he then may attribute the loss to not having purchased quite enough tickets or to having bought them at the "wrong" ticket outlet. This person was motivated to buy the tickets by his belief that he was destined to win. He justified his bad luck by attributing the cause to factors other than fate.

Personality and Motivation

Personality studies (discussed further in Chapter 11) provide a wealth of information about what motivates people. *Personality,* the way people respond to situations most of the time, influences just about everything people do. Thus, although motivated to succeed, a person who has personality characteristics of shyness may be inhibited and reticent about taking a chance in front of people. A person who is outgoing, in contrast, may be far more willing to assert herself or himself in a group situation.

Some aspects of personality may even have health consequences. Friedman and Rosenman (1974) proposed classifying people according to two distinct personality styles or behavior patterns that can be used to predict the likelihood of suffering a heart attack. They designated people who had a great sense of urgency about all things and were impatient, aggressive, easily roused to anger, and extremely achievement oriented as Type A individuals (who are at greater risk for heart attacks). All other people are Type B. Although their primary goal was to help Type A people become Type B people (Kahn, et al., 1982), their research also provided information on what motivates people.

Using behavior patterns such as Type A and Type B, psychologists can infer a great deal about individuals' motivations and how they will respond to various situations. Type A people, for example, possess an intense desire to control their environment, and they become irritated and show emotional distress when others slow down their rapid pace (Suarez & Williams, 1989; Suls & Wan, 1989). Furthermore, they find it difficult to develop new motives and new behaviors to help them slow down and relax. Type B people do not seem to be motivated by the same desires for mastery and success. When they desire greatness or achievement, they are willing to pursue these objectives at a far more deliberate pace.

You will see in Chapter 13 that the Type A–Type B classification system has become popular, but it lacks rigorous scientific support (e.g., Langeluddecke, Fulcher, Jones, & Tennant, 1988). It does, however, frame certain key questions for motivation researchers. Among these questions are "Who is likely to be motivated?" "When are people likely to be motivated?" "Can motivation predict behavior?"

Expectancy Theories and Predicting Behavior

Learning Objective 19.4
Identify the mechanistic and cognitive elements of expectancy theories, and explain how expectancy theories are used to predict behavior.

One strength of achievement motivation and expectancy theories is their relative precision, which enables psychologists to predict people's behavior. Once they know whether a person's need for achievement is high or low, they can predict the person's behavior in achievement-related activities. For example, once we know that a ball player's need for achievement is very high, we can predict that the athlete will work hard to achieve a goal of winning. Expectancy theories in general achieve precision because they focus on a specific set of behaviors (see Building Table 19.1).

Expectancy theories are cognitive in the sense that people's expectations of success or failure provide the context in which choices are made. Yet, because they retain certain mechanistic details and descriptions, they do not make the full leap into contemporary cognitive psychology, which places much more emphasis on the causal role of thought in behavior.

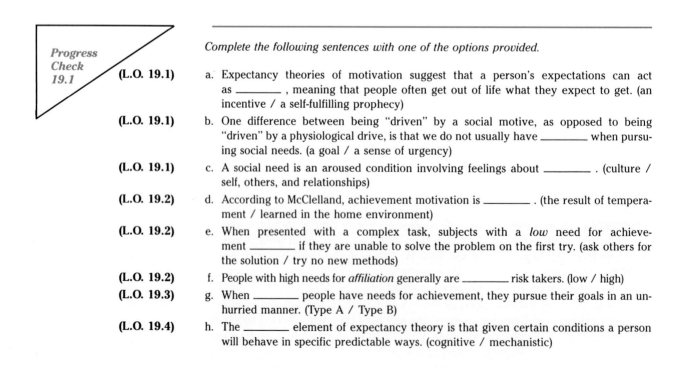

Progress Check 19.1

Complete the following sentences with one of the options provided.

(L.O. 19.1) a. Expectancy theories of motivation suggest that a person's expectations can act as ________ , meaning that people often get out of life what they expect to get. (an incentive / a self-fulfilling prophecy)

(L.O. 19.1) b. One difference between being "driven" by a social motive, as opposed to being "driven" by a physiological drive, is that we do not usually have ________ when pursuing social needs. (a goal / a sense of urgency)

(L.O. 19.1) c. A social need is an aroused condition involving feelings about ________ . (culture / self, others, and relationships)

(L.O. 19.2) d. According to McClelland, achievement motivation is ________ . (the result of temperament / learned in the home environment)

(L.O. 19.2) e. When presented with a complex task, subjects with a *low* need for achievement ________ if they are unable to solve the problem on the first try. (ask others for the solution / try no new methods)

(L.O. 19.2) f. People with high needs for *affiliation* generally are ________ risk takers. (low / high)

(L.O. 19.3) g. When ________ people have needs for achievement, they pursue their goals in an unhurried manner. (Type A / Type B)

(L.O. 19.4) h. The ________ element of expectancy theory is that given certain conditions a person will behave in specific predictable ways. (cognitive / mechanistic)

Building Table 19.1

Drive and expectancy theories of motivation

Theory	Theorist(s)	Principally explains	Key idea	View of behavior
Drive	a. Nisbett b. Schachter c. Hebb	a. Obesity b. Hunger and obesity c. Optimal arousal	a. Number of fat cells determines obesity. b. External cues energize eating behavior. c. Performance depends on level of arousal.	a. Mechanistic: obesity is biologically determined. b. Partially mechanistic but recognizes the role of learning. c. Mostly mechanistic: The efficiency of behavior is determined by level of physiological arousal.
Expectancy	a. McClelland b. Friedman & Rosenman	a. Achievement motivation b. The people prone to Type A behavior associated with coronary heart attack	a. Humans learn the need to achieve. b. Time urgency leads to a competitive, unending search for mastery and success, and to heart disease.	a. Partly cognitive, partly mechanistic: achievement is a learned behavior. b. Partly cognitive, partly mechanistic: Type A behavior is initiated early in life through reinforcement and punishment.
Cognitive				

Cognitive Theory

Learning Objective 19.5 Describe the cognitive theory of motivation, and cite the results of a study that investigated the degree of cognitive control we have over physiological reactions.

cognitive theory: An explanation of behavior that emphasizes the role of thoughts and individual choices regarding life goals and the means of achieving them.

The **cognitive theory** of motivation asserts that people are actively and regularly involved in determining their goals and their means for achieving them. Even more than expectancy theory, cognitive theory focuses on thoughts as initiators and determiners of behavior. It emphasizes the role of decision making in all areas of life. For example, you are actively involved in deciding how much time you will spend studying for a psychology exam, how hard you will work to become an accomplished pianist, or how much you will dedicate yourself to a new diet or exercise program.

As early as 1949, Donald Hebb anticipated how cognitive theory would influence psychology to move away from mechanistic views of motivation and behavior. Hebb recognized that mechanistic drive- or need-reduction theories were incomplete and that other factors, such as arousal and attention, are important determinants of motivation. As a result of Hebb's brilliant theorizing, contemporary researchers emphasize the role of active decision making and the human capacity for abstract thought. These cognitive theorists assume that individuals set their goals and decide how to achieve them.

Cognitive Controls

It may seem like common sense that if you are aware of—and think about—your behavior, motivation, and emotions, and you attempt to alter your thoughts, you can control your behavior. Cognitive psychologists maintain that if human beings are aware of their thought patterns, they can control their reasoning and ultimately their overt behavior. When explaining motivation, cognitive psychologists show that arousal (which Hebb and other researchers equated with drive) is under voluntary (that is, cognitive) control.

In what is now regarded as a classic study, Lazarus and Alfert (1964) monitored subjects' levels of arousal under conditions capable of inducing great stress. Subjects watched a film showing a primitive ritual called subincision (which involves deeply cutting the penises of adolescents). During the film, which showed five operations, one group of subjects, the *denial commentary* group, heard a commentary during the film that denied that pain and harm were associated with the operation. Another group of subjects, the *denial orientation* group, heard the same commentary before the film. A third group saw the film but did not hear any commentary.

The electrodermal response (EDR)—a measure of arousal—of subjects who saw the film with no commentary increased at once (see Figure 19.2). More important, the increase in EDR for subjects who heard the denial commentary during the film was less than the no-commentary subjects, and the increase was lowest for subjects who heard the denial before the film began (the denial orientation group). Lazarus and Alfert believed that the denial orientation group was able to build up their psychological defenses against the potentially stressful content of the film. In other words, they had some degree of cognitive control over their physiological reactions. Through instruction and self-help techniques, people can alter their behavior by changing their thoughts and thus changing their expectancies (e.g., Norris, 1989). That our thoughts can alter our behavior also becomes evident when people think about reinforcements, their intrinsic and extrinsic motivations.

Learning Objective 19.6 Describe intrinsically motivated behavior, and explain how extrinsic rewards affect these behaviors.

Intrinsic and Extrinsic Motivation

People engage in a wide variety of behaviors for the fun of it, behaviors that bring no external tangible rewards. Infants play with mobiles, children build erector

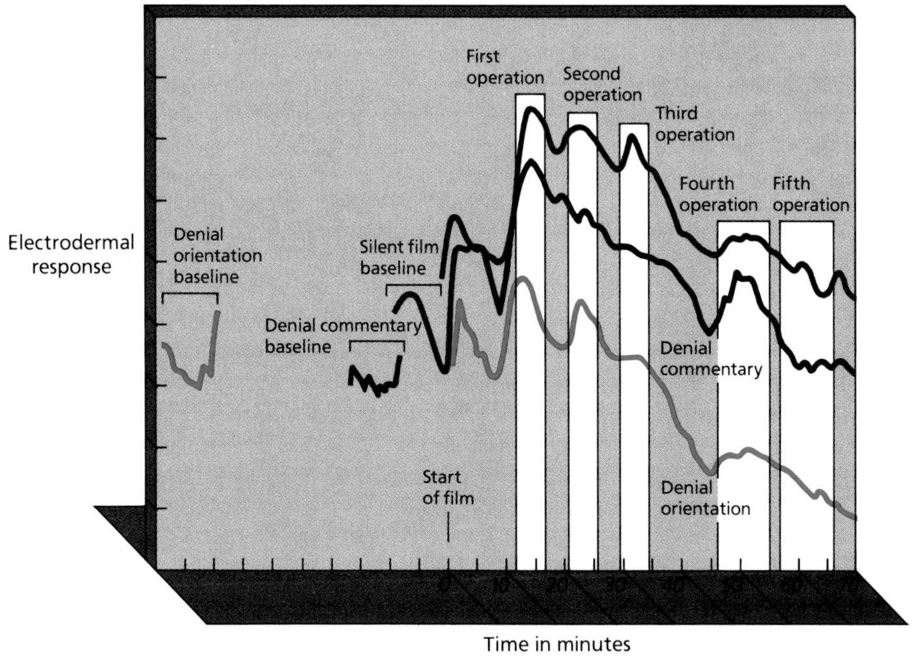

Figure 19.2

Lazarus and Alfert measured the electrodermal response (EDR) of subjects viewing a film of stress-inducing operations. The baseline indicates the level of EDR before the film was shown; with the start of the film, EDR increased in all groups. The increase was greatest in subjects who did not hear a commentary denying the pain. (Lazarus & Alfert, 1964, p. 199. Copyright 1964 by the American Psychological Association. Reprinted by permission.)

set cities and then take them down and adults do crossword and jigsaw puzzles. Psychologists call behaviors performed for no apparent reward except the pleasure of the activity itself, **intrinsically motivated behaviors.** Edward Deci (1975) suggests that people perform intrinsically motivated behaviors for two reasons: to achieve stimulation and to achieve a sense of accomplishment, competence, and mastery over their environment.

In studies focusing on intrinsic motivation, Deci compared two groups of college-age subjects engaged in puzzle solving. One group received no (external) rewards, and the other group received rewards. He found that subjects who were initially given rewards generally spent less time solving puzzles when rewards were no longer given. Those who were never rewarded, on the other hand, spent the same amount of time solving puzzles on all trials (Deci, 1971, 1972). Similar studies of younger children yielded comparable results (Lepper, Greene, & Nisbett, 1973) and also showed that if rewards are expected before the activity is performed, the effect of not giving them is even greater (Ryan, Mims, & Koestner, 1983). Building Table 19.2 on the next page adds Deci's cognitive theory to the summary of motivation theories.

Other research (e.g., McGraw & Fiala, 1982) shows that offering rewards for engaging in an already attractive task results in a lower level of involvement and often permanent disengagement. Lepper and Greene (1978) refer to this phenomenon as the *hidden cost of reward.* When people think about the causes of their actions, it can alter their behavior.

Extrinsic rewards come from the external environment: Praise, a high grade, or money for a particular behavior are extrinsic rewards. Such rewards can strengthen existing behaviors, provide people with information about their performance, and increase feelings of self-worth and competence. On the other hand, when extrinsic rewards are given in a way that will alter a person's motivational orientation, they can decrease intrinsic motivation (Pittman & Heller, 1987). Also, verbal extrinsic rewards (such as praise) are less likely to interfere with intrinsic motivation than are tangible rewards (such as money) (Anderson, Manoogian, & Reznick, 1976).

intrinsically motivated behaviors: [in-TRIN-zick-lee] Behaviors that a person performs in order to feel more competent, satisfied, and self-determined.

extrinsic reward: [ecks-TRIN-zick] A reward that comes from the external environment.

Drive, expectancy, and cognitive theories of motivation

Building Table 19.2

Theory	Theorist(s)	Principally explains	Key idea	View of behavior
Drive	a. Nisbett b. Schachter c. Hebb	a. Obesity b. Hunger and obesity c. Optimal arousal	a. Number of fat cells determines obesity. b. External cues energize eating behavior. c. Performance depends on level of arousal.	a. Mechanistic: obesity is biologically determined. b. Partially mechanistic but recognizes the role of learning. c. Mostly mechanistic: The efficiency of behavior is determined by level of physiological arousal.
Expectancy	a. McClelland b. Friedman & Rosenman	a. Achievement motivation b. The people prone to Type A behavior associated with coronary heart attack	a. Humans learn the need to achieve. b. Time urgency leads to a competitive, unending search for mastery and success, and to heart disease.	a. Partly cognitive, partly mechanistic: achievement is a learned behavior. b. Partly cognitive, partly mechanistic: Type A behavior is initiated early in life through reinforcement and punishment.
Cognitive	Deci	Intrinsic motivation	Intrinsic motivation is self-rewarding because it makes people feel competent.	Cognitive: Motivation is inborn, but extrinsic rewards often decrease it; decision making is crucial.
Humanistic				

Humanistic Theory

Learning Objective 19.7
Describe Abraham Maslow's theory of human motivation.

One of the appealing aspects of the humanistic theory is that it recognizes the interplay of behavior theories and incorporates some of the best elements of the drive, expectancy, and cognitive approaches for explaining behavior.

Humanistic theory emphasizes the entirety of life rather than the components of behavior. Humanistic psychologists insist that individuals' behavior must be viewed within the framework of their environment and their values. These psychologists focus both on the dignity of individual choice and freedom and on an individual's feelings of self-worth.

humanistic theory: An explanation of behavior that emphasizes the role of human qualities such as dignity, individual choice, and self-concept.

self-actualization: The process of realizing one's uniquely human potential for good; the process of achieving everything that one is capable of achieving.

As was shown in Chapter 1, one of the leaders and founders of the humanistic approach is Abraham Maslow (1908–1970), who assumed that people are essentially good, that they possess an innate inclination to develop their potential and to seek beauty, truth, and harmony. Like other humanistic theorists, Maslow believed that people are innately open and trusting and can experience the world in truly healthy ways. In his words, people are innately motivated toward **self-actualization.** Self-actualized, self-fulfilled people fulfill their true (positive) natures and their potentials.

Maslow listed the characteristics that he felt distinguished self-actualized people. Although few people have all the following traits, according to Maslow, all people strive (and are directed) toward acquiring them. He believed that self-actualized people

- Are realistically oriented
- Have thoughts that are unconventional and spontaneous
- Have a need for privacy
- Have a fresh appreciation of people
- Identify with people
- Are democratic
- Have good senses of humor
- Appreciate the natural environment
- Accept themselves
- Are problem centered and solution oriented
- Are independent
- Have spiritual experiences
- Have intimate relationships
- Do not confuse the means with ends
- Are creative and nonconformist

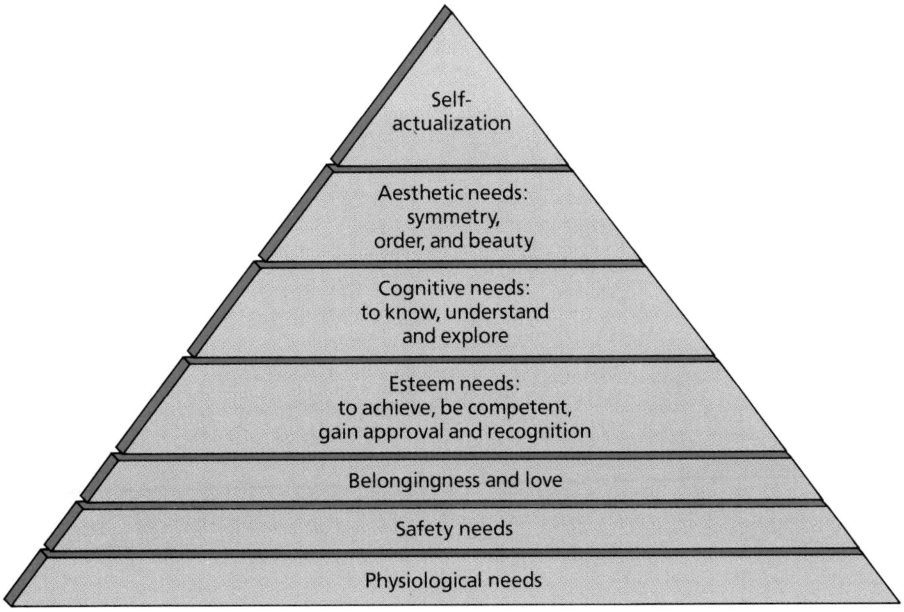

Figure 19.3

Maslow's pyramid of needs: Physiological needs are at the base; successive layers reflect increasingly learned social needs.

Drive, expectancy, cognitive, and humanistic theories of motivation

Building Table 19.3

Theory	Theorist(s)	Principally explains	Key idea	View of behavior
Drive	a. Nisbett b. Schachter c. Hebb	a. Obesity b. Hunger and obesity c. Optimal arousal	a. Number of fat cells determines obesity. b. External cues energize eating behavior. c. Performance depends on level of arousal.	a. Mechanistic: obesity is biologically determined. b. Partially mechanistic but recognizes the role of learning. c. Mostly mechanistic: The efficiency of behavior is determined by level of physiological arousal.
Expectancy	a. McClelland b. Friedman & Rosenman	a. Achievement motivation b. The people prone to Type A behavior associated with coronary heart attack	a. Humans learn the need to achieve. b. Time urgency leads to a competitive, unending search for mastery and success, and to heart disease.	a. Partly cognitive, partly mechanistic: achievement is a learned behavior. b. Partly cognitive, partly mechanistic: Type A behavior is initiated early in life through reinforcement and punishment.
Cognitive	Deci	Intrinsic motivation	Intrinsic motivation is self-rewarding because it makes people feel competent.	Cognitive: Motivation is inborn, but extrinsic rewards often decrease it; decision making is crucial.
Humanistic	Maslow	Learned needs for fulfillment and for feelings of self-actualization	Self-actualization	Cognitive: Humans seek to self-actualize after they have fulfilled basic needs for food and security; conscious decisions determine all higher goals.

Maslow's influential theory conceived of people's motives as forming a pyramid-shaped structure, with fundamental physiological needs at the base and needs for love, achievement, and understanding near the top (see Figure 19.3 on page 375). According to Maslow, as low-level needs are satisfied, people strive for the next higher level, culminating in self-actualization aspirations. He claimed that once someone's basic physiological needs are met, the person is in a better position to satisfy emotional needs. He did not claim that a person's basic physiological needs have to be satisfied completely before he or she can achieve a higher level of fulfillment. However, unless their basic physiological needs are met, people are unlikely to grow and develop physically or to acquire social and aesthetic motives that might direct behavior. Only if people's needs for food, shelter, and physical safety are met can they attend to developing a sense of self-respect or a sense of beauty.

Abraham Maslow believed in the humanistic approach, and suggested that people strive for self-actualization.

Although Maslow's theory provides an interesting way to organize aspects of motivation and behavior and their relative importance, its global nature makes experimental verification difficult. Moreover, his levels of motivation seem closely tied to middle-class American cultural experience, so the theory may not be valid in all cultures or socioeconomic strata. Maslow's theory, like many other motivation theories, does not explain how other components of our lives interact with behavior. For example, how does motivation to self-actualize affect our emotional experiences? Building Table 19.3 presents an overview of the theories of motivation that we have discussed thus far in this chapter.

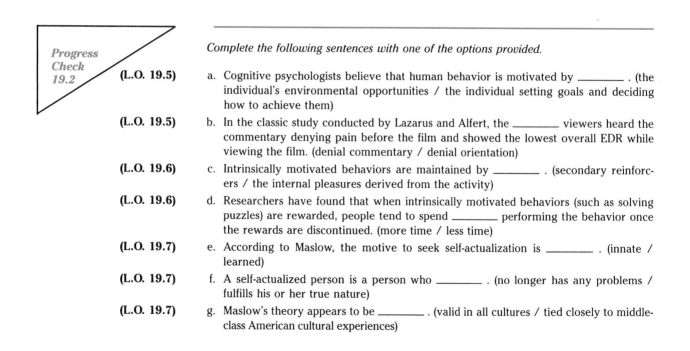

Progress Check 19.2

Complete the following sentences with one of the options provided.

(L.O. 19.5) a. Cognitive psychologists believe that human behavior is motivated by ________ . (the individual's environmental opportunities / the individual setting goals and deciding how to achieve them)

(L.O. 19.5) b. In the classic study conducted by Lazarus and Alfert, the ________ viewers heard the commentary denying pain before the film and showed the lowest overall EDR while viewing the film. (denial commentary / denial orientation)

(L.O. 19.6) c. Intrinsically motivated behaviors are maintained by ________ . (secondary reinforcers / the internal pleasures derived from the activity)

(L.O. 19.6) d. Researchers have found that when intrinsically motivated behaviors (such as solving puzzles) are rewarded, people tend to spend ________ performing the behavior once the rewards are discontinued. (more time / less time)

(L.O. 19.7) e. According to Maslow, the motive to seek self-actualization is ________ . (innate / learned)

(L.O. 19.7) f. A self-actualized person is a person who ________ . (no longer has any problems / fulfills his or her true nature)

(L.O. 19.7) g. Maslow's theory appears to be ________ . (valid in all cultures / tied closely to middle-class American cultural experiences)

Module Summary

Learned Motives

- *Expectancy theory* focuses on people's need for achievement and success; the theory suggests that people's expectations of success and their valuation of it may direct their behavior. (p. 366)
- A *social motive* is a condition that directs people toward establishing or maintaining relationships with others and toward feelings about themselves and others (p. 366).

Cognitive and Humanistic Theories

- *Cognitive theories* and *humanistic theory* move away from mechanistic descriptions of behavior and focus on the role of human choice and expression (p. 372).
- *Intrinsically motivated behaviors* are behaviors that a person performs in order to feel competent and self-determining. *Extrinsic rewards* decrease the recurrence of intrinsically motivated behavior (pp. 372–373).
- Maslow's *humanistic motivation theory* assumes that people are basically good and that they strive for self-actualization, the process of fulfilling one's positive potential to the greatest degree possible. It is the process of achieving everything one is capable of (p. 375).

KEY TERMS

cognitive theory, p. 372
expectancy theory, p. 366
extrinsic reward, p. 373
humanistic theory, p. 375
intrinsically motivated behaviors, p. 373
motive, p. 366
need for achievement, p. 366
self-actualization, p. 375
social motive, p. 366
social need, p. 366

SELF-TEST

Module 19

- Before taking the self-test, **recite** and **review.**
- Use the key at the back of the text to *correct* your answers.
- *Restudy* pages that correspond to any questions you answered incorrectly.

1. Expectancy theory asserts that behavior is energized by
   a. social needs.
   b. potential rewards.
   c. faith.
   d. self-confidence.
2. High achievement needs are most pronounced in adults who
   a. were firstborn children.
   b. had parents who provided physical and emotional reward for achievement.
   c. grew up in a home that stressed excellence.
   d. all of the above
3. When people use their general views about the causes of failure or success to interpret things they have done, psychologists say they are making
   a. excuses.
   b. new goals.
   c. attributions.
   d. an adjusted proposal.
4. A strength of achievement motivation and expectancy theories is that they
   a. emphasize the concept of free will.
   b. describe random behaviors that occur as a result of chance.
   c. allow psychologists to predict what specific individuals will do under specific conditions.
   d. all of the above
5. The results of Lazarus and Alfert's study in which subjects watched a film showing a primitive ritual called "subincision" indicate that people
   a. do not enjoy watching subject matter that is difficult to understand.
   b. will find ways to deny what they have seen.
   c. believe what they see and hear.
   d. have some degree of cognitive control over their physiological reactions.
6. The phrase *hidden cost of reward* refers to
   a. responsibilities that accompany individual freedom and choice.
   b. being obligated to return a favor when someone has done you a favor.
   c. reduced involvement in intrinsically attractive tasks because external rewards have been linked to the task.
   d. the tendency for a person to become too self-assured.
7. Maslow suggested that it is easier for a person to satisfy love and belongingness needs if ________ needs have been fulfilled.
   a. physiological and safety
   b. esteem and cognitive
   c. aesthetic and transcendent
   d. self-actualization
8. Abraham Maslow's humanistic theory of motivation
   a. rejects drive theories.
   b. has been verified through scientific experimentation.
   c. suggests that people will be happier if they focus on social needs rather than on physiological needs.
   d. incorporates the best elements of drive, expectancy, and cognitive theories.

Module 20

Emotion

LEARNING OBJECTIVES

When you have mastered the material in this module, you will be able to

Definition and Theories of Emotion (pp. 381–384)

20.1 Describe the nature of emotion and state the three basic elements of an emotion (p. 381).

20.2 Describe the James–Lange, Zajonc, and Cannon–Bard biological explanations of emotion (p. 382).

20.3 Describe Schachter–Singer, Valins, Shaver, and Frijda's cognitive explanations of emotion (p. 383).

Development of Emotional Responses (pp. 385–388)

20.4 Discuss inborn and environmental conditions that contribute to normal emotional development (p. 385).

Expression of Emotions (pp. 386–391)

20.5 Explain how brain asymmetry and various social variables have been found to influence behavioral expression of emotion (p. 386).

20.6 Describe the role of the autonomic nervous system in the study of emotions and explain why lie detector tests may not be valid (p. 387).

20.7 Describe the self-regulation view of emotion, including how thought, arousal, and cultural expectations influence the expression of emotion (p. 387).

SQ3R
- ▲ **Survey** to set goals for studying.
- ▲ Ask **questions** as you **read.**
- ▲ Stop occasionally to **recite** and **review.**

plus
- ▲ **Write** a summary of key points.
- ▲ **Reflect** on the hypotheses, evidence, and implications of this material and on the relevance it has to *your* life.

The Saturday evening news sometimes seems filled with stories of angry lovers who fought and hurt one another. Warring nations hurl not only accusations, but bombs. Anger can cause us to hurl an object across the room or to lash out at a friend. Happiness can make us smile all day, donate change to the Salvation Army, or stop to help a motorist with a flat tire. Strong emotions may motivate us to work hard for a particular grade, pay increase, or respect from a parent. Fear can make our legs pump faster as we sprint down a dark, shadowy alley. Emotions, including love, joy, fear, disgust, and anger, can direct people's behavior. Most of us can agree on a long list of emotional states, but such categories remain fuzzy.

Definition and Theories of Emotion

Learning Objective 20.1 Describe the nature of emotion, and state the three basic elements of an emotion.

To some extent, the word *emotion* is an umbrella term referring to a wide range of subjective states, such as love, fear, hate, or disgust. We all have emotions, talk about them, and agree on what represents an emotion such as fear, but this is not scientific. The psychological investigation of emotion has led to a more precise definition. An **emotion** is a subjective response, usually accompanied by a physiological change, which is interpreted by the individual, then readies the individual toward some action, and is associated with a change in behavior. People cry when they are sad, find increased energy when they are excited, and breathe faster, sweat, feel nauseous, and salivate less (causing a dry mouth) when they are afraid. Some physiological changes precede an identifiable emotional response. For example, just before a collision in an automobile accident, people show physiological arousal, muscle tension, and avoidance responses—that is, they brace themselves in anticipation. Other changes are evident only after an emotion-causing event. It is only after the auto accident that people shake with fear, disbelief, or rage.

People often respond to physiological changes by altering their behavior. When they are afraid, they scream. When they are angry, they may seek revenge or retribution. When they are in love, they act tenderly toward others. In some situations, people think about acting out such behaviors but may not express them in directly observable ways. Also, an emotional expression sometimes seems contradictory, as in Juliet's claim that "parting is such sweet sorrow." Although emotions may seem written all over people's faces, appearances can be deceiving and difficult to interpret.

Many psychologists acknowledge that emotion consists of three elements: feelings, physiological responses, and behaviors. People experience the same kinds of emotions, but the intensity or quality of those emotions vary. One person's sense of joy is different from another's. Thus, emotions have a private, personal, and unique component. This subjective element is called *feeling.*

emotion: A subjective response, usually accompanied by a physiological change that is interpreted by the individual, then readies the individual toward some action, and is associated with a change in behavior.

Subjective feelings are difficult to measure, so most researchers focus on the other two aspects of emotion—physiological response and behavior. This focus shifts research from the internal process to action or readiness toward action. Physiological responses, such as heart rate and blood pressure, and behavioral responses, such as smiling and crying, are observable and measurable. Not every researcher considers all elements of a definition of emotion in his or her studies. One may focus on emotional expression; another may focus on emotional experiences. Physiological psychologists sometimes trace pathways and confine their research to brain mechanisms such as the hypothalamus. We consider next those theories that focus on the biological bases of emotion.

Biological Theories of Emotion

Learning Objective 20.2 Describe the James–Lange, Zajonc, and Cannon–Bard biological explanations of emotion.

The wide range of emotions that human beings express is in large part controlled by a series of neurons located in an area deep within the brain: the *limbic system.* The limbic system is composed of cells in the hypothalamus, the amygdala, and other cortical and subcortical areas. Studies of these crucial areas began in the 1920s with two major physiological approaches to the study of emotion: the James–Lange theory and the Cannon–Bard theory. Both are concerned with the physiology of emotions and whether physiological change or emotional feelings occur first.

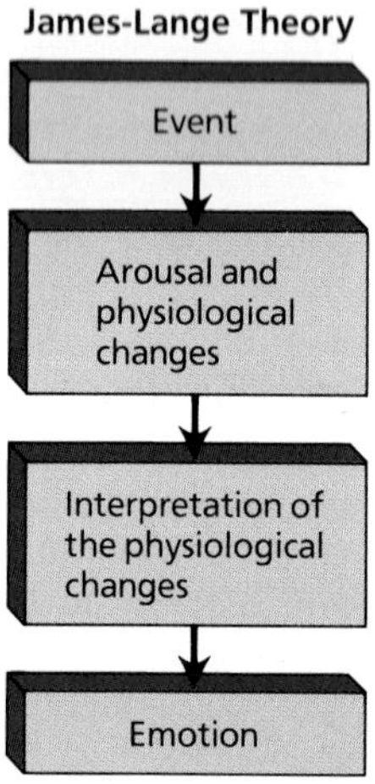

Figure 20.1

According to the James–Lange theory, arousal precedes interpretation, which precedes emotion.

The James–Lange Theory. According to a theory proposed by William James (1842–1910) and developed with Carl Lange (1834–1900), people experience physiological changes and then interpret them as emotional states (see Figure 20.1). People do not cry because they feel sad; they feel sad because they cry. People do not perspire because they are afraid; they feel afraid after they perspire. In other words, the James–Lange theory says that people do not experience an emotion until after their bodies become aroused and begin to respond with physiological changes. That is, feedback from the body produces feelings or emotions (James, 1884; Lange, 1885/1922). For this approach, *feeling* is the essence of emotion; thus, James (1890) wrote, "every one of the bodily changes whatsoever it be is felt, acutely or obscurely, the moment it occurs" (p. 1004).

A modern physiological approach suggests that facial movements, by their actions, create emotions. In some ways, this approach is similar to the James–Lange theory. For example, when some specific facial movements create a change in blood flow and temperature in the brain, pleasant feelings occur. Thus, when a facial movement happens, such as a smile or an eye movement, according to Zajonc, Murphy, and Inglehart (1989), this may release the appropriate emotion-linked neurotransmitters. Some neurotransmitters may bring about pleasant, and others unpleasant, emotions. Zajonc and his colleagues argue that facial movements alone are capable of inducing emotions—even movements associated with breathing. This theory is still relatively new and has not yet been tested extensively by other researchers.

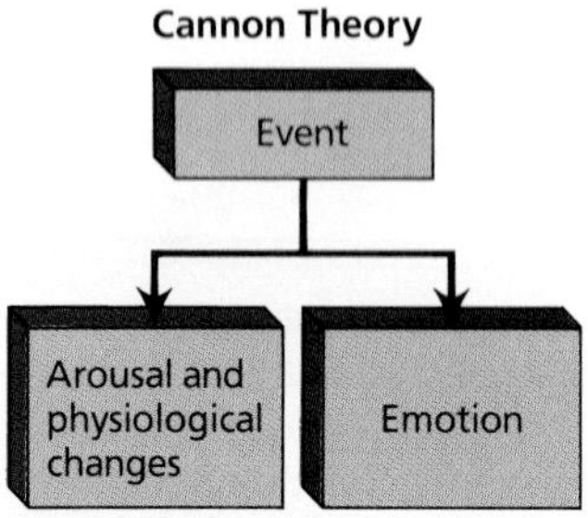

Figure 20.2

According to Cannon's theory, arousal and emotion occur simultaneously.

The Cannon–Bard Theory. Physiologists, notably Walter Cannon (1871–1945), were critical of the James–Lange theory. Cannon and P. Bard, a colleague, argued that the physiological changes in many emotional states were identical. They reasoned that if increases in blood pressure and heart rate accompany feelings of both anger and joy, how can people determine their emotional state simply from their physiological state?

Cannon argued that when a person is emotional, two areas of the brain—the thalamus and the cerebral cortex—are stimulated simultaneously (he did not realize the full nature of the limbic system). Stimulation of the cortex produces the emotional component of the experience; stimulation of the thalamus produces physiological changes in the sympathetic nervous system. According to Cannon (1927), emotional feelings *accompany* physiological changes (see Figure 20.2), they do not produce it. A problem with the Cannon–Bard approach is that physiological changes in the brain do not happen exactly simultaneously; further, people report that they often have an experience and then have physiological and emotional reactions to it. Neither the James–Lange nor the Cannon–Bard approach considered the idea that people's interpretation or thoughts about a situation might alter their physiological reactions and emotional responses.

Cognitive Theories of Emotion

Learning Objective 20.3 Describe Schachter–Singer, Valins, Shaver, and Frijda's cognitive explanations of emotion.

Cognitive theories of emotion developed in response to the older biological approaches. They focus on interpretations as well as physiology to explain emotions. They follow logically in the history of psychology because thought processes have become extremely influential in the past three decades. Continually, new research shows that thought and emotional responses are constantly interacting, although they are also independent processes (Murphy & Zajonc, 1990).

The Schachter–Singer Approach. The Schachter–Singer view of emotion is a cognitive approach that focuses on emotional activation, incorporating elements of both the James–Lange and the Cannon–Bard theories. Stanley Schachter and Jerome Singer observed that people do indeed interpret their emotions but not solely from bodily changes. They argued that people interpret their physical sensations within a specific context. An observer who might watch a tape of a person's face cannot interpret what a person's crying means unless the observer knows the situation in which that behavior occurs. If a man cries at a funeral, we suspect he is sad; if he cries at his daughter's wedding, we expect that he is joyful.

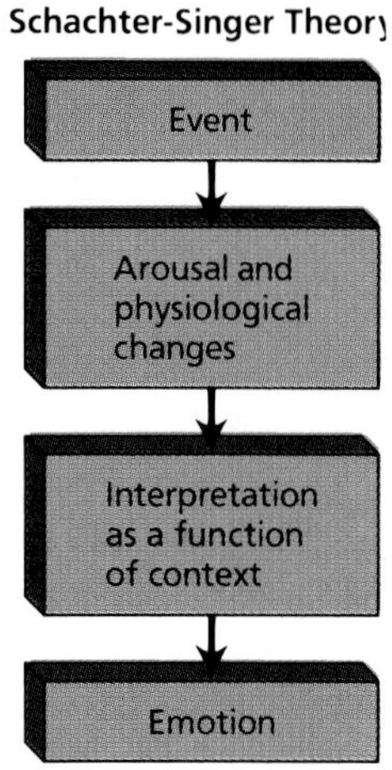

Figure 20.3

According to Schachter and Singer, people's interpretations of arousal depend on the context in which they find themselves.

To prove their contention, Schachter and Singer (1962) injected volunteer subjects with epinephrine, a powerful stimulant (sometimes called adrenaline) that increases signs of arousal such as heart rate, excitement, energy, and even sensations of butterflies in the stomach. The subjects were not aware of the usual results of the injection. To see if they could affect how subjects interpreted their aroused state, Schachter and Singer manipulated the setting in which the subjects experienced their arousal. They hired undergraduates and paid them to act either happy and relaxed or sad, depressed, and angry. These hired subjects—called stooges—pretended that they, too, were volunteers in the drug study. However, they were given injections of saltwater, not epinephrine. Their emotional behavior was strictly an act. The happy stooges shot wads of paper into a wastepaper basket and flew airplanes around the room. The unhappy stooges complained about the questionnaire they had to fill out and voiced their dissatisfaction with the experiment.

All the experimental subjects showed increased physiological arousal. Those with the happy stooges reported that the drug made them feel good; those with the angry stooges reported feeling anger. Schachter and Singer reasoned that when people have no immediate explanation for their physiological arousal, they will label their feelings in terms of the thoughts available to them. The physiological feelings that accompany both joy and anger are the same, but the label attached to the emotion depends on the person's situation (see Figure 20.3).

The cognitive view receives support from anecdotal data as well as experiments. When people first smoke marijuana or take other psychoactive drugs, for example, they tend to approach the experience with definite expectations. If told the drug will produce feelings of hunger, new users will report feeling hunger; if told the drug is a downer, users often interpret their bodily sensations as depressive. In Schachter and Singer's view, people thus experience internal arousal, become aware of the arousal, seek an explanation for it, identify an external cue, and then label the arousal. This labeling determines the emotion that is felt. This view has not gone unchallenged: Valins (1966) and Reisenzein (1983) challenged Schachter and Singer's view. Valins showed that thoughts *alone* are sufficient to produce emotional behavior.

To understand emotional behavior, Shaver identified six basic emotions that all people recognize and experience: love, joy, anger, fear, sadness, and surprise.

Shaver and Others. Phillip Shaver and his colleagues have sought to identify the basic emotions that all people experience and the ways in which they are experienced. Shaver showed that there are six emotions that almost all people will describe when asked to identify emotions: love, joy, anger, sadness, fear, and surprise (Shaver, Schwartz, Kirson, & O'Connor, 1987). Of course, these six categories can overlap, and many other emotional states can be grouped under these six basic categories.

Shaver asserts that people understand and interpret emotional events by comparing the events to basic emotional concepts. For example, when a mother sees her child fall and start to cry, she rushes toward the child. The mother sees this event and *assumes* that the child is frightened and possibly hurt. This inference is based on general knowledge about fear and love. Schwartz and Shaver (1987) claim that people make use of implicit learned knowledge to understand and manage social interactions. Only by understanding this structure of emotion can we begin to place cognitive interpretations within a reasonable framework.

Frijda: Appraisal and Readiness. Another view of emotion sees appraisal as important but also considers the idea that people ready themselves for action. Frijda asserts that every emotional experience is not only a cognitive appraisal of a situation, but also a set of action tendencies or behaviors that are prepared as the cognitive appraisal takes place. For Frijda, when a situation is potentially threatening, a person prepares to flee or attack, and autonomic nervous system arousal is invoked (Frijda, Kuipers, & ter Schure, 1989). This approach looks again at how emotions develop—an area of research that has often followed different avenues.

Development of Emotional Responses

Learning Objective 20.4
Discuss inborn and environmental conditions that contribute to normal emotional development.

People's ability to express emotion develops from birth through adulthood. Some aspects seem to be learned, others to be inborn. Naturalistic observations of human infants indicate that they follow a relatively fixed pattern of emotional development. They are born with a startle, or Moro, reflexive response; they smile, coo, and gurgle at about 6 weeks; they develop fear of strangers at 6–9 months. Attachment behaviors encouraged in the early weeks and months of life are also nurtured during adolescence and adulthood, when people form close loving bonds with others.

Emotional expressions appear in all cultures; fear, joy, surprise, sadness, anger, and disgust are common expressions. These expressions are also found in deaf and blind people and in people without limbs, who therefore have more limited touch experiences (Izard & Saxton, 1988; cf. Ortony & Turner, 1990). Because of these findings, most researchers consider those emotional expressions innate even though they unfold slowly over the first year of life and are reinforced by caregivers.

Emotional Development in Rhesus Monkeys

To find out how people develop emotional responses, Harry Harlow (1905–1981), a psychologist at the University of Wisconsin, focused on the development of emotion in rhesus monkeys. Harlow initially studied the nature of early interactions among monkeys. He found that monkeys raised from birth in isolated bare-wire cages, away from their mothers, did not survive, even though they were well fed. Other monkeys, raised in the same conditions but with scraps of terry cloth (the fabric used for bath towels) in their cages, survived.

Terry cloth is hardly a critical variable in the growth and development of monkeys, yet its introduction into a wire cage made the difference between life and death for rhesus monkeys. Harlow inferred that the terry cloth provided some measure of security. That conclusion led him to attempt to discover whether infant monkeys had an inborn desire for love or warmth that might be satisfied by soft, warm objects such as terry cloth.

In a classic experiment, Harlow placed infant monkeys in cages, along with two wire-covered shapes resembling adult monkeys. One figure was covered with terry cloth; the other was left bare. Both could be fitted with bottles to provide milk. In some cases, the wire mother surrogate had the bottle of milk; in other cases, the terry cloth mother surrogate had the bottle. Harlow found that the infant monkeys clung to the terry cloth mother surrogates whether or not they provided milk. He concluded that the wire mother surrogate, even with a bottle of milk, could not provide the comfort that a terry cloth–covered mother surrogate could provide (Harlow & Zimmerman, 1958).

Another result of Harlow's experiment was that neither group of monkeys grew up to be totally normal. Both groups of Harlow's monkeys were more aggressive and fearful than normally raised monkeys. They were also unable to engage in normal sexual relations. Further, some of the infants raised with wire mother surrogates engaged in self-destructive behaviors (Harlow, 1962).

Harlow next suggested that the emotions of fear, curiosity, and aggression are inborn and that the brain mechanisms underlying them develop over time and in a specific sequence. To test this idea, he isolated monkeys of various ages for different periods of time. As Harlow expected, some specific behaviors, such as attachment and nurturing, were more affected by early isolation, and others

Harlow studied the emotional development of rhesus monkeys. He discovered that young monkeys raised in sterile environments would not thrive as well as those raised with a terrycloth-covered wire surrogate mother.

were more affected by later isolation. When monkeys were deprived of social contacts with other monkeys from ages 18–24 months, for example, their later social behaviors relating to mating were essentially normal. Harlow concluded that nature and nurture must interact at specific times (when the relevant brain mechanisms are ready to mature) for normal emotional and social development to occur.

Emotional Development in Human Beings

Although it is a broad leap from Harlow's monkeys to human infants, it is reasonable to assume that human infants, like monkeys, have an inborn need for social stimulation. Klaus and Kennell (1983) assert that the first minutes and hours of an infant's life constitute a sensitive period during which close contact allows bonding—that is, attachment between parents and child; their assertion is that the presence or absence of bonding may exert an extraordinary influence later in life (Bornstein, 1989).

Human newborns respond to their mothers through body and eye movements and have a regular communication system (Tronick, 1989). Such responses may strengthen the mother's attachment bond to her child—a bond already affected by hormonal changes, prevailing cultural biases, and the mother's personal experiences. This early opportunity to form a strong parent-infant attachment may significantly influence both the parent's ability to care effectively for the child and the infant's ability to give and receive affection and love. Parent-infant attachment can be seen on the faces of new parents and on their newborn children, even in the earliest moments of life (Brazelton & Crammer, 1990).

Expression of Emotions

Learning Objective 20.5 Explain how brain asymmetry and various social variables have been found to influence behavioral expression of emotion.

Psychologists have long recognized that facial expressions provide reliable clues to people's feelings. This *behavioral expression* of emotions is easily observed and interpreted by others. Most important, facial expressions are generally an accurate index of a person's emotional state. Recent research suggests that there are asymmetries in facial expressions in infants and adults, and that adults can easily discern those differences. Best and Queen (1989) found that the left side of the face (controlled by the right side of the brain in most people) may be more expressive than the right side of the face, especially in adults (Rothbart, Taylor, & Tucker, 1989). They argue that the right side of the face may be more readily under control by the left side of the brain, and people are able to inhibit right-face expression more easily than left-face expression. Nonetheless, though facial expressions (either side) are good indicators of emotion, they are only indicators; real emotions can be masked by a happy face or a turned-down mouth.

People also display emotion through gestures, body language, and voice tone and volume (Izard & Saxton, 1988). For example, psychologists have studied the emotional expression of store clerks and their responses to customers. In one study (Rafaeli, 1989), a range of variables was considered: clerk gender, wearing a smock with a name tag, presence of other clerks, and customer gender. Although the results were complicated, the emotional expression of the clerks was affected by nearly all the variables. Female clerks displayed positive emotions more often than males; male customers received positive emotional responses more often than female customers; and when especially aware of their role (wearing a smock), clerks were more expressive. The expression of emotion was thus affected by context and by subtle variables that are still being investigated.

Physiological Expressions of Emotions: Lie Detectors

Learning Objective 20.6
Describe the role of the autonomic nervous system in the study of emotions, and explain why lie detector tests may not be valid.

Many physiological changes that accompany emotions are due to an increase in autonomic nervous system activity. Fear, for example, may slow or halt digestion, increase blood pressure and heart rate, deepen breathing, dilate pupils, decrease salivation (causing a dry mouth), and tense muscles. Researchers recognize that the autonomic nervous system provides direct, observable, measurable responses that can be quantified in a systematic manner. This realization led to the development of what is commonly called a lie detector.

A polygraph test (meaning recordings of many physiological records), or lie detector, is perhaps the most widely recognized recorder of emotion. This device records changes in the autonomic nervous system activity of subjects. Most autonomic nervous system activity is involuntary, and lying is usually associated with an increase in autonomic activity. A trained polygraph operator compares a person's autonomic responses to a series of relatively neutral questions to his or her responses to questions about the issue being explored. During noncontroversial questions (such as requests for the person's name or address), autonomic activity remains at what is considered baseline level. During critical questions (such as whether the person used a knife as a holdup weapon), however, a person with something to hide usually shows a dramatic increase in autonomic nervous system activity.

A lie detector test can be useful in indicating whether a person is lying. Not all people, however, show marked autonomic nervous system changes when emotionally aroused. Habitual liars show little or no change in autonomic activity when they lie; they seem to be able to lie without becoming emotionally aroused. Equally important is the finding that some people who tell the truth may register changes in autonomic nervous system activity because of anxiety. This means that a truthful individual who takes a lie detector test might be called a liar when the individual is in fact telling the truth. In summary, lie detectors are subject to significant errors in both directions (Kleinmuntz & Szucko, 1984; Patrick & Iacono, 1989).

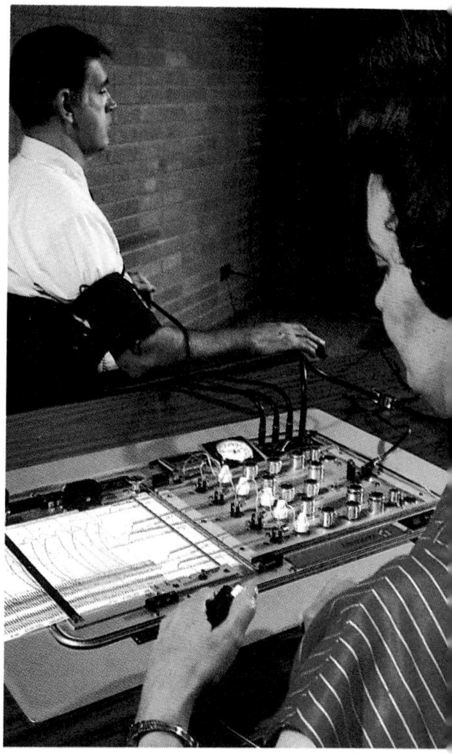

The lie detector test was originally designed to measure physiological responses to emotions, but psychologists today assert that the validity of its findings is highly questionable.

Today, most states do not accept the lie detector as valid evidence in court, especially in criminal cases. A federal law now restricts businesses from using the polygraph to test prospective employees. The American Psychological Association has also expressed reservations about the use of polygraph tests, asserting that they may cause psychological damage to innocent persons. The association's concerns stem in part from the knowledge that some people can control their emotions and do not respond automatically to external stimuli, and other people are less able to control their emotions and may overreact to external stimuli.

Controlling Emotions

Learning Objective 20.7
Describe the self-regulation view of emotion, including how thought, arousal, and cultural expectations influence the expression of emotion.

The self-regulation view of emotional expression, another aspect of cognitive theory, emphasizes that people are not passive, that they do not respond automatically to environmental or internal stimuli. This view asserts that people manage or determine their emotional state in purposeful ways by constantly evaluating their environment and feelings. Through this appraisal of the environment, individuals alter their level of arousal.

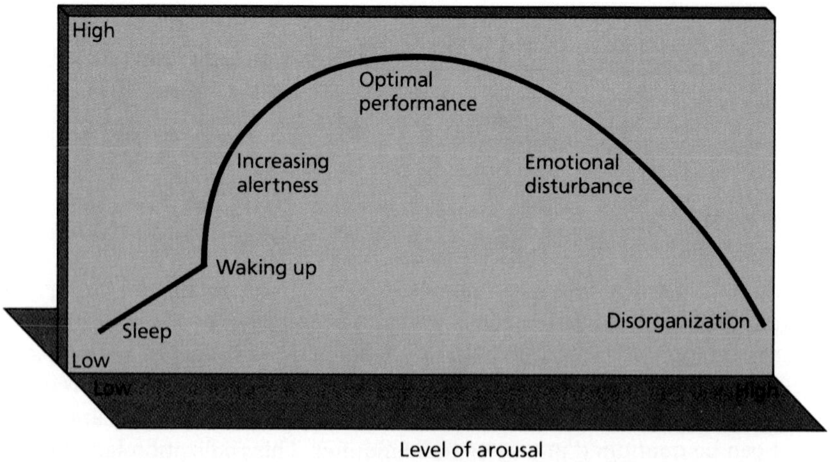

Figure 20.4

In accordance with the Yerkes-Dodson law (see p. 359), increases in motivation and arousal often bring increases in emotional feelings. Most important, these increases in arousal change the effectiveness of a person's behavior. (From *Textbook of Psychology,* Third Edition by D. Hebb, copyright © 1972 by Saunders College Publishing, reprinted by permission of the publisher.)

Arousal. Arousal is an essential component in emotion, and researchers show that people can use cognitive means to control their arousal level and therefore their emotions. Even young infants show some forms of emotional restraint and control, and an infant's control of emotion continues to develop, especially at the end of the first year (Kopp, 1989). For psychologists studying the behavior of disturbed individuals, the interaction of arousal, emotion, and thought has become increasingly important. Even in normal individuals, too high a level of arousal can produce extreme emotional responses and can lead to disorganized behavior (see Figure 20.4). Many maladjusted individuals, such as those suffering from the manic stages of a bipolar disorder, have so high a level of arousal that they cannot organize their thinking or behavior (see Chapter 13, p. 540).

Responses to Emotions. Some studies show that people can control their body's biochemistry. In the study by Lazarus and Alfert (1964) discussed earlier, for example, subjects were able to manipulate their EDR (electrodermal response) when told in advance about a subincision ritual shown in a film. People also control their emotions because of strong cultural expectations. By using conscious and directed thought, people can control their behavior and wait until the proper time and place to express emotions. The suppression of existing ideas and thoughts can be useful and can lead us to avoid emotions that are out of place (Wegner, Shortt, Blake, & Page, 1990). Thus, emotion and its expression reflect a person's motivations and basic biochemistry (Carver & Scheier, 1990).

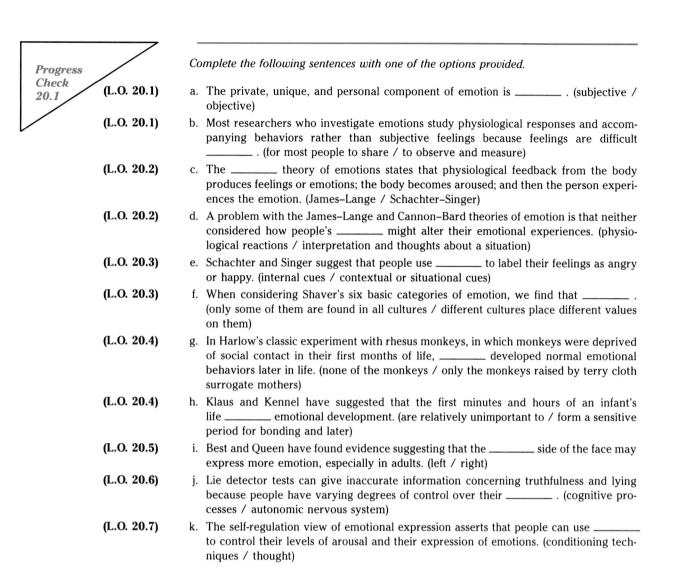

Progress Check 20.1

Complete the following sentences with one of the options provided.

(L.O. 20.1) a. The private, unique, and personal component of emotion is ________ . (subjective / objective)

(L.O. 20.1) b. Most researchers who investigate emotions study physiological responses and accompanying behaviors rather than subjective feelings because feelings are difficult ________ . (for most people to share / to observe and measure)

(L.O. 20.2) c. The ________ theory of emotions states that physiological feedback from the body produces feelings or emotions; the body becomes aroused; and then the person experiences the emotion. (James–Lange / Schachter–Singer)

(L.O. 20.2) d. A problem with the James–Lange and Cannon–Bard theories of emotion is that neither considered how people's ________ might alter their emotional experiences. (physiological reactions / interpretation and thoughts about a situation)

(L.O. 20.3) e. Schachter and Singer suggest that people use ________ to label their feelings as angry or happy. (internal cues / contextual or situational cues)

(L.O. 20.3) f. When considering Shaver's six basic categories of emotion, we find that ________ . (only some of them are found in all cultures / different cultures place different values on them)

(L.O. 20.4) g. In Harlow's classic experiment with rhesus monkeys, in which monkeys were deprived of social contact in their first months of life, ________ developed normal emotional behaviors later in life. (none of the monkeys / only the monkeys raised by terry cloth surrogate mothers)

(L.O. 20.4) h. Klaus and Kennel have suggested that the first minutes and hours of an infant's life ________ emotional development. (are relatively unimportant to / form a sensitive period for bonding and later)

(L.O. 20.5) i. Best and Queen have found evidence suggesting that the ________ side of the face may express more emotion, especially in adults. (left / right)

(L.O. 20.6) j. Lie detector tests can give inaccurate information concerning truthfulness and lying because people have varying degrees of control over their ________ . (cognitive processes / autonomic nervous system)

(L.O. 20.7) k. The self-regulation view of emotional expression asserts that people can use ________ to control their levels of arousal and their expression of emotions. (conditioning techniques / thought)

Module Summary

Definition and Theories of Emotion

- *Emotions* are aroused internal states that may occur in response to either internal or external stimuli; they are usually accompanied by marked physiological change and are interpreted events (p. 381).
- The *James–Lange theory* of emotion states that people interpret their emotions in response to physiological changes. The *Cannon–Bard* theory states that when people experience emotions, two areas of the brain are stimulated simultaneously, one creating an emotional response and the other creating physiological change (p. 382).
- According to the *Schachter–Singer* approach, people interpret physiological changes within the context of a situation and infer emotions from these cues. Shaver asserts that those interpretations come from a broader understanding of emotional categories (p. 383).
- Shaver showed that there are six emotions that most people will describe: love, joy, anger, sadness, fear, and surprise. These six categories can overlap, and many other emotional states can be grouped under these basic categories (p. 384).

Development of Emotional Responses

- Infants show several emotional responses at birth, but some emotions develop through warm attachments during infancy, and many others continue to develop due to learning across the life span (p. 386).

Expression of Emotion

- Both facial expressions and physiological expressions of emotion appear to influence emotions, and both are influenced by thoughts, as well as by emotions (p. 386).

KEY TERMS

emotion, p. 381

SELF-TEST

Module 20

- Before taking the self-test, **recite** and **review.**
- Use the key at the back of the text to *correct* your answers.
- *Restudy* pages that correspond to any questions you answered incorrectly.

1. The subjective component of an emotion is
   a. called a *feeling.*
   b. how others describe the way a particular individual is feeling.
   c. an action or overt response that accompanies a feeling.
   d. always expressed in behavior.

2. "I am frightened because my heart is beating quickly" characterizes the ________ theory of emotion.
   a. James–Lange
   b. Cannon–Bard
   c. Schachter–Singer
   d. Shaver prototype

3. According to Frijda, emotional experience is the result of
   a. general knowledge about life situations.
   b. a cognitive appraisal of a situation accompanied by preparations for action.
   c. labeling feelings of arousal.
   d. physiological changes that are interpreted by the person.

4. Based on his experiments with rhesus monkeys, what was Harry Harlow's conclusion concerning the conditions necessary for normal emotional development?
   a. If basic physiological needs (such as food and water) are satisfied, normal emotions will develop.
   b. Nature and nurture must interact at specific times when relevant brain mechanisms are ready to mature.
   c. Normal emotional expression can be taught at any age during early childhood.
   d. Normal emotional expression is innate, and the environment has little if any effect on its development.

5. In a study investigating the emotional expression of store clerks, one researcher found that
   a. clerks who wore a smock were more emotionally expressive than those who did not wear one.
   b. male clerks were more emotionally expressive than female clerks.
   c. both male and female clerks avoided emotional expression.
   d. female clerks seemed to give more positive emotional expression to female customers.

6. Best and Queen argue that people are able to inhibit or mask emotional expression on the right side of the face because
   a. muscles on the right side of the face are more flexible.
   b. emotions are generated from the right side of the brain.
   c. the right side of the face is under the influence of the more easily controlled left side of the brain.
   d. most people are right-handed and right-eyed, so when they look in the mirror, they observe the expressions on the right side of the face more than the left.

7. Which of the following statements concerning lie detector tests is the most accurate?
   a. Most states accept the lie detector as valid evidence in court.
   b. A federal law requires the use of lie detector tests when hiring prospective employees for interstate commerce, which affects about 35% of all employees.
   c. Lie detector tests are extremely accurate at detecting lies told by habitual liars, but often inaccurate when measuring the responses of infrequent liars.
   d. The American Psychological Association believes that lie detector tests can cause psychological damage to innocent people.

8. The ________ of emotional expression focuses on one's ability to alter levels of arousal through thought and active appraisal of the environment.
   a. expectancy view
   b. self-regulation view
   c. biochemical maintenance view
   d. behavioral expression view

Connections

If you are interested in . . .	Turn to . . .	To learn more about . . .
The role of motivation in learning, memory, and intelligence	◆ Chapter 5, p. 178	How an organism in a need state (such as hunger) learns more quickly and better in classical conditioning
	◆ Chapter 6, p. 228	Ways to improve your memory
	◆ Chapter 11, p. 454	The relationship between innate intelligence and motivation to succeed on a test
How thoughts influence motives and behavior	◆ Chapter 5, p. 190	How cognitive learning takes place without specific observable motives or reinforcement
	◆ Chapter 10, p. 426	How personality theorists are introducing thought into the equation of how a person develops and maintains a personality
	◆ Chapter 14, p. 578	The way in which treatment approaches to various disorders consider the role of motivation and a person's appraisal of situations in determining behavior
The emotional responses people make to various situations	◆ Chapter 4, p. 142	How a person can learn to manipulate his or her body's response and subsequent emotions through techniques such as hypnosis and biofeedback
	◆ Chapter 12, p. 482	How people's health can be affected by their overall emotional responses when faced with stressful situations
	◆ Chapter 13, p. 545	The interaction between physiological disorders and emotional responses

Because human behavior is motivated and most of it does not occur by chance, the relationship of motivation to other sub-specialties is especially important. Biological drives such as hunger and thirst help initiate behavior and they are controlled in sections of the hypothalamus (Chapter 2, p. 65). Our ability to change our consciousness (Chapter 4, p. 142) and learn about the world (Chapter 5) happen only when we are motivated to do so. While parents may seek to optimize their child's development (Chapter 8, p. 277) a child must be motivated for new experiences to have positive effects on personality (Chapter 10). A person's health and adjustment (Chapter 12, p. 481) and whether they will develop psychological disorders (Chapter 13, p. 519) all are dependent on how an individual relates to other people (Chapter 15, p. 621) and his or her desire to seek various kinds of goals. When well motivated and exposed to the appropriate circumstances a person's emotional life can be rich and fulfilled and their range of emotional expression (Chapter 12, p. 504) can be varied and appropriate.

Module 21 ► INSIGHT THEORIES 396

Module 22 ► TRAIT AND BEHAVIORAL THEORIES 420

Chapter 10

Personality

Personality is a set of relatively enduring behavioral characteristics that describe how a person reacts to the environment. This chapter focuses on the various approaches to personality, each using different concepts to explain the sources and development of personality. The first module, Module 21, presents psychoanalytic and humanistic theories, which focus on the individual. Psychoanalytic theories view personality as the result of competing internal drives for gratification and acceptance. Psychoanalytic theories are shown in a historical context, showing how Freud's early ideas have been modified by neo-Freudians (*neo* means "new"), and how other theories have evolved that are loosely rooted in Freud's original ideas. In contrast to Freudian theories are humanistic ones, which view personality as the successful expression of an individual's innermost talents and abilities; this directly contrasts with a Freudian notion of inner conflict and biological based aggression.

In Module 22, behavioral theories are presented, which see personality as social behavior developed in response to learning or observational experiences. The behavioral theories of today bear little resemblance to earlier ones, primarily because behaviorists such as Bandura and Mischel have shown that thought is an important vehicle for shaping, altering, and maintaining personality. Also presented in this module are trait theories and cognitive perspectives of personality.

Each of these approaches focus on specific behaviors, but because none of these theories alone satisfactorily explains all aspects of personality for all people, most psychologists use an eclectic approach, combining aspects of various theories when considering personality. In addition, microtheories have been especially useful in increasing psychologists' understanding of day-to-day behavior. For example, a microtheory about *locus* (location/focus) of control helps in understanding whether people perceive their environment as controlling them (*external* locus of control) or as under their control (*internal* locus of control). This eclecticism also allows for flexibility in therapy so that the type of approach used depends in some measure on the person's problem. For someone having a problem with self-image, the therapist may use a fulfillment approach, which emphasizes enhancement of self-image. For a person with feelings of guilt about sexuality, a more Freudian approach may seem appropriate. The combination of smaller well-researched theories with some of the global theories (which are more difficult to confirm experimentally) probably holds the key to understanding personality.

Module 21

Insight Theories

LEARNING OBJECTIVES

When you have mastered the material in this module, you will be able to

Introduction (p. 397)

21.1 Explain both what psychologists mean by the term *personality* and why it is a complex topic of study (p. 397).

Psychoanalytic Theory (pp. 398–406)

21.2 Distinguish between psychodynamic theory and psychoanalysis and discuss the main ideas of Freud's theory (p. 398).

21.3 Describe the three levels of consciousness and three psychic forces used by Freud to explain the causes of behavior (p. 399).

21.4 Describe Freud's psychosexual-stage theory of personality development (p. 400).

21.5 Explain how fixations affect development and describe how people use defense mechanisms to reduce anxiety caused by unresolved conflicts (p. 402).

21.6 Discuss ways in which Freud contributed to modern-day psychology, describe some of the criticisms of his theories, and share interesting aspects of his personal life (p. 403).

Psychoanalytic Theory: Neo-Freudians—Dissent and Revision (pp. 406–408)

21.7 Describe a neo-Freudian and compare and contrast Jung's analytic theory and Freud's theory (p. 406).

21.8 Describe Adler's theory of personality and tell both how it differs from Freud's theory and how it has contributed to the field of psychology (p. 407).

Humanistic Approaches (pp. 409–414)

21.9 Describe humanistic theories and how they differ from Freudian-based theories, and summarize Maslow's theory (p. 409).

21.10 Describe Rogers's theory of personality and explain how it differs from Freud's theory (p. 409).

SQ3R
- **Survey** to set goals for studying.
- Ask **questions** as you **read.**
- Stop occasionally to **recite** and **review.**

plus
- **Write** a summary of key points.
- **Reflect** on the hypotheses, evidence, and implications of this material and on the relevance it has to *your* life.

Week after week, television evangelist Jim Bakker exhorted his viewers to shun worldly evils, to seek and pursue peace—and he then asked for generous donations to help finance his growing ministry. With wife and children at his side, Bakker had a boyish charm that many considered infectious and sincere. The downfall of Bakker and his compatriots followed weeks of scandalous headlines on the nightly news: misuse of funds, overbooking of hotel rooms promised to people who pledged money, then the reports that Bakker had a romantic affair with Jessica Hahn. The nasty details spewed forth: motel rooms, cover-up money, lies, and a wildly extravagant life-style. Before long, Jim Bakker was arrested for misuse of church funds. During his lengthy trial, critics and colleagues proposed a variety of explanations for his behavior. Some said the evangelist was a lecher hiding beneath a pious facade; others proclaimed him a saint who suffered a moral lapse; still others declared the man an egomaniac who believed he could do no wrong. Which of these personality assessments is correct? Could each be partly true? Are those who label the evangelist a hypocrite being cynical . . . or just realistic? Did Bakker change, or was he always this way?

No other phenomenon is so complex, so resistant to easy definition and assessment as the human character. Most people describe the way they respond to the world by using catchwords: They say they are shy, or sensitive, or outgoing, or concerned, or aggressive. They also use these words to describe their personalities.

Learning Objective 21.1 Explain both what psychologists mean by the term *personality* and why it is a complex topic of study.

Psychologists describe personality, but they do so in a systematic and scientific way. For psychologists, **personality** is a set of relatively enduring behavioral responses and internal predispositions that characterize how a person reacts to the environment. That is, someone's personality can be defined as the individual's behavior in a variety of situations over time. However, psychologists also recognize that an individual's behavior is not consistent all the time or in every situation; A person may not "be herself" on a particular day; a television evangelist may "suffer a moral lapse."

What makes people consistent in their behavior? To answer this question, some personality theorists focus on the day-to-day behaviors that characterize people; others focus on the inner conflicts that shape personality. Some see a human being as an individual who reacts to the environment. Others emphasize the internal, even genetic, influences that impel a person to action. Personality theorists must consider social psychological theories such as attitude theories, motivational theories such as expectancy theories, and even biological theories such as those suggesting biological predispositions toward some personality characteristics (e.g., shyness). We begin by examining an approach to personality—psychoanalytic theory—that focuses on the unconscious and how thought and ideas con-

personality: A set of relatively enduring behavioral characteristics and internal predispositions that describe how a person reacts to the environment.

tained therein direct day-to-day behavior. This approach is the well-known and widely disputed theory of Sigmund Freud.

Psychoanalytic Theory

Learning Objective 21.2 Distinguish between psychodynamic theory and psychoanalysis, and discuss the main ideas of Freud's theory.

Freud's influence on psychology is so great that some of his basic ideas and concepts are often taken for granted. However, when Freud first introduced his ideas, he was seen as strange, heretical, and simply off base. Studying the unconscious and suggesting that children have sexual experiences were, to say the least, out of the mainstream.

Sigmund Freud (1856–1939) was an Austrian physician who used hypnosis to treat people with physical and emotional problems. Most of Freud's patients were from the middle and upper classes of Austrian society. Many were society matrons who, because they lived in a repressive society, had limited opportunities for the release of anxiety and tension. Freud noticed that many of them needed to discuss their problems and often felt better after having done so. From his studies of hypnosis and work with these patients, Freud began to conceptualize a theory of behavior, and many of his early conclusions focused on the role of sexual frustrations in producing physical symptoms. Over time, Freud developed an elaborate theory of personality and an accompanying approach to therapy. His approach to personality came to be called *psychoanalytic theory;* his method of therapy, *psychoanalysis.*

Key Concepts

Many psychological theories have a key concept around which the theory grows. Freud's theory had two such key concepts: psychic determinism and unconscious motivation. **Psychic determinism** suggests that all thoughts, feelings, actions, gestures, and speech are determined by some action or event that happened to an individual in the past. Adults, for example, do not have accidental slips of the tongue, nor do they frown or change mood by accident; instead, past events affect all of today's actions. Moreover, most of a person's thoughts and behavior are determined by **unconscious motivation**—thoughts and feelings buried in the mind, or unconscious. By definition, people are unaware of the contents of the unconscious and are even unaware of its very existence. These two ideas—that behavior is caused by previous events and that people are no longer aware of these events—guided much of Freud's theory.

In addition to these two key concepts, Freud theorized that people are energized and able to act the way they do because of two basic instinctual drives—*life,* which prominently features sex and sexual energy, and *death,* which features aggression. These instincts are buried deep within the unconscious and are not always socially acceptable. Freud wrote little about aggression until late in his life; he focused mainly on sexual instincts, which he termed the **libido** (later in his writings Freud referred to the **libido** as *life energy*). His critics assert that he was preoccupied with sexual matters.

When people exhibit socially unacceptable behaviors or have feelings that they consider socially unacceptable, especially sexual feelings, they often experience self-punishment, guilt, and anxiety. Freud's theory thus describes a conflict between a person's instinctual (often unconscious) needs for gratification and the demands of society for socialization. In other words, it paints a picture of human beings caught in a conflict between basic sexual and aggressive desires and soci-

psychic determinism: [SIE-kick] A psychoanalytic assumption that everything a person feels, thinks, and does has a purpose and that all behaviors are caused by past events.

unconscious motivation: A psychoanalytic assumption that behavior is determined by desires, goals, and internal states of which an individual is unaware.

libido: [lih-BEE-doe] In Freud's theory, the instinctual life force that energizes the id. Supports the pleasure principle and seeks immediate gratification; usually sexual in nature.

ety's demands. For Freud, a person's basic desire is to maximize instinctual gratification while minimizing punishment and guilt.

Structure of Personality

In his theory, Freud considered the sources and consequences of conflict and how people deal with it. For Freud, a person's source of energy to deal with conflict is biologically determined, complex, and lies in the structure of consciousness.

Learning Objective 21.3
Describe the three levels of consciousness and three psychic forces used by Freud to explain the causes of behavior.

Structure of Consciousness. According to Freud, consciousness consists of three levels. The first level, **conscious** awareness, consists of the thoughts, feelings, and actions of which people are aware. The second level, **preconscious** awareness, includes mental activities that people can become aware of only if they closely attend to them. The third level, the **unconscious,** involves mental activities that people are unaware of and can only become aware of through some specific therapeutic techniques, such as dream analysis. To illustrate how these behavior levels differ, suppose that a woman decides to become a psychotherapist for a *conscious* reason—the reason she gives family and friends: She wants to help people. Later, during an introspective moment, she realizes that her *preconscious* motivation for becoming a psychotherapist stems from a desire to resolve her own unhappiness. Finally, through psychoanalysis, she discovers that she hungers for love and intimacy, which her parents denied her. *Unconsciously,* she hopes that her future patients will satisfy that hunger by making her feel needed. Freud's theory focuses on people's unconscious level and how it influences their behavior.

Id, Ego, and Superego. According to Freud's theory, the primary structural elements of personality are three forces that reside, fully or partially, in the unconscious: the id, the ego, and the superego. Each force accounts for a different aspect of functioning. It is important to keep in mind that the id, ego, and superego are concepts of mental forces, not physical structures of the brain.

The **id** is the source of a person's instinctual energy, which, according to Freud, is either sexual or aggressive. The id works through the *pleasure principle,* whereby it tries to maximize immediate gratification through satisfaction of raw impulses. Deep within the unconscious, the demanding, irrational, and selfish id seeks only pleasure. It does not care about morals, society, or other people. Freud might argue that it was Jim Bakker's id that propelled him toward a sexual liaison despite his religious exhortations to others.

While the id seeks to maximize pleasure and obtain immediate gratification, the **ego** (which grows out of the id) works via the *reality principle* and seeks to satisfy the individual's instinctual needs in accordance with reality. The ego acts as a manager, adjusting cognitive and perceptual processes to balance the person's functioning, to control the id, and to stay in touch with reality. For example, the id of a boy who wakes up shivering may tell him to steal a blanket from his older brother, sleeping on the bottom bunk. However, the boy's ego tells him that his older brother might punish him for stealing the blanket. Working on the reality principle, the boy realizes that he can gratify his id more safely by asking his parents for another blanket.

The **superego** is the moral aspect of mental functioning, taught by parents and society. The superego tells the id and the ego whether gratification in a particular instance is ethical. It attempts to control the id by internalizing parental authority (whether rational or irrational) through the process of socialization and by punishing transgressions with feelings of guilt and anxiety. The superego may tell the boy that stealing a blanket from his brother, who may then become cold, is immoral. By asking his parents for another blanket, the boy can satisfy his id

conscious: [KON-shus] Freud's first level of awareness, which refers to behaviors (feelings and actions) of which a person is aware.

preconscious: Freud's second level of awareness, which refers to mental activity that a person can become aware of by attending to it.

unconscious: Freud's third level of awareness, which refers to mental activity beyond a person's normal awareness, but which can be made available through psychoanalysis.

id: In Freud's theory, the source of instinctual energy, which works on the pleasure principle.

ego: [EE-go] In Freud's theory, the part of personality that seeks to satisfy both the id and the superego, in accordance with reality.

superego: [SUP-er-EE-go] In Freud's theory, the moral branch of mental functioning, comprising the ego ideal and conscience and taught by parents and society.

TABLE 21.1 Freud's view of mental structures

Structure	Consciousness	Contents and function
Id	Unconscious	Basic impulses (sex and aggression); seek immediate gratification; immediate, irrational, impulsive
Ego	Mostly conscious	Executive mediating between id impulses and superego inhibitions; tests reality; rational
Superego	Both conscious and unconscious	Ideals and morals; strives for perfection; incorporated from parents; becomes a person's conscience

without feeling guilty, fearful, or anxious. The ego and superego attempt to modulate the id and direct it toward more appropriate ways of behaving (see Table 21.1).

Development of Personality

Learning Objective 21.4 Describe Freud's psychosexual-stage theory of personality development.

Freud strongly believed that if people look at the development of their behavior, they can gain insight into their current behavior, and he used this principle with his patients. This belief led him to an elaborate stage theory of personality development. Freud believed that the core aspects of personality are established early, remain stable throughout life, and change only with great difficulty. Freud argued that all people pass through five critical stages of personality development: oral, anal, phallic, latency, and genital.

oral stage: Freud's first stage of personality development (birth to about age 2 years), during which infants obtain gratification primarily through the mouth.

anal stage: Freud's second stage of personality development (ages 2 years to about 3), during which children learn to control the immediate gratification obtained through defecation and become responsive to the demands of society.

Oral Stage. The first stage is the **oral stage,** based on the fact that newborns' instincts are focused on their mouths—their primary pleasure-seeking center. They receive oral gratification through feeding, thumb sucking, and cooing; during the early months of life, people's basic feelings about the world are established. Freud relied heavily on symbolism, and he contended that an adult who considers the world a bitter place (referring to the mouth and taste senses) probably had difficulty during the oral (location of the taste buds) stage of development. Adults who had difficulty in the oral stage of development would tend to have problems that focus on nurturing and on receiving warmth and love.

Anal Stage. The second major stage of development is the **anal stage.** At about 2 or 3 years of age, children learn to respond to some of society's demands. One parental demand is that children control their bodily functions of urination and defecation. Most 2- and 3-year-olds experience pleasure in moving their bowels, with the anal area the focus of pleasurable feelings. This stage therefore establishes the basis for conflict between the id and the ego, between the desire for infantile pleasure and the demand for adult, controlled behavior. Freud claimed that during the anal stage, children develop certain lasting personality characteristics regarding control, such as neatness and extreme orderliness, that reflect their toilet training. Thus, adults who had difficulty in the anal stage would tend to have problems that focus on orderliness and also might be compulsive in many behaviors.

Phallic Stage. Freud's third stage, the **phallic stage,** centers on the genitals. At about age 4 or 5 years, children become aware of their sexuality. Freud claimed that during this stage, numerous feelings are repressed so deeply that children, and later adults, are unaware of many of their sexual urges. Nonetheless, sex-role development begins during this period.

The **Oedipus complex,** which develops in the phallic stage, is a boy's love for his mother, hostility toward his father, and the consequent fear of castration and punishment by the father. In resolving the Oedipus complex, he eventually accepts his father's close relationship with his mother. Rather than feel excluded by it, he chooses to gratify his need for his mother's attention by identifying with his father. In this way, a young boy begins to identify with and model his behavior after that of his father.

For females, Freud argued that the Oedipus complex, sometimes termed the *Electra complex,* follows a slightly different course. Freud held that when a young girl realizes that she has no penis, she develops what Freud called *penis envy.* He then suggested that by attaching her love to her father, she can symbolically acquire a penis. A young girl then may ask her father to marry her so that they can raise a family together. When she realizes that this is unlikely, she may identify with her mother and copy her mother's behavior as a means of obtaining (or sharing in) her father's affection. Like the young male, the young female identifies with the parent of the same sex in the hope of obtaining affection from the parent of the opposite sex. For both boys and girls, the critical component in resolving the Oedipus complex is the development of identification with the parent of the same sex.

The existence of an Oedipus complex is controversial and widely debated, especially because many people find it sexist and degrading to women. There is no doubt about Freud's views of women; he saw women as weaker and less rational than men and believed that they should be subservient to men. Today, most researchers believe that Freud's notion of penis envy was imaginative but unconvincing (Stagner, 1988).

Latency Stage. Freud's fourth stage of development, the **latency stage,** lasts from about age 7 years until puberty. During latency, children develop physically, but sexual urges are inactive (latent). Libidinal urges, sexual fears, and frustrations are repressed, and much of a child's energy is channeled into social or achievement-related activities. Some modern psychoanalysts (considered in the next section) believe that this stage has disappeared from American society because of the fast-paced maturation of children into adolescence. They assert that children move from the phallic stage directly to the genital stage.

Genital Stage. When people reach the last stage of development, the **genital stage,** the sexuality, fears, and repressed feelings of earlier stages are once again exhibited (see Figure 21.1 on the next page). Many of an adolescent's repressed feelings of sexuality toward his or her mother and father resurface. During the genital stage, the adolescent shakes off dependence on parents and learns to deal with members of the opposite sex in socially and sexually mature ways. Members of the opposite sex, who may have been ignored during the latency stage, are now seen as attractive and desirable.

During the genital stage, many unresolved conflicts and repressed urges affect behavior. Ideally, if previous stages of development were maneuvered without major incident, people will develop conventional relations with members of the opposite sex. If not, a person may continue to have a series of unresolved conflicts within his or her unconscious.

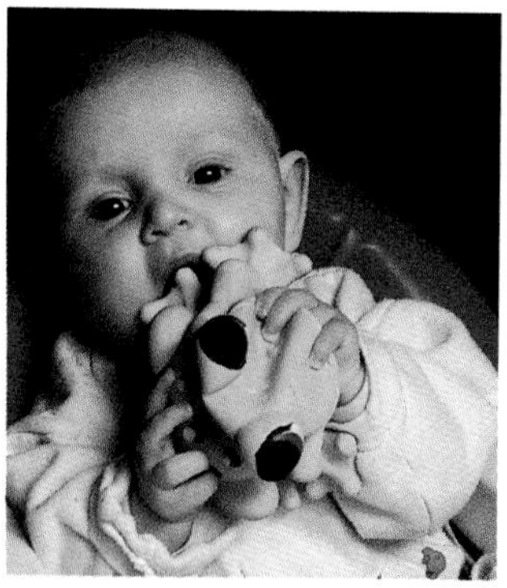

Freud believed that the first stage of development is the *oral stage* during which an infant focuses on oral gratification.

phallic stage: [FAAL-ick] Freud's third stage of personality development (ages 3 to 7 years), during which children obtain gratification primarily from the genitals; includes passing through the Oedipus (or Electra) complex.

Oedipus complex: [ED-dip-us] Occurs during the phallic stage: Feelings of rivalry with the parent of the same sex and love of the parent of the opposite sex; ultimately resolved through identification with the parent of the same sex. *Electra complex* specifically refers to this process in women.

latency stage: [LAY-ten-see] Freud's fourth stage of personality development (age 7 years until puberty), during which sexual urges are inactive.

genital stage: [JEN-it-ul] Freud's last stage of personality development, during which the sexual conflicts of childhood resurface at puberty and are resolved in adulthood.

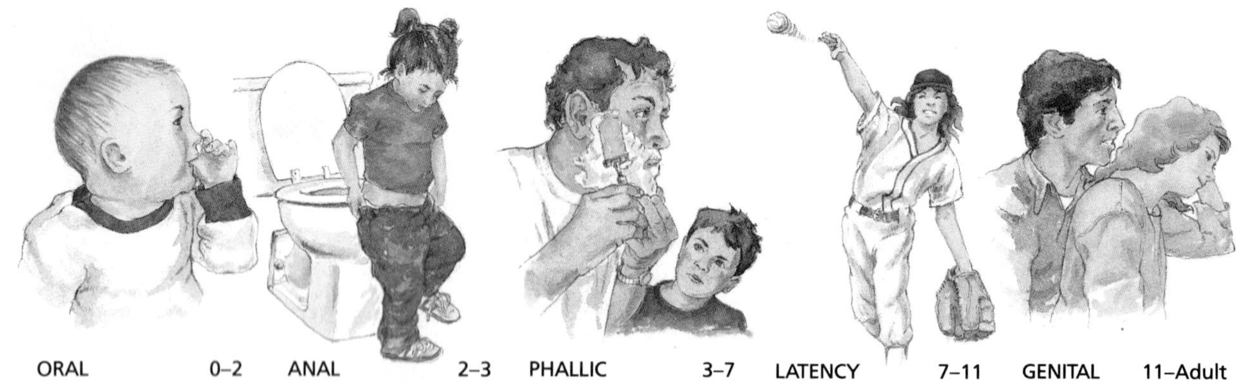

ORAL 0–2
Infant achieves gratification through oral activities such as feeding, thumb sucking, and cooing.

ANAL 2–3
The child learns to respond to some of the demands of society (such as bowel and bladder control).

PHALLIC 3–7
The child learns to realize the differences between males and females and becomes aware of sexuality.

LATENCY 7–11
The child continues his or her development, but sexual urges are relatively quiet.

GENITAL 11–Adult
The growing adolescent shakes off old dependencies and learns to deal maturely with the opposite sex.

Figure 21.1

Freud described five psychosexual stages of development.

Unresolved Conflicts

Learning Objective 21.5
Explain how fixations affect development, and describe how people use defense mechanisms to reduce anxiety caused by unresolved conflicts.

Fixation. As children proceed from one developmental stage to the next, they adjust their views of the world. However, if they do not successfully pass through a stage, a fixation occurs. A **fixation** is an excessive attachment to some person or object that is only appropriate at an earlier level of development. When a person becomes fixated, he or she is said to be arrested at a particular stage of development. Fixation at one developmental stage does not prevent all further development, but unless people master each stage successfully, they cannot fully master the later stages. Someone troubled by an unresolved conflict who develops a fixation will find successful completion of later stages more difficult. For example, according to Freud, a child who does not successfully pass through the phallic stage probably has not resolved the Oedipus complex and may feel hostility toward the parent of the same sex. The child may suffer the consequences of this unresolved conflict throughout life.

According to Freud, healthy personality adjustment generally involves a balance among competing forces: the child, and later the adult, is neither too self-centered nor too moralistic. Restrictive, punitive, and overbearing parents or parents who are indifferent, smothering, or overindulgent produce emotionally disturbed children who have a difficult time coping with life because of the resulting fixations. Fixations or partial fixations usually occur because of frustration or overindulgence that hinders the expression of sexual or aggressive energy at a particular psychological stage. What happens when a person becomes fixated? According to Freud, the person develops defense mechanisms and sometimes maladjustment.

fixation: Arrested or halted personality development at a particular stage. Also may involve an excessive attachment to some person or object that is only appropriate to an earlier level of development.

defense mechanism: A way of reducing anxiety by distorting perceptions of reality.

Defense Mechanisms. For each of us, **defense mechanisms** are largely unconscious ways of reducing anxiety by distorting our perceptions of reality. Everyone defends against anxiety from time to time. Defense mechanisms allow the ego to deal with the uncomfortable feelings that anxiety produces. In fact, people are typically unaware that they are using defense mechanisms. Nonetheless, people who use defense mechanisms to such an extent that reality is sharply distorted can become maladjusted.

Freud described many kinds of defense mechanisms but identified **repression** as the most important. In repression, anxiety-provoking behavior or thoughts are totally relegated to the unconscious. When people repress a feeling or desire, they become unaware of it. Thus, a young girl who was taught that assertiveness is inappropriate in women may repress her own assertiveness. In addition to repression, Freud observed five other key defense mechanisms:

- **Projection**—People attribute their own undesirable traits to others. An individual who unconsciously recognizes his or her aggressive tendencies may then see other people acting in an excessively aggressive way. Jim Bakker may have used projection, calling other people sinners against God.
- **Denial**—A person refuses to accept reality. Someone with strong sexual urges may deny interest in sex rather than deal with those urges.
- **Reaction formation**—A person defends against anxiety by adopting behaviors opposite to his or her true feelings. A classic example of reaction formation is the behavior of someone with strong sexual urges who becomes extremely chaste, perhaps by becoming a priest. Another example is someone who censures pornographic literature, but has strong desires to read it.
- **Sublimation**—Energy from an impulse that might be considered taboo is channeled or redirected into a socially desirable form; thus, a man who has sexual desires for someone whom he knows may be off limits (perhaps a cousin) channels that sexual energy or drive into painting nudes.
- **Rationalization**—A person tries to reinterpret undesirable behavior to make it appear acceptable. For example, a thief may rationalize that her victims acquired their wealth through illegal or immoral means or that she needs the money more than they do. Jim Bakker may have rationalized that his followers wanted him to lead a lavish life-style. When people rationalize, they try to make unreasonable feelings or behaviors seem reasonable.

When defense mechanisms take over and reality becomes distorted and maladaptive, a person must be concerned about using them; it is our over-reliance upon defense mechanisms that leads to maladjustment.

repression: A defense mechanism by which people block anxiety-provoking feelings from conscious awareness and push them into the unconscious.

projection: A defense mechanism by which people attribute to other people or objects their own undesirable traits.

denial: A defense mechanism by which people refuse to accept the true source of their anxiety.

reaction formation: A defense mechanism by which people behave in a manner opposite to their true but anxiety-provoking feelings.

sublimation: [sub-li-MAY-shun] A defense mechanism by which people redirect socially unacceptable impulses into acceptable ones.

rationalization: A defense mechanism by which people reinterpret behavior in terms that render it acceptable.

Freud Today

Learning Objective 21.6
Discuss ways in which Freud contributed to modern-day psychology, describe some of the criticisms of his theories, and share interesting aspects of his personal life.

When Freud's psychosexual theory of development was first published around 1900, it received both favorable and unfavorable attention. It was considered absurd that young children had sexual feelings toward their parents. Freud's theory, however, has to be considered in a cultural context. Austrian society, with its rigid standards of behavior, and Freud's wealthy patients biased him in directions that few theorists would adopt today.

Yet, as we watch young children and the way in which they identify with their parents, we can see that there are elements of truth to this conception of how personality development proceeds. Little girls do tend to idolize their fathers, and little boys often become strongly attached to their mothers. However, Freud was not nearly as interested in normal development as he was in the pathology, or disorder, that appeared as a result of imperfect development. In many ways, Freud's developmental theory paved the way for other developmental stage theorists, such as Piaget, Levinson, and Erikson, who made more specific predictions about specific behaviors and whose theories are accepted more readily in many psychological circles (see Figure 21.2).

Freud's theories have been sharply criticized for a number of reasons. Some psychologists object to his basic conception of human nature, its emphasis on sexual urges, and his idea that human behavior is biologically determined; others reject his predictions about psychosexual stages and fixations. Psychologists assert that his theory does not account for changing situations and the contexts in which people find themselves. Many people find Freud's ideas about women patently offensive. At a minimum, his ideas are controversial, and many psychologists do not regard them as valid. Almost all agree that his theory makes specific predictions about individual behaviors almost impossible. Regardless of whether Freud's theory is right or wrong, his influence on psychology and on Western culture

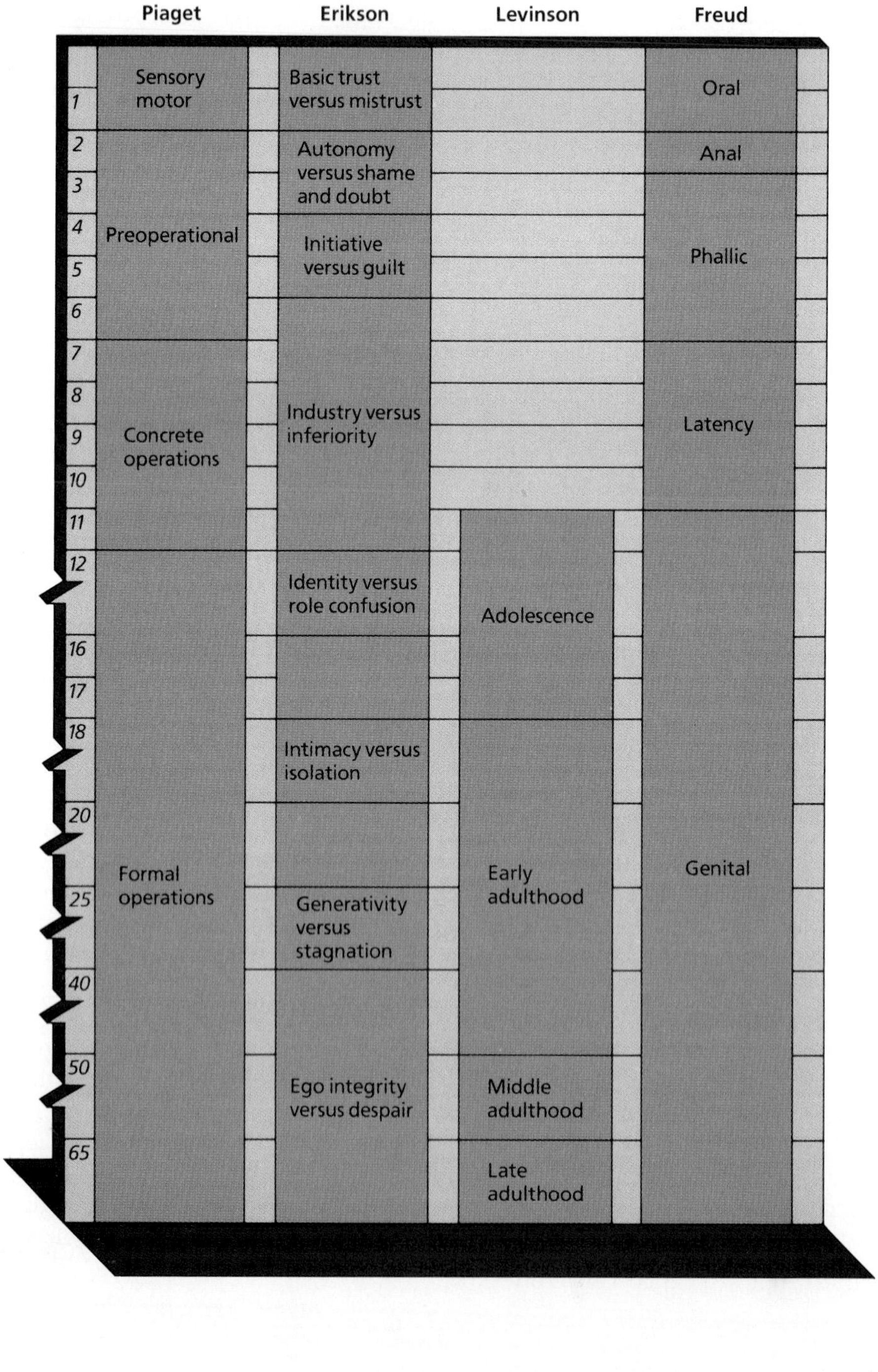

Figure 21.2

The stage theories of Piaget, Erikson, Levinson, and Freud all suggest that individuals must master each stage before they can pass successfully through the next. Notice the similarities among all four theories.

exceeds that of any other personality theorist, present or past. It weaves together his clinical experiences with patients, his speculations about human nature, and his own extraordinary personality, which the next section describes.

Sigmund Freud is best known for his psychoanalytic theory and the therapy method derived from it, psychoanalysis.

The Life of Sigmund Freud

Sigmund Freud is the best-known personality theorist of all time. His mark on psychological thinking was extraordinary, and his insights were unparalleled. The life and personality of Freud were as complex as his theory was profound. He was unhappy, quarrelsome, rebellious, and vindictive. Yet he was also energetic, loving, thoughtful, and a superb clinician. Many biographers have attempted to portray the complexity of Freud and his theory, but Yale professor Peter Gay has done it best in his 1988 book, *Freud—A Life for Our Time.*

Gay conducted extensive research into Freud's beliefs, life, and papers and letters (many of which were unpublished). Gay acknowledged Freud's *The Interpretation of Dreams,* published in 1899, as "an autobiography at once candid and canny, as tantalizing in what it omits as in what it discloses" (1988, p. 104). In this autobiographical work, Freud laid out the keys to psychoanalysis and distinguished between the manifest and the latent content of dreams. The *manifest content* is what people remember when they awake; the *latent content* is the deeper, encoded meaning, which requires decoding. From Freud's view, a dream is the disguised fulfillment of a repressed wish. Gay also showed how Freud's extensive reading and study of art, literature, and history affected his theorizing. From 1908 to 1914, Freud worked on papers that dealt with literary characters, including Oedipus, and used the information to build theories on character development, especially ego development.

Gay looked closely at Freud's personal life and recounted Freud's revelation that his father's death was the most significant event, the most decisive loss of his life. Gay noted also that Freud's failure to deal with the loss of his mother was also important. Gay wrote, "Should it really be true that a mother's death is any less poignant? Freud was very much his father's son, dreaming and worrying more about paternal than about maternal relations" (p. 89).

The life of Sigmund Freud must be considered in its historical and cultural context. From his birth in 1856 until his death in 1939, Freud's world underwent vast economic and social changes. He was born into a world of order, but his theorizing took place during a turbulent time—the emergence of World War I. "Freud, a man astonished at very little, was astonished at the hideous spectacle of human nature at war" (p. 353). This experience had an impact later on his views of preparing for death.

Gay's book allows us to peer into little-known realms of Freud's personal life. Until about 1920, Freud was often seen as radical and extreme—considered an outcast by many. However, by the mid-1920s, his celebrity was secure, and Freud acknowledged that he had become a household word. For example, in 1925, Hollywood mogul Samuel Goldwyn asked Freud to write a love story for him, but Goldwyn's extravagant financial offer was refused. The one gratification Freud desired but never achieved was a Nobel prize—a bitter disappointment, according to Gay.

On more than one occasion, Freud destroyed his notes and letters, to discourage future biographers, Nonetheless, his expansive correspondence and the volumes he wrote about his theories provided a legacy to document an important chapter of psychology's history. Gay's biography is a sympathetic portrait of Freud and will be a classic because it examines in detail and in an historical context some of the milestone ideas Freud put forth, including fixations, defense mechanisms, and the issue of unresolved conflicts.

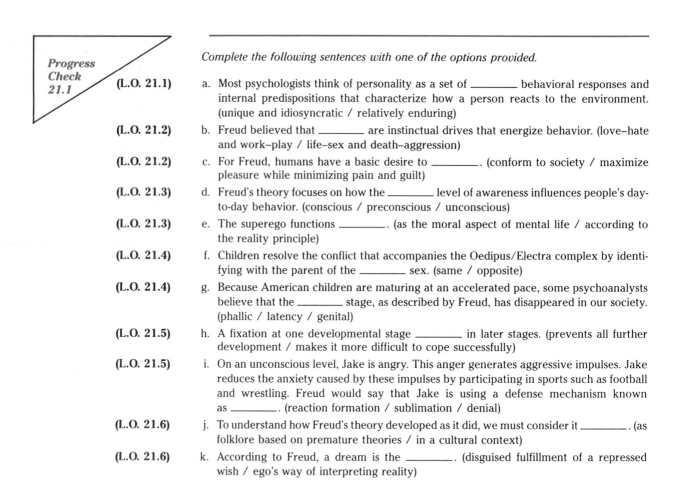

Progress Check 21.1

Complete the following sentences with one of the options provided.

(L.O. 21.1) a. Most psychologists think of personality as a set of ______ behavioral responses and internal predispositions that characterize how a person reacts to the environment. (unique and idiosyncratic / relatively enduring)

(L.O. 21.2) b. Freud believed that ______ are instinctual drives that energize behavior. (love–hate and work–play / life–sex and death–aggression)

(L.O. 21.2) c. For Freud, humans have a basic desire to ______. (conform to society / maximize pleasure while minimizing pain and guilt)

(L.O. 21.3) d. Freud's theory focuses on how the ______ level of awareness influences people's day-to-day behavior. (conscious / preconscious / unconscious)

(L.O. 21.3) e. The superego functions ______. (as the moral aspect of mental life / according to the reality principle)

(L.O. 21.4) f. Children resolve the conflict that accompanies the Oedipus/Electra complex by identifying with the parent of the ______ sex. (same / opposite)

(L.O. 21.4) g. Because American children are maturing at an accelerated pace, some psychoanalysts believe that the ______ stage, as described by Freud, has disappeared in our society. (phallic / latency / genital)

(L.O. 21.5) h. A fixation at one developmental stage ______ in later stages. (prevents all further development / makes it more difficult to cope successfully)

(L.O. 21.5) i. On an unconscious level, Jake is angry. This anger generates aggressive impulses. Jake reduces the anxiety caused by these impulses by participating in sports such as football and wrestling. Freud would say that Jake is using a defense mechanism known as ______. (reaction formation / sublimation / denial)

(L.O. 21.6) j. To understand how Freud's theory developed as it did, we must consider it ______. (as folklore based on premature theories / in a cultural context)

(L.O. 21.6) k. According to Freud, a dream is the ______. (disguised fulfillment of a repressed wish / ego's way of interpreting reality)

Psychoanalytic Theory: Neo-Freudians—Dissent and Revision

Learning Objective 21.7 Describe a neo-Freudian, and compare and contrast Jung's analytic theory and Freud's theory.

There is no question that Freud had an enormous impact on psychological thought. Nonetheless, his theory has been attacked by modern theorists, including some of his students who felt that there were serious omissions, errors, and obvious biases in Freudian theory. Many have developed new ideas loosely based on Freud's original conception.

Freud's powerful intellect and key concepts fascinated many psychologists and psychoanalysts. They were not ready to throw good ideas out with bad ones, and where they dissented from Freud, they revised his theories. They became known as **neo-Freudians.** Carl Jung is one of the best-known theorists who broke with Freud over key issues, and we explore his influential theory next.

neo-Freudian: Persons who modified variations of the basic ideas of Freud, usually attributing a greater influence to cultural and interpersonal factors than Freud did.

Jung's Analytical Psychology

Carl Gustav Jung (1875–1961) was a psychiatrist who became a close friend and follower of Freud. However, Jung, a brilliant thinker, ultimately broke with Freud over several key issues. Jung placed relatively little emphasis on sex, at least compared to Freud. He focused on people's desires to blend their basic drives (including sex) with real-world demands; thus, Jung saw people's behavior as less rigidly fixed and determined. Jung emphasized the search for meaning in life. When he declared his disagreements with Freud in 1917, he and Freud severed relationships; Freud was intolerant of followers who deviated too much from his position.

Jung chose to differentiate his approach from Freud by terming it an *analytic* approach rather than *psycho*analytic approach. Like Freud, Jung emphasized unconscious processes as determiners of behavior, and he believed that each person houses past events in the unconscious. Jung's version of the unconscious was slightly different, however; he held that the unconscious anticipates the future and redirects a person when the person is leaning too much in one psychological direction. In addition, Jung developed a new concept central to his ideas, that of the *collective unconscious*, a layer of unconscious that is even more primitive and deeply hidden from direct examination. The **collective unconscious** is a storehouse, a collection of ideas and images inherited from our ancestors. These inherited ideas and images are called *archetypes* and are passed from generation to generation. **Archetypes** are emotionally charged ideas and images that have rich meaning and symbolism and are contained within a person's collective unconscious. The archetypes of our collective unconscious emerge in art, in religion, and especially in dreams.

Carl Gustav Jung deviated from Freud in concentrating on people's attempts to successfully match their basic desires against real-life demands.

For example, one especially important archetype is the mandala; the *mandala* is considered a mystical symbol, generally circular in form, and in Jung's view represents the striving for unity within a person's self. Jung pointed out that many religions have mandalalike symbols; indeed, Hinduism and Buddhism use mandala symbols as aids to meditation. Another archetype is the concept of mother; each person is born with a predisposition to react to certain types of people or institutions as mother figures. Mother figures are considered warm, accepting, and nurturing—the Virgin Mary, one's alma mater, or the earth. There are archetypes for wise older men and wizards. Jung found rich symbolism in dreams, and used symbols such as the mandala and mothers to help people understand their own mental processes and behavior.

collective unconscious: In Jung's theory, a storehouse (collection) of primitive ideas and images in the unconscious, which are inherited from our ancestors.

archetypes: [AR-ki-types] In Jung's theory, emotionally charged ideas and images that have rich meaning and symbolism and are contained within the collective unconscious.

Carl Jung's ideas are widely read but not widely accepted by mainstream psychologists. Although his impact on psychoanalysis is important, he never achieved prominence in leading psychological thought because his ideas, even more than Freud's, cannot be verified. Some even view them as mere poetic speculation. Another psychologist who broke with Freud but who made a more lasting impact on psychological thought was Alfred Adler, considered next.

Alfred Adler: A Break from Freud

Learning Objective 21.8 Describe Adler's theory of personality, and tell both how it differs from Freud's theory and how it has contributed to the field of psychology.

Alfred Adler (1870–1937) was heavily influenced by Freud, and some psychologists consider his theory an extension of Freud's. Adler was a Viennese physician who remembered having an unhappy childhood. He recalled being compared to his older brother, who seemed to be better liked because of his physical prowess and attractiveness. Perhaps his unhappy childhood and feelings of inferiority led Adler to believe that people strive to become the best they can be. When Adler broke with Freudian traditions, he focused much more on human values and social interactions.

Key Concepts. At the turn of the century, physicians believed that diseases attacked weak, or inferior, organs. As a physician, Adler subscribed to this notion of "organ inferiority" and used it in his personality theory. Adler suggested that people try to strengthen weaknesses both in their organs and their personality. Thus, a key concept of Adler's theory is that people develop a striving for physical, mental, and psychological superiority; later in his writing, he spoke about striving for completion and perfection.

Another key concept of Adler's theory is that people strive to better themselves by focusing not simply on the self (as Freud thought) but on the self *as a*

Alfred Adler deviated from psychoanalysis moving toward a more humanistic approach to behavior.

member of society. Adler maintained that people are inherently social beings who seek goals and values that are social in nature. Adler believed that from birth on, people interact with parents, family, and society of their own free will. These innate social qualities temper people's drives for perfection.

Adler differed with Freud on two key points. First, Adler viewed human beings as striving to overcome obstacles toward fulfilling themselves, not as striving for pleasure. Second, Adler viewed the social nature of human beings as much more important than did Freud. Adler met with Freud on a weekly basis, but in 1911, Freud denounced him because of sharp, irreconcilable differences in their views of personality.

Structure of Personality. According to Adler, people are motivated, or energized, by natural feelings of inferiority, which lead them to strive for completion, superiority, and ultimately perfection. Thus, feelings of inferiority are not always detrimental. A sense of inferiority can compel people to strive for and thereby express their core tendencies, both as individuals and as members of society. Adler recognized that people seek to express their needs for superiority in different areas of life. Some seek to be superior artists; others seek to be superior social advocates, parents, teachers, or corporate executives. Adler eventually sought to develop an "individual" psychology, arguing that people have to be analyzed as unique human beings.

Adler stressed fulfillment through striving toward specific goals. Some life goals, which Adler called *fictional finalism,* are not realistic and are unlikely to be achieved by most, such as winning the Nobel prize for literature, becoming a billionaire, or earning worldwide fame (Adler, 1929/1969). However, it is these fictional goals (often unconscious) that motivate people and set up unique patterns of striving.

Development of Personality. Adler felt that children's social interactions are particularly important in determining eventual personality characteristics (later, Carl Rogers would come to the same conclusion). Adler and his followers relied heavily on the idea that early relationships with siblings, parents, and other family members determine what life-style an individual eventually chooses. It therefore follows that birth order is important. A firstborn child, for example, is likely to have a different relationship with people, and thus develop a different life-style, from that of a thirdborn child. Firstborns are pushed by parents toward success, leadership, and independence and thus tend to have high needs for achievement. Their early experiences make it likely that they will choose a life-style reflecting high needs for achievement, such as that of a corporate president or U.S. Senator. Thirdborn children, on the other hand, are usually more relaxed about achievement. A young child who feels competitive with an older sibling, however, may develop strong needs for success, mastery, and achievement that drive that child toward success.

Foundations for Other Theories. To a great extent, psychologists see Adler as stressing an interpersonal route to fulfillment. Adler's ideas of an inferiority complex and of life-style have made their way into popular theories of psychology. In addition, Adler's key ideas also serve as the foundation of many Adlerian child care development centers. Adler's theory can be thought of as the parent of humanistic theories, such as Carl Rogers's, because it was developed 20 years earlier and laid the foundation for these theories. Adler emphasized an innate social need motivated by feelings of inferiority to strive toward perfection and superiority, whereas humanistic theories (considered next) stressed self-actualization.

Humanistic Approaches

Learning Objective 21.9 Describe humanistic theories and how they differ from Freudian-based theories, and summarize Maslow's theory.

Unlike Freudians and neo-Freudians, who wanted to understand relationships between children and parents, theorists such as Abraham Maslow and Carl Rogers were more interested in people's conceptions of themselves and what they would like to become. In general, *humanistic theories* assume that people are motivated by internal forces to achieve personal goals. Humanistic psychology does not focus on disturbed individuals but rather on understanding how healthy people cope with human motives such as self-esteem.

Humanistic theories, which emphasize fulfillment, developed partly in response to Freud's theory, which stresses the conflict of inner forces. Whereas Freud saw people in conflict warding off evil thoughts and desires with defenses, humanists see people as basically decent and worthwhile (although some of their specific behaviors might not be). Moreover, humanistic fulfillment theories enable theoreticians and practitioners to make predictions about specific behaviors.

Sometimes, humanistic theories are also called *phenomenological approaches* because they focus on the individual and his or her unique ways of interpreting the world (phenomena). Humanistic or phenomenological approaches are more likely to examine immediate experiences than past ones and are more likely to deal with an individual's perception of the world than with a therapist's perception of the individual. Finally, they focus on self-determination; people carve their own destinies, from their own vantage points, and in their own ways. The humanistic approach is represented by two well-known psychologists, Maslow and Rogers, whose theories are examined next.

Abraham Maslow

No single individual is more closely associated with humanistic phenomenological psychology than Abraham Maslow (1908–1970). Chapter 9 examined Maslow's theory of motivation (pp. 375–377), which states that human needs are arranged in a pyramidal hierarchy in terms of importance and potency. Lower needs are powerful and drive people toward fulfilling them—food and water, for example. At the middle of the pyramid of needs are safety, then belongingness, and self-esteem. At the top of the pyramid is self-actualization. The higher the need on the hierarchy, the more distinctly human the need.

As a humanist, Maslow felt that human beings were born healthy and undamaged, and he had a strong bias toward studying healthy human beings, rather than those wrapped up in maladjustment. He spoke about personality in terms of human uniqueness and the human need for **self-actualization,** the process of growth, the realization of human potential. He focused not on what was missing from personality or life, but what might be achieved in realizing one's full potential. The process of realizing potential, and of growing, is the process of becoming self-actualized.

self-actualization: The process of realizing one's innate human potential, to become the best one can be.

Critics of Maslow find his notions too fuzzy and diffuse (as they do Freud's). His approach to psychology is viewed as romantic and never fully developed. A more complete and scientific humanistic approach was presented by Carl Rogers.

Carl Rogers and Self Theory

Learning Objective 21.10 Describe Rogers's theory of personality, and explain how it differs from Freud's theory.

Carl Rogers (1902–1987) began to formulate his personality theory during the first years of his practice as a clinician in Rochester, New York. He listened to thousands of patients and was one of the first psychologists to record and transcribe interactions with patients. Given the opportunity, Rogers' patients talked about

UNDERSTANDING THE RESEARCH PROCESS

Women's Personality Changes

Does personality change over time, or does it stay the same from adolescence through old age? Are personality changes the same for men and women? Trait theorists assume that personality remains much the same over the life span. Shy people stay shy; high school pranksters become retirement home pranksters. Erik Erikson and adult stage theorists such as Daniel Levinson (Chapter 8), on the other hand, contend that people change during the life span. These psychologists believe in an adult life cycle.

Unfortunately, most personality and adult life-cycle studies have been conducted with men—who represent less than half the population. Do women's personalities change in a similar way? Do the personalities of career-oriented women change and family-oriented women stay the same? Helson and Moane (1987) from the University of California at Berkeley asked these questions of a group of women starting at college age and continuing to midlife. Their primary objective was to discover whether personality changes are obvious across different life paths and whether those changes support theories of adult development and personality. A second goal was to compare the life cycles of men and women because of the failure of previous long-term studies to address the vital issue. They asked whether life cycles in adulthood need to be rethought. Do women have midlife transitions as men do?

Helson and Moane began their work in 1958 at Mills College, a private women's college located in Oakland, California. They gathered information from the same 81 women at ages 21, 27, and 43. (In using this longitudinal method, they studied a single group of people at different times, to determine whether changes have occurred over time; for a review of this method, see Chapter 8, p. 278). The researchers used several measures of personality, including the California Psychological Inventory, or CPI. The CPI, commonly used to study people from mid-adolescence to old age, is a test of normal personality. Designed to assess effectiveness in interpersonal functioning, it examines confidence, independence, responsibility, socialization, self-control, tolerance, and flexibility, among other dimensions.

The results, reported as correlations between the different measures of personality, showed interesting stabilities and changes. For example, when the women were between ages 21 and 27, they took control of their lives, acknowledged differences in the way the world ought to be and the way it was, and scored higher on tolerance, social maturity, and femininity than they did later in life. At ages 27–43, they scored higher in the areas of dominance, independence, and confidence, but lower on flexibility and femininity. The changes from ages 27 to 43 were greater than the changes from 21 to 27. As the women grew older, they became more organized, committed, and work-oriented, but less open to change.

their experiences and thoughts and about themselves. From his experiences with patients, Rogers made three basic assumptions about behavior:

- Behavior is goal-directed and worthwhile.
- People are innately good, so they will almost always choose adaptive, enhancing, and self-actualizing behaviors.
- How a person sees his or her world determines how that person will behave.

fulfillment: In Rogers's personality theory, an inborn tendency directing people toward actualizing their inherited natures and thus attaining their potentials.

Key Concepts. Rogers believed that personal experiences provide an individual with a unique, subjective internal frame of reference and world view. He believed that **fulfillment**—an inborn tendency directing people toward actualizing their inherited nature and thus attaining their potential—is the motivating force of personality development. Thus, people strive naturally to express their capabilities, potential, and talents to the fullest extent.

Rogers' personality approach is *unidirectional* because it always moves in the direction of fulfillment. This does not mean that a person's personality undergoes

The results of this study are consistent with adult life-cycle theories of development that have focused on men. From ages 21 to 43, there were increases in self-discipline and commitment to duties; this also typically occurs with men. The women became more confident, independent, and work-oriented. Until age 27, changes were small, but after age 27, the women became less feminine, focusing less on gender-specific tasks, such as child care, and more on gaining independence and confidence and on developing a career.

Helson and Moane (1987) maintain that women's personalities change in consistent and predictable ways between ages 21 (young adulthood) and 43 (middle age). They feel, for example, that a career requires a woman to develop skills, confidence, and insight into others—things that were not necessary at earlier life stages. From Helson and Moane's view, personality is not static but a constantly evolving, developing set of skills and abilities acquired to cope with the demands and dilemmas that face maturing individuals. This is consistent with some stage theorists who have focused on men, but it presents problems for trait theorists who assert that personality is stable across the life span.

Helson and Moane conducted their studies during a time of rapid change in women's roles in society, from 1960 through 1985. Were changes that occurred during this time similar to the changes taking place now or to changes that will occur in the next 20 years? Is the U.S. likely to experience a decade similar to the one that saw the Vietnam War? Today, women may not show the same patterns. Today's women have experienced the war in the Persian Gulf and the August 1991 coup in the Soviet Union, for example.

Helson and Moane used a longitudinal method, a procedure that has problems. There were a limited number of subjects, and those subjects changed as the times did; also, some dropped out of the research project. Further, after repeated testing on the same task (even though years apart), some of the subjects may have shown spurious results because of prior practice on the same tests.

In addition, there are life-style variations that this research did not specifically address (e.g., many women now opt for careers first and families later). Socioeconomic status and societal changes determine so many life-style, educational, and work issues that this too needs to be examined. Further research must consider results within a historical context, taking into account changing political, social, and moral values. Last, it will take a longitudinal study of college women of the 1980s traced over 20 years to determine whether Helson and Moane's findings are still valid for today's generation.

- ***What was the fundamental question that Helson and Moane asked in their research?***
- ***The researchers used a correlational approach; why might this limit the results or the implications of their study?***
- ***Because many women opt for careers first and family later, what are the implications of this age-related childbearing phenomenon for the results of the Helson and Moane study? Does it alter their conclusions? Will they find different conclusions, depending on when women have children?***

uninterrupted growth. During some periods, no growth is evident. However, for Rogers, a person's core tendency is to actualize, maintain, and enhance the experiencing organism. Rogers liked the analogy of a seed, which if watered grows into a plant—a strong, healthy plant, a representative sample of other members of its species.

Structure of Personality. Rogers' theory of personality is structured around the concept of self. What he means by **self** are those perceptions individuals have of themselves and their relationships to people and aspects of life. The self is how people see their own behavior and internal characteristics. As mentioned before, his theory assumes that individuals are constantly engaged in the process of fulfilling their potential, that is, of actualizing their true selves.

Rogers suggested that each person has a concept not only of self, but also of an ideal self. An **ideal self** is the self a person would like to be, such as a competent professional, devoted mate, or loving parent. According to Rogerian theory, each person's happiness lies within his or her conception of self. A person is gener-

self: The main structural component of Rogers's theory of personality. Perceptions that characterize an individual and his or her relationship to other people and to other aspects of his or her life.

ideal self: The self that a person would ideally like to be.

Carl Rogers developed a personality theory based on his belief in the concept of *self.*

ally happy when agreement exists between the real (Rogers used the term *phenomenal*) self and the ideal self; great discrepancies between the real and the ideal selves create unhappiness and dissatisfaction, and in extreme cases, major maladjustment.

Rogers' focus on the self led him to his basic principle, which is that people have a tendency to maximize their self-concept through *self-actualization.* In this process, the self grows, expands, and becomes social. People are self-actualized when they have expanded their self-concepts and developed their potential to approximate their ideal selves. When people's self-concepts are not what they would like them to be, anxiety develops. Like Freud, Rogers saw anxiety as useful because it motivates people to try to actualize their best selves, to become all they are capable of being.

Development of Personality. Unlike Freud, Rogers suggested that development occurs continuously, not in stages. He contended that personality development involves learning self-assessment techniques to master the process of self-actualization—which takes a lifetime.

Rogers was particularly aware that children develop basic feelings about themselves early in life, which led him to understand the role of social influences in the development of self-concepts. The self-assessments of children who are told that they are beautiful, intelligent, and clever are radically different from those of children who are told that they are bad, dirty, shameful, and a general nuisance. Rogers did not claim that negative feelings toward children's behavior should not be expressed. He suggested that children must grow up in an atmosphere in which they can experience life fully. This involves their recognizing both the good and bad sides of their behavior.

Self-concepts. People with rigid self-concepts guard themselves against potentially threatening feelings and experiences. Rogers suggested that these people become unhappy when they are unable to fit new types of behavior into their existing self-concepts. They then distort their perceptions of their behavior in order to make the perceptions compatible with their self-concepts. A person whose self-concept includes high moral principles, rigid religious observances, and strict self-control, for example, probably becomes anxious when he feels envy. Such a feeling is inconsistent with his self-concept. To avoid anxiety, he denies or distorts what he is truly experiencing. He may deny that he feels envy, or he may insist that he is entitled to the object he covets.

When a person is faced with a changing world, it may threaten his or her self-concept. The person may then screen out difficult ideas or thoughts, creating a narrow view, a limited conception of the world, and a restriction on personal growth. However, individuals can reduce or eliminate their fear by broadening their frame of reference and by considering alternative behaviors. People with healthy self-concepts can allow new experiences into their lives and can accept or reject them. Such people move in a positive direction. With each new experience, their self-concepts become stronger and more defined, and the goal of self-actualization is brought closer.

Individual Development. Rogers' concept of personality shows an abiding concern for *individual development.* Rogers stressed that each person must evaluate his or her own situation from a personal (internal) frame of reference, not from the external framework of others.

Freud's and Rogers' theories of personality make fundamentally different assumptions about human nature and how personality is expressed. Freud saw a biologically driven human being in conflict; Rogers saw human beings as inher-

Psychoanalytic and humanistic theories

Building Table 21.1

Approach	Major proponent	Core of personality	Structure of personality	Development	Behavior pathology because of
Psycho-analytic	Sigmund Freud	Maximizes gratification while minimizing punishment or guilt; instinctual urges direct behavior	Id, ego, superego	Five stages: oral, anal, phallic, latency, genital	Imbalances between the id, ego, and superego resulting in fixations
Humanistic	Carl Rogers	Actualizes, maintains, and enhances the experiences of life through the process of self-actualization	Self	Process of cumulative self-actualization	Wide discrepancy between concept of self and of ideal self
Trait					

ently good and trying to be everything they can be. Where Freud was strongly deterministic, humanists are strongly oriented toward free will. Humanists believe that people can rise above their biologically inherited traits and can use decision-making processes to guide behavior. (See Building Table 21.1 for a summary of psychoanalytic and humanistic approaches.) The treatment procedures that developed from the theories of Freud and Rogers—psychoanalysis and client-centered therapy (discussed in Chapter 14)—are fundamentally different. Module 22 describes approaches to personality that focus on traits and on the specific behavioral responses that individuals make throughout their lives.

Progress Check 21.2

Complete the following sentences with one of the options provided.

(L.O. 21.7) a. According to Jung, the unconscious ________ and redirects a person when psychological energies are out of balance. (recalls the painful past / anticipates the future)

(L.O. 21.7) b. Carl Jung said that the collective unconscious contained ________. (memories from birth through death / primitive images inherited from our ancestors)

(L.O. 21.8) c. Adler's theory is based on the idea that people strive for physical, mental, and psychological ________. (balance / superiority, completion, and perfection)

(L.O. 21.8) d. Adler focused on the self as a member of society because he believed that human beings are ________ social. (forced to be / conditioned to be / inherently)

(L.O. 21.8) e. According to Adler, birth order and social interactions within one's family of origin strongly influence ________. (intellectual development / the life-style a person chooses)

(L.O. 21.9) f. Humanistic psychology focuses on how people ________. (acquire healthy self-esteem / develop unhealthy maladjustments)

(L.O. 21.9) g. The word *phenomenological* refers to the way people ________ in the lives. (perceive and interpret immediate events / make use of psychic phenomena, such as ESP)

(L.O. 21.9) h. According to Maslow, the higher the location of a need on the pyramidal hierarchy of needs, the more ________ the need. (mechanistic and drive-based / distinctly human)

(L.O. 21.10) i. Carl Rogers believed that ________ is the motivating force for personal growth and personality development. (freedom from psychological pain / fulfillment)

(L.O. 21.10) j. Rogers refers to the self that a person would like to be as the ________ self. (total / ideal / real)

Module Summary

Psychoanalytic Theory

- Freud's structure of personality includes the id, the ego, and the superego. The id, which works on the pleasure principle, is the source of human instinctual energy. The ego tries to satisfy the id in accordance with reality. The superego acts as the moral aspect of mental functioning (p. 399).
- Freud described the development of personality in terms of five consecutive stages: oral, anal, phallic, latency, and genital. Fixation at any single stage results in major conflict and anxiety (p. 400).
- Defense mechanisms, such as projection, rationalization, denial, sublimation, and reaction formation, are ways in which people reduce anxiety by distorting reality. For Freud, the most important defense mechanism is repression (p. 402).

Psychoanalytic Theory: Neo-Freudians—Dissent and Revision

- According to neo-Freudians, there were serious omissions and errors and obvious biases in Freudian theory. They felt that Freud stressed sex too much and left out many key issues dealing with the meaning of life (p. 406).
- Carl Jung emphasized unconscious processes as determiners of behavior and believed that each person houses past events in the unconscious. In Alfred Adler's theory, people's core tendency is to strive for superiority or perfection. This tendency is often prompted by feelings of inferiority. According to Adler, individuals develop a lifestyle that allows them to display their life goals (pp. 406–407).

Humanistic Approaches

- The humanistic approach of Carl Rogers states that an inborn tendency directs people toward fulfilling their inherited potentials. Personality development is the process of fulfilling those abilities (p. 410).
- For Rogers, personality is structured around the idea of self. An ideal self is the individual a person would like to be. According to Rogers's theory, the core tendency of individuals is to actualize, maintain, and enhance the experiencing organism through the process of self-actualization (p. 412).

KEY TERMS

anal stage, p. 400
archetypes, p. 407
collective unconscious, p. 407
conscious, p. 399
defense mechanism, p. 402
denial, p. 403
ego, p. 399
fixation, p. 402
fulfillment, p. 410
genital stage, p. 401
id, p. 399
ideal self, p. 411
latency stage, p. 401
libido, p. 398
neo-Freudian, p. 406
Oedipus complex, p. 401
oral stage, p. 400
personality, p. 397
phallic stage, p. 401
preconscious, p. 399
projection, p. 403
psychic determinism, p. 398
rationalization, p. 403
reaction formation, p. 403
repression, p. 403
self, p. 411
self-actualization, p. 409
sublimation, p. 403
superego, p. 399
unconscious, p. 399
unconscious motivation, p. 398

SELF-TEST

Module 21

- Before taking the self-test, **recite** and **review.**
- Use the key at the back of the text to *correct* your answers.
- *Restudy* pages that correspond to any questions you answered incorrectly.

1. Personality is a complex phenomenon to study because
   a. it is inconsistent and always changing.
   b. psychologists can study so many different aspects of it.
   c. psychologists cannot agree on a definition of "personality."
   d. there are no behavioral responses to measure because personality comprises solely internal predispositions.
2. Which of the following best describes Freud's view of the causes of human behavior?
   a. peoples' thoughts, feelings, and actions interact on a daily basis.
   b. culture and interpersonal relationships shape our behavior.
   c. behavior is determined by past events that we no longer remember.
   d. behavior is the result of individual decision making and the choices made.
3. According to Freud, the function of a well-developed ego is to
   a. provide a person with instinctual energy.
   b. direct the id toward appropriate and realistic behaviors.
   c. internalize parental authority and produce guilt when the id transgresses moral behavior.
   d. satisfy instinctual needs through the pleasure principle.
4. According to Freud's theory of personality development, adults who have trouble with nurturing others and with receiving warmth and love from others probably had difficulty during the ________ stage.
   a. oral
   b. anal
   c. phallic
   d. genital
5. Children who are frustrated by restrictive and overbearing parents or who are spoiled because of indifferent, smothering, or overindulgent parents are likely to
   a. have dehydrated libidos.
   b. develop a strong and resilient ego.
   c. skip the phallic stage of development.
   d. develop fixations or partial fixations.
6. Deep inside, Clayton does not trust himself because when he feels insecure, he goes back on his word and breaks commitments. To reduce anxiety caused by his lack of self-trust, Clayton often attacks others with comments such as, "I don't trust you." Clayton is using a defense mechanism known as
   a. projection.
   b. sublimation.
   c. reaction formation.
   d. rationalization.
7. Freud's theories have been criticized by some for
   a. placing too much emphasis on biological determinants.
   b. being sexist and degrading toward women.
   c. lacking precision for making specific predictions about behavior.
   d. all of the above

8. According to Jung, an archetype is
   a. a person with a very predictable personality.
   b. a person with a remarkably advanced and mature personality.
   c. an image that is emotionally charged, symbolic, and very meaningful.
   d. anything that can be represented by something else.
9. *Fictional finalism* is a phrase Adler used to describe
   a. specific goals that motivated behavior but probably could never be attained.
   b. the process by which people failed to fulfill their true potentials.
   c. the dynamics and pervasive influence of a family atmosphere.
   d. the relationship between the individual and society.
10. Which of the following describes the humanistic approach to personality development?
    a. People must defend themselves against biologically based evil thoughts.
    b. People actively determine their own destinies.
    c. What is important is to understand and accept the humanistic therapist's conception of self.
    d. Once people have had years of humanistic therapy, they become basically decent and worthwhile.
11. Carl Rogers believed that children develop healthy self-concepts if they are
    a. protected from negative feelings concerning their behavior.
    b. able to recognize both the good and bad sides of their behavior.
    c. told what to think and how to behave.
    d. provided with strong role models.
12. According to Rogers, unhappy people are people who
    a. express a *unidirectional* pattern of personality development.
    b. live their lives according to an internal frame of reference.
    c. have rigid self-concepts that cannot accommodate unfamiliar feelings and experiences.
    d. rely on free will and individual choice as a way of experiencing life.

Module 22

Trait and Behavioral Theories

LEARNING OBJECTIVES

When you have mastered the material in this module, you will be able to

Trait and Type Theories (pp. 419–422)

22.1 Distinguish between personality *traits* and personality *types* (p. 419).

22.2 Describe Allport's three categories of personality traits, Cattell's technique for understanding traits, and Eysenck's personality type theory (p. 419).

22.3 Explain why trait and type theories are useful and list five reasons why they are criticized (p. 421).

Behavioral Approaches (pp. 422–426)

22.4 Describe the behavioral approach to personality development and tell how it differs from other personality theories (p. 422).

22.5 Explain how classical conditioning, operant conditioning, and observational learning contribute to the development of personality (p. 424).

Cognitive Approaches (pp. 426–431)

22.6 Explain how the cognitive approach to personality development adds a new dimension to our understanding of it (p. 426).

22.7 Identify the advantage of microtheories and discuss the features of Rotter's locus-of-control theory (p. 426).

22.8 Explain both the importance of having a strong sense of self-efficacy and how this aspect of personality develops (p. 427).

22.9 Explain why Mischel is considered an interactionist and describe how people make adjustments in behavior to suit a current situation (p. 429).

SQ3R
- ▲ **Survey** to set goals for studying.
- ▲ Ask **questions** as you **read.**
- ▲ Stop occasionally to **recite** and **review.**

plus
- ▲ **Write** a summary of key points.
- ▲ **Reflect** on the hypotheses, evidence, and implications of this material and on the relevance it has to *your* life.

Both ancient philosophers and medieval physicians believed that the proportion of bodily fluids (called humors) determined a person's temperament and personality. Cheerful, healthy people, for example, were said to have a *sanguine* (hopeful and self-confident) personality because blood was their primary humor, while those who had a preponderance of yellow bile were considered hot-tempered. Like their medieval counterparts, some early psychologists based their personality theories on the behaviors people openly exhibit, such as shyness, impulsiveness, and aggressiveness. Research shows that many of these easily observed characteristics predict other behaviors—for example, extremely shy people are more like to be anxious, lonely, and have low self-esteem (DePaulo, Dull, Greenberg, & Swaim, 1989). Theories based on these observations—personality trait and type theories—make intuitive sense and thus have been very popular.

trait: Any readily identifiable stable behavior that characterizes the way in which an individual differs from other individuals.

types: Broad collections of personality traits tied together loosely and interrelated.

Trait and Type Theories

Trait theorists study specific behaviors, or traits. A **trait** is any readily identifiable behavior that characterizes the way an individual differs from other people. Someone might characterize John F. Kennedy as having been energetic and forward looking and Margaret Thatcher as having been tough and practical. Such characterizations present specific ideas about these people's behaviors—that is, their traits. Traits can be evaluated on a continuum, so a person can be extremely shy, very shy, shy, or just occasionally shy. Traits become especially important because for some personality theorists, such as Buss (1989), they are the stuff that personality is made of.

Learning Objective 22.1 Distinguish between personality *traits* and personality *types.*

Type theorists group together traits common to specific personalities. **Types,** therefore, are broad collections of traits tied together and interrelated. Although the distinction between traits and types sometimes blurs, according to Gordon Allport (1937), "A man can be said to *have* a trait; but he cannot be said to *have* a type. Rather he *fits* a type" (p. 295). This section examines the theories of two well-known trait psychologists, Gordon Allport and Raymond Cattell, and then examines the broader personality type theory of Hans Eysenck.

Learning Objective 22.2 Describe Allport's three categories of personality traits, Cattell's technique for understanding traits, and Eysenck's personality type theory.

Allport's Trait Theory

The distinguished psychologist Gordon Allport (1897–1967) was a leading trait theorist who suggested that each individual has a unique set of personality traits.

Psychologist Gordon Allport was especially well-known as a trait theorist.

According to Allport (1937), if a person's traits are known, it is possible to predict how he or she will respond to various environmental stimuli. Allport quickly discovered that there are thousands of ways—or traits—to characterize people's behavior, but some seemed more dominant than others.

Allport eventually decided that people's behavior could be categorized into three kinds of traits: cardinal, central, or secondary. *Cardinal traits* are ideas and behaviors that determine the direction of a person's life. A clergyman's cardinal trait may be devotion to God; a philosopher's, the need to investigate and explain knowledge; a civil rights leader's, the desire to rectify social and political injustices. Allport noted that many people have no such overall guiding behavior or idea.

The more common *central traits* are reasonably easy to identify behaviors that characterize a person's daily interactions. They are the basic units of personality. Allport believed that central traits, including such characteristics as control, apprehension, tension, self-assuredness, forthrightness, and practicality, adequately describe many personalities. For example, boxing legend Muhammad Ali could be characterized as forthright and self-assured; Woody Allen's typical film persona could be described as tense and apprehensive.

Secondary traits are specific behaviors that occur in response to specific situations. For example, a person may have a secondary trait of prejudice toward minorities, a keen interest in psychology lectures, or a love of spectator sports. Being less characteristic of an individual's behavior than central traits, secondary traits are more easily modified and are not necessarily shown on a daily basis.

Everyone has different combinations of traits, which is why Allport claimed that each person is unique. To identify a person's traits, Allport recommended an in-depth study of that individual. If Allport's theory is true, knowing a person's traits would allow a psychologist to predict how that person would respond to the environment—that is, what his or her behavior would be.

Cattell's Factor Theory

Psychologists such as Allport and Raymond B. Cattell (1905–) argue that it is possible to tell a great deal about a person just by knowing a few of his or her traits. Cattell (1965) used the technique of *factor analysis,* a statistical procedure in which groups of variables (factors) are analyzed to detect which are related, to show that groups of traits tend to cluster together. Thus, people who describe themselves as warm and accepting also tend to rate themselves as high on nurturance and tenderness but low on aggression, suspiciousness, and apprehensiveness. Researchers also see patterns within professions; for example, artists may see themselves as creative, sensitive, and open, while accountants may describe themselves as careful, serious, conservative, and thorough-minded. Cattell termed the obvious, day-to-day cluster of traits *surface traits,* and the more encompassing cluster of traits *source traits.*

Hans Eysenck developed a *type* theory of personality.

Eysenck's Type Theory

Whereas Allport and Cattell focused on the trait level, Hans Eysenck (1916–) focused on higher levels of trait organization, or what he called *types.* Eysenck (1970) argued that all personality traits can be reduced to three basic dimensions: emotional stability or instability, introversion or extroversion, and psychoticism.

Emotional stability refers to the extent to which people have control over their feelings. People can be spontaneous, genuine, and warm, or they can be controlled, calm, flat, unresponsive, and stilted. *Introversion* or *extroversion* refers to the extent to which people are socially withdrawn or open. Introverts are socially withdrawn and shy; extroverts are socially outgoing and open and like to meet new people. Eysenck's third dimension, *psychoticism*, is sometimes called tough- or tender-mindedness. At one extreme, people are troublesome, antiauthority, sensation seeking, insensitive, and risk takers; at the other end, they are warm, gregarious, and tender (see also Howarth, 1986). Each type incorporates elements at a lower level (traits), and each trait incorporates lower-order qualities (habits).

Eysenck argues that personality has a biological basis but emphasizes that learning and experience also shape an individual's behavior. For example, he says that introverts and extroverts possess different levels of arousal in the cortex of the brain. Accordingly, persons of each type seek the amount of stimulation necessary to achieve their preferred level of arousal. For example, a person with a low level of arousal, where stimulation is less intense, may become a security guard or a librarian; a person with a high level of arousal, which is reflected in his or her outward behavior, may become a race-car driver or a politician.

Criticisms of Trait and Type Theories

Learning Objective 22.3
Explain why trait and type theories are useful, and list five reasons why they are criticized.

Trait and type theories are appealing because they characterize people in important dimensions and, therefore, provide simple explanations for how individuals behave. However, psychologists have criticized these theories on five basic fronts. First, is trait theory actually a personality theory? Does it make predictions about a behavior and explain why that behavior occurs? Some psychologists claim that trait theory is merely a list of behaviors arranged into a hierarchy. Second, most trait theories do not tell which personality characteristics last a lifetime and which are transient.

Third, if an individual's behavior depends on the situation or context, how can traits predict the individual's acts or behaviors (Epstein & O'Brien, 1985)? Some contend that the failure of trait theory to account for situational differences is a crucial weakness. Fourth, trait theory does not account for changing cultural differences; if you test the same persons at intervals 10 years apart, their traits are likely to be different, but society is also different—values change, and people adopt new ideas. Trait and type theories do not account for these changing cultural norms. Finally, trait and type theories do not explain why people develop traits or why traits change.

Although trait and type theories continue to evolve, psychologists want a theory that explains (a) the development of personality, (b) the ways in which personality theory can predict maladjustment, and especially (c) the reasons that a person's behavior can be dramatically different in different situations. Theories that attempt to describe, explain, and predict behavior with precision tend to be behavioral ones, the next major group of theories discussed.

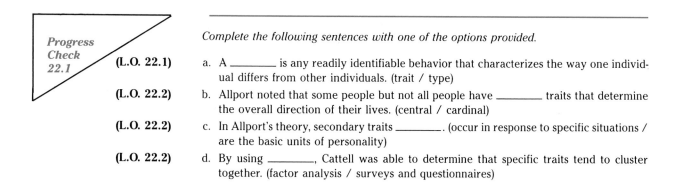

Progress Check 22.1

Complete the following sentences with one of the options provided.

(L.O. 22.1) a. A ________ is any readily identifiable behavior that characterizes the way one individual differs from other individuals. (trait / type)

(L.O. 22.2) b. Allport noted that some people but not all people have ________ traits that determine the overall direction of their lives. (central / cardinal)

(L.O. 22.2) c. In Allport's theory, secondary traits ________. (occur in response to specific situations / are the basic units of personality)

(L.O. 22.2) d. By using ________, Cattell was able to determine that specific traits tend to cluster together. (factor analysis / surveys and questionnaires)

(L.O. 22.2) e. Eysenck's ______ dimension of personality measures whether a person isolates from others by being "tough" or connects with others by being "tender-minded." (introversion–extroversion / psychoticism)

(L.O. 22.2) f. According to Eysenck, ______ have an important role in determining variations in personality. (biological levels of arousal / cultural values)

(L.O. 22.3) g. One criticism of trait and type theories is that they ______ behavior. (do not predict / provide overly simple explanations of)

Behavioral Approaches

Learning Objective 22.4
Describe the behavioral approach to personality development, and tell how it differs from other personality theories.

The concepts on which some personality theorists focus—inner drives, psychic urges, need for self-actualization—are hard to define, referring to some inner personal characteristic. Building Table 22.1 presents a summary of the theories discussed so far. However, another group of personality theorists—the behaviorists—assert that inner forces, hard-to-define constructs, and psychic urges are not the proper subject matter of personality study. Behavioral theorists are practical. They believe that people often need to change aspects of their lives quickly and efficiently and that many do not have the time, money, or energy for a lengthy therapy or personality analysis.

Key Behavioral Concepts

Behavioral personality theorists assert that personality develops as people learn from their environments. The key word is *learn*. According to behaviorists, personality characteristics are not long-lasting or enduring, but are modifiable and subject to change. Thus, personality is the sum of a person's learned tendencies. Behaviorists look at personality very differently from any other theorists described so far. They generally do not look inward; they look only at overt behavior. Behavioral approaches are often viewed as a reaction to the vagaries of traditional personality theories.

Precisely Defined Elements. Behavioral theories tend to center on precisely defined elements, such as the relationship between stimuli and responses, the strength of stimuli, and the strength, duration, and timing of a reinforcer. All these can be tested in a laboratory or clinical setting. By focusing on stimuli and responses, behaviorists avoid conceptualizing human nature and concentrate instead on predicting behavior in specific circumstances. As a result, their assertions are more easily tested. Behaviorists see the development of personality simply as a change in response characteristics—a person learns new behaviors in response to new environments and stimuli.

Responses to Stimuli. For most behaviorists, the structural unit of personality is the response to stimuli. Any behavior, regardless of the situation, is seen as a response to stimuli or a response awaiting reinforcement (or punishment). When an identifiable stimulus leads to an identifiable response, researchers predict that every time that stimulus occurs, so will the response. This stimulus–response relationship helps explain the constancy of personality. If, for example, every time a teenager complains about his financial predicament, his father talks about sports, the teenager may stomp out of the room and slam the bedroom door as he hears his father pronounce, "Teenagers are so moody these days." If this scene is re-

Building Table 22.1

Psychoanalytic, humanistic, and trait theories

Approach	Major proponent	Core of personality	Structure of personality	Development	Behavior pathology because of
Psycho-analytic	Sigmund Freud	Maximizes gratification while minimizing punishment or guilt; instinctual urges direct behavior	Id, ego, superego	Five stages: oral, anal, phallic, latency, genital	Imbalances between the id, ego, and superego resulting in fixations
Humanistic	Carl Rogers	Actualizes, maintains, and enhances the experiences of life through the process of self-actualization	Self	Process of cumulative self-actualization	Wide discrepancy between concept of self and of ideal self
Trait	Gordon Allport	A series of interrelated hierarchically arranged traits that characterize the day-to-day behaviors of the individual	Traits	Process of learning new traits	Having learned faulty or inappropriate traits
Behavioral					

peated often, it becomes predictable—the stimulus of avoidance (sports talk) leads to the response of withdrawal.

Behavior Patterns. Using a behavioral analysis, psychologists can discover how people develop behavior patterns (such as eating their vegetables or being hostile) and why behavior is in constant flux. The behavioral approach suggests that learning is the process that shapes personality and that learning takes place through experience. Because new experiences happen all the time, a person is constantly learning about the world and changing response patterns accordingly. Just as there are several learning principles involving the use of stimuli, responses, and reinforcement (for a review, see Chapter 5), there are several behavioral personality theories, based on classical conditioning, operant conditioning, or observational learning.

Classical Conditioning

Learning Objective 22.5
Explain how classical conditioning, operant conditioning, and observational learning contribute to the development of personality.

Most people are fearful or anxious at some time. Some are fearful more often than not. How do people become fearful? What causes constant anxiety and apprehension? Many behavioral psychologists maintain that people develop anxiety and fear through classical conditioning, in which a neutral stimulus is paired with another stimulus that elicits some response. Eventually, the neutral stimulus can elicit the response on its own. For example, many people fear rats. Because rats are often encountered in dark cellars, people may learn to fear dark cellars—dark cellars become a feared stimulus. Later, the person may develop a generalized fear of dark places. If the first time a person sees a train, it's in a darkened station that looks like a cellar, the person may learn to fear trains. Classical conditioning thus allows a researcher to explain the predictability of a person's responses when presented with a specific stimulus; it describes the relationship between one stimulus and a human being's expectation of another, and the response that the person makes (Rescorla, 1988).

Operant Conditioning

In operant conditioning, spontaneous behavior is followed with a consequence, such as reinforcement or punishment. According to behaviorists, personality can be explained as spontaneous behavior that is reinforced. When a person is affectionate and that behavior is reinforced, the person is likely to continue to be affectionate.

Behavioral psychologists often use the operant learning principles of reward and punishment to help children control themselves and to shape their personalities. Consider the problem of discipline in school, specifically of a 10-year-old child in the Florida public school system who frequently used obscenities. In an hour's time, the child would utter as many as 150 obscene words and phrases. Each time the child uttered an obscene word, Lahey, McNees, and McNees (1973) took him out of the classroom for a minimum of 5 minutes and placed him in a well-lit, empty room. The child was told he would be placed in the time-out room every time he made an obscene statement. In a few days, the number of obscenities decreased dramatically, from two a minute to fewer than five an hour. Using a behavioral technique, the researcher modified an element of personality.

The time-out procedure is often used in learning situations in both classrooms and laboratories. As with any reinforcement or punishment procedure, the subject learns that the procedure is contingent on behavior. In the example, time-out was punishing. The child found it rewarding to be in the classroom and punishing to be in the time-out room. Thus, to remain in the classroom and avoid being put in the time-out room, he learned not to utter obscenities.

Violence on television may actually teach children that violence is acceptable and sometimes even admirable behavior.

Observational Learning

Observational learning theories assume that people learn new behaviors simply by watching others. The theory contends that an observer will imitate the specific behaviors of a model and thus develop a set of personality characteristics. Personality is thus seen as developing through the process of observation and imitation.

The theory stresses the importance of the relationship between the observer and the model in eliciting imitative behavior. When children view the behavior of a parent or other important figure, their imitative behavior will be significantly more extensive than when they observe the actions of someone less important to them. A son is more likely to adopt his father's hurried behavior than his neighbor's relaxed attitude.

People can learn abnormal, as well as acceptable, behavior and personality characteristics through imitation. In fact, the most notable behavior that people observe and then imitate may be violence on television. As is shown in Chapter 15, ample evidence shows that children who observed aggressive violent television programs were more willing to hurt others after watching the program. If children observe people who are reinforced for violent, aggressive behavior, they are more likely to imitate that behavior rather than more socially desirable behaviors.

Observational learning theories assume that learning a new response can occur independent of reinforcement. However, although personality develops as a function of imitating the behavior of other people, later reinforcement acts to maintain such learned behaviors. Most people, for example have observed aggressive, hostile behavior in others but still choose different ways to express emotions. Together, the imitative aspects of observational learning theory and the reinforcement properties of conditioned learning can account for most behaviors. For example, a daughter may become logical and forthright by watching her lawyer mother prepare arguments for a court case and seeing her win.

Researchers who focus on observational learning recognize that people choose to show some behaviors some of the time and to omit other behaviors. Accordingly, some researchers focus on observational learning in combination with another element—thought. These ideas constitute cognitive theory, a natural reaction to behavioral theory. The cognitive emphasis is on the interaction of a person's thoughts and behavior.

Cognitive Approaches

Learning Objective 22.6
Explain how the cognitive approach to personality development adds a new dimension to our understanding of it.

In some important ways, cognitive approaches to personality appeared as a reaction to strict behavioral models, adding a new dimension. The cognitive emphasis is on the interaction of a person's thoughts and behavior. It considers the uniqueness of human beings, especially their thought processes, and it assumes that human beings are decision makers, planners, and evaluators of behavior (strict behavioral approaches did not consider thought processes). Cognitive views have been influenced by the humanistic idea that people are essentially good and strive to be better. Many researchers now claim that people can change their behavior, their conceptions of themselves, and their personalities in a short time if they are willing to change their thoughts.

Key Cognitive Concepts

From a cognitive point of view, the mere association of stimuli and responses is not enough for conditioning and learning to occur in human beings—thought processes have to be involved. According to cognitive theory, people exhibit learned behavior based on their situation and personal needs at a particular time. If thought and behavior are closely intertwined, then when something affects a person's thoughts, it should also affect behavior. The man who mentally yells "STOP!" whenever his thoughts become hostile should realize some success in quelling his violent behaviors.

Rotter's Locus of Control

Learning Objective 22.7
Identify the advantage of microtheories, and discuss the important features of Rotter's locus-of-control theory.

Many classic theories that attempt to explain all aspects of personality and behavior have been criticized because they are difficult to study scientifically. The ego in Freud's theory, for example, is not a physiological structure or state that can be manipulated, studied, or examined. Similarly, the concepts of self and of maximizing potential in Rogers' theory are difficult to measure and assess. As a reaction to imprecise grand theories, psychologists have developed smaller, more well-researched theories. These *microtheories,* some of which follow a cognitive approach, account for specific behaviors in specific situations. Because of their smaller scope, they are easier to test.

One such widely studied cognitive-behavioral theory is locus of control, developed by Julian Rotter (1916–). *Locus of control* involves the extent to which individuals believe that they or that external factors control their lives. Rotter focused on whether people place their locus of control inside themselves (internal) or in their environments (external). Locus of control influences how people view the world and how they identify the causes of success or failure in their lives. In an important way, people's locus of control reflects their personality—their view of the world and their reactions to it. To examine locus of control, Rotter developed a test consisting of a series of statements about oneself and other people. Answering the following questions will help you determine your locus of control:

With enough effort, we can wipe out political corruption.	*versus*	It is difficult to have much control over the things politicians do in office.
There is a direct connection between how hard I study and the grade I get.	*versus*	Sometimes I can't understand how teachers arrive at the grades they give.
What happens to me is my own doing.	*versus*	Sometimes I feel that I don't have enough control over the direction my life is taking.
People's misfortunes result from the mistakes they make.	*versus*	Many of the unhappy things in people's lives are partly due to bad luck.

Julian Rotter

These statements reflect either an internal (the statements on the left) or an external (the statements on the right) locus of control. People classified as internal (by their choice of statements) feel that they need to control their environment. People with an external locus of control believe that they have little control over their lives. A college student may attribute his or her poor grade to a lousy teacher, feeling there was nothing he or she could have done to get an A. In contrast, individuals who develop an internal locus of control feel that they can master any course they take because they believe that through hard work, they can do well in any subject. People develop expectations based on their beliefs about the sources of reinforcement in their environments. These expectations lead to specific behaviors, described as personality. Reinforcement of these behaviors in turn strengthens expectancy and leads to increased belief in internal or external control.

Locus of control elegantly integrates personality theory, expectancy theory, reinforcement theory, and cognitive theory (see Figure 22.1 on page 429). Locus of control describes several specific behaviors, but it is not comprehensive enough to explain all or even most of an individual's behavior. Bandura's theory, discussed next, specifically addresses people's convictions (thoughts) about their own effectiveness, and the Applying Psychology box on the next page shows how some behaviors may have a biological origin.

Albert Bandura

Bandura's Self-efficacy

Learning Objective 22.8 Explain both the importance of having a strong sense of self-efficacy and how this aspect of personality develops.

One of the most influential cognitive theories of personality was developed by Albert Bandura (1925–), a former president of the American Psychological Association. His conception of personality began with observational learning theory and the idea that human beings observe, think about, and imitate behavior (Bandura, 1977a). Bandura played a major role in reintroducing thought processes into learning and personality theory.

In 1977, Bandura argued that people's expectations of mastery and achievement and their convictions about their own effectiveness determine the types of behavior they will engage in and the amount of risk they will undertake (Bandura, 1977a, 1977b). He called this *self-efficacy.* **Self-efficacy** is a person's belief about whether he or she can successfully engage in and execute a specific behavior. Judgments about self-efficacy determine how much effort people will expend and how long they will persist in the face of obstacles (Bandura, 1982a, 1982b). A strong sense of self-efficacy allows people to feel free to select, influence, and even construct the circumstances of their own lives. Also, if a person feels she

self-efficacy: A person's belief about whether he or she can successfully engage in and execute a specific behavior.

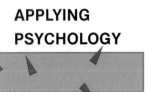

APPLYING PSYCHOLOGY

Overcoming Shyness

About 40% of adults report being shy, and for at least 2 million adults, **shyness** is a serious behavior problem that inhibits personal, social, and professional growth. Shy people show extreme anxiety in social situations; they are extremely reticent and often overly concerned with how they look and sound and how others view them. They fear looking, sounding, or acting foolish; as a consequence, they may develop clammy hands, dry mouth, excessive perspiration, trembling, nausea, blushing, and a need to go to the bathroom frequently. Shyness keeps people away from social situations and makes them speak softly, when they speak at all. Shy people not only hold back from approaching other people, but avoid them (Asendorpf, 1989). Most shy people report that they have always been shy, and half of all shy people feel that they are more shy than other people in similar situations (Carducci & Stein, 1988).

Personality researchers contend that certain personality traits, including shyness, are long-lasting. Jerome Kagan found that 2- and 3-year-olds who were extremely cautious and shy tended to remain that way for years (Kagan, 1989). Daniels and Plomin (1985) also found an important relationship between biological mothers' shyness and adopted infants' shyness at 2 years of age. These findings suggest that genetic factors play an important role in shyness.

Although Kagan suggests that extreme shyness may have a biological basis, we also know that shyness emerges because people develop distorted self-concepts and negative views about their competencies and their self-efficacy. Such individuals view themselves in a poor light and see themselves as having few if any social graces. These thoughts combined with actions such as withdrawal and nervousness set a person up for social failure. When such events occur, the person then says "See, I was right." A person's thoughts about his or her shyness, body reactions, and social behaviors thus help maintain the shyness.

People who are shy believe that they can overcome it with some help, and treatment programs exist (Carducci & Stein, 1988). If you are shy, there are some things you can do to help overcome your shyness.

- Rehearse what you want to say before speaking.
- Build your self-esteem by focusing on your good points.
- Accept who you are, and think about your distinctive, positive traits.
- Practice smiling and making eye contact.
- Use social learning theory concepts—observe the behavior of others whom you admire, and copy their behavior.
- Think about how others feel; remember that about 40% of all people feel the way you do.
- Engage in relaxation training, which might include self-hypnosis, yoga, or even biofeedback.
- Read self-help books on putting your best foot forward.
- Think positively; a positive attitude about yourself and other people can go a long way toward helping to overcome shyness.

- ***What is the evidence that leads researchers to believe that shyness may be biologically based?***
- ***What are the implications of the finding that behaviors that are found in a person during infancy are also found in that person in later childhood or adolescence?***
- ***This module has focused on approaches to personality suggesting that personality is learned; if this is the case, what are the implications for a shy person, in terms of overcoming shyness?***

shyness: Extreme anxiety in individuals who are socially reticent and often overly concerned with how they look and sound to others; this anxiety leads to avoidance of social situations.

can control a situation, this increases her perceived self-efficacy to manage it (Bandura & Wood, 1989). Thus, when she has a high level of self-efficacy, she is more likely to attribute success to variables within herself rather than to chance factors and is more likely to pursue a task (Bandura, 1988; McAuley, Duncan, & McElroy, 1989). Because people can think about their motivation, and even their own thoughts, they can affect changes in themselves and persevere during tough times (Bandura, 1989).

Bandura's theory is optimistic. It is a long way from Freud's deterministic theory, which argues that conflicting biologically based forces determine human

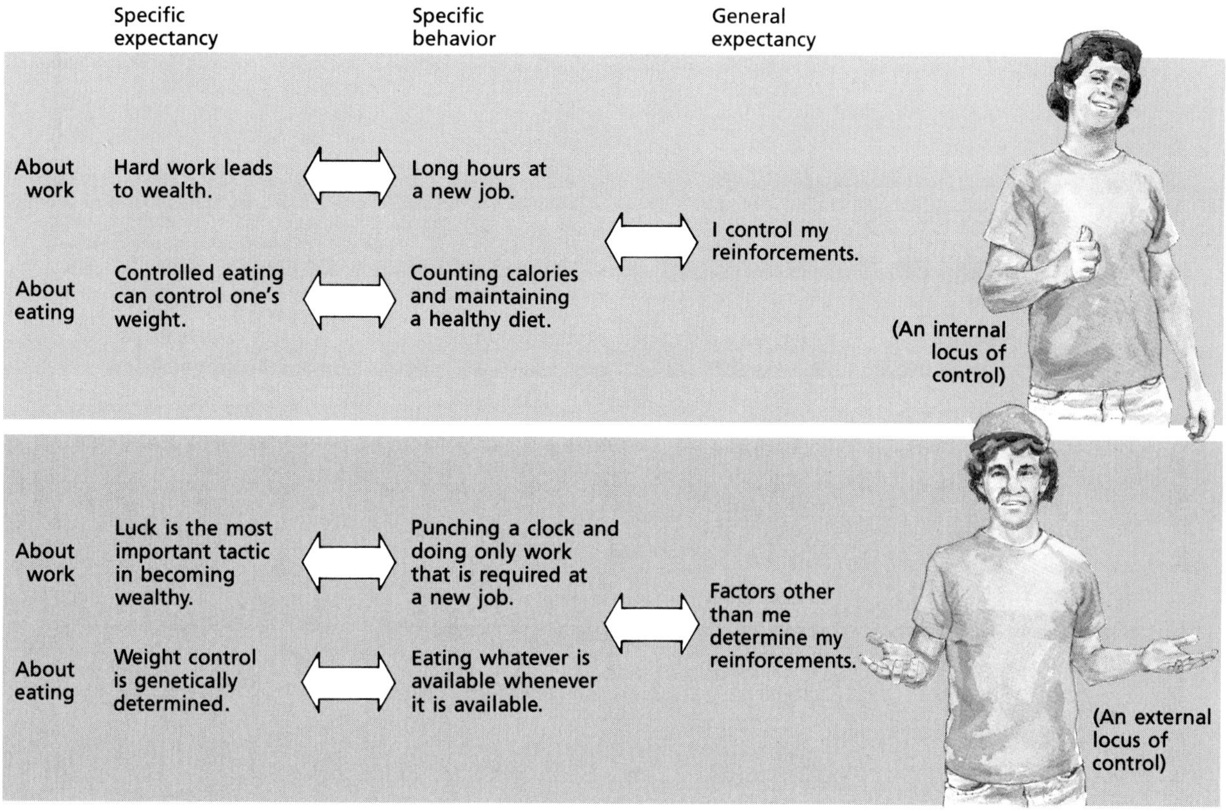
Specific expectancy
Specific behavior
General expectancy
About work
Hard work leads to wealth.
Long hours at a new job.
I control my reinforcements.
About eating
Controlled eating can control one's weight.
Counting calories and maintaining a healthy diet.
(An internal locus of control)
About work
Luck is the most important tactic in becoming wealthy.
Punching a clock and doing only work that is required at a new job.
Factors other than me determine my reinforcements.
About eating
Weight control is genetically determined.
Eating whatever is available whenever it is available.
(An external locus of control)

Figure 22.1

A person's general expectations about life are determined in a three-stage process: specific expectancies lead to behaviors, which are reinforced. This cycle eventually leads to a general expectancy about life and to an internal or external locus of control.

behavior. It is also a long way from a strict behavioral theory, which suggests that environmental contingencies shape behavior. Bandura believes that human beings have choices, that they direct the course of their lives. He also believes that society, parents, experiences, and even luck help shape those lives.

Bad luck or nonreinforcing experiences can damage a developing sense of self-efficacy. Observation of positive, prosocial models during the formative years, on the other hand, can help people to develop a strong sense of self-efficacy that will encourage and reinforce them to direct their own lives. Bandura's theory allows individual flexibility in behavior. People are not locked into specific responses to specific stimuli, as some strict behaviorists might assert. According to Bandura, people choose the behaviors they will imitate, and they are free to adapt their behavior to any situation. Because self-efficacy both determines and flows from feelings of self-worth, a person's sense of self-efficacy may not match the person's efficacy as perceived by others. For example, a person whom others view as successful may not share that view, and a person who has achieved little of note to society may consider himself a capable and worthy person. Unfortunately, this means that people often develop disproportionately negative thoughts about themselves and develop poor senses of self-efficacy. Also, a sense of poor self-esteem might not be shown in all circumstances; Mischel highlights this idea in the next section.

Learning Objective 22.9
Explain why Mischel is considered an interactionist, and describe how people make adjustments in behavior to suit a current situation.

Mischel's Cognitive Social Learning

Like Bandura, Walter Mischel (1930–) claims that thought is crucial in determining human behavior, but he also believes that both past experiences and current rein-

Psychoanalytic, humanistic, trait, behavioral, and cognitive theories

Building Table 22.2

Approach	Major proponent	Core of personality	Structure of personality	Development	Behavior pathology because of
Psychoanalytic	Sigmund Freud	Maximizes gratification while minimizing punishment or guilt; instinctual urges direct behavior	Id, ego, superego	Five stages: oral, anal, phallic, latency, genital	Imbalances between the id, ego, and superego resulting in fixations
Humanistic	Carl Rogers	Actualizes, maintains, and enhances the experiences of life through the process of self-actualization	Self	Process of cumulative self-actualization	Wide discrepancy between concept of self and of ideal self
Trait	Gordon Allport	A series of interrelated hierarchically arranged traits that characterize the day-to-day behaviors of the individual	Traits	Process of learning new traits	Having learned faulty or inappropriate traits
Behavioral	B. F. Skinner	Reduction of social and biological needs that energize behavior through the emission of learned responses	Responses	Process of learning new responses	Having learned faulty or inappropriate behaviors
Cognitive	Several, including Rotter, Bandura, and Mischel	Learned responses depend on a changing environment, and person responds after thinking about context of the environment	Changing responses	Process of thinking about new responses	Inappropriate thoughts or faulty reasoning

forcement are important. What's more, Mischel is an *interactionist*—he focuses on the interaction of people and their environment (Mischel, 1983). Mischel and other cognitive theorists (e.g., Cantor & Kihlstrom, 1982) argue that people respond flexibly to various situations. They change their responses, based on their past experiences and their current assessment of the situation, to suit the present situation. This process of adjustment is called *self-regulation.* People make subtle adjustments in their tone of voice and overt behavior (their personality), depending on the context in which they find themselves. Those who tend to be warm, caring, and attentive, for example, can become hostile and aggressive, depending on the situation.

People's personalities and particularly their responses to a stimulus are determined by *competencies,* what they know and can do; *encoding strategies,* the way they process, attend to, and select information; *expectancies,* their anticipation of outcomes; *personal values,* the importance they attach to various situations; and *self-regulatory systems,* the systems of rules people have established for themselves to guide their behavior (Mischel, 1979). (Building Table 22.2 on the facing page summarizes the information on personality theories described in this chapter.)

Walter Mischel is a cognitive theorist who believes that the interaction of people and their environment shapes day-to-day behavior.

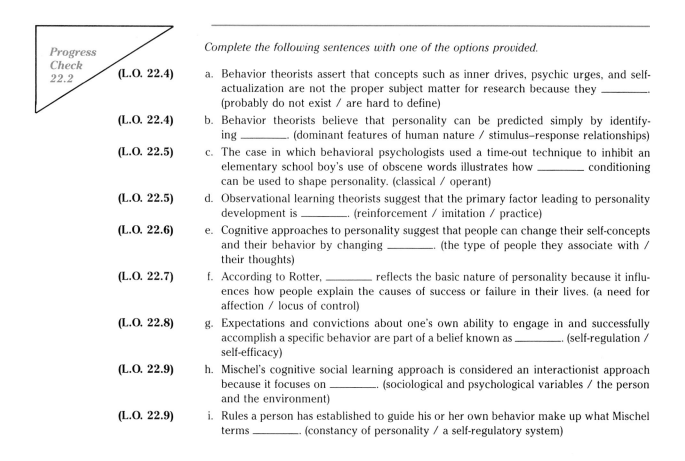

Progress Check 22.2

Complete the following sentences with one of the options provided.

(L.O. 22.4) a. Behavior theorists assert that concepts such as inner drives, psychic urges, and self-actualization are not the proper subject matter for research because they ________. (probably do not exist / are hard to define)

(L.O. 22.4) b. Behavior theorists believe that personality can be predicted simply by identifying ________. (dominant features of human nature / stimulus–response relationships)

(L.O. 22.5) c. The case in which behavioral psychologists used a time-out technique to inhibit an elementary school boy's use of obscene words illustrates how ________ conditioning can be used to shape personality. (classical / operant)

(L.O. 22.5) d. Observational learning theorists suggest that the primary factor leading to personality development is ________. (reinforcement / imitation / practice)

(L.O. 22.6) e. Cognitive approaches to personality suggest that people can change their self-concepts and their behavior by changing ________. (the type of people they associate with / their thoughts)

(L.O. 22.7) f. According to Rotter, ________ reflects the basic nature of personality because it influences how people explain the causes of success or failure in their lives. (a need for affection / locus of control)

(L.O. 22.8) g. Expectations and convictions about one's own ability to engage in and successfully accomplish a specific behavior are part of a belief known as ________. (self-regulation / self-efficacy)

(L.O. 22.9) h. Mischel's cognitive social learning approach is considered an interactionist approach because it focuses on ________. (sociological and psychological variables / the person and the environment)

(L.O. 22.9) i. Rules a person has established to guide his or her own behavior make up what Mischel terms ________. (constancy of personality / a self-regulatory system)

Module Summary

Trait and Type Theories

- *Personality* is a set of relatively enduring behavioral characteristics that describe how a person reacts to the environment. Personality theorists attempt to explain people's internal dispositions and the ways in which their behavior changes in response to environmental demands (p. 397).
- *Traits* are any readily identifiable behaviors that characterize the way an individual differs from other people; *types* are broad collections of traits loosely tied together and interrelated. Trait and type theories are appealing because they characterize people on important dimensions and therefore provide simple explanations for an individual's behavior (p. 419).

Behavioral Approaches

- For behaviorists, the structural unit of personality is the response. All behaviors are seen as responses to stimuli or as responses waiting for reinforcement (p. 422).
- Behavioral theories claim that personality development is a gradual process of growth in which some behaviors are reinforced and others are not. Disturbed behavior is considered the result of faulty learning patterns (p. 424).
- Observational learning theory assumes that people can learn new behaviors by watching others. Unlike classical learning theory, observational learning theory states that (1) learning can occur independent of reinforcement, and (2) thought processes play a significant role in human behavior (p. 425).

Cognitive Approaches

- The cognitive theories of Bandura, Mischel, and Rotter have reintroduced thought into the equation of personality and situational variables. They have especially focused on how people interpret the situations in which they find themselves and how they then alter their behavior (p. 426).

KEY TERMS

self-efficacy, p. 427
shyness, p. 428
trait, p. 419
types, p. 419

SELF-TEST

Module 22

- Before taking the self-test, **recite** and **review.**
- Use the key at the back of the text to *correct* your answers.
- *Restudy* pages that correspond to any questions you answered incorrectly.

1. A "type" is defined by a personality theorist as
   a. any readily identifiable stable behavior.
   b. a specific behavior that occurs in response to a specific event.
   c. behaviors that characterize a person's day-to-day interactions.
   d. a broad collection of traits that are linked and interrelated.
2. The difference between introverts and extroverts is that
   a. introverts are gregarious, whereas extroverts are reserved.
   b. introverts are emotionally stable, whereas extroverts are emotionally unstable.
   c. introverts prefer to be alone, whereas extroverts like to meet new people.
   d. introverts are risk takers, whereas extroverts are sensation seekers.
3. Which of the following is a criticism of trait and type theories?
   a. They do not account for changing cultural norms.
   b. They fail to account for situational differences.
   c. They give no indication about which personality characteristics endure and which are transient.
   d. all of the above
4. For a behavior theorist, personality is
   a. the recognition of the real self.
   b. the sum of a person's learned behaviors.
   c. not enduring, but rather subject to change.
   d. both b and c
5. Behavioral approaches to personality differ from traditional personality theories, in that behavioral approaches
   a. are easier to test through scientific study.
   b. give comprehensive explanations to explain why we behave as we do.
   c. are generally imprecise "grand" theories.
   d. make use of hypothetical constructs and abstract conceptualizations.
6. Classical conditioning allows a behavior theorist to predict the response a person will make in a specific situation by describing
   a. a particular stimulus, the person's expectation that will be associated with it, and the way in which the person will respond.
   b. behaviors that are intrinsically reinforcing.
   c. internal reactions to environmental stimuli.
   d. all of the above
7. Cognitive approaches to personality assume that human beings are
   a. controlled by environmental demands.
   b. decision makers who strive to improve themselves.
   c. inconsistent when it comes to integrating thought and behavior.
   d. "thinkers," not "doers."
8. Which of the following claim that personality and associated behavior can be changed in a relatively short time?
   a. trait and type theories
   b. behavioral and cognitive theories
   c. global and interactive theories
   d. humanistic and neo-Freudian theories

9. People who have an ________ locus of control believe they have little control over their own lives.
   a. introverted
   b. extroverted
   c. internal
   d. external
10. Which of the following would be most likely to be observed in a person with a weak sense of self-efficacy. The person would
    a. feel free to select and construct the circumstances of his or her life.
    b. demonstrate the basic coping skills needed for solving simple day-to-day problems.
    c. attribute success to chance, rather than to her or his own actions.
    d. have a good sense of self-esteem.
11. Which of the following would Mischel probably consider *least* important in predicting how a person would respond to a particular situation?
    a. competency—what a person knows and can do.
    b. luck—being in the right place at the right time.
    c. encoding—how a person processes, attends to, and selects information.
    d. expectancy and values—anticipated outcomes and the importance a person places on the situation.

Connections

If you are interested in . . .	Turn to . . .	To learn more about . . .
Freud's psychoanalytic approach and the broad array of theories that developed from it	◆ Chapter 8, p. 320	Erik Erikson's stage theory of adult development
	◆ Chapter 12, p. 505	How psychologists who teach people to deal with stress realize that people often use defense-oriented coping skills—some of which are Freudian in nature
	◆ Chapter 14, p. 560	How Freudian approaches to the treatment of abnormal behavior focus on helping people uncover hidden motivations and biological urges
The relationship between personality and stress	◆ Chapter 9, p. 368	People who are motivated to compete against others
	◆ Chapter 12, p. 501	How people with Type A personalities may be at risk for adverse health consequences
	◆ Chapter 14, p. 581	Stress management, which may involve talking to oneself and trying to maintain composure

In important ways, the study of personality reflects not only people's inherited structures (Chapter 2, p. 39) and learning experiences (Chapter 5, p. 161), but also their motivation (Chapter 9, p. 351), and level of awareness (Chapter 4, p. 127). Personality, reflecting the usual way in which people respond to the world, can be characterized from remarkably different perspectives. Some theorists focus on maladjustment (Chapter 13), others on how personality affects how we view other people (Chapter 15, p. 603). Personality affects how we change during development (Chapter 8, p. 317), and how we respond to stressors in the environment (Chapter 12, p. 493). Of course, determining which comes first, personality or thought and personality or responses to other people, is difficult to discern, and each of the personality theories discussed in this chapter show that personality affects many areas of psychology, and these many areas help shape personality theory.

Module 23 ► WHAT IS INTELLIGENCE? 438

Module 24 ► EXCEPTIONALITY AND ASSESSMENT 462

Chapter 11

Intelligence and Assessment

Everyone seems to be able to judge other people's abilities, but psychologists attempt to do so systematically, with precision, and with a goal of making predictions about future behavior. This chapter is about intelligence and assessment. The chapter's first module, Module 23, presents an analysis of the nature of intelligence and of how tests are developed, and it presents an overview of some of the important intelligence tests. The module highlights how intelligence tests such as the Stanford-Binet and the Wechsler Adult Intelligence Scale—Revised (WAIS-R) have become more sophisticated, reliable, and valid since 1905, when intelligence testing began. Throughout the first module, it is emphasized that standardized intelligence tests cannot tell the whole story. An evaluator must also take into account a person's family background, motivation, and socioeconomic status. Only with such information can interpreters of test scores make relatively accurate predictions about future performance, especially in academic settings. The module also presents the controversy of testing: Although intelligence tests have been criticized for cultural or racial bias, scientific research has shown that differences in measured IQ between racial groups on tests are the same differences found between siblings of any race or ethnic group.

Differences among people are especially evident when psychologists consider particularly exceptional individuals. These differences are part of the focus of Module 24. Gifted children are those who show outstanding intellectual, leadership, or artistic abilities. Only about 3% of children can be considered gifted, yet few of these receive any special training. As a whole, American society has not yet addressed the needs of the gifted and talented. At the other end of the spectrum are the mentally retarded. The mentally retarded not only have low IQs but also have trouble adapting socially to changes in their environment. People with mild mental retardation can largely overcome their deficits through training. Increasingly, these individuals are being mainstreamed early into regular classroom settings, in an attempt to normalize their experience and to help them achieve maximal educational and social adjustment. Module 24 concludes with a presentation of assessment techniques. Assessment of intelligence tells a clinician important information, but there is more to be learned through other types of objective and projective tests. Along with behavioral assessment and intelligence testing, a researcher or clinician can gather a comprehensive picture of intellectual and personality functioning.

Module 23

What Is Intelligence?

LEARNING OBJECTIVES

When you have mastered the material in this module, you will be able to

Introduction (p. 439)

23.1 Explain both why intelligence is difficult to measure and how psychologists overcome such difficulties (p. 439).

What Is Intelligence (pp. 440–443)

23.2 List three concepts shared by all definitions of intelligence and give Wechsler's definition of intelligence (p. 440).

23.3 Describe the basic features of five influential theories of intelligence (p. 441).

Testing (pp. 443–449)

23.4 Describe how and why the first intelligence test was developed (p. 443).

23.5 Explain how psychologists go about developing standardized tests; also describe the scores that can be obtained from these tests (p. 445).

23.6 Explain how diagnostic tests are evaluated for reliability and validity and discuss the importance of accurate test-score interpretation (p. 448).

Three Important Intelligence Tests (pp. 450–451)

23.7 Discuss the history, uses, and strengths of the Stanford-Binet, Wechsler, and Kaufman intelligence tests (p. 450).

Testing Controversy: Validity and Cultural Biases (pp. 452–454)

23.8 Identify two controversial areas concerning intelligence testing and discuss both five criticisms of and defenses for the validity of intelligence tests (p. 452).

23.9 Describe the controversy concerning cultural bias in intelligence testing and discuss the current predominant opinion regarding the appropriate use of intelligence tests (p. 453).

Intelligence: Nature Versus Nurture (pp. 454–459)

23.10 Describe the nature-versus-nurture controversy as it applies to intelligence (p. 454).

23.11 Discuss how comparisons are made among races and child-rearing environments to explore the relative contributions of nature and nurture on intelligence (p. 455).

23.12 Explain why differences in test scores between blacks and whites and between males and females are getting smaller (p. 457).

SQ3R
- **Survey** to set goals for studying.
- Ask **questions** as you **read.**
- Stop occasionally to **recite** and **review.**

plus
- **Write** a summary of key points.
- **Reflect** on the hypotheses, evidence, and implications of this material and on the relevance it has to *your* life.

Learning Objective 23.1 Explain both why intelligence is difficult to measure and how psychologists overcome such difficulties.

Maria Vega waits anxiously but quietly as her high school adviser examines her school records. Finally, the adviser tells Maria that her intelligence test score is well above average and high enough for the accelerated physics class; students in that class are required to have an IQ test score of 125 or more, a recommendation from the school psychologist, and permission from the instructor. The adviser notes that Maria excels in creative pursuits and knows that she is keenly interested in science and has always received A's in science. The adviser seeks the approval of the physics teacher, and Maria is thrilled when the teacher grants her request.

Through diligent studying, Maria manages to score consistently in the top third of the class on the course exams. Beyond this, her best talents are revealed when the physics class is divided into groups and assigned projects for the school science fair. Maria is nominated leader of her group, and she thinks of an especially creative experiment that wins first place. Estimating intellectual capabilities is a complex task, but there is more to intelligence than a single test score. Intelligence tests do not measure several mental characteristics that are important to success, such as motivation, creativity, and leadership skills.

Intelligence is difficult to measure because it is hard to define. Consider many of the generalized, and often inaccurate, attributes some people use to evaluate intelligence. Sometimes shy, quiet people or unusually attractive ones are assumed to be slow-witted, while others, perhaps because they earn a high income, are judged to be bright. Yet looks, income, and talkativeness provide little or no gauge of an individual's intelligence. People demonstrate effective and intelligent behavior in many ways, but not necessarily in all areas. Some people, for example, can write a complicated computer program but not a short story or an essay. Moreover, intelligence must be defined in terms of the situation in which people find themselves. Intelligent behavior for a dancer is very different from intelligent behavior for a scientist, and both types of behavior are different from intelligent behavior for a child with a learning disability.

What all this means is that no single test—such as a test of verbal ability, English literature, or math—is a clear measure of intelligence. Psychologists therefore use a variety of tests, as well as other data such as interviews, teacher evaluations, and writing and drawing samples, to evaluate an individual's current standing, to make predictions about future performance or behavior, and to offer suggestions for remedial work or therapy. Also, in spite of their drawbacks, tests have strong predictive value; for example, intelligence tests can *generally* predict academic achievement, and achievement tests can *generally* predict whether someone will profit from further training in a specific area.

The focus of this chapter is intelligence: theories, tests, and controversies about intelligence. We also examine two special populations with respect to intelligence: the gifted and the mentally retarded. We begin with the question, "What is intelligence?"

What Is Intelligence?

Learning Objective 23.2 List three concepts shared by all definitions of intelligence, and give Wechsler's definition of intelligence.

Why do two students who study the same material for the same amount of time get different scores on an examination? Why do some people succeed in medical school and others have difficulty finishing high school? One factor might be that one person is more intelligent than the other, and high intelligence enhances a person's chances to succeed academically.

Intelligence is one of the most widely used yet highly debated concepts in science and everyday life. In 1921, a group of psychologists attempting to answer the question, "What is intelligence?" could not come to an agreement. Sixty-five years later, Sternberg and Detterman (1986) posed the same question to 25 respected researchers, but they still could not reach an agreement.

Definitions of Intelligence

For some, *intelligence* refers to all mental abilities; for others, to the basic general factor necessary for all mental activity; for still others, it refers to a group of specific abilities. McNemar (1964) contended that "All intelligent people know what intelligence is—it is the thing that the other guy lacks!" Various definitions of intelligence all share certain concepts:

- Intelligence is defined in terms of observable, objective behavior.
- Intelligence takes in both an individual's capacity to learn and his or her acquired knowledge.
- A sign of intelligence is one's ability to adapt to the environment.

intelligence: According to Wechsler, "the aggregate or global capacity of the individual to act purposefully, to think rationally, and to deal effectively with the environment."

Perhaps the most widely accepted definition of **intelligence** is that of the well-known test constructor David Wechsler: *Intelligence is the aggregate or global capacity of the individual to act purposefully, to think rationally, and to deal effectively with the environment* (1958, p. 7). In Wechsler's definition, intelligence is expressed behaviorally—It is the way people act, and their ability to learn new things and to use previously learned knowledge. Most important, intelligence deals with peoples's ability to adapt to the environment. Wechsler's definition has had far-reaching effects on how test developers devise intelligence tests and investigate the nature of intelligence.

Theories of Intelligence

Learning Objective 23.3 Describe the basic features of five influential theories of intelligence.

Humans beings show intelligent behavior in a variety of ways, and sometimes they choose not to act intelligently. We cannot say that all people are intelligent all of the time, nor can we specify the exact conditions under which people will exhibit their intelligence. This realization of individual differences in behavior has been a problem for psychology from its beginnings. Today, the most influential approaches to the study of intelligence are Piaget's and Wechsler's theories, factor theories, Jensen's two-level theory, and the relatively new theory of intelligence proposed by Sternberg.

Piaget. According to Jean Piaget, intelligence is a reflection of a person's adaptation to the environment, with intellectual development consisting of changes in the way the individual accomplishes that adaptation. Every child goes through invariant (in terms of sequence) stages in intellectual development, with different levels of cognitive processes determining the types of intellectual tasks the child can accomplish. (This developmental process is examined in Chapter 8.) Three-year-olds cannot learn calculus because they are not ready to perform the mental operations needed to grasp the necessary concepts. Piaget's theory of intellectual development focuses on the interaction of biological readiness and learning. In Piaget's view, neither predominate in the development of intelligence; they work together.

Wechsler. As one of the developers of a widely used and widely respected intelligence test, Wechsler knew well that tests were made up of many subparts, each measuring a different aspect of a person's functioning and resourcefulness. He therefore examined closely the components of intelligence and argued that intelligence tests involving spatial relations and verbal comprehension reveal little about someone's *overall* capacity to deal with the world. In Wechsler's view, psychologists need to remember that intelligence is more than simply mathematical or problem-solving ability; it is the broad ability to deal with the world.

Factor Theories. Factor theories of intelligence use a correlation technique known as **factor analysis** to discover what makes up intelligence. Verbal comprehension, spelling, and reading speed, for example, usually correlate highly, suggesting that some underlying attribute of verbal abilities determines a person's score on those three tests.

Early in this century, Charles E. Spearman (1863–1945) used factor analysis to show that intelligence really consisted of two parts: a general factor affecting all tasks and several specific factors necessary to perform specific tasks. According to Spearman, some amounts of both the general and specific factors were necessary for the successful performance of any task. This basic approach to intelligence is the *two-factor theory of intelligence.*

Louis L. Thurstone (1887–1955) developed Spearman's work further by postulating a general factor analogous to Spearman's, as well as seven other factors, each of which represented a unique mental ability. His theory is known as the **factor-theory approach to intelligence.** In it, he developed a computational scheme for sorting out the seven factors that he considered to be the abilities of human beings: verbal comprehension, word fluency, number facility, spatial visualization, associative memory, perceptual speed, and reasoning.

Thurstone's factor-theory approach, with its seven abilities, led to and culminated in J.P. Guilford's multifactor approach to intelligence testing. He is concerned with developing a testable scheme of intelligence. Guilford gave large numbers of tests to diverse populations and found a whole range of factors that seemed appropriate to describe intelligence. He looked for a structure, a rational

factor analysis: A statistical procedure designed to discover the mutually independent elements (factors) in any set of data.

factor-theory approach to intelligence: Theories of intelligence based on factor analysis.

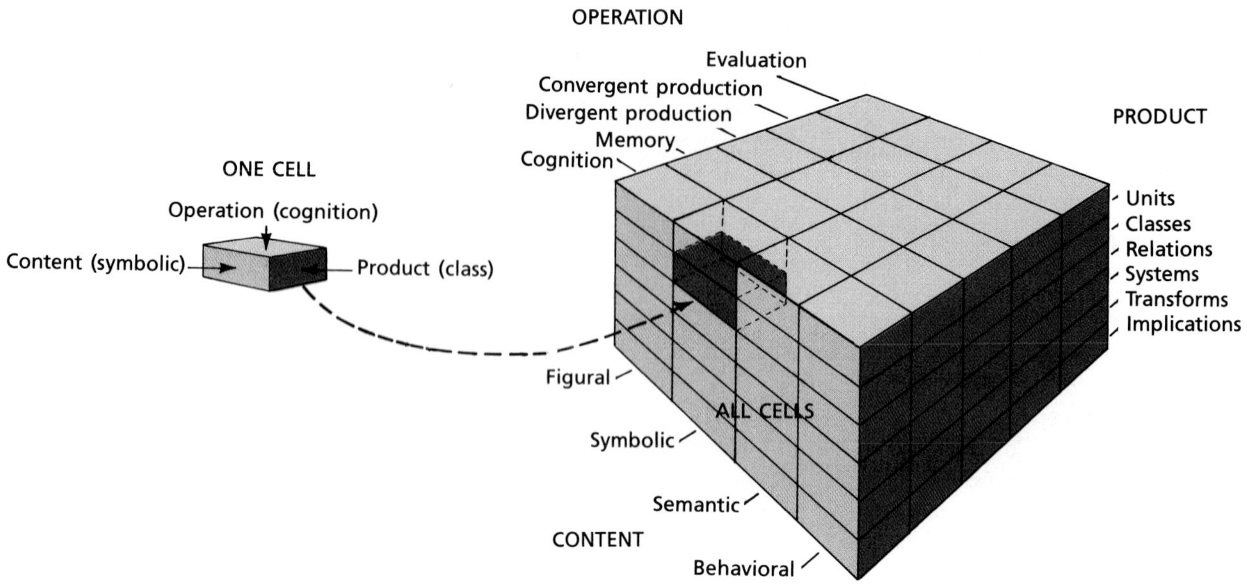

Figure 23.1

Each of Guilford's three dimensions of intellectual abilities—operations, products, and content—has many attributes. Through various combinations, these dimensions and their attributes produce 120 separate factors.

scheme of grouping them together, and he eventually described a *structure-of-intellect model.* According to Guilford (1967), human intellectual abilities and activities can be described in terms of three major dimensions: the mental operations performed, the content of those operations, and the resulting product of the operations. As Figure 23.1 shows, Guilford's three-dimensional model produces 120 factors, 98 of which have been demonstrated experimentally. Guilford (1985) contends that several scores are necessary for a correct assessment of an individual's intellectual abilities, not just one or two, or even four. He also asserts that intelligence should be defined as "a systematic collection of abilities or functions for processing information of different kinds in different forms" (p. 231). Research supports Guilford's theory and suggests that optimally weighted composite scores may best predict achievement, school learning, and work performance (Guilford, 1985).

Jensens's Two-Level Theory. Arthur Jensen approaches intelligence testing not from the view of a test constructor, but from the view of a theoretician. Jensen (1969, 1970) suggests that intellectual functioning consists of associative abilities and cognitive abilities. *Associative abilities* enable us to connect stimuli and events; they require little reasoning or transformation. Questions testing associative abilities include asking someone to repeat from memory a seven-digit number sequence or to name the first president of the United States. *Cognitive abilities,* on the other hand, deal with reasoning and problem solving. Solving word problems and defining new words or concepts are examples of cognitive ability tasks.

Jensen's idea is not new; even the founders of the testing movement suggested that different kinds of intellectual functioning are involved in intelligence. What is new is Jensen's claim that associative and cognitive abilities are inherited, adding more information to the nature-versus-nurture controversy about intelligence (discussed later in this chapter).

Sternberg's View. Robert J. Sternberg takes an information-processing view of intelligence. His view is *triarchic,* dividing intelligence into three dimensions: componential, experiential, and contextual. His aim is to relate a person's intelligence to his or her internal and external world. Sternberg's ideas, which are relatively new in the domain of theories of intelligence, are presented in the following box. Like other researchers, he believes in multiple types of intelligence e.g., Gardner, 1983 and his ideas are explored in more detail in the Understanding the Research Process box at the top of the next page.

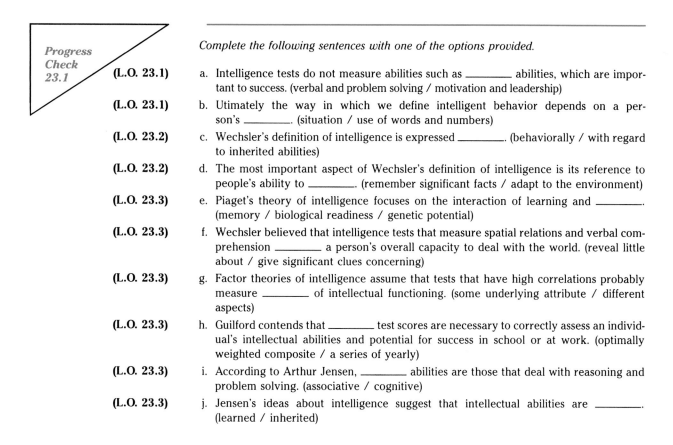

Progress Check 23.1

Complete the following sentences with one of the options provided.

(L.O. 23.1) a. Intelligence tests do not measure abilities such as ________ abilities, which are important to success. (verbal and problem solving / motivation and leadership)

(L.O. 23.1) b. Utimately the way in which we define intelligent behavior depends on a person's ________. (situation / use of words and numbers)

(L.O. 23.2) c. Wechsler's definition of intelligence is expressed ________. (behaviorally / with regard to inherited abilities)

(L.O. 23.2) d. The most important aspect of Wechsler's definition of intelligence is its reference to people's ability to ________. (remember significant facts / adapt to the environment)

(L.O. 23.3) e. Piaget's theory of intelligence focuses on the interaction of learning and ________. (memory / biological readiness / genetic potential)

(L.O. 23.3) f. Wechsler believed that intelligence tests that measure spatial relations and verbal comprehension ________ a person's overall capacity to deal with the world. (reveal little about / give significant clues concerning)

(L.O. 23.3) g. Factor theories of intelligence assume that tests that have high correlations probably measure ________ of intellectual functioning. (some underlying attribute / different aspects)

(L.O. 23.3) h. Guilford contends that ________ test scores are necessary to correctly assess an individual's intellectual abilities and potential for success in school or at work. (optimally weighted composite / a series of yearly)

(L.O. 23.3) i. According to Arthur Jensen, ________ abilities are those that deal with reasoning and problem solving. (associative / cognitive)

(L.O. 23.3) j. Jensen's ideas about intelligence suggest that intellectual abilities are ________. (learned / inherited)

Testing

Learning Objective 23.4 Describe how and why the first intelligence test was developed.

Like Maria Vega, who was profiled at the beginning of this chapter, you probably have taken one or more intelligence tests during your school years. The results of intelligence tests—often rendered in precise numbers—may have determined your educational curriculum from elementary school onward. Psychologists are among the first to admit that intelligence tests have shortcomings, and researchers continue to revise them to correct inadequacies.

Intelligence tests have had a long and interesting history. In the late 19th and early 20th century, Alfred Binet (1857–1911), a Frenchman, became interested in psychology and began to study the relationship of physiology and behavior. He later employed Theodore Simon (1873–1961), a physician, and their friendship and collaboration became famous.

Binet and Simon are well known as the founders of the psychological testing movement. In 1904, Binet was commissioned to identify procedures for the educa-

UNDERSTANDING THE RESEARCH PROCESS

A New Theory of Intelligence

A psychologist in search of a field for important research with far-ranging practical implications could confidently choose intelligence and intelligence testing. Robert J. Sternberg of Yale University did—and his life has never been the same. Fully aware that traditional theories of intelligence are purported to be the building blocks of today's intelligence tests, Sternberg has criticized most widely used tests.

Sternberg (1986a) finds intelligence tests too narrow and contends that they don't adequately account for intelligence in the everyday world. He argues that researchers have focused for too long on *how* to measure intelligence, rather than on the more important question of "What is intelligence, how does it change, and what can individuals do to enhance it?" Sternberg reasons that some tests measure individual mental abilities while other tests measure the way the individual operates in the environment. Sternberg asserts that a solid theory of intelligence must account for both individual mental abilities and the ability of the person to use his or her capabilities in the environment.

Sternberg (1985, 1986a) described his new triarchic theory of intelligence in his book *Beyond IQ.* Sternberg's theory's three dimensions can be viewed as three subparts or subtheories, each dealing with a different aspect of intelligence—contextual, experiential, and componential intelligence.

The *contextual* subtheory deals with an individual's ability to use intelligence to prepare for problem solving in specific situations. This part of the triarchic theory focuses on how people shape their environments so that their competencies can be best utilized. For example, an individual might organize problems in a meaningful way, perhaps by grouping similar items together. This first subtheory, contextual, does not refer to any mental operations that are necessary to carry out problem solving.

The second subtheory, *experiential,* deals with the individual and his or her external world. According to this theory, a test measures intelligence if it assesses a person's ability to master handling novel tasks in an automatic manner. Such a task might involve learning to remember all words containing the letter T in a paragraph. Initially, finding and remembering such words is tedious, but with much practice, the task becomes automatic.

The third subtheory, *componential,* is the glue that holds the other two subtheories together. The componential subtheory describes the mental mechanisms that underlie what are commonly considered intelligent behaviors. A *component* is a basic method of information processing. It includes a person's ability to determine what tasks need to be done, to determine subtasks that need to be undertaken first, to analyze their subparts; to decide what information should be processed, and to monitor performance. Tasks that can be used to measure the elements of the componential subtheory are analogies, vocabulary, and syllogisms (see Figure 23.2).

To be intelligent, a behavior has to involve all three components—all three subtheories of intelligence. For example, Sternberg suggests that eating is a behavior that is adaptive but does not show novelty or use of nontrivial abilities. Similarly, turning on a light switch is adaptive but it is automatic and does not demonstrate the components of intelligence. Few behaviors involve all three components, and so Sternberg asserts that various tasks measure intelligence to a different extent.

Does Sternberg support the continued use of IQ tests? Yes, if the tests are used prudently. Sternberg argues that existing IQ tests do not do justice to the theo-

tion of children with mental retardation in Paris. Binet was chosen for the task because he had been lobbying for action to help the schools; only recently had schools been made public and open to all, and disadvantaged children were doing poorly and dropping out. In 1905, Binet and Simon set a goal to separate normal children from children with mental retardation. Binet and Simon were concerned only with measuring general intelligence in children, not with why some children were retarded in intellectual development or what their future might be.

Binet coined the phrase *mental age,* meaning the age level at which a child is functioning cognitively. He and Simon developed everyday tasks, such as countries from which they evolved and that new tests examining all aspects of intelligent behavior need to be estabished. Existing IQ tests measure some people's intelligence some of the time, but they are often misleading. This is especially true when viewed by nonpsychologists or those without expertise in testing. From Sternberg's view, new batteries of tests are needed to analyze fully the three basic subcomponents of intelligent behavior.

- ***What is the key weakness that Sternberg finds with existing intelligence tests that made him want to develop a new test?***
- ***What evidence can be used to suggest that existing IQ tests measure some people's behavior only some of the time?***
- ***If Sternberg is correct about the limitations of existing IQ tests, what are the implications for psychological practitioners?***

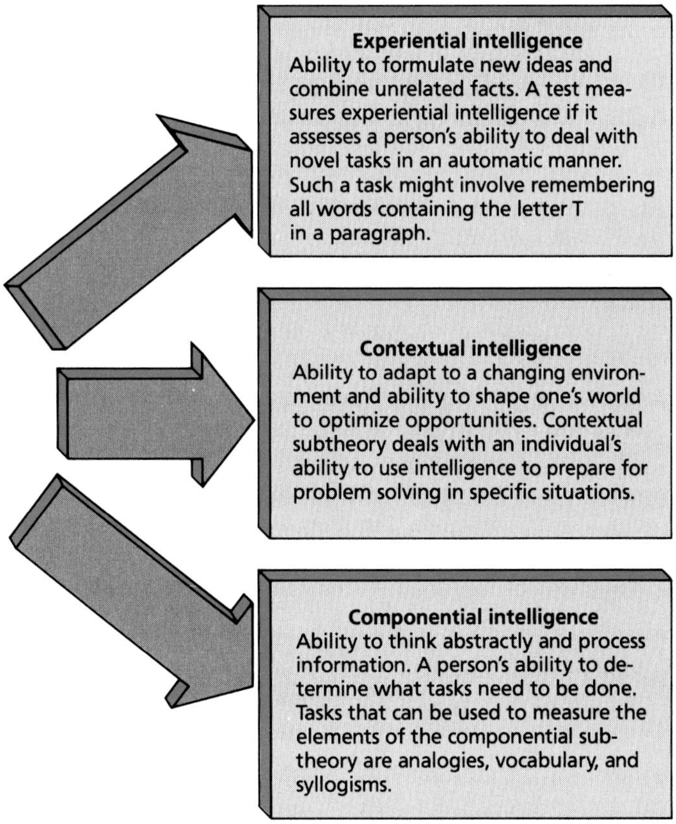
Experiential intelligence
Ability to formulate new ideas and combine unrelated facts. A test measures experiential intelligence if it assesses a person's ability to deal with novel tasks in an automatic manner. Such a task might involve remembering all words containing the letter T in a paragraph.
Contextual intelligence
Ability to adapt to a changing environment and ability to shape one's world to optimize opportunities. Contextual subtheory deals with an individual's ability to use intelligence to prepare for problem solving in specific situations.
Componential intelligence
Ability to think abstractly and process information. A person's ability to determine what tasks need to be done. Tasks that can be used to measure the elements of the componential subtheory are analogies, vocabulary, and syllogisms.

Figure 23.2

Sternberg's triarchic theory of intelligence.

ing, naming, and using objects, to determine mental age. The scale they developed can be considered the first useful and practical test of intelligence.

Principles of Test Development

Learning Objective 23.5 Explain how psychologists go about developing standardized tests; also describe the types of scores that can be obtained from these tests.

Imagine that you are a 7-year-old child taking an intelligence test and you come to a question that asks, "Which one of the following tells you the temperature?" Below the question are pictures of the sun, a radio, a thermometer, and a pair of mittens. Is the thermometer the only correct answer? Suppose that there are no

standardization: The process of developing a uniform procedure for the administration and scoring of a test, based on developing norms from a large, representative sample.

representative sample: A sample of individuals who match the population with whom they are to be compared, with regard to key variables such as age.

norms: The score and corresponding percentile ranks or standard scores of each subgroup of persons on whom the test was standardized.

thermometers in your home, but you often hear the temperature given on radio weather reports. Or imagine instead that you "test" the temperature each morning by standing outside to feel the sun's strength, or that you know it's cold outside when your parents tell you to wear mittens. According to your experiences, any one of the answers to the question might be an appropriately intelligent response.

What Does a Test Measure? The ambiguity and cultural biases of this hypothetical test question illustrate the complexity of intelligence-test development. In general, we say that a *test* is a standardized device for examining a person's responses to specific stimuli, usually questions or problems. Because there are many potential pitfalls in creating a test, psychologists follow an elaborate set of guidelines and procedures to make certain that their questions are properly constructed (see Figure 23.3).

First, a psychologist must decide what the test is to measure. For example, will it measure musical ability, or knowledge of geography, mathematics, or psychology? Second, he or she needs to construct and evaluate items for the test, that will give an examiner some reasonable expectation that success on the test means something. Third, the test must be standardized.

Standardization. **Standardization** is the process of developing a uniform procedure for administering and scoring a test and for establishing norms. **Norms** are the scores and corresponding percentile ranks of a large and **representative sample** of subjects from the population for whom the test was designed. The people in the sample are matched with regard to variables such as socioeconomic status and age (this idea is also discussed in the appendix). Thus, a test designed for college freshmen might be given to 2,000 freshmen, with an equal number of men and women, 16- to 20-year olds, from large and small high schools, and from different areas of the country. Standardization ensures that there is a basis for comparing future test results with those of a standard reference group.

After a test is designed and administered to a representative sample, the results are examined to establish norms for different segments of the test population, such as for children, adolescents, and adults, or for psychologists, musicians,

Figure 23.3

Procedures for constructing a standardized test. (Source: Adapted from Rudman, 1977)

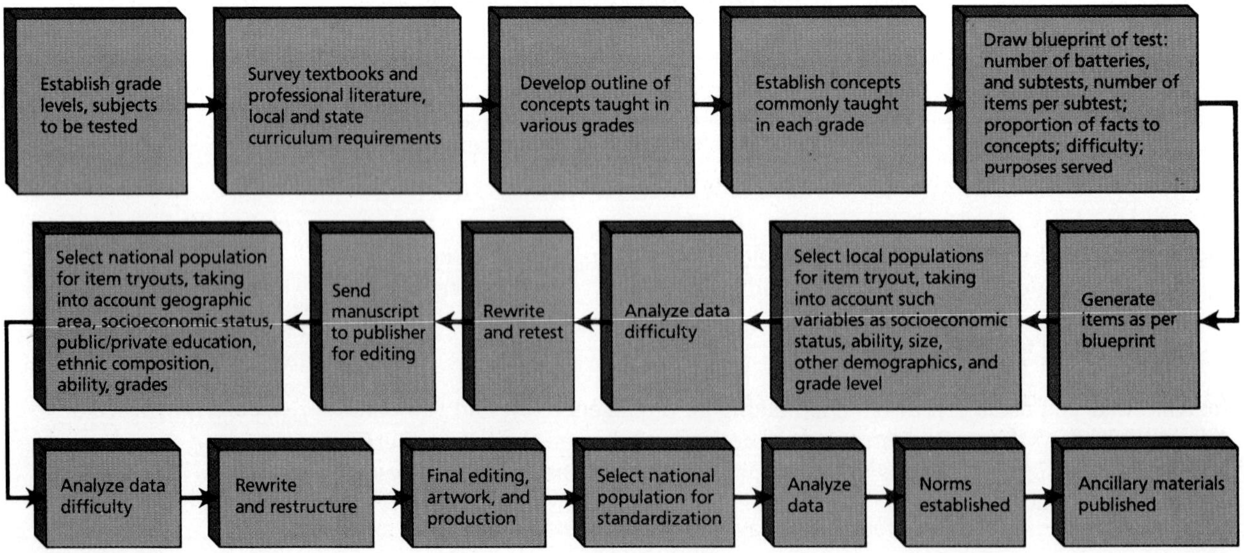

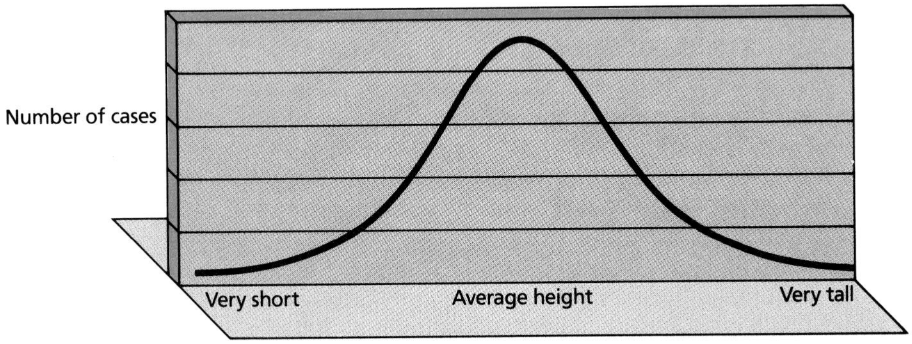

Figure 23.4

This bell-shaped curve shows the normal distribution of height in the general population. As with normal distributions of weight or even intelligence, very few people are represented at the extremes.

or geographers. Knowing how people in the representative sample have done allows psychologists and educators to interpret future test results properly. In other words, the scores of those in the samples serve as a reference point for comparing individual scores.

Normal Curve. Test developers generally plot the scores of the representative sample on a graph that shows how frequently each score occurs. On most tests, some people do very well, some score very poorly, and most score in the middle. When test scores are distributed that way, psychologists say the data are normally distributed or fall on a normal curve. A **normal curve** is a bell-shaped graphic representation of data arranged so that a certain percentage of the population falls under each part of the curve. As Figure 23.4 shows, most people are in the middle range, with a few at each extreme. Tests are often devised so that comparisons can be made of individual scores against a normal distribution. (The appendix discusses the normal distribution in detail on p. 664.

Scores. The simplest score on a test is the **raw score**—that is, the number of correct answers. However, the raw score is seldom a true indicator of a person's ability. On many tests, particularly intelligence tests, raw scores need to be adjusted to take into account a person's age, sex, and grade level. Such scores are commonly expressed in terms of a **standard score,** indicating an individual's position relative to others. If, for example, a 100-item intelligence test is administered to students in the 3rd and 11th grades, we would expect those in the 11th grade to answer more items correctly than those in the 3rd grade. To adjust for the differences, after the test, each student's score is compared to the score typically achieved by other students at the same grade level. Thus, if 11th-graders typically answer 70 questions correctly, an 11-grader who answers 90 questions correctly will have done better than most other students at that grade level. Similarly, if 3rd-graders usually answer 25 questions correctly, then a 3rd-grader who answers 15 questions correctly will have performed worse than most other students at that grade level.

A standard score is generally a **percentile score,** which indicates the percentage of other students taking the test who obtain a lower score. If, for example, someone's percentile score is 84, then 84% of people taking the test obtained a lower score than that person.

normal curve: A bell-shaped curve arranged so that a certain percentage of the population falls under each part of the curve.

raw score: An examinee's unconverted score on a test (such as the number of correct answers).

standard score: A score that expresses an individual's position relative to the mean, based on standard deviation; often derived by converting a raw score to one interpretable on the basis of a population variable (such as age or grade).

percentile score: A score indicating what percentage of the test population would obtain a lower score.

The Earliest Tests Were Intelligence Tests. Perhaps the oldest and most widely recognized test is the intelligence test. In the early 1900s, intelligence was measured by a simple formula. An intelligence quotient, or IQ, was calculated by dividing a person's mental abilities, or mental age, by his or her chronological age and multiplying the result by 100. Mental ages of children were calculated from the number of correct answers on a series of test items; the higher the number answered correctly, the higher the mental age.

These variations make predictions and comparisons difficult. To simplify measures of IQ, psychologists and testers began using **deviation IQ,** a standard score for which the mean and standard deviation remain constant at all ages. Thus, a child of 9 years and a child of 16, each with an IQ of 115, have the same position relative to others who have taken the same IQ test. Both are in the 84th percentile; that is, both scored better than 84% of all others their age who took the same IQ test.

Reliability and Validity

Learning Objective 23.6 Explain how diagnostic tests are evaluated for reliability and validity, and discuss the importance of accurate test-score interpretation.

Of all the achievements by psychologists in making tests useful, perhaps the most important is to ensure that tests are both reliable and valid. If a student obtains different scores on two versions (or forms) of the same test, which score is correct? Furthermore, does the test measure what it is supposed to measure and *only* that?

Reliability. **Reliability** refers to the consistency of test scores. In other words, a test is reliable if it yields the same (or very similar) score for the same person in repeated testing, or the same score for the same person using different versions of the test. (Consistency of test scores assumes that the person is in the same emotional and physiological state at each time of administration.) If a test's results are not consistent from one testing session to another, or for two comparable groups of people, meaningful comparisons are impossible.

There are several ways to determine whether a test is reliable. The simplest, termed **test–retest,** is to administer the same test to the same person on two or more occasions. If, for example, the person achieves a score of 90 one day and 135 another, the test is probably not reliable. Nonetheless, keep in mind the possibility that the person might have remembered some of the test items from one occasion to the next. To avoid that problem, testers use the **alternative-form** method, which involves giving two different versions of the same test. If the two forms test the same characteristic and differ only in their items, both should yield the same result.

Even the most reliable test will not yield identical results each time it is taken, but a good test will have a relatively small standard error of measurement. The **standard error of measurement** is the number of points a score varies because of imperfect reliability. Consider an intelligence test that has a standard error of measurement of 3, for example. If someone scores 115 on that IQ test, a practitioner can state with a high degree of confidence that the individual's real score is between 112 and 118—within 3 points above or below the obtained score.

Validity. If your psychology exam includes questions such as "What is the square root of 647?" and "Who wrote *The Grapes of Wrath*?" it is probably not a valid measure of your knowledge of psychology. That is, it is not measuring what it is supposed to measure. To be useful, in addition to reliability, a test must have **validity**—it should measure what it is supposed to measure and predict what it is supposed to predict. *Content validity* refers to the test's ability to measure the knowledge or behavior it is intended to measure. A test designed to measure musical aptitude should not include items that assess mechanical aptitude or personality characteristics. Similarly, an intelligence test should measure only intelligence, not musical training, cultural experiences, or socioeconomic status. In addition to content validity, a test should have *predictive validity*—it should be able to predict a person's future achievements with at least some degree of accuracy. Table 23.1 shows four types of validity.

deviation IQ: A standard IQ test score that has the same mean and standard deviation at all ages.

reliability: The ability of a test to yield the same score for the same individual through repeated testings.

test–retest: A method of assessing reliability by administering a test to the same group of examinees on two different occasions and computing the similarity between the scores.

alternative form: A method of assessing reliability by administering two forms of a test and computing the similarity between the scores.

standard error of measurement: Based on statistical formulas, the number of points that a score may vary because of imperfect reliability.

validity: The ability of a test to measure only what it is supposed to measure.

TABLE 23.1 Types of validity used to assess tests

Validity	Aspect measured
Content validity	The extent to which a test reflects a sample of the actual behavior to be measured
Face validity	The extent to which a test "looks" appropriate just from a reading of the items
Predicitive validity	The extent to which a test can predict a person's behavior in some other setting
Construct validity	The extent to which a test actually measures a particular trait (such as intelligence, anxiety, or musical ability)

Interpretation

Tests are generally made up of different subtests or subscales, each yielding a score. There may also be one general score for the entire test. All these scores require knowledgeable interpretation; that is, test scores must be given in a context that is meaningful to the person who receives the information, perhaps a parent of a teacher. Without such a context, the score is little more than a number.

Many intelligence tests provide a single IQ score. These tests, however, contain far more information than that single score. Consider one of the most popular IQ tests for children, the Wechsler Intelligence Scale for Children—Revised, or WISC-R (mentioned in the introduction to this chapter). In addition to an overall IQ score, the WISC-R test yields scores for verbal IQ, performance IQ (measuring visuospatial ability, numerical memory, and other nonverbal abilities), and various other subtests. Although single and multiple scores are useful, researcher Alan Kaufman (1979) suggests that to evaluate an individual accurately, global or overall IQ scores should be deemphasized and test examiners should look instead at the components of the IQ score.

Binet worked with Simon and initiated some of the first psychological testing in the 20th century.

Progress Check 23.2

Complete the following sentences with one of the options provided.

(L.O. 23.4) a. The purpose of the first intelligence test developed by Binet and Simon was to ________ in children. (measure general intelligence / determine the cause of mental retardation)

(L.O. 23.5) b. A test is said to be ________ when norms and a uniform procedure for administering and scoring the test have been established. (standardized / valid)

(L.O. 23.5) c. A graphic representation of data arranged so that most of the population falls in the middle and smaller percentages of the population extend out from the middle is a ________. (deviation IQ / normal curve)

(L.O. 23.5) d. A ________ score is the number of correct answers given on a test before it is converted into a meaningful score. (raw / standard)

(L.O. 23.5) e. Before the deviation IQ was developed, an intelligence quotient (IQ score) was calculated by ________ and multiplying the result by 100. (totaling the correct answers / dividing mental age by chronological age)

(L.O. 23.6) f. A problem with the ________ method of determining test reliability is that a person might remember some of the test items from one occasion to the next. (test–retest / alternative-form)

(L.O. 23.6) g. A standard error of measurement refers to the number of points a test score may vary from the real score because ________. (of imperfect reliability / an alternate form of the test was used)

(L.O. 23.6) h. When a test measures the knowledge or behavior it is intended to measure, we say it has ________ validity. (content / predictive)

Three Important Intelligence Tests

Learning Objective 23.7 Discuss the history, uses, and strengths of the Stanford-Binet, Wechsler, and Kaufman intelligence tests.

What is the best intelligence test? What does it measure? Can you study for an intelligence test to get a higher score? As in other areas in science, theory leads to application; many intelligence theorists applied their theoretical knowledge to test development. The three tests we examine briefly here are all based on the theories of their developers.

Stanford-Binet Intelligence Scale

Most people associate the beginning of intelligence testing with Alfred Binet and Theodore Simon. Their original test was actually 30 short tests, arranged in order of difficulty, consisting of tasks such as distinguishing food from nonfood or pointing to objects and naming them. Decades of psychologists used the original and later revised versions of the test now called the Stanford-Binet (Stanford refers to Stanford University, where the test was further developed). The Stanford-Binet has traditionally been a good predictor of academic performance, and many of its simplest tests correlate highly with one another. A new version of the Stanford-Binet was published in 1986, with items that minimize gender and racial characteristics. It comprises four major subscales and one overall IQ score, and it tests individuals ages 2 through 23 years.

The new Stanford-Binet is a potent test; one great strength is that it can be used over a wide range of ages and abilities. However, like all tests it has limitations, especially in that not all examinees are given the same battery of tests across age levels. This makes comparison of individuals difficult; nonetheless, the new Stanford-Binet correlates well with the old one, as well as with the WISC-R and the Kaufman Assessment Battery for Children, which are discussed next.

In the 1930s, Wechsler developed a widely used intelligence test for adults. The latest revision of that test is known as the WAIS-R.

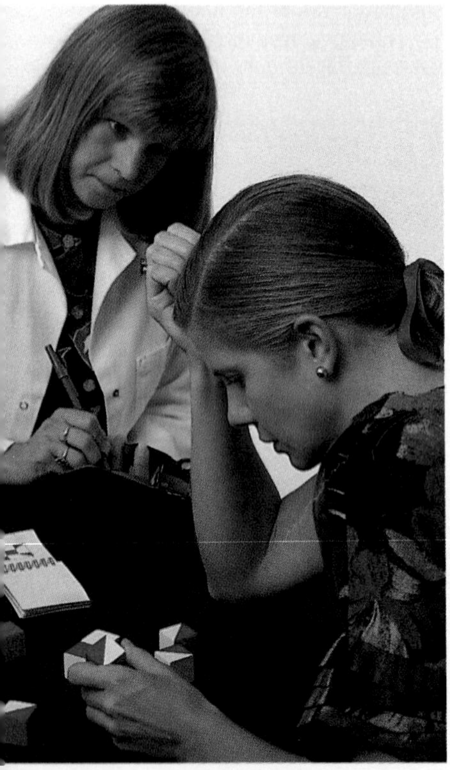

Wechsler Scales

In the 1930s, David Weschler (1896–1981) recognized that the Stanford-Binet was inadequate to test the IQ of adults. He also maintained that some of the Stanford-Binet items lacked validity. In 1939, Wechsler developed the Wechsler-Bellevue Intelligence Scale to test the IQ of adults. In 1955, the Wechsler Adult Intelligence Scale (WAIS) was published, which eliminated some technical difficulties of the Wechsler-Bellevue. The 1981 revision of the test is the WAIS-R.

Wechsler also developed the Wechsler Intelligence Scale for Children, the WISC, which is for children ages 6 through 16 years. It was revised in 1974 as the WISC-R, and then in 1991 as the WISC-III. Table 23.2 shows the typical subtests included. In 1967, the Wechsler Preschool and Primary Scale of Intelligence (WPPSI) was developed for children ages 4 to $6\frac{1}{2}$ years and was revised in 1989 as the WPPSI-R.

The Wechsler scales group test items by content: For example, all the information questions are presented together and all the arithmetic problems are presented together. The Wechsler scales have been well researched; thousands of studies have been conducted to assess their reliability and validity. They are valid cross-culturally (Insua, 1983), for special education students (Covin & Sattler, 1985), for learning disabled students (Clarizio & Veres, 1984), and for clinical populations (Eppinger, Craig, Adams, & Parsons, 1987).

The Kaufman Assessment Battery for Children

Many intelligence tests have been criticized for being biased, with some questions geared toward the white middle-class male experience. Psychologists Alan and Nadeen Kaufman contend that their Kaufman Assessment Battery for Children (K-ABC) uses tasks that tap the experience of all people, regardless of their backgrounds. A memory task in the K-ABC, for example, might have a subject look at a picture of a face and a few moments later pick it out from among pictures of other faces.

The K-ABC, like the Stanford-Binet and the Wechsler Scales, is individually administered, and it was designed especially for assessment, intervention, and remediation of school problems. School psychologists, who are the primary users of the K-ABC, act as evaluators and consultants to families and schools, helping them to set and achieve appropriate educational goals. The K-ABC consists of four global scales: Three measure mental processing abilities (sequential processing, simultaneous processing, and a composite of the two); the fourth assesses achievement. The Kaufmans believe that the sequential- and simultaneous-processing scales measure abilities synonymous with intelligence—that is, the ability to process information and to solve problems (A. S. Kaufman, 1983).

Although early research on the K-ABC shows it to be a promising IQ test (Zins & Barnett, 1983), it is not without its critics. Kaufman (1984) argues that his test is valid and reliable and that it is evolving to continue to get better. He wants it to be an alternative to the WISC-III and the Stanford-Binet. Many practitioners consider it child-oriented and easy to administer. Final evaluations of the K-ABC are still probably a decade away.

TABLE 23.2 Typical subtest on the WISC-R

Verbal test		Performance test	
Subtest	**Type of task**	**Subtest**	**Type of task**
Information	Given a question, recall a general fact that has been acquired in both formal and informal school settings.	Picture completion	Given an incomplete picture, point out the part that is missing.
Similarities	Given two ideas, use another concept in describing how both are alike.	Picture arrangement	Given a series of pictures that tell a story, put them in the right sequence.
Arithmetic	Given a word problem, solve it without pencil and paper.	Block design	Given a picture of a block design, use real blocks to reproduce it.
Digit span	Given an orally presented string of digits, recall them.	Oject assembly	Given a jigsaw-type puzzle, put the pieces together to form a complete object.
Vocabulary	Given a vocabulary word, define it.	Coding	Given a key that matches numbers to geometric shapes, fill in a blank form with the shapes that go with the numbers.
Comprehension	Given a question requiring practical judgment and common sense, answer it.		

Testing Controversy: Validity and Cultural Biases

Learning Objective 23.8 Identify two controversial areas concerning intelligence testing, and discuss both five criticisms of and defenses for the validity of intelligence tests.

In 1986, a federal court in California upheld a 1979 ruling barring administration of IQ tests to black students in the state. According to the judge who made the original ruling, the tests are culturally biased and therefore discriminate against blacks for "special education" purposes, resulting in a disproportionate number of blacks being assigned to classes for the mentally retarded. The California court case illustrates the political, cultural, and scientific issues involved in the debate over what intelligence tests actually measure. Minority groups have joined psychologists and educators in challenging the usefulness of testing in general, and of intelligence testing in particular. The controversy focused on two major issues: the validity and the cultural bias of intelligence tests.

Test Validity

There are five basic criticisms of—and defenses for—the validity of tests and testing. The first is that there is no way to measure intelligence because no clear, agreed-upon definition of intelligence exists. The defense against this argument, by Mercer (1977) and other researchers, is that although different IQ tests seem to measure different abilities, the major tests have face validity. **Face validity** is the appropriateness of test items "on their face"—that is, do they seem appropriate to experts? Intelligence tests have face validity; that is, they generally contain items requiring problem solving and rational thinking, which in white middle-class society is an appropriate test of intelligence.

The second criticism is that because IQ test items usually consist of *learned information,* they reflect the quality of a child's schooling, rather than the child's actual intelligence. The response to this challenge is that most vocabulary items on IQ tests are learned in the general environment, not in school; moreover, the ability to learn vocabulary and facts seems to depend on the ability to reason verbally.

The third criticism is that *school settings* may adversely affect IQ and other test scores, not only because tests are often administered inexpertly, but also because of halo effects. A **halo effect** is the tendency to allow preconceived attitudes about an individual to influence evaluation. A teacher or test administrator can develop a negative (or positive) feeling about a person, a class, or a group of students that might carry over and influence his or her teaching or the administration or interpretation of test scores. People who defend testing against this charge acknowledge that incorrectly administered tests are likely to result in inaccurate IQ test scores, but they claim that these effects are less powerful than opponents claim.

face validity: The appropriateness of test items "on their face"—that is, do they seem appropriate to experts?

halo effect: The tendency to let one of an individual's characteristics influence the evaluation of other characteristics.

The two other criticisms of testing are less directly related to the issue of validity. One is that some people are *test wise.* These individuals make better use of their time than others do, they guess the tester's intentions, and they find clues in the test. Practice in taking tests improves these people's performance. The usual responses are that the items on IQ tests are unfamiliar even to experienced test-takers and that the effects of previous practice are seldom or never evident on IQ tests. The final criticism is that individuals' scores often depend on their *motivation to succeed* rather than on actual intelligence. Defenders of IQ tests agree that examinees' attitudes toward a test and their motivation are important, but they deny that the IQ tests themselves influence motivation.

Cultural Biases

Learning Objective 23.9 Describe the controversy concerning cultural bias in intelligence testing, and discuss the current predominant opinion regarding the appropriate use of intelligence tests.

Another major argument against IQ testing is that tests are culturally biased and thus are used to discriminate against individuals who do not come from the test-makers' environments, usually white, middle-class, and suburban. A test item or subscale is considered culturally biased when, with all other factors held constant, its content is more difficult for members of one group than for another (Kaufman, 1982). To understand how a test can be culturally biased, imagine that an impoverished migrant worker's child is asked the temperature problem posed earlier. If the child is unfamiliar with thermometers and radios, he or she may choose the sun as the best answer. Based on experiments that have shown some tests to be culturally or racially biased (Shimberg, 1929; Williams, 1970; see also Table 23.3 on the next page), some educators and parents have urged banning tests in all public schools, especially IQ tests. They argue that some groups of individuals who are not exposed to the same education and experiences as the middle-class group for whom the tests were designed are bound to perform less well.

Clearly, those who interpret IQ tests must be particularly sensitive to any potential biases. Nonetheless, although researchers find differences among the IQ test scores of various racial and cultural groups, they find no conclusive evidence of bias in the tests themselves.

Jensen (1976) examined the WISC-R scores of a random sample of 600 white and 600 black California school children in grades 5 through 12; he found that whites scored an average of 12 points higher, but he also found an average 12-point difference between siblings. The difference between siblings was as great as the difference between racial groups; the variability is as great between individuals as between groups. After examining several other important variables in widely used standardized tests of intelligence, Jensen concluded that "The notion that IQ tests discriminate largely in terms of race or social class is a myth" (p. 340). Jensen does not claim that biases cannot exist—only that they do not exist on tests such as the WISC-R. Other well-respected psychologists support his view (Sattler, 1988).

IQ testing has been criticized for not taking cultural differences into account. Faced with the same test questions, two culturally divergent men, such as these British and aboriginal men, are unlikely to perform equally well due to their differing interpretation of the questions posed.

Conclusions

IQ tests cannot predict or explain all types of intellectual behavior. They are derived from a small sample of a restricted range of cognitive activities. As Sattler noted (1988), intelligence can be demonstrated in many ways; an IQ test tells little about someone's ability to be flexible in new situations and to function in mature and responsible ways. Intelligence tests reflect many aspects of a person's environment—how much they are encouraged to express themselves verbally, how much time they spend reading, and the extent to which parents have urged them to engage in academic pursuits.

In the past two decades, the public, educators, and psychologists have scrutinized the weaknesses of IQ tests and have attempted to eliminate bias from testing by creating better tests and by establishing better norms for comparison. However, even the courts acknowledge the complexity of the issues involved in tests and testing (Elliott, 1987). In isolation, IQ scores mean little. Information about an individual's home environment, personality, socioeconomic status, and special abilities is crucial to understanding his or her intellectual functioning.

Critics of standardized testing have been vocal and persuasive, and their arguments cannot be discounted. Research into test construction, test validation, and the causes of differences among individuals' scores continues. Overall, experts see tests as adequately measuring the most important elements of intelligence, despite the flaws of these tests (Snyderman & Rothman, 1987). The components of tests, their subscales, and specific questions not only help researchers evaluate their validity, but also help sort out the components that are most affected by nature from those most affected by nurture. Table 23.4 summarizes some misconceptions about intelligence and testing.

Intelligence: Nature Versus Nurture

Learning Objective 23.10
Describe the nature-versus-nurture controversy as it applies to intelligence.

Scientists now can visualize how hard someone is thinking. In a study conducted at the University of California Irvine, eight volunteers took a 36-item abstract-reasoning test that required them to complete patterns made by geometric designs. At the start of the test, each volunteer was injected with radioactive glucose, which made the most active parts of the working brains light up on positron emission test (PET) scans. Contrary to what you might expect, the brains of those who scored well on the test showed *less* activity overall than those who did poorly. In others words, the high-scorers seemed to be more efficient thinkers, while the low-scorers seemed to use more brain area to solve the puzzles. Did the high-scorers inherit superior mental circuitry, or did they learn to use their brains more efficiently, or both?

Some people believe that intelligence cannot be increased with special training, that people are born with all the intelligence they will ever have and that programs such as Head Start, designed to boost scholastic achievement among minorities and the culturally disadvantaged, are a waste of time and money. These people subscribe to the genetic, or *nature,* point of view. Proponents of the genetic view generally assert that intelligence tests portray intelligence accurately.

Other people believe that intelligence is subject to experience and training and is a fluid, changing concept. They believe in the environmental, or *nurture,* point of view. Proponents of this view believe that today's intelligence tests are inadequate—that they do not measure a person's adaptation to a constantly changing environment. That environment is crucial to a person's IQ development

TABLE 23.3 Assessments for urban versus rural children

Test A	Test B
1. What are the colors in the American flag? *2.* Who is the president of the United States? *3.* What is the largest river in the United States? *4.* How can banks afford to pay interest on the money you deposit? *5.* What is the freezing point of water? *6.* What is a referendum in government?	*1.* Of what is butter made? *2.* Name a vegetable that grows above ground. *3.* Why does seasoned wood burn more easily than green wood? *4.* About how often do we have a full moon? *5.* Who was president of the U.S. during the World War? *6.* How can you locate the pole star?

Myra Shimberg (1929) standardized two tests on urban and rural schoolchildren in New York state. Each test contained 25 questions. These examples show clearly that they test for different kinds of information. Shimberg found that rural children scored significantly lower than urban children on Test A but higher than urban children on Test B. The difference between the scores of the two groups was in part a function of the tests themselves, not of any real difference in the children's intellectual capacities: Test A was biased toward urban children, Test B toward rural children.

TABLE 23.4 Some misconceptions about intelligence tests and testing

Misconception	Reality
Intelligence tests measure innate intelligence.	IQ scores measure some of an individual's interactions with the environment; they never solely measure innate intelligence.
IQs are fixed and never change.	People's IQs change throughout life, but especially from birth through age 6 years. Even after this age, significant changes can occur.
Intelligence tests provide perfectly reliable scores.	Test scores are only estimates. Every test score should be reported as a statement of probability, such as: "There is a 90% chance that the child's IQ falls between X and Y."
Intelligence tests measure all we need to know about a person's intelligence.	Most intelligence tests do not measure the entire spectrum of abilities related to intellectual behavior. Some stress verbal and nonverbal intelligence but do not adequately measure other areas, such as mechanical skills, creativity, and social intelligence.
A battery of tests can tell us everything we need to know in making judgments about a person's competence.	No battery of tests can give a complete picture of any person. A battery can only illuminate various areas of functioning.

Source: Adapted from Sattler, 1988.

seems obvious, because even so basic an intellectual capability as speech must be learned. Nonetheless, Arthur Jensen strongly endorses the *nature* point of view.

Arthur Jensen on the Side of Nature

Learning Objective 23.11 Discuss how comparisons are made among races and childrearing environments to explore the relative contributions of nature and nurture on intelligence.

Psychologists have long recognized that both biological capacities established even before birth (nature) and people's life experiences (nurture) play an important role in intelligence. However, as in other areas of psychology, researchers have debated the relative importance of nature and nurture. Arthur Jensen entered the debate in 1969 on the side of nature when he published a controversial article in the *Harvard Educational Review.*

Jensen addressed the issue of the difference in measured IQ scores between blacks and whites. In a study of 1200 California school children, Jensen found that on the average blacks scored 16 points lower on IQ tests than whites. Jensen concluded that genetic factors are strongly implicated in the difference, thus proposing heredity causes racial differences in intelligence.

The scientific community's response to Jensen's claim was immediate. Psychologists criticized his logic and challenged the accuracy of the studies he cited and the validity of IQ tests in general. Jensen was called a biased researcher. Despite these objections, since 1969, Jensen has continued to maintain that genetic heritage contributes significantly more than environmental factors to the development of intelligence (Jensen, 1976, 1977, 1980). Is Jensen's idea correct?

Environmental Studies

Another way in which researchers study the relative influence of environment and heredity is by investigating childrearing environments. One type of study compares the intellectual abilities of adopted children with the abilities of their adoptive parents (J. M. Horn, 1983). Many of these studies use identical twins who were separated at birth; because the twins share the same genetic heritage, any differences in IQ test scores must be the result of environmental influences.

One French adoption study showed a 14-point increase in IQ test scores in children whose biological parents were unskilled workers but whose adoptive parents were in a higher socioeconomic class (Schiff, Duyme, Dumaret, & Tomkiewicz, 1982). This study demonstrated that the effect of the environment is clearly potent. However, other data strongly suggest that home environment has a much *smaller* effect on a child's IQ than the genetic influence of the mother's IQ test score (Bouchard, Lykken, McGue, Segal, & Tellegen, 1990; McGue & Bouchard, 1989).

A classic environmental study administered IQ tests to children reared in different communities in the Blue Ridge Mountains, an isolated area 100 miles west of Washington, DC. (Sherman & Key, 1932). Most of the adults in each community were illiterate, and communication with the outside world was limited. The investigators concluded that lack of language training and school experience accounted for the children's poor scores on standardized tests, particularly on tests involving calculation and problem solving. Moreover, because the IQ scores of the children were highest in communities with the best social development and lowest in communities with the least social development, the researchers concluded that the children's IQ developed only as their environment demanded development. Angoff (1988) has similarly asserted that children from impoverished homes can achieve more on IQ tests, the Scholastic Aptitude Test (SAT), and other standardized tests if "cognitive training begins early in life and continues for an extended period . . . and is carried out in a continuously supportive and motivating atmosphere" (p. 717).

There is a myth that if a behavior or characteristic is genetic, then it cannot be changed. However, as Weinberg (1989) asserts, genes do not fix behavior; they establish a range of possible reactions. Environments determine whether the full range of genetic potential is expressed. Table 23.5 summarizes the correlations between IQ scores and childrearing environments for both related and unrelated children in two different studies. If genetics were the sole factor in determining IQ test scores, the correlation for identical twins should be 1.0 whether they were raised together or apart. Also, the correlation should not decrease when any two

TABLE 23.5 Median correlations between IQs of persons of various relationships, raised together or apart

Relationship and upbringing	Median correlation: Study 1	Median correlation: Study 2
Identical twins (monozygotic), reared together	.88	.85
Identical twins (monozygotic), reared apart	.75	.67
Fraternal twins (dizygotic), reared together	.53	.58
Siblings, reared together	.49	.45
Siblings, reared apart	.46	.24
Unrelated children, reared together	.17	.30

Sources: Study 1, Loehlin, Lindzey, & Spuhler, 1975; Study 2, Bouchard & McGue, 1981.

siblings (twins or not) are brought up apart from one another. However, identical twins raised together or apart do not have identical IQ scores—although their scores are similar (Bouchard et al., 1990). Researchers such as Bouchard conclude that about half of the similarities between identical twins can be accounted for by genetics. This finding lends strong support to the idea that genetics must play an important role—but not the sole role—in determining IQ scores. Based on these twin and home environment studies, we can conclude that Jensen's findings concerning the genetic component of intelligence are not entirely wrong, but that they provide only part of the explanation.

Environment and Intelligence

Learning Objective 23.12 Explain why differences in test scores between blacks and whites and between males and females are getting smaller.

An inspiring English teacher, a stimulating television series, or a neighbor with a chemistry set may be variables that affect differences between the IQ scores of siblings (McCall, 1983). Although siblings are often very similar to one another on a number of dimensions, they are also very different from one another (Dunn & Plomin, 1990). Siblings experience the same or similar environment differently. If an array of variables affect differences between brothers and sisters, it could be very difficult to estimate how they may affect differences among racial or ethnic groups.

Black–white differences in IQ scores, SAT scores, and other measures of achievement or ability are narrowing. This may be due to a generation of desegregation, more equal opportunities under the law, federal intervention programs for the culturally disadvantaged, or socioeconomic factors that affect home environments. Further, differences within groups are often greater than differences between groups, a fact that minimizes the importance of between-group differences (Zuckerman, 1990).

The fact remains that to a great extent, rather than measuring innate intellectual capacity, IQ tests measure the degree to which people adapt to the culture in which they live. All individuals have special capabilities, and how those capabilities are regarded depends on the social environment. Being a genius in Africa may mean being a fine hunter or a good storyteller; in the United States, it may mean being an astute and aggressive sales manager. Too often, the concept of giftedness is attached to high academic achievement alone. This limited conception of intelligence is one reason that educators in some settings are placing less emphasis on IQ test scores.

Researchers today assert that typical tests of intelligence are too limited because they do not take into account the many forms of intelligent behavior that occur outside of the testing room (Frederiksen, 1986). Frederiksen suggests that real-life problem situations might be used to supplement the usual psychological tests. This view is consistent with Sternberg's (1986a) idea that intelligence must be evaluated on many levels, including the environment in which a person lives and works. This means examining how people solve problems in their world and how they deal with novel situations and everyday problem-solving situations.

Gender Differences

Remember Maria: She excelled at science and her adviser suggested that she take an accelerated physics class. Was Maria's success in science genetically based? As a girl, is she more analytical? Are girls better than boys at some tasks; are boys better than girls at some tasks; or are they equal?

The consensus of psychologists has always been that gender differences exist in verbal ability, with girls exceeding boys in most verbal tasks in the early school years. However, how much of this finding is due to the cultural expectations of parents and teachers? At least some of the differences have been due to expectations. For example, parents and teachers alike have encouraged boys more than girls in spatial, mechanical tasks. Two interesting events have occurred in the past two decades. First, parents have been encouraging girls *and* boys in math, verbal, and spatial skills—there has been less gender stereotyping. Second, the observed cognitive differences between boys and girls have been diminishing each year. It turns out that the old consensus about gender differences is at a minimum exaggerated, and probably wrong. In general, differences between the test scores of males and females are disappearing (Feingold, 1988b).

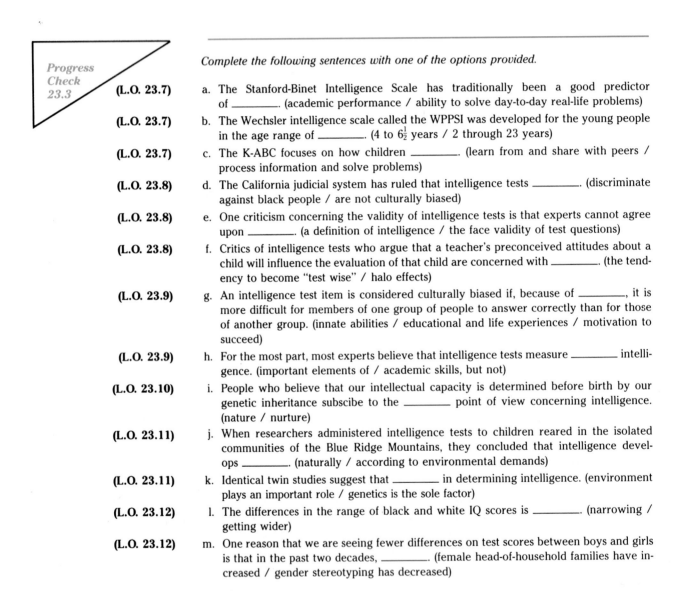

Progress Check 23.3

Complete the following sentences with one of the options provided.

(L.O. 23.7) a. The Stanford-Binet Intelligence Scale has traditionally been a good predictor of ________. (academic performance / ability to solve day-to-day real-life problems)

(L.O. 23.7) b. The Wechsler intelligence scale called the WPPSI was developed for the young people in the age range of ________. (4 to $6\frac{1}{2}$ years / 2 through 23 years)

(L.O. 23.7) c. The K-ABC focuses on how children ________. (learn from and share with peers / process information and solve problems)

(L.O. 23.8) d. The California judicial system has ruled that intelligence tests ________. (discriminate against black people / are not culturally biased)

(L.O. 23.8) e. One criticism concerning the validity of intelligence tests is that experts cannot agree upon ________. (a definition of intelligence / the face validity of test questions)

(L.O. 23.8) f. Critics of intelligence tests who argue that a teacher's preconceived attitudes about a child will influence the evaluation of that child are concerned with ________. (the tendency to become "test wise" / halo effects)

(L.O. 23.9) g. An intelligence test item is considered culturally biased if, because of ________, it is more difficult for members of one group of people to answer correctly than for those of another group. (innate abilities / educational and life experiences / motivation to succeed)

(L.O. 23.9) h. For the most part, most experts believe that intelligence tests measure ________ intelligence. (important elements of / academic skills, but not)

(L.O. 23.10) i. People who believe that our intellectual capacity is determined before birth by our genetic inheritance subscibe to the ________ point of view concerning intelligence. (nature / nurture)

(L.O. 23.11) j. When researchers administered intelligence tests to children reared in the isolated communities of the Blue Ridge Mountains, they concluded that intelligence develops ________. (naturally / according to environmental demands)

(L.O. 23.11) k. Identical twin studies suggest that ________ in determining intelligence. (environment plays an important role / genetics is the sole factor)

(L.O. 23.12) l. The differences in the range of black and white IQ scores is ________. (narrowing / getting wider)

(L.O. 23.12) m. One reason that we are seeing fewer differences on test scores between boys and girls is that in the past two decades, ________. (female head-of-household families have increased / gender stereotyping has decreased)

Module Summary

What Is Intelligence?

- Intelligence must be defined in terms of observable, objective behavior, it must consider both an individual's capacity to learn and his or her acquired knowledge, and it must indicate the person's ability to adapt to the environment. A widely accepted definition of intelligence is Wechsler's: The aggregate or global capacity of the individual to act purposefully, to think rationally, and to deal effectively with the environment (p. 440).
- According to Guilford, human intellectual abilities and activities can be described in terms of three major dimensions: the mental operations performed, the content of those operations, and the resulting product of the operations (p. 444).

Testing

- Standardization is the process of developing a uniform procedure for the administration and scoring of a test (p. 446).
- Standardization includes the development of norms: the scores and corresponding percentile ranks of the large representative sample of subjects on whom the test was standardized (p. 447).

Three Important Intelligence Tests

- The Stanford-Binet has been a good predictor of academic performance, and many of its tests correlate highly with one another (p. 450).
- The Wechsler scales group test items by content while the K-ABC consists of four global scales: Three measure mental-processing abilities (sequential processing, simultaneous processing, and a composite of the two); the fourth assesses achievement (p. 451).

Testing Controversy: Validity and Cultural Biases

- There are five basic criticisms of—and defenses for—the validity of tests and testing. The first focuses on the *definition of intelligence*. The second focuses on *learned information*. The third criticism is that *school settings* may adversely affect IQ. The remaining criticisms of testing focus on the *issue of validity* and people's *motivation to succeed* (p. 452).
- Although researchers find differences among the IQ test scores of various racial and cultural groups, they find no conclusive evidence of bias in the tests themselves (p. 453).

Intelligence: Nature Versus Nurture

- Proponents of the genetic view generally assert that intelligence tests portray intelligence accurately. Proponents of the nurture view believe that today's intelligence tests are inadequate, that they do not measure a person's adaptation to a constantly changing environment (p. 455).
- The evidence of many studies conducted with a variety of intelligence tests and ethnic minority groups indicates that currently used intelligence tests are not culturally biased (p. 456).

KEY TERMS

alternative form, p. 448
deviation IQ, p. 448
face validity, p. 452
factor-theory approach to intelligence, p. 441
factor analysis, p. 441
halo effect, p. 452
intelligence, p. 440
normal curve, p. 447
norm, p. 447
percentile score, p. 447
raw score, p. 447
reliability, p. 448
representative sample, p. 446
standard error of measurement, p. 448
standard score, p. 447
standardization, p. 446
test–retest validity, p. 448
validity, p. 448

SELF-TEST

Module 23

- Before taking the self-test, **recite** and **review.**
- Use the key at the back of the text to *correct* your answers.
- *Restudy* pages that correspond to any questions you answered incorrectly.

1. In order to predict a person's potential for achieving in school, psychologists rely on
   a. reading, writing, and math assessment scores.
   b. intelligence test scores obtained from standardized tests.
   c. characteristics such as talkativeness, looks, and income.
   d. a variety of test scores, interviews, teacher evaluations, and writing and drawing samples.
2. Which of the following is *not* a concept that is included in most definitions of intelligence?
   a. observable, objective behavior
   b. capacity to learn and knowledge already acquired
   c. mathematical and social skills
   d. ability to adapt to the environment
3. Spearman's two-factor theory of intelligence suggests that intelligence consists of
   a. divergent and convergent thought.
   b. general and specific abilities.
   c. content and product.
   d. operations and content.
4. Robert Sternberg, the psychologist who has criticized the validity of most existing intelligence tests, suggests that the three dimensions of intelligence are
   a. contextual, experiential, and componential
   b. associative, cognitive, and interactive
   c. novel, original, and appropriate
   d. operations, content, and product
5. The first useful and practical intelligence test was developed
   a. by David Wechsler.
   b. by Alfred Binet and Theodore Simon.
   c. in the United States.
   d. Both b and c
6. Vincent's teacher informed him that 92% of his classmates scored lower than he did on an intelligence test. The number 92 represents
   a. an intelligence quotient.
   b. a deviation IQ.
   c. a percentile score.
   d. a raw score.
7. Jill took an intelligence test at her college, and a month later, while applying for a job, she was asked to take the same intelligence test. The first time she took the test, her deviation IQ was 127; the second time it was 92. Based on this information, we can say that
   a. one of the tests was not interpreted accurately.
   b. the test was not reliable.
   c. she felt more stress over qualifying for a job than she felt qualifying for college.
   d. Jill's intelligence decreased one standard deviation in 1 month.
8. Elias achieves a deviation IQ of 121. The school psychologist tells him she is confident his real IQ scores falls somewhere between 117 and 125. This indicates that the IQ test
   a. is valid.
   b. was standardized to a population that does not adequately represent Elias.
   c. cannot be used to predict achievement or success.
   d. has a standard error of measurement of 4.

9. The Kaufman Assessment Battery for Children (K-ABC) was designed
   a. to assess, intervene, and remediate children experiencing learning problems in school.
   b. to measure the intellectual abilities of preschoolers.
   c. so that intelligence can be measured while children are engaged in pleasurable activities such as drawing and painting.
   d. Both a and c
10. The Wechsler intelligence scales probably would *not* give reliable and valid results if used to measure the intellectual abilities of
    a. children under the age of 3 years.
    b. cross-cultural populations.
    c. learning-disabled students.
    d. people with psychiatric/clinical diagnoses.
11. A criticism concerning the validity of intelligence tests is that
    a. they reflect the quality of a child's schooling rather than actual intelligence.
    b. they contain test items that require the use of common sense.
    c. they make use of vocabulary words learned in the general environment.
    d. the items on intelligence tests are often unfamiliar even to experienced test-takers.
12. Jensen says that it is a myth to think that IQ tests discriminate according to race and social class because in his research he found that differences between IQ scores
    a. was as great between siblings as it was between racial groups.
    b. among blacks and whites was insignificant.
    c. narrows once children begin to go to school.
    d. had more to do with attitudes than with race or social class.
13. Which of the following best explains the relative contributions of nature and nurture to intelligence?
    a. Some people are born winners; others are born losers.
    b. Genes establish a range of potential; environments determine to what degree that potential is actually expressed.
    c. Genetic potential is fixed; environmental factors are fluid.
    d. Genetic heritage determines intelligence; environmental factors determine academic skills.
14. Based on twin and home environment studies, we can conclude that Jensen's assertion about genetics contributing more than environments to the development of intelligence is
    a. accurate.
    b. completely inaccurate.
    c. only a partial explanation.
    d. prejudicial and unethical.
15. Behavior that is considered intelligent behavior must be defined
    a. in a social and cultural context.
    b. according to white middle-class standards.
    c. with regard to the type of questions and tasks that can be used on standardized intelligence tests.
    d. by developing a clear understanding of the skills that lead to high academic achievement.

Module 24

Exceptionality and Assessment

LEARNING OBJECTIVES

When you have mastered the material in this module, you will be able to

Introduction (p. 463)

24.1 Discuss the types of evaluation and classification that take place in grade school and explain what is meant by the term *exceptional* (p. 463).

Giftedness (pp. 463–464)

24.2 Explain what it means to be "gifted" and discuss some problems a gifted child might encounter in the public schools (p. 463).

Mental Retardation (pp. 464–467)

24.3 Characterize mental retardation and describe the four levels used when diagnosing the mentally retarded (p. 464).

24.4 Discuss changes that have taken place in schools as a result of the Education for All Handicapped Children Act and describe the concept of mainstreaming (p. 465).

Psychological Assessment (pp. 467–472)

24.5 Explain why psychologists are interested in assessing individuals and describe some of the well-known assessment tests that they use (p. 467).

24.6 Name, describe, and cite examples of four popular behavioral assessment techniques used by psychologists (p. 470).

SQ3R
- ▲ **Survey** to set goals for studying.
- ▲ Ask **questions** as you **read.**
- ▲ Stop occasionally to **recite** and **review.**

plus
- ▲ **Write** a summary of key points.
- ▲ **Reflect** on the hypotheses, evidence, and implications of this material and on the relevance it has to *your* life.

Learning Objective 24.1
Discuss the types of evaluation and classification that take place in grade school, and explain what is meant by the term *exceptional.*

Aileen Weiss is a former member of the President's commission on mental retardation. In that role, she became an advocate of the needs of exceptional individuals. Her passion and concern were driven in part by her personal understanding of special needs. She said it best in her own words:

> I am the mother of a twenty-year old mentally retarded daughter. Twenty years ago I had no training for raising a developmentally disabled child, but it didn't take long before I realized that raising her would take courage, persistence, ingenuity, good humor, commitment, and fight—just to get her the very things that every human being takes for granted.
>
> Vicki was diagnosed as severely and profoundly retarded, and you would have thought that she had a dread disease. For some reason everything she needed was called "special"—special schools, special medical treatment, special job training, special work.
>
> My daughter Vicki will be twenty-one years old in July, and there is no way her mother and father will outlive her; therefore, Vicki now has another need. I am asking all of you to be Vicki's advocate. Advocacy is a tough business, but you must not back down from your commitment to fulfill her basic human needs and rights. The law is a great promise; but the fact is that the passage of new legislation will not bring about easy or quick changes. Due process, legal provisions won't add up to instant solutions to problems that have been around a long time. Change is going to take a lot of work, but when that change comes, we well realize that the needs of developmentally disabled persons were never special needs at all. They just are the needs of other human beings.

Vicki Weiss is doing well, and her parents and many other educators and legislators are working diligently to help those with different abilities and needs. American society is oriented toward educating, testing, and looking for the special or exceptional child. As early as the first weeks of the first grade, most students take some kind of reading readiness test; by the end of the fourth grade, they are usually labeled and classified as to their projected future development, again largely on the basis of tests. The term *exceptional* refers to people who are gifted as well as to those who have learning disabilities, physical impairments, and mental retardation.

Giftedness

Learning Objective 24.2
Explain what it means to be "gifted," and discuss some problems a gifted child might encounter in the public schools.

In the movie *Amadeus,* the court composer Salieri is intensely jealous of the musical gifts of his rival, Mozart. Salieri is obviously a very intelligent man, an eloquent conversationalist, and an accomplished musician. He is cunning in his attempts to ruin Mozart. Conceivably, Salieri would have scored at least as high as Mozart on a traditional IQ test. Yet Mozart's musical talent dwarfed Salieri's. What made Mozart so different?

J.P. Guilford, one of the leading researchers in intelligence testing, whom we discussed earlier, developed a theory about the nature of intellectual functioning. He argued that there is more to intelligence than a high score on a subtest of the WISC-III. He contended that some people are exceptional in traditionally defined ways, such as those measurable by a high IQ score, but that others are exceptional

mental retardation: Below-average intellectual functioning as measured on an IQ test, accompanied by an impairment in adaptive behavior originating during childhood.

in nontraditional ways (e.g., Mozart, who displayed his genius musically, and Madame Curie, who displayed hers in science).

Gifted individuals represent one end of the continuum of intelligent and talented behavior. However, exceptional ability is not limited to cognitive skills. Most 6-year-olds enrolled in a ballet class will probably show average ability; dance teachers report that only an occasional child has a natural proclivity for and ability to dance. In the same way, many children and adults learn to play the piano, but few excel. Over a wide range of behaviors, some people excel in a particular area far beyond normal expectations but in other areas are rather average.

The phenomenon of gifted children has been recognized and discussed for centuries. Some, like Mozart, display their genius musically. Others display it in science; many great scientists made their most important theoretical discoveries very early in their careers. Although there is no universally accepted definition of giftedness (just as there is no universally agreed-upon definition of intelligence), one was given in the Gifted and Talented Children's Act of 1978:

> The term *gifted and talented* means children, and whenever applicable, youth who are identified at the preschool, elementary, or secondary level as possessing demonstrated or potential abilities that give evidence of high performance responsibility in areas such as intellectual, creative, specific academic or leadership ability, or in the performing visual arts and who by reason thereof require services or activities not ordinarily provided by the school. (Section 902)

Thus, gifted children may have superior cognitive, leadership, or performing arts abilities. Moreover, gifted individuals require special education that goes beyond the ordinary classroom. Without special schooling, these children may not realize their potentials.

The United States has a special love-hate relationship with gifted individuals. Although everyone wants the gifted to succeed and realizes that their successes represent breakthroughs in science and the arts, public schools are designed for the average child and may isolate and even cause ridicule of students who are unique. Moreover, even though the federal government acknowledges the need for special education for gifted individuals, states and communities bear the major financial burden for their education (about 92%). Most do not offer gifted programs for all grades (Reis, 1989); however, like the needs of students with mental retardation (considered next), the special needs of students who are gifted should not be addressed only 1 day a week or only in Grades 1 through 6.

Mental Retardation

Learning Objective 24.3 Characterize mental retardation, and describe the four levels used when diagnosing the mentally retarded.

Mental retardation covers a wide range of behaviors, from slow learning to severe mental and physical impairment. Many people with mental retardation are able to cope well with their environments. Most learn to walk and to feed and dress themselves; many learn to read and are able to work. There are a variety of causes for mental retardation from deprived environments (especially for those with mild retardation) to genetic abnormalities, infectious diseases, and physical trauma (including drugs taken by pregnant women).

Levels of Retardation

A diagnosis of **mental retardation** involves three criteria: a lower-than-normal (below 70) IQ test score, as measured on a standardized test such as the WISC-III or the WAIS-R; difficulty adapting to the environment; and the presence of such problems before age 18 years. There are four basic levels of mental retardation, each corresponding to a different range of scores on a standardized IQ test (see Table 24.1).

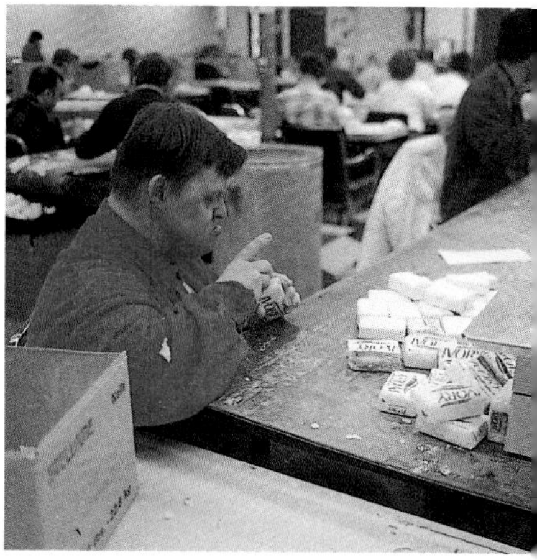

With proper training, many retarded adults are able to successfully get and keep a job.

Mild Retardation. People with mild mental retardation (Wechsler IQs of 55–69) account for approximately 90% of people classified as mentally retarded. Through special programs, they are able to acquire academic and occupational skills but generally need some supervision in their work (e.g., Allington, 1981). As adults, people with mild mental retardation function intellectually at the level of a 10-year-old. Thus, with some help from family and friends, most people with mild mental retardation can cope successfully with their environments.

Moderate Retardation. People with moderate mental retardation (Wechsler IQs of 40–54) account for approximately 6% of those classified as mentally retarded. Most live in institutions or as dependents of their families. Those who are not institutionalized need special classes; some can hold simple jobs, although few are employed. People with moderate mental retardation are able to speak, write, and interact with friends, but their motor coordination, posture, and social skills are clumsy. Their intellectual level is equivalent to that of a 5- to 6-year-old.

Severe Retardation. Only about 3% of people with mental retardation display severe retardation (Wechsler IQs of 25–39). People with severe mental retardation show great motor, speech, and intellectual impairment and are almost totally dependent on others to take care of their basic needs. Severe retardation often results from birth disorders or traumatic injury to the brain.

Profound Retardation. About 1% of people with mental retardation are classified as profoundly retarded (IQs below 25). These people are unable to master even simple tasks and require total supervision and constant care. Their motor development and intellectual development is minimal, and many are physically underdeveloped. Physical deformities and other congenital defects (such as deafness, blindness, and seizures) often accompany profound mental retardation.

The Law and Education

Learning Objective 24.4
Discuss changes that have taken place in schools as a result of the Education for All Handicapped Children Act, and describe the concept of mainstreaming.

Until recently, thousands of children used to be given substandard educations after doing poorly on an intelligence test. Labeled as slow learners or perhaps mentally retarded, these children were given neither special education nor special attention. But in 1975 the federal government passed Public Law 94-142 (PL 94-142),

TABLE 24.1 Types of distribution of mental retardation, as measured on the Stanford-Binet and Wechsler tests

Classification	Stanford-Binet IQ	Wechsler IQ	Percentage of the mentally retarded	Educational level possible
Mild	52–68	55–69	90	Sixth grade
Moderate	36–51	40–54	6	Second to fouth grade
Severe	20–35	25–39	3	Limited speech
Profound	Below 20	Below 25	1	Unresponsive to training

APPLYING PSYCHOLOGY

Employing Workers with Mental Retardation

Companies are realizing that if people with mild mental retardation are placed in the right job, are properly trained, and are effectively motivated, they can be counted on to be good workers. As a result, many companies now hire workers with mental retardation who were once thought unemployable.

Drawbacks do exist in hiring workers with mental retardation. One is that training them often requires extra patience. A more detailed and carefully defined training program is usually necessary; behavioral techniques such as those described in Chapter 5 are used extensively. Even a relatively simple task may be broken down into 30 or 40 individual steps. Workers with mental retardation sometimes need help to keep them focused on their job, such as prompts from supervisors or a checklist. In addition, they may work more slowly than others in the same position and may require training in social skills as well, for example in being friendly and smiling at coworkers. Also, workers who have lower IQs and may be less adept at personal grooming and may not read, write, tell time, or handle money well.

Nonetheless, there are also great successes. Those workers who have been brought through training programs do exceptionally well. Workers with mental retardation are likely to stay with jobs that others tire of. They may be more dependable, motivated, and industrious than other workers. After they are trained, they have few problems adjusting to the routine of a nine-to-five job. Owners of fast-food restaurants who hire workers with mental retardation (e.g., McDonalds) report that these workers never come in late and are rarely sick. They consider their new workers reliable and dependable. Marriott Corporation employs more than 1,000 workers who are mentally retarded. In addition, the federal government provides tax benefits to employers of the mentally or physically handicapped. People labelled as mentally retarded and unemployable are working, earning a wage, and handling their lives impressively. They do far better in their lives outside of their jobs than they ever did before—because of the law and mainstreaming.

The federal government has taken an extensive role in the education and support of individuals with mental retardation and provides Supplemental Social Security Income payments to unemployed workers with mental retardation. Advocates of indivuals with mental retardation are concerned because the costs of such support programs are rising very quickly. This makes work training programs even more valuable; various states are providing funds heretofore reserved only for institutions to businesses and colleges for the purpose of training mentally retarded workers. Such programs are money-savers for local government; workers who earn money pay taxes and do not require support payments. The task for government is substantial, and the challenge, in terms of numbers of persons and financial cost, is formidable.

Educators and parents are pushing hard for reform, government support, innovative training programs, and the active support of businesses. Businesses can help move people with mental retardation from the welfare rolls to the employment rolls. Promoting change is difficult, especially in large corporations, but it is possible.

- ▲ ***Identify the difficulties associated with hiring workers with mental retardation.***
- ▲ ***What are the implications in terms of costs to the state and federal government when employers hire the mentally retarded.***

the Education for All Handicapped Children Act. Originally conceived to improve school programs for physically handicapped children, its passage insured individualized testing and educationally relevant programs for all children.

The law holds that all school aged children must be provided an appropriate, free public education. After testing, children with special needs are not to be grouped separately unless they have severe handicaps. Tests for identification and placement be unbiased. Further, educational programs must be arranged to make them as close to normal as possible, with the unique needs of each child considered. An individualized educational plan (or program; an IEP) must be arranged by school in consultation with the parents. The law also mandates that schools must follow specific procedures: an explanation of rights, evaluation procedures, regular reevaluation, and reasons for any changes in a student's status.

PL 94-142 significantly increased the amount of testing in the public school systems, leading to more labeling and classification; many see this is a disadvantage. However, the implementation of the law has also guaranteed thousands of children with special needs an appropriate education. This is costly for local school districts, but when students need special education, they can rely on the courts to make sure that the school system provides it.

Since the passage of PL 94-142, there has been a shift toward **mainstreaming,** the integration of all children with special needs into regular classroom settings whenever appropriate. (Technically, the law requires students to be placed in the least restrictive—or unusual—environment feasible.) Its purpose is to make life as normal as possible for these children by requiring that they and their teachers and classmates cope with their current skill level and expand upon it as much as possible. In mainstreaming, children are assigned to a regular class for at least half of their school day. For the rest of the day, they are often in special education classrooms or in vocational training situations. Although research studies on mainstreaming have produced conflicting data on its effectiveness, psychologists and educators generally support it.

mainstreaming: The administrative practice of placing exceptional children in regular classroom settings with the support of special education services.

assessment: The process of evaluating individual differences among human beings by using tests and direct observation of behavior. The role of the clinician is central in assessment techniques.

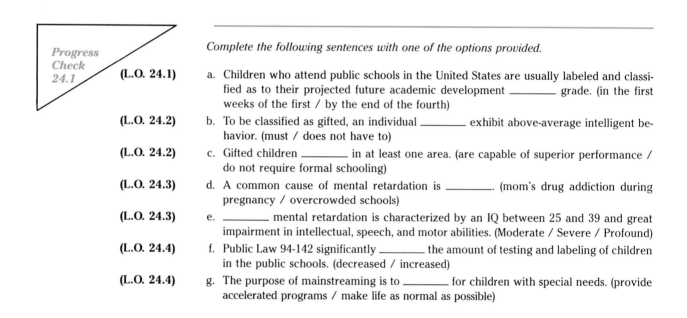

Progress Check 24.1

Complete the following sentences with one of the options provided.

(L.O. 24.1) a. Children who attend public schools in the United States are usually labeled and classified as to their projected future academic development ________ grade. (in the first weeks of the first / by the end of the fourth)

(L.O. 24.2) b. To be classified as gifted, an individual ________ exhibit above-average intelligent behavior. (must / does not have to)

(L.O. 24.2) c. Gifted children ________ in at least one area. (are capable of superior performance / do not require formal schooling)

(L.O. 24.3) d. A common cause of mental retardation is ________. (mom's drug addiction during pregnancy / overcrowded schools)

(L.O. 24.3) e. ________ mental retardation is characterized by an IQ between 25 and 39 and great impairment in intellectual, speech, and motor abilities. (Moderate / Severe / Profound)

(L.O. 24.4) f. Public Law 94-142 significantly ________ the amount of testing and labeling of children in the public schools. (decreased / increased)

(L.O. 24.4) g. The purpose of mainstreaming is to ________ for children with special needs. (provide accelerated programs / make life as normal as possible)

Psychological Assessment

Psychologists are constantly seeking ways to evaluate people in order to explain behavior, to diagnose and classify maladjusted people, and to develop treatment plans when necessary (Haynes, 1984). **Assessment** is the process of evaluating individual differences that occur among human beings, using methods such as intelligence tests, interviews, observations, and recordings of physiological processes. A number of tests and techniques are used to help assess an individual's intelligence and personality; often more than one assessment procedure must be used to provide all the necessary information. Therefore, many psychologists administer a group or a battery of tests.

Learning Objective 24.5 Explain why psychologists are interested in assessing individuals, and describe some of the well-known assessment tests that they use.

A psychologist may assess personality with the Minnesota Multiphasic Personality Inventory—2nd edition (MMPI-2), intelligence with the WAIS-R, and a specific skill, such as coordination, with some other specific test. More confidence can be placed in the data from several tests than in data from a single test; further, with several measures, current levels of functioning are better characterized. It is interesting to note that hundreds of psychological tests exits; there are over 100 tests just for measuring the various elements of anxiety. The purpose of the testing determines the type of tests administered, and the comprehensiveness of the battery increases the likelihood that their use will be valued, such as in courtroom settings (Matarazzo, 1990).

Intelligence Tests

Often, the first test given in a psychological assessment is an *intelligence test.* These tests provide specific information about a person's level of intellectual functioning and, therefore, can be good predictors of academic achievement—an important part of personality development. They may give an overall IQ score, separate verbal IQ and performance IQ scores (e.g., in the WISC-III), or all three types of scores. However, intelligence tests are limited because they provide only a general indication of a person's behavior pattern.

Objective Personality Tests

Next to intelligence tests, the most widely given tests are *objective tests* of personality. These tests, sometimes termed *personality inventories,* generally consist of true–false or check-the-best-answer questions. The aim of objective personality tests varies. Cattell developed a test called the *16PF* to screen job applicants or to examine individuals who fall within a normal range of functioning. The California Personality Inventory (CPI) is used primarily to identify and assess normal aspects of personality. Using a large sample of normal subjects as a reference group, it examines personality traits such as sociability, self-control, and responsibility.

One of the most widely used and well-researched personality tests is the MMPI. The original MMPI was widely used, and the new MMPI-2 published in 1989 is considered a significant and major revision. The MMPI-2 consists of 567 true–false statements that focus on attitudes, feelings, motor disturbances, and bodily complaints. A series of subscales examine different aspects of functioning and measure the truthfulness of the subject's responses. Typical statements are as follows:

- ▲ I tire easily.
- ▲ I become very anxious before examinations.
- ▲ I worry about sex matters.
- ▲ I become bored easily.

The MMPI-2 can be administered individually or to a group. The test takes 90 minutes to complete and can be scored in less than $\frac{1}{2}$ hour. It provides a profile that lets psychologists assess an individual's current level of functioning and characteristic way of dealing with the world, and it provides a description of some specific personality characteristics. The MMPI-2 also enables psychologists to make reasonable predictions about a person's ability to function in specific situations, such as working in a mental hospital or as a security guard.

Generally, the MMPI-2 is used as a screening device for maladjustment. The norms for the MMPI-2 are based on the profiles of thousands of normal people and a smaller group of psychiatric patients. Each scale tells how most normal individuals score; a score far above or below normal is an important indicator. In general, a score significantly above normal may be considered evidence of maladjustment.

Nearly 5000 published studies have examined the validity and reliability of the original MMPI. For the most part, these studies have supported the MMPI as a valid and useful predictive tool. The MMPI-2 now has a better representative sample of minorities that reflects the overall population, a much larger (2600) sample of subjects for standardization (also, the subjects were more representative of the population than were the initial group of subjects used for standardization). The MMPI-2 adds questions that focus on eating disorders and drug abuse. Older questions that had a gender bias were revised. Newer studies will soon evaluate the MMPI-2; because many of the traditional features of the test remain unchanged, the refinements and modifications should only improve the test's predictive validity.

projective test: A variety of devices or instruments used to assess personality, in which an examinee is shown a standard set of ambiguous stimuli and asked to respond in an unrestricted manner.

Projective Tests

The fundamental idea underlying the use of a **projective test** is that a person's unconscious motives direct daily thoughts and behavior. To uncover those motives, researchers provide ambiguous stimuli to which examinees can provide responses that might reflect their unconscious. The examinee thus reflects or projects unconscious feelings, drives, and motives onto the ambiguous stimuli. Clinicians assess the deeper levels of a person's personality structure and detect motives of which the examinee is not aware. Projective tests are used when it is particularly important to determine whether the examinee is trying to hide something from the psychologist. They tend to be less reliable than objective personality tests, but they help complete a picture of psychological functioning.

Rorschach Inkblot Test. A widely used projective test is the Rorschach Inkblot Test. Ten inkblots are shown, one at a time, to an examinee. Five are black and white, two have some red ink, and three have various pastel colors. They are symmetrical, with a specific shape or form (see Figure 24.1).

After the 10 inkblots have been shown, the examiner asks specific questions, such as "Describe the facelike figures" or "What were the figures talking about?" Subjects tell the clinician what they see in the design; a detailed report of the response is made for later interpretation. Although norms are available for responses, skilled interpretation and good clinical judgment are necessary for placing a subject's responses in a meaningful context. Long-term predictions can be formulated only with great caution (Exner, Thomas, & Mason, 1985).

Thematic Apperception Test. The *Thematic Apperception Test,* or TAT (which was discussed in Chapter 10 as one way to assess a person's need for achievement), is much more structured than the Rorschach. The TAT consists of black-

Figure 24.1

In a Rorschach test, the psychologist asks the subject to describe what he or she sees in an inkblot such as the one above. From these descriptions, the psychologist makes inferences about the subject's drives, motivations, and unconscious conflicts.

and-white pictures depicting one or more people in ambiguous situations, and subjects are asked to tell a story describing the situation in each picture. Specifically, they are asked what led up to the situation, what will happen in the future, and what the people are thinking and feeling.

The TAT is particularly useful as part of a battery of tests to examine a person's characteristic way of dealing with others and of interacting with the world. To some extent, projective tests have a bad reputation among nonpsychologists. Some people feel that interpretation of pictures is too subjective and prone to error, and others even suspect a bit of hocus-pocus.

Behavioral Assessment

Learning Objective 24.6 Name, describe and cite examples of four popular behavioral assessment techniques used by psychologists.

Traditionally, *behavioral assessment* focused on overt behaviors that could be examined directly. Today, practitioners and researchers examine cognitive activity as well. Their aim is to gather information both to diagnose maladjustment and to prescribe treatment. Four popular and widely used behavioral assessment techniques are behavioral assessment interviews, naturalistic observation, self-monitoring, and neuropsychological assessment.

Behavioral Assessment Interviews. It is likely that any psychological assessment begins with an interview. Interviews are personal, giving a client (and the client's family) an opportunity to express feelings, facts, and experiences that might not be expressed through other assessment procedures. Interviews yield important information about a client's family situation, occupational stresses, and other events that affect the behavior being examined. They also allow psychologists to evaluate a client's motivations, as well as inform the client about the assessment process.

Behavioral assessment interviews tend to be systematic and structured, focusing on overt and current behaviors and paying attention to the situations in which these behaviors occur. An interviewer will ask an examinee about the events that led up to a specific response, how the examinee felt as he or she made the response, and whether the same response might occur in other situations. The clinician has the opportunity to select the problems to be faced in therapy and to set treatment goals. Many clinicians consider their first interview with a client a key component in the assessment process.

Interviews reveal only what the interviewee wishes to disclose, however, and are subject to bias on the part of the interviewer. Nonetheless, together with other behavioral measures, interviews are a good starting point.

The Thematic Apperception Test (TAT) requires subjects to relate an imagined story to an ambiguous illustration. Responses are interpreted with the intention of gaining a better understanding of the way they deal with people and real-life situations.

Naturalistic Observation. In behavioral assessment, *naturalistic observation* involves two or more observers entering a client's natural environment and recording the occurrence of specified behaviors at predetermined intervals. In a personality assessment, for example, psychologists might observe how often a child in a classroom uses obscene words or how often a hospitalized patient refers to his or her depressed state. The purpose of naturalistic observation as a behavioral assessment technique is to observe people without interference by or the influence of a psychologist. The strength of the approach is in providing information that might otherwise be unavailable or difficult to piece together. For example, it can help psychologists realize the sequence of actions that may lead up to an outburst of depressed feelings or to antisocial behaviors.

Naturalistic observation is not without its problems, however. How does a researcher record behavior in a home setting without being observed? Do naturalistic samples of behavior represent interactions in other settings? Does the observer have any biases, make inaccurate judgments, or collect enough data? Although naturalistic observation is not perfect, it is a powerful technique of behavioral assessment.

Self-Monitoring. **Self-monitoring** is an assessment procedure in which a person systematically counts and records the frequency and duration of specific behaviors in himself or herself. A person might record the number and duration of specific personality traits or symptoms, such as migraine headaches, backaches, or feelings of panic. Another person might self-monitor eating or sleeping patterns, sexual behavior, or smoking.

self-monitoring: An assessment procedure in which a person systematically records the frequency and duration of specific behaviors in himself or herself.

Self-monitoring is inexpensive to conduct, easy to do, and applicable for a variety of problems. It reveals information that might otherwise be inaccessible and enables practitioners to probe the events that preceded the monitored activity to see whether some readily identifiable pattern exists. In addition, self-monitoring helps a person become more aware of his or her own behaviors and the situations in which they occur.

Neuropsychological Assessment. The newest branch of assessment is *neuropsychological assessment.* Whereas *neurologists* are physicians who study the physiology of the brain and its disorders, *neuropsychologists* are psychologists who study the brain and its disorders as they relate to behavior. Though neuropsychology is a traditional area in experimental psychology, practitioners now routinely watch for signs of neuropsychological disorders; in the past, such monitoring was uncommon.

Often, low I.Q. test scores, personality changes, and some forms of maladjustment result from some type of brain disorder or malfunction in the nervous system. The signs may be evident from traditional assessment devices, such as histories (history of headaches), intelligence tests (slow reaction times), or observation of the client during a session (head motions or muscle spasms). Thus, when a child is making obscene gestures or remarks frequently and inappropriately, and these are accompanied by facial tics, a practitioner may wonder whether the cause may be neurological disorder Gilles de la Tourette syndrome, in which such behaviors are often evident, is the cause. When psychologists see evidence of a neuropsychological deficit, they often refer a client to a neuropsychologist or neurologist for further evaluation.

Professionals are often called in to assess the coping mechanisms and the overall effectiveness of office workers.

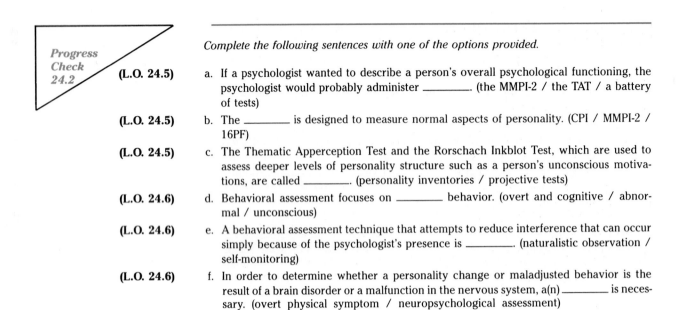

Progress Check 24.2

Complete the following sentences with one of the options provided.

(L.O. 24.5) a. If a psychologist wanted to describe a person's overall psychological functioning, the psychologist would probably administer ________. (the MMPI-2 / the TAT / a battery of tests)

(L.O. 24.5) b. The ________ is designed to measure normal aspects of personality. (CPI / MMPI-2 / 16PF)

(L.O. 24.5) c. The Thematic Apperception Test and the Rorschach Inkblot Test, which are used to assess deeper levels of personality structure such as a person's unconscious motivations, are called ________. (personality inventories / projective tests)

(L.O. 24.6) d. Behavioral assessment focuses on ________ behavior. (overt and cognitive / abnormal / unconscious)

(L.O. 24.6) e. A behavioral assessment technique that attempts to reduce interference that can occur simply because of the psychologist's presence is ________. (naturalistic observation / self-monitoring)

(L.O. 24.6) f. In order to determine whether a personality change or maladjusted behavior is the result of a brain disorder or a malfunction in the nervous system, a(n) ________ is necessary. (overt physical symptom / neuropsychological assessment)

Module Summary

Giftedness

- Gifted children are those with superior cognitive, leadership, or artistic abilities (p. 464).
- Almost 2 million children in American public schools could be classified as gifted (p. 464).

Mental Retardation

- *Mental retardation* is below-average intellectual functioning, together with an impairment in adaptive behavior, originating before age 18 years. There are four basic categories of mental retardation, each corresponding to a specific range of scores on a standardized test of intelligence. The behaviors associated with mental retardation vary from slow learning to an inability to care for oneself due to impaired physical, motor, and intellectual development (pp. 464–465).
- *Mainstreaming* is the integration of exceptional children—especially children with mental retardation—into a regular classroom setting. The purpose of mainstreaming is to help normalize the life experiences of such children (p. 467).

Psychological Assessment

- *Assessment* is the process of evaluating individual differences that occur among human beings, using techniques of intelligence tests, interviews, observations in natural settings, and the recordings of physiological measures (p. 467).
- Behavioral assessment uses diagnosis, evaluation, and suggestions for treatments in which direct observation, self-evaluation, and interviews and components (p. 470).

KEY TERMS

assessment, p. 467
mainstreaming, p. 467
mental retardation, p. 464
projective test, p. 469
self-monitoring, p. 471

SELF-TEST

Module 24

- Before taking the self-test, **recite** and **review.**
- Use the key at the back of the text to *correct* your answers.
- *Restudy* pages that correspond to any questions you answered incorrectly.

1. The term *exceptional* refers to people who are
   a. are gifted.
   b. are mentally retarded.
   c. have learning disabilities or physical impairments.
   d. all of the above.
2. A gifted person will demonstrate a superior level of performance in
   a. intellectual or creative thinking abilities.
   b. performing visual arts.
   c. specific academic or leadership abilities.
   d. abilities in all or one of the above areas or in some other area.
3. In the United States,
   a. most states offer special classes for the gifted in kindergarten through 12th grade.
   b. gifted children are privileged children; they get the best of all the resources a school system can offer.
   c. schools are designed and funded with the average child in mind.
   d. all of the above.
4. Choose the statement would be most helpful in diagnosing a person as mentally retarded.
   a. The symptoms must be present before the age of 12 years.
   b. The person must be educated in a specialized environment, away from normal children.
   c. The person's behavior appears erratic, eccentric, or emotional.
   d. The person must score below 70 on a standardized intelligence test.
5. A mildly retarded person
   a. can achieve an intellectual level comparable to a 13-year-old.
   b. is able to work in occupational skill areas with some supervision.
   c. takes care of personal hygiene, but cannot learn to read or write.
   d. scores under 55 on the Wechsler Intelligence Scales.
6. Public Law 94-142 requires public schools to
   a. separate and group all children with special needs into classes with other children who have similar needs.
   b. provide all children with educationally relevant school programs.
   c. follow specific procedures to ensure individual rights, proper evaluation, and placement.
   d. Both b and c
7. Psychological assessment refers to
   a. a process of evaluating an individual to determine how the person differs from others in certain areas of behavior and mental processing.
   b. determining an appropriate label or diagnosis for characterizing a person's behavior.
   c. evaluating the professional demeanor of a clinical psychologist.
   d. helping a person overcome problems that resulted from a harsh and abusive childhood.

8. Which of the following statements concerning the MMPI is true?
   a. The test has a built-in measure for determining the "truthfulness" of the person's answers.
   b. To complete the test, a person answers 567 multiple-choice questions.
   c. The test is a projective test.
   d. The test allows psychologists to accurately predict exactly how a person will function in any situation.
9. A test that is especially useful because it provides information concerning a person's characteristic way of interacting with others is the
   a. Minnesota Multiphasic Personality Inventory.
   b. California Personality Inventory.
   c. Thematic Apperception Test.
   d. Rorschach Inkblot Test.
10. A benefit of having a person monitor his or her own behavior is that
    a. the person can keep track of behaviors that the professional would be unable to observe and count.
    b. the person becomes aware of his or her own behavior and the situations in which they occur.
    c. self-monitoring is inexpensive.
    d. all of the above.
11. If a psychologist assessed the behavior of a child who has a facial tic and a pattern of making frequent and inappropriate obscene gestures and remarks, the psychologist's next step probably would be to
    a. design an elaborate behavior modification plan to eliminate the tic and increase the child's self-esteem.
    b. suspect Gilles de la Tourette syndrome and refer the case to a neuropsychologist.
    c. ask the child to self-monitor his or her hostile behavior.
    d. prescribe a medication to eliminate the tic.

Connections

If you are interested in . . .	Turn to . . .	To learn more about . . .
The role intelligence plays in psychological theory	◆ Chapter 2, p. 39	How the study of the biological basis of human behavior focuses on the extent to which inherited structures determine intelligence
	◆ Chapter 8, p. 296	How theories of child development often focus on intellectual functioning
	◆ Chapter 8, p. 336	The ways in which developmental psychologists examine growth and maturation by examing issues such as the decline of intellectual functioning that occurs with advanced age or with diseases such as Alzheimer's
The influence of environment in the development of intelligence	◆ Chapter 8, p. 300	The ways in which early childhood interactions with parents are important for intellectual functioning
	◆ Chapter 8, p. 318	How gender differences in social development are often translated into performance differences in intelligence, the workplace, and the classroom
	◆ Chapter 15, p. 598	How many of a person's basic attitudes toward work, school, and intellectual tasks are determined by parents in the early developmental years
How personality and intelligence are evaluated by psychologists	◆ Chapter 11, p. 469	How personality can be examined through projective tests such as the TAT
	◆ Chapter 11, p. 450	The ways in which three important tests of intelligence and their various subscales were constructed, and how they are administered
	◆ Chapter 8, p. 296	How Piaget examined intellectual development in children and incorporated these measures into his theory of intellectual development
	◆ Chapter 14, p. 562	How some therapies require that individuals be motivated and capable of abstract reasoning

Intelligence is so widely debated, such as in the nature-versus-nurture concept, that the idea of measuring intelligence and personality traits pervades psychology. It had its roots in the earliest psychological studies that examined individual differences. It is a topic of wide popular debate, and every school child has some idea about what psychological assessment is about.

The relationship of intelligence and assessment to other areas of psychology is so profound that hardly a chapter in this text, or a lecture in a psychology course does not use the term intelligence at one point or another. Learning helps determine intelligence (Chapter 5, p. 192), and the process of maturation and development is crucial to normal intellectual development (Chapter 8, p. 296). Without being motivated, however, a person may be intelligent but may not show intelligence in her behavior (Chapter 9, p. 387). Nonetheless, intelligence has a biological basis (Chapter 2, p. 39) and may underlie aspects of personality (discussed Chapter 10, p. 419). When we assess personality characteristics we often make attributions about the causes of a person's behavior (discussed in social psychology—Chapter 15, p. 603), and assessment is often necessary in diagnosing and classifying maladjustment and prescribing treatments for it (discussed in Chapters 13 and 14, p. 522 and p. 558).

Module 25 ► HEALTH PSYCHOLOGY AND SEXUAL BEHAVIOR 480

Module 26 ► STRESS, HEALTH PSYCHOLOGY, AND COPING 492

Chapter 12

Health, Stress, and Coping

The relationship between people's health and their welfare is subtle, complex, and affected by a wide range of variables, including the stress in their life and their ability to cope—this is the focus of this chapter. In the first module of this chapter, Module 25, the idea is presented that psychologists look at health as a positive state, not just the absence of disease. With this frame of reference, specific behaviors and events can help shape a person's health; when health deteriorates, specific behaviors can make disease more tolerable, or at least less noxious. The variables that affect health and illness are presented, as are normal sexual responses and the course of deteriorating sexual functioning. A person's headaches, high blood pressure, and inability to sleep are affected by job pressures, family relationships, and even love affairs. Wellness programs, stress-management programs, and various types of therapy for specific illnesses such as weight problems or cholesterol-related problems are regularly offered in community settings.

So many health problems are related to stress that practitioners and theoreticians have taken a special interest in the sources of stress and in therapeutic options for helping people deal with stress. The focus of the second module of the chapter, Module 26, is what is the relationship of stress to coping with the day-to-day demands faced by human beings. Stress is described as an overall response, and then its relationship to coping and failures in coping are presented. Major theoretical formulations (such as those developed by Hans Selye) have helped shape the research. Much of the research has lead to a better understanding of coping mechanisms and of how people adjust to life's day-to-day problems, as well as their long-term adaptations. Some of the major studies of stress have focused on failures in coping and especially suicide—the most dramatic example of a failure in coping. Suicide happens at an alarming rate, and its multiple causes do not provide a clear convincing single *etiology* (cause or originating set of conditions leading to a disease or other health problem). The idea is presented that people who commit suicide are usually depressed, and when a person suggests that he or she is considering suicide, one should not take such a statement lightly.

Module 25

Health Psychology and Sexual Behavior

LEARNING OBJECTIVES

When you have mastered the material in this module, you will be able to

Health Psychology (pp. 481–486)

25.1 Describe the field of health psychology and explain what contemporary physicians and psychologists mean by the term *health* (p. 481).

25.2 Explain how personality, cognitions, social environment, and sociocultural variables are related to health and illness (p. 482).

25.3 Define *sick role,* describe several social expectations regarding illness, and identify factors that influence whether a person will seek health care and comply with medical advice (p. 483).

25.4 Identify and give examples of three ways that health psychologists take an active role in improving the quality of people's lives (p. 485).

Sexual Behavior (pp. 487–489)

25.5 Explain how the human sex drive differs from the sex drive of animals and describe the four stages of the human sexual response cycle (p. 487).

25.6 Describe the causes and characteristics of sexual dysfunctions experienced by men and women (p. 488).

SQ3R
- ▲ **Survey** to set goals for studying.
- ▲ Ask **questions** as you **read.**
- ▲ Stop occasionally to **recite** and **review.**

plus
- ▲ **Write** a summary of key points.
- ▲ **Reflect** on the hypotheses, evidence, and implications of this material and on the relevance it has to *your* life.

Michael Murray is 34 years old and has just become a new father. His 2-month-old daughter is a source of constant joy, and he is amazed by her developing abilities. Yet sometimes he feels as if the walls are closing in. Although his marriage is strong, he and his wife are beginning to suffer from the strain of balancing two careers with child care, running an enlarged household, and coping with the demands of a new baby. Michael is often tired and irritable. Lately, he has begun to depend on several gin and tonics to help him relax at night.

health psychology: Psychological subfield concerned with the use of psychological ideas and principles in health enhancement, illness prevention, diagnosis and treatment of disease, and rehabilitation processes.

Carolyn Boal is proud of her success. In the 5 years since she graduated from college, she has worked her way up the corporate ladder to the position of senior marketing analyst, the youngest employee to hold such an important position. There are never enough hours in the day, though, and she feels constantly rushed. Because of her demanding schedule, her social life is nonexistent, and she has begun to suffer from migraines during the day and insomnia at night.

Tony Munn returned from Vietnam in 1969 and has worked hard to put the war behind him. He is married, the father of two sons, and holds a good job as a computer programmer. Recently, though, (especially after the Persian Gulf War) he has begun waking up in the middle of the night drenched in a cold sweat. His dreams are terrifying re-creations of the horrors he witnessed in the war. He has become depressed, unable to concentrate at work, and increasingly withdrawn from his family.

As a student, you may face some special stresses in your life: studying for three final exams in one week, delivering a speech, juggling your studies with a part-time job to help with your tight finances, and getting along with your roommate in a small apartment or dorm room. Stress, ranging from the minor hassle of being caught in a traffic jam to the major trauma of war, is a reality for all of us. This chapter examines the nature of stress, the many means of coping with stress, and the relationship between health and stress. It highlights the ways in which motivation, learning, and personality work together to influence people's day-to-day lives.

Health Psychology

Learning Objective 25.1 Describe the field of health psychology, and explain what contemporary physicians and psychologists mean by the term *health.*

At least half of all deaths in the United States are the result of unhealthy lifestyles. In the past, most people died from causes beyond their control—influenza, tuberculosis, and pneumonia, for example. Today, the leading causes of death—heart disease, cancer, stroke, and accidents—can be largely controlled by environmental and behavioral variables. Psychologists believe that there is a direct relationship between people's health and their behavior. **Health psychology** is the study of ideas from many fields that enhance health, prevent illness, diagnose and treat disease, and rehabilitate people.

Traditionally, physicians have looked at health as the absence of disease. If a person was not infected with a virus, bacterial infection, cold, and so on, he or she was considered healthy. Now, however, doctors and psychologists acknowledge that *health* refers not to the absence of disease, but to the total welfare of a person in terms of social, physical, and mental well-being. Health and welfare are now seen as conditions people can actively pursue by eating well, exercising regularly, and managing stress effectively (Cowen, 1991). Unlike medicine, which focuses on specific diseases, health psychology looks at the psychosocial mechanisms that influence the development of disease (Taylor, 1990).

Learning Objective 25.2
Explain how personality, cognitions, social environment, and sociocultural variables are related to health and illness.

Variables That Affect Health and Illness

Health and illness are not single entities affected by single variables. A person's health is affected by complex interrelationships among many events. Accordingly, health researchers have explored four variables that correlate strongly with health and illness: personality, cognitions, social environment, and sociocultural variables (Rodin & Salovey, 1989).

Personality. Do certain personality types predispose people to illness? Or does illness predispose people to a specific personality? Some evidence suggests that angry, hostile people are more prone to illness, and optimists are less prone. But which comes first? Perhaps lack of illness causes optimism, or at least positive life-styles. The role of personality variables in illness and health is still unclear, and much more research is needed, as you saw when we examined the role of Type A behavior in heart disease (p. 369). One personality variable that seems important is the extent to which people feel that they control their lives, health, and illness. When people have a sense that they can control their own health, they are more likely to engage in health-conscious behaviors, such as eating lots of complex carbohydrates, decreasing their consumption of saturated fat, or exercising more (Taylor, 1990).

Cognitions. People's thoughts and beliefs about themselves, other people, and situations affect health-related behaviors. For example, people with an internal locus of control (discussed in Chapter 10, p. 426) are more likely to take charge of their illnesses and attempt to get better than people with an external locus of control, who believe that there is nothing that they can do to affect their health. People who feel they have control over their health are more likely to lead healthy life-styles.

Social Environment. Family, close friends, and work can be sources of social support—a key element in maintaining health and recovering from illness. Greater self-esteem, positive feelings about the future, and a sense of control are characteristic of people with strong social support. Adults in stable long-term relationships such as marriage are less likely to have illnesses than are people devoid of strong social support networks; in addition, the children of parents who are married are also likely to be healthier (Gottman & Katz, 1989). Support from coworkers and supervisors in the work environment may also facilitate health (Repetti, Matthews, & Waldron, 1989). Individuals with support are more likely to engage in preventive dental health, proper eating habits, and the use of safety practices, such as seat belts.

Sociocultural Variables. Gender, age, ethnic group, and socioeconomic class are also important variables that affect health. Women tend to visit physicians more often than men, although in some non-Western cultures, the quality of their treatment is not equal to that given men. With advancing age, some people are more likely to become ill, but there is great individual variation. Often, illness among the elderly is affected by other variables, such as loneliness, widowhood, and isolation from family. Ethnic minorities and people from lower socioeconomic groups may lack knowledge, funds, or access to preventive care. In addition, older, less educated, and less affluent individuals are far less likely to engage in exercise, which helps to prevent illness. Disease prevention is the focus of many health psychologists. Recently, preventing the spread of AIDS, considered in the Applying Psychology box on page 482, has been of great concern.

Health psychologists are attempting to assist individuals and families affected by devastating illnesses and diseases such as AIDS.

The Psychology of Being Sick

Learning Objective 25.3 Define *sick role,* describe several social expectations regarding illness, and identify factors that influence whether a person will seek health care and comply with medical advice.

When a person is sick with an illness that impairs his or her day-to-day functioning, the effects can be devastating. The impact on the individual can be profound both psychologically and economically. Illness seriously affects both the sick person and his or her family members. Health psychologists are concerned not only with the links between stress and health, but also with how people cope with illness when it occurs.

Seeking Health Care. When do people seek health care? What are the variables that prompt a person to become well and healthy? Most people avoid medical care and advice except when absolutely necessary. Usually, when a person has a visible symptom (rashes, cuts, swelling, fever) and the symptom appears threatening, painful, and persistent, he or she seeks professional help. People are more likely to seek professional treatment when they are sure that the problem is physical rather than psychological and when medical attention will provide a cure. If they think that medical attention will be a waste of time, or if they dread a diagnosis, they often delay seeking help.

The Sick Role. When people do what they feel will help them get well, we say that they are adopting a *sick role.* For most people, this means taking specific steps to get well, relieving themselves of normal responsibilities, and realizing that they are not at fault for their illness. (Of course, a person can adopt behaviors associated with illness, when in fact there is no illness or pathology.) Unfortunately, many people blame the ailing person for being sick, even though the illness may be totally unrelated to any preventive measures a person might have taken. When sick, a person usually is relieved of normal responsibilities, such as working or taking care of the family. Although our society fosters an approach that says to be cheerful when you are sick, it is normal for people to be slightly depressed or even angry (Lazarus, 1984). Because sickness is generally seen as a

APPLYING PSYCHOLOGY

AIDS (Acquired Immune Deficiency Syndrome)

A major concern of health psychologists is AIDS (acquired immune deficiency syndrome). People who contract this deadly infectious disease generally die within 2 years of diagnosis because their immune systems can no longer fight off germs and diseases. A great deal is known about AIDS, but at present, there are no vaccines or cures and few treatments to slow its destructive course. Moreover, some people, fearing contamination, shun AIDS victims. Because many AIDS victims acquired the disease through homosexual contact or intravenous drug use, some see it as a moral stigma. For all these reasons, AIDS is accompanied by devastating psychological consequences (Schofferman, 1988).

Reports from the Center for Disease Control and the U.S. Department of Health and Human Services (1990) show that more than 100,000 deaths due to AIDS have occurred in the United States, and an estimated 1.5 million U.S. inhabitants are infected with the human immunodeficiency virus (HIV—the virus that causes AIDS). Worldwide, 5 million persons are infected. The U.S. Department of Health and Human Services projects that by 1993, at least 450,000 adults in the Untied States will have been diagnosed with AIDS. Moreover, AIDS-infected mothers will have passed the disease to another 10,000 children by that date (American Psychological Association, 1989). Most AIDS victims are between 20 and 49 years of age, and although at present, some states, such as New York and California, have a greater percentage of cases than others, most experts believe that this unevenness will disappear in time.

Few other diseases are accompanied by so many losses. AIDS patients face the loss of physical strength, mental acuity, ability to work and care for their families, self-sufficiency, social roles, income and savings, housing, the emotional support of friends and loved ones, and ultimately life itself. Some schools have prohibited from attending classes any children who have AIDS or even who have family members with AIDS. People with AIDS have been fired, co-workers have quit their jobs to avoid them, and judges have held legal hearings on closed-circuit television to avoid contact with AIDS victims. For many AIDS victims, self-esteem fades rapidly as they blame themselves for having contracted the disease. This self-blame leads to depression, anxiety, self-anger, and a negative outlook on life. Families and friends become similarly affected as they cope with a dying loved one and face their own inability to understand the disease.

Psychologists pay particular attention to high-risk behaviors in AIDS prevention. High-risk behaviors directly expose people to the blood or semen of others who are more likely to have been exposed to the virus—in other words, to other people who are likely to have engaged in high-risk behaviors. Often, individuals who have engaged in high-risk behaviors are sexually promiscuous people, homosexual and bisexual men, or present and past intravenous drug abusers. In addition, heterosexuals who have had sexual contact with carriers of AIDS are at risk. Ethnic minorities, particularly blacks (24%) and Hispanics (14%), make up a disproportionately large share of AIDS cases in the United States (Peterson & Marin, 1988).

Health professionals agree that the only way to control the spread of AIDS is to decrease the behaviors that put people at risk. People are not likely to get AIDS if they make conscientious decisions about their personal behaviors. Individuals who are not in long-term monogamous relationships must use condoms and must avoid both oral and anal sex, and intravenous drug users must avoid sharing needles.

Health psychologists can play a major role in setting up AIDS prevention programs, especially for hard-hit high-risk groups. Adolescents are especially at risk because they more than adults are likely to engage in unprotected sexual activity, and AIDS education aimed at this group is critically important (Flora and Thoresen, 1988). Although AIDS education and prevention campaigns have, in fact, resulted in profound behavior changes among gay men, still not enough is being done to educate other high-risk groups and the general population, and people are still engaging in casual sex with strangers (Clark, 1990). Interestingly, women who have had a previous sexually transmitted disease are more likely than men to alter their high-risk behaviors, though men seem to alter their behavior when they experience cognitive changes, such as fear of the disease (Cochran and Mays, 1989). Thoughts and ideas play an important role both in disease prevention and in how people respond to becoming sick.

- ▲ ***What are the implications of the vast number of new AIDS patients that are emerging each year?***
- ▲ ***What is meant by the term* high-risk behavior?**
- ▲ ***What is the implication of the finding that men seem more affected than women by cognitive (thought) changes such as fear of AIDS?***

temporary state, we expect people to get well and to work toward that end—taking medication, sleeping, and especially, complying with medical advice.

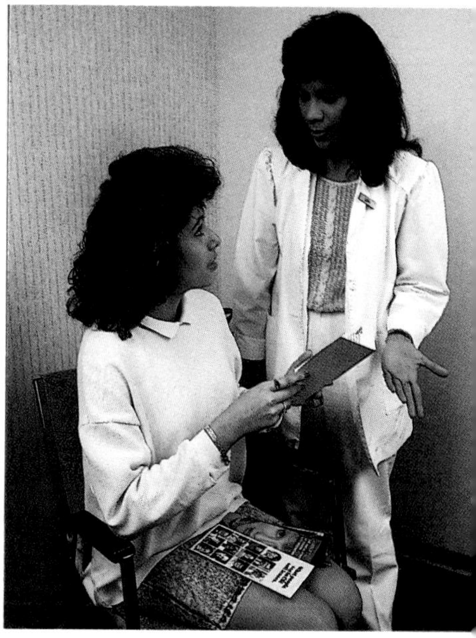

Health workers are trained to assist clients in identifying problems, dealing with decisions, and managing stress.

Compliance with Medical Advice. Getting people to adhere to a health regimen has long been a focus of health psychologists. Clients will comply with specific recommendations for a specific disease, such as "Take three tablets a day for 10 days." However, they are less likely to adhere to general recommendations for diet, exercise, and overall health conditions, such as quitting smoking or relaxing more. The impact of many of the recommendations of physicians is great; for example, a 10% weight reduction in men ages 35–55 through diet and exercise would produce an estimated 20% reduction in heart attacks (American Heart Association, 1984). However, research shows that clients are more receptive to medical advice and treatment when the treatments are specific, simple, easy to do, and have minimal side effects.

Compliance with medical advice depends on the severity of a problem. When seeking a cure or relief of specific symptoms, people are more likely to be cooperative than when merely seeking wellness or prevention. When exercise is the prescribed treatment, most people drop out of a program within 6 months. If an illness causes pain or discomfort, people are more likely to comply with a regimen of treatment to alleviate the discomfort.

Compliance to a health care regimen is increased when tailored to the life-style and habits of a patient. Even written agreements between practitioners and clients can be helpful. Health psychologists have found clients more likely to adhere to treatments when the doctor's influence and family support system are substantial. Social support from family and friends turns out to be especially valuable in getting even very sick people to comply with a guidelines for treatment (DiMatteo & DiNicola, 1984). The next section shows that health psychologists try to help people to be adaptive and to cope with their situations.

Health Psychology and Adaptive Behavior

Learning Objective 25.4
Identify and give examples of three ways that health psychologists take an active role in improving the quality of people's lives.

Health psychologists focus on adaptive behaviors that will improve people's day-to-day lives. They encourage preventive programs at work and educate people about ways to manage stress and other positive approaches toward health that will enhance and prolong life. They frequently conduct stress-management workshops to help managers and workers cope with increasing pressures and work loads, and they are involved in helping people quit smoking, control their alcohol intake, follow exercise programs, and practice good nutrition.

Today, health psychologists attempt to change people's behavior *before* it gets out of hand. Health psychology is an action-oriented discipline, and in the 1990s, many men and women seek more healthful life-styles, and psychologists are playing an instrumental role in that quest. Sometimes, they focus on preventive behaviors—using sunscreens when sunbathing, using condoms to prevent the spread of AIDS, exercising regularly, and so on. At other times, they help people deal with existing problems such as obesity, diabetes, and high stress levels. We now examine three of these areas: behavioral interventions, pain management, and stress management.

Behavioral Interventions. To manage existing health disorders and to help prevent disease, behavioral interventions are necessary and important. Health psychologists know that many problems are clearly subject to change and modification—these are often considered life-style problems and include obesity, smoking, hypertension, and alcohol and other drug abuse.

Consider drug abuse. One sure way to destroy a person's normal health and behavior is through drug use that impairs memory, alertness, and achievement.

The principal place where people are introduced to drugs is school, in both city and suburban settings. As a result, in the mid-1980s—under the direction of then Secretary of Education William J. Bennett—a national plan was laid out for achieving drug-free schools. To a great extent, the plan was an effort to help students cope without drugs.

Pain Management. Severe and disabling pain is symptomatic of some specific illnesses and can take three forms: (1) *chronic* pain is long-lasting and ever-present; (2) *periodic* pain comes and goes; (3) *progressive* pain is always present and increases in severity as an illness progresses. Pain management is especially important because many people have chronic pain, such as headache pain, lower back pain, and arthritis. Some pain can be treated with drugs, surgery, or other medical interventions; but other types of chronic pain, such as pain caused by arthritis and cancer, sometimes call for nontraditional, psychological techniques.

Stress Management. Because stress exists in all our lives, whether it's from school exams, parent or peer pressures, natural disasters, illness, death, divorce, inflation, or financial difficulties, many health psychologists focus on stress and its management. With the help of health psychologists, employers are sponsoring programs that focus on managing stress in the workplace (Glasgow & Terborg, 1988). The programs usually involve education, exercise, nutrition classes, and counseling. The results show fewer work days lost to illness and lower health-care costs. When patients who were hospitalized for heart attacks were treated for stress symptoms after their release from the hospital, they had fewer subsequent heart attacks, compared to a control group that did not receive specific stress treatments (Frasure-Smith & Prince, 1989).

The task of managing stress in people's daily lives is becoming greater each day as new and potent forces impinge on people's health (Ilgen, 1990). In the 1990s, people are concerned not only about managing day-to-day illness and stress, but also about potential threats in the environment and in the food supply.

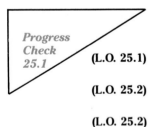

Progress Check 25.1

Complete the following sentences with one of the options provided.

(L.O. 25.1) a. Contemporary physicians and psychologists view health as ________. (the absence of illness or disease / a state of well-being)

(L.O. 25.2) b. A person's health is affected by ________ variables. (biological / a complex interrelationship among many)

(L.O. 25.2) c. A person with an ________ locus of control is more likely to take charge of his or her illness and to get better. (internal / external)

(L.O. 25.2) d. People who have strong social support networks and people who are young, educated, and affluent are more likely to be healthy because they are more likely to engage in behaviors that ________ illness. (keep them from being exposed to / prevent)

(L.O. 25.3) e. When a person realizes that he or she is not at fault for feeling ill, relinquishes normal responsibilities, and does what is necessary to get well, we say the person ________. (has adopted the sick role / is a hypochondriac)

(L.O. 25.3) f. People are more likely to follow medical advice when they are seeking ________. (suggestions for staying well / a cure for specific symptoms)

(L.O. 25.4) g. Because health psychology focuses on prevention of illness and elimination of life-threatening conditions such as stress and obesity, it is considered ________ discipline. (an action-oriented / a medical / a developmental)

Sexual Behavior

In the 1990s, sexual discussions are open, more honest than in past years, and certainly frequently aired through the mass media. This focus on sexuality has implications for psychologists. Psychologists study sexuality and often see clients who have various types of sexual problems. Unlike animals, the sexual drive in human beings is no longer considered solely or even primarily under physiological control, but is to a great extent under psychological control. In contrast, the sexual behavior of lower organisms is controlled largely by their physiological and hormonal systems. (See Chapter 2 for a review of hormones).

When hormones are released, they exert profound effects on behavior. If the hormone-generating testes of male rats are removed, the animals show a marked decrease in sexual activity. Similarly, most female lower organisms are sexually responsive only when hormones are released into the bloodstream—that is, when they are "in heat." Human beings, on the other hand, can choose whether to respond sexually to encounters at any given time. In fact, in human beings, removal of hormone-generating organs may not affect sexual behavior at all (depending on the person's age at removal).

Generally, the higher the organism on the phylogenetic ladder (evolutionary hierarchy of species), the more important sexual experience and learning is to normal sexual behavior later in life. In rats, for example, early social experience is not necessary for adult sexual function. The human sexual response cycle is far more complex and is made up of a series of stages.

Learning Objective 25.5
Explain how the human sex drive differs from the sex drive of animals, and describe the four stages of the human sexual response cycle.

Sexual Response Cycle

When human beings become sexually aroused, they go through a series of four stages, known as the *sexual response cycle.* In the **excitement phase,** there is increased heart rate, blood pressure, and respiration. A key characteristic of the excitement phase is **vasoconstruction** or engorgement of the blood vessels. In the female, breasts swell and vaginal lubrication increases; in males, there is an erection. The excitement phase is anticipatory and may last from a few minutes to a few hours; it may be initiated by physical contact, fantasy, or any of the senses.

In the **plateau phase,** both men and women are prepared for orgasm. Autonomic nervous system (ANS) activity increases, such as with heart rate increasing. In women, the vagina becomes engorged and at its full extension; in men, the penis is fully erect and turns a darker color. In the **orgasm phase,** ANS activity reaches its peak, and muscle contractions throughout the body occur in spasms. An *orgasm* is the peak of sexual activity in which muscular contractions occur, especially in the genital area. In men, muscles throughout the reproductive system help to expel semen; in women, muscles surrounding the outer vagina contract. Although men experience only one orgasm during each sexual response cycle, women are capable of multiple orgasms. Orgasms are an all-or-none activity lasting only a few seconds; once a threshold for orgasm is reached, it occurs.

After orgasm, a **resolution phase** occurs in which the body naturally returns to its resting or normal state; this takes from 1 to several minutes and varies considerably from person to person. During the resolution phase, men are usually unable to achieve an erection for a period of time, called a *refractory period.* Like many other physiological responses, the sexual response cycle is subject to considerable variation. Some people have a lengthy plateau phase, while others have a longer resolution phase. When people are unable normally to experience pleasure from sexual activity, and they consider sexual behavior to be difficult, painful, or aversive, they may suffer from a sexual dysfunction.

excitement phase: The stage of the sexual response cycle in which there are initial increases in heart rate, blood pressure, and respiration. *Vasoconstriction,* vaginal lubrication, and erections occur during this stage.

vasoconstriction: [VAS-oh-kun-STRICK-shun] In the sexual response cycle, an engorgement of the blood vessels, particularly in the genital area.

plateau phase: The stage of the sexual response cycle in which both men and women are preparing for orgasm. Autonomic nervous system (ANS) activity and vasoconstriction increases. In women, the vagina becomes engorged and at its full extension; in men, the penis is fully erect and turns a darker color.

orgasm phase: The stage of the sexual response cycle in which ANS activity peaks and spasmic muscle contractions occur throughout the body. In orgasm in men, muscles through the reproductive system help expel semen; in women, muscles surrounding the outer vagina contract.

resolution phase: The stage of the sexual response cycle in which the body naturally returns to its resting or normal state; this takes 1 to several minutes and varies considerably from person to person.

Learning Objective 25.6
Describe the causes and characteristics of sexual dysfunctions experienced by men and women.

Sexual Dysfunctions

Sexual dysfunction is the inability to obtain satisfaction from sexual behavior, often accompanied by the inability to experience orgasm. Sexual dysfunctions sometimes occur from too much alcohol or other drugs; sometimes, they occur due to fatigue or some other physical ailment. Additionally, some sexual dysfunctions are the result of early experience in which faulty sexual behaviors or attitudes are learned. Most people experience some type of sexual problem at one time or another, and generally these problems are temporary.

Sexual problems have been carefully researched. Starting with the work of Masters and Johnson (1966, 1970), psychologists and physicians have been attempting to help people with sexual dysfunctions. The Masters and Johnson approach has a strong commitment toward treating pairs of people. Thus, when a man or a woman comes for treatment, a typical procedure is to treat not only the client but also his or her partner.

A man is said to suffer from **erectile dysfunction** when he is unable to attain or maintain an erection of sufficient strength to allow him to engage in sexual intercourse. Erectile dysfunction can be caused by anatomical defects, damage to the central nervous system, or the excessive use of alcohol and other drugs. Most often, however, erectile dysfunction is caused by emotional problems.

There are two kinds of erectile dysfunction. A man who suffers from **primary erectile dysfunction** has never had an erection of sufficient strength to have engaged in sexual intercourse; this dysfunction is relatively rare. Masters and Johnson argue that fear and unusual sensitivity or anxiety regarding sexual incidents that may have happened early in a man's life generally contribute to primary erectile dysfunction.

The other kind of erectile dysfunction, secondary erectile dysfunction occurs more frequently. Those with **secondary erectile dysfunction** have had successful sexual intercourse in the past but are now incapable of consistently engaging in sexual intercourse. When a man fails to achieve penile erection in 25% of his sexual attempts, he is categorized as having secondary erectile dysfunction. One of the key symptoms and major blocks to curing those with secondary erectile dysfunction is that once a man has had a problem in achieving or maintaining an erection, he becomes overly sensitive and maintains a distinct memory of the incident. The next time he tries to have an erection, he may fail completely because he fears that he might not be able to maintain it.

Another common sexual dysfunction is premature ejaculation. **Premature ejaculation** occurs when a man cannot delay ejaculation long enough to satisfy his sexual partner during at least half of his sexual encounters. Instead, ejaculation occurs at, just before, or just following insertion of the penis. Many people have assumed that premature ejaculation is caused by either an abnormally sensitive penis or an inability of the man to control himself. However, premature ejaculation is usually caused by emotional and psychological factors; with the cooperation of his partner, a man can learn to withhold orgasm until he wants it to happen. Fear and anxiety caused by previous failures often deprive the man of his "staying power," just as fear can cause secondary erectile dysfunction. Masters and Johnson report a 98% success rate in the treatment of premature ejaculation.

Sexual dysfunctions are not limited to men. When a woman is unable to obtain an orgasm she is said to have orgasmic dysfunction. A woman who has **primary orgasmic dysfunction** never achieves an orgasm through any method of sexual stimulation. Many causes for primary orgasmic dysfunction are physical, but more often, they are psychological and are due to extreme religious orthodoxy, unfavorable communication about sexual activities, or some childhood trauma.

sexual dysfunction: The inability to obtain satisfaction from sexual behavior, often accompanied by the inability to experience orgasm.

erectile dysfunction: The inability of a man to attain or maintain an erection of sufficient strength to allow sexual intercourse.

primary erectile dysfunction: Occurs when a man has never been able to achieve or maintain an erection of sufficient strength for sexual intercourse.

secondary erectile dysfunction: Occurs when a man fails to achieve an erection in 25% or more (but not all) of his sexual attempts.

premature ejaculation: The condition in which a man cannot delay ejaculation long enough to satisfy his sexual partner in 50% or more of his sexual encounters.

primary orgasmic dysfunction: The condition in which a woman has never achieved orgasm by any means at any time.

Most orgasmic dysfunctions are categorized as secondary (or situational) orgasmic dysfunctions. **Secondary orgasmic dysfunction** is the inability of a woman who has achieved orgasm by one technique or another in the past to achieve it in a given situation. Thus, a woman who has had an orgasm, even if it is not during a heterosexual encounter, does not suffer from primary orgasmic dysfunction. Very often, the secondary orgasmic dysfunction occurs when a woman is unable to accept her mate because she finds him or her sexually unattractive, undesirable, or in some other way unacceptable. In addition, many women find that orgasm brings about feelings of guilt, shame, and fear. Like her male counterpart (who suffers from secondary erectile dysfunction), the woman may have experienced traumatic sexually related events that inhibit her sexual feelings and may bring about fear. For example, she may fear the sexual encounter because it brings about memories of previous sexual abuse in her childhood.

secondary orgasmic dysfunction: A woman's inability to achieve orgasm, even though she has achieved orgasm in the past by one technique or another.

Progress Check 25.2

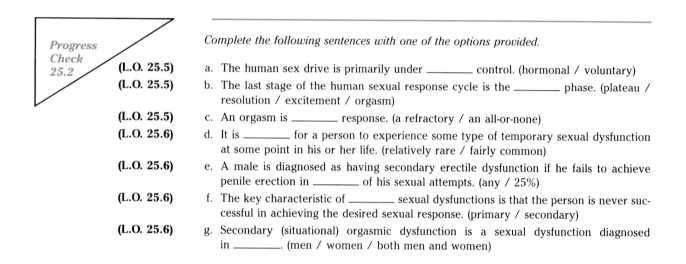

Complete the following sentences with one of the options provided.

(L.O. 25.5) a. The human sex drive is primarily under ______ control. (hormonal / voluntary)

(L.O. 25.5) b. The last stage of the human sexual response cycle is the ______ phase. (plateau / resolution / excitement / orgasm)

(L.O. 25.5) c. An orgasm is ______ response. (a refractory / an all-or-none)

(L.O. 25.6) d. It is ______ for a person to experience some type of temporary sexual dysfunction at some point in his or her life. (relatively rare / fairly common)

(L.O. 25.6) e. A male is diagnosed as having secondary erectile dysfunction if he fails to achieve penile erection in ______ of his sexual attempts. (any / 25%)

(L.O. 25.6) f. The key characteristic of ______ sexual dysfunctions is that the person is never successful in achieving the desired sexual response. (primary / secondary)

(L.O. 25.6) g. Secondary (situational) orgasmic dysfunction is a sexual dysfunction diagnosed in ______. (men / women / both men and women)

Module Summary

Health Psychology

- Health psychologists employ ideas and principles from many fields to enhance health, prevent illness, diagnose and treat disease, and rehabilitate people. Health is now seen as a condition people can actively pursue by eating right, exercising, and managing stress effectively (p. 481).
- When people undertake specific behaviors that they feel will help them get well, we say they are adopting a "sick role." Compliance with medical advice depends on the severity of a problem. When seeking a cure, people are more likely to be compliant with a regimen of activities than when seeking wellness or preventive medical goals. Research shows that clients are more receptive to medical treatments when the treatments are specific and simple, with minimal side effects (p. 483).
- More than 78,000 cases of AIDS have been diagnosed in the United States, and an estimated 2 million U.S. inhabitants are infected with the human immunodeficiency virus. Psychologists highlight the distinction between high-risk and low-risk behavior in AIDS prevention (p. 484).

Sexual Behavior

- Sexual dysfunction is the inability to obtain satisfaction from sexual behavior, often accompanied by the inability to experience orgasm (p. 487).
- Often, sexual dysfunctions are the result of early experience in which faulty sexual behaviors or attitudes are learned (p. 488).
- Most people experience some type of sexual problem at one time or another, but most sexual dysfunctions are treatable (p. 488).

KEY TERMS

erectile dysfunction, p. 488
excitement phase, p. 487
health psychology, p. 481
orgasm phase, p. 487
plateau phase, p. 487
premature ejaculation, p. 488
primary erectile dysfunction, p. 488
primary orgasmic dysfunction, p. 488
resolution phase, p. 487
secondary erectile dysfunction, p. 488
secondary orgasmic dysfunction, p. 489
sexual dysfunction, p. 488
vasoconstriction, p. 487

SELF-TEST

Module 25

- Before taking the self-test, **recite** and **review.**
- Use the key at the back of the text to *correct* your answers.
- *Restudy* pages that correspond to any questions you answered incorrectly.

1. The main focus of health psychology is the
   a. etiology of specific diseases.
   b. symptoms of specific diseases.
   c. best treatment or cure for specific diseases.
   d. psychosocial mechanisms that contribute to disease.
2. Who is *least* likely to become ill?
   a. a married person
   b. an ethnic minority
   c. a widow
   d. a poor person
3. A social expectation regarding illness is that
   a. illness is a temporary state, and people should do what it takes to get well.
   b. a person should act cheerful even though he or she feels ill.
   c. the ailing person is at fault in some way for being ill because we expect people to be well.
   d. all of the above.
4. A person is *least* likely to comply with a physician's advice when
   a. the illness or physical problem is very severe.
   b. general recommendations such as diet, exercise, and relaxation are given.
   c. the treatment is simple, easy, has minimal side effects, and relieves discomfort.
   d. the doctor's influence and family support are substantial.
5. When a person learns to relax with feelings of pain, the person
   a. may be jeopardizing his or her overall health because physical symptoms are dismissed.
   b. probably has a high biological tolerance for pain.
   c. is making use of behavior modification and cognitive therapy techniques.
   d. increases the probability that he or she will begin to experience stress-related diseases over time.
6. The excitement phase of the human sexual response cycle
   a. occurs when the autonomic nervous system reaches a peak.
   b. can be initiated by physical contact, fantasies, or any of the body's senses.
   c. is accompanied by intense muscle contractions in both men and women.
   d. is the second stage of the human sexual response cycle.
7. During the human sexual response cycle,
   a. men have one orgasm, while women are capable of multiple orgasms.
   b. vasoconstriction takes the same form in both men and women.
   c. men cycle through the plateau phase, but women usually do not.
   d. women experience a resolution phase, where men generally do not.
8. Although erectile dysfunction and premature ejaculation can be caused by any of the following, the *primary* cause for both of these dysfunctions is
   a. an abnormally insensitive or sensitive penis.
   b. psychological or emotional problems.
   c. the excessive use of alcohol or drugs.
   d. a physical problem.

Module 26

Stress, Health Psychology, and Coping

LEARNING OBJECTIVES

When you have mastered the material in this module, you will be able to

Stress (pp. 493–504)

26.1 Describe the relationships among stressors, stress, and anxiety; also explain what determines whether an event is experienced as stressful (p. 493).

26.2 Describe and give examples of three *types* of stress, and identify and describe three *sources* of stress (p. 494).

26.3 Describe physical, emotional, and behavioral responses to stress that people experience (p. 496).

26.4 Explain how stress and arousal affect *motivation, burnout, disease,* and *children* (p. 497).

26.5 Describe the three stages of Selye's general adaptation syndrome (p. 498).

26.6 Describe the Holmes–Rahe Social Readjustment Scale and explain why some psychologists challenge its validity (p. 499).

26.7 Discuss how work-related stress, certain behavior patterns, and physiological reactivity relate to heart disease (p. 499).

26.8 Characterize post-traumatic stress disorder and identify the people who are likely to be victims of this disorder (p. 502).

Coping and Adjustment (504–511)

26.9 List five features of coping behavior and identify important factors that influence how well people cope (p. 504).

26.10 Describe defense-oriented and task-oriented coping strategies and discuss the effectiveness of each (p. 505).

26.11 Discuss suicide rates in the United States, identify some of the warning signs given by potential suicide victims, and discuss the causes of suicide and the ways that we can help to prevent it from occurring (p. 508).

SQ3R
- ▲ **Survey** to set goals for studying.
- ▲ Ask **questions** as you **read.**
- ▲ Stop occasionally to **recite** and **review.**

plus
- ▲ **Write** a summary of key points.
- ▲ **Reflect** on the hypotheses, evidence, and implications of this material and on the relevance it has to *your* life.

"My son has flipped out" declared an angry and upset Brenda Playman. A string of adjectives then followed, which described her utter frustration with her 21-year-old son, Gordon. Gordon, with his girlfriend of 3 weeks, was quitting college to take to the highway on his Yamaha. His ultimate plan was to open up a Yamaha dealership and motorcycle repair shop. Brenda Playman was beside herself; she was having migraine headaches. She was sure that Gordon had to be taking drugs. She questioned whether he had fallen in with a religious cult. Was Gordon's girlfriend leading him astray? Was he losing his mind?

Brenda Playman was under strain; her questioning, fears, and speculations about her son were placing her under a great deal of pressure. She was feeling enraged, upset, and no longer in control of a part of her life. She had become nervous, critical of others, and was irritable all of the time. Her tension caused her blood pressure to rise. She was arguing with her husband, and she was short-tempered at work. She told herself that she was "stressed-out." She was taking responsibility for her son's life. She felt stressed, angry, infuriated, and helpless. While she might have considered Gordon's decision foolish, she should have realized that college students are growing, changing, and developing. Everyone has a different way of responding to his environment and its stresses. Brenda Playman was responding to the changes in her son's life with headaches, chest pains, and shortness of breath.

stressor: An environmental stimulus that affects an organism in ways that are either physically or psychologically injurious, usually producing anxiety, tension, and physiological arousal.

stress: A nonspecific, often global response by an organism to real or imagined demands made on it; a person has to appraise a situation as stressful for it to be stressful.

anxiety: A generalized feeling of fear and apprehension that might be related to a particular event or object and is often accompanied by increased physiological arousal.

Stress

Learning Objective 26.1 Describe the relationship among stressors, stress, and anxiety; also explain what determines whether an event is experienced as stressful.

Brenda Playman's reactions may have been somewhat extreme, but they were well within the broad range of normal reactions to stress. Human beings' responses to stress vary greatly and depend on people's biological state, their genetic inheritance, and their accumulated learning experiences. Brenda Playman's neighbors or coworkers may be able to manage the same amount of stress in more positive ways, without suffering negative health consequences. Herein lies an important difference: Stress can be evaluated and handled in different ways, depending on the person.

What Is Stress?

A **stressor** is an environmental stimulus that acts (or might act) on an organism in physically or psychologically injurious ways. Stressors *may* induce a response of **stress** in an organism, producing anxiety, tension, and psychological arousal. **Anxiety** is a generalized feeling of fear and apprehension that might be related to a particular event or object and is often accompanied by increased physiological arousal. Whenever something negatively affects someone, physically or psychologically, the person may experience the effect as a stress. The key is that not all people view a stimulus or a situation in the same way; *a person has to appraise a situation as stressful for it to be stressful.* This broad definition recognizes that everyone experiences stress at some time, but that stress is an interpreted state, a response on the part of a person.

Appraisal: A Key Component

A key component of stress is that a person has to appraise a situation as stressful for it to be stressful. (What is stressful for me, such as a track meet, may be of little consequence for you.) What determines whether a particular event is stressful? When does a person see someone, something, or some time as dangerous or threatening? The answer lies in the extent to which people are familiar with an event, how much they had anticipated the event, and how much they can control the event and themselves.

Your first date, your first speech, and your first day in school are all more threatening than the second date, speech, and day in school. This is partly because when we are familiar with an event, we can predict with some accuracy what will happen, how we will feel, and how others will react to us. Knowing that a test will be hard because we have taken another similar test before helps us deal with our fears. If you took the written portion of a drivers' license examination more than once, you probably remember that your apprehension was much greater the first time than the second time—you were probably less stressed the second time. When people can predict events, they feel that they are more in control and can have some impact on the future. This is a two-step process: First, you decide whether a situation is threatening to your well-being, then you decide whether you can cope with it or handle it well.

Types and Sources of Stress

Learning Objective 26.2 Describe and give examples of three types of stress, and identify and describe three sources of stress.

There are three broad types of stress: *frustrations,* which result when people are impeded in meeting their goals; *conflicts,* which result when people must make difficult decisions; and *pressures,* which result from the need to achieve goals.

Frustration. When people are hindered from meeting their goals, they often feel frustrated. **Frustration** is an emotional state that is said to occur when any goal—work, family, or personal—is thwarted or blocked. When people feel that they cannot achieve a goal (often due to situations beyond their control), they may experience frustration and stress. When you are unable to obtain a summer job because of a lack of experience, it can cause feelings of stress; when a grandparent becomes ill, you may feel helpless, and this causes stress. People who seek to get ahead by hard work and education may feel frustrated when opportunities are blocked because of a lack of funds.

Some frustrations are externally caused, and there is little a person can do to alleviate them. Your lack of experience for a specific job, your grandparent's illness, or your family's lack of money are external events over which you have little control. Other frustrations are caused by specific people; your boss may be unfair in his appraisal of you, your roommate may be too stingy to chip in for new furniture, or your instructor may be too lenient with people who goof off. You can sometimes alleviate the frustration of dealing with other people by taking some personal action; these actions, however, often place you in conflict, which also causes stress.

frustration: The emotional state or condition resulting from a situation when a goal is thwarted or blocked.

Conflict. When people must make difficult decisions, we say that they are in a state of **conflict** and that this conflict results in feelings of arousal and stress. Consider the difficult decision of those American draftees who did not want to fight in the Vietnam war but did not want to flee to Canada or face imprisonment. What happens if a person's goals and needs conflict—if someone must choose between two equally desirable desserts or two equally difficult academic courses? One of the first psychologists to describe and quantify such conflict situations was Neal Miller (1944, 1959). Miller developed hypotheses about how animals and human beings behave in situations that have both positive and negative aspects. In general, he described three types of situations that involve competing demands.

Approach–approach conflicts arise when a person must choose one of two equally pleasant alternatives, such as two wonderful jobs or two good movies. This conflict generates discomfort and a stress response, but people can usually tolerate it because either alternative is pleasant. **Avoidance–avoidance conflicts** occur when a choice involves two equally distasteful alternatives, such as mowing the lawn or painting the garage. **Approach–avoidance conflicts** occur when a particular situation has both appealing and repellant aspects. Studying for an exam, which can lead to good grades but is boring and difficult, is an approach–avoidance situation. All these conflict situations lead to stress.

Miller developed descriptions to predict behavior in conflict situations, particularly in approach–avoidance situations. (1) The closer a subject is to a goal, the stronger the tendency is to approach the goal. (2) When two incompatible responses are available, the stronger one will be expressed. (3) The strength of the tendency to approach or avoid is correlated with the strength of the motivating drive (thus a child who is both hungry and thirsty will seek food if he or she is more hungry than thirsty). People face such conflict situations regularly. In such situations, they may become anxious and upset. Moreover, if their conflicts affect their day-to-day behavior, they may exhibit symptoms of maladjustment.

Pressure: Work, Time, and Life Events. When people feel **pressure** or expectations from others for certain behaviors or results, arousal and stress occur.

conflict: The emotional state or condition in which a person has to make difficult decisions about two or more competing motives, behaviors, or impulses.

approach–approach conflict: The result of having to choose between two equally attractive alternatives or goals.

avoidance–avoidance conflict: The result of having to choose between two equally distasteful alternatives or goals.

approach–avoidance conflict: The result of having to choose a goal that has both attractive and repellent aspects.

pressure: The emotional state or condition resulting from expectations for success, or specific behaviors or results; the feelings that result from coercion.

Certain jobs, such as this air traffic controller's involve stress levels that not every personality could successfully manage.

Neal Miller described conflict by identifying situations which evoke competing demands.

Although individual situations differ, certain sources of stress are common to almost everyone; these *sources of stress* are most often associated with work, time, and life events.

Work that is either too burdensome or too light (and therefore understimulating) can cause stress. Work-related stress also can come from fear of retirement, being passed over for promotion, and organizational changes. In addition, the physical work setting may be overstimulating (too noisy or crowded) or understimulating and isolated. Work-related pressure—deadlines, competition, professional relationships—can cause a variety of physical problems. People suffering from work stress may experience migraines, ulcers, sleeplessness, hunger for sweets, overeating, and intestinal distress. Stress at work often leads to illness, resulting in lost efficiency and absenteeism.

Individuals with high-stress jobs, particularly when stress is constant, show the effects convincingly. Air traffic controllers and surgeons, for example, are responsible for the lives of other people every day and must be alert and organized at all times. If they work too many hours without relief, they may even make a fatal mistake. Other high-stress jobs include inner-city high school teachers, customer service agents, waiters and waitresses, and emergency workers, to name just a few.

Lack of time is another common source of stress. Everyone faces deadlines: Students must complete tests before class ends, auto workers must keep pace with the assembly line, and tax returns must be filed by April 15th. A sense of urgency and competitiveness drives some people to speed up their pace continually.

People have only a limited number of hours each day in which to accomplish tasks; therefore, most people carefully allocate their time to reduce time pressure. They may establish routines, make lists, set schedules, leave optional meetings early, and set aside leisure time in which to rid themselves of stressful feelings. If they do not handle time pressures successfully, they may begin to feel overloaded and stressed.

A third common stress source involves the stages of life, which may be both positive and stressful at the same time. Consider marriage. Marriage gives people a partner, a companion, a lover, a friend, and a person with whom to share future aspirations. Nonetheless, adjusting to married life means becoming familiar with new experiences, responding to unanticipated events, and having less control over many aspects of day-to-day experiences, all of which may be stressful, Also, at times, interpersonal discord arises: One partner may not be fulfilling marital or role obligations or may be causing his or her spouse to feel left out, both of which may bring about stress. Parents feel the joy of watching their children mature, learn from experiences, and become sensitive, responsible adults. On the other hand, the rearrangement of schedules and added responsibilities of having a child can cause great stress. We discuss stressful life events in more detail on page 500.

Responding to Stress

Learning Objective 26.3 Describe physical, emotional, and behavioral responses to stress that people experience.

People react to stress in a wide variety of ways. Some experience modest increases in physiological arousal, while others may exhibit significant physical symptoms. In extreme cases, people become so aroused, anxious, and disorganized that their behavior becomes maladaptive or maladjusted.

Emotion, Physiology, and Behavior. When psychologists study stress, they typically break down a person's stress reactions into emotional, physiological, and behavioral components. *Emotionally,* people's reactions often depend on their frustration, their work-related pressures, and their day-to-day conflicts. When frustrated, people became angry and annoyed; when pressured, they become aroused

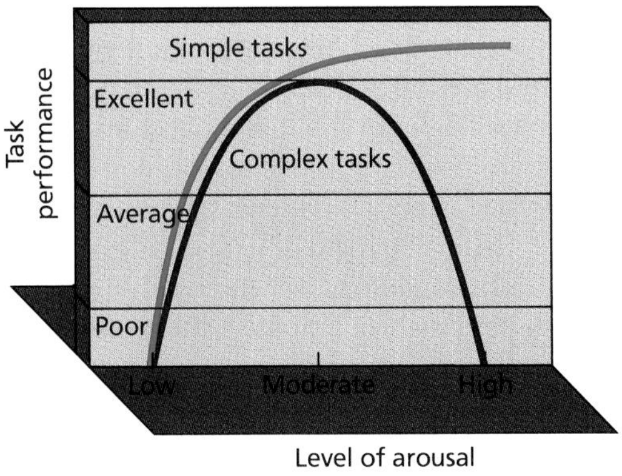

Figure 26.1

When arousal is low, task performance is poor or nonexistent. Performance is usually best at moderate levels of arousal; at high levels of arousal, on complex tasks, performance usually deteriorates.

and anxious; when placed in situations of conflict, they may vacillate or become irritable and sometimes hostile.

Physiologically, the stress response is characterized by arousal. When psychologists refer to arousal, they usually mean changes in the autonomic nervous system, including increased heart rate, breathing, and blood pressure; sweating of the palms; and dilation of the pupils. Arousal is often the first change that occurs when a person feels stressed.

Behaviorally, stress and its arousal response are related. As we saw in Chapter 9, psychologist Donald Hebb (1972) argued that effective behavior depends on a person's state of arousal. When people are moderately aroused, they behave with optimal effectiveness; when underaroused, they lack stimulation to behave effectively. Overarousal tends to produce disorganized behavior in which people do not use their most effective skills (see Figure 26.1), particularly if the tasks they undertake are complex.

A moderate amount of stress is necessary and desirable. Stress and its accompanying arousal is what keeps us active and involved. It impels students to study, drives athletes to excel during competition, and helps businesspeople to strive toward greater heights. In short, stress and arousal can help people achieve their potentials. See Figure 26.2 for an overview of the responses to stressors that occur after an appraisal.

Learning Objective 26.4 Explain how stress and arousal affect *motivation, burnout, disease,* and *children.*

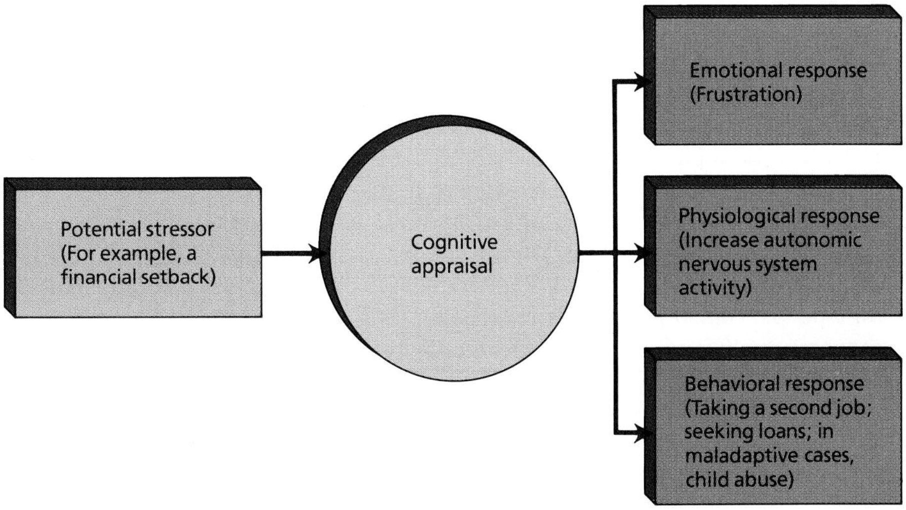

Figure 26.2

After a threat is evaluated, its impact can be seen emotionally, physiologically, and behaviorally.

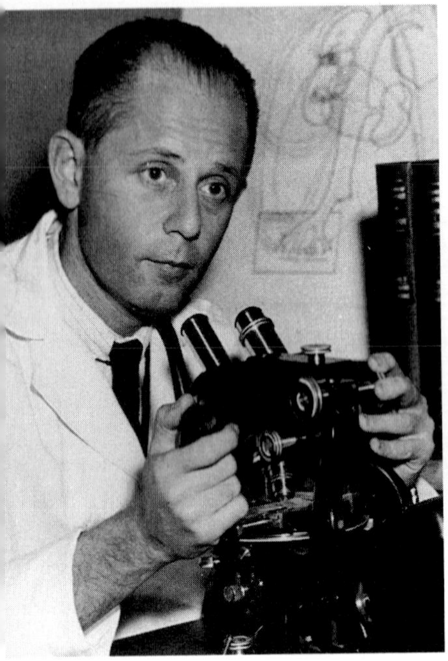

Hans Selye undertook a systematic study of stressors and stress and theorized a *general adaptation syndrome.*

Burnout. A stress reaction especially common to people with high standards is **burnout,** a state of emotional and physical exhaustion, lowered productivity, and feelings of isolation, often due to work-related pressures (Kalimo & Mejman, 1987). People who daily face high stress levels, often feel enervated, hopeless, and emotionally drained and may eventually stop trying. Although work-related problems and stress are most often the cause of burnout, family, financial, and social pressures can create the same feelings. Burnout victims develop negative self-concepts because they are unable to maintain the high standards they have set for themselves. People with burnout often cease to be concerned about others and have physical as well as social problems.

Health Consequences. Stress does not cause disease, but it contributes to many diseases, including the six major causes of death in the United States: heart disease, cancer, lung ailments, accidental injuries, cirrhosis of the liver, and suicide. In general, stress affects the immune system, making people more vulnerable to disease (Cohen & Williamson, 1991). It may cause headaches, backaches, decreased productivity, and family arguments; at a minimum, stress-related illnesses are causing an increase in medical costs for both individuals and employers. Extreme stress, in addition to other psychological challenges, can be implicated in sudden heart attacks (Kamarck & Jennings, 1991)

Stress afflicts children, as well as adults. Children are usually unable to change or control the circumstances in which they find themselves (Band & Weisz, 1988). Children may experience stress in school, stress caused by an abusive parent, stress from their parents' divorce, or stress from peer pressure. Children, like adults, often show their stress response in physical symptoms.

Studying Stress: Focus on Physiology

Laypersons and psychologists alike want to know how today's increasingly harried life-styles affect individual physical and psychological well-being. Does intense competition make businesspeople more susceptible to heart attacks? How can psychologists help people cope with life stresses, such as having a baby? How can therapists help veterans who are traumatized by war or other disasters?

Learning Objective 26.5
Describe the three stages of Selye's general adaptation syndrome.

Selye's General Adaptation Syndrome. In the 1930s, Hans Selye (1907–1982) began a systematic study of stressors and stress. He investigated the physiological changes in people who were experiencing various amounts of stress. Selye conceptualized people's responses to stress in terms of a *general adaptation syndrome* (1956, 1976). (A *syndrome* is a set of responses. In the case of stress, it is a set of behaviorally defined physical symptoms.) Selye's work initiated thousands of studies on stress and stress reactions, and Selye himself published more than 1600 articles on the topic.

According to Selye, people's response to a stressor can be divided into three stages: (1) an initial short-term stage of alarm, (2) a longer period of resistance, and (3) a final stage of exhaustion. During the initial *alarm stage,* people experience increased physiological arousal. They become excited, anxious, or frightened. Because people cannot stay highly aroused for long periods of time, the initial alarm response usually gives way to *resistance.* During this stage, physiological and behavioral responses become more moderate and sustained. People in the resistance stage often are irritable, impatient, and angry, and they may experience chronic fatigue. This stage can persist for a few hours, several days, or even years. The final stage of Selye's three-part syndrome is *exhaustion.* Stress saps psychological energy; if people don't relieve their stress, they can become too exhausted to

burnout: A state of emotional and physical exhaustion, lowered productivity, and feelings of isolation, often due to work-related pressure.

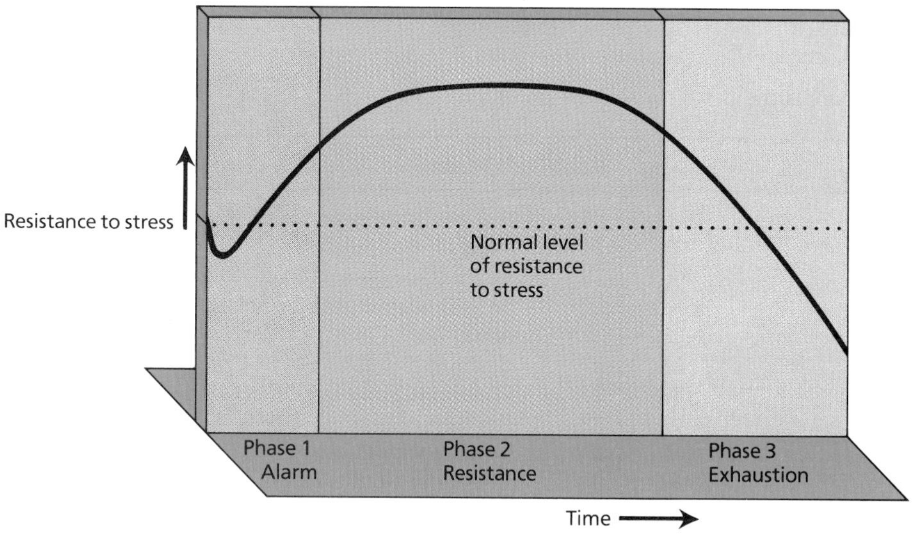

Figure 26.3

The *general adaptation syndrome,* according to Selye. During the first phase, the body mobilizes its resources. In the second phase, resistance levels off and eventually begins to decline. In the third phase, resistance is depleted, leading to exhaustion.

adapt. At that point, they again become extremely alarmed, and they finally give up. Maladjustment, withdrawal, or, in extreme cases, death may follow. See Figure 26.3 for a graphic view of Selye's three-part syndrome.

Learning Objective 26.6
Describe the Holmes–Rahe Social Readjustment Scale, and explain why some psychologists challenge its validity.

Selye inspired others to attempt to identify stressors and refine his theory; one such attempt attributes more specificity to stress than did Selye (Smith, 1989). Another product of continued research is Holmes and Rahe's (1967) Social Readjustment Rating Scale, shown in Table 26.1 on the next page. This 1960s scale recognized that there are both positive and negative stressful experiences in life. Holmes and Rahe's basic assumption is that stressful life events to which people must adapt, especially in combination, will damage health. *Stressful life events* are prominent changes in a person's day-to-day circumstances that necessitate change. The scale has been widely used, hotly debated, and revised, and it has become a source of new and important research. Rahe (1989) now uses a list with more than 71 life events.

The Holmes–Rahe scale includes only major life events. The stressors faced by most people are seldom crises; they are the day-to-day hassles and irritations that add up over the years (Kanner et al., 1981). Table 26.2 on the next page presents the 10 most frequent hassles people worry about. The results of a study of the effect of major life events and daily hassles on reported health of elderly subjects showed that hassles are more closely related to psychological and physical health than are major life events (Chamberlain & Zika, 1991; Weinberger, Hiner, & Tierney, 1987).

Health Psychology, Heart Disease, and Stress

Learning Objective 26.7
Discuss how work-related stress, certain behavior patterns, and physiological reactivity relate to heart disease.

Heart disease and high blood pressure account for more than half the deaths each year in the United States. Among U.S. blacks, high blood pressure is the number one health problem (N. Anderson, 1989). Physicians and psychologists view this silent killer as a disorder of life-style and quality of life (Kaplan, 1988). Three components of day-to-day life that are particularly important in heart disease are worksite stress, Type A personality factors, and physiological reactivity. Intense research into each of these biobehavioral factors has altered heart patient treatment.

Worksite Stress. The likelihood that you will have a heart attack increases significantly if you are an air traffic controller or a surgeon. This occurs because

TABLE 26.1 The social readjustment rating scale

Rank	Life event	Value	Rank	Life event	Value
1	Death of spouse	100	23	Son or daughter leaving home	29
2	Divorce	73	24	Trouble with in-laws	29
3	Marital separation	65	25	Outstanding personal achievement	28
4	Jail term	63	26	Second wage-earner begins or stops work	26
5	Death of close family member	63	27	Begin or end school	26
6	Personal injury or illness	53	28	Change in living conditions	25
7	Marriage	50	29	Revision of personal habits	24
8	Fired at work	47	30	Trouble with boss	23
9	Marital reconciliation	45	31	Change in work hours or conditions	20
10	Retirement	45	32	Change in residence	20
11	Change in health of family member	44	33	Change in schools	20
12	Pregnancy	40	34	Change in recreation	19
13	Sex difficulties	39	35	Change in church activities	19
14	Gain of new family member	39	36	Change in social activities	18
15	Business readjustment	39	37	Mortgage or loan less than $10,000	17
16	Change in financial state	38	38	Change in sleeping habits	16
17	Death of close friend	37	39	Change in number of family get-togethers	15
18	Change to different line of work	36	40	Change in eating habits	15
19	Change in number of arguments with spouse	35	41	Vacation	13
20	Mortgage over $10,000	31	42	Christmas	12
21	Foreclosure of mortgage or loan	30	43	Minor violations of the law	11
22	Change in responsibilities at work	29			

Holmes and Rahe, Social readjustment rating scale, *Journal of Psychosomatic Research* 11 (1967): 213–18, copyright 1967, Pergamon Press plc.

these kinds of work are loaded with potential stressors; other jobs may demand too little or too much of a worker. Stress is also affected by autonomy, the extent to which a person controls the speed, flow, and level of work. A position with high demands and low controls increases stress. A factory worker, for example, has no control over his work and may experience stress. Worksite stress increases the prevalence of heart attacks (Levi, 1990).

TABLE 26.2 Ten most frequent hassles

Day-to-day hassles create stress as do major events in a person's life
1. Concerns about weight
2. Health of a family member
3. Rising prices of common goods
4. Home maintenance
5. Too many things to do
6. Misplacing or losing things
7. Yard work or outside home maintenance
8. Property, investment, or taxes
9. Crime
10. Physical appearance

Source: Kanner et al., 1981.

Gender differences in heart disease prevalence are apparent. Until the past decade or so, women were more likely to be in jobs (often secretarial) with high demands, low controls, and low pay—key ingredients for stress and stress-related illness (Baruch, Biener, & Barnett, 1987). Placed in similar life situations, however, men and women seem to respond similarly in developing heart disease (Hamilton & Fagot, 1988).

Type A behavior: Characterized by individuals who are competitive, impatient, hostile, and always striving to do more in less time.

Type B behavior: Characterized by people who are calmer, more patient, and less hurried than Type A behavior individuals.

Type A Behavior. In the late 1950s, two physicians (Friedman & Rosenman, 1974, studied briefly in Chapter 11) identified a pattern of behavior that they believe contributes to heart disease—Type A behavior. **Type A behavior** occurs in individuals who are competitive, impatient, hostile, and always striving to do more in less time. (Alternatively, **Type B behavior** people are calmer, more patient, less hurried.) Do you see yourself as a Type A or a Type B person? Do you know anyone who is Type A?

Early studies of Type A behavior showed a positive association with heart disease; that is, Type A individuals were more likely to have heart attacks. However, more-recent research suggests that no such relationship exists (Matthews, 1988). Some elements of Type A behavior seem related to hear disease or angina (Byrne & Reinhard, 1989), but not the overall Type A behavior pattern. For example, hostility and anger have been related to heart disease (Krantz et al., 1988), as have suspiciousness and mistrust (Weidner et al., 1989).

Has all the Type A research been discredited? No. People who are extremely anxious, depressed, angry, and unhappy have a higher rate of heart disease than normally adjusted people. Type A behavior patterns exist, but a direct relationship to heart disease is minimal or nonexistent. Rather, components of the type A personality (e.g., hostility) may predict heart disease (Friedman & Booth-Kewley, 1988; Matthews, 1988).

Physiological Reactions. A possible third factor relating stress to heart disease is how our bodies react to stress. This is called *reactivity,* or *physiological reactivity.* A situation interpreted as stressful may cause our bodies to react physiologically, triggering processes that lead to heart disease. Research shows that Type A behavior patterns are associated with increased physiological reactivity (Contrada, 1989), long-lasting emotional distress (Suls & Wan, 1980a and b), and feelings of anger and hostility (Suarez & Williams, 1989). It is still not clear whether people predisposed to heart disease show reactivity, or whether reactivity predisposes them to heart disease. Further, people who are physically fit react better physiologically to stressful situations than those who are not fit.

Although worksite stress, some components of Type A behavior, and physiological reactivity each may be individually linked to coronary heart disease, the research appears to suggest that they are interactive (Krantz et al., 1988). From a psychologist's viewpoint, these are important indications requiring further investigation. First, much more research is needed to sort out all of the factors involved. Second, behavioral factors contribute (although we are not sure how much) to heart disease. Third, and most important, psychologists can suggest interventions that will deter or lessen conditions such as stress and significantly alter the likelihood of heart disease.

Still another variable, controlling cigarette smoking, is being addressed by health psychologists with a number of methods (Burling et al., 1989) but with only moderate success because quitting smoking is so difficult for most people (Epstein & Perkins, 1988). The challenges exist, the research continues, and we all await preventive measures that will help combat both the harmful effects of stress and heart disease. Stress affects many areas of a person's life, such as in the disorder we consider next, post-traumatic stress disorder.

Learning Objective 26.8
Characterize posttraumatic stress disorder, and identify the people who are likely to be victims of this disorder.

Post-traumatic Stress Disorder

In 1989, a group of army veterans returned with several therapists to Vietnam, where they had waged war more than two decades earlier. This time, however, their mission was not to fight an enemy but to heal their own psychological wounds. One veteran reported that he had been haunted for years by nightmares of his combat experiences. His return to Vietnam helped him lay those nightmares to rest.

Origins and Symptoms. Sometimes stress-related disorders are severe; psychologists now designate a category of mental disorders evident after a person has undergone the stress of some type of disaster: **post-traumatic stress disorder.** Victims of rape, natural disasters (tornadoes, earthquakes, hurricanes, floods), and human-made disasters (wars, train wrecks, toxic chemical spills) often suffer from this disorder. Many survivors of the San Francisco earthquake still fear the double-decker freeways of California, which took a heavy toll in the quake; post-traumatic stress disorder is still evident after the 1980 volcanic eruption of Mt. St. Helens (Shore, Vollmer, & Tatum, 1989).

Common symptoms of post-traumatic stress disorder include vivid, intrusive recollections or reexperiences of the traumatic event and occasional lapses of normal consciousness. People may develop anxiety, depression, or exceptionally aggressive behavior; they may avoid situations that resemble the traumatizing events. Such behaviors eventually interfere with daily functioning, family interactions, and health. Research on post-traumatic stress disorder is scanty, with only a few studies focusing on natural disasters such as tornadoes (e.g., Madakasira & O'Brien, 1987) or floods (Solomon et al., 1987); there have been many more studies on Vietnam veterans (e.g., Pitman et al., 1990).

post-traumatic stress disorder: A mental disorder occurring after a person has undergone a trauma: common symptoms include vivid, intrusive recollections or re-experiences of the traumatic event and occasional lapses of normal consciousness.

The Vietnam Veteran. Vietnam veterans, such as Tony (introduced at the beginning of this chapter) are vulnerable to post–traumatic stress disorder. Thousands of the 600,000 Americans who served in that war still suffer feelings of

Stress is an unavoidable part of our lives. The loss of a home through fire or the assumption of the responsibilities accompanying marriage are both high stress situations.

alienation, sleeping problems, reliving of painful experiences, and concentration difficulties. Most veterans do not suffer from the disorder; of those who do, many did not experience symptoms until months or even years after their return home. Those who suffer from the disorder seem more likely to have other stressful events in their lives, which in turn make the disorder worse—a vicious cycle (Solomon et al., 1988).

The Vietnam war created unique psychological problems (Kaylor, King, & King, 1987). Survival—not patriotism—was the primary concern of many military personnel who served. Some servicemen turned to drugs such as alcohol to alleviate fear. Moreover, combatants knew that many people in the United States vehemently opposed the conflict. Finally, unlike the 1991 conflict in the Persian Gulf, many Vietnam veterans were whisked home without ceremony or a chance to reacclimate gradually (Walker & Cavenar, 1982).

For a number of complicated psychological, political, and social reasons, mental health practitioners have tended to be unresponsive to individuals suffering from post–traumatic stress disorder. Too often, clients have been held responsible for how they react to stress. Now that psychologists recognize the disorder, special help in the form of workshops and therapy is becoming available, and drug therapies are being assessed (Lerer et al., 1987). Clients who feel disoriented and disheartened have options; they need not consider their lives a waste or their situations hopeless. When people feel doomed, they often consider or attempt reckless acts such as suicide, considered in the next section.

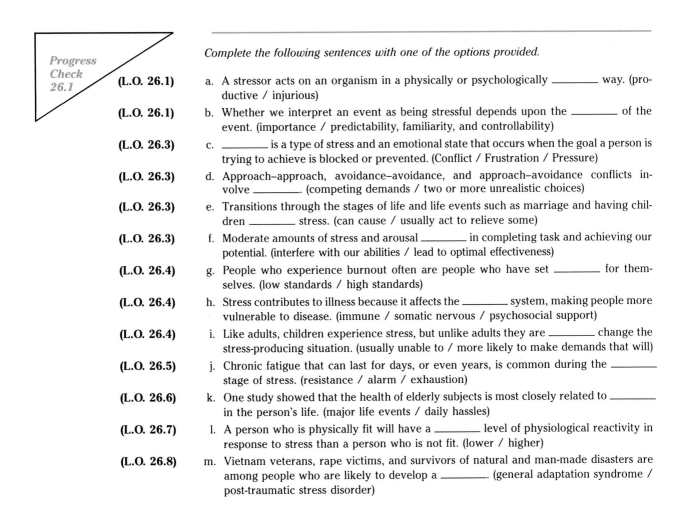

Progress Check 26.1

Complete the following sentences with one of the options provided.

(L.O. 26.1) a. A stressor acts on an organism in a physically or psychologically ________ way. (productive / injurious)

(L.O. 26.1) b. Whether we interpret an event as being stressful depends upon the ________ of the event. (importance / predictability, familiarity, and controllability)

(L.O. 26.3) c. ________ is a type of stress and an emotional state that occurs when the goal a person is trying to achieve is blocked or prevented. (Conflict / Frustration / Pressure)

(L.O. 26.3) d. Approach–approach, avoidance–avoidance, and approach–avoidance conflicts involve ________. (competing demands / two or more unrealistic choices)

(L.O. 26.3) e. Transitions through the stages of life and life events such as marriage and having children ________ stress. (can cause / usually act to relieve some)

(L.O. 26.3) f. Moderate amounts of stress and arousal ________ in completing task and achieving our potential. (interfere with our abilities / lead to optimal effectiveness)

(L.O. 26.4) g. People who experience burnout often are people who have set ________ for themselves. (low standards / high standards)

(L.O. 26.4) h. Stress contributes to illness because it affects the ________ system, making people more vulnerable to disease. (immune / somatic nervous / psychosocial support)

(L.O. 26.4) i. Like adults, children experience stress, but unlike adults they are ________ change the stress-producing situation. (usually unable to / more likely to make demands that will)

(L.O. 26.5) j. Chronic fatigue that can last for days, or even years, is common during the ________ stage of stress. (resistance / alarm / exhaustion)

(L.O. 26.6) k. One study showed that the health of elderly subjects is most closely related to ________ in the person's life. (major life events / daily hassles)

(L.O. 26.7) l. A person who is physically fit will have a ________ level of physiological reactivity in response to stress than a person who is not fit. (lower / higher)

(L.O. 26.8) m. Vietnam veterans, rape victims, and survivors of natural and man-made disasters are among people who are likely to develop a ________. (general adaptation syndrome / post-traumatic stress disorder)

Coping and Adjustment

Most people need a way to cope with anxiety and the physical ailments produced by stress. Some people seek medical and psychological help; others turn to alcohol and other drugs. From your own experience, do you know some coping techniques that are more effective than others?

What Is Coping?

Learning Objective 26.9 List five features of coping behavior, and identify important factors that influence how well people cope.

In general, *coping* means dealing with a situation. However, for a psychologist, **coping** is the process by which a person takes some action to manage environmental and internal demands that cause, or might cause, stress and that will tax the individual's inner resources. This definition of coping involves five important components. First, coping is constantly changing and being evaluated, and is therefore a *process* or *strategy.* Second, coping involves *managing* situations, not necessarily bringing them under complete control. Third, coping is *effortful;* it does not happen automatically. Fourth, coping aims to manage *behavioral* as well as *cognitive* events. Finally, coping is a *learned* process.

Many types of coping strategies exist; a person may use one, two, or many of them. Coping begins at the biological level. People's bodies respond to stress with specific reactions, including changes in hormone levels, autonomic nervous system activity, and the amount of neurotransmitters in the brain. Effective coping strategies occur at the psychological level when people learn new ways of dealing with their vulnerabilities.

Vulnerability, Coping Skills, and Social Support

A crucial factor that determines how well people cope with their problems is vulnerability. **Vulnerability** is the extent to which people are easily impaired by an event and thus respond maladaptively. A person who is vulnerable is not very resiliant. Whether a person is vulnerable depends on his or her coping skills. **Coping skills** are the techniques people use to deal with stress and changing situations. People who have effective coping skills to guide them are prepared to deal with stress-related situations and are thus less vulnerable (Wieze, 1991). On the other hand, people with poor coping skills may be extremely vulnerable and not able to deal well with stress at all. In some cases, they even develop a sense of *learned helplessness,* which results from learning that rewards and punishments are not contingent on their behavior, so they learn not to try to cope, thereby remaining helpless. Faced with poor coping skills and a loss of control, some people stop responding. (We discuss learned helplessness further in Chapters 13 and 15).

A person's vulnerability is affected by the extent to which he or she has social support. **Social support** is the availability of comfort, recognition, approval, and encouragement from other people. When people feel supported by others with emotional concern and displays of caring, such as a phone call or a note, they can cope better with extraordinary pressure, especially when the support is offered by someone who is considered important to the vulnerable person (Dakof & Taylor, 1990). In addition to, and sometimes in place of, friends and family, group therapy (Chapter 14) can be especially effective in alleviating anxiety. In group therapy, other people in similar situations can offer emotional concern and support. According to psychologist Richard Lazarus (1982), people faced with constant stress, whether supported or not, use either defense- or task-oriented coping strategies, considered next.

coping: The process by which a person manages environmental and internal demands that do, or even that might, cause stress.

vulnerability: The extent to which people are easily impaired by an event, and thus respond maladaptively to external or internal demands being placed upon them.

coping skills: The techniques people use to deal with stress and changing situations.

social support: Comfort, recognition, approval, and encouragement provided to a person by others, including friends, family, organizations, and co-workers.

Defense-Oriented Coping Strategies

Learning Objective 26.10
Describe defense-oriented and task-oriented coping strategies, and discuss the effectiveness of each.

Defense-oriented coping strategies do not reduce the stress, but they help people to protect themselves from its effects. These strategies ease distress, thereby enabling people to tolerate and deal with disturbances. As we saw in Chapter 12, Freud and other personality theorists described defense mechanisms by which people distort reality in order to defend themselves against life's pressures. One such mechanism is *rationalization,* whereby people reinterpret reality to make it more palatable. If your boyfriend or girlfriend dumps you, you might cope by telling your friends that you "never really liked him (or her) anyway!" Similarly, a person who is turned down for a job may rationalize that he didn't want to work for the company after all. Another defense mechanism is *reaction formation.* A woman who raves about her new job but is feeling a lot of stress and fear has developed a reaction formation. She is expressing a feeling that is the opposite her true one.

Task-Oriented Coping Strategies

Stress management is becoming increasingly important to highly stressed individuals. Counselors commonly treat stress by identifying the source and then by helping the client modify his or her behavior to cope with it. Through therapy, a person troubled by stressful situations can learn to cope by untangling personal feelings, understanding the sources of the stress, and then modifying his or her behavior to alleviate it.

Students about to enter college, for example, often show signs of stress. They're worried about academic pressures, social life, and overall adjustment. At some schools, incoming college students can receive counseling to learn how to deal with their stress. Similarly, stress-management seminars, in which psycholo-

People who cope with stress successfully alleviate their concern over an issue by taking positive action and seeking others' support.

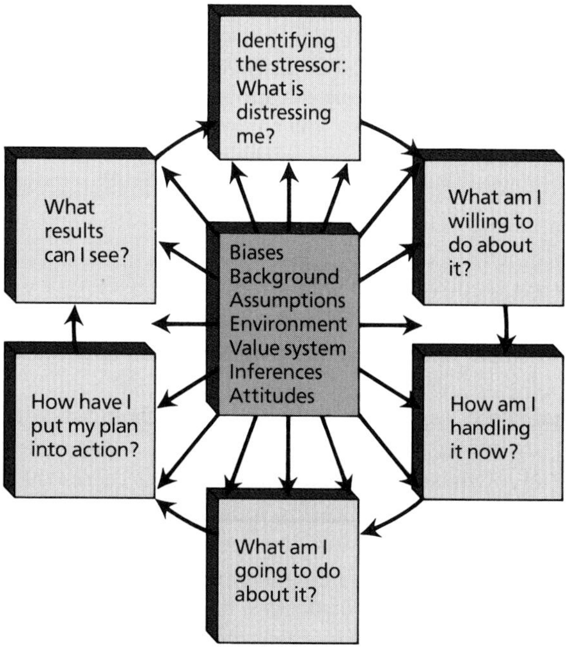

Figure 26.4

The steps involved in developing a stress-reduction program.

APPLYING PSYCHOLOGY

Coping, Health, and a Positive Attitude

Applied psychologists claim that simply maintaining a positive attitude can have beneficial effects on coping with stress and reducing physical symptoms. People who feel that they have control over their lives, health, and well-being are more relaxed than those who do not (Rodin, 1986). An upbeat mood, a positive sense of personal control, and even a self-serving bias (discussed in Chapter 15) can facilitate worthwhile behaviors, such as helping others and evaluating people more favorably. Some researchers suggest that people who have positive attitudes may even live longer. People say, "Look on the bright side," with the aim of reframing a situation to make it appear better, and to change a person's attitude and thus his or her behavior.

Sometimes, reframing or rethinking a situation is a rationalization (see Chapter 10) to make it less anxiety-producing. Taking a positive approach and believing in your own abilities helps you to ward off stress and to avoid the fear and arousal that come from feelings of despair and low self-esteem (Bandura et al., 1988). Seligman (1988) argues that optimism helps people achieve goals and cope more effectively—for example, optimistic salespeople substantially outsell their pessimistic colleagues.

People can develop a positive attitude by conserving resources. Hobfoll (1989) suggests that people strive to retain, protect, and build resources because the potential or actual loss of these valued resources is threatening. A person's home, marriage, or status as a community leader are all resources; and from Hobfoll's view, when these resources are under attack, people try to defend themselves against these attacks. They attempt to ward off the attack or replace the loss of resources by seeking a new marriage or new leadership position, or by gaining some new area of competence or financial strength. Treatment might mean shifting a person's focus of attention and reinterpreting the threat, replacing the lost resources (e.g., finding a new job), and reevaluating the threat. Hobfoll argues (1989) that a new more modern view of stress should go beyond the idea of stress as a reaction. His alternative is the conservation-of-resources model.

One effect of a positive approach is that it may harness the body's own defense mechanisms. Recent studies of **psychoneuroimmunology** (PNI)—the relationship between the immune system and behavior—have shown that the immune system (which fights disease) responds to a person's moods, stress, and basic attitudes about life. According to PNI researchers, the brain provides information to the immune system about how and when to respond. The two systems seem to be linked together, with each producing substances that alter the other's functions. The brain sends signals to the immune system that trigger its disease-fighting ability. The immune system sends signals to the brain that alter its functioning (Glaser & Kiecolt-Glaser, 1988). Thus, the immune system of a person with a positive, upbeat attitude, responds better and faster than that of a person who is depressed and lethargic, whose depressed immune system slows down (Kiecolt-Glaser & Glaser, 1988). Consider people who have recently lost loved ones to death; they consistently show higher rates of illness. Today, many AIDS patients are provided counseling to bolster their immune systems by improving their attitudes, which may help them live longer.

gists help business executives deal with stress in the corporate world, are becoming increasingly popular. The aim of both programs is the same: to modify a person's response to stress and to replace maladaptive responses with more useful ones.

psychoneuroimmunology: [SIE-ko-NEW-ro-IM-u-NOLL-oh-gee] (PNI) The study of how psychological processes and the nervous system affect and are affected by the body's natural defense system—the immune system.

Most psychologists, especially behavioral psychologists, recommend *task-oriented coping strategies* that often involve stress management. The general strategy usually involves several steps (see Figure 26.4 on the previous page). These can be simplified to the following four steps: (1) *Identifying the source of stress*—because stress-producing situations exist in many areas, identifying the source of stress is often difficult. (2) *Choosing an appropriate course of action for stress reduction*—Once the source of stress is found, people need to choose among several coping strategies. (3) *Implementing the plan*—Helping people prepare for stressful situations. (4) *Evaluating the plan's success*—A well-designed coping plan

Some psychologists find it difficult to accept the fact that the immune system responds to mental attitudes. The concept is not behavioral, in the sense that it can easily be trained, shaped, or measured. Researchers, however, are beginning to acknowledge that people can harness the power of positive thinking (O'Leary, 1990). Though positive attitudes and illusions can be beneficial, they can only go so far (DeAngelis, 1988) and help some people (Manuck, et al., 1991). Sometimes, having a positive attitude and practicing hypnosis, meditation, and the other traditional techniques fail to reduce stress. Sometimes, it is because they are tried half-heartedly; at other times, they are attempted inexpertly. More often, people just lack coping skills or even knowledge that such skills exist. Wearing rose-colored glasses from time to time can be beneficial, but continuous self-deception can lead to maladjustment, lies, and a truly distorted view of reality. Unfortunately, some individuals turn to chemical substances to alleviate their pain, stress, fatigue, and anxiety—and these substances often lead to abuse.

Effective coping strategies: There are a number of steps you can take to cope, manage stress, and stay healthy.

- **Increase exercise.** People cope better when they improve physical fitness, usually through exercise. In addition, increased exercise will lower blood pressure, reducing the risk of heart disease.
- **Eat well.** People feel better and cope better when they eat well and have a balanced diet. This also means not being overweight.
- **Sleep well.** People react better to life when they have had a good night's sleep—reaction time improves, as does judgment.
- **Learn to relax.** In our fast-paced society, few people take the time to relax and let uncomfortable ideas and feelings leave them. Learn meditation, yoga, or deep breathing. Schedule some time each day for yourself.
- **Be flexible.** Our lives are unpredictable; accept that fact, and day-to-day surprises will be easier to handle.
- **Keep stress at school or the office.** Work-related pressures should be kept in a work environment. Bringing stress and pressure home will only make the problem worse; people are more likely to be involved in substance abuse and domestic violence when they bring stress home with them.
- **Communicate.** Share your ideas, feelings, and thoughts with the significant people in your life. This will decrease misunderstanding, mistrust, and stress.
- **Seek support.** Social support from family, friends, and self-help groups helps you to appraise a situation differently. Remember, you have to appraise a situation as stressful for it to be stressful—social support helps you keep stressful situations in perspective.

- ***What is the fundamental assumption that many applied psychologists maintain about health and well-being?***
- ***What is the evidence that the immune system is implicated in the relationship of attitudes and health?***
- ***Because people often lack adequate coping skills, they often take steps that are deleterious to their physical health; what are the implications for applied psychologists in terms of providing advice and counseling to help patients and even people who are not making drastic mistakes but not doing as well as they might?***

involves evaluating the plan's success. Have the techniques been effective? Is there still more do do? Are new or further actions needed?

One way in which to help people prepare for stressful situations is by providing them with new ideas is called stress inoculation. Sometimes **stress inoculation** involves a single technique such as breathing deeply and regularly. At other times it is more elaborate, involving graded exposure to various levels of threats or providing detailed information about a forthcoming procedure (Janis, 1985). Janis likens stress inoculation to an antibiotic dose given to ward off disease. It helps people to defend themselves and to cope with an event when it occurs. Stress inoculation increases the predictability of stressful events, fosters coping skills, generates positive self-talking, encourages confidence about successful outcomes, and builds a commitment to personal action and responsibility for an adaptive course of action.

stress inoculation: [in-OK-you-LAY-shun] The procedure of giving people realistic warnings, recommendations, and reassurances to help them prepare for and cope with impending dangers or losses.

Almost everyone who commits suicide shows signs of depression prior to the attempt.

Failures in Coping: Suicide

Learning Objective 26.11 Discuss suicide rates in the United States, identify some of the warning signs given by potential suicide victims, discuss the causes of suicide and the ways that we can help to prevent it from occurring.

Most people who think about suicide do not actually commit the act. However, as in *Hamlet,* the processes of deciding, contemplating, and evaluating can take a heavy toll. When people are depressed during such contemplation, the likelihood that they will actually commit suicide increases. Suicide is traditionally studied in the context of sociology, the study of the structure, function, and organization of society. However, suicide is as much a psychological as a sociological phenomenon. Today, researchers examine suicide from the point of view of sociology and psychology—in this case, the disciplines meld.

According to sociologists, each day, about 80 people in the United States commit suicide—that's 30,000 people each year. These individuals are often lonely, guilty, and depressed. They feel that things cannot and will not get better, and that suicide is their best option. A distinction must be drawn between attempters and completers. *Attempters* try to commit suicide but are unsuccessful; they tend to be young, more often women, impulsive, and more likely to make nonfatal attempts, such as wrist slashing. *Completers* take their lives successfully; they tend to be male and older, and they use highly lethal techniques of self-destruction, such as hand guns. Nonetheless, all suicide attempts are cause for grave concern.

Suicide rates in the United States are alarming. More than three times as many men as women actually commit suicide, although four times as many women attempt it (U.S. Department of Health and Human Services, 1986). Among adolescents, suicide is the second leading cause of death (after accidents); 1 out of every 1000 adolescents attempts suicide each year, and nearly 5000 young people between the ages of 15 and 24 years are successful (Stivers, 1988). The elderly, divorced, and former patients with psychological disorders have a higher likelihood of attempting and committing suicide. In fact, the elderly make up 23% of those who commit suicide (U.S. Department of Health and Human Services, 1986). People who have been suffering from major depression are more likely to attempt suicide while they are recovering, when their energy level is higher. At the depths of depression, a person is usually too weak, divided, and lacking in energy to commit suicide. Although only 15% of depressed people are suicidal, most suicide-prone individuals are depressed.

Are there warning signs of suicide? Psychologists point to several indicators: changes in personal appearance, dramatic drop in schoolwork, changes in drug abuse patterns, decreased appetite, giving away prized possessions, and most important, a depressed attitude. Nearly everyone who is suicidal exhibits depression; such individuals show changes in sleeping patterns, diminished ability to concentrate, fatigue, and feelings of worthlessness. In addition, 86% of those who are successful have attempted suicide before. Clearly, suicide attempters may become suicide completers if no one intervenes.

Most suicide completers talked about their death in advance and gave signs to those around them that it was a possibility. For some, suicide follows a tragic event; for others, it is an attempt to relieve suffering and pain. For still others, it is an attempt to make a political, religious, or social statement; for the Japanese kamikaze fighters in World War II, suicide was a way to achieve honor.

Causes. The causes of suicide are as complex as the people who commit suicide and may lie both within the individual (psychological) and outside the individual in society (sociological). For some individuals, societal pressures serve as a catalyst, leading them to take their own lives. For others, the catalysts are ill parents, substance abuse that impairs judgment, or traumatic events. For still other people, a long-standing series of psychological disorders may predispose them to suicide.

Psychologists cite a broad array of factors that may influence a suicide attempt. *Biological* psychologists assert that certain neurotransmitters have been linked to disorders that predispose an individual to suicide (e.g., Ray, 1991). *Behavioral* psychologists suggest that past experiences with suicide (by observing the effects of suicides on other people) make the behavior reinforcing. Other people who have taken their lives may also serve as models for the behavior (Davidson et al., 1989)—this idea is controversial because it is not always the case (Kessler et al., 1989).

Psychodynamically oriented psychologists suggest that a person is turning hostility and anger inward. Freud might argue that the act of suicide is the ultimate release of aggressive instinct. *Cognitive* psychologists assert that suicide is the failure of a person's problem-solving abilities in response to stress, or alternatively, that a person's cognitive assessment is that his or her future is hopeless. *Humanists* see suicide as a waste of a human being's potential, and they attempt to help suicidal and depressed patients focus on the meaning in their lives so that they might fulfill rather than destroy themselves. Many theorists, regardless of orientation, focus on a person's attempt to escape from aversive self-awareness (Baumeister, 1990).

Sociologists tend to focus on society and its role in suicide and its prevention. In particular, adolescent suicide has received a great deal of attention. Adolescents who attempt suicide often see a wide discrepancy between their high personal ambitions and meager results. The causes of adolescent suicide are still not fully understood, but the increasing pressures and stress faced by adolescents today certainly contribute to the rising number of suicides. Adolescents face an extremely competitive work force, a social situation teeming with violence, crime, and drugs, and alternating pressure to conform and to be an individual. Often, angry and frustrated adolescents exhibit other self-destructive behaviors (Stivers, 1988) in addition to feeling hopeless (Kashani, Reid, & Rosenberg, 1989) and low self-esteem (Stivers, 1990).

Adaptive behaviors, such as working out on a regular basis, are preventive measures that protect an individual's overall health. Many companies are recognizing this and provide exercise facilities to their personnel.

Prevention. Most individuals who attempt suicide want to live, but their stress and sense of helplessness about the future tells them that death is the only way

TABLE 26.3 Facts and fables about suicide

Numerous false beliefs persist about suicide. The following list is compiled from numerous sources, but especially from the continuing work of the two most noted names in suicide research, Edwin Shneidman and Norman Farberow.

Fable	Fact
1. Suicide happens without warning.	1. Suicidal individuals give many clues; 80% have to some degree discussed with others their intent to commit suicide.
2. Once people become suicidal, they remain so.	2. Suicidal persons remain so for limited periods, thus the value of temporary restraint.
3. Suicide occurs almost exclusively among affluent or very poor individuals.	3. Suicide tends to occur proportionately in all economic levels of society.
4. Virtually all suicidal individuals are mentally ill.	4. As already noted, this is not so.
5. Suicidal tendencies are inherited or run in families.	5. There is no evidence for a direct genetic factor.
6. Suicide does not occur in primitive cultures.	6. Suicide occurs in almost all societies and cultures.
7. Ritual suicide is common in Japan.	7. Ritual suicide is rare in modern Japan; the most common method is barbiturate overdose.
8. Writers and artists have the highest suicide rates because they are "a bit crazy to begin with."	8. Physicians and police officers have the highest suicide rates; they have access to the most lethal means, and their work involves a high level of frustration.
9. Once a person starts to come out of a depression, the risk of suicide dissipates.	9. The risk of suicide is highest in the initial phase of an upswing from the depth of depression.
10. People who attempt suicide fully intend to die.	10. People who attempt suicide have a diversity of motives.

Source: Meyer & Salmon, 1988.

out—this is even more true of adults than of adolescents (Cole, 1989). Some are helped by crisis intervention and hot lines (at which a crisis worker might help a person avoid taking his or her life). Sociologists and psychologists often focus their research efforts on high-risk groups—people suffering from depression or substance abuse. Those who were recently seriously depressed, those who have had a traumatic loss, or those who have been forced into retirement or are suffering ill health are all at greater risk. See Table 26.3 for some facts and fables about suicide.

When a person makes a suicide threat, take it seriously. Because most people who commit suicide leave clues to their intentions ahead of time, people need to be aware of such clues. Statements such as "I don't want to go on" or "I'm a burden to everyone, so maybe I should end it all" should be taken as warning signs. When people begin to give things away or to write letters with ominous tones to relatives and friends, these too are signs.

If you know someone you think may be contemplating suicide, here are some steps that Curran (1987) suggests you can take:

- ▲ Talk. Don't be afraid to talk with your friend or relative about suicide; it will not influence him or her to commit suicide.
- ▲ Talk with a person who is at risk about stressors; the more an individual talks, the better.
- ▲ Help a person who is contemplating suicide to seek out a psychologist, counselor, or parent. A person thinking of suicide needs counseling.
- ▲ Tell your friend's spouse, parent, guardian, or counselor. Unless you are certain that these people know, you should tell someone responsible for your friend's welfare.
- ▲ Do not keep a contemplated suicide a secret. Resist your friend's attempt to keep you quiet about his or her confidences. Despite a friend's wishes for secrecy, be responsible, and tell the friend's relatives or guardian.

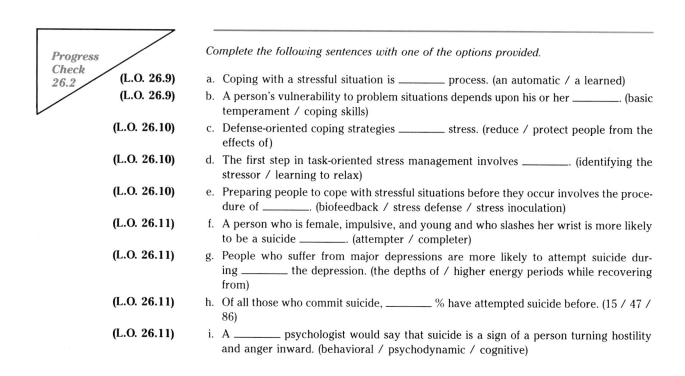

Progress Check 26.2

Complete the following sentences with one of the options provided.

(L.O. 26.9) a. Coping with a stressful situation is ________ process. (an automatic / a learned)

(L.O. 26.9) b. A person's vulnerability to problem situations depends upon his or her ________. (basic temperament / coping skills)

(L.O. 26.10) c. Defense-oriented coping strategies ________ stress. (reduce / protect people from the effects of)

(L.O. 26.10) d. The first step in task-oriented stress management involves ________. (identifying the stressor / learning to relax)

(L.O. 26.10) e. Preparing people to cope with stressful situations before they occur involves the procedure of ________. (biofeedback / stress defense / stress inoculation)

(L.O. 26.11) f. A person who is female, impulsive, and young and who slashes her wrist is more likely to be a suicide ________. (attempter / completer)

(L.O. 26.11) g. People who suffer from major depressions are more likely to attempt suicide during ________ the depression. (the depths of / higher energy periods while recovering from)

(L.O. 26.11) h. Of all those who commit suicide, ________ % have attempted suicide before. (15 / 47 / 86)

(L.O. 26.11) i. A ________ psychologist would say that suicide is a sign of a person turning hostility and anger inward. (behavioral / psychodynamic / cognitive)

Module Summary

Stress

- A *stressor* is a stimulus that acts on an organism in either physically or psychologically injurious ways. Stressors can produce anxiety, tension, and especially physiological arousal (p. 493).
- Physiologically, the stress response is characterized by arousal. Behaviorally, stress and its arousal response are related; when people are moderately aroused, they behave with optimal effectiveness; when underaroused they lack stimulation to behave effectively. Emotionally, people's reactions often depend on their frustration, their work-related pressures, and their day-to-day conflicts (p. 494).
- People exposed to high levels of stress for long periods of time may develop stress-related disorders, including physical illness. *Post-traumatic stress disorder* is a category of mental disorders evident after a person has undergone some type of trauma; common symptoms include vivid, intrusive recollections or reexperiences of the traumatic event and even occasional lapses of normal consciousness (p. 502).

Coping and Adjustment

- *Coping* is the process by which a person manages environmental and internal demands that cause, or that might cause, stress and will tax his or her inner resources. Coping skills are the techniques people use to come to grips with the sources of stress they encounter (p. 504).
- *Defense-oriented coping* strategies do not reduce stress but instead help people protect themselves from its effects. Most psychologists, especially behavioral psychologists, recommend *task-oriented coping* strategies, which often involve stress management (p. 505).
- A distinction should be drawn between suicide attempters and completers. An *attempter* tries to commit suicide but is unsuccessful; *completers* take their lives successfully, though attempters often can become completers. Suicide is the second leading cause of death among adolescents; the peak age for suicide attempts is between 25 and 29 years of age. Most suicide completers have talked about their death in advance; most want to live, but their sense of helplessness about the future tells them that death is the only way out (p. 508).

KEY TERMS

SELF-TEST

Module 26

- Before taking the self-test, **recite** and **review.**
- Use the key at the back of the text to *correct* your answers.
- **Restudy** pages that correspond to any questions you answered incorrectly.

1. Which of the following is the most accurate definition for the term *stress?*
   a. A state of emotional and physical exhaustion.
   b. An increase in automatic nervous system activity.
   c. A generalized feeling of fear and apprehension.
   d. A nonspecific, often global response to life's demands.
2. In order for an event to be considered a stressor, an individual must
   a. feel intense anxiety for at least 5 minutes.
   b. appraise the event as being stressful.
   c. have competing needs.
   d. have other things on his or her mind.
3. According to Miller, if a person is in an approach–avoidance conflict, the person will
   a. avoid the entire situation.
   b. choose to approach if he or she is close to achieving a goal.
   c. find a way to make the avoidance part of the conflict more palatable.
   d. more than likely, flip a coin or make a decision based on some fleeting whim of thought.
4. A person's work situation can cause stress if the work
   a. setting is noisy or crowded.
   b. is too light or sparse.
   c. involves making frequent critical decisions.
   d. all of the above
5. Which of the following is the first change that occurs when a person is stressed?
   a. Behavior becomes disorganized.
   b. Automatic nervous system becomes aroused.
   c. The person becomes annoyed or angry.
   d. The person's emotions vacillate.
6. Complete the following statement: People who experience burnout
   a. feel emotionally drained and often stop trying to achieve.
   b. express heightened concern about others.
   c. have emotional and social problems, but no physical ones.
   d. have the experience immediately after returning from a vacation or leave of absence.
7. Hans Selye's conceptualization of a progressive three-stage response to stress is called the
   a. social readjustment scale.
   b. general adaptation syndrome.
   c. stress–rest cycle.
   d. transactional model of stress.
8. According to Holmes and Rahe, "stressful life events"
   a. are major changes in a person's day-to-day circumstances that necessitate change.
   b. occur when minor daily hassles add up over several years.
   c. can be avoided by most people.
   d. both b and c.

9. Heart disease
   a. is directly related to Type A behavior.
   b. may be related to some components of Type A behavior, such as anger, hostility, and unhappiness.
   c. occurs more often in Type B people than in Type A people.
   d. seems to have no relationship to behavior or personality types.
10. Which statement best describes post-traumatic stress disorder?
   a. Victims experience vivid recollections of the traumatic event.
   b. The disorder is frequently accompanied by anxiety, depression, and exceptionally aggressive behavior.
   c. Occasional lapses of normal consciousness can occur.
   d. All of the above.
11. A person who has poor coping skills and lacks a sense of control
   a. would be classified as a "vulnerable" person.
   b. may develop learned helplessness and stop responding.
   c. would benefit from having a strong social support system.
   d. all of the above.
12. Coping strategies that make use of defense mechanisms
   a. involve an unconscious distortion of reality.
   b. eliminate environmental stressors.
   c. are ineffective, though they are frequently taught in stress-management training sessions.
   d. all of the above.
13. Suicide seems to be
   a. caused by psychological and sociological factors.
   b. an easy way of avoiding responsibility.
   c. a self-destructive behavior exhibited only by people who have severe psychological disorders.
   d. a very private event; most suicide completers give no warning signs.
14. The best way to behave in a situation where you are concerned about a friend who seems suicidal is
   a. watch from a distance so he or she can have time to work out emotional problems.
   b. ignore statements about suicide so that you do not reinforce immature, attention-seeking behaviors.
   c. try to help your friend feel better, but keep his or her problems and suicidal warnings confidential.
   d. talk to your friend, give guidance to your friend, and tell someone who is responsible for your friend's welfare of your concerns.

Connections

If you are interested in . . .	Turn to . . .	To learn more about . . .
The role of stress in every day life	◆ Chapter 9, p. 359	The relationship between arousal and stress
	◆ Chapter 13, p. 523	How certain psychological disorders have a strong component of anxiety
	◆ Chapter 15, p. 630	How frustration can lead to stress and ultimately agression
How people cope with everyday problems	◆ Chapter 4, p. 142	Various coping techniques (such as biofeedback and self-hypnosis), which can be practiced at home to effectively manage stressors
	◆ Chapter 11, p. 387	How people can learn to control their emotional responses to situations through self-instruction
	◆ Chapter 13, p. 540	How seriously depressed people often feel there is no hope and that they cannot cope any longer
	◆ Chapter 14, p. 578	Cognitive therapy, which focuses on changing people's distorted ideas of reality and helps them to develop positive self-esteem
Psychology's role in health and wellbeing	◆ Chapter 5, p. 168	How the immune system can be conditioned to respond to environmental stimulation
	◆ Chapter 8, p. 333	The inevitable physical deterioration that occurs with aging
	◆ Chapter 13, p. 527	Various disorders that affect both physical and mental health

The relationship of stress, health, and coping to the various subdisciplines of psychology is readily evident. People's health is dependent on their body and biological mechanisms working properly (Chapter 2, p. 43). When health is poor or level of stress is high, people may have trouble sleeping and unfortunately often turn to substances to elevate pain (Chapter 4, p. 145). How people interpret stress is dependent on both their cognitive level of development (Chapter 8, p. 296) and how well they have passed through various adult life cycles (Chapter 8, p. 321). How people interpret stress and cope also depends on their personality (Chapter 10, p. 494), their intelligence (Chapter 11, p. 444), and the attitudes that they have developed about other people and institutions (Chapter 15, p. 598). Whether people cope effectively in response to stress not only affects their health and adjustment, but in severe cases may lead to maladjustment (Chapter 13, p. 527).

Module 27 ► ABNORMALITY, MALADJUSTMENT, AND ANXIETY DISORDERS 518

Module 28 ► SERIOUS BEHAVIOR DISORDERS 534

Chapter 13

Psychological Disorders

Behavior characterized as (1) atypical, (2) socially unacceptable, (3) distressing, (4) maladaptive, or (5) the result of distorted thoughts is the focus of this chapter. The first module of this chapter, Module 27, pays special attention to these five distinguishing characteristics of abnormal behavior. The system that psychologists use to classify maladjustment, presented in a work that is abbreviated as *DSM-III-R,* is described, and the strengths and weakness of this system are discussed. The module introduces the topic of anxiety—feelings of fear and apprehension, often accompanied by increased physiological arousal, which might be related to particular events or object. The unit concludes with a presentation of anxiety disorders and somatoform disorders, two types of problems that have anxiety as a central and underlying symptom.

The second module of this chapter, Module 28, presents some of the major behavioral disorders that seriously impair functioning. When a person is suffering from some form of maladjustment, the person's life is often turned upside-down. Normal functioning becomes difficult, thoughts become confusing, and sometimes people become unable to evaluate reality. Personality disorders are presented; these are disorders in which behavior appears odd or eccentric, fearful or anxious, or dramatic, emotional, and erratic. Sexual deviations are another form of maladjustment; these are sexual practices directed toward objects rather than people, sexual encounters involving real or simulated suffering or humiliation, or sexual activities with nonconsenting partners. Depression is introduced as part of a section on mood disorders; depression is so common in our society that it is covered in depth. Last, schizophrenia, an especially serious behavior disorder, is presented. The various subtypes of schizophrenia are characterized, and recovery rates and causes are considered.

Module 27

Abnormality, Maladjustment, and Anxiety Disorders

LEARNING OBJECTIVES

When you have mastered the material in this module, you will be able to

What Is Abnormal Behavior? (p. 519)

27.1 Identify the percentage of U.S. citizens who exhibit symptoms of abnormality, describe five characteristics of abnormal behavior, and distinguish between *maladjustment* and *abnormal behavior* (p. 519).

27.2 Describe the medical–biological, psychodynamic, humanistic, behavioral, cognitive, sociocultural, and eclectic models of abnormal behavior (p. 520).

Diagnosing Abnormal Behavior: DSM-III-R (p. 522)

27.3 Describe the *DSM-III-R,* explain what it is used for, and discuss some of the controversy surrounding it (p. 522).

Anxiety Disorders (pp. 523–527)

27.4 Discuss Horney and Freud's views on anxiety, explain how contemporary psychologists view anxiety, and characterize generalized anxiety disorders (p. 524).

27.5 Describe the type of people who develop phobias and characterize agoraphobia, social phobia, and simple phobias (p. 524).

27.6 Characterize obsessive–compulsive disorders and identify three possible causes of the disorder (p. 527).

Somatoform and Dissociative Disorders (pp. 527–529)

27.7 Characterize three somatoform disorders (p. 527).

SQ3R
- ▲ **Survey** to set goals for studying.
- ▲ Ask **questions** as you **read.**
- ▲ Stop occasionally to **recite** and **review.**

plus
- ▲ **Write** a summary of key points.
- ▲ **Reflect** on the hypotheses, evidence, and implications of this material and on the relevance it has to *your* life.

Under a 1987 directive issued by Mayor Edward Koch to help New York City's mentally ill homeless, Joyce Brown was forcibly committed to Bellevue Hospital. The 40-year-old former secretary had lived on a Manhattan sidewalk for a year, feeding herself on seven dollars a day and huddling over a hot-air vent in winter to stay warm. She was dirty and incoherent, cursed at passersby, defecated in her clothes, and tore up and burned dollar bills given to her. Brown, however, didn't want to be "helped." "Some people are street people," she said. "That's the life they choose to lead."

abnormal behavior: Behavior characterized as atypical, socially unacceptable, distressing, maladaptive, or the result of distorted cognitions.

Brown took her battle to court, and the judge found her to be educated, intelligent, and fiercely independent. In explaining her odd behavior, Brown said that after she had eaten enough for the day, she burned any excess money because carrying cash at night was dangerous. She attributed her filthy condition to the inaccessibility of public toilets. Neither suicidal nor malnourished, Brown seemingly posed little threat to herself or others. Three psychiatrists hired by Brown's attorneys testified that the woman was odd but not crazy. Four psychiatrists for the city said she was insane.

The judge ruled in Brown's favor, noting that street life may be aesthetically offensive but the mentally ill are as entitled as everyone else to freedom.

Brown's case raises an old question about mental illness: How different must a person's behavior be to qualify as abnormal? Is Brown's behavior any stranger than that of an old woman who leaves a multimillion-dollar fortune to her cats? Is it any more eccentric than taking a midwinter bath in an ice-covered lake (as do members of the Polar Bear Club) or undergoing extensive cosmetic surgery to obtain a perfect face and body?

What Is Abnormal Behavior?

Learning Objective 27.1 Identify the percentage of U.S. citizens who exhibit symptoms of abnormality, describe five characteristics of abnormal behavior, and distinguish between *maladjustment* and *abnormal behavior.*

Is Joyce Brown's behavior merely odd, or is she abnormal? To some extent, it depends on where you live, because every society has its own definition of abnormal behavior. In the Soviet Union, for example, people were once regularly placed in mental institutions for political dissent (Farone, 1982). Generally, however, people classified as abnormal have lost touch with reality—their behavior is more than odd. Recent data suggest that in any 1 month about 15% of the U.S. population 18 and over meet the criteria for a mental disorder—that is, they exhibit symptoms of abnormality (Reiger et al., 1988). **Abnormal behavior** is behavior characterized as atypical, socially unacceptable, distressing, maladaptive,

model: A perspective or approach derived from data in one field, used to help describe data in another field.

abnormal psychology: The field of psychology concerned with the assessment, treatment, and prevention of maladaptive behavior.

or the result of distorted cognitions. Let us consider these five distinguishing characteristics of abnormal behavior.

First, abnormal behavior is *atypical.* Many behaviors are unusual, but abnormal behaviors tend to be so unusual as to be statistically rare. For example, you would not consider ear piercing among teenage boys to be abnormal because the practice is fairly common in our society today. However, washing one's hands every few minutes during the day until they are raw is abnormal. (Keep in mind that not all atypical behavior is necessarily abnormal. The Olympic feats of runner Florence Griffith-Joyner are statistically uncommon, but not abnormal.)

Second, in addition to being atypical, abnormal behavior is also *socially unacceptable.* Society is fickle. Ideas about what is normal and abnormal vary according to cultural values that are in a constant state of flux. What is normal in one culture may be labeled abnormal in another; consider the Islamic practice of polygamy. Similarly, behavior that was considered abnormal 10 years ago, such as male ear piercing, may be considered normal today. For behavior to be judged abnormal, it must be unacceptable to society.

Third, abnormal behavior often causes *distress* or *discomfort* to the person or to those around him or her. While feelings of anxiety are a normal reaction in many situations, prolonged distress may indicate abnormal behavior. You may feel anxious when preparing to speak in front of a group, but constant, unrelenting anxiety, avoidance of any situations that might require public speaking, and fear of people in general suggests abnormal behavior.

Fourth, many psychologists also define abnormal behavior as *maladaptive* or self-defeating to the person exhibiting it. Maladaptive behaviors, such as depression or drug abuse, are harmful and nonproductive. They often lead to more misery and prevent the person from making positive changes in his or her life.

Last, abnormal behavior is often the result of *distorted cognitions.* For example, a young man with distorted cognitions (thoughts) may falsely believe that people are out to get him. A woman suffering from major depression may believe that she is worthless, stupid, and unlovable.

In recent years, psychologists have begun to describe behavior in terms of *maladjustment* rather than *abnormality.* The distinction is important because it implies that a person with a maladaptive behavior can, with treatment, adapt and become productive. The term *maladjustment* also emphasizes specific behaviors rather than labeling the entire person.

To summarize, abnormal behavior is characterized as atypical, socially unacceptable, distressing, maladaptive, and the result of distorted cognitions. There are, of course, exceptions to this definition; one or more of these characteristics may be absent in some cases. For example, we do not hesitate to label drug abuse as abnormal, but unfortunately that behavior is not as atypical as it once was. Nevertheless, this definition provides psychologists with a solid framework from which to explore abnormal behavior and its treatment.

Learning Objective 27.2 Describe the medical–biological, psychodynamic, humanistic, behavioral, cognitive, sociocultural, and eclectic models of abnormal behavior.

Before prescribing treatment, mental health practitioners want to know why a person is maladjusted, because the cause of a disorder can sometimes help define a treatment plan. Therefore, they often turn to theories and models that attempt to explain the causes of abnormality. A **model** is an analogy that helps scientists discover relationships among data; it uses a structure from one field to help describe data in another. Psychologists use models to make predictions about behavior. These models form the basis of **abnormal psychology,** the field of psychology concerned with the assessment, treatment, and prevention of maladaptive behavior. Several models help explain abnormal behavior: medical–biological, psychodynamic, humanistic, behavioral, cognitive, sociocultural, and eclectic or eclectic–interactionist.

The *medical–biological model* focuses on the biological and physiological conditions that initiate abnormal behaviors. It focuses on genetic abnormalities, problems in the central nervous system, and hormonal changes. It also helps explain and treat individuals with substance abuse problems and with schizophrenia, two disorders that may have a strong biological component. The medical model assumes that abnormal behavior, like other illnesses, can be diagnosed, treated, and cured. However, the medical approach has not gone unchallenged. Its critics say that the model does not take advantage of modern psychological insights, such as those of learning theory.

In the 18th and 19th centuries, Philippe Pinel insisted on treating mental patients as recoverable subjects. His humane treatment of patients fostered a new era of change in the treatment of psychological disorders.

The *psychodynamic* approach to explaining abnormal behavior is loosely rooted in Freud's theory of personality (discussed in Chapter 11). Psychodynamic theories assume that psychological disorders result from anxiety produced by unresolved conflicts and forces of which a person may not be aware. They assert that maladjustment occurs when a person relies on too many defense mechanisms or when defense mechanisms fail. Like psychodynamic theorists, *humanists* assume that inner psychic forces are important in establishing and maintaining a normal life-style. However, unlike psychodynamic theorists, humanists believe that people have much more cognitive control over their lives. They focus on individual uniqueness and decision making.

The *behavioral model* states that abnormal behaviors are caused by faulty or ineffective learning and conditioning patterns. Two fundamental assumptions of learning theorists are that disordered behavior can be reshaped and that more appropriate, worthwhile behaviors can be substituted through traditional learning techniques (see Chapter 5). Learning theorists assume that events in a person's environment reinforce or punish various behaviors selectively, and in doing so, they shape personality and may create maladjustment. The *cognitive* perspective asserts that human beings engage in both prosocial and maladjusted behaviors because of ideas and thoughts. As thinking organisms, individuals decide how to behave, with abnormal behavior based on false assumptions or unrealistic situations. Practitioners with the cognitive perspective treat people with psychological disorders by helping them develop new thought processes that instill new values.

People develop abnormalities within a context—the context of family, the community, and society—some practitioners therefore adopt a *sociocultural perspective.* Researchers, especially cross-cultural researchers, have shown that people's personality development and their disorders reflect their cultures, the stressors in their societies, and the type of disorders prevalent in their societies. As researchers examine the frequency and types of disorders that occur in different societies, they note some sharp differences not only between societies, but also within societies, as a function of the decade being examined and the age and gender of the clients.

The *legal perspective* defines abnormal behavior differently. Think about John W. Hinckley, Jr., the man who attempted to assassinate President Ronald Reagan. A jury declared him "not guilty by reason of insanity," and he was acquitted of murder charges. During the public outcry that followed, states sought to prohibit the insanity plea. At least half the states changed their insanity pleas, 12 adopted a new plea—"guilty but mentally ill," and three chose to eliminate the insanity plea altogether.

No one model can explain every kind of abnormal behavior, but each has value. For some disorders (such as phobias), learning theory explains the cause and prescribes an effective course of treatment. For other disorders (such as schizophrenia), medical–biological theories explain a significant part of the problem. Consequently, many psychologists take an *eclectic,* or eclectic–interactionist position, drawing on all these perspectives. For example, a therapist could treat

TABLE 27.1 DSM-III-R

Major classifications in *DSM-III-R*	
Disorders of infancy, childhood, and adolescence	Anxiety disorders
Organic mental disorders	Somatoform disorders
Psychoactive substance use disorders	Dissociative disorders
Schizophrenia	Sexual disorders
Delusional disorders	Sleep disorders
Psychotic disorders	Factitious disorders
Mood (affective) disorders	Disorders of impulse control
Personality disorders	Adjustment disorders

Note: Each classification is further broken down into subtypes (with some minor modifications).

a depressed patient by arranging for antidepressant drugs (medical–biological model); helping the patient develop new, optimistic thought processes (cognitive model); and teaching the patient adaptive behaviors to eliminate depression-inducing stress (behavioral model). As you examine each of the psychological disorders presented in this chapter, think about why you favor one of the explanations of maladjustment over another. Considered next is the system developed to aid practitioners in making diagnoses, which is presented in the work known as the *DSM-III-R.*

Diagnosing Abnormal Behavior: DSM-III-R

Learning Objective 27.3 Describe the *DSM-III-R,* explain what it is used for, and discuss some of the controversy surrounding it.

Three psychiatrists hired by Joyce Brown's attorneys testified that she was odd but not crazy. Four other psychiatrists (for the city) said she was insane. This controversy underscores the fact that diagnosing maladjusted behavior is a complicated process. Therefore, the American Psychiatric Association has devised a system for diagnosing maladjusted behavior, is described in the *Diagnostic and Statistical Manual of Mental Disorders,* the most recent edition of which was published in 1987 and is abbreviated as the *DSM-III-R* (referring to the third [III] edition, revised [R]). The goal of *DSM-III-R* is to improve the reliability of diagnoses by categorizing disorders according to observable behaviors. The system designates 19 major categories of maladjustment and more than 200 subcategories. Table 27.1 lists some of the 19 major classifications in the *DSM-III-R. DSM-III-R* also cites the *prevalence* of each disorder: the percentage of the population displaying a disorder during any specified period.

You might think that a diagnostic manual is straightforward, like an encyclopedia of mental disorders. However, *DSM-III-R* has met resistance and controversy (Millon, 1983). Some psychologists applaud its increased recognition of social and environmental influences on behavior (Linn & Spitzer, 1982). Others argue that it is too precise; still others that it is too complicated. Some assert that it is vague and not precise enough. Some claim a sexist bias against women (Kaplan, 1983). Others feel that the *DSM-III-R* should go beyond diagnosis and include problem-oriented and problem-solving information rather than just symptoms (Longabaugh et al., 1986). Many psychologists are unhappy with the continued use of psychiatric terms that perpetuate the use of a medical rather than a behavioral model.

Overall, the psychological community would rather have *DSM-III-R* than not have it (McReynolds, 1989), though *DSM-III-R* it is by no means the final word in diagnosing maladjustment, and its reliability is not completely know. It is an evolving system, and psychologists and psychiatrists are hard at work preparing *DSM-IV* (the fourth edition). We now explore some of the most important disorders in *DSM-III-R* and their consequences, beginning with anxiety disorders.

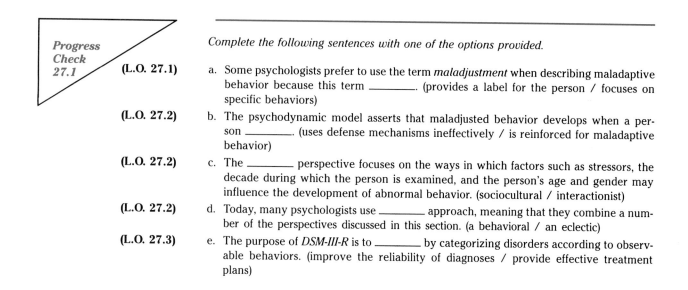

Progress Check 27.1

Complete the following sentences with one of the options provided.

(L.O. 27.1) a. Some psychologists prefer to use the term *maladjustment* when describing maladaptive behavior because this term ________. (provides a label for the person / focuses on specific behaviors)

(L.O. 27.2) b. The psychodynamic model asserts that maladjusted behavior develops when a person ________. (uses defense mechanisms ineffectively / is reinforced for maladaptive behavior)

(L.O. 27.2) c. The ________ perspective focuses on the ways in which factors such as stressors, the decade during which the person is examined, and the person's age and gender may influence the development of abnormal behavior. (sociocultural / interactionist)

(L.O. 27.2) d. Today, many psychologists use ________ approach, meaning that they combine a number of the perspectives discussed in this section. (a behavioral / an eclectic)

(L.O. 27.3) e. The purpose of *DSM-III-R* is to ________ by categorizing disorders according to observable behaviors. (improve the reliability of diagnoses / provide effective treatment plans)

Anxiety Disorders

It had been a stress-filled week for Conrad, and now he was arguing with his wife on the phone. Suddenly, he became short of breath and his heart began to pound vigorously. Certain that he was having a heart attack, Conrad hung up and called an ambulance. At the hospital, the examining doctor informed Conrad that he had suffered nothing more than acute anxiety.

Psychologists know that almost everyone experiences anxiety. Most people feel anxious in specific situations, such as before taking an examination, competing in a swim meet, or delivering a speech. Although anxiety can be a positive, motivating force, its effects can be debilitating and, left untreated, may eventually impair a person's health and lead to hospitalization. Given that anxiety disorders are so common in the general population, they warrant special consideration. Interestingly, research into anxiety disorders is not extensive and there is a paucity of research on special populations, for example African Americans (Neal & Turner, 1991).

Defining Anxiety

Learning Objective 27.4
Discuss Horney and Freud's views on anxiety, explain how contemporary psychologists view anxiety, and characterize generalized anxiety disorders.

Karen Horney, a neo-Freudian renowned for her work on anxiety, described anxiety as the central factor in both normal and abnormal behavior (Horney, 1937). **Anxiety** is customarily considered a generalized feeling of fear and apprehension, often accompanied by increased physiological arousal, which might be related to a particular event or object. Freud saw anxiety as the result of constant conflict among the id, ego, and superego, and he called nearly all forms of behavior associated with anxiety *neurotic*. Freud's term *neurosis* has made its way into everyday language, and nonpsychologists tend to describe any behavioral quirk as neurotic. Today, psychologists believe that as a catchall, the term *neurosis* is neither appropriate nor efficient. However, psychologists recognize anxiety as a key symptom of maladjustment—not necessarily the cause of maladjustment. Apprehension, fear, and its accompanying autonomic nervous system arousal are caused by thoughts, environmental stimuli, or perhaps some long-standing and as-yet-unresolved conflict. This is clearly the case with generalized anxiety disorders, considered next.

anxiety: A generalized feeling of fear and apprehension that might be related to a particular event or object, often accompanied by increased physiological arousal.

generalized anxiety disorder: Characterized by persistent anxiety for at least 1 month, sometimes with problems in motor tension, autonomic hyperactivity, apprehension, and concentration.

free-floating anxiety: Persistent anxiety not clearly related to any specific object or situation, accompanied by a sense of impending doom.

phobic disorder: Characterized by fear and subsequent attempted avoidance of specific objects or situation, acknowledged by the person as unreasonable.

Generalized Anxiety Disorder

Every disorder represents a different pattern of behavior and maladjustment, and *DSM-III-R* classifies them under a variety of diagnostic categories. Those in which anxiety is the prominent feature are designated as **generalized anxiety disorders.** People with a generalized anxiety disorder feel anxious almost constantly. They often report sleep disturbances, excessive sweating, muscle tension, headaches, and insomnia. They are tense and irritable, unable to concentrate, have difficulty making decisions, and may hyperventilate (Rapee, 1986).

For this diagnosis, *DSM-III-R* states that a person must show persistent anxiety for at least 1 month. When such chronic anxiety has no obvious source, it is **free-floating anxiety.** On the other hand, the source of such extreme anxiety may be, and often is, specific stressors in the environment, such as being in a prisoner-of-war camp.

Psychologists describe three areas of functioning in which people with a generalized anxiety disorder show impairment. One is *motor tension,* whereby the person is unable to relax and exhibits jumpiness, restlessness, and tension. The second is *autonomic hyperactivity,* whereby the person sweats, has a dry mouth, has a high resting pulse rate, urinates frequently, and may complain of a lump in the throat. The third is impaired *vigilance,* whereby the person has difficulty concentrating and is irritable and impatient. Unlike people who feel anxious almost constantly, those who suffer from phobic disorders, considered next, have far more focused anxiety and fear.

Phobic Disorders

Learning Objective 27.5
Describe the type of people who develop phobias, and characterize agoraphobia, social phobia, and simple phobias.

Do you know someone who is petrified at the thought of an airplane ride, who avoids crowds at all cost, or who shudders at the sight of a harmless garden snake? A **phobic disorder** is an anxiety disorder involving the irrational fear of, and consequent attempt to avoid, specific objects or situations. People with phobic disorders exhibit avoidance and escape behaviors, show increased heart rate and breathing patterns, and report thoughts of disaster and severe embarrassment. Many psychologists agree that, once established, phobias are maintained by the relief a person derives from escaping or avoiding the feared situation.

One key to diagnosing a phobic disorder is that the fear must be disproportionate to the situation. Most people who fear heights would not avoid visiting a

In extreme cases, people suffering from agoraphobia are afraid to leave the safety of their own homes. They are often isolated and depressed.

friend who lived on the top floor of a tall building, but a person with a phobia of heights would. Fear alone does not distinguish a phobia; both fear *and* avoidance must be evident.

Mild phobic disorders occur in about 7.5% of the population. They are, in fact, relatively common in well-adjusted people. Severe disabling phobias occur in less than 0.05% of the population and typically appear in patients with other disorders (Seif & Atkins, 1979). Phobias occur most frequently between the ages of 30 and 60 years and about equally in men and women (Marks, 1977). There are an infinite number of objects and situations toward which people could become fearful. Because of their diversity and number, *DSM-III-R* classifies three basic kinds of phobias: agoraphobia, social phobia, and simple phobia; we consider them next.

Agoraphobia. **Agoraphobia** is a marked fear of being alone or isolated in open and public places from which escape might be difficult. It is accompanied by avoidance behaviors that may eventually interfere with normal activities. It can become so debilitating that it prevents the individual from going into any open space, traveling in airplanes, or being in crowds. People with severe cases may decide to never leave their homes. Agoraphobia is often brought on by stress, particularly interpersonal stress. It is far more common in women than in men and is often accompanied by other disorders.

The disorder brings about hyperventilation, extreme tension, and even cognitive disorganization (Zitrin, 1981). Agoraphobics feel weak and dizzy when they have an attack and often suffer from severe panic attacks (*panic attacks* are characterized as acute anxiety that is not triggered by a specific event). They often are seriously depressed (Breier, Charney, & Heninger, 1984).

Agoraphobia is complicated, incapacitating, and extraordinarily difficult to treat. According to Freud and other psychoanalysts, traumatic childhood experiences may cause people to avoid particular objects, events, and situations that produce anxiety. Freudians speculate that agoraphobics may have feared abandonment by a cold or nonnurturing mother, and the fear has generalized to a fear

agoraphobia: [AG-or-uh-FOE-bee-uh] A disorder characterized by fear and avoidance of being in public places from which escape might be difficult.

TABLE 27.2 Some common forms of simple object phobias

Name	Object(s) feared
Acrophobia	High places
Agoraphobia	Open places
Ailurophobia	Cats
Algophobia	Pain
Anthropophobia	Men
Aquaphobia	Water
Astraphobia	Storms, thunder, and lightning
Claustrophobia	Enclosed places
Cynophobia	Dogs
Hematophobia	Blood
Mysophobia	Contamination
Nyctophobia	Darkness
Pathophobia	Disease
Pyrophobia	Fire
Thanatophobia	Death
Xenophobia	Strangers
Zoophobia	Animals

of abandonment or helplessness. Most researchers today find Freudian explanations of phobic behavior unconvincing. As an alternative, modern learning theory suggests that agoraphobia may develop because people avoid situations they have found painful or embarrassing. Failed coping strategies and low self-esteem have been implicated (Williams, Kinney, & Falbo, 1989). Despite much research, no simple cause for the disorder has been found.

Social Phobia. While a person with agoraphobia may avoid all situations involving other people, a person with a **social phobia** tends to avoid situations in which he or she may be exposed to the scrutiny of other people. A person with a social phobia fears behaving in an embarrassing or humiliating way and avoids eating in public or speaking before other people. The person with a social phobia avoids evaluation by refusing to deal with people or situations in which evaluation might occur.

social phobia: [FOE-bee-uh] A disorder characterized by fear of, and desire to avoid, situations in which the person might be exposed to scrutiny by others and might behave in an embarrassing or humiliating way.

simple phobia: A disorder characterized by irrational and persistent fear of an object or situation, along with a compelling desire to avoid it.

Simple Phobias. *DSM-III-R* classifies all specific phobias other than agoraphobia and social phobia as a **simple phobia.** A person with a simple phobia shows an irrational and persistent fear of an object or a situation, along with a compelling desire to avoid it. Most people are familiar with simple phobias; they include *claustrophobia*—fear of closed spaces, *hematophobia*—fear of the sight of blood, and *acrophobia*—fear of heights. Table 27.2 lists some common simple phobias. Many develop in childhood, adolescence, or early adulthood. Most people who have fears of heights, small spaces, water, doctors, or flying can calm themselves and deal with their fears; those who cannot (true phobics) often seek the help of a therapist when the phobia interferes with their health or with day-to-day functioning. Treatment using behavior therapy is typically effective.

Obsessive–Compulsive Disorders

Being orderly and organized is an asset for most people in today's fast-paced, complex society. However, when orderliness becomes the primary concern in a person's life, he or she may be suffering from an obsessive–compulsive disorder. **Obsessive–compulsive disorders** are characterized by the presence of unwanted thoughts, urges, and actions that focus on maintaining order and control.

Learning Objective 27.6 Characterize obsessive–compulsive disorders, and identify three possible causes of the disorder.

People with obsessive–compulsive disorders combat anxiety by carrying out ritual behaviors that reduce tension. For example, a man obsessed with avoiding germs may wash his hands 100 times a day and may wear white gloves to avoid touching contaminated objects. If these compulsive acts are not performed, the person may develop severe anxiety. A woman obsessed with punctuality may become extremely anxious if dinner guests arrive five minutes late. A person may write notes about every detail of every task compulsively before permitting her- or himself to take any action.

Freud and other psychodynamic theorists believed that the obsessive–compulsive disorder comes largely from difficulties during the anal stages of development when orderliness and cleanliness are often stressed. Learning theorists argue that bringing order to a person's environment reduces uncertainty and risk and thus is reinforcing. Because reinforced behaviors tend to recur, these behaviors become exaggerated during times of stress. Biologically oriented theorists believe that factors such as chronic elevated levels of arousal are implicated (Turner, Beidel, & Nathan, 1985).

Practitioners report that true obsessive–compulsive disorders are relatively rare. Treatment often includes drugs, (such as Prozac®, which may cause serious side effects if used indiscriminately), in combination with relaxation exercises. This helps to change their ideas about stress and the consequences of anxiety (e.g., Christensen, Hadzi-Pavlovic, Andrews, & Mattick, 1987). While obsessive–compulsive disorders are rare, they are relatively easy to understand; today, self-help groups and a greater awareness of the disorder are leading to treatment. Somatoform and dissociative disorders, discussed next, are also rare, but in some important ways, they are harder to understand and treat.

obsessive–compulsive disorder: [ob-SESS-iv kom-PULS-iv] Characterized by persistent and uncontrollable thoughts and irrational beliefs that cause performance of compulsive rituals that interfere with daily life.

somatoform disorder: [so-MAT-oh-form] Characterized by real physical symptoms not under voluntary control and for which no evident physical cause exists.

somatization disorder: Characterized by recurrent and multiple complaints of several years' duration for which medical attention is ineffective.

Somatoform and Dissociative Disorders

If you were a television writer for a soap opera, you might have on your desk a copy of *DSM-III-R,* with the page turned to somatoform and dissociative disorders. These disorders are relatively rare and are studied less than other disorders, but they make for fascinating reading and study. They are naturals for interesting television storylines.

Learning Objective 27.7 Characterize three somatoform disorders.

Somatoform Disorders

Somatoform disorders involve real physical symptoms, often pain, that are not under voluntary control and for which no apparent physical cause exists. Evidence suggests that the causes are psychological. Three types of somatoform disorders are somatization disorder, conversion disorder, and hypochondriasis.

Somatization Disorder. **Somatization disorders** involve recurrent and multiple complaints of several years' duration for which medical attention has not been

APPLYING PSYCHOLOGY

Dissociative Disorders

Dissociative disorders involves a sudden but temporary alteration in consciousness, identity, or memory. These disorders are quite noticeable and vivid, although relatively rare.

Psychogenic amnesia, one of several dissociative disorders, used to be grouped with hysterical neuroses. Today, however, psychologists recognize it as a separate disorder. **Psychogenic amnesia** is the sudden inability to recall important personal information. The memory loss is too extensive to be explained by ordinary forgetfulness. Often, the amnesia is brought on by traumatic incidents involving threat of physical injury or death. The condition, relatively rare, is more common during wars or natural disasters and is assumed to be caused by high levels of stress or extreme reactions to a traumatic life event such as an accident, a war, or a personal disaster.

Another form of dissociative disorder, often associated with psychogenic amnesia but presenting a dramatically different kind of behavior, is multiple personality. A diagnosis of **multiple personality** is made when two or more distinct personalities, each of which is dominant at particular times, exist in a single person. Each personality has a unique style with different memories and behavioral patterns. For example, one personality may be adaptive and efficient at coping with life, while another may exhibit maladaptive behavior. Some people's alternate personalities are of the opposite sex.

Each personality is usually unaware of any other one, although in some cases, they eavesdrop on each other (Schacter, et al., 1989). The different personalities (when active) acknowledge that time has passed but cannot account for it. The switch from one to the other is usually brought on by stress.

Despite popular movies and books, such as *The Three Faces of Eve* and *Sybil,* multiple personality as a diagnosed disorder is extremely rare, with less than 300 actual recorded cases in history. The mass media and lay people often confuse multiple personality with schizophrenia, a much more common disorder discussed later in this chapter. Psychologists have few data on the causes of multiple personality and debate how it might be classified (see Greaves, 1980). There is even controversy as to whether multiple personality actually exists. Some psychologists think that some people invent multiple personalities to avoid taking responsibility for their own behavior, especially in criminal cases; other researchers think that some therapists subtly encourage patients to show symptoms of this disorder so that they (the therapists) might achieve some recognition. Multiple personality is a well-known disorder, vivid and interesting, and much more research is needed before comprehensive theories and effective treatments are available. Multiple personality is sometimes confused with personality disorders that exhibit a different set of symptoms. We consider them in the next module.

▲ ***What is the fundamental symptom of a dissociative disorder?***

▲ ***What is the evidence to suggest that a person is displaying the symptoms of a multiple personality dissociative disorder?***

dissociative disorder: Characterized by a sudden temporary alteration in consciousness, identity, or motor behavior.

psychogenic amnesia: [sie-ko-JEN-ick] A disorder characterized by the sudden and extensive inability to recall important personal information.

effective. Those with the disorder, however, tend to seek medical attention at least once a year. The disorder typically begins before age 30 years and is diagnosed in only about 1% of females and is even rarer in males. Patients feel sickly for a good part of their lives and may report muscle weakness, double vision, memory loss, and hallucinations. Other commonly reported symptoms include gastrointestinal problems, such as vomiting and diarrhea; painful menstrual periods with excessive bleeding; sexual indifference; and pains in the back, chest, and genitals. Patients are often beset by anxiety and depression. Individuals with somatization disorders often have a host of emotional problems that cause their medical complaints; unfortunately, some of the medical conditions are not psychologically caused, and physicians must be especially careful to treat medically those conditions that need treatment and not dismiss all the patient's problems as psychological.

Conversion Disorder. **Conversion disorders** are the loss or alteration of physical functioning for no apparent physiological reason. People suffering from conversion disorders often lose the use of their arms, hands, or legs, or their vision or another sensory modality. They may develop a combination of ailments. For example, a patient may become not only blind but also deaf, mute, or totally paralyzed.

Although the patient may be unaware of the relationship, conversion disorders are generally considered a way to escape or avoid upsetting situations. Also, the huge amount of attention and support patients sometimes receive because of the symptoms may cause them to maintain the disorder. Conversion disorders are often associated with a history of psychosomatic illness. Men and women are equally likely to develop a conversion disorder, but, like somatization disorder, it is rare.

Hypochondriasis. When a person spends a lot of time going to a physician with all types of bodily complaints for which the physician can find no cause, psychologists suspect hypochondriasis. **Hypochondriasis** is the inordinate preoccupation with health and illness, coupled with an excessive concern and anxiety about disease. Such individuals feel that they have grave afflictions. They become preoccupied with minor aches and pains and often miss work and create alarm among family members. Every ache, every minor symptom is examined, interpreted, and feared.

Psychodynamic views of hypochondriasis focus on how the symptoms of the illness keep the person from dealing with some other painful source of stress in his or her life. Behavioral psychologists focus on how the illness can be reinforcing: People are given extra attention and care, and the illness diverts attention from other tasks at which the individual may not be succeeding. By focusing on his or her illness, a person may avoid marital problems, financial affairs, and educational goals. Of course, to the hypochondriac, the fears and anxiety are real, and only through therapy can the true causes of the overattention to symptoms be handled.

multiple personality: A disorder characterized by the existence within an individual of two or more different personalities, each of which is dominant and directs the individual's behavior at distinct times.

conversion disorder: Characterized by the loss or alteration of physical functioning not due to a physiological disorder, but apparently due to internal psychological conflict.

hypochondriasis: [HYE-po-kon-DRY-a-sis] A disorder characterized by inordinate preoccupation with health and illness, coupled with excessive anxiety about disease.

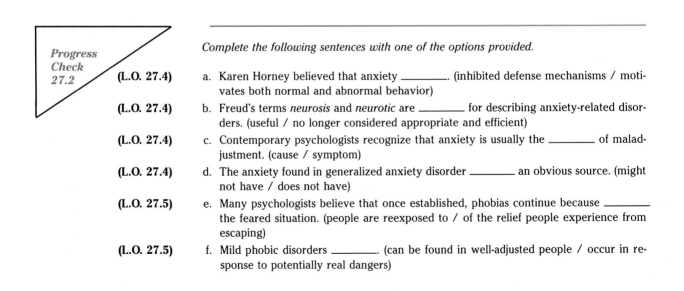

Progress Check 27.2

Complete the following sentences with one of the options provided.

(L.O. 27.4) a. Karen Horney believed that anxiety ________. (inhibited defense mechanisms / motivates both normal and abnormal behavior)

(L.O. 27.4) b. Freud's terms *neurosis* and *neurotic* are ________ for describing anxiety-related disorders. (useful / no longer considered appropriate and efficient)

(L.O. 27.4) c. Contemporary psychologists recognize that anxiety is usually the ________ of maladjustment. (cause / symptom)

(L.O. 27.4) d. The anxiety found in generalized anxiety disorder ________ an obvious source. (might not have / does not have)

(L.O. 27.5) e. Many psychologists believe that once established, phobias continue because ________ the feared situation. (people are reexposed to / of the relief people experience from escaping)

(L.O. 27.5) f. Mild phobic disorders ________. (can be found in well-adjusted people / occur in response to potentially real dangers)

(L.O. 27.5) g. Agoraphobics often suffer from ________. (hypochondriasis / panic attacks)

(L.O. 27.5) h. An extreme fear of being alone or isolated in open and public places from which escape might be difficult is termed ________. (agoraphobia / a social phobia)

(L.O. 27.5) i. All specific phobias other than agoraphobia and social phobia are categorized as ________ in the *DSM-III-R*. (simple phobias / phobic reactions / acrophobias)

(L.O. 27.6) j. Unavoidable thoughts, ideas, and urges are called ________. (obsessions / compulsions)

(L.O. 27.6) k. Freud and other psychodynamic theorists believed that obsessive–compulsive disorder is the result of a fixation in the ________ stage of development. (oral / anal / phallic)

(L.O. 27.7) l. People who are preoccupied by minor aches and pains, experience excessive concern and anxiety about disease, and, as a result, miss work and alarm others have ________ disorder. (somatization / hypochondriasis)

(L.O. 27.7) m. Disorders such as conversion disorder and hypochondriasis seem to be maintained by ________. (knowing how to "fake it" / attention and the avoidance of difficult situations)

Module Summary

What Is Abnormal Behavior?

- There are five distinguishing characteristics of abnormal behavior: (1) atypical, (2) socially unacceptable, (3) distressing or discomforting to the person exhibiting the behavior or to those around him on her, (4) maladaptive or self-defeating to the person exhibiting it, and often (5) the result of distorted cognitions (p. 519).
- A wide range of behavior exists on a continuum from normal to abnormal. There are many ways of classifying behavior as abnormal, including the statistical, psychodynamic, medical, humanistic, behavioral, cognitive, sociocultural, interactionist, and legal approaches (p. 520).

Diagnosing Abnormal Behavior: DSM-III-R

- The diagnostic categories of the *DSM-III-R*, compiled and published by the American Psychiatric Association, are helpful because they describe behavior in terms of its characteristics rather than solely in terms of its frequency (p. 522).
- Though widely accepted and used, the *DSM-III-R* has also received criticism from many sources (p. 522).

Anxiety Disorders

- *Anxiety* is a generalized feeling of fear and apprehension, often accompanied by increased physiological arousal, which might be related to a specific event or object. The fear and apprehension are usually disproportionate (p. 524).
- A *generalized anxiety disorder* is characterized by persistent anxiety of at least 1 month's duration. It can include problems in motor tension, autonomic hyperactivity, apprehension, and concentration (p. 524).
- Individuals with an *obsessive–compulsive disorder* have persistent and uncontrollable thoughts and irrational beliefs, causing them to perform compulsive rituals that interfere with normal daily functioning (p. 527).

Somatoform and Dissociative Disorders

- *Somatization disorder* and *conversion disorder* are somatoform disorders. They are characterized by real physical symptoms not under voluntary control and for which no evident physical cause exists. Evidence suggests that psychological conflicts are the cause (pp. 527–529).
- *Psychogenic amnesia* and *multiple personality disorder* are examples of rare dissociative disorders. Dissociative disorders are characterized by a sudden temporary alteration in consciousness, identity, or motor behavior (p. 528).

KEY TERMS

abnormal behavior, p. 519
abnormal psychology, p. 520
agoraphobia, p. 525
anxiety, p. 524
conversion disorder, p. 529
dissociative disorder, p. 528
free-floating anxiety, p. 524
generalized anxiety disorder, p. 524
hypochondriasis, p. 529
model, p. 520
multiple personality, p. 529
obsessive–compulsive disorder, p. 527
phobic disorder, p. 524
psychogenic amnesia, p. 528
simple phobia, p. 526
social phobia, p. 526
somatization disorder, p. 527
somatoform disorder, p. 527

SELF-TEST

Module 27

- Before taking the self-test, **recite** and **review.**
- Use the key at the back of the text to *correct* your answers.
- *Restudy* pages that correspond to any questions you answered incorrectly.

1. Which of the following is a primary characteristic of abnormal behavior?
   a. Abnormal behavior varies according to cultural values.
   b. Abnormal behavior is statistically atypical.
   c. Abnormal behavior is often the result of distorted cognitions.
   d. All of the above.
2. Which of the following is an assumption made by the behavioral model of abnormal behavior?
   a. Maladaptive behavior is the result of false or unrealistic thoughts and ideas.
   b. People who have serious behavior disorders and who commit crimes should be found "guilty and mentally ill."
   c. Psychological disorders are the result of anxiety produced by unresolved conflicts.
   d. Behavior can be reshaped and worthwhile behaviors substituted for maladaptive behaviors.
3. *DSM-III-R* has been criticized for
   a. not recognizing social and environmental influences on behavior.
   b. perpetuating the medical model by using psychiatric terms that label a person as having a disease.
   c. having a sexist bias against women.
   d. both b and c.
4. The chronic anxiety often found in generalized anxiety disorder
   a. is highly focused and directed toward a specific person or situation.
   b. results from an irrational fear.
   c. is characterized by motor tension, autonomic hyperactivity, and impaired vigilance.
   d. must be present for at least 1 year before a diagnosis can be given.
5. Free-floating anxiety
   a. has no obvious source.
   b. is caused by a specific stressor that has become generalized.
   c. is a symptom in most phobic disorders.
   d. is the kind of anxiety we feel momentarily just before doing something risky.
6. A person who avoids certain normal every day activities because of a fear that others may evaluate his or her behavior would be diagnosed as having ______.
   a. agoraphobia
   b. hematophobia
   c. a simple phobia
   d. a social phobia
7. If a person with an obsessive–compulsive disorder is prevented from performing the compulsive rituals associated with the disorder, the
   a. obsessions will cease.
   b. person may experience severe anxiety.
   c. person will develop a new set of stereotyped behaviors.
   d. disorder will gradually extinguish.

8. Which of the following characterizes a somatization disorder?
   a. The person examines, interprets, and fears every ache and minor physical symptom.
   b. The person becomes blind, mute, deaf, or paralyzed for no apparent physiological reason.
   c. The person has recurrent and multiple physical complaints of long duration, for which medical treatment has not been effective.
   d. The person worries about contacting germs and becomes preoccupied with cleanliness.

Module 28

Serious Behavior Disorders

LEARNING OBJECTIVES

When you have mastered the material in this module, you will be able to

Personality Disorders (pp. 536–537)

28.1 Characterize paranoid, dependent, histrionic, narcissistic, and antisocial personality disorders and identify causes of antisocial personality (p. 536).

Sexual Disorders (pp. 537–539)

28.2 Characterize the common paraphilias and explain what causes them and how they are treated (p. 537).

Mood Disorders (pp. 539–543)

28.3 Characterize bipolar disorder and major depression and discuss their prevalence in today's society (p. 539).

28.4 Discuss the causes of depression according to the biological, learning, cognitive, and learned-helplessness theories (p. 541).

Schizophrenia (pp. 543–549)

28.5 Characterize schizophrenic disorder and identify categories of people who are likely to be diagnosed as having this disorder (p. 543).

28.6 List five features that must be present for a diagnosis of schizophrenia and characterize five types of schizophrenia (p. 544).

28.7 Discuss biological and environmental factors that contribute to the development of schizophrenia and state the most likely cause of this disorder (p. 545).

SQ3R ▲ **Survey** to set goals for studying.
▲ Ask **questions** as you **read.**
▲ Stop occasionally to **recite** and **review.**

plus ▲ **Write** a summary of key points.
▲ **Reflect** on the hypotheses, evidence, and implications of this material and on the relevance it has to *your* life.

His good friends knew that Carl was changing. He had become sad, depressed, and extremely moody. The mere mention of his father (who had been dead for 10 years) now caused tears, and mention of his estranged sister would produce half an hour of angry outbursts. Carl's childhood had been difficult. He had been shipped from one foster home to another, beaten by an alcoholic father, and taunted by older children because he was short. All that seemed to have straightened itself out: Carl went to college, became a successful accountant, married well, and had two nice kids. Now, however, the past seemed to be catching up with him. Carl found himself discussing the past frequently. The periods of sadness that resulted were growing longer and were no longer alleviated by the tranquilizers his physician prescribed. Carl began missing work. He stayed in bed for days at a time. He lost interest in everything, and his energy disappeared. Even sex became simply a dutiful chore. When Carl spoke of the future, it was always in tones of despair. Slowly, and yet all too quickly, life seemed to have lost its zest. Carl's wife knew that something was wrong, but she didn't know what to do. She watched helplessly as her husband underwent a change she never conceived possible. Carl's wife was watching the onset of a serious depression. Although it was slow in developing, it was serious in nature: It affected his work, his family relationships, and his feelings about himself and the future. Carl was suffering from what psychologists call a *major depression.*

Sometimes, people like Carl become so sad and depressed that their problems obliterate the good things in their lives—their family, their friends, and their accomplishments. Some depressed or troubled individuals experience a distinct break with reality; they may begin to hallucinate, experience delusions, or develop bizarre ideas and behaviors. The behavior of a person who is seriously depressed is abnormal. Often, laypeople say that someone they know is "paranoid," "depressed," or "obsessive," but such everyday descriptions of behavior usually are exaggerated or inaccurate. These terms have precise clinical meanings that are not known by most nonpsychologists. Many people experience some of the symptoms of serious behavior disorders, but most of these people would not be diagnosed by a mental health practitioner as having a major disorder. Everyone experiences periods of depression or anxiety or periods in which they may act in a slightly paranoid manner, but such occasional lapses do not satisfy the *DSM-III-R* criteria. In the disorders discussed in this module, the individual's behavior is considered extreme. Most professionals agree that these behavior disorders require the special attention of mental health practitioners. They often have a complex origin and are difficult to treat.

Personality Disorders

Learning Objective 28.1 Characterize paranoid, dependent, histrionic, narcissistic, and antisocial personality disorders, and identify causes of antisocial personality.

People who are inflexible and have long-standing maladaptive ways of relating to the environment may be diagnosed as having a **personality disorder.** Often, these disorders begin in childhood or adolescence and persist throughout adulthood. People with personality disorders are easy to spot but difficult to treat because they often do not see their symptoms as a problem—they are just being themselves.

Types of Personality Disorders

People with personality disorders are divided into three broad types: those whose behavior appears (1) odd or eccentric, (2) fearful or anxious, or (3) dramatic, emotional, and erratic. We now consider five specific personality disorders: paranoid, dependent, histrionic, narcissistic, and antisocial.

People who have unwarranted feelings of persecution and who mistrust almost everyone are said to have *paranoid personality disorder.* They are hypersensitive to criticism and have a restricted range of emotional responses. They have strong fears of losing control and of independence. Sometimes they appear cold, humorless, and even scheming. As you might expect, people with paranoid personality disorder are seldom able to form close, intimate relationships with others.

Fearful or anxious behaviors are characteristic of people with a *dependent personality disorder.* Such people let others make all important decisions in their lives. They try to appear pleasant and agreeable at all times. They act meek, humble, and affectionate in order to keep their protectors. Battered wives often suffer from the dependent personality disorder.

The *histrionic personality disorder* is characterized by dramatic, emotional, and erratic behaviors. These people seek attention by exaggerating situations in their lives. They have stormy personal relationships, are excessively emotional, and demand reassurance and praise.

Closely related to the histrionic personality disorder is the *narcissistic personality disorder.* People with this disorder have an extremely exaggerated sense of self-importance, an expectation of special favors, and a constant need for attention. They show a lack of caring for others, and they react to criticism with rage, shame, or humiliation.

personality disorder: Inflexible, long-standing, maladaptive behaviors in dealing with the environment, which typically cause stress and social or occupational problems.

antisocial personality disorder: Characterized by continuous and chronic behavior that violates the rights of other people and by lack of feelings of guilt, understanding of other people, responsible behavior, and fear of punishment, as well as by egocentrism (often).

Antisocial Personality Disorder

Perhaps the most widely recognized personality disorder is the **antisocial personality disorder.** Such individuals are generally superficially charming, so their destructive and often reckless behavior may go unnoticed.

A person who frequently changes jobs, does not take proper care of his or her children, is arrested often, fails to pay bills, and lies constantly displays behaviors described in the *DSM-III-R* as typical of antisocial personality disorder. Such people are relatively unsocialized adults, unwilling to conform to and live by society's rules, and their behavior often brings them into conflict with society. Antisocial people consistently blame others for their behavior. They seldom feel guilt or learn from experience or punishment. The disorder occurs six times more often in men than in women. Extreme forms of this disorder are displayed by cold-blooded killers like Charles Manson or Ted Bundy, although most antisocial personalities reveal their sociopathy through less deadly and sensational means.

Adopted children separated at birth from antisocial parents are likely to show antisocial behavior later in life (Cadoret, 1978). This suggests a genetic contribution to the disorder. Another fact that suggests a genetic cause is that the nervous systems of people diagnosed as having antisocial personality disorders may be different from those of normal people. When normal people do something wrong, their autonomic nervous system reacts with symptoms of anxiety, such as fear, heart palpitations, and sweating. Evidence suggests that decreased autonomic arousal is characterized in persons with antisocial personality disorders (Waid, 1976). These people do not function at sufficiently high levels of autonomic nervous system arousal, do not experience the physiological symptoms of anxiety, and thus do not learn to associate those symptoms with antisocial behavior.

On the nurture side, some psychologists believe that childrearing practices and unstable family situations render individuals with an antisocial personality disorder unable to learn fear, guilt, and punishment avoidance. Such people seem to have learned maladaptive behaviors from their family situations and consequently to have developed inappropriate behaviors. If the environmental viewpoint is correct, then antisocial personality disorder may be a learned behavior. The symptoms of antisocial personality disorder often are seen first in a person's home environment in interactions with family members. Unfortunately, family relationships become strained, and some people suffering with the disorder may become involved in criminal behavior such as rape, discussed in the Applying Psychology box on page 538.

sexual disorder: Sexual practices directed toward objects rather than people, sexual encounters involving real or simulated suffering or humiliation, or sexual activity with a nonconsenting partner.

fetishism: A sexual disorder in which sexual arousal and gratification are brought about by objects such as shoes, underwear, or toilet articles.

Sexual Disorders

Learning Objective 28.2 Characterize the common paraphilias, and explain what causes them and how they are treated.

Few behaviors arouse more anxiety, fear, and superstition than those involving human sexuality. However, many sexual problems, such as orgasmic dysfunction, are often temporary symptoms of some other type of problem that is not sexual in nature, such as anxiety or poor communication between partners. We considered the sexual response cycle in Chapter 12 when we examined sexual motivation (p. 487). We now consider disorders referred to as *sexual disorders* that focus on sexual behavior.

Sexual disorders or deviations (called *paraphilias* in *DSM-III-R*) are sexual practices directed toward objects rather than people, sexual encounters involving real or simulated suffering or humiliation, or sexual activities with nonconsenting partners. *DSM-III-R* classifies only a few true sexual disorders; some researchers, however, maintain that there are many more (Money, 1984). A diagnosis of sexual disorder is made when the causes are psychological rather than physical and when these behaviors are the primary source of sexual stimulation or gratification for the individual.

The following are some unconventional sexual activities that characterize sexual disorders. **Fetishism,** which is more common in men, involves sexual arousal and gratification brought about by objects rather than by people. For example, a man may have a fetish about a woman's shoes and may receive sexual gratification from them instead of from her.

In **transvestic fetishism,** also known as transvestism or *cross-dressing,* a male receives sexual gratification by dressing in the clothing of a woman. (The number of females so diagnosed is very small.) Interference with this cross-dressing produces frustration. Transvestites consider themselves of their own sex, and most are not homosexual.

A person who achieves sexual satisfaction by watching other people in different states of undress or sexual activity is practicing **voyeurism.** Most voyeurs, or "peeping Toms," are men. Because voyeurs generally do not want to be seen, some researchers suggest that they are excited by the risk of discovery involved in watching other people. Another unconventional sexual activity is **exhibitionism,** in which adult males expose their genitals to unsuspecting observers, who

transvestic fetishism: A sexual disorder characterized by recurrent and persistent cross-dressing for the purpose of achieving sexual excitement.

voyeurism: A sexual disorder in which the preferred method of sexual gratification consists of repetitive observations of people in different states of undress or sexual activity.

exhibitionism: A sexual disorder in which the preferred method of sexual stimulation and gratification consists of repetitive acts of exposing the genitals to strangers.

APPLYING PSYCHOLOGY

Studies of Rape

Rape is not a *DSM-III-R* classification. Rape is a crime, often involving an individual with an antisocial personality disorder. **Rape** is forcible sexual assault of an unwilling partner, usually, but not always, a woman (cf. Myers, 1989). Most rapes are planned, often in a meticulous manner; they are generally not impulsive acts prompted by a spur-of-the-moment sexual or aggressive feeling. According to experts, rape should be considered a violent crime rather than a sexual crime. Labeling rape a sexual assault obscures the violent, brutal nature of the crime and often places the woman on the defensive in the courtroom—*even though she was the victim.*

More than 91,000 cases of rape were reported during 1987, according to the FBI, but many experts assert that this is only one fourth of the actual number. For example, one research study found that 27% of college women had experienced situations in which rape was attempted, and 7.5% of college men reported initiating acts that meet the definition of rape (Koss, Gidycz, & Wisniewski, 1987). Although these results are not generalizable to the entire population, rape or attempted rape seems to be far more common than previously believed. Today, on college campuses, rape or attempted rape by an acquaintance—sometimes known as *date rape*—is receiving increased attention; many rape victims know (or dated) their assailants. Date rape on campuses is far too common and is even promoted by some fraternities, but it is not limited to a campus setting (Sanday, 1990).

Because rape is such a violent crime, it has come under the critical eye of researchers who have sought to understand the characteristics and motivations of the rapist. Several facts about rapists are coming into focus. They tend to be young, often between 15 and 25 years old (Sadock, 1980). Often, rapists are poor, culturally disadvantaged, and uneducated. Many have willing sexual partners, and half are married, although their high level of aggressiveness probably precludes a happy and stable marriage or other relationship.

Rapists may have some history of sexual dysfunctions, but this finding is not consistent across all studies. Rapists often have committed another sex-related offense, although this finding also is not consistent across all studies (Furby, Weinrott, & Blackshaw, 1989). They tend to be more inclined toward violence than are other men (Quinsey et al., 1984) and less able to understand cues and messages from women who say no. Levels of maladjustment of rapists vary from slight to extreme when measured on psychological tests (Kalichman, Szymanowski, McKee, Taylor, & Craig, 1989), and men who assault women and rape them often do not view their attack as rape, but rather as a "mere" assault (Bourque, 1989). Rape is an act of violence; it is not considered a sexual disorder like the ones considered in the section on sexual disorders.

- ▲ ***What is implied by the term* date rape?**
- ▲ ***Why is rape not considered a sexual, spur-of-the-moment act?***
- ▲ ***What is the evidence to suggest that rape is widespread and should be receiving increased research and media attention?***
- ▲ ***What are the implications of the fact that many rapists know their victims and do not view their attacks as rape?***

are almost always female. Exhibitionists find the startled reactions of their victims sexually arousing.

Some people derive sexual satisfaction through sexual contact with children, a disorder known as **pedophilia.** Most pedophiles are well acquainted with the child; sometimes they are even close relatives. Many are married and seemingly well adjusted, both sexually and socially. Pedophiles may suffer from loneliness or schizophrenia (Regestein & Reich, 1978). Fifty percent were themselves sexually abused as children.

Two other types of paraphilia are **sexual sadism** and **sexual masochism.** A *sadist* achieves sexual gratification by inflicting pain on a sexual partner. A *masochist* achieves sexual gratification from experiencing pain inflicted by someone else. Sadists and masochists are often sexual partners; the sadist provides the pain for the masochist, and both achieve sexual satisfaction. The pain involved can be physical or emotional.

rape: Forcible, sexual assault of an unwilling partner who is usually a woman.

pedophilia: A sexual disorder in which the preferred method of sexual stimulation and gratification consists of repetitive sexual activity with children.

Most psychologists agree that sexual disorders are learned behaviors. According to Freudians, problems during the Oedipal period create sexual problems later in life. Most behavioral practitioners agree in part with Freud, saying that people with sexual disorders are people whose normal sex-role stereotyping when haywire early in their lives. They argue that a difficult adolescence and a poor emerging self-concept are learning factors that may predispose an individual to sexual disorders. Individuals who had a difficult time with their parents and peers, for example, may exhibit some of those problems through sexual disorders when they are adults. Often, anger, hostility, shame, and doubt are present in people who suffer from sexual disorders.

Unfortunately, the causes and treatment of sexual disorders have not been studied much. Thus, psychologists know less than they would like to know about biological and environmental contributions. Most practitioners focus on behavioral treatments and teaching people new, more adaptive ways of expressing feelings, fears, and sexual urges. These techniques can be effective and do not require hospitalization or drug therapy, unlike treatment for some of the more debilitating disorders considered in the remainder of this chapter.

sexual sadism: A sexual disorder in which an individual inflicts physical or psychological pain on another person in order to achieve sexual excitement.

sexual masochism: A sexual disorder in which an individual seeks physical or psychological pain, often including humiliation or being bound or beaten, to achieve sexual excitement.

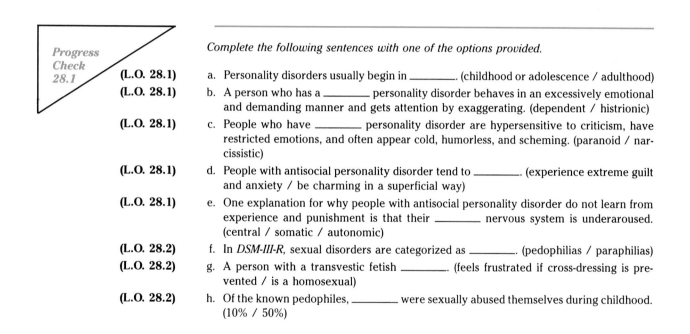

Progress Check 28.1

Complete the following sentences with one of the options provided.

(L.O. 28.1) a. Personality disorders usually begin in ________. (childhood or adolescence / adulthood)

(L.O. 28.1) b. A person who has a ________ personality disorder behaves in an excessively emotional and demanding manner and gets attention by exaggerating. (dependent / histrionic)

(L.O. 28.1) c. People who have ________ personality disorder are hypersensitive to criticism, have restricted emotions, and often appear cold, humorless, and scheming. (paranoid / narcissistic)

(L.O. 28.1) d. People with antisocial personality disorder tend to ________. (experience extreme guilt and anxiety / be charming in a superficial way)

(L.O. 28.1) e. One explanation for why people with antisocial personality disorder do not learn from experience and punishment is that their ________ nervous system is underaroused. (central / somatic / autonomic)

(L.O. 28.2) f. In *DSM-III-R,* sexual disorders are categorized as ________. (pedophilias / paraphilias)

(L.O. 28.2) g. A person with a transvestic fetish ________. (feels frustrated if cross-dressing is prevented / is a homosexual)

(L.O. 28.2) h. Of the known pedophiles, ________ were sexually abused themselves during childhood. (10% / 50%)

Mood Disorders

Learning Objective 28.3 Characterize bipolar disorder and major depression, and discuss their prevalence in today's society.

All of us experience depression at one time or another. Ending a long-term intimate relationship, feeling overwhelmed during final exams, mourning the death of a close friend, and experiencing serious financial problems are all sources of depression. When people become so depressed or sad that a change occurs in their outlook and overt behavior, they may be suffering from depression. Depression is considered by *DSM-III-R* to be a type of mood disorder (previously known as affective disorders). Depression is often caused or at least initiated by a specific event, although for many individuals, the symptoms occur gradually. There are two major types of mood disorders that involve depression: bipolar disorders and depressive disorders.

bipolar disorder: Characterized by vacillation between two extremes, mania and depression.

depressive disorders: A general category of disorders in which people show extreme and persistent sadness, despair, and loss of interest in life's usual activities.

major depression: A disorder characterized by loss of interest in almost all usual activities as evidenced by a sad, hopeless, or discouraged mood. Other symptoms include sleep disturbance, loss of appetite, loss of energy, and feelings of unworthiness and guilt; a subtype of depressive disorders.

delusions: False beliefs, inconsistent with reality, held in spite of evidence to the contrary.

Bipolar Disorders

Bipolar disorder gets its name from the fact that patients' behavior vacillates between two polar extremes—mania and depression. The *manic phase* is characterized by rapid speech, inflated self-esteem, distractibility, impulsiveness, and decreased need for sleep. Patients in a manic phase are easily distracted, get angry when things do not go their way, and seem to have boundless energy. A person in the *depressed phase,* which often follows the manic phase, is moody and sad, with feelings of hopelessness.

Almost 2 million Americans suffer from bipolar disorders, which typically begin in early adulthood and continue throughout life. Patients can be relatively normal for a few days, weeks, or months between episodes of excitement and depression, or they can rapidly vacillate between excitement and depression. The key component of bipolar disorders is the shift from mania or excited states to depressive states of sadness and hopelessness. People who suffer bipolar disorders are often in their late twenties before they begin to manifest symptoms. The disorder seems to have a biological basis (Leber, Beckham & Danker-Brown, 1985), with patients responding fairly well to drug treatment, especially to lithium (which is discussed in the next chapter).

Depressive Disorder: Major Depression

Bonnie Strickland, former president of the American Psychological Association, said during 1988 APA meetings, "Depression has been called the common cold of psychological disturbances . . . which underscores its prevalence, but trivializes its impact." Strickland noted that at any one time, there are about 14 million people suffering from this disabling disorder. The main difference between **depressive disorders** and bipolar disorders is that people with depressive disorders show no vacillation between excitement and depression; they tend to be depressed constantly. **Major depression,** one of a series of depressive disorders, is eight times more common than bipolar disorders.

The essential characteristics of major depression are a depressed, sad, hopeless mood and a loss of interest in all or almost all usual activities and pastimes. Someone experiencing a major depression is not experiencing merely fleeting anxiety with sadness, but displays a relatively extreme reaction to a specific event, such as the loss of a loved one, job, or home, or a failure in life. People experiencing a major depression show at least some impairment of social and occupational functioning, although their behavior is not necessarily bizarre.

Symptoms. Depressed individuals experience symptoms such as poor appetite, insomnia, weight loss, loss of energy, feelings of worthlessness, intense guilt, inability to concentrate, difficulty sleeping, and sometimes thoughts of death and suicide. They have a gloomy outlook on life, especially slow thought processes, an extremely distorted view of current problems, and a tendency to blame themselves. Depressed people often withdraw from social and physical contact with others. Every task seems to require a greater effort.

Depressed people may also have **delusions** or false beliefs that induce feelings of guilt, shame, and persecution. Seriously disturbed patients show even greater disruptions in thought and motor processes and a total lack of spontaneity and motivation. Such patients typically report that they have no hope for themselves or the world; nothing seems to interest them. Some feel responsible for serious world problems such as economic depression, disease, or hunger. They report strange diseases and may insist that their body is disintegrating or that their brain is being eaten from the inside out. Most people who exhibit symptoms of a major depression can describe their reasons for feeling sad and dejected, but they may be unable to explain why their response is so deep and so prolonged.

Psychologists say that people suffering from major depression are poor at reality testing. *Reality testing* is a person's ability to accurately judge the demands of the environment and his or her ability to deal with those demands. People with poor reality testing are unable to cope with the demands of life in rational ways because their reasoning ability is grossly impaired.

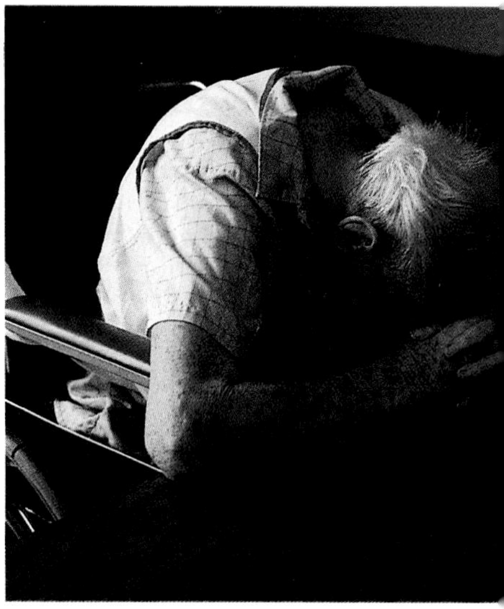

With few positive reinforcements in their lives, the elderly often become depressed and further alienate those people who could be caring for them.

Onset and Duration. A major depressive episode can occur at any age, although major depression usually first occurs before age 40. Symptoms are rapidly apparent and last for a few days, weeks, or months. Episodes may occur once or many times. Sometimes, depressive episodes are separated by years of normal functioning, followed by two or three brief episodes of depression a few weeks apart. Stressful life events are not good predictors of depression (Swindle, Cronkite, & Moos, 1989). It is important to recognize that depression is not exclusively an adult disorder; many researchers find evidence of depression in children and young adolescents (Larson et al., 1990).

Prevalence. Women, as teenagers and adults, are twice as likely as men to be diagnosed as depressed and are more likely to express feelings of depression openly (Allgood-Merten, Lewinsohn, & Hops, 1990). In the United States, about 19–23% of women and 8–11% of men have experienced a major depressive episode at some time. About 6% of women and 3% of men have experienced episodes sufficiently severe to require hospitalization. Some practitioners assert that women, more than men, respond to depressing life events differently—with men cutting off depressing feelings before they get out of hand (Nolen-Hoeksema, 1990). Seligman (1988) suggests that the increased incidence of depression in the United States stems from too much emphasis on the individual, coupled with a loss of faith in such supportive institutions as family, country, and religion.

Theories of Depression

Learning Objective 28.4 Discuss the causes of depression according to the biological, learning, cognitive, and learned-helplessness theories.

Most psychologists believe that depression is caused by a combination of biological, learning, and cognitive factors. Biological theories suggest that chemical and genetic processes can account for depression. Learning theories suggest that people develop faulty behaviors. Cognitive theories suggest that irrational ideas guide behavior. We next examine each theory in more detail.

Biological Theories. Are people born with a predisposition to depression? Depression may be biologically or genetically based, according to Tsuang and Faraone (1990). Tsuang and Faraone found that children of depressed patients are more likely to be depressed themselves. Other researchers discovered the *norepinephrine hypothesis,* which states that an insufficient amount of *norepinephrine* (a neurotransmitter in the brain; see Chapter 2) may cause depression. Research has shown that if the level of norepinephrine at the receptor site in the brain is increased, depression is alleviated. Because aversive stimuli decrease norepinephrine levels, however, being in a stressful situation could bring about depression. Other evidence for a biological explanation of depression is that antidepressant drugs (tricyclics) seem to help certain types of depressed patients. Recent research suggests that although the norepinephrine hypothesis is not false, the biological underpinnings of depression are more complex. That is, depression may be caused by many other substances in the brain, in addition to norepinephrine, that are not functioning properly, or because of a genetic heritage, or both (Faraone, Kremen, & Tsuang, 1990).

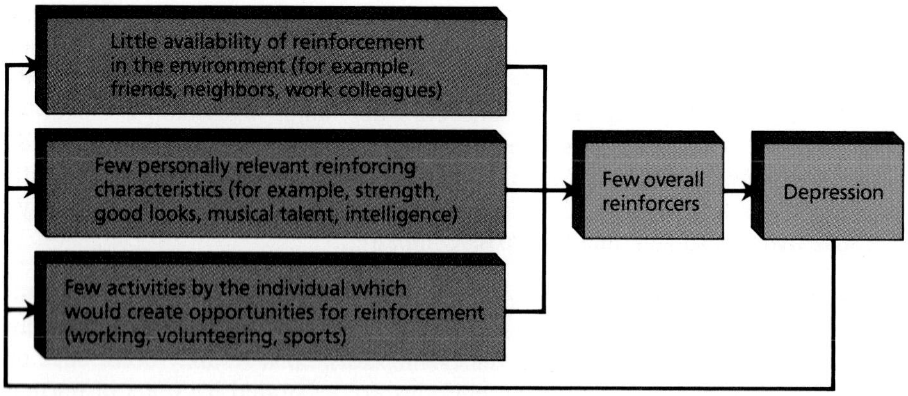

Figure 28.1

According to Lewinsohn, few reinforcers in the environment are available for some people, and this causes depression, which then leads to even fewer reinforcers.

Learning and Cognitive Theories. Learning and cognitive theorists argue that people who are depressed learn depressive behaviors and thoughts. People with poor social skills who never learn to express prosocial behaviors and who are punished for the behaviors they do exhibit experience the world as aversive and depressing. In support of this idea is the finding that children of depressed parents are more likely to be depressed (Downey & Coyne, 1990). In addition, Peter Lewinsohn (1974) believes that people who have few positive reinforcements in their lives (often the old, sickly, and poor) become depressed. Other people find them unpleasant and avoid them, thus creating a nonreinforcing environment (Lewinsohn & Talkington, 1979). Lewinsohn stresses that depressed people often lack the social skills needed to obtain reinforcement, such as asking a neighbor or friend for help with a problem. See Figure 28.1 for a summary of this process.

Psychiatrist Aaron Beck has proposed an influential cognitive-learning theory. Beck suggests that depressed people already have negative views of themselves, the environment, and the future, which cause them to magnify their errors. They compare themselves to other people, usually unfairly, and when they come up short, they see the difference as disastrous. They see the human condition as universally wretched, become angry (Riley, Treiber, & Woods, 1989), and view the world as a place that defeats positive behavior. Their poor self-concept, along with negative expectations about the world, produce negative future expectations that lead to depression. Beck (1976) believes that depression does not cause negative feelings, but that negative feelings and expectations *cause* depression. Beck's theory is influential among psychologists because it is consistent with the notion that depression stems from a lack of appropriate (positive) reinforcements in people's environments and because it acknowledges both cognitive *and* environmental variables.

learned helplessness: The behavior of giving up or not responding, exhibited by subjects exposed to negative consequences or punishment over which they have no control.

Learned Helplessness. What happens when a person's hopes and dreams are constantly thwarted, regardless of his or her behavior? What would you do if you failed every exam you took, regardless of your efforts? **Learned helplessness** (discussed in more detail in Chapter 15) results when a people learn that rewards and punishments are not contingent on their behavior. Faced with a loss of control, some people stop responding.

In one version of learned helplessness, Seligman (1976) suggested that people's beliefs about the causes of their successes or failures determine whether they become depressed. When they attribute their mistakes or failures to unalterable conditions within themselves ("my own weakness, which is unlikely to change"), they come to regard themselves with low self-esteem (Raps et al., 1982).

That is, when they believe that eventual outcomes are unrelated to anything in their control, people develop learned helplessness. For example, a man who comes to believe that his effort to meet new people by being outgoing and friendly never works may stop trying. Eventually, he will choose not to respond to the environment because he has learned that his behavior makes no difference (Peterson & Seligman, 1984). Seligman (1988) argues that the environment, rather than genetics, is the cause of depression and helplessness, especially when people believe they are the cause of long-standing failures in many areas of their lives.

The effects of helplessness and depression are poignant and painful. They influence the day-to-day life of the individual, the work environment, and the person's family. These factors and more become especially apparent when studying an even more disabling disorder, schizophrenia, the next subject in this chapter.

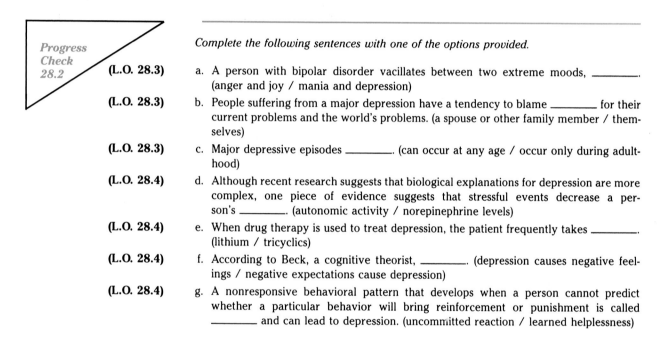

Progress Check 28.2

Complete the following sentences with one of the options provided.

(L.O. 28.3) a. A person with bipolar disorder vacillates between two extreme moods, ________. (anger and joy / mania and depression)

(L.O. 28.3) b. People suffering from a major depression have a tendency to blame ________ for their current problems and the world's problems. (a spouse or other family member / themselves)

(L.O. 28.3) c. Major depressive episodes ________. (can occur at any age / occur only during adulthood)

(L.O. 28.4) d. Although recent research suggests that biological explanations for depression are more complex, one piece of evidence suggests that stressful events decrease a person's ________. (autonomic activity / norepinephrine levels)

(L.O. 28.4) e. When drug therapy is used to treat depression, the patient frequently takes ________. (lithium / tricyclics)

(L.O. 28.4) f. According to Beck, a cognitive theorist, ________. (depression causes negative feelings / negative expectations cause depression)

(L.O. 28.4) g. A nonresponsive behavioral pattern that develops when a person cannot predict whether a particular behavior will bring reinforcement or punishment is called ________ and can lead to depression. (uncommitted reaction / learned helplessness)

Schizophrenia

Learning Objective 28.5
Characterize schizophrenic disorder, and identify categories of people who are likely to be diagnosed as having this disorder.

Schizophrenia is considered the most devastating, complex, and frustrating of all mental disorders; people with the disorder lose touch with reality and are often unable to function in a world that makes no sense to them. We often say that such individuals are psychotic; the term **psychotic** refers to the fact that the impairment is wide ranging, it usually includes a lack of reality testing and it hinders an individual's ability to meet the ordinary demands of life. Schizophrenia begins slowly, with more symptoms developing as time passes.

psychotic: [sie-KOT-ick] A gross impairment of reality testing that interferes with an individual's ability to meet the ordinary demands of life.

Schizophrenia affects one of every 100 people in the United States. Almost 25% of patients admitted to mental hospitals each year are diagnosed as schizophrenic (Sartorious, 1982). The diagnosis occurs more frequently among lower socioeconomic groups and nonwhites (Lindsey & Paul, 1989) and more frequently among younger rather than older people. Men who are diagnosed as schizophrenic at an early age exhibit and more negative symptoms, and they have

schizophrenic disorders: [SKIT-soh-FREN-ick] A group of disorders characterized by lack of reality testing and deterioration of social and intellectual functioning, and often by serious personality disintegration with significant changes in thought, mood, perception, and behavior.

hallucinations: [ha-LOOSE-in-AY-shuns] Compelling perceptual experiences without a real physical stimulus. They may be visual, tactile, olfactory, or most commonly in schizophrenia, auditory.

affect: A person's emotional response.

a poorer chance of recovery than women who are diagnosed at an early age (Goldstein & Tsuang, 1990).

Essential Characteristics of Schizophrenia

People with **schizophrenic disorders** display sudden changes in thought, perception, emotion (affect), and overall behavior. Those changes are often accompanied by distortions of reality. Further, there is usually an inability to respond appropriately in thought, perception, or emotion.

Thought Disorders. One of the first signs of schizophrenia is difficulty in maintaining logical thought and coherent conversation. People with schizophrenia show disordered thinking and impaired memory. They may have *delusions* (false beliefs held even in the face of contrary evidence). Many have delusions of persecution and believe that the world is a hostile place.

Delusions of persecution are often accompanied by *delusions of grandeur:* the patient believes that he or she is a particularly important person. This importance becomes the reason for his or her persecution. Sometimes, for example, the patient takes on the role of an important character in history—Boris Yeltsin, Jesus Christ, Norman Schwarzkopf, or the Queen of England—and deludes him or herself that people are conspiring to harm him or her.

Perceptual Disorders. Another sign of schizophrenia is the presence of **hallucinations,** which may be visual, tactile, olfactory, or most commonly, auditory. The patient reports hearing voices originating outside his or her head. The voices may comment on the patient's behavior or direct the patient to behave in certain ways (Bentall, 1990). For example, convicted murderer David Berkowitz (known to the media as Son of Sam) claimed that his neighbor's dog told him to kill.

Emotional Disorders. One of the most striking characteristics of schizophrenia is the display of inappropriate emotional responses, or **affect.** A patient with schizophrenia, for example, may become depressed and cry when her favorite food falls on the floor yet laugh hysterically at the death of a close friend or relative. Some patients show no emotion (either appropriate or inappropriate) and seem incapable of experiencing a normal range of feeling. Their emotional range is constricted, or *flat.* They show blank, expressionless faces, even when presented with a deliberately provocative remark or situation. Other patients show *ambivalent* affect. They have a wide range of emotional behaviors in a brief period, seeming happy one moment and sad and dejected the next. An ambivalent affect is usually caused by internal conflicts.

Types of Schizophrenia

Learning Objective 28.6 List five features that must be present for a diagnosis of schizophrenia, and characterize five types of schizophrenia.

There are five types of schizophrenia, each with different symptoms, diagnostic criteria, and causes: disorganized, paranoid, catatonic, residual, and undifferentiated. According to *DSM-III-R,* a diagnosis of schizophrenia, regardless of the subtype, requires the presence of the following features:

- ▲ lack of reality testing,
- ▲ involvement of more than one area of psychological functioning,
- ▲ deterioration in social and intellectual functioning,
- ▲ onset of illness generally before age 45, and
- ▲ duration of illness for at least 6 months.

Disorganized Type. The **disorganized type** of schizophrenia is characterized by severely disturbed thought processes. Patients have hallucinations and delusions and are frequently incoherent. They may exhibit bizarre emotions, with periods of giggling, crying, or irritability for no apparent reason. Their behavior can be silly, inappropriate, or even obscene. Such patients exhibit a severe disintegration of normal personality, a loss of reality testing, and often poor personal hygiene. Their chances for recovery are poor.

disorganized type: A major subtype of schizophrenia, characterized by frequent incoherence, absence of systematized delusions, and blunted, inappropriate, or silly affect.

paranoid type: [PAIR-uh—noid] A major subtype of schizophrenia, characterized by delusions, hallucinations of persecution and/or grandeur, and sometimes irrational jealousy.

catatonic type: [CAT-uh-TAWN-ick] A major subtype of schizophrenia, characterized by stupor, in which the individual is mute, negative, and basically unresponsive, or by displays of excited or violent motor activity.

residual type: A schizophrenic disorder characterized by inappropriate affect, illogical thinking, or eccentric behavior but with the patient generally in touch with reality.

undifferentiated type: A schizophrenic disorder characterized by a mixture of symptoms.

Paranoid Type. **Paranoid-type** schizophrenics are among the most difficult to identify and study because their outward behavior often seems appropriate to the situation. They may actively seek out other people and not show extreme withdrawal from social interaction. The degree of disturbance of paranoid type patients varies over time.

Paranoid patients may be alert, intelligent, and responsive, but their delusions and hallucinations impair their ability to deal with reality (see Kendler, 1980), and their behavior is often unpredictable and sometimes hostile. Patients diagnosed as paranoid types may see bizarre images and are likely to have auditory hallucinations. They may feel that they are being chased by ghosts or intruders from another planet. Paranoid-type patients have extreme delusions of persecution and, occasionally, of grandeur. Though harder to identify and study, patients diagnosed as paranoid schizophrenics have a better chance of recovery than do patients with other subtypes of schizophrenia.

Catatonic Type. There are actually two subtypes of **catatonic type** schizophrenia—excited and withdrawn, both of which involve extreme overt behavior. *Excited* catatonic patients show excessive activity. They may talk and shout continuously and engage in seemingly uninhibited, agitated, and aggressive motor activity. These episodes usually appear and disappear suddenly. *Withdrawn* catatonic patients tend to appear stuporous, mute, and negative. Although they occasionally exhibit signs of the excited phase, they usually show a high degree of muscular rigidity. They are not immobile but have a decreased level of speaking, moving, and responding, although they are usually aware of events around them. Catatonic type patients may use immobility and unresponsiveness to maintain control over their environment because their behavior relieves them of the responsibility of responding to external stimuli.

Residual and Undifferentiated Type. People who show symptoms attributable to schizophrenia but who remain in touch with reality are characterized as **residual type.** Such patients show inappropriate affect, illogical thinking, or eccentric behavior. They have a history of at least one previous schizophrenic episode.

Sometimes, it is difficult to determine which category most appropriately describes a patient (Gift et al., 1980). Some patients exhibit all the essential features of schizophrenia—prominent delusions, hallucinations, incoherence, and grossly disorganized behavior—but do not fall into the categories of disorganized, catatonic, paranoid, or residual type. These individuals are classified as **undifferentiated type.**

Learning Objective 28.7
Discuss biological and environmental factors that contribute to the development of schizophrenia, and state the most likely cause of this disorder.

Causes of Schizophrenia

What causes people to lose their grasp on reality with such devastating results? Are people born with schizophrenia, or do they develop it as a result of painful childhood experiences? Theories of schizophrenia take markedly different posi-

Catatonic patients limit their physical movements until they are actually rigid. This behavior is accompanied by a general decrease in responsiveness even though they retain an awareness of the world around them.

tions about its origins. Biologically oriented psychologists focus on chemicals in the brain and a person's genetic heritage—the basic argument is that schizophrenia is a brain disease (D. L. Johnson, 1989). Learning theorists argue that a person's environment and early experiences cause schizophrenia. The arguments for each approach are compelling, and there are data to support each of the various theories.

Biological Causes. Evidence exists to suggest the presence of some kind of biological determinant or predisposition to schizophrenia (Farone & Tsuang, 1985). People born with that predisposition have a greater probability of developing schizophrenia than do other people; it is now generally accepted that schizophrenia runs in families (Gottesman, 1991). The children and siblings of schizophrenic patients are more likely to exhibit maladjustment and schizophrenic symptoms than are other people (Walker & Emory, 1983). About 1% of the U.S. population are schizophrenic, but when one parent has schizophrenia, the probability that an offspring also will have it increases to between 3 and 14%. If both parents have schizophrenia, children have about a 35% probability of developing it (D. Rosenthal, 1970).

However, if schizophrenia were totally genetic, then the likelihood that identical (monozygotic) twins, who have identical genes, would show the disorder would be 100%. This likelihood is referred to as the **concordance rate**. Studies of schizophrenia in identical twins show concordance rates from 0 to 86% (Dalby, Morgan, & Lee, 1986), with most suggesting a rate of about 48%—this suggests that there are *other* factors involved besides genetics. In an important study of identical twins, analysis of brain structures showed subtle but important brain abnormalities in a schizophrenic individual whose identical twin did not show the abnormality. This study argues that *nongenetic* factors must exert an important influence on schizophrenia (Suddath et al., 1990) and are critical in its development (Gottesman, 1991).

Nevertheless, most researchers agree that genetics is a fundamental cause of the disorder. The concordance rate for schizophrenia in monozygotic (identical) twins is almost five times that in dizygotic (fraternal) twins. Moreover, studies of monozygotic twins reared apart from their natural parents and from each other show a higher concordance rate than fraternal twins or control subjects (Stone, 1980).

The Genain quadruplets, all of whom developed some manifestation of schizophrenic disorder, are a classic example of genetic influence.

concordance rate: The percentage of occasions when two groups or individuals show the same trait.

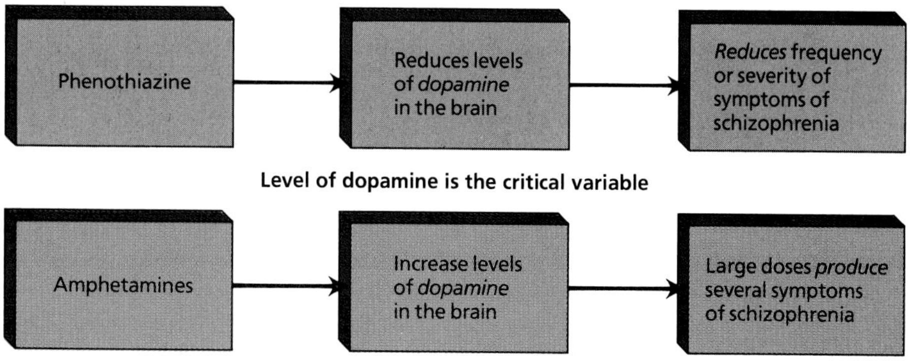

Figure 28.2

In the dopamine hypothesis, schizophrenia is assumed to develop in part from an excess of dopamine in the brain.

Other support for a biological basis of schizophrenia comes from researchers who discovered that chemicals in the bloodstream may contribute to the development of schizophrenia. Several studies support the importance of the neurotransmitter dopamine. Dopamine pathways are considered one of the main sites of biochemical disturbance in the brain. Drugs called *phenothiazines* appear to block receptor sites in the dopamine pathways. When patients with schizophrenia are given phenothiazines, many of their disturbed thought processes and hallucinations disappear. Conversely, drugs that stimulate the dopamine system (such as amphetamines) aggravate existing schizophrenic disorders. (See Figure 28.2.) Evidence now shows that certain portions of the brains of schizophrenic patients have abnormalities (although it is not yet clear whether schizophrenia causes the brain changes or the brain changes cause schizophrenia). For example, the brain *ventricles,* hollow areas normally filled with fluid, are enlarged in some schizophrenic patients (Suddath et al., 1990), (Raz & Raz, 1990).

Environmental Factors. Some psychologists believe that in addition to genetics, environmental interactions determine the development of schizophrenia. Freudian psychologists, for example, suggest that early childhood relationships determine whether a person will become fixated at the oral stage and develop a disorder such as schizophrenia. Such a person has not developed an ego and will make judgments based on the id's pleasure principle. Lacking the ego, which uses the reality principle in making judgments, the individual will seek immediate gratification and thus be unable to deal effectively with reality. Freudian psychologists assert that a person who has successfully passed through the oral stage and has developed a strong ego is unlikely to suffer from schizophrenia.

Behavioral explanations of schizophrenia rely on traditional learning principles such as those discussed in Chapter 5. This approach argues that faulty reinforcement and extinction procedures, as well as social learning processes, can account for schizophrenia. Imagine a child brought up in a family where the parents constantly argue, where the father is an alcoholic, and neither parent shows much caring or affection for each other or for anyone else. Such a child, receiving no reinforcement for interest in events, people, and objects in the outside world, may become withdrawn and begin to exhibit schizophrenic behavior. Lidz (1973) argues that children who grow up in such homes adopt the family's faulty view of the world and relationships and thus are likely to expect reinforcement for abnormal behaviors. Growing up in such an emotionally fragmented environment may predispose individuals to emotional disorder and eventual schizophrenia. In addition, if parents themselves are schizophrenic and they mistreat the child, this increases the likelihood of behavior problems such as schizophrenia in the child's future (Walker, Downey, & Bergman, 1989).

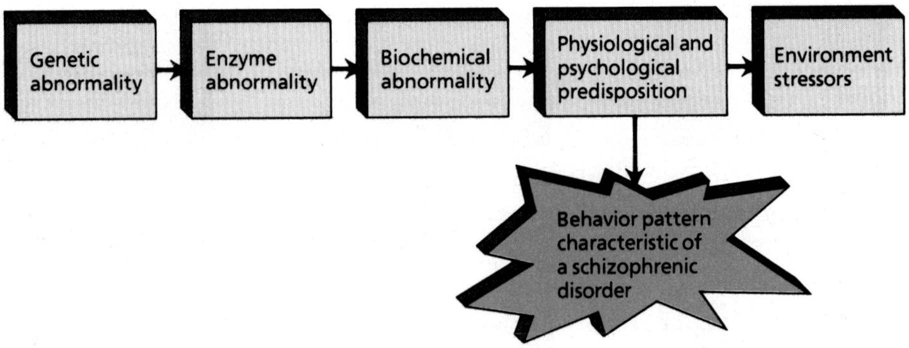

Figure 28.3

According to the biological view of schizophrenia, the environment triggers behaviors in people who are predisposed to schizophrenia. Thus, for people who opt for the combined view of nature and nurture, genetic abnormalities lead to situations in which environmental stressors trigger the behavioral pattern of schizophrenia.

Even in families in which marital conflict is absent, parents sometimes confuse their children. Some parents, for example, place their children in situations that offer two competing messages: a **double bind.** Initially proposed by Gregory Bateson, double-bind situations usually occur between individuals with a strong emotional attachment, such as that of a child and parents (Mishler & Waxler, 1968). In play, parents may hold up a toy and say, "No, you may not have this," while smiling and giving other nonverbal assurances that the child may have the toy. Generally, the child understands that the parent is teasing. However, not all children understand this, and not all situations are so clearly cued. Games such as this, if played consistently, may shape an environment of confusion conducive to the development of schizophrenia.

Learning theory suggests that schizophrenics are likely to develop and maintain the disorder because of faulty reinforcement patterns. A person who receives a great deal of attention for behaviors that other people see as bizarre is likely to continue those behaviors. People who fail to develop effective social skills are more at risk (Meusser et al., 1990). Other reinforcement theories suggest that bizarre behavior and thoughts are themselves reinforcing because they allow the person to escape from both acute anxiety and an overactive autonomic nervous system.

Nature or Nurture? Many variables determine whether an individual will develop schizophrenia. Some people, because of family environment, genetic history, or brain chemistry, are more vulnerable than others (see Figure 28.3). The more **vulnerable** the individual, the less necessary are environmental stress or other disorders (such as anxiety) to the initiation of a schizophrenic episode. When a person develops the disorder, the effect on the individual and his or her family is devastating; the strains on family life are formidable (Lefley, 1989).

Although the causes of schizophrenia are still undetermined, research suggests the following:

- A connection exists between genetics and schizophrenia, although genetics alone cannot account for its development.
- Specific types of chemical substances in the brain are associated with schizophrenia.
- Environmental factors (such as the presence of marital conflict and double binds) contribute to the development of schizophrenia. Among these factors, early childhood relationships may be especially important.
- The most likely cause of schizophrenia is a biological predisposition in the individual, aggravated by a climate of emotional immaturity, lack of communication, and emotional instability.

double bind: A situation in which an individual is given two different and inconsistent messages.

vulnerable: A person's diminished ability to deal with demanding life events.

Progress Check 28.3

Complete the following sentences with one of the options provided.

(L.O. 28.5) a. A person who is diagnosed schizophrenic ________. (shows a serious disintegration of personality / developed the symptoms suddenly)

(L.O. 28.5) b. Hearing voices or seeing things that are not being perceived by other people are ________. (delusions / hallucinations)

(L.O. 28.5) c. A schizophrenic who exhibits no emotion and seems incapable of experiencing a normal range of feelings is described as having ________ affect. (inappropriate / flat / ambivalent)

(L.O. 28.6) d. To be diagnosed as schizophrenic, the person must show ________. (the symptoms before age 16 / impairment in more than one area of psychological functioning)

(L.O. 28.6) e. When comparing the subtypes of schizophrenia, a person who has ________ schizophrenia has the best chance for recovery. (catatonic / disorganized / paranoid)

(L.O. 28.6) f. Two types of catatonic schizophrenia are ________. (excited and withdrawn / dependent and independent)

(L.O. 28.6) g. People who show symptoms of schizophrenia but remain in touch with reality are diagnosed as having ________ type schizophrenia. (residual / undifferentiated)

(L.O. 28.6) h. A paranoid schizophrenic who believes that she or he will be *the* person chosen by aliens to deliver a special message to earthlings is having delusions of ________. (persecution / grandeur)

(L.O. 28.7) i. If both parents have schizophrenia, the probability of offspring developing the disorder is about ________. (3% / 14% / 35%)

(L.O. 28.7) j. Genetic research concerning the causes of schizophrenia has shown that the concordance rate for identical twins is ________ than that for fraternal twins. (no different / three times lower / five times higher)

(L.O. 28.7) k. Several studies suggest that too much of the neurotransmitter ________ plays an influential role in the development of schizophrenia. (acetylcholine / dopamine / norepinephrine)

(L.O. 28.7) l. According to Freud, schizophrenia develops because the person is fixated in the ________. (oral stage and has not developed an ego / phallic stage and has not developed a superego)

(L.O. 28.7) m. A *double-bind* situation may contribute to the development of schizophrenia because the child ________. (cannot please both parents / becomes confused by competing messages)

(L.O. 28.7) n. A learning theorist might suggest that the bizarre thoughts and behaviors of a schizophrenic continue because they ________. (are entertaining / allow escape from acute anxiety)

Module Summary

Personality Disorders

- People who have unwarranted feelings of persecution and who mistrust almost everyone are said to have *paranoid personality disorder.* Fearful or anxious behaviors are characteristic of people who have a *dependent personality disorder.* Dramatic, emotional, and erratic behaviors are characteristic of the *histrionic personality disorder* (p. 536).
- Antisocial personality disorder is usually exhibited before age 15 years and characterized by a history of behavior that violates the rights of others. Persons with antisocial personality disorders come into conflict with society because they lack feelings of guilt and any real understanding of others (p. 536).

Sexual Disorders

- *Sexual deviation* is a sexual practice directed toward objects rather than people, or involving real or simulated suffering, humiliation, or nonconsenting partners (p. 537).

Mood Disorders

- Patients diagnosed as having a *major depression* disorder have a gloomy outlook on life, especially slow thought processes, an exaggerated view of current problems, and a tendency to blame themselves. *Psychotic behavior* shows gross impairment in reality testing, which usually interferes with an individual's ability to meet the ordinary demands of life (p. 540).
- The *norepinephrine hypothesis* suggests that an insufficient amount of norepinephrine at receptor sites causes depression. If the substance level is increased, depression will be alleviated. Learning theories (such as those of Lewinsohn, Beck, and theorists who emphasize the role of learned helplessness) stress that reinforcement—and where, how, and when it is delivered—determines the course and nature of depression (p. 541).

Schizophrenia

- *Schizophrenia* is a group of disorders characterized by lack of reality testing and by deterioration of social and intellectual functioning. It begins before age 45 years and lasts for at least 6 months. Individuals with this diagnosis often show serious personality disintegration, with significant changes in thought, mood, perception, and behavior. Patients diagnosed as schizophrenic have problems with various aspects of behavior, particularly with attention, emotions, perceptions, and motor behavior (p. 543).
- Biological studies suggest that the cause of schizophrenia must be to some extent genetic. Environmental studies suggest that home environment and early interactions in life (such as in double-bind situations) affect whether a person will develop schizophrenia (pp. 546–547).

KEY TERMS

affect, p. 544
antisocial personality disorder, p. 536
bipolar disorder, p. 540
catatonic type, p. 545
concordance rate, p. 546
delusions, p. 540
depressive disorders, p. 540
disorganized type, p. 545
double bind, p. 548
exhibitionism, p. 537
fetishism, p. 537
hallucinations, p. 544
learned helplessness, p. 542
major depression, p. 540
paranoid type, p. 545
pedophilia, p. 538
personality disorder, p. 536
psychotic, p. 543
rape, p. 538
residual type, p. 545
schizophrenic disorders, p. 544
sexual disorder, p. 537
sexual masochism, p. 539
sexual sadism, p. 539
transvestic fetishism, p. 537
undifferentiated type, p. 545
voyeurism, p. 537
vulnerable, p. 548

SELF-TEST

Module 28

- Before taking the self-test, **recite** and **review.**
- Use the key at the back of the text to *correct* your answers.
- *Restudy* pages that correspond to any questions you answered incorrectly.

1. A person who acts meek and humble, tries to be agreeable at all times, and looks to others to make important life decisions would be diagnosed as having a
   a. paranoid personality disorder.
   b. dependent personality disorder.
   c. histrionic personality disorder.
   d. narcissistic personality disorder.
2. A primary characteristic of a person with antisocial personality disorder is that the person
   a. has unwarranted feelings of persecution.
   b. behaves like a hermit, isolating himself from others.
   c. is unwilling to conform to society's rules.
   d. demands to have reassurance and praise from others.
3. The sexual satisfaction gained from voyeurism may involve
   a. the risk of being discovered.
   b. the startle response of their victims.
   c. feeling powerful over objects.
   d. enjoying the experience of pain.
4. Most psychologists agree that sexual disorders
   a. develop as a result of learned experiences in childhood or adolescence.
   b. are a by-product of other serious behavior disorders.
   c. are the result of physiological dysfunctions.
   d. must be treated while the person is confined in a hospital or corrections facility.
5. Bipolar disorders
   a. are more common than depressive disorders.
   b. have a biological basis and are generally treated with drugs.
   c. involve moments of high anxiety, followed by moments of deep relaxation.
   d. first appear during childhood or adolescence.
6. During the manic phase of bipolar disorder, the person
   a. shows few signs of the disorder and behaves relatively normally.
   b. is moody and sad, lacks energy, and feels hopeless.
   c. has rapid speech and an inflated sense of self-esteem, is easily distracted, and behaves impulsively.
   d. is deeply depressed.
7. A depressed person who makes inaccurate judgments about life's demands and her or his own ability to cope with them
   a. is having delusions.
   b. is paranoid.
   c. has poor reality-testing skills.
   d. is about to enter a manic episode.

8. Lewinsohn, a learning theorist, suggests that depression occurs
   a. when people learn that the rewards and punishments they receive have nothing to do with how hard they tried.
   b. in people who have negative thoughts and expectations.
   c. because the depressed person lacks the skills needed to obtain reinforcement.
   d. when people compare themselves to others and then feel "less than" another person.
9. Three areas of psychological impairment found in schizophrenics involve
   a. creativity, intelligence, and memory.
   b. vocalization, attention, and persistence.
   c. thought, perception, and emotion.
   d. fine motor coordination, concentration, and resiliency.
10. ________ schizophrenics are among the most difficult to identify because their outward behavior frequently seems appropriate to the situation.
    a. Disorganized
    b. Paranoid
    c. Catatonic
    d. Undifferentiated
11. When schizophrenics are given ________, many of their symptoms disappear.
    a. amphetamines
    b. phenothiazines
    c. dopamine
    d. tricyclics
12. The most probable explanation for the cause of schizophrenia suggests that
    a. a virus acts on a genetic predisposition and causes schizophrenia.
    b. a biological predisposition is aggravated by an environmental climate of emotional immaturity.
    c. structural changes in the brain cause schizophrenia.
    d. schizophrenics were not allowed to play during childhood.

Connections

If you are interested in . . .	Turn to . . .	To learn more about . . .
The role of anxiety in normal behavior and in maladjustment	◆ Chapter 9, p. 359 ◆ Chapter 12, p. 496	How behavior is affected when a person is feeling anxious and aroused How a person's health can deteriorate due to continually high levels of anxiety, stress, and autonomic nervous system arousal
The role of learning in the development of various forms of maladjustment	◆ Chapter 5, pp. 190–195 ◆ Chapter 10, p. 427 ◆ Chapter 15, pp. 598, 604	How children's behavior, both good and bad, is learned through conditioning procedures How self-esteem and self-efficacy—often learned in the formative years of childhood—affect the ability to cope with simple as well as complex demands of life How attitudes and self-perceptions develop through a process of repeated experiences
The biological bases of psychological disorders	◆ Chapter 2, p. 42 ◆ Chapter 9, pp. 352–358 ◆ Chapter 14, pp. 587–589	Hormonal and genetic influences on behavior How overeating, or even eating the wrong foods, can affect behavior The use of drugs to treat various forms of maladjustment

Students of psychology often are surprised to find that psychological disorders and their treatment are not principle topics of study for psychologists. Psychological disorders are, however, a mainstay of psychology, and their relationship to other disciplines is longstanding. The study of mood disorders and schizophrenia depends upon the study of biological mechanisms (Chapter 2, p. 51). Psychological disorders often alter people's consciousness (Chapter 4, p. 127) and their thought processes (Chapter 7, p. 240). Although biology plays an important role, researchers all agree that learning plays a vital role in the development of many disorders (Chapter 5, p. 193); this ultimately effects a person's motivation (Chapter 9, p. 365), a person's personality structure (Chapter 10, p. 422), and eventually the person's health and adjustment (Chapter 12, p. 496). Psychological disorders are usually not considered alone. People need to be considered within their social world (Chapter 15, p. 596) before treatment for various disorders is considered (Chapter 13, p. 519).

Module 29 ► INSIGHT APPROACHES 556

Module 30 ► BEHAVIORAL AND COGNITIVE APPROACHES 572

Chapter 14

Approaches to Treatment

Many types of treatment are available for people who are having difficulty coping with life. There are literally dozens of treatments, and this chapter presents a broad overview of those methods. First, Module 29 provides an overview of the therapeutic process and methods used to evaluate the outcomes of therapy. Commonalities and differences between the various treatment methods are highlighted. Much of the rich history of therapy comes from the psychodynamic tradition—Freud's approach—this approach to treatment is discussed in detail, and its natural outgrowth, humanistic therapy, is then presented. Key methods and procedures in psychodynamic and humanistic approaches are presented as well as expected changes that occur through therapy.

The diversity of therapeutic approaches is next highlighted by considering the reactions that occurred in the post-World War II era to traditional therapeutic approaches. The second module of this chapter, Module 30, presents three key alternatives to psychodynamic and humanistic approaches, which often prove to be equally as effective as, or even more effective than, the traditional approaches. Behavior therapy relies heavily on learning theory; cognitive therapy focuses on thought processes; and group therapy uses a variety of approaches to help groups of people who share similar problems. These approaches are presented as more time efficient, concise, and popular alternatives to traditional psychodynamic approaches. The module also describes the role of mental health practitioners in the delivery of psychological services to individuals in the community—the focus of community psychology. The module concludes with an overview of biologically based therapies, which rely heavily on drugs.

Module 29

Insight Approaches

LEARNING OBJECTIVES

When you have mastered the material in this module, you will be able to

Therapy Comes in Many Forms (pp. 557–560)

29.1 Distinguish between somatic therapy and psychotherapy (p. 557).
29.2 Briefly describe seven major types of psychotherapy (p. 557).
29.3 Identify some important features of effective therapy, discuss the placebo effect, and comment on research findings concerning the effectiveness of psychotherapy (p. 558).

Psychodynamic Therapy (pp. 560–565)

29.4 Distinguish between psychoanalysis and psychodynamic therapy and state the major assumptions and goals of these types of therapy (p. 560).
29.5 Describe the techniques used in psychoanalysis and two common patient responses that occur during the process (p. 562).
29.6 Explain how ego analysis differs from psychoanalysis and discuss some of the criticisms made about Freudian-based therapies (p. 564).

Humanistic Therapy (pp. 565–569)

29.7 Describe the assumptions, goals, techniques, and common criticisms of client-centered therapy (p. 565).
29.8 Describe the assumptions, goals, and common criticisms of Gestalt therapy (p. 567).

SQ3R
- ▲ **Survey** to set goals for studying.
- ▲ Ask **questions** as you **read.**
- ▲ Stop occasionally to **recite** and **review.**

plus
- ▲ **Write** a summary of key points.
- ▲ **Reflect** on the hypotheses, evidence, and implications of this material and on its relevance to *your* life.

Ricky Estevez was depressed about his monthly sales totals—at least that's what he told his coworkers. He invited them to join him for a couple of beers after work. Most declined, knowing that Ricky was suffering another bout of depression. Outside the bar, Ricky telephoned his wife to say he was going to be home late. His wife lectured him; this led to harsh words, and Ricky began shouting, then abruptly hung up. Ricky soon began to come into work late and sometimes skipped out altogether. Angry and anxious about his sales performance, losing sleep, losing weight, and verging on alcoholism, Ricky made an appointment with a counselor at the hospital's Psychological Service Center.

psychotherapy: [SIE-ko-THER-uh-pee] The treatment of emotional or behavioral problems through psychological techniques.

Psychologists recognize that people are vulnerable to numerous coping problems related to stress, maladjustment, peer pressure, and drug (including alcohol) abuse. Everyone suffers to some degree, but for some people, these problems become overwhelming. They afflict Ricky so intensely that he has become unhappy and maladjusted. In such severe cases, the afflicted person may seek professional help.

Therapy Comes in Many Forms

Learning Objective 29.1
Distinguish between somatic therapy and psychotherapy.

Many types of treatment are available for people such as Ricky Estevez who are having difficulty coping with life. When a person seeks help from a physician, mental health counseling center, or drug treatment center, an initial working diagnosis is necessary. Does the person have medical problems? Should the person be hospitalized? Is the person dangerous to himself or others? If talking therapy is in order, what type of practitioner is best suited for the person? There are two broad types of therapy: somatic therapy and psychotherapy.

Somatic therapy refers to therapies for the body, including therapies that affect hormones and the brain (see Chapter 2). For example, severely depressed individuals may need tranquilizers; those diagnosed as having a schizophrenic disorder may need antipsychotic drugs; those with less severe disorders may be advised to change their diets and to exercise more. These somatic therapies are biologically based therapies. We examine some of these biological therapies later in this chapter; now, however, explore the broad array of psychological therapies that are available for people suffering from maladjustment.

Psychotherapy is the treatment of emotional or behavioral problems through psychological techniques. It is a *change-oriented* process. The goal of psychotherapy is to help people cope better and to achieve more emotionally satisfying life-styles, often by helping them relieve stress, improve interpersonal communication, and modify their faulty ideas about the world. Psychotherapy helps people improve their self-images and adapt to new and challenging situations.

Types of Psychotherapy

Learning Objective 29.2
Briefly describe seven major types of psychotherapy.

There are about 200 different forms of therapy. Some focus on treating individuals, some on groups of individuals *(group therapy)*, and others on families *(family therapy)*. Some psychologists even deal with whole communities. Community psychologists focus on helping individuals, groups, and communities develop a more action-oriented approach to individual and social adjustment.

A therapist's training will usually determine the type of treatment approach taken. Rather than using just one type of psychotherapy, many therapists take an

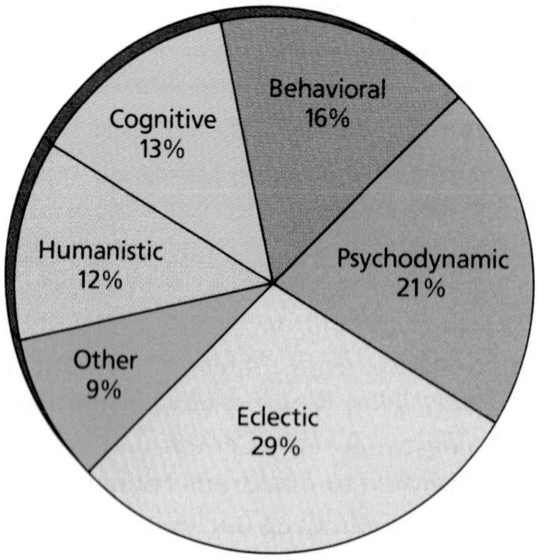

Figure 29.1

The primary orientation of 579 clinical psychologists who belong to the American Psychological Association. (Source: Based on data from Norcross, Prochaska, & Gallagher, 1989.) Reprinted by permission from the *Clinical Psychologist,* 1989, 42, 45–52.

eclectic approach—that is, they combine a number of different techniques in their treatment. Here is an overview of the psychotherapeutic approaches in use today.

Some practitioners use *psychodynamically based approaches* that loosely or closely follow Freud's basic ideas. Their aim is to help patients understand the motivations underlying their behavior. They assume that maladjustment and abnormal behavior occur when people do not understand themselves adequately. *Humanistic* therapists assume that people are essentially good—that they have an innate disposition to develop their potential and to seek beauty, truth, and goodness. Humanistic therapy is oriented toward helping people realize their full potential and find meaning in life. In contrast, *behavior therapy* is based on the assumption that most behaviors, whether normal or abnormal, are learned. Behavior therapists encourage their clients to learn new adaptive behaviors. Growing out of behavior therapy and the heavy influence of cognitive psychology is *cognitive therapy.* Cognitive therapy focuses on changing a client's thoughts and perceptions. See Figure 29.1 for a graphic representation of the primary orientations of clinical psychologists.

Which Therapy, Which Therapist?

Learning Objective 29.3
Identify some important features of effective therapy, discuss the placebo effect, and comment on research findings concerning the effectiveness of psychotherapy.

The appropriate type of therapy and its effectiveness vary with the type of disorder being treated and the goal of the client. For example, individual psychodynamic therapy has a good success rate for people with anxiety and adjustment disorders, but it is less successful for those with schizophrenic disorders. Long-term group therapy is more effective than short-term individual therapy for people with personality disorders. Behavior therapy is usually the most effective approach with children. Thus, Ricky Estevez could receive effective treatment from a variety of therapists. One therapist might focus on discovering the root causes of Ricky's maladjustment, while another therapist might concentrate on eliminating symptoms—depression, drinking, and poor work performance. Research on treatment methods is often conducted for specific disorders, such as for depression (Robinson, Berman, & Neimeyer, 1990).

In addition to differing therapeutic approaches, other therapist characteristics affect the treatment: the therapist's gender, personality, level of experience, and degree of empathy. Although there are differences among the various psychotherapies and therapists, there are also some commonalities. In all the therapies, clients usually expect a positive outcome, which helps them strive for change. In addition, they receive attention, which helps them maintain a positive attitude. Moreover, no matter what type of therapy is involved, certain characteristics must be present in both therapist and client for therapeutic change to occur. For example, good therapists communicate interest, understanding, respect, tact, maturity, and ability to help. They use suggestion, encouragement, interpretation, examples, and perhaps rewards to help clients change or rethink their situations. If a therapist is knowledgeable, accepting, and objective, he or she can facilitate behavior change, but the client is the one who makes the changes (Lafferty, Beutler, & Cargo, 1989). Therapists also must address special obstacles facing clients of racial and other minority groups (Sue, 1988), and in general, a therapist and client must form an alliance, a joint desire to work purposefully together (Luborsky, Barber, & Crits-Christoph, 1990). Table 29.1 presents some of the generally recognized and agreed-upon signs of good progress in therapy.

placebo effect: [pluh-SEE-bo] A nonspecific therapeutic change that occurs as a result of a person's expectations of change rather than as a direct result of any specific treatment.

Challenges to Psychotherapy

Is therapy really necessary? Some researchers note that many clients could achieve relief from their symptoms without psychotherapy. Others assert that psychotherapy is more art than science; still others feel that psychotherapy only provides transitory placebo effects.

Placebo Effects. A **placebo effect** is a change in behavior that occurs as a result of a person's *expectations* rather than as a result of a specific treatment. Physicians report that sometimes people experience relief from their symptoms when they are given sugar pills and told that the pills will help them. In much the same way, patients in psychotherapy may show relief from their symptoms simply because they have entered therapy and now expect change. For some people, just the attention of a therapist and the chance to express their feelings can be therapeutic. It is important to note that placebo effects in psychotherapy are likely to be transient. Any long-lasting therapeutic effects will generally come about from the client's and therapist's efforts (Horvath, 1988).

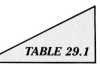

TABLE 29.1 Therapeutic Progress

Signs of good progress in therapy
▲ The client is providing personally revealing and significant material.
▲ The client is exploring the meaning of feelings and occurrences.
▲ The client is exploring material avoided earlier in therapy.
▲ The client is expressing significant insight into personal behavior.
▲ The client's method of communicating is active, alive, and energetic.
▲ There is a valued client–therapist working relationship.
▲ The client feels free to express strong feelings toward the therapist—either positive or negative.
▲ The client is appropriately expressing strong feelings outside of therapy.
▲ The client moves toward a different set of personality characteristics.
▲ The client is showing improved functioning outside of therapy.
▲ The client indicates a general state of well-being, good feelings, and positive attitudes.

Source: Mahrer & Nadler, 1986. Copyright 1986 by the American Psychological Association. Reprinted by permission.

psychoanalysis: [SIE-ko-uh-NAL-uh-siss] A lengthy insight therapy developed by Freud that aims at uncovering conflicts and unconscious impulses.

psychodynamically based therapies: [SIE-ko-die-NAM-ick-lee] Therapies based loosely on Freud's theory of psychoanalysis, using a part of the approach; some practitioners reject some elements of Freud's theory.

insight therapy: A therapy that attempts to discover relationships between unconscious motivations and current behavior; assumes that abnormal behavior results from failure to understand unconscious motivations and needs; given understanding of motivations, behavior should change.

Learning Objective 29.4
Distinguish between psychoanalysis and psychodynamic therapy, and state the major assumptions and goals of these types of therapy.

Psychotherapy Research. In 1952, an important paper by Eysenck challenged the effectiveness of psychotherapy, claiming that it produces no greater change in maladjusted individuals than do naturally occurring life experiences. Thousands of studies followed that attempted to investigate the effectiveness of therapy.

Research shows what clients and therapists have known for decades. Using sophisticated statistical techniques to analyze large amounts of data, Smith and Glass found psychotherapy effective (Smith, Glass, & Miller, 1980). Although many psychologists challenge the data, techniques, and conclusions of these analyses, most are still convinced that psychotherapy is effective (e.g., Matt, 1989). Many researchers contend that most psychotherapies are equally effective; that is, regardless of the approach a therapist uses, the results are often the same. New, more complete psychotherapy research strategies are under development, and as more studies are completed, there will be a clearer picture of how various approaches are best used to treat certain disorders with particular types of clients. Before surveying the therapies, identify some things that you think should happen as a result of treatment. What would you expect to gain, lose, or change during therapy? As you consider these questions, consider the processes of evaluating research, which is considered in the Understanding the Research Process box on the facing page.

Psychodynamic Therapy

Classical Freudian **psychoanalysis** focuses on helping the client uncover the unconscious motivations that lead to psychological conflict and maladaptive behavior; it is practiced by therapists who are specifically trained in its theory and practice. There are about 3000 practicing psychoanalysts in the United States, and many other psychologists use a therapy loosely connected to or rooted in Freudian theory. Psychologists refer to these as **psychodynamically based therapies**—that is, they use theory, approach, or techniques that derive from Freud.

Sigmund Freud believed that the exchange of words in psychoanalysis causes therapeutic change. Freud's therapy is an **insight therapy;** insight therapies share two basic assumptions. The first is that becoming aware of one's motivations helps a person change and become more adaptable; the second is that the causes of maladjustment are unresolved conflicts, which the patient was unaware of and therefore was unable to deal with. The goal of insight therapy is to treat the *causes* of abnormal behavior rather than the *behaviors* themselves. In general, insight therapists try to help people see life from a different perspective so that they can choose more adaptive life-styles. Because psychoanalysis is based on the development of a unique relationship between the therapist and the patient, compatibility is especially critical; the patient and therapist usually decide within the first few sessions whether they feel comfortable working with each other.

Goals of Psychoanalysis

Many individuals who seek psychotherapy are unhappy with their behavior but are unable to change. The general goal of psychoanalysis is to help patients understand the unconscious motivations that direct their behavior. Only when patients become aware of those motivations can they begin to choose behaviors that will let them lead more fulfilling lives. In psychoanalysis, patients are encouraged to express healthy impulses, strengthen day-to-day functioning based on reality, and perceive the world as a positive rather than a punishing place.

UNDERSTANDING THE RESEARCH PROCESS

Outcomes of Therapy

Throughout this text, we present research studies that describe experiments in which a treatment is given to one group, which is then compared with a control group. The same procedure is used in evaluating therapy outcomes. The general question is, "Is a certain type of therapy effective?" The specific question is usually more precise. For example, the researchers may ask, "Is systematic desensitization more effective than client-centered therapy in treating phobias?" Researchers evaluate the research by asking questions such as: "Are there enough subjects?" "Is there a control group?" "Have the studies been repeated?"

Usually, there are at least three groups of subjects. One group is treated with systematic desensitization; another is treated with client-centered therapy; and the third is placed on a waiting list to receive therapy. The aim is to let time pass and then compare the two experimental groups with the untreated or control group. The control group usually receives treatment after the other two groups have been treated (it would be unethical not to provide treatment for all the participants). Another element of research on the outcomes of therapy is that all clients are usually tracked after the termination of therapy. Six-month and 1-year follow-ups are common. By these means, a researcher can determine whether the effects of therapy are long-lasting.

Outcome studies are difficult. Clients have to be recruited. Therapists have to be trained in specific techniques. Clients have to be evaluated before treatment begins. Clients then must be treated, usually over a 10- to 16-week period. Posttreatment evaluations must be conducted, as well as follow-ups 6 months later. Only then can the results be evaluated. Sometimes, a therapy study concerns families, not single individuals. This complicates recruitment, scheduling, retention of subjects, and outcome measures—for example, who has changed, on what dimensions, and to what extent.

As you read about a specific therapy, you might ask, "Is it effective?" This is a reasonable question, often asked by professional psychologists. Three researchers at the University of Missouri asked the question about family therapy (Hazelrigg, Cooper, & Borduin, 1987). They searched the psychological literature of the previous 18 years to find every article that dealt with family therapy. In reviewing those articles, they found that family therapy had positive effects as measured by family interactions and behavior ratings. However, they also found that at the time of posttreatment follow-up, many of the advances exhibited by clients during their therapy had diminished somewhat. The researchers concluded that there is a need for more systematic research.

Family therapy is effective; in some situations, it is more effective than any other treatment procedure, including traditional individual therapy. It took research to show that this is true and to persuade skeptical practitioners to believe it. This is part of the joy of psychology: developing hypotheses about a topic of special interest, testing those hypotheses, publishing the results, reevaluating other psychologists' research, and making meaningful breakthroughs that help improve the human condition.

- ▲ ***What is the purpose of having multiple groups of subjects being tested in a therapy outcome study?***
- ▲ ***What are the implications of subjects dropping out from a research study? How does their loss affect results?***
- ▲ ***What are the implications of the phrase "in some situations" when describing the effectiveness of family therapy or any other therapy?***

To illustrate the psychoanalytical approach, suppose Ricky (our module opener example) seeks the help of a counselor who uses a psychodynamically based therapy. The psychologist might attempt to discover the source of Ricky's problems by asking him to describe how he relates to his parents. From this description, the psychologist learns that Ricky's father has long expected his son to take over the family business. He also learns that Ricky has sought his father's

Freud's study in London contained the couch which would later become the symbol of psychoanalysis.

approval all his life; in fact, that's why he is in the family business. However, Ricky is not sure he wants to be in sales and has always resented his father's insistence that he become a sales manager.

Through therapy, Ricky realizes he is torn between his desire to please his father and his dislike of sales. In fact, Ricky thinks he might prefer being a photographer. Ricky also discovers that he has been incapable of expressing anger toward his father; frustrated, he has lost interest in work and begun using alcohol to numb the pain of his diminishing self-esteem.

Learning Objective 29.5 Describe the techniques used in psychoanalysis and two common patient responses that occur during the process.

Techniques of Psychoanalysis

Psychoanalysis uses specific techniques designed to help the patient and therapist examine the conflicting demands of the patient's personality, such as those exhibited by Ricky Estevez. In general, psychoanalytic techniques are geared toward the exploration of early experiences, on the assumption that current behaviors result from unconscious motivations that may have their basis in early childhood experiences.

In traditional psychoanalysis, the patient lies on a couch, and the therapist sits in a chair out of the patient's view. Freud believed that this arrangement would allow the patient to be more relaxed and less threatened than he or she would be in viewing the therapist. However, many contemporary followers of Freud prefer to face patients rather than use the couch, feeling that this factor was overrated.

free association: A psychoanalytic technique in which a person reports to the therapist his or her thoughts and feelings as they occur, regardless of illogical order or content.

Two major techniques used in psychoanalysis are free association and dream analysis. In **free association,** the patient is asked to report whatever comes to mind, regardless of how trivial it might seem or how disagreeable it might feel. A therapist might say, "I can help you best if you say whatever thoughts and feelings come to your mind, even if they seem irrelevant, immaterial, foolish, embarrassing, upsetting, or even if they're about me, even very personally, just as they come, without censoring or editing" (Lewin, 1970, p. 67). The purpose of free association is to help patients learn to recognize connections and patterns among their thoughts and to allow the unconscious to express itself freely.

In **dream analysis,** patients are asked to describe their dreams in detail. Sometimes lifelike, sometimes chaotic, sometimes incoherent, dreams periodically replay a person's life history and at other times venture into a person's current problems. Freud believed that dreams represent some element of the unconscious seeking expression. Psychodynamically oriented therapists see much symbolism in dreams. They assert that the overt content of the dream hides the true meaning; many therapists use patients' dreams to understand their current problems. The goal of dream analysis is to disclose unconscious desires and motivations by discovering the meaning of the patient's dreams.

Both free association and dream analysis involve **interpretation** by therapists. In psychoanalysis, therapists try to make unconscious ideas, feelings, and impulses conscious by providing a context for them; they try to find common threads in a patient's behavior and thoughts. When patients use *defense mechanisms* (techniques to mask or avoid dealing with anxiety, examined in Chapter 10), this is often a sign of an area that may need to be explored. For example, if a patient becomes jittery every time he speaks about women, the therapist may speculate that the patient's nervousness results from early difficulties with women, perhaps with his mother. The therapist may then encourage the patient to explore his attitudes and feelings about women in general and about his mother in particular.

Two processes central to psychoanalysis are resistance and transference. **Resistance** is a patient's unwillingness to cooperate with the therapist, sometimes to the point of becoming belligerent. For example, disturbed by his counselor's unsettling interpretations, Ricky might become angry and start resisting treatment by missing appointments. Analysts usually interpret these behaviors as meaning that the patient wishes to avoid discussing a particular subject, or that an especially difficult stage in therapy has been reached. To minimize resistance, they try to accept the patient's behavior. When the therapist does not judge but merely listens, the patient is more likely to describe feelings thoroughly.

In **transference,** patients transfer feelings from earlier relationships to the therapist. For example, if Ricky's therapist is a man, Ricky may act hostile or competitive toward him, while another client may behave lovingly toward the same therapist. Psychoanalysts would say that in both cases, the patients are acting as if the therapist were their father. Because the therapist will respond differently from the way Ricky's father might have, Ricky can experience the conflict differently, leading to a better understanding of the issue. By permitting transference, the therapist gives patients a new opportunity to understand their feelings and can guide them in the exploration of repressed or difficult material. The examination of thoughts or feelings that were previously considered unacceptable (and therefore were often repressed) helps patients understand and identify the underlying conflicts that direct their behavior.

Therapy, with its slowly gained insights into the unconscious, is gradual and continual. Through their gradual insights, often frequently repeated, patients learn new ways of coping with instinctual urges and develop more mature ways of dealing with anxiety and guilt. The entire process of interpretation, resistance to interpretation, and transference is sometimes referred to as **working through.**

dream analysis: A psychoanalytic technique in which a patient's dreams are interpreted; used to gain insight into the individual's unconscious motivations.

interpretation: In Freud's theory, the technique of providing a context, meaning, or cause of a specific idea, feeling, or set of behaviors; the process of tying a set of behaviors to an unconscious determinant.

resistance: In psychoanalysis, an unwillingness to cooperate: a patient signals this by withholding information or otherwise not helping the therapist to understand or interpret a situation.

transference: A psychoanalytic procedure in which a therapist becomes the object of a patient's emotional attitudes about an important person in his or her life, such as a parent.

working through: The gradual, often repetitive, slow process in therapy of interpretation, resistance to interpretation, and transference.

Ego Analysts

Learning Objective 29.6
Explain how ego analysis differs from psychoanalysis, and discuss some of the criticisms made about Freudian-based therapies.

Freud's theory has not been universally accepted; even his followers have disagreed with him. One group of psychoanalysts, referred to as **ego analysts,** or ego psychologists, have modified some of Freud's basic ideas about psychoanalysis. Like Freud, they assume that psychoanalysis is the appropriate method for treating patients with emotional problems. Unlike Freud, however, they assume that people have voluntary control over when, whether, and in what way their biological urges will be expressed.

A major disagreement has to do with the role of the id and the ego. Whereas traditional psychoanalysts begin by focusing on unconscious material in the id and only later try to increase the patient's ego control, ego analysis aims at helping clients develop stronger control of their egos. (Recall from Chapter 10 that the *ego* is the part of the personality that operates on the reality principle and tries to control impulsive behavior by responding realistically to the demands of the environment.) From an ego analyst's point of view, a weak ego may cause maladjustment, due to failure to understand and control the id. Thus, by learning to master and develop their egos—including moral reasoning and judgment—people gain greater control over their lives.

Criticisms of Psychoanalysis

Some critics of psychoanalysis contend that the approach is unscientific, imprecise, and subjective; they assert that its concepts, such as id, ego, and superego, are not linked to real things or day-to-day behavior. Other critics object to Freud's biologically oriented approach, which suggests that human beings are bundles of energy caught in conflict and driven toward some hedonistic goal. These critics want to know where is the free will in human behavior. Also, some elements of Freud's theory are sexist and untestable. Freud's critics are often harsh and unforgiving (e.g., Masson, 1990).

The effectiveness of psychoanalysis is also open to question. Research shows that psychoanalysis is selectively effective: It is more effective, for example, for people with anxiety disorders than for those diagnosed as schizophrenic. Also, younger patients improve more than older ones. In general, studies show that psychoanalysis can be as effective as other therapies, but it is no more so (Garfield & Bergin, 1986).

ego analysts: Psychoanalytic practitioners who assume that the ego has greater control over behavior than Freud suggested; they are more concerned with reality testing and control over the environment than with unconscious motivations and processes.

One major drawback of psychoanalysis is that it is not suitable for all patients. The problems addressed in psychoanalysis are difficult, and a patient must be highly motivated and articulate to grasp the complicated and subtle relationships explored. Also, because traditional psychoanalysis involves meeting individually with the therapist for 1 hour, five days a week, for approximately 5 years, a typical psychoanalysis might cost $100,000. Many people who seek therapy do not want or cannot afford the money or time for this type of therapy.

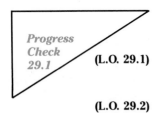

Progress Check 29.1

Complete the following sentences with one of the options provided.

(L.O. 29.1) a. Therapy designed to treat mental health disorders that involves biologically based methods such as prescribing drugs or changing a person's diet is sometimes termed ______. (psychotherapy / somatic therapy)

(L.O. 29.2) b. A psychotherapist who combines a number of techniques from various types of psychotherapy uses ______ approach. (an eclectic / a humanistic)

(L.O. 29.3) c. In effective psychotherapy, the one who makes the changes in a client's behavior is the ________. (therapist / client)

(L.O. 29.3) d. Usually, the most effective type of psychotherapy for children is ________ therapy. (psychodynamic / behavior)

(L.O. 29.3) e. A placebo effect refers to changes in behavior that occur because of the client's ________, rather than as a result of a specific treatment. (courage and efforts to understand / expectations)

(L.O. 29.4) f. Psychoanalysis and psychodynamic therapies are sometimes termed ________ therapies because they focus on helping the patient become aware of unconscious motivations and conflicts. (insight / consciousness-raising)

(L.O. 29.5) g. One goal of free association is to help the patient ________. (relax / make connections among thoughts / make friends)

(L.O. 29.5) h. Freud believed that dreams represent some element of the ________. (unconscious seeking expression / libido flooding over)

(L.O. 29.5) i. Psychoanalytic and psychodynamic therapists use ________ to find a common thread among a patient's thoughts and behaviors. (interpretation / guided imagery / empathetic understanding)

(L.O. 29.5) j. Resistance can be minimized if the therapist ________ the patient's unwillingness to cooperate. (confronts / ignores / accepts)

(L.O. 29.6) k. Ego analysts differ from traditional psychoanalysts in that they focus on ________. (the pleasure principle / reality testing and control)

(L.O. 29.6) l. One drawback of psychoanalysis is that it is ________. (ineffective 50% of the time / time-consuming and expensive)

Humanistic Therapy

Humanistic therapies, unlike psychoanalytic therapies, emphasize the uniqueness of the human experience and the idea that human beings have free will to determine their destinies. Humanistic psychologists assert that human beings are conscious, creative, and born with an innate desire to fulfill themselves. To some extent, humanistic approaches are an outgrowth of psychodynamically based insight therapies: They help people understand the causes of their behavior. Client-centered therapy and Gestalt therapy are two types of humanistic therapies.

Learning Objective 29.7
Describe the assumptions, goals, techniques, and common criticisms of client-centered therapy.

Client-Centered Therapy

Client-centered therapy, also termed *person-centered therapy,* was developed by Carl Rogers (1902–1987). Rogers was a quiet, caring man who turned the psychoanalytic world upside down when he introduced his approach. He focused on the person, he listened intently to his clients, and he encouraged them to define their own "cures." Rogers saw people as basically good, competent, social beings who move forward and grow. Throughout life, they move toward their ideal selves, maturing into fulfilled individuals through the process of self-actualization.

Rogerian therapists hold that problem behaviors occur when the environment prevents a person from developing his or her innate potential. If children are given love and reinforcement only for their achievements, for example, as adults they may see themselves and others only in terms of achievement. Rogerian treatment involves helping people to evaluate the world from their own perspective and develop improved self-regard. For example, a Rogerian therapist might treat Ricky by encouraging him to explore his goals, desires, and expectations, and then asking whether he can achieve these through sales, photography, or some other option. Ricky may come to realize that he can be a good son even if he

client-centered therapy: An insight therapy that seeks to help people evaluate the world and themselves from their own perspective by providing a nondirective environment and unconditional positive regard for the client.

TABLE 29.2 Carl Rogers's assumptions about human beings

Carl Rogers made assumptions about human beings which shaped his therapeutic approach.
▲ People are innately good and are effective in dealing with their environments. ▲ Behavior is purposeful and goal-directed. ▲ Healthy people are aware of all their behavior; they choose their behavior patterns. ▲ A client's behavior can be understood only from his or her own point of view. Even if a client has misconstrued the events in the world, the therapist must understand how the client sees those events. ▲ Effective therapy occurs only when a client modifies his or her own behavior, not when the therapist manipulates it.

doesn't become a sales manager. Table 29.2 presents the basic assumptions underlying Rogers's approach to treatment.

Techniques of Client-Centered Therapy. Because its goal is to help clients discover and actualize their as-yet-undiscovered selves, client-centered therapy is nondirective. In **nondirective therapy,** the therapist does not dominate the client, but instead encourages the client's search for growth. The use of the word *client* rather than *patient* is a key aspect of Rogers's approach to therapy. In psychoanalysis, therapists *direct* the patient's cure and help them to understand their behavior; in Rogerian therapy, therapists *guide* clients and help them to realize what the client feels is right for them. The client directs the conversation, and the therapist helps the client organize thoughts and ideas simply by asking the right questions, responding with words such as "Oh," and reflecting back the client's feelings. Even a small movement, such as a nod or gesture, can help the client stay on the right track. The client learns to evaluate the world from his or her own vantage point, with little interpretation by the therapist.

A basic tenet of client-centered therapy is that the therapist must be a warm, accepting person who projects positive feelings toward the client. To counteract clients' negative experiences with people who were unaccepting, and who thus taught them that they are bad or unlikable, client-centered therapists accept clients as they are, with good and bad points; they respect them for their worth as individuals and show them positive regard and respect. *Empathic understanding,* whereby therapists communicate acceptance and recognition of clients' emotions and encourage them to discuss whatever feelings they have, is an important part of the therapeutic relationship.

Client-centered therapy can be viewed as a consciousness-raising process that helps people expand their awareness. Initially, clients tend to express attitudes and ideas they have adopted from other people. Thus, Ricky might say, "I should get top sales figures," implying "because my father counts on my success." As therapy progresses and Ricky experiences the empathic understanding of the therapist, he will begin to use his own ideas when evaluating himself (Rogers, 1951). As a result, he will talk about himself in more positive ways and try to please himself rather than others. He may say, "I should make top sales figures only if they mean something to me," reflecting a more positive, more accepting attitude about himself. As Ricky feels better about himself, he will eventually suggest to the therapist that he knows how to deal with the world and may be ready to leave therapy.

nondirective therapy: A form of therapy in which the client determines the direction of therapy while the therapist remains permissive (almost passive) and accepts totally the client's feelings and behavior.

Criticisms of Client-Centered Therapy. Client-centered therapy is widely acclaimed for its focus on the therapeutic relationship. No other therapy seems to make clients feel so warm, accepted, and safe. These are important characteristics of any therapy, but critics argue that they may not be enough to bring about long-lasting change. Critics of client-centered therapy assert that lengthy discussions about past problems do not necessarily help people with their present difficulties, and that an environment of unconditional positive regard may not be enough to bring about behavior change. They feel that Rogerian therapy may be making therapeutic promises that cannot be fulfilled and that it focuses on concepts that are hard to define, such as self-actualization.

Gestalt therapy: [Gesh-TALT] An insight therapy that emphasizes the importance of a person's being aware of current feelings and situation.

Gestalt Therapy

Learning Objective 29.8 Describe the assumptions, goals, and common criticisms of Gestalt therapy.

With the aim of creating an awareness of a person's whole self, **Gestalt therapy** differs significantly from psychoanalysis. It assumes that human beings are responsible for themselves and their lives and that they need to focus not on the past, but on the present. As such, Gestalt therapy is concerned with current feelings and behaviors and their representation in a meaningful coherent whole.

Frederick S. ("Fritz") Perls (1893–1970), a physician and psychoanalyst trained in Europe, was the founder and principal proponent of Gestalt therapy. He was a dynamic, charismatic therapist, and many psychologists followed him and his ideas closely. Perls assumed that the best way to help clients come to terms with anxiety and other unpleasant feelings was to focus on their current understanding and awareness of the world, not on past situations and experiences.

The goals of Gestalt therapy are to help people resolve old conflicts and enable them to resolve future conflicts. It aims at expanding clients' awareness of their current attitudes and feelings so they can respond more fully and appropriately to current situations. Gestalt therapy does not attempt to cure people; rather, it helps them become complete and enables them to continue to adapt in the future. Gestalt psychologists help people deal with feelings of what Perls termed *incomplete Gestalts*—that is, unfinished business or unresolved conflicts, such as previously unrecognized feelings of anger toward a spouse or envy of a brother or sister.

From Perls's point of view, the client needs to expand his or her conscious awareness by reconnecting fragments of past and current experience. He argued

Frederick Perls's Gestalt therapy concentrates on present experiences and feelings.

that people develop false lives and are not in touch with their real selves. Only when people become aware of the here and now can they become sensitive to the tensions and repressions that made their previous behavior maladaptive. Also, once they become aware of their current feelings and accept themselves, clients can understand early behaviors and plan appropriate future behaviors. From a Gestalt viewpoint, healthy people are in touch with their feelings and reality. Thus, a major goal of therapy is to get people in touch with their feelings so that they can construct an accurate picture of their psychological world.

Guided by a Gestalt-oriented therapist, Ricky may explore his current relationship with his parents. He may realize that his anger, drinking, and poor sales reflect low self-esteem and hostile feelings toward his father. After constructing an accurate picture of his psychological world, Ricky can adopt new behaviors that will help him explore other careers while continuing his sales work.

Gestalt therapy encourages clients to be in touch with their feelings through a variety of techniques. This approach is seen as both a strength and a weakness. Some critics feel that Perls was too focused on individuals' happiness and growth, that he encouraged the attainment of these goals at the expense of other goals. Gestalt therapy is also criticized for focusing too much on feelings and not enough on thought and decision making. Some psychologists think that Gestalt therapy might work best for healthy people who want to grow, and that it might not be as successful with severely maladjusted people who cannot make it through the day.

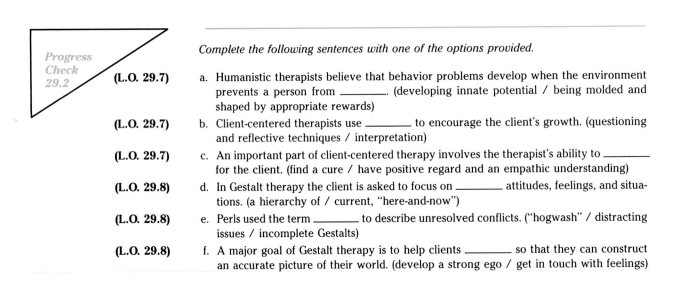

Progress Check 29.2

Complete the following sentences with one of the options provided.

(L.O. 29.7) a. Humanistic therapists believe that behavior problems develop when the environment prevents a person from ________. (developing innate potential / being molded and shaped by appropriate rewards)

(L.O. 29.7) b. Client-centered therapists use ________ to encourage the client's growth. (questioning and reflective techniques / interpretation)

(L.O. 29.7) c. An important part of client-centered therapy involves the therapist's ability to ________ for the client. (find a cure / have positive regard and an empathic understanding)

(L.O. 29.8) d. In Gestalt therapy the client is asked to focus on ________ attitudes, feelings, and situations. (a hierarchy of / current, "here-and-now")

(L.O. 29.8) e. Perls used the term ________ to describe unresolved conflicts. ("hogwash" / distracting issues / incomplete Gestalts)

(L.O. 29.8) f. A major goal of Gestalt therapy is to help clients ________ so that they can construct an accurate picture of their world. (develop a strong ego / get in touch with feelings)

Module Summary

Therapy Comes in Many Forms

- *Psychotherapy* is the treatment of emotional or behavioral problems through psychological techniques. The goal of psychotherapy is to help people cope better and to achieve more emotionally satisfying life-styles, often by helping them relieve stress, improve interpersonal communication, and modify faulty ideas about the world (p. 557).

Psychodynamic Therapy

- *Insight therapists,* such as those who are psychodynamically based, assume that maladjustment or abnormal behavior is caused by failure to understand one's own motivations and needs. *Behavior therapists* apply learning principles to produce specific changes in behavior. Growing out of behavior therapy and the heavy influence of cognitive psychology is cognitive therapy (p. 560).
- According to Freudian theory, conflicts among a person's unconscious thoughts and processes produce maladjusted behavior; the general goal of psychoanalysis is to help patients understand the unconscious motivations that direct their behaviors (p. 560).
- Ego analysis is a psychoanalytic approach to therapy that assumes that the ego should have greater control over behavior than Freud suggested. This approach is more concerned with reality testing and control over the environment than with unconscious motivations and processes (p. 564).

Humanistic Therapy

- Client-centered therapy, a humanistic approach developed by Carl Rogers, aims at helping clients to realize their potential by learning to evaluate the world and themselves from their own point of view. It is nondirective; the therapist allows the client to determine the direction of therapy (p. 565).
- Gestalt therapy, also an insight-oriented, humanistic therapy, which was developed by Fritz Perls, encourages individuals to get in touch with their current feelings and to become aware of their current situations. Gestalt techniques are designed to help clients become more alert to significant sensations in themselves and their surroundings (p. 567).

KEY TERMS

client-centered therapy, p. 565
dream analysis, p. 563
ego analysts, p. 564
free association, p. 562
Gestalt therapy, p. 567
insight therapy, p. 560
interpretation, p. 563
nondirective therapy, p. 566
placebo effect, p. 559
psychoanalysis, p. 560
psychodynamically based therapies, p. 560
psychotherapy, p. 557
resistance, p. 563
transference, p. 563
working through, p. 563

SELF-TEST

Module 29

- Before taking the self-test, **recite** and **review.**
- Use the key at the back of the text to *correct* your answers.
- *Restudy* pages that correspond to any questions you answered incorrectly.

1. Psychotherapy involves
   a. the manipulation of diet and exercise to promote mental health.
   b. methods such as lobotomies, electroconvulsive shock, and prescribing drugs.
   c. using psychological techniques to treat emotional and behavioral problems.
   d. all of the above.
2 Psychologists apply psychotherapeutic techniques when they are working with
   a. individuals.
   b. families and other small groups of people.
   c. whole communities of people.
   d. all of the above.
3. Which statement describes a component found in effective psychotherapy?
   a. change is facilitated through suggestion, encouragement, and reward.
   b. the therapist and client form an alliance.
   c. the therapist is sensitive to obstacles that are special to particular minority groups.
   d. all of the above
4. Most research investigating the effectiveness of psychotherapy indicates that
   a. natural maturation through life stages is just as effective as psychotherapy.
   b. psychotherapy is effective, but clarification is needed to determine which approach is most effective for particular disorders.
   c. psychotherapy is too complex to be studied scientifically.
   d. psychotherapy needs to advance to more sophisticated levels before it can be considered effective.
5. Therapeutic techniques that are similar to psychoanalysis because they are loosely rooted in Freudian theory are called ________ therapies.
   a. psychiatric
   b. psychodynamic
   c. eclectic
   d. transformational
6. Lynn's therapist is understanding and very attentive, and yet Lynn responds to him as if he will not hear, care about, or accept what she has to say. Eventually, Lynn realizes that as a child her parents subtly, but powerfully, transmitted the message, "children should be seen and not heard." This insight lets Lynn realize that people will hear her if she gives them a chance to do so. Lynn's early behavior toward the therapist illustrates
   a. free association.
   b. resistance.
   c. transference.
   d. reaction formation.
7. Ego analysts help their patients
   a. develop stronger control over their egos.
   b. maximize pleasure by gaining control of the id.
   c. avoid emotional pain by strengthening the superego.
   d. discover the relationship between the id, ego, and superego.

8. Psychoanalytic and psychodynamic therapies seem to be most effective when used with
   a. schizophrenics.
   b. older people who have never been in therapy before.
   c. younger people with anxiety disorders.
   d. all of the above
9. A goal in client-centered therapy is to help the client learn to
   a. express attitudes that will make an impression on others.
   b. conform to society by behaving in ways that are considered acceptable.
   c. evaluate the world from his or her own vantage point.
   d. live with internal conflicts that cannot be resolved.
10. Some psychologists believe that Gestalt therapy is most effective for people who
    a. experience psychological pain on a daily basis.
    b. need to become more analytical and decisive about problems in their lives.
    c. want to learn to put the happiness and welfare of others before their own.
    d. are psychologically healthy and want to grow.
11. Client-centered and Gestalt therapy are two forms of
    a. ego analysis.
    b. humanistic therapy.
    c. behavior therapy.
    d. brief therapy.

Module 30

Behavioral and Cognitive Approaches

LEARNING OBJECTIVES

When you have mastered the material in this module, you will be able to

Behavior Therapy (pp. 574–578)

30.1 Describe the assumptions, goals, and basic techniques of behavior therapy; also, comment on the debate concerning symptom substitution (p. 574).

30.2 Explain how the principles of operant conditioning are used in behavior therapy (p. 575).

30.3 Describe two techniques based on classical conditioning that involve counterconditioning (p. 577).

30.4 Explain how observational learning is used in behavior therapy (p. 578).

Cognitive Therapy (pp. 578–582)

30.5 State the major goal and three basic propositions of cognitive therapy (p. 578).

30.6 Describe the approaches used by Ellis, Beck, and Meichenbaum (p. 579).

Group Therapy (582–584)

30.7 Explain why group therapy and self-help groups are popular (p. 582).

30.8 Describe the goals and techniques of traditional group therapy (p. 582).

30.9 Describe the assumptions, goals, and techniques used by psychologists and social workers involved in family therapy (p. 584).

Community Psychology (pp. 584–587)

30.10 Describe the general aims, key elements, and special focus of community psychology (p. 584).

30.11 Describe the importance of neighborhood clinics, crisis intervention centers, and sensitivity to human diversity (p. 586).

Biologically Based Therapies (pp. 587–589)

30.12 Describe biologically based therapies and explain why they are sometimes used along with talking therapies (p. 587).

30.13 Discuss the past and present use of psychosurgery and electroconvulsive shock (p. 587).

30.14 Identify four types of psychotropic drugs and state the types of disorders for which they are prescribed (p. 588).

SQ3R
- **Survey** to set goals for studying.
- Ask **questions** as you **read.**
- Stop occasionally to **recite** and **review.**

plus
- **Write** a summary of key points.
- **Reflect** on the hypotheses, evidence, and implications of this material and on the relevance it has to *your* life.

At 57 years of age, Tom Gredler was proud to say he was a self-made man. He was also proud to say that pulling oneself up by one's own bootstraps was the way to solve personal problems. However, Tom Gredler's bootstraps had worn thin, his usual coping mechanisms were failing, and he was facing a crisis. Tom had been retired for six years; he had planned to make the most of his retirement, but he found that his free time was driving him into bouts of depression. The plant at which he had made paper products had been his life. He had worked so hard for so many years that he had never developed any hobbies or outside activities. Now, 6 years into his retirement, he was having anxiety attacks followed by periods of intense sadness.

Tom Gredler had never heard of an anxiety attack, but the panic he felt—his fast heartbeat, increased blood pressure, and the lump in his throat—were classic symptoms of an acute anxiety attack. Tom was not unusual: many retirees experience feelings of stress during a period in their life when they are supposed to be reaping the benefits of years of hard work. For some people, however, retirement can be a time of crisis, of distress, of looking back and realizing mistakes as well as successes. During retirement, many individuals ask themselves whether their current situation is or their past life has been meaningful. Periodic questioning and self-doubt are normal. Many people use such periods to identify what is important to them and to get organized before going on to meet other challenges.

Sometimes, people have problems, such as fear of heights, anxiety about public speaking, marital conflicts, or sexual dysfunction, that may not warrant an indepth discussion of early childhood experiences, an exploration of unconscious motivations, a lengthy discussion about current feelings, or a resolution of inner conflicts. In these cases, behavior therapy may be more appropriate than psychodynamically based or humanistic therapy.

Behavior Therapy

Learning Objective 30.1 Describe the assumptions, goals, and basic techniques of behavior therapy; also, comment on the debate concerning *symptom substitution.*

Behavior therapy, sometimes termed *behavior modification,* uses learning principles to help people replace maladaptive behaviors with new ones. Behavior therapists assume that people's behavior is influenced by changes in their environments, in the way they respond to that environment, and in the way they interact with other people. Unlike psychodynamic therapy, behavior therapy does not aim to discover the origins of a behavior, only to alter it. For a person with a nervous twitch, for example, the goal would be to eliminate the twitch. Thus, behavior therapists treat people by having them first unlearn old, faulty behaviors and then learn new, more effective ones.

Goals of Behavior Therapy

Behavior therapists do not always focus on the problems that caused the client to seek therapy. If they see that the client's problem is caused by some other situation, they may focus on changing that situation. A client may, for example, seek therapy because of a faltering marriage. However, the therapist may discover that the marriage is suffering because of the client's excessive arguments with his spouse, each of which is followed by a period of heavy drinking. The therapist may then discover that both the arguments and the drinking are brought on by extreme frustration at work, aggravated by his client's excessive expectations regarding his performance (Goldfried & Davison, 1976). In this situation, the therapist might focus on helping the client to develop standards consistent with his capabilities, past performance, and realistic future performance, which will ease the original cause of the problem—the tension felt at work.

Unlike psychodynamic or humanistic therapy, behavior therapy does not encourage clients to interpret past events to find their meaning. Although a behavior therapist may uncover a chain of events leading to a specific behavior, that discovery will not generally prompt a close examination of the client's early experiences.

When people enter behavior therapy, many aspects of their behavior may change, not just those specifically being treated. Thus, a person who is being treated for extreme shyness might find not only that the shyness decreases, but also that he can engage more easily in discussions about emotional topics and perform better on the job. Behaviorists argue that once a person's behavior has changed, it may be easier to manage attitudes, fears, and intrapsychic conflicts. What are some other aspects of people's lives that might change when they enter behavior therapy?

Most insight therapists, especially those who are psychodynamically based, assume that if only *overt* behavior is treated, as is often done in behavior therapy, symptom substitution may occur. **Symptom substitution** is the appearance of one behavior to replace another that has been eliminated by treatment. Thus, insight therapists argue that if a therapist eliminates a nervous twitch without examining its underlying causes, the client will express the disorder by developing some other symptom, such as a speech impediment. Behavior therapists, on the other hand, contend that symptom substitution does not occur if treatment involves proper use of behavioral principles. Research shows that behavior therapy is at least as effective as insight therapy and in some cases is more effective (e.g., Snyder & Wills, 1989; Snyder, Wills, & Grady-Fletcher, 1991).

behavior therapy: A therapy based on the application of learning principles to human behavior. Synonymous with *behavior modification,* it focuses on changing overt behaviors rather than on understanding subjective feelings, unconscious processes, or motivations.

symptom substitution: The appearance of one symptom to replace another that has been eliminated.

Techniques of Behavior Therapy

Behavior therapy uses an array of techniques to help people change their behavior, among them: operant conditioning, counterconditioning, and modeling, often in combination. In addition to using several behavioral techniques, the therapist may use some insight techniques. A good psychotherapist will use whatever combination of techniques will help a client most efficiently and effectively. The more complicated the disorder being treated, the more likely it is that a practitioner will use a mix of therapeutic approaches—a *multimodal approach,* an approach often taken by an eclectic psychologist (e.g., Blanchard et al., 1990).

Behavior therapy usually involves three general procedures: (1) identifying the problem behavior and its frequency; (2) treating the client, perhaps by reeducation, communication training, or some type of counterconditioning; and (3) assessing whether there is a lasting behavior change. If the client exhibits the new behavior for several weeks or months, the therapist concludes that treatment was effective. We now discuss the major behavior therapy techniques—operant conditioning, counterconditioning, and modeling—in more detail.

token economy: An operant conditioning procedure in which tokens are given to the patient to reinforce socially acceptable behavior. The tokens are later exchanged for desirable items or privileges.

Operant Conditioning

Learning Objective 30.2 Explain how the principles of operant conditioning are used in behavior therapy.

Operant conditioning procedures are used with different people in different settings to achieve a wide range of desirable behaviors, including increased reading speed, improved classroom behaviors, and the maintenance of personal hygiene. As explained in Chapter 5, operant conditioning to establish new behaviors depends on a reinforcer, defined as any event that increases the probability that a particular response will recur.

One of the most effective uses of operant conditioning is with children who are antisocial, slow learners, or in some way maladjusted. Operant conditioning is also effective with patients in mental hospitals. Ayllon and Haughton (1964), for example, instructed staff members to reinforce hospitalized patients for psychotic verbalizations during one period and for neutral verbalizations during another. As expected, the frequency of psychotic verbalizations increased when they were reinforced and decreased when they were not reinforced (see Figure 30.1).

Token Economies. Token economies are one way of rewarding adaptive behavior. In a **token economy,** participants receive tokens when they engage in appropriate behavior. Patients can exchange the tokens for desired items or activi-

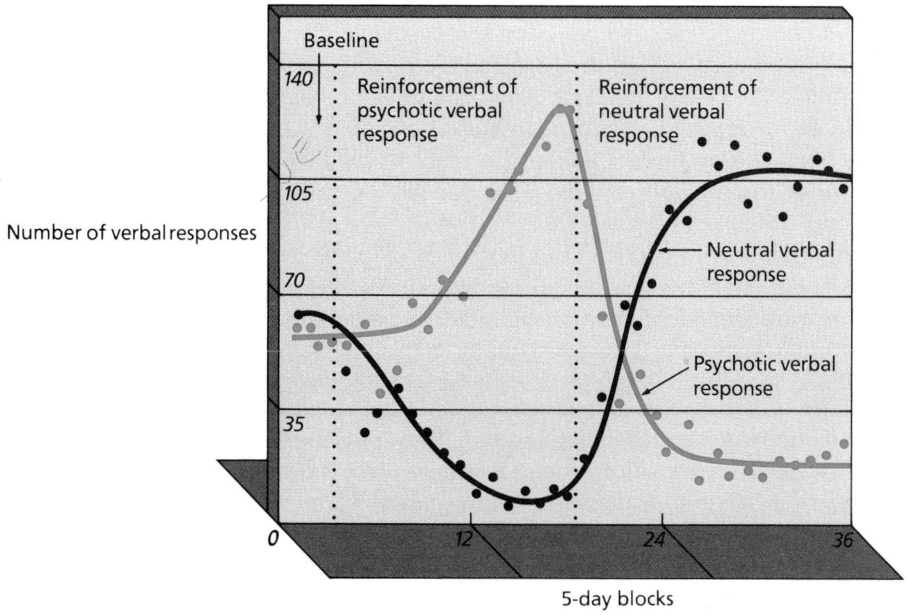

Figure 30.1

A study by Allyon and Haughton (1964) found that reinforcement affected the frequency of psychotic and neutral verbal behavior in hospitalized patients. (Reprinted with permission from T. Allyon and E. Haughton, Modification of symptomatic verbal behavior of mental patients, *Behavior Research and Therapy* 2, pp. 87–97, Copyright 1964, Pergamon Press plc.)

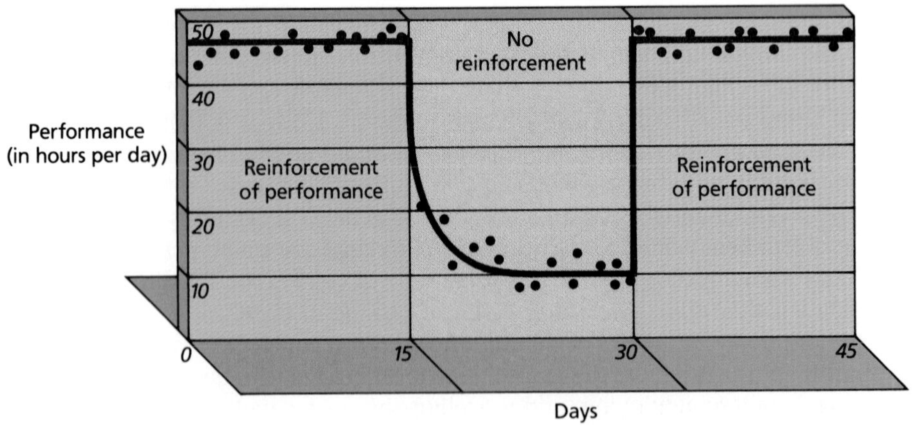

Figure 30.2

Allyon and Azrin (1965) found that tokens increased the number of hours worked by patients. (From T. Allyon and N. H. Azrin, The measurement and reinforcement behavior of psychotics. *Journal of the Experimental Analysis of Behavior,* 8 (1965): 357–383. Copyright 1965 by the Society for the Experimental Analysis of Behavior, Inc.)

ties, such as candy, new clothes, games, or time with important people in their lives. The more tokens people earn, the more items or privileges they can obtain.

Token economies are used to modify behavior in social settings, usually with groups of people. They aim to strengthen behaviors that are compatible with social norms. For example, a patient in a mental hospital might receive tokens for cleaning tables, helping in the hospital laundry, and maintaining certain standards of personal hygiene and appearance. The number of tokens earned is determined by the level of difficulty of the behavior or job and how long the person performs it. Thus, patients might receive 3 tokens for brushing their teeth but 40 tokens for engaging in prosocial helping behaviors. Allyon and Azrin (1965) monitored the performance of a group of patients for 45 days. They found that when tokens (reinforcement) were contingent on performance, the patients produced about four times as much work per day as when tokens were not delivered. (See Figure 30.2.) Such techniques become especially effective when combined with other behavioral techniques (Miller, Cosgrive, & Doke, 1990), such as extinction and time-out procedures, discussed next.

Extinction and Punishment. As explained in Chapter 5, extinction and punishment are conditioning techniques that can decrease the frequency of an undesired behavior. If reinforcers are withheld, extinction of a behavior will occur. Suppose a six-year-old refuses to go to bed at the designated time. When she is taken to her bedroom, she cries and screams violently. A therapist might suggest the following approach. If the parents give in and allow her to stay up, they are reinforcing the crying behavior: The child cries, the parents give in. One way to eliminate the crying behavior is to stop reinforcing it by insisting that the child go to bed and stay there. Chances are that the child will cry loudly and violently for two or three nights, but the behavior will eventually be extinguished (C. D. Williams, 1959).

Another way to decrease the frequency of undesired behavior is to punish it. Punishment often involves the presentation of an aversive stimulus. In the laboratory, researchers might provide slight electric shocks to get adult subjects to stop performing a specific behavior. Usually, punishment for undesired behaviors is combined with positive reinforcement for prosocial and desired behaviors.

time-out: A punishment procedure in which a person is removed from a desired or reinforcing situation to decrease the likelihood that an undesired behavior will recur.

Time-Out. As mentioned in Chapter 5, **time-out,** the physical removal of a person from sources of reinforcement, is widely used. It decreases the occurrence of undesired behaviors. Suppose a child regularly throws a temper tantrum each time she wants a piece of candy, an ice-cream cone, or her little brother's toys, and out of frustration and embarrassment her parents often give in. In the time-out procedure, whenever the child misbehaved, she would be placed in a room without toys, television, or other people, or otherwise away from the rest of her family. She would be kept in the restricted area (such as a chair or the time-out room) for a short period, such as 5 or 10 minutes; if she left, more time would be added. (Generally speaking, as a guideline many practitioners assert that the maximum time for a time-out should be 1 minute for each year of the child's age until the child is 5 years old, and then 2 minutes per year thereafter.) Not only is the child not getting what she wants, but she is also removed from any potential source of reinforcement. Time-out is especially effective when combined with positive reinforcers for appropriate behavior and administered by a child-care specialist (Crespi, 1988).

Counterconditioning

Learning Objective 30.3 Describe two techniques based on classical conditioning that involve counterconditioning.

A second major approach to behavior therapy, **counterconditioning** or reconditioning, teaches people new, more adaptive responses to familiar situations. For example, anxiety is one of the first responses people show when they are maladjusted, fearful, or lacking in self-esteem, so if a therapist can inhibit anxiety by conditioning a person to respond with something other than fear—that is, by *counter*conditioning the person—a real breakthrough in therapy will be achieved.

Joseph Wolpe (1915–) was one of the initial proponents of counterconditioning. His work in classical conditioning, especially situations in which animals show conditioned anxiety responses, led him to attempt to inhibit or decrease anxiety as a response in human beings. His therapeutic goal was to replace anxiety with some other response, such as relaxation, amusement, or pleasure.

Wolpe's work has had a profound impact on behavior therapists. Behavior therapy using counterconditioning begins with a specific stimulus (S_1) that elicits a specific response (R_1). After the person undergoes counterconditioning, the same stimulus (S_1) should elicit a new response (R_2) (Wolpe, 1958). There are two basic approaches to counterconditioning: systematic desensitization and aversive counterconditioning.

counterconditioning: A process of reconditioning in which a person learns a new response to a familiar stimulus.

systematic desensitization: A counterconditioning procedure in which a person first learns deep relaxation and then imagines a series of progressively more vivid approximations of fearful situations, learning to feel relaxation rather than fear as a new response to a formerly fearful stimulus.

aversive counterconditioning: A counterconditioning technique that pairs an aversive or noxious stimulus with a stimulus that elicits undesirable behavior so that the subject will adopt new behaviors in response to the original stimulus.

Systematic Desensitization. **Systematic desensitization** is a three-stage process in which people are taught to relax when presented with stimuli that formerly elicited anxiety. First the subject learns how to relax; then the subject describes the specific situations that arouse anxiety; and finally the subject, while deeply relaxed, imagines increasingly vivid scenes of the situations that elicit anxiety. In this way the subject is gradually, step by step, exposed to the source of anxiety, usually by imagining a series of progressively more fearful or anxiety-provoking situations. Eventually, this imaginal desensitization is transferred to approaching the actual situation.

Flying in an airplane, for example, is a stimulus situation (S_1) that can bring about an inappropriate fear response (R_1). With systematic desensitization therapy, the idea of flying (S_1) can eventually elicit a response of curiosity or even relaxation (R_2). The therapist might first ask the client to imagine sitting in an airplane on the ground, then to imagine the airplane taxiing, and eventually to imagine flying through the billowing clouds. As the client realizes that imagining the scene will not result in harm or isolation, he or she becomes able to tolerate more stressful imagery and may eventually perform the imagined behavior, in this case, *flying* in an airplane. Systematic desensitization is most successful for people with impulse-control problems, anger control, or who exhibit forms of anxiety, such as phobias.

Aversive Counterconditioning. The second major type of counterconditioning is **aversive counterconditioning,** which is used with a pleasant or neutral stimulus that elicits undesirable behavior. That is, before therapy, a client doesn't avoid a stimulus that prompts inappropriate behavior. Treatment involves pairing this stimulus with a noxious or aversive stimulus. As with systematic desensitization, the objective is to teach a new response to the original stimulus. A behavior therapist, for example, might use aversive counterconditioning to teach someone like Tom Gredler a new response to alcohol. The first step might be to teach him to associate alcohol (the original stimulus) with the sensation of nausea (a noxious stimulus). If verbal instruction is not enough, the therapist might administer a drug that causes nausea whenever alcohol is consumed. The goal is to make the drinking of alcohol—the undesirable behavior—unpleasant. Eventually, the treatment will make the client experience nausea just at the thought of consuming alcohol, thus learning avoidance behavior (the new response).

Modeling

Learning Objective 30.4
Explain how observational learning is used in behavior therapy.

Both children and adults learn behaviors by watching and imitating other people—in other words, by observing models. Children learn table manners, toilet behavior, and appropriate responses to animals by observing and imitating their parents and other models. Similarly, the music you listen to, the clothing styles you wear, and the social or political causes you support are determined, in part, by the people around you. By watching the behavior of others, people learn to exhibit more adaptive and appropriate behavior. Bandura, Blanchard, and Ritter (1969), for example, asked people with snake phobias to watch other people handling snakes. Afterward, the subjects' fear of snakes was reduced.

One problem with modeling is that people may observe and imitate the behavior of inappropriate models. Many studies show that people imitate violent behaviors that they have observed on television and in movies. Further, many adolescents become involved in alcohol and other drug abuse because they imitate their peers. Such imitation often occurs because of faulty thinking about situations, people, or lifelong goals. When people have developed a faulty set of expectations that guide their behavior, cognitive therapy may be in order.

Cognitive Therapy

Learning Objective 30.5
State the major goal and three basic propositions of cognitive therapy.

Cognitive psychologists have had a profound impact on many areas of psychology, especially in therapy. In the past, most behavior therapists were concerned only with overt behavior, but many now incorporate thought processes into their treatments. Researchers now suggest that the thought process may hold the key to managing many forms of maladjustment. Therapists who use *cognitive restructuring,* for example, are interested in modifying the faulty thought patterns of disturbed people. Cognitive restructuring as a therapeutic technique is effective for people who have attached overly narrow or otherwise inappropriate labels to certain situations; for example, they may feel that sex is dirty or that assertiveness is unwomanly. Whenever they are presented with a situation that involves sex or assertiveness, they respond in a way that is determined by their thoughts about the situation, rather than by facts of the situation.

There are three basic propositions of cognitive therapy (Dobson & Block, 1988): (1) Cognitive activity affects behavior; (2) cognitive activity can be monitored; and (3) behavior changes can be effected through cognitive changes. Like other forms of behavior therapy, cognitive restructuring therapy focuses on current behavior and current thoughts. It is not especially concerned with uncovering forgotten childhood experiences, although it can be used to alter thoughts about childhood experiences.

Rational–Emotive Therapy

The best-known cognitive therapy is **rational–emotive therapy,** developed by researcher Albert Ellis (1913–) more than 30 years ago. Most behavior therapists assume that abnormal behavior is caused by faulty and irrational behavior patterns. Ellis and his colleagues, however, assume that it is caused by faulty and irrational thinking patterns (Ellis, 1970; Ellis & Harper, 1961). They believe that if faulty thought processes can be replaced with rational ideas, maladjustment and abnormal behavior will disappear.

Learning Objective 30.6
Describe the approaches used by Ellis, Beck, and Meichenbaum.

According to Ellis, psychological disturbance is a result of events in a person's life that give rise to irrational beliefs, leading to negative emotions and behaviors. Moreover, they are a breeding ground for further irrational ideas (Dryden & Ellis, 1988). Ellis argues that people place dogmatic demands on themselves and on other people, and they rigidly hold onto them no matter how unrealistic and illogical they are (Ellis, 1988).

Thus, a major goal of rational–emotive therapy is to help a person examine the past events that produced the irrational beliefs. Ellis, for example, tries to zero in on a client's basic philosophy of life and how it is inevitably self-defeating. He thus tries to uncover the client's thought patterns and help the client recognize that his or her underlying beliefs are faulty. In other words, the therapist tries to alter irrational beliefs and thought patterns. When rational–emotive therapy is successful, the client adopts different behaviors based on new, more rational thought processes. Cognitive behavior therapy has been used effectively to treat depression, bulimia, weight loss, anger, and adolescent behavior problems (e.g.,

rational–emotive therapy: A cognitive behavior therapy that emphasizes the importance of logical, rational thought processes.

TABLE 30.1 Ten irrational assumptions outlined by Albert Ellis

Because people think irrationally they behave irrationally according to Albert Ellis
1. It is a necessity for an adult to be loved and approved by almost everyone for virtually everything.
2. A person must be thoroughly competent, adequate, and successful in all respects.
3. Certain people are bad, wicked, or villainous and should be punished for their sins.
4. It is catastrophic when things are not going the way one would like.
5. Human unhappiness is externally caused. People have little or no ability to control their sorrows or to rid themselves of negative feelings.
6. It is right to be terribly preoccupied with and upset about something that may be dangerous or fearsome.
7. It is easier to avoid facing many of life's difficulties and responsibilities than it is to undertake more rewarding forms of self-discipline.
8. The past is all-important. Because something once strongly affected someone's life, it should continue to do so indefinitely.
9. People and things should be different from the way they are. It is catastrophic if perfect solutions to the grim realities of life are not immediately found.
10. Maximal human happiness can be achieved by inertia and inaction or by passively and without commitment "enjoying oneself."

Source: From the book, *A Guide to Rational Living* by Albert Ellis, Ph.D., and Robert A. Harper, Ph.D. © 1989, 1961. Used by permission of the publisher, Prentice Hall/A division of Simon & Schuster, Inc., Englewood Cliffs, N.J.

Butler et al, 1991; Deffenbacher, 1988). Table 30.1 on page 579 lists 10 irrational assumptions that, according to Ellis, cause emotional problems and maladaptive behaviors.

Other Cognitive Approaches: Beck and Meichenbaum

Another cognitive restructuring therapy that focuses on irrational ideas is that of Aaron Beck (1963). As described in Chapter 13, Beck's theory assumes that depression is caused by people's distorted cognitive views of reality, which lead to negative views about the world, themselves, and the future, and often to gross overgeneralizations. A man who thinks that he has no future, that all of his options are blocked, and who undervalues his intelligence is likely to be depressed. Such individuals form appraisals of situations, especially self-appraisals, that are distorted and based on insufficient (and sometimes wrong) data. The goal of therapy, therefore, is to help people develop realistic rather than distorted appraisals of the situations they encounter, and to solve problems the way they do in the rest of their lives (Beck, 1991). The therapist acts as a trainer and co-investigator, providing data to be examined and guidance for understanding how cognitions influence behavior (Beck & Weishaar, 1989).

Some researchers, such as Donald Meichenbaum, believe that what people

TABLE 30.2 Summary of key issues in psychoanalysis, humanistic therapy, behavior therapy, and cognitive therapy

	Psychoanalysis	**Humanistic**	**Behavior therapy**	**Cognitive therapy**
Nature of psychopathology	Maladjustment reflects inadequate conflict resolution and fixation in early development, which leave overly weak ego controls or strong impulses	Pathology reflects an incongruity between the real self and the potential, desired self; the person is overly dependent on others for gratification and self-esteem	Symptomatic behavior stems from faulty learning or learning of maladaptive behaviors. The symptom is the problem; there is no underlying disease	Maladjustment occurs because of faulty irrational ideas and thinking about the world
Goal of therapy	Attainment of psychosexual maturity, strengthened ego functions, and reduced control by unconscious and repressed impulses	Fostering self-determination, authenticity, and integration by releasing human potential and expanding awareness	Relieving symptomatic behavior by suppressing or replacing maladaptive behaviors	To change the way subjects think about themselves and the world
Role of therapist	An *investigator,* uncovering conflicts and resistances	An *authentic, empathetic person* in true encounter with patient, sharing experience	A *trainer,* helping subject unlearn old behaviors and learn new ones	A *trainer and coinvestigator,* helping the client learn new rational ways to think about the world
Techniques	Analyst takes an active role in interpreting the patterns of dreams and free associations	Patient is asked to see the world from a different perspective and is encouraged to focus on current situations rather than past ones	Subjects learn new responses; used to establish new behaviors and eliminate faulty or undesirable ones	Subjects learn to think situations through logically and to reconsider many of their irrational assumptions

Albert Ellis developed a cognitive therapy known as rational-emotive therapy. He believed that maladjustment was caused by faulty or irrational assumptions.

Aaron Beck based his cognitive restructuring therapy on the theory that individuals may appraise themselves and their life decisions using faulty data.

say to themselves determines what they will do. Therefore, a goal of therapy is to change the things people say to themselves. According to Meichenbaum, the therapist has to change the client's self-instructions.

A strength of Meichenbaum's theory is that self-instruction can be used in many settings for many different problems (Dobson & Block, 1988). It can help people who are shy or impulsive, people with speech impediments, and even those who are schizophrenic (Meichenbaum, 1974). Rather than attempting to change irrational beliefs, clients learn a repertoire of activities that they can use to make their behavior more adaptive. For example, they may learn to conduct a private monologue in which they work through adaptive ways of thinking and coping with situations. They can then discuss with a therapist the quality of these self-instructional statements and their usefulness. They may learn to organize their responses to specific situations in an orderly, more easily exercised set of steps. Cognitive therapy continues to make enormous strides and influences an increasing number of theorists and practitioners who conduct both long-term therapy and brief therapy, which is considered in the Applying Psychology box on page 583.

Table 30.2 provides an overall summary of the cognitive, humanistic, behavioral, and psychoanalytic approaches to individual therapy. Considered next is group therapy, which focuses on treating groups of people rather than individuals.

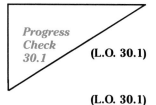

Progress Check 30.1

Complete the following sentences with one of the options provided.

(L.O. 30.1) a. Insight therapists argue that symptom substitution is likely to occur if a person is treated with behavior therapy because the ________ the behavior have not been examined. (underlying causes of / consequences that shaped)

(L.O. 30.1) b. The more complicated the disorder being treated, the more likely that the therapist will use a ________ approach. (strict behavioral / multimodal)

(L.O. 30.1) c. The first step in any plan for behavior therapy involves ________ the problem behavior. (understanding the client's feelings about / identifying and knowing the frequency of)

(L.O. 30.2) d. In a token economy, a person receives objects that ________. (are intrinsically reinforcing / can be traded for something special)

(L.O. 30.2) e. The goal of a token economy is to increase behaviors that are compatible with ______. (social norms / a person's self-image)

(L.O. 30.2) f. In behavior therapy, when extinction, punishment, and time-out are used to decrease the frequency of undesired behaviors, ______ is also used to strengthen appropriate and desired behaviors. (stimulus control / positive reinforcement)

(L.O. 30.3) g. The main goal in counterconditioning is to teach the client to have ______. (increased willpower / a new response to a specific stimulus)

(L.O. 30.3) h. Systematic desensitization is especially effective in treating behavior problems such as ______. (excessive anger and phobias / psychosis and interpersonal conflict)

(L.O. 30.3) i. In aversive counterconditioning, ______ stimulus is paired with a stimulus that elicits undesired behavior. (a noxious / an improbable)

(L.O. 30.4) j. When a therapist teaches a client adaptive and appropriate behavior by having the client observe others, the therapist is using a technique termed ______. (mirroring / modeling)

(L.O. 30.5) k. Cognitive restructuring is an effective therapeutic technique for people who have ______ certain life events. (attached inappropriate labels to / non-conventional ideas concerning)

(L.O. 30.6) l. In Ellis' rational–emotive therapy, the sentence "I must be thoroughly competent, adequate, and successful in all possible respects," would ______. (be used as a therapeutic self-statement / be considered irrational)

(L.O. 30.6) m. Aaron Beck's focus on cognitive restructuring is geared toward helping clients use ______ to appraise their life situations and themselves. (realistic and accurate data / feedback from others)

Group Therapy

Learning Objective 30.7
Explain why group therapy and self-help groups are popular.

When several people meet to receive psychological help, the treatment is referred to as **group therapy.** This technique was introduced around the turn of the century and has become increasingly popular since World War II. One reason for its popularity is that the demand for therapists exceeds the number available. Individually, a therapist can generally see up to 40 clients a week for 1 hour each, but in a group, the same therapist might see 8 or 10 clients in just 1 hour. Another reason for the popularity is that the therapist's fee is shared among the members of the group, making it less expensive than individual therapy.

Group therapy is often more effective than individual therapy in the treatment of such problems as interpersonal conflicts. The social pressures that operate in a group can help shape the members' behavior; in addition, group members provide useful models of behavior for each other. Successful helping organizations such as Weight Watchers, Gamblers Anonymous, and Alcoholics Anonymous practice a form of group therapy; such self-help groups continue to grow in popularity each year. About 6 million American adults are currently members of self-help groups, and researchers see the self-help group as an important method for coping with some mental health problems (Jacobs & Goodman, 1989).

group therapy: A treatment of emotional and behavioral problems in which several people meet as a group with a therapist.

Techniques, Goals, and Format of Group Therapy

Learning Objective 30.8
Describe the goals and techniques of traditional group therapy.

The techniques used by a therapy group are determined largely by the nature of the group and the orientation of its therapist. The group may follow a psychoanalytic, client-centered, Gestalt, behavior therapy, or other approach. No two groups are alike, and no two groups deal with individual members in the same way.

APPLYING PSYCHOLOGY

Brief Therapy

There is a new therapy in town—and it is often a cognitive therapy. Brief therapy rejects many of the traditional ideas of the various therapies just discussed. Proponents of brief therapy reject the concept of an ideal therapist who can do all things for all people, the idea that one therapeutic approach can help all people with any behavior or emotional problem, the belief that a person's unconscious or life history must be understood fully before the client can end therapy, and the concept that the therapist and client have only one chance to resolve past or future psychological problems.

In an award-winning address to the American Psychological Association, Nicholas Cummings (1986) described a new model for psychotherapy, **brief intermittent therapy** throughout the life cycle, which is based on a blend of psychotherapeutic orientations and skills. A basic goal of brief therapy is to give clients what they need. The therapy therefore focuses on treating client's problems efficiently and getting them back on their own as quickly as possible. One of its objectives is to save clients time and money, with the knowledge that they can and will return if they need help in the future. There are, however, no limits on the number of sessions, and the client remains in therapy as long as he or she feels it is necessary. The key distinction of this changing approach to therapy is that today more and more therapists think in terms of *planned* short-term treatments (Wells & Phelps, 1990).

In the first session of brief therapy, the therapist makes sure that treatment begins. He or she strives to perform an *operational diagnosis* that answers the question, "Why is the client here today instead of last week or last month, last year, or next year?" The answer indicates to the therapist the specific problem for which the client is seeking help. Also in the first session, "Every client makes a therapeutic contract with every therapist" (Cummings, 1986, p. 430; Goulding, 1990). The goals of therapy are established and agreed on by the client and the therapist—the therapy is precise with no unnecessary extra steps (Lazarus & Fay, 1990).

Because it is relatively new, there is not a great deal of published research on the effectiveness of brief psychotherapy, but what is published is very encouraging (e.g., Zeig & Gilligan, 1990). Research has been limited to relatively few clients with a narrow range of problems. Nonetheless, researchers have found brief therapy to be effective when treatment goals and procedures are tailored to the client's needs and the time available (Brom, Kleber, & Defares, 1989). It can be especially effective when combined with thought restructuring (Ellis, 1990) and has been shown to be effective for relapse prevention for alcoholics (Sandahl & Ronnberg, 1990).

▲ ***What does Cummings suggest is the goal and approach of brief intermittent therapy?***

▲ ***If brief therapy is especially effective, what are the implications for traditional therapists who practice long-term psychodynamic or humanistic therapy?***

In traditional group therapy, from 6 to 12 clients meet on a regular basis (usually once a week) with a therapist in a clinic, hospital, or therapist's office. Generally, the therapist selects members on the basis of what they can gain from and offer to the group. The goal is to construct a group whose members are compatible (but not necessarily the same) in terms of age, needs, and problems.

The format of traditional group therapy varies, but generally each member describes his or her problems to the other members, who in turn relate their experiences with similar problems and how they coped with them. This gives individuals a chance to express their fears and anxieties to other people who are warm and accepting; each member eventually realizes that every person has emotional problems. Group members also have opportunities to role play, or try out, new behaviors in a safe but evaluative environment. In a Vietnam outreach center, for example, a therapist might help members relive past traumas and cope with their continuing fears. Finally, in group therapy, members can exert pressure on an individual to behave in more appropriate ways, or at least more like the

brief intermittent therapy: A therapy approach that focuses on identifying the client's current problem and treating it with the most effective treatment as quickly as possible.

group norms. Sometimes, the therapist is directive in helping the group cope with a specific problem. At other times, he or she allows the group to work through its problems independently.

Family Therapy

Learning Objective 30.9
Describe the assumptions, goals, and techniques used by psychologists and social workers involved in family therapy.

A special form of group therapy is **family therapy,** in which two or more members of a family are treated at once. A *family* is defined as any group of people who are committed to each other's well-being, preferably for life (Bronfenbrenner, 1989). Widely used by a large number of practitioners, especially social workers, family therapy aims to change the ways in which family members interact. From a family therapist's point of view, the real patient in family therapy is the family's structure and organization (Jacobson & Bussob, 1983). While parents may identify one member of their family, perhaps a delinquent child, as the problem, family therapists believe that the person, in many cases, may simply be a scapegoat. The so-called problem member diverts the family's attention from other problems that are more difficult to confront. Sometimes, family therapy is termed *relationship therapy* because this is often the focus of the intervention (Becvar & Becvar, 1988).

family therapy: Therapy in which two or more people who are committed to each other's well-being are treated at once; attempts to change *family systems* and assumes that individuals affect family processes and family processes affect individuals.

community psychology: A branch of psychology that seeks to reach out to society to provide services such as community mental health centers and especially to effect social change through planning, prevention, intervention, research, and evaluation; emphasizes empowerment of individuals.

Social workers and family therapists attempt to change *family systems.* This means that treatment takes place within an ongoing, active social system such as a marriage or family. Therapists assume that there are multiple sources of psychological influence: Individuals within a family affect family processes and family processes affect individuals—it is an interactive system. The family systems approach has become especially popular in universities that have social work colleges, in departments of psychology, and even in colleges of medicine where patients are often seen in a family setting.

A major technique used in family therapy is to actually *restructure* the family's interactions. If a son is responding too submissively to his domineering mother, for example, the therapist may suggest that the son be assigned household chores only by his father. Many psychologists, social workers, and psychiatrists use family therapy to help individuals and families change. However, not all families profit equally from such interventions. Family therapy is difficult, for example, with families that are disorganized or in which not all members participate.

Some researchers feel that the family systems approach is as effective as individual therapy and in some situations more effective (Bednar, Burlingame, & Masters, 1988). A clinician who is presented with a person with some type of adjustment problem must also consider the impact of this problem on other people, one of the main focuses of codependence, the topic we consider in the Applying Psychology box on the facing page.

Community Psychology

Learning Objective 30.10
Describe the general aims, key elements, and special focus of community psychology.

The therapies described in this chapter are based on the assumption that people need help to adapt to society in healthy and productive ways. However, some psychologists try to help people in a broader way. **Community psychology** has emerged in response to a widespread desire for a more action-oriented approach to individual and social adjustment.

The general aims of community psychology are to strengthen existing social support networks and to stimulate the formation of new networks to meet new challenges (Gonzales et al., 1983). A key element is community involvement to effect social change. A church or synagogue group, for example, could mobilize

APPLYING PSYCHOLOGY

Codependence

Recently, practitioners have been focusing on families and how families often become wrapped up in a patient's problems—depression, alcoholism, drug abuse, child abuse, or anxiety disorders—that become devastating for them. This focus on the problem of one family member is termed *codependence.* Codependence is not a *DSM-III-R* disorder; in fact, the families of people with disorders such as substance abuse have often gone relatively unnoticed. Although practitioners often treat whole families, not just a person suffering from maladjustment, they are facing codependence as a new type of adjustment problem, not for the patient, but for his or her family and friends.

In codependence, families often cling to a person with serious problems in a dependent way. The codependent—the family member or friend—is often plagued by intense feelings of shame, fear, anger, or pain but cannot express those feelings because of an intense desire to please and care for the person suffering from a disorder or addiction. Codependent people hope to be perfect in helping the person with the disorder; they feel that if they are perfect, they can help the individual. In some cases, people actually need for the patient to stay disordered; for example, families sometimes unwittingly want a patient to maintain dependence on them so that they can stay in a controlling position. A practitioner often has a patient who is facing alcoholism or a cocaine addiction and a friend or family member who is codependent.

Codependency has long been recognized by psychologists, but Pia Mellody and colleagues have brought it before practitioners again in a book, *Facing Codependence* (1989). They assert that families often need therapy and that people who suffer from codependence lack the necessary skills to lead mature, satisfying adult lives. Codependents have difficulty experiencing positive self-esteem; they have difficulty setting psychological boundaries between themselves and others; and they have difficulty defining and meeting day-to-day needs. They become wrapped up in another person and in doing so suffer themselves and retard the growth of the original patient. The problem of codependence is just being realized and evaluated; Mellody suggests a therapeutic approach for treating codependency, and future research will evaluate these ideas scientifically. We now recognize that disorders, both mild and severe, affect a person's life, coworkers, family members, and ultimately the community.

▲ ***What led psychologists to hypothesize the existence of codependency?***

▲ ***What is the evidence that a researcher could use to tell if family members are being codependent?***

▲ ***What is implied by the phrase "setting psychological boundaries"?***

its senior citizens for a foster grandparent program and could set up support groups of family and friends for patients released from mental hospitals.

Another key element of community psychology is **empowerment,** that is, helping people to enhance existing skills and develop new skills, knowledge, and motivation so they can gain control over their own lives (Rappaport, 1987). Community psychology focuses on prevention, early intervention, planning, research, and evaluation. Community psychologists work in schools, churches, planning commissions, and prisons. They plan and set up programs for bringing psychological skills and knowledge into the community.

empowerment: Facilitating the development of skills, knowledge, and motivation in individuals so that they can act for themselves and gain mastery over their own affairs.

A special focus of community psychology is *primary prevention*—that is, lowering the rate of new cases of a disorder or counteracting harmful circumstances that might lead to maladjustment. Primary prevention usually works on groups rather than on individuals. It may focus on an entire community, on mild-risk groups (such as children from families of low socioeconomic status), or on high-risk groups (such as children of schizophrenic parents).

Community Mental Health Programs

Learning Objective 30.11 Describe the importance of neighborhood clinics, crisis intervention centers, and sensitivity to human diversity and explain why they are sometimes used along with talking therapies.

In response to growing public awareness of mental health problems, a special kind of service agency—*the neighborhood clinic*—has been developed. Such clinics help communities cope with problems created by mental illness, unemployment, and lack of education. Some clinics provide free, confidential treatment for problems such as drug addiction, alcoholism, and emotional and psychological disorders.

Centers offer various services, including partial hospitalization programs for people who require hospitalization during the day, and outpatient care for people who live at home while receiving therapy. They also offer consultation, education programs, and lectures and literature on topics such as therapy, family planning, and drug rehabilitation.

Crisis intervention centers help people deal with short-term, stressful situations that require immediate therapeutic attention. Often, the crisis is a specific event; for example, a man may lose his job, a child may be seriously ill, or a woman may be raped. The focus of crisis intervention is on the immediate circumstances, not on past experiences. Psychologists know that a crisis is a turning point at which things will get better or worse—a point at which change is possible (Pittman, Flomenhaft, & DeYoung, 1990). Some studies show that crisis intervention therapy can be especially effective (Sawicki, 1988). One problem in evaluating crisis therapy is that a variety of techniques are used, making controlled comparisons difficult (Slaikeu, 1990).

Applied psychologists often seek to develop human service programs. Although many community psychologists focus on research, many are also involved in intervention, consultation, and development of existing resources. Whether they work in the juvenile justice system, in helping communities deal with the impact of toxic waste, or in the direct delivery of mental health services, community psychologists are generally considered applied psychologists.

Human Diversity

Community psychologists have been especially sensitive to *human diversity*—that is, the fact that people are not alike and do not have the same needs. A society is made up of individuals from many different cultures, races, religions, and regional heritages. Each subgroup has developed its own style of living, which may vary considerably from that of the majority culture (Snowden, 1987) and may lead to marked ethnic-related differences in mental health (Snowden & Cheung, 1990).

Crisis intervention centers such as this battered women's shelter provide immediate assistance to people in need.

One special population, the elderly, forms a growing percentage of the general population. During the early 1990s, more than 30 million Americans will be age 65 years or older. The proportion of elderly people is expected to increase by the year 2030, and the number of Americans over age 65 years will exceed 60 million. Community psychologists are developing programs that focus on the special needs of the elderly for social support, physical and psychological therapy, and continuing education.

Another special group, women, accounts for somewhat more than half the general population. However, much more than half of the people seen by mental health practitioners are women. Men are less likely to seek therapy. On reason for this difference may be that changes in sex roles have placed severe stresses on women, many of whom combine the roles of mother, spouse, and wage earner. In addition, as a group, women are paid less than their male counterparts. Single mothers, older women, women members of minority groups, and women homosexuals often have great difficulty getting a job that can adequately support a family, and finding their own place in a world where societal values and expectations are constantly changing. Of course, generalizations about women cannot necessarily be applied universally to individual women, just as generalizations about Afro-Americans or Hispanics or other special populations should not be considered as truisms for specific individuals within those populations.

Community psychologists are paying special attention to the thousands of mental patients who have been discharged from state hospitals—deinstitutionalized—and are making their way, sometimes quite unsuccessfully, in the outside world (Johnson, 1990); they now comprise a substantial proportion of the American homeless population. Some researchers (Isaac & Armat, 1990) assert that we have abandoned the mentally ill and their needs and have avoided sometimes simple biological treatments that can help the mentally ill; we discuss this approach next.

electroconvulsive shock therapy: [eel-ECK-tro-con-VUL-siv] A treatment for severe mental illness in which a brief (less than a second) application of electricity is used to produce a generalized seizure.

Biologically Based Therapies

Learning Objective 30.12 Describe biologically based therapies and explain why they are sometimes used along with talking therapies.

When an individual is referred to a practitioner for help, the usual approach involves some form of psychological treatment. This usually means a talking therapy that may be based on psychodynamic, behavior, cognitive, or humanistic theories. However, for some patients, talking therapy is not enough. Some are too depressed; others may be exhibiting symptoms of bipolar disorders (see Chapter 13); others may need hospitalization because they are suicidal.

Biologically based therapies may include medication, hospitalization, and the involvement of physicians. Biologically based approaches are generally not used alone, but in combination with traditional forms of therapy—a multimodal approach. Biological therapies fall into broad classes that vary from those rarely if ever used to those used frequently: psychosurgery, electroconvulsive shock therapy, and drug therapies.

Psychosurgery

Learning Objective 30.13 Discuss the past and present use of psychosurgery and electroconvulsive shock.

Psychosurgery is brain surgery that was once used to alleviate symptoms of mental disorders. In the 1940s and 1950s, *prefrontal lobotomies* were common; this procedure involved removing or surgically severing parts of a patient's frontal lobes from other parts of the brain. Severing the frontal lobes, which were thought to control emotions, destroyed connections within the brain, making patients docile. Patients lost the symptoms of their mental disorders but also became calm and wholly unemotional; some became unable to control their impulses, and an estimated 1 to 4% died from the operation.

Today, despite advances in technology and the precision of the operation, psychosurgery is rarely, if ever, used, for three basic reasons. First, drug therapy has proven more effective than such surgical procedures; second, the long-term effects of psychosurgery are questionable; and most important, the procedure is irreversible and morally objectionable to most practitioners, patients, and their families. Its widespread use earlier in this century is considered by many to have been a serious mistake.

Electroconvulsive Shock Therapy

Shock treatment, or **electroconvulsive shock therapy** (ECT), was once a widely used treatment for depressed individuals. ECT is a treatment for severe mental illness in which a brief application of electricity is used to produce a generalized seizure. The duration of the shock is less than a second; patients are treated in 3–12 sessions over several weeks. In the 1940s and 1950s, ECT was routinely given to severely disturbed patients in mental hospitals. Unfortunately, it was often used with patients who did not need it—far more often with women—and by overzealous physicians to control unruly patients in mental institutions.

Today ECT is not a common treatment. According to the National Institutes of Health, fewer than 2.5% of all psychiatric hospital admissions are treated with ECT, about 30,000 patients each year. Is ECT effective at all? Could drug therapy or traditional psychotherapy be used in its place?

ECT is effective in the *short-term* management of severely depressed individuals and is sometimes used when a patient is at risk of suicide. However, its effects are transient if it is not followed by drug therapy and psychotherapy. Generally speaking, ECT should be used as a last resort when other forms of drug treatment and psychotherapy are ineffective. ECT is not appropriate in the treatment of schizophrenia or to manage unruly behavior or symptoms of other disorders.

The medical risk of death during the administration of ECT is low. However, there is potential for memory loss and a decreased ability to learn and retain new information, which may endure for several weeks. In addition, ECT may frighten patients and can leave feelings of shame and stigma.

Much more research is needed to determine the effects of ECT and the subgroups for whom the treatment is beneficial, if any. If practitioners determine that ECT is warranted, the law requires (and medical ethics demand) that a patient has the right to accept or reject the treatment.

Drug Therapies

Learning Objective 30.14 Identify four types of psychotropic drugs, and state the types of disorders for which they are prescribed.

Drug therapy attempts to manage psychological problems through the use of drugs. By administering various doses of drugs, therapists can help people who are experiencing symptoms of anxiety, mania, depression, and schizophrenia. Their symptoms are lessened. Drugs for the relief of mental problems are sometimes termed *psychotropic drugs* and are usually grouped into four classes: antianxiety, antidepressant, antimania, and antipsychotics.

Antianxiety Drugs. Calming and anxiety reducing, these tranquilizers are mood-altering substances. Widely used in the United States (and probably overprescribed by physicians), these drugs (technically termed *anxiolytics*) reduce stressful feelings, calm patients, and lower excitability. Tranxene, Librium, Valium, and Miltown are some of the most widely used. To help a person deal with his anxiety on a temporary basis, a physician may prescribe an antianxiety drug such as Tranxene. However, long-term continued use of antianxiety drugs without some adjunct therapy is usually ill-advised.

Antidepressant Drugs. As their name suggests, antidepressants, sometimes considered mood elevators, are used to treat individuals who are extremely depressed. People who take antidepressants (technically termed *thymoleptics*) become more optimistic, less sad, and often redevelop a sense of purpose. These medications allow people to function outside of a hospital setting. They can take as long as 4 weeks to reach their full effectiveness, and a daily dosage is necessary to maintain its benefit.

Antidepressants are from two categories of drugs, *tricylics* and *monoamine oxidase (MAO) inhibitors.* Both potent drugs, the tricylics are prescribed much more often because they pose less danger of medical complications (patients on MAO inhibitors have to adhere to special diets and some other restrictions, to prevent adverse physical reactions to the drug). Although they have side effects that include drowsiness, antidepressants lift the spirits of people who are depressed and are an important aid in the recovery of people with mood disorders, such as depression and some anxiety disorders (Swedo et al., 1989). The drugs work by altering levels of neurotransmitters in the brain.

Antimania Drugs: Lithium. Another drug, lithium carbonate, has come into wide use. Lithium carbonate (technically also a thymoleptic) is widely used with bipolar disorders—it relieves the manic elements. Psychiatrists find that when a daily maintenance dose is taken, lithium is especially helpful in warding off future episodes of mania. The dosage of any drug is important, but in the case of lithium, it is especially important. Too much produces noxious side effects, while too little has no effect.

Antipsychotic Drugs. Antipsychotic drugs are used mainly with people who suffer from the disabling disorder of schizophrenia. Such drugs (technically termed *neuroleptics*) reduce hostility and aggression in violent patients and make their disorders more manageable. These drugs reduce delusions and in some cases allow a person to manage life outside of a hospital setting. Antipsychotic drugs are usually *phenothiazines* (the most common of these is *chlorpromazine*). They seem to work by altering the level of brain neurotransmitter substances and their uptake—but we are not sure (Goldenberg, 1990). As in antimania drugs, dosages of antipsychotic drugs are crucial. Further, if patients are maintained on antipsychotic drugs for too long, other problems can emerge, including facial ticks and involuntary movements of the mouth and shoulders. This problem is termed *tardive dyskinesia.*

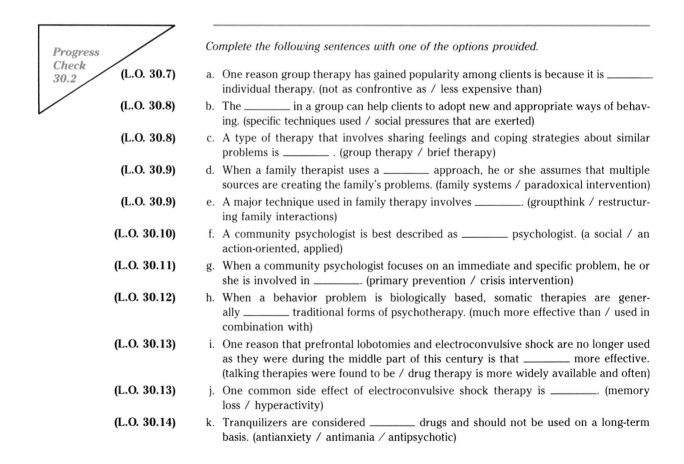

Progress Check 30.2

Complete the following sentences with one of the options provided.

(L.O. 30.7) a. One reason group therapy has gained popularity among clients is because it is ________ individual therapy. (not as confrontive as / less expensive than)

(L.O. 30.8) b. The ________ in a group can help clients to adopt new and appropriate ways of behaving. (specific techniques used / social pressures that are exerted)

(L.O. 30.8) c. A type of therapy that involves sharing feelings and coping strategies about similar problems is ________ . (group therapy / brief therapy)

(L.O. 30.9) d. When a family therapist uses a ________ approach, he or she assumes that multiple sources are creating the family's problems. (family systems / paradoxical intervention)

(L.O. 30.9) e. A major technique used in family therapy involves ________. (groupthink / restructuring family interactions)

(L.O. 30.10) f. A community psychologist is best described as ________ psychologist. (a social / an action-oriented, applied)

(L.O. 30.11) g. When a community psychologist focuses on an immediate and specific problem, he or she is involved in ________. (primary prevention / crisis intervention)

(L.O. 30.12) h. When a behavior problem is biologically based, somatic therapies are generally ________ traditional forms of psychotherapy. (much more effective than / used in combination with)

(L.O. 30.13) i. One reason that prefrontal lobotomies and electroconvulsive shock are no longer used as they were during the middle part of this century is that ________ more effective. (talking therapies were found to be / drug therapy is more widely available and often)

(L.O. 30.13) j. One common side effect of electroconvulsive shock therapy is ________. (memory loss / hyperactivity)

(L.O. 30.14) k. Tranquilizers are considered ________ drugs and should not be used on a long-term basis. (antianxiety / antimania / antipsychotic)

Module Summary

Behavior Therapy

- *Behavior therapy* uses learning principles to help people replace maladaptive behaviors with new ones; behavior therapists treat people by having them first unlearn old, faulty behaviors and then learn new ones (p. 574).
- Behavior therapy usually involves at least three procedures: (1) identifying the problem behavior and its frequency; (2) treating the client; and (3) assessing whether there is a lasting behavior change (p. 575).

Cognitive Therapy

- There are three basic propositions of cognitive therapy: (1) Cognitive activity affects behavior; (2) cognitive activity can be monitored; and (3) behavior changes can be brought about through cognitive changes (p. 578).
- *Rational–emotive therapy,* a cognitive therapy developed by Albert Ellis, emphasizes the role of logical, rational thought processes in behavior. It assumes that irrational assumptions are the cause of maladjustment (p. 579).

Group Therapy

- Group therapy is used to treat several people simultaneously for emotional and behavioral problems (p. 582).
- Group therapy is often more effective than individual therapy in the treatment of such problems as interpersonal conflicts (p. 582).

Community Psychology

- Community psychology provides mental health services on a continuous basis in an attempt to reach people who might not otherwise seek psychological help (p. 584).
- The general aims of community psychology are to strengthen existing social support networks, to stimulate the formation of new networks to meet new challenges, and to empower members of the community (p. 586).

Biologically Based Therapies

- Electroconvulsive shock therapy (ECT) is a treatment for severe mental illness in which a brief application of electricity is used to produce a generalized seizure. ECT is appropriate for a very narrow range of disorders and should be used only as a last resort—when no other available treatment has been effective (p. 587).
- Drugs for the relief of mental problems are called *psychotropic drugs* and are usually grouped together into four classes: antianxiety drugs, antidepressant drugs, antipsychotics, and antimania drugs (p. 588).

KEY TERMS

aversive counterconditioning, p. 577
behavior therapy, p. 574
brief intermittent therapy, p. 583
community psychology, p. 584
counterconditioning, p. 577
electroconvulsive shock therapy, p. 587
empowerment, p. 585
family therapy, p. 584
group therapy, p. 582
rational–emotive therapy, p. 579
symptom substitution, p. 574
systematic desensitization, p. 577
time-out, p. 576
token economy, p. 575

SELF-TEST

Module 30

- Before taking the self-test, **recite** and **review.**
- Use the key at the back of the text to *correct* your answers.
- *Restudy* pages that correspond to any questions you answered incorrectly.

1. A behavior therapist knows that treatment has been effective when
   a. insight is achieved.
   b. the patient describes a new coping skill.
   c. follow-up observations show that the new behavior is still occurring.
   d. the patient is able to identify reinforcers in his or her life.
2. When extinction is used in behavior therapy,
   a. reinforcers that had been given for an undesired behavior are withheld.
   b. the person is removed from a reinforcing environment.
   c. a privilege or special possession is taken away for misbehavior.
   d. an aversive stimulus, such as a spanking, is given.
3. When systematic desensitization is used, the client
   a. is reinforced for a new behavior.
   b. learns to relax while imaging situations that had previously produced anxiety.
   c. is directly exposed to an anxiety-producing situation until it no longer causes fear.
   d. learns to avoid fear-producing stimuli.
4. A therapeutic technique that allows a child's fear of dogs to diminish simply because the child observes others playing with dogs is
   a. operant conditioning.
   b. modeling.
   c. cognitive restructuring.
   d. play therapy.
5. A basic proposition of cognitive therapy is
   a. forgotten childhood experiences influence behavior.
   b. thoughts can be monitored.
   c. thought processes have little to do with overt behavior.
   d. thoughts are elusive.
6. Meichenbaum's approach to cognitive restructuring makes use of techniques such as
   a. resocialization and constructive brainwashing.
   b. self-instructions and private monologues.
   c. anchoring and reframing.
   d. positive regard and empathetic understanding.
7. One reason that self-help groups such as Weight Watchers and Alcoholics Anonymous are effective is that
   a. members provide useful models of behavior for one another.
   b. they are free, and attendance is voluntary.
   c. trained psychologists provide guidance on how to help one's self while helping others.
   d. all of the above
8. A type of therapy in which several clients might act out situations, feelings, and roles is
   a. a self-help group.
   b. biotherapy.
   c. group therapy.
   d. modeling.

9. From a family therapist's point of view, the patient in family therapy is
   a. the family member who is used as a scapegoat.
   b. the family member or members who do the scapegoating.
   c. the person who actually causes the problem.
   d. the family's structure and organization.
10. Which of the following might community psychologists be found doing?
    a. identifying potential problems, such as the spread of AIDS, and implementing programs to prevent them from occurring.
    b. strengthening social support networks and facilitating social change.
    c. providing people in the community with a sense of empowerment.
    d. all of the above
11. Community mental health centers and neighborhood clinics offer
    a. affordable part-time hospitalization and outpatient care.
    b. consultation and therapy for people who have emotional problems or who are having trouble coping with life events.
    c. education and literature on topics related to mental health.
    d. all of the above
12. When biologically based therapies are used for psychological treatment, the person being treated
    a. does not need to see a psychotherapist.
    b. is usually also involved in some type of talking therapy.
    c. will experience an immediate change for the better.
    d. is mentally ill.
13. Today, electroconvulsive shock therapy is used
    a. as a treatment for schizophrenia.
    b. as a way of controlling unruly patients in mental hospitals.
    c. on severely depressed or suicidal patients when drug therapy and psychotherapy have been ineffective.
    d. all of the above
14. ________ is a psychotropic drug that is used to suppress episodes of mania in a person who has bipolar disorder.
    a. Chlorpromazine
    b. Librium
    c. Lithium carbonate
    d. Monoamine oxidase

Connections

If you are interested in . . .	Turn to . . .	To learn more about . . .
Freud's theory of psychoanalysis as a therapeutic approach	◆ Chapter 10, pp. 398–406	Freud's theory of personality, which later developed into a full-blown treatment approach
	◆ Chapter 10, p. 402	How defense mechanisms are often overused by individuals in need of therapy
The behavioral approach to therapy	◆ Chapter 1, p. 18	How early behaviorists focused only on overt, observable behavior
	◆ Chapter 5, p. 160	Classical conditioning, operant conditioning, and modeling, which can help explain long-standing behaviors—some of which may become maladaptive
	◆ Chapter 13, pp. 540–543	How disorders such as depression often have a cognitive basis, which requires a change in thought processes and overt behavior
Biological approaches to therapy	◆ Chapter 2, pp. 42–46	How certain chemicals in the blood and brain which affect behavior can be used as part of a multimodal treatment approach
	◆ Chapter 12, p. 496	How stress can lead to a number of health-related issues that can be alleviated, in part, through psychotherapy, and in part, through drug treatments
	◆ Chapter 13, p. 541	Depression's biological basis and how it can sometimes be alleviated through drug therapy

The treatment of psychological disorders involves studying diverse subspecialties in psychology. Clearly, a study of abnormality is necessary to understand treatment processes (Chapter 13, p. 522). However, in addition to the study of maladjustment, a comprehensive understanding of treatment processes requires psychologists to understand the assessment process (Chapter 11, p. 467) and normal personality (Chapter 10, p. 397). Before undertaking a study of treatment, psychologists realize that a knowledge of the biological basis of behavior (Chapter 2, p. 51) is necessary, as is a study of learning processes (Chapter 5, p. 160). Today, treatment not only involves biological mechanisms but also thought processes (Chapter 7, p. 240). Practitioners are especially sensitive to developmental processes in children and adults (Chapter 8, p. 306), as well as motivational causes for specific disorders (Chapter 9, p. 355). No study of treatment processes can be complete without understanding the nature of stress (Chapter 12, p. 496) and social interactions (Chapter 15, p. 621). Treatment is thus a multimodal process involving many of the subdisciplines of psychology.

Module 31 ► THE SOCIAL WORLD 596

Module 32 ► SOCIAL INTERACTIONS 620

Module 33 ► APPLIED PSYCHOLOGY 638

Chapter 15

Social Psychology

Social psychologists study how individual behavior is affected by the behavior of other people; because most of us interact with dozens or hundreds of people in any one week their behavior can have profound implications on day-to-day thoughts and actions. This chapter focuses on those interactions and on human responses to other people. The first module of the chapter, Module 31, focuses on how people affect our attitudes not only about other individuals, but also about ourselves. Our attitudes are shaped by early interactions and affected by many subtle interpersonal variables, but they are also modifiable across our life span. Attitudes and self-perception are the first two topics introduced in this chapter. Just being with others can have profound effects on our willingness to go along with them, conform, obey, work harder, or even slack off—a phenomenon known as "social loafing." The topics in Module 31 focus on social influence and the study of behavior in groups.

People develop complex relationships with one another, and these relationships are determined by physical and social factors. The chapter's second module, Module 32, focuses on these human interactions and on those interpersonal variables that affect liking, helping, prejudice, and aggressive behaviors. With some persons and in some situations, we may be provoked to aggression. In addition, our interactions with other people are not confined to interpersonal situations. In our larger social world, we are affected both by factors in the physical environment, such as room arrangements, the space available to us, and room temperature, and by the expectations that society (and employers) have concerning what we must do to be productive and responsible citizens.

The chapter concludes in the third module, Module 33, with an examination of environmental psychology, which focuses on interpersonal space, crowding, and preserving the natural environment, and the study of industrial and organizational psychology. Industrial/organizational psychologists focus on how individual behavior is affected by the work environment, by coworkers, and by organizations. How well people can be chosen for jobs and how well individuals perform their duties and relate to one another is a concern of industrial/organizational psychologists. Accordingly, the third module also examines performance appraisal, a major area of industrial/organizational psychology.

Module 31

The Social World

LEARNING OBJECTIVES

When you have mastered the material in this module, you will be able to

Introduction (pp. 597–598)

31.1 Describe the subject matter of social psychology (p. 597).

Attitudes (pp. 598–602)

31.2 Describe three dimensions of attitudes and three ways in which attitudes are learned (p. 598).

31.3 Discuss four factors that are important when trying to persuade people to change their attitudes (p. 599).

31.4 Discuss the cognitive dissonance, self-perception, balance, and reactance theories of attitude and behavior change (p. 600).

Social Cognition (pp. 602–607)

31.5 Define social cognition and explain how various forms of nonverbal communication contribute to the impressions we form of others (p. 602).

31.6 Describe the attribution process, explain two common attribution errors, and discuss how we are influenced by the "just-world belief" (p. 603).

31.7 Explain how self-perceptions develop and how they affect our perceptions of others (p. 604).

31.8 Explain how self-serving biases influence our self-esteem (p. 605).

31.9 Explain how learned helplessness develops (p. 606).

Social Influence (pp. 607–612)

31.10 Describe Asch's classic conformity experiment and identify variables that influence a person's need to conform (p. 608).

31.11 Describe Milgram's classic obedience study, identify factors that influenced the results, and discuss the ethics of studies such as this one (p. 609).

Behavior in Groups (pp. 613–616)

31.12 Identify the characteristics of a group; describe social facilitation, social loafing, group polarization, and groupthink; and explain why each of these phenomena occur (p. 613).

SQ3R
- ▲ **Survey** to set goals for studying.
- ▲ Ask **questions** as you **read.**
- ▲ Stop occasionally to **recite** and **review.**

plus
- ▲ **Write** a summary of key points.
- ▲ **Reflect** on the hypotheses, evidence, and implications of this material and on the relevance it has to *your* life.

In 1978, a team of 40 eminent scientists assembled in Turin, Italy, to study a yellowed, 14-foot strip of linen bearing the ghostly imprint of a bearded man wearing a crown of thorns. Purported to be Christ's burial cloth, the Shroud of Turin has been worshiped by multitudes since its earliest known exhibit in 1354. After 6 days of extensive testing—including X-ray fluorescence, surface sampling, photographic computer analysis, and image enhancement—the scientists announced that the cloth's imprint was not paint or pigment and may have resulted from a brief flash of radiation emanating from a body. In a news service interview, the scientific team's leader said, "Every one of the scientists I have talked to believes the cloth is authentic." Convinced that the shroud was genuine, one Jewish member of the scientific team converted to Christianity.

social psychology: The study of how people influence and are influenced by the thoughts, feelings, and behaviors of other people; the focus is on individual behavior.

In the fall of 1988, the Vatican permitted small swatches of the shroud to be submitted to a new carbon-14 dating technique (earlier carbon-14 procedures would have destroyed too much of the cloth). All three laboratories that analyzed the linen concluded it was woven between 12 and 13 centuries after Christ's death. One expert declared the shroud to be the work of a brilliant medieval hoaxer. However, the new scientific proof didn't shake the faith of those who ardently believed in the shroud legend. Some believers questioned the accuracy of carbon-14 dating, others said that the image—regardless of its age—was created by a miracle.

The Shroud of Turin case exemplifies how humans acquire, maintain, and change their attitudes. On one hand, preliminary "proof" of the shroud's authenticity convinced a well-educated man to change his long-standing religious beliefs. Yet even stronger scientific evidence debunking the shroud proved unpersuasive to others. Why would people hold such strong and different attitudes about a piece of cloth?

Learning Objective 31.1 Describe the subject matter of social psychology.

Social psychology is the study of how people influence and are influenced by the thoughts, feelings, and behaviors of other people. Your behavior, although it may not always be apparent, is directly affected by the social world in which you live. Social psychologists focus on *individual behavior,* on how individuals form attitudes and feelings about themselves and other people, and on individuals'

attitude: A pattern of relatively enduring feelings, beliefs, and behavior tendencies toward other people, ideas, or objects.

responses to others. Our social world influences us powerfully, directly, and from the moment we are born. This module focuses on how individual behavior is affected by other people. This is especially evident in the formation of attitudes, our first topic.

Attitudes

Learning Objective 31.2 Describe three dimensions of attitudes and three ways in which attitudes are learned.

Attitudes determine whether you will respond to a given situation positively or negatively, with enthusiasm or with reluctance. **Attitudes** are lasting patterns of feelings, beliefs, and behavior tendencies toward other people, ideas, or objects. These patterns are shaped by how other people perceive us, and by how we think other people see us. Social psychologists are concerned with how the behavior and attitudes of other people influence an individual's behavior. The scientist who underwent the religious conversion while studying the Shroud of Turin was undoubtedly influenced by the beliefs of his fellow investigators. Moreover, his attitudes toward the shroud were shaped by professional training that made the existing scientific proofs very convincing.

Dimensions of Attitudes

People's attitudes comprise different dimensions. Most psychologists contend that there are three basic dimensions to attitudes: cognitive, emotional, and behavioral. The *cognitive dimension* of attitudes consists of thoughts and beliefs, such as the belief that science or religious faith can reveal truths. The *emotional dimension* involves feelings of like or dislike. For example, a person may like the idea that the Shroud of Turin is authentic because it makes her or him feel more spiritual. The third dimension, *behavior,* is how people show their beliefs and feelings, such as publicly announcing the shroud's authenticity or taking steps to show a religious conversion. When people have strongly held attitudes and adopt a specific belief, they are said to have a *conviction.* Once people acquire a conviction, they think about it, become involved with it, and may become emotional over it (which makes convictions long-lasting and resistant to change).

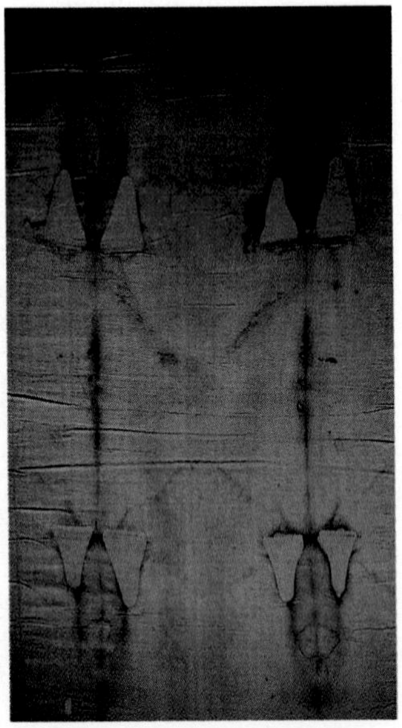

The Shroud of Turin presents a dilemma to believers and unbelievers alike as new evidence corroborates, then denies that this is the shroud of Christ.

Forming Attitudes

Attitudes are acquired through learning, beginning early in life. Thus, psychologists rely on learning theories to explain how children form attitudes. Three learning theory concepts (discussed in detail in Chapter 5) that help explain attitude formation are classical conditioning, operant conditioning, and social-observational learning.

The pairing of people, events, and ideologies with attitudes often goes unnoticed because it is so effortless in classical conditioning. However, such pairings can shape children's views and emotional responses to the world, thereby forming the basis of children's (and later adults') attitudes (see Figure 31.1). A key principle of operant conditioning states that reinforced behaviors are likely to recur, which helps explain how attitudes are maintained over time. In socializing children, parents express and reinforce ideas and behaviors consistent with their own perception of the correct view of the world. The social learning point of view asserts that people establish attitudes by watching the behavior of someone whom they consider significant, and then by imitating it. The new attitudes people learn eventually become their own.

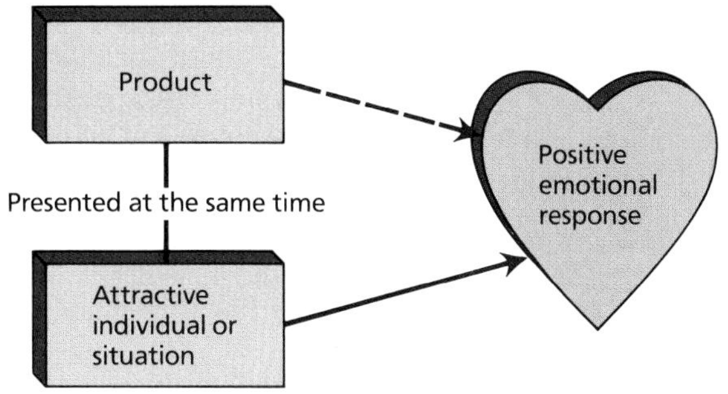

Figure 31.1

In attempting to induce positive feelings toward a product or idea, advertisers use classical conditioning techniques—they pair their product or idea with an attractive, desirable state, person, or situation, to evoke a pleasant response.

Changing Attitudes

Learning Objective 31.3 Discuss four factors that are important when trying to persuade people to change their attitudes.

It is important to remember that people's attitudes are not always reflected in their behavior, and attitudes can change. Just as people learn attitudes, they can unlearn them and learn new ones. New attitudes may impel a person to try a particular brand of soap, to vote Democratic, or to undergo a religious conversion. A common avenue by which people's attitudes change is the mass media, particularly television. The goal of television commercials is to change or to reinforce people's behavior. Commercials exhort viewers to drink Pepsi, not Coke; to drive a Volvo instead of a Saab; to say "no" to drugs; or to vote for Mr. Bush. Their appeal may be cognitive (one product tastes better than the other) or emotional (owning this product will make you feel proud).

To change an attitude, a person must be motivated and receptive. Moreover, the person who wishes to effect the change—the communicator—must be persuasive. Social psychologists have often listed four components of attitude change: the communicator, the communication, the medium, and the audience.

The Communicator. To be persuasive, a communicator—the person trying to influence the attitude change—must project integrity, credibility, and trustworthiness. If people don't trust, respect, or like the communicator, they are unlikely to change their attitudes. An unknown conservationist is less likely to convince an audience of the importance of preserving wildlife than a well-known scientist such as Carl Sagan.

The prestige of entertainers and sports figures makes them very effective as communicators—a fact on which advertisers are quick to capitalize.

The Communication. Presenting a clear, convincing, and logical argument is the most effective tool for changing attitudes. Changing attitudes is more likely when the targeted attitude is not too different from an existing one and when the audience is not highly involved with a particular point of view (Johnson & Eagly, 1989). Research also shows that people who expect to receive the content of a new idea are likely to exhibit attitude changes and those changes will persist (Boninger et al., 1990). Researchers also find that if people hear an argument, commercial, or political view often enough, they begin to believe it, regardless of its value. Repeated exposure to situations can change attitudes (Bornstein, 1989).

The Medium. The way in which communication is presented—its medium—influences people's receptiveness to change. For example, face-to-face communication has more impact than communication through television or in writing. Thus, although candidates for public office rely on TV, radio, and printed ads, meeting people face-to-face is a stronger persuasion tool. Also, because friends are more trusted than the communications media, information received from friends is considered even more influential.

The Audience. From time to time, people actually *want* to have their attitudes changed; they seek out alternative views. At other times, they fold their arms across their chest and announce, "It's going to take an act of Congress to change my mind." Changing people's attitudes, and ultimately their behavior, can be difficult if they have well-established habits (which often come with advancing age) or are highly motivated in the opposite direction.

The Search for Cognitive Consistency

Learning Objective 31.4 Discuss the cognitive dissonance, self-perception, balance, and reactance theories of attitude and behavior change.

Although basic ideas about life and morals are established early, attitudes continually develop and change. Some people seek change, trying to keep pace with friends or relatives; others are resistant. Most people try to maintain consistency between their various attitudes and between their attitudes and behavior. Consistency leads to orderly living and enables people to make decisions about future behavior more easily without having to filter through numerous alternatives (Cialdini, 1988).

Cognitive Dissonance. Image the dilemma faced by the scientist who, after discovering preliminary proof of the Shroud of Turin's authenticity in 1978, converted to Christianity. As a scientist, he must have found the physical evidence of the shroud compelling; as a Jew, he must have been bewildered by the apparent proof of Christ's divinity. How could he reconcile these two opposite attitudes? Moreover, what further confusion did he suffer when he later learned that the cloth was only six centuries old?

Whenever people realize that their attitudes conflict with each other or with their behavior, they feel uncomfortable. For example, if a student believes he should be saving part of his income toward tuition but spends every dime of it, his attitudes and behavior conflict. He may feel uncomfortable or even upset. Leon Festinger (1919–1989) termed this feeling as *dissonance,* the discomfort that results when a discrepancy exists among two or more of a person's beliefs or between the person's beliefs and her or his overt behavior.

Based on the concept that people seek to reduce dissonance, Festinger (1957) proposed a **cognitive dissonance** theory. According to the theory, when people experience conflict between their attitudes and their behavior (or other attitudes), they are motivated to change either their attitudes or their behavior. For example, suppose you are a strong proponent of animal rights. You support the ASPCA and Greenpeace, refrain from eating meat, and are repulsed by women in mink coats. Then you win in a raffle and are awarded an expensive black leather coat—just like the one worn by your favorite rock star. Wearing the coat goes against all your beliefs, but it feels good, you know it looks great on you, and all your friends admire it. According to cognitive dissonance theory, you are experiencing conflict between your attitudes (animal rights) and your behavior (wearing the coat). To relieve the conflict, you either stop wearing the coat or modify your beliefs. (Some psychologists consider cognitive dissonance theory a type of motivation theory because people become energized to do something.)

cognitive dissonance: [COG-nuh-tiv DIS-uh-ninss] A state in which individuals feel uncomfortable because they hold two or more thoughts, attitudes, or behaviors that are inconsistent with one another.

self-perception theory: An approach to attitude formation by which people are assumed to infer their attitudes based on observations of their own behavior.

An Alternative to Cognitive Dissonance Theory. Although cognitive dissonance theory has wide popularity, not all psychologists subscribe to it. Social psychologist Daryl Bem (1972) claims that people do not change their attitudes because of internal states such as dissonance. He contends that people often do not understand the causes of their own behavior, that they infer their attitudes and emotional states from the situations in which they find themselves. According to Bem, people can perceive their behavior only after the fact and in the context in which it occurred; that is, they can interpret their behavior only in a situational

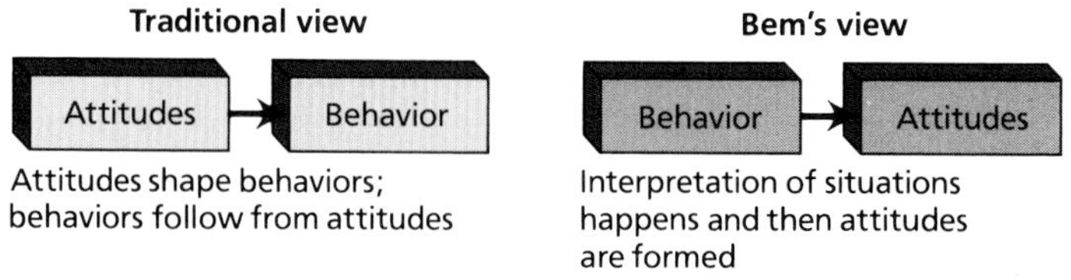

Figure 31.2

In a traditional view of attitudes and dissonance, behavior follows from attitudes. In Bem's approach, attitudes are determined *after* a person appraises his or her behavior in a situation.

context. His approach is **self-perception theory.** It suggests that people do not so much change their attitudes after inconsistent behavior but that they simply look at their behavior and say, "If I behaved in this way, I must have had this (consistent) attitude." See Figure 31.2 for an overview of the traditional view of attitude formation compared with Bem's view.

Balance Theory. **Balance theory** states that we prefer satisfying and harmonious relationships between our beliefs and the beliefs of others whom we like. For instance, if Don likes Paula and Don likes heavy metal music, he will feel a state of cognitive balance if he thinks Paula also likes heavy metal music. However, he will feel a state of imbalance if he thinks Paula does not like heavy metal music (see Figure 31.3). Like cognitive dissonance theory, balance theory can be considered a motivation theory. The unpleasant tension state that results from disagreement motivates people to change. Also, like cognitive dissonance theory, it assumes that people are decision makers whose thoughts ultimately determine their behavior.

balance theory: An attitude theory stating that people prefer to hold consistent beliefs and try to avoid incompatible beliefs.

Reactance Theory. Have you ever been ordered to do something (perhaps by a parent) that caused you to want to do the exact opposite? According to social psychologist Jack W. Brehm (1966), whenever people feel their freedom of choice is unjustly restricted, they are motivated to reestablish that freedom. Brehm terms this form of negative influence *reactance.* In reactance, what is inconsistent is the image of ourselves as free to choose and the realization that someone is trying to force us to choose an alternative.

Reactance theory is derived from the old notion of forbidden fruit. Whenever people are forbidden to do something, that activity often becomes more attractive. Choosing the forbidden fruit may provide an individual with a sense of autonomy. Thus, if an adolescent is told he cannot be friends with members of a minority group (thereby limiting his freedom of choice), he might seek out members of that group more often; thus, when coercion is used, resistance follows.

According to reactance theory, the extent of reactance is usually directly related to the extent of the restrictions on behavior. If the person does not consider the behavior to be very important and the restriction is slight, little reactance

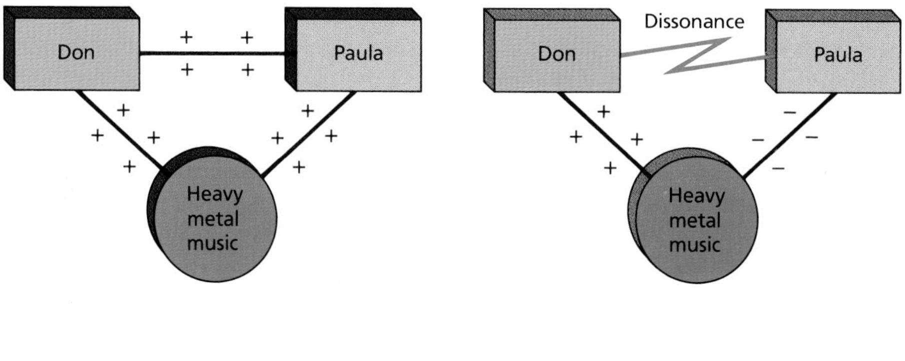

Figure 31.3

When Don and Paula both like the same things (heavy metal music, for example), we say their relationship is in balance (plus signs indicate liking; minus signs indicate disliking). However, when Don realizes that Paula doesn't like heavy metal music, he feels some dissonance—an imbalance exists.

develops. The wording or delivery of the restriction also affects the extent of reactance. A person who is told that she *must* respond in a certain way is more likely to react negatively than if she merely receives a suggestion or is given a relatively free choice in responding.

Social Cognition

Learning Objective 31.5
Define social cognition, and explain how various forms of nonverbal communication contribute to the impressions we form of others.

After meeting someone for the first time, you might say, "I really like him!" or "I can't explain why, but she rubs me the wrong way." Often, first impressions are based on nothing more than the other person's appearance, body language, and speech patterns. Yet these impressions can have lasting effects. How do we form attitudes about others?

Social cognition is the process of making sense of events and people, including ourselves, by analyzing and interpreting those people and events. Social cognition is a thought process that focuses on social information in memory and how it affects judgments, choices, evaluations, and ultimately our behavior (Sherman, Judd, & Park, 1989). The process often begins with our attempts to understand other people's communications, which can be verbal (through words) or nonverbal (through gazes, gestures, body movements, and other means of expression), and to form impressions of them. The process by which people use the behavior and appearance of others to infer their internal states and intentions is known as **impression formation;** usually, but not always, the impressions are accurate.

Nonverbal Communication

Impression formation often begins with **nonverbal communication** or messages. When a person "rubs you the wrong way," it may be due to a gesture, a grimace, or an averting of the eyes that generated your bad feelings. Nonverbal communication comes from many sources: the face, body movements, physical contact, and eye contact.

social cognition: The thought process of making sense through the interpretation of events, people, ourselves, and the world in general.

impression formation: A process by which people use the behavior and appearance of others to infer their internal states and intentions.

nonverbal communications: Information provided by cues or actions that involve movements of the body, especially the face, and sometimes the vocal cords (e.g., tone).

body language: The communication of information through body positions and gestures.

Facial Expressions. Many of the conclusions we draw from other people's communications are based on their facial expressions. Smiling expresses happiness; furrowed brows and eye twitching suggest anger, disgust, or fear. Recall from Chapter 9 that researchers find some people better at interpreting these expressions; similarly, people differ in their ability to convey information through nonverbal mechanisms. Nonetheless, most people can distinguish six basic emotions in the facial expressions of other people—love, joy, anger, sadness, fear, and surprise (Shaver et al., 1987).

Body Language. Facial expressions are not the only way people communicate nonverbally. They also convey information about their moods and attitudes through body position and gestures—a phenomenon termed **body language.** Body movements such as crossing the arms, lowering the head, and standing rigidly can all communicate negative attitudes.

Although differences in body language may be small, such differences exist, based on age and gender. The way in which younger people walk makes them appear sexier, more carefree, and happier than the way older people walk (Montepare & Zebrowitz-McArthur, 1988). Additionally, research shows that women are often better than men at communicating and interpreting nonverbal messages, especially facial expressions (Hall, 1979). Women are more likely to send nonverbal facial messages but are also more cautious in interpreting nonverbal messages sent to them by men (Rosenthal & DePaulo, 1979).

Eye Contact. Researchers are well aware of another form of nonverbal communication—the *eyes* convey a surprising amount of information about feelings. When a person looks at you, he or she may gaze briefly or may stare. You might glance or stare back. Psychologists term this process *making eye contact.* You would probably gaze tenderly at someone you find attractive but avoid eye contact with someone you do not trust or like or do not know well (Teske, 1988). When people are looked at, they accept it as a sign of being liked. Frequent eye contact between a man and a woman may indicate that they are sexually attracted to each other.

We tend to judge people by the eye contact they make with us. Generally, people prefer modest amounts of eye contact rather than constant or no eye contact. Job applicants, for example, are rated more favorably when they make moderate amounts of eye contact, and speakers who make more rather than less eye contact are preferred. We know that other people judge us by superficial characteristics such as our clothes, our weight, or the car we drive. People spend significant amounts of time and money trying to manage the impression that they make on others through spiffy clothes, dieting, and just the right auto to make the desired impression.

Facial expressions and eye contact convey as much about our attitudes and intentions as do our spoken words.

Attribution

Learning Objective 31.6 Describe the attribution process, explain two common attribution errors, and discuss how we are influenced by the "just-world belief."

If it's noon and you see people eating hamburgers and french fries, you can be fairly certain that they are eating because they are hungry. Similarly, if you see a man at the bus stop reading the Muslim holy book, the Koran, you might infer that he is a devout Moslem. In getting to know other people, we often infer the causes of their behavior. When we do, we are making attributions.

Attribution is the process by which someone infers or decides about other people's motives and intentions from observing their behavior, deciding whether the causes of behavior are *dispositional* (internal) or *situational* (external). Through attribution, people decide how they will react toward others; they attempt to evaluate and to make sense of their social world.

At first, attribution seems like a fairly straightforward process based on common sense. However, keep in mind that it must take into account internal as well as external causes of behavior. If someone makes an *internal attribution,* he or she feels that the behavior comes from within the person, from the individual's personality or abilities. If someone makes an *external attribution,* he or she believes that the person's behavior is caused by outside events, such as the weather or luck. In other words, if internal causes seem to predominate, a person's behavior will be attributed to his or her personality or abilities; if external causes predominate, the behavior is attributed to the situation.

attribution: The process by which someone infers other people's motives and intentions from observing their behavior; a key focus is whether the causes of behavior are considered *dispositional* (internal) or *situational* (external).

Errors in Attribution. Social psychologists have found that we are often mistaken or biased in our attributions. Some of the most common types of errors have been identified, including the fundamental attribution error and the actor–observer effect. When people commit the **fundamental attribution error,** they assume that a person's behavior is caused by internal dispositons—which may or may not be true. They underestimate situational influences and overestimate dispositional influences upon other people's behavior. A man may have lost his temper after being overcharged for an item; a woman may have become hostile because the waiter spilled soup on her and did not apologize.

fundamental attribution error: The tendency to attribute behavior to individual dispositional (internal) causes rather than to situational (external) causes; usually occurs when explaining the behavior of other people.

Another kind of error in attribution is the **actor–observer effect,** or the tendency for people to attribute the behavior of others to dispositional causes, but to attribute their own behavior to situational causes. When a young child gets hurt, he or she often says, "You made me hurt myself." However, when a friend gets hurt, the same child may say, "You're clumsy." If you fail an exam, you may blame it on your roommate whose radio kept you from concentrating on your studies. However, when someone else fails an exam, you may wonder about the person's intelligence.

A Just World? According to Melvin Lerner (1970), many people believe that an appropriate relationship exists between what they do and what happens to them. In other words, they believe that the world is just, that people get what they deserve. A negative consequence of the *just-world belief* is that victims of crime, poverty, illness, and other misfortune are often treated as if they brought these things on themselves (Connors & Heaven, 1989). People may blame female rape victims for wearing seductive clothing or too much makeup, for acting too friendly toward men, or for going out alone after dark (see McCaul et al., 1990). The realization that bad things can happen to good people threatens our belief that the world is just. The ability to see that someone else has been treated unfairly can upset an individual's belief in a just world and perhaps motivate him or her to rectify the situation or compensate someone who was unfairly punished, thus trying to reestablish justice.

Self-perception

Learning Objective 31.7
Explain how self-perceptions develop and how they affect our perceptions of others.

How would you describe yourself? **Self-perceptions** are people's attitudes toward and beliefs about themselves, and they are greatly affected by how other people perceive them. Thus, when social psychologists study self-perception, they examine how other people and social situations affect how people see themselves, and how that perception influences everyday behavior. Social psychologists study self-perceptions through surveys, interviews, naturalistic observation, and traditional experimental methods.

actor–observer effect: The tendency for people to attribute the behavior of other people to dispositional causes, while attributing their own behavior to situational causes.

self-perception: Attitudes toward and beliefs about oneself, largely formed during childhood and adolescence and often a reflection of other people's perceived attitudes.

role: A set of behaviors expected from a certain category of individuals; a person's roles may change depending on the context of the social group.

Developing Self-perceptions. Established early in life and reevaluated frequently, self-perceptions develop over time and from experience. At first, children get answers to questions such as, "Mommy, am I pretty?" or "Mommy, do you like me?" to help form self-perceptions. Adolescents then reassess their early self-perceptions, which enables them to establish a firm identity consistent with both previous attitudes and new values. Successful completion of adolescence (which Erikson calls the identity crisis) results in a person's ability to adapt to new situations while retaining a firm understanding of self and personal values.

Over the years, people develop a sense of themselves by combining aspects of their family, occupational, recreational, and gender roles. A **role** is a set of behaviors expected from a specific group of individuals. Our culture, for example, has certain expectations for men, women, various ethnic groups, leaders, and those in various social positions. Roles for individuals are sometimes established on the basis of prominent physical cues, such as height, where people expect tall men and women to play basketball and do not expect shorter people to enjoy or play it; in some ways, people are lazy about paying attention to other aspects of a person's behavior (Fiske, 1989). People also develop self-perceptions by comparing themselves to others and seeing how they measure up. Thus, athletes compare themselves to better athletes, as well as to less competent ones, and high school juniors compare their academic and social skills both to other juniors and to sophomores and seniors.

Perceiving Others. We perceive others in relation to our own value systems and ideas—our self-perceptions. An assertive person, for example, may view other assertive people as expressing normal, appropriate behavior. A quiet, shy, and passive person, on the other hand, may view assertive people as inappropriate, loud, or even aggressive. A person's frame of reference usually starts with himself or herself, and a comparison is made. Then the person compares an individual to other people, or an absolute standard, and makes an overall evaluation.

Physical Appearance. Many factors determine a person's self-perception, including physical appearance, work habits, athletic abilities, and success as a parent or mate. According to a substantial body of literature, one of these factors—physical appearance—sharply affects people's attitudes toward others. In turn, those attitudes, expressed in behavior, influence how people perceive themselves.

In general, attractive people are judged to have more positive traits and characteristics than are unattractive people, especially when appearance is the first information provided (Benassi, 1982). For example, teachers believe that attractive children get higher marks and misbehave less than do unattractive children. Attractive children are also predicted to have more successful careers. The same process occurs with adults: Attractive people are granted more freedom and liberties and perceived as more fair and competent than unattractive people (Cherulnik, Turns, & Wilderman, 1990). Thus, attractive college professors are seen as better teachers and are less likely to be blamed if a student receives a failing grade in a course (Romano & Bordieri, 1989).

It is unfortunate that people's self-concepts and their status in other people's eyes may be largely determined by superficial characteristics such as physical attractiveness, which can set them up for a lifelong pattern of reinforcement or punishment. Physically unattractive and different people tend to be isolated, to be ignored by members of both sexes, and to have negative traits attributed to them, and this makes employers less likely to hire them (Forsythe, 1990). In addition, people who perceive themselves as physically unattractive are more likely to have anxiety problems in dealing with members of the opposite sex.

Learning Objective 31.8 Explain how self-serving biases influence our self-esteem.

Self-serving Biases. Social psychologists have found that most people are not realistic in evaluating themselves, their capabilities, or their behavior. The **self-serving bias** refers to people's tendency to evaluate their own behavior as worthwhile, regardless of the situation. Most people consider themselves more charitable, more giving, more intelligent, more considerate, more sensitive, more likely to succeed, and more of a leader than they consider most other people.

Errors in attribution, discussed earlier, contribute to self-serving biases. People tend to take credit for their successes and blame others for their failures; e.g., people assume that good things happen to them because they deserve them and that bad things happen to other people because, in a just world, they deserve them. When something bad happens to you, you may blame it on bad luck or circumstances. When something bad happens to others, you may blame it on their careless or reckless behavior. This combination of attribution errors and a self-serving bias helps some people maintain self-esteem and appear competent. Such an attitude, however, may inhibit people from having realistic goals, thus setting them up for disappointment. They may develop and exhibit maladjusted or abnormal behavior, as we saw in Chapter 14. One reason that people may use self-serving attribution biases and errors is to develop a sense of control that enables

self-serving bias: People's tendency to evaluate their own behavior as worthwhile, regardless of the situation.

Feeling overwhelmed and without resources, some people give up on changing the negative aspects of their lives, a behavior known as learned helplessness.

them to maintain self-esteem and belief in their own ability to succeed and be happy. Therefore, although people misrepresent reality through attribution biases and errors, they feel that they gain control over their lives and their ability to get what they need.

Learned Helplessness

Learning Objective 31.9 Explain how learned helplessness develops.

Most people feel they can control their environment to a reasonable extent. They develop a successful internal locus of control (Rotter 1991). What happens to people in a situation in which they feel they have little control, though? How do they react when negative things happen to them? Assume that you are a subject in an experiment in which you have to solve puzzles. The puzzles appear relatively simple, yet no matter what you, do, you cannot find the correct sequence. You probably become frustrated.

Real-life situations in which people have no control over events also create frustration. A university instructor who wants to use audiovisual presentations, for example, may find that the university will not purchase a projector. She will undoubtedly feel some frustration. A student blocked from taking courses she needs to graduate will similarly feel frustrated and helpless.

Research has shown that both people and animals, when put in situations in which they have no control over the negative things happening to them, often stop responding. Martin Seligman (1975) and his colleagues showed, for example, that dogs first exposed to a series of inescapable shocks and then given a chance to escape further punishment fail to learn the escape response. Seligman termed this behavior **learned helplessness.** According to Seligman, the major cause of learned helplessness is an organism's belief that its response will not affect what happens to it in the future. In such cases, anxiety, depression, and eventually nonresponsiveness result. Of course, the opposite of learned helplessness is *learned optimism,* a sense that the world has positive outcomes over which people can see happy positive outcomes in their lives (Seligman, 1991)—in both cases Seligman argues that learning is the key to a sense of doom or optimism.

learned helplessness: The behavior of giving up or not responding, exhibited by subjects exposed to negative consequences or punishment over which they have no control.

Progress Check 31.1

Complete the following sentences with one of the options provided.

(L.O. 31.1) a. Social psychologists are primarily interested in the behavior of ________ and how such behavior is influenced by the thoughts, feelings, and behaviors of people. (individuals / groups / cultures)

(L.O. 31.2) b. Sending a donation to your favorite charity represents the ________ dimension of the attitude, "It is good to help those who are less fortunate." (cognitive / emotional / behavioral)

(L.O. 31.3) c. If people hear a particular argument, advertisement, or political view often enough, they begin to believe it ________ value. (regardless of its / because they can finally understand why it has)

(L.O. 31.3) d. People are more likely to be persuaded by new information if they receive it from ________. (a friend / a popular television news program)

(L.O. 31.4) e. Attitude and behavior changes made in an attempt to reduce cognitive dissonance occur because people need to have a sense of ________ in their lives. (consistency / success)

(L.O. 31.4) f. Cognitive dissonance theory and balance theory can both be considered ________ theories because they describe how unpleasant feelings energize people to change. (motivation / social)

(L.O. 31.5) g. Most people are able to distinguish ________ basic emotions through facial expressions. (6 / 10)

(L.O. 31.5) h. Research has found that ________ are generally better at communicating and interpreting nonverbal facial expressions. (men / women)

(L.O. 31.6) i. You will be more likely to attribute an individual's behavior to personality or ability if it seems that ________ factors had a primary influence on motivating the person. (internal / external)

(L.O. 31.6) j. When we accuse someone of having an explosive character without considering the situational factors that surrounded the person's expression of anger, we may be making an error in attribution termed the ________. (fundamental attribution error / actor—observer effect)

(L.O. 31.6) k. When attributing causes to our own behavior, we tend to focus on ________ causes. (dispositional / situational)

(L.O. 31.7) l. Feedback concerning ________ seems to have the greatest influence on a person's self-perception. (physical appearance / potential)

(L.O. 31.8) m. People with self-serving biases are generally ________ (unrealistic about themselves and their goals / motivated to please others)

(L.O. 31.9) n. When people are placed in situations in which they have no control over the negative things happening to them, they frequently ________. (conform to conventional norms / stop responding)

Social Influence

Social influence is the way in which one or more people alter the attitudes or behavior of others. For example, parents try to instill specific values in their children. An adolescent may notice the hairstyle or mannerism of an attractive peer and decide to adopt it. Professors urge students to shed preconceived ideas. The behavior and appearance of a celebrity may be emulated by adoring fans. Religious leaders exhort their followers to live in certain ways. A person who has observed esteemed scientists adopt a new belief in the validity of the Shroud of Turin may come to believe in its authenticity. People exert a powerful influence on others, and psychologists have attempted to understand how this influence

social influence: The way in which one or more people alter the attitudes or behavior of others.

operates. Studies of social influence have focused on two topics: conformity and obedience.

Conformity

Learning Objective 31.10
Describe Asch's classic conformity experiment, and identify variables that influence a person's need to conform.

People conform to the behaviors and attitudes of their peer or family groups. A successful young executive might wear conservative dark suits and drive a BMW in order to fit in with office colleagues. Similarly, the desire to conform can induce people to do things they might not do otherwise.

Conformity occurs when a person changes his or her attitudes or behaviors to be consistent with other people or with social norms. The behaviors they might adopt include positive, prosocial behaviors such as wearing seatbelts, volunteering time and money for a charity, or buying only products that are safe for the environment. Sometimes, however, people conform to counterproductive, antisocial behaviors, such as becoming involved in drug use, hazing in fraternities, or becoming part of an angry mob.

Conformity Experiment. Suppose you have agreed to participate in an experiment of line discriminations. You are seated at the end of a table next to four other students. The experimenter holds up a card and asks each of you to pick which of two lines is longer, A or B. You quickly discover that the task is simple. The experimenter proceeds to hold up successive pairs of lines, with each participant correctly identifying the longest. Suddenly, after several rounds, you notice that the first person has chosen line A instead of line B, which is obviously longer. You are surprised when the second person also chooses line A, then the third, then the fourth. Your turn is next. You are sure that line B is longer. What do you do?

In 1951, Solomon Asch performed a similar experiment to explore conformity. Seven to nine subjects were brought into a room and told that they would be participating in an experiment involving visual judgment, such as that found in Figure 31.4; subjects had to judge which of three lines matched a standard. However, only one group member was a naïve subject; the others were collaborators of

Conformity is the course most people choose to take, but some individuals prefer a greater degree of independence and are willing to risk social disapproval for it.

the researcher, and they deliberately gave false answers to try to influence the naïve subject. Asch found that the naïve subject will generally go along with the group, even though the majority answer is obviously wrong and even though the group exerts no explicit or directly observable pressure to do so.

Although only some of the naïve subjects conformed in Asch's experiments, enough did so that psychologists have researched the phenomenon further. They have found the number of people in the group to be a critical variable. When one or two individuals collaborate with the researcher, the tendency to conform is considerably less than when 10 do. Another important variable is the number of dissenting votes—if even 1 of 15 people disagrees with the other collaborating subjects, the naïve subject is more likely to choose the correct line.

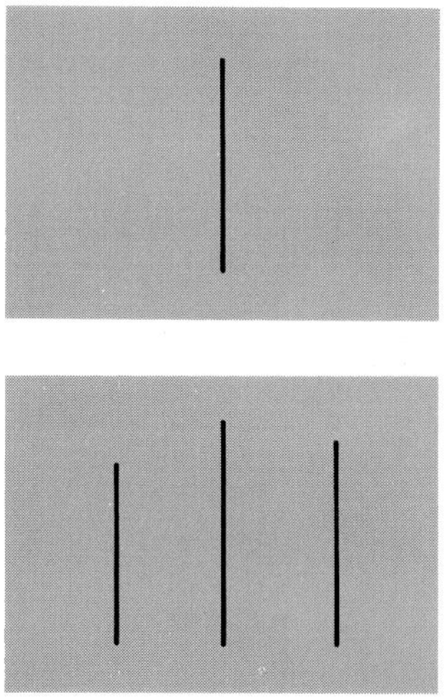

Figure 31.4

Asch's line-drawing task. Subjects were shown these cards and asked to choose the line in the picture on the bottom that was the same length as the line in the picture on the top.

Variables in Conformity. How do groups influence individual behavior? One variable is the amount of information provided when a decision is made. When people are uncertain of how to behave in ambiguous situations, they seek the opinions of others. For example, when they are unsure of how they should vote in an election, people often ask trusted friends for advice.

Another important variable that determines the degree of conformity is the relative competence of the group. People are more likely to conform to the decision of a group if they perceive its members as more competent than themselves. This pressure becomes stronger as group size increases. The extent to which behavior is public also determines people's responses. Individuals are more willing to make decisions that are inconsistent with those of their group when behavior is private.

Both everyday experience and research show that *dissenting opinions* help counteract group influence and conformity. Even one or two people in a large group can seriously influence decision making. Moreover, when group decision making occurs, a consistent minority can exert substantial influence, even when it is devoid of power, status, or even competence (Mungy, 1982).

Obedience and Milgram's Study

Learning Objective 31.11 Describe Milgram's classic obedience study, identify factors that influenced the results, and discuss the ethics of studies such as this one.

According to psychologists, **obedience** is the process by which a person complies with the orders of another person or group. Stanley Milgram's (1933–1984) studies on obedience are classic. Today, his results and interpretations still generate debate.

Milgram's work focuses on the extent to which an individual obeys a significant person. His studies, which showed that ordinary people were remarkably willing to comply with the wishes of others, especially if the others were seen as important, reveals a great deal about the social world, about social influence in general, and about obedience in particular. They also reveal something about an individual's self-perception, values, and early interactions in life.

Milgram (1963) appeared to bring two subjects into a laboratory and told them that they were participating in an experiment on paired-associate learning. The subjects drew lots to determine who would be the teacher and who would be the learner. In actuality, the drawing was rigged; one subject was collaborating with the experimenter. The naïve subject was always the teacher; the collaborator was always the learner.

The learner–collaborator was taken to an adjoining room, where the teacher–naïve subject could not see her or him. The teacher–naïve subject was shown a shock-generator box containing 30 switches, each labeled with varying shock intensities from low shock to danger—severe shock. The teacher–naïve subject was told to shock the learner by hitting one of the switches every time he or she made an error.

obedience: The process by which a person complies with the orders of another person or group of people.

A social psychologist and an assistant, both wearing white lab coats, encouraged the naïve subject to increase the shock voltage one level each time the learner made a mistake. As the shock level rose, the learner–collaborator screamed *as if* suffering increasing pain. When the shock intensity reached the point of severe shock, the learner stopped responding vocally to the paired-associate stimulus and pounded on the walls of the experimental booth. The psychologist directed the teacher to treat the learner's lack of response as an error and to continue to administer increasing levels of shock. As Figure 31.5 shows, 65% of the subjects continued to shock the learner until all the shock levels were delivered. (You may have guessed by now that the learner–collaborators were not actually receiving shocks; they were only pretending to be in pain.)

Not all Milgram's subjects were obedient. Moreover, the presence of other subjects who refused to participate reduced the probability of obedience to as little as 10% (Milgram, 1965a). These data suggest that behavior is sensitive to both authority and peer behavior. An individual's ability to resist coercion in the presence of an ally who also refuses to participate indicates the importance of social influences on behavior.

Explaining Milgram's Results. Why did so many subjects in Milgram's experiments obey the wishes of the authority figure? One reason is that the subjects were volunteers, and volunteers often bring undetected biases to an experimental situation, and one such bias is to go along with authority. Another is that the experimental situation can itself bias the outcome. Perhaps the subjects were willing to administer the shocks only because they knew they were participating in an experiment or because they were instructed to do so by the experimenter, and they might not act the same way without being told to do so or when outside the experimental context.

Obedience to authority figures can also be explained by learning theories. Children learn that authority figures, such as teachers and parents, know more than they do and that taking their advice generally proves beneficial. As adults, they maintain those beliefs, with the authority figures being employers, judges, government leaders, and so on.

Not only do we obey those in authority, we also take directives from people who look authoritative. People who take on the trappings of power (expensive clothes, uniforms, prestigious cars, fancy offices) are often treated as authority

Milgram's studies questioned to what degree behavior is sensitive to both authority and peer pressure. Surprisingly, most subjects were willing to deliver extreme levels of shock when told to do so. The man on the right was one of the few subjects who quit the experiment rather than deliver such shocks.

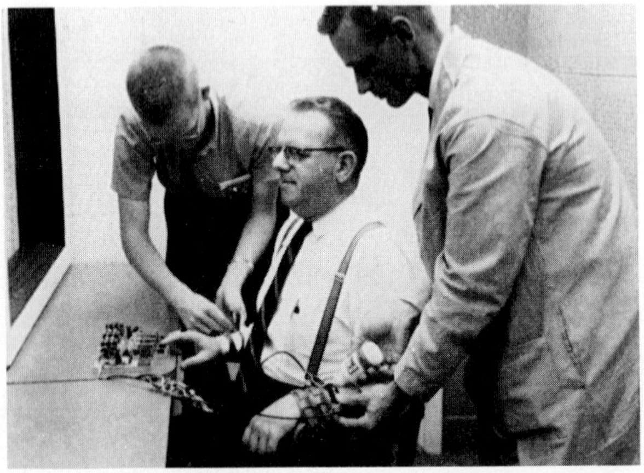

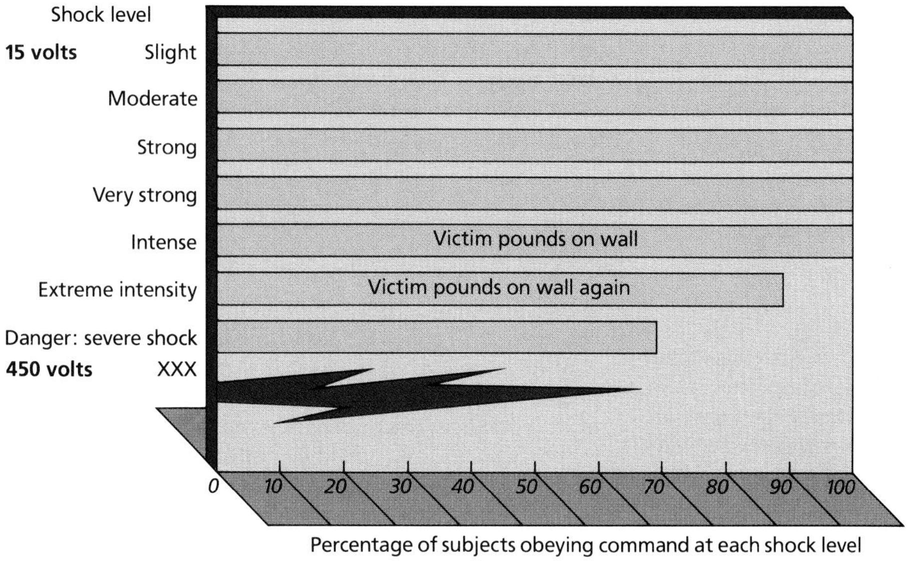

Figure 31.5

In a study by Milgram, 65% of the subjects were willing to use the highest levels of shock intensity. Virtually all subjects were willing to provide shocks they thought to be of moderate or strong intensity. (Source: Data from Milgram, 1963)

figures. We are more likely to heed security guards who dress in uniforms that look like police garb than those who wear clothing of a less official appearance. As we saw in Milgram's conformity studies, people rely on symbols to make quick decisions, although the decisions are sometimes irrational.

Ethical Issues. Milgram's experimental methods raise several ethical questions. The primary issue is deception and potential harm to the subjects who participated. Obtaining unbiased responses in psychological research often requires deceiving naïve subjects. After the experiment, subjects are then debriefed. **Debriefing** informs subjects about the true nature of the experiment after its completion. Debriefing preserves both the validity of the responses and ethical considerations; of course, debriefing must be done carefully, because if done poorly, it can do more harm than good.

Milgram's subjects were fully debriefed and shown that they had not actually harmed the other person. Nevertheless, critics argue, the subjects realized that they were capable of inflicting severe pain on other people. Milgram therefore had a psychiatrist interview a sample of his obedient subjects a year after the study. No evidence was found of psychological trauma or injury. Moreover, one study reported that subjects viewed participation in the obedience experiment as a positive experience. They did not regret having participated, nor did they report any short-term negative psychological effects (Ring, Wallston, & Corey, 1970).

Implications. Milgram's studies have important implications for social psychologists. They show how people of authority can change the course of events and even influence history; people in positions of power tend to be obeyed. Milgram's findings are cross-cultural and apply to men and women, old and young; they show that the social world and our interactions within it are strongly affected by other people. Powerful people in positions of authority can change the course of events and indeed potentially influence history (consider Hitler, Khaddafi, or the Pope). Milgram's studies challenge social psychologists to know why people obey and why people in lower positions in a hierarchy (e.g., government, a school, or an industry) will not challenge authority. They also encourage us to ask how do other people influence us to comply with their wishes, the topic considered in the Applying Psychology box on the next page.

debriefing: A procedure to inform subjects about the true nature of an experiment after its completion.

APPLYING PSYCHOLOGY

Influence Techniques

How can we influence others? How can others influence us? What techniques facilitate compliance or at least attitude change? Managers, salespeople, parents, and politicians all apply the principles of social psychology and influence people daily by using social psychological techniques, such as foot in the door, door in the face, ask and you shall be given, low balling, modeling, and incentives.

Foot in the Door. To get someone to change an attitude or grant a favor, begin by asking for a small attitude change or a small favor. In other words, get your foot in the door. Ask to borrow a quarter today, a dollar next week, and money for your tuition within a month.

The essence of the *foot-in-the-door* effect is that if a person grants a small request, he or she is more likely to comply with a larger request later. It only works, however, if the person first grants the small favor, and it works best if there is some time between the first small request and the later large one. If the person says no to the first favor, it may be even easier to say no to subsequent ones. Although the foot-in-the-door effect is relatively easy to find in American society, cross-cultural studies show that it does not occur as easily in all countries (Kilbourne, 1989).

Door in the Face. To use the *door-in-the-face* technique, first ask for something outrageous; then later ask for something much smaller and more reasonable. That is, use reverse psycholgy. Ask a friend to lend you $100; after being turned down, ask to borrow $5. Your friend may be relieved to grant the smaller favor.

The principle of the door-in-the-face effect is that a person is more likely to grant a small request if he or she has previously turned down a larger one. It appears to work because people do not want to be seen turnig down someone twice, and it works best if there is little time in between requests. To look good and maintain a positive self-image, they agree to the lesser of two requests.

Ask and You Shall Be Given. When people ask for money for a good cause, whether the request is large or small, they usually will get a positive response. Ask someone who has given before, and the request is even more likely to be granted (Doob & McLaughlin, 1989). Fund raisers for universities, churches, and museums know that asking usually will get a positive response.

Lowballing. *Lowballing* is a compliance technique by which a person is influenced to make a decision or commitment because of the low stakes associated with it. Once the decision is made, the stakes might increase, but the person will likely stick with the original decision. For example, if a man agrees to buy a car for $9000, he may still buy it even if the saleswoman increases the price to $10,000. Lowballing works because people tend to stick to their commitments, even if the stakes are raised. Changing one's mind may suggest a lack of good judment, cause stress, and make the person feel as if he or she were violating an (often imaginary) obligation.

Modeling. Showing someone good behavior, such as conserving energy or saying "no" to drugs, increases the likelihood that the person will behave similarly. The person being observed is a model for the desired behavior. *Modeling,* which was discussed in Chapter 5, is a powerful technique by which people learn and adopt new behaviors and attitudes by witnessing others engaged in those behaviors and then expressing those attitudes themselves. When well-known athletes publicly declare their attitudes about the scourge of drugs, they act as models for youngsters who aspire to careers such as theirs.

Incentives. Nothing succeeds in eliciting a particular behavior better than a desired incentive. Offering a 16-year-old unlimited use of the family car if he or she sets the table every day for dinner usually results in a neatly set dinner table. Offering a large monetary bonus to a sales agent for year-end sales performance usually boosts sales efforts.

We can influence others and induce attitude change by using techniques that researchers have studied in the laboratory. Researchers have shown that the way a request is framed, the approach that a person takes, or the incentives that are offered can be critical in determining whether people will comply. Shopkeepers, parents, and politicians all apply these principles to convince and persuade other people. In studies of groups, many other factors operate to influence individual behavior.

- ***On what principle does the foot-in-the-door effect rely?***
- ***What evidence exists to show that modeling is a way of inducing compliance?***
- ***On what principle does the idea that increased incentives affect behavior rely?***

Behavior in Groups

Learning Objective 31.12
Identify the characteristics of a group; describe social facilitation, social loafing, group polarization, and groupthink; and explain why each of these phenomena occur.

"Membership has its privileges," according to American Express. By appealing to people's desire to be part of a group, the charge-card company is employing psychological principles to sell its product and engender loyalty. To make the American Express group as attractive as possible, the company runs magazine ads featuring famous athletes, actors, politicians, and businesspeople who are card members. Who wouldn't want to identify with such an elite group?

Membership does confer certain advantages, which is why people belong to all kinds of groups. There are formal groups, such as the American Association of University Students, and informal ones, such as peer groups. A **group** can be either a large number of people working toward a common purpose or a small number of people, even two, who are loosely related and have some common goals or interests. Members of groups share characteristics and goals and recognize their relationship with one another and a sense of shared purpose. By joining a group, people indicate that they agree with or have a serious interest in its purpose. If a major function of the American Cancer Society is to raise money for cancer research, a person's membership indicates willingness to raise money for this purpose.

group: A number of individuals (two or more) who are loosely or cohesively related and share some common characteristics and goals.

social facilitation: The change in task performance that occurs when people believe they are in the presence of other people.

Social Facilitation

Individual behavior is affected not only by joining a group but also by the presence of a group. One effect of the presence of a group is **social facilitation**—a change in performance, either better or worse, because of the presence (or imagined presence) of other people. For example, someone practicing a new sport such as basketball with a degree of success may do even better when other people enter the court. Another person, however, may do worse when other people are around. How the presence of others changes our behavior, and whether it changes for better or worse, is illustrated in Figure 31.6, which is based on the generally accepted theory of Robert Zajonc (1965).

According to Zajonc, the presence of others produces heightened arousal, which leads to a greater likelihood of performing likely responses. Bond and Titus

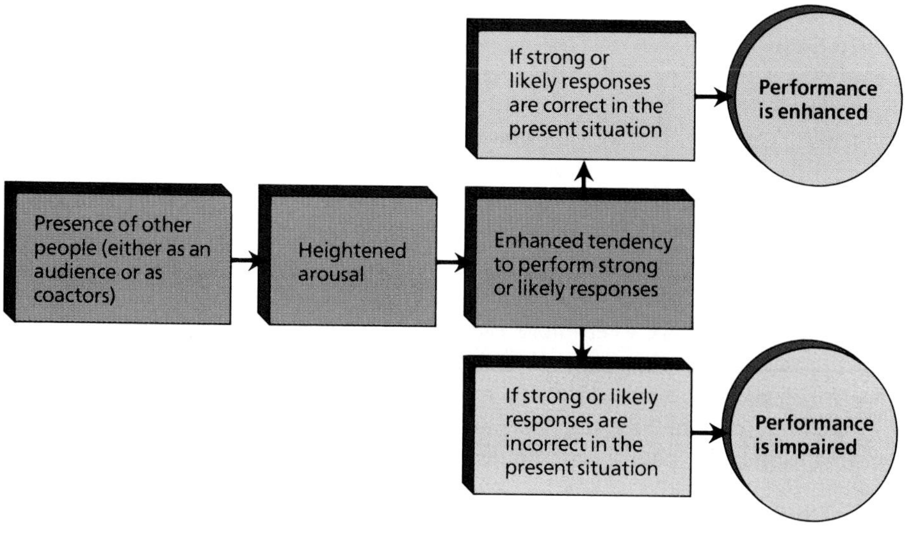

Figure 31.6

According to the *drive theory* of social facilitation, the presence of other people increases our level of motivation or arousal, which, in turn, enhances the performance of our strongest or most likely responses in a given situation. If these responses are correct, performance is enhanced. If they are incorrect, performance is impaired.

social loafing: The decrease in productivity that occurs when an individual works in a group instead of alone.

group polarization: The exaggeration of individuals' preexisting attitudes as a result of group discussion.

(1983) suggest that the effects of social facilitation are often overestimated, and the effects of believing oneself to be observed are often underestimated. They caution that a model of social facilitation must take into account the actual and believed presence of observers, as well as the perceived importance of the evaluation by the perceived observers.

Social Loafing

A decrease in an individual's effort and productivity as a result of working in a group is **social loafing.** Social loafing was shown in an early experiment, in which individuals had to pull on a rope, either alone or with help: They exerted more effort alone than when other people helped. Similarly, in an experiment in which individuals were instructed to clap their hands and cheer, they clapped and cheered less loudly when they were part of a group (Latane, Williams, & Harkins, 1979).

Most psychologists claim that social loafing occurs when individual performance within a group cannot be evaluated: Poor performance may go undetected, and exceptional performance may go unrecognized. Consequently, people feel less pressure to work hard or efficiently. One study showed that as group size increased, individual members felt their own efforts were more dispensable—the group could function without their help. "Let George do it!" became the prevailing attitude (Kerr & Bruun, 1983).

Social loafing is minimized when the task is attractive and rewarding and the group is committed to high task performance (Zaccaro, 1984). It is also less apparent when a group is small, when the members know each other well, and when a group leader calls on individuals by name or lets it be known that individual performance may be evaluated (Williams, Harkins, & Latane, 1981). Some researchers have noted decreased social loafing when people have the opportunity to evaluate their own performance relative to other people's, despite the fact that no one else evaluated them (Szymanski & Harkins, 1987), as well as when people evaluated their performance against an objective standard, again when no one else evaluated them (Harkins & Szymanski, 1988).

Group Polarization

In groups people are often willing to adopt behaviors slightly more extreme than their individual behaviors. They are willing to make decisions that are risky or even daring. A person who by himself is unwilling to invest money in a venture may change his mind on hearing that other members of the group are investing. Some early research on group decision making focused on the willingness of individuals to accept more risky alternatives when other members of the group did so. Such formulations described individuals as making a *risky shift* in their decisions.

People in a group initially perceive themselves as being more extreme than the other members of the group. They believe they are more fair, more right-minded, more liberal, and so on. When they discover that their positions are not very different from those of others in the group, they shift, or become *polarized,* to show that they are even more right-minded, more fair, or more liberal. They often become more assertive in expressing their views. This phenomenon is known as **group polarization.** If a group becomes polarized, there are two exaggerated opposing opinions. When such an event occurs (as it often does with government officials), people sometimes fall into a trap called *groupthink* discussed next.

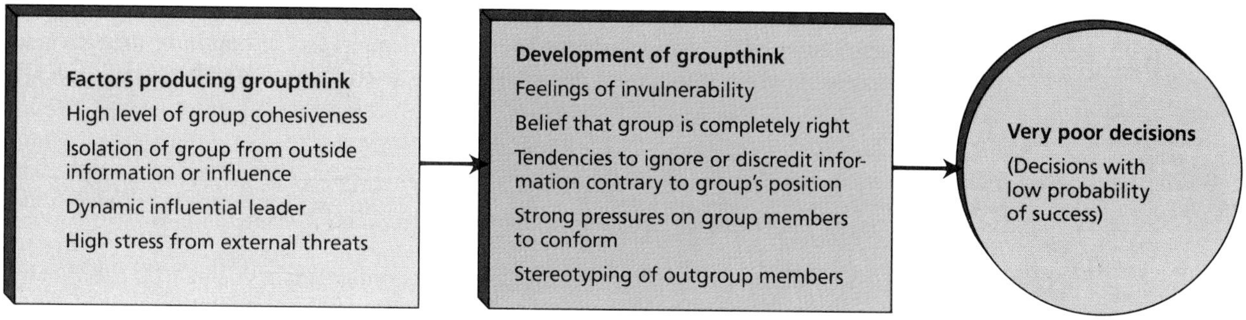

Factors producing groupthink
High level of group cohesiveness
Isolation of group from outside information or influence
Dynamic influential leader
High stress from external threats
Development of groupthink
Feelings of invulnerability
Belief that group is completely right
Tendencies to ignore or discredit information contrary to group's position
Strong pressures on group members to conform
Stereotyping of outgroup members
Very poor decisions
(Decisions with low probability of success)

Figure 31.7

Factors leading to the development of *groupthink*.

Groupthink

Studies of decision making in government have relied heavily on a concept from the social psychology laboratory. The concept is **groupthink,** the tendency of people in a group to seek concurrence with each other when reaching a decision, usually prematurely. Groupthink occurs when group members reinforce commonly held beliefs in the interest of getting along, rather than effectively evaluating alternative solutions to the problem. The group does not allow its members to disagree or to take dissenting opinions and evaluate options realistically (Janis, 1983). It discredits or ignores information not held in common. See Figure 31.7 for a summary of the factors producing groupthink.

Social psychologist Ivan Steiner (1982) suggests that groupthink occurs when members' overriding concern is to maintain group cohesiveness and harmony. Others maintain that it occurs when individuals in a group feel a sense of cohesiveness and believe that the group cannot make mistakes. Strong leaders often insulate a group from information or other people to keep the group thinking in one direction (McCauley, 1989). Although groupthink is not inevitable, it is common enough so that social psychologists consider it an important issue in group influence on decision making. They look at it in terms of group behavior, social in-

groupthink: The phenomenon of people in a group reinforcing each other and seeking concurrence and group cohesiveness, rather than effectively evaluating choices and reasoning.

Deindividuation of members within a group encourages conformity, even at the expense of personal qualms.

fluence, and a self-serving and self-reinforcing mechanism. Students of political science, government, and history can use the concept of groupthink to train new leaders to avoid unplanned decision making and to avoid irrational behaviors.

Progress Check 31.2

Complete the following sentences with one of the options provided.

(L.O. 31.10) a. Asch found that an individual tends to go along with a group's opinion ________. (even when it is obviously wrong / only when it appears to be accurate)

(L.O. 31.10) b. A small, consistent minority that has little or no power, status, or competence ________ influence on the decision-making process of a large group. (generally has little / can have substantial)

(L.O. 31.11) c. Milgram found that the probability of obedience dropped significantly when subjects ________. (were certain that the shocks were real / had allies that refused to participate)

(L.O. 31.11) d. ________ is a procedure used to protect subjects who participated in a psychological experiment involving deception. (Psychotherapy / Debriefing)

(L.O. 31.11) e. Milgram's findings concerning obedience to authority seem to ________. (apply across cultures, gender, and age groups / be limited to timid people)

(L.O. 31.12) f. Two or more people constitute what is called a "group" as long as they ________. (are together in the same location / have a shared purpose)

(L.O. 31.12) g. Social facilitation seems to influence an individual's behavior because ________. (observers provide encouragement / arousal increases when others are present)

(L.O. 31.12) h. Social loafing occurs because individual performance within a group ________. (cannot be evaluated / is indispensable)

(L.O. 31.12) i. ________ occurs when individuals within a group exaggerate their initial opinions. (Group polarization / Groupthink)

Module Summary

Attitudes

- *Social psychology* is the study of how people influence and are influenced by the thoughts, feelings, and behaviors of other people. Social psychologists focus on individual behavior, on how individuals form attitudes and feelings about themselves and other people, and on individuals' responses to others (p. 598).
- *Attitudes* are lasting patterns of feelings, beliefs, and behavior tendencies toward other people, ideas, or objects. Most psychologists contend that attitudes have three basic dimensions—cognitive, emotional, and behavioral (p. 598).

Social Cognition

- *Social cognition* is the process of making sense of events and people, including ourselves, by analyzing and interpreting those people and events. The process by which people use the behavior and appearance of others to infer their internal states and intentions is impression formation (p. 602).
- *Attribution* is the process by which someone infers other people's motives and intentions from observing their behavior. The focus is usually on deciding if the causes of behavior are dispositional or situational (p. 603).

Social Influence

- *Social influence* is the way in which one or more people alter the attitudes or behavior of others (p. 607).
- *Conformity* occurs when a person changes his or her attitudes or behaviors to be consistent with other people or with social norms. The social conformity approach states that people conform to avoid the stigma of being wrong, deviant, out of line, or different from others (p. 608).
- *Obedience* is the process by which a person complies with the orders of another person or group of people. Obedience studies showed that ordinary people were remarkably willing to comply with the wishes of others, especially if the others were seen as authorities (p. 609).

Behavior in Groups

- Social psychologists have shown that individual and group behavior is dramatically affected by the presence of other people. People's attitudes are not always readily apparent; often, these attitudes are conveyed to other people through small, subtle gestures (p. 613).
- *Social facilitation* is a change in performance because of the presence of other people. The change can be either positive or negative. *Social loafing* is the decrease in an individual's productivity as a result of working in a group (p. 613).

KEY TERMS

actor–observer effect, p. 604
attitude, p. 598
attribution, p. 603
balance theory, p. 601
body language, p. 602
cognitive dissonance, p. 600
debriefing, p. 611
fundamental attribution error, p. 603
group, p. 613
group polarization, p. 614
groupthink, p. 615
impression formation, p. 602
learned helplessness, p. 606
nonverbal communications, p. 602
obedience, p. 609
role, p. 604
self-perception, p. 604
self-perception theory, p. 600
self-serving bias, p. 605
social cognition, p. 602
social facilitation, p. 613
social influence, p. 607
social loafing, p. 614
social psychology, p. 597

SELF-TEST

Module 31

- Before taking the self-test, **recite** and **review.**
- Use the key at the back of the text to *correct* your answers.
- *Restudy* pages that correspond to any questions you answered incorrectly.

1. Social psychologists study
   a. how behavioral traditions develop in different cultures.
   b. the effects cultures have on group behavior.
   c. individual differences in life-style and opportunity.
   d. how social situations and other people influence individual behavior.
2. Which of the following represents the *cognitive dimension* of the attitude "Children should be respected as human beings?"
   a. Believing that children are worthy of all the respect you would give an adult.
   b. Feeling upset when an adult infringes on the rights of a child.
   c. Praising a child for holding his or her own opinion even though it differs from your own.
   d. Having pride in children who write letters to promote children's rights.
3. Attitudes learned through classical conditioning occur
   a. because a person is reinforced for having a particular belief.
   b. with such little effort that the conditioning process frequently goes unnoticed.
   c. when someone observes and imitates the attitudes of another.
   d. when a person has the opportunity to express an attitude freely.
4. The most effective medium for communicating persuasive messages is
   a. the television.
   b. newspapers.
   c. billboards and flyers.
   d. face-to-face communication.
5. Daryl Bem disagrees with cognitive dissonance theory and suggests that rather than making attitude changes because of a need for consistency, people change their attitudes based on
   a. observations of their own behavior in a situational context.
   b. the reinforcers or punishers associated with change.
   c. harmonious relationships that allow beliefs to be shared.
   d. a need for freedom of choice.
6. If Mindy's father tells her she has to go to college and Mindy responds by moving out of the house, taking a job at a fast-food restaurant, and spending her free time doing aerobic exercises, reactance theory would emphasize that she
   a. has an unhealthy and rebellious attitude.
   b. found her father's ideas inconsistent with her long-term goals.
   c. behaved as she did in order to maintain a sense of autonomy.
   d. was not open to parental advice or suggestions.
7. In most social interactions, people generally prefer ________ eye contact with the other people.
   a. little or no
   b. moderate amounts of
   c. almost constant
   d. constant

8. Those who believe that "people get what they deserve"
   a. make very few attribution errors.
   b. have made the fundamental attribution error.
   c. believe in a just world.
   d. are self-centered.
9. Self-perceptions develop when people
   a. ask others to evaluate them.
   b. take on roles and compare themselves to others.
   c. move into adulthood and assess who and what they are.
   d. focus on their own lives rather than the lives of others.
10. When people evaluate their own behavior as worthwhile regardless of the situation, we say they are showing
    a. altruism.
    b. high self-esteem.
    c. egocentric behavior.
    d. a self-serving bias.
11. Learned helplessness develops when a person
    a. wants attention.
    b. believes her actions will make no difference.
    c. finds ways to get others to do things for him that he should learn to do himself.
    d. tries too hard to help someone who does not want help.
12. A person's tendency to conform to group opinion *declines*
    a. when a situation is ambiguous.
    b. if the group members exert pressures to conform.
    c. if there is at least one other person in the group with a dissenting opinion.
    d. if the person is asked to voice his or her opinion publicly.
13. In Milgram's obedience-to-authority study, ________ of the subjects delivered the most intense level of shock to the collaborator-learner.
    a. 12%
    b. 37%
    c. 65%
    d. 86%
14. Groupthink seems to be the result of
    a. an excessive need to evaluate alternative solutions.
    b. wanting above all else to maintain group cohesiveness and harmony.
    c. a weak leader and a group that has no sense of purpose.
    d. "too many cooks in the kitchen."

Module 32

Social Interactions

LEARNING OBJECTIVES

When you have mastered the material in this module, you will be able to

Relationships and Attraction (pp. 621–624)

32.1 Explain how proximity, physical characteristics, and shared attitudes contribute to interpersonal attraction (p. 621).

32.2 Discuss the characteristics of friendships and the importance of equity in friendships (p. 623).

32.3 Discuss the characteristics of intimate relationships and love relationships (p. 624).

Prejudice (pp. 625–628)

32.4 Distinguish between prejudice and discrimination and describe several behaviors that perpetuate discrimination (p. 625).

32.5 Summarize the four theoretical explanations of the causes of prejudice (p. 626).

32.6 Identify a number of ways that we can work toward reducing and eliminating prejudice (p. 627).

Prosocial Behavior (pp. 628–630)

32.7 Discuss the characteristics and developmental process of prosocial behaviors such as altruism (p. 628).

32.8 Describe *bystander apathy* and the conditions under which it is likely and unlikely to occur (p. 629).

Aggression (pp. 630–634)

32.9 Characterize aggression and discuss three explanations concerning aggressive behavior in humans (p. 630).

SQ3R
- ▲ **Survey** to set goals for studying.
- ▲ Ask **questions** as you **read.**
- ▲ Stop occasionally to **recite** and **review.**

plus
- ▲ **Write** a summary of key points.
- ▲ **Reflect** on the hypotheses, evidence, and implications of this material and on the relevance it has to *your* life.

We killed, killed, killed. The Malays would stop and go through people's pockets and take their watches and money. We did not think of watches or money. We thought only of killing. . . . truly we were drunk with blood.

interpersonal attraction: The tendency of one person to evaluate another person (or a symbol of another person) in a positive way.

A Semai soldier told that tale to American anthropologist Robert K. Dentan (1968), who lived with the man's tribe for more than a year. What is most remarkable about the story is that the Semais are among the most gentle people on earth. Not a single murder has been recorded among this central Malayan tribe, adults never physically attack one another, children are taught to be nonviolent, and they have no police force. The Semai even regret having to kill their chickens for food.

Despite their pacifist heritage, Semai tribesmen were recruited and trained by the British to fight Communist guerrillas in the early 1950s. When their comrades fell in battle, the Semai became "blood drunk" and avenged themselves on the enemy with terrible ferocity. One veteran even reported drinking the blood of a man he killed. Upon their return home, however, the Semai soldiers returned to their pacifist ways.

Like all human beings, the Semai can be either loving or ferocious. Whether an individual is kind or aggressive, sociable or withdrawn, capable or incapable, depends in part on social and other environmental influences, both past and present. The previous chapter examined how grand-scale, long-term social factors help shape individual attitudes and how, in turn, those attitudes mold general behavior patterns. This chapter focuses on more personal social and environmental interactions that influence whom we love, like, or fight.

Social psychologists have shown that human behavior is affected by sometimes subtle, but powerful, social interactions. One aspect of such interaction is relationships and attraction. Another is the way people are hurtful and helpful. We take up each of these topics in turn.

Relationships and Attraction

Learning Objective 32.1 Explain how proximity, physical characteristics, and shared attitudes contribute to interpersonal attraction.

What is it about your friends that attracts you and makes you want to maintain a relationship with them? We saw in Chapter 9 that people develop relationships to fulfill their needs for warmth, understanding, and emotional security. Social psychologists study **interpersonal attraction**—the tendency of one person to evaluate another person (or symbol or image of a person) in a positive way. Psychologists know that people are attracted to those they consider good looking, who share their attitudes, and with whom they spend time.

Physical attraction is defined by the culture in which we live.

Proximity

People are more likely to develop a relationship with a neighbor than with someone who lives several blocks or miles away. Three decades of research show that the closer people are to someone geographically—whether it is where they work or where they live—the more attracted they will be to that person. A simple explanation is that they are likely to see that person often, and repeated exposure leads to familiarity, which leads to attraction. Another reason is that attraction is facilitated by anticipating a relationship with someone one encounters frequently. In addition, if people are members of a group, such as a computer club, a volunteer organization, or an aerobics class, they perceive themselves as sharing the same feelings, attitudes, and values as others in the group. That belief leads to attraction.

Physical Characteristics

In addition to liking people who like us, who have views similar to our own, and who live or work close by, we tend to like people we find physically attractive. Numerous experiments have shown that people ascribe more power, status, competence, and personal regard to individuals they find physically attractive than to those they don't; we saw this in Module 31 in examining who can best change people's attitudes (Dion, Pak, & Dion, 1990). Volumes of research show that people are attracted romantically, at least at first, to those whom they find attractive, but research also shows that physical attraction in romantic relationships is only one important element among many others (Feingold, 1988a). If physical attraction is only one characteristic of attraction, what are others?

Liking Those Who Like Us and Share Our Attitudes

Learning theorists contend that men and women are attracted to and form relationships with those who give them positive reinforcement and dislike those who punish them. The basic idea is simple: People like individuals who like them. Moreover, if someone likes an individual, he or she tends to assume (sometimes incorrectly) that the individual likes him or her in return and that they share similar qualities.

Another attribute that affects the development of relationships is real or perceived similarity in attitudes and opinions. If you perceive someone's attitudes as similar to your own, there is an increased probability that you will like that person. Having similar values, interests, and background is a good predictor of a likely friendship (e.g., Miller, 1990). Similarly, voters who are in agreement with a particular candidate tend to rate him or her as more honest, friendly, and persuasive than politicians with whom they disagree.

These phenomena are explained by cognitive consistency theory, which suggests that sharing similar attitudes reduces cognitive dissonance, the phenomenon discussed earlier. To avoid dissonance, people feel attracted to those they believe share similar attitudes. Shared attitudes in turn lead to attraction and liking. Learning theories also suggest that we like people with similar attitudes because similar attitudes are reinforcing to us. As long as we feel the other person's attitudes are genuine, such liking will continue.

Friendships and the Role of Equity

Learning Objective 32.2 Discuss the characteristics of friendships and the importance of equity in friendships.

Friendship is a special two-way relationship between people. A key component of a close relationship such as a friendship is the extent to which people are connected with one another's lives. According to one influential group of researchers (Kelley et al., 1983), if two people's behaviors, emotions, and thoughts are related, then the people are dependent on one another, and we can say a relationship exists. Closeness is reported by many researchers as the key variable that defines a relationship, although *close* must be defined clearly so that all researchers mean the same thing when they use the word (Berscheid, Snyder, & Omoto, 1989).

Variables in Friendships. Ideally, friends participate as equals, enjoy each other's company, have mutual trust, provide mutual assistance, accept each other as they are, respect each other's judgment, feel free to be themselves spontaneously, understand each other in fundamental ways, are intimate, and share confidences (Davis & Todd, 1984). Reciprocity and commitment between people who see themselves as equals are essentials of friendship (Hartup, 1989). Compared with casual friends, close friends interact more frequently across a greater range of settings and are more exclusive and offer each other more benefits (Hays, 1989).

As we saw in Chapter 8, friendships among children tend to be of the same sex; cross-sex friendships are rare. With youngsters, friendships lead to cooperation rather than competition, at least more than with nonfriends (Hartup, 1989). Among adults, friendships between two women differ from those between two men; both differ from friendships between a man and a woman. Women talk more about family, personal matters, and doubts and fears than men do; men talk more about sports and work than women do; cultural expectations for specific gender-based behaviors often determine such interactions.

Equity. Equity plays an important role in relationships. *Equity theory* states that people attempt to maintain stable, consistent, interpersonal relationships in which the ratio of each member's contribution is equal to that of the other members. This ensures that all members are treated fairly. People in close relationships usually have a sense of balance in these relationships and believe they will stay together for a long time (Clark & Reis, 1988).

According to equity theory, one way in which people maintain a balanced relationship is to make restitution when it is demanded. Apologies help restore a sense of autonomy to the injured individual: If you harm me, I need an apology. Similarly, people who do favors expect favors in return. When a politician running for reelection responds to her constituents' desires and has a playground built, she expects their votes on election day. People use the principles of equity theory unconsciously in day-to-day life; for example, you do a favor because you know you will need one in the future.

Intimate Relationships and Love

Learning Objective 32.3
Discuss the characteristics of intimate relationships and love relationships.

Intimacy. People involved in a close relationship may be intimate with one another. *Intimacy* generally refers to the willingness of one person to be self-disclosing and to express important feelings and information to another person; in response, the other person usually acknowledges the first person's feelings, making the individual feel valued and cared for (Reis & Shaver, 1988). Self-disclosure and emotional openness are important, key elements in intimate relationships. Self-disclosure comes through direct reports, nonverbal messages, and even touching. Self-disclosure tends to be reciprocal, not a one-way process, so that people who self-disclose to others are usually the recipients of intimate information.

Unfortunately, there is little research on intimate relationships outside of marriage. Communication, affection, consideration, and self-disclosure between friends have been studied relatively little. Important individual and gender differences exist in friendships. For example, men are more self-disclosing with a woman than they are with another man (Derlega et al., 1985), and in general, men are less likely to be self-disclosing and intimate than are women (Aukett, Ritchie, & Mill, 1988). Psychologists know much more about intimate relationships between men and women where sex, marriage, and love become involved.

People in intimate relationships often express feelings in unique ways—they give flowers, take moonlight walks, write lenghty letters, and have romantic dinners. Love, emotional commitment, and sex may be a part of an intimate relationship. According to psychologists, love has psychological, emotional, and social factors.

Elements in a Love Relationship. Researchers have identified some common elements in love relationships. *Love* usually involves the idealization of another person; people see their loved ones in a positive light. It also involves caring for another person and being fascinated with that person. Love also involves trust, respect, liking, honesty, companionship, and sexual attraction. A central element in love is commitment; however, researchers disagree as to whether love and commitment can be separated, because one usually follows from, or is part of, the other (Fehr, 1988; Fehr & Russell, 1991).

Love may be a state of mind, but it is also a series of behaviors.

Many classifications of love have been suggested and all have some overlapping components. One influential classification is Sternberg's (1986b) view, which sees love as having three components: intimacy, commitment, and passion. *Intimacy* is a sense of emotional closeness. *Commitment* refers to the extent to which a relationship is permanent and long-lasting. *Passion* refers to arousal, some of it sexual, some intellectual, and some motivational.

Love is a state, but it also is an act and a series of behaviors. Thus, although a person may be in love, most psychologists think of love in terms of the behaviors that demonstrate it, including remaining faithful sexually and showing caring behaviors (Buss, 1988). Love can be considered a process. It begins with infatuation, often based on physical attraction. As people get to know one another, the physical attraction leads toward shared interests, liking, companionship, and perhaps sexual intimacy. When a person reaches out to other people, many old ideas and fears disappear—ideas that may have their roots in prejudice, our next topic.

Prejudice

People involved in close relationships know each other well, are attracted to one another, and share ideas, values and activities. What happens, though, when you do not share ideas, values, or activities with another person or another group of people? What happens when you do not know another group of people well, or at all? Why do some people form negative evaluations of certain groups, such as blacks, Asians, Jews, or homosexuals? What is prejudice? How does it arise? How can it be prevented?

Learning Objective 32.4 Distinguish between prejudice and discrimination, and describe several behaviors that perpetuate discrimination.

What is Prejudice?

Prejudice is a negative evaluation of an entire group of people typically based on unfavorable ideas about the group. The negative evaluation is generally based on a small sample of experience, and sometimes on no experience, with an individual from the group being evaluated. People sometimes develop prejudices because of stereotypes about others they do not know well. **Stereotypes** are fixed, simple ideas, often about traits, attitudes, and behaviors, of groups of people; usually, these attributions are oversimplified and wrong. Often, such stereotypes are negative and are generalizations. People hold stereotyped ideas about American Indians, Catholics, women, or mountain folk; such stereotypes can lead to prejudice. Stereotypes usually have a historical basis; for example, the idea that all blacks are natural musicians or athletes probably stems from the fact that historically blacks were barred from avenues of upward mobility except for the entertainment and sports industries.

Prejudice is an attitude; when prejudice is translated into behavior, it is called discrimination. **Discrimination** is behavior targeted at a person with the aim of holding that person (or group) apart, treating the person differently.

Sometimes, people are prejudiced but do not show that attitude in behavior—that is, they do not discriminate. Merton (1949) referred to such individuals as cautious bigots, compared to true bigots, who are prejudiced and who discriminate. Also, sometimes people show *reverse discrimination,* in which they bend over backward to treat some individual favorably—more positively than they should, based on that person's performance—solely based on preexisting biases or stereotypes (Chidester, 1986). Thus, someone prejudiced toward blacks may treat a black person oversolicitously and may evaluate the person favorably, based on lower standards, in the workplace. This, too, is discrimination and has been demonstrated in laboratory studies (Fajardo, 1985). In *tokenism,* prejudiced people engage in positive but trivial actions toward members of a group they dislike. A man may make a token gesture toward the women on his staff, or a manager may hire a token Hispanic. By engaging in tokenism, a person often attempts to put off more important actions, such as in overall hiring practices. The trivial behavior justifies, in this person's mind, the idea that he or she has done something for this minority group. Tokenism has negative consequences for the minority person and perpetuates discrimination.

prejudice: A negative evaluation of an entire group of people, usually based on a set of negative (and often wrong) ideas about the group.

stereotypes: Fixed, overly simple ideas, often about traits, attitudes, and behaviors (and often wrong), that are attributed to groups of people.

discrimination: Behavior targeted at a person or group, with the aim of holding them apart and treating them differently.

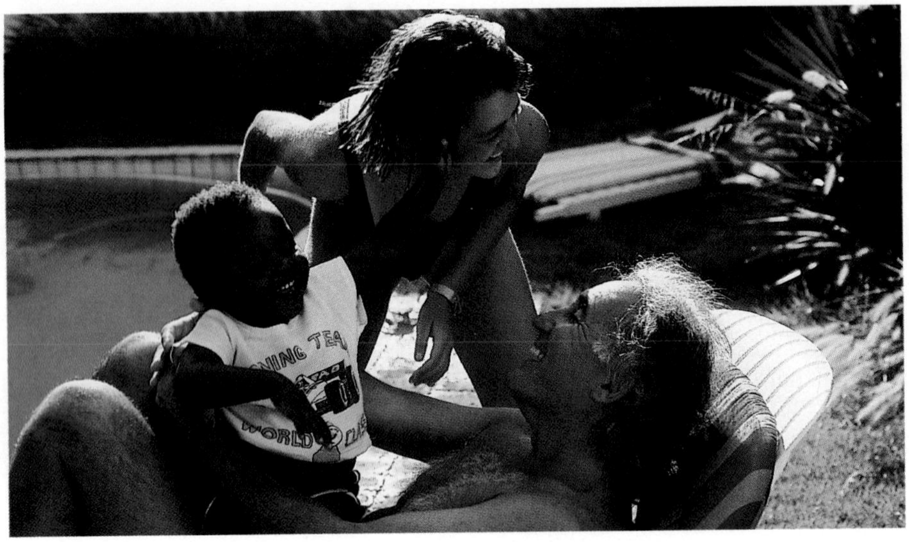

We learn attitudes such as racial tolerance. The father shown here has set an example of racial acceptance which his daughter is likely to accept and follow.

What Causes Prejudice?

Learning Objective 32.5
Summarize the four theoretical explanations of the causes of prejudice.

The causes of prejudice cannot be tied to a single theory or explanation. Like so many other psychological phenomena, prejudice has multiple causes. We consider four theories used to explain prejudice: social learning theory, motivational theory, cognitive theory, and personality theory.

Social Learning Theory. According to social learning theory, we learn to be prejudiced; we watch our parents, neighbors, and relatives engaged in acts of discrimination, which often includes stereotyped judgments and racial slurs, and we then incorporate those ideas into our own behavioral repertoire. After a child has observed such behaviors, the child is then reinforced (operant conditioning techniques) for exhibiting similar behaviors to classmates or relatives. Thus, through imitation and reinforcement, a prejudiced view is transmitted from parents to children, and from one generation to the next.

Motivational Theory. Motivational theory asserts that individuals learn to dislike specific individuals (competitors) and then generalize that dislike to whole classes of similar individuals (races, religion, or colors). This helps make those groups of people (often seen as competitors) into scapegoats—such as the Jews in Nazi Germany, and blacks in South Africa. Competition for jobs among immigrants can also create prejudice, particularly in times of economic hardship.

Cognitive Theory. Cognitive theorists assert that people think about individuals and the groups that they come from as a way of organizing the world. Cialdini (1988) argues that there are so many events, circumstances, and changing variables in our lives that we cannot easily analyze all the relevant data. People thus devise shortcuts to help them make decisions. One of those shortcuts is to stereotype individuals and the groups that they belong to—all Hispanics, all yuppies, all men, all attorneys. By devising such shortcuts in thinking, people develop ideas about who is in an *in-group*—that is, who is a member of a group to which they belong or want to belong. People tend to see themselves and other members of an in-group in a favorable light (Wilder & Thompson, 1980). As we saw earlier, when judging other people, individuals make fundamental attribution errors. They assume that other people's behavior is caused by internal dispositions—

which might not be true—and that other people are all alike (Judd & Park, 1988). They underestimate situational influences and overestimate dispositional influences on other people's behavior, and then they use those behaviors as evidence for their attitudes (prejudices).

Personality Theory. Some psychologists assert that people develop prejudices because they have a prejudice-prone personality. Some personality tests examine the extent to which people are likely to be prejudiced. For example, one personality trait that appears to be prevalent is the *authoritarian personality.* People with authoritarian personalities were fearful and anxious as children and may have been raised by cold, love-withholding parents who regularly used physical punishment. To gain control and mastery as adults, such individuals become aggressive and controlling over others. They see the world in absolutes—good versus bad, black versus white. They also tend to blame others for their problems and become prejudiced toward those people. The relationship between personality traits and prejudice has its roots in psychoanalytic theory, but it is not widely accepted by many theorists who study prejudice today. However, the idea that some people have traits that lead them toward prejudice has guided some personality theory research.

Reducing and Eliminating Prejudice

Learning Objective 32.6 Identify a number of ways that we can work toward reducing and eliminating prejudice.

To reduce and eliminate prejudice, we can teach rational thinking, judge people by their behavior, and promote equality. Once people have worked on a community project with an attorney, lived with a person of another race, or prayed with members of a different church, their views of them as individuals change.

As a society, we can pass laws that mandate equal treatment for all people, that eliminate discrimination in the workplace, housing market, and social situations. We can elect officials based on their competence, throw them out of office based on their incompetence, and make gender-neutral judgments of performance. Margaret Thatcher, former Prime Minister of Great Britain, was judged by her performance (e.g., "a tough old coot"), not by her gender.

As students of psychology, we can become especially sensitive to thinking about *individuals* rather than about groups. Through examining individuals, we can be sensitive to the wide diversity of human behavior. Although it is tempting to derive broad generalizations about behavior and people when making attributions about the causes of behavior we can focus on men and women as individuals, not as members of any particular group. When we focus on individuals, we see that human beings are engaged in a whole array of behaviors—some of them destructive and harmful, and others prosocial, worthwhile, and helpful.

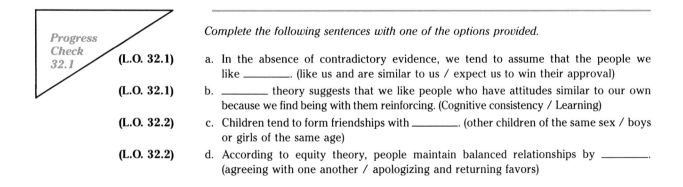

Progress Check 32.1

Complete the following sentences with one of the options provided.

(L.O. 32.1) a. In the absence of contradictory evidence, we tend to assume that the people we like ________. (like us and are similar to us / expect us to win their approval)

(L.O. 32.1) b. ________ theory suggests that we like people who have attitudes similar to our own because we find being with them reinforcing. (Cognitive consistency / Learning)

(L.O. 32.2) c. Children tend to form friendships with ________. (other children of the same sex / boys or girls of the same age)

(L.O. 32.2) d. According to equity theory, people maintain balanced relationships by ________. (agreeing with one another / apologizing and returning favors)

(L.O. 32.3) e. Intimacy refers to ________ closeness. (physical / emotional)

(L.O. 32.3) f. A man is most likely to be self-disclosing with a ________ friend. (male / female)

(L.O. 32.4) g. Stereotypes, preexisting ideas used to evaluate or categorize others, are generally ________. (quite reliable / oversimplified and wrong)

(L.O. 32.4) h. When an individual is overly generous and accepting when evaluating the performance of a minority person, we say the individual is involved in ________. (reverse discrimination / tokenism)

(L.O. 32.5) i. The idea that we turn certain groups of people into scapegoats because we see them as competitors for important resources supports the ________ theory of what causes prejudice. (motivational / cognitive)

(L.O. 32.5) j. Contemporary psychologists who study prejudice find the ________ theory to be the least convincing explanation of what causes prejudice. (social learning / personality)

(L.O. 32.6) k. One situation that is effective in reducing prejudice occurs when people who hold a particular prejudice ________ with the people toward whom they are prejudiced. (are not forced to interact / participate in shared activities or have common goals)

Prosocial Behavior

Learning Objective 32.7 Discuss the characteristics and developmental process of prosocial behaviors such as altruism.

Are country people more helpful than city people? It turns out that they are (Steblay, 1987), but what factors are at work? Under what conditions are people helpful? If a woman is walking down the street with a bag of groceries and drops them, what is the likelihood that someone will help her pick them up? If a man approaches someone for change to make a phone call, will the person give it to him? Will someone do something if he or she observes a serious accident or crime? Psychologists who ask these questions want to find out when, and under what conditions, someone will help a stranger. They are examining the likelihood of prosocial behavior. **Prosocial behavior** is some act that benefits someone else or society but generally has no obvious benefit to the person doing it and might even involve some personal risk or sacrifice.

Altruism: Helping Without Rewards

Why does Peter Beneson, the founder of Amnesty International, devote so much time and effort to helping "prisoners of conscience" around the world? What compels Mother Teresa to wander Calcutta's streets and attend to the wounds and diseases of people no one else will touch? Who were the people who risked their lives to help the Jews hide from the SS and escape the Nazi death camps during World War II?

Altruistic acts are those behaviors that benefit other people and for which there is no discernible reward, recognition, or appreciation. When a person helps someone in need and there is no obvious reward, he or she is generally referred to as being altruistic (Quigley, Gaes, & Tedeschi, 1989). However, does an altruistic person truly expect *no* reward for his or her good acts? Isn't the feeling of well-being one enjoys after performing an altruistic act a reward? Does the altruist expect a reward in an afterlife?

prosocial behavior: An act that benefits someone else and often has no obvious benefit to the person doing it; the act might even involve some personal risk or sacrifice.

altruistic act: [ahl-true-ISS-tick] Behavior that benefits other people for which there is no discernible extrinsic reward, recognition, or appreciation.

Behavioral Explanations. Behavioral psychologists have a difficult time explaining altruism, because altruistic acts are performed without overt reinforcement or even anticipated reinforcement. Many behaviorists contend that a personality element develops that directs people to seek social approval by helping; for example, self-monitoring individuals tailor their behavior to help other people

(White & Gerstein, 1987). People with a high need for achievement are also more likely to be helpful (Puffer, 1987). Some people may develop altruistic behaviors because such actions are self-reinforcing. Research also shows that when we have a relationship with a person, we are more likely to be caring and helpful (Batson, 1990). Intrinsically rewarding activities tend to become powerful behavior initiators. Thus, intrinsically rewarding behaviors become established as regular activities, and people are later impelled to help others, such as the homeless, disadvantaged senior citizens, and orphans.

bystander apathy: The unwillingness of witnesses to an event to help; the effect increases when there are more observers.

diffusion of responsibility: The feeling of individuals in a group that they cannot be held individually responsible for the group's actions.

Bystander Apathy: Failing to Help

Learning Objective 32.8 Describe *bystander apathy* and the conditions under which it is likely and unlikely to occur.

The study of helping behavior has taken some interesting twists and turns. For example, psychologists have found that in large cities where potentially lethal emergencies (accidents, thefts, stabbings, rapes, and murders) occur frequently, people exhibit bystander apathy—they watch but seldom help. Bibb Latané and John Darley (1970) investigated **bystander apathy** in a long series of studies. They found that in situations requiring uncomfortable responses, people must choose between helping or standing by apathetically. They must decide whether to introduce themselves into a situation, especially when there are other bystanders.

The Classic Study. Latané and Darley reasoned that when people are aware of other bystanders in an emergency situation, they might be less likely to help because they experience a **diffusion of responsibility**—they do not take individual responsibility for an action. To test their hypothesis, they brought college students to a laboratory and told them they were going to be involved in a study of people who were interested in discussing college life. The researchers told the students that in the interest of preserving people's anonymity, a group discussion would be held over an intercom system rather than face to face, and that each person in the group would talk in turn. In fact, there was only one true subject in each experimental session. All the other conversations were prerecorded from assistants who worked for the researchers.

Observing someone in need and failing to come to their aid is a common phenomenon. Studies show that the greater the number of observers, the less the chances are that an individual will choose to help.

The independent variable in this study was the number of people the naïve subject thought were in the discussion group. The dependent variable was whether the subject helped, and the speed with which the naïve subject reported the emergency when one of the assistants appeared to have a serious nervous seizure.

The future seizure victim spoke first; he talked about his difficulties getting adjusted to New York City and mentioned that he was prone to seizures, particularly when studying hard. Next, the naïve subject spoke, followed by the prerecorded discussions of assistants. Then the seizure victim talked again. After a few relatively calm remarks, his speech became increasingly loud and incoherent; he stuttered and indicated that he needed help because he was having "a-a-a real problerm-er-right now and I-er-if somebody could help me out it would-it would-er-er sh-sure be good." At this point, the experimenter began timing the speed of the naïve subject's response.

The naïve subjects were led to believe that their discussion group contained two, three, or six people. In the two-person group, they believed they were the only bystanders, while in the three-person group, they thought there was one other bystander. When the subjects thought they were the only bystanders, 85% of the naïve subjects responded before the end of the seizure. With one other bystander, 62% of the naïve subjects responded by the end of the seizure. When subjects thought there were four other bystanders, only 31% responded by the

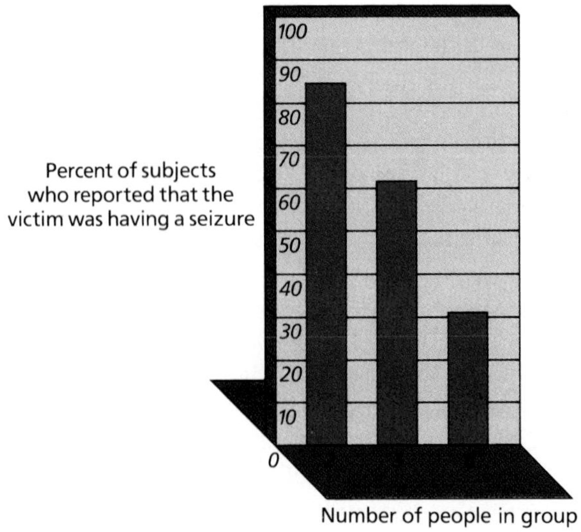

Figure 32.1

In the bystander apathy studies, as the number of people in the group increased, the willingness of naïve subjects to inform the experimenter that the victim had suffered a seizure decreased.

end of the seizure. (Some of the results of this study are presented in Figure 32.1.) Thus, cast in the role of bystanders to an emergency, the naïve subjects were less likely to respond if they thought other people were present who might help. In general, Latané (1981) found that speed of assistance decreases as the number of bystanders believed to be present increases.

Did these subjects not help because they were cold and callous? Apparently not. They seemed to be very concerned about the seizure victim. Why did they not respond? Latané and Darley suggest that they were worried about the guilt and shame they would feel if they did not help, but they also feared making fools of themselves if they did help.

In general, research has shown that bystanders will help under some conditions. For one thing, people's self-concepts and previous experiences affect their willingness to intercede. Bystanders who see themselves as being especially competent in emergencies (such as doctors or nurses) are likely to help a victim regardless of the number of people present. If the person who needs help has a relationship with the person who can offer help, help is more likely to be given (Batson, 1990). Also, personality characteristics of the individual involved in a bystander situation are important. Tice and Baumeister (1985) found, for example, that subjects who had a high degree of masculinity were less likely to respond. Researchers contended that highly masculine subjects might be especially fearful of embarrassment. In our society, the personality characteristics of men, in general, emphasize strength and aggression (our next topic) rather than sensitivity.

Learning Objective 32.9
Characterize aggression, and discuss three explanations concerning aggressive behavior in humans.

Aggression

The Yanomamo Indians of Brazil and Venezuela are among the most violent people on earth: Their murder rate is three times that of the city of Detroit's, and an estimated 44% of the men ages 25 or older have participated in at least one killing. Yet other South American Indian tribes are as peaceful as the Yanomamo are violent. The Semai soldiers discussed at the beginning of the chapter were both brutal killers and compassionate social beings. If people can be either loving or violent, what compels them to act one or the other?

aggression: Any behavior that has as its goal to harm another person or thing.

When people feel unable to control situations that affect their lives, they may become frustrated, angry, and aggressive. Social psychologists define **aggression** as any behavior designed to harm another person or thing. An aggressive person may attempt to harm others physically through force; verbally, through gossip, rumors, or irritating comments; emotionally, by withholding love; or, on a larger scale, by acts of war. Psychologists study aggression to determine what behaviors people are capable of and why those behaviors occur. They have examined three major sources to explain aggressive behavior: instincts, acquired drives, and social learning.

Instincts

Some psychologists believe that many aspects of behavior, including aggression, are inborn (see Di Lalla & Gottesman, 1991). These *nativists* believe that people are genetically predisposed toward aggression. One nativist, Nobel laureate Konrad Lorenz (1903–1989), investigated aggressive behavior through naturalistic observation. He noted that although animals of the same species fight with each other, they have signals that tell them to stop fighting well before death occurs. In other words, most animals generally do not attempt to kill members of their

After watching an adult model take aggressive action against a "Bobo" doll, children became actively aggressive in their own interactions with the doll.

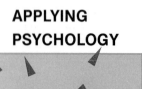

APPLYING PSYCHOLOGY

Television and Aggressive Stimuli

Danny is engrossed in watching Andre the Giant in a professional wrestling match on a Saturday afternoon. Almost without realizing it, Danny lurches over and tackles his sister, Lori. Lori screams, prompting their mother to burst into the room and turn off the TV.

From a psychologist's viewpoint, Danny's mother did the right thing. When children are in situations for which they have not established their own standard responses, they copy the behaviors of others. Thus, they imitate characters they see in the movies or on television. According to Bandura, aggressive behavior can be both established and eliminated through *observational learning.* Bandura argues that children are not born with aggressive instincts but learn aggression (or nonaggression) by seeing other people, including parents, teachers, and peers, exhibiting such behavior. A child will learn to be aggressive by imitating another child usng a toy gun or by watching parents or teachers act aggressively. On the other hand, a child will learn to be nonaggressive if he or she sees parents act nonaggressively or someone being punished for aggressive behavior. Similarly, Semai children learn gentleness from their parents, then as Semai soldiers, they were taught to kill by the British.

In a classic study, Bandura, Ross, and Ross (1963) found that children who viewed aggression (either live, on films, or in TV cartoons) were nearly twice as aggressive in subsequent play as those who did not view it. (See Chapter 5 for more on observational learning.) Much research supports Bandura's findings (Wood, Wong, & Chacheee, 1991). Worchel, Hardy, and Hurley (1976), for example, had adult subjects view films with either violent or nonviolent content and then interact with a series of research assistants. One research assistant was directed to assume a bumbling and inadequate manner by purposely committing mistakes. After the subjects had viewed and interacted with the assistants, they were asked to rate them to help determine which of the assistants would be rehired. The subjects who had viewed the violent films rated the bumbling assistant lower than those who had viewed the nonviolent films; they also were the only ones to recommend not rehiring. Their judgments were more aggressive.

Most children spend more hours watching television than they spend in any other activity except sleep (A.C. Nielsen Co., 1988). Children have a great deal of unstructured time and are often indiscriminate viewers of television (Kubey & Csikszentmihalyi, 1990). Because children watch so much television, it serves as a major source of models for imitative behavior and may alter their overall views of life (Cairns, 1990). The fact that television portrays so much aggressive behavior concerns parents and educators, as well as social psychologists.

In general, research supports the contention that children who frequently watch violent television programs are more likely to be aggressive than children

own species. Human beings are the exception. According to Lorenz (1964), aggression is instinctive and spontaneous. He contends that the aggressive instinct serves to maximize the use of food, space, and resources. Lorenz stresses the social implications of people's aggressive instincts, focusing on their adaptive rather than maladaptive values.

Acquired Drives

frustration–aggression hypothesis: The view that frustration of goal-directed behavior leads to aggression.

Another explanation for aggressive behavior is the **frustration–agression hypothesis,** initially proposed by Dollard et al. (1939). This theory relies on the everyday experience demonstrating that people involved in goal-oriented tasks often become aggressive or angry when frustrated. Ordinarily, a driver is unlikely to become upset if another car pulls out into traffic in front of her. However, if who see less television violence. The American Psychological Association and many other professional organizations have endorsed this conclusion. Further, one study found that children exposed to large doses of television violence are less likely to help a real-life victim of violence, and another found that viewers of violence were less sympathetic to victims than nonviewers of violence (Linz, Donnerstein, & Penrod, 1988). They also are more fearful of becoming victims of violent acts. Children who play violent video games also seem to act more aggressively at later ages (Schutte et al., 1988), and even infants can be affected by watching television (Meltzoff, 1988).

How does watching violence on television affect viewers? How can it increase the likelihood of a person committing violent acts? Baron and Byrne (1987) describe four primary effects of viewing television violence:

- It weakens the inhibitions of viewers.
- It may suggest new ideas and techniques to the uninitiated.
- It may prime or stimulate existing aggressive ideas.
- It may reduce a person's overall emotional sensitivity to violence.

Television can also have positive effects on children. Children exposed to shows such as *Sesame Street* and *Mister Rogers's Neighborhood,* which focus on topics such as sharing and caring are more likely to engage in prosocial behavior with other children. Children can also learn vocabulary and language structures from television (Rice & Woodsmall, 1988).

Generally researchers have focused on the outcomes of watching television. Recently, however, the causes of why children watch so much television have been explored. While environmental reasons are important (parents and brothers and sisters watch a lot), so are genetic reasons. Children of adoptive parents watched a great deal of television if their biological parents did! This is a surprising finding and is currently undergoing more extensive research (Plomin, Corley, DeFries, & Fulker, 1990).

Research on the effects of television has been more extensive and had important social implications. Children under the age of 5 years believe what they see on television to be the truth, and thus the content of television shows influences chldren in profound ways. Further, researchers are concerned about the widespread availability of cable television, which has programs that portray violence more frequently and explicitly than network television does. Such shows can act as a cue for children who might already be aggressive (Josephson, 1987). Social psychologists interested in public policy making are suggesting requirements for minimum amounts of educational programming for children on every station and controls to protect children from advertising that exploits their special vulnerability (Huston, Watkins, and Junkel, 1989).

- ***What is the hypothesis with which Bandura began working?***
- ***What does Bandura's approach do that others do not?***
- ***What are the implications of using a social learning approach for research in aggression?***

the woman is in a hurry to get to work, she might honk angrily at the other driver. On a larger scale, the violence between Catholics and Protestants in Northern Ireland is fueled in part by intense competition for decent jobs in a depressed economy.

Berkowitz (1989) examined the evidence for the frustration–aggression hypothesis and proposed that frustrations generate aggressive inclinations to the extent that they arouse negative feelings in the person affected (Berkowitz, 1989). These negative feelings can change the way people experience and then express anger (Berkowitz, 1990). Berkowitz's conception accounts for the reason people don't always become aggressive when frustrated. Many psychologists find the frustration–aggression hypothesis too simple, but it is beneficial, in part, because it has led to other research that helps describe behavior, such as social learning theory.

Progress Check 32.2

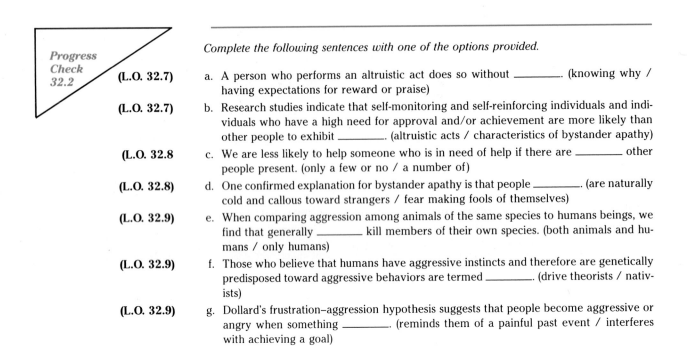

Complete the following sentences with one of the options provided.

(L.O. 32.7) a. A person who performs an altruistic act does so without ________. (knowing why / having expectations for reward or praise)

(L.O. 32.7) b. Research studies indicate that self-monitoring and self-reinforcing individuals and individuals who have a high need for approval and/or achievement are more likely than other people to exhibit ________. (altruistic acts / characteristics of bystander apathy)

(L.O. 32.8 c. We are less likely to help someone who is in need of help if there are ________ other people present. (only a few or no / a number of)

(L.O. 32.8) d. One confirmed explanation for bystander apathy is that people ________. (are naturally cold and callous toward strangers / fear making fools of themselves)

(L.O. 32.9) e. When comparing aggression among animals of the same species to humans beings, we find that generally ________ kill members of their own species. (both animals and humans / only humans)

(L.O. 32.9) f. Those who believe that humans have aggressive instincts and therefore are genetically predisposed toward aggressive behaviors are termed ________. (drive theorists / nativists)

(L.O. 32.9) g. Dollard's frustration–aggression hypothesis suggests that people become aggressive or angry when something ________. (reminds them of a painful past event / interferes with achieving a goal)

Module Summary

Relationships and Attraction

- *Interpersonal attraction* refers to the tendency to evaluate another person (or a symbol of another person) in a positive way. The process of attraction involves the characteristics of both the people involved and the situation variables such as proximity (p. 621).
- From Sternberg's view, *love* has three components: intimacy, commitment, and passion. *Intimacy* is a sense of emotional closeness. *Commitment* refers to the extent to which a relationship is permanent. *Passion* refers to arousal, some of it sexual, some intellectual, and some motivation. (p. 624).

Prejudice

- *Prejudice* is a negative evaluation of an entire group of people that is usually based on a set of negative (and often wrong) ideas about the group. Such ideas are usually based on stereotypes, or fixed, simple ideas, often about traits, attitudes, and behaviors that are attributed to groups of people (p. 625).
- Prejudice has multiple causes and can be accounted for, at least to some extent, by learning theory, motivational theory, cognitive theory, and personality theory (p. 626).

Prosocial Behavior

- *Prosocial behavior* is some act that benefits someone else but generally has no obvious benefit to the person doing it and might even involve some personal risk or sacrifice (p. 628).
- *Bystander apathy* is the unwillingness of witnesses to an event to help, especially when there are a number of observers; the effect increases when there are more observers. (p. 629).

Agression

- Aggressive behavior is any behavior that has as a goal to harm another person or thing. Not all aggressive acts are physical. Aggression can be viewed as an instinct, an acquired drive, a learned social behavior, or a response to frustration or aggressive stimulation (p. 631).
- Research supports the contention that children who frequently watch violent television programs are more likely to be aggressive than children who see less television violence. Viewing television violence may weaken inhibitions of viewers, suggest new ideas and techniques to the uninitiated, prime or stimulate existing aggressive ideas, and reduce a person's overall emotional sensitivity to violence (p. 632).

KEY TERMS

aggression, p. 631
altruistic acts, p. 628
bystander apathy, p. 629
diffusion of responsibility p. 629
discrimination, p. 625
frustration–aggression hypothesis, p. 632
interpersonal attraction, p. 621
prejudice, p. 625
prosocial behavior, p. 628
stereotypes, p. 625

SELF-TEST

Module 32

- Before taking the self-test, **recite** and **review.**
- Use the key at the back of the text to *correct* your answers.
- *Restudy* pages that correspond to any questions you answered incorrectly.

1. Research shows that you are most likely to like someone who
   a. likes you.
   b. plays hard to get.
   c. has opinions that challenge your own opinions.
   d. all of the above
2. Friendships require all of the following *except:*
   a. being connected through behaviors, emotions, and/or shared attitudes.
   b. reciprocity and commitment.
   c. mutual trust.
   d. passion.
3. Love is
   a. a state of mind involving idealization, passion, and intimacy.
   b. a process beginning with infatuation and growing toward long-lasting commitment.
   c. a series of behaviors such as remaining sexually faithful and being kind to the other person.
   d. all of the above.
4. Which statement describes prejudice and discrimination?
   a. Prejudice and discrimination are both emotional states.
   b. Reverse discrimination occurs when a bigot is treated with prejudice and discrimination.
   c. Prejudice is an attitude, and discrimination is a behavior.
   d. People who are prejudiced, but do not discriminate, are called "nonprejudiced bigots."
5. Cognitive theorists suggest that prejudice is the result of
   a. attitudes and behaviors passed from one generation to the next through imitation and reinforcement.
   b. disliking a specific individual and then generalizing that dislike to whole classes of similar individuals.
   c. using stereotypes as a shortcut for organizing our world views.
   d. having an authoritarian personality.
6. One way to work toward the reduction and elimination of prejudice is to
   a. make generalizations about behavior and people.
   b. become sensitive to individual differences in behavior.
   c. focus on people as individuals rather than as members of a particular group.
   d. both b and c.
7. An example of a prosocial behavior is
   a. interpersonal attraction.
   b. reverse discrimination.
   c. altruism.
   d. the foot-in-the-door effect.

8. Which of the following factors allow a person to take charge and help victims in an emergency?
   a. Seeing one's self as being competent to handle the emergency.
   b. Having a high degree of masculinity in one's personality.
   c. Witnessing a large group of people who are observing the crisis but apparently finding it unnecessary to help, even though it is obvious help is needed.
   d. all of the above.
9. Based on the text's definition of aggression, which of the following would *not* be considered an aggressive act?
   a. Withholding love or attention from a person because he or she did not live up to your expectations.
   b. Spreading rumors about someone when you have no first hand evidence about the gossip.
   c. Hitting, kicking, biting, or shooting a person.
   d. Breaking a teammate's foot by unintentionally jumping on it while trying to make the final spike to win the championship game.

Module 33

Applied Psychology

LEARNING OBJECTIVES

When you have mastered the material in this module, you will be able to

Introduction (p. 639)

33.1 Describe the subject matter of environmental psychology (p. 639).

Environmental Psychology (pp. 639–643)

33.2 Discuss how environmental variables such as temperature and noise can act as stressors (p. 639).

33.3 Identify the conditions that contribute to feeling crowded and the feelings people have when in these conditions (p. 640).

33.4 Explain how we use personal space and spatial zones to control the nature of our interactions with others (p. 640).

33.5 Explain why privacy is important and how people establish a sense of privacy (p. 642).

33.6 Describe some of the research aimed at finding ways to encourage people to conserve and protect natural resources (p. 642).

Industrial and Organizational Psychology (pp. 644–649)

33.7 Describe the subject matter of industrial/organization (I/O) psychology (p. 644).

33.8 Explain how I/O psychologists approach the task of selecting personnel (p. 644).

33.9 Identify some common problems with performance appraisal procedures and explain why performance appraisals are important (p. 645).

33.10 Identify several factors that contribute to job motivation and performance, and distinguish between job motivation and job satisfaction (p. 645).

33.11 Describe three styles of management that are used to motivate employees (p. 648).

SQ3R ▲ **Survey** to set goals for studying.
▲ Ask **questions** as you **read.**
▲ Stop occasionally to **recite** and **review.**

plus ▲ **Write** a summary of key points.
▲ **Reflect** on the hypotheses, evidence, and implications of this material and on the relevance it has to *your* life.

Suppose it is a cool spring day and you are relaxing on a park bench when the baby of the woman seated next to you begins to cry. Now, imagine that it is 90 degrees on a very crowded, stuffy airplane and you have been trying for 15 minutes to get to your assigned seat when suddenly, the baby of the woman standing next to you starts bawling. The infant in the park was unhappy and needed loving attention; the baby on the airplane is a screaming, irritating brat. Environmental conditions influence reactions. The study of **environmental psychology** is twofold: how physical settings affect human behavior and how people change the environment—often to make it more comfortable and acceptable.

Learning Objective 33.1 Describe the subject matter of environmental psychology.

Environmental Psychology

Environmental psychologists study the physical and social aspects of the environment, how the individual behaves in it, and how it might be changed. The studies are often conducted in institutional settings, such as schools, hospitals, and churches. For example, consider the design of a nurses' station in a hospital. In traditional hospital floor plans, the nurses' station is the center of activity on each floor and is usually placed between two long corridors. An alternative is to place the nurses' station at the hub of a wheel-like arrangement of rooms.

environmental psychology: The study of how physical settings affect human behavior and how human behavior affects the environment.

The environment represents more than the shape of a building, the layout of a nurses' station, or a dormitory, or the arrangement of buildings in a housing project or shopping mall. It represents variables such as size, shape, furniture and fixtures, climate, noise level, and the number of people per square foot. Environmental psychology is the study of the relationships among such variables.

Environmental Variables

Whether a room is perceived as crowded, for example, is determined not only by the number of people in it but also by the room's size and shape, furniture layout, ceiling height, number of windows, wall colors, lighting, and the time of day. Researchers who look at global environment systems, such as cities, communities, and neighborhoods, must consider all these variables and more. Two of the easiest environmental variables to control to assure well-being are temperature and noise.

Learning Objective 33.2 Discuss how environmental variables such as temperature and noise can act as stressors.

Temperature. The consequences of severe climatic environments on behavior—those with very hot or very cold climates—can range from annoyance to

stressor: A stimulus that elicits uncomfortable feelings such as anxiety, tension, and physiological arousal.

crowding: The perception that one's space is too restricted.

personal space: The area around an individual that is considered private and around which the person feels an invisible boundary

inability to function. New England industrial workers, for example, would never survive the winter without proper shelter, heating, and clothes, and southern industrial workers would be less productive without air conditioning during the summer.

Environmental variables that impair work performance are stressors. A **stressor** is a stimulus that elicits uncomfortable feelings such as anxiety, tension, and physiological arousal. Temperature can be a stressor and can affect behaviors, including academic performance, driving an automobile, and being attracted toward others. In general, performance is optimal at moderate temperatures and becomes progressively worse at high or low temperatures.

Noise. Another environmental variable that can affect performance is noise. *Noise* is unwanted sound, a stressor that can stimulate people to uncommonly high levels of arousal and poor performance. Some noises, such as that of a buzzing fluorescent light, a humming refrigerator, an opening and closing door, a chirping bird, passing cars, or people talking are almost always present in the environment. They are continuous and not too loud, and although they may be unwanted, they are usually not too disruptive, nor are they stressors. Rarely do such noises raise levels of arousal or interfere with daily activities. However, loud uncontrolled noise, such as a marching band practicing outside your window, a dog barking, or a car honking can impair human performance, especially when concentration is required, as when studying.

Crowding

Learning Objective 33.3 Identify the conditions that contribute to feeling crowded and the feelings people have when in these conditions.

Another environmental variable is the number of people who are around. In some situations in which there are myriad people, you may feel closed in and crowded. In other situations, the excitement of a crowd may make you feel exhilarated. It is not the size of a space or the number of people that causes you to feel crowded. It is the perception that your space is too limited. Thus, **crowding** is a psychological state. One person might feel crowded and uncomfortable in a mall filled with Christmas shoppers, while someone else may feel that the throngs promote a holiday ambience.

Crowding is affected by both social and spatial density. *Social density* refers to the number of people in a given space; *spatial density* refers to the size of a space with a fixed number of people in it. (See Figure 33.1.) For example, in an empty theater, a person may feel lonely, but she may feel crowded when the theater is full, or even half-full. Similarly, the first few people who arrive at a party often feel awkward and ill-at-ease. yet within an hour, with perhaps only 20 people there, they may feel closed in. Researchers must be careful to separate the variables of social and spatial density (Baum, 1987).

Controlling the Environment

Although the effects of crowding are not consistent across all situations or populations, certain effects seem to be universal. In high-density situations, people feel stressed, overloaded, and sometimes overaroused. They may feel alone or anonymous and withdraw from the situation. They may become apathetic, exhibit impaired task performance, and sometimes become hostile. Maintaining a sense of control seems to be a crucial variable (Fleming, Baum, & Weiss, 1987; Ruback & Pandey, 1991).

Learning Objective 33.4 Explain how we use personal space and spatial zones to control the nature of our interactions with others.

Personal Space. To help assert individuality and maintain a sense of personal control, human beings generally try to establish appropriate personal spaces. **Personal space** is the area or invisible boundary around an individual that he or she considers private. Encroachment on that space causes displeasure and often withdrawal.

The size of your personal space can change, depending on the situation and the people near you. For example, you may walk arm in arm with a family member but avoid physical contact with a stranger. You may stand close to a friend and whisper in his or her ear, but will keep a certain distance from an elevator operator or a store clerk.

Anthropologist Edward Hall (1966) suggested that personal space is a mechanism by which people communicate with others. He proposed that people adhere to established norms of personal space that are learned in childhood. Hall also observed that the use of personal space varies from culture to culture. In the United States, especially in suburban and rural areas, people are used to generous space and large homes. In Japan, on the other hand, where there is little space available per person, people are used to small homes that provide little private space. In general Western cultures insist on a fair amount of space for people, reserving proximity for intimacy and close friends, but Arab cultures allow much smaller distances between strangers.

To understand the concept of personal space, Hall classified four *spatial zones,* or distances, used in social interactions with other people: An *intimate distance* (from 0 to 18 inches) is reserved for people who have great familiarity with one another. It is acceptable for comforting someone who is hurt, for lovers, for physicians, and for contact sports. The closeness enables a person to hold another person, examine the other's hair and eyes, and hear the other's breath. It also permits opposing team members to tackle each other or a soldier to engage an enemy in hand-to-hand fighting.

An acceptable distance for close friends and everyday interactions is *personal distance* ($1\frac{1}{2}$ to 4 feet). It is the distance used for most social interactions. At $1\frac{1}{2}$–2 feet, someone might tell a spicy story to a close friend. At 2 feet, people can walk together while conversing. At 2–4 feet, they maintain good contact with a coworker without seeming too personal or impersonal.

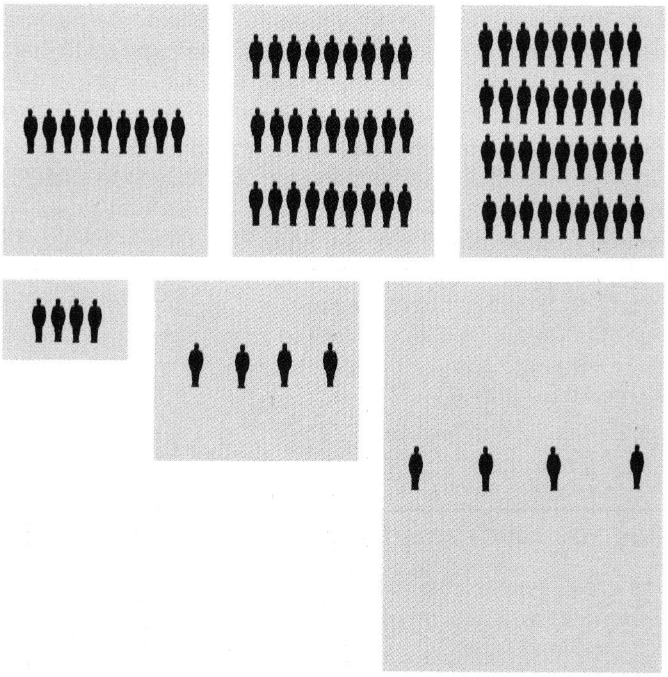

Figure 33.1

Manipulations of *social density* are manipulations of the number of people in the same size space. Manipulations of *spatial density* are manipulations of the size of the space, with the number of people held constant.

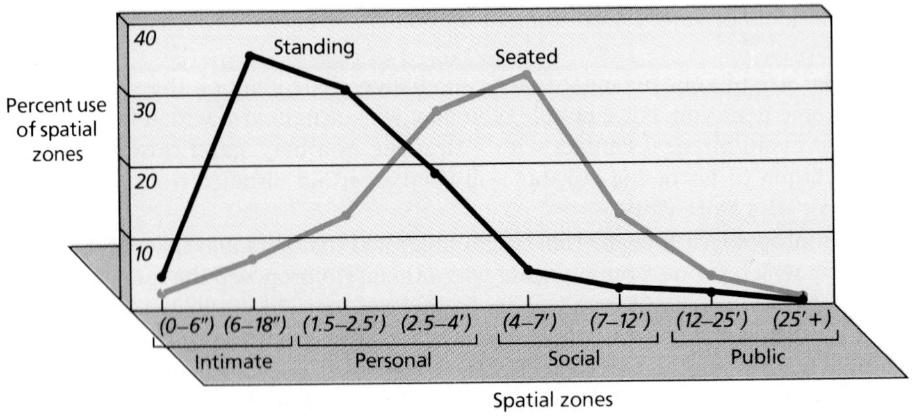

Figure 33.2

While standing, people use primarily the personal and intimate zones. While seated, they use primarily the personal and social zones. (Source: Altman & Vinsel, 1977)

privacy: The process of limiting the access of other people by controlling the boundaries between those people and oneself.

Social distance (4–12 feet) is used for business and interactions with strangers. At 4–6 feet, people are close enough to communicate their ideas effectively while far enough away to remain separated. Personal space in the social zone may be controlled by physical barriers, such as a desk to separate a clerk, receptionist, or teacher from the people with whom he or she interacts.

Public distance (12–25 feet) minimizes personal contact. It is the distance at which politicians speak at lunch clubs, teachers instruct classes of students, and actors and musicians perform. Public distance is sufficiently great to eliminate personal communication between individuals and their audiences. See Figure 33.2 for a presentation of the space that people use when seated or standing.

Learning Objective 33.5 Explain why privacy is important and how people establish a sense of privacy.

Privacy. Altman (1975) suggests that the key to understanding why people feel crowded and need personal space is privacy. **Privacy** is the process of controlling boundaries between people so that access is limited. Everyone needs privacy. According to Altman, privacy allows people to develop and nurture a sense of self. Without it, people feel they have no control over who and what can intrude on them. This sense of helplessness can lead to lowered self-esteem and poor social adaptations. Understanding people's need for privacy is central to understanding the behavior of human beings in their environment.

One way in which people maintain a sense of privacy is to change their immediate environment. When a teenager goes into a room and closes the door, she closes herself off from other people; she limits their access to her. The teenager has set up a boundary—a closed door—behind which she can do what she wants when she wants to. Similarly, two people may enter a room and close the door, thereby controlling other people's access to them. Groups of people, such as a study group or a therapy group, may also desire privacy and set themselves apart from others. The President of the United States uses Camp David as a retreat for privacy. Sometimes the only privacy a parent of young children can find is in the shower.

Learning Objective 33.6 Describe some of the research aimed at finding ways to encourage people to conserve and protect natural resources.

Preserving the Environment

An emerging area of environmental research is in controlling people's behavior in the environment, such as littering. Research studies by Scott Geller at Virginia

Polytechnic Institute found that littering can be significantly reduced by providing instructions for proper disposal of objects; the more specific the instructions, the less littering (Geller, 1975; Geller, Witmer, & Tuso, 1977).

Another area of research is finding out what variables make people want to preserve the environment. Consider energy conservation, including driving smaller, more fuel-efficient cars and investing in solar panels for the home. Research on these issues has shown that tax laws (tax savings for energy-efficient homes), signs (turn light off when leaving room), and new equipment (thermostats that automatically turn themselves on and off) help people adopt energy-saving behaviors. As in the littering issue, when given specific instructions and prompts, people are more likely to comply (Geller, Winett, & Everett, 1982). This was clearly shown in a study that prompted people to use seatbelts in automobiles.

Specific behaviors can be changed with methods derived from environmental research. Nonetheless, there are tremendous problems that must be solved in our world. Geller (1989) suggests that principles from marketing be added to knowledge provided by psychology to solve these bigger problems. First, promoting socially beneficial ideas and behaviors must be advanced; this helps move people to intend to do such things as wearing seatbelts (Stasson & Fishbein, 1990). This means promoting a product or idea by making it affordable, accessible, and desirable. It also means that psychologists must analyze the wants, needs, and perceptions of the people being targeted for change. After the target population is analyzed and strategies are developed, only then should specific interventions be applied. After going through these steps, the results should be evaluated to see whether the strategy has been effective. Geller claims that behavioral interventions combined with a social marketing strategy can provide an integrative program for environmental preservation.

The workplace is an environment where stressors are often apparent, and the burden of an unproductive, disorganized employee often falls on other employees, and ultimately on management and stockholders. Discussed next are psychologists' efforts to help businesses and organizations with such problems.

Acceptable amounts of personal space differs between cultures. Arab cultures typically allow strangers to conduct business in much closer physical proximity than do Western cultures.

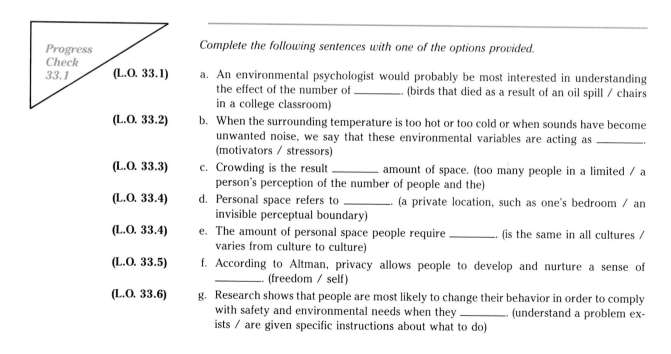

Progress Check 33.1

Complete the following sentences with one of the options provided.

(L.O. 33.1) a. An environmental psychologist would probably be most interested in understanding the effect of the number of ________. (birds that died as a result of an oil spill / chairs in a college classroom)

(L.O. 33.2) b. When the surrounding temperature is too hot or too cold or when sounds have become unwanted noise, we say that these environmental variables are acting as ________. (motivators / stressors)

(L.O. 33.3) c. Crowding is the result ________ amount of space. (too many people in a limited / a person's perception of the number of people and the)

(L.O. 33.4) d. Personal space refers to ________. (a private location, such as one's bedroom / an invisible perceptual boundary)

(L.O. 33.4) e. The amount of personal space people require ________. (is the same in all cultures / varies from culture to culture)

(L.O. 33.5) f. According to Altman, privacy allows people to develop and nurture a sense of ________. (freedom / self)

(L.O. 33.6) g. Research shows that people are most likely to change their behavior in order to comply with safety and environmental needs when they ________. (understand a problem exists / are given specific instructions about what to do)

Industrial and Organizational Psychology

industrial/organizational (I/O) psychologists: Applied psychologists who work in industry, government, and public agencies and focus on how individual behavior is affected by the work environment, coworkers, and organizational practices.

Many business experts thought that Sharp Corporation of Japan made a big mistake when they built an electronics factory in Memphis. In 1966, RCA Corporation had built a TV plant in that city, but wildcat strikes, product sabotage, and abysmal quality control forced RCA to shut the factory down. The Japanese plant proved successful, however. What made the difference? A possible explanation is that the Japanese bosses treated their American employees like family while demanding the highest quality control. In return, the employees were motivated and found their work fulfilling.

Industry, Organizations, and Applications

Learning Objective 33.7 Describe the subject matter of industrial/organizational (I/O) psychology.

As productivity becomes increasingly important to American industry, industrial/organizational psychologists are playing more important roles. **Industrial/organizational (I/O) psychologists** focus on how individual behavior is affected by the work environment, coworkers, and organizations. I/O psychology is often thought of as an applied discipline that spans several areas of psychology, including those that deal with work, fatigue, personnel selection, evaluation of programs, consumer surveys, small-group processes, and pay and efficiency. I/O psychology has reached out to government, hospitals, universities, and public-service agencies, in addition to traditional settings, such as businesses. In all these environments, how well individuals perform their duties and relate to one another is a key concern.

Psychology and Business: Selecting Personnel

Learning Objective 33.8 Explain how I/O psychologists approach the task of selecting personnel.

An important task of I/O psychologists is to help businesses select well-trained, qualified individuals for specific positions. Today, finding the right people for jobs occurs within the context of an organization's or business's *strategic planning.* This means forecasting the future needs of an organization, establishing specific

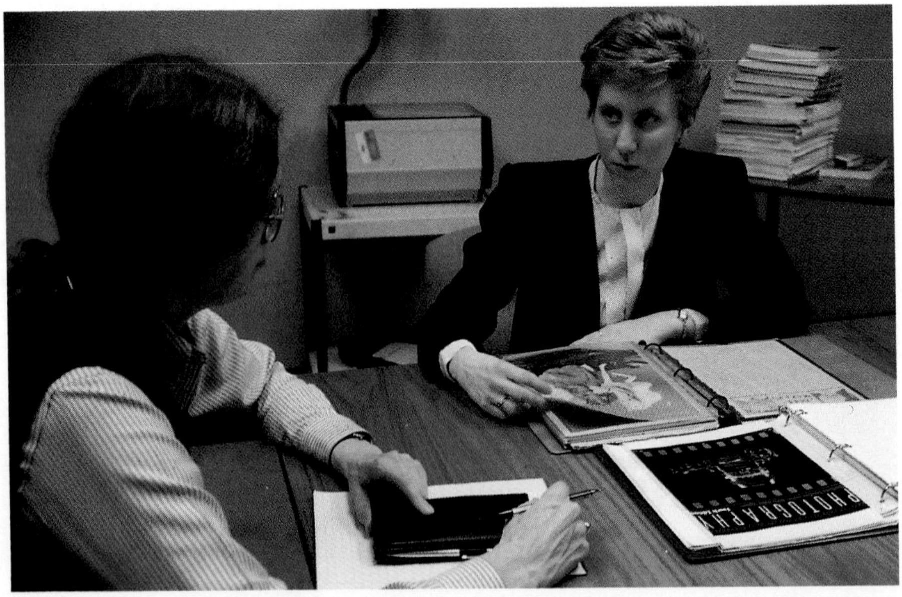

Interviewers are warned not to allow subtle variables such as their own mood to interfere with the interview process.

objectives, and implementing programs to ensure that appropriate people will be available when the organization needs them (Jackson & Schuler, 1990). Employers want people who will enjoy their work, suit the company's needs, and be productive. To find such employees, I/O psychologists apply learning and motivational theories to the workplace. Using specific selection procedures, including interviews and a series of standardized tests, I/O psychologists strive to produce the best match between employers and employees. The selection procedure for a job with a large firm is often complicated and time-consuming. Unfortunately, even a complex selection process can result in serious hiring mistakes.

performance appraisal: The process by which a supervisor evaluates the performance of a subordinate on a periodic basis.

Selection procedures are aimed at one basic task—predicting the success of a job candidate. The key factor is standardization. Employers and researchers alike stress that to compare individuals, they have to use applications, interviews, work samples, and tests that are alike if reasonable comparisons are to be made. Subtle factors can be at work in selection procedures, and interviewers have to pay particular attention to these factors to make sure that such things as their own moods do not influence their evaluations (Baron, 1987).

Standardized cognitive tests, such as those for general ability and specific knowledge, can be good predictors of academic success. However, the widespread use of tests in industry has raised questions for I/O psychologists concerning whether the tests are valid predictors of job performance. This has become especially important, given the large number of lawsuits by people who feel that the tests have discriminated against them; these lawsuits challenge the use of tests as selection devices (Guion & Gibson, 1988).

Performance Appraisal

Learning Objective 33.9 Identify some common problems with performance appraisal procedures, and explain why performance appraisals are important.

Have you ever been evaluated by an employer? Did your boss appreciate your hard work, dedication to details, and unstinting loyalty? Bosses are sometimes good at making an appraisal of work, but they sometimes forget your good efforts and remember only your mistakes, or their poor social skills may not allow them to convey to you accurately how they feel about your performance. What makes a boss good at evaluating employees? How could a psychologist assess whether a manager is good at his or her assigned task—managing and evaluating?

Performance appraisal is the process by which a supervisor periodically evaluates the performance of a subordinate. Supervisors have been making such appraisals since there have been supervisors, and researchers in the past 70 years have tried to find ways to do it systematically. Performance appraisals are especially important because they are so often used in salary determinations (Cleveland, Murphy, & Williams, 1989). The problem with performance appraisal is that it is generally done inaccurately by people with few skills in evaluation and with few good diagnostic aids. Supervisors generally report that they dislike conducting evaluations. They don't like to review their subordinates; they often acknowledge that they do not have strong evaluative skills; furthermore, some managers have sexist and other biases (Swim, Borgida, Maruyama, & Myers, 1989). Many companies require periodic evaluations, but reluctant managers do it as infrequently as possible, sometimes in a cursory manner. They often evaluate everybody about the same—average, or perhaps very good. This often leaves employees feeling unappreciated. Ways to improve the process typically involve more active thinking on the part of a supervisor; we see this in the Understanding the Research Process box on the next page.

Learning Objective 33.10 Identify several factors that contribute to job motivation and performance, and distinguish between job motivation and job satisfaction.

Motivating Workers

In addition to selecting and appraising personnel, another task of I/O psychologists is to motivate workers. One obvious motivator is economics. People need

UNDERSTANDING THE RESEARCH PROCESS

Performance Appraisal

"I distinctly remember you goofing off last Thursday; on Friday, I saw you behaving rudely to a customer! Don't do it again, do you hear?" exhorted The Boss to an intimidated employee. The frightened clerk shook his head and walked away muttering. He had been out sick on Thursday; further, his boss didn't know the nature of the interaction with the customer who yelled, insulted, and did everything but slap him. He felt that his performance appraisal was inaccurate because of the boss's poor memory (he was off last Thursday) and lack of information (the rudeness episode).

Managers have to observe employees, code and store in memory their performance, remember it after intervening activities have taken place, and then recall specific behaviors accurately. In general, cognitive processes have been assumed to be crucial in making a performance appraisal (DeNisi & Williams, 1988).

Research shows that when a person makes a performance appraisal of an individual's work, the most recent work has a strong biasing effect. That is, although people's work may be at a distinct level of performance, a good (or bad) period of performance just before an appraisal can bias an observer toward a good or poor decision. Steiner and Rain (1989) argue that there are recency effects in performance appraisals, just as there are in memory studies (see Chapter 6). This means that frequent performance appraisals are less likely to be affected by a single episode than a performance appraisal done after a long period of time, when the performance of the past day or two might disproportionately affect results. Are there other memory effects in performance appraisal?

Realizing that memory effects are potentially important in performance appraisal, DeNisi, Robbins, and Cafferty (1989) asked subjects to watch videotapes of carpenters who were sawing, sanding, and staining. They were to evaluate the carpenter's performance. The subjects were provided with a guide to the correct performance and a set of diary cards with tabs on them. The tabbed cards had either the names of the carpenters, the task names, or they were blank. There were four groups of subjects; three who used diaries that tracked performance *by task, by person,* and a *blank* set of cards with no particular orientation, and a *control group* with no diary.

Results showed that the diary conditions produced better recall and improved ratings. Keeping a diary provided a structure for the raters that organized information and made them less dependent on memory. This would obviously help eliminate recency effects found by Steiner and Rain. Performance appraisals are a cognitive task affected by traditional cognitive variables, such as intervening activity, memory loss, and recency effects. Keeping a diary can minimize the negative effects, but of course, raters need to look at their diaries to make better appraisals. The research shows that the practical considerations of diary keeping may improve performance appraisals.

Because laws have been passed to protect employees from discrimination according to age, race, gender, and religion, employers have been forced to be more responsive to employees by doing regular performance appraisals. In the process, larger companies with better trained staffs are helping workers by specifying behavioral objectives. Employees are given specific tasks to master during the next appraisal period. I/O psychologists have also worked to develop better rating forms, to train managers to evaluate more effectively and especially to help managers who regularly conduct performance appraisals do so without preconceived biases. They have set up on-the-job training programs for eliminating the biases that might exist. All this can be especially beneficial in motivating workers and helping them to find satisfaction in their work.

- ▲ ***What evidence suggests that more frequent performance appraisals affect the quality of appraisals?***
- ▲ ***What evidence suggests that managers may make different types of performance appraisals if they keep diaries of performance?***
- ▲ ***According to the research, what type of special efforts could managers make to ensure that performance appraisals are fair, understood, and unbiased?***

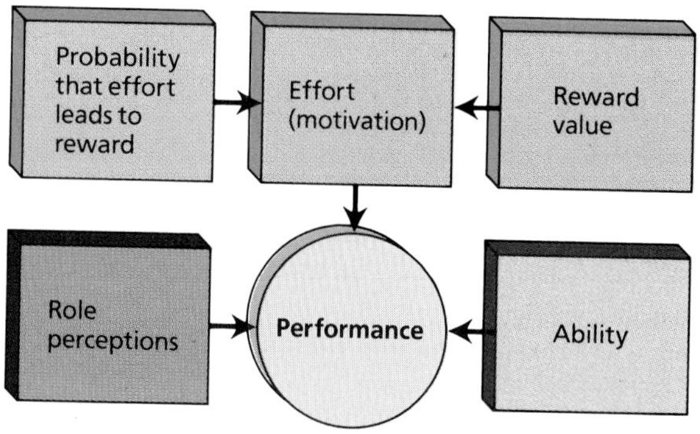

Figure 33.3

According to Lawler and Porter's (1967) managerial model, ability, motivation, and role perceptions determine work performance, and the values of a reward and the probability that an effort will be successful affect motivation level. The Lawler and Porter modification of the Vroom expectancy model is widely accepted, but probably not the final word on the variables that affect work performance.

money to live. Nonetheless, a successful employer–employee relationship relies on other factors in addition to economic motivation. Performance is also affected by *intrinsically motivated behavior*—that is, behavior engaged in strictly because it brings pleasure. (We examined intrinsic and extrinsic motivation in Chapter 9).

Psychologists know that when intrinsically motivated behaviors are constantly reinforced with direct external rewards (such as money), productivity drops. In addition, we know that an extremely well-paid plumber may find her work tedious and unfulfilling and thus be sloppy. In contrast, a lower-paid clerical worker who finds his job important and challenging will perform well and increase his responsibilities.

Employers, often with the help of I/O psychologists, are constantly trying to find ways to motivate employees to be more productive and hence provide the company with more profit. One theory, initially proposed by Vroom (1964), suggests that job performance is determined by both motivation and ability. Vroom's is an expectancy theory (we examined expectancy theories in Chapter 9); it states that motivation is determined by what people expect to get from performing a task—a rewarding experience or a frustrating one. According to Vroom, a person must first have the ability to perform the task; without that, the experience will be frustrating and hence nonmotivating.

Lawler and Porter (1967) modified and expanded Vroom's theory. They contend that performance is determined by motivation, ability, and *role perception*—the way people think about themselves and their jobs (see Figure 33.3). Lawler and Porter believe that workers must fully understand the nature of their positions and all that is required of them in performing their jobs. Too often, people fail not because of lack of effort (motivation) or ability, but because they do not know what is expected of them or how to achieve a sense of control or power in an organization (Ragins & Sundstrom, 1989). Today, researchers claim that motivation to work is explained by integrating theories that focus on goals, expectancies, and thoughts (Locke & Latham, 1990).

Job Satisfaction. Job satisfaction is different from job motivation because performance may or may not be affected by job satisfaction. Motivation, which refers to the internal conditions that direct a person to act, is always shown in behavior. Job satisfaction, which is a person's attitude about his or her work and workplace, may not be shown in behavior. A tired, bored, and overworked person may feel discouraged and angry—she may even hate her job—but she can still be motivated to work. Her motivation may stem from the high pay she receives, her obligation to complete a job, or from some other reason. Her motivation and job perform-

TABLE 33.1 Key factors in job satisfaction

Some key factors related to job satisfaction shown to be important across a variety of research studies
▲ The work is interesting.
▲ There is adequate recognition.
▲ The work contributes to self-esteem.
▲ There are opportunities for advancement.
▲ The pay is perceived as adequate and equitable.
▲ There is job security.
▲ There are good relationships with supervisory personnel.
▲ There are opportunities for enjoyable social interactions.
▲ There is a positive attitude toward the work environment.
▲ The work is perceived to be challenging.
▲ There are opportunities to apply one's own judgment.
▲ There is some degree of autonomy.
▲ Opportunities exist to influence company policy and procedures.
▲ There is adequate information and equipment.
▲ There is authority to ensure that a job is completed.

ance are high—as seen in her work. Thus, although her job satisfaction is low, it does not affect her performance.

Job satisfaction must be viewed within the context of the work setting and the worker's standards (Locke & Latham, 1990). Workers' motivations and values have to be consistent with opportunities and resources that are available, thus facilitating potential advancement and satisfaction (Katzell & Thompson, 1990). People's level of satisfaction depends on the extent to which they see a discrepancy between their expectations for satisfaction and actual satisfaction. This depends on various facets of a job; people can be pleased or dissatisfied about hours, pay, client contact, promotion opportunities, and other specific facets of a job (Algera, 1990). People have standards for comparison that determine the extent to which they feel they are doing well or poorly (Rice, McFarlin & Bennett, 1989). Table 33.1 presents factors that have been shown to be important across a variety of research studies.

Learning Objective 33.11 Describe three styles of management that are used to motivate employees.

Motivation Management. Both employers and psychologists know that people can be motivated by different variables. Monetary rewards are important, for example, but so is the likelihood of success. Psychologists recognize three basic approaches to motivating people, or motivation management: paternalistic, behavioral, and participatory.

The fundamental idea of *paternalistic management* is that a company takes care of its employees' needs and desires in a fatherly manner. This management approach was common in the mining companies of Appalachia, which provided housing, schools, recreation, and churches for employees, not because of individual job performance but simply because they were employees.

The paternalistic management approach is contrary to most psychologists' views on behavior. Instrumental conditioning studies show that for a behavior (such as work) to be established and maintained, reinforcement must be contingent on performance. In a paternalistic system, all employees—productive as well as nonproductive—are given reinforcement. Reinforcement without contingency does not encourage people to work hard.

Behavioral approaches to motivation assume that people will work only if they receive tangible rewards for specific task performance. Examples include paying a factory worker by the piece and a typist by the page. In such a system, hard-working employees obtain more rewards—commissions, salary raises, bonuses, and so on—because they produce more.

Participatory management is based on the belief that individuals who have a say in the decisions that affect their lives are more motivated to work. Participation, it is argued, provides a setting in which managers and employees can exchange information to solve problems (Tjosvold, 1987). Supporters of this approach believe that a sense of competence and self-determination is likely to increase individuals' levels of motivation. "Quality circles," whereby workers of all levels assemble to discuss ways to promote excellence, is one technique employers use to involve workers in the management process (Matsui & Onglatco, 1990). Many variables affect the success of participatory management programs: the work setting, the individuals involved, the kind of decisions to be made, and the hiring policies. If you were setting up your own company, which type of management style would you use? Would you be the paternalistic boss, would you set objectives to be met, or would you have more participatory management?

In participatory management programs, employees are offered a chance to comment on the business operations that affect them.

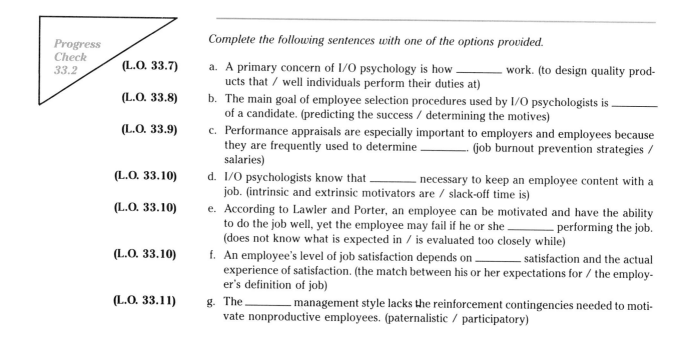

Progress Check 33.2

Complete the following sentences with one of the options provided.

(L.O. 33.7) a. A primary concern of I/O psychology is how ________ work. (to design quality products that / well individuals perform their duties at)

(L.O. 33.8) b. The main goal of employee selection procedures used by I/O psychologists is ________ of a candidate. (predicting the success / determining the motives)

(L.O. 33.9) c. Performance appraisals are especially important to employers and employees because they are frequently used to determine ________. (job burnout prevention strategies / salaries)

(L.O. 33.10) d. I/O psychologists know that ________ necessary to keep an employee content with a job. (intrinsic and extrinsic motivators are / slack-off time is)

(L.O. 33.10) e. According to Lawler and Porter, an employee can be motivated and have the ability to do the job well, yet the employee may fail if he or she ________ performing the job. (does not know what is expected in / is evaluated too closely while)

(L.O. 33.10) f. An employee's level of job satisfaction depends on ________ satisfaction and the actual experience of satisfaction. (the match between his or her expectations for / the employer's definition of job)

(L.O. 33.11) g. The ________ management style lacks the reinforcement contingencies needed to motivate nonproductive employees. (paternalistic / participatory)

Module Summary

Environmental Psychology

- Environmental psychologists study how physical settings affect human behavior and how people change their environments to meet their psychological needs (p. 639).
- *Crowding* is the psychological feeling that one's space is too restricted, given the number of people in the space. *Social density* refers to the number of people in the same size of space. *Spatial density* refers to the variable size of a space containing the same number of people (p. 640).

Industrial and Organizational Psychology

- Industrial/organizational psychology attempts to apply psychological principles in the workplace. When I/O psychologists help develop selection procedures, they generally use tools such as standardized applications, interviews, work samples, and tests (p. 644).
- *Performance appraisal* is the process by which a supervisor periodically evaluates the performance of a subordinate. I/O psychologists have developed better rating forms, have trained managers to evaluate more effectively, and especially have helped managers to evaluate work performance without biases (p. 645).

KEY TERMS

crowding, p. 640
environmental psychology, p. 639
industrial/organizational (I/O) psychologists, p. 644
performance appraisal, p. 645
personal space, p. 640
privacy, p. 642
stressor, p. 640

SELF-TEST

Module 33

- Before taking the self-test, **recite** and **review.**
- Use the key at the back of the text to *correct* your answers.
- *Restudy* pages that correspond to any questions you answered incorrectly.

1. Environmental psychology is the study of how
   a. global pollution will affect future generations.
   b. physical settings influence human behavior.
   c. to motivate people to conserve natural resources and protect the natural environment.
   d. both b and c.
2. Environmental stressors such as uncomfortable temperatures or noise
   a. cause a decline in human performance.
   b. are annoying, but have little or no effect on our overall behavior.
   c. motivate people to work harder and faster so that they can complete the task and get away from the stressor.
   d. seem to impair the performance of some people and motivate the performance of other people.
3. If a psychologist observes a group of 100 people in a 1,000-square-foot room and then moves the group to a 10,000-square-foot room and observes them there, the psychologist is studying the effects of
   a. crowding.
   b. social density.
   c. spatial density.
   d. social and spatial density.
4. The spatial zone that Hall termed *intimate distance*
   a. is commonly found in contact sports.
   b. would be observed frequently in an average friendship.
   c. is found only in romantic relationships.
   d. would be maintained while a person told another person a spicy story.
5. People establish a sense of privacy by
   a. ignoring other people.
   b. limiting access to their immediate environment.
   c. maintaining a personal-distance spatial zone.
   d. reprimanding someone who invades their personal space.
6. According to Geller, environmental psychologists can encourage people to preserve the environment by
   a. finding ways to eliminate unnecessary stressors.
   b. using social marketing strategies to apply behavioral interventions to targeted populations.
   c. using scare tactics.
   d. creating public policies.
7. I/O psychologists are concerned with how business organizations, work environments, and employees influence
   a. the economy.
   b. demands for quality control.
   c. affirmative action policies.
   d. individual employee behavior.

8. When selecting personnel for an employer, I/O psychologists
   a. attempt to standardize all selection procedures in order to make valid comparisons among job applicants.
   b. must not allow their own moods to influence their evaluations.
   c. pay particular attention to the physical attractiveness of potential candidates.
   d. both a and b.
9. Which of the following is a common problem with performance appraisal procedures?
   a. No research has been done to determine a systematic way of appraising performance.
   b. Supervisors often do not have the evaluative skills needed to appraise their employees.
   c. Supervisors frequently exaggerate the differences among their employees in terms of performance evaluation.
   d. Sexism and racism always bias the evaluation process.
10. Which of the following lists factors that are important to job performance, according to Vroom and Lawler and Porter?
    a. motivation, ability, expectation, and role perception
    b. personality, intelligence, skill, and academic training
    c. salary, benefits, vacation time, and sick leave
    d. recognition, schedule flexibility, task variation, and promotions
11. A management style that attempts to motivate employees by providing commissions, salary raises, bonuses, and other tangible rewards is
    a. paternalistic management.
    b. motivation management.
    c. employee-centered management.
    d. the behavioral management approach.
12. Participatory management increases employee's motivation because
    a. it gives employees a sense of competence and self-determination.
    b. the company takes care of the employee's basic living needs.
    c. specific tasks are well-defined and rewarded upon completion.
    d. each employee writes his or her own job description.

Connections

If you are interested in . . .	Turn to . . .	To learn more about . . .
The formation of attitudes	◆ Chapter 5, p. 193	How social (observational) learning theory claims that people learn attitudes by observing the behavior and attitudes of others
	◆ Chapter 8, pp. 306, 317	The way children's and adolescents' developing attitudes, which are often based on sex-role stereotypes, have their roots in childhood learning
The way people form self-concepts	◆ Chapter 8, pp. 306, 317	How early interactions with parents, friends, and relatives help shape a child's developing self-concept
	◆ Chapter 10, p. 409	How humanists such as Carl Rogers focused their theories around the idea of an emerging and satisfying self-concept
	◆ Chapter 14, pp. 578–581	How cognitive psychologists claim that a person's self-concept can be bolstered through cognitive (thought) reshaping
Industrial and organizational psychology and the use of tests in the workplace	◆ Chapter 11, pp. 467–472	Using tests to predict specific behaviors, such as academic achievement or mechanical aptitude
	◆ Chapter 9, pp. 365–370	How a person's motivation and expectations for success change test results and work performance
	◆ Chapter 11, p. 468	How personality tests such as the MMPI-2 are used to screen people for maladjustment

Because social psychologists study the influence of other people on specific individuals, it is not surprising that the relationship of social psychology to other areas of psychology is vast. Our perception of the world (Chapter 3, p. 78) is affected by learning in particular (Chapter 5, p. 192). People's ability to make performance appraisals has been shown to be affected by memory (Chapter 6, p. 213). Our social relationships start in our childhood development (Chapter 8, p. 306) and proceed through adolescence and adulthood (Chapter 8, p. 317). Our social world is affected by our personality (Chapter 10, p. 426), how we handle stress (Chapter 12, p. 496), and whether we are affected by any psychological disorders. Social psychology has taken on a strong cognitive emphasis (Chapter 7, p. 240) and has acknowledged the importance of individual differences (Chapter 11, p. 441) and motivation (Chapter 9, p. 372).

Appendix

Scientific and Statistical Methods

Until recently, Shirley could not hold a job because she suffered from debilitating schizophrenic symptoms, including disordered thinking and bizarre auditory hallucinations. Now, however, Shirley works 40 productive hours a week at a floral shop, and she rarely experiences the mental aberrations that once made her life a living hell. Shirley's improvement is due in part to phenothiazine, a drug that helps control the brain's use of the neurotransmitter dopamine, and in part to a caring psychotherapist. However, credit must also be given to researchers who discovered that children of schizophrenic parents have a statistically greater risk for developing schizophrenia. By helping to uncover the disorder's biological connection, they spurred the search for drugs such as phenothiazine.

Scientific progress is in many ways directly linked to our ability to measure and quantify data. In the physical sciences, the need to measure time, weight, and distance precisely has given rise to terms describing mind-boggling minuteness, including femtosecond (one quadrillionth of a second), nanogram (one billionth of a gram), and angstrom (one ten-billionth of a meter). Examining behavioral phenomena in numerical terms enables scientists to be more exact, consistent, and objective.

Statistics is a branch of mathematics that deals with collecting, classifying, and analyzing data. To rule out coincidence and discover the true causes of behavior, psychologists control the variables in experiments, then use statistics to describe, summarize, and present results.

statistics: The branch of mathematics that deals with collecting, classifying, and analyzing data.

Conducting Experiments

The following account of a therapy experiment helps to illustrate how proper methodology and statistics help scientists to interpret results. A psychologist was interested in determining whether a new therapeutic technique he had been using was effective with couples who were experiencing marital conflict. The approach he used focused on relaxation. For three years, he had been teaching couples relaxation techniques to help them cope better, and he found it effective—the couples were better able to communicate after they had gone through relaxation exercises. Now, he wanted to show it in an experiment; he wanted to show that relaxation training *caused* the marital improvement.

Hypotheses

He *hypothesized*—that is, developed a tentative idea—that relaxation training can be crucial to communication in marriage. A **hypothesis** is a tentative statement about a causal relationship between two variables or situations, which is usually meant to be evaluated in an experiment. Recall that an **experiment** is a procedure in which a researcher systematically manipulates certain variables in order to describe objectively the relation between the variables of concern and the resulting behavior. Well-designed experiments permit inferences about cause and effect.

The psychologist advertised in the newspaper for couples experiencing marital problems. He told the couples who answered the ad that they would be participating in a study of "therapy for marriage difficulties." He informed the potential clients that all of the couples would receive effective therapy, although not all at the same time or in the same order, and some would have to be on a waiting list for a few months.

Variables

The psychologist wanted to know whether his therapeutic technique (relaxation) would be effective—thus, the independent variable in his study would be the delivery of therapy. Recall from Chapter 1 that the **independent variable** is the one that is directly and purposefully manipulated by the experimenter to see what effect differences in it will have on the variables under study. The **dependent variable** is the behavior measured by an experimenter in order to assess whether changes in the independent variable affect the behavior under study. The dependent variable in this study would be scores in three areas: the couples' level of anxiety, marital satisfaction, and frequency of sexual contact.

To know whether his treatment would be effective, the psychologist asked each of the couples in the study to fill out a battery of questions that measured their anxiety, the level of marital satisfaction, and the frequency of sexual contact. With these, he could later assess whether his subjects changed over the course of treatment.

The psychologist divided 75 couples into three groups. He put every third couple in a control group and told them that they would have to wait several months for therapy to begin. This **control group** provides a standard for comparison. The couples in the other two groups would be compared to those in the control group to see whether relaxation produced any measurable effect. These second and third groups were **experimental groups;** they received training in relaxation over a 6-month period. One of the experimental groups received relaxation training alone, and the other received both relaxation training and communication exercises.

Every week for 20 weeks, the couples in the two experimental groups were treated. At the end of the study, the researcher again examined the 75 couples' level of anxiety, their marital satisfaction, and level of sexual activity. He expected

hypothesis: A tentative statement about a causal relationship between two variables or situations to be evaluated in an experiment.

experiment: A procedure in which a researcher systematically manipulates certain variables to describe objectively the relation between the variables of concern and the resulting behavior. Well-designed experiments permit inferences about cause and effect.

independent variable: The variable in an experiment that is directly and purposefully manipulated by the experimenter to see what effect the differences in it will have on the variables under study.

dependent variable: The behavior measured by an experimenter to assess whether changes in the independent variable affect the behavior under study.

control group: In an experiment, the group of subjects that does not receive the treatment under investigation. The control group is used for comparison purposes so that the observed effects can be traced to the variable under study.

experimental group: In an experiment, the group of subjects that receives the treatment under investigation.

sample: A group of subjects or participants who generally represent the population about which an inference is being made.

those who received the experimental treatments to do better than the control group. (At the end of 20 weeks, the control group was then given treatment that involved relaxation and communication.)

The researcher found, as expected, that the control group changed very little (or not at all) over the course of the experiment. However, the relaxation training groups produced strong effects when compared with the control group. Those who had received relaxation treatment—especially when it was combined with communication training—were less anxious, happier in their marriages, and had more frequent sexual contact. The researcher concluded that the independent variable (the relaxation training) caused a change in the subjects' lives. This experiment is a simple one. Though there are other things that the researcher might do to make it better, it has the elements of a good experiment.

Carefully Conducted Experiments

What makes a good experiment? As mentioned in Chapter 1, to be generalizable to a population, a good experiment must have a sufficient number of carefully selected subjects in each group. Experiments have one or more experimental groups and a control group.

Inferences. If researchers are to make valid inferences from the data that is collected, it is important that the subjects come from the same larger population. With human beings, this may mean that the subjects should come from the same socioeconomic status, perhaps even the same community, or be nearly the same age; the goal is to provide a balanced group or sample with regard to important characteristics. Thus, a **sample** is a group of subjects or participants who are generally representative of the population about which an inference is being made. Any differences among the groups must be due only to the experimental manipulation. If other variables in the study were properly controlled (i.e., held constant), the researchers could conclude that any difference in the couples' marital relationship at the end of the experiment was a result of therapy. If the sample was not carefully balanced, then it would be difficult or impossible to conclude that therapy alone made the difference.

Subject Selection. Proper selection is a key element of good research. Sometimes, subjects are selected randomly; for example, researchers may administer a newly developed achievement test to randomly chosen members of the general population in order to derive an average test score. At other times, subjects are chosen with respect to a specific variable, such as gender or age. In any case, experimental subjects must be representative of the population to which they will be compared, and the researchers must make enough observations to ensure that the behaviors observed are representative and not uncharacteristic.

Carefully Defined Variables. The description of the independent and dependent variables is especially important. The independent variable has to be spelled out accurately, and how it is administered or delivered to subjects has to be equally painstakingly specified. If, for example, the variable is a particular drug dosage, the dosage must be specified carefully. If an experiment states that rats receive 10 milligrams of a drug for each kilogram of body weight, then regardless of its weight, each rat would receive the proper amount of the drug. Similarly, the dependent variable has to be carefully defined; how is it to be measured, with what instruments, how frequently, and by whom? Some dependent variables, such as running speed, are easily specified; others, such as arousal, anxiety, and depression, are more difficult to define precisely. In those cases, researchers offer an

operational definition of the variable—that is, they provide a concrete description of how the variable being studied will be measured. In the therapy example, marital adjustment could be operationally defined as scores on an adjustment scale or anxiety scale, or self-reports monitored on a weekly basis. If the behavior being measured is anxiety, it can be defined operationally as a change in the electrodermal response (a measure of nervous system arousal).

After researchers have specified the variables and chosen the subjects, they conduct the experiment, hoping it will yield interpretable, meaningful results. However, extraneous or irrelevant variables can affect the results, making interpretation difficult. *Extraneous variables* are factors that affect the results of an experiment but are not of interest to the experimenter. A lightning storm that occurs during an experiment in which anxiety is being measured through electrodermal response is an extraneous variable. It would be difficult or impossible for the researchers to ascertain which parts of the increased electrodermal response were due to manipulations of the independent variable and which parts were due to anxiety associated with lightning storms. When extraneous variables occur during an experiment (or just before it), they may *confound* the results, making the data difficult to interpret.

operational definition: A definition based on a set of concrete steps used to define a variable.

descriptive statistics: A general set of procedures used to describe and summarize samples of data.

frequency distribution: A chart or an array, usually arranged from the highest to lowest score, showing the number of instances of each obtained score.

frequency polygon: A graph of a frequency distribution that shows the number of instances of obtained scores; usually, data points are connected by straight lines.

Descriptive Statistics

Statistics is a branch of mathematics that researchers use to evaluate and organize experimental data. Specifically, researchers use **descriptive statistics** to summarize, condense, and describe data. Descriptive statistics make it possible for researchers to interpret the results of their experiment. Similarly, your professors use descriptive statistics to interpret exam results. For example, a statistical description of a 100-point midterm exam may show that 10% of a class scored more than 60 points, 70% scored between 40 and 60 points, and 20% scored fewer than 40 points. Based on this statistical description, the professor might conclude that the test was exceptionally difficult and arrange the grades so that anyone who earned 61 points or more receives an A. However, before inferences can be drawn or before grades can be arranged, the data from a research study must be organized in a meaningful way.

Organization of Data

When psychologists do research, they often produce large amounts of data that must be assessed. Suppose a social psychologist asks parents to monitor the number of hours their children watch television. The parents might report between 0 and 20 hours of television watching a week.

The first step in making these numbers meaningful is to organize them so that we can see the number of times each score occurs. This type of organization is known as a **frequency distribution.** As the frequency distribution in Table A.1 (on the next page) shows, the number 9 occurs more frequently than any other, indicating that more children (in this sample) watched 9 hours of TV a week than any other number of hours.

Researchers often construct graphs from the data in a frequency distribution. such a graph, a **frequency polygon,** shows the possible scores (e.g., the number of hours children watched TV) on the horizontal axis, or *abscissa,* and the frequency of each score (e.g., the number of children who watched TV for those

TABLE A.1 A frequency distribution for TV hours watched by 100 children

Number of hours of TV watching	Number of individuals watching	Total number of individuals
0	1	1
1	1 1 1	3
2	1 1 1	3
3	1 1 1 1	4
4	1 1 1 1 1	5
5	1 1 1 1 1 1	6
6	1 1 1 1 1 1 1	7
7	1 1 1 1 1 1 1	7
8	1 1 1 1 1 1 1 1 1	9
9	1 1 1 1 1 1 1 1 1 1	10
10	1 1 1 1 1 1 1 1 1	9
11	1 1 1 1 1 1 1	7
12	1 1 1 1 1 1	6
13	1 1 1 1 1	5
14	1 1 1 1	4
15	1 1 1 1	4
16	1 1 1	3
17	1 1 1	3
18	1 1	2
19	1	1
20	1	1

Note: Few individuals score very high or very low; most individuals have scores in the middle range.

hours) on the vertical axis, or *ordinate*. Figure A.1 is a frequency polygon of the data from the frequency distribution in Table A.1. Straight lines connect the data points.

Measures of Central Tendency

People use the term *average* to describe a variety of commonalities or tendencies. A wife asks a clerk to help her find a sweater for her average-sized husband. The owner of a new sedan boasts that his car averages 40 miles to a gallon of gasoline. A doctor tells her patient that his serum cholesterol level is average because it falls halfway between low and high measurements. In each of these cases, a person is using "average" to depict a type of norm. A descriptive statistic that tells us which single score best represents an entire set of scores is referred to as a **measure of central tendency.** It is used to summarize and condense data. Also, because almost every group has members who score high or lower than the group, researchers often use a measure of central tendency to describe the group as a whole.

measure of central tendency: An index of the average or typical value of a distribution of scores.

Consider the statement, "Men are taller than women." Because we know that some women are taller than some men, we assume that the statement means, "On the average, men are taller than women." In other words, if we take all the men and all the women in the world and compare their heights, on the average men will be taller.

Mean. How would someone investigate the truth of the statement, "Men are taller than women"? One way would be to measure the height of thousands of men and women, taking a careful sample from each country, race, and age group. One could then calculate the average heights of the men and women in the sample and plot the results on a graph. For each group, the heights of the subjects were measured, added together, and divided by the number of subjects in the group. The resulting number, the **mean,** represents the arithmetic average in terms of height for a person in the group. The mean is the most frequently used measure of central tendency.

Mode. Another statistic used to describe the central tendency of a set of data is the mode. The **mode** is the data point most frequently observed. Figure A.2 plots the frequency of different heights for a series of individuals. It shows that only one person is 58 inches tall, three are 79 inches, and more people are 70 inches tall than any other height. The mode of that group therefore is 70 inches.

Median. The **median** is the 50% point: Half the observations fall above the median and the other half fall below it. Figure A.3 on the next page arranges a series of data from lowest to highest. It shows that half the data fall above 68 and half fall below 68. The median of the data set, therefore, is 68. You probably have read news reports about median income in the United States being on the rise. For example, a typical news report might be "According to the U.S. Census Bureau, the median income in the United States rose to $31,000 in 1992"; half of the families earn more than this amount, and half earn less.

Table A.2 on the next page presents a set of data from an experiment on memory. The scores are the number of correctly recalled items. There are three groups of subjects: A control group received no special treatment; the second group received task-motivating instructions (such as, "think hard," "Focus your attention"), and the third group was hypnotized and told under hypnosis that they would recall better. The results of the study show that the task-motivating group did slightly worse than the control group (the mean was 10.3 compared with the control group mean of 10.6), but the hypnosis group recalled 15.4 words on average, compared with the control group's recall of 10.6 words, a difference of 4.8 words. Hypnosis seemed to have a positive effective on memory—or did it?

mean: A measure of central tendency calculated by dividing the sum of the scores by the number of scores; the arithmetic average.

mode: A measure of central tendency; the most frequently observed value or measurement.

median: A measure of central tendency; the point at which 50% of all observations occur either above or below.

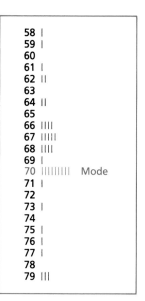

58 |
59 |
60
61 |
62 ||
63
64 ||
65
66 ||||
67 |||||
68 ||||
69 |
70 ||||||||| Mode
71 |
72
73 |
74
75 |
76 |
77 |
78
79 |||

Figure A.2

The *mode* is the data point that occurs with the greatest frequency.

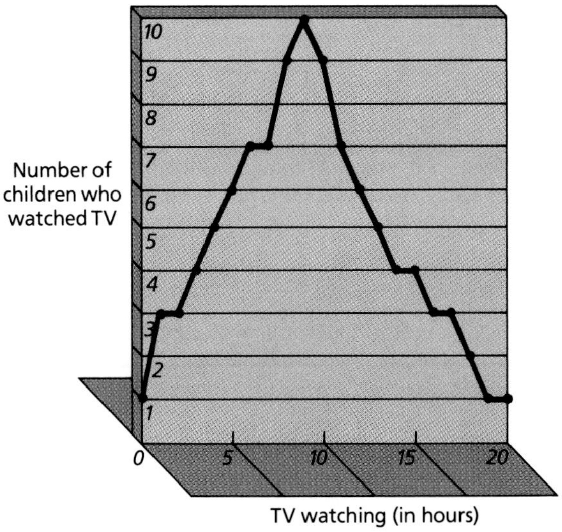

Figure A.1

This frequency polygon shows the number of hours of TV watched by 100 children. Frequency is shown on the ordinate or vertical axis; the actual scores occur on the abscissa or horizontal axis.

TABLE A.2 Calculations of mean and median for three groups of subjects

Subject	Control group	Experimental I (task motivating)	Experimental II (hypnosis)
1	10	11	16
2	12	13	14
3	14	14	16
4	10	12	12
5	11	12	10
6	9	8	9
7	5	10	15
8	12	5	12
9	16	10	18
10	7	8	32
Sum	106	103	154
Mean	10.6	10.3	15.4
Median	10.5	10.5	14.5

Control group (scores are reordered)

$$\text{Mean} = \frac{5 + 7 + 9 + 10 + 10 + 11 + 12 + 12 + 14 + 16}{10} \quad \frac{106}{10} = 10.6$$

Median = 5 7 9 10 [10 11] 12 12 14 16
↓
10.5

The point at which half the scores fall above and half the scores fall below is 10.5; that is, 10.5 is the median.

Experimental I (scores are reordered)

$$\text{Mean} = \frac{5 + 8 + 8 + 10 + 10 + 11 + 12 + 12 + 13 + 14}{10} \quad \frac{103}{10} = 10.3$$

Median = 5 8 8 10 [10 11] 12 12 13 14
↓
10.5

The point at which half the scores fall above and half the scores fall below is 10.5; that is, 10.5 is the median.

Experimental II (scores are reordered)

$$\text{Mean} = \frac{9 + 10 + 12 + 12 + 14 + 15 + 16 + 16 + 18 + 32}{10} \quad \frac{154}{10} = 15.4$$

Median = 9 10 12 12 [14 15] 16 16 18 32
↓
14.5

The point at which half the scores fall above and half the scores fall below is 14.5; that is, 14.5 is the median.

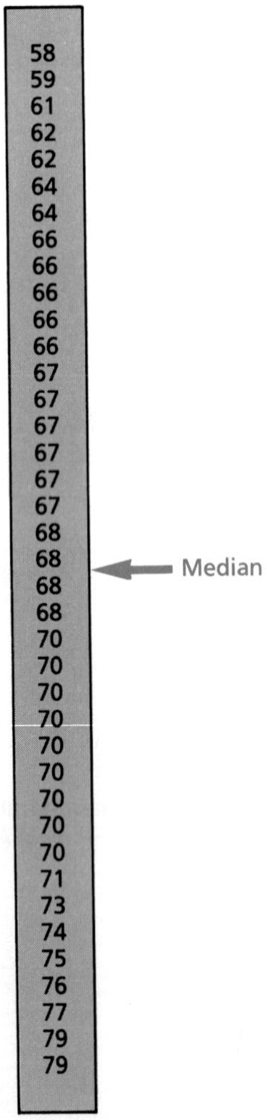

Figure A.3

The *median* is the 50% point. It is the point at which half the points fall above and half the points fall below.

The medians for the control and task-motivating group were equal—that is, 10.5 words. If you examine medians, the difference between the control group and the hypnosis group was 4 words. The median difference (4 words) is smaller than the mean difference (4.8 words). This occurred because the median discounts very high or very low scores. For example, if you average a zero in with five other test scores (where the average score is about 70), it will drop your *average* substantially; averaging in a 60 would not have as big an impact. However, with medians, an extreme score (be it a 0 or a 60) would count the same. With a small sample like this one, where a single score can have a big impact, the median is often a better measure of central tendency.

The mean, mode, and median are descriptive statistics that are measures of central tendency. They each tell researchers something about the average (or typical) subject. Sometimes, they are the same number, but more often there exists enough variability (one very tall person, two very short ones) that each central tendency measure yields a slightly different result. You should use the measure most appropriate to your situation. If, for example, you had to guess the height of a woman you had never met, a good guess would be the mean, the average height for women. If you were a buyer for a clothing store and had to pick one size of dress or shoe to order, you might be more likely to pick the modal size, the size that will occur more often than any other.

variability: A measure of the extent to which scores differ from one another and especially the extent to which they differ from the mean.

range: A measure of variability that describes the spread of scores within a group, calculated by subtracting the lowest score from the highest score.

Measures of Variability

A measure of central tendency is a single number that describes a hypothetical average subject. In real life, however, people do not always have scores that reflect the central tendency. Consequently, knowing how an average subject might score is more useful when we know how the scores in the group are distributed relative to one another. If you know that the mean of a group of numbers is 150, you do not know how widely dispersed are the scores that are averaged to calculate that mean.

A statistic that describes the extent to which scores differ from one another in a distribution is called a *measure of variability.* **Variability** is a measure of the extent to which scores differ from one another and especially the extent to which they differ from the mean. If all the subjects obtain the same score, no variability exists; this, however, is very unlikely to occur. It is more usual that in any group of subjects being tested or measured in some way, personal and situational characteristics will cause some to score high and some to score low. If researchers know the extent of that variation, they can estimate the extent to which subjects differ from the mean or the average subject.

Range. One measure of variability, the **range,** shows the spread of scores in a distribution. The range is calculated by subtracting the lowest score from the highest score. If the lowest score on a test was 20 points, and the highest was 85, the range was 65 points. Whether the mean was 45, 65, or 74 points, the range remained 65. There was always a 65-point spread from the lowest score to the highest.

The range is a relatively crude measure of the extent to which subjects vary within a group. In a group of 100 students, for example, nearly all may have scored within 10 points of the mean score of 80. However, if the lowest score was 20 and the highest was 85, the range would be 65. More precise measures of the spread of scores within a group are available, however. They indicate how scores are distributed as well as the extent of their spread.

Standard Deviation. Consider a reaction-time study that measures how quickly subjects press a button when a light is flashed. The following list gives the

standard deviation: A descriptive statistic that measures the variability of data from the mean of the sample.

number of milliseconds it took each of 30 tenth-graders chosen at random to press a button when a light was flashed; clearly, the reaction times vary.

450	490	500
610	520	470
480	492	585
462	600	490
740	700	595
500	493	495
498	455	510
470	480	540
710	722	575
490	495	570

A person who was told only that the mean reaction time is 540 would assume that 540 is the best estimate of how long it takes a tenth-grade student to respond to the light. However, these data are variable—not everyone took 540 milliseconds. Some took longer and some took less time. Psychologists say that the data were variable, or that there existed variability.

To find out how much variability exists among data, and to quantify it in a meaningful manner, we need to know the standard deviation. A **standard deviation** is a descriptive statistic that shows the variability of data from the mean of the sample; the standard deviation is calculated by figuring the extent to which each score differs from the mean.

Table A.3 shows the reaction times for two new groups of subjects responding to a light. The mean is the same for both groups, but Group 1 shows a large degree of variability, while Group 2 shows little variability. The standard deviation (i.e., estimate of variability) for Group 1 subjects will therefore be substantially higher than that for Group 2 subjects because the scores differ from the mean much more in the first group than in the second.

A standard deviation gives information about all the members of a group, not just an average member. Knowing the standard deviation—that is, the variability

TABLE A.3 Reaction times in milliseconds for two groups of subjects.

Group 1	Group 2
380	530
400	535
410	540
420	545
470	550
480	560
500	565
720	570
840	575
930	580
Mean = 555	Mean = 555
Standard deviation = 197	Standard deviation = 17

Note: Group 1 shows a wider range of scores and thus greater variability. Group 2, by contrast, shows a narrow range of scores and little variability.

associated with each mean—enables a researcher to make more accurate predictions. Because the standard deviation for subjects in Group 2 is small, a researcher can more confidently predict that a subject will respond to light in about 555 milliseconds (the mean response time). However, the researcher cannot confidently make the same prediction for subjects in Group 1 because that group's standard deviation is high.

Confidence in predictions turns out to be a key issue for statisticians; they want to be as sure as possible that the mean of a group actually represents the mean of the larger population that group (sample) represents. This concern is important because researchers want to make inferences that a difference between a control and an experimental group are due to the manipulation of the experimenter, not to chance factors, extraneous variables, or one or two scores that are deviant. It turns out that many of the manipulations and controls that researchers devise are necessary if they wish to make sound inferences, the topic we consider next.

Inferential Statistics and the Normal Curve

Researchers use a branch of statistics known as **inferential statistics** in making decisions about data. Inferential statistics are procedures used to reach generalizations about larger populations from a small sample of data, with a minimal degree of error. There are usually two issues to be explored. First, does the mean of a sample, a small group of subjects, actually reflect the mean of a larger population? Second, is a difference found between two means (for example, between a control group and an experimental group) a real and important difference, or is it a result of chance? Psychologists hope to find a **significant difference,** which means that a difference in performance between two groups can be repeated experimentally using similar groups of subjects and is not a result of chance variations. Generally, psychologists assume that a difference is statistically significant if the likelihood of its occurring by chance is less than 5 out of 100 times. However, many researchers assume a significant difference only if the likelihood of its occurring by chance is fewer than 1 out of 100 times.

It is sometimes difficult to decide whether a difference is significant. We now refer back to Table A.2 on page 660 where calculations were performed for a set of data. The data represent scores from a memory study in which the participants had to learn lists of unrelated words. There were three groups of subjects: One was given task-motivating instructions to concentrate deeply (Group 1), a second group was hypnotized (Group 2), and a third group was given no special instructions (the control group). The dependent variable was the average number of words correctly recalled by each subject. The results showed that the task-motivated groups recalled no more words, on the average, than the control group (in fact, 0.3 words less). The hypnosis group recalled 4.8 more words than the control group, on the average.

The hypnosis group did better than the control group. Can we conclude that hypnosis is a beneficial memory aid? Did the hypnosis group do significantly better than the control group? Was a 4.8-word difference *significant?* It is easy to see that *if* the difference between recall was 10 words, and if the variability within the groups was very small, the difference would be considered significant. However, a one- or two-word difference would not be considered significant if the variability within the groups was large. In the present case, 4.8-word difference was not

inferential statistics: Procedures used to reach conclusions (generalizations) about larger populations from a small sample of data with a minimal degree of error.

significant difference: A statistically determined likelihood that a behavior has not occurred because of chance alone. A result is said to be significant (trustworthy) if the probability of its occurrence by chance alone is less than 5 times out of 100, or less than 5%.

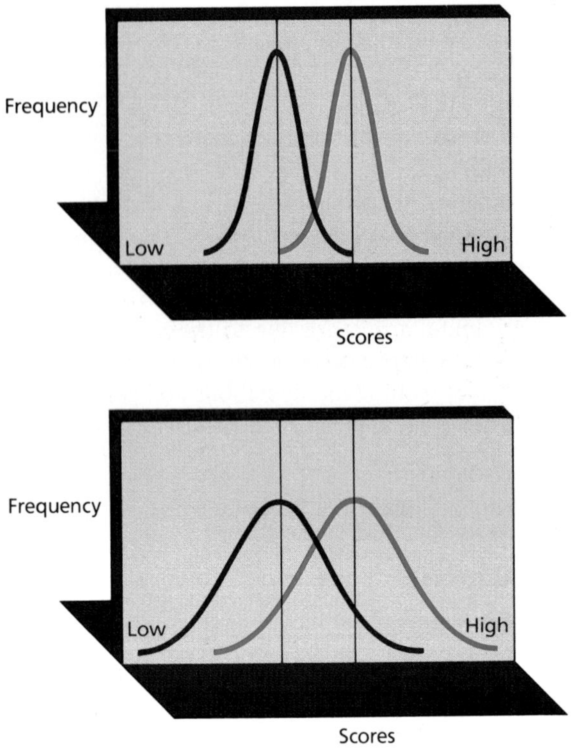

Figure A.4

The possible outcomes of two experiments are shown in the two graphs. In both cases, the means are identical. In the first, the scores all cluster around the means—there is little variability. The difference between the means in the first graph is likely to be significant. However, the means in the second graph (although identical to the first) are unlikely to be significantly different—the scores are too widely distributed. In the second graph, there is too much variability; the means may be affected by an extreme score—thus, a scientist is unlikely to accept them as significantly different from one another.

significant; the scores were highly variable, and only a small sample of subjects was used. When scores are variable (widely dispersed), both statistical tests and researchers are unlikely to view a small difference between two groups as being significant or important (see Figure A.4).

Even if statistically significant differences are obtained, most researchers require that an experiment be repeated with the same results. Repeating an experiment to verify a result is termed *replicating* the experiment. If, after replicating an experiment, the same statistically significant results are obtained, a researcher will generally say that the observed difference between the two groups is important.

Definition of the Normal Curve

When a large number of scores are involved, a frequency polygon often takes the form of a bell-shaped curve termed a **normal distribution,** or *normal curve.* Normal distributions usually have a few scores at each end and progressively many more scores toward the center. Height, for example, is approximately normally distributed: There are more people of average height than very tall or very short people (see Figure A.5). In addition to height, characteristics such as weight, shoe size, intelligence, and scores on psychology exams tend to be normally distributed.

normal distribution: A bell-shaped (symmetrical) curve that depicts the distribution of scores when using, a very large representative sample; also termed *normal curve.* Generally, the mean, mode, and median are equal.

Characteristics of a Normal Curve

A normal curve has some specific characteristics. The mean, mode, and median are assumed to be the same, and the distribution of scores around that central point is symmetrical. Also, most individuals have a score that occurs within six

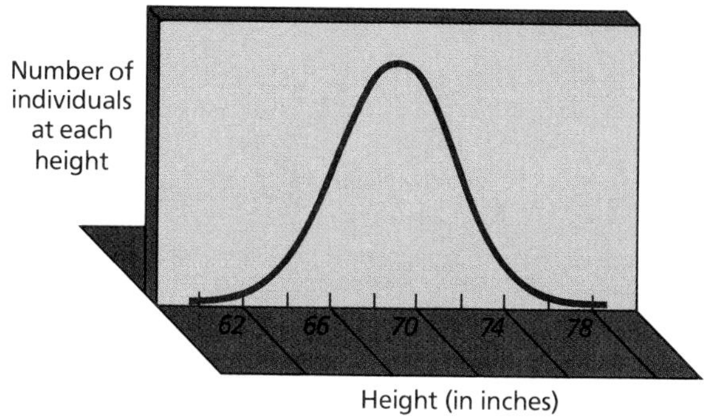

Figure A.5

In a normal distribution, or a normal curve, there are many more people of average height, weight, or intelligence than people at the extremes.

standard deviations—three above the mean and three below it (see Figure A.6). To explain, Figure A.7 shows a normal curve for test scores. The mean is 50, and the standard deviation is 10. Note how each increment of 10 points above or below the mean accounts for fewer and fewer individuals. Scores between 50 and 60 account for 34.13% of those tested; scores of 60–70 account for 13.59%; and scores above 70 account for only about 3%. The sum of these percentages (34.13 + 13.59 + 2.14 + 0.13) represents 50% of the scores.

When you know the mean and standard deviation of a set of data, you can estimate where an individual in the sample population stands, relative to others. In Figure A.8 on page 666, Dennis, for example, is 74 inches tall. His height is one standard deviation above the mean, which means that he is taller than 84% of

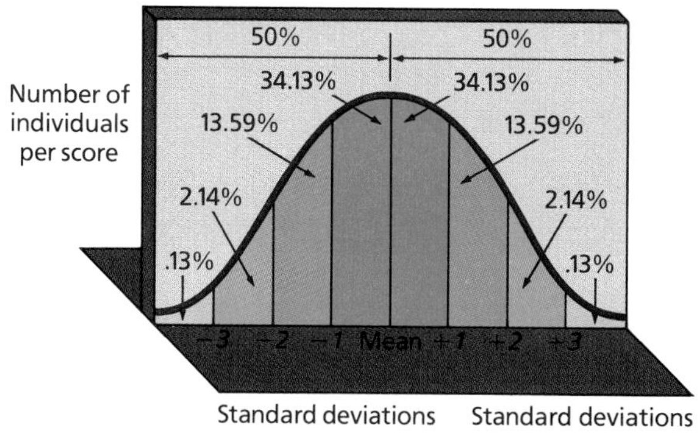

Figure A.6

In a normal distribution, or a normal curve, most individuals score within six standard deviations, three on either side of the mean; each standard deviation accounts for a different proportion of the population.

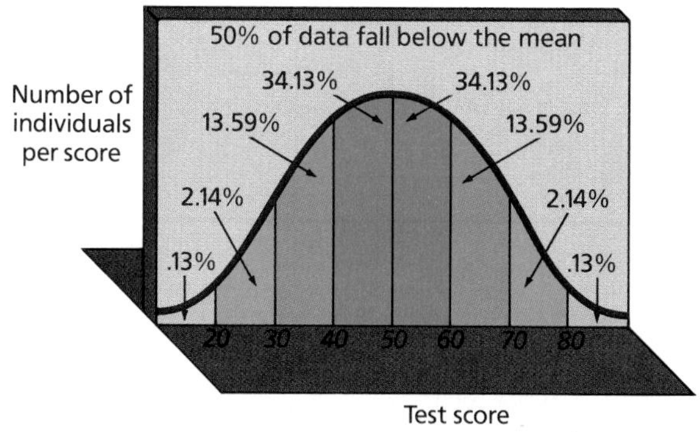

Figure A.7

In this normal curve, the standard deviation is 10 points.

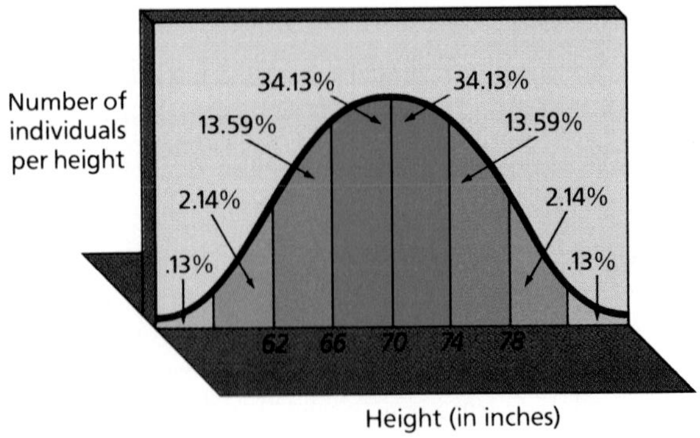

Figure A.8

When the mean distribution of height is 70 and the standard deviation is 4, Dennis, who is 74 inches tall, is taller than 84% of the sample population (0.13 + 2.14 + 13.59 + 34.13 + 34.13 = 84.12), whereas Rob, who is 66 inches tall, is taller than only 16% of the population (0.13 + 2.14 + 13.59 = 15.86).

the population (0.13 + 2.14 + 13.59 + 34.13 + 34.13 = 84.12%). Rob, who is 66 inches tall, is taller than only 16% of the population. His height is one standard deviation below the mean.

correlation coefficient: A number that expresses the degree (higher = stronger correlation) and direction (positive or negative) of a relationship between two variables; the number ranges from −1.0 (a perfect negative correlation) to +1.0 (a perfect positive correlation), and 0 (zero) indicates no correlation.

Correlation

Sometimes, researchers wish to compare data that were gathered in different surveys and questionnaires. To do so, they perform a *correlation study.* A correlation implies that an increase in the value of one variable will be accompanied by an increase or a decrease in the value of a second variable. The degree of relationship between two variables is expressed by a numerical value termed the **correlation coefficient.** Correlation coefficients go from −1, through 0, to +1. Any correlation greater or less than 0, regardless of its sign, indicates that the variables are related. When two variables are perfectly correlated, they are said to have a

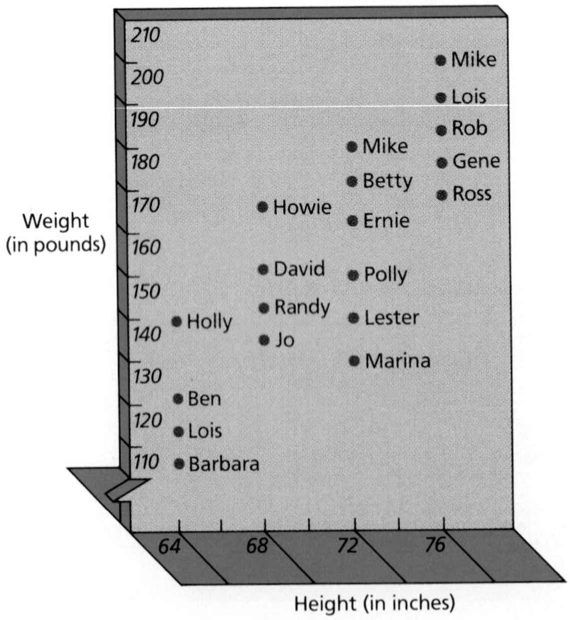

Figure A.9

When two variables are related, knowing the value of one helps a person predict the value of the other. A perfect prediction is not available unless the correlation is a correlation of 1 (or −1).

correlation of 1. A *perfect correlation* occurs when knowing the value of one variable allows one to predict *precisely* the value of the second, but this rarely occurs in psychological phenomena.

Most variables are not perfectly correlated; for example, they may have a correlation of 0.6. Consider height and weight. Although tall people generally weigh more than short people, some tall people weigh less than some short people. Figure A.9 illustrates the fact that knowing a person's height does not enable one to predict his or her weight exactly. The two variables, height and weight, have a correlation of only 0.65.

Another example of imperfectly correlated variables is found in the incidence of children of schizophrenic parents. If a parent is schizophrenic, the likelihood that the child will be schizophrenic increases sharply. Thus, there is a correlation between parents and children with respect to schizophrenia. Because this correlation is not perfect—that is, not every child born to a schizophrenic parent will develop the disorder—psychologists believe that genetics is only one of several contributing factors in the development of the disorder.

When one variable shows an increase in value, and a second shows an increase, the two variables are positively related, and the relationship is known as a *positive correlation.* Height and weight show a positive correlation: Generally, as height increases, so does weight. On the other hand, if one variable decreases as the other increases, the direction of the correlation is changed to *negative correlation.*

The relationship between number of hours of therapy and extent of anxiety shows a negative correlation. As the number of hours of therapy increases, anxiety decreases. These variables have a negative correlation of about -0.6 or -0.7 (see Figure A.10).

Another example of a negative correlation exists between time and memory. A person might be able to recall an entire list of 10 words immediately after reading it; the next day, he may remember only 5 of the words, and a week later, only 1 word. As time increases, memory decreases. Similarly, people who live close to an airport report that aircraft noise is painfully loud; those who live farther away report less noise. The loudness of the aircraft noise is negatively correlated to distance from the airport: As distance increases, loudness decreases.

It is important to remember that a correlation of $+0.7$ is no stronger than one of -0.7. The *direction,* not the strength, of the relationship is changed by the plus or minus sign. The strength is determined by the number: The larger the

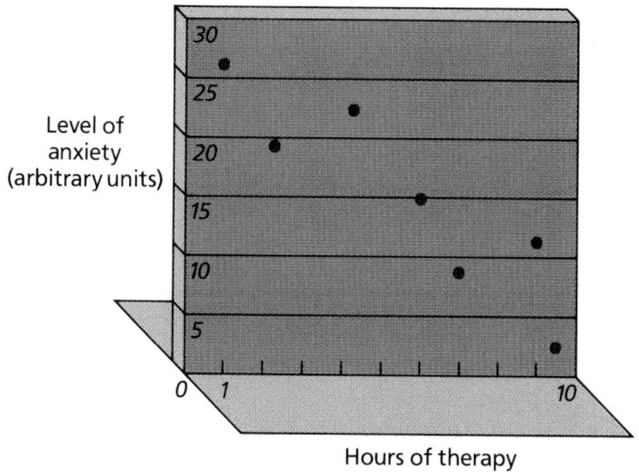

Figure A.10

An increase in one variable does not always mean an increase in the other. In a negative correlation, an increase in one variable is associated with a decrease in the other.

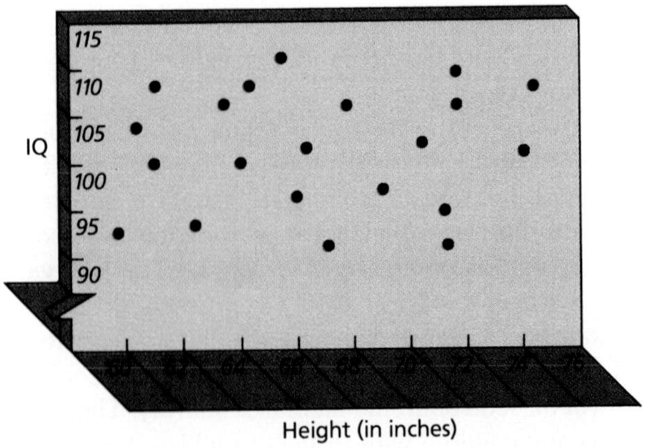

Figure A.11

When two variables show no relationship, they have a correlation of 0 (zero). Weight and height are correlated, but IQ and height have a correlation of 0.

number, the greater the strength of the correlation. A correlation of −0.8 is greater than one of +0.7; a correlation of +0.6 is greater than one of −0.5.

Some variables show absolutely no correlation; this is expressed by a correlation coefficient of 0. Figure A.11, plots data for height and IQ. The figure shows no correlation between IQ and height, so the two variables have a correlation of 0 (see Figure A.12).

As was pointed out in Chapter 1, correlation studies make no statements regarding cause and effect. They simply show that if there is an increase in one variable, there will probably be an increase or decrease in another variable. It is only through experimental studies that researchers can make cause-and-effect statements. Many of the studies reported in this text are correlational, but far more are experimental. Whenever possible, researchers wish to draw causal inferences.

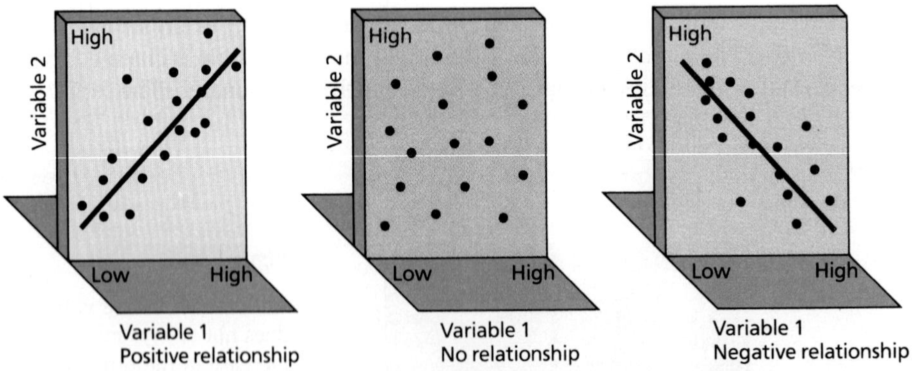

Figure A.12

The left panel shows a *positive correlation:* An increase in one variable is associated with an increase in the other. The right panel shows a *negative correlation:* An increase in one variable is associated with a decrease in the other. The middle panel shows a *0 (zero) correlation,* with one variable not related to the other.

Study Guide Answers

Chapter 1

MODULE 1 ▸

Progress Check Answers

1.1 a. healthy skepticism b. mental processes c. are not d. theory e. medical doctors f. Clinical psychologists g. Psychoanalysis h. doctoral

1.2 a. applied b. community c. A school d. health e. a set of techniques used to examine behavior

Self-test

Answer	Learning Objective	Answer	Learning Objective
1. d	1.1	5. b	1.2
2. c	1.1	6. a	1.3
3. a	1.1	7. c	1.4
4. c	1.2	8. d	1.4

MODULE 2 ▸

Progress Check Answers

2.1 a. school of psychological thought b. Wundt, in Germany c. introspection d. functionalism e. Gestalt f. John B. Watson g. thoughts h. The biological perspective i. eclectic

2.2 a. 7% b. correlation c. significant difference d. independent e. A hypothesis f. control g. a self-fulfilling prophecy h. double-blind i. ask additional questions j. that the target behavior may not be exhibited k. reliable

Self-test

Answer	Learning Objective	Answer	Learning Objective
1. b	2.1	6. a	2.3
2. c	2.1	7. b	2.4
3. a	2.1	8. b	2.5
4. c	2.1	9. c	2.6
5. d	2.2	10. d	2.7

Chapter 2

MODULE 3 ▸

Progress Check Answers

3.1 a. nature b. nurture c. chromosome d. may not be expressed outwardly in e. the 23rd pair of chromosomes f. fraternal g. the relative contributions of nature and nurture h. an extra chromosome or partial chromosome on the 21st pair i. secrete hormones into the bloodstream j. pituitary k. islets of Langerhans l. hypoglycemia m. absence of n. normal amounts

3.2 a. combine the activities of b. hold neurons in place c. an axon d. electrochemical e. Polarization f. acetylcholine g. ions to penetrate the cell membrane h. can have either inhibitory or i. Parkinson's disease

Self-test

Answer	Learning Objective	Answer	Learning Objective
1. b	3.1	6. d	3.6
2. a	3.2	7. c	3.7
3. c	3.3	8. d	3.7
4. a	3.4	9. a	3.7
5. d	3.5	10. d	3.8

MODULE 4 ▸

Progress Check Answers

4.1 a. involuntary, physiological changes b. sympathetic c. the heart beats at a normal rate d. the spinal cord e. do not require f. single unit recording g. alpha h. MRI i. brain lesions

4.2 a. hindbrain and midbrain b. reticular formation and pons c. amygdala d. basal ganglia are e. corpus callosum f. electrical stimulation g. parietal h. speech and language production i. calcium j. some

Self test

Answer	Learning Objective	Answer	Learning Objective
1. b	4.1	5. d	4.4
2. c	4.2	6. a	4.4
3. b	4.3	7. d	4.4
4. a	4.4	8. b	4.5

Chapter 3

MODULE 5 ▸

Progress Check Answers

5.1 a. sensation b. an active, constructive c. wavelengths ranging from 400 to 750 nanometers d. iris e. convergence f. fovea g. resolution capacity h. almost 30 minutes i. more j. The optic chiasm takes k. more

5.2 a. Brightness b. do not possess c. duller d. wide e. all f. trichromatic g. opponent-process

h. lateral geniculate nucleus i. Monochromats j. lack specific color-absorbing pigments k. mothers to their sons

5.3 a. surrounding objects give us perceptual cues b. monocular c. kinetic depth effect d. accommodation e. Ponzo f. in the background g. perceptual processes reflect brain organization h. continuity i. different j. attenuation theory k. limited capacity

Self test

Answer	Learning Objective	Answer	Learning Objective
1. c	5.1	9. b	5.7
2. d	5.2	10. c	5.8
3. a	5.3	11. c	5.9
4. a	5.3	12. b	5.10
5. b	5.4	13. d	5.11
6. b	5.4	14. b	5.12
7. c	5.5	15. a	5.13
8. b	5.6	16. a	5.14

MODULE 6 ►

Progress Check Answers

6.1 a. interact with b. during crucial periods c. what they expect to experience d. can be used to help modify habits e. mechanical and electrochemical f. frequency or pitch g. can have either a high or a low h. middle i. tiny bones j. displacement of hair cells k. combine the best of l. sensorineural m. sounds in the high-frequency range

6.2 a. papillae b. sweet c. sensory adaptation d. olfactory rods e. epidermis f. there are more receptor cells g. free nerve endings h. whether gates are fully or partially open or closed i. has yielded inconclusive results j. Enkephalin k. the vestibular sense l. telepathy

Self test

Answer	Learning Objective	Answer	Learning Objective
1. a	6.1	7. d	6.7
2. a	6.2	8. b	6.7
3. c	6.3	9. b	6.8
4. a	6.4	10. b	6.9
5. a	6.5	11. d	6.10
6. d	6.6	12. a	6.11

Chapter 4

MODULE 7 ►

Progress Check Answers

7.1 a. levels b. receptive c. around a day d. slow or late e. about the same amount of f. eye movements g. four h. 90 minutes i. Stage 4 j. aware k. catch up on REM and Stage 4

7.2 a. tend to involve thinking b. that awaken us c. incorporate sounds from the environment into the d. watching an object in e. latent content f. the pons and the cortex

Self test

Answer	Learning Objective	Answer	Learning Objective
1. b	7.1	5. c	7.5
2. a	7.2	6. a	7.6
3. a	7.3	7. d	7.6
4. d	7.4	8. d	7.7

MODULE 8 ►

Progress Check Answers

8.1 a. rats b. induction c. conscious and aware, but d. relaxation, attitudes, and expectations lead e. intense concentration f. At least 1/3 g. psychoactive drugs h. addictive i. tolerance j. substance

8.2 a. can destroy a person's life and family structure b. depressant c. the female will have a greater d. 0.10% e. creates medical, social, and psychological problems f. four g. once an alcoholic, always an alcoholic h. added to i. respiratory j. are polydrug users k. blocks the effect of l. interferes with m. are highly n. stimulant o. ice

Self test

Answer	Learning Objective	Answer	Learning Objective
1. d	8.1	9. a	8.8
2. d	8.2	10. b	8.9
3. c	8.3	11. d	8.10
4. d	8.4	12. c	8.11
5. d	8.4	13. a	8.12
6. a	8.5	14. c	8.10 & 8.12
7. d	8.6	15. d	8.6–8.12
8. d	8.7		

Chapter 5

MODULE 9 ►

Progress Check Answers

9.1 a. observing behavior and measuring physiological changes b. involuntarily c. weaker d. emotional responses e. a complex network of conditioned f. unconditioned g. half a second before and should overlap with h. predictability i. no longer paired with the conditioned stimulus j. spontaneous recovery k. discrimination

Self test

Answer	Learning Objective	Answer	Learning Objective
1. c	9.1	5. b	9.5
2. c	9.2	6. a	9.6
3. c	9.3	7. c	9.7
4. d	9.4	8. d	9.8

MODULE 10 ►

Progress Check Answers

10.1 a. voluntary b. consequence that follows c. often used as synonymous terms d. cumulative recorder e. shaping f. escape g. the Premack principle h. need or want it i. superstitious j. primary k. often return to l. time-out

10.2 a. an interval b. variable-ratio c. generalization d. extinction e. eventually disappears completely f. cross an electrified grid to receive

10.3 a. without conditioning and reinforcement b. discovery c. not be forgotten d. latent learning e. generative f. be aggressive and violent g. whom they perceive as powerful h. the setting and the perceived expectations i. dominant or nurturing

Self test

Answer	Learning Objective	Answer	Learning Objective
1. a	10.1	7. a	10.7
2. b	10.2	8. d	10.8
3. c	10.3	9. a	10.9
4. b	10.4	10. a	10.10
5. d	10.5	11. b	10.11
6. b	10.6	12. c	10.12

Chapter 6

MODULE 11 ▸

Progress Check Answers

11.1 a. separate, but interdependent b. could relearn c. Distributed d. von Restorff effect e. recall f. paired-associate g. developing schemas h. amazingly accurate

11.2 a. Encoding b. perform initial coding of and briefly store c. echoic d. icon e. count backwards and then recall f. active integration g. associating ideas with elaborative h. chooses from all possibilities i. rehearsal and importance j. declarative k. declarative l. give full attention to m. a limited image space n. the image o. storage process

Self test

Answer	Learning Objective	Answer	Learning Objective
1. d	11.1	7. b	11.6
2. a	11.2	8. b	11.7
3. b	11.3	9. a	11.7
4. a	11.4	10. c	11.8
5. d	11.5	11. d	11.8
6. c	11.6	12. a	11.9

MODULE 12 ▸

Progress Check Answers

12.1 a. memory trace b. is not c. of crowding of information d. Proactive inhibition e. encoding-specificity f. motivated forgetting g. Anterograde h. memory enhancement i. consolidation j. branch out with new dendrites and synapses k. is a

Self test

Answer	Learning Objective	Answer	Learning Objective
1. b	12.1	4. d	12.3
2. b	12.2	5. d	12.4
3. d	12.3	6. d	12.5

Chapter 7

MODULE 13 ▸

Progress Check Answers

13.1 a. we actively construct our reality b. can be c. depth and spread d. concept e. dimensions f. internal bridging g. hypothesis-testing h. global focusing

13.2 a. logic b. truth c. The compensatory model d. estimating probabilities e. can be influenced by psychological factors f. recognize that a problem exists g. to a psychological set h. high-quality i. divergent thinking j. artificial intelligence k. Heuristics l. subgoal analysis

Self test

Answer	Learning Objective	Answer	Learning Objective
1. b	13.1	7. d	13.6
2. c	13.2	8. d	13.7
3. b	13.2	9. c	13.8
4. c	13.3	10. a	13.9
5. a	13.4	11. d	13.10
6. c	13.5	12. d	13.10

MODULE 14 ▸

Progress Check Answers

14.1 a. thought shapes language b. 45 c. ma d. is not e. Syntax f. are born with the ability g. differently from h. surface i. more than one

14.2 a. genetic inheritance b. conditioning c. how we generate an infinite number of sentences d. a genetic blueprint e. brain lateralization f. maturation of neurological capacities g. 160 h. learned i. concrete, specific, and limited

Self test

Answer	Learning Objective	Answer	Learning Objective
1. b	14.1	5. d	14.4
2. a	14.2	6. b	14.5
3. b	14.2	7. d	14.5
4. b	14.3	8. a	14.5

Chapter 8

MODULE 15 ▸

Progress Check Answers

15.1 a. cross-sectional b. a Fallopian tube c. placenta d. is formed e. second trimester f. the intelligence test scores of g. before the mother is even aware of being pregnant

15.2 a. well developed b. Babinski c. 12 d. complex e. visual cliff f. make decisions based on g. begins to use language h. 7 i. curious and self-directed j. process of emotional attachment k. the physical attractiveness of the infant l. throughout one's life m. genetics and childrearing practices

Self test

Answer	Learning Objective	Answer	Learning Objective
1. a	15.1	6. b	15.5
2. a	15.2	7. b	15.6
3. b	15.2	8. c	15.6
4. a	15.3	9. b	15.7
5. a	15.4	10. d	15.8

MODULE 16 ▸

Progress Check Answers

16.1 a. thought processes or "how" b. assimilated c. A sense of intention d. sensorimotor e. decentration f. make appearance–reality distinctions g. concrete operations h. recognizing and providing stimulation for i. repeat the same sounds j. rigid and rule bound k. moral relativity l. justice m. reward and punishment n. conscience o. look for alternatives or a compromise p. opportunities for role-taking

16.2 a. alone or alongside b. do not understand c. their shared gender d. 24 e. longer f. are cared for in a home environment g. are providing mixed results h. do not seem to differ

Self test

Answer	Learning Objective	Answer	Learning Objective
1. c	16.1	9. b	16.5
2. c	16.1	10. c	16.6
3. b	16.1	11. b	16.7
4. b	16.2	12. c	16.8
5. c	16.2	13. b	16.9
6. b	16.3	14. b	16.10
7. c	16.4	15. a	16.11
8. c	16.5		

MODULE 17 ▸

Progress Check Answers

17.1 a. and yet, only 11% b. white, middle-class American teenagers c. puberty ends d. both boys and girls e. satisfying involvement in athletics f. behavioral and cognitive g. Sex roles h. the parent of the same sex i. a normal part of growing up j. they are uninformed about reproduction k. form our self-image l. failed to form an identity m. on a continuum of doing one's best n. intimacy versus isolation

17.2 a. growth b. 30 c. Personality and coping skills d. psychology has been a male-dominated profession e. unique patterns of interacting with life events f. early adulthood g. in irregular sequences h. the role of motherhood

17.3 a. 74.7 b. limited c. appearance d. heredity e. reversible dementias f. terminal drop g. the tests are timed h. denial i. an insightful discussion of shared feelings

Self test

Answer	Learning Objective	Answer	Learning Objective
1. d	17.1	13. b	17.11
2. d	17.2	14. c	17.11
3. c	17.3	15. a	17.12
4. b	17.4	16. c	17.12
5. d	17.5	17. b	17.12
6. d	17.5	18. a	17.13
7. b	17.6	19. b	17.13
8. b	17.6	20. d	17.14
9. d	17.7	21. c	17.15
10. a	17.8	22. d	17.16
11. a	17.9	23. d	17.17
12. d	17.10	24. a	17.17

Chapter 9

MODULE 18 ▸

Progress Check Answers

18.1 a. initiates and maintains goal-directed behavior b. mechanistic c. need d. brain detects a low blood-sugar level e. ventromedial f. size g. exercise

18.2 a. middle- and upper-class adolescent females b. 50% c. binge eating and purging d. pituitary gland and kidneys e. cellular dehydration f. even though it is not caused g. a specific optimal h. an internal response to a stimulus

Self test

Answer	Learning Objective	Answer	Learning Objective
1. d	18.1	5. b	18.5
2. c	18.2	6. b	18.6
3. a	18.3	7. a	18.7
4. b	18.4	8. b	18.8

MODULE 19 ▸

Progress Check Answers

19.1 a. a self-fulfilling prophecy b. a sense of urgency c. self, others, and relationships d. learned in the home environment e. try no new methods f. low g. Type B h. mechanistic

19.2 a. the individual setting goals and deciding how to achieve them b. denial orientation c. the internal pleasures derived from the activity d. less time e. innate f. fulfill his or her true nature g. tied closely to middle-class American cultural experiences

Self test

Answer	Learning Objective	Answer	Learning Objective
1. a	19.1	5. d	19.5
2. d	19.2	6. c	19.6
3. c	19.3	7. a	19.7
4. c	19.4	8. d	19.7

MODULE 20 ▸

Progress Check Answers

20.1 a. subjective b. to observe and measure c. James–Lange d. interpretation and thoughts about a situation e. contextual or situational cues f. different cultures place different values on them g. none of the monkeys h. form a sensitive period for bonding and later i. left j. autonomic nervous system k. thought

Self test

Answer	Learning Objective	Answer	Learning Objective
1. a	20.1	5. a	20.5
2. a	20.2	6. c	20.5
3. b	20.3	7. d	20.6
4. b	20.4	8. b	20.7

Chapter 10

MODULE 21 ►

Progress Check Answers

21.1 a. relatively enduring b. life–sex and death–aggression c. maximize pleasure while minimizing pain and guilt d. unconscious e. as the moral aspect of mental functioning f. same g. latency h. makes it more difficult to cope successfully i. sublimation j. in a cultural context k. disguised fulfillment of a repressed wish

21.2 a. anticipates the future b. primitive images inherited from our ancestors c. superiority, completion, and perfection d. inherently e. the life-style a person chooses f. acquire healthy self-esteem g. perceive and interpret immediate events h. distinctly human i. fulfillment j. ideal

Self test

Answer	Learning Objective	Answer	Learning Objective
1. b	21.1	7. d	21.6
2. c	21.2	8. c	21.7
3. b	21.3	9. a	21.8
4. a	21.4	10. b	21.9
5. d	21.5	11. b	21.10
6. a	21.5	12. c	21.10

MODULE 22 ►

Progress Check Answers

22.1 a. trait b. cardinal c. occur in response to specific situations d. factor analysis e. psychoticism f. biological levels of arousal g. do not predict

22.2 a. are hard to define b. stimulus–response relationships c. operant d. imitation e. their thoughts f. locus of control g. self-efficacy h. the person and the environment i. a self-regulatory system

Self test

Answer	Learning Objective	Answer	Learning Objective
1. d	22.1	7. b	22.6
2. c	22.2	8. b	22.4 & 22.6
3. d	22.3	9. d	22.7
4. d	22.4	10. c	22.8
5. a	22.4	11. b	22.9
6. a	22.5		

Chapter 11

MODULE 23 ►

Progress Check Answers

23.1 a. motivation and leadership b. situation c. behaviorally d. adapt to the environment e. biological readiness f. reveal little about g. some underlying attribute h. optimally weighted composite i. cognitive j. inherited

23.2 a. measure general intelligence b. standardized c. normal curve d. raw e. dividing mental age by chronological age f. test–retest g. of imperfect reliability h. content

23.3 a. academic performance b. 4 to $6\frac{1}{2}$ years c. process information and solve problems d. discriminate against black people e. a definition of intelligence f. halo effects g. educational and life experiences h. important elements of i. nature j. according to environmental demands k. environment plays an important role l. narrowing m. gender stereotyping has decreased

Self test

Answer	Learning Objective	Answer	Learning Objective
1. d	23.1	9. d	23.7
2. c	23.2	10. a	23.7
3. b	23.3	11. a	23.8
4. a	23.3	12. a	23.9
5. b	23.4	13. a	23.10
6. c	23.5	14. c	23.11
7. b	23.6	15. a	23.12
8. d	23.6		

MODULE 24 ►

Progress Check Answers

24.1 a. by the end of the fourth b. does not have to c. are capable of superior performance d. mom's drug addiction during pregnancy e. Severe f. increased g. make life as normal as possible

24.2 a. a battery of tests b. CPI c. projective tests d. overt and cognitive e. naturalistic observation f. neuropsychological assessment

Self test

Answer	Learning Objective	Answer	Learning Objective
1. d	24.1	7. a	24.5
2. d	24.2	8. a	24.5
3. c	24.2	9. c	24.5
4. d	24.3	10. d	24.6
5. b	24.3	11. b	24.6
6. d	24.4		

Chapter 12

MODULE 25 ►

Progress Check Answers

25.1 a a state of well-being b. a complex interrelationship among many c. internal d. prevent e. has adopted the sick role f. a cure for specific symptoms g. an action-oriented

25.2 a. voluntary b. resolution c. an all-or-none d. fairly common e. 25% f. primary g. women

Self test

Answer	Learning Objective	Answer	Learning Objective
1. d	25.1	5. c	25.3
2. a	25.2	6. b	25.4
3. d	25.3	7. a	25.5
4. b	25.3	8. b	25.6

MODULE 26 ►

Progress Check Answers

26.1 a. injurious b. predictability, familiarity, and controllability c. Frustration d. competing demands

e. can cause f. lead to optimal effectiveness g. high standards h. immune i. usually unable to j. resistance k. daily hassles l. lower m. posttraumatic stress disorder

26.2 a. a learned b. coping skills c. protect people from the effects of d. identifying the stressor e. stress inoculation f. attempter g. higher-energy periods while recovering from h. 86 i. psychodynamic

Self test

Answer	Learning Objective	Answer	Learning Objective
1. d	26.1	8. a	26.6
2. b	26.1	9. b	26.7
3. b	26.2	10. d	26.8
4. d	26.2	11. d	26.9
5. b	26.3	12. a	26.10
6. a	26.4	13. a	26.11
7. b	26.5	14. d	26.11

Chapter 13

MODULE 27 ▸

Progress Check Answers

27.1 a. focuses on specific behaviors b. uses defense mechanisms ineffectively c. sociocultural d. an eclectic e. improve the reliability of diagnoses

27.2 a. motivates both normal and abnormal behavior b. no longer considered appropriate and efficient c. symptom d. might not have e. of the relief people experience from escaping f. can be found in well-adjusted people g. panic attacks h. agoraphobia i. simple phobias j. obsessions k. anal l. hypochondriasis m. attention and the avoidance of difficult situations

Self test

Answer	Learning Objective	Answer	Learning Objective
1. d	27.1	5. a	27.4
2. d	27.2	6. d	27.5
3. d	27.3	7. b	27.6
4. c	27.4	8. c	27.7

MODULE 28 ▸

Progress Check Answers

28.1 a. childhood or adolescence b. histrionic c. paranoid d. be charming in a superficial way e. autonomic f. paraphilias g. feels frustrated if cross-dressing is prevented h. 50%

28.2 a. mania and depression b. themselves c. can occur at any age d. norepinehrine levels e. trycyclics f. negative expectations cause depression g. learned helplessness

28.3 a. shows a serious disintegration of personality b. hallucinations c. flat d. impairment in more than one area of psychological functioning e. paranoid f. excited and withdrawn g. residual h. grandeur i. 35% j. five times higher k. dopamine l. oral stage and has not developed an ego m. becomes confused by competing messages n. allow escape from acute anxiety

Self test

Answer	Learning Objective	Answer	Learning Objective
1. b	28.1	7. c	28.3
2. c	28.1	8. c	28.4
3. a	28.2	9. c	28.5
4. a	28.2	10. b	28.6
5. b	28.3	11. b	28.7
6. c	28.3	12. b	28.7

Chapter 14

MODULE 29 ▸

Progress Check Answers

29.1 a. somatic therapy b. an eclectic c. client d. behavior e. expectations f. insight g. make connections among thoughts h. unconscious seeking expression i. interpretation j. accepts k. reality testing and control l. time consuming and expensive

29.2 a. developing innate potential b. questioning and reflective techniques c. have positive regard and an empathetic understanding d. current, "here-and-now" e. incomplete Gestalts f. get in touch with feelings

Self test

Answer	Learning Objective	Answer	Learning Objective
1. c	29.1	7. a	29.6
2. d	29.2	8. c	29.6
3. d	29.3	9. c	29.7
4. b	29.3	10. d	29.8
5. b	29.4	11. b	29.7& 29.8
6. c	29.5		

MODULE 30 ▸

Progress Check Answers

30.1 a. underlying causes of b. multimodal c. identifying and knowing the frequency of d. can be traded for something special e. social norms f. positive reinforcement g. a new response to a specific stimulus h. excessive anger and phobias i. a noxious j. modeling k. attach inappropriate labels l. be considered irrational m. realistic and accurate data

30.2 a. less expensive than b. encounter group therapy c. social pressures that are exerted d. family systems e. restructuring family interactions f. an action-oriented, applied g. crisis intervention h. used in combination with i. drug therapy is more widely available and often j. memory loss k. antianxiety

Self test

Answer	Learning Objective	Answer	Learning Objective
1. c	30.1	8. c	30.8
2. a	30.2	9. d	30.9
3. b	30.3	10. d	30.10
4. b	30.4	11. d	30.11
5. b	30.5	12. b	30.12
6. b	30.6	13. c	30.13
7. a	30.7	14. c	30.14

Chapter 15

MODULE 31 ▸

Progress Check Answers

31.1 a. individuals b. behavioral c. regardless of its d. a friend e. consistency f. motivation g. 6 h. women i. internal j. fundamental attribution error k. situational l. physical appearance m. unrealistic about themselves and their goals n. stop responding

31.2 a. even when it is obviously wrong b. can have substantial c. had allies that refused to participate d. Debriefing e. apply across cultures, gender, and age groups f. have a shared purpose g. arousal increases when others are present h. cannot be evaluated i. Group polarization

Self test

Answer	Learning Objective	Answer	Learning Objective
1. d	31.1	8. c	31.6
2. a	31.2	9. b	31.7
3. b	31.2	10. d	31.8
4. d	31.3	11. b	31.9
5. a	31.4	12. c	31.10
6. c	31.4	13. c	31.11
7. b	31.5	14. b	31.12

MODULE 32 ▸

Progress Check Answers

32.1 a. like us and are similar to us b. Learning c. other children of the same sex d. apologizing and returning favors e. emotional f. female g. oversimplified and wrong h. reverse discrimination i. motivational j. personality k. participate in shared activities or have common goals

32.2 a. having expectations for reward or praise b. altruistic acts c. a number of d. fear making fools of themselves e. only humans f. nativists g. interferes with achieving a goal

Self test

Answer	Learning Objective	Answer	Learning Objective
1. a	32.1	6. d	32.6
2. d	32.2	7. c	32.7
3. d	32.3	8. a	32.8
4. c	32.4	9. d	32.9
5. c	32.5		

MODULE 33 ▸

Progress Check Answers

33.1 a. chairs in a college classroom b. stressors c. a person's perception of the number of people and the d. an invisible perceptual boundary e. varies from culture to culture f. self g. are given specific instructions about what to do

33.2 a. well individuals perform their duties at b. predicting the success c. salaries d. intrinsic and extrinsic motivators are e. does not know what is expected in f. the match between his or her expectations for g. paternalistic

Self test

Answer	Learning Objective	Answer	Learning Objective
1. d	33.1	7. d	33.7
2. a	33.2	8. d	33.8
3. c	33.3	9. b	33.9
4. a	33.4	10. a	33.10
5. b	33.5	11. d	33.11
6. b	33.6	12. a	33.11

References

A. C. Nielsen Co. (1988). *1988 Nielsen report on television.* Northbrook, IL: Author.

Adelmann, P. K., Antonucci, T. C., Crohan, S. E., & Colemen, L. M. (1989). Empty nest, cohort, and employment in the well-being of midlife women. *Sex Roles, 20,* 173–180.

Adler, A. (1969). *The science of living.* Garden City, NY: Anchor Books. (Original work published 1929)

Ainscough, C. E. (1990). Premenstrual emotional changes a prospective study of symptomatology in normal women. *Journal of Psychosomatic Research, 34,* 35–45.

Ainsworth, M. D. S. (1979). Infant–mother attachment. *American Psychologist, 34,* 932–937.

Algera, J. A. (1990). The job characteristics model of work motivation revisited. In U. Kleinbeck, H. Quast, H. Thierry, & H. Hacker (Eds.), *Work motivation,* Hillsdale, NJ: Erlbaum.

Alkon, D. L. (1989). Memory storage and neural systems. *Scientific American, July,* 42–50.

Allgood-Merten, B., Lewinsohn, P. M., & Hops, H. (1990). Sex differences and adolescent depression. *Journal of Abnormal Psychology, 99,* 55–63.

Allington, R. L. (1981). Sensitivity to orthographic structure in educable mentally retarded children. *Contemporary Educational Psychology, 6,* 135–139.

Allport, G. W. (1937). *Personality: A psychological interpretation.* New York: Holt.

Allyon, T., & Azrin, N. H. (1965). The measurement and reinforcement behavior of psychotics. *Journal of the Experimental Analysis of Behavior, 8,* 357–383.

Allyon, T., & Haughton, E. (1964). Modification of symptomatic verbal behavior of mental patients. *Behavior Research and Therapy, 2,* 87–97.

Altman, I. (1975). *The environment and social behavior.* Monterey, CA: Brooks/Cole.

Altman, I., & Vinsel, A. M. (1977). Personal space: An analysis of E. T. Hall's proxemics framework. In I. Altman, A. Rapoport, & J. F. Wohlwill (Eds.), *Human Behavior and environment: Vol. 2. Advances in theory and research.* New York: Plenum Press.

American Heart Association. (1984). *Exercise and your heart.* Dallas, TX: Author.

American Psychological Association. (1989). Pediatric AIDS and human immunodeficiency virus infection: Psychological issues. *American Psychologist, 44*(2), 258–264.

Ames, L. D., Gillespie, C., Haines, J., & Ilg, F. L. (1979). *The Gesell Institute's child from one to six.* New York: Harper & Row.

Anderson, C. A. (1989). Temperature and aggression: Ubiquitous effects of heat on occurrence of human violence. *Psychological Bulletin, 106,* 74–96.

Anderson, K. J. (1990). Arousal and the inverted-U hypothesis: A critique of Neiss's "reconceptualizing arousal." *Psychological Bulletin, 107,* 96–100.

Anderson, R., Manoogian, S., & Reznick, J. (1976). Undermining and enhancing of intrinsic motivation in preschool children. *Journal of Personality and Social Psychology, 34,* 915–922.

Andrews, J. D. W. (1989). Integrating visions of reality: Interpersonal diagnosis and the existential vision. *American Psychologist, 44,* 803–817.

Angoff, W. H. (1988). The nature–nurture debate, aptitudes, and group differences. *American Psychologist, 43,* 713–720.

Aoki, C., & Siekevitz, P. (1988). Plasticity in brain development. *Scientific American, 12,* 56–64.

Asch, S. E. (1951). Effects of group pressure upon the modification and distortion of judgments. In J. Guetzkow (Ed.), *Groups, leadership, and men.* Pittsburgh: Carnegie Press.

Asendorpf, J. B. (1989). Shyness as a final common pathway for two different kinds of inhibition. *Journal of Personality and Social Psychology, 57,* 481–492.

Ashcraft, M. H. (1989). *Human memory and cognition,* Glenview, IL: Scott Foresman.

Atkinson, M. A., & Maclaren, N. K. (1990). What causes diabetes? *Scientific American, July,* 62–71.

Attie, I., & Brooks-Gunn, J. (1989). Development of eating problems in adolescent girls: A longitudinal study. *Developmental Psychology, 25,* 70–79.

Aukett, R., Ritchie, J., & Mill, K. (1988). Gender differences in friendship patterns. *Sex Roles, 19,* 57–63.

Azrin, N. H., & Holtz, W. C. (1966). Punishment. In Werner K. Honig (Ed.), *Operant behavior: Areas of research and application.* New York: Appleton-Century-Crofts.

Backer, T. E., & Richardson, D. (1989). Building bridges: Psychologists and families of the mentally ill. *American Psychologist, 44,* 546–550.

Baddeley, A. D., & Hitch, G. (1974). Working memory. In G. Bower (Ed.), *Recent advances in learning and motivating* (Vol. 8). New York: Academic Press.

Baddeley, A. D., & Longman, D. J. A. (1966). The influence of length and frequency of training session on rate of learning to type. In A. D. Baddeley (Ed.), *The psychology of memory.* New York: Basic Books.

Baddeley, A. D., & Warrington, E. K. (1970). Amnesia and the distinction between long- and short-term memory. *Journal of Verbal Learning and Verbal Behavior, 9,* 176–189.

Bahrick, H. P., & Hall, L. K. (1991). Lifetime Maintenance of High School Mathematics Content. *Journal of Experimental Psychology: General, 120,* 20–33.

Baillargeon, R., & Graber, M. (1988). Evidence of location memory in 8-month-old infants in a nonsearch AB task. *Developmental Psychology, 24,* 502–511.

Baird, J. C., Wagner, M., & Fuld, K. (1990). A simple but powerful theory of the moon illusion. *Journal of Experimental Psychology: Human Perception and Performance, 16,* 675–677.

Baltes, P. B. Reese, H. W., & Lipsitt, L. P. (1980). Life-span developmental psychology. *Annual Review of Psychology, 31* 65–110.

Banaji, M. R., & Crowder, R. G. (1989). The bankruptcy of everyday memory. *American Psychologists, 44,* 1185–1193.

Band, E. B., & Weisz, J. R. (1988). How to feel better when it feels bad: Children's perspectives on coping with everyday stress. *Developmental Psychology, 24,* 247–253.

Bandura, A. (1969). *Principles of behavior modification.* New York: Holt, Rinehart and Winston.

Bandura, A. (1977a). Self-efficacy: Toward a unifying theory of behavioral change. *Psychological Review, 84,* 191–215.

Bandura, A. (1977b). *Social learning theory.* Englewood Cliffs, NJ: Prentice-Hall.

Bandura, A (1982a). The psychology of chance encounters and life paths. *American Psychologist, 37,* 747–755.

Bandura, A. (1982b). Self-efficacy: Mechanism in human agency. *American Psychologist, 37,* 122–147.

Bandura, A. (1988). Self-regulation of motivation and action through goal systems. In V. Hamilton, G. H. Bower, & N. H. Frijda (Eds.), *Cognitive perspectives on emotion and motivation* (pp. 37–61). Dordrecht, Netherlands: Kluwer Academic Publishers.

Bandura, A. (1989). Human agency in social cognitive theory. *American Psychologist, 44,* 1175–1184.

Bandura, A., Blanchard, E. B., & Ritter, B. (1969). Relative efficacy of desensitization and modeling approaches for inducing behavioral, affective, and attitudinal changes. *Journal of Personality and Social Psychology, 13,* 173–199.

173–199.

Bandura, A., Cioffi, D., Taylor, B., & Brouillard, M. E. (1988). Perceived self-efficacy in coping with cognitive stressors and opioid activation. *Journal of Personality and Social Psychology, 55*(3), 479–488.

Bandura, A., & Menlove, F. L. (1968). Factors determining vicarious extinction of avoidance through symbolic modeling. *Journal of Personality Development, 8,* 99–108.

Bandura, A., Ross, D., & Ross, S. A. (1963). Imitation of film-mediated aggressive models. *Journal of Personality and Social Psychology, 66,* 3–11.

Bandura, A., & Walters, R. (1963). *Social learning and personality development.* New York: Holt, Rinehart and Winston.

Bandura, A., & Wood, R. (1989). Effect of perceived controllability and performance standards on self-regulation of complex decision making. *Journal of Personality and Social Psychology, 56,* 805–814.

Barclay, C. R., & Wellman, H. M. (1986). Accuracies and inaccuracies in autobiographical memories. *Journal of Memory and Language, 25,* 93–103.

Bardon, J. I. (1983). Psychology applied to education: A specialty in search of an identity. *American Psychologist, 38,* 185–196.

Barnes, D. M. (1988). Drugs: Running the numbers. *Science, 240,* 1729–1731.

Baron, R. A. (1987). Interviewer's moods and reactions to job applicants: The influence of affective states on applied social judgments. *Journal of Applied Social Psychology, 17,* 911–926.

Baron, R. A., & Byrne, D. (1987). *Social psychology: Understanding human interaction* (5th ed.). Boston: Allyn & Bacon.

Baruch, G. K., Biener, L., & Barnett, R. C. (1987). Women and gender in research on work and family stress. *American Psychologist, 42*(2), 130–136.

Batson, C. D. (1990). How social an animal? *American Psychologist, 45,* 336–346.

Baum, A. (1987). Crowding. In D. Stokols & I. Altman (Eds.). *Handbook of environmental psychology.* New York: Wiley.

Baumeister, R. F. (1990). Suicide as escape from self. *Psychological Review, 97,* 90–113.

Beck, A. T. (1963). Thinking and depression: I. Idiosyncratic content in cognitive distortions. *Archives of General Psychiatry,* 9, 324–333.

Beck, A. T. (1976). *Cognitive therapy and emotional disorders.* New York: International Universities Press.

Beck, A. T. (1991). Cognitive therapy. *American Psychologist, 46,* 368–375.

Beck, A. T., & Weishaar, M. (1989). Cognitive therapy. In A. Freeman, K. M. Simon, L. E. Beutler, & H. Arkowitz (Eds.), *Comprehensive handbook of cognitive therapy.* New York: Plenum Press.

Becvar, D. S., & Becvar, R. J. (1988). *Family therapy: A systemic integration.* Boston MA: Allyn & Bacon.

Bednar, R. L., Burlingame, G. M., & Masters, K. S. (1988). Systems of family treatment: Substance or semantics? *Annual Review of Psychology, 39,* 401–434.

Behar, D., Rapoport, J. L., Adams, A. J., Berg, C. J., & Cornblath, M. (1984). Sugar challenge testing with children considered behaviorally "sugar reactive." *Nutrition and Behavior, 1,* 277–288.

Bekerian, D. A., & Bowers, J. M. (1983). Eyewitness testimony: Were we misled? *Journal of Experimental Psychology: Learning, Memory, and Cognition, 9,* 139–145.

Belsky, J. (1990). Parental and nonparental child care and children's socioemotional development: A decade in review. *Journal of Marriage and the Family, 52,* 885–903.

Belsky, J., & Rovine, M. J. (1988). Nonmaternal care in the first year of life and the security of infant-parent attachment. *Child Development, 59,* 157–167.

Belsky, J., & Steinberg, L. D. (1978). The effects of day care: A critical review. *Child Development, 49,* 929–949.

Bem, D. J. (1972). Self-perception theory. In L. Berkowitz (Ed.), *Advances in experimental social psychology.* New York: Academic Press.

Benassi, M. A. (1982). Effects of order of presentation, primacy, and attractiveness on attributions of ability. *Journal of Personality and Social Psychology, 43,* 48–58.

Bentall, R. P. (1990). The illusion of reality: A review and integration of psychological research on hallucinations. *Psychological Bulletin, 107,* 82–95.

Berkowitz, L. (1989). Frustration–aggression hypothesis: Examination and reformulation. *Psychological Bulletin, 106,* 59–73.

Berkowitz, L. (1990). On the formation and regulation of anger and aggression. *American Psychologist, 45,* 494–503.

Berlin, B., & Kay, P. (1969). *Basic color terms: Their universality and evolution.* Berkeley: University of California Press.

Bernstein, I. L. (1988, September 9). *What does learning have to do with weight loss and cancer?* Paper presented at a science and Public Policy Seminar sponsored by the Federation of Behavioral, Psychological and Cognitive Sciences, Washington, DC.

Berscheid, E., Snyder, M., & Omoto, A. M. (1989). The relationship closeness inventory: Assessing the closeness of interpersonal relationships. *Journal of Personality and Social Psychology, 57,* 792–807.

Best, C. T., & Queen, H. F. (1989). Baby, it's in your smile: Right hemiface bias in infant emotional expressions. *Developmental Psychology, 25,* 264–276.

Bexton, W. H., Heron, W., & Scott, T. H. (1954). Effects of decreased variation in the sensory environment. *Canadian Journal of Psychology, 8,* 70–76.

Bishop, J. E. (1986). Technology: Researchers track pain's path, develop new kind of reliever. *The Wall Street Journal,* p. 23.

Bjorklund, A., Dunnett, S. B., Lewis, M. E., & Iversen, S. D. (1980). Reinnervation of the denervated striatum by substantia nigra transplants: Functional consequences as revealed by pharmacological and sensorimotor testing. *Brain Research, 199,* 307–333.

Blanchard, E. B., Appelbaum, K. A., Radnitz, C. L., Michultka, D., Morrill, B., Kirsch, C., Hillhouse, J., Evans, D. D., Guarnieri, P., Attanasio, V., Andrasik, F., Jaccard, J., & Dentinger, M. P. (1990). Placebo-controlled evaluation of abbreviated progressive muscle relaxation and of relaxation combined with cognitive therapy in the treatment of tension headache. *Journal of Consulting and Clinical Psychology, 58,* 210–215.

Bloom, F. E. (1981). Neuropeptides. *Scientific American, 10,* 148–168.

Blum, K., Noble, E. P., Sheridan, P. J., et al. (1990). Allelic association of human dopamine D_2 receptor gene in alcoholism. *Journal of the American Medical Association, 263,* 2055–2060.

Bohannon, J. N. III (1988). Flashbulb memories for the space shuttle disaster: A take of two theories. *Cognition, 29,* 179–196.

Bond, C. F., Jr., & Titus, L. J. (1983). Social facilitation: A meta-analysis of 241 studies. *Psychological Bulletin, 94,* 265–292.

Boninger, D. S., Brock, T. C., Cook, T. D., Gruder, C. L., & Romer, D. (1990). Discovery of reliable attitude change persistence resulting from a transmitter tuning set. *American Psychological Society, 1,* 268–271.

Borg, E., & Counter, S. A. (1989). The middle-ear muscles. *Scientific American,* 9, 74-80.

Bornstein, M. H. (1989). Sensitive periods in development: Structural characteristics and causal interpretations. *Psychological Bulletin, 105,* 179–197.

Bornstein, R. F. (1989). Exposure and affect: Overview and meta-analysis of research, 1968–1987. *Psychological Bulletin, 196,* 265–289.

Bouchard, T. J., Jr., Lykken, D. T., McGue, M., Segal, N. L., & Tellegen, A. (1990). Sources of human psychological differences: The Minnesota study of twins reared apart. *Science, 250,* 223–250.

Bouchard, T. J., Jr., & McGue, M. (1981). Familial studies of intelligence: A review. *Science, 212,* 1055–1058.

Bourque, L. B. (1989). *Defining rape.* Durham, NC: Duke University Press.

Bower, G. H. (1981). Mood and memory. *American Psychologist, 36,* 126–148.

Boynton, R. M. (1988). Color vision. In M. R. Rosenzweig & L. W. Porter (Eds.), *Annual Review of Psychology* (Vol. 39). Palo Alto, CA: Annual Reviews.

Boysen, S. T., & Berntson, G. G. (1989). Numerical competence in a chimpanzee (Pan troglodytes). *Journal of Comparative Psychology, 103,* 23–31.

Boysen, S. T., & Berntson, G. G. (1990). The development of numerical skills in chimpanzee (Pan troglodytes). In S. T. Parker and K. R. Gibson (eds.) *"Language" and Intelligence in Monkeys and Apes,* New York, NY: Cambridge University Press.

Brazelton, T. B., & Cramer, B. G. (1990). *The earliest relationship,* Reading, MA: Addison-Wesley.

Brehm, J. W. (1966). *A theory of psychological reactance.* New York: Academic Press.

Breier, A., Charney, D., & Heninger, G. R. (1984). Major depression in patients with agoraphobia and panic disorder. *Archives of General Psychiatry, 41,* 1129–1135.

Bretschneider, J. G., & McCoy, N. L. (1988). Sexual interest and behavior in healthy 80- to 102-year-olds. *Archives of Sexual Behavior, 17,* 109–129.

Broberg, A., Lamb, M. E., & Hwang, P. (1990). *Child Development, 61,* 1153–1163.

Brody, E. M., Lawton, M. P., & Liebowitz, B. (1984). Senile dementia: Public policy and adequate institutional care. *American Journal of Public Health, 74,* 1381–1383.

Brom, D., Kleber, R. J., & Defares, P. B. (1989). Brief psychotherapy for post-traumatic stress disorders. *Journal of Consulting and Clinical Psychology, 57,* 607–612.

Bronfenbrenner, U. (1989, September 7). *Who cares for children?* Invited address, UNESCO, Paris.

American Psychologist, 44, 249–257.

Brown, B. B. (1990). Peer groups and peer cultures. In S. S. Feldman & G. R. Elliot (eds.) *At the Threshold,* Cambridge, MA: Harvard University Press.

Brown, R. (1970). The first sentences of child and chimpanzee. In R. Brown (Ed.), *Psycholinguistics: Selected papers.* New York: Free Press.

Brown, R., & Kulik, J. (1977). Flashbulb memories. *Cognition, 5,* 73–99.

Bruner, J. (1990). *Acts of meaning,* Cambridge, MA: Harvard University.

Bryant, R. A., & McConkey, K. M. (1989). Hypnotic blindness: A behavioral and experiential analysis. *Journal of Abnormal Psychology, 98,* 71–77.

Burling, T. A., Marotta, J., Gonzalez, R., Moltzen, J. O., Eng, A. M., Schmidt, G. A., Welch, R. L., Ziff, D. C., & Reilly, P. M. (1989). Computerized smoking cessation program for the worksite: Treatment outcome and feasibility. *Journal of Consulting and Clinical Psychology, 57,* 619–622.

Burman, B. Mednick, S. A., Machon, R. A., Parnas, J., & Schulsinger, F. (1987). Children at high risk for schizophrenia: Parent and offspring perceptions of family relationships. *Journal of Abnormal Psychology, 96,* 364–366.

Burr, D. C., Morrone, M. C., & Spinelli, D. (1989). Evidence for edge and bar detectors in human vision. *Vision Research, 29,* 419–431.

Bushman, B. J., & Cooper, H. M. (1990). Effects of alcohol on human aggression:,An integrative research review. *Psychological Bulletin, 107,* 341–354.

Buss, A. H. (1989). Personality as traits. *American Psychologist, 44,* 1378–1388.

Buss, D. M. (1988). Love acts: The evolutionary biology of love. In R. J. Sternberg & M. L. Barnes (Eds.), *The psychology of love.* New Haven, CT: Yale University Press.

Butler, G., Fennell, M., Robson, P., & Gelder, M. (1991). Comparison of behavior therapy and cognitive behavior therapy in the treatment of generalized anxiety disorder. *Journal of Consulting and Clinical Psychology, 59,* 167–175.

Byrne, D. G., & Reinhart, M. I. (1989). Occupation, Type A behavior and self-reported angina pectoris. *Journal of Psychosomatic Research, 33,* 609–619.

Cadoret, R. J. (1978). Psychopathology in adopted-away offspring of biologic parents with antisocial behavior. *Archives of General Psychiatry. 35,* 176–184.

Cadoret, R. J., Troughton, E., & O'Gorman, T. W. (1987). Genetic and environmental factors in alcohol abuse and antisocial personality. *Journal of Studies on Alcohol, 48,* 1–8.

Cairns, E. (1990). Impact of television news exposure on children's perceptions of violence in northern Ireland. *The Journal of Social Psychology, 130,* 447–452.

Caldera, Y. M., Huston, A. C., & O'Brien, M. (1989). Social interactions and play patterns of parents and toddlers with feminine, masculine, and neutral toys. *Child Development, 60,* 70–76.

Cannon, W. B. (1927). The James–Lange theory of emotion: A critical examination and an alternative theory. *American Journal of Psychology, 39,* 106–124.

Cantor, N., & Kihlstrom, J. F. (1982). Cognitive and social processes in personality. In G. T. Wilson and C. M. Franks (Eds.), *Contemporary behavior therapy.* New York: Guilford Press.

Carducci, B. J., & Stein, N. D. (1988, April). *The personal and situational pervasiveness of shyness in college students: A nine-year comparison.* Paper presented at the annual meeting of the Southeastern Psychological Association, New Orleans.

Carlson, R. A., Sullivan, M. A., & Schneider, W. (1989). Practice and working memory effects in building procedural skill. *Journal of Experimental Psychology: Learning, Memory, and Cognition, 15,* 517–526.

Carver, C. S., & Scheier, M. F. (1990). Origins and functions of positive and negative affect: A control-process view. *Psychological Review, 97,* 19–35.

Caspi, A., Elder, G. H., & Bem, D. J. (1988). Moving away from the world: Life-course patterns of shy children. *Developmental Psychology, 24*(6), 824–831.

Cattell, R. B. (1965). *The scientific analysis of personality.* Baltimore: Penguin.

Cavanagh, P., & Leclerc, Y. G. (1989). Shape from shadows. *Journal of Experimental Psychology: Human Perception and Performance, 15,* 3–27.

Ceci, S. J., & Bronfenbrenner, U. (1991). On the demise of everyday memory. *American Psychologist, 46,* 27–31.

Cermak, L. S. (1975). *Improving your memory.* New York: W. W. Norton.

Chamberlain, K., & Zika, S. (1990). The minor events approach to stress: Support for the use of daily hassles. *British Journal of Psychology, 81,* 469–481.

Cherry, E. C. (1953). Some experiments on the recognition of speech with one and with two ears. *Journal of the Acoustical Society of America, 25,* 975–979.

Cherulnik, P. D., Turns, L. C., & Wilderman, S. K. (1990). Physical Appearance and Leadership: Exploring the role of appearance-based attribution in leader emergence. *Journal of Applied Social Psychology, 20,* 1530–1539.

Chidester, T. R. (1986). Problems in the study of interracial interaction: Pseudo-interracial dyad paradigm. *Journal of Personality and Social Psychology, 50,* 74–79.

Child, I. L. (1985). Psychology and anomalous observations: The question of ESP in dreams. *American Psychologist, 40,* 1219–1230.

Chomsky, N. (1957). *Syntactic structures.* The Hague, Netherlands: Mouton.

Christensen, H., Hadzi-Pavlovic, D., Andrews, G., & Mattick, R. (1987). Behavior therapy and tricyclic medication in the treatment of obsessive-compulsive disorder: A quantitative review. *Journal of Consulting and Clinical Psychology, 55,* 701–771.

Cialdini, R. B. (1988). *Influence: Science and practice* (2nd ed.). Glenview, IL: Scott Føresman.

Clarizio, H., & Veres, V. (1984). A short-form version of the WISC-R for the learning disabled. *Psychology in the Schools, 21,* 154–157.

Clark, M. S., & Reis, H. T. (1988). Interpersonal processes in close relationships. In M. R. Rosenzweig & L. W. Porter (Eds.), *Annual Review of Psychology* (Vol. 39). Palo Alto, CA: Annual Reviews.

Clark, R. D. III (1990). The impact of AIDS on gender differences in willingness to engage in casual sex. *Journal of Applied Social Psychology, 20,* 771–782.

Clarke-Stewart, K. A. (1989). Infant day care: Maligned or malignant? *American Psychologist, 44,*(2), 266–273.

Clarke-Stewart, A., Friedman, E. G., & Koch, I (1985). *Child development: A topical approach.* New York: Wiley.

Cleveland, J. N., Murphy, K. R., & Williams, R. E. (1989). Multiple uses of performance appraisal: Prevalence and correlates. *Journal of Applied Psychology, 74,* 130–135.

Cochran, S. D., & Mays, V. M. (1989). Women and AIDS-related concerns. *American Psychologist, 44,* 529–535.

Cohen, J. F., & Tronick, E. Z. (1983). Three-month-old infants' reaction to simulated maternal depression. *Child Development, 54,* 185–193.

Cohen, R. M., Weingartner, H., Smallberg, S., Pickar, D., & Murphy, D. L. (1982). Effort and cognition in depression. *Archives of General Psychiatry, 39,* 593–597.

Cohen, S., & Williamson, G. M. (1991). Stress and infectious disease in humans. *Psychological Bulletin, 109,* 5–24.

Cohn, D. A. (1990). Child–mother attachment of six-year-olds and social competence at school. *Child Development, 61,* 152–162.

Cohn, L. D. (1991). Sex differences in the course of personality development: A meta-analysis. *Psychological Bulletin, 109,* 252–266.

Cole, D. A. (1989). Psychopathology of adolescent suicide: Hopelessness, coping beliefs, and depression. *Journal of Abnormal Psychology, 98,* 248–255.

Connors, J., & Heaven, P. C. L. (1990). Belief in a just world and attitudes toward AIDS sufferers. *The Journal of Social Psychology, 130,* 559–560.

Contrada, R. J. (1989). Type A behavior, personality hardiness, and cardiovascular responses to stress. *Journal of Personality and Social Psychology, 57,* 895–903.

Conway, M. A. (1991). In defense of everyday memory. *American Psychologist, 46,* 19–26.

Coppola, D. M., & O'Connell, R. J. (1988). Behavioral responses of peripubertal female mice toward puberty-accelerating and puberty-delaying chemical signals. *Chemical Senses, 13*(3), 407–424.

Coren, S., & Halpern, D. F. (1991). Left-handedness: A marker for decreased survival fitness. *Psychological Bulletin, 109,* 90–106.

Cornsweet, T. N. (1970). *Visual perception.* New York: Academic Press.

Covin, T. M., & Sattler, J. M. (1985). A longitudinal study of the Stanford-Binet and WISC-R with special education students. *Psychology in the Schools, 22,* 274–276.

Cowan, E. L. (1991). In pursuit of wellness. *American Psychologist, 46,* 404–408.

Cowan, N. (1988). Evolving conceptions of memory storage, selective attention, and their mutual constraints within the human information-processing system. *Psychological Bulletin, 104,* 163–191.

Craik, F. I. M., & Lockhart, R. S. (1972). Levels of processing: A framework for memory research. *Journal of Verbal Learning and Verbal Behavior, 11,* 671–784.

Craik, F. I. M., & Tulving, E. (1975). Depth of processing and the retention of words in episodic memory. *Journal of Experimental Psychology: General, 104,* 268–294.

Crespi, T. D. (1988). Effectiveness of time-out: A comparison of psychiatric, correctional and day-treatment programs. *Adolescence, 23,* 805–811.

Cummings, N. A. (1986). The dismantling of our health system: Strategies for the survival of psychological practice. *American Psychologist, 41,* 426–431.

Curran, D. K. (1987). *Adolescent suicidal behavior.* Washington, DC: Hemisphere Publishing.

Cutler, W. B., Preti, G., Krieger, A., Huggins, G. R., Garcia, C. R., & Lawley, H. J. (1986). Human axillary secretions influence women's menstrual cycles: The role of donor extract from men. *Hormones & Behavior, 20,* 463–473.

Dakof, G. A., & Taylor, S. E. (1990). Victim's perceptions of social support: What is helpful from whom? *Journal of Personality and Social Psychology, 58,* 80–89.

Dalby, J. T., Morgan, D., & Lee, M. L. (1986). Single case study: Schizophrenia and mania in identical twin brothers. *The Journal of Nervous and Mental Disease,* 174, 304–308.

Dalton, K. (1984). *The premenstrual syndrome and progesterone therapy.* Chicago: Year Book Medical Publishers.

Damon, W. (1988). *The moral child.* New York: The Free Press.

Daniels, D., & Plomin, R. (1985). Origins of individual differences in infant shyness. *Developmental Psychology, 21,* 118–121.

Davidson, L. E., Rosenberg, R. L., Mercy, J. A., Franklin, J., & Simmons, J. T. (1989). An epidemiologic study of risk factors in two teenage suicide clusters. *Journal of the American Medical Association, 262,* 2687–2692.

Davis, J. H. (1989). Psychology and law: The last 15 years. *Journal of applied social psychology, 19,* 199–230.

Davis, K., & Todd, M. J. (1984). Prototypes, paradigm cases, and relationship assessment: The case of friendship. In S. Duck and D. Perlman (Eds.), *Sage series in personal relationships* (Vol. 1). Beverly Hills, CA: Sage Publications.

Dawson, G., Grofer, L., Panagiotides, H., Hill, D., & Spieker, S. (1990). *Frontal lobe activity and affective behavior of infants of mothers with depressive symptoms.* Manuscript submitted for publication.

Dawson, G., Grofer, L., Panagiotides, H., Hill, D., & Spieker, S. (1991). Frontal lobe activity and affective behavior of infants of mothers with depressive symptoms. Submitted manuscript.

Day, R. H., & McKenzie, B. E. (1977). Constancies in the perceptual world of the infant. In W. Epstein (Ed.), *Stability and constancy in visual perception.* New York: Wiley.

DeAngelis, T. (1988). In praise of rose-colored specs. *APA Monitor, 19*(1), 11.

Deci, E. L. (1971). Effect of externally mediated rewards on intrinsic motivation. *Journal of Personality and Social Psychology, 18,* 105–115.

Deci, E. L. Effects of contingent and non-contingent rewards and controls on intrinsic motivation. *Organizational Behavior and Human Performance, 8,* 217–229.

Deci, E. L. (1975). *Intrinsic motivation* New York: Plenum Press.

Deffenbacher, J. L. (1988, August). *Cognitive-behavioral approaches to anger reduction: Some treatment considerations.* Paper presented at 96th annual convention of the American Psychological Association at Atlanta, GA.

DeLeon, P. H. (1988). Public policy and public service. *American Psychologist, 43,* 309–315.

DeLuca, R. V., & Holborn, S. W. (1990). Effects of fixed-interval and fixed-ratio schedules of token reinforcement on exercise with obese and non-obese boys. *The Psychological Record, 40,* 67–82.

Dement, W. C., & Kleitman, N. (1957). The relation of eye movements during sleep to dream activity: An objective method for the study of dreaming. *Journal of Experimental Psychology, 53,* 339–346.

Dement, W., & Wolpert, E. A. (1958). The relation of eye movements, body motility, and external stimuli to dream content. *Journal of Experimental Psychology, 55,* 543–553.

DeNisi, A. S., Robbins, T., & Cafferty, T. P. (1989). Organization of information used for performance appraisals: Role of diary-keeping. *Journal of Applied Psychology, 74,* 124–129.

DeNisi, A. S., & Williams, K. J. (1988). Cognitive approaches to performance appraisal. *Personnel and Human Resources Management, 6,* 109–155.

Dentan, R. K. (1968). *The Semai: A nonviolent people of Malaya.* New York: Holt, Rinehart and Winston.

DePaulo, B. M., Dull, W. R., Greenberg, J. M., & Swaim, G. W. (1989). Are shy people reluctant to ask for help? *Journal of Personality and Social Psychology, 56,* 834–844.

Derlega, V. J., Winstead, B. A., Wong, P. T. P., Hunter, S. (1985). Gender effects in an initial encounter: A case where men exceed women in disclosure. *Journal of Soc Pers Relat 2,* 25–44.

Dershowitz, A. M. (1986). *Reversal of fortune inside the Von Bulow case.* New York: Random House.

DeValois, R. L., & Jacobs, G. H. (1968). Primate color vision. *Science, 162,* 533–540.

DeValois, R. L., Thorell, L. G., & Albrecht, D. G. (1985). Periodicity of striate-cortex-cell receptive fields. *Journal of the Optical Society of America (A),* 1115–1123.

De Vries, B., & Walker, L. J. (1986). Moral reasoning and attitudes toward capital punishment. *Developmental Psychology, 22,* 509–513.

Dewsbury, D. A. (1990). Early interactions between animal psychologists and animal activists and the founding of the APA committee on precautions in animal experimentation. *American Psychologists, 45,* 315–327.

Deyo, R. A., Straube, K. T., & Disterhoft, J. F. (1989). Nimodipine facilitates associative learning in aging rabbits. *Science,* 2/10/89, Vol. *243,* 809–811.

DiLalla, L. F., & Gottesman, I. I. (1991). Biological and genetic contributors to violence—widom's untold tale. *Psychological Bulletin, 109,* 125–129.

DiNicola, D. D., & DiMatteo, M. R. (1984). Practitioners, patients, and compliance with medical regimens: A social psychological perspective. In A. Baum, S. E. Taylor, & J. E. Singer (Eds.), *Handbook of psychology and health: Vol. 4. Social psychological aspects of health.* Hillsdale, NJ: Erlbaum.

Dion, K. K., Pak, A. W., & Dion, K. L. (1990). Stereotyping physical attractiveness. *Journal of Cross-Cultural Psychology, 21,* 158–179.

Dobson, K. S., & Block, L. (1988). Historical and philosophical bases of the cognitive-behavioral therapies. In Keith S. Dobson (Ed.) *Handbook of cognitive behavioral therapies.* New York: Guilford Press.

Dollard, J., Doob, L. W., Miller, N. E., Mowrer, O. H., & Sears, R. R. (1939). *Frustration and aggression.* New Haven, CT: Yale University Press.

Doob, A. N., & McLaughlin, D. S. (1989). Ask and you shall be given: Request size and donations to a good cause. *Journal of Applied Social Psychology, 19,* 1049–1056.

Downey, G., & Coyne, J. C. (1990). Children of depressed parents: An integrative review. *Psychological Bulletin, 108,* 50–76.

Drake, R. E., Osher, F. C., & Wallach, M. A. (1989). Alcohol use and abuse in schizophrenia. *The Journal of Nervous and Mental Disease, 177,* 408–413.

Dryden, W., & Ellis A. (1988). Rational–emotive therapy. In Keith S. Dobson (Ed.), *Handbook of cognitive-bahavioral therapies.* New York: Guilford Press.

Dunant, Y., & Israel, M. (1985). The release of acetylcholine. *Scientific American, 252,* 58–83.

Duncan, J. (1980). The locus of interference in the perception of simultaneous stimuli. *Psychological Review, 87,* 272–300.

Dunn, J., & Plomin, R. (1990). *Separate lives,* Basic Books.

Dutton, D. G. (1988). *The domestic assault of women.* Boston, MA: Allyn & Bacon.

Duyme, M. (1988). School success and social class. An adoption study. *Developmental Psychology, 24,* 203–209.

Eich, E., & Metcalf, J. (1989). Mood dependent memory for internal versus external events. *Journal of Experimental Psychology: Learning, Memory, and Cognition, 15,* 443–455.

Eisdorfer, C., & Wilkie, F. (1977). Stress, disease, aging, and behavior. In J. E. Birren & K. W. Schaie (Eds.), *Handbook of the psychology of aging.* New York: Van Nostrand Reinhold.

Elkind, D. (1981b). *The hurried child.* Reading, MA: Addison-Wesley.

Elkind, D. (1987). *Miseducation.* New York: Alfred A. Knopf.

Ellingson, R. J. (1975). Ontogenesis of sleep in human. In C. G. Lairy & Salzarula (Eds.), *The experimental study of human sleep: Methodological problems.* Amsterdam: Elsevier Press.

Elliot, R. (1987). *Litigating intelligence IQ tests, special education, and social science in the courtroom.* Dover, MS: Auburn House.

Ellis, A. (1970). *The essence of rational psychotherapy: A comprehensive approach to treatment.* New York: Institute for Rational Living.

Ellis, A. (1988, August). *The philosophical basis of rational-emotive therapy (RET).* Paper presented at the 96th annual meeting of the American Psychological Association in Atlanta, GA.

Ellis, A. (1990). How can psychological treatment aim to be briefer and better? The rational–emotive approach to brief therapy. In J. K. Zeig & S. G. Gilligan (Eds.), *Brief therapy myths, methods, and metaphors,* New York, NY: Brunner/Mazel.

Ellis, A., & Harper, R. A. (1961). *A guide to rational living.* North Hollywood, CA: Wilshire Book.

Emery, R. E. (1989a). Family violence. *American Psychologist, 44,* 321–328.

Emery, R. E. (1989b, September 15). *Family violence: Has science met its match?* Edited transcript of a Science and Public Policy Seminar presented by the Federation of Behavioral, Psychological and Cognitive Sciences in the Rayburn House Office Building in Washington, DC.

Eppinger, M. G., Craig, P. L., Adams, R. L., & Parsons, O. A. (1987). The WAIS-R index for estimating premorbid intelligence: Cross-validation and

WAIS-R index for estimating premorbid intelligence: Cross-validation and clinical utility. *Journal of Consulting and Clinical Psychology, 55,* 86–90.

Epstein, L. H., & Perkins, K. A. (1988). Smoking, stress, and coronary heart disease. *Journal of Consulting and Clinical Psychology, 56,* 342–349.

Epstein, S., & O'Brien, E. J. (1985). The person-situation debate in historical and current perspective. *Psychological Bulletin, 98,* 513-537.

Ericksen, C. W., Webb, J. M., & Fournier, L. R. (1990). How much processing do nonattended stimuli receive? Apparently very little, but . . . . *Perception & Psychophysics, 47,* 477–488.

Erickson, E. H. (1968). *Identity: Youth and crisis.* New York: W. W. Norton.

Etaugh, C. (1980). Effects of nonmaternal care on children. *American Psychologist, 35,* 309–319.

Evans, D. A., Funkenstein, H. H., Albert, M. S., Sherr, P. A., Cook, N. R., Chown, M. J., Hebert, L. E., Hennekens, C. H., & Taylor, J. O. (1989). *Journal of the American Medical Association, 262,* 2551–2556.

Exner, Jr., J. E., & Mason, B. (1985). Children's Rorschachs: Description and prediction. *Journal of Personality Assessment, 49,* 13–14.

Eysenck, H. J. (1952). The effects of psychotherapy: An evaluation. *Journal of Consulting and Clinical Psychology, 16,* 319–324.

Eysenck, H. J. (1970). *The structure of human personality* (3rd ed.). London: Methuen.

Fagan, T. K. (1986). School psychology's dilemma. *American Psychologist, 41,* 851-861.

Fajardo, D. M. (1985). Author race, essay quality, and reverse discrimination. *Journal of Applied Social Psychology, 15,* 255–268.

Fantz, R. L. (1961). The origin of form perception. *Scientific American, 204,* 66–72.

Faraone, S. V., Kremen, W. S., & Tsuang, M. T. (1990). Genetic transmission of major affective disorders: Quantitative models and linkage analyses. *Psychological Bulletin, 108,* 109–127.

Farone, S. (1982). Psychiatry and political repression in the Soviet Union. *American Psychologist, 37,* 1105–1112.

Farone, S. V., & Tsuang, M. T. (1985). Quantitative models of the genetic transmission of schizophrenia. *Psychological Bulletin, 98,* 41–66.

Feeney, D. M. (1987). Human rights and animal welfare. *American Psychologist,* 42, 593–599.

Fehr, B. (1988). Prototype analysis of the concepts of love and commitment. *Journal of Personality and Social Psychology, 55,* 557–579.

Fehr, B., & Russell, J. A. (1991). The concept of love viewed from a prototype perspective. *Journal of Personality and Social Psychology, 60,* 425–438.

Feingold, A. (1988a). Cognitive gender differences are disappearing. *American Psychologist, 43* 95–103.

Feingold, A. (1988b). Matching for attractiveness in romantic partners and same-sex friends: A meta-analysis and theoretical critique. *Psychological Bulletin, 104,* 226–235.

Feingold, B. F. (1976). Hyperkinesis and learning disabilities linked to the ingestion of artificial food colors and flavors. *Journal of Learning Disabilities, 9*(9), 19–27.

Feiring, C., Fox, N. A., Jaskir, J., & Lewis, M. (1987). The relation between social support, infant risk status and mother–infant interaction. *Developmental Psychology, 3,* 400–405.

Ferguson, H. B., Stoddart, C., & Simeon, J. G. (1986). Double-bind challenge studies of behavioral and cognitive effects of sucrose–aspertame ingestion in normal children. *Nutrition Reviews, 44* (Suppl.), 144–150.

Festinger, L. (1957). *A theory of cognitive dissonance.* Evanston, IL: Row, Petersen.

Fillion, T. J., & Blass, E. M. (1986). Infantile experience with suckling odors determines adult sexual behavior in male rats. *Science, 231,* 729–731.

Fine, A. (1986). Transplantation in the central nervous system. *Scientific American, 255,* 52–67.

Finke, R. A., Pinker, S., & Farah, M. J. (1989). Reinterpreting visual patterns in mental imagery. *Cognitive Science, 13,* 51–78.

Finn, P. R., & Pihl, R. O. (1987). Men at high risk for alcoholism: The effect of alcohol on cardiovascular response to unavoidable shock. *Journal of Abnormal Psychology, 96,* 230–236.

Fisher, J. F. (1988). Possible effects of reference group-based social influence on AIDS-risk behavior and AIDS prevention. *American Psychologist, 43,* 914–920.

Fiske, S. T. (1989, August 13). *Interdependence and stereotyping: From the laboratory to the Supreme Court (and back).* Paper presented at the American Psychological Association Convention, New Orleans.

Flavell, J. H. (1963). *The development psychology of Jean Piaget.* New York: Van Nostrand Reinhold.

Flavell, J. H., Green, F. L., & Flavell, E. R. (1989). Young children's ability to differentiate appearance–reality and Level 2 perspectives in the tactile modality. *Child Development, 60,* 201–213.

Fleming, I., Baum, A., & Weiss, L. (1987). Social density and perceived control as mediators of crowding stress in high-density residential neighborhoods. *Journal of Personality and Social Psychology, 52,* 899–906.

Fleming, J. D. (1974). Field report: The state of the apes. *Psychology Today, 7,* 31–46.

Flor, H., & Turk, D. C. (1989). Psychophysiology of chronic pain: Do chronic pain patients exhibit symptom-specific psychophysiological responses? *Psychological Bulletin, 105,* 215–259.

Flora, J. A. & Thoresen, C. E. (1988). Reducing the risk of AIDS in adolescents. *American Psychologist, 43,* 965–970.

Forbes, G. B. (1990). Do obese individuals gain weight more easily than nonobese individuals? *American Journal of Clinical Nutrition, 52,* 224–227.

Forsythe, S. M. (1990). Effect of applicant's clothing on interviewer's decision to hire. *Journal of Applied Social Psychology, 20,* 1579–1595.

Fox, N., Kagan, J., & Weiskopf, S. (1979). The growth of memory during infancy. *Genetic Psychology Monographs, 99,* 91–130.

Frankenberg, W. K., & Dodds, J. B. (1967). The Denver Developmental Screening Test. *Journal of Pediatrics, 71,* 181–191.

Frasure-Smith, N., & Prince, R. (1989). Long-term follow-up of the ischemic heart disease life stress monitoring program. *Psychosomatic Medicine, 51,* 485–513.

Frederiksen, N. (1986). Toward a broader conception of human intelligence. *American Psychologist, 41,* 445–452.

Freud, S. (1933). *New introductory lectures on psycho-analysis.* New York: W. W. Norton.

Freud, S. (1953). The interpretation of dreams. In J. Strachey (Ed.), *The standard edition of the complete psychological works of Sigmund Freud* (Vols. 4 and 5). London: Hogarth. (Original work published 1900)

Frezza, M., di Padova, C., Pozzato, G., Terpin, M., Baraona, E., & Lieber, C. S. (1990). High blood alcohol levels in women. *The New England Journal of Medicine, 322,* 95–99.

Friedman, H. S., & Booth-Kewley, S. (1988). Validity of the Type A construct: A reprise. *Psychological Bulletin, 104,* 381–384.

Friedman, M., & Rosenman, R. H. (1974). *Type A behavior and your heart.* Greenwich, CT: Fawcett.

Frijda, N. H., Kuipers, P., & ter Schure, E. (1989). Relations among emotion, appraisal, and emotional action readiness. *Journal of Personality and Social Psychology, 57,* 212–228.

Furby, L., Weinrott, M. R., & Blackshaw, L. (1989). Sex offender recidivism: A review. *Psychological Bulletin, 105,* 3–30.

Furstenberg, F. F., Jr., Brooks-Gunn, J., & Chase-Lansdale, L. (1989). Teenaged pregnancy and childbearing. *American Psychologist, 44,* 313–320.

Gackenbach, J., & Bosveld, J. (1989). *Control your dreams.* New York: Harper & Row.

Gallup, G. G., Jr., & Suarez, S. D. (1985). Alternatives to the use of animals in psychological research. *American Psychologist, 40,* 1104–1111.

Galotti, K. M. (1989). Approaches to studying formal and everyday reasoning. *Psychological Bulletin, 105,* 331–351.

Garcia, J., Gustavson, C. R., Kelly, D. J., & Sweeney, M. (1976). Preylithium aversions: I. Coyotes and wolves. *Behavioral Biology, 16,* 61–72.

Garcia, J., & Koelling, R. A., (1971). The use of ionizing rays as a mammalian olfactory stimulus. In H. Autrum, R. Jung, W. R. Loewenstein, D. M. MacKay, H. L. Teuber (Eds.), *Handbook of sensory physiology: Vol. 4. Chemical senses* (Part 1). Springer-Verlag: New York.

Gardner, H. (1983). *Frames of mind.* New York: Basic Books.

Gardner, R. A., & Gardner, B. T. (1969). Teaching sign language to a chimp. *Science, 165,* 664–672.

Gardner, W., Scherer, D., & Tester, M. (1989). Asserting scientific authority: Cognitive development and adolescent legal rights. *American Psychologist, 6,* 895–902.

Garfield, S. L., & Bergin, A. E. (1986). *Handbook of psychotherapy and behavior change* (3rd ed.). New York: Wiley.

Garza, R. T., & Borchert, J. E. (1990). Maintaining social identity in a mixed-gender setting: Minority/majority status and cooperative/competitive feedback. *Sex Roles, 22,* 679–691.

Gay, P. (1988). *Freud–A life for our time.* New York: W. W. Norton.

Gazzaniga, M. S. (1983). Right hemisphere language following brain bisection: A 20-year perspective. *American Psychologist, 38,* 525–537.

Gazzaniga, M. S. (1989). Organization of the human brain. *Science, 245,* 947–952.

Geller, E. S. (1975). Increasing desired waste disposals with instructions. *Man Environment Systems, 5,* 125–128.

Geller, E. S. (1989). Applied behavior analysis and social marketing: An integration for environmental preservation. *Journal of Social Issues, 45,* 17–36.

Geller, E. S., Kalsher, M. J., Rudd, J. R., & Lehman, G. R. (1989). Promoting safety belt use on a university campus: An integration of commitment and incentive strategies. *Journal of Applied Social Psychology, 19,* 3–19.

Geller, E. S., Winett, R. A., & Everett, P. B. (1982). *Preserving the environment: New strategies for behavior change.* New York: Pergamon Press.

Geller, E. S., Witmer, J. F., & Tuso, M. E. (1977). Environmental intervention for litter control. *Journal of Applied Psychology, 62,* 344–351.

Gevins, A. S., Bressler, S. L., Cutillo, B. A., Illes, J., Miller, J. C., Stern, J., & Jex, H. R. (1990). Effects of prolonged mental work on functional brain topography. *Electroencephalography and Clinical Neurophysiology, 76,* 339–350.

Gevins, A. S., Morgan, N. H., Bressler, S. L., Cutillo, B. A., White, R. M., Illes, J., Greer, D. S., Doyle, J. C., & Zeitlin, G. M. (1987). Human neuroelectric patterns predict performance accuracy. *Science, 235,* 580–585.

Gibbons, B. (1986). The intimate sense of smell. *National Geographic, 9,* 324–360.

Gibson, E. J. (1988). Exploratory behavior in the development of perceiving, acting, and the acquiring of knowledge. *Annual Review of Psychology, 39,* 1–41.

Gift, T. E., Strauss, J. S., Ritzler, B. A., Kokes, R. F., & Harder, D. W. (1980). How diagnostic concepts of schizophrenia differ. *Journal of Nervous and Mental Disease, 168,* 3–8.

Gilligan, C. (1982). *In a different voice: Psychological theory and women's development.* Cambridge, MA: Harvard University Press.

Glaser, R. (1989, June 16). *The fourth R: The ability to reason.* Presented by the Federation of Behavioral, Psychological and Cognitive Sciences in the House Rayburn Building.

Glaser, R., & Kiecolt-Glaser, J. (1988). Stress-associated immune suppression and acquired immune deficiency syndrome (AIDS). In T. P. Bridge, A. F. Mirsky, & F. K. Goodwin (Eds.), *Psychological, neuropsychiatric, and substance abuse aspects of AIDS.* New York: Raven Press.

Glasgow, R. E., & Treborg, J. R. (1988). Occupational Health Promotion Programs to Reduce Cardiovascular Risk. *Journal of Consulting and Clinical Psychology, 56,* 365–373.

Gloor, P., Olivier, A., Quesney, L. F., Andermann, F., & Horowitz, S. (1982). The role of the limbic system in experimental phenomena of temporal lobe epilepsy. *Ann Neurol 12,* 129–144.

Goldenberg, M. M. (1990). *Pharmacology for the psychotherapist.* Muncie, IN: Accelerated Development.

Goldfried, M. R., & Davison, G. C. (1976). *Clinical behavior therapy.* New York: Holt, Rinehart and Winston.

Goldstein, J. M., & Tsuang, M. T. (1990). Gender and schizophrenia: An introduction and synthesis of findings. *Schizophrenia Bulletin, 16,* 179–183.

Gonzales, L. R., Hays, R. B., Bond, M. A., & Kelly, J. G. (1983). Community mental health. In M. Hersen, A. E. Kazdin, & A. S. Bellack (Eds.), *The clinical psychology handbook.* New York: Pergamon Press.

Gorham, J. (1988). The relationship between verbal teacher immediacy behaviors and student learning. *Communication Education, 37,* 40–53.

Gottesman, I. I. (1991). *Schizophrenia genesis,* New York, NY: W. H. Freeman & Company.

Gottman, J. M., & Katz, L. F. (1989). Effects of marital discord on young children's peer interaction and health. *Developmental Psychology, 25,* 373–381.

Goulding, M. M. (1990). Getting the important work done fast: Contract plus redecision. In J. K. Zeig & S. G. Gilligan (Eds.), *Brief therapy myths, methods, and metaphors.* New York: Brunner/Mazel.

Graham, J. R., & Strenger, V. E. (1988). MMPI characteristics of alcoholics: A review. *Journal of Consulting and Clinical Psychology, 56,* 197–205.

Greaves, G. B. (1980). Multiple personality: 165 years after Mary Reynolds. *Journal of Nervous and Mental Disease, 168,* 577–596.

Greene, R. L. (1987). Effects of maintenance rehearsal on human memory. *Psychological Bulletin, 102,* 403–413.

Greenfield, P. M., & Savage-Rumbaugh, E. S. (1990). Grammatical combination in Pan paniscus: Processes of learning and invention in the evolution and development of language. In S. T. Parker and K. R. Gibson (Eds.) *"Language" and Intelligence in Monkeys and Apes,* New York, NY: Cambridge University Press.

Greeno, J. G. (1989). A perspective on thinking. *American Psychologist, 44,* 134–141.

Greenwald, A. G., Spangenberg, E. R., Pratkanis, A. R., & Eskenazi, J. (1990). *Double-bind tests of subliminal self-help audiotapes.* Paper presented in a Division 23 Symposium at the annual meeting of the American Psychological Association.

Grossman, F. K., Pollack, W. S., Golding, E. (1988). Fathers and children: Predicting the quality and quantity of fathering. *Developmental Psychology, 1,* 92–91.

Guilford, J. P. (1967). *The nature of human intelligence.* New York: McGraw Hill.

Guilford, J. P. (1985). The structure of intellect model. In B. B. Wolman (Ed.), *Handbook of intelligence: Theories, measurements, and applications,* New York: Wiley.

Guion, R. M., & Gibson, W. M. (1988). Personnel selection and placement. In M. R. Rosenzweig & L. W. Porter (Eds.), *Annual Review of Psychology.* Palo Alto, CA: Annual Reviews.

Haaf, R. A., Smith, P. H., & Smitley, S. (1983). Infant response to facelike patterns under fixed-trial and infant-control procedures. *Child development, 54,* 172–177.

Haber, R. N. (1969). Eidetic images. *Scientific American, 220*(4), 36–44.

Haber, R. N. (1979). Twenty years of haunting eidetic imagery: Where's the ghost? *Behavioral and Brain Sciences, 2,* 583–629.

Haith, M. M., & McCarty, M. E. (1990). Stability of visual expectations at 3.0 months of age. *Developmental Psychology, 26,* 68–74.

Halgren, E., Walter, R. D., Cherlow, A. G., & Crandall, Ph.H. (1978). Mental phenomena evoked by electrical stimulation of the human hippocampal formation and amygdala. *Brain, 101,* 83–117.

Hall, E. T. (1966). *The hidden dimension.* Garden City, NY: Doubleday.

Hall, J. A. (1979). Gender, gender roles, and nonverbal communication skills. In R. Rosenthal (Ed.), *Skill in nonverbal communication.* Cambridge, MA: Oelgeschlager, Gunn & Hain.

Hall, S. M., Havassy, B. E., & Wasserman, D. A. (1990). Commitment to abstinence and acute stress in relapse to alcohol, opiates, and nicotine. *Journal of Consulting and Clinical Psychology, 58,* 175–181.

Hamilton, S., & Fagot, B. I. (1988). Chronic stress and coping styles: A comparison of male and female undergraduates. *Journal of Personality and Social Psychology, 5,* 819–823.

Harkins, S. G., & Szymanski, K. (1988). Social loafing and self-evaluation with an objective standard. *Journal of Experimental Social Psychology, 24,* 354–365.

Harlow, H. F. (1962). The heterosexual affectional system in monkeys. *American Psychologist, 17,* 1–9.

Harlow, H. F., & Zimmerman, R. R. (1958). The development of affectional responses in infant monkeys. *Proceedings of the American Philosophic Society, 102,* 501–509.

Hartup, W. W. (1989). Social relationships and their developmental significance. *American Psychologist, 44,* 120–126.

Haskins, R. (1989). Beyond metaphor: The efficacy of early childhood education. *American Psychologist, 44*(2), 274–282.

Hauser, S. T., & Bowlds, M. K. (1990). Stress, coping, and adaptation. In S. S. Feldman & G. R. Elliott (Eds.) *At the Threshold,* Cambridge, MA: Harvard University Press.

Haynes, S. N. (1984). Behavioral assessment of adults. In G. Goldstein & M. Hersen (Eds.), *Handbook of Psychological Assessment.* New York: Pergamon Press.

Hays, R. B. (1989). The day-to-day functioning of close versus casual friendships. *Journal of Social and Personal Relationships, 6,* 21–37.

Hazelrigg, M. D., Cooper, H. M., & Borduin, C. M. (1987). Evaluating the effectiveness of family therapies: An integrative review and analysis. *Psychological Bulletin, 101,* 428–442.

Heatherton, T. F., Polivy, J., & Herman, C. P. (1991). Restraint, weight loss, and variability of body weight. *Journal of Abnormal Psychology, 100,* 78–83.

Hebb, D. O. (1949). *Organization of behavior.* New York: Wiley.

Hebb, D. O. (1972). *Textbook of psychology* (3rd ed.). Philadelphia: W. B. Saunders.

Heckler, M. M. (1985). Psychology in the public forum: The fight against Alzheimer's disease. *American Psychologist, 40,* 1240–1244.

Heider, E. R. (1971). "Focal" color areas and the development of color names. *Developmental Psychology, 4,* 447–455.

Heilbrun, A. B., Jr., Wydra, D., & Friedberg, L. (1989). Parent identification and gender schema development. *Journal of Genetic Psychology, 150*(3), 293–299.

Held, R., & Hein, A. (1963). Movement produced stimulation in the development of visually guided behavior. *Journal of Comparative and Physiological Psychology, 56,* 872–876.

Hirsch, J., & Leibel, R. L. (1988). New light on obesity. *The New England Journal of Medicine, 318,* 509–510.

Hobfoll, S. E. (1989). Conservation of resources: A new attempt at conceptualizing stress. *American Psychologist, 44,* 513–524.

Hobson, J. A. (1989). *Sleep.* New York: W. H. Freeman.

Hobson, J. A., & McCarley, R. W. (1977). The brain as a dream state generator: An activation–synthesis of the dream process. *American Journal of Psychiatry, 134,* 1335–1348.

Hochberg, J. E. (1974). Organization and the Gestalt tradition. In E. C. Carterette & M. P. Friedman (Eds.), *Handbook of perception.* New York: Academic Press.

Hochberg, J. E. (1979). Sensation and perception. In E. Hearst (Ed.), *The first century of experimental psychology.* New York: Wiley.

Holder, M. D., Yirmiya, R., Garcia, J., & Raizer, J. (1989). Conditioned taste aversions are not readily disrupted by external excitation. *Behavioral Neuroscience, 103,* 605–611.

Holland, M. K. (1975). *Using psychology: Principles of behavior and your life.* Boston: Little, Brown.

Holmes, T. H., & Rahe, R. H. (1967). The social readjustment rating scale. *Journal of Psychosomatic Research, 11,* 213–218.

Hom, H. L., Jr., & Arbuckle, B. (1988). Mood induction effects upon goal setting and performance in young children. *Motivation and Emotion, 12,* 113–122.

Horn, J. M. (1983). The Texas Adoption Project: Adopted children and their intellectual resemblance to biological and adoptive parents. *Child Development, 54,* 268–275.

Horne, J. (1988). *Why we sleep.* New York: Oxford University Press.

Horney, K. (1937). *The neurotic personality of our time.* New York: W. W. Norton.

Horvath, P. (1988). Placebos and common factors in two decades of psychotherapy research. *Psychological Bulletin, 204,* 214–225.

Howard, K. I., Kopta, S. M., Krause, M. S., & Orlinsky, D. E. (1986). The dose–effect relationships in psychotherapy. *American Psychologist, 41,* 159–164.

Howarth, E. (1986). What does Eysenck's psychoticism scale really measure? *British Journal of Psychology, 77,* 223–227.

Hoyt, I. P., Nadon, R., Register, P. A., Chorny, J., Fleeson, W., Grigorian, E. M., & Otto, L. (1989). Daydreaming, absorption, and hypnotizability. *The International Journal of Clinical and Experimental Hypnosis, 37,* 332–342.

Hubel, D. H., & Wiesel, T. N. (1962). Receptive fields, binocular interaction, and functional architecture in the cat's visual cortex. *Journal of Physiology, 160,* 106–164.

Hurvich, L., & Jameson, D. (1974). Opponent processes as a model of neural organization. *American Psychologist, 30,* 88–102.

Huston, A. C., Watkins, B. A., & Kunkel, D. (1989). Public policy and children's television. *American Psychologist, 44,* 424–433.

Hyde, J. S., Fennema, E., & Lamon, S. J. (1990). Gender differences in mathematic performance: A meta-analysis. *Psychological Bulletin, 107,* 139–155.

Hyde, J. S., & Linn, M. C. (1988). Gender differences in verbal ability: A meta-analysis. *Psychological Bulletin, 104,* 53–69.

Ilgen, D. R. (1990). Health issues at work: Opportunities for industrial/organizational psychology. *American Psychologist, 45,* 273–283.

Ingbar, D. H., & Gee, J. B. L. (1985). Pathophysiology and treatment of sleep apnea. *Annual Review of Medicine, 36,* 369–395.

Insua, A. M. (1983). WAIS-R factor structures in two cultures. *Journal of Cross-Cultural Psychology, 14,* 427–438.

Isaac, R. J., & Armat, V. C. (1990). *Madness in the streets.* New York: The Free Press.

Isabella, R. A., Belsky, J., & von Eye, A. (1989). Origins of infant–mother attachment: An examination of interactional synchrony during the infant's first year. *Developmental Psychology, 25,* 12–21.

Izard, C. E., & Saxton, P. M. (1988). Emotions. In R. C. Atkinson, R. J. Herrnstein, G. Lindzey, & R. D. Luce (Eds.), *Stevens handbook of experimental psychology Vol. 1. Perception and motivation* (1st ed.). New York: Wiley.

Jackson, S. E., & Schuler, R. S. (1990). Human resource planning: Challenges for industrial/organizational psychologists. *American Psychologist, 45,* 223–239.

Jacobs, M. K., & Goodman, G. (1989). Psychology and self-help groups. *American Psychologist, 44,* 536–545.

Jacobson, N. S., & Bussob, N. (1983). Marital and family therapy. In M. Hersen, A. E. Kazdin, & A. S. Bellack. *The clinical psychology handbook.* New York: Pergamon Press.

James, W. (1884). What is an emotion? *Mind, 9,* 188–205.

James, W. (1890). *Principles of psychology.* New York: Dover Publications.

Janis, I. L. (1983). The role of social support in adherence to stressful decisions. *American Psychologist, 38,* 142–160.

Janis, I. L. (1985). Stress inoculation in health care: Theory and research. In A. Monat & R. S. Lazarus (Eds.), *Stress and coping* (2nd ed.). New York: Columbia University Press.

Jaynes, J. (1976). *The origin of consciousness in the breakdown of the bicameral mind.* Boston: Houghton Mifflin.

Jenkins, H. M., & Harrison, R. H. (1960). Effect of discrimination training on auditory generalization. *Journal of Experimental Psychology, 59,* 244–253.

Jensen, A. R. (1969). How much can we boost IQ and scholastic achievement? *Harvard Educational Review, 39,* 1–123.

Jensen, A. R. (1970). Can we and should we study race differences? In J. Hellmuth (Ed.), *Disadvantaged child* (Vol. 3). New York: Brunner/Mazel.

Jensen, A. R. (1976). Test bias and construct validity. *Phi Delta Kappan, 58,* 340–346.

Jensen, A. R. (1977). Cumulative deficit in IQ of blacks in the rural south. *Developmental Psychology, 3,* 194–191.

Jensen, A. R. (1980). Can we be neutral about bias? *Contemporary Psychology, 25,* 868–871.

Johnson, A. B. (1990). *Out of bedlam,* New York: Basic Books.

Johnson, B. T., & Eagly, A. H. (1989). Effects of involvement on persuasion: A meta-analysis. *Psychological Bulletin, 106,* 290–314.

Johnson, C., & Larson, R. (1982). Bulimia: An analysis of moods and behavior. *Psychosomatic Medicine, 44,* 341–351.

Johnson, D. L. (1989). Schizophrenia as a brain disease. *American Psychologist, 44,* 553–555.

Johnson, L. C., Slye, E. S., & Dement, W. (1965). Electronencephalographic and autonomic activity during and after prolonged sleep deprivation. *Psychosomatic Medicine, 27,* 415–423.

Johnson, M. A. (1989). Variables associated with friendship in an adult population. *The Journal of Social Psychology, 129*(3), 379–390.

Jones, S. S., & Raag, T. (1989). Smile production in older infants: The importance of a social recipient for the facial signal. *Child Development, 60,* 811–818.

Josephson, W. L. (1987). Television violence and children's aggression: Testing the priming, social script, and disinhibition predictions. *Journal of Personality and Social Psychology, 53,* 882–890.

Judd, C. M., & Park, B. (1988). Out-group homogeneity: Judgments of variability at the individual and group levels. *Journal of Personality and Social Psychology, 54,* 778–788.

Jussim, L. (1989). Teacher expectations: Self-fulfilling prophecies, perceptual biases, and accuracy. *Journal of Personality and Social Psychology, 57,* 469–480.

Kagan, J. (1989). Temperamental contributions to social behavior. *American Psychologist, 44,* 668–674.

Kagan, J., Reznick, J. S., & Gibbons, J. (1989). Inhibited and unhibited types of children, *Child Development, 60,* 838–845.

Kagan, J., Reznick, J. S., & Snidman, N. (1987). The physiology and psychology of behavioral inhibition in children. *Child Development, 58,* 1459–1473.

Kahn, J. P., Kornfield, D. S., Blood, D. K., Lynn, R. B., Heller, S. S., & Frank, K. A. (1982). Type A behavior and the thallium stress test. *Psychosomatic Medicine, 44,* 431–436.

Kaitz, M., Meschulach-Sarfaty, O., & Auerbach, J. (1988). A reexamination of newborns' ability to imitate facial expressions. *Developmental Psychology,1,* 3–7.

Kales, A., Tan, T. L., Kollar, E. J., Naithoh, P., Preson, T. A., & Malmstrom, E. J. (1970). Sleep patterns following 205 hours of sleep deprivation. *Psychosomatic Medicine, 32,* 189–200.

Kalichman, S. C. (1989). Sex roles and sex differences in adult spatial performance. *The Journal of Genetic Psychology, 150,* 93–100.

Kalichman, S. C., Craig, M. E., & Follingstad, D. R. (1989). Factors influencing the reporting of father–child sexual abuse: Study of licensed practicing psychologists. *Professional Psychology: Research and Practice, 20,* 84–89.

Kalichman, S. C., Szymanowski, D., McKee, G., Taylor, J., & Craig, M. E. (1989). Cluster analytically derived MMPI profile subgroups of incarcerated adult rapists. *Journal of Clinical Psychology, 45,* 149–155.

Kalil, R. E. (1989). Synapse formation in the developing brain. *Scientific American,* 76–85.

Kalimo, R., & Mejman, T. (1987). Psychological and behavioral responses to

Kalimo, R., & Mejman, T. (1987). Psychological and behavioral responses to stress at work. In R. Kalimo, M. A. El-Batawi, & C. L. Cooper (Eds.), *Psychosocial factors at work and their relation to health.* Geneva: World Health Organization.

Kamarck, T., & Jennings, J. R. (1991). Biobehavioral factors in sudden cardiac death. *Psychological Bulletin, 109,* 42–75.

Kanner, A. D., Coyne, J. C., Schaefer, C., & Lazarus, R. S. (1981). Comparison of two modes of stress measurement: Daily hassles and uplifts versus major life events. *Journal of Behavioral Medicine, 4,* 1–39.

Kaplan, A. S., & Woodside, D. B. (1987). Biological aspects of anorexia nervosa and bulimia nervosa. *Journal of Consulting and Clinical Psychology, 55,* 645–653.

Kaplan, C. A., & Simon, H. A. (1990). In search of insight. *Cognitive Psychology, 22,* 374–419.

Kaplan, M. (1983). A woman's view of *DSM-III. American Psychologist, 38,* 786–792.

Kaplan, R. M. (1988). Health-related quality of life in cardiovascular disease. *Journal of Consulting and Clinical Psychology, 56*(3), 382–392.

Karlsson, T., Backman, L., Herlitz, A., Nilsson, L. G., Winblad, B., & Osterlind, P. O. (1989). Memory improvement at different stages of Alzheimer's disease. *Neuropsychologia, 27,* 737–742.

Kashani, J. H., Reid, J. C., & Rosenberg, T. K. (1989). Levels of hopelessness in children and adolescents: A developmental perspective. *Journal of Consulting and Clinical Psychology, 57,* 496–499.

Katchadourian, H. (1990). Sexuality. In S. S. Feldman & G. R. Elliot (Eds.) *At the Threshold,* Cambridge, MA: Harvard University Press.

Katzell, R. A., & Thompson, D. E. (1990). Work motivation. *American Psychologist, 45,* 144–153.

Kaufman, A. S. (1979). *Intelligent testing with the* WISC-R. New York: Wiley.

Kaufman, A. S. (1982). The impact of *WICS-R* research for school psychologists. In C. R. Reynolds & T. B. Gutkin (Eds.), *The handbook of school psychology.* New York: Wiley.

Kaufman, A. S. (1983). Some questions and answers about the Kaufman Assessment Battery for Children (K-ABC). *Journal of Psychoeducational Assessment, 1,* 205–218.

Kaufman, A. S. (1984). K-ABC and controversy. *The Journal of Special Education, 18,* 409–444.

Kaylor, J. A., King, D. W., & King, L. A. (1987). Psychological effects of military service in Vietnam: A meta-analysis. *Psychological Bulletin, 102,* 257–271.

Keesey, R. E., & Powley, T. L. (1986). The regulation of body weight. In M. R. Rosenzweig & L. W. Porter (Eds.), *Annual Review of Psychology.* Palo Alto, CA: Annual Reviews.

Kelley, H. H., Berscheid, E., Christensen, A., Harvey, J. H., Huston, T. L., et al. (1983). *Close relationships.* New York: W. H. Freeman.

Kelley, C., & Goodwin, G. C. (1983). Adolescents' perception of three styles of parental control. *Adolescence, 18,* 567–571.

Kendler, K. S. (1980). The nosologic validity of paranoia (simple delusional disorder): A review. *Archives of General Psychiatry, 37,* 699–706.

Kerr, N., & Brunn, S. E. (1983). Dispensability of member effort and group motivation losses: Free-rider effects. *Journal of Personality and Social Psychology, 44,* 78–94.

Kessler, R. C., Downey, G., Stipp, H., & Milavsky, J. R. (1989). Network television news stories about suicide and short-term changes in total U.S. suicides. *The Journal of Nervous and Mental Disease, 177,* 551–555.

Kiecolt-Glaser, J., & Glaser, R. (1988). Major life changes, chronic stress, and immunity. In T. P. Bridge, A. F. Mirsky & F. K. Goodwin (Eds.), *Psychological, neuropsychiatric, and substance abuse aspects of AIDS.* New York: Raven Press.

Kilbourne, B. K. (1989). A cross-cultural investigation of the foot-in-the-door compliance induction procedure. *Journal of Cross-Cultural Psychology, 20,* 3–38.

Kimmel, D. C. (1980). *Adulthood and aging: An interdisciplinary view* (2nd ed.). New York: Wiley.

Kingsbury, S. J. (1987). Cognitive differences between clinical psychologist and psychiatrists. *American Psychologist, 42,* 152–156.

Kirshnit, C. E., Richards, M. H., & Ham, M. (1988, August). *Athletic participation and body-image during early adolescence.* Paper presented at the 96th annual convention of the American Psychological Association, Atlanta, GA.

Kitwood, T. (1990). *Concern for others,* New York, NY: Routledge.

Klatzky, R. L. (1991). Let's be friends. *American Psychologist, 46,* 43–45.

Klaus, M. H., & Kennell, J. H. (1983). In Antonia W. Hamilton (Ed.), *Bonding: The beginnings of parent–infant attachment* (rev. ed.). New York: New American Library.

Kleinmuntz, B., & Szucko, J. J. (1984). Lie detection in ancient and modern times: A call for contemporary scientific study. *American Psychologist, 39,* 766–776.

Kohlberg, L. (1963). The development of children's orientation toward a moral order: Sequence in the development of moral thought. *Vita Humana, 6,* 11–33.

Kohlberg, L. (1969). The cognitive-developmental approach to socialization. In D. A. Goslin (Eds.), *Handbook of socialization theory and research.* Chicago: Rand McNally.

Kohlberg, L. (1971). From *is* to *ought:* How to commit the naturalistic fallacy and get away with it in the study of moral development. In T. Mischel (Ed.), *Cognitive development and epistemology.* New York: Academic Press.

Kohlberg, L. (1976). Moral stages and moralization: The cognitive-developmental approach. In T. Likcona (Eds.), *Moral development and behavior.* New York: Holt, Rinehart and Winston.

Kohn, A. (1976). *No contest: The case against competition.* Boston, MA: Houghton Mifflin.

Kolb, B. (1989). Brain development, plasticity, and behavior. *American Psychologist, 44,* 1203–1212.

Kopp, C. B. (1989). Regulation of distress and negative emotions: A developmental view. *Developmental Psychology, 25,* 343–354.

Koss, M. P. (1990). The women's mental health research agenda. *American Psychologist, 45,* 374–380.

Koss, M. P., Gidycz, C. A., & Wisniewski, N. (1987). The scope of rape: Incidence and prevalence of sexual aggression and victimization in a national sample of higher education students. *Journal of Consulting and Clinical Psychology, 55,* 162–170.

Kosslyn, S. M. (1975). Information representation in visual images. *Cognitive Psychology, 7,* 341–370.

Kosslyn, S. M. (1978). Measuring the visual angle of the mind's eye. *Cognitive Psychology, 7, 10,* 356–385.

Kosslyn, S. M. (1987). Seeing and imagining in the cerebral hemispheres: A computational approach. *Psychological Review, 2,* 148–175.

Koulack, D. (1991). *To catch a dream.* Albany, NY: State University of New York Press.

Krantz, D. S., Contrada, R. J., Hill, D. R., & Friedler, E. (1988). Environmental stress and biobehavioral antecedents of coronary heart disease. *Journal of Consulting and Clinical Psychology, 56,* 333–341.

Kubey, R., & Csikszentmihalyi, M. (1990). *Television and the quality of life.* Hillsdale, NJ: Erlbaum.

Laessle, R. G., Tuschl, R. J., Waadt, S., & Pirke, K. M. (1989). The specific psychopathology of bulimia nervosa: A comparison with restrained and unrestrained (normal) eaters. *Journal of Consulting and Clinical Psychology, 57,* 772–775.

Lafferty, P., Beutler, L. E., & Crago, M. (1989). Differences between more and less effective psychotherapists: A study of select therapist variables. *Journal of Consulting and Clinical Psychology, 57,* 76–80.

Lahey, B. B., McNees, M. P., & McNees, M. C. (1973). Control of an obscene "verbal tic" through timeout in an elementary school classroom. *Journal of Applied Behavior Analysis, 6,* 101–104.

Lamb, M. E., Hwang, C., Bookstein, F. L., Broberg, A., Hult, G., & Frodi, M. (1988). Determinants of social competence in Swedish preschoolers, *Developmental Psychology, 1,* 58–70.

Landers, S. (1988b). Survey verifies teen risk-taking. *American Psychological Association Monitor, 19,* 11, 30.

Lange, C. G. (1922). *The emotion* (Trans.). Baltimore: Williams & Wilkins. (Original work published 1885)

Langeluddecke, P., Fulcher, G., Jones, M., & Tennant, C. (1988). Type A behavior and coronary atherosclerosis. *Journal of Psychosomatic Research, 32,* 77–84.

Langlois, J. H. Roggman, L. A., & Rieser-Danner, L. A. (1990). Infants' differential social responses to attractive and unattractive faces. *Developmental Psychology, 26,* 153–159.

Langman, B., Cockburn, A. (1975). Sirhan's gun. *Harper's, 250*(1496), 16–27.

Larrick, R. P., Morgan, J. N., & Nisbett, R. E. (1990). Teaching the use of cost-benefit reasoning in everyday life. *American Psychological Society, 1,* 362–369.

Larson, R. W., Raffaelli, M., Richards, M. H., Ham, M., & Jewell, L. (1990). Ecology of depression in late childhood and early adolescence: A profile of daily states and activities. *Journal of Abnormal Psychology, 99,* 92–102.

Latane, B., & Darley, J. M. (1970). *The unresponsive bystander: Why doesn't he help?* New York: Meredith.

Latane, B., Williams, K., & Harkins, S. (1979). Many hands make light work:

Social Psychology, 37, 822–832.

Lawler, E. E., & Porter, L. W. (1967). Antecedent attitudes of effective managerial performance. *Organizational Behavior and Human Performance, 2,* 122–142.

Lazarus, A. A., & Fay, A. (1990). Brief psychotherapy: Tautology or oxymoron? In J. K. Zeig & S. G. Gilligan (Eds.), *Brief theraphy myths, methods, and metaphors,* New York: Brunner/Mazel.

Lazarus, R. S. (1982). The psychology of stress and coping, with particular reference to Israel. In C. D. Spielberger, I. G. Sarason, & N. A. Milgram (Eds.), *Stress and anxiety* (Vol. 8). Washington, DC: Hemisphere Publishing.

Lazarus, R. S. (1984). The trivialization of distress. In B. L. Hammonds & C. J. Scheirer (Eds.), *Psychology and health: The master lecture series.* Washington, DC: American Psychological Association.

Lazarus, R. S., & Alfert, E. (1964). Short-circuiting of threat by experimentally altering cognitive appraisal. *Journal of Abnormal and Social Psychology, 69,* 195–205.

Leber, W. R., Beckham, E. E., & Danker-Brown, P. (1985). Diagnostic criteria for depression. In E. E. Beckham & W. R. Leber (Eds.), *Handbook of depression: Treatment, assessment, and research.* Homewood, IL: Dorsey Press.

Lee, V. E. , Schnur, E., & Brooks-Gunn, J. (1988). Does Head Start work? A 1-year follow-up comparison of disadvantaged children attending Head Start, no preschool, and other preschool programs. *Developmental Psychology, 24,* 210–222.

Lefley, H. P. (1989). Family burden and family stigma in major mental illness. *American Psychologist, 44,* 556–560.

Leiner, H. C. , Leiner, A. L. , & Dow, R. S. (1986). Does the cerebellum contribute to mental skills? *Behavioral Neuroscience, 100,* 443–454.

Lenneberg, E. H. (1967). *Biological foundations of language.* New York: Wiley.

Lepper, M. R., & Greene, D. (1978). Overjustification research and beyond: Toward a means–end analysis of intrinsic motivation. In M. R. Lepper & D. Greene (Eds.), *The hidden cost of reward.* Hillsdale, NJ: Erlbaum.

Lepper, M. R., Greene, D., & Nisbett R. E. (1973). Undermining children's intrinsic interest with extrinsic reward: A test of the overjustification hypothesis. *Journal of Personality and Social Psychology, 28,* 129–137.

Lerer, B., Bleich, A., Kotler, M., Garb, R., Hertzberg, M., & Levin, B. (1987). Posttraumatic stress disorder in Israeli combat veterans. *Archives of General Psychiatry, 44,* 976–978.

Lerner, M. J. (1970). The desire for justice and reactions to victims. In J. Macaulay & L. Berkowitz (Eds.), *Altruism and helping behavior: Social psychological studies of some antecedents and consequences.* New York: Academic Press.

LeVere, T. E., Brugler, T., Sandin, M., & Gray-Silva, S. (1989). Recovery of function after brain damage: Facilitation by the calcium entry blocker nimodipine. *Behavioral Neuroscience, 103,* 561–565.

Levi, L. (1990). Occupational stress. *American Psychologist, 45,* 1142–1145.

Levin, D. J. (1990). *Alcoholism.* New York: Hemisphere Publishing.

Levine, M. (1975). *Hypothesis testing: A cognitive theory of learning.* Hillsdale, NJ: Erlbaum.

Levinson, D. J. (1978). *The seasons of a man's life.* New York: Alfred A. Knopf.

Levinson, D. J. (1980). Toward a conception of the adult life course. In N. J. Smelser & E. H. Erikson (Eds.), *Themes of work and love in adulthood.* Cambridge: Harvard University Press.

Levy-Leboyer, C. (1988). Success and failure in applying psychology. *American Psychologist,43,* 779–785.

Lewin, K. K. (1970). *Brief psychotherapy.* St Louis: Warren H. Green.

Lewinsohn, P. M. (1974). Classical and theoretical aspects of depression. In I. S. Calhoun, H. E. Adams, & K. M. Mitchell (Eds.), *Innovative treatment methods in psychopathology.* New York: Wiley Interscience.

Lewinsohn, P. M., & Talkington, J. (1979). Studies on the measurement of unpleasant events and relations with depression. *Applied Psychological Measurement, 3,* 83–101.

Lewis, M., & Feiring, C. (1989). Infant, mother, and mother–infant interaction behavior and subsequent attachment. *Child Development, 60,* 831–837.

Lewis, R. S. (1989). Remembering and the prefrontal cortex. *Psychonomic Society, 17*(1), 102–107.

Lidz, T. (1973). *The origin and treatment of schizophrenic disorders.* New York: Basic Books.

Lilly, J. C. (1956). Mental effects of reduction of ordinary levels of physical stimuli in intact, healthy persons. *Psychiatric Research Reports, 5,* 1–28.

Lindsey, K. P., & Paul, G. L. (1989). Involuntary commitments to public mental institutions: Issues involving the overrepresentation of blacks and assessment of relevant functioning. *Psychological Bulletin, 106,* 171–183.

Linn, L., & Spitzer, R. L. (1982). *DSM-III:* Implications for liaison psychiatry and psychosomatic medicine. *Journal of the American Medical Association, 247,* 3207–3209.

Linz, D. G., Donnerstein, E. D., & Penrod, S. (1988). Effects of long-term exposure to violent and sexually degrading depictions of women. *Journal of Personality and Social Psychology, 55,* 758–768.

Locke, E. A., & Latham, G. P. (1990). Work motivation: The high performance cycle. In U. Kleinbeck, H. Quast, H. Thierry, & H. Hacker (Eds.), *Work motivation.* Hillsdale, NJ: Erlbaum.

Locke, E. A., & Latham, G. P. (1990). Work motivation and satisfaction: Light at the end of the tunnel. *American Psychological Society, 1,*240–246.

Locke, E. A., & Schweiger, D. M. (1979). Participation in decision-making: One more look. In B. M. Staw (Ed.), *Research in organizational behavior* (Vol. 1). Greenwich, CT: JAI Press.

Lockhart, R. S., & Craik, F. I. M. (1990). Levels of processing: A retrospective commentary on a framework for memory research. *Canadian Journal of Psychology, 44,* 87–112.

Loehlin, J. C., Lindzey, G., & Spuhler, J. N. (1975). *Race differences in intelligence.* San Francisco: W. H. Freeman.

Loftus, G. S., Shimamura, A. P., & Johnson, C. (1985). How much is an icon worth? *Journal of Experimental Psychology: Human Perception and Performance, 11,* 1–13.

Logue, C. M., & Moos, R. H. (1986). Perimenstrual symptoms: Prevalence and risk factors. *Psychosomatic Medicine, 48,* 388–414.

Longabaugh, R., Stout, R., Kriebel, G. W., Jr., McCullough, L., & Bishop, D. (1986). *DSM-III* and clinically identified problems as a guide to treatment. *Archives of General Psychiatry, 43,* 1097–1103.

Lorenz, K. (1964). Ritualized fighting In J. D. Carthy & F. J. Ebling (Eds.), *The natural history of aggression.* New York: Academic Press.

Lowell, E. L. (1952). The effect of need for achievement on learning and speed of performance. *Journal of Psychology, 33,* 31–40.

Luborsky, L., Barber, J. P., & Crits-Christoph, P. (1990). Theory-based research for understanding the process of dynamic psychotherapy. *Journal of Consulting and Clinical Psychology, 58,* 281–287.

Lynch, G., & Baudry, M. (1984). The biochemistry of memory: A new and specific hypothesis. *Science, 224,* 1057–1063.

Maccoby, E. E. (1990). Gender and relationships. *American Psychologist, 45,* 513–520.

Maccoby, E. E., & Jacklin, C. N. (1987). Gender segregation in childhood. *Advances in Child Development and Behavior, 20,* 239–287.

MacNichol, E. F. (1964). Three-pigment color vision. *Scientific American, 211,* 48–56.

Madakasira, S., & O'Brien, K. F. (1987). Acute posttraumatic stress disorder in victims of a natural disaster. *The Journal of Nervous and Mental Disease, 175,* 286.

Maier, N. R. F., & Klee, J. B. (1941). Studies of abnormal behavior in the rat: XVII. Guidance versus trial and error and their relation to convulsive tendencies. *Journal of Experimental Psychology, 29,* 380–389.

Manuck, S. B., Cohen, S., Rabin, B. S., Muldoon, M. F., & Bachen, E. A. (1991). Individual differences in cellular immune response to stress. *American Psychological Society, 2,* 111–115.

Margraf, J., Ehlers, A., Roth, W. T., Clark, D. B., Sheikh, J., Agras, W. S., & Taylor, C. B. (1991). How "blind" are double-blind studies? *Journal of Consulting and Clinical Psychology, 59,* 184–187.

Marks, I. M. (1977). Clinical phenomena in search of laboratory models. In J. D. Maser & M. E. P. Seligman (Eds.), *Psychopathology experimental models.* San Francisco: W. H. Freeman.

Marks, W. B., Dobell, W. H., & MacNichol, J. R. (1964). The visual pigments of single primate cones. *Science, 142,* 1181–1183.

Marlatt, G. A., Baer, J. S., Donovan, D. M., & Kivlahan, D. R. (1988). Addictive behaviors: Etiology and treatment. *Annual Review of Psychology, 39,* 223–252.

Marschark, M., Yuille, J. C., Richman, C. L., & Hunt, R. R. (1987). The role of imagery in memory: On shared and distinctive information. *Psychological Bulletin, 102,* 28–41.

Maslow, A. H. (1962). *Toward a psychology of being.* New York: Van Nostrand.

Maslow, A. H. (1969). Toward a humanistic biology. *American Psychologist, 24,* 734–735.

Masson, J. M. (1990). *Final analysis,* Reading, MA: Addison-Wesley Publishing Company.

Masters, W. H., & Johnson, V. E. (1966). *Human sexual response.* Boston, MA: Little, Brown.

Masters, W. H., & Johnson, V. E. (1970). *Human sexual inadequacies.* Boston, MA: Little, Brown.

Matarazzo, J. D. (1990). Psychological assessment versus psychological testing. *American Psychologist, 45,* 999–1017.

Matsui, T., & Onglatco, M. L. U. (1990). Relationships between employee quality circle involvement and need fulfillment in work as moderated by work type: A compensatory or a spillover model? In U. Kleinbeck, H. Quast, H. Thierry, & H. Hacker (Eds.), *Work motivation.* Hillsdale, NJ: Erlbaum.

Matt, G. E. (1989). Decision rules for selecting effect sizes in meta-analysis: A review and reanalysis of psychotherapy outcome studies. *Psychological Bulletin, 105,* 106–115.

Matthews, K. A. (1988). Coronary heart disease and Type A behaviors: Update on and alternative to the Booth-Kewley and Friedman (1987) quantitative review. *Psychological Bulletin, 104,* 373–380.

Matthies, H. (1989). Neurobiological aspects of learning and memory. *Annual Review of Psychology, 40,* 381–404.

May, J., & Kline, P. (1987). Measuring the effects upon cognitive abilities of sleep loss during continuous operations. *The British Psychological Society, 78,* 443–455.

McAuley, E., Duncan, T. E., & McElroy, M. (1989). Self-efficacy cognitions and causal attributions for children's motor performance: An exploratory investigation. *The Journal of Genetic Psychology, 150*(1), 65–73.

McCall, R. B. (1983). Environmental effects on intelligence: The forgotten realm of discontinuous nonshared within-family factors. *Child Development, 54,* 408–415.

McCaul, K. D., Veltum, L. G., Boyechko, V., & Crawford, J. J. (1990). Understanding attributions of victim blame for rape: Sex, violence, and foreseeability. *Journal of Applied Social Psychology, 20,* 1–26.

McClelland, D. C. (1961). *The achieving society.* Princeton, NJ: Van Nostrand.

McClelland, D. C. (1987). Characteristics of successful entrepreneurs. *The Journal of Creative Behavior, 21,* 219–233.

McClelland, D. C. (1989). Motivational factors in health and disease. *American Psychologist, 44,* 675–683.

McKlintock, M. K. (1971). Menstrual synchrony and suppression. *Nature, 229,* 244–245.

McConkey, K. M., & Kinoshita, S. (1988). The influence of hypnosis on memory after one day and one week. *Journal of Abnormal Psychology, 97,* 48–53.

McGaugh, J. L. (1983). Preserving the presence of the past: Hormonal influences on memory storage. *American Psychologist, 38,* 161–174.

McGinty, D., & Szymusiak, R. (1988). Neuronal unit activity patterns in behaving animals: Brainstem and limbic system. *Annual Review of Psychology, 39,* 135–168.

McGraw, K. O., & Fiala, J. (1982). Undermining the Zeigarnik effect: Another hidden cost of reward. *Journal of Personality, 50,* 58–66.

McKeachie, W. J. (1988). Teaching thinking. *Update: National Center for Research to Improve Postsecondary Teaching and Learning, 2,* 1.

McKeachie, W. J., Pintrich, P. R., & Lin, Y. (1985). Learning to learn. In G. d'Ydewalle (Ed.), *Cognition, information processing, and motivation.* North Holland: Elsevier Science Publishers.

McNemar, Q. (1964). Lost: Our intelligence—Why? *American Psychologist, 19,* 871–882.

McReynolds, P. (1989). Diagnosis and clinical assessment: Current status and major issues. *Annual Review of Psychology, 40,* 83–108.

Medin, D. L. (1989). Concepts and conceptual structure. *American Psychologist, 44,* 1469–1481.

Mednick, S. A., Parnas, J., & Schulsinger, F. (1987). The Copenhagen High-Risk Project, 1962–86. *Schizophrenia Bulletin, 13,* 485–495.

Meichenbaum, D. (1974). *Cognitive behavior modification.* Morristown, NJ: General Learning Press.

Mellody, P., Miller, A. W., & Miller, J. K. (1989). *Facing codependence.* New York: Harper & Row.

Melton, G. B. (1987). Bringing psychology to the legal system. *American Psychologist, 42,* 488–495.

Meltzoff, A. N. (1988). Imitation of televised models by infants. *Child Development, 59,* 1221–1229.

Melzack, R. (1990). The tragedy of needless pain. *Scientific American, 262,* 27–33.

Melzack, R. & Loeser, J. D. (1978). Phantom body pain in paraplegics: Evidence for a central "pattern generating mechanism" for pain. *Pain,* 4, 195–210.

Melzack, R. & Wall, P. D. (1970). Psychophysiology of pain. *International Anesthesiology Clinics, 8,* 3–34.

Mercer, J. R. (1977). The struggle for children's rights: Critical juncture for school psychology. *School Psychology Digest, 6,* 4–19.

Mercer, R. T., Nichols, E. G., & Doyle, G. C. (1989). *Transitions in a woman's life: Focus on Women* (Vol. 12). New York: Springer.

Merton, R. K. (1949). Merton's typology of prejudice and discrimination. In R. M. MacIver (Ed.), *Discrimination and National Welfare.* New York: Harper & Row.

Messer, S. C., Wuensch, K. L., & Diamond, J. M. (1989). Former latchkey children: Personality and academic correlates. *Journal of Genetic Psychology, 150*(3). 301–309.

Meyer, R. G., & Salmon, P. (1988). *Abnormal psychology* (2nd ed.). Boston: Allyn & Bacon.

Meyers, A. F., Sampson, A. E., Wetzman, M., Rogers, B. L., & Kayne, H. (1989). School breakfast program and school performance. *American Journal of Diseases of Children, 143,* 1234–1239.

Mikulincer, M., Babkoff, H., Caspy, T., & Sing, H. (1989). The effects of 72 hours of sleep loss on psychological variables. *British Journal of Psychology, 80,* 145–162.

Milgram, S. (1963). Behavioral study of obedience. *Journal of Abnormal and Social Psychology, 67,* 371–378.

Milgram, S. (1965a). Liberating effects of group pressure. *Journal of Personality and Social Psychology, 1,* 127–134.

Miller, G. A. (1956). The magic number seven, plus or minus two: Some limits on our capacity for processing information. *Psychological Review, 63,* 81–97.

Miller, G. A. (1965). Some preliminaries to psycholinguistics. *American Psychologist, 20,* 15–20.

Miller, K. F., & Baillargeon, R. (1990). Length and distance: Do preschoolers think that occlusion brings things together? *Developmental Psychology, 26,* 103–114.

Miller, L. C. (1990). Intimacy and liking: Mutual influence and the role of unique relationships. *Journal of Personality and Social Psychology, 59,* 50–60.

Miller, N. E. (1944). Experimental studies of conflict. In J. McV. Hunt (Ed.), *Personality and behavioral disorders* (Vol. 1). New York: Ronald Press.

Miller, N. E. (1959). Liberalization of basic S–R concepts: Extensions to conflict behavior, motivation, and social learning. In S. Koch (Ed.), *Psychology: A study of a science* (Vol. 2). New York: McGraw-Hill.

Miller, N. E. (1969). Learning of visceral and glandular responses. *Science, 163,* 434–445.

Miller, P. H., & Aloise, P. A., (1989). Young children's understanding of the psychological causes of behavior: A review. *Child Development, 60,* 257–285.

Miller, R. P., Cosgrove, J. M., & Doke, L. (1990). Motivating adolescents to reduce their fines in a token economy. *Adolescence, 25,* 97–104.

Millon, T. (1983). The *DSM-III:* An insider's perspective. *American Psychologist, 38,* 804–814.

Milner, B. (1966). Amnesia following operation on the temporal lobes. In C. W. M. Whitty & O. L. Zangwill (Eds.), *Amnesia.* London: Butterworth.

Milner, P. M. (1989). A cell assembly theory of hippocampal amnesia. *Neuropsychologia, 27,* 23–30.

Mischel, W. (1979). On the interface of cognition and personality: Beyond the person–situation debate. *American Psychologist, 34,* 740–754.

Mischel, W. (1983). Alternatives in the pursuit of the predictability and consistency of persons: Stable data that yield unstable interpretations. *Journal of Personality, 51,* 578–604.

Mishler, E. G., & Waxler, N. E. (1968). Family interaction processes and schizophrenia: A review of current theories. In E. G. Mishler & N. E. Waxler (Eds.), *Family processes and schizophrenia.* New York: Science House.

Money, J. (1984). Paraphilias: Phenomenology and classification. *American Journal of Psychotherapy, 38,* 164–168.

Montepare, J. M., & Zebrowitz-McArthur, L. (1988). Impressions of people created by age-related qualities of their gaits. *Journal of Personality and Social Psychology, 55,* 547–556.

Montgomery-St. Laurent, T., Fullenkamp, A. M., & Fisher, R. B. (1988). A role for the hamster's flank gland in heterosexual communication. *Physiology & Behavior, 44*(6), 759–762.

Morrison, D. M. (1985). Adolescent contraceptive behavior: A review. *Psychological Bulletin, 98,* 538–568.

Moskowitz, B. A. (1978). The acquisition of language. *Scientific American, 239*(5), 92–108.

Mungy, G. (1982). The power of minorities. In H. Tajfel (Ed.), *European monographs in social psychology* (Vol 31). London: Academic Press.

Murphy, S. T., & Zajonc, R. B. (1990). *Effective primacy and affective priming of preferences.* Paper presented at the American Psychological Association in Boston, MA August 1990.

Mussen, P. H., & Distler, L. (1959). Masculinity, identification, and father–son relationships. *Journal of Abnormal and Social Psychology, 59,* 350–356.

Muuss, R. E. (1989). Carol Gilligan's theory of sex differences in the development of moral reasoning during adolescence. *Adolescence, 23,* 229–243.

Myers, M. F. (1989). Men sexually assaulted as adults and sexually abused as boys. *Archives of Sexual Behavior, 18,* 203–215.

Naar, R. (1990). Psychodrama in short-term psychotherapy. In R. A. Wells & V. J. Giannetti (Eds.), *Handbook of the brief psychotherapies.* New York: Plenum Press.

Nace, E. P. (1987). *The treatment of alcoholism.* New York: Brunner/Mazel.

Nash, M. (1987). What, if anything, is regressed about hypnotic age regression? A review of the empirical literature. *Psychological Bulletin, 102,* 42–52.

Nathan, P. E., & Skinstad, A. H. (1987). Outcomes of treatment for alcohol problems: Current methods, problems, and results. *Journal of Consulting and Clinical Psychology, 55,* 332–340.

Nathans, J. (1989). The genes for color vision. *Scientific American, 260,* 42–49.

Navon, D. (1990). How critical is the accuracy of an eyewitness's memory? Another look at the issue of lineup diagnosticity. *Journal of Applied Psychology, 75,* 506–510.

Neal, A. M., & Turner, S. M. Anxiety disorders research with African Americans: Current status. *Psychological Bulletin, 109,* 400–410.

Nemeroff, C. B., Knight, D. L., Kirshnan, R. R., Slotkin, T. A., Bissette, G., Melville M. L., Blazer, D. G. (1988). Marked reduction in the number of platelet-tritiated imipramine binding sites in geriatric depression. *Archives of General Psychiatry, 45,* 919–923.

Newlin, D. B., & Thomson, J. B. (1990). Alcohol challenge with sons of alcoholics: A critical review and analysis. *Psychological Bulletin, 108,* 383–402.

Nisbett, R. E. (1972). Hunger, obesity, and the ventromedial hypothalamus. *Psychological Review, 79,* 433–453.

Nolen-Hoeksema, S. (1990). *Sex differences in depression,* Stanford, CA: Stanford University Press.

Norcross, J. C., Prochaska, J. O., & Gallagher, K. M. (1989). Clinical psychologists in the 1980s: II. Theory, research, and practice. *The Clinical Psychologist, 42,* 45–52.

Norris, J. (1989). Normative influence effects on sexual arousal to nonviolent sexually explicit material. *Journal of Applied Social Psychology, 19,* 341–352.

Norris, R. V., & Sullivan, C. (1983). *PMS/Premenstrual syndrome.* New York: Rawson Associates.

Novak, M. A., & Suomi, S. J. (1988). Psychological well-being of primates in captivity. *American Psychologist, 43,* 765–773.

Oetting, E. R., & Beauvais, F. (1990). Adolescent drug use: Findings of national and local surveys. *Journal of Consulting and Clinical Psychology, 58,* 385–394.

Ogilvie, R. D., McDonagh, D. M., & Stone, S. N. (1988). Eye movements and the detection of sleep onset. *Psychophysiology, 25,* 81–91.

Olds, J. (1955). Physiological mechanisms of reward. *Nebraska Symposium on Motivation, 3,* 73–139.

Olds, J. (1969). The central nervous system and the reinforcement of behavior. *American Psychologist, 24,* 114–132.

Olds, J. & Milner, P. (1954). Positive reinforcement produced by electrical stimulation of septal area and other regions of rat brain. *Journal of Comparative and Physiological Psychology, 47,* 419–427.

O'Leary, A. (1990). Stress, emotion, and human immune function. *Psychological Bulletin, 108,* 363–382.

O'Leary, K. D., Barling, J., Arias, I., Rosenbaum, A., Malone, J., & Tyree, A. (1989). Prevalence and stability of physical aggression between spouses: A longitudinal analysis. *Journal of Consulting and Clinical Psychology, 57,* 263–268.

Omura, Y. (1977). Critical evaluation of the methods of measurement of "tingling threshold," "pain threshold," and "pain tolerance" by electrical stimulation. *Acupuncture & Electro-Therapeutic Research International Journal, 2,* 161–236.

Ornstein, R. E. (1977). *The psychology of consciousness* (2nd ed.). New York: Harcourt Brace Jovanovich.

Ortony, A, & Turner, T. J. (1990). What's basic about basic emotions? *Psychological Review, 97,* 315–331.

Osterweis, M., & Townsend, J. (1988). *Health professionals and the bereaved.* Rockville, MD: National Institute of Mental Health.

Owens, M. E., Bliss, E. L., Koester, P., & Jeppsen, E. A. (1989). Phobias and hypnotizability: A reexamination. *The International Journal of Clinical and Experimental Hypnosis, 37,* 207–216.

Pagano, R. W., Rose, R. M., Stivers, R. M., & Warrenburg, S. (1976). Sleep during transcendental meditation. *Science, 191,* 308–310.

Paivio, A. (1971). *Imagery and verbal processes.* New York: Holt, Rinehart and Winston.

Papini, M. R., & Bitterman, M. E. (1990). The role of contingency in classical conditioning. *Psychological Review, 97,* 396–403.

Parker, D. E. (1980). The vestibular apparatus. *Scientific American, 243,* (5), 118–135.

Patrick, C. J., & Iacono, W. G. (1989). Psychopathy, threat, and polygraph test accuracy. *Journal of Applied Psychology, 74,* 347–355.

Pavlov, I. P. (1927). *Conditioned reflexes.* London: Oxford University Press.

Peele, S. (1984). The cultural context of psychological approaches to alcoholism: Can we control the effects of alcohol? *American Psychologist, 39,* 1337–1351.

Penfield, W. (1958). *The excitable cortex in conscious man.* IL: Thomas.

Penfield, W., & Perot, P. (1963). The brain's record of auditory and visual experience. *Brain, 86,* 595–696.

Pesut, D. J. (1990). Creative thinking as a self-regulatory metacognitive process—A model for education, training and further research. The *Journal of Creative Behavior, 24,* 105–110.

Peterson, A. C. (1988). Adolescent development. In M. R. Rosenzweig & L. W. Porter (Eds.), *Annual review of psychology* (Vol 39). Palo Alto, CA: Annual Reviews.

Peterson, C., & Seligman, M. E. P. (1984). Causal explanations as a risk factor for depression: Theory and evidence. *Psychological Review, 91,* 347–374.

Peterson, C., Seligman, M., & Vaillant, G. E. (1988). Unpublished research. (Cited by T. DeAngelis, 1988). In praise of rose-colored specs. *Monitor, 19,* 22.

Peterson, J. L., & Marin, G. (1988). Issues in the prevention of AIDS among black and Hispanic men. *American Psychologist, 43,* 871–877.

Peterson, L. R., & Peterson, M. J. (1959). Short-term retention of individual verbal items. *Journal of Experimental Psychology, 58,* 193–198.

Piaget, J. (1932). *The moral judgment of the child.* London: Routlege & Kegan Paul.

Pihl, R. O., Peterson J., & Finn, P. (1990). Inherited predisposition to alcoholism: Characteristics of sons of male alcoholics. *Journal of Abnormal Psychology, 99,* 291–301.

Pion, G. M., Bramblett, J. P., Jr., & Wicherski, M. (1987). *Preliminary report: 1985 doctorate employment survey.* Washington, DC: American Psychological Association.

Pirenne, M. H. (1967). *Vision and the eye.* London: Science Paperbacks.

Pitman, R. K., Orr, S. P., Forgue, D. F., Altman, B., de Jong, J. B., & Herz, L. R. (1990). Psychophysiologic responses to combat imagery of Vietnam veterans with posttraumatic stress disorder versus other anxiety disorders. *Journal of Abnormal Psychology, 99,* 49–54.

Pittman, F. S., III, Flomenhaft, K., & DeYoung, C. D. (1990). Family crisis therapy. In R. A. Wells & V. J. Gianetti (Eds.), *Handbook of the brief psychotherapies.* New York: Plenum Press.

Pittman, T. S., & Heller, J. F. (1987). Social motivation. In M. R. Rosenzweig & L. W. Porter (Eds.), *Annual review of psychology.* Palo Alto, CA: Annual Review.

Plomin, R. (1989). Environment and genes: Determinants of behavior. *American Psychologist, 44*(2), 105–111.

Plomin, R., Corley, R., DeFries, J. C., & Fulker, D. W. (1990). Individual differences in television viewing in early childhood: Nature as well as nurture. *American Psychological Society, 1,* 371–377.

Pomerleau, A., Bolduc, D., Malcuit, G., & Cossette, L. (1990). Pink or blue: Environmental gender stereotypes in the first two years of life. *Sex Roles, 22,* 359–367.

Povinelli, D. J., Nelson, K. E., & Boysen, S. T. (1990). Inferences about guessing and knowing by chimpanzees. *Comparative Psychology, 3,* 203–210.

Powell, D. A., Milligan, W. L., & Furchtgott, E. (1980). Peripheral autonomic changes accompanying learning and reaction time performance in older people. *Journal of Gerontology, 35,* 57–65.

Powers, S. I., Hauser, S. T., Kilner, L. A. (1989). Adolescent mental health. *American Psychologist, 44,* 200–208.

Powley, T. L. (1977). The ventromedical hypothalamic syndrome, satiety, and a cephalic phase hypothesis. *Psychological Review, 84,* 89–126.

Premack, D. (1962). Reversibility of the reinforcement relation. *Science, 136,*

255–257.

Premack, D. (1965). Reinforcement theory. In D. Levine (Ed.), *Nebraska symposium on motivation* (Vol. 13, pp. 123–180). Lincoln: University of Nebraska Press.

Premack, D. (1971). Language in chimpanzees? *Science, 172,* 808–822.

Presser, H. B. (1989). Some economic complexities of child care provided by grandmothers. *Journal of Marriage and the Family, 51,* 581–591.

Preti, G., Cutler, W. B., Garcia, C. R., Huggins, G. R., & Lawley, H. J. (1986). Human axillary secretions influence women's menstrual cycles: The role of donor extract of females. *Hormones and Behavior, 20,* 474–482.

Price, D. D., et al. (1984). A psychophysical analysis of acupuncture analgesia. *Pain, 19,* 27–42.

Prinz, P. N., Vitello, M. V., Raskind, M. A., & Thorpy, M. J. (1990). Geriatrics: Sleep disorders and aging. *The New England Journal of Medicine, 323,* 520–526.

Prinz, R. J., & Riddle, D. B. (1986). Associations between nutrition and behavior in five-year-old children. *Nutrition Reviews, 44* (Suppl.), 151–157.

Puffer, S. M. (1987). Prosocial behavior, noncompliant behavior, and work performance among commission salespeople. *Journal of Applied Psychology, 72,* 615–621.

Quigley, B., Gaes, G. G., & Tedeschi, J. T. (1989). Does asking make a difference? Effects of initiator, possible gain, and risk on attributed altruism. *The Journal of Social Psychology, 129,* 259–267.

Quinsey, V. L., Chaplin, T. C., & Upfold, D. (1984). Sexual arousal to nonsexual violence and sadomasochism themes among rapist and non-sex-offenders. *Journal of Consulting and Clinical Psychology, 52,* 651.

Rafaeli, A. (1989). When clerks meet customers: A test of variables related to emotional expressions on the job. *Journal of Applied Psychology, 74,* 385–393.

Ragins, B. R., & Sundstrom, E. (1989). Gender and power in organizations: A longitudinal perspective. *Psychological Bulletin, 105,* 51–88.

Rahe, R. H. (1989). Recent life change stress and psychological depression. In T. W. Miller (Ed.), *Stressful life events.* Madison, WI: International Universities Press.

Rapee, R. (1986). Differential response to hyperventilation in panic disorder and generalized anxiety disorder. *Journal of Abnormal Psychology, 95,* 24–28.

Rappaport, J. (1987). Terms of empowerment/exemplars of prevention: Toward a theory for community psychology. *American Journal of Community Psychology, 2,* 121–148.

Raps, C. S., Reinhard, K. E., Peterson, C., Abramson, L. Y., & Seligman, M. E. P. (1982). Attributional style among depressed patients. *Journal of Abnormal Psychology, 91,* 102–108.

Raz, S., & Raz, N. (1990). Structural brain abnormalities in the major psychoses: A quantitative review of the evidence from computerized imaging. *Psychological Bulletin, 208,* 93–108.

Reed, C. F. (1984). Terrestrial passage theory of the moon illusion. *Journal of Experimental Psychology: General, 113,* 489–516.

Regestein, Q. R., & Reich, P. (1978). Pedophilia occurring after onset of cognitive impairment. *The Journal of Nervous and Mental Disease, 166,* 794–798.

Reiger, D. A., Boyd, J. H., Burke, J. D., Rae, D. S., Myers, J. K., Kramer, M., Robins, L. N., George, L. K., Karno, M., & Locke, B. Z. (1988). One-month prevalence of mental disorders in the United States. *Archives of General Psychiatry, 45,* 977–986.

Reinert, H. (1976). One picture is worth a thousand words? Not necessarily! *The Modern Language Journal. 60*(4), 160–168.

Reis, H. T., & Shaver, P. (1988). Intimacy as an interpersonal process. In S. Duck (Ed.), *Handbook of personal relationships: Theory, relationships and interventions.* Chichester: Wiley.

Reis, S. M. (1989). Reflections on policy affecting the education of gifted and talented students. *American Psychologist, 44,* 399–408.

Reisenzein, R. (1983). The Schachter theory of emotion: Two decades later. *Psychological Bulletin, 94,* 239–264.

Repetti, R. L., Matthews, K. A., & Waldron, I. (1989). Employment and women's health. *American Psychologist, 44,* 1394–1401.

Rescorla, R. A. (1977). Pavlovian 2nd-order conditioning: Some implications for instrumental behavior. In H. Davis & H. Herwit (Eds.), *Pavlovian–operant interactions.* Hillsdale, NJ: Erlbaum.

Rescorla, R. A. (1988). Pavlovian conditioning: It's not what you think it is. *American Psychologist, 43,* 151–160.

Restle, F. (1970). Moon illusion explained on the basis of relative size. *Science, 167,* 1092–1096.

Rice, M. L., & Woodsmall, L. (1988). Lessons from television: Children's word learning when viewing. *Child Development, 59,* 420–429.

Rice, R. W., McFarlin, D. B., & Bennett, D. (1989). Standards of comparison and job satisfaction. *Journal of Applied Psychology, 74,* 591–598.

Richardson, J. T. E., & Zucco, G. M. (1989). Cognition and olfaction: A review. *Psychological Bulletin, 105,* 352–360.

Richardson-Klavehn, A., & Bjork, R. A. (1988). Measures of memory. In M. R. Rosenzweig & L. W. Porter (Eds.), *Annual review of psychology* (Vol 39). Palo Alto, CA: Annual Reviews.

Riley, W. T., Treiber, F. A., & Woods, M. G. (1989). Anger and hostility in depression. *The Journal of Nervous and Mental Disease, 177,* 668.

Ring, K., Wallston, K., & Corey, M. (1970). Mode of debriefing as a factor affecting subjective reaction to a Milgram-type obedience experiment: An ethical inquiry. *Representative Research in Social Psychology, 1,* 67–88.

Roberts, G. W. (1988). Immunocytochemistry of neurofibrillary tangles in dementia pugilistica and Alzheimer's disease: Evidence for common genesis. *The Lancet,* December 24/31, 1456–1457.

Robinson, F. P. (1970). *Effective study* (4th ed). New York: Harper & Row.

Robinson, L. A., Berman, J. S., & Neimeyer, R. A. (1990). Psychotherapy for the treatment of depression: A comprehensive review of controlled outcome research. *Psychological Bulletin, 108,* 30–49.

Robinson, N. M., & Robinson, H. B. (1976). *The mentally retarded child* (2nd ed.). New York: McGraw Hill.

Rodin, J. (1981). Current status of the internal–external hypothesis for obesity: What went wrong? *American Psychologist, 36,* 361–372.

Rodin, J. (1986). Aging and health: Effects of the sense of control. *Science, 233,* 1271–1276.

Rodin, J., & Salovey, P. (1989). Health psychology. In M. R. Rosenzweig & L. W. Porter (Eds.), *Annual review of psychology* (Vol 40). Palo Alto, CA: Annual Reviews.

Rodman, H., Prato, D. J., & Nelson, R. S. (1988). Toward a definition of self-care children: A commentary on Steinberg (1986). *Developmental Psychology, 24,* 292–294.

Roehrs, T., Timms, V., Zwyghuizen-Doorenbos, A., & Roth, T. (1989). Sleep extension in sleepy and alert normals. *Sleep, 12,* 449–457.

Rogers, C. R. (1951). *Client-centered therapy.* Boston: Houghton Mifflin.

Romano, S. T., & Bordieri, J. E. (1989). Physical attractiveness stereotypes and students' perceptions of college professors. *Psychological Reports, 64,* 1099–1102.

Rosch, E. (1973). Natural categories. *Cognitive Psychology, 4,* 328–350.

Rosenthal, R., & Depaulo, B. M. (1979). Sex differences in accommodation in nonverbal communication. In R. Rosenthal (Ed.), *Skill in nonverbal communication.* Cambridge, MA: Oelgeschlager, Gunn & Hain.

Ross, H., & Taylor, H. (1989). Do boys prefer daddy or his physical style of play? *Sex Roles, 20,* 23–26.

Roth, J. D., & Kosslyn, S. M. (1988). Construction of the third dimension in mental imagery. *Cognitive Psychology, 20,* 344–361.

Rothbart, M. K., Taylor, S. B., & Tucker, D. M. (1989). Right-sided facial asymmetry in infant emotional expression. *Neuropsychologia, 27,* 675–687.

Rotter, J. B. (1990). Internal versus external control of reinforcement. *American Psychologist, 45,* 489–493.

Roy, A., Segal, N. L., Ceterwall, B. S., & Robinette, C. D. (1991). Suicide in twins. *Archives of General Psychiatry, 48,* 29–32.

Ruback, R. B., & Pandey, J. (1991). Crowding, perceived control, and relative power: An analysis of households in India. *Journal of Applied Social Psychology, 21,* 315–344.

Rudman, H. C. (1977). The standardized test flap. *Phi Delta Kappan, 59,* 179–185.

Rumbaugh, D. M., Gill, T. V., & Von Glaserfeld, E. D. (1973). Reading and sentence completion by a chimpanzee (PAN). *Science, 182,* 731–733.

Rumbaugh, D. M., & Savage-Rumbaugh, S. (1978). Chimpanzee language research: Status and potential. *Behavior Research Methods and Instrumentation, 10,* 119–131.

Russo, N. F., & Denmark, F. L. (1987). Contributions of women to psychology. In M. R. Rosenzweig & L. W. Porter (Eds.), *Annual review of psychology* (Vol 38). Palo Alto, CA: Annual Reviews.

Ryan, R. M., Mims, V., & Koestner, R. (1983). Relation of reward contingency and interpersonal context to intrinsic motivation: A review and test using cognitive evaluation theory. *Journal of Personality and Social Psychology, 45,* 736–750.

Sadock, V. (1980). Special areas of interest. In H. Kaplan, A. Freeman, &

B. Sadock (Eds.), *Comprehensive textbook of psychiatry* (Vol. 3). Baltimore: Williams & Wilkins.

Sandahl, C., & Ronnberg, S. (1990). Brief group psychotherapy in relapse prevention for alcohol dependent patients. *International Journal of Group Psychotherapy, 40,* 453–476.

Sanday, P. R. (1990). *Fraternity gang rape.* New York: New York University Press.

Sanders, R. J. (1985). Teaching apes to ape language: Explaining the imitative and nonimitative signing of a chimpanzee (Pan troglodytes). *Journal of Comparative Psychology, 99,* 197–210.

Sappington, A. A. (1990). Recent psychological approaches to the free will versus determinism issue *Psychological Bulletin, 108,* 19–29.

Sartorious, N. (1982). Epidemiology and mental health policy. In M. O. Wagenfeld, P. V. Lemkau, & B. Justice (Eds.), *Public mental health: Perspectives and prospects.* Beverly Hills, CA: Sage Productions.

Sattler, J. M. (1982). *Assessment of children's intelligence and special abilities* (2nd ed.). Boston: Allyn & Bacon.

Sattler, J. M. (1988). *Assessment of children* (3rd ed.). San Diego, CA: Jerome M. Sattler.

Savage-Rumbaugh, S. (1987). A new look at ape language: Comprehension of vocal speech and syntax. In R. A. Dienstbier & D. W. Leger, *Comparative perspectives in modern psychology.* Lincoln, NE: University of Nebraska Press.

Savage-Rumbaugh, E. S., Pate, J. L., Lawson, J., Smith, S. T., & Rosenbaum, S. (1983). Can a chimpanzee make a statement? *Journal of Experimental Psychology: General, 112,* 457–492.

Scarr, S., Phillips, D. & McCartney, K. (1990). Facts, fantasies and the future of child care in the United States. *American Psychological Society, 1,* 26–35.

Schachter, S., Goldman, R., & Gordon, A. (1968). Effects of fear, food deprivation, and obesity on eating. *Journal of Personality and Social Psychology, 10,* 91–97.

Schachter, S., & Singer, J. E. (1962). Cognitive social, and physiological determinants of emotional state. *Psychological Review, 69,* 379–399.

Schachter, D. L., Kihlstrom, J. F., Kihlstrom, L. C., & Berren, M. B. (1989). Autobiographical memory in a case of multiple personality disorder. *Journal of Abnormal Psychology, 98,* 508–514.

Schaie, K. W., & Willis, S. L. (1986). *Adult development and aging* (2nd ed.). Boston: Little, Brown.

Sherer, D. G., & Reppucci, N. D. (1988). Adolescents' capacities to provide voluntary informed consent. *Law and Human Behavior,* 12, 123–141.

Schiff, M., Duyme, M., Dumaret., & Tomkiewicz, S. (1982). How much could we boost scholastic achievement and IQ scores? A direct answer from a French adoption study. *Cognition,* 12, 165–196.

Schindler, P. J., Moely, B. E., & Frank, A. L. (1987). Time in day care and social participation of young children. *Developmental Psychology, 2,* 255–261.

Schlundt, D. G., & Johnson, W. G. (1990). *Eating disorders,* Boston, MA: Allyn & Bacon.

Schneiderman, N., Fuentes, I., & Gormenzano, I. (1962). Acquisition and extinction of the classically conditioned eyelid response in the albino rabbit. *Science, 136,* 650–652.

Schofferman, J. (1988). Care of the AIDS patient. *Death Studies, 12,* 433–449.

Schutte, N. S., Malouff, J. M., Post-Gorden, J. C., & Rodasta, A. L. (1988). Effects of playing videogames on children's aggressive and other behaviors. *Journal of Applied Social Psychology, 18,* 454–460.

Schwartz, J. C., & Shaver, P. (1987). Emotions and emotion knowledge in interpersonal relations. *Advances in Personal Relationship, 1,* 197–241.

Schwartz, P. (1983). Length of day-care attendance and attachment behavior in eighteen-month-old infants. *Child Development, 54,* 1073–1078.

Schweickert, R., & Boruff, B. (1986). Short-term memory capacity: Magic number or magic spell? *Journal of Experimental Psychology: Learning, Memory, and Cognition, 12,* 419–425.

Sejnowski, T. J., Koch, C., & Churchland, P. S. (1988). Computational neuroscience. *Science,* 1299–1306.

Seligman, M. E. P. (1975). *Helplessness.* San Francisco: W. H. Freeman.

Seligman, M. E. P. (1976). *Learned helplessness and depression in animals and humans.* Morristown, NJ: General Learning Press.

Seligman, M. (1988, August). G. Stanley Hall lecture presented at the annual meeting of the American Psychological Association, Atlanta, GA.

Seligman, M. E. P. (1991). *Learned optimism.* New York: Alfred A. Knopf Inc.

Selye, H. (1956). *The stress of life.* New York: McGraw Hill.

Selye, H. (1976). *Stress in health and disease.* London: Butterworth.

Shaver, P., Schwartz, J., Kirson, D., & O'Connor, C. (1987). Emotion knowledge: Further exploration of a prototype approach. *Journal of Personality and Social Psychology, 52,* 1061–1086.

Sheridan, M. S. (1985). Things that go beep in the night. Home monitoring for apnea. *Health and Social Work,* 63–70.

Sherman, M., & Key, C. B. (1932). The intelligence of isolated mountain children. *Child Development, 3,* 279–290.

Sherman, S. J., Judd, C. M., & Park, B. (1989). Social cognition. *Annual Review of Psychology, 40,* 281–326.

Sherman, T. M. (1985). Learning improvement programs. *Journal of Higher Education, 56,* 85–100.

Shimamura, A. P., & Squire, L. R. (1986). Memory and metamemory: A study of the feeling-of-knowing phenomenon in amnesic patients. *Journal of Experimental Psychology: Learning, Memory, and Cognition,* 12, 452–460.

Shimberg, M. E. (1929). An investigation into the validity of norms with special reference to urban and rural groups. *Archives of Psychology, 104,* 1–62.

Shneidman, E. (1989). The Indian summer of life: A preliminary study of septuagenarians. *American Psychologist, 44,* 684–694.

Shore, J. H., Vollmer, W. M., & Tatum, E. L. (1989). Community patterns of posttraumatic stress disorders. *The Journal of Nervous and Mental Disease, 177,* 681–685

Siegel, E. F. (1979). Control of phantom limb pain by hypnosis. *American Journal of Clinical Hypnosis, 21,* 285–286.

Silberman, E. K., Weingartner, H., & Post, R. M. (1983). Thinking disorder in depression: Logic and strategy in an abstract reasoning task. *Archives of General Psychiatry, 40,* 775–780.

Simonton, D. K. (1988). Age and outstanding achievement: What do we know after a century of research? *Psychological Bulletin, 104,* 251–267.

Singer, D. G., & Singer, J. L. (1990). *The house of make-believe,* Cambridge, MA: Harvard University Press.

Skinner, B. F. (1983). Intellectual self-management in old age. *American Psychologist, 38,* 239–244.

Skinner, B. F. (1989). The origins of cognitive thought. *American Psychologist, 44,* 13–18.

Skinner, B. F. (1990). Can psychology be a science of mind? *American Psychologist, 45,* 1206–1210.

Skitka, L. J., & Maslach, C. (1990). Gender roles and the categorization of gender-relevant behavior. *Sex Roles, 22,* 133–150.

Slaikeu, K. A. (1990). *Crisis intervention.* Boston: Allyn & Bacon.

Slobin, D. I. (1975). On the nature of talk to children. In E. H. Lenneberg & E. Lenneberg (Eds.), *Foundations of language development: A multidisciplinary approach* (Vol. 1). New York: Academic Press.

Smith, C. A. (1989). Dimensions of appraisal and physiological response in emotion. *Journal of Personality and Social Psychology, 56,* 339–353.

Smith, M. L., Glass, G. V., & Miller, T. I. (1980). *The benefits of psychotherapy.* Baltimore: Johns Hopkins University Press.

Snowden, L. R. (1987). The peculiar successes of community psychology: Service delivery to ethnic minorities and the poor. *American Journal of Community Psychology, 5,* 575–586.

Snowden, L. R. & Cheung, F. K. (1990). Use of inpatient mental health services by members of ethnic minority groups. *American Psychologist, 45,* 347–355.

Snyder, D. K., & Wills, R. M. (1989). Behavioral versus insight-oriented marital therapy: Effects on individual and interspousal functioning. *Journal of Consulting and Clinical Psychology, 57,* 39–46.

Snyder, D. K., Willis, R. M., & Grady-Fletcher, A. (1991). Long-term effectiveness of behavioral versus insight-oriented marital therapy: A 4-year follow-up study. *Journal of Consulting and Clinical Psychology, 59,* 138–141.

Snyder, S. H. (1980). Brain peptides as neurotransmitters. *Science, 209,* 976–983.

Snyderman, M., & Rothman, S. (1987). Survey of expert opinion on intelligence and aptitude testing. *American Psychologist, 42,* 137–144.

Sobal, J., & Stunkard, A. J. (1989). Socioeconomic status and obesity: A review of the literature. *Psychological Bulletin, 105,* 260–275.

Sobell, M. B., & Sobell, L. C. (1982). Controlled drinking: A concept coming of age. In K. R., Blanstein & J. Polivy (Eds.), *Self-control and self-modification of emotional behavior.* New York: Plenum Press.

Solomon, S. D., Smith, E. M., Robins, L. N., & Fischbach, R. L. (1987). Social involvement as a mediator of disaster-induced stress. *Journal of Applied Social Psychology, 17,* 1092–1112.

Solomon, Z., Mikulincer, M. & Flum, Hanoch, F. (1988). Negative life events, coping responses, and combat-related psychopathology: A prospective study. *Journal of Abnormal Psychology, 97*(3), 302–307.

Sorce, J. F., & Emde, R. N. (1981). Mother's presence is not enough: Effect of emotional availability on infant exploration. *Developmental Psychology, 17,*

737–745.
Sorce, J. F., Emde, R. N., Campos, J., & Klinnert, M. D. (1985). Maternal emotional signaling: Its effect on the visual cliff behavior of 1-year-olds. *Developmental Psychology, 21,* 195–200.
Soskis, D. A., Orne, E. C., Orne, M. T., & Dinges, D. F. (1989). Self-hypnosis and meditation for stress management: A brief communication. *The International Journal of Clinical and Experimental Hypnosis, 37,* 285–289.
Spanos, N. P., Perlini, A. H., & Robertson, L. A. (1989). Hypnosis, suggestion, and placebo in the reduction of experimental pain. *Journal of Abnormal Psychology, 98,* 285–293.
Sperling, G. (1960). The information available in brief visual presentations. *Psychological Monographs, 15,* 201–293.
Sperry, R. W. (1985). Consciousness, personal identity, and the divided brain. In D. F. Benson & E. Zaidel (Eds.), *The dual brain: Hemispheric specialization in humans* (pp. 11–26). New York: Guilford Press.
Spring, B., Chiodo, J., & Bowen, D. J. (1987). Carbohydrates, tryptophan, and behavior: A methodological review. *Psychological Bulletin, 102,* 234–256.
Squire, L. R. (1987). *Memory and brain.* New York: Oxford.
Stagner, R. (1985). Aging in industry. In J. E. Birren & K. W. Schaie (Eds.), *Handbook of the psychology of aging* (2nd ed.). New York: Van Nostrand Reinhold.
Stagner, R. (1988). *A history of psychological theories.* New York: MacMillan.
Stall, R. D., Coates, T. J., & Hoff, C. (1988). Behavioral risk reduction for HIV infection among gay and bisexual men. *American Psychologist, 43,* 878–885.
Stapp, J., Fulcher, R., & Wicherski, M. (1984). Human resources in psychology: The employment of 1981 and 1982 doctorate recipients in psychology. *American Psychologist, 39,* 1408–1423.
Stapp, J., Tucker, A. M., & VandenBos, G. R. (1985). Human resources in psychology: Census of psychological personnel—1983. *American Psychologist, 40,* 1317–1351.
Stasson, M., & Fishbein, M. (1990). The relation between perceived risk and preventive action. A within-subject analysis of perceived driving risk and intentions to wear seatbelts. *Journal of Applied Social Psychology, 20,* 1541–1557.
Steblay, N. M. (1987). Helping behavior in rural and urban environments: A meta-analysis. *Psychological Bulletin, 102,* 346–356.
Steiner, D. D., & Rain, J. S. (1989). Immediate and delayed primacy and recency effects in performance evaluation. *Journal of Applied Psychology, 74,* 136–142.
Steiner, I. D. (1982). Heuristic models of groupthink. In M. Brandstatter, J. H. Davis, & G. Stocker-Kreichgauer (Eds.), *Group decision making.* New York: Academic Press.
Stephan, C. W., & Langlois, J. H. (1984). Baby beautiful: Adult attributions of infant competence as a function of infant attractiveness. *Child Development, 55,* 576–585.
Stephenson, J. S. (1985). *Death, grief, and mourning: Individual and social realities.* New York: Macmillan.
Sternberg, R. J. (1985). *Beyond IQ,* Cambridge, MA: Cambridge University Press.
Sternberg, R. J. (1986a). *Intelligence applied: Understanding and increasing your intellectual skills.* New York: Harcourt Brace Jovanovich.
Sternberg, R. J. (1986b). A triangular theory of love. *Psychological Review, 93,* 119–135.
Sternberg, R. J. & Detterman, D. L. (Eds.) (1986). *What is intelligence? Contemporary viewpoints on its nature and definition.* Norword, NJ: Ablex.
Stets, J. E., & Pirog-Good, M. A. (1989). Sexual aggression and control in dating relationships. *Journal of Applied Social Psychology, 19,* 1392–1412.
Stivers, C. (1988). Adolescent suicide: An overview. *Marriage and Family Review, 12,* 135–142.
Stivers, C. (1990). Promotion of self-esteem in the prevention of suicide. *Death Studies, 14,* 303–327.
Stone, M. H. (1980). *The borderline syndromes.* New York: McGraw Hill.
Straus, M. A., & Gelles, R. J. (1986). Societal change in family violence from 1975 to 1985 as revealed by two national surveys. *Journal of Marriage and the Family, 48,* 465–479.
Streissguth, A. P., Barr, H. M., & Martin, D. C. (1983). Maternal alcohol use and neonatal habituation assessed with the Brazelton scale. *Child Development, 54,* 1109–1118.
Streissguth, A. P., Barr, H. M., Sampson, P. D., Darby, B. L., & Martin, D. C. (1989). IQ at age 4 in relation to maternal alcohol use and smoking during pregnancy. *Developmental Psychology, 25*(1), 3–11.
Striegel-Moore, R. H., Silberstein, L. R., & Rodin, J. (1986). Toward an understanding of risk factors for bulimia. *American Psychologist, 41,* 246–263.
Strober, M., & Humphrey, L. L. (1987). Familial contributions to the etiology and course of anorexia nervosa and bulimia. *Journal of Consulting and Clinical Psychology, 55,* 654–659.
Stunkard, A., Coll, M., Lundquist, S., & Meyers, A. (1980). Obesity and eating style. *Archives of General Psychiatry, 37,* 1127–1129.
Suarez, E. C., & Williams, R. B. (1989). Situational determinants of cardiovascular and emotional reactivity in high and low hostile men. *Psychosomatic Medicine, 51,* 404–418.
Suddath, R. L., Christinson, G. W., Torrey, E. F., Casanova, M. F., & Weinberger, D. R. (1990). Anatomical abnormalities in the brains of monozygotic twins discordant for schizophrenia. *The New England Journal of Medicine, 322,* 789–794.
Sue, S. (1988). Psychotherapeutic services for ethnic minorities. *American Psychologist, 43,* 301–308.
Suedfeld, P., & Coren, S. (1989). Perceptual isolation, sensory deprivation, and rest: Moving introductory psychology texts out of the 1950s. *Canadian Psychology, 30,* 17–29.
Sugarman, D. B., & Hotaling, G. T. (1989). Violent men in intimate relationships: An analysis of risk markers. *Journal of Applied Social Psychology, 19,* 1034–1048.
Suls, J., & Wan, C. K. (1989a). Effects of sensory and procedural information on coping with stressful medical procedures and pain: A meta-analysis. *Journal of Consulting and Clinical Psychology, 57,* 372–379.
Suls, J., & Wan, C. K. (1989b). The relation between Type A behavior and chronic emotional distress: A meta-analysis. *Journal of Personality and Social Psychology, 57,* 503–512.
Swedo, S. E., Leonard, H. L., Rapoport, J. L., Lenane, M. C., Goldberger, E. L., & Cheslow, D. L. (1989). A double-blind comparison of clomipramine and desipramine in the treatment of trichotillomania (hair pulling). *The New England Journal of Medicine, 321,* 497–501.
Swim, J., Borgida, E., Maruyama, G., & Myers, D. G. (1989). Joan McKay versus John McKay: Do gender stereotypes bias evaluations? *Psychological Bulletin, 105,* 409–429.
Swindle, R. W., Jr., Cronkite, R. C., & Moos, R. H. (1989). Life stressors, social resources, coping, and the 4-year course of unipolar depression. *Journal of Abnormal Psychology, 98,* 468-477.
Szymanski, K., & Harkins, S. G. (1987). Social loafing and self-evaluation with a social standard. *Journal of Personality and Social Psychology, 53,* 891–897.

Taylor, C. W. (1988). Various approaches to and definitions of creativity. In R. J. Sternberg (Ed.), *The nature of creativity.* New York: Cambridge University Press.
Taylor, S. H. (1990). Health psychology. *American Psychologist, 45,* 40–50.
Teevan, R. C., & McGhee, P. E. (1972). Childhood development of fear of failure motivation. *Journal of Personality and Social Psychology, 21,* 345–348.
Terrace, H. S. (1980). *Nim.* New York: Alfred A. Knopf.
Terrace, H. S. (1985). In the beginning was the "name." *American Psychologist, 40,* 1011–1028.
Teske, J. A. (1988). Seeing her looking at you: Acquaintance and variation in the judgment of gaze depth. *American Journal of Psychology, 101,* 239–257.
Tilley, A., & Warren, P. (1983). Retrieval from semantic memory at different times of day. *Journal of Experimental Psychology: Learning, Memory, and Cognition, 9,* 718–724.
Tjosvold, D. (1987). Participation: A close look at its dynamics. *Journal of Management, 13,* 739–750.
Tjosvold, D. & Chia, L. C. (1989). Conflict between managers and workers: The role of cooperation and competition. *The Journal of Social Psychology, 129,* 235–247.
Treisman, A. M. (1969). Strategies and models of selective attention. *Psychological Review, 76,* 282–295.
Tronick, E. Z. (1989). Emotions and emotional communication in infants. *American Psychologist, 44,* 112–119.
Tsuang, M. T., & Faraone, S. V. (1990). *The genetics of mood disorders.* Baltimore, MD: The Johns Hopkins University Press.
Tsuang, M. T., & Vandermey. (1980). *Genes and the mind.* City: Oxford University Press.
Tulving, E. (1972). Episodic and semantic memory. In E. Tulving and W. Donaldson (Eds.), *Organization and memory.* New York: Academic Press.
Turner, A. M., & Greenough, W. T. (1985). Differential rearing effects on rat visual cortex synapses. I. Synaptic and neuronal density and synapses per neuron. *Brain Research, 329,* 195–203.

Turner, S. M., Beidel, D. C., & Nathan, R. S. (1985). Biological factors in obsessive–compulsive disorders. *Psychological Bulletin, 97,* 430–450.

U.S. Bureau of the Census (1989). *Single parents and their children* (Statistical Brief, No. SB-3-89). Washington, DC: U.S. Government Printing Office.

U.S. Bureau of the Census (1987). *Statistical Brief,* Survey of Income and Program Participation, SB-2-87, May 1987.

U.S. Bureau of the Census (1990, June). *Time off for babies: Maternity leave arrangements.* U.S. Department of Commerce.

U.S. Congress, Office of Technology Assessment. (1987). *Losing a million minds: Confronting the tragedy of Alzheimer's disease and other dementias* (Report OTA-BA-323). Washington DC: U.S. Government Printing Office.

U.S. Department of Health and Human Services (1986). *Suicide.* Rockville, MD: National Institute of Mental Health.

U.S. Department of Health and Human Services (1988). *Facts for the 1987 national high school senior survey.* Washington, DC: Alcohol, Drug Abuse, and Mental Health Administration.

Usdin, G., & Hofling, C. K. (1978). *Aging: The process and the people.* New York: Brunner/Mazel.

Vaillant, G. E., & Milofsky, E. S. (1982). The etiology of alcoholism: A prospective view. *American Psychologist, 37,* 494–503.

Valins, S. (1966). Cognitive effects of false heart-rate feedback. *Journal of Personality and Social Psychology, 4,* 400–408.

Vandell, D. L., & Corasaniti (1988). The relation between third graders' after-school care and social academic, and emotional function. *Child Development, 59,* 868–875.

Vitiello, M. V. (1989). *Unraveling sleep disorders of the aged.* Paper presented at the annual meeting of the Association of Professional Sleep Societies in Washington DC.

Vroom, V. H. (1964). *Work and motivation.* New York: Wiley.

Waid, W. M. (1976). Skin conductance response to both signaled and unsignaled noxious stimulation predicts level of socialization. *Journal of Personality and Social Psychology, 34,* 923–929.

Walker, E., Downey, G., & Bergman, A. (1989). The effects of parental psychopathology and maltreatment of child behavior: A test of the diathesis-stress model. *Child Development, 60,* 15–24.

Walker, E., & Emory, E. (1983). Infants at risk for psychopathology: Offspring of schizophrenic parents. *Child Development, 54,* 1269–1285.

Walker, J. I., & Cavenar, J. O. (1982). Vietnam veterans: Their problems continue. *The Journal of Nervous and Mental Disease, 170,* 174–180.

Walker, L. E. A. (1989). Psychology and violence against women. *American Psychologist, 44,* 695–702.

Walsh, B. T., Roose, S. P., Glassman, A. H., Gladis, M., & Sadik, C. (1985). Bulimia and depression. *Psychosomatic Medicine, 47,* 123–131.

Washton, A. M. (1989). *Cocaine addiction.* New York: W. W. Norton.

Webb, W. B., & Agnew, H. W. Jr. (1975). The effects on subsequent sleep of an acute restriction of sleep length. *Psychophysiology, 12,* 367–370.

Wechsler, D. (1958). *The measurement and appraisal of adult intelligence* (4th ed.). Baltimore: Williams & Wilkins.

Wegner, D. M., Shortt, J. W., Blake, A. W., & Page, M. S. (1990). The suppression of exciting thoughts. *Journal of Personality and Social Psychology, 58,* 409–418.

Weidner, G., Friend, R., Ficarrotto, T. J., & Mendell, N. R. (1989). Hostility and cardiovascular reactivity to stress in women and men. *Psychosomatic Medicine, 51,* 36–45.

Weinberg, R. A. (1989). Intelligence and IQ. *American Psychologist, 44,* 98–104.

Weinberger, M., Hiner, S. L., & Tierney, W. M. (1987). In support of hassles as a measure of stress in predicting health outcomes. *Journal of Behavioral Medicine, 10,* 19–31.

Weingartner, H., Adefris, W., Eich, J. E., & Murphy, D. L. (1976). Encoding-imagery specificity in alcohol state-dependent learning. *Journal of Experimental Psychology, 2,* 83–87.

Weingartner, H., Cohen, R. M., Murphy, D. L., Martello, J., & Gerdt, C. (1981). Cognitive processes in depression. *Archives of General Psychiatry, 38,* 42–47.

Weintraub, S. (1987). Risk factors in schizophrenia: The Stony Brook High-Risk Project. *Schizophrenia Bulletin, 13,* 439–443.

Wells, R. A., & Phelps, P. A. (1990). The brief psychotherapies: A selective overview. In R. A. Wells & V. J. Giannetti (Eds.), *Handbook of the brief psychotherapies.* New York: Plenum Press.

West, M. (1982). Meditation and self-awareness: Physiological and phenomenological approaches. In G. Underwood (Ed.), *Aspects of consciousness: Vol. 3. Awareness and self-awareness.* London: Academic Press.

White, M. J., & Gerstein, L. H. (1987). Helping: The influence of anticipated social sanctions and self-monitoring. *Journal of Personality, 55,* 41–55.

Whorf, B. L. (1956). J. B. Carroll (Ed.), *Language, thought, and reality: Selected writings of Benjamin Lee Whorf.* New York: Wiley.

Wiebe, D. J. (1991). Hardiness and stress moderation: A test of proposed mechanisms. *Journal of Personality and Social Psychology, 60,* 89–99.

Wilcox, C. (1989). Risk taking and presidential voting: Gambling on McGovern and Carter. *The Journal of Social Psychology, 129,* 161–168.

Wilder, D. A., & Thompson, J. E. (1980). Intergroup contact with independent manipulations of in-group and out-group interaction. *Journal of Personality and Social Psychology, 38,* 589–603.

Williams, A. F. (1986). Raising the legal purchase age in the United States: Its effects on fatal motor vehicle crashes. *Alcohol, Drugs, and Driving, 2,* 1–12.

Williams, C. D. (1959). Case report: The elimination of tantrum behavior by extinction procedures. *Journal of Abnormal and Social Psychology, 59,* 269.

Williams, K., Harkins, S., & Latane, B. (1981). Identifiability as a deterrent to social loafing: Two cheering experiments. *Journal of Personality and Social Psychology, 40,* 303–311.

Williams, R., Karacan, I., & Hursch, C. (1974). *EEG of human sleep.* New York: John Wiley & Sons.

Williams, R. L. (1970). Black pride, academic relevance, and individual achievement. *Counseling Psychologist, 2,* 18–22.

Williams, S. L., Kinney, P. J., & Falbo, J. (1989). Generalization of therapeutic changes in agoraphobia: The role of perceived self-efficacy. *Journal of Consulting and Clinical Psychology, 57,* 436–442.

Wilson, M. N. (1989). Child development in the context of the black extended family. *American Psychologist, 44* (2), 380–385.

Wise, R. A., & Bozarth, M. A. (1987). A psychomotor stimulant theory of addiction. *Psychological Review, 94,* 469–492.

Wittrock, M. C. (1987, August 29). *The teaching of comprehension.* Thorndike Award Address presented at the annual meeting of the American Psychological Association, New York.

Wolpe, J. (1958). *Psychotherapy by reciprocal inhibition.* Stanford, CA: Stanford University Press.

Wolraich, M. L., Milich, R., Stumbo, P., & Schultz, F. (1985). The effects of sucrose ingestion on the behavior of hyperactive boys. *Journal of Pediatrics, 106,* 862–867.

Wood, W., Wong, F. Y., & Chachere, J. G. (1991). Effects of media violence on viewers' aggression in unconstrained social interaction. *Psychological Bulletin, 109,* 371–383.

Woodhead, M. (1988). When psychology informs public policy: The case of early childhood intervention. *American Psychologist, 6,* 443–454.

Woodward, W. R. (1982). The "discovery" of social behaviorism and social learning theory, 1870–1980. *American Psychologist, 37,* 396–410.

Woolfolk, R. L., & McNulty, T. F. (1983). Relaxation treatment for insomnia: A component analysis. *Journal of Consulting and Clinical Psychology, 51,* 495–503.

Worchel, S., Hardy, T. W., & Hurley, R. (1976). The effects of commercial interruption of violent and nonviolent films on viewers' subsequent aggression. *Journal of Experimental Social Psychology,* 12, 220–232.

Worell, J. (1978). Sex roles and psychological well-being. Perspectives on methodology. *Journal of Consulting and Clinical Psychology, 46,* 777–791.

Wynne, L. C., Cole, R. E., & Perkins, P. (1987). University of Rochester Child and Family Study: Risk research in progress. *Schizophrenia Bulletin, 13,* 463–467.

Wyszecki, G., & Stiles, W. S. (1967). *Color science: Concepts and methods, quantitative data and formulas.* New York: Wiley.

Yerkes, R. M., & Dodson, J. D. (1908). The relation of strength of stimulus to rapidity of habit formation. *Journal of Comparative Neurology and Psychology, 18,* 459–482.

York, R., Freeman, E., Lowery, B., & Strauss, J. F. (1989). Characteristics of premenstrual syndrome. *Obstetrics and Gynecology, 73,* 601–605.

Young, K. T. (1990). American conceptions of infant development from 1955 to 1984: What the experts are telling parents. *Child Development, 61,* 17–28.

Young, S. N., Smith, S., Pihl, R. O., & Ervin, F. R. (1985). Tryptophan depletion causes a rapid lowering of mood in normal males. *Psychopharmacology, 87,* 173–177.

Yuille, J. C., & Cutshall, J. L. (1986). A case study of eyewitness memory of a crime. *Journal of Applied Psychology, 71,* 291–301.

Yussen, S. R. (1977). Characteristics of moral dilemmas written by adolescents. *Developmental Psychology, 13,* 162–163.

Zaccaro, S. J. (1984). Social loafing: The role of task attractiveness. *Personality and Social Psychology Bulletin, 10,* 99–106.

Zajonc, R. B. (1965). Social facilitation. *Science, 149,* 269–274.

Zajonc, R. B., Murphy, S. T., & Inglehart, M. (1989). Feeling and facial efference: Implications of the vascular theory of emotion. *Psychological Review, 96,* 395–416.

Zeig, J. K., & Gilligan, S. G. (1990). *Brief therapy myths, methods, and metaphors.* New York: Brunner/Mazel.

Zigler, E. F. (1987). Formal schooling for four-year-olds? No. *American Psychologist, 42,* 254–260.

Zins, J. E., & Barnett, D. W. (1983). The Kaufman Assessment Battery for Children and school achievement: A validity study. *Journal of Psychoeducational Assessment, 1,* 235–241.

Zitrin, C. M. (1981). Combined pharmacological and psychological treatment of phobias. In M. Navissakalian & D. H. Barlow (Eds.), *Phobias: Psychological and pharmacological treatments.* New York: Guilford Press.

Zola-Morgan, S., Squire, L. R., & Mishkin, M. (1982). The neuroanatomy of amnesia: Amygdala–hippocampus versus temporal stem. *Science, 218,* 1337–1339.

Zuckerman, M. (1969). Variables affecting deprivation results and hallucinations, reported sensations, and images. In J. P. Zubek (Ed.), *Sensory deprivation.* Appleton-Century-Crofts.

Zuckerman, M. (1990). Some dubious premises in research and theory on racial differences. *American Psychologist, 45,* 1297–1303.

Name Index

Subject Index

(*Continued from copyright page*)
Click, Chicago; 41R: L. T. Rhodes/TSW-Click, Chicago. 49: Biophoto-Science Library/Photo-Researchers Inc. 62L: Superstock; 62R: New York Hospital/Peter Arnold. 64: A. Glauberman/Photo Researchers Inc. 77: Superstock. 80: J. & L. Weber/Peter Arnold. 90: T. Farmer/TSW-Click, Chicago. 91: Superstock. 92: R. Schwerzel/Stock, Boston. 98: Shostal/Superstock. 109: G. Zimbel/Monkmeyer Press Photo. 118: B. Barnhart/Offshoot Stock. 131: R. Morsch/The Stock Market. 132: G. Hunter/TSW-Click, Chicago. 142: B. Daemmrich/Stock, Boston. 147: A. Glauberman/Photo-Researchers Inc. 150: A. Collins/Monkmeyer Press Photo. 151: R. Morsch/The Stock Market. 164: Psychology Archives. 177: Woodfin Camp & Assoc. 180: J. Brown/OffShoot Stock. 181: AP/Wide World Photos. 185: M. Winter/Stock, Boston. 193: R. Kopstein/Monkmeyer Press Photo. 204: The Bettmann Archive. 212: D. Schaefer/Monkmeyer Press Photo. 213: C. Morrow/Stock, Boston. 214: Courtesy of NASA. 226: D. Dempster/Allyn and Bacon. 227: DVW/Stock, Boston. 230: J. Parsons/Stock, Boston. 240: T. Wurl/Stock, Boston. 241: S. Sutton/Duomo. 247: R. Isear/Photo-Researchers Inc. 248: R. Das/Monkmeyer Press Photo. 261: Corroon/Monkmeyer Press Photo. 263: B. Gallery/Stock, Boston. 266: S. Kuklin/Photo-Researchers Inc. 279: Science Library/Photo-Researchers Inc. 280T: P. Format-Science Library/Photo-Researchers Inc. 280B: J. Stevenson-Science Library/Photo-Researchers Inc. 284T: Dr. David Linton. 297: B. Anderson/Monkmeyer Press Photo. 298: D. Goodman/Monkmeyer Press Photo. 307: G. Goodwin/Monkmeyer Press Photo. 308: C. Parksa/The Stock Market. 309: J. Caccavo/The Picture Group. 316: H. Rainier/OffShoot Stock. 319: El Herwig/Stock, Boston. 320: Courtesy of Harvard University News. 325: Allyn and Bacon. 326: Superstock. 331: M. Heron/Woodfin Camp & Assoc. 333: D. Krakel III/Photo-Researchers Inc. 335: I. Wyman/Sygma. 337: P. Menzel/Stock, Boston. 338: K. Horan/The Picture Group. 353: Arizona Historical Society Library. 354: Superstock. 358: G. Zimbel/Monkmeyer Press Photo. 359: R. Morsch/The Stock Market. 367: C. Gupton/Stock, Boston. 377: Historical Picture Service. 384TL: G. Palmer/The Stock Market; TC: K. Harrison/The Image Works; TR: R. Hutchings/Photo-Researchers Inc.; BL: Sygma; BC: R. Morsch/The Stock Market; BR: B. Alper/Stock, Boston. 385: M. Rogers/TSW-Click, Chicago. 387: TSW-Click, Chicago. 401: A. Canavesio/Photo-Researchers Inc. 405: Archive/Photo-Researchers. 407: Archive/Photo-Researchers Inc. 408: UPI/Bettmann Archive. 412: Research Library. 420T: UPI/Bettmann Archive. 420B: Historical Picture Service. 425: D. Dempster/Allyn and Bacon. 427T: Historical Picture Service. 427B: Historical Picture Service. 449: Psychology Archives. 450: W. McIntyre/Photo-Researchers Inc. 453: R. Schleipman/OffShoot Stock. 465: J. Coletti, Stock, Boston. 470: D. Dempster/Allyn and Bacon. 471: D. Dempster/Allyn and Bacon. 483: D. Hudson/Sygma. 485: J. Caccavo/The Picture Group. 495: J. Brown/Offshoot Stock. 498: UPI/Bettmann Archives. 502L: G. Smith/Stock, Brown, Boston: 502R: C. Fishman/Woodfin Camp & Assoc. 505: Sudhir/The Picture Group. 508: P. Chauvel/Sygma. 509: A Grace/Stock, Boston. 521: Mary Evans Picture Library/Photo-Researchers Inc. 525: D. Dempster/Offshoot Stock. 541: B. Daemmrich. 546: Grunnitus/Monkmeyer Press Photo. 546B: The Genain Estate. 562: Mary Evans Picture Library. 567: Research Library. 581L: The Bettmann Archive. 581R: Research Library. 586: B. Daemmrich. 598: Tortoni/Photo-Researchers Inc. 599: D. Lyn/Shooting Star. 603: R. Sydney/Stock, Boston. 606: D. Grossman/Photo-Researchers Inc. 608: B. Daemmrich. 610: The Milgrim Estate. 615: P. Conklin/Monkmeyer Press Photo. 622L: J. Curtis/Offshoot Stock. 622R: D. Dempster/Offshoot Stock. 624: Superstock. 626: J. Curtis/Offshoot Stock. 631: C. Wolinsky/Stock, Boston. 643: D. Gardner/Offshoot Stock. 644: D. Dempster/Offshoot Stock. 649: G. Palmer/The Stock Market.